3/98

Contemporary Theatre, Film and Television

Explore your options!

Gale databases are offered in a variety of formats

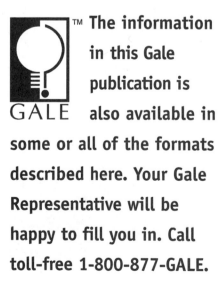 ™ The information in this Gale publication is also available in some or all of the formats described here. Your Gale Representative will be happy to fill you in. Call toll-free 1-800-877-GALE.

GaleNet

A number of Gale databases are now available on GaleNet, our new online information resource accessible through the Internet. GaleNet features an easy-to-use end-user interface, the powerful search capabilities of BRS/SEARCH retrieval software and ease of access through the World Wide Web.

Diskette/Magnetic Tape

Many Gale databases are available on diskette or magnetic tape, allowing systemwide access to your most-used information sources through existing computer systems. Data can be delivered on a variety of mediums (DOS-formatted diskettes, 9-track tape, 8mm data tape) and in industry-standard formats (comma-delimited, tagged, fixed-field).

CD-ROM

A variety of Gale titles are available on CD-ROM, offering maximum flexibility and powerful search software.

Online

For your convenience, many Gale databases are available through popular online services, including DIALOG, NEXIS, DataStar, ORBIT, OCLC, Thomson Financial Network's I/Plus Direct, HRIN, Prodigy, Sandpoint's HOOVER, the Library Corporation's NLightN and Telebase Systems.

ISSN 0749-064X

Contemporary Theatre, Film and Television

A Biographical Guide Featuring Performers, Directors, Writers, Producers, Designers, Managers, Choreographers, Technicians, Composers, Executives, Dancers, and Critics in the United States, Canada, Great Britain and the World

Kathleen J. Edgar, Senior Editor

Joshua Kondek, Pam Zuber, Associate Editors

Volume 18

Includes Cumulative Index Containing References to
Who's Who in the Theatre and *Who Was Who in the Theatre*

GALE

DETROIT · NEW YORK · TORONTO · LONDON

STAFF

Kathleen J. Edgar, *Senior Editor*

Joshua Kondek and Pam Zuber, *Associate Editors*

Nancy A. Edgar, Janet L. Hile, Deborah Kondek, Terry Kosdrosky, Annette Petrusso, Lynn M. Spampinato, Arlene True, Hilary Weber, and Carole L. Whitaker, *Sketchwriters*

Patti A. Tippett, *Contributor*

Christine Tomassini, *Editorial Research Consultant*

Pamela Willwerth Aue and James P. Draper, *Managing Editors*

Victoria B. Cariappa, *Research Manager*

Andrew Guy Malonis, *Research Specialist*

Julia C. Daniel, Research Coordinator

Michele P. LaMeau, Barbara McNeil, Maureen Richards, and Gary Oudersluys, *Research Specialists*

Tamara C. Nott, Tracie A. Richardson, and Norma Sawaya, *Research Associates*

Phyllis Blackman, Jeffrey D. Daniels, Talitha A. Jean, and Corrine A. Stocker, *Research Assistants*

This book is printed on acid-free paper that meets the minimum requirements of American National Standard for Information Sciences Permanence Paper for Printed Library Materials, ANSI Z39.48-1984.

Library of Congress Catalog Card Number 84-649371

ISBN 0-7876-2056-4
ISSN 0749-064X

Printed in the United States of America

10 9 8 7 6 5 4 3 2 1

Contents

Preface

Provides Broad, Single-Source Coverage in the Entertainment Field

Contemporary Theatre, Film and Television (*CTFT*) is a biographical reference series designed to provide students, educators, researchers, librarians, and general readers with information on a wide range of entertainment figures. Unlike single-volume reference works that focus on a limited number of artists or on a specific segment of the entertainment field, *CTFT* is an ongoing publication that includes entries on individuals active in the theatre, film, *and* television industries. Before the publication of *CTFT*, information-seekers had no choice but to consult several different sources in order to locate the in-depth biographical and credit data that makes *CTFT's* one-stop coverage the most comprehensive available on the lives and work of performing arts professionals.

Scope

CTFT covers not only performers, directors, writers, and producers, but also behind-the-scenes specialists such as designers, managers, choreographers, technicians, composers, executives, dancers, and critics from the United States and Great Britain. With nearly 400 entries in *CTFT 17*, the series now provides biographies on approximately 8,000 people involved in all aspects of theatre, film, and television.

CTFT gives primary emphasis to people who are currently active. New entries are prepared on major stars as well as those who are just beginning to win acclaim for their work. *CTFT* also includes entries on personalities who have died but whose work commands lasting interest.

Compilation Methods

CTFT editors identify candidates for inclusion in the series by consulting biographical dictionaries, industry directories, entertainment annuals, trade and general interest periodicals, newspapers, and on-line databases. Entries are compiled from published biographical sources and then mailed to the listees or their agents for review and verification.

Revised Entries

To ensure *CTFT's* timeliness and comprehensiveness, entries from previous volumes, as well as from Gale Research's *Who's Who in the Theatre*, are updated for individuals who have been active enough to require revision of their earlier biographies. Such individuals will merit revised entries as often as there is substantial new information to provide. Obituary notices for deceased entertainment personalities already listed in *CTFT* are also published.

Accessible Format Makes Data Easy to Locate

CTFT entries, modeled after those in Gale's highly regarded *Contemporary Authors* series, are written in a clear, readable style designed to help users focus quickly on specific facts. The following is a summary of the information found in *CTFT* sketches:

  ENTRY HEADING: the form of the name by which the listee is best known.

- *PERSONAL:* full or original name; dates and places of birth and death; family data; colleges attended, degrees earned, and professional training; political and religious affiliations when known; avocational interests.

- *ADDRESSES:* home, office, agent, publicist and/or manager addresses.

- *CAREER:* tagline indicating principal areas of entertainment work; resume of career positions and other vocational achievements; military service.

- *MEMBER:* memberships and offices held in professional, union, civic, and social organizations.

- *AWARDS, HONORS:* theatre, film, and television awards and nominations; literary and civic awards; honorary degrees.

- *CREDITS:* comprehensive title-by-title listings of theatre, film, and television appearance and work credits, including roles and production data as well as debut and genre information.

- *RECORDINGS:* album, single song, video, and taped reading releases; recording labels and dates when available.

- *WRITINGS:* title-by-title listing of plays, screenplays, scripts, and musical compositions along with production information; books, including autobiographies, and other publications.

- *ADAPTATIONS:* a list of films, plays, and other media which have been adapted from the listee's work.

- *SIDELIGHTS:* favorite roles; portions of agent-prepared biographies or personal statements from the listee when available.

- *OTHER SOURCES:* books and periodicals where interviews or feature stories can be found.

Access Thousands of Entries Using *CTFT*'s Cumulative Index

Each volume of *CTFT* contains a cumulative index to the entire series. As an added feature, this index also includes references to all seventeen editions of *Who's Who in the Theatre* and to the four-volume compilation *Who Was Who in the Theatre.*

Available in Electronic Format

Online. Recent volumes of *CTFT* are available online as part of the Gale Biographies (GALBIO) database accessible through LEXIS-NEXIS. For more information, contact LEXIS-NEXIS, P.O. Box 933, Dayton, OH 45401-0933; phone (937) 865-6800, toll-free: 800-346-9759.

Suggestions Are Welcome

Contemporary Theatre, Film and Television is intended to serve as a useful reference tool for a wide audience, so comments about any aspect of this work are encouraged. Suggestions of entertainment professionals to include in future volumes are also welcome. Send comments and suggestions to: The Editor, *Contemporary Theatre, Film and Television,* Gale Research Inc., 835 Penobscot Bldg., 645 Griswold St., Detroit, MI 48226-4094; call toll-free at 1-800-347-GALE; or fax to 1-313-961-6599.

Contemporary Theatre, Film and Television

* Indicates that a listing has been compiled from secondary sources believed to be reliable, but has not been personally verified for this edition by the listee.

AAMES, Willie 1960-

PERSONAL

Original name Albert William Upton; born July 15, 1960, in Newport Beach, CA; married Victoria Weatherman (marriage ended); married Maylo McCaslin (an actress), 1986; children: (first marriage) Christopher; (second marriage) Harleigh (daughter).

Addresses: *Home*—Olathe, Kansas.

Career: Actor. Producer and director for a video company in Kansas City, MO.

CREDITS

Television Appearances; Series:
Kenny Platt, *We'll Get By*, CBS, 1975.
Fred Robinson, *Swiss Family Robinson*, ABC, 1975-76.
Tommy Bradford, *Eight Is Enough*, ABC, 1977-81.
Robbie Hamlin, *The Edge of Night*, NBC, 1983.
Voice of Hank, *Dungeons and Dragons* (animated), CBS, 1983-87.
Buddy Lembeck, *Charles in Charge*, CBS, 1984-85, then syndicated, 1987-88.

Television Appearances; Miniseries:
Wesley Jordache, *Rich Man, Poor Man*, ABC, 1976.

Television Appearances; Pilots:
Kenny Platt, *We'll Get By*, CBS, 1974.
Adam Morgan, *Doctor Dan*, CBS, 1974.
Tom Swift, *The Tom Swift and Linda Craig Mystery Hour*, ABC, 1983.

Television Appearances; Episodic:
Leonard Unger, "Win One for Felix," *The Odd Couple*, ABC, 1971.
"P.S. Murry Christmas," *Gunsmoke*, CBS, 1971.
Harold, "The Karate Story," *The Courtship of Eddie's Father*, ABC, 1972.
Harold, "In the Eye of the Beholder," *The Courtship of Eddie's Father*, ABC, 1972.
"A Quiet Day in Dodge," *Gunsmoke*, CBS, 1973.
"The Enemies," *Medical Center*, CBS, 1974.
"Runaway on the Rogue River," *World of Disney*, NBC, 1974.
"Credit Risk," *Adam-12*, NBC, 1974.
"Torment," *Medical Center*, CBS, 1975.
T. J. Latimer, "Jury Duty," *Family*, ABC, 1976.
"Injun Kid," *Little House on the Prairie*, NBC, 1977.
"The First Time," *Family*, ABC, 1977.
"Labors of Love," *Family*, ABC, 1977.
"Doc's Nephew," *The Love Boat*, ABC, 1982.
Chip, "Love and New Year's Eve," *The New Love, American Style*, ABC, 1985.
"Love and Halley's Comet," *The New Love, American Style*, ABC, 1986.
"Revenge of the Esperanza," *Blacke's Magic*, NBC, 1986.
"Peter McGovern," *An American Portrait*, CBS, 1986.
"Love and Chartreuse," *The New Love, American Style*, ABC, 1986.

Voice characterization in *Wait 'til Your Father Gets Home* (animated), syndicated.

Television Appearances; Movies:
William Frankenstein, *Frankenstein*, ABC, 1973.
Gum, *Unwed Father*, ABC, 1974.
Donny, *The Family Nobody Wanted*, ABC, 1975.
Tommy Bradford, *Eight Is Enough: A Family Reunion*, NBC, 1987.
Tommy Bradford, *An Eight Is Enough Wedding*, NBC, 1989.

Television Appearances; Specials:
ABC team member, *Battle of the Network Stars VII,* ABC, 1979.
ABC team member, *Battle of the Network Stars IX,* ABC, 1980.
Bob Hope's All-Star Look at Television's Prime Time Wars (also known as *Bob Hope's Special: Bob Hope's All-Star Look at Television's Prime Time Wars*), NBC, 1980.
Host, *We're Movin',* syndicated, 1982.
The Tenth Annual Circus of the Stars (also known as *Circus of the Stars*), CBS, 1985.
Super Bloopers and New Practical Jokes, NBC, 1989.
The 14th Annual Circus of the Stars (also known as *Circus of the Stars*), CBS, 1989.
The Hollywood Christmas Parade, 1989.

Film Appearances:
Kenny Stevens, *Scavenger Hunt,* Twentieth Century-Fox, 1979.
Hog Wild, Avco Embassy, 1980.
David, *Paradise,* Avco Embassy, 1982.
Peyton Nichols, *Zapped!,* Avco Embassy, 1982.
Goma-2, Golden Sun, 1984.
Tony, *Killing Machine* (also known as *Maquina de Matar*), Embassy Home Entertainment, 1985.
Tommy, *Cut and Run* (also known as *Inferno in Diretta, Amazon: Savage Adventure,* and *Amazonia*), New World, 1986.

Also appeared in *Bull from the Sky.*

RECORDINGS

Videos:
Bibleman/Miles Peterson, "Big Big Book," *The Bibleman Show* (Christian video for children), Sparrow and Pamplin Entertainment, 1996.
Bibleman/Miles Peterson, "Back to School" *The Bibleman Show* (Christian video for children), Sparrow and Pamplin Entertainment, 1996.

OTHER SOURCES

Periodicals:
People, July 17, 1995, p. 43.

Other:
http://www.acloserlook.com/9601ac1/ children_youth/thebiblemanshow.html, September 24, 1997.*

ADAMS, Brooke   1949-

PERSONAL

Born February 8, 1949, in New York, NY; daughter of Robert K. (an actor and producer) and Rosaland (an actress; maiden name, Gould) Adams; married Tony Shalhoub, 1992. *Education:* Attended High School of Performing Arts and Institute of American Ballet; studied acting with Lee Strasberg.

Addresses: *Agent*—Susan Smith & Associates, 121 N. San Vicente Blvd., Beverly Hills, CA 90211-2303.

Career: Actress.

CREDITS

Stage Appearances:
Carol, *Split,* Second Stage, New York, 1980.
Lisa, *Key Exchange,* WPA, New York, 1982.
Julia, *The Philanderer,* Yale Repertory, New Haven, CT, 1983.
Carol, *Linda Hur,* Second Stage, New York, 1984.
Heidi Holland, *The Heidi Chronicles,* Plymouth The-atre, New York City, 1990.
Bella, *Lost in Yonkers,* Center Theatre Group/ Ahmanson Theatre, Los Angeles, CA, 1991-92.
Jolly, *The Old Neighborhood,* American Repertory Theatre, Cambridge, MA, 1997.

Also made her New York debut as Gabrielle, *The Petrified Forest,* St. Clements.

Film Appearances:
Car Wash, Universal, 1976.
Rose, *Shockwaves* (also known as *Shock Waves, Almost Human,* and *Death Corps*), 1977.
Abby, *Days of Heaven,* Paramount, 1978.
Elizabeth Driscoll, *Invasion of the Body Snatchers,* United Artists, 1978.
Stacy Bishop, *A Man and a Woman and a Bank,* Avco Embassy, 1979.
Alexandra Pulido, *Cuba,* United Artists, 1979.
The Great Train Robbery (also known as *The First Great Train Robbery*), United Artists, 1979.
Jeannie, *Tell Me a Riddle,* 1980.
Marion Edwards, *Utilities,* 1981.
Sarah Bracknell, *The Dead Zone,* Paramount, 1983.
Erica Boyer, *Almost You,* Twentieth Century-Fox, 1985.
Guest star in "Stuff commercials," *The Stuff,* 1985.
Lisa Simon, *Key Exchange,* 1985.

Jane Belletto, *Man on Fire* (also known as *Absinthe*), TriStar, 1987.

Virginia Marshall, *The Unborn,* Califilm, 1991.

Nora, *Gas Food Lodging,* IRS Releasing/TriStar, 1992.

Young Missy, *My Boyfriend's Back,* Buena Vista, 1993.

Sleepless, 1994.

Narrator, *The Fire This Time,* Blacktop Films, 1994.

Elizabeth Thomas Brewer, *The Baby-Sitter's Club,* TriStar, 1995.

Film Director:

Two Faced, Theater 1761, 1995.

Television Appearances; Series:

Cynthia Crackerby, *O.K. Crackerby,* ABC, 1965-66.

Television Appearances; Miniseries:

Pagan Tralone, *Lace,* ABC, 1984.

Pagan Tralone, *Lace II,* ABC, 1985.

Television Appearances; Movies:

Mae, *The Daughters of Joshua Cabe,* ABC, 1972.

F. Scott Fitzgerald and *"The Last of the Belles,"* ABC, 1974.

Mae, *The Daughters of Joshua Cabe Return,* ABC, 1975.

Vera Franklin, *Murder on Flight 502,* ABC, 1975.

Diane Fowler, *Who Is the Black Dahlia?,* NBC, 1975.

Beverly, *James Dean: Portrait of a Friend* (also known as *James Dean* and *The Legend*), NBC, 1976.

Sarah Dacos, *Nero Wolfe,* ABC, 1979.

Julia Newell, *The Innocents Abroad,* PBS, 1983.

Diane Dupuy, *Special People: Based on a True Story,* CBS, 1984.

Grace Danet, *The Lion of Africa,* HBO, 1987.

Pat McClinton, *Bridesmaids,* CBS, 1989.

Sally Norman, *Sometimes They Come Back* (also known as *Stephen King's "Sometimes They Come Back"*), CBS, 1991.

Anna Dunne, *The Last Hit* (also known as *The Long Kill*), USA Network, 1993.

Television Appearances; Pilots:

Jennifer, *Black Bart,* CBS, 1975.

Frannie Rosello, *Flatbush/Avenue J,* ABC, 1976.

Meg Robbins, *A Girl's Life,* ABC, 1989.

Television Appearances; Episodic:

"Angela," *Police Woman,* NBC, 1976.

"The Boy Next Door," *Bob Newhart Show,* CBS, 1976.

Judy Trowbridge, Walter's Law Clerk, "The Law Clerk," *Tony Randall Show,* ABC, 1976.

"Dead Again," *Kojak,* CBS, 1976.

"Acts of Love," *Family,* ABC, 1977.

"Echoes of Love," *Family,* ABC, 1978.

"Haunted," *American Playhouse,* PBS, 1984.

"Paul Reiser: Out on a Whim," *On Location,* HBO, 1987.

"The Stork Club," *Moonlighting,* ABC, 1988.

"Fetal Attraction," *Moonlighting,* ABC, 1988.

"Maddie Hayes Got Married," *Moonlighting,* ABC, 1988.

"And the Flesh Was Made Word," *Moonlighting,* ABC, 1988.

Guest, *The Tonight Show,* NBC, 1988.

Susana, *Touched by An Angel,* CBS, 1994.

Guest Caller Marilyn, *Frasier,* NBC, 1995.

Angie Varnas, "Song of Songs," *Picture Windows,* Showtime, 1995.

Nun, *Wings,* NBC, 1996.

Joyce, *Gun,* ABC, 1997.*

ADAMS, Edie   1929(?)-

PERSONAL

Born Elizabeth Edith Enke, April 16, 1929 (some sources say 1927), in Kingston, PA; daughter of Sheldon and Ada (Adams) Enke; married Ernie Kovacs (an actor and comedian), 1955 (died in a car crash, 1962); married Marty Mills, 1964 (a photographer; divorced); married Pete Candoli (an entertainer), 1972 (divorced); children: (first marriage) Mia Susan (died, 1981); stepchildren: (first marriage) two daughters. *Education:* Attended Juilliard School of Music and Columbia University; trained in design at the Traphagen School of Fashion Design. *Avocational Interests:* Dressmaking, interior decoration.

Addresses: *Contact*—c/o Roger Richman Agency, 9777 Wilshire Blvd., Suite 700, Beverly Hills, CA 90212.

Career: Actress.

Awards, Honors: Antoinette Perry Award, 1956, for *Li'l Abner.*

CREDITS

Television Appearances; Movies:

Flossie, *Evil Roy Slade,* 1972.

Massage Parlor Owner, *The Return of Joe Forrester* (also known as *Cop on the Beat*), 1975.

Joyce, *Superdome,* 1978.
Connie Burton, *Fast Friends,* 1979.
Kate Loves a Mystery (also known as *Mrs. Columbo: Word Games*), NBC, 1979.
Tessie, *A Cry for Love,* 1980.
Francine Sherman, *Make Me an Offer,* 1980.
Mrs. Kennedy, *Portrait of an Escort,* 1980.
Hazel, *Shooting Stars,* ABC, 1983.
Mae West, *Ernie Kovacs: Between the Laughter,* 1984.
Lady (Booster), *Jake Spanner, Private Eye* (also known as *Jack Spanner, Back on the Case, The Old Dick,* and *Hoodwinked*), USA Network, 1989.

Television Appearances; Series:
Edith Adams, *Ernie in Kovacsland,* NBC, 1951.
The Ernie Kovacs Show, CBS, 1952-53, then NBC, 1956.
The Chevy Show, NBC, 1958.
Panelist, *Take a Good Look,* ABC, 1960-61.
The Edie Adams Show (also known as *Here's Edie*), ABC, 1963-64.
Take Charge!, PBS, 1988.

Also appeared as Rosanne, *As the World Turns,* CBS, and as a guest on *Kovacs Unlimited,* WCBS.

Television Appearances; Miniseries:
Flora Cato, *The Seekers,* 1979.
Ruby Miller, *Armistead Maupin's "Tales of the City"* (also known as *Tales of the City*), PBS, 1994.

Television Appearances; Specials:
Cinderella, 1959.
The Bob Hope Show, 1970.
The Don Adams Special: Hooray for Hollywood, CBS, 1970.
The Bob Hope Show, 1971.
Madame Zenia, *The Haunting of Harrington House,* 1981.
Ernie Kovacs: Television's Original Genius, (cable), 1982.
The Screen Actors Guild 50th Anniversary Celebration, 1984.
Flo, *Neat and Tidy* (also known as *Adventures Beyond Belief*), 1986.
The Television Academy Hall of Fame, 1987.

Television Appearances; Pilots:
Lillian Sinclair, *Bosom Buddies* (pilot), 1980.

Television Appearances; Episodic:
Herself, "Lucy Meets the Moustache," *The Lucy-Desi Comedy Hour,* CBS, 1960.
Angela, "Sourdough Suite," *Vega$,* ABC, 1981.

Appeared on *U.S. Steel Hour, Miss U.S. Television, Kovacs on the Corner, Three to Get Ready, The Jack Paar Show, The Ed Sullivan Show, The Perry Como Show, G.E. Theatre, The Dinah Shore Show, The Pat Boone Show, Colgate Comedy Hour,* and *Palace.*

Film Appearances:
Miss Olsen, *The Apartment,* United Artists, 1960.
Rebel Davis, *Lover, Come Back,* Universal, 1962.
Irene, *Under the Yum-Yum Tree,* Columbia, 1963.
Monica Crump, *It's a Mad, Mad, Mad, Mad World,* United Artists, 1963.
Frederica Larsen, *Call Me Bwana,* 1963.
Barbie, Barbara of Seville, *Love with the Proper Stranger,* Paramount, 1964.
Mabel Cantwell, *The Best Man,* United Artists, 1964.
Irene Chase, *Made in Paris,* Metro-Goldwyn-Mayer, 1966.
Trina Yale, *The Oscar,* Embassy, 1966.
Merle McGill, *The Honey Pot* (also known as *Anyone for Venice?* and *It Comes up Murder*), United Artists, 1967.
Tempest Stoner, *Cheech & Chong's "Up in Smoke"* (also known as *Up in Smoke*), 1978.
Leslie, *Racket,* 1979.
The Happy Hooker Goes to Hollywood, 1980.
Carolyn, *Boxoffice,* 1982.

Film Work:
Production assistance, *Kovacs,* 1971.

Stage Appearances:
(Debut) *Blithe Spirit,* Chapel Theatre, Ridgewood, NJ, 1947.
(New York debut) Eileen, *Wonderful Town,* Winter Garden Theatre, 1953.
Daisy Mae, *Li'l Abner,* St. James Theatre, NY, 1956.
Sweet Bird of Youth, 1960.
Free as a Bird, 1960.
Sadie Thompson, *Rain,* Packard Music Hall, Warren, OH, 1963.
Title role, *La Perichole,* Opera House, Seattle, WA, 1972.
Best Little Whorehouse in Texas, Falmouth Playhouse, ME, 1983.
The Merry Widow, Long Beach Civic Light Opera, CA, 1986.
Happy Birthday, Mr. Abbott! or Night of 100 Years, Palace Theatre, New York City, 1987.

Tours:
The Merry Widow, U.S. Cities, 1959.
Reno Sweeney, *Anything Goes,* U.S. Cities, 1974.
Lovely Lowell, *The Cooch Dancer,* U.S. Cities, 1975.

Cabaret:
It's a Bird, It's a Plane, It's Edie and Peter, 1973.
Broadway, My Way, St. Regis Hotel, NY, 1982.

Also appeared in *Mame* and *Where's Charley?*

WRITINGS

For Film:
Kovacs, 1971.

Books
(With Robert Windeler), *Sing a Pretty Song: The "Offbeat" Life of Edie Adams, Including the Ernie Kovacs Years,* Morrow, 1990.*

ADAMS, Mason   1919-

PERSONAL

Born February 26, 1919, in New York, NY; married Margot Adams (a writer), 1958; children: Betsy, Bill. *Education:* University of Wisconsin, B.A., 1940, M.A., 1941; trained for the stage at the Neighborhood Playhouse.

Addresses: *Agent*—Paul Kohner, 9300 Wilshire Blvd., Suite 555, Beverly Hills, CA 90212.

Career: Actor. On-camera and voice spokesperson for television commercials, including commercials for Nuprin pain reliever and Smuckers products.

Awards, Honors: Emmy Award nominations, supporting actor in a drama series, 1979, 1980, and 1981, all for *Lou Grant.*

Member: Actors' Equity Association, Screen Actors Guild, American Federation of Television and Radio Artists, Players Club, Delta Sigma Rho, Phi Kappa Phi.

CREDITS

Television Appearances; Series:
Love of Life, CBS, 1951.
Charlie Hume, *Lou Grant,* CBS, 1977-82.
Gordon Blair, *Morning Star, Evening Star,* NBC, 1985-86.
Everett Daye, *Knight and Daye,* NBC, 1989.

Television Appearances; Pilots:
Peter Braden, *Hope Divison* (also known as *Shades of Blue*), ABC, 1987.

Television Appearances; Movies:
Bill Cairns, *The Deadliest Season,* CBS, 1977.
Dr. Eliot Losen, *And Baby Makes Six,* NBC, 1979.
Dr. Ed Johnson, *A Shining Season,* CBS, 1979.
Elmo Tyson, *Flamingo Road,* NBC, 1980.
Willie the Wino, *Murder Can Hurt You!,* ABC, 1980.
Wally, *The Revenge of the Stepford Wives,* NBC, 1980.
Harry Tannenbaum, *The Kid with the Broken Halo,* NBC, 1982.
Father Ryan, *Rage of Angels,* 1982.
Ray Mellette, *Adam,* NBC, 1983.
Solomon Northup's Odyssey (also known as *Half-Slave, Half-Free*), 1984.
Ron Sandler, *Passions,* CBS, 1984.
Sumner Murdock, *The Night They Saved Christmas,* ABC, 1984.
Dr. Karl Janss, *Northstar,* ABC, 1986.
Geoffrey Wiggins, *Under Siege,* 1986.
Under the Influence, CBS, 1986.
Dr. Gordon, *Who Is Julia?,* CBS, 1986.
Father Ryan, *Rage of Angels: The Story Continues,* NBC, 1986.
Frank Halloran, *Perry Mason: The Case of the Maligned Mobster* (also known as *The Case of the Maligned Mobster*), NBC, 1991.
Judge Colbert, *Jonathan: The Boy Nobody Wanted* (also known as *Who Speaks for Jonathan?*), NBC, 1992.
Henry Hyde, *Assault at West Point* (also known as *Conduct Unbecoming: The Court-Martial of Johnson Whittaker*) Showtime, 1994.
Dr. Frederick Rochelle, *Not of This Earth* (also known as *Roger Corman Presents: Not of This Earth*), Showtime, 1995.

Also appeared in *Freedom to Speak* and *Buying a Landslide.*

Television Appearances: Miniseries:

Appeared in *The Quiet Conspiracy,* [England].

Television Appearances; Episodic:
"The Case of the Phantom Fire," *The Man behind the Badge,* CBS, 1954.
The Love Boat, ABC, 1981.
Announcer, *Moonlighting,* ABC, 1985.
Professor Lloyd Rhodes, *Family Ties,* NBC, 1986.
Bob Ranier, "The Heiress," *Matlock,* NBC, 1988.
Roger Philby, *Murder, She Wrote,* CBS, 1989.
"A New Woman," *Monsters,* syndicated, 1990.
"Chute First, Ask Questions Later," *Civil Wars,* ABC, 1992.

"Citizen's Court judge," *Family Matters*, ABC, 1997.
"Diary of a Serial Killer," *Murder One*, ABC, 1997.

Television Appearances; Specials:
Clyde Hawthorne, *Peking Encounter*, syndicated, 1982.
Voice, *The Grinch Grinches the Cat in the Hat*, 1982.
Narrator, *Great Day*, 1983.
Narrator, *The Whimsical World of Oz*, 1985.
Narrator, *Arnold of the Ducks*, 1985.
Dr. Parke, *You Are the Jury*, 1986.
Narrator and Host, *Norman Rockwell: An American Portrait*, PBS, 1987.
Narrator, *Challenge on the Coast* (also known as *Conserving America*), PBS, 1989.

Stage Appearances:
(Broadway debut) Joe Rigga, *Get Away Old Man*, Cort Theatre, 1943.
(London debut) Playwright, bed salesman, and Herbert, *You I Can't Hear You When the Water's Running*, New Theatre, 1968.
Paradise Lost, Mirror Repertory Company, Theatre at St. Peter's Church, New York City, 1984.
Time of Your Life, Mirror Repertory Company, Theatre at St. Peter's Church, 1985.
Danger: Memory!, Lincoln Center, New York City, 1987.
Budge/Arno Klein, *The Day Room*, Manhattan Theatre Club, City Center Stage, New York City, 1987-88.
Lou Gold, *The Rose Quartet*, Circle Repertory Company, New York City, 1991.
The Ryan Interview, or How It Was Around Here (part of *Marathon '95*), Ensemble Studio Theatre, 1995.

Appeared in productions at the Hilltop Theatre, Baltimore, summer, 1940; appeared in productions on Broadway, including *Career Angel, Public Relations, Violet, Shadow of My Enemy, Inquest, The Sign in Sidney Brustein's Window, Tall Story, Foxfire*, and *The Trial of the Catonsville Nine*; also appeared in *The Shortchanged Review*, New York Shakespeare Festival, New York City. Appeared off-Broadway in *Checking Out, Meegan's Game*, and *The Soft Touch*.

Film Appearances:
The Happy Hooker, Cannon, 1975.
Voice, *Raggedy Ann and Andy* (animated), 1976.
Obstetrician, *Demon* (also known as *God Told Me To*), 1977.
President of the United States, *The Final Conflict* (also known as *Omen III: The Final Conflict*), Twentieth Century-Fox, 1981.

Colonel Mason, *F/X* (also known as *F/X—Murder by Illusion* and *Murder by Illusion*), Orion, 1986.
Deputy Director Brown, *Toy Soldiers*, TriStar, 1991.
Walter Sr., *Son-in-Law*, Buena Vista, 1993.
Mr. Pike, *Houseguest*, Buena Vista, 1995.
Father Nestor, *Touch*, Metro-Goldwyn-Mayer/United Artists, 1997.
Hudson River Blues, 1997.

Radio Appearances:
Title role, *Pepper Young's Family*, 1946-60.

Performed on most major radio shows originating in New York; radio voiceovers for WPLJ-FM radio in New York City, 1995.*

AGUTTER, Jenny 1952-

PERSONAL

Surname is pronounced with emphasis on the first syllable; born Jennifer Ann Agutter, December 20, 1952, in Taunton, England; daughter of Derek Brodie (a live entertainment organizer) and Catherine (Lynam) Agutter; married Johan Tham (a hotel owner); children: one son. *Education:* Trained for the stage at the Elmhurst Ballet School.

Addresses: *Agent*—The Gersh Agency, 232 North Canon Dr., Beverly Hills, CA 90210.

Career: Actress.

Awards, Honors: Most Promising Artiste Award, Variety Club of Great Britain, 1971; Emmy Award, best supporting actress, 1971, for *The Snow Goose;* Best Actress nomination, New York British TV Scout, 1972, for *A War of Children;* British Academy of Film and Television Arts and Sciences Award, best supporting actress, 1977, for *Equus.*

Member: British American Academy of Dramatic Art.

CREDITS

Stage Appearances:
(Debut) Lady Teazle, *The School for Scandal*, Castle Theatre, Farnham, Surrey, 1972.
(London debut) *Rooted*, Hampstead Theatre Club, 1973.
Raina, *Arms and the Man*, Manchester '73 Festival, 1973.

The Ride across Lake Constance, Hampstead Theatre Club, 1973.

Miranda, *The Tempest,* National Theatre, 1974.

Thea, *Spring's Awakening,* National Theatre, 1974.

Hedda, *Hedda Gabler,* Round House, London, 1980.

Emma, *Betrayal,* Charles Playhouse, Boston, MA, 1980.

Alice Arden, *Arden of Faversham,* Royal Shakespeare Company, 1982.

Fontanelle, (Edward Bond's) *Lear,* Royal Shakespeare Company, 1982.

The Other Place, Royal Shakespeare Company, 1982.

Regan, *King Lear,* Royal Shakespeare Company, 1982-83.

Grace, *The Body,* Royal Shakespeare Company, 1983.

(Broadway debut) Pat Green, *Breaking the Code,* Neil Simon Theatre, 1987-88, then John F. Kennedy Center for the Performing Arts, 1988.

Princess of France, *Love's Labour's Lost,* Barbican Theatre, London, 1995.

Also appeared in *Shrew,* Los Angeles, and *Mothers and Daughters.*

Film Appearances:

(Debut) Asua, *East of Sudan,* 1963.

Ballerina, 1965.

Linda Frazier, *A Man Could Get Killed,* 1966.

Maud, *Gates of Paradise* (also known as *Vrata raja* and *Pforten des Paradieses*), 1967.

Pamela, *Star!* (also known as *Those Were Happy Times*), Twentieth Century-Fox, 1968.

Wynne, *I Start Counting,* United Artists, 1970.

Girl, *Walkabout,* Twentieth Century-Fox, 1971.

Roberta/Bobbie, *The Railway Children,* Universal, 1971.

Shelley, 1972.

Jessica, *Logan's Run,* United Artists, 1976.

Molly Prior, *The Eagle Has Landed,* Columbia, 1977.

Jill Mason, *Equus,* Warner Bros., 1977.

Anne Ballard, *Dominique* (also known as *Avenging Spirit* and *Dominique Is Dead*), 1978.

Catherine, *Clayton and Catherine* (also known as *China 9, Liberty 37, Gunfire,* and *Love, Bullets, and Frenzy*), 1978.

Clara Dollman, *The Riddle of the Sands,* 1979.

Ann Walton, *Sweet William,* 1980.

Miss Hobbs, *The Survivor,* 1980.

Amy Medford, *Amy* (also known as *Amy on the Lips*), 1981.

Nurse Alex Price, *An American Werewolf in London,* Universal, 1981.

Miss Lowrie, *Secret Places,* 1984.

Cleopatra, "Antony and Cleopatra Promo," *Amazon Women on the Moon* (also known as *Cheeseburger Film Sandwich*), 1987.

Miss Right, 1988.

Hannah Coke, *King of the Wind,* 1988.

Carolyn Page, *Dark Tower,* Spectrafilm, 1989.

Joanne Simpson, *Child's Play 2,* Universal, 1990.

Burn doctor (uncredited), *Darkman,* Universal, 1990.

Voice of Daffers, *Freddie as F.R.O.7* (also known as *Freddie the Frog;* animated), Miramax, 1992.

Guinevere/Mary Fenton, *Blue Juice,* 1995.

Television Appearances; Series:

The All New Alexei Sayle Show, BBC, 1994.

Connie Fairbrother Spencer, *And the Beat Goes On,* BBC, 1996.

Television Appearances; Miniseries:

Lizzie Corlay, *Beulah Land,* NBC, 1980.

Jill Albery, *Not a Penny More, Not a Penny Less,* USA Network, 1990.

Idina Hatton, *The Buccaneers,* PBS, 1995.

Television Appearances; Movies:

Johanna, *Long after Summer,* 1967.

The Great Inimitable Mr. Dickens, 1970.

Fritha, *The Snow Goose,* NBC, 1971.

Anya, *The Cherry Orchard,* BBC, 1971.

Maureen Tomelty, *A War of Children,* BBC, then CBS, 1972.

Kiss Me and Die, ABC, 1974.

Dominie Lanceford, *The Savage Curse,* 1974.

Melanie, *A Legacy,* BBC, 1975.

Sue, *The Waiting Room,* Thames TV, 1975.

Louise De La Valliere, *The Man in the Iron Mask,* NBC, 1977.

Poppy Jackson, *School Play,* BBC, 1979.

Pricilla Mullins, *The Mayflower, Voyage of the Pilgrims* (also known as *Mayflower: The Pilgrims' Adventure*), CBS, 1979.

Desdemona, *Othello,* 1981.

A Dream of Alice, BBC, 1982.

Rosaline, *Love's Labour's Lost,* BBC, 1984, later as part of *The Shakespeare Plays,* PBS, 1985.

Pam Fawce, *This Office Life,* BBC, 1984.

Nancy Lammeter, *Silas Marner: The Weaver of Raveloe,* PBS, 1987.

Lady Capulet, *Romeo and Juliet,* PBS, 1994.

Isobel Balmerino, *September* (also known as *Rosamunde Pilcher's "September"*), Showtime, 1996.

Television Appearances; Episodic:

Beth, "As Many As Are Here Present," *The Ten Commandments,* Yorkshire TV, 1971.

Mary Shelley, *Omnibus,* BBC, 1971.

Dr. Leah Russell, "Deadly Countdown: Part 1," *The Six Million Dollar Man,* ABC, 1974.

Dr. Leah Russell, "Deadly Countdown: Part 2," *The Six Million Dollar Man,* ABC, 1974.

Hedvig, "The Wild Duck," *Classic Theatre,* PBS, 1975.

Dr. Leah Russell, *Six Million Dollar Man,* ABC, 1977.

"Little Games," *Magnum P.I.,* CBS, 1984.

Morgan Le Fay, "The Last Defense of Camelot," *The Twilight Zone,* CBS, 1986.

"The White Rose for Death," *Murder, She Wrote,* CBS, 1986.

"Voices in the Earth," *The Twilight Zone,* CBS, 1987.

Lauren Demeter, "The Visitation," *The Equalizer,* CBS, 1989.

Kate Milverton, "Needle in a Haystack," *TECX,* 1990.

Kate Milverton, "A Soldier's Death," *TECX,* 1990.

Kate Milverton, "Rock a Buy Baby," *TECX,* 1990.

Woman who wanted to have a child with our hero, *Dream On,* HBO, 1990.

The Outsiders, Fox, 1990.

Professor Mamet, "Psirens," *Red Dwarf,* 1993.

Voice, "The Winter's Tale," *Shakespeare: The Animated Tales,* HBO, 1996.

Also appeared in *Dear John,* NBC.

Other Television Appearances:

Appeared as Grace Hubbard, *Alexander Graham Bell;* Nurse, *A House in Regent Place;* Kristy Kerr, *The Newcomers; The Two Ronnies; Boon; Love Hurts;* and *Heartbeat.*

Radio Appearances:

(Debut) *There's Love and Love,* BBC, 1973.

WRITINGS

Snap: Observations of Los Angeles and London (nonfiction), Quartet Books, 1983.

OTHER SOURCES

Periodicals:

Times, February 3, 1995, p. 14; March 12, 1996, p. 15.*

AIMEE, Anouk   1932(?)-

PERSONAL

Born Francoise Sorya Dreyfus, April 27, 1932 (some sources say 1934), in Paris, France; daughter of Henri (an actor; professional name Murray) and Genevieve Sorya (Durand) Dreyfus; married Edouard Zimmermann, 1949 (divorced); married Nico Papatakis (a director), 1951 (divorced, 1954); married Pierre Barouh, 1966 (divorced); married Albert Finney (an actor), 1970 (divorced, 1978); children: (second marriage) Manuela. *Education:* Studied dance at Marseilles Opera; studied theater in England, then at Cours Bauer-Therond.

Addresses: *Agent*—c/o Agents Associes, 201 rue du Faubourg St. Honore, F-75008 Paris, France.

Career: Actress.

Awards, Honors: Academy Award nomination, best actress, 1966, British Academy of Film and Television Arts Award, best actress, 1967, and Golden Globe Award, best actress in a drama, 1967, all for *Un Homme et une femme;* Cannes International Film Festival Award, best actress, 1980, for *Salto nel vuoto;* Studios International Circle of Achievement, 1985.

CREDITS

Film Appearances:

(Film debut) Anouk, *La Maison sous la mer,* 1946.

La Fleur de l'age, 1947.

The Golden Salamander, General Films, 1949.

Georgia Maglia, *Les Amants de Verone* (also known as *The Lovers of Verona*), Souvaine Selective, 1951.

Conquetes du froid, 1951.

Noche de tormenta, 1951.

Le Rideau cramoisi (also known as *The Crimson Curtain*), 1951.

Jeanne, *La Bergere et le ramoneur* (also known as *The Paris Express* and *The Man Who Watched Trains Go By*), Raymond Stross/George Schaefer, 1953.

Forever My Heart (also known as *Happy Birthday*), British Lion, 1954.

Elena Vargas, *Contraband Spain,* British Pathe, 1955.

Ich suche dich, 1955.

Les Mauvaises Rencontres (also known as *The Bad Liasons*), 1955.

Nina, 1956.

Stresemann, 1956.

Tous peuvent me tuer (also known as *Anyone Can Kill Me*), 1957.

Marie Pichon, *Pot bouille* (also known as *The House of Lovers*), 1957.

Stephanie, *La Tete contre les murs* (also known as *The Keepers*), 1958.

Carve Her Name with Pride, J. Arthur Rank, 1958.

Eva, *The Journey* (also known as *Some of Us May Die*), Metro-Goldwyn-Mayer, 1959.

Jeanne, *Les Dragueurs* (also known as *The Chasers* and *The Young Have No Morals*), 1959.

Helene LaRouche, *Le Farceur* (also known as *The Joker*), Lopert, 1961.

Maddalena, *La Dolce Vita,* Astor/American International, 1961.

Title role, *Donna Di Vita* (also known as *Lola*), Rome Paris/Euro International/Films-Around-the-World, 1961.

Jeanne Hebuterne, *Modigliani of Montparnasse* (also known as *Montparnasse 19* and *The Lovers of Montparnasse*), Franco-London/Astra-Pallavicina/Continental Distributing, 1961.

L'imprevisto, 1961.

Quai Notre Dame, 1961.

Il guidizio universale (also known as *The Last Judgment*), 1961.

Queen Bera, *Sodome et Gomorrhe* (also known as *Sodom and Gomorrah, Sodom e Gomorra,* and *The Last Days of Sodom and Gomorrah*), Titanus/Pathe Cinema/ S.G.C./Twentieth Century-Fox, 1962.

Luisa Anselmi, *Otto e mezzo* (also known as *8 1/2* and *Fellini's 8 1/2*), Embassy, 1963.

Mita Palumbo, *Liola* (also known as *A Very Handy Man*), Federiz-Francinex-Cinecitta/Rizzoli, 1963.

Il giorno piu corto (also known as *The Shortest Day*), 1963.

Il terroista, 1963.

Il successo, 1963.

Anna, *Les Grands Chemins* (also known as *Of Flesh and Blood* and *Il Baro*), Copernic-Saphrene-Dear/Times, 1964.

Lorenza, *Le Sexe des Anges* (also known as *Le voci bianche, I castrati, Undercover Rouge,* and *White Voices*), Franca-Federiz-Francoriz/Rizzoli, 1965.

Il morbidone, 1965.

Luisa, *La Fuga,* Cine 3/International Classics (Fox), 1966.

Anne Gauthier, *Un Homme et une femme* (also known as *A Man and a Woman*), Les Films 13/Allied Artists, 1966.

Mita, *La stagione del nostro amore* (also known as *A Very Handy Man*), Federiz-Francinex-Cinecitta/Rizzoli, 1966.

Lo scandalo, 1966.

Anne, *Un Soir, un train* (also known as *One Night . . . a Train*), Parc-Fox Europa Films du Siecle/Twentieth Century-Fox, 1968.

Carla, *The Appointment,* Metro-Goldwyn-Mayer, 1969.

Title role, *Justine,* Twentieth Century-Fox, 1969.

Lola, *The Model Shop,* Columbia, 1969.

Sarah, *Si c'etait a refaire* (also known as *Second Chance* and *If It Were To Do Over Again*), United Artists, 1976.

Jane (Mother), *Mon Premier Amour* (also known as *My First Love*), 7 Films/Gaumont, 1978.

Marta Ponticelli, *Salto nel vuoto* (also known as *A Leap in the Dark* and *Leap Into the Void*), Summit, 1982.

Barbara, *Tragedia di un uomo ridiculo* (also known as *The Tragedy of a Ridiculous Man*), Warner Bros., 1982.

Helene, *Qu-est-ce qui fait courir David?* (also known as *What Makes David Run?*), Columbia/EMI Warners/MK2-Diffusion, 1982.

Countess Betsy, *Le General de l'Armee Morte* (also known as *The General of the Dead Army*), WMF/Union Generale Cinematographique, 1983.

Monique de Fontaine, *Success Is the Best Revenge,* Gaumont, 1984.

Viva la Vie! (also known as *Long Live Life*), Union Generale Cinematographique, 1984.

Flagrant Desire, Hemdale, 1985.

Anne Gauthier, *Un Homme et une femme: Vingt ans deja* (also known as *A Man and a Woman: 20 Years Later*), Films 13/Warner Bros., 1986.

Arrivederci e Grazie (also known as *Goodbye and Thank You*), Medusa Distribuzione, 1988.

La Table tournante, 1989.

Il y a des jours . . . et des lunes (also known as *There Were Days and Moons*), JP2 Audiousvel/AFMD-Roissy, 1990.

Marie-France Coudaire, *Bethune—The Making of a Hero,* 1990.

Francoise, *Les Marmottes* (also known as *The Groundhogs*), 1993.

Simone Lowenthal, *Ready to Wear* (also known as *Pret-a-Porter*), Miramax, 1994.

Actor for a Day, *Les cent et une nuits* (also known as *A Hundred and One Nights*), Mecure Distribution, 1995.

Dis-Moi Oui (also known as *Say Yes*), Lumiere Pictures, 1995.

Herself, *L'Univers de Jacques Demy* (also known as *The Universe of Jacques Demy;* documentary), [France], 1995.

Hommes, femmes: mode d'emploi (also known as *Men, Women: A User's Manual*), UFD, 1996.

Les Menteurs (also known as *The Liars*), Lumiere Pictures, 1996.

Television Appearances:

Une Page d'amour (movie), 1979.

Haute Couture: The Great Designers (special), PBS, 1987.
Des voix dans le jardin (also known as *Voices in the Garden*), 1991.

Stage Appearances:
Sud, 1954.*

ALBERT, Eddie 1908-

PERSONAL

Born Edward Albert Heimberger, April 22, 1908, in Rock Island, IL; son of Frank Daniel (a realtor) and Julia (Jones) Heimberger; married Maria Margarita Guadalupe Teresa Estella Bolado Castilla y O'Donnell (an actress and singer; professional name, Margo Albert), December 5, 1945 (deceased, 1985); children: Edward (an actor), Maria. *Education:* Attended the University of Minnesota, 1927-29. *Avocational interests:* Organic gardening, reading philosophical works, playing the guitar, beachcombing, designing and making movies and glass paintings.

Addresses: *Contact*—Agency for the Performing Arts, 9000 Sunset Blvd., Suite 1200, Los Angeles, CA 90069. *Agent*—Gold/Marshak/Liedtke Talent & Literary Agency, 3500 West Olive Ave., Suite 1400, Burbank, CA 91505.

Career: Actor, singer, and producer. Founder, Eddie Albert Productions (a production company specializing in educational films), 1945; appeared in a nightclub act with wife, Margo Albert, 1954; also singer with the Threesome, performing on radio and on stage throughout the United States; theater manager in Minneapolis, MN; lecturer on ecology, 1969-70; performed concerts at Plaza de la Raza. Special World Envoy, Meals for Millions, 1963; consultant, United Nations Food Conference, Rome, Italy, 1974, and to the governor of Pennsylvania; also chairperson, Eddie Albert World Trees Foundation; trustee, National Arbor Day Foundation; national conservation chairperson, Boy Scouts of America; trustee, Alaska Pacific University, Anchorage, AK; director, U.S. Committee on Refugees; member of board of directors, Film Council; trustee, National Recreation and Parks Association; board of directors, solar lobby; and member of consumer advisory board, U.S. Department of Energy. Speaker at U.S. Navy's 222nd Anniversary ceremonies, Washington, DC, 1997. *Military service:* U.S. Navy, lieutenant, served during World War II.

Awards, Honors: Academy Award nomination, best supporting actor, 1955, for *Roman Holiday;* Academy Award nomination, best supporting actor, and National Film Critics' Award, both 1972, for *The Heartbreak Kid;* Golden Globe Award nomination, best supporting actor, 1975, for *The Longest Yard;* Southern Illinois University, honorary D.F.A., 1982; Presidential World Without Hunger Award, 1984.

Member: Actors' Equity Association, Screen Actors Guild, American Federation of Television and Radio Artists, National Recreation and Parks Association (board of trustees), Bohemian Club (San Francisco).

CREDITS

Film Appearances:
(Debut) Bing Edwards, *Brother Rat,* Warner Bros., 1938.
Dr. Clinton Forrest, Jr., *Four Wives,* Warner Bros., 1939.
Phil Dolan, Jr., *On Your Toes,* Warner Bros., 1939.
Peter Coleman, *An Angel from Texas,* Warner Bros., 1940.
Bing Edwards, *Brother Rat and a Baby* (also known as *Baby Be Good*), Warner Bros., 1940.
Max Stargardt, *A Dispatch from Reuters* (also known as *This Man Reuter*), Warner Bros., 1940.
Dusty Rhodes, *My Love Came Back,* Warner Bros., 1940.
Clint Forrest, *Four Mothers,* Warner Bros., 1941.
Dreamy, *The Great Mr. Nobody,* Warner Bros., 1941.
George Watkins, *Out of the Fog,* Warner Bros., 1941.
Eddie Barnes, *Thieves Fall Out,* Warner Bros., 1941.
Matt Varney, *The Wagons Roll at Night,* Warner Bros., 1941.
Leckie, *Eagle Squadron,* Universal, 1942.
Terry Moore, *Lady Bodyguard,* Paramount, 1942.
Bill "Panama Kid" Kingsford, *Treat 'em Rough,* Universal, 1942.
Tom Hughes, *Bombardier,* RKO, 1943.
Wacky Walters, *Ladies' Day,* RKO, 1943.
Chris Thomson, *Strange Voyage,* Signal, 1945.
Gil Cummins, *The Perfect Marriage,* Paramount, 1946.
Rendezvous with Annie, Republic, 1946.
Kip Walker, *Hit Parade of 1947,* Republic, 1947.
Steve Nelson, *Smash-Up: The Story of a Woman* (also known as *A Woman Destroyed* and *Smash-Up*), Universal, 1947.
Jake Bullard, *Time Out of Mind,* Universal, 1947.
Mermaid barker (uncredited), *Unconquered,* 1947.
Daniel Bone, *The Dude Goes West,* Allied Artists, 1948.

Bullets Booker, *You Gotta Stay Happy,* Universal, 1948.

Harry Proctor/Old Joe, *Every Girl Should Be Married,* 1948.

Humphrey Briggs, *The Fuller Brush Girl* (also known as *The Affairs of Sally*), Columbia, 1950.

Christopher Leeds, *Meet Me After the Show,* Twentieth Century-Fox, 1951.

Lieutenant Bill Barron, *You're in the Navy Now* (also known as *U.S.S. Tea Kettle*), Twentieth Century-Fox, 1951.

Orlando Higgins, "Woman of Sin" in *Actors and Sin,* United Artists, 1952.

Charles Drouet, *Carrie,* Paramount, 1952.

Irving Radovich, *Roman Holiday,* Paramount, 1953.

Eliot Atterbury, *The Girl Rush,* Paramount, 1955.

Burt McGuire, *I'll Cry Tomorrow,* Metro-Goldwyn-Mayer, 1955.

Ali Hakim, *Oklahoma!,* Magna Theatres, 1955.

Captain Erskine Cooney, *Attack!,* United Artists, 1956.

Captain McLean, *The Teahouse of the August Moon,* Metro-Goldwyn-Mayer, 1956.

Austin Mack, *The Joker Is Wild* (also known as *All the Way*), Paramount, 1957.

Bill Gorton, *The Sun Also Rises,* Twentieth Century-Fox, 1957.

Hanagan, *The Gun Runners,* United Artists, 1958.

Major MacMahon, *Orders to Kill,* United Motion Picture, 1958.

Abe Fields, *The Roots of Heaven,* Twentieth Century-Fox, 1958.

Carter, *Beloved Infidel,* Twentieth Century-Fox, 1959.

Harry Davis, *The Two Little Bears,* Twentieth Century-Fox, 1961.

Dr. Charles Dornberger, *The Young Doctors,* United Artists, 1961.

Colonel Tom Newton, *The Longest Day,* Twentieth Century-Fox, 1962.

Harvey Ames, *Madison Avenue,* Twentieth Century-Fox, 1962.

Clint Morgan, *Who's Got the Action?,* Paramount, 1962.

Colonel Norval Algate Bliss, *Captain Newman, M.D.,* Universal, 1963.

Rider Otto, *Miracle of the White Stallions* (also known as *The Flight of the White Stallions*), Buena Vista, 1963.

Ben, *The Party's Over,* Allied Artists, 1966.

Charles Pether, *Seven Women* (also known as *Women*), Metro-Goldwyn-Mayer, 1966.

Mr. Corcoran, *The Heartbreak Kid,* Twentieth Century-Fox, 1972.

Warden Hazen, *The Longest Yard,* Paramount, 1974.

Captain Ed Kosterman, *McQ,* Warner Bros., 1974.

Chief Berrigan, *The Take,* Columbia, 1974.

Dr. Samuel Richards, *The Devil's Rain,* Bryanston, 1975.

Jason O'Day, *Escape to Witch Mountain,* Buena Vista, 1975.

Leo Sellars, *Hustle,* Paramount, 1975.

Colonel Lockyer, *Whiffs* (also known as *W.H.I.F.S.* and *C.A.S.H.*), Twentieth Century-Fox, 1975.

Pa Strawacher, *Birch Interval,* Gamma III, 1976.

Alex Warren, *Moving Violation,* Twentieth Century-Fox, 1976.

Eli Sande, *The Concorde—Airport'79* (also known as *Airport '79, The Concorde Affair,* and *Airport '80: The Concorde*), Universal, 1979.

Moffat, *The Border* (also known as *Border Cop* and *The Blood Barrier*), 1979.

Daggett, *Foolin' Around,* Columbia, 1980.

Max, *How to Beat the High Cost of Living,* American International, 1980.

Bert Kramer, *Yesterday,* Cinepix, 1980.

Samuel Ellison, *Take This Job and Shove It,* Avco-Embassy, 1981.

This Time Forever (also known as *The Victory*), 1981.

Henry Pollack, *Yes, Giorgio,* Metro-Goldwyn-Mayer/United Artists, 1982.

Harry, *The Act* (also known as *Bless 'em All*), Film Ventures, 1984.

The President, *Dreamscape,* Twentieth Century-Fox, 1984.

Dean Bradley, *Stitches,* International Film Marketing, 1985.

Helmes, *Head Office,* TriStar, 1986.

Turnaround, Rose Productions/A-S-Major, 1987.

Captain Danny Jackson, *Terminal Entry,* United Film, 1988.

Police Chief Maloney, *Brenda Starr,* New World, 1989.

Emcee, *The Big Picture,* Columbia, 1989.

Headless!, [USA], 1994.

Illusion Infinity, 1997.

Film Work; Song Performer:
"Green Acres Theme," *Son-in-Law,* Buena Vista, 1993.

Television Appearances; Series:
Larry Tucker, *Leave It to Larry,* CBS, 1952.

Host, *Nothing But the Best,* ABC, 1953.

Host, *The Eddie Albert Show,* CBS, 1953.

Host, *Saturday Night Revue,* NBC, 1954.

Host, *On Your Account,* CBS, 1954-56.

Oliver Wendell Douglas, *Green Acres,* CBS, 1965-71.

Frank McBride, *Switch,* CBS, 1975-78.
Carlton Travis, *Falcon Crest,* CBS, 1987.
Uncle Bill Scofield, *Okavango,* 1992-93.

Also appeared on *General Hospital,* ABC.

Television Appearances; Miniseries:
Ogden Towery, *The Word,* CBS, 1978.
Brian Murphy, *Evening in Byzantium,* syndicated, 1978.
Felix Kendrick, *Beulah Land,* NBC, 1980.
Festus, *Peter and Paul,* CBS, 1981.
Admiral Wiley Sloan, *Goliath Awaits,* syndicated, 1981.
Breckinridge Long, *War and Remembrance,* ABC, 1988.

Television Appearances; Pilots:
Oliver Douglas, *Carol,* CBS, 1967.
Howdy, ABC, 1970.
Bob Randall, *Daddy's Girl,* CBS, 1973.
Frank McBride, *Switch* (also known as *Las Vegas Roundabout*), CBS, 1975.
Carroll Yeager, *Trouble in High Timber Country* (also known as *The Yeagers*), ABC, 1980.
Vincent Slattery, *Living in Paradise,* NBC, 1981.
Jason O'Day, *Beyond Witch Mountain,* CBS, 1982.

Television Work; Pilots:
Theme performer, "That's the Way I Am," *Living in Paradise,* NBC, 1981.

Television Appearances; Movies:
The Lieutenant, NBC, 1963.
Dr. Thomas Spencer, *See the Man Run,* ABC, 1971.
Colonel Douglas Graham, *Fireball Forward,* ABC, 1972.
Pop, *Promise Him Anything,* ABC, 1975.
Captain Dunn, *Crash* (also known as *The Crash of Flight 401*), ABC, 1978.
Coach Homer Sixx, *The Oklahoma City Dolls,* ABC, 1981.
Reverend Harlan Barnum, *Rooster,* ABC, 1982.
Father Dietrich, *The Demon Murder Case* (also known as *The Rhode Island Murders*), NBC, 1983.
Will Larson, *Burning Rage,* CBS, 1984.
Judge Hand, *Dress Gray,* NBC, 1984.
Bill White, *In Like Flynn,* ABC, 1985.
Joe Varon, *Mercy or Murder?,* NBC, 1987.
Nutcracker: Money, Madness, Murder, NBC, 1987.
Oliver Douglas, *Return to Green Acres,* 1990.
Charles, *The Girl from Mars,* 1991.
Ernest Gower, *The Barefoot Executive,* ABC, 1995.

Television Appearances; Episodic:
"Revenge," *Kraft Suspense Theatre,* NBC, 1949.
Teller of Tales (also known as *The Somerset Maugham TV Theatre*), CBS, 1950.
"Mutiny Below," *Kraft Suspense Theatre,* NBC, 1953.
"The Little Wife," *Revlon Mirror Theatre,* NBC, 1953.
"Outlaw's Reckoning," *The Motorola TV Hour,* CBS, 1953.
"Journey to Nowhere," *Philip Morris Playhouse,* CBS, 1953.
"Tin Wedding," *U.S. Steel Hour,* CBS, 1953.
"Stage to Tucson," *Zane Grey Theatre* (also known as *Dick Powell's Zane Grey Theatre*) CBS, 1956.
"A Fugitive," *Zane Grey Theatre* (also known as *Dick Powell's Zane Grey Theatre*) CBS, 1956.
"A Gun for My Bride," *Zane Grey Theatre* (also known as *Dick Powell's Zane Grey Theatre*) CBS, 1956.
"The Vaunted," *Zane Grey Theatre* (also known as *Dick Powell's Zane Grey Theatre*) CBS, 1956.
The David Niven Theatre, NBC, 1959.
"Apple of His Eye," *U.S. Steel Hour,* CBS, 1959.
"Famous," *U.S. Steel Hour,* CBS, 1961.
"A Break in the Weather," *U.S. Steel Hour,* CBS, 1962.
Phil, "Doughboy," *Combat!,* ABC, 1963.
Land of the Giants, ABC, 1964.
Andy Thorne, "Cry of Silence," *The Outer Limits,* ABC, 1964.
Dr. Fred Wilson, "Eleven Days to Zero," *Voyage to the Bottom of the Sea,* 1964.
"The Golden Ocean," *The Rogues,* NBC, 1965.
Hippodrome, CBS, 1966.
Major General Martin J. Hollister, "Dead Weight," *Columbo,* NBC, 1971.
Dr. George Baxter, "Blood of the Dragon," *Kung Fu,* ABC, 1974.
Turandot, PBS, 1982.
Mack Erickson, *Hotel,* ABC, 1985.
Sen. Corky McCorkindale, "Jonathan Smith Goes to Washington," *Highway to Heaven,* NBC, 1986.
Jackson Lane, "The Body Politic," *Murder, She Wrote,* CBS, 1988.
Roger Simpson Leads, "Dream Me a Life," *The Twilight Zone,* CBS, 1988.
Charlie Weston, *thirtysomething,* ABC, 1989.
Jonathan Hughes, "A Touch of Petulance," *The Ray Bradbury Theatre,* HBO and USA Network, 1990.
Noah, "Treasure of the Ages," *Time Trax,* syndicated, 1993.
Himself, "One Flu over the Cuckoo's Nest," *The Jackie Thomas Show,* ABC, 1993.
Adrian Toomes/The Vulture, "Shriek of the Vulture," *Spider-Man,* Fox, 1996.

Also appeared in episodes of "1984," *Studio One,* CBS; *Your Show of Shows,* NBC; *Alcoa Premiere,* ABC; *Playhouse 90,* CBS; *Schlitz Playhouse of Stars,* CBS; *Chrysler Medallion Theatre,* CBS; *Ford Theatre Hour,* NBC; *Front Row Center,* CBS; *Lights Out,* NBC; *The Loretta Young Theatre,* NBC; *The Alcoa Hour,* NBC; *Chevrolet Tele-Theatre,* NBC; *Dupont Show of the Week,* NBC; *Goodyear Television Playhouse,* NBC; *The Virginian,* NBC; *Wagon Train,* NBC; *Sam Benedict,* NBC; *Wide Country,* NBC; *The Naked City,* ABC; *Dr. Kildare,* NBC; *The Love Boat,* ABC; *The Fall Guy,* ABC; *Golden Palace,* CBS; and *Dr. Quinn, Medicine Woman,* CBS.

Television Appearances; Specials:
Bumerli, *The Chocolate Soldier,* NBC, 1955.
Martin Barret, *A Connecticut Yankee,* NBC, 1955.
Dr. Jack Davidson, *Johnny Belinda,* CBS, 1955.
Host, *The Night of Christmas,* NBC, 1959.
Paul Hughes, *The Ballad of Louie the Louse,* CBS, 1959.
Hollywood Sings, NBC, 1960.
Albert Warren, "The Spiral Staircase," *Theatre '62,* NBC, 1961.
Cameo, *Li'l Abner,* NBC, 1971.
Narrator, *Dr. Seuss' "The Lorax,"* CBS, 1972.
Pod Clock, "The Borrowers," *Hallmark Hall of Fame,* NBC, 1973.
Title role, *The Lives of Ben Franklin: The Ambassador,* CBS, 1974.
Host, *Siegfried and Roy,* NBC, 1980.
Guest, *Parade of Stars,* ABC, 1983.
Sylvia Fine Kaye's Musical Comedy Tonight III: The Spark and the Glue, PBS, 1985.
Bill Watson, "Daddy Can't Read," *ABC Afterschool Specials,* ABC, 1988.
Christmas with the Stars: An International Earthquake Benefit, 1989.
The Legend of the Beverly Hillbillies, CBS, 1993.
Host, *A Norman Rockwell Christmas,* Discovery Channel, 1994.
Himself, *Art Linkletter on Positive Aging: Alternative Living, Senior Rip-Offs, and Grandparenting,* PBS, 1994.
Interviewee, *Victory in the Pacific,* CBS, 1995.
Voice, *Extreme Ghostbusters,* 1997.

Stage Appearances:
(Broadway debut) *O, Evening Star!,* Empire Theatre, 1936.
Bing Edwards, *Brother Rat,* Biltmore Theatre, New York City, 1936.
Leo Davis, *Room Service,* Cort Theatre, New York City, 1937.

Antipholus, *The Boys from Syracuse,* Alvin Theatre, New York City, 1938.
Horace Miller, *Miss Liberty,* Imperial Theatre, New York City, 1949.
Title role, *Reuben, Reuben,* Shubert Theatre, Boston, MA, 1955.
Jack Jordan, *Say, Darling,* American National Theatre and Academy Theatre, New York City, 1958.
Harold Hill, *The Music Man,* Majestic Theatre, New York City, 1960.
George Bartlett, *No Hard Feelings,* Martin Beck Theatre, New York City, 1973.
Martin Vanderhof, *You Can't Take It with You,* Plymouth Theatre, New York City, 1983.
The Stagehand, *Parade of Stars Playing the Palace,* Palace Theatre, New York City, 1983.

Also appeared in *Seven Year Itch* and *Our Town.* Appeared with Circus Moderno in Mexico, 1941, and with the Hagenbeck Circus in Europe, 1965. Performed with the San Francisco Opera, 1982.

Radio Appearances; Series:
Eddie, *The Honeymooners—Grace and Eddie,* NBC, 1935.

RECORDINGS

Videos:
Voice, *Mouse on the Mayflower,* Family Home Entertainment, 1993.*

ALBERT, Edward 1951-
(Edward Albert Jr.)

PERSONAL

Full name, Edward Laurence Albert; born February 20, 1951, in Los Angeles, CA; son of Eddie (an actor) and Margo (an actress, singer, and dancer; full name, Maria Margarita Guadalupe Bolado Castilla y O'Donnell) Albert; married Kate Woodville, 1978; children: Thais Carmen Woodville. *Education:* Attended University of California at Los Angeles, and Oxford University; studied acting in Stratford-upon-Avon, England. *Avocational interests:* Ranching and raising horses, raising organic fruits and vegetables.

Addresses: *Agent*—Henderson/Hogan Agency, 850 Seventh Ave., Suite 1003, New York, NY 10019.

Career: Actor. Performed with his father on radio. Pop musician and composer; photographer and freelance writer, with photography exhibits in Los Angeles.

Awards, Honors: Golden Globe Award nomintion, best actor in a musical or comedy, Hollywood Foreign Press Association, 1973, for *Butterflies Are Free;* Nosostros Golden Eagle Award for Highest Career Achievement.

CREDITS

Film Appearances:

George Mellish, *The Fool Killer* (also known as *Violent Journey*), Allied Artists, 1965.

Don Baker, *Butterflies Are Free,* Columbia, 1972.

Peter Latham, *Forty Carats,* Columbia, 1973.

Lieutenant Tom Garth, *Midway* (also known as *The Battle of Midway*), Universal, 1976.

Jerry, *Un Taxi Mauve* (also known as *The Purple Taxi*), Parafrance, 1977.

Ross Pine, *The Domino Principle* (also known as *The Domino Killings*), Avco-Embassy, 1977.

Nico Tomasis, *The Greek Tycoon,* Universal, 1978.

Michael Rogan, *A Time to Die* (also known as *Seven Graves for Rogan*), Almi, 1979.

Jeff, *The Squeeze* (also known as *Diamond Thieves, The Heist,* and *The Rip-Off*), Maverick, 1980.

Brian, *When Time Ran Out* (also known as *Earth's Final Fury*), Warner Bros., 1980.

Cabren, *Galaxy of Terror* (also known as *Mindwarp, An Infinity of Terror,* and *Planet of Horrors*), New World, 1981.

Wash Gillespie, *Butterfly,* Analysis, 1982.

Ted, *The House Where Evil Dwells,* Metro-Goldwyn-Mayer/United Artists, 1982.

Tom, *Ellie,* Film Ventures, 1984.

"Tag" Taggar, *Getting Even* (also known as *Hostage: Dallas*), American Distribution Group, 1986.

Captain Danny Jackson, *Terminal Entry,* Celebrity Home Entertainment, 1986.

Danny Warren, *The Underachievers,* Lightning, 1988.

Commander Merrill, *The Rescue,* Buena Vista, 1988.

Jason Marks, *Distortions,* Cori/Academy Entertainment, 1988.

Eddie Powers, *Accidents,* Trans-World Entertainment, 1988.

A Puno Limpio, 1988.

Dana Lund, *Mind Games,* Metro-Goldwyn-Mayer/United Artists, 1989.

Harry "Punchy" Moses, *Fist Fighter,* LIVE Home Video, 1989.

Colonel Lavara, *Wild Zone,* Columbia TriStar Home Video, 1990.

Filipe Soto, *Exiled in America,* Prism Entertainment, 1992.

Broken Trust, Monarch Home Video, 1993.

Mr. C, *Shootfighter: Fight to the Death,* Columbia TriStar Home Video, 1993.

Jeffrey West, *The Ice Runner,* Borde Releasing, 1993.

(As Edward Albert, Jr.) Chief of examiners, *Hard Drive,* Triboro Entertainment Group, 1994.

(As Edward Albert, Jr.) Barry Carlisle, *Guarding Tess,* TriStar, 1994.

(As Edward Albert, Jr.) Remy Grilland, *Demon Keeper,* New Horizons Home Video, 1994.

Richard, *Sexual Malice,* A-Pix Entertainment, 1994.

Howard, *Sorceress* (also known as *Temptress II*), Triboro Entertainment Group, 1994.

Max Maxwell, *The Secret Agent Club,* Cabin Fever Entertainment, 1996.

Frank, *Kid Cop,* Image Organization/Brainstorm Media, 1996.

Film Work:

Production assistant, *Patton,* Twentieth Century-Fox, 1970.

Executive producer, *Strictly Ballroom,* Miramax, 1993.

Television Appearances; Series:

Quisto Champion, *The Yellow Rose,* NBC, 1983-84.

Jeff Wainwright, *Falcon Crest,* CBS, 1986.

Arthur DeRhodes, *Profiler* (also known as *Insight*), NBC, 1996.

Taylor Griffin, *Walker, Texas Ranger,* CBS, 1996.

Dr. Bennett Devlin, *Port Charles,* ABC, 1997—.

Television Appearances; Miniseries:

The Legend of the Black Hand, ABC, 1978.

Ron "Dal" Dalrymple, *The Last Convertible,* NBC, 1979.

Television Appearances; Movies:

Edward Van Bohlen, *Killer Bees,* ABC, 1974.

James Radney, *Death Cruise,* ABC, 1974.

Lewis Barry, *Black Beauty,* NBC, 1978.

Captain Dunn, *Crash* (also known as *Crash of Flight 401* and *Crash, the True Story of Flight 401*), ABC, 1978.

Tom Buchanan, *Silent Victory: The Kitty O'Neil Story,* CBS, 1979.

Phil Wharton, *Blood Feud,* syndicated, 1983.

Kurt Williams, *Sight Unseen* (also known as *Out of Sight, Out of Mind* and *Out of Sight, Out of Her Mind*), syndicated, 1991.

Dan, *The Girl from Mars,* The Family Channel, 1991.

Charles Stella, *Body Language,* USA Network, 1992.

Federal agent, *Red Sun Rising,* HBO, 1994.
Captain Gray, *Space Marines,* Showtime, 1996.

Television Appearances; Episodic:
"A Terribly Strange Bed," *Orson Welles' Great Mysteries,* syndicated, 1973.
"Blood of the Dragon," *Kung Fu,* ABC, 1974.
"Nightmare," *The Rookies,* ABC, 1975.
"A Life in the Balance," *Medical Story,* NBC, 1975.
"The Test of Brotherhood," *Police Story,* NBC, 1976.
"The Adventure of Caesar's Last Sleep," *Ellery Queen,* NBC, 1976.
"Afternoon Waltz," *Gibbsville,* NBC, 1976.
"The Little People," *The Love Boat,* ABC, 1978.
"Kidnapped," *Walking Tall,* NBC, 1981.
"Bank Job," *Today's FBI,* ABC, 1982.
"Hit, Run, and Homicide," *Murder, She Wrote,* CBS, 1984.
"Man at the Window," *The Hitchhiker,* HBO, 1985.
Fame, Fortune, and Romance, ABC, 1986.
Oliver Alden, "Deadly Connection," *The New Mike Hammer,* CBS, 1987.
Lester Farnum, "North of the Border," *Houston Knights,* CBS, 1987.
Brothers, Showtime, 1987.
Elliot Burch, "Siege," *Beauty and the Beast,* CBS, 1987.
Elliot Burch, "Shades of Grey," *Beauty and the Beast,* CBS, 1988.
Elliot Burch, "Ozymadias," *Beauty and the Beast,* CBS, 1988.
"Legacy," *In the Heat of the Night,* CBS, 1993.
Zayra, "A Man Alone," *Star Trek: Deep Space Nine,* syndicated, 1993.
Dr. William Burke, "Where the Heart Is," *Dr. Quinn, Medicine Woman,* CBS, 1994.
Voice of Matt Murdock/Daredevil, "Framed," *Spider-Man* (animated), syndicated, 1996.
Dan Singleton, "Vanishing Act," *The Sentinel,* UPN, 1997.

Other Television Appearances:
Paul Matthews, *The Millionaire* (pilot; also known as *The New Millionaire*), CBS, 1978.
Battle of the Network Stars XV (special), ABC, 1983.
"Daddy Can't Read," *ABC Afterschool Special,* ABC, 1988.

Host of the programs *Viva, Different Point of View,* and *On Call.*

Stage Appearances:
Mr. McGee, *Very Warm for May,* Carnegie Hall/Weill Hall, New York City, 1994.

Made London debut as Don, *Terribly Strange Bed;* appeared as Fortinbras, *Hamlet,* Mark Taper Forum, Los Angeles; and as Jim O'Connor, *The Glass Menagerie,* Manhattan Theater Club, New York City; also appeared in *Our Town* and *Room Service.**

ALBERT, Edward, Jr.
    See ALBERT, Edward

ALDA, Rutanya   1942-
    (Ruth Alda)

PERSONAL

Born Rutanya Skrastins, October 13, 1942, in Riga, Latvia; daughter of Janis (a poet) and Vera (a businesswoman; maiden name, Ozolins) Skrastins; married Richard Bright (an actor), June 11, 1977. *Education:* University of Northern Arizona, B.S.; studied acting with Barbara Loden and Paul Mann in New York City.

Addresses: *Agent*—Greene & Associates, 8899 Beverly, Suite 705, Los Angeles, CA.

Career: Actress.

Member: Actors' Equity Association, Screen Actors Guild, American Federation of Radio and Television Artists.

CREDITS

Television Appearances; Movies:
Rachel, *Can Ellen Be Saved?,* ABC, 1975.
Jess, *Battered,* NBC, 1978.
Mrs. Linderman, *The Day the Kids Took Over,* 1986.
Dr. Kroyden, *Laguna Heat,* HBO, 1987.
Mrs. Paretti, *Winnie* (also known as *Winnie: My Life in the Institution*), NBC, 1988.
Marge Crawford, *Rainbow Drive* (also known as *City of Angels*), Showtime, 1990.
Sue Madelhurst, *They* (also known as *They Watched*), Showtime, 1993.
Minnie Sayre, *Zelda,* TNT, 1993.
Gabriel Neuland, *Double Jeopardy,* CBS, 1996.
Maureen, *Childhood Sweetheart?,* CBS, 1997.

Also appeared in *Nobody Ever Died of Old Age,* PBS.

Television Appearances; Miniseries:
Lorraine Taylor, *Innocent Victims,* ABC, 1996.
Beth, *Seduced by Madness: The Diane Borchardt Story* (also known as *Murderous Passion: The Diane Borchardt Story*), NBC, 1996.

Television Appearances; Episodic:
Mrs. Cheney, *Law & Order,* NBC, 1994.
Clara Munday, *Gun,* ABC, 1996.
Mrs. Harridan, *JAG,* CBS, 1996.

Also appeared on *Doc Elliot,* ABC; Mrs. Degnan, *Cannon,* CBS; *As the World Turns,* CBS; and *General Hospital,* ABC.

Film Appearances:
(Debut; as Ruth Alda) Linda, *Greetings,* Sigma III, 1969.
(As Ruth Alda) *Hi Mom,* Sigma III, 1970.
Nurse Anne, *Panic in Needle Park,* Twentieth Century-Fox, 1971.
Hippie, *Scarecrow,* Warner Bros., 1973.
Rutanya Sweet, *The Long Goodbye,* 1973.
Assassination Team B, *Executive Action,* National General, 1973.
Ruthie Lee, *Pat Garrett and Billy the Kid,* Metro-Goldwyn-Mayer, 1973.
Apple Mary, *Deadly Hero,* Avco-Embassy, 1976.
Kristen, *The Fury,* Twentieth Century-Fox, 1978.
Angela, *The Deer Hunter,* Universal, 1978.
Mrs. Mandrakis, *When a Stranger Calls,* Columbia, 1979.
Carol Ann, *Mommie Dearest,* Paramount, 1981.
Dolores, *Amityville II: The Possession,* Orion, 1982.
Vicki, *Vigilante,* Films Around the World, 1982.
Mrs. Nash, *Racing with the Moon,* Paramount, 1983.
Girls' Nite Out, Aries International, 1984.
Cecilia, *Rappin',* Cannon Films, 1985.
Georgia Kristidis, *Hot Shot,* Twentieth Century-Fox, 1986.
Irene, *Black Widow,* Twentieth Century-Fox, 1986.
Alma, *The Long Lost Friend,* 1986.
Mrs. Vandemeeer, *Defense Play,* 1988.
Irene, *Black Widow,* Twentieth-Century Fox, 1987.
Elma Kelly, *Apprentice to Murder,* New World, 1988.
Aunt Sarah, *Prancer,* Orion, 1989.
Mama Slovak, *Gross Anatomy,* Buena Vista, 1989.
Georgette's Mother, *Last Exit to Brooklyn,* 1989.
Palmer Hospital Nurse, *Leaving Normal,* Universal, 1992.
Ann Travis, *Article 99,* Orion, 1992.
Miriam Cowley, *The Dark Half,* Orion, 1993.
Linda, *The Ref* (also known as *Hostile Hostages*), Buena Vista, 1994.
Safe Passage, 1994.

Also appeared in *The Nap* (short).

Stage Appearances:
(Debut) Ellen, *Sunday in New York,* Yarmouth Playhouse, Cape Cod, MA, 1965.
Teresa, *Every Place Is Newark,* Theatre at St. Clements, New York City, 1980.

Also appeared as Julia, *A Thing Called Child* and Sister Johanna, *The Cradle Song,* both at the Berkshire Playhouse, MA; Ellen, *Luv,* Cellar Theatre, Los Angeles; the Actress, *The Exercise,* Actors Studio, Los Angeles; Falidia, *And They Put Handcuffs on the Flowers,* Inner City Cultural Center, Los Angeles; Jennifer, *Middle Class White,* Los Angeles Actors Theatre; Esther, *A Cat in the Ghetto,* Whole Theatre Company, Montclair, NJ; Miss Gilpin, *The Straw,* Barbara Loden Workshop, New York City; Ern, *Sacraments,* Harold Clurman Theatre, New York City.

Stage Work:
Also director of *And They Put Handcuffs on the Flowers,* Inner City Cultural Center, Los Angeles.

SIDELIGHTS

Rutanya Alda earlier told *CTFT:* "Growing up in displaced persons camps after World War II, I saw my first play, a fairy tale, done in the camps. It showed a better life than I was living in, it was magical and I said to myself then and there, that's what I want to do. . . . My favorite role is the one I'm currently working on, whatever it may be. But there are some that stand out—Angela in *The Deer Hunter,* Linda in *Greetings,* the 'be black baby sequence' in *Hi Mom,* Carol Ann in *Mommie Dearest,* and Alma in *The Long Lost Friend.*"*

ALDA, Ruth
   See ALDA, Rutanya

ALEXANDER, Jane   1939-

PERSONAL

Born Jane Quigley, October 28, 1939, in Boston, MA; daughter of Thomas Bartlett (a doctor) and Ruth Elizabeth (Pearson) Quigley; married Robert Alexander (an actor and director), July 23, 1962 (divorced, 1969); married Edwin Sherin (a director), March 29,

1975; children: (first marriage) Jason, Jane. *Education:* Attended Sarah Lawrence College, 1957-58; attended University of Edinburgh, 1959-60.

Addresses: *Agent*—William Morris Agency, 1350 Avenue of the Americas, New York, NY 10019.

Career: Actress, producer, and writer. Member, Charles Playhouse Boston, 1964-65; member, Arena Stage acting company, Washington, DC, 1965-68; associated with the American Shakespeare Festival; appointed chairperson of the National Endowment of the Arts, 1993.

Awards, Honors: Antoinette Perry Award, Drama Desk Award, and *Theatre World* Award, all best supporting actress, all 1969, for *The Great White Hope;* Academy Award nomination, best supporting actress, 1970, for *The Great White Hope;* Golden Globe Award, most promising newcomer—female, 1971; Antoinette Perry Award nomination, best actress (dramatic), 1973, for *Six Rms Riv Vu;* Antoinette Perry Award nomination, best actress (dramatic), 1974, for *Find Your Way Home;* Emmy Award nomination, best actress in a drama or comedy special, 1976, for *Eleanor and Franklin;* Academy Award nomination, best supporting actress, 1976, for *All the President's Men;* Television Critics Circle Award and Emmy Award nomination, best actress in a drama or comedy special, both 1977, for *Eleanor and Franklin: The White House Years;* St. Botolph Club Achievement in Dramatic Arts, 1979; Antoinette Perry Award nomination, best actress (dramatic), 1979, for *First Monday in October;* Academy Award nomination and Golden Globe Award nomination, both best supporting actress, both 1979, for *Kramer vs. Kramer;* Emmy Award, outstanding supporting actress in a limited series or a special, 1981, for *Playing for Time;* Israel Cultural Award, 1982; Academy Award nomination and Golden Globe Award nomination, both best actress, both 1983, for *Testament;* Emmy Award nomination, best actress in a limited series or special, 1984, for *Calamity Jane;* Helen Caldicott Leadership Award, 1984; Western Heritage Wrangler Award, 1984; Emmy Award nomination, best actress in a limited series or special, 1985, for *Malice in Wonderland;* Living Legacy Award, Women's International Center, San Diego, 1988; Obie Award, best performance, 1993, for *The Sisters Rosensweig;* Environmental Leadership Award, Eco-Expo.

Member: Actors' Equity Association, Screen Actors Guild, American Federation of Television and Radio Artists, Women's Action for Nuclear Disarmament (board of directors, 1981-88), Wildlife Conservation International (board of directors, 1984—), Film Forum (board of directors, 1985-90), National Stroke Association (board of directors, 1985—), New York Zoological Society (advisory board, 1991—, board of directors, 1991).

CREDITS

Stage Appearances:
(Broadway debut) Eleanor Bachman, *The Great White Hope,* Alvin Theatre, 1968.

Katrina, *Mother Courage and Her Children,* Arena Stage, Washington, DC, 1970.

Mistress Page, *The Merry Wives of Windsor,* American Shakespeare Festival, Stratford, CT, 1970.

Lavinia, *Mourning Becomes Electra,* American Shakespeare Festival, 1970.

Title role, *Major Barbara,* American Shakespeare Festival, 1971.

Kitty Duval, *The Time of Your Life,* Eisenhower Theatre, Kennedy Center, Washington, DC, then Philadelphia, Chicago, and the Huntington Hartford Theatre, Los Angeles, all 1972.

Anne Miller, *Six Rms Riv Vu,* Helen Hayes Theatre, New York City, 1972.

Jacqueline Harrison, *Find Your Way Home,* Brooks Atkinson Theatre, New York City, 1974.

Liz Essendine, *Present Laughter,* Eisenhower Theatre, Kennedy Center, Washington, DC, 1974.

Gertrude, *Hamlet,* Vivian Beaumont Theatre, Lincoln Center, New York City, 1975.

Catherine Sloper, *The Heiress,* Broadhurst Theatre, New York City, 1976.

Hilda, *The Master Builder,* Eisenhower Theatre, Kennedy Center, Washington, DC, 1977.

Judge Ruth Loomis, *First Monday in October,* Majestic Theatre, New York City, 1978.

Joanne, *Losing Time,* Manhattan Theatre Club, New York City, 1979.

Natalia, *Goodbye Fidel,* Ambassador Theatre, New York City, 1980.

Cleopatra, *Antony and Cleopatra,* Alliance Theatre, Atlanta, 1981.

Title role, *Hedda Gabler,* Hartman Theatre, Stamford, CT, then Boston, 1981.

Annie, *Monday After the Miracle,* Spoleto Festival, Charleston, SC, then Eisenhower Theatre, Kennedy Center, Washington, DC, both 1982, then Eugene O'Neill Theatre, New York City, 1983.

Anna, *Old Times,* Roundabout Theatre, Stage One, New York City, 1983-84.

Maxine Faulk, *Night of the Iguana,* Circle in the Square Theatre, New York City, 1988.

Charlotte Blossom, *Approaching Zanzibar,* Second Stage, New York City, 1989.

Nurse, *Mystery of the Rose Bouquet,* Center Theatre Group, Mark Taper Forum, Los Angeles, CA, 1989.

Joy Davidman, *Shadowlands,* Brooks Atkinson Theatre, 1990.

Claire Zachanassian, *The Visit,* Criterion Center Stage Right, 1992.

Sara Goode, *The Sisters Rosensweig,* Lincoln Center Theatre, New York City, then Ethel Barrymore Theatre, New York City, both 1993.

Film Appearances:

(Debut) Eleanor Bachman, *The Great White Hope,* Twentieth Century-Fox, 1970.

Nora Tenneray, *A Gunfight,* Paramount, 1971.

Dorothy Fehler, *The New Centurions,* Columbia, 1972.

Bookkeeper, *All the President's Men,* Warner Bros., 1976.

Alicia Hardeman, *The Betsy,* Allied Artists, 1978.

Margaret Phelps, *Kramer vs. Kramer,* Columbia, 1979.

Lillian Gray, *Brubaker,* Twentieth Century-Fox, 1980.

Doris Strelyzk, *Night Crossing,* Buena Vista, 1982.

Carol Wetherly, *Testament,* Paramount, 1983.

Addy, *City Heat,* Warner Bros., 1984.

Juanelle, *Square Dance* (also known as *Home Is Where the Heart Is*), Island Pictures, 1987.

Anna Willing, *Sweet Country,* Cinema Group, 1987.

Mrs. Shaw, *Glory,* TriStar, 1989.

Narrator, *Building Bombs* (documentary), Tara Releasing, 1991.

Women Don't Want To (also known as *Le Donne non Vogliono Piu*), 1993.

Princess, *The Star Maker* (also known as *L'Uomo Delle Stelle*), Miramax, 1995.

Film Work:

Executive producer, *Square Dance* (also known as *Home Is Where the Heart Is*), Island Pictures, 1987.

Script supervisor, *Immortal,* 1995.

Television Appearances; Miniseries:

Eleanor Roosevelt, *Eleanor and Franklin,* ABC, 1976.

Eleanor Roosevelt, *Eleanor and Franklin: The White House Years,* ABC, 1977.

Doris Ashley, *Blood and Orchids,* CBS, 1986.

Blanche Kettman, *Stay the Night,* ABC, 1992.

Television Appearances; Movies:

Anne Palmer, *Welcome Home Johnny Bristol,* CBS, 1971.

Karen Walker, *Miracle on 34th Street,* CBS, 1973.

Sarah Shaw, *This Is the West that Was,* NBC, 1974.

Frances Gunther, *Death Be Not Proud,* ABC, 1975.

Mary MacCracken, *A Circle of Children,* CBS, 1977.

Mary MacCracken, *Lovey: A Circle of Children, Part II,* CBS, 1978.

Dear Liar, PBS, 1978.

Barbara Moreland, *A Question of Love* (also known as *A Purely Legal Matter*), NBC, 1978.

Alma Rose, *Playing for Time,* CBS, 1980.

Sandy Caldwell, *In the Custody of Strangers,* ABC, 1983.

Title role, *Calamity Jane,* CBS, 1984.

Nora Strangis, *When She Says No,* ABC, 1984.

Hedda Hopper, *Malice in Wonderland,* CBS, 1985.

Sybil Stockdale, *In Love and War,* NBC, 1987.

Ginny Carlson, *Open Admissions,* CBS, 1987.

Hannah Dournevald, *A Friendship in Vienna* (also known as *The Devil in Vienna*), The Disney Channel, 1988.

Peggy Ryan, *Daughter of the Streets* (also known as *My Daughter of the Streets*), ABC, 1990.

Television Appearances; Episodic:

Voice of Emily Dickinson, "Emily Dickinson," *Voices & Visions,* PBS, 1988.

Narration, "Dr. Spock the Baby Doc," *Nova,* PBS, 1995.

Interviewee, "James Earl Jones," *Biography,* Arts and Entertainment, 1995.

Television Appearances; Specials:

Host, *Generations,* 1987.

Herself, *The 41st Annual Tony Awards,* 1987.

Herself, *Drug Free Kids: A Parent's Guide,* PBS, 1988.

Narration, *Sea Turtles' Last Dance,* PBS, 1988.

Narration, *Sea Turtles: Ancient Nomads,* PBS, 1989.

Narration, *They're Doing My Time,* PBS, 1989.

Herself, *Night of 100 Stars III,* NBC, 1990.

Georgia O'Keeffe, "A Marriage: Georgia O'Keeffe and Alfred Stieglitz," *American Playhouse,* PBS, 1991.

Herself, *The 47th Annual Tony Awards,* 1993.

Herself, *The Kennedy Center Honors: A Celebration of the Performing Arts,* CBS, 1993.

Presenter, *The 48th Annual Tony Awards,* 1994.

Honoree, accepting on behalf of the NEA, *The Kennedy Center Honors: A Celebration of the Performing Arts,* CBS, 1994.

Herself, *The 49th Annual Tony Awards,* 1995.

Host, *24th International Emmy Awards,* 1996.

Television Pilots:
Elsie Robertson, *New Year,* 1993.

Television Work:
Co-producer, *Calamity Jane* (movie), CBS, 1984.
Executive producer, "A Marriage: Georgia O'Keeffe and Alfred Stieglitz," *American Playhouse,* PBS, 1991.
Segment producer, "The Power of Dance," "Lord of the Dance," "Dance at Court," "Dance Centerstage," *Dancing* (series), PBS, 1992-93.

RECORDINGS

Has recorded the audio books *Wuthering Heights,* Random House; and *Rebecca,* Warner.

WRITINGS

(With Greta Jacobs) *The Bluefish Cookbook,* Globe Pequot (Chester, CT), 1980.
(With Tom Alexander) *Mountain Fever,* Bright Mountain (Asheville, NC), 1995.

Author, with Sam Engelstad, of the play *The Master Builder;* author of the teleplays for *The Time of Your Life* and *Find Your Way Home.**

ALLEN, Nancy 1950-

PERSONAL

Born June 24, 1950, in New York, NY; married Brian De Palma, 1979 (divorced, 1983); married Craig Shoemaker, 1992. *Education:* Attended High School for the Performing Arts.

Addresses: *Agent*—Don Buchwald & Associates, 9229 Sunset Blvd., Suite 710, Los Angeles, CA 90069.

Career: Actress.

CREDITS

Film Appearances:
(Film debut) Nancy, *The Last Detail,* Columbia, 1973.
Chris Hargenson, *Carrie,* United Artists, 1976.
Pam Mitchell, *I Wanna Hold Your Hand,* Universal, 1978.
Kristina, *Home Movies,* United Artists, 1979.
Donna, *1941,* Universal, 1979.
Liz Blake, *Dressed to Kill,* Filmways, 1980.

Sally, *Blow Out,* Filmways, 1981.
Betty Walker, *Strange Invaders,* Orion, 1983.
Carrie, *The Buddy System,* Twentieth Century-Fox, 1984.
Lois, *Not for Publication,* Thorn-EMI, 1984.
Allison, *The Philadelphia Experiment,* New World Pictures, 1984.
Forced Entry (also known as *The Last Victim*), Century International, 1984.
Terror in the Aisles, 1984.
Anne Lewis, *Robocop,* Orion, 1987.
Jillian Grey, *Sweet Revenge,* Concorde, 1987.
Patricia Gardner, *Poltergeist III,* Metro-Goldwyn-Mayer/United Artists, 1988.
Casey Falls, *Limit Up,* MCEG, 1989.
Anne Lewis, *Robocop 2,* Orion, 1990.
Anne Lewis, *Robocop 3,* Orion, 1993.
Mexico—The Weightlifter, *Mod F— Explosion,* 1994.
Catherine Pelman, *Les Patriotes* (also known as *The Patriots*), 1994.
Out of Sight, 1998.

Television Appearances; Movies:
Susan Neville, *The Gladiator,* 1986.
Jennifer Gordon, *Memories of Murder* (also known as *Passing Through Veils*), Lifetime, 1990.
Cathy Thomas, *Acting on Impulse* (also known as *Eyes of a Stranger*), Showtime, 1993.
Jesse Gallardo, *The Man Who Wouldn't Die* (also known as *The Gift;* pilot), ABC, 1995.

Television Appearances; Episodic:
Rachel Rose, "Valerie 23," *The Outer Limits,* Showtime/syndicated, 1995.
Megan, *Touched by an Angel* (also known as *Someone to Watch Over Me* and *Angel's Attic*), CBS, 1994-95.*

ALVARADO, Trini 1967-

PERSONAL

Full name, Trinidad Alvarado; born January 10, 1967, in New York, NY; daughter of Domingo (a flamenco dancer) and Sylvia (a flamenco dancer) Alvarado; married Robert McNeill (an actor). *Education:* Attended Professional Children's School; attended Fordham University.

Addresses: *Contact*—J. Michael Bloom, 233 Park Ave. South, 10th Floor, New York, NY 10003.

Career: Actress. Performed as a flamenco dancer in her parents' dance troupe at age seven.

CREDITS

Film Appearances:
Franny Phillips and performer of song, "Happy Ida and Broken-Hearted John," *Rich Kids,* United Artists, 1979.
Pamela "Pammy" Pearl and performer of song, "Your Daughter Is One," *Times Square,* Associated Film Distribution, 1980.
Irene Soffel, *Mrs. Soffel,* Metro-Goldwyn-Mayer/United Artists, 1984.
Molly Garber, *Sweet Lorraine,* Angelika, 1987.
May "Mooch" Stark, *Satisfaction* (also known as *Girls of Summer*), Twentieth Century-Fox, 1988.
Jenny Claire, *Stella,* Buena Vista, 1990.
Lisa Titus, *The Chair* (also known as *Hot Seat*), Imperial Entertainment, 1991.
Lorraine, *American Blue Note* (also known as *Fakebook*), Panorama Entertainment, 1991.
Helen Woodford-Ruth, *The Babe,* Universal, 1992.
Miss Elinor Hartley, *American Friends,* Castle Hill, 1993.
Meg March, *Little Women,* Columbia, 1994.
Teresa Perez, *The Perez Family,* Samuel Goldwyn, 1995.
Lucy Lynskey, *The Frighteners,* Universal, 1996.

Television Appearances; Movies:
Teresa, *Dreams Don't Die,* ABC, 1982.
Lisa Castello, *Jacobo Timerman: Prisoner without a Name, Cell without a Number* (also known as *Prisoner without a Name, Cell without a Number*), NBC, 1983.
Anna Rogna, *Frank Nitti: The Enforcer* (also known as *Nitti*), ABC, 1988.

Beth, *The Christmas Tree,* ABC, 1996.

Television Appearances; Specials:
Jump rope girl, "The Magic Pony Ride," *Unicorn Tales,* NBC, 1977.
Goldilocks, "Big Apple Birthday," *Unicorn Tales,* NBC, 1978.
Dena McKain, "A Movie Star's Daughter," *ABC Afterschool Special,* ABC, 1979.
Alicia Marin, "Starstruck," *ABC Afterschool Special,* ABC, 1981.
"Private Contentment," *American Playhouse,* PBS, 1982.
Younger Elinor Blair, "Sensibility and Sense," *American Playhouse,* PBS, 1990.

Television Appearances; Episodic:
Mindy, "Winning," *Kate and Allie,* CBS, 1986.
Sarah, "The Big Vacation," *Kay O'Brien,* CBS, 1986.
Laurie Kincaid, "Sleepless Dreams," *Spenser: For Hire,* ABC, 1987.
Elizabeth "Betsey" Wood, *The Human Factor,* CBS, 1992.
Behind the Scenes, E! Entertainment Television, 1996.

Stage Appearances:
Becca, 1976.
(Broadway debut) Melinda, *Runaways,* New York Shakespeare Festival, Plymouth Theatre, also produced at Public Theatre, New York City, both 1978.
Anne Frank, *Yours, Anne,* Playhouse 91, New York City, 1985.
Maggie, *Maggie Magalita,* Lamb's Theatre, New York City, 1986.
Godspell, off-Broadway, 1988.

Also appeared in *I Love You, I Love You Not, Reds,* and *The Magic Show.*

Radio Appearances:
The Frighteners, WFSB, 1996.

RECORDINGS

Soundtracks; Plays:
"Your Daughter Is One," *Times Square,* 1980.
Yours, Anne, 1986.

Soundtracks; Films:
"For the Beauty of the Earth," *Little Women,* Sony Classical, 1994.

Albums; Background Vocals:
"String of Pearls," "Caged Rat," and "Tell Me When," *Let Your Dim Light Shine,* by Soul Asylum, Columbia, 1995.

OTHER SOURCES

Periodicals:
Detroit News, July 13, 1996.
Maclean's, June 6, 1994.
People, February 26, 1990, p. 58.*

ANA-ALICIA   1956(?)-
(Robin)

PERSONAL

Full name, Ana-Alicia Ortiz; born December 12 (some sources say December 10), 1956 (some sources say 1957), in Mexico City, Mexico; father, in business; mother, a clothing manufacturing executive, name Alicia Ortiz. *Education:* University of Texas at El Paso, B.A. (drama); attended Wellesley College for one year; studied law at Southwestern Law School; studied acting with Kim Stanley, Vivian Mason, Milton Katselas, and Julie Bovasso. *Avocational interests:* Race car driving, motorcycle riding, scuba diving, horseback riding, tennis.

Addresses: *Contact*—SDB Partners Inc., 1801 Avenue of the Stars, Los Angeles, CA 90067-5902.

Career: Actress. Zitro Productions, founder; Twelfth Night Repertory Company, member of company. Humane Society of the United States, national spokesperson; National Association for the Hispanic Elderly, national spokesperson; Association for Retarded Citizens, spokesperson. Also worked as a real estate broker and as a Los Angeles Police Reserve trainee.

Member: Screen Actors Guild, American Federation of Television and Radio Artists, Actors' Equity Association.

Awards, Honors: Golden Eagle Award, best television actress, 1984 and 1989, for *Falcon Crest;* Equitable Award, 1985; LULAC Award, National Hispanic Hall of Fame, 1986; Cesar Award, 1987.

CREDITS

Television Appearances; Series:
Alicia Nieves, *Ryan's Hope,* NBC, 1977-78.
Melissa Agretti Cumson Gioberti, *Falcon Crest,* CBS, 1982-89.

Television Appearances; Episodic:
Next Step Beyond, syndicated, 1978.
Aurora, "Take the Celestra," *Battlestar Galactica,* ABC, 1979.
Falina Redding, "Vegas in Space," *Buck Rogers in the 25th Century,* NBC, 1979.
Galactica 1980, ABC, 1980.
"No Way to Treat a Patient," *Quincy, M.E.,* NBC, 1980.

"Seven Lady Captives," *B. J. and the Bear,* NBC, 1981.
"A Matter of Honor," *McClain's Law,* NBC, 1982.
"My Mother, My Chaperone," *The Love Boat,* ABC, 1984.
Mary, "And the Flesh Was Made Word," *Moonlighting,* ABC, 1988.
Samantha Ross, "Resurrection," *Falcon Crest,* CBS, 1989.
Linda Davidson, "Easy Riders," *Acapulco H.E.A.T.,* syndicated, 1994.
Doctor, "Sheriff Reno," *Renegade,* syndicated, 1994.
Sergeant Hilda Dupont, *Murder, She Wrote,* CBS, 1994.
Angela Baptista, "Hard Evidence," *Renegade,* syndicated, 1996.

Appeared in episodes of *Hotel,* ABC; *The Hardy Boys Mysteries,* ABC; and *Lobo,* NBC.

Television Appearances; Movies:
Yolanda Suarez, *Roughnecks,* syndicated, 1980.
Thelma Messenkott, *Condominium,* HBO, 1980.
Lisa Saldonna, *The Ordeal of Bill Carney,* CBS, 1981.
Violet, *Coward of the County,* CBS, 1981.
Veronica, *Happy Endings,* CBS, 1983.
Michelle Honda, *Miracle Landing,* CBS, 1990.
Dolores Santillan, *Rio Shannon,* ABC, 1993.

Television Appearances; Miniseries:
Drusilla Alvarado, *Louis L'Amour's The Sacketts* (also known as *The Sacketts*), NBC, 1979.

Television Appearances; Specials:
CBS team member, *Battle of the Network Stars XV,* ABC, 1983.
Philadelphia host, *CBS All-American Thanksgiving Day Parade,* CBS, 1985.
Walt Disney World host, *The Second Annual CBS Easter Parade,* CBS, 1986.
Host, *The CBS Cotton Bowl Parade,* CBS, 1986.
Texas 150: A Celebration Special, CBS, 1986.
Sex Symbols: Past, Present, and Future, syndicated, 1987.
Host, *CBS Tournament of Roses Parade,* CBS, 1988.
Host, *The World's Greatest Stunts III,* Fox, 1991.

Film Appearances:
Janet, *Halloween II,* Universal, 1981.
Arista Zelada, *Romero,* Four Seasons Entertainment, 1989.
Voice of Kathy's mother, *To Die, to Sleep* (also known as *Mortal Danger* and *Turn Your Pony Around*), Imperial Entertainment, 1992.

Stage Appearances:
Appeared in *Gaslight, The Odd Couple, Busybody, The Sound of Music,* and *Boeing, Boeing,* all at Adobe Horseshoe Dinner Theatre, in Texas, between 1973 and 1976; also appeared in *A Midsummer's Night Dream, You Can't Take It with You, Everything in the Garden, Brigadoon, Kiss Me Kate,* and *Crawling Around,* all with Twelfth Night Repertory Company.

WRITINGS

Nonfiction:
(Under the pseudonym Robin, with others) *You'll Never Make Love in This Town Again,* edited by Jennie Louise Frankel, Terrie Maxine Frankel, and Joanne Parent, Dove Books (Beverly Hills, CA), 1995.*

ANDERSON, Laurie   1947-

PERSONAL

Born in 1947, in Glenn Ellyn (some sources say Wayne), IL; daughter of Arthur T. and Mary Louise (Rowland) Anderson. *Education:* Barnard College, B.A. (magna cum laude), art history, 1969; Columbia University, M.F.A., sculpture, 1972.

Addresses: *Office*—530 Canal St., New York, NY 10013. *Agent*—Monterey Peninsula Artists, 509 Hartnell St., Monterey, CA 93940.

Career: Performance artist, sculptor, and composer. South Bank Centre, London, artistic director of Meltdown concert, 1997. As a performance artist and musician (electronic keyboard and electric violin), has appeared in numerous solo shows in the United States, England, and Japan, including performances at Harold Rivkin Gallery, Washington, DC, 1973; and Queens Museum, Queens, NY, 1984. City College of the City University of New York, instructor in art history, 1973-75; ZBS Media, artist in residence, 1975. Critic for such magazines as *Art News* and *Art Forum.* Designing a theme park called Real World in Barcelona, Spain, scheduled to open in 2000.

Participated in individual exhibitions, including Barnard College, New York, 1970; Harold Rivkin Gallery, Washington, DC, 1973; Artists Space, New York, 1974; Holly Solomon Gallery, New York, and Hopkins Center, Dartmouth College, Hanover, NH, both 1977; And/Or Gallery, Seattle, WA, Projects

Gallery, Museum of Modern Art, New York, and Matrix Gallery, Harford Atheneum, CT, all 1978; University of California Art Museum, Berkeley, 1979; "Dark Dogs, American Dreams," Holly Solomon Gallery, New York, 1980; "Scenes from 'United States,'" Holly Solomon Gallery, New York, 1981; "Retrospective," Institute of Contemporary Arts, London, 1982; Institute of Contemporary Art, Philadelphia (then Los Angeles, CA, Houston, TX, and Flushing, NY), 1983; and Laforet Museum, Akasaka, Tokyo, Nihon Seinehkau, Tokyo, Sankei Hall, Osaka, Japan, and Kyoto Kaikan, Tokyo, all 1984.

Selected group exhibitions include: "Thought Structure," Pace University, New York, 1973; "New Work, New York," Fine Arts Gallery, California, and State University, Los Angeles, both 1976; "Surrogates/Self-Portraits," Holly Solomon Gallery, New York, and "Words at Liberty," Museum of Contemporary Art, Chicago, both 1977; "American Narrative Story Art," Contemporary Art Museum, Houston (then University of California Art Museum, Berkeley), 1978; "10 Artists: Artists' Space," Neuberger Museum, State University of New York at Purchase (then New Museum, New York), 1979; "Drawings: The Pluralist Decade," at the Biennale, Venice (also toured Europe and appeared at the Institute of Contemporary Art, Philadelphia, 1980; "Avant-Garde in the Eighties," Los Angeles County Museum of Art, 1987.

Member: Phi Beta Kappa.

Awards, Honors: Grants from National Endowment for the Arts, 1974, 1977, and 1979, and New York State Council on the Arts, 1974 and 1977; Villager Award, 1981; Guggenheim fellowship, 1983; honorary doctorate from San Francisco Art Institute, 1980.

CREDITS

Stage Appearances; Performance Art Pieces:
Automotive, Town Green, Rochester, VT, 1972.
Story Show, 1972.
O-Range, Lewisohn Stadium, City College of the City University of New York, New York City, 1973.
Duets on Ice, New York City, 1973.
How to Yodel, The Kitchen, New York City, 1974.
Songs and Stories for the Insomniac, Artists Space, New York City, 1975.
Songs and Stories for the Insomniac . . . Continued, Oberlin College, Oberlin, OH, 1975.
Out of the Blue, University of Massachusetts, Amherst, 1975.

Dearreader, Holly Solomon Gallery, New York City, 1975.

Dearreader-2, Sarah Lawrence College, Bronxville, NY, 1975.

Dearreader-3, Rhode Island School of Design, Providence, 1975.

Fast Food, Artists Space, 1976.

Stereo Stories, M. L. D'Arc Gallery, New York City, 1976.

Engli-SH, Akademie der Kunst, Berlin, Germany, 1976, Louisiana Museum, Humleback, Denmark, 1976.

Road Songs, St. Mark's Poetry Center, New York City, 1976.

Songs, New School, New York City, 1976.

Refried Beans for Instants, 1976.

For Instants, Part 5: Songs for Lines, Songs for Waves, The Kitchen, 1977.

Audio Talk, School of Visual Arts, New York City, 1977.

Some Songs, International Cultural Center, Brussels, Belgium, 1977, And/Or Gallery, Seattle, WA, 1978, Mills College, Oakland, CA, 1978.

That's Not the Way I Heard It, Documenta, Kassel, West Germany, 1977.

On Dit, Paris Biennale, Paris, 1977.

That's Not the Way I Heard It-2, Galleria Salvatore Ala, Milan, Italy, 1977.

For Instants-Continued, Otis Art Gallery, Los Angeles, 1978.

Like a Stream, The Kitchen, 1978.

Like a Stream-3, with St. Paul Chamber Orchestra, Walker Art Center, Minneapolis, MN, 1978.

Down Here, Texas Opry House, Houston, 1978.

Some Songs-2, Portland Center for the Visual Arts, Portland, OR, 1978.

For Instants-6, DC Space, Washington, DC, 1978.

A Few Are. . ., Art Gallery of Ontario, Toronto, 1978.

Songs for Self-Playing Violin, Contemporary Art Center, Cincinnati, OH, 1978, Real Art Ways, Hartford, CT, 1978.

Handphone Table, Museum of Modern Art, New York City, 1978.

Some Are. . ., benefit for Hallwalls, Buffalo, NY, 1978.

Americans on the Move—Preview, Carnegie Recital Hall, NY, 1979.

Americans on the Move, The Kitchen, 1979.

Blue Horn File, Mudd Club, New York City, 1979.

(With David van Tieghem and Peter Gordon) *Commerce,* U.S. Customs House, New York City, 1979.

Fuer Augen und Ohren, Akademie der Kunst, 1980.

New Music America, Walker Art Center, Minneapolis, 1980.

Privates, New York City, 1981.

Bonds, New York City, 1981.

It's Cold Outside, Alicy Tully Hall, New York, 1981.

United States, Moore Theatre, Seattle, WA, 1982.

United States, Parts I-IV, Park West, Chicago, IL, 1982, then Brooklyn Academy of Music, Brooklyn, NY, 1983.

Empty Places, Next Wave Festival, Brooklyn Academy of Music, 1989.

Voices from Beyond, 1992.

Stories from the Nerve Bible, 1993.

Other performance art pieces include *It's Cold Outside* and *Born, Never Asked.*

Tours:

Mister Heartbreak, U.S., Canadian, and Japanese cities, 1984-85.

Home of the Brave, U.S. cities, 1986.

Nerve Bible Tour (solo show), U.S. cities, including Washington, D.C., and Seattle, 1995.

Film Appearances:

Home of the Brave, Cinecom International, 1986.

Heavy Petting, Academy Entertainment, 1988.

Hotel Deutschland, 1991.

Film Work:

"Closed Circuit," *System Ohne Schatten,* 1983.

Music performer, *Nicaragua: No Pasaran,* 1984.

Co-producer, director, and soundtrack co-producer, *Home of the Brave,* Cinecom International, 1986.

Song performer, "Strange Angels," *The Doctor,* Buena Vista, 1991.

Television Appearances; Series:

Host, *Alive from Off Center,* PBS, 1987.

Television Appearances; Specials:

"John Cage: I Have Nothing to Say and I'm Saying It," *American Masters,* PBS, 1990.

Presenter, *The 2nd International Rock Awards,* ABC, 1990.

CyberSpace, The Disney Channel, 1995.

Television Appearances; Episodic:

Herself, "Art Show," *Space Ghost Coast to Coast,* Cartoon Network, 1996.

WRITINGS

Performance Art Pieces; Writer, Composer, and Visual Designed, Except Where Indicated:

Automotive, Town Green, Rochester, VT, 1972.

Story Show, 1972.

O-Range, Town Green, Rochester, VT, 1973.

Duets on Ice, Town Green, Rochester, VT, 1973.

Songs and Stories for the Insomniac, Town Green, Rochester, VT, 1975.

Refried Beans for Instants, 1976.

For Instants, Part 5, The Kitchen, New York City, 1977.

Handphone Table, Museum of Modern Art, New York City, 1978.

Americans on the Move, The Kitchen, 1979.

United States, Parts I-IV, Brooklyn Academy of Music, Brooklyn, NY, 1983.

Home of the Brave (concert performance), U.S. cities, 1986.

Composer only, *Alcestis,* American Repertory Theatre, Cambridge, MA, 1986.

Empty Places, Next Wave Festival, Brooklyn Academy of Music, 1989.

Other works include *Like a Stream—3, It's Cold Outside,* and *Born, Never Asked.*

Films; Composer, Except Where Indicated:

Writer, *Fourteen Americans,* 1979.

Writer, *Film du silence,* 1981.

(With John Cale) *Something Wild* (also known as *Dangereuse sous tous rapports*), Orion, 1986.

And writer, *Home of the Brave,* Cinecom International, 1986.

Swimming to Cambodia, Cinecom International, 1987.

"Angel Fragments" in *Wings of Desire,* 1987.

Monster in a Box, Fine Line, 1991.

"Strange Angels" in *The Doctor,* Buena Vista, 1991.

Other Writings:

The Package, 1971.

October, 1972.

Transportation Transportation, 1973.

The Rose and the Stone, 1974.

Notebook, 1976.

Typisch Frau, 1981.

Artifacts at the End of a Decade, 1981.

Composer, "Bad Blood" in *Bill Cosby Salutes Alvin Ailey* (television special), 1989.

The Ugly One with the Jewels, 1995.

Author of the book *Stories from the Nerve Bible: A Retrospective, 1972-1992,* published by HarperPerennial. Contributor to periodicals, including *October* and *Hotel.*

RECORDINGS

Albums:

It's Not the Bullet That Kills You, It's the Hole, 1977.

Airwaves, 1977.

New Music for Electronic and Recorded Media, 1978.

Big Ego, 1979.

Walk the Dog, O Superman, 1981.

Big Science, Warner Bros., 1982.

(Contributor) *You're the Guy I Want to Share My Money With,* 1982.

Mr. Heartbreak, Warner Bros., 1984.

United States Live, Warner Bros., 1985.

Strange Angels, Warner Bros., 1989.

Bright Red, Warner Bros., 1994.

The Speed of Darkness, 1997.

CDROMs:

Puppet-Motel, Voyager, 1995.

OTHER SOURCES

Periodicals:

American Theatre, July-August, 1995, p. 48.

Entertainment Weekly, February 24, 1995, p. 125.

Interview, September, 1994, p. 49; March, 1997, p. 144.*

ANDERSON, Loni   1945(?)-

PERSONAL

Born August 5, 1945 (some sources say 1946, 1947 or 1950), in St. Paul, MN; daughter of Klaydon (an environmental chemist) and Maxine (a model) Anderson; married Bruce Hasselberg (a salesperson), 1964 (divorced, 1966); married Ross Bickell (an actor), 1974 (divorced, 1981); married Burt Reynolds (an actor), April 29, 1988 (divorced, 1993); children: (first marriage) Deidre Hoffman; (third marriage) Quinton Anderson (adopted). *Education:* Received B.A. in art and drama from the University of Minnesota.

Addresses: *Agent*—Innovative Artists, 1999 Avenue of the Stars, Suite 2850, Los Angeles, CA 90067.

Career: Actress. Worked as a school teacher prior to acting career.

Awards, Honors: Emmy nominations, best supporting actress in a comedy, variety, or music series, 1980 and 1981, for *WKRP in Cincinnati.*

CREDITS

Television Appearances; Series:

Lindsay (Sue's roommate), *Harry O,* ABC, 1974.

Jennifer Marlowe, *WKRP in Cincinnati,* CBS, 1978-82.

Sydney Kovak, *Partners in Crime,* NBC, 1984.

L. K. McGuire, *Easy Street,* NBC, 1986-87.

Casey MacAfee, *Nurses,* NBC, 1993-94.

Teri Carson, *Melrose Place,* Fox, 1995-96.

Television Appearances; Movies:

Miss Daroon, *The Magnificent Magical Magnet of Santa Mesa,* NBC, 1977.

Angela Ross, *Three on a Date,* ABC, 1978.

Title role, *The Jayne Mansfield Story,* CBS, 1980.

Julie Davis, *Sizzle,* ABC, 1981.

Mollie Dean Purcell, *Country Gold,* CBS, 1982.

Ellen Blake, *My Mother's Secret Life,* ABC, 1984.

Lora Mae Holloway, *A Letter to Three Wives,* NBC, 1985.

Stacy Tweed, *Stranded,* NBC, 1986.

Ellen Berent, *Too Good to Be True,* NBC, 1988.

Lauren LaSalle, *Necessity,* CBS, 1988.

Liz Bartlett, *A Whisper Kills,* ABC, 1988.

Angela Stevenson, *Sorry, Wrong Number,* USA Network, 1989.

Leah Crawford, *Coins in the Fountain,* 1990.

Title role, *White Hot: The Mysterious Murder of Thelma Todd,* NBC, 1991.

Lacey Stewart, *The Price She Paid* (also known as *Plan of Attack*), CBS, 1992.

Without Warning (also known as *July 13*), CBS, 1994.

Martha, *Deadly Family Secrets* (also known as *Family Secrets*), NBC, 1995.

Television Appearances; Miniseries:

Fanny Porter, *Gambler V: Playing for Keeps,* CBS, 1994.

Television Appearances; Specials:

Circus of the Stars, CBS, 1979.

Host, *Merry Christmas from the Grand Ole Opry* (also known as *Christmas in Opryland*), ABC, 1979.

Host, *The Fantastic Funnies,* CBS, 1980.

Bob Hope's All-Star Look at TV's Prime Time Wars, NBC, 1980.

Siegfried and Roy, NBC, 1980.

Host, *The New and Spectacular Guinness Book of World Records,* ABC, 1980.

Bob Hope's All-Star Comedy Birthday Party, NBC, 1980.

The Bob Hope Christmas Special, NBC, 1980 and 1981.

Bob Hope's Spring Fling of Comedy and Glamour, NBC, 1981.

Host, *The Candid Camera Special,* NBC, 1981.

Bob Hope's All-Star Comedy Look at the Fall Season: It's Still Free and Worth It!, NBC, 1981.

Host, *Magic with the Stars,* NBC, 1982.

Bob Hope's Women I Love—Beautiful But Funny, NBC, 1982.

Bob Hope's Christmas Special, NBC, 1982.

Host, *Sunday Funnies,* NBC, 1983.

Bob Hope's Wicki-Wacky Special from Waikiki, NBC, 1984.

Dom DeLuise and Friends—Part IV, ABC, 1986.

Voice of Blondie, *Blondie and Dagwood* (animated), CBS, 1987.

Friday Night Surprise! (also known as *Surprise!*), 1988.

Voice of Blondie, *The Blondie and Dagwood's Second Wedding Workout* (animated), CBS, 1989.

Host, *New and Improved Kids* (documentary; also known as *Raising Good Kids in Bad Times*), syndicated, 1990.

Bob Hope's 1990 Christmas Show from Bermuda, 1990.

Host, *The 1991 King Orange Jamboree Parade,* 1991.

A Party for Richard Pryor, 1991.

Ringmaster, *The All New Circus of the Stars & Side Show XVII* (also known as *The 17th Annual All New Circus of the Stars & Side Show*), CBS, 1992.

What About Me? I'm Only 3!, CBS, 1992.

Bob Hope's Bag Full of Christmas Memories, NBC, 1993.

The Return of TV's Censored Bloopers 2, NBC, 1993.

People's 20th Birthday, ABC, 1994.

Also appeared on the *Shaun Cassidy Special.*

Television Appearances; Awards Presentations:

The 43rd Annual Primetime Emmy Awards Presentation, 1991.

The 17th Annual People's Choice Awards, 1991.

Presenter, *The 8th Annual American Comedy Awards,* ABC, 1994.

Presenter, *The 51st Annual Golden Globe Awards,* TBS, 1994.

Presenter, *The 31st Annual Academy of Country Music Awards,* NBC, 1996.

Television Appearances; Pilot:

Swenson, *Winner Take All,* CBS, 1977.

Tom Snyder's Celebrity Spotlight, NBC, 1980.

Television Appearances; Episodic:

Leslie Greely, "Carlin's New Suit," *The Bob Newhart Show,* CBS, 1977.

Lead Model, "Of Models and Murder," *The Incredible Hulk*, CBS, 1978.

The Stewardess Two-Timing Jack, *Three's Company*, ABC, 1978.

Whodunnit?, NBC, 1979.

Guest, *The Merv Griffin Show*, syndicated, 1979.

Cupid, "Guilt Trip," *Amazing Stories*, NBC, 1985.

Win, Lose, or Draw, syndicated, 1987.

Dawn St. Clair, "Grand Theft Hotel," *B. L. Stryker*, ABC, 1990.

Guest, *The Extraordinary*, syndicated, 1994.

Claudia Loring, "Who Killed the Highest Bidder?," *Burke's Law*, CBS, 1995.

Herself, "Women in Film," *Women of the House*, CBS, 1995.

Guest, *The Oprah Winfrey Show*, syndicated, 1995.

Also appeared on *The Love Boat*, ABC; *Barnaby Jones*, CBS; *Phyllis*, CBS; and *S.W.A.T.*, ABC.

Film Appearances:

Pembrook Feeney, *Stroker Ace*, Universal/Warner Bros., 1983.

Cameo, *The Lonely Guy*, Universal, 1984.

Voice of Flo, *All Dogs Go to Heaven* (animated), United Artists, 1989.

Cathy, *Munchie* (also known as *Munchie Strikes Back*), Concorde, 1992.

Stage Appearances:

Appeared in regional and dinner theater productions as Billie Dawn, *Born Yesterday*, Tzeitel, *Fiddler on the Roof*, and Sophie, *The Star Spangled Girl;* also appeared in productions of *Never Too Late, The Can-Can, The Threepenny Opera, Any Wednesday, Send Me No Flowers,* and *The Secret Life of Walter Mitty.*

WRITINGS

Books:

(With Warren Larkin) *My Life in High Heels* (autobiography), Morrow, 1995.

OTHER SOURCES

Periodicals:

Good Housekeeping, September, 1993, p. 56; November, 1995, pp. 116-119.

People's Weekly, June 28, 1993, p. 60; September 13, 1993, p. 80; November 8, 1993, p. 100; November 20, 1995, pp. 42-45, 46-49.

Redbook, May, 1994, p. 97.*

ANDRESS, Ursula   1936-
(Ursula Parker)

PERSONAL

Born March 19, 1936, in Berne, Switzerland; married John Derek (an actor and director), 1957 (divorced, 1966); children: (with Harry Hamlin; an actor) Dimitri.

Addresses: *Agent*—c/o Mike Greenfield, Charter Management, 9000 Sunset Blvd., Suite 1112, Los Angeles, CA 90069.

Career: Actress. Sometimes billed as Ursula Parker.

Awards, Honors: Golden Globe Award, most promising newcomer—female, 1964.

CREDITS

Film Appearances:

Le Avventure di Giacomo Casanova (also known as *Adventures of Giacomo Casanova, The Loves of Casanova,* and *Sins of Casanova*), Iris Film/Orso Film, 1954.

Un Americano a Roma (also known as *An American in Rome*), 1954.

La Catena Dell'Odio, 1955.

The Tempest Has Gone (also known as *La Tempesta e Passata*), 1955.

Honey Ryder, *Dr. No*, United Artists, 1963.

Maxine Richter, *Four for Texas* (also known as *4 for Texas*), Warner Bros., 1963.

Margarita Dauphine, *Fun in Acapulco*, Paramount, 1963.

Ayesha (she who must be obeyed), *She*, Metro-Goldwyn-Mayer, 1965.

Caroline Meredith, *The Tenth Victim* (also known as *La Decima Vittima*), Embassy, 1965.

Rita, *What's New, Pussycat?* (also known as *Quoi de Neuf, Pussycat?*), United Artists, 1965.

Alexandrine, *Les Tribulations d'un Chinois en Chine* (also known as *Chinese Adventures in China* and *Up to His Ears*), Vide, 1965.

Alex, *Once Before I Die*, Warner Bros., 1965.

Wife, *Nightmare in the Sun*, 1965.

Countess Kaeti, *The Blue Max*, Twentieth Century-Fox, 1966.

Norma, *Anyone Can Play* (also known as *Le Dolci Signore*), 1967.

Vesper Lynd, *Casino Royale*, Columbia, 1967.

Erica Kramer, *The Southern Star*, Columbia, 1969.

Britt, Lady Dorset, *Perfect Friday*, Chevron, 1970.

Cristina, *Red Sun* (also known as *Soleil Rouge* and *Sole Rosso*), National General, 1972.

Five Against Capricorn, 1972.

Nora, *Loaded Guns* (also known as *Stick 'em Up, Darlings* and *Colpo in Canna*), Cineproduzioni Daunia 70, 1974.

Stateline Motel (also known as *Last Chance, Last Chance for a Born Loser*, and *L'Ultima Chance*), 1975.

Josephine De Beauharnais, *The Loves and Times of Scaramouche* (also known as *Scaramouche* and *Le Avventure e Gli Amori di Scaramouche*), 1975.

Madeline Cooper, *Africa Express* (also known as *Tropical Express*), Deutsche Fox Film/Tritone Cinematografica, 1975.

40 Gradi Sotto il Lenzuolo, 1976.

Safari Express, 1976.

The Nurse (also known as *I Will If You Will, The Secrets of a Sensuous Nurse, The Sensuous Nurse,* and *L'Infermiera*), 1976.

Casanova e Compagnia, 1976.

Marina, *Spogliamoci Cosi Senza Pudor* (also known as *Love in Four Easy Lessons*), 1977.

Mountain of Cannibal Gods (also known as *Prisoner of the Cannibal God, Slave of the Cannibal God,* and *Montagna del Dio Cannibale*), 1978.

Princess Dell'Orso, *Double Murder on Via Governo Vecchio* (also known as *Double Murders* and *Doppio Delitto*), R.E.C.F./Primex, 1978.

Tigers in Lipstick (also known as *Four Tigers in Lipstick, Wild Beds, Camas Calientes,* and *Letti Selvaggi*), 1978.

Mademoiselle De La Valliere, *The Fifth Musketeer* (also known as *Behind the Iron Mask* and *The 5th Musketeer*), 1979.

Una Strana Coppia di Gangsters, 1979.

Speed Driver, 1980.

Aphrodite, *Clash of the Titans*, United Artists, 1981.

Mabel Dodge, *Mexico in Flames* (also known as *Red Bells, Campanas Rojas,* and *Krasnye Kolokola*), 1982.

Dieci Giorni che Sconvolsero il Mondo, 1982.

Marie Antoinette, *Liberty, Equality, Sauerkraut* (also known as *Liberte, Egalite, Choucroute*), 1985.

Class Reunion (also known as *Class Meeting, Klassezamekunft,* and *Klassentreffen*), Condor Films, 1988.

Alles Gelogen, 1996.

Queen, *Cremaster 5,* 1997.

Also appeared in *The Nineteenth Victim, Primitive Desires, Reporters,* and *Toys for Christmas.*

Television Appearances; Miniseries:

Athalie, *Peter the Great*, NBC, 1986.

Xellesia, *Cave of the Golden Rose III* (also known as *Fantaghiro III*), 1993.

Xellesia, *Cave of the Golden Rose IV* (also known as *Fantaghiro IV*), 1994.

Television Appearances; Pilots:

"Manimal," *Manimal*, NBC, 1983.

Television Appearances; Movies:

Another Falling Star (also known as *Il Professore-Diva*), 1989.

Betty Starr, *Man Against the Mob: The Chinatown Murders* (also known as *Man Against the Mob II: Man in Cement* and *The Chinatown Murders: Man Against the Mob*), NBC, 1989.

Television Appearances; Episodic:

Luana, "La Strega," *Thriller*, NBC, 1960.

Herself, *The Fall Guy*, ABC, 1981.

"The Pledge," *The Love Boat*, ABC, 1983.

"Hornet's Nest," *Falcon Crest*, CBS, 1988.

"King's Gambit," *Falcon Crest*, CBS, 1988.

"Telling Tales," *Falcon Crest*, CBS, 1988.

Television Appearances; Specials:

The Bob Hope Show, NBC, 1970.

The Bob Hope Show, NBC, 1971.

Bob Hope Special: Bob Hope's Women I Love—Beautiful But Funny, NBC, 1982.

Elvis: The Echo Will Never Die (documentary), syndicated, 1986.

Rich and Famous 1988 World's Best, syndicated, 1988.

Elvis: The Fans—A Perspective (also known as *Elvis: The Fans*), TNN, 1989.

Presenter, *The 1994 World Music Awards*, 1994.*

ANDREWS, Anthony   1948-

PERSONAL

Born January 12 (some sources say December 1), 1948, in London, England; married Georgina Simpson, 1971; children: Joshua, Jessica, Amy-Samantha. *Education:* Attended Royal Masonic School, Hertfordshire, England.

Addresses: *Agent*—Peters, Fraser & Dunlop, Fifth Floor, The Chambers, Chelsea Harbour, Lot's Rd., London SW10 0XF, England. *Contact*—Paradigm, 200 West 57th St., Suite 900, New York, NY 10019.

Career: Actor. Stagescreen Productions, founder (with Derek Granger and Jeffrey Taylor), 1984.

Awards, Honors: Golden Globe nomination, best actor in a television miniseries or motion picture, 1993, for *Danielle Steel's Jewels.*

CREDITS

Television Appearances; Miniseries:
Fortunes of Nigel, BBC, 1973.
Lord Silverbridge, *The Pallisers,* BBC, 1974, then PBS, 1977.
Lord Stockbridge, *Upstairs Downstairs,* London Weekend Television, then PBS, 1975.
Lieutenant Brian Ash, "Danger UXB," *Masterpiece Theatre,* PBS, 1978.
Sebastian Flyte, *Brideshead Revisited,* Granada, 1980, then PBS, 1982.
Nero, *A.D.* (also known as *A.D.—Anno Domini*), NBC, 1985.
William Whitfield, *Danielle Steel's Jewels* (also known as *Jewels*), NBC, 1992.

Television Appearances; Movies:
Reg Hogg, *A War of Children,* CBS, 1972.
Stephen Kelno, *QB VII,* ABC, 1974.
Buckley, *Mistress of Paradise,* ABC, 1981.
Sir Percy Blakeney (title role), *The Scarlet Pimpernel,* CBS, 1982.
Wilfred of Ivanhoe (title role), *Ivanhoe,* CBS, 1982.
Tony Browne, *Agatha Christie's Sparkling Cyanide* (also known as *Sparkling Cyanide*), CBS, 1983.
Edward VII, Prince of Wales, *The Woman He Loved,* CBS, 1988.
Michael Fitzgerald, *Bluegrass,* CBS, 1988.
Eliot Blake, "Columbo Goes to the Guillotine" (also known as "Columbo" and "The Return of Columbo"), *The ABC Mystery Movie,* ABC, 1989.
Professor James Moriarty, *Hands of a Murderer* (also known as *Sherlock Holmes and the Prince of Crime* and *The Napoleon of Crime*), CBS, 1990.
The Law Lord [England], 1992.
Luke Crossland, *Heartstones,* BBC, 1996.

Television Appearances; Episodic:
Harry, "The Beast with Two Backs," *Wednesday Play,* BBC, 1968.
Marcus Carrington, "Lottie's Boy," *The Duchess of Duke Street,* BBC, 1978.
Johnnie Aysgarth, "Suspicion," *American Playhouse,* PBS, 1988.

Dr. Henry Jekyll/Mr. Edward Hyde, "The Strange Case of Dr. Jekyll and Mr. Hyde," *Nightmare Classics,* Showtime, 1989.
"About Face," *Tales from the Crypt,* HBO, 1996.

Appeared as the school prefect, "Alma Mater," *Play for Today,* BBC; as Basil and actor, "As the Actress Said to the Bishop," *Mating Machine,* London Weekend Television; and in *Play of the Month.*

Television Appearances; Series:
Paul Richard, *Dixon of Dock Green,* BBC, 1972.

Television Appearances; Specials:
Woodstock, 1972.
Follyfoot, 1973.
Carlos, *A Day Out,* 1973.
Steerforth, *David Copperfield,* 1974.
Claudio, *Much Ado about Nothing,* [England], 1977.
The Country Wife, 1977.
French without Tears, 1977.
Mercutio, *Romeo and Juliet,* PBS, 1979.
Z for Zachariah, BBC, 1983.
Backstage at Masterpiece Theatre: A 20th Anniversary Special, PBS, 1991.

Also appeared in *London Assurance, The Judge's Wife,* and *A Superstition.*

Stage Appearances:
Forty Years On, New Shakespeare Company, Chichester Festival Theatre, Chichester, England, then Apollo Theatre, London, 1968.
Chief Stoat and Mr. Turkey, *Toad of Toad Hall,* Duke of York's Theatre, London, 1970.
Mustardseed, *A Midsummer Night's Dream,* Regent's Park Open Air Theatre, London, 1971.
Balthasar, *Romeo and Juliet,* Regent's Park Open Air Theatre, 1971.
Douglas Blake, *The Dragon Variation,* Duke of York's Theatre, 1977.
One of Us, 1986.
Neville, *Coming In to Land,* National Theatre Company, Lyttelton Theatre, London, 1987.

Made regional stage debut in 1967.

Film Appearances:
Doomwatch, Tigon, 1972.
Hugo Flaxman, *Take Me High* (also known as *Hot Property United Kingdom*), EMI, 1973.
It's Not the Size That Counts (also known as *Percy's Progress*), 1974.

The Adolescents (also known as *Les Adolescentes*), 1976.

Joseph Gabcik, *Operation Daybreak* (also known as *Seven Met at Daybreak* and *The Price of Freedom*), Warner Bros., 1976.

Call Girl, 1976.

Himself, *Observations from under the Volcano* (documentary), Teleculture, 1983.

Himself, *Notes from under the Volcano* (documentary), 1983.

Hugh Firmin, *Under the Volcano,* Universal, 1984.

Johann Tennyson von Tiebolt, *The Holcroft Covenant,* EMI/Universal, 1985.

Major Hanlon, *The Second Victory,* J & M, 1986.

Major Meinertzhagen, *The Lighthorsemen,* Cannon, 1987.

Squadron leader McCormack, *Hanna's War,* Cannon, 1988.

Andrei Miller/Cowboy, *Lost in Siberia* (also known as *Zatyeryanny v Sibri*), 1991.

Robert Mariell, *Haunted,* Evergreen Entertainment, 1995.

Film Work:

(With Lewis Gilbert) Producer, *Haunted,* Evergreen Entertainment, 1995.*

ANSPACH, Susan 1939(?)-

PERSONAL

Born November 23, 1939 (some sources say 1945), in New York, NY; married Mark Goddard (an actor), 1970 (divorced, 1977); married Sherwood Ball, 1983; children: (with Steve Curry) one daughter; (with Jack Nicholson) Caleb Goddard (a producer and writer). *Education:* Attended Catholic University of America.

Addresses: *Agent*—c/o Sharon Kemp Talent Agency, Los Angeles, CA.

Career: Actress.

Member: Actors' Equity Association, American Federation of Television and Radio Artists, Screen Actors Guild.

CREDITS

Film Appearances:

(Film debut) Susan Enders, *The Landlord,* United Artists, 1970.

Catherine Van Ost, *Five Easy Pieces,* Columbia, 1970.

Nancy, *Play It Again Sam,* Paramount, 1972.

Nina Blume, *Blume in Love,* Warner Bros., 1973.

Lila, *The Big Fix,* Universal, 1978.

Janet, *Running,* Universal, 1979.

Penny Hart, *The Devil and Max Devlin,* Buena Vista, 1981.

Jane Beardsley, *Gas,* Paramount, 1981.

Marilyn Jordan, *Montenegro,* 1981.

Lilly, *Misunderstood,* Metro-Goldwyn-Mayer, 1984.

Rosalind Winfield, *Into the Fire* (also known as *The Legend of Wolf Lodge*), 1987.

Karen McKeon, *Heaven and Earth,* [USA], 1987.

Dr. Judith Glass, *Blue Monkey* (also known as *Green Monkey*), Spectrafilm, 1988.

Widow, *Blood Red,* Hemdale, 1990.

Madeline Hix, *Back to Back,* Concorde/Vertex, 1990.

Kate Simpson, *The Rutanga Tapes,* Shapiro Glickenhaus Home Video, 1991.

Television Appearances; Movies:

Donna Jo Martelli, *I Want to Keep My Baby,* 1976.

Wilma, *The Secret of Life of John Chapman,* 1976.

Beverly Dresden, *Rosetti & Ryan: Men Who Love Women,* 1977.

Christian Sebastiani, *Mad Bull,* 1977.

Betty Leslie-Melville, *The Last Giraffe,* 1979.

Jordan West, *Portrait of an Escort,* 1980.

Lucy Dillon, *The First Time,* 1982.

Chris Butler, *Deadly Encounter* (also known as *American Eagle*), 1982.

Gone Are the Days, 1984.

Deborah Nelson, *Cagney & Lacey: The Return,* CBS, 1994.

Television Appearances; Series:

Grace McKenzie, *The Yellow Rose,* NBC, 1983.

Annie Maxwell, *The Slap Maxwell Story,* ABC, 1987-88.

Television Appearances; Other:

Elinor Grant, *James A. Michener's Space* (also known as *Space;* miniseries), CBS, 1985.

"Dead Man's Curve," *Hitchhiker* (episodic), HBO, 1986.

Stage Appearances:

A Coupla White Chicks Sitting Around Talking, Hollywood Playhouse, Los Angeles, 1985.

Performed in Off-Broadway productions in early career.

OTHER SOURCES

Periodicals:
People Weekly, July 1, 1996, p. 46.*

ANTON, Susan   1950(?)-

PERSONAL

Born October 12, 1950 (some sources say 1951), in Yucaipa (some sources say Oak Glen), CA; daughter of Wally (a detective) and Lou Anton; married Jack Stein (divorced, 1979); married Jeff Lester, 1992. *Education:* Attended Bernadino College.

Addresses: *Agent*—c/o International Creative Management, 8942 Wilshire Blvd., Beverly Hills, CA 90211.

Career: Actress and singer. Won title of Miss California, 1969, and tied for second runner-up in the 1970 Miss America pageant. Appeared in advertisements for Muriel cigars, 1976. Performer in nightclubs in Las Vegas, NV; toured the country with Kenny Rogers's concert tour. American Cancer Society, honorary chair; California Special Olympics, honorary chair; U.S. Women's Olympic Volleyball Team, honorary captain.

Awards, Honors: Golden Globe Award nomination, best new female star of the year, 1980, for *Goldengirl.* Japanese gold record for single "Killin' Time."

Member: Actor's Equity Association, Screen Actors Guild, American Federation of Television and Radio Artists.

CREDITS

Film Appearances:
Goldine Serafin and performer of song "Slow Down, I'll Find You," *Goldengirl,* Avco-Embassy, 1979.
Stevie Castle, *Spring Fever* (also known as *Sneakers*), Comworld Pictures, 1983.
Jill, *Cannonball Run II,* Warner Bros., 1984.
Making Mr. Right, Orion, 1987.
Herself, *Options,* Vestron, 1989.
Sara, *Lena's Holiday,* Prism Entertainment, 1991.

Television Appearances; Series:
Cohost, *Mel & Susan Together,* ABC, 1978.

Susan Williams, *Cliff Hangers: Stop Susan Williams* (also known as *Cliff Hangers* and *Stop Susan Williams*), NBC, 1979.
Host, *Presenting Susan Anton,* NBC, 1979.
True Confessions, 1986.
Cohost, *Home,* ABC, 1989.
Jackie Quinn, *Baywatch,* syndicated, 1992-94.
Lainie Lane, *Nick Freno: Licensed Teacher* (also known as *The Teacher* and *What Rules?*), The WB, 1996-97.

Television Appearances; Pilots:
That's TV, NBC, 1982.
Guest judge, *Battle of the Beat,* syndicated, 1983.
Charlotte "Charlie" Montgomery, *Hardesty House,* ABC, 1986.
Julie Brown: The Show, CBS, 1989.

Television Appearances; Movies:
Betty Sue Allen, the previous year's queen, *The Great American Beauty Contest,* ABC, 1973.

Television Appearances; Episodic:
"The Costa Rica Connection," *Hunter,* CBS, 1977.
"For Broke," *Switch,* CBS, 1977.
Host of second program, *The Shape of Things,* NBC, 1982.
"East Meets West," *The Love Boat,* ABC, 1983.
"Deadly Prey," *Mickey Spillane's Mike Hammer* (also known as *The New Mike Hammer*), CBS, 1984.
"Corned Beef and Carnage," *Murder, She Wrote,* CBS, 1986.
"Separation," *Mr. Belvedere,* ABC, 1987.
"Past Tense/All the King's Men," *Hotel,* ABC, 1987.
It's Garry Shandling's Show, Showtime, 1987.
"Memories," *My Secret Identity,* syndicated, 1988.
Diane Lewis, "Animal Lovers," *Alfred Hitchcock Presents,* USA Network, 1988.
"No Baby, No Shower," *It's Garry Shandling's Show,* Fox, 1988.
"The Talk Show," *Night Court,* NBC, 1989.
Herself, *The Pat Sajak Show,* CBS, 1989.
Herself, *Attitudes,* Lifetime, 1989.
"Teddy Falls in Love," *The Famous Teddy Z,* CBS, 1989.
Herself, *The Ben Stiller Show,* Fox, 1992.
Women Aloud (also known as *Funny Ladies*), Comedy Central, 1992.
Herself, "The Breakdown," *The Larry Sanders Show,* HBO, 1993.

Also appeared in episodes of *Blossom,* NBC; *The Merv Griffin Show; Quantum Leap,* NBC; and *The Tonight Show,* NBC.

Television Appearances; Specials:

The Magic of David Copperfield, CBS, 1981.

Bob Hope's Stand up and Cheer for the National Football League's 60th Year, NBC, 1981.

The Suzanne Somers Special, CBS, 1982.

The Boy Who Loved Trolls, 1984.

Placido Domingo . . . Stepping out with the Ladies, ABC, 1985.

How to Be a Man, 1985.

The Academy of Country Music's 20th Anniversary Reunion, 1986.

"Jonathan Winters: On the Ledge" (also known as "The Jonathan Winters Show," *Showtime Comedy Spotlight,* Showtime, 1987.

Candid Camera . . . Funny Money, CBS, 1990.

All New Circus of the Stars and Side Show, CBS, 1991.

(With Ana-Alicia, Roy Firestone, and Kathy Ireland) Host, *The World's Greatest Stunts III,* Fox, 1991.

Miss America: Their Untold Stories (also known as *Miss Americas . . . Where Are They Now?* and *There She Was . . . Miss America*), NBC, 1993.

The World's Greatest Magic II (also known as *The 2nd Annual World's Greatest Magic*), NBC, 1995.

Candid Camera across America, CBS, 1997.

Host, *Las Vegas!,* The Travel Channel, 1997.

Also appeared in the *Anthony Newley Special.*

Television Appearances; Awards Presentations:

The 39th Annual Tony Awards, 1985.

The 40th Annual Tony Awards, 1986.

The Golden Eagle Awards, 1987.

Song performer, "Our Favorite Son," *The Kennedy Center Honors: A Celebration of the Performing Arts* (also known as *The 14th Annual Kennedy Center Honors: A Celebration of the Performing Arts*), CBS, 1991.

Stage Appearances:

Darlene, *Hurlyburly,* New York City, 1985.

Maude Mix, *A Coupla White Chicks Sitting around Talking,* State Theatre, Cleveland, OH, 1985, then Proctor's Theatre, Schenectady, NY, 1986.

Xmas a Go-Go, off-Broadway, 1992.

Ziegfeld's favorite, *The Will Rogers Follies,* Palace Theatre, New York City, 1992.

Also appeared in *They're Playing Our Song.*

Major Tours:

Great Radio City Music Hall Spectacular, U.S. cities, 1994.

Also appeared in *They're Playing Our Song,* U.S. cities.

RECORDINGS

Albums:

Recorded *The First Time* (country and western).

Singles:

"Killin' Time" and "Foxy" (country and western).*

ARBEIT, Herman O. 1925-

PERSONAL

Born April 19, 1925; son of Max (a candystore keeper, packer, and sewing machine operator) and Katie (Zweibel) Arbeit; married Sylvia Newfeld (a receptionist), February 16, 1958; children: Barbara Rachel. *Education:* City College of New York Business School, for three years; studied for the theater at the Neighborhood Playhouse, Herbert Berghof Studios and the Shakespeare Festival, with Sanford Meisner, Morris Carnovsky, Aaron Frankel, and Bobby Lewis.

Addresses: *Contact*—c/o 14055 34th Ave., Apt. 1B, Flushing, NY 11354-3029.

Career: Actor. *Military:* Served in U.S. Army during World War II.

CREDITS

Stage Appearances:

(Debut) Doc, *Come Back, Little Sheba,* Playrads Drama Group, City College of New York, 1952.

Tarleton, *Misalliance,* Cragsmoor, NY, 1954.

Kendall, *Little Scandal,* Cragsmoor, NY, 1954.

(New York debut) Reverend, *Climate of Eden,* Actors Playhouse, New York, NY, 1955.

Doctor, *Boy Meets Girl,* Equity Library, NY, 1955.

Lawyer, *A Dream Play,* Minor Latham, NY, 1957.

Paravicini, *The Mouse Trap,* Rockland County Playhouse, NY, 1959.

Papa, *The Happy Time,* Rockland County Playhouse, NY, 1959.

Sheriff Talbott, *Orpheus Descending,* Rockland County Playhouse, NY, 1959.

Uncle Max, *A Hole in the Head,* Rockland County Playhouse, NY, 1959.

Barney, *Summer of the Seventeenth Doll,* Rockland County Playhouse, NY, 1959.

Bellhop, *The Girls in 509,* Rockland County Playhouse, NY, 1959.

Otto Frank, *Diary of Anne Frank,* Rockland County Playhouse, NY, 1959.

Noah, *The Flowering Peach,* Rockland County Playhouse, NY, 1959.

Walter, *Time Remembered,* Woodstock Playhouse, NY, 1960.

Milgrim, *The Disenchanted,* Woodstock Playhouse, NY, 1960.

Rabbi David and Aaron, *The World of Sholom Aleichem,* Woodstock Playhouse, NY, 1960.

Gant, *Look Homeward, Angel,* Woodstock Playhouse, NY, 1960.

Hunk, *Dead End,* Equity Library, NY, 1960.

Professor, *The Lesson,* Center Stage, Baltimore, MD, 1963.

Brabantio, *Othello,* Corning Summer Theatre, NY, 1963.

Dodds, *Calculated Risk,* Corning Summer Theatre, NY, 1963.

Sidney Black, *Light Up the Sky,* Center Stage, Baltimore, MD, 1963-64.

Chausable, *The Importance of Being Earnest,* Center Stage, Baltimore, MD, 1963-64.

Senator, *The Respectful Prostitute,* Center Stage, Baltimore, MD, 1963-64.

Bert, *The Room,* Center Stage, Baltimore, MD, 1963-64.

Alonzo, *The Tempest,* Washington Theatre Club, Washington, DC, 1965.

Title role, *The Prisoner,* Erie Civic Theatre Association, Erie, PA, 1967.

Peter Stockmann, *An Enemy of the People,* Equity Library, NY, 1968.

Sgt. Carlino, *Wait Until Dark,* Corning Summer Theatre, NY, 1968.

Gilbert, *Everything in the Garden,* Corning Summer Theatre, NY, 1968.

The Merchant, *The Exception and the Rule,* Assembly, NY, 1970.

Duncan, porter, and Hecate, *Macbeth,* North Shore Music Theatre, Beverly, MA, 1972.

Harry Brock, *Born Yesterday,* Firehouse Dinner Theatre, Omaha, NE, 1973.

Uncle Murray, *Moonchildren,* Charles St. Playhouse, Boston, MA, 1974.

Reb Alter, *Yentl,* Chelsea, NY, 1974-75.

Yekel, *God of Vengeance,* Masterworks Laboratory, Brooklyn, NY, 1975.

Reb Alter, *Yentl,* Eugene O'Neill, NY, 1975-76.

Wiseman, Cohn, and understudy Abe, *Knock Knock,* Biltmore, NY, l976.

Dankel, *Marathon '33,* Lion, NY, 1976.

Abe, *Knock Knock,* Center Stage, Baltimore, MD, 1977.

Oscar Wolfe, *The Royal Family,* Seattle Repertory, Seattle, WA, 1977-78.

Loach, *The National Health,* Seattle Repertory, Seattle, WA, 1977-78.

Uncle Morty, *Awake and Sing,* Playwrights Horizons, NY, 1978.

Harry Edison, *The Prisoner of Second Avenue,* Playwrights Horizons, NY, 1978.

Dodge, *Buried Child,* GeVa, Rochester, NY, 1979.

Uncle David, *Me and Molly,* Jewish Repertory, NY, 1980.

Soloway, *The Goodbye People,* PAF, NY, 1981.

Dr. Edward Peller, *In the Matter of J. Robert Oppenheimer,* American Jewish Theatre, NY, 1981.

Ranger Three, *Who Killed Johnny Granger,* Columbia University, NY, 1982.

Zog, *The Seventh Day,* Quaigh, NY, 1983.

Max Glass, *Taking Steam,* Jewish Repertory, NY, 1983.

Judge, *Christopher Blake,* Quaigh, NY, 1983.

Harpagon, *The Miser,* University of Maryland, College Park, MD, 1983.

Cymberline, Globe Playhouse, Los Angeles, CA, 1986-87.

Understudy Ben/Jack, *Broadway Bound,* St. Paul's Ordway Music Theatre, 1988, then Providence Performing Arts Center, 1989.

Mordechai Weiss, *A Shayna Maidel,* Delaware Theatre Company, Wilmington, DE, 1990-91.

Sam, *Black Forest,* Vineyard Theatre/26th Street, New York, NY, 1994.

Participated in a public reading of two unproduced Tennessee Williams' plays, Kathryn Bache Miller Theatre, 1995.

Tours:

Bellamy, *The Fantasticks,* Bermudiana Hotel, Bahamas, 1964.

Mayor, *Never Too Late,* summer tour, Barnesville, PA, then Detroit, MI, 1965.

Doc, *West Side Story,* Beverly, Cohasset, and Hyannis, MA, 1968.

Understudy Gregory Solomon, *The Price,* U.S. cities, 1969-70.

Willy Loman, *Death of a Salesman,* National Theatre Company, 1970-71.

Murray, *The Odd Couple,* Chateau de Ville Dinner Theatre productions tour, MA and CT, 1973-74.

Professor Lyman, *Bus Stop,* ACT tour, KY and IL, 1981.

Television Appearances; Episodic:
(Debut) Waiter, *Concerning Miss Marlowe,* NBC, 1954.
Juror, *Another World,* NBC, 1965.
Superintendent, *Edge of Night,* ABC, 1981.
Police Sergeant, *As the World Turns,* CBS, 1982.
Desk Sergeant, *The Guiding Light,* CBS, 1983.

Other Television Appearances:
Scott Candless, *It's My Body, It's My Life* (special), WCVB, Boston, 1974.
Harry Fine, *Law & Order* (episodic), NBC, 1991.

Film Appearances:
(Debut) Detective, *Cop Haters,* 1964.
Desk Clerk, *Headin' for Broadway,* 1980.

SIDELIGHTS

Herman O. Arbeit earlier told *CTFT:* "In addition to learning and growing in a craft, acting proved to be enormous personal therapy, not only giving me insights to personal problems but challenging me to take the strength garnered onstage and incorporate it into my daily life."*

ARKIN, Alan 1934-
(Robert Short)

PERSONAL

Full name, Alan Wolf Arkin; born March 26, 1934, in Brooklyn, NY; son of David I. (an artist and teacher) and Beatrice (a teacher; maiden name, Wortis) Arkin; married second wife, Barbara Dana (an actress and author), June 16, 1964; children: (first marriage) Adam (an actor), Matthew; (second marriage) Anthony. *Education:* Attended Los Angeles City College, 1951-52, Los Angeles State College (now California State University, Los Angeles), 1952-53, and Bennington College, 1953-55; studied acting with Benjamin Zemach, 1952-55.

Addresses: *Agent*—William Morris Agency, 151 El Camino Dr., Beverly Hills, CA 90212.

Career: Actor, director, composer, and writer. Member of folksinging group the Tarriers, 1957-59; actor in improvisational theatre with the Compass Players, St. Louis, MO, 1959, and (as an original member) with Second City, Chicago, IL, 1960; director of theatrical revues in the early 1960s; member of

children's music group the Babysitters. Worked briefly in vacuum cleaner repair and as a clerical worker.

Member: American Federation of Television and Radio Artists; American Federation of Musicians; American Society of Composers, Authors, and Publishers; Actors' Equity Association; Screen Actors Guild.

Awards, Honors: Antoinette Perry Award, best supporting actor, *Theatre World* Award, and *Variety* New York Drama Critics Poll Award, all 1963, for *Enter Laughing;* Emmy Award nomination, outstanding single performance by an actor in a leading role in a drama, 1966, for *ABC Stage 67;* Golden Globe Award, best actor in a musical or comedy, and Academy Award nomination, best actor, both 1967, for *The Russians Are Coming, the Russians Are Coming;* Academy Award nomination and New York Critics Award, both best actor, 1968, for *The Heart Is a Lonely Hunter;* Drama Desk Award, outstanding director, 1969, for *Little Murders;* Academy Award nomination, best live action short subject, 1969, for *People Soup;* Drama Desk Award, outstanding director, and Obie Award, distinguished directing, both 1970, for *The White House Murder Case.*

Golden Globe Award nomination, best motion picture actor—drama, 1970, for *Popi; Tony's Hard Work Day* listed as a book of the year by the Child Study Association of America, 1972; Antoinette Perry Award nomination, best director, 1973, for *The Sunshine Boys;* New York Critics Award, best supporting actor, 1975, for *Hearts of the West; The Lemming Condition* listed as a book of the year by the Child Study Association of America and named an outstanding book of the year by the *New York Times,* both 1976; Genie Award, best performance by a foreign actor, 1982, for *Improper Channels;* Genie Award, best actor in a supporting role, 1986, for *Joshua Then and Now;* Emmy Award nomination, outstanding actor in a miniseries or special, 1987 and Simon Wiesenthal Center Distinguished Service Award for the Performing Arts, 1989, both for *Escape from Sobibor.*

CREDITS

Stage Appearances:
Singer, *Heloise,* Gate Theatre, New York City, 1958.
Compass Players, Crystal Palace, St. Louis, MO, 1959.

Member of ensemble, *From the Second City* (revue), Royale Theatre, New York City, 1961, then off-Broadway, 1962.

Jimmy, *Man Out Loud, Girl Quiet* and *The Spanish Armada* (double-bill), Cricket Theatre, New York City, 1962.

Seacoast of Bohemia: Alarums and Excursions, Second City, Square East Theatre, New York City, 1962.

David Kolowitz, *Enter Laughing,* Henry Miller Theatre, New York City, 1963.

Member of ensemble, *A View from under the Bridge* (revue), Second City, Square East Theatre, 1964.

Harry Berlin, *Luv,* Booth Theatre, New York City, 1964.

The Opening, 1972.

Also appeared in *The Sunshine Boys* and *The Sorrows of Stephen.*

Major Tours:
David Kolowitz, *Enter Laughing,* U.S. cities, 1964.

Stage Director:
(As Robert Short) *Eh?,* Circle in the Square Theatre, New York City, 1966.

Hail Scrawdyke!, Booth Theatre, 1966.

Little Murders, Circle in the Square Theatre, 1969.

The White House Murder Case, Circle in the Square Theatre, 1970.

The Sunshine Boys, Broadhurst Theatre, New York City, 1972.

Molly, Alvin Theatre, New York City, 1973.

Joan of Lorraine, 1974.

Rubbers and *Yanks 3 Detroit 0, Top of the Seventh* (double-bill), American Place Theatre, New York City, 1975.

The Soft Touch, Wilbur Theatre, Boston, MA, 1975.

Joan of Lorraine, Hartman Theatre, Stamford, CT, 1976.

Sorrows of Stephen, Burt Reynolds Dinner Theatre, Jupiter, FL, 1984.

Room Service, Roundabout Theatre, New York City, 1986.

Forgive Me, Evelyn Bunns, Asolo State Theatre, Sarasota, FL, 1986.

Film Appearances:
(As part of musical group the Tarriers) *Calypso Heat Wave,* Columbia, 1957.

That's Me (short film), 1963.

The Last Mohican (short film), 1965.

Lieutenant Rozanov, *The Russians Are Coming, the Russians Are Coming* (also known as *The Rus-*

sians Are Coming! The Russians Are Coming!), United Artists, 1966.

Various roles, including Fred, *Woman Times Seven* (also known as *Sept Fois Femme* and *Sette Volte Donna*), Embassy, 1967.

Harry Roat Jr., *Wait until Dark,* Warner Bros.-Seven Arts, 1967.

John Singer, *The Heart Is a Lonely Hunter,* Warner Bros.-Seven Arts, 1968.

Chief Inspector Jacques Claus, *Inspector Claus,* United Artists, 1968.

Himself, *The Monitors,* Commonwealth United Entertainment, 1969.

Abraham Rodriguez, *Popi,* United Artists, 1969.

Captain John Yossarian, *Catch-22,* Filmways, 1970.

Detective, *Little Murders,* Twentieth Century-Fox, 1971.

Barney Cashman, *Last of the Red Hot Lovers,* Paramount, 1972.

Bean, *Freebie and the Bean,* Warner Bros., 1974.

Kessler, *Hearts of the West* (also known as *Hollywood Cowboy*), United Artists, 1975.

Gunny Rafferty, *Rafferty and the Gold Dust Twins* (also known as *Rafferty and the Highway Hustlers*), Warner Bros., 1975.

Ezra Fikus, *Fire Sale,* Twentieth Century-Fox, 1977.

Sigmund Freud, *The Seven-per-cent Solution* (also known as *Seven Per Cent Solution* and *The Seven Percent Solution*), Universal, 1977.

Sheldon Kornpett, *The In-Laws,* Warner Bros., 1979.

Yasha Mazur, *The Magician of Lublin,* Cannon, 1979.

Simon Mendelssohn, *Simon,* Warner Bros., 1980.

Flash, *Chu Chu and the Philly Flash,* Twentieth Century-Fox, 1981.

Jeffrey Martley, *Improper Channels,* Rank-Crown International, 1981.

Cooper, *Deadhead Miles,* Paramount, 1982.

Dr. Jacob Brand, *Full Moon High,* Filmways, 1982.

Voice of Schmendrick the Magician, *The Last Unicorn* (animated), ITC, 1982.

Captain Invincible, *The Return of Captain Invincible* (also known as *Legend in Leotards*), Seven Keys, 1983.

Dr. Ramon Madera, *Bad Medicine,* Twentieth Century-Fox, 1985.

Reuben Shapiro, *Joshua Then and Now,* Twentieth Century-Fox, 1985.

Leonard Hoffman, *Big Trouble,* Columbia, 1986.

Fred Libner, *Coupe de Ville,* Universal, 1990.

Bill Boggs, *Edward Scissorhands,* Twentieth Century-Fox, 1990.

Joe Volpi, *Havana,* Universal, 1990.

Peevy, *The Rocketeer,* Buena Vista, 1991.

George Aaronow, *Glengarry Glen Ross,* New Line, 1992.

Uncle Lou, *Indian Summer,* Touchstone, 1993.
So I Married an Axe Murderer, TriStar, 1993.
The director, *Samuel Beckett Is Coming Soon,* I'mnd Productions/Tiny Baby Productions, 1993.
Tommy Canard, *Taking the Heat,* FoxVideo, 1993.
Lazarro, *The Jerky Boys,* Buena Vista, 1994.
Judge Buckle, *North,* Columbia, 1994.
Lou Perilli, *Steal Big, Steal Little,* Savoy Pictures, 1995.
George Kraft, *Mother Night,* Fine Line Features, 1996.
Dr. Oatman, *Grosse Pointe Blank,* Buena Vista, 1997.
Charles Elbrick, *Four Days in September* (also known as *O Que E Isso, Companheiro?*), Miramax, 1997.
Hugo Coldspring, *Gattaca* (also known as *The Eighth Day*), Sony Pictures Entertainment, 1997.
Hugo Pool, BMG Independents, 1997.
The Slums of Beverly Hills, Fox Searchlight Pictures, 1998.
Jakob the Liar, TriStar, 1998.
Arigo, True Crime Productions, 1998.

Film Work:
Producer, *That's Me* (short film), 1963.
Producer, *The Last Mohican* (short film), 1965.
Director, *Thank God It's Friday* (short film; also known as *T.G.I.F.*), Columbia, 1967.
Director and producer, *People Soup* (short film), Columbia, 1969.
Director, *Little Murders,* Twentieth Century-Fox, 1971.
Director, *Fire Sale,* Twentieth Century-Fox, 1977.
Executive producer, *The In-Laws,* Warner Bros., 1979.
Director and producer, *Samuel Beckett Is Coming Soon,* I'mnd Productions/Tiny Baby Productions, 1993.
Director, *Arigo,* True Crime Productions, 1998.

Television Appearances; Series:
Harry Porschak, *Harry,* CBS, 1987.

Television Executive Producer; Series:
(With others) *Harry,* CBS, 1987.

Television Appearances; Movies:
It Couldn't Happen to a Nicer Guy, 1974.
Frank Dole, *The Other Side of Hell* (also known as *Escape from Hell*), NBC, 1978.
Simas Kudirka, *The Defection of Simas Kudirka,* CBS, 1978.
Harold Kaufman, *A Deadly Business,* CBS, 1986.
Leon Feldhandler, *Escape from Sobibor,* CBS, 1987.
Harry Willette, *Cooperstown,* TNT, 1993.
Tommy Canard, *Taking the Heat,* Showtime, 1993.

Yossi, *Doomsday Gun,* HBO, 1994.
Dogcatcher, *Heck's Way Home* (also known as *The Long Way Home*), Showtime, 1996.

Television Appearances; Specials:
"The Love Song of Barney Kempinski," *ABC Stage 67,* ABC, 1966.
Husband, "Double Trouble," *The Trouble with People,* NBC, 1972.
Lawrence, "Natasha Kovolina Pipishinsky," *Love, Life, Liberty, and Lunch,* ABC, 1976.
To America, CBS, 1976.
Flagg Purdy, "A Matter of Principle," *American Playhouse,* PBS, 1984.
Bo, "The Emperor's New Clothes," *Faerie Tale Theater* (also known as *Faerie Tale Theater: The Emperor's New Clothes*), Showtime, 1985.
Orontes, *The Fourth Wise Man,* ABC, 1985.
The Second City Twenty-fifth Anniversary Special, 1985.
Archie Correlli, "Necessary Parties," *WonderWorks,* PBS, 1988.
The Kennedy Center 25th Anniversary Celebration, PBS, 1996.
Interviewee, "Catch-22," *Great Books,* TLC, 1996.
Presenter, *The 49th Annual Primetime Emmy Awards,* CBS, 1997.

Television Work; Specials:
(With Clark Jones) Director, *Twigs,* CBS, 1975.
(With others) Producer, "Necessary Parties," *WonderWorks,* PBS, 1988.

Television Appearances; Episodic:
(With Second City) *The David Susskind Show,* syndicated, 1962.
"The Beatnik and the Politician," *East Side/West Side,* CBS, 1964.
The Les Crane Show, ABC, 1964.
The Les Crane Show, ABC, 1965.
Busting Loose, CBS, 1977.
Himself, *The Muppet Show,* syndicated, 1979.
"The Ties that Bind," *St. Elsewhere,* NBC, 1983.
"Newheart," *St. Elsewhere,* NBC, 1983.
"E.M. 7, Raiders Minus Three and a Half for a Nickel," *A Year in the Life,* NBC, 1987.
Tully, "Soir Bleu," *Picture Windows,* Showtime, 1995.

Also appeared as Zoltan Karpathein, "The Son Also Rises," *Chicago Hope,* CBS; in *Sesame Street,* PBS; and *Captain Kangaroo,* CBS.

Television Director; Episodic:
"The Visit," *Trying Times,* PBS, 1987.
"The Boss," *Trying Times,* PBS, 1989.

Television Director; Pilots:
(With others) *Fay,* NBC, 1975.

Other Television Work:
Director of a number of short films.

RECORDINGS

Albums; Cast Recordings:
Luv: A New Comedy, Columbia, 1965.

Albums with the Babysitters:
The Babysitters, 1958.
Songs and Fun with the Babysitters, 1960.
The Family Album, 1965.
The Babysitters Menagerie, 1968.

Singles with the Tarriers:
"The Banana Boat Song," 1957.

Also recorded other projects with the Tarriers.

WRITINGS

Stage Music:
Man Out Loud, Girl Quiet, Cricket Theatre, 1962.
(And author of lyrics and sketches) *A View from under the Bridge,* Square East Theatre, 1964.

Composer of songs, including "Cuddle Bug," "That's Me," and "Best Time of the Year."

Screenplays:
People Soup (short film), Columbia, 1969.

Teleplays; Specials:
(With others) "Necessary Parties," *WonderWorks,* PBS, 1988.

Juvenile Fiction:
Tony's Hard Work Day, illustrated by James Stevenson, Harper, 1972.
The Lemming Condition, illustrated by Joan Sandin, Harper, 1976.
The Clearing, Harper, 1986.

Also author of *Some Fine Grandpa.*

Autobiographies:
Halfway through the Door: An Actor's Journey toward the Self, Harper, 1979.

Other Writings:
Contributor to periodicals, including *Galaxy.*

OTHER SOURCES

Books:
Contemporary Authors, Volume 112, Gale (Detroit, MI), 1985, pp. 30-32.
Something about the Author, Volume 59, Gale, 1990, pp. 1-8.

Periodicals:
New York Times, February 9, 1986.*

ARMSTRONG, Gillian   1950-

PERSONAL

Full name, Gillian May Armstrong; born December 18, 1950, in Melbourne, Australia; father in real estate, mother a schoolteacher; married John Pffefer (a film editor); children: two daughters. *Education:* Studied stage and costume design at Swinbourne College; studied filmmaking at Australian Film and Television School.

Addresses: *Home*—Sydney, Australia. *Agent*—Creative Artists Agency, 9830 Wilshire Blvd., Beverly Hills, CA 90212.

Career: Director, producer, art director, and screenwriter. Director of television commercials; also worked as production assistant, assistant designer, and assistant editor of industrial and educational films. Worked as a waitress. Associated with Women's Film Group, Sydney, Australia.

Awards, Honors: Sydney Film Festival Award, best short film, 1976, for *The Singer and the Dancer;* British Critics' Award, best first feature, and seven Australian Film Institute Awards, including best film and best director, all 1980, for *My Brilliant Career;* FACTS Award, best travel commercial, 1982, for an American Express television commercial; eleven award nominations, Australian Film Institute, 1993, for *The Last Days of Chez Nous;* Victoria Teachers Federation award for the documentary trilogy of *Smokes and Lollies, Fourteen's Good, Eighteen's Better,* and

Bingo, Bridesmaids, and Braces; Australian Film Festival award nomination, best documentary, 1996, for *Not Fourteen Again.*

CREDITS

Film Work; Director, Except Where Indicated:
Old Man and Dog (short film), 1970.
Roof Needs Mowing (short film), 1971.
Gretel (short film), 1973.
Satdee Night (short film), 1973.
One Hundred a Day (also known as *100 a Day;* short film), 1973.
Art director, *Promised Woman,* BC Productions, 1974.
Assistant art director, *The Removalists,* 1975.
Art director, *The Trespassers,* Filmways, 1975.
Smokes and Lollies (documentary), 1975.
And producer, *The Singer and the Dancer,* Columbia, 1976.
My Brilliant Career, Analysis, 1979.
And co-producer, *Fourteen's Good, Eighteen's Better* (documentary), 1980.
A Busy Kind of Bloke, 1980.
Touch Wood (documentary), 1980.
Starstruck, Cinecom, 1982.
Having a Go (documentary), 1983.
Not Just a Pretty Face, 1983.
Mrs. Soffel, Metro-Goldwyn-Mayer/United Artists, 1984.
High Tide, Hemdale, 1987.
And producer, *Bingo, Bridesmaids, and Braces* (short documentary), Big Picture, 1988.
Fires Within, Metro-Goldwyn-Mayer/United Artists Home Video, 1991.
The Last Days of Chez Nous, Fine Line, 1993.
Little Women, Columbia, 1994.
And producer, *Not Fourteen Again* (documentary; also known as *Now They Are Fourteen* and *Not 14 Again!*), Beyond Films, 1996.
Oscar and Lucinda, Fox Searchlight, 1997.

Director of the short film *Storytime,* the documentary *A Time and a Place,* and the documentary *Tassie Wood;* assisted on the short film *Zibido.*

Film Appearances:
Nurse, *Promised Woman,* BC Productions, 1974.
Interviewer, *Smokes and Lollies* (documentary), 1975.
Interviewer, *Fourteen's Good, Eighteen's Better* (documentary), 1980.
Herself, *A Busy Kind of Bloke,* 1980.

Television Work; Specials:
Producer and director, *Bob Dylan in Concert,* HBO, 1986.
Director, *Hard to Handle: Bob Dylan with Tom Petty and the Heartbreakers,* HBO, 1986.

WRITINGS

Films:
Gretel, 1973.
Smokes and Lollies (documentary), 1975.
(With John Pleffer) *The Singer and the Dancer,* Columbia, 1976.
Fourteen's Good, Eighteen's Better (documentary), 1980.
A Busy Kind of Bloke, 1980.
Touch Wood (documentary), 1980.
Not Just a Pretty Face, 1983.
Not Fourteen Again (documentary; also known as *Now They Are Fourteen* and *Not 14 Again!*), Beyond Films, 1996.

Other:
Contributor to periodicals, including *Films in Review.*

OTHER SOURCES

Periodicals:
American Film, January-February, 1985.
Film Comment, March, 1993.
Harper's Bazaar, March, 1993, pp. 102-103.
Los Angeles Times, March 21, 1993.
New Yorker, March 1, 1993.
New York Times, March 8, 1995.
Premiere, May, 1993.
Washington Post, April 4, 1993.*

ARNESS, James   1923-
　　(James Aurness)

PERSONAL

Real name, James Aurness; born May 26, 1923, in Minneapolis, MN; son of Rolf C. and Ruth (Duesler) Arness; married Virginia Chapman, February 12, 1948 (divorced, 1960); married Janet Surtees, 1978; children: (first marriage) Craig, Jenny Lee, Rolf; brother of Peter Graves (an actor). *Education:* Attended Beloit College.

Addresses: *Home*—Los Angeles and Santa Barbara, CA. *Contact*—P.O. Box 49599, Los Angeles, CA 90049.

Career: Actor. Also worked as an advertising executive, a real estate salesperson, and a carpenter. *Military service:* Served in the U.S. Army during World War II.

Member: American Federation of Television and Radio Artists, Screen Actors Guild.

CREDITS

Television Appearances; Series:
Matt Dillon, *Gunsmoke* (also known as *Marshall Dillon*), CBS, 1955-75.
Zeb Macahan, *How the West Was Won,* ABC, 1978-79.
Detective Jim McClain, *McClain's Law,* NBC, 1981-82.

Television Appearances; Miniseries:
Zeb Macahan, *How the West Was Won,* ABC, 1977.

Television Appearances; Movies:
Zeb Macahan, *The Macahans,* ABC, 1976.
Jim Bowie, *The Alamo: Thirteen Days to Glory,* NBC, 1987.
Matt Dillon, *Gunsmoke: Return to Dodge,* CBS, 1987.
Tom Dunson, *Red River,* CBS, 1988.
Matt Dillon, *Gunsmoke: The Last Apache,* CBS, 1990.
Matt Dillon, *Gunsmoke: To the Last Man,* CBS, 1992.
Matt Dillon, *Gunsmoke: The Long Ride,* CBS, 1993.
Matt Dillon, *Gunsmoke: One Man's Justice,* CBS, 1994.

Television Appearances; Specials:
Himself, *The 11th Annual Emmy Awards,* 1960.
Himself, *A Salute to Television's 25th Anniversary,* 1972.
Host, *John Wayne Standing Tall,* 1989.

Television Work; Executive Producer:
Gunsmoke: The Long Ride, CBS, 1993.
Gunsmoke: One Man's Justice, CBS, 1994.

Film Appearances:
(As James Aurness) Peter Holstrom, *Farmer's Daughter,* RKO Radio Pictures, 1947.
Ray, *Roses Are Red,* Twentieth Century-Fox, 1947.
Garby, *Battleground,* Metro-Goldwyn-Mayer, 1948.
The Man from Texas, Eagle-Lion, 1948.
Russell, *Wyoming Mail,* Universal, 1950.
Kirk Hamilton, *Two Lost Worlds,* Eagle-Lion, 1950.
Little Sam, *Sierra,* Universal, 1950.
Floyd Clegg, *Wagon Master* (also known as *Wagonmaster*), RKO Radio Pictures, 1950.

Double Crossbones, Universal, 1950.
Stars in My Crown, Metro-Goldwyn-Mayer, 1950.
Alex Malik, *Iron Man,* Universal, 1951.
Johnny O'Hara, *The People Against O'Hara,* Metro-Goldwyn-Mayer, 1951.
The Thing, *The Thing from Another World* (also known as *The Thing*), RKO Radio Pictures, 1951.
Belle le Grand, Republic, 1951.
Barth, *The Cavalry Scout,* Monogram, 1951.
Mal Baxter, *Big Jim McClain* (also known as *Jim McClain*), Warner Bros., 1952.
Tiny McGilligan, *Horizons West,* Universal, 1952.
George Redfield, *Hellgate,* Lippert, 1952.
Matt, *The Girl in White* (also known as *So Bright the Flame*), Metro-Goldwyn-Mayer, 1952.
Leon Williams, *Carbine Williams,* Metro-Goldwyn-Mayer, 1952.
Ride the Man Down, Republic, 1952.
Gus Varden, *Lone Hand,* Universal, 1953.
Mutant crouching by Raygunner, *Invaders from Mars,* Twentieth Century-Fox, 1953.
McMullen, *Island in the Sky,* Warner Bros., 1953.
Lennie, *Hondo,* Warner Bros., 1953.
Targut, *The Veils of Bagdad,* Universal, 1953.
Robert Graham, *Them!,* Warner Bros., 1954.
Ralph Munsey, *Her Twelve Men,* Metro-Goldwyn-Mayer, 1954.
Esau Hamilton, *Many Rivers to Cross,* Metro-Goldwyn-Mayer, 1955.
Schlieter, *The Sea Chase,* Warner Bros., 1955.
Joel Kingdom, *The First Traveling Saleslady,* RKO Radio Pictures, 1956.
Rem Anderson, *Gun the Man Down* (also known as *Arizona Mission*), United Artists, 1956.
Kelly Rand, *Flame of the Islands,* Republic, 1958.
Matt Dillon, *Alias Jesse James,* United Artists, 1959.

OTHER SOURCES

Books:
Celebrity Register, 1990, Gale (Detroit, MI), 1990.*

AURNESS, James
    See ARNESS, James

AXTON, Hoyt   1938-

PERSONAL

Full name, Hoyt Wayne Axton; born March 25, 1938, in Duncan (one source says Comanche), OK; son of John Thomas and N. Mae (a writer of songs such as

Elvis Presley's "Heartbreak Hotel"; maiden name, Boren) Axton; married Kathy Roberts, 1963 (divorced, 1973); married Donna, 1980 (divorced, 1990); married Deborah Hawkins, August 28, 1997; children: Mark Roberts, Michael Stephen, April Laura, Matthew Christopher. *Education:* Attended Oklahoma State University, 1957-58. *Politics:* Democrat.

Addresses: *Home*—Hendersonville, TN. *Office*—Jeremiah Records, Inc., P.O. Box 1077, Hendersonville, TN 37075. *Email*—hoyt@sixcats .com. *Agent*—Charles Stern Agency, 11766 Wilshire Blvd., Suite 760, Los Angeles, CA 90028.

Career: Actor, composer, and singer. Chairperson, Jeremiah Records, 1979—. Spokesperson for American Heart Association, 1975, and UNICEF, 1975-76. Appeared in television commercials for companies such as McDonald's, 1970, Busch Beer, and Pizza Hut. Has been active in the political campaigns of Eugene McCarthy, George McGovern, Edmund Brown, and David Borean. Fundraiser for INTERPLAST, Free Clinics, Redwing Foundation, and Bread and Roses Foundation. *Military service:* U.S. Navy, 1958-62.

Member: Screen Actors Guild, American Federation of Television and Radio Artists, American Federation of Musicians, Country Music Association, Broadcast Music Inc., Oklahoma Cattlemen's Association.

Awards, Honors: Bread and Roses Foundation Award, 1984.

CREDITS

Television Appearances; Series:
Cactus Jack Slade, *The Rousters,* NBC, 1983-84.
Rip Steele, *Domestic Life,* CBS, 1984.

Television Appearances; Miniseries:
Voice, *The Civil War,* PBS, 1990.
Voice of John B. Gordon, *Smithsonian's Great Battles of the Civil War,* TLC, 1994.

Television Appearances; Pilots:
Cyrus Flint, *Skinflint,* 1979.
Hoyt Axton Show, NBC, 1981.
Red, *Steel Collar Man,* CBS, 1985.
Walter "Doodle" Pierce, *Doodle's,* ABC, 1988.

Television Appearances; Movies:
Silous Huddleston, *Act of Vengeance* (also known as *Act of Violence*), HBO, 1986.

Aaron Southworth, *Dallas: The Early Years,* CBS, 1986.
Charlie Hartford, *Guilty of Innocence: The Lenell Geter Story* (also known as *The Lenell Geter Story* and *Justice Delayed: The Lenell Geter Story*), CBS, 1987.
Al Bensinger, *Christmas Comes to Willow Creek* (also known as *Christmas Comes to Copper Creek*), CBS, 1987.
Sheriff Ben Tree, *Desperado: Avalanche at Devil's Ridge,* NBC, 1988.
Sheriff Sam Eberly, *Buried Alive* (also known as *Till Death Do Us Part*), USA Network, 1990.
Jake, *Doorways,* 1993.
Huey P. Long, Sr., *Kingfish: A Story of Huey P. Long,* TNT, 1995.

Television Appearances; Episodic:
"Dead and Gone," *Bonanza,* NBC, 1965.
Bob Hope Presents the Chrysler Theatre, NBC, 1965.
Bull, "Fastest Gun in the East," *I Dream of Jeannie,* NBC, 1966.
"Right of Way through Paradise," *Iron Horse,* ABC, 1966.
Guest, *Smothers Brothers Show,* CBS, 1975.
Midnight Special, NBC, 1975-77.
Dinah Shore Show (four appearances), 1975-77.
"Road to Nashville," *Bionic Woman,* ABC, 1976.
McCloud, NBC, 1976.
The Tonight Show (ten appearances), NBC, 1976 and 1977.
Hee Haw, syndicated, 1977, 1979, 1982, and 1984.
"Great Expectations," *Flying High,* CBS, 1978.
T. J. Watson, "I Do, I Do . . . For Now," *WKRP in Cincinnati,* CBS, c. 1978.
Nashville on the Road, syndicated, 1980-81.
Barbara Mandrell and the Mandrell Sisters, NBC, 1981.
"Good Neighbors Duke," *Dukes of Hazzard,* CBS, 1981.
Flo, CBS, 1982.
Cooper Johnson, *Seven Brides for Seven Brothers,* CBS, 1983.
"Goldilocks and the Three Bears," *Faerie Tale Theater,* Showtime, 1984.
Domestic Life, CBS, 1984.
Star Search, syndicated, 1984.
"Death in Vogue," *Cover up,* CBS, 1984.
Nashville Now, TNN, 1984.
Wes McKinney, "Sam's Father," *Diff'rent Strokes,* NBC, 1984.
Wes McKinney, "A Camping We Will Go," *Diff'rent Strokes,* NBC, 1985.
"Game of Hearts," *Trapper John, M.D.,* CBS, 1985.

"The Runaway," *Glitter,* ABC, 1985.
Guest, *Today's Country,* TNN, 1997.

Also appeared on *Music Hall America.*

Television Appearances; Specials:
The Hoyt Axton Country Western, Boogie Woogie, Gospel, Rock and Roll Show, 1975.
The All-Star Salute to Mother's Day, 1981.
Fairs and Festivals: Fan Fair/Nashville, TNN, 1990.
Narration, *Harley-Davidson: The American Motorcycle,* TNT, 1993.
The America's Awards, TNN, 1993.
The Legend of the Beverly Hillbillies, CBS, 1993.
Host, *The Life and Times of Conway Twitty,* TNN, 1995.
Host, *The Life and Times of Hank Williams,* TNN, 1995.
Host, *The Life and Times of Marty Robbins,* TNN, 1995.

Film Appearances:
The Story of a Folk Singer, 1963.
Fred, *Smoky,* Twentieth Century-Fox, 1966.
Silous Huddleston, *Act of Vengeance,* 1974.
Alec's father, *The Black Stallion,* United Artists, 1980.
Cecil Duncan, *Liar's Moon,* 1981.
Junkman, 1982.
Ben Morgan, *Endangered Species,* Metro-Goldwyn-Mayer/United Artists, 1982.
Tex Roque, *Heart Like a Wheel,* Twentieth Century-Fox, 1983.
Deadline Autotheft, 1983.
Rand Peltzer, *Gremlins,* Warner Bros., 1984.
Lt. Ashley, *Retribution,* United, 1988.
Clarence Laidlaw, *Dixie Lanes,* 1988.
Father Levesque, *We're No Angels,* Paramount, 1989.
Sheriff Henault, *Disorganized Crime,* Buena Vista, 1989.
Bill Stratton, *Harmony Cats,* Triboro Entertainment Group, 1994.
"Big" Upton, *Season of Change,* Monarch Home Video, 1995.
Lt. Joe Halsey, *Number One Fan,* Orion Home Video, 1995.

Stage Appearances:
Ernest Tubb Record Shop, Nashville, 1974-75.

Appeared at the Grand Ole Opry, Nashville, TN, 1974-76, 1980, 1982-83; Ernest Tubb Record Shop, Nashville, 1974-75, 1979; Ralph Emery Show, Nashville, 1974-76; Inaugural Ball for President Jimmy Carter, 1977.

WRITINGS

Songs:
(With Ken Ramsey), "Greenback Dollar," recorded by the Kingston Trio, 1962.
"The Pusher," recorded by Steppenwolf, 1964.
"Snowblind Friend," recorded by Steppenwolf, 1967.
"Joy to the World (Jeremiah)," recorded by Three Dog Night, also recorded by Axton, 1971.
"Never Been to Spain," recorded by Three Dog Night, 1972.
"Ease Your Pain," 1973.
"When the Morning Comes," recorded by Linda Ronstadt and Axton, 1974.
"Boney Fingers," recorded by Renee Armand and Axton, 1974.
"Lion in the Winter," 1974.
"The No, No Song," recorded by Ringo Starr, 1975.
"Flash of Fire," 1976.
"You're the Hangnail in My Life," 1977.

Also author of "Fearless," "Free Sailin'," "Life Machine," "My Griffin Is Gone," "Evangelina," and "Wild Bull Rider."

Stage Musicals:
The Happy Song, 1972.

Film Soundtracks:
Outlaw Blues, 1977.
Junkman, 1982.

Books:
Line Drawings, Volumes I-V, 1974-78.

Songbooks:
Life Machine, 1973.
Southbound, 1974.
Less Than the Song, 1977.

RECORDINGS

Albums:
Less Than the Song, A&M, 1973.
Life Machine, A&M, 1974.
Southbound, A&M, 1975.
Fearless, A&M, 1976.
Road Songs, A&M, 1977.
A Rusty Old Halo, Jeremiah Records, 1979.
Spin of the Wheel, 1990.
Snowblind Friend, MCA, 1995.
Free Sailin', MCA, 1996.
Hoyt Axton, Youngheart Music, 1996.

Also *Hoyt Axton Live* and *Pistol Packin' Mama,* both Jeremiah Records; *Heartbreak Hotel,* Accord; *Where Did the Money Go?;* and *Hoyt Axton's Greatest Hits.*

Singles:
Also "Fearless the Wonder Dog," "Evangelina," "Torpedo," "So Hard to Give It All Up," "Smile as You Go By," "Where Did the Money Go?," "Jealous Man," "She's Too Lazy to Be Crazy," "There Stands the Glass," "James Dean and the Junkman," "The Devil," "(When You Dance) You Do Not Tango," and "Wild Bull Rider."

SIDELIGHTS

Favorite part: Alec's father in *Black Stallion.* Hoyt's song "The Pusher" won him acclaim in the film *Easy Rider.*

OTHER SOURCES

Websites:
http://www.sixcats.com/axton/hoyt.htm.

B

BABCOCK, Barbara 1937-

PERSONAL

Born February 27, 1937, in Fort Riley, KS; raised in Japan; daughter of a general in the U.S. Army and an actress; married twice. *Education:* Wellesley College, B.A.; language certificates from University of Lausanne and University of Milan. *Avocational interests:* Attending archaeological and anthropological research expeditions in Africa and South America.

Addresses: *Agent*—c/o Paradigm, 10100 Santa Monica Blvd., 25th floor, Los Angeles, CA 90067.

Career: Actress. Claremont Graduate School, member of board of trustees, 1983—.

Awards, Honors: Emmy Award, outstanding lead actress in a drama series, 1981, for *Hill Street Blues;* Annual Cable Excellence Television Award, best actress in a dramatic series, 1987, for *Alfred Hitchcock Presents.*

CREDITS

Television Appearances; Series:
Liz Craig, *Dallas,* CBS, 1978-82.
Grace Gardner, *Hill Street Blues,* NBC, 1981-85.
Lorraine Elliot, *The Four Seasons,* CBS, 1984.
Mrs. June Swinford, *Mr. Sunshine,* ABC, 1986.
Ellie McGinnis, *The Law and Harry McGraw,* CBS, 1987-88.
Mae Hackett, *Wings,* NBC, 1990.
Sisters, NBC, 1992.
Dorothy Jennings, *Dr. Quinn, Medicine Woman,* CBS, 1993—.

Also appeared in *Search for Tomorrow.*

Television Appearances; Movies:
Shelley Drumm, *The Last Child,* ABC, 1971.
Rachel Sullivan, *A Christmas Miracle in Caufield, U.S.A.* (also known as *The Christmas Coal Mine Miracle*), NBC, 1977.
Lorna Sims, *The Survival of Dana,* CBS, 1979.
June Petrie, *Salem's Lot* (also known as *Blood Thirst, Salem's Lot: The Miniseries,* and *Salem's Lot: The Movie*), CBS, 1979.
Louise Lowry, *Memories Never Die,* CBS, 1982.
Judy Maida, *Quarterback Princess,* CBS, 1983.
Jane Dutton, *Attack on Fear,* CBS, 1984.
Joanne Steckler, *News at Eleven,* CBS, 1986.
Quinn Collins, *A Family for Joe* (also known as *Family Man* and *One Man's Family*), NBC, 1990.
Martha Robertson, *Perry Mason: The Case of the Poisoned Pen* (also known as *The Case of the Poisoned Pen* and *Perry Mason: The Case of the Murder Mystery Murder*), NBC, 1990.
Rhonda Devon, *Fugitive Nights: Danger in the Desert,* NBC, 1993.
Louise Mitchell, *A Mother's Instinct,* CBS, 1996.
Rose Carlson, *Childhood Sweetheart?,* CBS, 1997.

Television Appearances; Episodic:
Woman at Savoy, "The Quiet Warrior," *Combat,* ABC, 1962.
Pamela Osborne, "The Devil and Dobie Gillis," *The Many Loves of Dobie Gillis,* CBS, 1963.
"Bats of a Feather," *The Munsters,* CBS, 1965.
"Katy's New Job," *The Farmer's Daughter,* ABC, 1965.
Voice of Trelayne's mother, "The Squire of Gothos," *Star Trek,* NBC, 1966.
"Programmed for Death," *The Green Hornet,* ABC, 1966.
"The Frog Is a Deadly Weapon," *The Green Hornet,* ABC, 1966.
Voice, "Assignment: Earth," *Star Trek,* NBC, 1967.
Mea 349, "A Taste of Armageddon," *Star Trek,* NBC, 1967.

"Corpse of the Year," *The Green Hornet,* ABC, 1967.

"Citizen Ritter," *Judd, for the Defense,* ABC, 1967.

"To Love and Stand Mute," *Judd, for the Defense,* ABC, 1967.

"One in Every Crowd," *Hogan's Heroes,* CBS, 1967.

Philana, "Plato's Stepchildren," *Star Trek,* NBC, 1968.

Major Maria Felder, "The Cardinal," *Mission: Impossible,* CBS, 1968.

"The Need of a Friend," *Mannix,* CBS, 1968.

"Oh, to Be in England," *Family Affair,* CBS, 1969.

"Happy Birthday, Dear Hogan," *Hogan's Heroes,* CBS, 1969.

"The Experts," *Hogan's Heroes,* CBS, 1970.

"The Carrier," *Bold Ones: The Law Enforcers,* NBC, 1970.

Flora Alden, "Brenda," *Night Gallery,* NBC, 1970.

"The Test," *The FBI,* ABC, 1972.

"Coffin, Coffin in the Sky," *The Sixth Sense,* ABC, 1972.

"Time to Kill," *Banyon,* NBC, 1972.

"The Dead Samaritan," *Cannon,* CBS, 1973.

"To Quote a Dead Man," *Mannix,* CBS, 1973.

"Love and the Opera Singer," *Love, American Style,* ABC, 1973.

"The Deadly Madonna," *Mannix,* CBS, 1973.

"Nightmare," *Medical Center,* CBS, 1973.

Judith "Judy" Tyrell, "The Cat's Paw," *The Streets of San Francisco,* ABC, 1975.

"The Omaha Tiger," *Starsky and Hutch,* ABC, 1976.

"Homicide Is a Fine Art," *Jigsaw John,* NBC, 1976.

"Affair of the Heart," *McMillan,* NBC, 1977.

"A Good Smack in the Mouth," *Quincy, M.E.,* NBC, 1977.

"A Point of View," *Rafferty,* CBS, 1977.

"Irving the Explainer," *The Rockford Files,* NBC, 1977.

Flo, CBS, 1981.

Karen, "Like Father, Like Son," *Taxi,* ABC, 1981.

"A Time of Peril," *McClain's Law,* NBC, 1981.

"Frog's First Gunfight," *Best of the West,* ABC, 1982.

"Frog Gets Lucky," *Best of the West,* ABC, 1982.

Lana Marshall, "Now Pitching: Sam Malone," *Cheers,* NBC, 1983.

"Promises," *Hotel,* ABC, 1985.

"Tough Guys Don't Die," *Murder, She Wrote,* CBS, 1985.

"Fox and Hounds," *Crazy like a Fox,* CBS, 1985.

Steambath, Showtime, 1985.

Paula, "And the Winner Is," *Mary,* CBS, 1986.

Rosaline Gardner, "The Perfect Foil," *Murder, She Wrote,* CBS, 1986.

Marisa, "Steeled with a Kiss" (two-part episode), *Remington Steele,* NBC, 1987.

Cissie Enright, "Conversation over a Corpse," *Alfred Hitchcock Presents,* NBC, 1987.

"The Gift," *China Beach,* ABC, 1989.

"The First Time . . . Again," *Empty Nest,* NBC, 1989.

Television Appearances; Pilots:

Jean Lawrence, *Operating Room,* NBC, 1979.

Lily Maxwell, *Benson,* ABC, 1979.

Lori Fitzgerald, *The Big Easy,* NBC, 1982.

Velma, *Bliss,* ABC, 1984.

Film Appearances:

Angie Warfield, *Day of the Evil Gun,* Metro-Goldwyn-Mayer, 1968.

Mrs. Andrews, *Heaven with a Gun,* Metro-Goldwyn-Mayer, 1969.

Team owner, *Bang the Drum Slowly,* Paramount, 1973.

Lenore Chrisman, *Chosen Survivors,* Columbia, 1974.

Madeline Whitfield, *The Black Marble,* Avco-Embassy, 1980.

Rickey's mom, *Back Roads,* Warner Bros., 1981.

Abigail, *The Lords of Discipline,* Paramount, 1983.

Mrs. Douglas, *That Was Then . . . This Is Now,* Paramount, 1985.

Coralee Claibourne, *Heart of Dixie,* 1989.

Ruth Carpenter, *Happy Together,* Apollo Pictures, 1990.

Nora Christie, *Far and Away,* Universal, 1992.

Stage Appearances:

Kathleen Hogan, *Park Your Car in Harvard Yard,* Los Angeles Actors Theatre, Los Angeles, CA, 1982.

Eleanor, *Passion Play,* Center Theatre Group, Mark Taper Forum, Los Angeles, CA, 1985.

Appeared in summer theatre productions of *The Chairs* and *Sweet Bird of Youth.*

OTHER SOURCES

Periodicals:

People Weekly, May 9, 1994, p. 105.

BACH, Catherine   1954-

PERSONAL

Real name, Catherine Bachman; born March 1, 1954, in Warren, OH; raised in Faith, SD, and Los Angeles, CA; daughter of Bernard Bachman (a rancher) and Norma Kucera (an acupuncturist); married David Shaw, 1976 (divorced, 1982); married Peter Lopez (an attorney); children: Sophie Isabelle; stepchildren: Michael. *Education:* Studied acting at the University of California, Los Angeles.

Addresses: *Manager*—Mischel, Rubin, Iosu, and Akpovi, 16830 Ventura Blvd., Suite 415, Encino, CA 91436.

Career: Actress. World Wildlife Foundation, spokesperson, testified to Congress about animal conservation, 1991; animal rights activist.

CREDITS

Television Appearances; Series:
Daisy Duke, *The Dukes of Hazzard,* CBS, 1979-85.
Voice of Daisy Duke, *The Dukes* (animated), CBS, 1983.
Margo Dutton, *African Skies,* The Family Channel, 1992-94.

Television Appearances; Movies:
Alice, *Matt Helm,* ABC, 1975.
Lara, the guide, *Strange New World,* ABC, 1975.
Linda, *Murder in Peyton Place,* NBC, 1977.
Trisha Parker, *White Water Rebels,* CBS, 1983.
Daisy Duke, *The Dukes of Hazzard: Reunion!* (also known as *Dukes of Hazzard: Reunion* and *Reunion in Hazzard*), CBS, 1997.

Television Appearances; Episodic:
The Love Boat, ABC, 1983.
"Drive, She Said," *Trying Times,* PBS, 1987.
"Urges," *Space Ghost Coast to Coast,* The Cartoon Network, 1995.

Television Appearances; Specials:
Battle of the Network Stars VI, ABC, 1979.
CBS' Happy New Year America 1979, CBS, 1979.
Celebrity Challenge of the Sexes IV, CBS, 1979.
Battle of the Network Stars VIII, ABC, 1980.
Celebrity Challenge of the Sexes V, CBS, 1980.
The Nashville Palace, ABC, 1980.
The Magic of David Copperfield, CBS, 1981.
Battle of the Network Stars XII, ABC, 1982.
Circus of the Stars VI, CBS, 1982.
Night of 100 Stars, ABC, 1982.
Herself, *Bob Hope's Merry Christmas Show,* NBC, 1983.
CBS All-American Thanksgiving Day Parade, CBS, 1983.
Blondes vs. Brunettes, ABC, 1984.

CBS All-American Thanksgiving Day Parade, CBS, 1984.
George Burns' How to Live to Be 100, NBC, 1984.
The 21st Annual Academy of Country Music Awards, NBC, 1986.
Willie Nelson's Picnic, syndicated, 1987.
Stand-Up Comics Take a Stand!, The Family Channel, 1990.
Host, *The World's Greatest Stunts II,* Fox, 1991.
Voices That Care, Fox, 1991.
Welcome Home, America!—A USO Salute to America's Sons and Daughters, ABC, 1991.
Presenter, *Ninth Annual Genesis Awards,* 1995.

Film Appearances:
Nicole, *Genesis Home Video,* 1972.
Natalie Clayborne, *The Midnight Man,* Universal, 1974.
Melody, *Thunderbolt and Lightfoot,* United Artists, 1974.
Peggy Summers, *Hustle,* Paramount, 1975.
Marcie, *Cannonball Run II,* Warner Bros., 1984.
Tamarra, *Street Justice,* Lorimar, 1989.
Pam Weiss, *Criminal Act* (also known as *Tunnels*), 1989.
Harry, *Driving Force,* Academy Entertainment, 1989.
Kitty Wheeler, *Masters of Menace,* RCA/Columbia Pictures Home Video, 1991.
Captain Murdock, *Rage and Honor* (also known as *Rage & Honor*), Columbia TriStar Home Video, 1992.
Asylum attendant, *The Nut House* (also known as *The Nutty Nut*), Capella/Triboro Entertainment Group, 1992.

Also appeared in *Music City Blues* and *The Widow.*

Stage Appearances:
Night of 100 Stars, Radio City Music Hall, New York City, 1982.
Extremities, The Burt Reynolds Dinner Theatre, Jupiter, FL, 1985.

Major Tours:
Toured with the USO.

OTHER SOURCES

Periodicals:
Entertainment Weekly, April 25, 1997, p. 54.
People Weekly, July 25, 1994, pp. 139-140; April 21, 1997, p. 20.*

BAMMAN, Gerry 1941-

PERSONAL

Born September 18, 1941, in Independence, KS; son of Harry W. (a salesman) and Mary M. (Farrell) Bamman; married Emily Mann (a writer and director), August 12, 1981; children: Nicholas. *Education:* Xavier University, B.S.; New York University, M.F.A.

Career: Actor and writer. Co-founder, Manhattan Project; acting teacher, New York University, 1983-85; member, Guthrie Theatre resident company, 1985-86. *Military service:* U.S. Army, 1964-65.

Awards, Honors: CBS/Dramatists Guild National Award, 1983, for *Ecco!*

CREDITS

Stage Appearances:
(Debut) Fag, *The Rivals,* Edgecliff Theatre, Cincinnati, OH, 1965.
(New York debut) March Hare and White Knight, *Alice in Wonderland,* Virginia Theatre, 1970.
As You Like It, American Repertory Theatre, Cambridge, MA, 1980.
Thomas, *The Recruiting Officer* and Dr. Relling, *The Wild Duck,* Brooklyn Academy of Music (BAM) Theatre Company, 1981.
Understudy, *The Good Parts,* Astor Place Theatre, New York City, 1982.
Macbeth, *Macbeth,* Cincinnati Playhouse, OH, 1982.
Rip Van Winkle or "The Works," Yale Repertory Theatre, New Haven, CT, 1982.
Buckingham, *Richard III,* Delacorte Theatre, New York City, 1983.
Jack, *All Night Long,* McGinn/Cazale Theatre, New York City, 1984.
Thomas F. Norman, prosecuting attorney, *Execution of Justice,* Virginia Theatre, New York City, 1986, then Guthrie Theatre, Minneapolis, MN, 1986.
Torvald, *A Doll's House,* Hartford Stage Company, Hartford, CT, 1987.
Arnolphe, *The School for Wives,* Hartford Stage Company, 1988.
Eddie's Father/Jerry, *Road,* Lincoln Center Theatre/La Mama E.T.C. Annex, New York City, 1988.
Harpagon, *The Miser,* Hartford Stage Company, 1989.
Orgon, *Tartuffe,* Hartford Stage Company, 1993.
Ilya Ilyich Telyegin, *Uncle Vanya,* Circle in the Square Uptown, New York City, 1995.
Richard Nixon, *Nixon's Nixon,* MCC Theater, New York City, then Westside Theatre Downstairs, New York City, both 1996.

Also appeared in *Oedipus Rex, He and She, Johnny on the Spot, Museum, Henry V, Our Late Night, Sea Gull, Endgame, Accidental Death of an Anarchist,* and *Dwarfman.*

Film Appearances:
(Debut) *Lightning over Water* (documentary; also known as *Nick's Movie—Lightning over Water*), Image Entertainment, 1980.
Mr. Sloan, *Old Enough,* Midwest Films, 1984.
Mr. Stevens, *Hiding out* (also known as *Adult Education*), DEG, 1987.
Art Thomas, *The Secret of My Success,* Universal, 1987.
Tourist, *Cocktail,* Buena Vista, 1988.
Brian Nevins, *True Believer* (also known as *Fighting Justice*), Columbia, 1989.
Buddy, *Pink Cadillac,* Warner Bros., 1989.
Inspector McNamara, *Bloodhounds of Broadway,* Columbia, 1989.
Ed Tallent, *Desperate Hours,* Metro-Goldwyn-Mayer/United Artists, 1990.
Uncle Frank, *Home Alone,* Twentieth Century-Fox, 1990.
Doctor Judalon, *Lorenzo's Oil,* Universal, 1992.
Ray Court, *The Bodyguard,* Warner Bros., 1992.
Uncle Frank, *Home Alone 2: Lost in New York,* Twentieth Century-Fox, 1992.
Arthur Everson, *Married to It,* Orion, 1993.
Viscott, *Robert A. Heinlein's The Puppet Masters* (also known as *The Puppet Masters*), Buena Vista, 1994.
CIA Man (uncredited), *The Long Kiss Goodnight,* New Line, 1996.

Television Appearances; Series:
Senator Norton Wylie, *The Monroes,* ABC, 1995.

Television Appearances; Miniseries:
Mark Lockwood, *Love, Lies, and Murder,* NBC, 1991.
Judge Brooks, *Murder in the Heartland* (also known as *Starkweather: Murder in the Heartland*), ABC, 1993.

Television Appearances; Movies:
Artie, *Sentimental Journey,* 1984.
George Whitman, *Brass* (also known as *Police Brass*), CBS, 1985.
Assistant U.S. Attorney, *Courage* (also known as *Mother Courage*), CBS, 1986.

Phil Thomas, *Manhunt: Search for the Night Stalker* (also known as *Hunt for the Night Stalker* and *Trackdown*), NBC, 1989.

Warburton, *Kojak: None So Blind* (also known as *None So Blind*), ABC, 1990.

Peter Orr, *The Chase,* NBC, 1991.

Gruenwald, *The 10 Million Dollar Getaway,* USA Network, 1991.

Television Appearances; Episodic:
"The Blue Wall," *Law and Order,* NBC, 1991.

Captain Walker, *Swans Crossing,* syndicated, 1991.

Dean Pollard, "Guardian," *Law and Order,* NBC, 1995.

Stan Gillum, "I.D.," *Law and Order,* NBC, 1996.

Dr. Martin, *Cosby,* CBS, 1996.

Other Television Appearances:
(Debut) *Concealed Enemies,* PBS, 1984.

Malouf, *Saigon,* Thames TV (England), 1985.

WRITINGS

Plays:
A Thousand Nights and a Night, Theatre of the Open Eye, NY, 1978.

Ecco!, Portland Stage Company, Portland, ME, 1983.

A Doll's House (author of English text for Irene B. Berman's translation of the play by Henrik Ibsen), produced by the Hartford Stage Company, Hartford, CT, 1987.

Peer Gynt (translator with Berman of the play by Ibsen), produced by the Hartford Stage Company, 1989.

The Wild Duck (translator with Berman of the play by Ibsen), produced at the Los Angeles Theatre Center, 1990-91.

The Master Builder (translator with Berman of the play by Ibsen), produced by the Hartford Stage Company, 1991.

OTHER SOURCES

Periodicals:
American Theatre, March, 1996, p. 4.*

BANCROFT, Anne   1931-
   (Anne Italiano, Anne Marno)

PERSONAL

Original name, Anna Maria Luisa Italiano; born September 17, 1931, in Bronx, NY; daughter of Michael (a dress pattern maker) and Mildred (a telephone operator; maiden name, DiNapoli) Italiano; married Martin A. May (a building contractor), July 1, 1953 (divorced, February 13, 1957); married Mel Brooks (a director, screenwriter, actor, and producer), 1964; children: (second marriage) Maximilian. *Education:* Trained for the stage at American Academy of Dramatic Arts, 1948-50, with Herbert Berghof, 1957, and at Actors' Studio, 1958; studied film directing at Woman's Directing Workshop, American Film Institute.

Addresses: *Office*—c/o Brooksfilms, 9336 West Washington, Culver City, CA 90232. *Agent*—International Creative Management, 8942 Wilshire Blvd., Beverly Hills, CA 90211. *Contact*—915 North Foothill Rd., Beverly Hills, CA 90210; P.O. Box 900, Beverly Hills, CA 90213; 2301 La Mesa Dr., Santa Monica, CA 90405.

Career: Actress, director, producer, and screenwriter. Actors' Studio, member. Worked as an English tutor, drugstore clerk, and receptionist.

Member: Actors' Equity Association, Screen Actors Guild, American Federation of Television and Radio Artists.

Awards, Honors: Antoinette Perry Award, best supporting or featured dramatic actress, *Variety* New York Drama Critics Poll Award, and *Theatre World* Award, all 1958, for *Two for the Seesaw;* New York Drama Critics Award, best performance by a straight actress, 1959, Antoinette Perry Award, best dramatic actress, 1960, American National Theatre and Academy Award, 1960, and New York Philanthropic League Award, 1960, all for *The Miracle Worker;* Academy Award, best actress, and British Academy Award, best foreign actress, British Academy of Film and Television Arts, both 1962, for *The Miracle Worker;* Golden Globe Award, best actress in a drama, British Academy Award, best foreign actress, Cannes Film Festival Award, best actress, and Academy Award nomination, best actress, all 1964, for *The Pumpkin Eater;* Golden Globe Award, best actress in a musical or comedy, and Academy Award nomination, best actress, both 1968, for *The Graduate;* Academy Award nomination, best actress, and Golden Globe Award nomination, best actress in a drama, both 1977, for *The Turning Point;* Antoinette Perry Award nomination, best actress in a play, 1978, for *Golda;* Golden Globe Award nomination, best actress in a musical or comedy, 1984, for *To Be or Not to Be;* Golden Globe Award nomination, best actress in a musical or comedy, 1985, for *Garbo Talks;* Academy Award nomination, best actress, and Golden Globe Award nomination, best actress in a drama, both 1986, for *Agnes of God;* Golden Globe Award nomination, best actress in a drama, 1987, for *'night Mother;* British Academy Award, best actress, 1988, for *84 Charing Cross Road.*

CREDITS

Film Appearances:
(Film debut) Lyn Leslie, *Don't Bother to Knock,* Twentieth Century-Fox, 1952.

Marian Foley, *The Kid from Left Field,* Twentieth Century-Fox, 1953.

Emma Hurok, *Tonight We Sing,* Twentieth Century-Fox, 1953.

Marie, *Treasure of the Golden Condor,* Twentieth Century-Fox, 1953.

Paula, *Demetrius and the Gladiators,* Twentieth Century-Fox, 1954.

Laverne Miller, *Gorilla at Large,* Twentieth Century-Fox, 1954.

Katy Bishop, *The Raid,* Twentieth Century-Fox, 1954.

Corinna Marston, *The Last Frontier* (also known as *Savage Wilderness*), Columbia, 1955.

Maria Ibinia, *A Life in the Balance,* Twentieth Century-Fox, 1955.

Rosalie Regalzyk, *The Naked Street,* United Artists, 1955.

Kathy Lupo, *New York Confidential,* Warner Bros., 1955.

The Brass Ring, 1955.

Marie Gardner, *Nightfall,* Columbia, 1956.

Tianay, *Walk the Proud Land,* Universal, 1956.

Beth Dixon, *Girl in Black Stockings,* United Artists, 1957.

Angelita, *The Restless Breed,* Twentieth Century-Fox, 1957.

Annie Sullivan, *The Miracle Worker,* United Artists, 1962.

Jo Armitage, *The Pumpkin Eater,* Columbia, 1964.

Inga Dyson, *The Slender Thread,* Paramount, 1965.

Dr. D. R. Cartwright, *Seven Women,* Metro-Goldwyn-Mayer, 1966.

Mrs. Robinson, *The Graduate,* Embassy, 1967.

Arthur Penn (documentary), 1970.

Lady Jennie Churchill, *Young Winston,* Columbia, 1972.

The Countess, *The Hindenburg,* Universal, 1975.

Edna Edison, *The Prisoner of Second Avenue,* Warner Bros., 1975.

Herself, *Silent Movie,* Twentieth Century-Fox, 1976.

Carla Bondi, *Lipstick,* Paramount, 1976.

Emma Jacklin, *The Turning Point,* Twentieth Century-Fox, 1977.

Madge Kendal, *The Elephant Man,* Paramount, 1980.

Antoinette, *Fatso,* Twentieth Century-Fox, 1980.

Anna Bronski, *To Be or Not to Be,* Twentieth Century-Fox, 1983.

Estelle Rolfe, *Garbo Talks,* Metro-Goldwyn-Mayer/ United Artists, 1984.

Mother Miriam Ruth, *Agnes of God,* Columbia, 1985.

Thelma Cates, *'night Mother,* Universal, 1986.

Helene Hanff, *84 Charing Cross Road,* Columbia, 1987.

Ma, *Torch Song Trilogy,* New Line Cinema, 1988.

Meredith Perlestein, *Bert Rigby, You're a Fool,* Warner Bros., 1989.

Madame Ruth, *Love Potion No. 9,* Twentieth Century-Fox, 1992.

Bea Singer, *Honeymoon in Vegas,* Columbia, 1992.

Amanda, *Point of No Return* (also known as *The Assassin, La Femme Nikita, Nikita,* and *The Specialist*), Warner Bros., 1993.

Dr. Catherine Holland, *Mr. Jones,* TriStar, 1993.

Ms. Claire Kennsinger, *Malice,* Columbia, 1993.

Gypsy woman, *Dracula: Dead and Loving It,* Columbia, 1995.

Adele Larson, *Home for the Holidays,* Paramount, 1995.

Gladys Joe, *How to Make an American Quilt,* Universal, 1995.

Dr. Renata Baumbauer, *Sunchaser* (also known as *The Sunchaser*), Warner Bros., 1996.

Senator Lillian DeHaven, *G.I. Jane* (also known as *In Pursuit of Honor, A Matter of Honor, Navy Cross,* and *Undisclosed*), Buena Vista, 1997.

Critical Care, Live Entertainment, 1997.

Ms. Nora Dinsmoor, *Great Expectations,* Twentieth Century-Fox, 1997.

Film Work:
Choreographer, "Anna Karenina" dance sequence, *The Turning Point,* Twentieth Century-Fox, 1977.

Producer and director, *Fatso,* Twentieth Century-Fox, 1980.

Director of unreleased film, *The August.*

Stage Appearances:
(Broadway debut) Gittel Mosca, *Two for the Seesaw,* Booth Theatre, New York City, 1958.

Annie Sullivan, *The Miracle Worker,* Playhouse Theatre, New York City, 1959.

Mother Courage, *Mother Courage and Her Children,* Martin Beck Theatre, New York City, 1963.

Prioress, *The Devils*, Broadway Theatre, New York City, 1965.

Regina Giddens, *The Little Foxes*, Vivian Beaumont Theatre, New York City, 1967.

Anne, *A Cry of Players*, Vivian Beaumont Theatre, 1968.

Golda Meir, *Golda*, Morosco Theatre, New York City, 1977.

Stephanie Abrahams, *Duet for One*, Royale Theatre, New York City, 1981.

Patient, *Mystery of the Rose Bouquet*, Center Theatre Group, Mark Taper Forum, Los Angeles, CA, 1989.

Television Appearances; Series
The Goldbergs, CBS, 1950-51.

Television Appearances; Miniseries:
Mary Magdalene, *Jesus of Nazareth*, NBC, 1977.
Signora Polo, *Marco Polo*, NBC, 1982.
Lucy Marsden at age one hundred, *The Oldest Living Confederate Widow Tells All*, CBS, 1994.

Television Appearances; Movies:
Kate Jerome, *Neil Simon's "Broadway Bound,"* ABC, 1992.
Abigail "Ab" Tillerman, *Homecoming*, Showtime, 1996.

Television Appearances; Episodic:
(Television debut, as Anne Italiano) "The Torrents of Spring," *Studio One*, CBS, 1950.
"To Live in Peace," *Kraft Television Theatre*, NBC, 1953.
"A Medal for Benny," *Lux Video Theatre*, CBS, 1954.
"Hired Wife," *Lux Video Theatre*, NBC, 1956.
"The Corrigan Case," *Lux Video Theatre*, NBC, 1956.
"Fear Is the Hunter," *Climax*, CBS, 1956.
"Key Largo," *The Alcoa Hour*, NBC, 1956.
"So Soon to Die" *Playhouse 90*, CBS, 1957.
"Invitation to a Gunfighter," *Playhouse 90*, CBS, 1957.
"Hostages to Fortune," *The Alcoa Hour*, NBC, 1957.
"The Mad Bomber," *Climax*, CBS, 1957.
"Episode in Darkness," *Zane Grey Theatre*, CBS, 1957.
"A Time to Cry," *The Frank Sinatra Show*, ABC, 1958.
The Perry Como Show, NBC, 1960.
Person to Person, CBS, 1960.
"Out on the Outskirts of Town," *Bob Hope Chrysler Theatre*, NBC, 1964.
Virginia, "I'm Getting Married," *ABC Stage '67*, ABC, 1967.

Entertainment Tonight, syndicated, 1988.
Good Morning America, ABC, 1989.
Today Show, NBC, 1989.
Voice of Dr. Zweig, "Fear of Flying," *The Simpsons* (animated), Fox, 1994.

Appeared in episodes of *Danger*, CBS; *Kraft Music Hall*, NBC; *Omnibus*, CBS; *Philco-Goodyear Playhouse*, NBC; *Suspense*, CBS; and *The Tom Jones Show*, ABC.

Television Appearances; Specials:
The Bob Hope Show, NBC, 1964.
The Perry Como Special, NBC, 1964.
The Bob Hope Show, NBC, 1968.
Host, *Annie, the Woman in the Life of a Man*, CBS, 1970.
Host, *Annie and the Hoods*, ABC, 1974.
The Stars Salute Israel at Thirty, ABC, 1978.
Variety '77—The Year in Entertainment, CBS, 1978.
Bob Hope's Women I Love—Beautiful but Funny, NBC, 1982.
Host, *That Was the Week That Was*, ABC, 1985.
Lillian Cage, the title role, "Mrs. Cage," *American Playhouse*, PBS, 1992.
Presenter, *The 65th Annual Academy Awards Presentation*, 1993.
Mrs. Fanning, "The Mother" (also known as "Paddy Chayefsky's 'The Mother'"), *Great Performances*, PBS, 1994.

Other Television Appearances:
Freddie and Max, Thames Television, 1990.

Television Work; Specials:
Director, *Annie, the Woman in the Life of a Man*, CBS, 1970.

WRITINGS

Screenplays:
Fatso, Twentieth Century-Fox, 1980.

Teleplays; Specials:
Annie, the Woman in the Life of a Man, CBS, 1970.

OTHER SOURCES

Periodicals:
Premiere, December, 1995, p. 58.*

BARBERA, Joseph 1911-

PERSONAL

Surname is pronounced "Bar-*bear*-uh"; full name, Joseph Roland Barbera; born March 24, 1911, in New York, NY; son of Vincente (a barber) and Frances Barbera; married Dorothy Earl (divorced, 1964); married Sheila Holden; children: (first marriage) Lynn Meredith, Jayne Earl, Neal Francis. *Education:* Graduated from the American Institute of Banking; also attended Pratt Institute, Art Students League, and New York University.

Addresses: *Office*—Hanna-Barbera Productions, 3400 West Cahuenga Blvd., Hollywood, CA 90068.

Career: Animator, producer, director, composer, and writer. Van Beuren Studio, New York City, storyboard writer and sketch artist, 1932-34; Terrytoons, New Rochelle, NY, animator, 1934-37; Metro-Goldwyn-Mayer, Hollywood, CA, animator, director, and producer, 1937-57, head of animation department (with William Hanna), 1955-57; Hanna-Barbera Productions, Hollywood, founder (with Hanna) and president, beginning in 1957, later chairperson; Great American Broadcasting, president, beginning in 1988. Huntington Hartford Theatre, Los Angeles, president of board of directors; James A. Doolittle Theatre, Hollywood, president. Irving Trust Company, New York City, banking clerk, 1930-32. Los Angeles Earthquake Preparedness Committee, co-chairperson; Greater Los Angeles Visitors and Convention Bureau, member of board of directors; St. Joseph's Medical Center, member of board of directors; Children's Village, member of board of directors; Wildlife Waystation, honorary member of board of directors.

Member: National Academy of Television Arts and Sciences, Academy of Motion Picture Arts and Sciences, Cousteau Society, Greek Theatre Association (Los Angeles; past president), Southern California Theatre Association (president).

Awards, Honors: All with William Hanna: Academy Award nominations, best animated short subject, 1940, for *Puss Gets the Boot,* and 1941, for *The Night Before Christmas;* Academy Awards, best animated short subject, 1943, for *Yankee Doodle Mouse,* 1944, for *Mouse Trouble,* 1945, for *Quiet, Please!,* and 1946, for *The Cat Concerto;* Academy Award nomination, best animated short subject, 1947, for *Dr.*

Jekyll and Mr. Mouse; Academy Award, best animated short subject, 1948, for *The Little Orphan;* Academy Award nominations, best animated short subject, 1949, for *Hatch Up Your Troubles,* and 1950, for *Jerry's Cousin;* Academy Awards, best animated short subject, 1951, for *The Two Mouseketeers,* and 1952, for *Johann Mouse;* Academy Award nominations, best animated short subject, 1954, for *Touche, Pussy Cat,* 1955, for *Good Will to Men,* and 1957, for *One Droopy Knight;* Emmy Award, outstanding achievement in the field of children's programming, 1960, for *The Huckleberry Hound Show;* Golden Globe Award, outstanding achievement in international television cartoons, Hollywood Foreign Press Association, 1965, for *The Flintstones;* Emmy Award, outstanding children's special, 1966, for *Jack and the Beanstalk;* Emmy Award, outstanding achievement in children's programming (informational/factual), 1973, for *Last of the Curlews;* Emmy Award, outstanding informational children's series, 1974, for *The Runaways;* Annie Award, 1977, for *Charlotte's Web;* Christopher Award and Emmy Award, outstanding special—drama or comedy, both 1978, for *The Gathering;* Emmy Award, outstanding children's entertainment series, 1982, for *The Smurfs;* Golden Reel Award, animation sound editing, and Bronze Award, best children's special, both from International Film and Television Festival of New York, 1982, for *The Smurfs' Springtime Special;* Emmy Award, outstanding children's entertainment series, 1983, for *The Smurfs;* Bronze Award, best children's special, 1984, for *The Smurfic Games;* Men of the Year Award, National Center for Hyperactive Children, 1986; Gold Angel Award, excellence in media, Religion in Media, 1986; Distinguished Service Award, National Religious Broadcasters, and Award of Excellence, Film Advisory Board, both 1987, for *The Greatest Adventure: Stories from the Bible;* Humanitas Prize, 1987, for "Lure of the Orb" episode of *The Smurfs;* Governor's Award, National Academy of Television Arts and Sciences, 1988; inducted into Television Academy Hall of Fame, 1994.

CREDITS

Film Work; Features, with William Hanna:
Animation director, *Anchors Aweigh,* Metro-Goldwyn-Mayer, 1945.
Animation director, *Holiday in Mexico,* Metro-Goldwyn-Mayer, 1946.
Animation director, *Neptune's Daughter,* Metro-Goldwyn-Mayer, 1949.
Animation director (also with Fred Quimby), *Dangerous When Wet,* Metro-Goldwyn-Mayer, 1953.

Animation director (also with Quimby), *Invitation to the Dance,* Metro-Goldwyn-Mayer, 1956.

Producer and director, *Hey There, It's Yogi Bear* (animated), Columbia, 1964.

Producer and director, *The Man Called Flintstone* (also known as *That Man Flintstone;* animated), Columbia, 1966.

Producer and animation director, *Project X,* Paramount, 1968.

Producer, *Charlotte's Web* (animated), Paramount, 1973.

Producer, *C.H.O.M.P.S.,* AID, 1979.

Executive producer, *Liar's Moon,* Crown International, 1982.

Producer, *Heidi's Song* (animated), Paramount, 1982.

Producer, *GoBots: Battle of the Rock Lords* (animated), Atlantic Releasing, 1986.

Executive producer, *The Greatest Adventure: Stories from the Bible* (home video release), 1986.

Co-director and co-producer, *Jetsons: The Movie,* 1990.

Creative consultant, *Tom & Jerry: The Movie,* Turner Entertainment, 1992.

Executive producer (also with Kathleen Kennedy, David Kirschner, and Gerald R. Molen), *The Flintstones,* Universal, 1994.

Also producer of *Forever Like a Rose.*

Film Work; Animated Shorts; Director (with Hanna):

Gallopin' Gals, Metro-Goldwyn-Mayer, 1940.

Swing Social, Metro-Goldwyn-Mayer, 1940.

Puss Gets the Boot, Metro-Goldwyn-Mayer, 1940.

Romeo in Rhythm, Metro-Goldwyn-Mayer, 1940.

The Goose Goes South, Metro-Goldwyn-Mayer, 1941.

Midnight Snack, Metro-Goldwyn-Mayer, 1941.

The Night Before Christmas, Metro-Goldwyn-Mayer, 1941.

Officer Pooch, Metro-Goldwyn-Mayer, 1941.

The Bowling-Alley Cat, Metro-Goldwyn-Mayer, 1942.

Dog Trouble, Metro-Goldwyn-Mayer, 1942.

Fine Feathered Friend, Metro-Goldwyn-Mayer, 1942.

Fraidy Cat, Metro-Goldwyn-Mayer, 1942.

Puss 'n' Toots, Metro-Goldwyn-Mayer, 1942.

Baby Puss, Metro-Goldwyn-Mayer, 1943.

Yankee Doodle Mouse, Metro-Goldwyn-Mayer, 1943.

Lonesome Mouse, Metro-Goldwyn-Mayer, 1943.

Sufferin' Cats!, Metro-Goldwyn-Mayer, 1943.

War Dogs, Metro-Goldwyn-Mayer, 1943.

The Bodyguard, Metro-Goldwyn-Mayer, 1944.

The Million Dollar Cat, Metro-Goldwyn-Mayer, 1944.

The Zoot Cat, Metro-Goldwyn-Mayer, 1944.

Puttin' on the Dog, Metro-Goldwyn-Mayer, 1944.

Mouse Trouble (also known as *Cat Nipped* and *Kitty Foiled*), Metro-Goldwyn-Mayer, 1944.

The Mouse Comes to Dinner (also known as *Mouse to Dinner*), Metro-Goldwyn-Mayer, 1945.

Flirty Birdy (also known as *Love Boids*), Metro-Goldwyn-Mayer, 1945.

Mouse in Manhattan (also known as *Manhattan Serenade*), Metro-Goldwyn-Mayer, 1945.

Quiet, Please!, Metro-Goldwyn-Mayer, 1945.

Tee for Two, Metro-Goldwyn-Mayer, 1945.

The Milky Waif, Metro-Goldwyn-Mayer, 1946.

Solid Serenade, Metro-Goldwyn-Mayer, 1946.

The Cat Concerto, Metro-Goldwyn-Mayer, 1946.

Springtime for Thomas, Metro-Goldwyn-Mayer, 1946.

Trap Happy, Metro-Goldwyn-Mayer, 1946.

The Invisible Mouse, Metro-Goldwyn-Mayer, 1947.

Part-Time Pal (also known as *Fair Weathered Friend*), Metro-Goldwyn-Mayer, 1947.

Cat Fishin', Metro-Goldwyn-Mayer, 1947.

A Mouse in the House, Metro-Goldwyn-Mayer, 1947.

Dr. Jekyll and Mr. Mouse, Metro-Goldwyn-Mayer, 1947.

Salt Water Tabby, Metro-Goldwyn-Mayer, 1947.

Kitty Foiled, Metro-Goldwyn-Mayer, 1948.

Old Rockin' Chair Tom, Metro-Goldwyn-Mayer, 1948.

The Little Orphan, Metro-Goldwyn-Mayer, 1948.

Professor Tom, Metro-Goldwyn-Mayer, 1948.

Make Mine Freedom, Metro-Goldwyn-Mayer, 1948.

Mouse Cleaning, Metro-Goldwyn-Mayer, 1948.

The Truce Hurts, Metro-Goldwyn-Mayer, 1948.

Polka Dot Puss, Metro-Goldwyn-Mayer, 1949.

Hatch Up Your Troubles, Metro-Goldwyn-Mayer, 1949.

The Cat and the Mermouse, Metro-Goldwyn-Mayer, 1949.

Heavenly Puss, Metro-Goldwyn-Mayer, 1949.

Jerry's Diary, Metro-Goldwyn-Mayer, 1949.

Love That Pup, Metro-Goldwyn-Mayer, 1949.

Tennis Chumps, Metro-Goldwyn-Mayer, 1949.

Framed Cat, Metro-Goldwyn-Mayer, 1950.

Tom and Jerry in the Hollywood Bowl, Metro-Goldwyn-Mayer, 1950.

Jerry and the Lion (also known as *Hold That Lion*), Metro-Goldwyn-Mayer, 1950.

Little Quacker, Metro-Goldwyn-Mayer, 1950.

Saturday Evening Puss (also known as *Party Cat*), Metro-Goldwyn-Mayer, 1950.

Jerry's Cousin (also known as *City Cousin* and *Muscles Mouse*), Metro-Goldwyn-Mayer, 1950.

Texas Tom, Metro-Goldwyn-Mayer, 1950.
Cue Ball Cat, Metro-Goldwyn-Mayer, 1950.
Safety Second (also known as *F'r Safety Sake*), Metro-Goldwyn-Mayer, 1950.
Casanova Cat, Metro-Goldwyn-Mayer, 1951.
Cat Napping, Metro-Goldwyn-Mayer, 1951.
His Mouse Friday, Metro-Goldwyn-Mayer, 1951.
Jerry and the Goldfish, Metro-Goldwyn-Mayer, 1951.
The Two Mouseketeers, Metro-Goldwyn-Mayer, 1951.
Nit-Witty Kitty, Metro-Goldwyn-Mayer, 1951.
Sleepy-Time Tom, Metro-Goldwyn-Mayer, 1951.
Slicked-Up Pup, Metro-Goldwyn-Mayer, 1951.
The Flying Cat, Metro-Goldwyn-Mayer, 1952.
Cruise Cat, Metro-Goldwyn-Mayer, 1952.
The Dog House, Metro-Goldwyn-Mayer, 1952.
The Duck Doctor, Metro-Goldwyn-Mayer, 1952.
Fit to Be Tied, Metro-Goldwyn-Mayer, 1952.
Johann Mouse, Metro-Goldwyn-Mayer, 1952.
Little Runaway, Metro-Goldwyn-Mayer, 1952.
Push-Button Kitty, Metro-Goldwyn-Mayer, 1952.
Smitten Kitten, Metro-Goldwyn-Mayer, 1952.
Triplet Trouble, Metro-Goldwyn-Mayer, 1952.
The Missing Mouse, Metro-Goldwyn-Mayer, 1953.
Jerry and Jumbo, Metro-Goldwyn-Mayer, 1953.
That's My Pup, Metro-Goldwyn-Mayer, 1953.
Just Ducky, Metro-Goldwyn-Mayer, 1953.
Two Little Indians, Metro-Goldwyn-Mayer, 1953.
Life with Tom, Metro-Goldwyn-Mayer, 1953.
Pet Peeve, Metro-Goldwyn-Mayer, 1954.
Little School Mouse, Metro-Goldwyn-Mayer, 1954.
Baby Butch, Metro-Goldwyn-Mayer, 1954.
Mice Follies, Metro-Goldwyn-Mayer, 1954.
Neapolitan Mouse, Metro-Goldwyn-Mayer, 1954.
Downhearted Duckling, Metro-Goldwyn-Mayer, 1954.
Posse Cat, Metro-Goldwyn-Mayer, 1954.
Hic-Cup Pup (also known as *Tyke Takes a Nap*), Metro-Goldwyn-Mayer, 1954.
Puppy Tale, Metro-Goldwyn-Mayer, 1954.
Touche, Pussy Cat, Metro-Goldwyn-Mayer, 1954.
Good Will to Men, Metro-Goldwyn-Mayer, 1955.
Pup on a Picnic, Metro-Goldwyn-Mayer, 1955.
Designs on Jerry, Metro-Goldwyn-Mayer, 1955.
Southbound Duckling, Metro-Goldwyn-Mayer, 1955.
Pecos Pest, Metro-Goldwyn-Mayer, 1955.
Smarty Cat, Metro-Goldwyn-Mayer, 1955.
That's My Mommie, Metro-Goldwyn-Mayer, 1955.
Mouse for Sale, Metro-Goldwyn-Mayer, 1955.
Tom and Cherie, Metro-Goldwyn-Mayer, 1955.
Barbecue Brawl, Metro-Goldwyn-Mayer, 1956.
The Flying Sorceress, Metro-Goldwyn-Mayer, 1956.
Blue Cat Blues, Metro-Goldwyn-Mayer, 1956.
Give and Take, Metro-Goldwyn-Mayer, 1956.

Busy Buddies (also known as *Busy Bodies*), Metro-Goldwyn-Mayer, 1956.
The Egg and Jerry, Metro-Goldwyn-Mayer, 1956.
Scat Cats, Metro-Goldwyn-Mayer, 1956.
Downbeat Bear, Metro-Goldwyn-Mayer, 1956.
Muscle Beach Tom, Metro-Goldwyn-Mayer, 1956.
One Droopy Knight, Metro-Goldwyn-Mayer, 1957.
Feedin' the Kiddie, Metro-Goldwyn-Mayer, 1957.
Mucho Mouse, Metro-Goldwyn-Mayer, 1957.
Timid Tabby, Metro-Goldwyn-Mayer, 1957.
Tom's Photo Finish, Metro-Goldwyn-Mayer, 1957.
Tops with Pops, Metro-Goldwyn-Mayer, 1957.
Happy Go Ducky (also known as *One Quack Mind*), Metro-Goldwyn-Mayer, 1958.
Royal Cat Nap, Metro-Goldwyn-Mayer, 1958.
Robin Hoodwinked, Metro-Goldwyn-Mayer, 1958.
Tot Watchers, Metro-Goldwyn-Mayer, 1958.
The Vanishing Duck, Metro-Goldwyn-Mayer, 1958.
Little Bo Bopped, Metro-Goldwyn-Mayer, 1958.
Wolf Hounded, Metro-Goldwyn-Mayer, 1958.
Creepy Time Pal, Columbia, 1960.
Tale of a Wolf, Columbia, 1960.
The Do-Good Wolf, Columbia, 1960.
Life with Loopy, Columbia, 1960.
Snoopy Loopy, Columbia, 1960.
No Biz Like Shoe Biz, Columbia, 1960.
Here Kiddie, Kiddie, Columbia, 1960.
Count Down Clown, Columbia, 1961.
Happy Go Loopy, Columbia, 1961.
Two-Faced Wolf, Columbia, 1961.
Catch Meow, Columbia, 1961.
Child Sock-Cology, Columbia, 1961.
Fee Fie Foes, Columbia, 1961.
Kooky Loopy, Columbia, 1961.
Loopy's Hare-Do, Columbia, 1961.
This Is My Ducky Day, Columbia, 1961.
Zoo Is Company, Columbia, 1961.
Bungle Uncle, Columbia, 1962.
Bearly Able, Columbia, 1962.
Beef-for and After, Columbia, 1962.
Bunnies Abundant, Columbia, 1962.
Chicken Fracas-see, Columbia, 1962.
Common Scents, Columbia, 1962.
Rancid Ransom, Columbia, 1962.
Slippery Slippers, Columbia, 1962.
Swash Buckled, Columbia, 1962.
Just a Wolf at Heart, Columbia, 1963.
Chicken-Hearted Wolf, Columbia, 1963.
Whatcha Watchin', Columbia, 1963.
A Fallible Fable, Columbia, 1963.
Drum-Sticked, Columbia, 1963.
Bear Up!, Columbia, 1963.
The Crook That Cried Wolf, Columbia, 1963.
Habit Rabbit, Columbia, 1963.

Not in Nottingham, Columbia, 1963.
Sheep Stealers Anonymous, Columbia, 1963.
Wolf in Sheepdog's Clothing, Columbia, 1963.
Elephantastic, 1964.
Bear Hug, 1964.
Bear Knuckles, 1964.
Trouble Bruin, 1964.
Raggedy Rug, 1964.
Habit Troubles, 1964.
Big Mouse-Take, Columbia, 1965.
Pork Chop Phooey, Columbia, 1965.
Crow's Fete, Columbia, 1965.
Horse Shoo, Columbia, 1965.

Film Appearances:
Cameo appearance, *The Flintstones,* Universal, 1994.

Television Work; Series (Animated, Except Where Indicated); Executive Producer, Except Where Indicated, with Hanna:
Producer (also with Bob Cottle), *The Ruff and Reddy Show,* NBC, 1957-64.
Producer and director, *The Huckleberry Hound Show* (also featuring *Pixie and Dixie, Hokey Wolf,* and *Yogi Bear*), syndicated, 1958-62.
Producer and director, *Yogi Bear* (also featuring *Snagglepuss* and *Yakky Doodle Duck*), syndicated, 1958-62.
Producer, *The Quick Draw McGraw Show* (also featuring *Snooper and Blabber* and *Augie Doggie and Doggie Daddy*), syndicated, 1959-62.
Producer and director, *The Flintstones,* ABC, 1960-66.
Producer and director, *Top Cat,* ABC, 1961-62.
Producer and director, *Lippy the Lion,* syndicated, 1962.
Producer and director, *Touche Turtle,* syndicated, 1962.
Producer and director, *Wally Gator,* syndicated, 1962.
Also director, *The Jetsons,* ABC, 1962-63.
Also director, *The Adventures of Jonny Quest* (also known as *Jonny Quest*), ABC, 1964-65.
Producer and director, *The Magilla Gorilla Show* (also featuring *Ricochet Rabbit* and *Punkin Puss and Mush Mouse*), syndicated, 1964-67.
Producer and director, *The Peter Potamus Show* (also featuring *Yippie, Yappie, and Yahooey* and *Breezly and Sneezly*), syndicated, 1964-67.
Producer and director, *The Atom Ant/Secret Squirrel Show* (also featuring *The Hillbilly Bears, Squiddly Diddly,* and *Precious the Dog*), NBC, 1965-68.
Producer, *Sinbad, Jr., the Sailor* (also known as *The Adventures of Sinbad, Jr.*), syndicated, 1966.

Producer and director, *The Abbott and Costello Cartoon Show,* syndicated, 1966.
Producer (also with Larry Harmon), *Laurel and Hardy,* syndicated, 1966-67.
Producer and director, *Space Kiddettes,* NBC, 1966-67.
Producer and director, *Space Ghost* (also featuring *Dino Boy*), CBS, 1966-68.
Producer and director, *Frankenstein, Jr. and the Impossibles,* CBS, 1966-68.
Producer, *Samson and Goliath,* NBC, 1967-68.
Producer and director, *Birdman and the Galaxy Trio,* NBC, 1967-68.
Producer and director, *The Herculoids,* CBS, 1967-69.
Producer, *Moby Dick and the Mighty Mightor,* CBS, 1967-69.
Producer and director, *Shazzan!,* CBS, 1967-69.
Also director, *The Fantastic Four,* ABC, 1967-70.
Here Come the Stars (live-action), syndicated, 1968.
Producer, *The New Adventures of Huck Finn* (live-action and animated), NBC, 1968-69.
Producer and director, *The Wacky Races,* CBS, 1968-70.
Producer, *The Banana Splits Adventure Hour* (live-action and animated; also featuring *The Micro Venture, Danger Island, The Three Musketeers, The Hillbilly Bears,* and *The Arabian Knights*), NBC, 1968-70.
Also director, *The Adventures of Gulliver* (also known as *The Adventures of Young Gulliver*), ABC, 1969-70.
Producer and director, *The Perils of Penelope Pitstop,* CBS, 1969-71.
Also director, *The Cattanooga Cats* (also featuring *It's the Wolf, Around the World in 79 Days,* and *Auto Cat and Motor Mouse*), ABC, 1969-71.
Also director, *Dastardly and Muttley in Their Flying Machines,* CBS, 1969-71.
Also director (with Charles A. Nichols), *Scooby-Doo, Where Are You?,* CBS, 1969-74.
Also director, *Where's Huddles?,* CBS, 1970-71.
Also director, *The Harlem Globetrotters,* CBS, 1970-73.
Also director, *Josie and the Pussycats,* CBS, 1970-72, 1974-76.
Pebbles and Bamm Bamm, CBS, 1971-72.
Also director, *Help! It's the Hair Bear Bunch,* CBS, 1971-72.
Also director, *The Funky Phantom,* ABC, 1971-72.
Producer and director, *Wait 'til Your Father Gets Home,* syndicated, 1972.
Sealab 2020, NBC, 1972-73.
The Roman Holidays, NBC, 1972-73.

Also director, *The Amazing Chan and the Chan Clan,* CBS, 1972-74.

Also director, *The Flintstone Comedy Hour,* CBS, 1972-74.

Also director (with Nichols), *Josie and the Pussycats in Outer Space,* CBS, 1972-74.

The New Scooby-Doo Movies, CBS, 1972-74.

Speed Buggy, CBS, 1973-74.

Also director, *Butch Cassidy and the Sundance Kids,* NBC, 1973-74.

Producer, *Peter Puck,* NBC, 1973-74.

Inch High, Private Eye, NBC, 1973-74.

Yogi's Gang, ABC, 1973-75.

Jeannie, CBS, 1973-75.

Goober and the Ghost Chasers, ABC, 1973-75.

The Addams Family, NBC, 1973-75.

Super Friends, ABC, 1973-83.

Wheelie and the Chopper Bunch, NBC, 1974-75.

The Partridge Family: 2200 A.D., CBS, 1974-75.

Korg: 70,000 B.C. (live-action), ABC, 1974-75.

Hong Kong Phooey, ABC, 1974-76.

These Are the Days, ABC, 1974-76.

Devlin, ABC, 1974-76.

Valley of the Dinosaurs, CBS, 1974-76.

Also director, *The Scooby-Doo/Dynomutt Hour,* ABC, 1976-77.

Mumbly, ABC, 1976-77.

The Clue Club, CBS, 1976-77.

Jabberjaw, ABC, 1976-78.

The Skatebirds (also featuring *The Robonic Stooges, Wonder Wheels, Woofer and Wimper,* and *Mystery Island*), CBS, 1977-78.

The Tom and Jerry/Great Grape Ape Show, ABC, 1977-78.

Also director, *The New Super Friends Hour,* ABC, 1977-78.

Scooby's All-Star Laff-a-Lympics, ABC, 1977-78.

Fred Flintstone and Friends, syndicated, 1977-78.

The C.B. Bears (also featuring *Blast Off Buzzard and Crazy Legs, Posse Impossible, Undercover Elephant, Shake, Rattle, and Roll,* and *Heyyyyyy, It's the King*), CBS, 1977-78.

The Hanna-Barbera Happiness Hour (live-action), NBC, 1978.

Yogi's Space Race, NBC, 1978-79.

The Galaxy Goofups, NBC, 1978-79.

Scooby's All Stars, ABC, 1978-79.

Challenge of the Super Friends, ABC, 1978-79.

Also director, *The World's Greatest Super Heroes,* ABC, 1978-80.

Godzilla (also known as *Godzilla and the Super 90* and *The Godzilla Power Hour;* also featuring *Jana of the Jungle*), NBC, 1978-81.

Producer, *The Three Robonic Stooges,* CBS, 1978-81.

The All-New Popeye Hour, CBS, 1978-81.

The New Shmoo, NBC, 1979.

Fred and Barney Meet the Thing, NBC, 1979.

Buford and the Ghost, NBC, 1979.

Scooby-Doo and Scrappy-Doo, ABC, 1979.

The Super Globetrotters, NBC, 1979.

The New Fred and Barney Show, NBC, 1979.

Casper and the Angels, NBC, 1979-80.

Fred and Barney Meet the Shmoo, NBC, 1979-80.

Captain Caveman and the Teen Angels, ABC, 1980.

Flintstone Family Adventures (also featuring *The Frankenstones* and *Captain Caveman*), NBC, 1980-81.

The Scooby-Doo and Scrappy-Doo Show, ABC, 1980-82.

The Drak Pack, CBS, 1980-82.

Fonz and the Happy Days Gang, ABC, 1980-82.

The Richie Rich Show, ABC, 1980-82.

The Flintstones, NBC, 1981.

Space Stars (featuring *Space Ghost, Teen Force, The Herculoids,* and *Astro and the Space Mutts*), NBC, 1981-82.

The Kwicky Koala Show (also featuring *Dirty Dawg, Crazy Claws,* and *The Bungle Brothers*), CBS, 1981-82.

Trollkins, CBS, 1981-82.

Private Olive Oyl, CBS, 1981-82.

Laverne and Shirley in the Army, ABC, 1981-82.

Daniel Boone, CBS, 1981-82.

The Flintstone Funnies, NBC, 1981-84.

The Smurfs, NBC, 1981-88.

Also director, *Jokebook,* NBC, 1982.

Laverne and Shirley with the Fonz, ABC, 1982-83.

Mork and Mindy, ABC, 1982-83.

Scooby, Scrappy, and Yabba Doo, ABC, 1982-83.

The Gary Coleman Show, NBC, 1982-83.

The Little Rascals, ABC, 1982-84.

The Shirt Tales, NBC, 1982-84.

Pac-Man, ABC, 1983-84.

The Biskitts, CBS, 1983-84.

(With Margaret Leosch) *Benji, Zax, and the Alien Prince* (live-action), CBS, 1983-84.

Monchhichis, ABC, 1983-84.

The Dukes, CBS, 1983-84.

Scooby and Scrappy-Doo, ABC, 1983-84.

The Pink Panther and Sons, NBC, 1984-85.

The New Scooby-Doo Mysteries, ABC, 1984-85.

Super Friends: The Legendary Super Powers Show, ABC, 1984-85.

(Also with Freddy Monnickendam) *Snorks,* NBC, 1984-86.

Challenge of the GoBots, syndicated, 1984-86.

Scooby's Mystery Funhouse, ABC, 1985.

The Thirteen Ghosts of Scooby-Doo, ABC, 1985-86.

The Super Powers Team: Galactic Guardians, ABC, 1985-86.

The New Jetsons, syndicated, 1985-88.

The Funtastic World of Hanna-Barbera (featuring *Yogi's Treasure Hunt, Paw Paws, Goltar and the Golden Lance,* and *The New Adventures of Jonny Quest*), syndicated, 1986-87.

The Flintstone Kids, ABC, 1986-87.

Pound Puppies, ABC, 1986-87.

Wildfire, CBS, 1986-87.

Foofur, NBC, 1986-87.

The Funtastic World of Hanna-Barbera (featuring *Yogi's Treasure Hunt, Sky Commanders, The New Adventures of the Snorks,* and *The New Adventures of Jonny Quest*), syndicated, 1987-88.

Popeye and Son, CBS, 1987-88.

(Also with Jay Wolpert) *Skedaddle* (live-action), syndicated, 1988-89.

The Completely Mental Misadventures of Ed Grimley, NBC, 1988-89.

Fantastic Max, 1988-89.

The Yogi Bear Show, 1988-89.

A Pup Named Scooby Doo, 1988-93.

The Adventures of Don Coyote and Sancho Panda, 1990-92.

Timeless Tales from Hallmark, 1990-91.

The Tom and Jerry Kids Show, 1990-94.

Yo! Yogi, 1991-92.

And producer, *Droopy: Master Detective,* 1993-94.

Television Work; Pilots (Live-Action, Except Where Indicated); Executive Producer, Except Where Indicated, with Hanna:

The Beach Girls, syndicated, 1977.

The Funny World of Fred and Bunni (live-action and animated), CBS, 1978.

Sergeant T.K. Yu, NBC, 1979.

(With Arthur Weinthel and W. C. Elliott) *The B.B. Beegle Show,* syndicated, 1980.

Television Work; Movies (Live-Action, Except Where Indicated); Executive Producer, Except Where Indicated, with Hanna:

Hardcase, ABC, 1972.

Shootout in a One-Dog Town, ABC, 1974.

The Gathering, ABC, 1977.

The Beasts Are on the Streets, NBC, 1978.

(With William M. Aucoin) *KISS Meets the Phantom of the Park* (also known as *Attack of the Phantoms*), NBC, 1978.

The Gathering, Part II, NBC, 1979.

(With Barry Krost) *Belle Starr,* CBS, 1980.

Lucky Luke (animated), syndicated, 1987.

Stone Fox, NBC, 1987.

Hollyrock-a-Bye Baby (animated), ABC, 1993.

I Yabba-Dabba Do! (animated), ABC, 1993.

Johnny's Golden Quest (animated), USA Network, 1993.

Johnny Quest versus the Cyber Insects (animated), TNT, 1995.

Television Appearances; Movies:

Voice, *I Yabba-Dabba Do!* (animated), ABC, 1993.

Television Work; Specials (Animated, Except Where Indicated); Executive Producer, Except Where Indicated, with Hanna:

Alice in Wonderland, ABC, 1966.

Jack and the Beanstalk (live-action and animated), NBC, 1967.

The Thanksgiving That Almost Wasn't, syndicated, 1971.

A Christmas Story, syndicated, 1971.

Producer, *Last of the Curlews,* ABC, 1972.

Yogi's Ark Lark, ABC, 1972.

Robin Hoodnik, ABC, 1972.

Oliver and the Artful Dodger, ABC, 1972.

Here Come the Clowns, ABC, 1972.

The Banana Splits in Hocus Pocus Park, ABC, 1972.

Gidget Makes the Wrong Connection, ABC, 1973.

Lost in Space, ABC, 1973.

20,000 Leagues under the Sea, syndicated, 1973.

Also director, *The Three Musketeers,* syndicated, 1973.

The Count of Monte Cristo, syndicated, 1973.

The Crazy Comedy Concert (live-action and animated), ABC, 1974.

The Runaways (live-action), ABC, 1974.

Cyrano de Bergerac, ABC, 1974.

The Last of the Mohicans, syndicated, 1975.

Phantom Rebel (live-action), NBC, 1976.

"Davy Crockett on the Mississippi" (animated), *Famous Classic Tales,* CBS, 1976.

Taggart's Treasure (live-action), ABC, 1976.

Five Weeks in a Balloon, CBS, 1977.

Yabba Dabba Doo! The Happy World of Hanna-Barbera (live-action and animated), CBS, 1977.

Energy: A National Issue, 1977.

A Flintstones' Christmas, NBC, 1977.

The Flintstones' Little Big League, NBC, 1978.

Hanna-Barbera's All Star Comedy Ice Revue (live-action and animated), CBS, 1978.

"It Isn't Easy Being a Teenage Millionaire" (live-action), *ABC Afterschool Specials,* ABC, 1978.

Yabba Dabba Doo II, CBS, 1978.

Black Beauty, CBS, 1978.

Super Heroes Roast, NBC, 1979.

Challenge of the Super Heroes, NBC, 1979.
America vs. the World (live-action), NBC, 1979.
Scooby Goes Hollywood, ABC, 1979.
Casper's First Christmas, NBC, 1979.
Popeye Valentine Special: The Sweethearts at Sea, CBS, 1979.
Gulliver's Travels, CBS, 1979.
Casper's Halloween Special: He Ain't Scary, He's Our Brother, NBC, 1979.
The Gymnast (live-action), ABC, 1980.
The Hanna-Barbera Arena Show (live-action), NBC, 1981.
Jogging Fever, NBC, 1981.
The Great Gilly Hopkins (live-action), CBS, 1981.
Yabba Dabba Doo (live-action and animated), CBS, 1982.
The Smurfs' Springtime Special, NBC, 1982.
The Smurfs' Christmas Special, NBC, 1982.
Christmas Comes to Pac-Land, ABC, 1982.
Yogi Bear's All-Star Christmas Caper, CBS, 1982.
My Smurfy Valentine, NBC, 1983.
The Secret World of Og, ABC, 1983.
The Amazing Bunjee Venture, CBS, 1984.
The Smurfic Games, NBC, 1984.
Smurfily-Ever After, NBC, 1985.
Star Fairies, syndicated, 1985.
The Flintstones' 25th Anniversary Celebration (live-action and animated), CBS, 1986.
The Smurfs' Christmas Special, NBC, 1986.
Ultraman! The Adventure Begins, syndicated, 1987.
Yogi and the Magical Flight of the Spruce Goose, syndicated, 1987.
Scooby and the Reluctant Werewolf, syndicated, 1987.
The Jetsons Meet the Flintstones, syndicated, 1987.
Top Cat and the Beverly Hills Cats, syndicated, 1987.
Rockin' with Judy Jetson (also known as *Judy Jetson and the Rockers*), syndicated, 1987.
Yogi's Great Escape, syndicated, 1987.
Scooby-Doo and the Ghoul School, syndicated, 1987.
'Tis the Season to Be Smurfy, NBC, 1987.
The Good, the Bad, and the Huckleberry Hound, syndicated, 1987.
Scooby-Doo Meets the Boo Brothers, syndicated, 1987.
Yogi and the Invasion of the Space Bears, syndicated, 1987.
The Flintstone Kids "Just Say No" Special, ABC, 1988.
Hanna-Barbera's 50th: A Yabba Dabba Doo Celebration (live-action and animated), TNT, 1989.
Hagar the Horrible, 1989.
"Fender Bender 500," Wake, Rattle, and Roll, syndicated, 1990.
A Flintstone Family Christmas, ABC, 1993.

A Flintstones Christmas Carol, syndicated, 1994.
Arabian Nights, syndicated, 1994.

Also producer, *Rock Odyssey.*

Television Appearances; Specials:
The Flintstones' 25th Anniversary Celebration (live-action and animated), CBS, 1986.
The 40th Annual Emmy Awards, Fox, 1988.
Hanna-Barbera's 50th: A Yabba Dabba Doo Celebration, TNT, 1989.
MGM: When the Lion Roars (also known as *The MGM Story;* documentary), TNT, 1992.
The 10th Annual Television Academy Hall of Fame, The Disney Channel, 1994.
The Television Academy Hall of Fame (also known as *The Academy of Television Arts and Sciences' Hall of Fame*), NBC, 1995.

WRITINGS

Screenplays:
(With William Hanna and Warren Foster) *Hey There, It's Yogi Bear* (animated), Columbia, 1964.
(With Dick Robbins and Duane Poole) *C.H.O.M.P.S.,* AID, 1979.
(With Robert Taylor and Jameson Brewer) *Heidi's Song* (animated), Paramount, 1982.
Composer, "Snagglepuss Song," *Crooklyn,* Universal, 1994.
Composer, "(Meet) the Flintstones" and "The Bedrock Twitch," *The Flintstones,* Universal, 1994.

Teleplays:
(With Hanna and Douglas Widley) *The Adventures of Jonny Quest* (animated series; also known as *Jonny Quest*), ABC, 1964-65.

Songs:
Composer, *The Three Musketeers,* syndicated, 1973.
Composer of theme music, *I Yabba-Dabba Do!* (animated movie), ABC, 1993.
Composer of theme music "Meet the Flintstones," *Hollyrock-a-Bye Baby* (animated movie), ABC, 1993.
Composer of theme "Johnny Quest," *Johnny's Golden Quest* (animated movie), USA Network, 1993.
Composer of theme music, *Johnny Quest versus the Cyber Insects* (animated movie), TNT, 1995.

Other Writings:
My Life in 'Toons: From Flatbush to Bedrock in under a Century (autobiography), Turner Publishing (Atlanta, GA), 1994.

Musical compositions (with William Hanna) have been recorded as *The Flintstones: Modern Stone-Age Melodies,* Rhino Records (Los Angeles, CA), 1994. Contributor of cartoons to magazines, including *Collier's.*

Adaptations: The animated television series *The Real Adventures of Johnny Quest* (also known as *The New Adventures of Johnny Quest*), broadcast by TBS/TNT/Cartoon Network, 1996-97, was based on the characters and theme song created by Barbera for the original series.

OTHER SOURCES:

Books:

Contemporary Authors, Volume 150, Gale (Detroit, MI), 1996.

Something about the Author, Volume 51, Gale, 1988.*

BARRY, Gene 1919-

PERSONAL

Original name, Eugene Klass; born June 14, 1919, in New York, NY; son of Martin and Eva (Conn) Klass; married Betty Claire Kalb, October 22, 1944; children: Michael Lewis, Fredric James, Elizabeth. *Education:* Attended public schools in New York City, and New Utrecht High School, Brooklyn, NY.

Addresses: *Agent*—William Morris Agency, 151 El Camino Dr., Beverly Hills, CA 90212.

Career: Actor in stage, film, and television. Best known for his portrayal of dapper, well-dressed leading characters in television series; also a nightclub performer.

Member: Actors Equity Association, Screen Actors Guild (past first vice president), Boy Scouts of America.

Awards, Honors: Golden Globe Award, best male TV star, 1965; Antoinette Perry Award nomination, best actor in a musical, 1983, for *La Cage aux Folles;* named ADL Man of the Year, 1986.

CREDITS

Television Appearances; Series:
Gene Talbot, *Our Miss Brooks,* CBS, 1955-56.

Title role, *Bat Masterson,* NBC, 1958-61.
Captain Amos Burke, *Burke's Law,* ABC, 1963-65.
Title role, *Amos Burke, Secret Agent,* ABC, 1965-66.
Glenn Howard, *The Name of the Game,* NBC, 1968-72.
Agent Gene Bradley, *The Adventurer,* syndicated, 1972.
Bat Masterson, *Paradise,* CBS, 1989.
Captain Amos Burke, *Burke's Law,* CBS, 1994-95.

Television Appearances; Miniseries:
Carl Osborne, *Aspen* (also known as *The Innocent and the Damned*), NBC, 1977.
Bat Masterson, *Luck of the Draw: The Gambler Returns,* NBC, 1991.

Television Appearances; Movies:
Michael London, *Istanbul Express,* NBC, 1968.
Murray Jarvis, *Do You Take This Stranger?,* NBC, 1971.
Rankin, *The Devil and Miss Sarah,* ABC, 1971.
Gordon Harris, *A Cry for Love,* NBC, 1980.
John Cockerill, *The Adventures of Nelly Bly,* NBC, 1981.
Glen Kilgallen, *Perry Mason: The Case of the Lost Love,* NBC, 1987.
John Forrest, *Turn Back the Clock* (also known as *Repeat Performance*), NBC, 1989.

Television Appearances; Pilots:
Sergeant Andy Pile, *War Correspondent,* CBS, 1959.
Captain Amos Burke, *Honey West: Who Killed the Jackpot?,* ABC, 1965.
Dr. Ray Flemming, *Prescription: Murder* (also known as *Columbo: Prescription Murder*), NBC, 1968.
Harry Darew, *Ransom for Alice,* NBC, 1977.
Andrew Stovall, *The Girl, the Gold Watch, and Dynamite,* syndicated, 1981.

Television Appearances; Specials:
Tiptoe through TV, CBS, 1960.
Variety: The World of Show Biz, CBS, 1960.
NBC's 60th Anniversary Celebration, NBC, 1986.
The 40th Annual Tony Awards, CBS, 1986.
The 38th Annual Emmy Awards, NBC, 1986.
Judge, *The 12th Annual Mrs. America Pageant,* ABC, 1988.

Television Appearances; Episodic:
Hollywood Screen Test, ABC, 1948.
"To Each His Own," *Lux Video Theatre,* CBS, 1950.
"The Blood Call," *Believe It or Not,* NBC, 1950.
"Something about Love," *The Loretta Young Show,* NBC, 1954.

"The Girl in Car Thirty Two," *Suspense,* CBS, 1954.

"A Touch of Spring," *Ford Theatre,* NBC, 1955.

"Spider, Incorporated," *Science Fiction Theatre,* syndicated, 1955.

"Ride the Comet," *Appointment with Adventure,* CBS, 1955.

"Something about George," *The Loretta Young Show,* NBC, 1955.

"The World Below," *Science Fiction Theatre,* syndicated, 1955.

Dell Delaney, "Triggers in Leash," *Alfred Hitchcock Presents,* CBS, 1955.

"Nailed Down," *Fireside Theatre,* NBC, 1955.

"Salvage," *Alfred Hitchcock Presents,* CBS, 1955.

"The Blue Ribbon," *Ford Theatre,* NBC, 1955.

"The Story of Steve Carey," *The Millionaire,* CBS, 1955.

"The Good Luck Kid," *Damon Runyon Theatre,* CBS, 1956.

"The Woman Who Dared," *Ford Theatre,* ABC, 1956.

"A Place on the Bay," *Jane Wyman Theatre,* NBC, 1956.

"The Pendulum," *Jane Wyman Theatre,* NBC, 1957.

"Threat to a Happy Ending," *The Twentieth Century-Fox Hour,* CBS, 1957.

"Ain't No Time for Glory," *Playhouse 90,* CBS, 1957.

"The Headline Hero: File Number 28," *The Walter Winchell File,* ABC, 1958.

"Dynamite Blows Two Ways," *Wagon Train,* NBC, 1958.

"Crossed Wires," *Pete and Gladys,* CBS, 1961.

"Seeds of April," *The Dick Powell Show,* NBC, 1962.

"The Roman Kind," *General Electric Theatre,* CBS, 1962.

"Dear Uncle George," *The Alfred Hitchcock Hour,* CBS, 1963.

"The Apology," *The Feather and Father Gang,* ABC, 1977.

"Angels in the Wings," *Charlie's Angels,* ABC, 1977.

Fantasy Island, ABC, 1978.

"Where Is It Written?," *The Love Boat,* ABC, 1978.

"The Story of Abraham," *The Greatest Heroes of the Bible,* NBC, 1979.

Fantasy Island, ABC, 1981.

"Hula Angels," *Charlie's Angels,* ABC, 1981.

"Vicki the Gambler," *The Love Boat,* ABC, 1981.

Aloha Paradise, ABC, 1981.

"Abraham's Sacrifice," *The Greatest Heroes of the Bible,* NBC, 1981.

"Lillian Russell," *Fantasy Island,* ABC, 1981.

"She Brought Her Mother Along," *The Love Boat,* ABC, 1982.

"Fox and Wolf," *Crazy Like a Fox,* CBS, 1986.

Jason Starr, "The Old Team," *Shell Game,* CBS, 1987.

"Time and Teresa Golowitz," *Twilight Zone,* CBS, 1987.

"Reservations," *Hotel,* ABC, 1987.

"You've Got a Friend," *My Secret Identity,* syndicated, 1988.

Henry Reynard, "Test of Wills," *Murder, She Wrote,* CBS, 1989.

Hearts Are Wild, CBS, 1992.

Appeared in episodes of *The Clock* and *TV Reader's Digest,* both ABC.

Film Appearances:

Dr. Frank Addison, *Atomic City,* Paramount, 1952.

Captain Beaton, *Girls of Pleasure Island,* Paramount, 1953.

Johnny Kisko, *Those Redheads from Seattle,* Paramount, 1953.

Dr. Clayton Forrester, *War of the Worlds,* Paramount, 1953.

Verne Williams, *Alaska Seas,* Paramount, 1954.

Raphael Moreno, *Red Garters,* Paramount, 1954.

Al Willis, *Naked Alibi,* Universal, 1954.

Captain Charles Laverne, *The Purple Mask,* Universal, 1955.

Louis Hoyt, *Soldier of Fortune,* Twentieth Century-Fox, 1955.

Ellis, *Back from Eternity,* RKO Radio Pictures, 1956.

Frank Duncan, *The Houston Story,* Columbia, 1956.

Brock, *China Gate,* Twentieth Century-Fox, 1957.

Wes Bonnell, *Forty Guns* (also known as *Woman with a Whip*), Twentieth Century-Fox, 1957.

Jonathan Clark, *The 27th Day,* Columbia, 1957.

Casey Reed, *Hong Kong Confidential,* United Artists, 1958.

Troy Barrett, *Thunder Road,* United Artists, 1958.

Simon Grant, *Maroc Seven,* Paramount, 1967.

Donovan, *Subterfuge,* Commonwealth United Entertainment, 1969.

Television commentator, *The Second Coming of Suzanne,* Barry, 1974.

Congressman Leo O'Brien, *Guyana: Cult of the Damned* (also known as *Guyana: Crime of the Century*), Universal, 1980.

Film Work; Executive Producer:

The Second Coming of Suzanne, Barry, 1974.

Stage Appearances:

Rosalinda, 44th Street Theatre, New York City, 1942.

Catherine Was Great, Shubert Theatre, New York City, 1944.

Bless You All, Mark Hellinger Theatre, New York City, 1950.

The Perfect Setup, Cort Theatre, New York City, 1962.

Watergate: A Musical, Alliance Theatre Company, Atlanta, GA, 1982.

Georges, *La Cage aux Folles,* Palace Theatre, New York City, then Pantages Theatre, Los Angeles, CA, 1983.

Give My Regards to Broadway, Carnegie Hall, New York City, 1991.

Appeared in the plays *Happy Is Larry, Spotlight, Kismet, Destry Rides Again, The Merry Widow, Idiot's Delight, Pins and Needles,* and *The Would-Be Gentleman;* also appeared in the solo revue *Gene Barry in One.*

OTHER SOURCES

Periodicals:
People, August 28, 1989, p. 106.

Electronic Sources:
http://www.xmission.com/~emailbox/barry.htm*

BATEMAN, Justine   1966-

PERSONAL

Born February 19, 1966, in Rye, NY; daughter of Kent (an acting coach and theatrical manager) and Victoria (a flight attendant) Bateman; sister of Jason Bateman (an actor).

Addresses: *Agent*—Creative Artists Agency, 9830 Wilshire Blvd., Beverly Hills, CA 90212-1825.

Career: Actress. Writes and performs poetry and performance art.

Awards, Honors: Emmy Award (tied with Rhea Perlman), 1986, and Emmy Award nomination, 1987, both outstanding supporting actress in a comedy series, for *Family Ties.*

CREDITS

Television Appearances; Series:
Mallory Keaton, *Family Ties,* NBC, 1982-89.
Sarah Stretton, *Men Behaving Badly,* NBC, 1996-97.

Television Appearances; Miniseries:
A Century of Women (also known as *A Family of Women*), TBS, 1994.

Television Appearances; Pilots:
"Night Elevator," *Scary Tales,* syndicated, 1986.

Television Appearances; Movies:
Deborah Jahnke, *Right to Kill?,* ABC, 1985.
Mallory Keaton, *Family Ties Vacation,* NBC, 1985.
Karin Nichols, *Can You Feel Me Dancing?,* NBC, 1986.
Megan Brennan, *The Fatal Image* (also known as *City of Lights*), CBS, 1990.
Lynn Carlson, *In the Eyes of a Stranger* (also known as *Strangers*), CBS, 1992.
Robin Andrews, *Terror in the Night* (also known as *The Hunter*), CBS, 1994.
Lisa Temple, *Another Woman,* CBS, 1994.
Carla, "A Bucket of Blood," *Roger Corman Presents,* Showtime, 1995.

Television Appearances; Episodic:
Susan Anderson, "Mookie and Pookie," *Tales from the Darkside,* syndicated, 1984.
"How You Look," *One to Grow On,* NBC, 1984.
"Slumber Party," *It's Your Move,* NBC, 1984.
"On Your Toes," *Glitter,* ABC, 1984.
Guest, *Fame, Fortune, and Romance,* ABC, 1986.
"Teamwork," *One to Grow On,* NBC, 1987.
Host, *Saturday Night Live,* NBC, 1988.
"Privacy," *One to Grow On,* NBC, 1988.
"Miss Piggy's Hollywood," *Jim Henson Hour,* NBC, 1989.
Guest, *The Arsenio Hall Show,* syndicated, 1989.
Sarah/Zara, "Through a Glass Darkly," *Lois and Clark: The New Adventures of Superman,* ABC, 1996.
Sarah/Zara, "Big Girls Don't Fly," *Lois and Clark: The New Adventures of Superman,* ABC, 1996.
Sarah/Zara, "Lord of the Flys," *Lois and Clark: The New Adventures of Superman,* ABC, 1996.
Sarah/Zara, "Battleground Earth," *Lois and Clark: The New Adventures of Superman,* ABC, 1996.

Television Appearances; Specials:
Sara White, "First the Egg," *ABC Afterschool Special,* ABC, 1985.
Host, *Whatta Year . . . 1986,* ABC, 1986.
Disney's "Captain Eo" Grand Opening, NBC, 1986.
The 39th Annual Emmy Awards, Fox, 1987.
Mickey's 60th Birthday Special, NBC, 1988.
Inside Family Ties: Behind the Scenes of a Hit, PBS, 1988.
MTV's 1988 Video Music Awards, MTV, 1988.
The 14th Annual People's Choice Awards, 1988.
Candid Camera: Eat! Eat! Eat!, CBS, 1989.
Funny Women of Television: A Museum of Television and Radio Tribute, NBC, 1991.

Linda, *Merry Christmas, Baby,* Arts and Entertainment, 1992.

Voice of Josie Earp, *The Wild West* (documentary), syndicated, 1993.

Host, *Wendy's Ski Family Challenge,* The Family Channel, 1995.

Film Appearances:

Jennie Lee, *Satisfaction* (also known as *Girls of Summer*), Twentieth Century-Fox, 1988.

Jessica Grant, *The Closer,* ION Pictures, 1991.

Darcy Link, *Primary Motive,* FoxVideo, 1992.

Marty, *Deadbolt,* New Line Home Video, 1992.

Janet Beehan, *The Night We Never Met,* Miramax, 1993.

The Bridal Shower, 1994.

Carla, *The Death Artist,* New Horizons, 1995.

Meradith, *God's Lonely Man,* Cinequanon Pictures International, 1996.

Kiss and Tell, Phaedra Cinema, 1997.

Strangers in Transit, 1997.

Stage Appearances:

Abagail Williams, *The Crucible,* Roundabout Theatre, New York City, 1990.

Susan, *Carnal Knowledge,* Kaufman Theatre, New York City, 1990.

Appeared in *Journey to the Day,* Birmingham, AL; also appeared in *Lulu, Self-Storage, Love Letters,* and *Speed-the-Plow.*

OTHER SOURCES

Periodicals:

Entertainment Weekly, September 27, 1996, p. 64.*

BATES, Alan   1934-

PERSONAL

Full name, Alan Arthur Bates; born February 17, 1934, in Allestree, Derbyshire, England; son of Harold Arthur (an insurance broker) and Florence Mary (a homemaker; maiden name, Wheatcroft) Bates; married Victoria Valerie Ward (an actress), 1970 (died, 1992); children: Benedick (an actor and model), Tristan (an actor and model; died, 1990). *Education:* Trained for the stage at Royal Academy of Dramatic Arts with Tom Courtenay, Albert Finney, and Peter O'Toole, and with Claude W. Gibson; studied voice with Gladys Lea. *Religion:* Church of En-

gland. *Avocational interests:* Tennis, squash, swimming, diving, traveling, reading.

Addresses: *Agent*—International Creative Management, 8942 Wilshire Blvd., Beverly Hills, CA 90211.

Career: Actor. *Military service:* Royal Air Force.

Member: Actors' Equity Association, British Actors' Equity Association.

Awards, Honors: Forbes Robinson Award, Royal Academy of Dramatic Art, and Clarence Derwent Award, both 1959, for *Long Day's Journey into Night;* Academy Award nomination, best actor, 1968, for *The Fixer; Evening Standard* Award, best actor, 1972, for London performance of *Butley;* Antoinette Perry Award, best dramatic actor, and Drama Desk Award, both 1973, for New York performance of *Butley;* Best Actor Award, Variety Club of Great Britain, 1975, for *Otherwise Engaged;* Best Actor Award, Variety Club of Great Britain, and Society of West End Theatre Managers Award, best actor in a revival, both 1983-84, for *A Patriot for Me;* British Academy Award, best actor, British Academy of Film and Television Arts, 1983, for *An Englishman Abroad.*

CREDITS

Stage Appearances:

(Stage debut) *You and Your Wife,* Midland Theatre Company, Coventry, England, 1955.

Simon Fellowes, *The Mulberry Bush,* Royal Court Theatre, London, 1956.

Hopkins, *The Crucible,* English Stage Company, Royal Court Theatre, 1956.

Cliff Lewis, *Look Back in Anger,* English Stage Company, Royal Court Theatre, 1956.

Mr. Harcourt, *The Country Wife,* English Stage Company, Royal Court Theatre, 1956.

Stapleton, *Cards of Identity,* English Stage Company, Royal Court Theatre, 1956.

Monsieur le Cracheton, *The Apollo de Bellac,* English Stage Company, Royal Court Theatre, 1957.

Dr. Brock, *Yes — and After,* English Stage Company, Royal Court Theatre, 1957.

Cliff Lewis, *Look Back in Anger,* English Stage Company, World Youth Festival, Moscow, U.S.S.R., 1957, then Edinburgh Festival, Edinburgh, Scotland, 1958.

(Broadway debut) Cliff Lewis, *Look Back in Anger,* Lyceum Theatre, New York City, 1958.

Edmund Tyrone, *Long Day's Journey into Night,* Edinburgh Festival, Lyceum Theatre, Edinburgh, then Globe Theatre, London, both 1958.

Mick, *The Caretaker,* Arts Theatre, then Duchess Theatre, both London, 1960, later Lyceum Theatre, New York City, 1961.

Richard Ford, *Poor Richard,* Helen Hayes Theatre, New York City, 1964.

Adam, *The Four Seasons,* Saville Theatre, London, 1965.

Mr. Ford, *The Merry Wives of Windsor,* Stratford Shakespearean Festival, Stratford, Ontario, Canada, 1967.

Title role, *Richard III,* Stratford Shakespearean Festival, 1967.

Andrew Shaw, *In Celebration,* Royal Court Theatre, 1969.

Jaffer, *Venice Preserved,* Bristol Old Vic Company, Royale Theatre, Bristol, England, 1969.

Title role, *Hamlet,* Nottingham Playhouse, Nottingham, England, 1971.

Ben Butley (title role), *Butley,* Criterion Theatre, London, 1971, then Morosco Theatre, New York City, 1972.

Petruchio, *The Taming of the Shrew,* Royal Shakespeare Company, Royal Shakespeare Theatre, Stratford-on-Avon, England, 1973.

Allott, *Life Class,* Royal Court Theatre, then Duke of York's Theatre, London, both 1974.

Simon Hench, *Otherwise Engaged,* Queen's Theatre, London, 1975.

Boris Trigorin, *The Seagull,* Duke of York's Theatre, 1976.

Robert, *Stage Struck,* Vaudeville Theatre, London, 1979.

Alfred Redl, *A Patriot for Me,* Chichester Festival Theatre, Chichester, England, then Haymarket Theatre Royal, London, both 1983, later Center Theatre Group, Ahmanson Theatre, Los Angeles, CA, 1984.

Nicholas, the inquisitor, *One for the Road,* Lyric (Hammersmith), London, 1984.

The cabbie, *Victoria Station* (double-bill with *One for the Road*), Lyric (Hammersmith), 1984.

Edgar, *The Dance of Death,* London, 1985.

Yonadab, King David's nephew (title role), *Yonadab,* National Theatre, London, 1985.

(With Patrick Garland) *Down Cemetery Road* (poetry recital), 1986.

Mark Melon (title role), *Melon,* Haymarket Theatre Royal, 1987.

Nikolai Ivanov (title role), *Ivanov,* Strand Theatre, London, 1989.

Benedick, *Much Ado about Nothing,* Strand Theatre, 1989.

A Muse of Fire (one person show), Edinburgh Festival, 1989.

Richard Fenchurch, *Stages,* Cottesloe Theatre, London, 1992.

Life Class, Royal Court Theatre, then Duke of York's Theatre, 1993.

Rat in the Skull, [London], 1993.

Bruscon, *The Showman,* Almeida Theatre, London, 1993.

Halvard Solness, *The Master Builder,* Haymarket Theatre Royal, then Royal Alexandra Theatre, Toronto, Ontario, Canada, both 1995.

Kuzovkin, *Fortune's Fool,* Chichester Festival Theatre, then Theatre Royal, Bath, England, both 1996.

Let's Keep in Touch (benefit revue for Tristan Bates Theatre), Actors Centre, Covent Garden, England, 1996.

Simon Hench, *Simply Disconnected* (sequel to *Otherwise Engaged*), Minerva Theatre, Chichester, England, then Malvern Festival Theatre, Malvern, England, both 1996.

J. G., *Life Support,* Aldwych Theatre, London, 1997.

Also appeared in *Look Back in Anger,* New York City, and in *Fortune's Fool.*

Major Tours:
Ben Butley (title role), *Butley,* U.S. cities, 1975.
J. G., *Life Support,* English cities, 1997.

Film Appearances:
It's Never Too Late, 1956.

Frank Rice, *The Entertainer,* Bryanston/British Lion, 1960.

Arthur Blakey, *Whistle Down the Wind,* Pathe, 1961.

Vic Brown, *A Kind of Loving,* Governor, 1962.

Stephen Maddox, *The Running Man* (also known as *Carol Reed's The Running Man*), Columbia, 1963.

Mick, *The Guest* (also known as *The Caretaker*), Janus, 1964.

Jimmy Brewster, *Nothing But the Best,* Royal, 1964.

Basil, *Zorba the Greek* (also known as *Alexis Zorbas*), International Classics, 1964.

Narrator, *Insh'Allah,* 1965.

Jos, *Georgy Girl,* Columbia, 1966.

Gabriel Oak, *Far from the Madding Crowd,* Metro-Goldwyn-Mayer, 1967.

Private Charles Plumpick, *Le Roi de Coeur* (also known as *King of Hearts* and *Tutti Pazzio Meno Lo*), Lopert/United Artists, 1967.

Hands Up! (also known as *Rece do Gory*), 1967.

Yakov Bok, *The Fixer,* Metro-Goldwyn-Mayer, 1968.

Rupert Birkin, *Women in Love,* United Artists, 1969.
Colonel Vershinin, *Three Sisters,* American Film Theatre, 1970.
Ted Burgess, *The Go-Between,* Columbia, 1971.
Bri, *A Day in the Death of Joe Egg,* Columbia, 1972.
Second Best (short film), 1972.
Harry, *L'Impossible Objet* (also known as *Impossible Object* and *Story of a Love Story*), Valoria, 1973.
Ben Butley (title role), *Butley,* American Film Theatre, 1974.
Mikis Theodorakis: A Profile of Greatness, 1974.
Andrew Shaw, *In Celebration,* American Film Theatre, 1975.
Rudi von Starnberg, *Royal Flash,* Twentieth Century-Fox, 1975.
Charles Crossley, *The Shout,* Films, Inc., 1978.
Saul Kaplan, *An Unmarried Woman,* Twentieth Century-Fox, 1978.
Rudge, *The Rose,* Twentieth Century-Fox, 1979.
Sergei Diaghilev, *Nijinsky,* Paramount, 1980.
H. J. Heidler, *Quartet,* New World, 1981.
Mr. Macready, *Brittania Hospital,* Universal, 1982.
Captain Chris Baldry, *Return of the Soldier,* Twentieth Century-Fox, 1983.
Captain Jerry Jackson, *The Wicked Lady,* Metro-Goldwyn-Mayer/United Artists, 1983.
David Cornwallis, *Duet for One,* Cannon, 1986.
Dandy Jack Meehan, *A Prayer for the Dying,* Goldwyn, 1987.
Frank Meadows, *We Think the World of You,* Cinecom, 1988.
Say Anything, Twentieth Century-Fox, 1989.
Malcolm Forrest, *Force Majeure* (also known as *Uncontrollable Circumstances*), 1989.
Inspector Felix Detweiler, *Mr. Frost,* Triumph, 1990.
Claudius, *Hamlet,* Warner Bros., 1990.
Dr. Marsfeldt and guru, *Club Extinction* (also known as *Dr. M.* and *Docteur M.*), Prism Entertainment, 1990.
John, *Secret Friends,* Briar Patch Film Corp., 1992.
James Prentis, *Shuttlecock,* 1992.
Eamon McCree, *Silent Tongue,* Trimark Pictures, 1994.
Sir Hugo Coal, *Gentlemen Don't Eat Poets* (also known as *The Grotesque* and *Grave Indiscretion*), LIVE Entertainment, 1995.

Film Work:
Coproducer, *Second Best* (short film), 1972.

Television Appearances; Miniseries:
Michael Henchard (title role), *The Mayor of Casterbridge,* BBC, then *Masterpiece Theatre,* PBS, 1978.
Oliver, "Oliver's Travels," *Mystery!,* PBS, 1996.

Television Appearances; Specials:
Duel for Love, ABC, 1959.
Three on a Gas Ring, ABC, 1959.
The Wind and the Rain, Granada Television, 1959.
The Square Ring, AR-TV, 1959.
The Juke Box, AR-TV, 1959.
A Memory of Two Mondays, Granada Television, 1959.
The Thug, ABC, 1959.
A Hero of Our Time, BBC, 1966.
Plaintiffs and Defendants, BBC, 1975.
Two Sundays, BBC, 1975.
James, *The Collection,* 1976.
Cliff Lewis, *Look Back in Anger,* BBC, 1976.
Where Adam Stood, BBC, 1976.
Sir Jock Mellor, *Very like a Whale,* 1981.
The Trespasser, 1981.
The son, *A Voyage 'round My Father,* PBS, 1982.
John Malcolm/Maj. Pollack, *Separate Tables,* HBO, 1983.
Guy Burgess, *An Englishman Abroad,* BBC, then PBS, 1983.
Jones, "Dr. Fischer of Geneva," *Great Performances,* PBS, 1985.
One for the Road, 1986.
Stewart, "Pack of Lies," *Hallmark Hall of Fame,* CBS, 1987.
Blair, *The Dog It Was That Died,* Granada Television, 1988.
Host, *One Man in His Time: A Tribute to Laurence Olivier,* Arts and Entertainment, 1990.
Classic Mel: The Making of Mel Gibson's "Hamlet," HBO, 1991.
Losing Track, BBC, 1991.
Hamish Partt, *Unnatural Pursuits,* 1991, Arts and Entertainment, 1994.
Josiah Bounderby, "Hard Times" (also known as "Charles Dickens' Hard Times"), *Masterpiece Theatre,* PBS, 1995.

Appeared as Mick, *The Caretaker.*

Television Appearances; Movies:
Narrator, *The Story of Jacob and Joseph,* ABC, 1974.
Marcel Proust, "102 Boulevard Haussmann," *A & E Stage,* Arts and Entertainment, 1991.
Reg Green, *Nicholas's Gift,* CBS, 1998.

Television Appearances; Episodic:
John Fabian, "And So Died Riabouchinska," *Ray Bradbury Theatre,* HBO, 1985.

RECORDINGS

Taped Readings:
Cassio, *Othello,* Caedmon, 1960, HarperCollins Audio, 1995.

Florizel, *A Winter's Tale,* Caedmon, 1961, HarperCollins Audio, 1995.

Mark Antony, *Julius Caesar,* Caedmon, 1964, HarperCollins Audio, 1995.

Babii Yar and Other Poems, Caedmon, 1967.

Michael Henchard (title role), *The Mayor of Casterbridge,* Listen for Pleasure, 1981.

Oliver, *Oliver's Travels,* Hodder Headline Audiobooks, 1994.

Poems of William Blake, Reed Audio, 1995.

A Shropshire Lad, Hyperion, 1995.

Enobarbus and Duke Senior, *The Prince's Choice,* HighBridge Audio, 1996.

Also appeared as Ben Butley (title role), *Butley,* Caedmon, and in *English Poets,* Argo.

OTHER SOURCES

Periodicals:
Premiere [United Kingdom], September, 1995.
Seventeen, May, 1963.

Other:
The Alan Bates Archive, http://www.tiac.net/users/claret/bio.html (web page), November 17, 1997.*

BEARSE, Amanda 1958-

PERSONAL

Born August 9, 1958, in Winter Park, FL. *Education:* Attended Birmingham Southern College; trained for the stage with Sanford Meisner at Neighborhood Playhouse. *Avocational interests:* Motorcycling along the California coast.

Addresses: *Agent*—William Morris Agency, 151 El Camino Dr., Beverly Hills, CA 90212.

Career: Actress and director.

CREDITS

Television Appearances; Series:
Amanda Cousins, *All My Children,* ABC, 1982-84.
Marcy Rhoades, *Married . . . with Children,* Fox, 1987-97.

Television Work; Series:
Director, *Married . . . with Children,* Fox, 1991-97.

Co-director, *Malcolm and Eddie* (also known as *Top of the Stairs*), UPN, 1996.
Co-director, *Pauly* (also known as *Mommy and Me*), Fox, 1997.

Television Appearances; Movies:
Karen, *First Affair,* CBS, 1983.
Cathy, *The Goddess of Love,* NBC, 1988.
Mrs. Pearl, *Here Come the Munsters,* Fox, 1995.

Television Appearances; Specials:
Host, *Out There II,* Comedy Central, 1994.
Co-host, *Ho Ho Ho: TV's All-Time Funniest Christmas Moments,* Fox, 1995.
My Favorite "Married," Fox, 1995.
TV's All-Time Funniest Holidays, Fox, 1996.

Television Appearances; Episodic:
Jean Haywood, "Triangles," *Hotel,* ABC, 1986.
Win, Lose, Draw, syndicated, 1989.

Film Appearances:
Soap opera actress, *Protocol,* Warner Bros., 1984.
Nicole Ferret, *Fraternity Vacation,* New World, 1985.
Amy Peterson, *Fright Night,* Columbia, 1985.
Barmaid, *The Doom Generation,* Samuel Goldwyn Co., 1995.

OTHER SOURCES

Periodicals:
Advocate, September 21, 1993, p. 38.*

BEDFORD, Brian 1935-

PERSONAL

Born February 16, 1935, in Morley, Yorkshire, England; son of Arthur and Ellen (O'Donnell) Bedford. *Education:* Attended St. Bede's School, Bradford, and Royal Academy of Dramatic Art. *Avocational interests:* Traveling, reading, going to the movies and theatre.

Addresses: *Agent*—Paradigm, 200 West 57th St., Suite 900, New York, NY 10019.

Career: Actor and director.

Awards, Honors: Obie Award for acting, *Village Voice,* 1964, for *The Knack;* Drama Desk Award, outstanding performance, 1969, for *The Misanthrope;*

Drama Desk Award, outstanding performance, 1970, for *Private Lives;* Antoinette Perry Award, best dramatic actor, and Drama Desk award, outstanding performance, both 1971, both for *The School for Wives;* Drama Desk Award, outstanding performance, 1974, for *Jumpers;* Antoinette Perry Award nomination, best performance by a leading actor in a play, and Drama Desk Award, outstanding performance, both 1992, both for *Two Shakespearean Actors;* Antoinette Perry Award nomination, best performance by a leading actor in a dramatic play, 1994, for *Timon of Athens;* Antoinette Perry Award nomination, best performance by a leading actor in a play, and Outer Critics Circle Award nomination, outstanding performance by an actor, both 1995, for *The Moliere Comedies;* inducted into the Theatre Hall of Fame, 1997; Antoinette Perry Award nomination, best performance by a leading actor in a play, 1997, for *London Assurance.*

CREDITS

Stage Appearances:

(Stage debut) Decius Brutus, *Julius Caesar,* Bradford Civic Theatre, 1951.

(London debut) Travis de Coppet, *The Young and the Beautiful,* Arts Theatre Club, London, 1956.

Rodolpho, *A View from the Bridge,* Comedy Theatre, London, 1956.

Arviragus, *Cymbeline,* Memorial Theatre, Stratford-upon-Avon, England, 1957.

Ariel, *The Tempest,* Memorial Theatre, then Drury Lane Theatre, London, 1957.

Clive Harrington, *Five Finger Exercise,* Comedy Theatre, 1958.

(New York debut) Clive Harrington, *Five Finger Exercise,* Music Box Theatre, 1959.

David Roddingham, *Write Me a Murder,* Lyric Theatre, London, 1962.

Derek Pengo, *Lord Pengo,* Royale Theatre, New York City, 1962.

Louis Dubedat, *The Doctor's Dilemma,* Haymarket Theatre, London, 1963.

Tchaik, *The Private Ear,* Morosco Theatre, New York City, then Wimbledon, England, 1963.

Tom, *The Knack,* New Theatre, New York City, 1964.

Tom, *The Knack,* The Establishment Theatre Company, Huntington Hartford Theatre, Hollywood, CA, 1966.

James, *The Astrakhan Coat,* Helen Hayes Theatre, New York City, 1967.

General, *The Unknown Soldier and His Wife,* Vivian Beaumont Theater, New York City, then George Abbott Theatre, 1967.

Edward Chamberlayne, *The Cocktail Party,* Lyceum Theatre, New York City, 1968.

Alceste, *The Misanthrope,* Lyceum Theatre, 1968.

Lot, *The Seven Descents of Myrtle,* Ethel Barrymore Theatre, New York City, 1968.

Title role, *Hamlet,* American Shakespeare Festival, Stratford, CT, 1969.

Tusenback, *Three Sisters,* American Shakespeare Festival, 1969.

Elyot Chase, *Private Lives,* Billy Rose Theatre, New York City, 1969.

Arnolphe, *The School for Wives,* Lyceum Theatre, 1971.

General, *The Unknown Soldier and His Wife,* New Theatre, London, 1973.

George Moore, *Jumpers,* Kennedy Center, Washington, DC, then Billy Rose Theatre, 1974.

Angelo, *Measure for Measure,* Stratford Shakespeare Festival, Stratford, Ontario, Canada, 1975.

Malvolio, *Twelfth Night,* Stratford Shakespeare Festival, 1975.

Actor, *The Guardsman,* Center Theatre Group, Ahmanson Theatre, Los Angeles, 1976, then Stratford Shakespeare Festival, 1977.

Title role, *Richard III,* Stratford Shakespeare Festival, 1977.

Jacques, *As You Like It,* Stratford Shakespeare Festival, 1977-78.

Leontes, *The Winter's Tale,* Stratford Shakespeare Festival, 1978.

Astrov, *Uncle Vanya,* Stratford Shakespeare Festival, 1978.

Elyot Chase, *Private Lives,* Stratford Shakespeare Festival, 1978.

Benedick, *Much Ado about Nothing,* Stratford Shakespeare Festival, 1980.

Trigorin, *The Seagull,* Stratford Shakespeare Festival, 1980.

Malvolio, *Twelfth Night,* Stratford Shakespeare Festival, 1980.

Charles, *Blithe Spirit,* Stratford Shakespeare Festival, then Royal Alexandra Theatre, Toronto, Ontario, Canada, 1981.

Alceste, *The Misanthrope,* Stratford Shakespeare Festival, 1981.

Isaac Newton, *The Physicists,* Kennedy Center, 1982.

Title role, *Tartuffe,* Kennedy Center, 1982.

Bluntschli, *Arms and the Man,* Stratford Shakespeare Festival, 1982.

Alceste, *The Misanthrope,* Circle in the Square, New York City, 1983.

Title role, *Richard II,* Stratford Shakespeare Festival, 1983.

Title role, *Tartuffe,* Stratford Shakespeare Festival, 1983-84.

Bottom, *A Midsummer Night's Dream,* Stratford Shakespeare Festival, 1984.

Vladimir, *Waiting for Godot,* Stratford Shakespeare Festival, 1984.

Henry, *The Real Thing,* Citadel Theatre, Edmonton, Alberta, Canada, 1984.

Prospero, *The Tempest,* Citadel Theatre, 1985.

Elyot Chase, *Private Lives,* Citadel Theatre, 1986.

Title role, *Richard II,* Old Globe Theatre, San Diego, CA, 1986.

Charles Gounod, *Opera Comique,* Kennedy Center, 1987.

Gay Easterbrook, *No Time for Comedy,* Berkshire Festival, Stockbridge, MS, 1987.

Shylock, *The Merchant of Venice,* Shakespeare Theatre at the Folger, Washington, DC, 1988.

Shylock, *The Merchant of Venice,* Stratford Shakespeare Festival, 1989.

Lord Foppington, *The Relapse,* Stratford Shakespeare Festival, 1989.

Title role, *Macbeth,* Stratford Shakespeare Festival, 1990.

Brutus, *Julius Caesar,* Stratford Shakespeare Festival, 1990.

Arnolphe, *The School for Wives,* Stratford Shakespeare Festival, 1991.

Dogberry, *Much Ado about Nothing,* Stratford Shakespeare Festival, 1991.

Title role, *Timon of Athens,* Stratford Shakespeare Festival, 1991.

William Charles Mac Ready, *Two Shakespearean Actors,* Cord Theatre, New York City, 1991-92.

The Duke, *Measure for Measure,* Stratford Shakespeare Festival, 1992.

Title role, *Timon of Athens,* Lyceum Theatre, 1993.

Twelfth Night, 1994.

Sganarelle, *The School for Husbands,* and Sganarelle, *The Imaginary Cuckold,* billed together as *The Moliere Comedies,* Roundabout Theatre Company, Criterion Center Stage Right, New York City, 1995.

Antonio Salieri, *Amadeus,* Festival Stage, Stratford Shakespeare Festival, 1996.

The Little Foxes, Stratford Shakespeare Festival, 1996.

Dr. Martin Dysart, *Equus,* Avon Theatre, Stratford Shakespeare Festival, 1997.

Sir Harcourt Courtly, *London Assurance,* Roundabout Theatre Company, Criterion Center, 1997.

Also appeared in *The Tavern,* Academy Festival Theatre.

Major Tours:

Title role, *Butley,* U.S. cities, 1973.

Martin Dysart, *Equus,* U.S. cities, 1975.

Sidney Bruhl, *Deathtrap,* North American cities, 1979-80.

Ken Harrison, *Whose Life Is It, Anyway?,* North American cities, 1980.

Henry, *The Real Thing,* U.S. cities, 1985.

One-man Shakespeare show, *The Lunatic, the Lover, and the Poet,* North American cities, 1989-93.

Stage Work:

Stager, *The Knack,* Hartford Theatre, Hollywood, CA, 1966.

Director, *Titus Andronicus,* Stratford Shakespeare Festival, 1978.

Director, *Titus Andronicus,* Stratford Shakespeare Festival, 1980.

Director, *Coriolanus,* Stratford Shakespeare Festival, 1981.

Director, *Blithe Spirit,* Stratford Shakespeare Festival, 1981.

Director, *Tartuffe,* Stratford Shakespeare Festival, 1982.

Director, *The Rivals,* Stratford Shakespeare Festival, 1982.

Director, *Much Ado about Nothing,* Old Globe Theatre, San Diego, CA, 1986.

Director, *Phaedra,* Stratford Shakespeare Festival, 1990.

Director, *Othello,* Avon Theatre, Stratford Shakespeare Festival, 1994.

Director, *Waiting for Godot,* Stratford Shakespeare Festival, 1996.

Director, *Equus,* Avon Theatre, Stratford Shakespeare Festival, 1997.

Film Appearances:

Man of the Moment, Group, 1955.

Johnny, *Miracle in Soho,* Rank, 1957.

Eddie Barrett, *The Angry Silence,* British Lion, 1960.

Jimmy Gale, *Number Six,* Anglo-Amalgamated, 1962.

Escort, *The Punch and Judy Man,* Warner Pathe, 1963.

Bob Handman, *The Pad and How to Use It,* Universal, 1966.

Scott Stoddard, *Grand Prix,* Metro-Goldwyn-Mayer, 1966.

Voice of Robin Hood, *Walt Disney's Robin Hood* (animated), Buena Vista, 1973.

Clyde Tolson, *Nixon,* Buena Vista, 1995.

Television Appearances; Series:

Anthony, *Coronet Blue,* CBS, 1967.

Television Appearances; Miniseries:

Sir John Morland, *Scarlett,* CBS, 1994.

Television Appearances; Movies:
Lentulus, *Androcles and the Lion,* NBC, 1967.
Dr. Castle, *The Last Best Year,* ABC, 1990.

Television Appearances; Episodic:
Sgt. Oliver Grant, "Bump and Run," *The Equalizer,* CBS, 1985.
"How to Recede in Business," *Cheers,* NBC, 1988.
Sherlock Holmes, "My Dear Watson," *Alfred Hitchcock Presents,* NBC, 1989.

Also appeared in *Bob* and *Murder, She Wrote,* both CBS.

Television Appearances; Specials:
Voice of Adolf Eichmann, *The Trial of Adolf Eichmann,* PBS, 1997.*

BELKNAP, Allen R. 1941-

PERSONAL

Born November 25, 1941, in New York City; son of Ellsworth (a stock manager) and Deane (a teacher; maiden name, Woods) Belknap. *Education:* University of Pennsylvania, B.A. (cum laude), 1963; Carnegie-Mellon University, M.F.A., 1965.

Addresses: *Office*—749 South Ogden Dr., #4, Los Angeles, CA 90036.

Career: Director. University of Washington, Seattle, instructor, 1965-68; Hunter College, Albany, NY, associate professor, 1968-74; Direct Theatre, NY, founder and artistic director, 1974-80; freelance director, U.S. and Japan, 1980-90; Twentieth Century-Fox/Stephen Bochco Productions, Los Angeles, CA, director, 1990—. Member of board of directors, Rachael Harms Dance Company, New York City, 1980-82; consultant, Atwood Richards Inc., New York City, 1984-89; advisory board member, Primary Stages Theatre Company, New York City, 1985-90.

Member: Society of Stage Directors and Choreographers, American Film Institute.

Awards, Honors: Fellow in directing, National Endowment for the Arts, 1984.

CREDITS

Stage Work; Director:
Pop, Players Theatre, New York City, 1974.

The Devils, Direct Theatre, NY, 1975.
Gilgamesh, Direct Theatre, 1975.
Columbus, Direct Theatre, 1976.
Nature and Purpose of the Universe, Direct Theatre, 1976.
Lulu, Direct Theatre, 1977.
Earth Spirit and Pandora's Box, Direct Theatre, 1977.
The Beasts, Direct Theatre, 1978.
Modigliani, Direct Theatre, 1978.
Approaching Zero, La Mama Etc. Theatre, New York City, 1978.
Nature and Purpose of the Universe, Direct Theatre, 1979.
Jaywalkin', Direct Theatre, 1979.
Modigliani, Astor Place Theatre, New York City, 1979.
The Interview, Direct Theatre, 1980.
Blau and Pignoli, Perry Street Theatre, New York City, 1980.
Beginner's Luck, Tiffany's Attic, Kansas City, MO, 1981.
Almost an Eagle, American Stage Festival, 1981.
Last of the Red Hot Lovers, Tiffany's Attic, 1982.
South Pacific, Fredericksburg Theater Company, 1982.
Princess Grace, Wisdoms Bridge, Chicago, IL, 1982.
Blood Moon, Production Company, NY, 1983.
Comedy of Errors, Fort Worth Shakespeare Festival, TX, 1983.
The Taming of the Shrew, Alabama Shakespeare Festival, 1983.
Without Apologies, Pittsburgh Playhouse, PA, 1983.
Blood Moon, Actors and Directors, NY, 1983.
The Killing of Sister George, Roundabout, New York City, 1983.
School for Scandal, Folger Shakespeare Festival, Washington, DC, 1984.
The Flight of the Earls, Westside Arts Theatre, NY, 1984.
They're Playing Our Song, Toho Productions, Tokyo, Japan, 1984.
Philco Blues, NY, 1984.
Diminished Capacity, GeVa Theatre, Rochester, NY, 1986.
A Lesson from Aloes, Pennsylvania Stage Company, Allentown, PA, 1987.
Alfred Stieglitz Loves O'Keefe, GeVa Theatre, 1987.
Equus, GeVa Theatre, 1987.
How the Other Half Loves, Pennsylvania Stage Company, 1988.
Established Price, Philadelphia Festival Theatre, Philadelphia, PA, 1988.
Heaven's Hard, The Alley Theatre, Houston, TX, 1989.

Little Shop of Horrors, George Street Playhouse, New Brunswick, NJ, then Pennsylvania Stage Company, 1989.

The Boys Next Door, GeVa Theatre, 1989.

Adult Fiction, GeVa Theatre, 1990.

A Piece of My Heart, Manhattan Theatre Club, Union Square Theatre, New York City, 1991.

Director of *Electra, The Guardsman, On Borrowed Time, Beowulf, The Art Lovers, Anele, A Phoenix Too Frequent, A Sleep of Prisoners, Brechon-Brecht, Tango, The Bacchae, The Days Between, Under Milkwood, A Musical Timepiece, Brand, Arms and the Man, Peer Gynt, Room, Collection, Slights Ache, Dial 'M' for Murder, The Rose Tattoo, The Hostage, The Way of the World, Two for the Seesaw, A Streetcar Named Desire, The Little Foxes, Look Back in Anger, Picnic, After the Fall, Private Ear/Public Eye, A Taste of Honey, Barefoot in the Park, Who's Afraid of Virginia Woolf?, The Imaginary Invalid, My Fair Lady, Richard III,* and *Threepenny Opera,* all 1965-72.

Film Work; Director:

Traveler's Rest, 1991.*

BELMONDO, Jean-Paul   1933-

PERSONAL

Born April 9, 1933, in Neuilly-sur-Seine, France; son of Paul Belmondo (a sculptor); married Elodie Constantin, 1952 (divorced, 1967); children: Patricia (deceased), Florence, Paul. *Education:* Attended College Pascal, Paris; trained for the stage at National Conservatory of Dramatic Art, Paris, and with Raymond Girard. *Avocational interests:* Sports.

Addresses: *Office*—Cerito Films, 5 rue Clement Marot, 75008 Paris, France. *Agent*—c/o Art Media, 10 avenue George-V, 75008 Paris, France.

Career: Actor and producer. Founder (with Annie Girardot and Guy Bedos) of a traveling theatre group, 1956-57; Cerito Films, founder during the 1960s; also appeared with Comedie Francaise and as a performer in Parisian cafes. Worked as a welterweight boxer, 1949; Les Polymuscles (soccer team), part-owner.

Member: Syndicat Francais des Acteurs (president, 1963-66).

Awards, Honors: Prix Citron, 1972; Cesar award (French Academy Award), best actor, Academie des Arts et Techniques du Cinema, 1988, for *Itineraire d'un Enfant Gate;* Chevalier de la Legion d'honneur; Chevalier l'Ordre national du Merite et des Arts et des Lettres.

CREDITS

Film Appearances:

Dimanche Nous Volerons, 1956.

Pierrot, *Sois Belle et Tais-Toi* (also known as *Blonde for Danger, Just Another Pretty Face, Be Beautiful but Shut Up,* and *Be Beautiful and Shut Up*), 1958.

Venin, *A Pied, a Cheval, et en Voiture* (also known as *A Piedi . . . A Cavallo . . . In Automobile*), 1958.

Patrick, *Drole du Dimanche* (also known as *Un Drole de Dimanche*), 1958.

Trebois, *Les Copains du Dimanche,* 1958.

Jean, the old boyfriend, *Charlotte et son Jules* (short film; also known as *Charlotte and Her Jules* and *Charlotte and Her Boyfriends*), 1958.

Lou, *Les Tricheurs* (also known as *The Cheaters* and *Peccatori in Blue Jeans*), Continental Distributing, 1958.

Michel Poiccard, alias Laszlo Kovacs, *Breathless* (also known as *A Bout de Souffle*), Imperia, 1959.

Laszlo Kovacs, *A Double Tour* (also known as *Web of Passion, A Doppia Mandator,* and *Leda*), 1959, released in the United States by Times, 1961.

Michel Barrot, *Ein Engel auf Erden* (also known as *Mademoiselle Ange* and *Angel on Earth*), 1959, released in United States by Comet, 1966.

Eric Stark, *Classe tous Risques* (also known as *The Big Risk*), 1960, released in the United States by United Artists, 1963.

Paul, *Les Distractions* (also known as *Trapped by Fear*), 1960.

Michele, *La Ciociara* (also known as *Two Women* and *Paysanne aux Pieds Nus*), Embassy, 1960.

Chauvin, *Moderato Cantabile* (also known as *Seven Days . . . Seven Nights*), Royal Films International, 1960.

Leon Morin, *Leon Morin, Pretre* (also known as *Leon Morin, Priest* and *The Forgiven Sinner*), 1961.

Un nomme la Rocca (also known as *A Man Named Rocca* and *Quelloche Spara per Primo*), 1961.

Gil, "L'adultere" (movie segment), *La Francaise et l'Amour* (also known as *Love and the Frenchwoman*), Auerbach/Kingsley, 1961.

Alfred Lubitsch, *Une Femme Est une Femme* (also known as *A Woman Is a Woman* and *Le Donna e Donna*), Pathe-Contemporary, 1961.

Cartouche, *Cartouche* (also known as *Swords of Blood*), FS-Vides, 1962.

Amerigo Casamunti, *La Viaccia* (also known as *The Love Makers*), Embassy, 1962.

Gabriel Fouquet, *Un Singe en Hiver* (also known as *A Monkey in Winter* and *It's Hot in Hell*), Metro-Goldwyn-Mayer, 1962.

Silien, *Le Doulos* (also known as *Doulos—The Finger Man* and *Fingerman*), Pathe-Contemporary, 1962.

I Don Giovanni Della Costa Azzurra, 1962.

Michel Maudet, *L'Aine des Ferchaux* (also known as *Magnet of Doom* and *Un Jeune Homme Honorable*), 1962.

Un Coeur gros Comme ca! (also known as *The Winner*), 1962.

Mare Matto (also known as *Mad Sea* and *La Mer a Boire*), 1963.

Il giorno piu corto (also known as *The Shortest Day* and *Il Giorno piu Corto Commedia Umoristica*), 1963.

Giuliano Verdi, *Lettere di una Novizia* (also known as *Rita, La Novice,* and *Letter from a Novice*), Colorama Features, 1963.

Raymond LeLegion, *Dragees au Poivre* (also known as *Sweet and Sour, The Sweet and Bitter,* and *Confetti al Pepe*), Pathe-Contemporary, 1964.

Adrien Dufourquet, *L'Homme de Rio* (also known as *That Man from Rio* and *L'Uomo di Rio*), Lopert, 1964.

David Ladislas, *Enchappement Libre* (also known as *Backfire*), Royal Films International 1965.

Michel, *Peau de Banane* (also known as *Banana Peel*), Pathe-Contemporary, 1965.

Rocco, *Cent Mille Dollars au Soleil* (also known as *Greed in the Sun, 100,000 Dollars au Soleil,* and *Centamila Dollari al Sole*), Gaumont/Metro-Goldwyn-Mayer, 1965.

Fernand, *La Chasse a l'Homme* (also known as *The Gentle Art of Seduction, Male Hunt,* and *Caccia al Maschio*), Pathe-Contemporary, 1965.

Par un Beau Matin d'Ete (also known as *Crime on a Summer Morning* and *One Bright Summer Morning*), 1965.

Pierroflot/Y. Morandat, *Is Paris Burning?* (also known as *Paris Brule-t-il?*), Paramount, 1966.

Arthur Lempereur, *Les Tribulations d'un chinois en Chine* (also known as *Up to His Ears, Chinese Adventures in China,* and *L'uomo di Hong Kong*), Lopert, 1966.

Sergeant Julien Maillat, *Week-end a Zuydcoote* (also known as *Weekend at Dunkirk*), Twentieth Century-Fox, 1966.

French legionnaire, *Casino Royale,* Columbia, 1967.

Tony Marechal, *Tendre voyou* (also known as *Tender Scoundrel* and *Un Avventuriero a Tahiti*), Embassy, 1967.

Georges Randal, *Le Voleur* (also known as *The Thief of Paris*), Lopert, 1967.

La Bande a Bebel, 1967.

Ho, *Ho!,* Cocinor, 1968.

Ferdinand Griffon (title role), *Pierrot le Fou,* Pathe-Contemporary/Corinth, 1968.

Arthur, *Le Cerveau* (also known as *The Brain*), Paramount, 1969.

Dieu a Choisi Paris, 1969.

Francois Capella, *Borsalino,* Paramount, 1970.

Henri, *Histoire d'Aimer* (also known as *Love Is a Funny Thing, Again a Love Story, Un Tipo Chi mi Piace, Un Homme Qui me Plait,* and *A Man I Like*), United Artists, 1970.

Louis Mahe, *La Sirene du Mississippi* (also known as *Mississippi Mermaid* and *La Mia Droga si Chiama Julie*), Lopert/United Artists, 1970.

Nicolas Philibert, *Les Maries de l'An Deux* (also known as *Les Maries de l'An II, The Married Couple of Year Two, The Scarlet Buccaneer, The Swashbuckler,* and *The Scoundrel*), Gaumont International, 1971.

Azad, *Le Casse* (also known as *The Burglars*), Columbia, 1972.

Dr. Paul Simay, *Docteur Popaul* (also known as *Scoundrel in White* and *High Heels*), CIC, 1972.

Barthelemy Cordell, *L'Heritier* (also known as *The Inheritor* and *The Heir*), Valoria, 1972.

Borgo, *La Scoumoune* (also known as *Killer Man* and *Hit Man*), Fox-Lira, 1972.

Bob Saint-Clair/Francois Merlin, *Le Magnifique* (also known as *The Magnificent One, Secret Agent,* and *How to Destroy the Reputation of the Greatest Secret Agent*), Cine III, 1974.

Serge Alexandre Stavisky, *Stavisky* (also known as *L'Empire d'Alexandre*), Cinemation, 1974.

Roger Pilard/title role, *L'Alpagueur* (also known as *The Predator* and *The Hunter Will Get You*), AMLF, 1975.

Le Commissaire Jean Letellier, *Peur sur la Ville* (also known as *Fear over the City* and *The Night Caller*), AMLF, 1975.

Francois Leclerq, *Le Corps de Mon Ennemi* (also known as *The Body of the Enemy*), AMLF, 1976.

Mike Gaucher and Bruno Fechner, *L'Animal* (also known as *The Animal* and *Stuntwoman*), AMLF/Roissy, 1977.

Commissaire Stan Borowitz/Angelo Crutti, *Flic ou Voyou* (also known as *Cop or Hood*), Gaumont International, 1979.

Victor, *L'Incorrigible* (also known as *Incorrigible*), EDP Films, 1980.

Alain Dupre, *Le Guignolo,* 1980.

I Piccioni di Piazza San Marco, 1980.

Joss Baumont, *Le Professionnel* (also known as *The Professional*), 1981.

Joe Cavalier, *L'As des As* (also known as *Ace of Aces* and *The Super Ace*), Gaumont International/ Cerito-Rene Chateau, 1982.

Commissaire Philippe Jordan, *Le Marginal* (also known as *The Outsider*), Roissy/Gaumont, 1983.

Pierre Augagneur, *Les Morfalous* (also known as *The Vultures*), AAA/Roissy/Cerito-Rene Chateau, 1983.

Stephane Margelle, *Joyeuses Paques* (also known as *Happy Easter*), Sara/Cerito, 1984.

Grimm, *Hold-Up,* AMLF, 1985.

Commissioner Stan Jalard, *Le Solitaire,* AMLF/Cerito, 1987.

Sam Lion, *Itineraire d'un Enfant Gate* (also known as *Itinerary of a Spoiled Child* and *Loewe*), AFDM/ Films 13, 1988.

Fleur de Rubis, 1990.

Loursat, *L'Inconnu dans la Maison* (also known as *Stranger in the House*), 1992.

Henry Fortin/Jean Valjean/Roger Fortin, *Les Miserables* (also known as *Les Miserables du Vingtieme Siecle*), Warner Bros., 1995.

Actor for a day, *A Hundred and One Nights* (also known as *Les Cent et Une Nuits, A Hundred and One Nights of Simon Cinema,* and *Les Cent et Une Nuits de Simon Cinema*), Mercure Distribution, 1995.

Desire, *Desire,* Le Studio Canal Plus, 1996.

Half a Chance (also known as *Une Chance sur Deux*), 1997.

Film Producer:

Le Corps de Mon Ennemi (also known as *The Body of the Enemy*), AMLF, 1976.

L'As des As (also known as *Ace of Aces* and *Super Ace*), Gaumont International/Cerito-Rene Chateau, 1982.

Joyeuses Paques (also known as *Happy Easter*), Sara/ Cerito, 1984.

(Co-producer) *Itineraire d'un Enfant Gate* (also known as *Itinerary of a Spoiled Child* and *Loewe*), AFDM/Films 13, 1988.

L'Inconnu dans la Maison (also known as *Stranger in the House*), 1992.

Stage Appearances:

Tildian, *Moliere,* 1955.

Caesar and Cleopatra, 1958.

Tresor-Party (also known as *Treasure Party*), 1958.

Oscar, 1958.

Title role, *Cyrano de Bergerac,* Paris, 1990.

Also appeared in *L'Hotel du Libre-Echange, Medee, Kean, Tailleur pour Dames,* and *La Megere Apprivoisee* ("The Taming of the Shrew").

Television Appearances; Series:

Lauzun, *Les Amours Celebres* [France], 1961.

Also appeared on French television in a broadcast of *The Three Musketeers.*

WRITINGS

Trente Ans et Vingt-Cinq Films (autobiography; title means "Thirty Years and Twenty-Five Films"), Union Generale d'Editions (Paris), 1963.

OTHER SOURCES

Books

International Dictionary of Film and Filmmakers, Volume 3: *Actors and Actresses,* St. James Press (Detroit, MI), 1997.*

BENNETT, Harve   1930-

PERSONAL

Full name, Harve Bennett Fischman; born August 17, 1930, in Chicago, IL; son of Yale (a lawyer) and Kathryn (a journalist; maiden name, Susman) Fischman; married Carole Oettinger (an agent); children: Christopher, Susan, Callie, Samantha. *Education:* University of California, Los Angeles, B.A., theatre arts.

Addresses: *Contact*—Altman, Greenfield, and Selvaggi, 11766 Wilshire Blvd., Suite 1610, Los Angeles, CA 90025.

Career: Producer and screenwriter. Bennett-Katleman Productions, president; CBS-TV, associate producer and special events producer; ABC-TV, vice-president; director of television commercials. Newspaper columnist, drama critic, and freelance writer. Civilian aide to the Secretary of the Army, 1988-90.

Member: Theatre Arts Alumni Association of the University of California, Los Angeles (president, 1985-90).

Awards, Honors: Golden Globe Award, best dramatic television series, Hollywood Foreign Press Association, 1977, for *Rich Man, Poor Man;* Emmy Award, outstanding drama special, 1982, for *A Woman Called Golda;* NAACP Image Award, National Association for the Advancement of Colored People, best miniseries, 1984, for *The Jesse Owens Story.*

CREDITS

Film Work:
Executive producer, *Star Trek II: The Wrath of Khan* (also known as *Star Trek II: The Vengeance of Khan*), Paramount, 1982.
Producer, *Star Trek III: The Search for Spock,* Paramount, 1984.
Producer, *Star Trek IV: The Voyage Home,* Paramount, 1986.
Producer, *Star Trek V: The Final Frontier,* Paramount, 1989.

Film Appearances:
Voice of flight recorder, *Star Trek III: The Search for Spock,* Paramount, 1984.
Star Fleet commander, *Star Trek V: The Final Frontier,* Paramount, 1989.

Television Work; Series; Executive Producer, Except Where Indicated:
Producer (with Tony Barrett), *The Mod Squad,* ABC, 1968-73.
And creator, *The Young Rebels,* ABC, 1970-71.
(With Allan Balter) *The Six Million Dollar Man,* ABC, 1973-78.
The Invisible Man, NBC, 1975-76.
The Gemini Man, NBC, 1976.
(With Harris Katleman) *The American Girls,* CBS, 1978.
(With Katleman) *Salvage 1,* ABC, 1979.
(With Katleman) *From Here to Eternity,* NBC, 1980.
(With Bruce Lansbury) *The Powers of Matthew Star,* NBC, 1982-83.
And creator and developer, *Time Trax,* syndicated, 1993-94.

Television Work; Miniseries; Executive Producer:
Rich Man, Poor Man, ABC, 1976.
(With Katleman) *From Here to Eternity,* NBC, 1979.

Television Work; Pilots; Executive Producer:
The Invisible Man, NBC, 1975.
Gemini Man (also known as *Code Name: Minus One*), NBC, 1976.

(With Katleman) *Go West, Young Girl!,* ABC, 1978.
(With Katleman) *The Legend of the Golden Gun,* NBC, 1979.
(With Katleman) *Salvage,* ABC, 1979.
(With Katleman) *Alex and the Doberman Gang,* NBC, 1980.
(With Katleman) *Nick and the Dobermans,* NBC, 1980.

Television Work; Episodic:
Producer, *The Bionic Woman,* ABC, 1976.
Director, "The Dream Team," *Time Trax,* syndicated, 1994.

Television Work; Movies; Executive Producer, Except Where Indicated:
Producer, *The Birdmen* (also known as *Escape of the Birdmen*), ABC, 1971.
Producer, *The Astronaut,* ABC, 1972.
Producer, *Family Flight,* ABC, 1972.
Producer, *Death Race,* ABC, 1973.
Producer, *Money to Burn,* ABC, 1973.
You'll Never See Me Again, ABC, 1973.
The Alpha Caper (also known as *Inside Job*), ABC, 1973.
Runaway!, 1973.
Houston, We've Got a Problem, ABC, 1974.
Heatwave!, ABC, 1974.
Guilty or Innocent: The Sam Sheppard Case, NBC, 1975.
The Jesse Owens Story, syndicated, 1984.

Television Work; Specials:
Executive producer, *A Woman Called Golda,* syndicated, 1982.

Radio Appearances:
Appeared as a regular on the series *The Quiz Kids.*

WRITINGS

Films:
Star Trek III: The Search for Spock, Paramount, 1984.
(With Steve Meerson, Peter Krikes, and Nicholas Meyer) *Star Trek IV: The Voyage Home,* Paramount, 1986.

Television Episodes:
The Mod Squad, ABC, 1968-73.
The Young Rebels, ABC, 1970-71.
Time Trax, syndicated, 1992.

Television Movies:
(With Gerald DiPego, Charles Kuenstle, and Robert S. Biheller) *The Astronaut,* ABC, 1972.

Crash Landing: The Rescue of Flight 232 (also known as *A Thousand Heroes*), ABC, 1992.

Adaptations: The films *Star Trek II: The Wrath of Khan*, 1982, and *Star Trek V: The Final Frontier*, 1989, are based on stories by Bennett. The television movie *The Invisible Man* is also based on a Bennett story.*

BENSON, Bobby
   See BENSON, Robby

BENSON, Robby   1956-
   (Bobby Benson, Robin Benson)

PERSONAL

Original name, Robin Segal; born January 21, 1956, in Dallas, TX; son of Jerry Segal (a writer) and Ann Benson (an actress and business promotions manager); married Karla DeVito (a rock singer and actress), 1982. *Education:* Attended American Academy of Dramatic Arts.

Addresses: *Agent*—Krost/Chapin, 9465 Wilshire Blvd., Suite 430, Beverly Hills, CA 90212.

Career: Actor, director, producer, and writer. Appeared in television commercials and in summer theater productions at the age of five; University of Southern California, film instructor; musician.

CREDITS

Film Appearances:
Title role, *Jory*, Avco-Embassy, 1972.
Title role (Jeremy Jones), *Jeremy*, United Artists, 1973.
Billy Webber, *Lucky Lady*, Twentieth Century-Fox, 1975.
Title role (Billy Joe McAllister), *Ode to Billy Joe*, Warner Bros., 1976.
Henry Steele, *One on One*, Warner Bros., 1977.
Priest, *The End*, United Artists, 1978.
Nick Peterson, *Ice Castles*, Columbia, 1978.
Emilio Mendez, *Walk Proud* (also known as *Gang*), Universal, 1979.
Pinsky, *Die Laughing*, Warner Bros., 1980.
Jud Templeton, *Tribute*, Twentieth Century-Fox, 1980.
Brent Falcone, "Municipalians" in *National Lampoon Goes to the Movies* (also known as *National*

Lampoon's Movie Madness), Metro-Goldwyn-Mayer/United Artists, 1981.
Danny Saunders, *The Chosen*, Contemporary, 1982.
Billy Mills, *Running Brave*, Buena Vista, 1983.
Howard Keach, *Harry and Son*, Orion, 1984.
Carver, *City Limits*, Atlantic, 1985.
Pitts, *Rent-a-Cop*, Kings Road, 1988.
Scott, *White Hot* (also known as *Crack in the Mirror* and *Do It Up*), Triax Entertainment/Paul International, 1989.
Greg, *Modern Love*, 1990.
Voice of Beast, *Beauty and the Beast* (animated), Buena Vista, 1991.
Max Pierce, *Deadly Exposure*, Crystal Sky Communications, 1993.
Roger Swade, *At Home with the Webbers* (also known as *The Webbers* and *Webber's World*), LIVE Home Video, 1994.

Also appeared in *The Apple War*.

Film Work:
Producer (with Mark Canton), *Die Laughing*, Warner Bros., 1980.
Director and song performer ("Bang My Drum . . . Slowly" and "What Planet Are You From"), *White Hot* (also known as *Crack in the Mirror* and *Do It Up*), Triax Entertainment/Paul International, 1989.
Producer and director, *Modern Love*, 1990.

Television Appearances; Series:
Bruce Carson, *Search for Tomorrow*, CBS, 1971-73.
Detective Cliff Brady, *Tough Cookies*, CBS, 1986.
Voice of Prince Valiant, *The Legend of Prince Valiant* (animated), The Family Channel, 1991-94.
Voice of Five-Card Cud, *Wild West C.O.W. Boys of Moo Mesa*, 1992.
Voice of Simabacca and Lieutenant J. T. Marsh, *Exosquad*, 1993.
Voice, *The Magic School Bus*, 1994.
Edward "Ted" Spellman, *Sabrina, the Teenage Witch*, ABC, 1996-97.

Television Appearances; Movies:
Leroy Small, *The Virginia Hill Story*, NBC, 1974.
Frankie Hodges, *Remember When* (also known as *Four Stars in the Window*), NBC, 1974.
John, *All the Kind Strangers* (also known as *Evil in the Swamp*), ABC, 1974.
Johnnie Gunther, *Death Be Not Proud*, ABC, 1975.
Title role (Richie Werner), *The Death of Richie*, NBC, 1977.
Nolie Minor, *Two of a Kind*, CBS, 1982.

Nathan Bowzer, *California Girls,* ABC, 1985.
Dr. David Whitson, *Homewrecker* (also known as *Programmed for Murder*), Sci-Fi Channel, 1992.
Alex Pruitt, *Invasion of Privacy,* USA Network, 1992.
Robert Sims, *Precious Victims,* CBS, 1993.

Television Appearances; Specials:
George Gibbs, *Our Town,* NBC, 1977.
John Denver in Australia, ABC, 1978.
Host, *The 2nd Annual CBS Easter Parade,* CBS, 1986.
Be Our Guest: The Making of Disney's "Beauty and the Beast," The Disney Channel, 1991.
The 49th Annual Golden Globe Awards, 1992.
Voice of William Osborn Stoddard, *Lincoln,* ABC, 1992.
Star-athon '92: A Weekend with the Stars, syndicated, 1992.
Walt Disney World Happy Easter Parade, 1992.
Host, *Pinocchio: The Making of a Masterpiece,* The Disney Channel, 1993.
Host, *American Express Presents Backstage Pass . . . Disney's "Beauty and the Beast" Goes to Broadway,* The Disney Channel, 1994.
Voice of Tom Thumb, *P. T. Barnum: America's Greatest Showman,* The Disney Channel, 1995.

Television Appearances; Episodic:
"Julie's Blind Date," *One Day at a Time,* CBS, 1976.
"The Last of Mrs. Lincoln," *Hollywood Television Theatre,* PBS, 1976.
Ed Bolling, "Method Actor," *Alfred Hitchcock Presents,* NBC, 1985.
Jonathan Ravenhurst Blackwell, *Avonlea* (also known as *The Road to Avonlea*), CBC/The Disney Channel, 1990.
Himself, *Caroline in the City,* NBC, 1996.

Appeared on soap operas as a child, sometimes as Robin Benson or Bobby Benson.

Television Director; Series:
Sabrina, the Teenage Witch, ABC, 1996-97.
Life with Roger, 1996.

Television Director; Episodic:
"Try Not to Remember," *Dream On,* HBO, 1990.
Ellen (also known as *These Friend of Mine*), ABC, 1994.
Thunder Alley, ABC, 1994.
Friends, NBC, 1994.
Bringing Up Jack, 1995.
The George Wendt Show, CBS, 1995.

Friends, NBC, 1996.
Common Law, ABC, 1996.
Pearl, CBS, 1996.

Director of episodes of *True Confessions, Good Advice, Muddling Through, Monty, Evening Shade* and *Family Album;* director of the pilot episode, *Game Night.*

Stage Appearances:
David Hartman, *Zelda,* Ethel Barrymore Theatre, 1969.
Third urchin, *The Rothschilds,* Lunt-Fontanne Theatre, New York City, 1970.
Frederic, *The Pirates of Penzance,* Minskoff Theatre, New York City, 1981.

Appeared on Broadway at age five in *The King and I;* toured Japan in a production of *Oliver!,* c. 1964; also appeared in *King of Hearts, Evita, Do Black Patent Leather Shoes Really Reflect Up?,* and *Dude.*

RECORDINGS

Taped Readings:
Conduct Unbecoming: Gays and Lesbians in the U.S. Military, by Randy Shilts, Publishing Mills, 1993.

WRITINGS

Films:
(With father, Jerry Segal) *One on One,* Warner Bros., 1977.
(With Don Peake) and composer, *Walk Proud,* Universal, 1979.
(With Segal and Scott Parker) and composer (with Segal), *Die Laughing,* Warner Bros., 1980.
Song composer, "We Are Not Alone," *The Breakfast Club,* Universal, 1985.
Song composer, "Bang My Drum . . . Slowly," "What Planet Are You From," "The Hard Way," and "Love I Can Taste," *White Hot* (also known as *Crack in the Mirror* and *Do It Up*), Triax Entertainment/Paul International, 1989.
Screenplay and composer of songs "Evelyn's Theme," "Falling in Love with You," and "Brahma Beach Cop," *Modern Love,* 1990.
(With wife, Karla DeVito) *Betrayal of the Dove,* Prism Entertainment, 1993.*

BENSON, Robin
See BENSON, Robby

BERGER, Keith 1952-

PERSONAL

Born September 18, 1952, in Los Angeles, CA; son of Raymond M. (a playwright) and Frances R. (a psychologist; maiden name, Lucow) Berger; married Sharon Diskin (an actress, mime, and teacher); children: Gideon. *Education:* Attended American Academy of Dramatic Arts and American Mime Theatre; trained for mime with Paul Curtis. *Religion:* Jewish.

Addresses: *Home*—Sherman Oaks, CA. *Agent*—c/o Arthur Shafman International, Ltd., P.O. Box 352, Pawling, NY 12564.

Career: Actor, writer, mime performer, and director. Oberlin Mime Company, Oberlin, OH, director. Performed as solo mime at Palais D'Europe for Princess Grace of Monaco, and for President Jimmy Carter's inauguration, Washington, DC, 1977. Featured performer at the Kennedy Center for the Performing Arts, Lincoln Center, and the Palm Beach Arts Festival. Toured as a solo mime performer at U.S. and European colleges and festivals for ten years. Toured (with Sharon Diskin) as a member of the performance team the Chameleons, various places, including La MaMa Theatre, New York City; Mark Taper Forum, Los Angeles, CA; the Edinburgh Festival, Edinburgh, Scotland; nightclubs in Los Angeles, CA; and cruise ships.

Member: Actors' Equity Association, American Federation of Television and Radio Artists, Screen Actors Guild.

Awards, Honors: Joseph Papp Street Performer Award.

CREDITS

Stage Appearances:
Rooty Kazooty, *Broken Toys,* Orpheum Theatre, later Actors' Playhouse, both New York City, 1982.

Made stage debut as silent actor, *The Advent,* Radio City West, Los Angeles, CA. Also appeared in *Ezekiel,* off-Broadway.

Major Tours:
(With Sharon Diskin) *The Chameleons,* Los Angeles Music Center Education Division, U.S. and world cities, 1990—.

Film Appearances:
Ray, *Angels,* 1974.
Street mime, *Crossover Dreams,* Miramax, 1985.
Angel Heart, TriStar, 1987.
First attendant, *The Suicide Club,* 1987.

Made film debut in *Keith,* Billy Budd Films.

Film Work:
Choreographer, *The Suicide Club,* 1987.

Television Appearances; Specials:
Mime, *Funny Faces/Red Skelton,* HBO, 1981.
"Gryphon," *WonderWorks,* PBS, 1988.

Television Appearances; Movies:
Robot, *Automatic,* HBO, 1995.

Television Appearances; Series:
Space Rangers, CBS, 1993.

Television Appearances; Episodic:
With Sharon Diskin, appeared in variety and talk shows in the United States and Great Britain.

WRITINGS

Plays:
Broken Toys, Orpheum Theatre, later Actors' Playhouse, 1982.

Other plays include *Dog and Pony Show,* Oberlin College, Oberlin, OH; *Interruptions,* Silent Theatre; and *Visitor from Space,* Silent Theatre.*

BERRY, David 1943-

PERSONAL

Full name, David Adams Berry; born July 8, 1943, in Denver, CO; son of Richard Lambert (a chemist) and Mary Elizabeth (a real estate broker; maiden name, Adams) Berry; married Robin Graham, May 1, 1971 (divorced, 1980); stepchildren: Julia Lee Barclay. *Education:* Wesleyan University, B.A. (history and theatre), 1968; Harvard University, certificate in business, 1972. *Politics:* Independent.

Addresses: *Contact*—c/o Writers Guild of America West, 7000 West Third St., Los Angeles, CA 90048.

Career: Playwright and teacher. O'Neill Theatre Center, CT, intern (stage manager, house manager, and actor) at National Playwrights Conference, 1968, assistant director at theatre, 1971-74; Worcester Polytechnic Institute, Assumption College, Worcester, MA, playwright in residence, 1977-78; Rhode Island State Council on the Arts, theatre specialist, 1975-76; National Theatre Institute, instructor in playwriting, 1980-83. *Military service:* U.S. Army, 1968-69, served in Vietnam.

Member: Dramatists Guild, Vietnam Veterans of America.

Awards, Honors: Obie Award, distinguished playwriting, *Village Voice,* and Drama Desk Award nomination, best new American play, both 1977, for *G. R. Point;* creative writing fellowship, National Endowment for the Arts, 1978.

WRITINGS

Plays:
G. R. Point, National Playwrights Conference, O'Neill Theatre Center, CT, 1976, published 1981.
The Whales of August, Center Stage, Baltimore, MD, 1980, published 1984.
Tracers, New York Shakespeare Festival, Public Theatre, New York City, 1985.

Screenplays:
The Whales of August (based on his stage play), Alive Films, 1987.*

BILLINGSLEY, Peter   1972-

PERSONAL

Original name, Peter Michaelson; born April 16, 1972, in New York, NY; son of Alwin (a financial consultant) and Gail Michaelson; grand-nephew of Sherman Billingsley (owner of the Stork Club in New York City). *Education:* Attended Phoenix College. *Avocational interests:* Golf.

Addresses: *Home*—Los Angeles, CA. *Contact*—The Theatrex Company, 9028 Sunset Blvd., Penthouse 1, Los Angeles, CA 90069.

Career: Actor, director, producer, and editor. Actor in more than one hundred television commercials, including Messy Marvin in Nestle's Quik ads. Directs, edits, and scripts music videos and short programs.

Awards, Honors: Emmy Award nomination, 1994, for "The Writing on the Wall," *CBS Schoolbreak Specials.*

CREDITS

Film Appearances:
Child, *If Ever I See You Again,* Columbia, 1978.
Tad, *Paternity,* Paramount, 1981.
Billy Kramer, *Honky Tonk Freeway,* Universal/Associated Film Distribution, 1981.
Billy, *Death Valley,* Universal, 1982.
Ralphie, *A Christmas Story,* Metro-Goldwyn-Mayer/United Artists, 1983.
Jack Simmons, *The Dirt Bike Kid* (also known as *Crazy Wheels*), Concorde/Cinema Group, 1985.
Adam, *Russkies,* New Century/Vista, 1987.
Scooter Miller, *Beverly Hills Brats,* Taurus Entertainment, 1989.
Nick, *Arcade,* Paramount Home Video, 1994.
No Deposit, No Return, 1997.

Television Appearances; Series:
Host, *Real People,* NBC, 1982-84.
Billy Baker, *Sherman Oaks,* Showtime, 1995-96.

Television Appearances; Pilots:
Host, *Real Kids,* NBC, 1981.
Christopher ("the Brain"), *Massarati and the Brain,* ABC, 1982.
Roland Krantz, Jr., *Carly's Web,* NBC, 1987.

Television Appearances; Episodic:
Gideon, "No Beast So Fierce," *Little House on the Prairie,* NBC, 1981.
Ridley, "The Monster," *Highway to Heaven,* NBC, 1984.
Bobby Walsh, "Double Date," *Who's the Boss?,* ABC, 1984.
Kevin, "Pecos Bill, King of the Cowboys," *Shelley Duvall's Tall Tales and Legends,* Showtime, 1986.
Richmond Matzie, *Punky Brewster,* NBC, 1986.

Television Appearances; Movies:
Shawn Tilford, *Memories Never Die,* CBS, 1982.
Marty Adamson, *The Last Frontier,* CBS, 1986.
Mark, Jr., "Family Reunion: A Relative Nightmare," *The ABC Family Movie,* ABC, 1995.

Television Appearances; Specials:
The Hoboken Chicken Mystery, 1984.
Joey Martelli, "The Fourth Man," *CBS Schoolbreak Specials,* CBS, 1990.

Tony, "The Writing on the Wall," *CBS Schoolbreak Specials,* CBS, 1994.

OTHER SOURCES

Periodicals:
Entertainment Weekly, December 20, 1996, p. 88.*

BLACK, Noel   1937-

PERSONAL

Full name, Noel Anthony Black; born June 30, 1937, in Chicago, IL; son of Samuel Abraham and Susan (Quan) Black; married Sandra MacPhail, December 2, 1967 (marriage ended); married Catherine Elizabeth Cownie, June 1, 1988; children: Marco Eugene, Nicole Alexandra, Carmen Elizabeth, Catherine Ellen. *Education:* Attended University of Chicago, 1954-1957; University of California, Los Angeles, B.A., 1959, M.A., 1964.

Addresses: *Office*—Starfish Productions, 126 Wadsworth Ave., Santa Monica, CA 90405-3510. *Agent*—Don Buchwald and Associates, 9229 Sunset Blvd., Suite 710, Los Angeles, CA 90069.

Career: Director, producer, and writer. New York University, New York City, assistant professor at Institute for Film and Television, Tisch School of the Arts, 1992-93.

Member: Academy of Motion Picture Arts and Sciences, Directors Guild of America, Academy of Television Arts and Sciences, Writers Guild of America.

Awards, Honors: Academy Award nomination, best short subject (cartoon), Grand Prix and technical Grand Prix, Cannes XX International Film Festival, Silver Medal, Moscow V International Film Festival, and Waterford Glass Award, Cork International XI Film Festival, all 1966, for *Skaterdater;* Lion of St. Mark Award, Venice XVIII International Film Festival, and first prize, Vancouver International Film Festival, both 1967, for *Riverboy;* Outstanding Young Director Award from the Monte Carlo International Festival of Television, and Dove Award from the International Catholic Society for Radio and Television, both 1967, for *Trilogy: The American Boy;* George Foster Peabody Award, 1982, for *The Electric Grandmother.*

CREDITS

Film Work; Director, Except Where Indicated:
(And producer, with Marshal Backlar) *Skaterdater* (animated short film), United Artists, 1966.
Riverboy (short film), 1967.
(And co-executive producer) *Pretty Poison,* Twentieth Century-Fox, 1968.
Cover Me Babe (also known as *Run Shadow Run*), Twentieth Century-Fox, 1970.
Jennifer on My Mind, United Artists, 1971.
Mirrors (also known as *Bad Dreams, Marianne*), 1974.
A Man, a Woman and a Bank, Avco-Embassy, 1979.
Private School, Universal, 1983.
Executive producer, *Mischief,* Twentieth Century-Fox, 1985.
Heart and Soul, 1985.

Television Director; Movies:
The Other Victim, CBS, 1981.
Prime Suspect, CBS, 1981.
Happy Endings, CBS, 1982.
Quarterback Princess, CBS, 1983.
Promises to Keep, 1985.
A Time to Triumph, CBS, 1986.
My Two Loves, ABC, 1986.
Conspiracy of Love, CBS, 1987.
"Meet the Munceys," *Disney Sunday Movie,* ABC, 1988.
The Town Bully (also known as *A Friendly, Quiet Little Town*), ABC, 1988.

Television Director; Specials:
Trilogy: The American Boy, ABC, 1968.
"I'm a Fool," *American Short Story,* PBS, 1976.
The World Beyond, 1978.
The Electric Grandmother, NBC, 1981.
"The Doctors Wilde" (also known as "Zoovets"), *CBS Summer Playhouse,* CBS, 1987.
"The Eyes of the Panther," *Nightmare Classics,* Showtime, 1989.
"The Hollow Boy," *American Playhouse,* PBS, 1991.

Also directed "The Golden Honeymoon," *American Short Story,* PBS.

Television Director; Episodic:
McCloud, NBC, 1970.
Amy Prentiss, NBC, 1974.
Switch, CBS, 1975.
Quincy, M.E. (also known as *Quincy*), NBC, 1976.
Big Hawaii, NBC, 1977.
Lanigan's Rabbi, NBC, 1977.
The Twilight Zone, CBS, 1985.

Television Director; Pilots:
Mulligan's Stew, NBC, 1977.

Television Director; Miniseries:
Deadly Intentions, 1985.

WRITINGS

Screenplays:
Skaterdater (animated short film), United Artists, 1966.
Mischief, Twentieth Century-Fox, 1985.

Teleplays; Specials:
Trilogy: The American Boy, ABC, 1968.*

BLOUNT, Lisa   1957-

PERSONAL

Born July 1, 1957, in Jacksonville, AR. *Education:* Attended University of Arkansas.

Addresses: *Agent*—William Morris Agency, 151 El Camino Dr., Beverly Hills, CA 90212.

Career: Actress.

CREDITS

Film Appearances:
Sam's Song (also known as *The Swap* and *Line of Fire*), Cannon, 1969.
Billie Jean, *9/30/55* (also known as *September 30, 1955* and *Twenty-Four Hours of the Rebel*), Universal, 1977.
Girl on the beach, *Dead and Buried,* Avco-Embassy, 1981.
Lynette Pomeroy, *An Officer and a Gentleman,* Paramount, 1982.
Paula Murphy, *Cease Fire,* CineWorld, 1985.
Fran Hudson, *Cut and Run* (also known as *Inferno in Diretta, Amazon: Savage Adventure,* and *Amazonia*), New World, 1986.
Miles Archer, *Radioactive Dreams,* De Laurentiis Entertainment Group, 1986.
Leslie Peterson, *What Waits Below* (also known as *Secrets of the Phantom Caverns*), Blossom, 1986.
Audrey Zale, *Nightflyers,* Vista/New Century, 1987.
Catherine, *Prince of Darkness,* Universal, 1987.
Anette, *South of Reno* (also known as *Darkness, Darkness*), Castle Hill, 1987.

Phyllis, *Out Cold,* Hemdale, 1989.
Lois Brown, *Great Balls of Fire,* Orion, 1989.
Annie Winchester, *Blind Fury,* TriStar, 1989.
Jenny Purge, *Femme Fatale* (also known as *Fatal Woman*), Republic Pictures/Gibraltar Entertainment, 1991.
Cora Rusk, *Needful Things,* 1993.
Janie, *Stalked,* Republic Pictures Home Video, 1995.
Purlene Dupre, *Box of Moonlight,* Trimark, 1996.

Television Appearances; Series:
Mary Ruth Hammersmith, *Sons and Daughters,* CBS, 1991.
Melanie Marino, *Picket Fences,* CBS, 1992.
Bobbi Stakowski, *Profit,* Fox, 1996.

Television Appearances; Movies:
Karen Stockwell, *Unholy Matrimony,* 1988.
Becky Meadows, "An American Story" (also known as "After the Glory" and "War in Athens"), *Hallmark Hall of Fame,* CBS, 1992.
Carmen, *In Sickness and in Health* (also known as *Hearts on Fire*), CBS, 1992.
Janet Myers, *Murder between Friends,* NBC, 1994.
District Attorney Theresa Lewis, *Judicial Consent* (also known as *My Love, Your Honor*), HBO, 1995.

Television Appearances; Pilots:
Michelle Jameson, *Mickey Spillane's Mike Hammer: Murder Me, Murder You,* CBS, 1983.
Sissy Rigetti, *Stormin' Home,* CBS, 1985.
Cindy, *The Annihilator,* NBC, 1986.
Pat Yaraslovsky, "Off Duty," *CBS Summer Playhouse,* CBS, 1988.

Television Appearances; Episodic:
Toby, "Sleep Talkin' Guy," *Moonlighting,* ABC, 1986.

Also appeared in episodes of *Magnum P.I.,* CBS; *Starman,* ABC; *Murder, She Wrote,* CBS; and *Hitchhiker,* HBO.*

BOCHNER, Hart   1956(?)-

PERSONAL

Born December 3, 1956 (some sources say 1957), in Toronto, Ontario, Canada (some sources say Los Angeles, CA); son of Lloyd Bochner (an actor). *Education:* University of California, San Diego, B.A., 1978.

Addresses: *Agent*—United Talent Agency, 9560 Wilshire Blvd., Suite 500, Beverly Hills, CA 90212.

Career: Actor, director, and writer.

Awards, Honors: DramaLogue Award, 1982, for *The Wager;* Emmy Award, 1989, for *Fellow Traveller*.

CREDITS

Film Appearances:
Tom, *Islands in the Stream,* Paramount, 1975.
Rod, *Breaking Away* (also known as *Bambino*), Twentieth Century-Fox, 1978.
Doc Manley, *Terror Train* (also known as *Train of Terror*), Twentieth Century-Fox, 1979.
Chris Adams, *Rich and Famous,* Metro-Goldwyn-Mayer, 1980.
Ethan, *Supergirl* (also known as *Supergirl: The Movie*), TriStar, 1984.
David Curtiss, *The Wild Life,* Universal, 1984.
Don, *Making Mr. Right,* Orion, 1987.
Ellis, *Die Hard,* Twentieth Century-Fox, 1988.
Jack Carney, *Apartment Zero,* Skouras, 1989.
Niles Pender, *Mr. Destiny,* Buena Vista, 1990.
Miller Brown, *Mad at the Moon,* Republic Pictures, 1993.
Voice of Councilman Arthur Reeves, *Batman: Mask of the Phantasm* (animated; also known as *Batman: The Animated Movie*), Warner Bros., 1993.
Russell, *The Innocent* (also known as *Und der Himmel Steht Still*), 1993.
The Breakup, forthcoming.

Film Work:
Producer and director, *The Buzz* (short film), 1992.
Director, *PCU* (also known as *PCU Pit Party*), Twentieth Century-Fox, 1994.
Director, *High School High,* Columbia/TriStar, 1996.

Television Appearances; Miniseries:
Aron Trask, *John Steinbeck's East of Eden* (also known as *East of Eden*), ABC, 1980.
Jake Barnes, *Ernest Hemingway's The Sun Also Rises* (also known as *The Sun Also Rises*), NBC, 1984.
Byron Henry, *War and Remembrance,* first installment, ABC, 1988.
Byron Henry, *War and Remembrance,* second installment, ABC, 1989.
Clifford Byrnes, *Fellow Traveller,* 1989.
Buck Walker, *And the Sea Will Tell,* CBS, 1991.
Shelby Hornbeck, *Children of the Dust* (also known as *A Good Day to Die*), CBS, 1995.

Television Appearances; Movies:
Bill Hayward, *Haywire,* CBS, 1979.
Jess Enright, *Having It All,* ABC, 1982.
Ray Dolan, *Complex of Fear,* CBS, 1993.

Television Appearances; Specials:
Title role, *Callahan,* 1982.
Dr. Bonner, "Teach 109," *American Playhouse,* PBS, 1990.

Stage Appearances:
(Stage debut) *The Wager,* Cast Theatre, Los Angeles, CA, 1982.

WRITINGS

The Buzz (short film), 1992.

OTHER SOURCES

Periodicals:
Entertainment Weekly, August 20, 1993, p. 27.
Hollywood Reporter, June 22, 1993, p. I4.
Premiere, March, 1994.*

BOCHNER, Lloyd   1924-

PERSONAL

Born July 29, 1924, in Toronto, Ontario, Canada; children: Hart (an actor).

Addresses: *Agent*—David Shapira and Associates, 15301 Ventura Blvd., Suite 345, Sherman Oaks, CA 91403.

Career: Actor.

CREDITS

Television Appearances; Series:
Captain Nicholas Lacey, *One Man's Family,* NBC, 1952.
Police Commissioner Neil Campbell, *Hong Kong,* ABC, 1960-61.
Regular, *The Richard Boone Show,* NBC, 1963-64.
Cecil Colby, *Dynasty,* ABC, 1981-82.
Channing Creighton "C. C." Capwell, *Santa Barbara,* NBC, 1984.
Mad Dog's father, *First and Ten: The Bulls Mean Business,* HBO, 1988.

Avonlea (also known as *The Road to Avonlea*), CBC/ The Disney Channel, 1990.

Voice of Mayor Hill, *The Adventures of Batman and Robin,* syndicated, 1992.

Senator Elliot Moses, *Dr. Quinn, Medicine Woman,* CBS, 1994.

Television Appearances; Pilots:

Joseph Campbell, *Arena* (broadcast as an episode of *The Richard Boone Show*), NBC, 1964.

John Pendennis, *Scalplock,* ABC, 1966.

Lawrence, *Braddock,* CBS, 1968.

A. B. Carr, *They Call It Murder,* NBC, 1971.

David, *Rex Harrison Presents Short Stories of Love,* NBC, 1974.

Davenport, *Richie Brockelman: Missing 24 Hours,* NBC, 1976.

Hank's aide, *The Eyes of Texas,* NBC, 1980.

Hotel, ABC, 1983.

Manimal, NBC, 1983.

Ritter, *Crazy Dan,* NBC, 1986.

Mama's Boy, NBC, 1987.

Television Appearances; Episodic:

"Loyalties," *Kraft Television Theatre,* NBC, 1951.

"Visitation," *Star Tonight,* ABC, 1955.

"Castaway on a Nearby Island," *The Further Adventures of Ellery Queen,* NBC, 1959.

"The War between the States," *Americans,* NBC, 1961.

"The Prisoner in the Mirror," *Thriller,* NBC, 1961.

Chambers, "To Serve Man," *The Twilight Zone,* CBS, 1962.

"Inside Track," *Cain's Hundred,* NBC, 1962.

"The Other Woman," *U.S. Steel Hour,* NBC, 1962.

"Horn of Plenty," *Dr. Kildare,* NBC, 1962.

"There Are Dragons in This Forest," *Eleventh Hour,* NBC, 1962.

"Guest in the House," *Alcoa Premiere,* ABC, 1962.

"Code Name: Christopher," *G.E. True,* CBS, 1962.

"Days of Glory," *The Dick Powell Show,* NBC, 1962.

"Commando," *G.E. True,* CBS, 1963.

"The War Called Peace," *The Lieutenant,* NBC, 1964.

Dr. Martin Davis, "The Fear Makers," *Voyage to the Bottom of the Sea,* ABC, 1964.

"Murder in the First," *Bob Hope Chrysler Theatre,* NBC, 1964.

"The Case of the Latent Lover," *Perry Mason,* CBS, 1964.

"The See Paris and Die Affair," *The Man from U.N.C.L.E.,* NBC, 1965.

"The War and Eric Kurtz," *Bob Hope Chrysler Theatre,* NBC, 1965.

Kirby Wyatt, "The Cry of the Fallen Bird," *12 O'Clock High,* ABC, 1965.

"Seized, Confined, and Detained," *For the People,* CBS, 1965.

"The Trains of Silence," *Kraft Suspense Theatre,* NBC, 1965.

"The Dead Man's Hand," *The Legend of Jesse James,* ABC, 1965.

"The Owl and the Eye," *Honey West,* ABC, 1965.

Major Thorne, "Evasion," *Combat,* ABC, 1965.

"Show Me a Hero, I'll Show You a Bum," *12 O'Clock High,* ABC, 1965.

General Hobson, "The Deadliest Game," *Voyage to the Bottom of the Sea,* ABC, 1965.

"$10,000 for Durango," *Branded,* NBC, 1965.

"The Reward," *A Man Called Shenandoah,* ABC, 1965.

"Night of the Puppeteer," *Wild, Wild West,* CBS, 1966.

"And Two If by Sea," *The Wackiest Ship in the Army,* NBC, 1966.

"The Trap," *Daniel Boone,* NBC, 1966.

"The Silent Gun," *The Green Hornet,* ABC, 1966.

"Fortress Weisbaden," *12 O'Clock High,* ABC, 1966.

"The Danish Blue Affair," *The Girl from U.N.C.L.E.,* NBC, 1966.

"Danger! Woman at Work," *Occasional Wife,* NBC, 1966.

"Marked for Death," *T.H.E. Cat,* NBC, 1966.

"Curtains for Miss Window," *T.H.E. Cat,* NBC, 1966.

"The Romany Lie Affair," *The Girl from U.N.C.L.E.,* NBC, 1966.

"Track of the Dinosaur," *Tarzan,* NBC, 1967.

"The Prince," *Bonanza,* NBC, 1967.

"The Summit-Five Affair," *The Man from U.N.C.L.E.,* NBC, 1967.

"Time after Midnight," *The Big Valley,* ABC, 1967.

"Ah Sing vs. Wyoming," *The Virginian,* NBC, 1967.

"Desperate Mission," *Custer,* ABC, 1967.

"The Secret Code," *Daniel Boone,* NBC, 1967.

"The Imposter," *Daniel Boone,* NBC, 1968.

Captain Roberts/Lieutenant Baumann, "Funny Thing Happened on the Way to London," *Hogan's Heroes,* CBS, 1968.

"Transplant," *Judd, for the Defense,* ABC, 1968.

"Ordeal," *Name of the Game,* NBC, 1968.

"The Day God Died," *Insight,* syndicated, 1969.

"No Tears for Kelsey," *Insight,* syndicated, 1969.

"Voices," *My Friend Tony,* NBC, 1969.

"The Girl Who Came in with the Tide," *Mannix,* CBS, 1969.

Major Nicholas Zelinko, "The Glass Cage," *Mission: Impossible,* CBS, 1969.

"Cat's Paw," *It Takes a Thief,* ABC, 1969.

"Marriage, Witch's Style," *Bewitched*, ABC, 1969.

"All the Social Graces," *The Outsider*, NBC, 1969.

"Jeopardy," *Medical Center*, CBS, 1969.

"The Inside Man," *The FBI*, ABC, 1969.

"Nothing But the Truth," *The Debbie Reynolds Show*, NBC, 1970.

"The Landlords," *Daniel Boone*, NBC, 1970.

"Project X," *It Takes a Thief*, ABC, 1970.

"Prosecutor," *Silent Force*, ABC, 1970.

"This Is Jerry. See Jerry Run? Run, Jerry, Run, Run, Run," *Storefront Lawyers*, CBS, 1970.

"Beautiful Screamer," *Hawaii Five-0*, CBS, 1970.

Mayor Steve Tallman, "Takeover," *Mission: Impossible*, CBS, 1971.

"The Town Killer," *Men from Shiloh*, NBC, 1971.

"The People vs. Edwards," *The D.A.*, NBC, 1971.

"Moment of Crisis," *The Bold Ones*, NBC, 1972.

"Problem," *Emergency*, NBC, 1972.

Ambrose, "Bitter Legion," *Cannon*, CBS, 1972.

General Oliver Benjamin Hammond, "The Deal," *Mission: Impossible*, CBS, 1972.

"The Green Feather Mystery," *Hec Ramsey*, NBC, 1972.

"Shadow Soldiers," *Ironside*, NBC, 1972.

"The Park Avenue Rustlers," *McCloud*, NBC, 1972.

"The Case of the Frenzied Feminist," *The New Perry Mason*, CBS, 1973.

"To Quote a Dead Man," *Mannix*, CBS, 1973.

Berosky, "The Most Dangerous Match," *Columbo*, NBC, 1973.

"The Loose Connection," *Barnaby Jones*, CBS, 1973.

"Man on Fire," *The Magician*, NBC, 1973.

"Day of the Robot," *The Six Million Dollar Man*, ABC, 1974.

"The Iron Blood of Courage," *Gunsmoke*, CBS, 1974.

Conrad Ackers, "Triangle of Terror," *Cannon*, ABC, 1974.

Chopper One, ABC, 1974.

Chief, *Police Story*, NBC, 1974.

"S.W.A.T.," *The Rookies*, ABC, 1975.

"The Treasure Chest Murder," *Adams of Eagle Lake*, ABC, 1975.

"Murder—Eyes Only," *Hawaii Five-0*, CBS, 1975.

"Double Vengeance," *Barnaby Jones*, CBS, 1975.

"The Adventure of Colonel Nivens Memoirs," *Ellery Queen*, NBC, 1975.

"The Cruise Ship Murders," *Switch*, CBS, 1975.

"Jesse Who?" *Barbary Coast*, ABC, 1975.

"Long Time Dying," *Bronk*, CBS, 1976.

"Night of the Shark," *McCloud*, NBC, 1976.

"The Nurse Killer," *The ABC Mystery of the Week*, ABC, 1976.

"The White Collar Killer," *Most Wanted*, ABC, 1977.

"Biofeedback," *The Bionic Woman*, ABC, 1977.

"Philip's Game," *McMillan*, NBC, 1977.

"Carnival of Spies," *The Six Million Dollar Man*, ABC, 1977.

"The Big Frame," *The Feathers and Father Gang*, ABC, 1977.

"Deadly Countdown," *The Six Million Dollar Man*, ABC, 1977.

San Pedro Beach Bums, ABC, 1977.

"The House on Possessed Hill," *Hardy Boys/Nancy Drew Mysteries*, ABC, 1978.

"Night of the Clones," *The Amazing Spider-Man*, CBS, 1978.

Lyle Galen, "Yes, My Darling Daughter," *Vega$*, ABC, 1978.

"The Story of Moses and the Ten Commandments," *The Greatest Heroes of the Bible*, NBC, 1978.

"Angels Belong in Heaven," *Charlie's Angels*, ABC, 1978.

Fantasy Island, ABC, 1978.

"Angel Hunt," *Charlie's Angels*, ABC, 1979.

Commandant Leiter, "Baltar's Escape," *Battlestar Galactica*, ABC, 1979.

Commandant Leiter, "Greetings from Earth," *Battlestar Galactica*, ABC, 1979.

"School for Assassins," *Hawaii Five-0*, CBS, 1980.

Trapper John, M.D., CBS, 1980.

Mel Blandan, "Consortium," *Vega$*, ABC, 1980.

Hawaii Five-0, CBS, 1980.

"Too Many Crooks Are Murder," *Hart to Hart*, ABC, 1980.

Alexander Waverly, "French Twist," *Vega$*, ABC, 1981.

"Cyrano," *Fantasy Island*, ABC, 1981.

"Daisies," *Darkroom*, ABC, 1981.

Logan Rinewood, *Dynasty*, ABC, 1981.

"Does Father Know Best?" *The Love Boat*, ABC, 1982.

"Shark Bait," *Matt Houston*, ABC, 1982.

"Room and Bard," *Fantasy Island*, ABC, 1983.

"Heritage," *Matt Houston*, ABC, 1983.

"Ladies Choice," *Fantasy Island*, ABC, 1984.

"On the Run," *Matt Houston*, ABC, 1984.

"Winnings," *Masquerade*, ABC, 1984.

Shawn, "Beverly Hills Assault," *The A-Team*, NBC, 1985.

"Rallying Cry," *Hotel*, ABC, 1985.

Vincent Mulligan, "If the Show Fits," *Crazy Like a Fox*, CBS, 1986.

Cameron Wheeler, *Hotel*, ABC, 1986.

Charles Linney, "The Lady in Green," *Fall Guy*, ABC, 1986.

Terence, "Unfinished Business," *Murder, She Wrote*, CBS, 1986.

George Tilman, "Who Killed Maxwell Thorn?," *The Love Boat*, ABC, 1987.

"Till Death Do Us Part," *Hotel,* ABC, 1988.

"Summer of '45," *The Highwayman,* NBC, 1988.

Jason Richards, "Deadpan," *Murder, She Wrote,* CBS, 1988.

Appeared in episodes of *Designing Women,* CBS; *Hart to Hart,* ABC; and *The Golden Girls,* NBC.

Television Appearances; Movies:

Mr. Gorman, *Stranger on the Run* (also known as *Lonesome Gun*), NBC, 1967.

Kevin Pierce, *Crowhaven Farm,* ABC, 1970.

Professor Delacroix, *Satan's School for Girls,* ABC, 1973.

Averill Harriman, *Collision Course,* 1976.

Dr. Roger Cabe, *Terraces,* NBC, 1977.

Paul Gilliam, *A Fire in the Sky,* NBC, 1978.

Chris Noel, *The Immigrants,* syndicated, 1978.

Bob Stockwood, *The Best Place to Be,* NBC, 1979.

Dr. Hamill, *The Golden Gate Murders* (also known as *Spectre on the Bridge*), CBS, 1979.

Matthew, *Mary and Joseph: A Story of Faith* (also known as *Story of Faith*), NBC, 1979.

Hall, *Rona Jaffe's "Mazes and Monsters"* (also known as *Dungeons and Dragons*), CBS, 1982.

Adrien Damvilliers, *Louisiana* (also known as *Louisiane*), Cinemax, 1984.

Special Agent Vaughn, "Double Agent," *Disney Sunday Movie,* ABC, 1987.

James Cullen Offen, "Blood Sport," *The Dick Francis Mysteries* (also known as *The Mystery Wheel of Adventure*), syndicated, 1989.

Don Pedro, *Fine Gold,* syndicated, 1990.

Television Appearances; Specials:

Orsino, *Twelfth Night,* NBC, 1957.

Jack Favall, "Rebecca," *Theatre '62,* NBC, 1962.

Sam Hall, *A Mouse, A Mystery, and Me,* NBC, 1987.

Lamb Chop's Special Chanukah, PBS, 1995.

Other Television Appearances:

Also appeared in *Race for the Bomb, Double Agent, Eagle One,* and *Our Man Flint.*

Film Appearances:

David Moore, *Drums of Africa,* Metro-Goldwyn-Mayer, 1963.

Man in the dream, *The Night Walker,* Universal, 1964.

Marc Peters, *Harlow,* Magna, 1965.

Bruce Stamford III, *Sylvia,* Paramount, 1965.

Frederick Carter, *Point Blank,* Metro-Goldwyn-Mayer, 1967.

Vic Rood, *Tony Rome,* Twentieth Century-Fox, 1967.

Dr. Wendell Roberts, *The Detective,* Twentieth Century-Fox, 1968.

Archer Madison, *The Horse in the Gray Flannel Suit,* Buena Vista, 1968.

Raymond Marquis Allen, *The Young Runaways,* Metro-Goldwyn-Mayer, 1968.

Dr. Cory, *The Dunwich Horror,* American International Pictures, 1970.

Del Ware, *Tiger by the Tail,* Commonwealth, 1970.

Captain Gates, *Ulzana's Raid,* Universal, 1972.

Burton, *It Seemed like a Good Idea at the Time* (also known as *Good Idea*), Ambassador, 1975.

Churchill, *The Man in the Glass Booth,* American Film Theatre, 1975.

Mr. No Legs, 1981.

Severo, *Hot Touch,* Astral, 1982.

Walter Thornton, *The Lonely Lady,* Universal, 1983.

Frank Newley, *Crystal Heart* (also known as *Corazon de cristal*), New World, 1987.

Walters, *Millennium,* 1989.

Baggett, *The Naked Gun 2-1/2: The Smell of Fear,* Paramount, 1991.

Deadly Deception, [France/Spain], 1991.

Lolita al desnudo (also known as *Lolita's Affair*), [Spain], 1991.

Bull Matterson, *Landslide,* [England], 1992.

Bob Collins, *Morning Glory,* Academy Entertainment, 1993.

Also appeared in the films *Berlin Lady* and *The Dozier Case.*

Stage Appearances:

George, *Richard III,* Stratford Shakespearean Festival, Stratford, Ontario, 1953.

Longaville, *All's Well That Ends Well,* Stratford Shakespearean Festival, 1953.

Vincentio, the Duke, *Measure for Measure,* Stratford Shakespearean Festival, 1954.

Vincentio, *The Taming of the Shrew,* Stratford Shakespearean Festival, 1954.

Cassius, *Julius Caesar,* Stratford Shakespearean Festival, 1955.

Salanio, *The Merchant of Venice,* Stratford Shakespearean Festival, 1955.

Callapine, *Tamburlaine the Great,* Stratford Shakespearean Festival, then Winter Garden Theatre, New York City, both 1956.

Rugby, *The Merry Wives of Windsor,* Stratford Shakespearean Festival, 1956.

Duke of Burgundy, *Henry V,* Stratford Shakespearean Festival, 1956.

Horatio, *Hamlet,* Stratford Shakespearean Festival, 1957.

Orsino, *Twelfth Night,* Stratford Shakespearean Festival, 1957.

Protheus, *Two Gentlemen of Verona,* Stratford Shakespearean Theatre, then Phoenix Theatre, New York City, both 1958.*

BOLT, Robert   1924-1995

OBITUARY NOTICE—See index for *CTFT* sketch: Born August 15, 1924, in Sale, Manchester, England; died February 20, 1995, in Hampshire, England. Educator, film director, screenwriter, and playwright. Bolt was a playwright and screenwriter whose talent for conveying human dramas against broad historical backdrops earned him critical and popular acclaim. His movie scripts for *Dr. Zhivago* and *A Man for All Seasons* won him successive Academy Awards in 1965 and 1966. A graduate of the University of Manchester, Bolt worked as a schoolteacher for several years while trying his hand at writing. He apprenticed as a radio dramatist, but it was the success of his stageplay *Flowering Cherry,* performed in London in 1958, that allowed him to write full time. Unlike some of his more innovative playwriting contemporaries, Bolt favored traditional plays with elegant language and discernable structure. In 1960 the dramatist had a resounding London success with his play *A Man for All Seasons;* this story of Lord Chancellor of England Sir Thomas More, who was executed by King Henry VIII for his loyalty to the church, enjoyed a long Broadway run, won the New York Drama Critics Circle Award and a Tony in 1962, and went onto numerous revivals. Bolt's solid craftsmanship and traditionalism also served him well in Hollywood: his long partnership with film director David Lean began when the playwright was asked to polish (and subsequently rewrite) the script for the epic *Lawrence of Arabia;* in cooperation with Lean, Bolt wrote the screenplays for Boris Pasternak's sweeping saga of the Russian Revolution, *Dr. Zhivago,* and his own *Ryan's Daughter.* Though stricken by a paralyzing stroke in 1979, Bolt continued to write for the stage, motion pictures, and television. His film drama *The Mission,* filmed by Roland Joffe and set in colonial South America, won the prestigious Palme d'Or at the Cannes Film Festival in 1986.

OBITUARIES AND OTHER SOURCES

Books:
Contemporary Dramatists, 5th edition, St. James Press, 1993.

Periodicals:
Los Angeles Times, February 23, 1995, p. A18.
Times (London), February 23, pp. 1, 19.*

BOOTHE, Powers   1949-

PERSONAL

Born in 1949, in Snyder, TX; married Pam Cole, 1986. *Education:* Attended Southern Methodist University.

Career: Actor.

Member: Actors' Equity Association, Screen Actors Guild, American Federation of Television and Radio Artists.

Awards, Honors: Emmy Award, outstanding lead actor in a limited series or special, 1980, for *The Guyana Tragedy: The Story of Jim Jones.*

CREDITS

Film Appearances:
Actor in *Richard III* cast, *The Goodbye Girl,* Warner Bros., 1977.
Hankie salesman, *Cruising,* United Artists, 1980.
David, *The Cold Eye,* Berlin Cinematheque, 1980.
Rifleman Charles Hardin, *Southern Comfort,* Twentieth Century-Fox, 1981.
Andy Tanner, *Red Dawn,* Metro-Goldwyn-Mayer/ United Artists, 1984.
Michael Walker, *A Breed Apart,* Orion, 1984.
Bill Markham, *The Emerald Forest,* Embassy, 1985.
Cash Bailey, *Extreme Prejudice,* TriStar, 1987.
Stalingrad, 1990.
Lieutenant Mace Ryan, *Rapid Fire,* Twentieth Century-Fox, 1992.
Curly Bill Brocius, *Tombstone,* Buena Vista, 1993.
Vince Johnson, *Blue Sky,* Orion, 1994.
Frost, *Bio-Force I* (also known as *Mutant Species*), WT Entertainment, 1995.
General Alexander M. Haig Jr., *Nixon,* Buena Vista, 1995.
Joshua Foss, *Sudden Death,* Universal, 1995.
Sheriff Potter, *U-Turn* (also known as *Stray Dogs*), TriStar, 1997.

Film Work:
Set designer, *The Cold Eye,* Berlin Cinematheque, 1980.

Television Appearances; Miniseries:
John A. Walker Jr., *Family of Spies: The Walker Spy Ring* (also known as *A Family of Spies*), CBS, 1990.
Bartlett McClure, *True Women,* CBS, 1997.

Television Appearances; Movies:
Reverend Jim Jones, *The Guyana Tragedy: The Story of Jim Jones* (also known as *The Mad Messiah*), CBS, 1980.
Dick Hawkins, *The Plutonium Incident,* CBS, 1980.
Tony Bonnell, *A Cry for Love,* NBC, 1980.
Jackson Swallow, *Into the Homeland* (also known as *Swallows Come Back* and *When the Swallows Come Back*), HBO, 1987.
Cassidy, *By Dawn's Early Light* (also known as *The Grand Tour*), HBO, 1990.
Preacher, *Wild Card* (also known as *Preacher*), USA Network, 1992.
Mace Moutron, *Marked for Murder* (also known as *The Sandman* and *Hard Time*), NBC, 1993.
Dr. Phillip Benesch, *Web of Deception* (also known as *Mind over Matter*), NBC, 1994.
Sam Creekmouth, *Dalva,* ABC, 1996.

Television Appearances; Specials:
"Sapphire Man," *Showtime 30-Minute Movie,* Showtime, 1991.
Narrator, "Eternal Enemies: Lions and Hyenas," *National Geographic Specials,* PBS, 1992.

Television Appearances; Series:
Jim Whalen, *Skag,* NBC, 1980.
Title role and narrator, *Philip Marlowe, Private Eye,* HBO, 1983, 1986.

Television Appearances; Pilot:
Jim Whalen, *Skag,* NBC, 1980.

Stage Appearances:
Roderigo, *Othello,* Roundabout Theatre, New York City, 1978.
Roy, *Lone Star,* Century Theatre, New York City, 1979.*

BOSSON, Barbara   1939(?)-

PERSONAL

Born November 1, 1939 (some sources say 1940), in Belle Vernon (some sources say Charleroi), PA; father, a tennis coach; married Steven Bochco (a television producer and writer), February 14, 1969 (marriage ended); children: Melissa, Jesse. *Education:* Attended Carnegie Institute of Technology (now Carnegie-Mellon University); studied acting with Milton Katselas and Herbert Berghof; also studied musical comedy. *Avocational interests:* Skiing, raising herbs and vegetables, dancing, crossword puzzles.

Addresses: *Home*—Los Angeles, CA. *Agent*—Paradigm, 200 West 57th St., Suite 900, New York, NY 10019.

Career: Actress. The Committee (improvisational comedy group), San Francisco, CA, member; American Conservatory Theatre, secretary; also appeared in summer theatre productions. Worked as a Playboy Club bunny, secretary, and television production assistant.

Awards, Honors: Emmy Award nomination, outstanding supporting actress in a drama series, 1981, for *Hill Street Blues;* four other Emmy Award nominations for *Hill Street Blues;* Emmy Award nomination, outstanding supporting actress in a drama series, 1996, for *Murder One.*

CREDITS

Television Appearances; Series:
Sharon Peterson, *Richie Brockelman, Private Eye,* NBC, 1978.
Fay Furillo, *Hill Street Blues,* NBC, 1981-85.
Captain Celeste "C.Z." Stern, *Hooperman,* ABC, 1987-89.
Mayor Louise Plank, *Cop Rock,* ABC, 1990.
Miriam Grasso, *Murder One,* ABC, 1995-97.

Television Appearances; Miniseries:
Miriam Grasso, *Murder One: Diary of a Serial Killer,* ABC, 1997.

Television Appearances; Episodic:
"The Ten Days That Shook Kid Curry," *Alias Smith and Jones,* ABC, 1972.
Ms. Cox, *Sunshine,* NBC, 1975.
"The Deadly Cure," *McMillan and Wife,* NBC, 1976.
Marie Rizon, "A Fox at the Races," *Crazy like a Fox,* CBS, 1986.
Stacey Gill, *L.A. Law,* NBC, 1986.
"Love and the Honeymoon Hotel," *The New Love American Style,* ABC, 1986.
"Requiem for Billy," *The New Mike Hammer,* CBS, 1986.

"Contest of Wills," *Hotel*, ABC, 1988.

Guest, *Body by Jake*, syndicated, 1988.

Diane Raymond, "Wearing of the Green," *Murder, She Wrote*, CBS, 1988.

Guest, *Win, Lose, or Draw*, syndicated, 1988.

Guest, *The New Hollywood Squares*, syndicated, 1988.

Judge, *Civil Wars*, ABC, 1991.

Mrs. Davis, "Simone Says," *NYPD Blue*, ABC, 1994.

Dr. Friskin, "Whine, Whine, Whine," *Lois and Clark: The New Adventures of Superman*, ABC, 1995.

Dr. Friskin, "Individual Responsibility," *Lois and Clark: The New Adventures of Superman*, ABC, 1995.

Television Appearances; Pilots:

Sharon Peterson, *Richie Brockelman: Missing 24 Hours*, NBC, 1976.

Operating Room, NBC, 1979.

Television Appearances; Movies:

Esther Crowley, *The Impatient Heart*, NBC, 1971.

Nancy, *The Calendar Girl Murders* (also known as *Insatiable* and *Victimized*), ABC, 1984.

Roberta Spooner, *Hostage Flight*, NBC, 1985.

Evelyn Brattner, *The Great American Sex Scandal* (also known as *Jury Duty: The Comedy*), ABC, 1990.

Television Appearances; Specials:

Donna Crandall, "Supermom's Daughter," *ABC Afterschool Special*, ABC, 1987.

Kathy Gluesenkamp, "Words to Live By," *CBS Schoolbreak Special*, CBS, 1989.

Twin Peaks and Cop Rock: Behind the Scenes, ABC, 1990.

Presenter, *The 1996 Emmy Awards*, 1996.

Film Appearances:

A Session with The Committee, 1969.

Emily, *Mame*, Warner Bros., 1974.

Ms. Cox, *Sunshine Part II*, 1976.

Alva Leacock, *Capricorn One*, Warner Bros., 1977.

Jane Rogan, *The Last Starfighter*, Universal, 1984.

The Education of Allison Tate (also known as *The Abduction of Allison Tate*), 1986.

Mom, *Little Sweetheart* (also known as *Poison Candy*), Nelson Entertainment, 1988.

WRITINGS

Television Episodes:

Family, ABC, 1976.*

BOWIE, David 1947-

PERSONAL

Original name, David Robert Hayward-Jones; born January 8, 1947, in Brixton, South London, England; son of Hayward Stenton and Margaret Mary (Burns) Jones; married Mary Angela Barnetty, March 19, 1970 (divorced, 1980); married Iman (a model and actress), 1992; children: (first marriage) Zowie Duncan Haywood. *Education:* Attended Bromley Technical High School.

Addresses: *Office*—Isolar Productions, 40 West 57th St., New York, NY 10019; Duncan Heath Associates, 162 Wardour St., London W1, England. *Agent*—International Creative Management, 8942 Wilshire Blvd., Beverly Hills, CA 90211.

Career: Singer, songwriter, actor, and producer. Beckenham Arts Lab (performance club), London, England, founder, 1969. Performed with bands, including Manish Boys, 1964-65, the Lower Third, 1965-66, Feathers, 1968, Hype, beginning in 1970, the Spiders, 1972, and Tin Machine, beginning in 1989; toured the United States with the Spiders, 1972; toured with Glass Spider, 1987, Sound and Vision World Tour, 1990, and Outside Tour, 1995. War Child (music industry charity), patron, 1994.

Awards, Honors: Novello Award, special award for originality, 1970, for *Space Oddity*; best actor award, U.S. Academy of Science Fiction, Fantasy, and Horror Films, 1977, for *The Man Who Fell to Earth*; Grammy Award nomination, best recording for children, National Academy of Recording Arts and Sciences, 1978, for *Peter and the Wolf*; Grammy Award nomination, best male rock vocal, 1983, for the song "Cat People (Putting out Fire)"; Grammy Award nomination, album of the year, 1983, and Novello Award, international hit of the year, 1984, both for *Let's Dance*; Grammy Award, best short-form music video, 1984, for *David Bowie*; Grammy Award nominations, best male rock vocal, 1984, for "Blue Jean," and best video album, 1984, for *Serious Moonlight*; BRIT Award, best British male artist, 1984; MTV Video Music Award, best male video, 1984, for *China Girl*; shared Video Vanguard Award, MTV Video Music Awards, 1984; MTV Video Music Award, best overall performance, 1986, for *Dancing in the Street*; Silver Clef Award for Outstanding Achievement, Nordoff Robbins Music Therapy, 1987; Novello

Award, outstanding contribution to British music, 1990; shared Inspiration Award, Annual Q Awards, 1995; inducted into Rock and Roll Hall of Fame, 1996; BRIT Award, outstanding contribution to British music, 1996; Grammy Award nomination, best concept music video, for *Day In, Day Out;* several gold and platinum records, Recording Industry Association of America.

CREDITS

Film Appearances:
Space Oddity, 1969.
The Virgin Soldiers, Columbia, 1969.
Ziggy Stardust, *Ziggy Stardust and the Spiders from Mars,* Twentieth Century-Fox, 1973.
Thomas Jerome Newton, *The Man Who Fell to Earth,* British Lion, 1976.
Paul von Przygodsky, *Just a Gigolo* (also known as *Schoener Gigolo, armer Gigolo*), United Artists Classics, 1979.
Himself, *Christiane F wir Kinder vom Bahnhof Zoo,* 1981.
Cat People, Universal, 1983.
Major Jack "Straffer" Celliers, *Merry Christmas, Mr. Lawrence* (also known as *Furyo* and *Senjou no Merii Kurisumasu*), Universal, 1983.
John, *The Hunger,* Metro-Goldwyn-Mayer/United Artists, 1983.
Wet sailor, *Yellowbeard,* Orion, 1983.
Colin Morris, *Into the Night,* Universal, 1985.
Vendice Partners, *Absolute Beginners,* Orion, 1986.
Jareth, *Labyrinth,* TriStar, 1986.
Himself, *Imagine: John Lennon,* Warner Bros., 1988.
Pontius Pilate, *The Last Temptation of Christ,* Universal, 1988.
Monte, *The Linguini Incident,* Academy, 1991.
Himself, *Travelling Light,* 1992.
Phillip Jeffries, *Twin Peaks: Fire Walk with Me* (also known as *Twin Peaks: Fire Walk with Me, Teresa Banks* and *The Last Seven Days of Laura Palmer*), New Line, 1992.
Andy Warhol, *Basquiat* (also known as *Build a Fort, Set It on Fire*), Miramax, 1996.
Himself, *Inspirations* (documentary), Clear Blue Sky Productions, 1997.

Also appeared in *The Image.*

Film Work; Executive Producer:
Magic Hunter (also known as *Buvos Vadasz* and *Der Freischutz*), Shadow Distribution, 1994.
Mesmer, Overseas Filmgroup, 1994.

Gentle into the Night (also known as *Passaggio per Il Paradiso* and *Lift to Heaven*), In Pictures, 1996.

Television Appearances; Specials:
Bing Crosby's Merrie Olde Christmas, 1977.
David Bowie—Serious Moonlight, 1984.
Tina Turner: Private Dancer, 1985.
Bugs Bunny/Looney Tunes All-Star 50th Anniversary, CBS, 1986.
Rolling Stone Magazine's 20 Years of Rock 'n' Roll (also known as *Rolling Stone Magazine's 20th Anniversary Special* and *Rolling Stone Presents 20 Years of Rock 'n' Roll*), ABC, 1987.
Cissy Houston: Sweet Inspiration, PBS, 1988.
David Bowie: Glass Spider Tour, 1988.
Tribute to John Lennon, syndicated, 1990.
Song performer, *A Concert for Life,* Fox/MTV, 1992.
David Bowie: Black Tie White Noise, The Disney Channel, 1993.
The Sounds of Summer, ABC, 1993.
Host, *George Michael's Concert of Hope,* The Disney Channel, 1994.
Ed Sullivan Presents: Rock 'n' Roll Revolution: The British Invade America, CBS, 1995.
The White Room New Year's Eve Special, C4TV (England), 1995.
David Bowie and Friends—A Very Special Broadway Concert, Cable pay-per-view, 1997.

Television Work; Specials:
Art director, *David Bowie—Serious Moonlight,* 1984.
Art director, *David Bowie and Friends—A Very Special Broadway Concert,* Cable pay-per-view, 1997.

Television Appearances; Episodic:
Gadzooks! It's All Happening, 1965.
"Cracked Actor" (documentary), *Omnibus,* BBC, 1975.
Soul Train, 1975.
The Dinah Shore Show, 1977.
Marc, ITV (England), 1977.
Top of the Pops, CBS, 1987.
Sir Rowland Moorecock, "The Second Greatest Story Ever Told," *Dream On,* HBO, 1990.
ABC in Concert, ABC, 1991.
Wogan, BBC, 1991.
Saturday Night Live, NBC, 1991.
Late Night with David Letterman, NBC, 1993.
Interviewee, *Rock and Roll,* PBS, 1995.
The History of Rock 'n' Roll, syndicated, 1995.

Television Appearances; Awards Presentations:
The 2nd International Rock Awards, 1990.

Song performer, *The BRIT Awards '96,* 1996.
The VH1 Fashion Awards, VH1, 1996.
The 24th Annual American Music Awards, 1997.

Other Television Appearances:
The Pistol Shot, BBC, 1968.
The Midnight Special, NBC, 1973.
Title role, *Baal,* BBC, 1982.

Stage Appearances:
Pierrot in Turquoise (mime production), Oxford, England, 1967.
John Merrick, the title role, *The Elephant Man,* Booth Theatre, New York City, 1980.

Radio Appearances; Episodic:
Mark Goodier Evening Show, 1991.

RECORDINGS

Albums:
Feelin' Good, Prestige, 1965.
Out of Sight, Prestige, 1965.
David Bowie—1966, Atlantic, 1966.
David Bowie, Deram, 1967.
Man of Words, Man of Music, Mercury, 1969, released in England as *Space Oddity,* Rykodisc, 1969.
The Man Who Sold the World, Rykodisc, 1970.
Hunky Dory, Rykodisc, 1971.
The Rise and Fall of Ziggy Stardust, Rykodisc, 1972.
Aladdin Sane, Rykodisc, 1973.
Pinups, Rykodisc, 1973.
Diamond Dogs, Rykodisc, 1974.
David Live, Rykodisc, 1974.
Young Americans, Rykodisc, 1975.
Station to Station, Rykodisc, 1976.
Low, Rykodisc, 1977.
Heroes, Rykodisc, 1977.
Starting Point, London, 1977.
Evening with David Bowie, RCA, 1978.
Bowie Now, RCA, 1978.
Lodger, Rykodisc, 1978.
Stage, Rykodisc, 1978.
Peter and the Wolf, Rykodisc, 1978.
1980 All Clear, RCA, 1979.
Golden Double, RCA, 1979.
Lodger, Rykodisc, 1979.
Scary Monsters and Super Creeps, Rykodisc, 1980.
The Best of David Bowie, K-Tel, 1981.
Another Face, Decca, 1981.
Don't Be Fooled By the Name, PRT, 1981.
Changes, RCA, 1981.
In Bertolt Brecht's Baal, RCA, 1982.

Christiane F Wir Kinder (soundtrack), RCA, 1982.
Second Face, Decca, 1983.
Let's Dance, Virgin, 1983.
Ziggy Stardust, RCA, 1983.
Portrait of a Star, RCA, 1984.
Wild Is the Wind, RCA, 1984.
Tonight, Capitol, 1984.
Fame and Fashion: All-Time Greatest Hits, RCA, 1984.
Love You Til Tuesday, Polygram, 1984.
Time Will Crawl, EMI America, 1987.
Day In, Day Out, EMI, 1987.
Never Let Me Down, 1987.
1966, Castle, 1988.
Tech Unit, Rykodisc, 1991.
Black Tie White Noise, Virgin, 1993.
The Singles Connection, EMI, 1993.
The Singles: 1969-1993, Featuring His Greatest Hits, Rykodisc, 1993.
Santa Monica '72, Golden Years, 1995.
Buddha of Suburbia, Virgin, 1995.
Outside, RCA, 1995.
Earthling, Virgin, 1997.

Singles include "I Pity the Fool," Parlophone, 1965; "Can't Help Thinking about Me," Warner Bros., 1966; "Do Anything You Say," 1966; "I Dig Everything," Pye, 1966; "Rubber Band," 1966; "The Laughing Gnome," 1967; "The Prettiest Star," 1970; "Memory of a Free Festival," 1970; "Holy Holy," 1971; "Changes," Rykodisc, 1972; "Starman," 1972; "Pink Rose," Atlantic, 1990; and "Fame."

Albums; Compilations:
Images: 1966-67, London, 1973.
Changesonebowie, RCA, 1976.
Changestwobowie, RCA, 1981.
Golden Years, RCA, 1983.
Collection, Castle, 1985.
Sound + Vision (boxed set), Rykodisc, 1989.
Changesbowie, Rykodisc, 1990.
Early On (1964-1966), Rhino, 1991.
Singles Collection, Vol. 1, Alex, 1993.
Singles Collection, Vol. 2, Alex, 1993.
Singles, 1969-1993, Rykodisc, 1993.
Forgotten Songs of David Robert Jones, SPQR, 1997.
Deram Anthology, 1966-1968, Deram, 1997.
Best of David Bowie: 1969-1974, Capitol, 1997.

Albums; with Tin Machine:
Tin Machine, Virgin, 1989.
Tin Machine II, Victory, 1991.
Oy Vey, Baby, Victory, 1991.

Albums; Contributing Vocals:
Lou Reed, *Transformer,* RCA, 1972.
Mott the Hoople, *Greatest Hits,* Columbia, 1975.
Iggy Pop, *Lust for Life,* RCA Victor, 1977.
Iggy Pop, *TV Eye,* RCA, 1978.
Giorgio Moroder, *Cat People,* MCA, 1982.
Queen, *Hot Space,* Elektra, 1982.
Various artists, *Falcon and the Snowman* (original soundtrack), EMI America, 1985.
Various artists, *Labyrinth* (original soundtrack), Atlantic, 1986.
Mick Ronson, *Heaven & Hull,* Epic, 1994.

Albums; Producer:
Mott the Hoople, *All the Young Dudes,* Columbia, 1972.
Lou Reed, *Transformer,* RCA, 1972.
Mott the Hoople, *Greatest Hits,* Columbia, 1975.
Iggy Pop, *Idiot,* Virgin, 1977.
Lou Reed, *Walk on the Wild Side: The Best of Lou Reed,* RCA, 1977.
Ian Hunter, *You're Never Alone with a Schizophrenic,* Razor & Tie, 1979.
Ian Hunter, *Shades of Ian Hunter and Mott the Hoople,* Columbia, 1979.
Queen, *Hot Space,* Elektra, 1982.
Iggy Pop, *Choice Cuts,* RCA, 1984.
Various artists, *Dance Mix,* EMI, 1985.
Various artists, *Falcon and the Snowman* (original soundtrack), EMI America, 1985.
Iggy Pop, *Blah Blah Blah,* A&M Records, 1986.
Various artists, *Labyrinth* (original soundtrack), Atlantic, 1986.
Various artists, *When the Wind Blows,* Virgin, 1987.
Various artists, *Rock Classics of the '70s,* Columbia, 1989.
Iggy Pop, *Livin' on the Edge of the Night* (EP), Atlantic, 1990.
Various artists, *Pretty Woman* (original soundtrack), EMI America, 1990.
Various artists, *Virgin Value Collector Series 8,* Virgin, 1990.
Queen, *Classic Queen,* Hollywood, 1992.
Lou Reed, *Between Thought and Expression,* RCA, 1992.
Mott the Hoople, *Ballad of Mott: A Retrospective,* Columbia, 1993.
Brian Eno, *Eno Box I,* Virgin, 1994.
Lulu, *From Crayons to Perfume: The Best of Lulu,* Rhino, 1994.
Various artists, *Sedated in the 80s, No. 2,* The Right Stuff, 1994.
Various artists, *Basquiat* (original soundtrack), Polygram, 1996.

Lou Reed, *Different Times: Lou Reed in the 70s,* RCA, 1996.
Various artists, *Trainspotting* (original soundtrack), EMI Premier, 1996.
Various artists, *Grosse Pointe Blank* (original soundtrack), Polygram, 1997.
Mott the Hoople, *Super Hits,* Sony, 1997.
Various artists, *The Saint* (original soundtrack), Virgin, 1997.

Videos:
Love You Til Tuesday, Polygram Video, 1969.
Ashes to Ashes, 1980.
David Bowie, Sony/Picture Music, 1984.
Serious Moonlight, Music Media, 1984.
Jazzin' for Blue Jean, Pioneer, 1984.
China Girl, 1984.
Dancing in the Street, 1986.
Glass Spider, Volumes 1 and 2, Baker & Taylor Video, 1988.
Black Tie White Noise, BMG Video, 1994.
Santa Monica Live, 1972, Limited Edition, (with book), Griffin McKay, 1995.
Bowie: Ziggy Stardust, Weaver-Finch, 1995.
David Bowie: Video Collection, Rykodisc, 1996.

Other videos include *Day In, Day Out,* Picture Music International/Sony.

Computer Software:
Bowie: Jump Interactive, Iona, 1996.

WRITINGS

Films:
Songwriter, *Ziggy Stardust and the Spiders from Mars,* Twentieth Century-Fox, 1973.
Composer, *James Dean, the First American Teenager,* 1975.
Composer, *Jane Bleibt Jane,* 1977.
Songwriter, "Revolutionary Song," *Just a Gigolo* (also known as *Schoener Gigolo, armer Gigolo*), United Artists Classics, 1979.
Songwriter, "Always Crashing in the Same Car" and "Heroes/Helden," *Radio On,* Unifilm, 1979.
Songwriter, *Christiane F wir Kinder vom Bahnhof Zoo,* 1981.
Lyricist and composer, "Theme from Cat People (Putting Out Fire)," *Cat People,* Universal, 1982.
Songwriter, "The Man Who Sold the World," *Party, Party,* Twentieth Century-Fox, 1982.
Composer, *Hero,* Maya/Channel 4, 1983.
Songwriter, "Funtime," *The Hunger,* Metro-Goldwyn-Mayer/United Artists, 1983.

Composer, *Boy Meets Girl,* Abilene, 1984.

Songwriter, "Lust for Life," *Desperately Seeking Susan,* Orion, 1985.

Songwriter, *The Falcon and the Snowman,* Orion, 1985.

Songwriter, "That's Motivation" and "Absolute Beginners," *Absolute Beginners,* Orion, 1986.

Songwriter, *Labyrinth,* TriStar, 1986.

Songwriter, *Mauvais sang* (also known as *Bad Blood* and *The Night Is Young*), AAA Classic, 1986.

Songwriter, "Fame," *Something Wild,* Orion, 1986.

Songwriter, *When the Wind Blows,* Kings Road, 1986.

Songwriter, *Alien Nation,* Twentieth Century-Fox, 1988.

Songwriter, "Fall in Love with Me," *Slaves of New York,* TriStar, 1989.

"Fame," *Pretty Woman,* Buena Vista, 1990.

Songwriter, *Cool World* (animated), Paramount, 1992.

Songwriter, "Stateside," *Dr. Giggles,* Universal, 1992.

Songwriter, "All the Young Dudes," *Amongst Friends,* Fine Line, 1993.

Songwriter, title song, *Decadence,* 1993.

Composer, *Breaking the Waves,* October Films, 1996.

Songwriter, *Sunchaser,* Warner Bros., 1996.

Songwriter, "Lust for Life," *Trainspotting,* Miramax, 1996.

Songwriter, *Grosse Pointe Blank,* Buena Vista, 1997.

Songwriter, *Lost Highway,* October Releasing, 1997.

Songwriter, *The Deli,* Redwood Communications, 1997.

Songwriter, *The Saint,* Paramount, 1997.

Television:

Songwriter, *David Bowie: Glass Spider Tour* (special), 1988.

Songwriter, theme song, *Stephen King's Golden Years* (series), CBS, 1991.

Composer of title song and incidental music, *The Buddha of Suburbia* (mini-series), BBC, 1993.

Nonfiction:

David Bowie Anthology, Hal Leonard, 1985.

In Other Words: David Bowie, Omnibus (New York City), 1986.

Ziggy Stardust: Limited Edition, Rykodisc, 1990.

OTHER SOURCES

Periodicals:

Guitar Player, June, 1997, p. 60.

Other:

All-Music Guide, http://205.186.189.2/cg/amg.exe

Official David Bowie home page, http://www.davidbowie.com*

BRADEN, William   1939-

PERSONAL

Original name, William C. McIlvride; born June 2, 1939, in Red Deer, Alberta, Canada; son of William Dunn (a mechanic) and Mabel Alice (Kenney) McIlvride; married Debora J. Reuter, August 22, 1979; children: William D., Michelle G., Christine D., John-Paul C. *Education:* H.K.U. School of Continuing Education, M.A.

Career: Producer and writer. Feature Films, Inc., producer and vice-president in charge of production; Dunatai Corp., worked as head of film and television programming, president, 1976-78; Avco Embassy Pictures, production executive, 1981; Completion Bond Co., production executive, 1982-83; Filmaker Completion, managing director in Australia, 1983-85; also worked as script editor. Worked as stunt performer in Hollywood early in his career.

Member: Directors Guild of America, Directors Guild of Canada, Producers and Directors Guild of Australia, Writers Guild of Australia.

CREDITS

Film Work:

Production executive, *Farewell My Lovely,* Avco Embassy, 1975.

Production executive, *Rancho Deluxe,* United Artists, 1975.

Production executive, *92 in the Shade,* United Artists, 1975.

Production executive, *Russian Roulette,* Avco Embassy, 1975.

Associate producer and production supervisor, *The Pyramid,* Pyramid Movie Associates, 1975.

Production executive, *Breakheart Pass,* United Artists, 1976.

Director and co-producer, *America: Life in the Family,* Pyramid Films, 1978.

Production executive, *Goldengirl,* Avco Embassy, 1979.

Supervising producer, *Bigshot,* GMT Productions, 1980.

Assistant director, *Death Valley,* Universal, 1980.

Producer, *Rest in Peace,* RIP Company, 1981.

Production executive, *The Seduction,* Avco Embassy, 1982.

Production executive, *Swamp Thing,* Avco Embassy, 1982.

Production executive, *Slapstick,* Film Finance Ltd., London, 1982.

Creator of *Dublin Murders* and *One Way Out;* production executive for *Undercover, Constance, Heart of the Stag,* and *Razorback,* all Completion Bond Company, between 1982 and 1983; assistant director of *Dogpound Shuffle.*

Television Work; Specials:
Producer, *If My People. . .,* 1975.

Executive producer of *Nothing Great Is Easy* and *King of the Channel;* co-producer of *I Believe.*

Other Television Work:
Assistant director, *Waikiki* (pilot), ABC, 1979.

Creator and producer for the series *Requiem for a Planet;* producer of the movie *He Wants Her Back.*

Stage Work:
Producer, *If My People. . .,* toured U.S. cities, 1976.

WRITINGS

Screenplays:
Troubled Waters, 1980.
(With J. Michael Smith) *Winds of Winter,* 1980.
(With Smith) *Somebody! Love Me,* 1980.
Deep Cover, 1984.
Birdie's Cowboys, 1984.*

BRAEDEN, Eric   1941-
   (Hans Gudegast)

PERSONAL

Born Hans Gudegast, April 3, 1941, in Kiel, Germany; son of Wilhelm (mayor of Bredenbek, Germany) and Matilde; married, wife's name, Dale; children: Christian. *Education:* Attended Montana State University; attended Santa Monica College. *Avocational interests:* Boxing, soccer, running, tennis, and skiing.

Addresses: *Agent*—David Windsor, Irv Schechter Company, 9300 Wilshire Blvd., Suite 400, Beverly Hills, CA 90212.

Career: Actor.

Awards, Honors: Best actor, *Soap Opera Digest,* 1988, two daytime Emmy Award nominations, outstanding lead actor in a drama series, 1996, and 1997, and *Daytime TV Magazine* poll winner, best new daytime star, all for *The Young and the Restless;* Federal Medal of Honor from the President of Germany, for promoting positive, realistic image of Germans in America.

CREDITS

Television Appearances; Series:
(As Hans Gudegast) Captain Hauptman Hans Dietrich, *The Rat Patrol,* ABC, 1966-68.
Victor Newman, *The Young and the Restless,* CBS, 1980—.

Television Appearances; Miniseries:
Dimitri Stanislopolous, *Jackie Collins' Lucky Chances,* NBC, 1990.

Television Appearances; Movies:
Frederico Caprio, *Honeymoon with a Stranger,* ABC, 1969.
Dr. Roan Morgan, *The Mask of Sheba,* NBC, 1970.
Stoeffer, *Death Race,* ABC, 1973.
Kosinsky, *Death Scream,* ABC, 1975.
Ross Ford, *Happily Ever After,* CBS, 1978.
David Morrison, *A Perry Mason Mystery: The Case of the Wicked Wives,* NBC, 1993.

Television Appearances; Pilots:
Anton Granicek, *The Judge and Jake Wyler,* NBC, 1972.
Emhardt, *Intertect,* ABC, 1973.
Arlen Findletter, *The Six Million Dollar Man,* ABC, 1973.
Kapitan Drangel, *The New Original Wonder Woman,* ABC, 1975.
Ernest Graeber, *Code Name: Diamond Head,* NBC, 1977.
Stephens, *The Power Within,* ABC, 1979.
Leonard Nero, *The Aliens Are Coming,* NBC, 1980.

Television Apearances; Episodic:
The Mary Tyler Moore Show, CBS, 1977.
Francis Britten, *How the West Was Won,* ABC, 1978.
Nick Kincaid, *Airwolf,* CBS, 1986.
Gerhardt Brunner, *Murder, She Wrote,* CBS, 1986.
Frank Bradley, *The Nanny,* CBS, 1993.

Also appeared in *Charlie's Angels,* ABC; *CHiPs,* NBC; *Combat,* ABC; *Diagnosis Murder,* CBS, 1994; *The Eddie Capra Mysteries,* NBC; *The Gallant Men,* ABC; *A Man Called Sloane,* NBC; *Project UFO,* NBC; and *Vega$,* ABC.

Television Appearances; Specials:
Guiding Light: The Primetime Special, CBS, 1992.
CBS Soap Break, CBS, 1996.

Television Appearances; Awards Presentations:
The 14th Annual Daytime Emmy Awards, 1987.
The 16th Annual Daytime Emmy Awards, 1989.
The Soap Opera Awards, 1990.
Ninth Annual Genesis Awards, 1995.
Host, *The 23rd Annual Daytime Emmy Awards,* 1996.

Film Appearances:
(As Hans Gudegast) Klaus, *Operation Eichmann,* Allied Artists, 1961.
(As Hans Gudegast) Radio operator, *Morituri* (also known as *The Saboteur: Code Name Morituri* and *The Saboteur*), Twentieth Century-Fox, 1965.
(As Hans Gudegast) Max Eckhart, *Dayton's Devils,* Cue, 1968.
(As Hans Gudegast) Von Klemme, *One Hundred Rifles,* Twentieth Century-Fox, 1969.
Dr. Charles Forbin, *Colossus: The Forbin Project* (also known as *The Forbin Project* and *Colossus 1980*), Universal, 1969.
Dr. Otto Hasslein, *Escape from the Planet of the Apes,* Twentieth Century-Fox, 1971.
Peter Brinker, *Lady Ice,* National General, 1973.
Roland, *The Ultimate Thrill* (also known as *The Ultimate Chase*), General Cinema, 1974.
Bruno Von Stickle, *Herbie Goes to Monte Carlo,* Buena Vista, 1977.
Doctor, *The Ambulance,* Triumph Releasing, 1993.
John Jacob Astor, *Titanic,* Twentieth Century Fox/Paramount, 1997.

Also appeared in *The Adultress,* 1976.

Stage Appearances:
(As Hans Gudegast) Kurt Schonforn, *The Great Indoors,* Eugene O'Neill Theatre, New York City, 1966.*

BRANDON, Michael   1945-

PERSONAL

Born Michael Feldman, 1945, in Brooklyn, NY; married Lindsay Wagner (an actress), December, 1976 (divorced).

Addresses: *Contact*—Shapiro/West & Associates, 141 El Camino Dr., Suite 205, Beverly Hills, CA 90212.

Career: Actor.

Member: Actors' Equity Association, Screen Actors Guild, American Federation of Television and Radio Artists.

CREDITS

Film Appearances:
Mike Vecchio, *Lovers and Other Strangers,* Cinerama, 1970.
Marcus, *Jennifer on My Mind,* United Artists, 1971.
Robert, *Four Flies on Grey Velvet* (also known as *Quarto mosche di velluto gris*), Paramount, 1972.
Voice characterization, *Heavy Traffic* (animated), American International Pictures, 1973.
Jeff Dugan, *FM* (also known as *Citizen's Band*), Universal, 1978.
Dr. Jim Sandman, *Promises in the Dark,* Warner Bros., 1979.
Pete Lachapelle, *A Change of Seasons,* Twentieth Century-Fox, 1980.
Max, *Rich and Famous,* Metro-Goldwyn-Mayer/United Artists, 1981.
Jeff Littman, *The Disappearance of Kevin Johnson,* Bedord Communications Group, 1996.

Also appeared as Lepski in *Sauf votre respect,* 1989; appeared in *Presume Dengereux,* and *Le Dernier du colt,* both 1990.

Television Appearances; Series:
David Marquette, *Emerald Point, N.A.S.,* CBS, 1983-84.
Lieutenant James Dempsey, *Dempsey and Makepeace,* syndicated, 1984.
Teddy Kramer, *Home Fires,* NBC, 1992.

Television Appearances; Miniseries:
Arlen Marshall, *Dynasty: The Reunion,* ABC, 1991.
David Protess, *Gone in the Night,* CBS, 1996.
Ambassador Courtland, *Robert Ludlum's The Apocalypse Watch,* ABC, 1997.

Television Appearances; Pilots:
Kirk, *Man in the Middle,* CBS, 1972.
Tony Scott, *Scott Free,* NBC, 1976.
Dr. Pete Marcus, *Venice Medical,* ABC, 1983.
Bryan Dobbs, *Divided We Stand,* ABC, 1988.

Television Appearances; Movies:
Frank Pescadero, *The Impatient Heart,* NBC, 1971.
Billy, *The Strangers in 7-A,* CBS, 1972.

David, *The Third Girl from the Left,* ABC, 1973.
Jim Conklin, *The Red Badge of Courage,* NBC, 1974.
Keith Miles, *Hitchhike!,* ABC, 1974.
Ben Holian, *Cage without a Key,* CBS, 1975.
Davis Asher, *Queen of the Stardust Ballroom,* CBS, 1975.
Bill Bast, *James Dean,* NBC, 1976.
Carl Wyche, *Red Alert,* CBS, 1977.
Paul Lester, *The Comedy Company,* CBS, 1978.
Alan, *A Vacation in Hell,* NBC, 1979.
Steve Triandos, *A Perfect Match,* CBS, 1980.
Bob Frazer, *Between Two Brothers,* CBS, 1982.
Keith Sindell, *The Seduction of Gina,* CBS, 1984.
Michael Krasnick, *Deadly Messages,* ABC, 1985.
Jeff Robins, *Rock 'n' Roll Mom,* ABC, 1988.
Ted Ricci, *Not in My Family,* ABC, 1993.
Arnie Hansen, *Murder or Memory? A Moment of Truth Movie* (also known as *Moment of Truth: Hypnotic Confession*), NBC, 1994.

Television Appearances; Episodic:
Stan, *The Nanny,* CBS, 1996.
U. S. Attorney Sam Nardoni, *JAG,* CBS, 1997.

Also appeared as Barry Sinclair, *The Marshal,* 1995.

Television Appearances; Specials:
Lindsay Wagner—Another Side of Me, ABC, 1977.
Mr. Hansen, *Love in the Dark Ages,* CBS, 1994.
Stage Appearances:
The Lady and the Clarinet, Long Wharf Theatre, New Haven, CT, 1983.*

BRENNER, David   1945-

PERSONAL

Born February 4, 1945, in Philadelphia, PA; son of Louis Yehuda (a vaudeville singer, dancer, and comedian) and Estelle Anne (Rosenfeld) Brenner; children: Cole Jay, Slade Lucas Moby, Wyatt Destry Slater. *Education:* Temple University, B.S., mass communications. *Religion:* Jewish.

Addresses: *Manager*—Conversation Company Ltd., 697 Middle Neck Rd., Great Neck, NY 11023. *Contact*—Bill Zysblat, RZO, 110 West 57th St., New York, NY 10019.

Career: Comedian and nightclub performer. Worked as producer for WBBM-TV, Chicago, IL; WRCV and KYW-TV, both Philadelphia, PA; and WNEW-TV and PBL-TV, both New York City. Also producer, director, and writer for television documentaries; appeared in television commercials. Owner of Amsterdam Billiard Clubs, New York City. *Military service:* U.S. Army, served during early 1960s; became corporal.

Awards, Honors: Named Artist Comedian of the Year, American Guild of Variety Actors, 1976; Las Vegas Entertainer of the Week Award, 1977; Atlantic City Comedian of the Year, 1984; College Campus Entertainer/Comedian of the Year, 1984.

CREDITS

Television Appearances; Specials:
Neil Sedaka Steppin' Out, 1976.
Steve Martin's The Winds of Whoopie, NBC, 1983.
I Ask for Wonder: Experiencing God, 1988.
But Seriously '94, Showtime, 1995.

Television Appearances; Episodic:
(Television debut) *The Tonight Show,* NBC, 1971.
Live! Dick Clark Presents, CBS, 1988.
Alan King: Inside the Comedy Mind, 1991.
Comics Only, Comedy Central, 1991.

Also appeared on *The Hollywood Squares;* over seventy-five guest host appearances, *The Tonight Show with Johnny Carson.*

Television Appearances; Movies:
Himself, *Ebony, Ivory, and Jade,* CBS, 1979.

Television Appearances; Series:
Host, *Nightlife,* syndicated, 1986-87.

Film Appearances:
Celebrity auctioneer, *Worth Winning,* Twentieth Century-Fox, 1989.

Stage Appearances:

Made stage debut, Pips, Sheepshead Bay, Brooklyn, NY. Has appeared in concert halls, colleges, nightclubs, since August, 1969; including *The Laughs and Times of David Brenner,* Criterion Theatre, 1990.

RECORDINGS

Videos:
Catch a Rising Star's 10th Anniversary Show, Columbia/TriStar, 1983.
Young at Heart Comedians, Paramount Home Video, 1988.

WRITINGS

Books:

Soft Pretzels with Mustard, Arbor House (New York City), 1983.
Revenge Is the Best Exercise, Arbor House, 1985.
Nobody Sees You Eat Tuna Fish, Arbor House, 1985.
If God Wanted Us to Travel. . ., Pocket Books (New York City), 1990.

OTHER SOURCES

Books:

Contemporary Authors, Volume 133, Gale (Detroit, MI), 1991.

BROAD, Jay   1930-

PERSONAL

Born August 5, 1930, in Newcastle, PA; son of Henry and Celia Broad. *Education:* Attended Westminster College and Pennsylvania State University.

Addresses: *Contact*—2210 Jackson Pl., Bellmore, NY 11710-1105.

Career: Director and playwright. Theatre Atlanta, director, 1965-70; PAF Playhouse, Huntington Station, NY, director, 1975-80; Yale School of Drama, New Haven, CT, visiting lecturer, 1978; Arizona State University, Tempe, AZ, playwright in residence, 1980-81; National Endowment for the Arts, consultant, 1981-82; University of Southern California, Los Angeles, CA, visiting director and professor, 1983-85.

Member: Society of Stage Directors and Choreographers, National Theatre conference (past president), Players, Theatre Communications Group.

Awards, Honors: Straw Hat Award, 1972, for *A Conflict of Interest.*

CREDITS

Stage Work; Director:

Are You Now or Have You Ever Been?, New York, 1973.
Play Me a Country Song, 1982.
Madness in Jerusalem, 1984.
The Barclay Decision, 1985.

Benefactors, Meadow Brook Theatre, Rochester, MI, 1995.

Television Work; Episodic:

Director, "Spies Like Us," *The New WKRP in Cincinnati,* syndicated, 1992.

WRITINGS

Stage Plays:

(With Don Tucker) *Red, White and Maddox* (musical), Theatre Atlanta, 1968, then Cort Theatre, New York City, 1969.
Balance, Theatre Atlanta, 1969.
The Great Big Coca-Cola Swamp in the Sky, Westport Country Playhouse, Westport, CT, 1971.
A Conflict of Interest, Arena Stage, Washington, DC, 1972, published by Samuel French (New York City), 1974.
The Killdeer, Public Theatre, NY, 1974, published by Samuel French, 1974.
To Kill a Mockingbird (adaptation), 1975.
Events from the Life of Ted Snyder, Off-Broadway, 1976.
White Pelicans, 1976, Theatre de Lys, 1978.
Uncle Eddy, 1978.
Play Me a Country Song, 1982.
Madness in Jerusalem, 1984.

Television Episodes:

"Spies Like Us," *The New WKRP in Cincinnati,* syndicated, 1992.*

BROCKSMITH, Roy   1945-

PERSONAL

Born September 15, 1945, in Quincy, IL; son of Otis E. (a mechanic) and Vera A. (Hartwig) Brocksmith; married Adele M. Albright, December 25, 1963; children: Blake. *Education:* Attended Hannibal LaGrange Junior College and Culver-Stockton College; Quincy University, graduated, 1970.

Addresses: *Agent*—Talent Group, Inc., 6300 Wilshire Blvd., Suite 2110, Los Angeles, CA 90048.

Career: Actor, director, and essayist. Progressive Playhouse (community theatre), director; Great River Theatre Workshop, founder; California Cottage Theatre, co-founder, 1987, partner and producing director, 1987-96. Flower Fifth Avenue Hospital, New

York City, librarian at Lilliam Morgan Hetrick Medical Library; American Association of Midwives, past member of board of directors.

Member: Actors' Equity Association.

Awards, Honors: Kudos Award, Minneapolis, MN, 1981, for *Don Juan*.

CREDITS

Film Appearances:
Rip Off, J. Cinemax, 1972.
Frinkuleschti, *King of the Gypsies,* Paramount, 1978.
Warehouse owner, *The Squeeze* (also known as *Diamond Thieves, The Heist,* and *The Rip-Off*), Warner Bros., 1978.
Ollie, *Killer Fish* (also known as *Deadly Treasure of the Piranha, The Naked Sun,* and *Treasure of the Piranha*), Associated Films, 1979.
Dick Lobel, *Stardust Memories,* United Artists, 1980.
Stan, *Rent Control,* Group S, 1981.
Fat park jogger, *Wolfen,* Warner Bros., 1981.
Bartender, *Tales of Ordinary Madness,* Fred Baker, 1983.
Crystal salesman, *Who's That Girl?,* Warner Bros., 1987.
Doctor Parker, *Big Business,* Buena Vista, 1988.
Mike the mailman, *Scrooged,* Paramount, 1988.
Mr. Fisk, *The War of the Roses,* Twentieth Century-Fox, 1989.
Federal Agent Davis, *Tango and Cash,* Warner Bros., 1989.
Coroner, *Relentless,* New Line Cinema, 1989.
Doctor Edgemar, *Total Recall,* TriStar, 1990.
Irv Kendall, *Arachnophobia,* Buena Vista, 1990.
Mr. Kornheiser, *Martians Go Home!,* Taurus Entertainment, 1990.
Deputy James and song performer, *Bill and Ted's Bogus Journey* (also known as *Bill and Ted Go to Hell*), Orion, 1991.
Sammy Thornton, *Nickel and Dime,* Columbia TriStar Home Video, 1992.
Death Ring, New Line Cinema, 1993.
Poultney Dab, *The Road to Wellville,* Columbia, 1994.
Junction City tailor, *Lightning Jack,* Savoy Pictures, 1994.
Assessor, *It Runs in the Family* (also known as *My Summer Story*), Metro-Goldwyn-Mayer, 1994.
Board member, *The Hudsucker Proxy,* Warner Bros., 1994.
Tu, *Kull the Conqueror,* Universal, 1997.

Television Appearances; Movies:
Jacobo Timerman: Prisoner without a Name, Cell without a Number (also known as *Prisoner without a Name, Cell without a Number*), NBC, 1983.
Sheriff Bledsoe, *Izzy and Moe,* CBS, 1985.
Mr. Solomon, *Killer Instinct* (also known as *Over the Edge*), NBC, 1988.
Colonel Roland Duggins, *Steel Justice* (also known as *Nash's Vision*), NBC, 1992.
Professor Trumbell, *A Walton Wedding* (also known as *John-Boy's Wedding*), CBS, 1995.
Guv'ner Twist, *White Dwarf,* Fox, 1995.
Kuranda, *Almost Dead* (also known as *Resurrection*), HBO, 1996.

Television Appearances; Specials:
Monsieur Loyal, "Tartuffe," *Great Performances,* PBS, 1978.
"Almost Partners," *WonderWorks,* PBS, 1987.
Martin, "The Price of Life" (also known as "Triple Play II"), *American Playhouse,* PBS, 1991.
Zwertlow Cruntagg, *Vidiots,* CBS, 1991.

Television Appearances; Episodic:
Soloman Marcus, "The Aztec Dagger," *The Wizard,* CBS, 1987.
Sirna Kolrami, "Peak Performance," *Star Trek: The Next Generation,* syndicated, 1989.
Vic, "The Man Who Was Death," *Tales from the Crypt,* HBO, 1989.
Vic, "Cutting Cards," *Tales from the Crypt,* HBO, 1990.
Vic, "The Switch," *Tales from the Crypt,* HBO, 1990.
Landlord, "The Nose Job," *Seinfeld,* NBC, 1991.
Judge, *Coach,* ABC, 1993.
Floyd, "Neverending Battle," *Lois and Clark: The New Adventures of Superman,* ABC, 1993.
Dr. Elliott Matheson, "Chapter Five," *Murder One,* ABC, 1995.
Nowhere Man, UPN, 1995.
Razka, "Indiscretion," *Star Trek: Deep Space Nine,* syndicated, 1995.
Brother Alwyn Macomber, "The Deconstruction of Falling Stars," *Babylon 5,* syndicated, 1997.

Appeared in "Charlie Smith and the Fritter Tree," an episode of *Nova,* PBS.

Other Television Appearances:
Orthwaite Frodo, *Starstuck* (pilot), CBS, 1979.
Michael Oslo (recurring role), *Picket Fences* (series), CBS, 1992-95.

Appeared in the pilot *The Streets,* NBC; also appeared in *3-2-1 Contact,* PBS; and *The Beggar's Opera,* a cable television production.

Stage Appearances:
(Stage debut) Jack in the box, *A Christmas Pageant,* Quincy Junior Theatre, Quincy, IL, 1950.
(New York debut) Cop, *The Whip Lady,* Hunter's Playwrights Project, 1971.
Louis XIII, *The Three Musketeers,* 1984.

Appeared in *The Stingiest Man in Town* (musical), New York Town Hall, New York City; as Sganarelle, *Don Juan,* Delacorte Theatre, New York City; appeared in multiple roles in the Broadway production of *Stages;* appeared in a California production of *A Woman of Mystery;* appeared in New York City productions as Dr. Roy, *Doctor Selavy's Magic Theatre;* in multiple roles, *Polly;* as Ben Budge/Peachum, *The Beggar's Opera;* as Varanushka, *The Master and Margarita;* as Worm, *In the Jungle of Cities;* as Green Father, *The Leaf People;* as Loyal, *Tartuffe;* and ballad singer, *The Threepenny Opera.* Appeared in regional theatre as Cauchon, *Joan of Lorraine,* Hartman, CT; as Baron, *The Lower Depths,* Arena; as Harry Donovan, *Swing,* John F. Kennedy Center for the Performing Arts, Washington, DC; as Petkoff, *Arms and the Man,* as Sganarelle, *Don Juan,* as Professor Willard, *Our Town,* as Touchstone, *As You Like It,* and as Semicolon, *Hang On to Me,* all Tyrone Guthrie Theatre, Minneapolis, MN. Toured as Thurio in the musical *Two Gentlemen of Verona.*

Stage Work:
Director, *Twelfth Night,* Alaska Repertory Theatre, Anchorage, 1985-86.

Directed *Africanis Instructus* at Lennox Arts Center, and *Flea in Her Ear* at Center Stage, Baltimore, MD; at California Cottage Theatre, directed *Box Prelude Opus No. 1, Matinee, The One Less Traveled, A Necessary End, Ripe Conditions,* and *Letters from Queens.*

WRITINGS

Plays:
Paraplanta Verite, La MaMa, New York City, 1977.

Adapter of *Flea in Her Ear,* Center Stage, Baltimore, MD; author of the plays *Box Prelude Opus No. 1* and *Letters from Queens,* both California Cottage Theatre.

Other:

Contributor to periodicals, including *Performing Arts Journal;* contributor to satirical newsletters under the pseudonym Billy Breeze.*

BURROUGHS, William S. 1914-1997
  (William Lee, Willy Lee)

OBITUARY NOTICE—See index for *CTFT* sketch: Born February 5, 1914, in St. Louis, MO; died following a heart attack, August 2, 1997, in Lawrence, KS. Artist and author. The grandson of the inventor of the adding machine, Burroughs defied his conventional, aristocratic upbringing to become one of the founding members of the Beat Generation of the 1950s, along with writers Jack Kerouac, Allen Ginsberg, and Herbert Huncke. The Beats took an unconventional approach to literature—which included writings on the experimentation with drugs, sex, and petty crime—and spawned the counterculture of the 1960s. Burroughs was the last surviving member of the original Beats and was known as "the big daddy of the Beats," according to a writer for the London *Times.* He discarded his privileged upbringing to experience life among the lower fringes of society, showing Kerouac and Ginsberg around some of New York City's seedy areas. He led a nomadic life, living in such places as Mexico, Tangier, South America, Paris, London, and Texas, among others. While his written work was reviled by some as filth, he earned critical praise for controversial writings such as *The Naked Lunch.* Some critics viewed the work as a social commentary on the evils and soullessness of humanity, while others perceived it as "gibberish masquerading as social commentary," as noted in the *Los Angeles Times.* Burroughs also became popular in the pop culture of the 1990s as the Beat Movement was revived. He appeared in a video by the rock group U2, performed with rap artists Disposable Heroes of Hiphoprisy, and hung out with groups such as The Rolling Stones.

Burroughs was born in St. Louis, Missouri, in 1914. He was educated in ethnology, poetry, anthropology, and yoga at Harvard and studied medicine at Vienna University. He served briefly in the U.S. Army during World War II, being discharged after only three months of service for physical reasons. Reportedly, his mother intervened to have him discharged. Following his service, he worked in a variety of jobs—bartender, pest controller, private detective, factory worker, etc. He also claimed to be on the fringe of crime. According to a *New York Times* contributor: "He spent years experimenting with drugs as well as with sex, which he engaged in with men, women and children." He described his drug use, particularly heroin, in *The Naked Lunch:* "I have smoked junk, eaten it, sniffed it, injected it in vein-skin-muscle, inserted it in rectal suppositories. The needle is not important." He once sold his typewriter to buy drugs. According to the *Washington Post,* after Burroughs kicked the heroine habit with the help of a British doctor, he "end[ed] what he said were years of 'staring at the toe of my foot.'"

Burroughs was married twice. His first wife was a German-Jewish woman who fled the Nazis by marrying him and coming to the United States. The marriage was ended shortly thereafter. His second marriage to Joan Vollmer ended in controversy. While living in Mexico, he asked Vollmer to play a game of "William Tell" with him before friends in 1951. Although he was reportedly drunk at the time, he suggested that Vollmer place a glass on her forehead so he could shoot it off like the legendary archer who could shoot an apple off of someone's head. Instead, Burroughs shot his wife through the forehead, killing her instantly. Mexican authorities ruled the shooting accidental. In his later years, he lived with his longtime companion James Grauerholz.

Burroughs wrote of his drug experiences in the 1953 book *Junkie: Confessions of an Unredeemed Drug Addict.* The work was issued under the name William Lee. In 1959 he published *The Naked Lunch,* which was allegedly titled "Naked Lust" in manuscript stage, until Ginsberg misread Burroughs's handwriting and thought the title was "Naked Lunch." The book, according to a *Los Angeles Times* writer, was "written in a stream of consciousness style, and the prose is meant to repel, even nauseate, the reader with descriptions of bodily functions, sex acts and grotesque medical procedures." The work became the subject of a lengthy court battle regarding obscenity in the United States, and was ultimately published by Grove Press in 1962. Burroughs continued with *The Soft Machine* and *The Ticket That Exploded.*

Burroughs also received notice for his writings that employed the "cut up" method—he intertwined his prose with that of other writers, cutting up the manuscript and reassembling it at will. Among his "cut up" books are *Minutes to Go,* written with Sinclair Beiles, Gregory Corso, and Brion Gysin, and *The Exterminator,* also written with Gysin. He also penned

screenplays, including *The Last Words of Dutch Schultz.* He appeared in films as well, such as *Twister* and *Drug Store Cowboy.* In his later years, Burroughs wrote what critics consider to be more conventional books, including *The Western Lands* and *The Place of Dead Roads.* He also collaborated on *The Black Rider,* a comic opera that featured the music of Tom Waits and Burroughs' libretto. He also appeared on *Saturday Night Live,* where he read from *The Naked Lunch,* and he made numerous recordings, including *Spare Ass Annie* in 1993.

Burroughs also lent his creative energies to art, putting together pieces that were bought by many of his admirers, including the late Nirvana singer Kurt Cobain. His art was featured in a show in Chicago in 1988 and in Los Angeles in 1996. He also was concerned with animal rights, the rain forest, and other environmental issues.

OBITUARIES AND OTHER SOURCES

Books:
Contemporary Theatre, Film and Television, Volume 10, Gale, 1991.
Who's Who in the World, Marquis, 1996.

Periodicals:
Chicago Tribune (electronic), August 4, 1997.
CNN Interactive (electronic), August 2, 1997.
Detroit News, August 3, 1997, p. A11.
Los Angeles Times, August 3, 1997, p. A1.
New York Times, August 4, 1997, p. B5; August 10, 1997, sec. 4, p. 7.
Times (London; electronic), August 4, 1997.
Washington Post, August 4, 1997, p. B4.

BURTON, Kate 1957-

PERSONAL

Full name Katherine Burton; born September 10, 1957, in Geneva, Switzerland; daughter of Richard (an actor) and Sybil (a producer; maiden name, Williams) Burton; married Michael Ritchie (a stage manager), June, 1985. *Education:* Attended Brown University, studying history and Russian, 1979; Yale University, M.F.A. (acting), 1982. *Politics:* Democrat.

Addresses: *Contact*—c/o Alan Duncan, SEM&M, 22 West Nineteenth St., New York, NY 10011.

Career: Actress.

Awards, Honors: *Theatre World* Awards, 1982-83, for *Present Laughter, Alice in Wonderland,* and *Winners.*

CREDITS

Television Appearances; Series:
Anne Kramer, *Home Fires,* NBC, 1992.
Fran Richardson, *Monty,* Fox, 1994.

Television Appearances; Miniseries:
Vanessa Ogden, *Ellis Island,* CBS, 1984.
Agatha Bradford, *Evergreen,* NBC, 1985.

Television Appearances; Movies:
Ophelia, *Uncle Tom's Cabin,* Showtime, 1987.
Deborah, *Love Matters,* Showtime, 1993.
Katherine Donohue, *Mistrial,* HBO, 1996.

Television Appearances; Specials:
(Television debut) Title role, "Alice in Wonderland," *Great Performances,* PBS, 1983.
Agnes O'Neill, "Journey into Genius" (also known as "Eugene O'Neill: Journey into Genius"), *American Playhouse,* PBS, 1988.
"Richard Burton: In from the Cold," *Great Performances,* PBS, 1989.
Brenda Gardner, "Notes for My Daughter," *ABC Afterschool Specials,* ABC, 1995.
Voice, "Buckminster Fuller: Thinking Out Loud," *American Masters,* PBS, 1996.
Abigail, "Ellen Foster," *Hallmark Hall of Fame,* CBS, 1997.

Television Appearances; Episodic:
"If You Knew Sammy," *Spenser: For Hire,* ABC, 1987.
"Play It Again, Sammy," *Spenser: For Hire,* ABC, 1988.
Nun, *Law and Order,* NBC, 1991.
District Attorney Susan Alexander, *The Practice,* ABC, 1997.

Film Appearances:
Margo Litzenberger, *Big Trouble in Little China,* Twentieth Century-Fox, 1986.
Mrs. Burns, *Life with Mikey* (also known as *Give Me a Break*), Buena Vista, 1993.
Helen Blathwaite, *August,* Samuel Goldwyn Co., 1996.
Woman in bed, *The First Wives Club,* Paramount, 1996.
Looking for Richard, Twentieth Century-Fox, 1996.

Dorothy Franklin, *The Ice Storm,* Fox Searchlight, 1997.

Stage Appearances:
(New York debut) Daphne, *Present Laughter,* Circle in the Square Theatre, New York City, 1982.
Alice, *Alice in Wonderland,* Virginia Theatre, New York City, 1983.
May, *Winners,* Roundabout Theatre, New York City, 1983.
J. J., *Doonesbury,* Biltmore Theatre, New York City, 1983.
Eva, *The Accrington Pals,* Hudson Guild Theatre, New York City, 1984.
Pegeen, *Playboy of the Western World,* Roundabout Theatre, 1985.
Plough and the Stars, Roundabout Theatre, 1985.
Alexandra, *On the Verge; or, The Geography of Learning,* Hartford Stage Company, Hartford, CT, 1985-86.
The Three Sisters, Hartman Theatre, Stamford, CT, 1985-86.
Sasha, *Wild Honey,* Virginia Theatre, 1986-87.
Isabella, *Measure for Measure,* Mitzi E. Newhouse Theatre, New York City, 1989.
Betty McNeil, *Some Americans Abroad,* Vivian Beaumont Theatre, New York City, 1990.
Alice, *Aristocrats,* Huntington Theatre Company, Boston, MA, 1990-91.
Julie, *Jake's Woman,* Neil Simon Theatre, New York City, 1992, then Center Theatre Group, James A. Doolittle Theatre, Los Angeles, 1992-93.
Lauren, Grace, and Annie, *London Suite,* Union Square Theatre, New York City, 1995.
Sarah, *Company,* Criterion Theatre/Center Stage Right, New York City, 1995.

Appeared off-Broadway in *Romeo and Juliet.*

RECORDINGS

Taped Readings:
All That Remains, 1992.*

BURTON, LeVar   1957-

PERSONAL

Full name, Levardis Robert Martyn Burton; born February 16, 1957, in Landsthul, Germany; son of Levardis Robert (a photographer in the U.S. Army Signal Corps) and Erma (an educator, social worker, and administrator; maiden name, Christian) Burton; married Stephanie Cozart (a makeup artist), October, 1992; children: Eian, Michaela. *Education:* Attended the University of Southern California.

Addresses: *Agent*—Marion Rosenberg Office, 8428 Melrose Pl., Los Angeles, CA 90069.

Career: Actor, producer, director, and writer. Founder and president of Eagle Nation Films. Established a scholarship at the University of Southern California.

Awards, Honors: Emmy Award nomination, outstanding actor in a single performance for a drama or comedy series, 1977, for *Roots;* Daytime Emmy Awards, outstanding performer in a children's program, 1990, 1993, 1996, and 1997, Daytime Emmy Awards, outstanding children's series, 1990, 1993, 1996, and 1997, Daytime Emmy Award nominations, outstanding performer in a children's program, 1988, 1991, 1992, 1994, and 1995, Daytime Emmy Award nominations, outstanding children's series, 1991, 1992, 1994, and 1995, all for *Reading Rainbow;* National Association for the Advancement of Colored People Image Award, best performance in an educational or informational youth or children's series or special, 1996, for *LeVar Burton Presents: A Reading Rainbow Special.*

CREDITS

Television Appearances; Series:
Host, *Rebop,* PBS, 1976-79.
Host, *Reading Rainbow,* PBS, 1983—.
Lieutenant Commander Geordi La Forge, *Star Trek: The Next Generation,* syndicated, 1987-94.
Voice of Kwame, *Captain Planet and the Planeteers* (animated), TBS/syndicated, 1990-93.
Voice of Kwame, *The New Adventures of Captain Planet* (animated), TBS/syndicated, 1993—.
Daniel "Dan" Scott, *Christy,* CBS, 1995.

Television Appearances; Miniseries:
Kunta Kinte, *Roots,* ABC, 1977.

Television Appearances; Movies:
Billy Peoples, *Billy: Portrait of a Street Kid* (also known as *Ghetto Child*), CBS, 1977.
Ron LeFlore, *One in a Million: The Ron LeFlore Story,* CBS, 1978.
Andrew Sinclair, *Battered,* NBC, 1978.
Donald Lang, *Dummy,* CBS, 1979.

Richard Jefferson, *Guyana Tragedy: The Story of Jim Jones* (also known as *The Mad Messiah*), CBS, 1980.
Rodney, *The Acorn People,* NBC, 1981.
Charles "Tank" Smith, *Grambling's White Tiger,* NBC, 1981.
Ray Walden, *Emergency Room,* syndicated, 1983.
Professor Slade Preston, *The Jesse Owens Story,* syndicated, 1984.
Vinnie Davis, *The Midnight Hour,* ABC, 1985.
Liberty, NBC, 1986.
Ben Sumner, *A Special Friendship,* CBS, 1987.
Lieutenant Commander Geordi La Forge, *Star Trek: The Next Generation—Encounter at Farpoint* (also known as *Encounter at Farpoint*), syndicated, 1987.
Kunta Kinte, *Roots: The Gift* (also known as *A Roots Christmas: Kunta Kinte's Gift*), ABC, 1988.
Fire Chief J. Allan Mather, *Firestorm: 72 Hours in Oakland* (also known as *Firestorm: A Catastrophe in Oakland*), ABC, 1993.
Dr. Franklin Carter, *Parallel Lives,* Showtime, 1994.
Yesterday's Target, Showtime, 1996.

Television Appearances; Episodic:
"A Salute to the Brownings," *Anyone for Tennyson?,* PBS, 1978.
"Almos' a Man," *American Short Story,* PBS, 1978.
"A Piece of the Action," *Trapper John, M.D.,* CBS, 1982.
"Edward," *Fantasy Island,* ABC, 1983.
"Love Is Blind," *The Love Boat,* ABC, 1984.
"Booker," *WonderWorks,* PBS, 1984.
"And the Children Shall Lead," *WonderWorks,* PBS, 1986.
Dave Robinson, "Death Takes a Dive," *Murder, She Wrote,* CBS, 1987.
Evans, "Bad Girl," *Houston Knights,* CBS, 1987.
Mr. Metcalf, "The Boss," *Deadly Games,* UPN, 1995.
Voice of Anansi, "Mark of the Panther," *Gargoyles,* The Disney Channel, 1996.

Appeared as the voice of Hayden Sloane, *Batman: The Animated Series,* The WB; voice also featured in "The Frog Prince," *Happily Ever After: Fairy Tales for Every Child,* HBO.

Television Appearances: Specials:
Battle of the Network Stars, ABC, 1976.
Battle of the Network Stars II, ABC, 1977.
Celebrity Challenge of the Sexes, CBS, 1977.
The Paul Lynde Comedy Hour, ABC, 1977.
Battle of the Network Stars V, ABC, 1978.

Celebrity Challenge of the Sexes, CBS, 1979.
The Celebrity Football Classic, NBC, 1979.
I Love Liberty, ABC, 1982.
Breathing Easy, PBS, 1984.
Living the Dream: A Tribute to Dr. Martin Luther King,
    1988.
The Star Trek 25th Anniversary Special, syndicated,
    1991.
It's a Wonderful Cyberlife: A Holiday Buying Guide,
    The Discovery Channel, 1996.
Star Trek: 30 Years and Beyond, UPN, 1996.
LeVar Burton Presents: A Reading Rainbow Special,
    PBS, 1996.

Television Appearances; Awards Presentations:
The 19th Annual NAACP Image Awards, 1987.
The 23rd Annual NAACP Image Awards, NBC, 1991.
The 18th Annual Daytime Emmy Awards, CBS, 1991.
The 19th Annual Daytime Emmy Awards, NBC,
    1992.
Host, *The American Television Awards,* ABC, 1993.
The 48th Annual Primetime Emmy Awards (also
    known as *The 1996 Emmy Awards*), ABC, 1996.
The 27th Annual NAACP Image Awards (also known
    as *NAACP Image Awards*), Fox, 1996.
The Screen Actors Guild Awards (also known as *1997
    Screen Actors Guild Awards* and *The 33rd Screen
    Actors Guild Awards,*) NBC, 1997.

Television Work; Series:
Executive producer and contributing producer, *Reading Rainbow,* PBS, 1983—.

Television Work; Episodic:
Director, "Pegasus," *Star Trek: The Next Generation,*
    syndicated, 1993.
Director, "Second Chances," *Star Trek: The Next
    Generation,* syndicated, 1993.

Also directed episodes of *Star Trek: Deep Space
Nine,* syndicated; and *Star Trek: Voyager,* UPN.

Film Appearances:
Cap Jackson, *Looking for Mr. Goodbar,* Paramount,
    1977.
Tommy Price, *The Hunter,* Paramount, 1980.
Private Michael Osgood, *The Supernaturals,* Republic Entertainment International, 1986.
Lieutenant Commander Geordi La Forge, *Star Trek:
    Generations* (also known as *Star Trek VII*), Paramount, 1994.
Lieutenant Commander Geordi La Forge, *Star Trek:
    First Contact* (also known as *Star Trek: Borg, Star
    Trek: Destinies, Star Trek: Future Generations,
    Star Trek: Generations II, Star Trek: Resurrection*),
    Paramount, 1996.

WRITINGS

Aftermath (novel), Aspect (New York), 1997.

Author of *Malidoma,* a screenplay.

OTHER SOURCES

Books:
Contemporary Black Biography, Volume 8, Gale
    (Detroit, MI), 1994,

Periodicals:
Booklist, November 1, 1996, p. 459.
Library Journal, December, 1996, p. 152.
NEA Today, November, 1995, p. 7.
People Weekly, March 7, 1988, p. 65.
Publishers Weekly, December 9, 1996, p. 64.
TV Guide, August 13, 1988, p. 12.*

C

CADELL, Simon   1950-1996

PERSONAL

Full name, Simon John Cadell; born July 19, 1950, in London, England; died of lymphatic cancer, March 6, 1996, in England; son of John (a theatrical agent) and Gillian (a drama school principal; maiden name, Howell) Cadell; grandson of Jean Cadell (a stage actress); married Rebecca Croft, 1986; children: two sons. *Education:* Trained for the stage at Bristol Old Vic Theatre School, 1967-69. *Avocational interests:* Travel, wine.

Career: Actor. Bristol Old Vic Theatre Company, Bristol, England, member of company, 1969-70; Nottingham Playhouse, Nottingham, England, member of company, 1971. Also worked in radio.

Member: Groucho, MCC, Tramps.

Awards, Honors: Olivier Award, best comedy performance, 1993, for *Travels with My Aunt.*

CREDITS

Stage Appearances:
The Betrothed, *Geneva,* Mermaid Theatre, London, 1971.
Simon Green, *Lloyd George Knew My Father,* Savoy Theatre, London, 1972-73.
Julian Underwood, *The Case in Question,* Haymarket Theatre, London, 1975.
Justin Jackson, *Lies,* Albery Theatre, London, 1975.
Dr. Harry Trench, *Widowers' Houses,* Actors' Company, Wimbledon Theatre, London, 1976.
William Featherstone, *How the Other Half Loves,* Actors' Company, Wimbledon Theatre, 1976.
Andre, Count de Grival, *The Amazons,* Actors' Company, Wimbledon Theatre, 1977.
Ernest, *You Should See Us Now,* Greenwich Theatre, London, 1983.
Noel, *Noel and Gertie,* King's Head Theatre, London, 1983.
Jeffrey Fairbrother, *Hi-De-Hi,* Victoria Palace Theatre, London, 1983.
Archie, *Jumpers,* Aldwych Theatre, London, 1985.
Charles, *Blithe Spirit,* Vaudeville Theatre, London, 1986.
Aubrey Henry Maitland Allington, *Tons of Money,* National Theatre Company, Lyttelton Theatre, London, 1986.
Benedict Hough, *A Small Family Business,* National Theatre Company, Olivier Theatre, London, 1987.
Double Act, Playhouse Theatre, 1988.
Noel Coward, *Noel and Gertie,* Comedy Theatre, London, 1989-90.
Don't Dress for Dinner, Apollo Theatre, London, 1991.
Henry Pulling and Augusta Bertram, *Travels with My Aunt,* Wyndham's Theatre, London, 1992-93.

Appeared as Oswald, *Ghosts,* and in title role, *Hamlet,* both Birmingham Repertory Theatre, Birmingham, England; in title role, *Raffles,* Watford Palace Theatre, Watford, England; in *A Close Shave, Antigone,* and *The Balcony,* all Nottingham Theatre, Nottingham, England; and in *Zigger Zagger,* National Youth Theatre. Also appeared in *Major Barbara, Macbeth, School for Scandal, The Importance of Being Earnest,* and *Arms and the Man,* all Bristol Old Vic Theatre, Bristol, England. Toured as Elyot, *Private Lives,* British cities.

Television Appearances; Series:
Hauptman Reinicke, *Enemy at the Door,* London Weekend Television, 1978.

Major John Aird, *Edward and Mrs. Simpson,* Thames, 1980.

Geoffrey Fairbrother, *Hi-De-Hi!,* BBC, 1980-84.

Dundridge, *Blott on the Landscape,* BBC, 1985, then Arts and Entertainment, 1986.

Larry Wade, *Life without George,* 1988.

Singles, 1991.

Television Appearances; Miniseries:
Appeared in *She Fell among Thieves,* BBC, then on *Mystery!,* PBS.

Television Appearances; Movies:
The Dame of Sark, Anglia Television, 1976.

Colin Wilson, *Pride and Extreme Prejudice,* USA Network, 1990.

Also appeared in *Two Sundays, Plaintiff and Defendant, The Trials of Oscar Slater,* and *Name for the Day,* all BBC; and *The Promise,* Anglia Television.

Television Appearances; Episodic:
Appeared in episodes of *Tales of the Unexpected,* Anglia Television, then syndicated; *The Glittering Prizes,* BBC; *When the Boat Comes In,* BBC; *Minder,* Euston Films; and *Bergerac,* BBC.

Other Television Appearances:
Hogbin, *The Dog It Was That Died,* 1988.

Brendan Rylands, *Circles of Deceit: Kalon,* 1996.

Also appeared in *Hadleigh* and *Hine.*

Film Appearances:
Voice of Blackberry, *Watership Down,* Avco Embassy, 1978.

Vladimir Kozant, *In the Cold Light of Day* (also known as *The Cold Light of Day*), 1994.

Radio Appearances:
Also appeared on radio programs.

OBITUARIES AND OTHER SOURCES

Periodicals:
Times (London), March 8, 1996.*

CALDWELL, Zoe   1933-

PERSONAL

Original name, Ada Caldwell; born September 14, 1933, in Hawthorn, Victoria, Australia; daughter of A. E. (a plumber) and Zoe (a singer and dancer) Caldwell; married Robert Whitehead (a producer), May 9, 1968; children: William Edgar (Sam), Charlie. *Education:* Attended Methodist Ladies College, Melbourne, Australia.

Addresses: *Office*—c/o Whitehead Stevens, 1501 Broadway, Suite 1614, New York, NY 10036.

Career: Actress and director. Neighborhood Playhouse, New York City, teacher of Shakespearean drama, 1970; Florida Atlantic University, Dorothy F. Schmidt Visiting Eminent Scholar in Theatre, 1989-93.

Awards, Honors: *Theatre World* Award, 1965-66; Antoinette Perry Award, best supporting dramatic actress, 1966, for *Slapstick Tragedy;* Drama League Distinguished Performance Award, 1968; Antoinette Perry Award, best dramatic actress, 1968, for *The Prime of Miss Jean Brodie;* Drama Desk Award, outstanding performance, 1970, for *Colette;* Order of the British Empire, 1970; Andrew Allen Award, best acting performance in radio, 1981; Drama Desk Award, best actress, and Antoinette Perry Award, best dramatic actress, both 1982, for *Medea;* Drama Desk Award, best actress in a play, Outer Critics Circle Award, outstanding performance by an actress, and Antoinette Perry Award, best actress, all 1996, all for her portrayal of Maria Callas, *Master Class.*

CREDITS

Stage Appearances:
Title role, *Major Barbara,* Union Theatre Repertory Company, Melbourne, Australia, 1953.

Bubba, *The Seventeenth Doll,* Elizabethan Theatre Trust, Sydney, Australia, 1954.

Ophelia, *Hamlet,* Elizabethan Theatre Trust, 1954.

Twelfth Night, Royal Shakespeare Company, Shakespeare Memorial Theatre, Stratford-upon-Avon, England, 1958.

Hamlet, Royal Shakespeare Company, Shakespeare Memorial Theatre, 1958.

Daughter of Antiochus, *Pericles,* Royal Shakespeare Company, Shakespeare Memorial Theatre, 1958.

Margaret, *Much Ado about Nothing,* Royal Shakespeare Company, Shakespeare Memorial Theatre, 1958.

Bianca, *Othello,* Royal Shakespeare Company, Shakespeare Memorial Theatre, 1959.

Cordelia, *King Lear,* Royal Shakespeare Company, Shakespeare Memorial Theatre, 1959.

Helena, *All's Well That Ends Well,* Royal Shakespeare Company, Shakespeare Memorial Theatre, 1959.

A fairy, *A Midsummer Night's Dream,* Winter Garden Theatre, New York City, 1959.

(London debut) Whore, "Cob and Leach," in *Trials by Logue* (double-bill), Royal Court Theatre, London, England, 1960.

Ismene, *Antigone,* Royal Court Theatre, 1960.

Isabella, *The Changeling,* Royal Court Theatre, 1961.

Jacqueline, *Jacques,* Royal Court Theatre, 1961.

Rosaline, *Love's Labour's Lost,* Stratford Shakespeare Festival of Canada, Stratford, Ontario, 1961.

Sonja Downfahl, *The Canvas Barricade,* Stratford Shakespeare Festival of Canada, 1961.

Pegeen Mike, *The Playboy of the Western World,* Manitoba Theatre Center, Winnipeg, 1961.

Title role, *Saint Joan,* Adelaide Festival of the Arts, Adelaide, Australia, 1962.

Ham Funeral, Elizabethan Theatre Trust, 1962.

Nola Boyle, *The Season at Sarsaparilla,* Union Theatre Repertory Company, Union Theatre, Melbourne, 1962.

Frosine, *The Miser,* Minnesota Theatre Company, Tyrone Guthrie Theatre, Minneapolis, 1963.

Natalia, *The Three Sisters,* Minnesota Theatre Company, Tyrone Guthrie Theatre, 1963.

Woman, *Death of a Salesman,* Minnesota Theatre Company, Tyrone Guthrie Theatre, 1963.

Elizabeth Von Ritter, *A Far Country,* Crest Theatre, Toronto, Ontario, 1964.

Title role, *Mother Courage,* Manitoba Theatre Center, 1964.

Countess Aurelia, *The Madwoman of Chaillot,* Goodman Memorial Theatre, Chicago, IL, 1964.

Millamant, *The Way of the World,* Minnesota Theatre Company, Tyrone Guthrie Theatre, 1965.

Grusha Vashnadze, *The Caucasian Chalk Circle,* Minnesota Theatre Company, Tyrone Guthrie Theatre, 1965.

Frosine, *The Miser,* Minnesota Theatre Company, Tyrone Guthrie Theatre, 1965.

(Broadway debut) Sister Jean, *The Devils,* Broadway Theatre, 1966.

Polly, "The Gnadiges Fraulein," in *Slapstick Tragedy* (double-bill), Longacre Theatre, New York City, 1966.

Orinthia, *The Apple Cart,* Shaw Festival, Niagara-on-the-Lake, Ontario, 1966.

Lena Szczepanowska, *Misalliance,* Shaw Festival, 1966.

Lady Anne, *Richard III,* Stratford Shakespeare Festival of Canada, 1967.

Mrs. Page, *The Merry Wives of Windsor,* Stratford Shakespeare Festival of Canada, 1967.

Cleopatra, *Antony and Cleopatra,* Stratford Shakespeare Festival of Canada, 1967.

Title role, *The Prime of Miss Jean Brodie,* Helen Hayes Theatre, 1968.

Title role, *Colette,* Ellen Stewart Theatre, New York City, 1970.

Emma, Lady Hamilton, *A Bequest to the Nation,* Haymarket Theatre, London, 1970.

Eve, *The Creation of the World and Other Business,* Shubert Theatre, New York City, 1972.

Love and Master Will, Opera House, John F. Kennedy Center for the Performing Arts, Washington, DC, 1973.

Alice, *Dance of Death,* Vivian Beaumont Theatre, Lincoln Center, New York, 1974.

Mary Cavan Tyrone, *Long Day's Journey into Night,* Eisenhower Theatre, John F. Kennedy Center for the Performing Arts, 1975, then Brooklyn Academy of Music/Opera House, New York City, 1976.

The Neighborhood Playhouse at 50: A Celebration, Shubert Theatre, 1978.

Title role, *Medea,* Cort Theatre, New York City, 1982, then Clarence Brown Company, Knoxville, TN, 1982.

Title role, *Lillian* (solo show), Ethel Barrymore Theatre, New York City, 1986.

Katharine Brynne, *A Perfect Ganesh,* Manhattan Theatre Club, New York City, 1993.

Come A-Waltzing with Me, 1993.

Maria Callas, *Master Class,* John Golden Theatre, New York City, 1995.

Toured the U.S.S.R. in *Hamlet, Twelfth Night,* and *Romeo and Juliet,* all 1958-59; also tours with her solo show.

Stage Work:

Director, *An Almost Perfect Person,* Belasco Theatre, New York City, 1977.

Director, *Richard II,* Stratford Shakespeare Festival of Canada, 1979.

Director, *These Men,* Harold Clurman Theatre, New York City, 1980.

Director, *Othello,* Winter Garden Theatre, 1981.

Director, *The Taming of the Shrew,* American Shakespeare Theatre, 1985.

Director, *Hamlet,* American Shakespeare Theatre, 1985.

Director, *Macbeth,* Mark Hellinger Theatre, New York City, 1988.

Director, *Park Your Car in Harvard Yard,* American National Theatre Academy, Music Box Theatre, New York City, 1991.

Director, *Vita and Virginia,* New York City, 1995.

Film Appearances:
Countess, *The Purple Rose of Cairo,* Orion, 1985.

Television Appearances; Movies:
Title role, *Sarah Bernhardt,* 1977.
Mrs. Kennedy, *Lantern Hill* (also known as *Jane of Lantern Hill*), The Disney Channel, 1990.

Television Appearances; Specials:
The 43rd Annual Tony Awards, CBS, 1989.
Avonlea, The Disney Channel, 1990.
The 50th Annual Tony Awards, CBS, 1996.

Other Television Appearances:
Witness to Yesterday, 1974.

Also appeared in television productions of *The Seagull, Sarah, The Apple Cart, Macbeth,* and *The Lady's Not for Burning.*

Radio Appearances:
Appeared as Arkadina, *The Seagull,* BBC; and as Sarah Bernhardt, *Sarah,* CBC (Canada).

OTHER SOURCES

Periodicals:
New York, September 11, 1995, p. 64; May 13, 1996, p. 48.

CAMERON, Kirk   1970(?)-

PERSONAL

Born October 20, 1970 (one source says 1971), in Canoga Park, CA; son of Robert (a junior high school physical education teacher) and Barbara (a business manager) Cameron; brother of Candace Cameron (an actress); married Chelsea Noble (an actress), 1991. *Avocational interests:* Working out at the gym, playing the guitar.

Addresses: *Agent*—United Talent Agency, 9560 Wilshire Blvd., Suite 500, Beverly Hills, CA 90212.

Career: Actor and director. Began his career in television commercials at age nine. Spokesperson for "Just Say No" anti-drug campaign.

Awards, Honors: Best Actor Award, Family Television and Film Awards Organization, 1988; People's Choice Awards, favorite young television performer,

Proctor and Gamble Productions, 1988 and 1989; Golden Globe Award nomination for *Growing Pains.*

CREDITS

Television Appearances; Series:
Eric Armstrong, *Two Marriages,* ABC, 1983-84.
Mike Seaver, *Growing Pains,* ABC, 1985-92.
Kirk Hartman, *Kirk* (also known as *Life Happens*), The WB, 1995-96.

Television Appearances; Pilots:
Bobby, *Mickey Spillane's Mike Hammer: More Than Murder* (also known as *More Than Murder*), CBS, 1984.

Television Appearances; Episodic:
"Just One of the Guys," *Full House,* ABC, 1988.

Also appeared on *Just the Ten of Us,* ABC.

Television Appearances; Movies:
Boy number one, *Bret Maverick: The Lazy Ace* (also known as *Bret Maverick*), 1981.
Goliath Awaits, syndicated, 1981.
Gary, *Star Flight: The Plane That Couldn't Land* (also known as *Starflight One*), ABC, 1983.
Mickey Chandler, *Children in the Crossfire,* NBC, 1984.
Wilson "Will" Loomis, *A Little Piece of Heaven* (also known as *Honor Bright*), NBC, 1991.
Runner Campbell, "Star Struck," *CBS Sunday Afternoon Showcase,* CBS, 1994.
Dexter Riley, *The Computer Wore Tennis Shoes* (also known as *The ABC Family Movie* and *Disney Family Films*), ABC, 1995.

Television Appearances; Specials:
The Woman Who Willed a Miracle, ABC, 1981.
The Wildest West Show of the Stars, CBS, 1986.
Bob Hopes High-Flying Birthday Extravaganza, NBC, 1987.
Happy Birthday, Bob! Fifty Stars Salute Your Fifty Years with NBC, NBC, 1988.
Host, *The Ice Capades with Kirk Cameron* (also known as *Kirk Cameron at the Ice Capades*), ABC, 1988.
Superstars and Their Moms (also known as *Superstars & Their Moms*), ABC, 1988.
Super Bloopers and New Practical Jokes, NBC, 1988.
The Hollywood Christmas Parade (also known as *The 57th Annual Hollywood Christmas Parade*), syndicated, 1988.

The Hollywood Christmas Parade (also known as *The 58th Annual Hollywood Christmas Parade*), syndicated, 1989.

Comic Relief III (also known as *Comic Relief 3*), HBO, 1989.

Bob Hope's Love Affair with Lucy, NBC, 1989.

Super Bloopers and New Practical Jokes, NBC, 1990.

Ole! It's Bob Hope's Acapulco Spring Fling of Comedy and Music, NBC, 1990.

Happy Birthday, Bugs: Fifty Looney Years (also known as *Hollywood Celebrates Bugs Bunny's 50th Birthday*), CBS, 1990.

The Greatest Practical Jokes of All Time, NBC, 1990.

America's All-Star Tribute to Oprah Winfrey (also known as *All-Star Tribute to Oprah Winfrey*), ABC, 1990.

Host from Hollywood, *Dick Clark's New Year's Rockin' Eve* (also known as *New Year's Rockin' Eve '90*), ABC, 1990.

Special events chairperson, *Children's Miracle Network Telethon,* syndicated, 1991.

Bob Hope: The First Ninety Years, NBC, 1993.

Host, *The Making of the Twilight Zone Tower of Terror,* The Disney Channel, 1994.

Host, *Teen Spirit* (documentary), ABC, 1994.

Also appeared in *Andrea's Story.*

Television Appearances; Awards Presentations:

The 39th Annual Emmy Awards (also known as *The Emmy Awards*), Fox, 1987.

The 41st Annual Emmy Awards (also known as *The Emmy Awards*), Fox, 1989.

The 15th Annual People's Choice Awards (also known as *The People's Choice Awards*), CBS, 1989.

The 4th Annual American Comedy Awards, ABC, 1990.

The 16th Annual People's Choice Awards (also known as *The People's Choice Awards*), CBS, 1990.

The 42nd Annual Primetime Emmy Awards Presentation (also known as *The 42nd Annual Emmy Awards* and *The Emmy Awards*), Fox, 1990.

"The Walt Disney Company Presents the American Teacher Awards," *The Magical World of Disney,* The Disney Channel, 1990.

The 17th Annual People's Choice Awards (also known as *The People's Choice Awards*), CBS, 1991.

Presenter, *The 48th Annual Golden Globe Awards* (also known as *Golden Globe Awards*), TBS, 1991.

The 43rd Annual Primetime Emmy Awards Presentation (also known as *The 43rd Annual Emmy Awards* and *The Emmy Awards*), Fox, 1991.

Presenter, *The 18th Annual People's Choice Awards* (also known as *The People's Choice Awards*), CBS, 1992.

The 25th Annual Dove Awards, The Family Channel, 1994.

Television Work:

Second assistant director, *Out of Sight, Out of Mind* (also known as *Sight Unseen*), syndicated, 1990.

Film Appearances:

Teddy, *The Best of Times,* Universal, 1986.

Chris Hammond, *Like Father, Like Son,* TriStar, 1987.

Tucker Muldowney, *Listen to Me,* Columbia, 1989.

Mike Seaver, *The Willies,* Paramount Home Video/ Prism Entertainment, 1991.

OTHER SOURCES

Periodicals:

People Weekly, December 15, 1986, p. 177; August 5, 1991, pp. 88-89.*

CAMP, Colleen   1953-
(Colleen Camp Wilson)

PERSONAL

Born in 1953 in San Francisco, CA.

Addresses: *Agent*—Gersh Agency, P.O. Box 5617, 232 North Canon Dr., Beverly Hills, CA 90212.

Career: Actress. Worked as a bird trainer at Busch Gardens.

CREDITS

Film Appearances:

Gilda Riener, *Cat in the Cage,* Genesis Home Video, 1968.

Battle for the Planet of the Apes, Twentieth Century-Fox, 1973.

The Last Porno Flick (also known as *The Mad, Mad Moviemakers*), Bryanston, 1974.

Mary Ann, *The Swinging Cheerleaders,* Monterey Home Video, 1974.

Billy's girl, *Funny Lady,* Columbia, 1975.

Connie Thompson—Miss Imperial County, *Smile,* United Artists, 1975.

The Gumball Rally, Warner Bros., 1976.

She Devils in Chains (also known as *Ebony, Ivory and Jade, Foxfire,* and *Foxforce*), Simitar Entertainment, 1977.

Donna, *Death Game* (also known as *The Seducers*), Levitt-Pickman, 1977.

Billie Jean, *Love and the Midnight Auto Supply,* Producers Capitol, 1978.

Playmate, *Apocalypse Now,* United Artists, 1979.

Ann Morris and song performer, *The Game of Death* (also known as *Goodbye Bruce Lee: His Last Game of Death*), Columbia, 1979.

Randy, *Who Fell Asleep?,* 1979.

Cindy, *Cloud Dancer,* Blossom, 1980.

Christy Miller and song performer, *They All Laughed,* Twentieth Century-Fox/United Artists, 1981.

Robin, *The Seduction,* Avco Embassy, 1982.

Dusty Trails, *Smokey and the Bandit, Part 3,* Universal, 1983.

Sarah Richman, *Valley Girl,* Atlantic, 1983.

Liberty Jean, *Loose Ends,* 1983.

Rose and song performer, *The City Girl,* Moon, 1984.

Liz Sampson, *Joy of Sex,* Paramount, 1984.

Tracy King, *The Rosebud Beach Hotel,* Almi, 1984.

Elaine Fox, *D.A.R.Y.L.,* Paramount, 1985.

Yvette, *Clue,* Paramount, 1985.

Nancy Catlett, *Doin' Time,* Ladd/Warner Bros., 1985.

Kirkland, *Police Academy 2: Their First Assignment,* Warner Bros., 1985.

Liberty Jean, *Screwball Academy* (also known as *Divine Light*), TransWorld Entertainment, 1986.

Mrs. Kirkland-Tackleberry, *Police Academy 4: Citizens on Patrol,* Warner Bros., 1987.

Rhonda Shand, *Walk Like a Man,* Metro-Goldwyn-Mayer/United Artists, 1987.

Arlanda, *Track 29,* Island, 1988.

Molly Gilbert and song performer, *Illegally Yours,* Metro-Goldwyn-Mayer/United Artists, 1988.

Jenny, *Wicked Stepmother,* Metro-Goldwyn-Mayer/United Artists, 1989.

Margaret Snow, *My Blue Heaven,* Warner Bros., 1990.

Herself, *Hearts of Darkness: A Filmmaker's Apocalypse,* Paramount Home Video, 1991.

Mrs. Vanderhoff, *Wayne's World,* Paramount, 1992.

Deborah, *Un-Becoming Age* (also known as *The Magic Bubble*), Monarch Home Video, 1992.

Judy Dansig, *The Vagrant,* Metro-Goldwyn-Mayer/United Artists Home Video, 1992.

Song performer, *The Thing Called Love,* Paramount, 1993.

Ratcliff, *The Last Action Hero,* Columbia, 1993.

Judy Marks, *Sliver,* Paramount, 1993.

Patti, *Greedy,* Universal, 1994.

Auditioner, *Naked in New York,* Fine Line, 1994.

Tracy, *The No-Tell Hotel,* Palm Beach Entertainment, 1994.

Connie Kowalski, *Die Hard with a Vengeance,* Twentieth Century-Fox, 1995.

Maureen McGill, *The Babysitter's Club,* Columbia, 1995.

Neighbor's wife, *Three Wishes,* Savoy Pictures, 1995.

Mrs. Burtis, *House Arrest,* Metro-Goldwyn-Mayer/United Artists, 1996.

Plump Fiction, 1996.

(As Colleen Camp Wilson) Detective Jones, *The Associate,* Buena Vista, 1996.

Debbie, *Speed 2: Cruise Control,* Twentieth Century-Fox, 1997.

Dr. Pasmier, *The Ice Storm,* Fox Searchlight, 1997.

Also appeared in *American Beauty Hostages.*

Film Work:
Associate producer, *The City Girl,* Moon, 1984.

Television Appearances; Series:
Kristin Shepard, *Dallas,* CBS, 1979.

Kara Wilhoit, *Tom,* CBS, 1993-94.

Television Appearances; Episodic:
Contestant, *The Dating Game,* ABC, 1972.

Herself, "Love, Exciting and New," *WKRP in Cincinnati,* CBS, 1978.

"The Case of the Red-Faced Thespian," *Magnum, P.I.,* CBS, 1983.

Korman's wife, "Korman's Kalamity," *Tales from the Crypt,* HBO, 1990.

Debrah, "melissa in wonderland," *thirtysomething,* ABC, 1991.

Secretary, "Crime and Punishment," *Roseanne,* ABC, 1993.

"The Last Thursday in November," *Roseanne,* ABC, 1995.

"Pampered to a Pulp," *Roseanne,* ABC, 1996.

Also appeared on (television debut) *The Dean Martin Show,* NBC; *Happy Days,* ABC; *The Dukes of Hazzard,* CBS; and *Murder, She Wrote,* CBS.

Television Appearances; Miniseries:
Vickie St. John, *Rich Man, Poor Man, Book II,* ABC, 1976-77.

Television Appearances; Movies:
Starlet, *Amelia Earhart,* NBC, 1976.

Rosette, *Lady of the House,* NBC, 1978.
Ellie Snyder, *Addicted to His Love* (also known as *Sisterhood*), ABC, 1988.
Laurie, *Backfield in Motion,* ABC, 1991.
Chris, *For Their Own Good,* ABC, 1993.
Jude, *Suddenly* (also known as *An Urban Legend* and *When Somebody Loves You*), ABC, 1996.
Mrs. Buford Lowry, *The Right to Remain Silent,* Showtime, 1996.

Television Appearances; Specials:
Appeared on *George Burns Comedy Week* and *Going Home Again.**

CAMPION, Jane   1954(?)-

PERSONAL

Born c. 1954, in Wellington, New Zealand; daughter of Richard (a director) and Edith (an actress) Campion; companion, Colin Englert; children: Jasper (deceased). *Education:* Victoria University, B.A. (anthropology), 1975; Chelsea School of Arts, Diploma of Fine Arts; Sydney College of the Arts, Diploma of Fine Arts (painting), 1979; Australian Film, Television, and Radio School, Diploma in Direction, 1984.

Addresses: *Home*—East Sydney, Australia. *Agent*—Creative Artists Agency, 9830 Wilshire Blvd., Beverly Hills, CA 90212-1804.

Career: Director and screenwriter. Worked in short film medium and television in mid-1980s.

Awards, Honors: Diploma of Merit, Melbourne Film Festival, 1983, Palme d'Or, best short film, Cannes International Film Festival, 1986, and finalist for Greater Union Award, Australian Film Institute, all for *Peel: An Exercise in Discipline;* Rouben Mamoulian Award, best overall short film, Sydney Film Festival, 1984, Unique Artist Merit, Melbourne Film Festival, 1984, first prize cinestud, Amsterdam Film Festival, 1985, and best direction, best screenplay, and best cinematography awards, Australian Film Institute, all 1984, for *A Girl's Own Story;* Best experimental film, Australian Film Institute, 1984, Unique Artist Merit, Melbourne Film Festival, 1984, most popular short film, Sydney Film Festival, 1985, all for *Passionless Moments;* Best short fiction award, Melbourne International Film Festival, and XL Elders Award, best short fiction, both 1985, for *After Hours;* Golden Plaque for Television, Chicago International Film Festival, and best director, best telemovie, and best screenplay awards, Australian Film Institute, all 1987, for *Two Friends;* Georges Sadoul Prize, best foreign film, 1988, New Generation Award, Los Angeles Film Critics, 1990, and Best Australian Feature Award and best director award, Australian Film Critics' Circle, both 1989, Spirit of Independence Award, best foreign film, 1990, all for *Sweetie;* Byron Kennedy Award, Critics Award, Toronto Film Festival, Spirit of Independence Award, best foreign film, Otto Debelius Prize, Berlin Film Festival international jury, Si Presci Award, best film from international critics, Elvira Notari Award, best woman director, Silver Lion and seven other prizes from Venice Film Festival, all 1991, for *An Angel at My Table;* Palme d'Or, Cannes International Film Festival, 1993, New York Film Critics' Circle Award, best direction and best screenplay writing, 1993, Academy Award, best original screenplay, Academy Award nomination, best director, Golden Globe Award nominations, best director and best screenplay, and Writers Guild Award, best screenplay written directly for the screen, all 1994, for *The Piano.*

CREDITS

Film Work; Director:
Tissues, 1981.
Peel: An Exercise in Discipline, Unexpected Film Company, 1982.
Mishaps of Seduction and Conquest, 1983.
A Girl's Own Story, Unexpected Film Company, 1983.
Passionless Moments, Unexpected Film Company, 1984.
After Hours, 1984.
Sweetie, Avenue Pictures, 1989.
An Angel at My Table (originally broadcast as a miniseries on Australian television; adaptation of New Zealand author Janet Frames autobiography), Circle Releasing, 1990.
The Piano, Miramax, 1993.
The Portrait of a Lady, Gramercy Pictures, 1996.

Film Work; Other:
Film editor, *Peel: An Exercise in Discipline,* Unexpected Film Company, 1982.
Producer, cinematographer, and camera operator, *Passionless Moments,* Unexpected Film Company, 1984.
Casting, *Sweetie,* Avenue Pictures, 1989.

Film Appearances:
The Audition, 1989.

Television Work; Director:
Two Friends, Australian Broadcasting Company, 1986.

WRITINGS

Screenplays:
Peel: An Exercise in Discipline, Unexpected Film Company, 1982.
A Girl's Own Story, Unexpected Film Company, 1983.
Passionless Moments, Unexpected Film Company, 1984.
After Hours, 1984.
(With Gerard Lee) *Sweetie* (based on Campion's idea), Avenue Pictures, 1989, published by University of Queensland Press (St. Lucia, Australia), 1991.
The Piano, Miramax, 1993, published by Miramax Books (New York City), 1993.

Teleplays:
Two Friends, Australian Broadcasting Company, 1986.

Books:
(With Kate Pullinger) *The Piano* (novel), Hyperion (New York City), 1994.

Film Music:
"Feel the Cold," *A Girl's Own Story,* Unexpected Film Company, 1983.

OTHER SOURCES

Books:
Contemporary Authors, Volume 138, Gale (Detroit, MI), 1993.

Periodicals:
Vanity Fair, December, 1996, pp. 210-214, 229-230.
Washington Post, March 4, 1990.*

CAREY, Harry Jr. 1921-

PERSONAL

Born May 16, 1921, in Saugus, CA; son of Harry (an actor) and Oliver (Fuller) Carey; married Marilyn Frances Fix, August 12, 1944; children: Steven, Melinda, Thomas, Patricia.

Career: Actor and writer. Performed in summer theatre productions, Lakewood Theatre, Skowhegan, ME, 1940; National Broadcasting Company (NBC), New York City, page boy. *Military service:* U.S. Navy, 1941-46.

Addresses: *Contact*—P.O. Box 3256, Durango, CO 81302.

CREDITS

Film Appearances:
Rolling Home, 1946.
Prentice McComber, *Pursued,* Warner Bros., 1947.
Dan Latimer, *Red River,* United Artists, 1948.
Jimmy Biff, *Moonrise,* Republic, 1948.
William Kearney ("The Abilene Kid"), *The Three Godfathers,* Metro-Goldwyn-Mayer, 1948.
Lieutenant Ross Pennell, *She Wore a Yellow Ribbon,* RKO, 1949.
Lieutenant Ord, *Copper Canyon,* Paramount, 1950.
Trooper Daniel "Sandy" Boone, *Rio Grande,* Republic, 1950.
Sandy Owens, *Wagonmaster,* RKO, 1950.
Captain Gregson, *Warpath,* Paramount, 1951.
Reporter, *Monkey Business,* Twentieth Century-Fox, 1952.
Sergeant Shaker Schuker, *The Wild Blue Yonder* (also known as *Thunder across the Pacific*), Republic, 1952.
Griff, *Beneath the Twelve Mile Reef,* Twentieth Century-Fox, 1953.
Winslow, *Gentlemen Prefer Blondes,* Twentieth Century-Fox, 1953.
Hunt, *Island in the Sky,* Warner Bros., 1953.
Taxi driver, *Niagara,* Twentieth Century-Fox, 1953.
Dobe, *San Antone,* Republic, 1953.
Jim Riley, *Sweethearts on Parade,* Republic, 1953.
Bert, *The Outcast,* Republic, 1954.
Johnson, *Silver Lode,* RKO, 1954.
John, *House of Bamboo,* Twentieth Century-Fox, 1955.
Dwight Eisenhower, *The Long Gray Line,* Columbia, 1955.
Stefanowski, *Mister Roberts,* Warner Bros., 1955.
William Bensinger, *The Great Locomotive Chase* (also known as *Andrews' Raiders*), Buena Vista, 1956.
Brad Jorgensen, *The Searchers,* Warner Bros., 1956.
Corporal Morrison, *Seventh Cavalry,* Columbia, 1956.
Deputy Lee, *Gun the Man Down* (also known as *Arizona Mission*), United Artists, 1957.
Roundtree, *Kiss Them for Me,* Twentieth Century-Fox, 1957.

Chet, *The River's Edge,* Twentieth Century-Fox, 1957.

Trueblood, *From Hell to Texas* (also known as *Manhunt*), Twentieth Century-Fox, 1958.

Travis, *Escort West,* United Artists, 1959.

Harold, *Rio Bravo,* Warner Bros., 1959.

Dr. Joseph Mornay, *The Great Imposter,* Universal, 1960.

Jim Ferguson, *Noose for a Gunman,* United Artists, 1960.

Ortho Clegg, *Two Rode Together,* Columbia, 1961.

Bill Martin, *A Public Affair,* Parade, 1962.

Trooper Smith, *Cheyenne Autumn,* Warner Bros., 1964.

Jellicoe, *The Raiders* (also known as *The Plainsman*), Universal, 1964.

Lieutenant Hudson, *Taggart,* Universal, 1964.

Jenkins, *Shenandoah,* Universal, 1965.

Corporal Peterson, *Alvarez Kelly,* Columbia, 1966.

Ben, *Billy the Kid vs. Dracula,* Embassy, 1966.

Jay C., *Cyborg 2087,* Features, 1966.

Ed Mabry, *The Rare Breed,* Universal, 1966.

McBee, *The Way West,* United Artists, 1967.

Captain Rose, *The Devil's Brigade,* United Artists, 1968.

Mooney, *Ballad of Josie,* Universal, 1968.

Cort Hyjack, *Bandolero,* Twentieth Century-Fox, 1968.

Reverend Rork, *Death of a Gunfighter,* Universal, 1969.

Webster, *The Undefeated,* Twentieth Century-Fox, 1969.

Stuart, *Dirty Dingus Magee,* Metro-Goldwyn-Mayer, 1970.

Stamper, *The Moonshine War,* Metro-Goldwyn-Mayer, 1970.

Pop Dawson, *Big Jake,* National General, 1971.

Red, *One More Train to Rob,* Universal, 1971.

Joe Pickens, *Something Big,* National General, 1971.

Father, *Trinity Is Still My Name,* Embassy, 1971.

Hank, *Cahill, United States Marshal,* Warner Bros., 1973.

Holy Joe, *A Man from the East,* United Artists, 1974.

Dumper, *Take a Hard Ride,* Twentieth Century-Fox, 1975.

Dobie, *Nickelodeon,* Columbia, 1976.

George Arthur, *The Long Riders,* United Artists, 1980.

Dr. Emmer, *Endangered Species,* Metro-Goldwyn-Mayer/United Artists, 1982.

Mr. Anderson, *Gremlins,* Warner Bros., 1984.

Red, *Mask,* Universal, 1985.

George Martin, *UFOria,* Universal, 1985.

Bartender, *Crossroads,* Columbia, 1986.

Joshua Brackett, *The Whales of August,* Alive, 1987.

Snappy Tom, *Cherry 2000,* Orion, 1988.

Wally, *Illegally Yours,* Metro-Goldwyn-Mayer/United Artists, 1988.

C. J. Lee, *Bad Jim,* 1989.

Shoes, *Breaking In,* Samuel Goldwyn Company, 1989.

Saloon Old Timer, *Back to the Future III,* Universal, 1990.

Father Kanavan, *The Exorcist III,* Twentieth Century-Fox, 1990.

Marshall Fred White, *Tombstone,* Buena Vista, 1993.

Himself, *Ben Johnson: Third Cowboy On the Right* (documentary), FBN, 1996.

Cashier, *Sunchaser,* Warner Bros., 1996.

Howard Hawks: American Artist, BFI-TV, Bravo, DocStar, Museum of Modern Art Film & Video, 1997.

Television Appearances; Episodic:

Bill Burnett, "Spin and Marty," *The Mickey Mouse Club,* ABC, 1955.

Bill Burnett, "The Further Adventures of Spin and Marty," *The Mickey Mouse Club,* ABC, 1957.

Bill Burnett, "The New Adventures of Spin and Marty," *The Mickey Mouse Club,* ABC, 1958.

Deesah, "Horse Deal," *Gunsmoke,* CBS, 1959.

Turloe, "Bad Sheriff," *Gunsmoke,* CBS, 1961.

Jim Grant, "Quint Asper Comes Home," *Gunsmoke,* CBS, 1962.

Jake, "Abe Blocker," *Gunsmoke,* CBS, 1962.

"Horse of a Slightly Different Color," *Banacek,* NBC, 1974.

Josh, "Not to drop a Drink," *Knight Rider,* NBC, 1982.

"Auntie Sue," *B. L. Stryker,* ABC, 1989.

Appeared in *Little House on the Prairie,* NBC.

Television Appearances; Miniseries:

Ben Jenkins, "Texas John Slaughter," *Walt Disney Presents,* ABC, 1958-61.

Mr. Bond, *Black Beauty,* NBC, 1978.

Television Appearances; Pilots:

Deputy Luke, *Kate Bliss and the Ticker Tape Kid,* ABC, 1978.

Television Appearances; Movies:

Fitz Bragg, *Wild Times,* syndicated, 1980.

Pa Traven, *Louis L'Amour's the Shadow Riders* (also known as *The Shadow Riders*), CBS, 1982.

Herald Fitch, *Once upon a Texas Train,* CBS, 1988.

Sanford, *Last Stand at Saber River,* TNT, 1997.

Television Appearances; Specials:

John Wayne Standing Tall, 1989.

Host, *Legends of the American West,* Arts and Entertainment, 1992.

Also appeared in *Cowboys,* AMC; *GI Joe: The Ernie Pyle Story,* PBS; *John Ford's America,* AMC; *John Ford,* British Film Institute; and *John Wayne: The Unquiet American,* BBC.

WRITINGS

Memoirs:
Company of Heroes: My Life as an Actor in the John Ford Stock Company, Scarecrow Press (Metuchen, NJ), 1994.

CAREY, Ron 1935-

PERSONAL

Born Ronald J. Cicenia, December 11, 1935, in Newark, NJ; son of John and Fanny Cicenia; married Sharon Boyeronus, November 11, 1967. *Education:* Seton Hall University, B.A., 1958.

Career: Actor and stand-up comedian. Appeared in more than 100 television commercials.

Member: Screen Actors Guild, American Federation of Television and Radio Artists, Actors' Equity Association.

CREDITS

Film Appearances:
(Film debut) Boston cab driver, *The Out-of-Towners,* Paramount, 1970.
Part of group, *Made for Each Other,* Twentieth Century-Fox, 1971.
Bartender, *Who Killed Mary What's 'er Name?* (also known as *Death of a Hooker*), Cannon, 1971.
Dynamite Chicken, EYR, 1972.
Devour, *Silent Movie,* Twentieth Century-Fox, 1976.
Brophy, *High Anxiety,* Twentieth Century-Fox, 1977.
Frankie, *Fatso,* Twentieth Century-Fox, 1980.
Swiftus Lazarus, *History of the World, Part I,* Twentieth Century-Fox, 1981.
Pat, *Johnny Dangerously,* Twentieth Century-Fox, 1984.
Voice of Joe Dalton, *Lucky Luke: Daisy Town* (animated), Adriana Chiesa Enterprises, 1991.
Sheriff Fox, *Troublemakers,* 1995.
Robert Lambert, *Killer per caso* (also known as *The Good Bad Guy*), [Italy], 1997.

Television Appearances; Series:
Regular, *The Garry Moore Show,* CBS, 1966-67.
Regular, *The Melba Moore-Clifton Davis Show,* CBS, 1972.
Donald Hooten, *The Corner Bar,* ABC, 1973.
Frank Montefusco, *The Montefuscos,* NBC, 1975.
Officer Carl Levitt, *Barney Miller,* ABC, 1976-82.
Father Vincent Paglia, *Have Faith,* ABC, 1989.

Television Appearances; Pilots:
Regular, *Twentieth Century Follies,* ABC, 1972.
Monk, *Peeping Times,* NBC, 1978.
Johnny Antonizzio, *Johnny Garage,* CBS, 1983.
Hugo, *Pumpboys and Dinettes on Television,* NBC, 1983.

Television Appearances; Episodic:
Ben Braxton, Carol's Boss, *Empty Nest,* NBC, c. 1988.

Appeared on *The New Love, American Style,* ABC; *The Jack Paar Show,* NBC; *The Johnny Carson Show,* NBC; *The Merv Griffin Show,* syndicated; *The Mike Douglas Show,* syndicated; *The Steve Allen Show.*

Television Appearances; Specials:
The Wonderful World of Aggravation, ABC, 1972.
Acts of Love and Other Comedies, ABC, 1973.
ABC's Silver Anniversary Celebration—25 and Still the One, ABC, 1978.
Candid Camera . . . Funny Money, CBS, 1990.

Stage Appearances:
(Broadway Debut) Jerry, *Lovers and Other Strangers,* Brooks Atkinson Theatre, 1968.

RECORDINGS

Albums:
The Slightly Irreverent Comedy of Ron Carey, 1966.*

CARLISLE, Kevin 1935-

PERSONAL

Full name, Kevin Bruce Carlisle; born December 24, 1935, in Brooklyn, NY; son of Theodore Daily and Ruth (Bardell) Carlisle. *Education:* Juilliard School of Music, graduated, 1956.

Career: Director, producer, and choreographer. Solid Gold Dancers, creator, 1979; Kevin Carlisle and Associates, Hollywood, CA, president. Choreographer of numerous videos, including exercise videos for Debbie Reynolds and Suzanne Somers.

Member: Society of Stage Directors and Choreographers, Actors' Equity Association, American Federation of Television and Radio Artists, Directors Guild of America, Association of Canadian Television and Radio Artists, American Society of Composers, Authors, and Publishers.

Awards, Honors: Antoinette Perry Award nomination, best choreography, 1968, for *Hallelujah, Baby!*; Emmy Award, best choreography for a single episode of a special program, 1979, for *The 3rd Barry Manilow Television Special*; honorary doctorate, Sierra University, 1987.

CREDITS

Television Work; Specials; Producer, Director, and Choreographer, Except Where Indicated:
The Tony Awards Show, 1970.
The Academy Awards Show, 1972.
The Grammy Awards Show, 1973.
The Jerry Lewis Telethon, 1974, 1976.
Tokyo Music Festival, 1974, 1983.
The Junior Miss Pageant, 1974-78.
State Fair America, 1977.
The Great American Music Celebration, 1977.
The Rich Little Christmas Carol, 1978.
The 2nd Barry Manilow Special, 1978.
Choreographer, *The 3rd Barry Manilow Special,* 1979.
Choreographer, *Solid Gold '79,* 1980.
Tuscaloosa's Calling Me But I'm Not Going, 1980.
The Karen Morrow and Nancy Dussault Special, 1980.
The John Schneider Special, 1980.
Choreographer, *The Beatrice Arthur Special,* 1980.
Choreographer, *Barry Manilow: One Voice,* 1980.
Solid Gold Christmas Special, 1982.
Choreographer, *The Rainbow Girl,* 1982.
Battle of the Beat, 1983.
Choreographer, *Pump Boys and Dinettes on Television,* 1983.
The Debbie Reynolds Exercise Show, 1983.
Barry Manilow in Concert, Showtime, 1983.
Barry in Japan, TBS, 1983.
Barry at Blenheim, BBC, 1983.
The John Sebastian Special, 1986.
Producer and director, *What a Day for a Daydream,* The Disney Channel, 1986.
Director, *The Mother-Daughter Pageant, 1987,* syndicated, 1987.

Choreographer, *Barry Manilow: Big Fun on Swing Street,* 1988.
Producer and director, *Barry Manilow: SRO on Broadway,* Showtime, 1989.
Choreographer, *Julie and Carol: Together Again* (also known as *AT & T Presents*), ABC, 1989.
Director, *The Jaleel White Special,* ABC, 1992.

Also producer, director, and choreographer of *Disney Golf Classic Variety Special, Disney Thanksgiving Special, The Jim Nabors Show, The Smothers Brothers Show, Nobody's Perfect, The Singers, The Sonny and Cher Show, Music for a Winter's Night, The Bing Crosby Special, The Jonathan Winters Special, Tennessee Ernie Ford Christmas Special, The Monty Hall Special, The Brass Are Coming, The Don Ho Special, The Bob Hope Special, Jack Benny Specials, Dick Van Dyke Meets Bill Cosby, The Doris Day Special, The Jose Feliciano Special, The Dinah Shore Telethon, Bell Telephone Hour, Chevrolet Special, The Tony Bennett Special,* and *Gypsy Fever.*

Foreign specials include *A Christmas Carol,* CBC; *Vienna Ice Show, Carousel,* and *Wonderful Town,* Belgium; *Krona Circus,* Germany; *The Modern Jazz Quartet,* France; *Roy Castle,* England; *Sabato Serra,* Italy; *La Pelirroja, La tia de Carlos,* Mexico; *La Pelirroja,* Spain; and *Siempre Domingo,* Austria.

Television Work; Series; Producer, Director, and Choreographer, Except Where Indicated:
Coliseum Variety, CBS, 1967.
Dance director, *What's It All About, World?,* ABC, 1969.
Choreographer, *Cos,* ABC, 1976.
Choreographer, *The Peter Marshall Variety Show,* syndicated, 1977.
Choreographer, *Sha Na Na,* syndicated, 1978.
The New Quiz Kids, 1978.
The Little Show, 1978.
Choreographer, *Solid Gold,* syndicated, 1980-83.
Alice, CBS, 1984.
Benson, ABC, 1984.
Choreographer, *Dream Girl USA,* syndicated, 1986.

Also producer, director, and choreographer of *The Garry Moore Show,* CBS; *The Dean Martin Show,* NBC; and *The Glen Campbell Show.*

Stage Work:
Choreographer, *Hallejuh Baby!,* 1968.
Choreographer, *Barry Manilow on Broadway,* 1983.
Director, *Barry Manilow's Showstoppers,* Paramount Theatre, New York City, 1992.

Director and choreographer, *Lamb Chop on Broadway*, Richard Rodgers Theatre, New York City, 1994. Choreographer, *Wonderful Town*, Freud Playhouse, University of California at Los Angeles, 1997.

Choreographer for the Broadway productions *Happy Time; Hallelujah, Baby!;* and *Harry Blackstone, Jr. on Broadway;* producer, director, and choreographer for concerts, including *Kevin Carlisle's Sold Gold Dancers;* Paul Anka, 1983; *Barry Manilow-The Concert at Blenheim Palace;* Melissa Manchester, 1983, 1984; Tammy Wynette, 1984; *Solid Gold at Riviera Hotel, Las Vegas,* 1984, 1985; Marilyn McCoo and Billy Davis Jr., 1984; Marilyn McCoo, 1984-87; Robert Guillaume, 1985-87; Cathy Rigby, 1985-86; Ed Bruce; Charly McClain; Group with No Name; Shari Lewis; Holly Lipton; Lettermen; Hank Williams Jr.; Judy Garland; *An Evening with George Burns;* The Mike Curb Congregation; Joey Heatherton; Liberace; Steve Lawrence and Eydie Gorme; Connie Stevens; Shields and Yarnell; Karen Morrow and Nancy Dussault; Peter Marshall; and Janie Fricke.

Tour work includes Barry Manilow's national tour, 1979-85; Barry Manilow's international tour, 1979-85; Shaun Cassidy's national tour, 1979-80; and Harry Blackstone, Jr., 1980.

Film Work:

Choreographer, *The Pebble and the Penguin* (animated), Metro-Goldwyn-Mayer/United Artists, 1995.*

CARRADINE, Keith 1949-

PERSONAL

Full name, Keith Ian Carradine; born August 8, 1949, in San Mateo, CA; son of John Richmond Reed (an actor) and Sonia Sorel (an actress and artist; maiden name, Henius) Carradine; brother of David (an actor) and Robert (an actor); married Sandra Will, February 6, 1982; children: Martha Campbell Plimpton, Cade Richmond, Sorel. *Education:* Studied drama at Colorado State University, 1967. *Politics:* Democrat. *Religion:* Episcopalian.

Addresses: *Agent*—William Morris Agency, 151 El Camino Dr., Beverly Hills, CA 90212.

Career: Actor, singer, songwriter. Appeared in music video "Material Girl," by Madonna; also, voice-overs for commercials.

Member: Academy of Motion Picture Arts and Sciences, Greenpeace Foundation, Cousteau Society, Sierra Club.

Awards, Honors: Academy Award, best song, and Golden Globe Award, best original song for a motion picture, 1975, both for *I'm Easy,* from the motion picture *Nashville;* Emmy Award nomination, outstanding supporting actor in a limited series or special, 1983, for *Chiefs;* Outer Critics Circle award, outstanding debut, 1983, for *Foxfire;* Antoinette Perry Award nomination, best performance by a leading actor in a musical, 1991, for *The Will Rogers Follies.*

CREDITS

Film Appearances:
Young gunfighter, *A Gunfight,* Paramount, 1971.
Cowboy, *McCabe and Mrs. Miller,* Warner Bros., 1971.
Cigaret, *Emperor of the North Pole* (also known as *Emperor of the North*), Twentieth Century-Fox, 1973.
John, *Antoine et Sebastien,* 1973.
Whizzer, *Hex,* Twentieth Century-Fox, 1973.
Joe, *Run, Run, Joe!* (also known as *Arrivano Joe e Margherito* and *Joe y Margherito*), 1974.
Bowie, *Thieves Like Us,* United Artists, 1974.
Arthur, *Idaho Transfer,* Cinemation, 1975.
Tom Frank and song performer, *Nashville,* Paramount, 1975.
You and Me, 1975.
David Foster, *Lumiere,* New World, 1976.
Carroll Barber and song performer, *Welcome to L.A.,* United Artists, 1976.
Antione d'Hubert, *The Duellists,* Paramount, 1977.
E. J. Bellocq, *Pretty Baby,* Paramount, 1978.
Cameo, *Sgt. Pepper's Lonely Hearts Club Band,* Universal, 1978.
Hal, *An Almost Perfect Affair,* Paramount, 1979.
Wayne Vantil, *Old Boyfriends,* Avco-Embassy, 1979.
Jim Younger, *The Long Riders,* United Artists, 1980.
Rifleman Lee Spencer, *Southern Comfort,* Twentieth Century-Fox, 1981.
Mickey Bolton, *Choose Me,* Island Alive, 1984.
Clarence Butts and song performer, *Maria's Lovers,* Cannon, 1985.
Coop, *Trouble in Mind,* Alive, 1985.
Tauro, *L'Inchiesta* (title means "The Inquest;" also known as *The Investigation* and *The Inquiry*), Sacis, 1986.
Nick Hart, *The Moderns,* Alive, 1988.
Michael, *Street of No Return* (also known as *Sans Espoir de Retour*), President Films, 1988.

Reed, *Backfire,* Vidmark, 1989.

Clarence, *Daddy's Dyin'* . . . *Who's Got the Will?,* Metro-Goldwyn-Mayer/United Artists, 1990.

Monte Latham, *Cold Feet,* Avenue, 1990.

Doctor Emil Grasler, *The Bachelor* (also known as *Mio Caro Dottor Graeslaer*), Triboro Entertainment Group, 1990.

Marvin Macy, *The Ballad of the Sad Cafe,* Angelika Films, 1991.

John Cross, *Crisscross,* Metro-Goldwyn-Mayer, 1992.

Will Rogers, *Mrs. Parker and the Vicious Circle* (also known as *Mrs. Parker and the Round Table*), Fine Line Features, 1994.

Harry Whitney, *Andre* (also known as *Andre the Seal*), Paramount, 1994.

Buffalo Bill Cody, *Wild Bill* (also known as *Wild Bill Hickok* and *Deadwood*), Metro-Goldwyn-Mayer/United Artists, 1995.

John Netherwood, *The Tie that Binds,* Buena Vista, 1995.

Detective Creighton, *2 Days in the Valley,* Metro-Goldwyn-Mayer/United Artists, 1996.

Ty Smith, *A Thousand Acres,* Buena Vista, 1997.

Television Appearances; Movies:

Middle Caine, *Kung Fu,* ABC, 1972.

Danny Brown, *Man on a String,* CBS, 1972.

Lieutenant Lewis, *The Godchild,* ABC, 1974.

John Boslett, *Scorned and Swindled,* CBS, 1984.

Allen Devlin/Ed Vinson, *Blackout,* HBO, 1985.

Pete Gray, *A Winner Never Quits,* ABC, 1986.

J.J., *Half a Lifetime,* HBO, 1986.

Jim Lee, *Eye on the Sparrow,* NBC, 1987.

Richard Everton, *Stones for Ibarra,* CBS, 1988.

Elmo R. Zumwalt III, *My Father, My Son,* CBS, 1988.

Captain Tom Watkins, *The Forgotten,* USA Network, 1989.

Pierre Guitry, *Judgment* (also known as *Sacraments* and *Vermillion Parish*), HBO, 1990.

Liam Devlin, *Confessional,* syndicated, 1990.

Peter "Mac" MacAllister, *Payoff,* Showtime, 1991.

Brad, *Is There Life Out There?,* CBS, 1994.

Owen Turner, *Trial By Fire,* ABC, 1995.

Captain Eugene Slader, *Special Report: Journey to Mars,* CBS, 1996.

Vern Kidston, *Last Stand at Saber River,* TNT, 1997.

Will Hallowell, *Keeping the Promise* (also known as *The Oath*), CBS, 1997.

Television Appearances; Miniseries:

Lt. Murph McCoy, *A Rumor of War,* CBS, 1980.

Foxy Funderburke, *Chiefs,* CBS, 1983.

John Rule, *Murder Ordained* (also known as *Broken Commandments* and *Kansas Gothic*), CBS, 1987.

Agent Michael Rourke, *The Revenge of Al Capone,* NBC, 1989.

Tom Leary, *In the Best of Families: Marriage, Pride and Madness* (also known as *Bitter Blood*), CBS, 1994.

Bigfoot Wallace, *Larry McMurtry's Dead Man's Walk* (also known as *Dead Man's Walk*), ABC, 1996.

Television Appearances; Series:

Voice, *The West* (documentary), PBS, 1996.

Dr. Richard Beckett, *Fast Track,* 1997.

Television Appearances; Episodic:

(Television debut) Ern, "Bushwacked," *Bonanza,* NBC, 1971.

The Fall Guy, ABC, 1984.

An American Portrait, CBS, 1986.

Narrator, "Annie Oakley," *American Heroes and Legends,* 1992.

Arthur Bristol, "Dream of Doom," *Perversions of Science,* 1997.

Also appeared in *Love, American Style.*

Television Appearances; Specials:

The Meaning of Life, CBS, 1991.

Song performer, *The 14th Annual Kennedy Center Honors: A Celebration of the Performing Arts,* CBS, 1991.

Star-athon '92: A Weekend with the Stars, syndicated, 1992.

Voice of William Herndon, *Lincoln* (documentary), ABC, 1992.

Narrator, "Hot on the Trail," *The Untold West,* TBS, 1993.

Voiceover, *Baseball* (documentary), 1994.

Host, "Rediscovering Will Rogers," *American Masters,* PBS, 1994.

Host, *A Capitol Fourth (1996),* PBS, 1996.

Television Appearances; Awards Presentations:

The 45th Annual Tony Awards, CBS, 1991.

The 34th Annual Grammy Awards, CBS, 1992.

Song performer, *The 66th Annual Academy Awards Presentation,* ABC, 1994.

Presenter and song performer, *The Newsweek American Achievement Awards,* CBS, 1995.

Presenter, *The 18th Annual CableAce Awards,* TNT, 1996.

Television Work:

Executive producer, *The Forgotten,* USA Network, 1989.

Stage Appearances:

Claude, *Hair,* Los Angeles, CA, 1969.

(Broadway debut) Woof (understudy), *Hair,* Biltmore Theater, New York City, 1969-70.

Dude, *Tobacco Road,* Alhambra Dinner Theatre, Jacksonville, FL, 1970.

Orpheus, *Wake Up, It's Time to Go to Bed,* New York Shakespeare Festival, LuEsther Theater, New York City, 1979.

Benjamin Hubbard, *Another Part of the Forest,* Seattle Repertory Theatre, Seattle, WA, 1981-82.

Dillard Nations, *Foxfire,* Ethel Barrymore Theatre, New York City, 1982-83, later at Ahmanson Theatre, Los Angeles, CA, 1985-86.

Charlie, *Detective Story,* Center Theatre Group, Ahmanson Theatre, 1983-84.

Will Rogers, *The Will Rogers Follies,* Palace Theatre, New York City, 1991-92.

RECORDINGS

Albums:

I'm Easy, Asylum, 1977.

Lost and Found, Asylum, 1978.

Contributed music to the film *Welcome to L.A.*

WRITINGS

Film Music:

"I'm Easy," *Nashville,* Paramount, 1975.

Welcome to L.A., United Artists, 1976.

Lyricist, "Maria's Song," *Maria's Lovers,* Cannon, 1985.

OTHER SOURCES

Periodicals:

New York Times, April 7, 1977.*

CARTWRIGHT, Veronica 1950-

PERSONAL

Born April 20, 1950, in Bristol (some sources say Altringham, Cheshire), England; married Richard Compton (a writer and director), October, 1982; sister of Angela Cartwright (an actress [*Lost in Space* TV series]). *Education:* Studied acting with Jack Garfein and Stephen Book.

Addresses: *Agent*—Metropolitan Talent Agency, 4526 Wilshire Blvd., Los Angeles, CA 90010-3801.

Career: Actress.

Awards, Honors: Emmy Award for *Tell Me Not in Mournful Numbers.*

CREDITS

Film Appearances:

(Film debut) Allie O'Neill, *In Love and War,* Twentieth Century-Fox, 1958.

Rosalie, *The Children's Hour* (also known as *The Loudest Whisper*), United Artists, 1961.

Cathy Brenner, *The Birds,* Universal, 1963.

Becky Spencer, *Spencer's Mountain,* Warner Bros., 1963.

Mary, *One Man's Way,* United Artists, 1964.

Harlene, *Inserts,* United Artists, 1975.

Hermine, *Goin' South,* Paramount, 1978.

Nancy Bellicec, *Invasion of the Body Snatchers,* United Artists, 1978.

Lambert, *Alien,* Twentieth Century-Fox, 1979.

Betty Grissom, *The Right Stuff,* Warner Bros., 1983.

Claire Houston, "Night of the Rat," *Nightmares,* Universal, 1983.

Elaine Swit, *My Man Adam,* 1985.

Helen Freeman, *The Flight of the Navigator,* Buena Vista, 1986.

Samantha Wisdom, *Wisdom,* Twentieth Century-Fox, 1986.

Felicia Alden, *The Witches of Eastwick,* Warner Bros., 1987.

Patricia Gibbs, *Valentino Returns,* Skouras, 1989.

Vera Errickson, *False Identity,* 1990.

Walking the Dog, 1991.

Helen Dextra, *Man Trouble,* Twentieth Century-Fox, 1992.

Sister Aja, *Mirror, Mirror 2: Raven Dance,* Orphan Entertainment, 1994.

Octavia Tarrant, *Candyman: Farewell to the Flesh* (also known as *Candyman 2*), Gramercy Pictures, 1995.

Connie Cipriani, *Money Talks,* New Line, 1997.

Television Appearances; Movies:

Marceline Jones, *Guyana Tragedy: The Story of Jim Jones* (also known as *The Mad Messiah*), CBS, 1980.

Sister Theresa, *The Big Black Pill* (also known as *Joe Dancer*), NBC, 1981.

Janice Staplin, *Prime Suspect,* CBS, 1982.

Still the Beaver, The Disney Channel, 1983.

Emily, *Intimate Encounters* (also known as *Encounters in the Night*), NBC, 1986.

Betty Petrie, *Desperate for Love* (also known as *Dying for Love*), CBS, 1989.

Dorothy Donaldson, *A Son's Promise* (also known as *The O'Kelley Brothers, Fire in the Heart,* and *The Terry O'Kelley Story*), ABC, 1990.

Patricia Benedict, *Hitler's Daughter,* USA Network, 1990.

Victoria Haines, *Dead in the Water,* USA Network, 1991.

Barbara, *It's Nothing Personal,* NBC, 1993.

Carla Hulin, *Triumph over Disaster: The Hurricane Andrew Story,* NBC, 1993.

The caller, *Dead Air* (also known as *Hit Radio*), USA Network, 1994.

Pat, *My Brother's Keeper,* CBS, 1995.

Mrs. Dunbar, *The Lottery,* NBC, 1996.

Myra, *Quicksilver Highway* (also known as *Chattery Teeth* and *The Body Politic*), Fox, 1997.

Television Appearances; Episodic:

Violet Rutherford, *Leave It to Beaver,* ABC, 1960.

Agatha, "I Sing the Body Electric," *Twilight Zone,* CBS, 1962.

Margaret Flanagan, *L.A. Law,* NBC, 1986.

Reporter, "Bagels with Bruce," *Tanner '88* (also known as *Tanner: A Political Fable*), HBO, 1988.

Reporter, "Moonwalker and Bookbag," *Tanner '88* (also known as *Tanner: A Political Fable*), HBO, 1988.

Reporter, "Night of the Twinkies," *Tanner '88* (also known as *Tanner: A Political Fable*), HBO, 1988.

Angela, "Dr. Death Takes a Holiday," *American Gothic,* CBS, 1995.

Betty, *Boston Common,* NBC, 1996.

Mrs. Huston, "Whose Appy Now?," *ER,* NBC, 1996.

Appeared in episodes of *Alcoa Presents* (also known as *One Step Beyond*), ABC; *Dragnet,* NBC; *The Mod Squad,* ABC; *The Name of the Game,* NBC; *Still the Beaver,* Disney; and *Alfred Hitchcock Presents.*

Television Appearances; Specials:

Kiri Rudek, *Who Has Seen the Wind?,* ABC, 1965.

Marjorie, *Bernice Bobs Her Hair,* PBS, 1976.

Caroline Morris, "Abby, My Love," *CBS Schoolbreak Specials,* CBS, 1991.

The Horror Hall of Fame II, syndicated, 1991.

Woman in grocery, "On Hope," *Directed By,* Showtime, 1994.

Molly, "Two Over Easy," *Showtime 30-Minute Movie,* Showtime, 1994.

Also appeared in *Tell Me Not in Mournful Numbers.*

Other Television Appearances:

Jemimia Boone, *Daniel Boone* (series), NBC, 1964-66.

Ethel Kennedy, *Robert Kennedy and His Times* (miniseries), CBS, 1985.

Stage Appearances:

Diane Newbury, *The Hands of Its Enemies,* Mark Taper Forum, Los Angeles, 1984.

"Mirror, Mirror," *The Triplet Connection,* Matrix Theatre, Los Angeles, 1985.

Aline Solness, *The Master Builder,* Hartford Stage Company, Hartford, CT, 1990-91.

Appeared as Sally Talley, *Talley's Folly,* Denver, CO; and in *Electra, Homesteaders,* and *Butterflies Are Free.**

CARVEY, Dana   1955-

PERSONAL

Born April 2, 1955, in Missoula, MT; married Paula Zwaggerman; children: Dex, Tom. *Education:* Studied communication arts at San Francisco State University.

Addresses: *Agent*—International Creative Management, 8942 Wilshire Blvd., Beverly Hills, CA 90211.

Career: Actor and stand-up comedian. Stand-up comedian in San Francisco and Los Angeles, CA.

Awards, Honors: Emmy Award nominations, outstanding individual performance in a variety or music program, 1989, 1990, and 1991, and American Comedy Awards, funniest supporting male in television, George Schlatter Productions, 1989, 1990, and 1991, all for *Saturday Night Live;* American Comedy Award, TV's Funniest Supporting Male Performer, 1990, 1991; Emmy Award, outstanding individual performance in a variety or music program, 1993, for *Saturday Night Live's Presidential Bash;* Emmy Award nomination, outstanding guest actor in a comedy series, 1993, for "Guest Host," *The Larry Sanders Show;* winner of San Francisco Stand-Up Comedy Competition.

CREDITS

Television Appearances; Series:

Adam Shields, *One of the Boys,* NBC, 1982.

Clinton "Jafo" Wonderlove, *Blue Thunder*, ABC, 1984.
Saturday Night Live, NBC, 1986-93.
The Dana Carvey Show, ABC, 1996.

Television Appearances; Pilots:
Michael Elliott, *Alone at Last*, NBC, 1980.
Simon, *Whacked Out*, NBC, 1981.

Television Appearances; Episodic:
"Guest Host," *The Larry Sanders Show*, HBO, 1992.
"Hank's New Assistant," *The Larry Sanders Show*, HBO, 1995.

Also appeared on *Dennis Miller Live*.

Television Appearances; Specials:
Comic Relief II, HBO, 1987.
Elliot Clinton, *Slickers*, NBC, 1987.
Host, *Superman's 50th Anniversary: A Celebration of the Man of Steel*, CBS, 1988.
Saturday Night Live 15th Anniversary, NBC, 1989.
The Tonight Show Starring Johnny Carson: 28th Anniversary Special, NBC, 1990.
Comic Relief IV, HBO, 1990.
Host/Garth, *Saturday Night Live Halloween Special*, NBC, 1991.
Saturday Night Live Goes Commercial, NBC, 1991.
The 19th Annual American Film Institute Life Achievement Award: A Salute to Kirk Douglas, CBS, 1991.
Lyle, *Toonces, The Cat Who Could Drive a Car* (also known as *Toonces and Friends*), NBC, 1992.
Back to School '92, CBS, 1992.
Host, *Saturday Night Live's Presidential Bash* (also known as *Saturday Night Live: Election Special*), NBC, 1992.
Saturday Night Live: All the Best for Mother's Day, NBC, 1992.
Host, *The 15th Annual Young Comedians Show—Hosted by Dana Carvey*, HBO, 1992.
1993: A Year at the Movies, CNBC, 1993.
Garth, *Wayne and Garth's Saturday Night Live Music a Go-Go*, NBC, 1993.
Dana Carvey: Critics' Choice, HBO, 1995.
Who Makes You Laugh?, ABC, 1995.

Also appeared on *Salute to the Improvisation* and *Superbowl of Comedy*.

Television Appearances; Awards Presentations:
The 2nd Annual American Comedy Awards, ABC, 1988.
The 41st Annual Emmy Awards, Fox, 1989.

The 4th Annual American Comedy Awards, ABC, 1990.
MTV's 1991 Video Music Awards, MTV, 1991.
1992 MTV Video Music Awards, MTV, 1992.
MTV Movie Awards, MTV, 1992.
The 64th Annual Academy Awards Presentation, ABC, 1992.
The 1993 Billboard Music Awards, Fox, 1993.

Television Work; Series:
Executive producer, *The Dana Carvey Show*, ABC, 1996.

Film Appearances:
Assistant, *Halloween II*, Universal, 1981.
Baby Face, *Racing with the Moon*, Paramount, 1984.
Mime waiter, *This Is Spinal Tap*, Embassy, 1984.
Richie Evans, *Tough Guys*, Buena Vista, 1986.
Brad Williams, *Moving*, Warner Bros., 1988.
Eddie Farrell, *Opportunity Knocks*, Universal, 1990.
Garth Algar, *Wayne's World*, Paramount, 1992.
Garth Algar, *Wayne's World 2*, Paramount, 1993.
Maurice Pogue, *Clean Slate* (also known as *Cool Slate*), Metro-Goldwyn-Mayer/United Artists, 1994.
Alvin Firpo, *Trapped in Paradise*, Fox Video, 1994.
George Kellogg, *The Road to Wellville*, Columbia, 1994.
Himself, *The Shot*, Bread and Water Productions, 1994.

WRITINGS

For Television:
(With others) *Saturday Night Live's Presidential Bash* (also known as *Saturday Night Live: Election Special*), NBC, 1992.
Dana Carvey: Critics' Choice, HBO, 1995.

OTHER SOURCES

Periodicals:
Entertainment Weekly, May 13, 1994, pp. 14-15.
Gentlemen's Quarterly, August, 1989, p. 230.
People Weekly, May 4, 1987, p. 101.
Rolling Stone, October 22, 1987, p. 29; May 13, 1993, pp. 47-52.
San Francisco, May, 1981, p. 61.*

CATES, Phoebe   1963(?)-

PERSONAL

Born July 16, 1963 (some sources say 1964), in New York, NY; daughter of Joseph Cates (a television producer and director); niece of Gilbert Cates (a producer and director); married Kevin Kline (an actor), March 5, 1989; children: Owen Joseph, Greta. *Education:* Attended Professional Children's School; attended Julliard School; studied with Actors Circle theatre group; studied ballet.

Addresses: *Agent*—William Morris Agency, 151 El Camino Dr., Beverly Hills, CA 90212.

Career: Actress. Worked as a model prior to 1984.

Member: Screen Actors Guild.

CREDITS

Film Appearances:
Linda Barrett, *Fast Times at Ridgemont High,* Universal, 1982.
Sarah, *Paradise,* Embassy, 1982.
Christine Ramsay, *Private School,* Universal, 1983.
Kate, *Gremlins,* Warner Bros., 1984.
Patty Winston, *Date with an Angel,* DEG, 1987.
Amanda, *Bright Lights, Big City,* Metro-Goldwyn-Mayer/United Artists, 1988.
Carson McBride, *Shag: The Movie* (also known as *Shag*), TriStar, 1988.
Aiken Reed, *Heart of Dixie,* TriStar, 1990.
Kate Beringer, *Gremlins 2: The New Batch,* Warner Bros., 1990.
Woman at discotheque bar, *I Love You to Death,* TriStar, 1990.
Elizabeth Cronin, *Drop Dead Fred,* New Line Cinema, 1991.
Carol, *Bodies, Rest and Motion* (also known as *Bodies, Rest & Motion*), Fine Line Features, 1993.
Herself, *My Life's in Turnaround,* Arrow Releasing, 1994.
Title role and Mary, *Princess Caraboo,* TriStar, 1994.

Film Work:
Performer of songs "How Do I Let You Know" and "Just One Touch," *Private School,* Universal, 1983.

Television Appearances; Movies:
Annie Burroughs, *Baby Sister,* ABC, 1983.

Television Appearances; Miniseries:
Lilli, *Lace,* ABC, 1984.
Lilli, *Lace 2,* ABC, 1985.

Television Appearances; Episodic:
Entertainment Tonight, syndicated, 1989.

Marguerite, "Vaclav Havel's Largo Desolato," *Great Performances,* PBS, 1990.

Television Appearances; Awards Presentations:
The 63rd Annual Academy Awards Presentation, ABC, 1991.

Television Appearances; Series:
Appeared in *Mr. and Mrs. Dracula.*

Stage Appearances:
Ariadna Koromyslova, *The Nest of the Wood Grouse,* New York Shakespeare Festival, Public Theatre, New York City, 1984.
Jill, *Rich Relations,* Second Stage Theatre, New York City, 1985.
Rosaria, *Women and Football,* Manhattan Punch Line, New York City, 1988.
Juliet, *Romeo and Juliet,* Goodman Theatre, Chicago, IL, 1988.
Hero, *Much Ado about Nothing,* New York Shakespeare Festival, New York City, 1988.
Evelyn Foreman, *The Tenth Man,* Vivian Beaumont Theatre, New York City, 1989.

OTHER SOURCES

Periodicals:
New York Post, June 28, 1984.
People Weekly, June 14, 1982, p. 36.*

CHER 1946-

PERSONAL

Full name, Cherilyn Sarkisian LaPiere; born May 20, 1946, in El Centro, CA; daughter of John Sarkisian and Georgia Holt (a model and actress); married Sonny Bono (a singer, restaurateur, and politician), October 27, 1964 (some sources say 1969; divorced, May 1975, some sources say February 20, 1974); married Gregg Allman (a musician), June, 1975 (divorced); children: (first marriage) Chastity; (second marriage) Elijah Blue. *Education:* Trained for the stage with Jeff Corey.

Addresses: *Agent*—International Creative Management, 8942 Wilshire Blvd., Beverly Hills, CA 90211.

Career: Actress and singer. Began career as backup singer for the Crystals and Ronettes; appeared with Sonny Bono as Caesar and Cleo, then as Sonny and

Cher, beginning in 1964; recorded and performed in duo Sonny and Cher, 1964-75 and 1977; member of rock band Black Rose, 1979-80; performer in night clubs in Las Vegas and Atlantic City. Head of independent film company, Isis Productions. Has appeared in commercials and infomercials. Sanctuary (catalog sales company), founder, 1994.

Awards, Honors: Grammy Award nomination, best female pop vocal, National Academy of Recording Arts and Sciences, 1971, for "Gypsies, Tramps, and Thieves;" Emmy Award nominations, outstanding single variety or musical program, 1972, and best variety musical series, 1972, 1973 and 1974, all for *The Sonny and Cher Comedy Hour;* Golden Globe Award, best actress in a television comedy or musical, Hollywood Foreign Press Association, 1974, for *The Sonny and Cher Comedy Hour;* Emmy Award nomination, best comedy-variety or music series, 1975, for *Cher.*

Academy Award nomination, best supporting actress, and Golden Globe Award, best actress in a supporting role in a motion picture, both 1983, for *Silkwood;* Palm d'Or, best actress, Cannes Film Festival, 1985, for *Mask;* Hasty Pudding Woman of the Year Award, 1985; Academy Award, best actress, and Golden Globe Award, best actress in a motion picture comedy or musical, both 1987, for *Moonstruck;* Golden Globe Award nomination, best performance by an actress in a supporting role in a series, miniseries, or motion picture, 1997, for *If These Walls Could Talk.*

CREDITS

Film Appearances:
Herself, *Good Times,* Columbia, 1967.
Title role, *Chastity,* American International, 1969.
Sissy, *Come Back to the Five and Dime, Jimmy Dean, Jimmy Dean,* Viacom, 1982.
Dolly Pelliker, *Silkwood,* Twentieth Century-Fox, 1983.
Rusty Dennis, *Mask,* Universal, 1985.
Kathleen Riley, *Suspect,* TriStar, 1987.
Alexandra Medford, *The Witches of Eastwick,* Warner Bros., 1987.
Loretta Castorini, *Moonstruck,* Metro-Goldwyn-Mayer/United Artists, 1987.
Rachel Flax, *Mermaids,* Orion, 1990.
As herself, *The Player,* Fine Line, 1992.
As herself, *Ready to Wear (Pret-a-Porter),* Miramax, 1994.
Margaret O'Donnell, *Faithful,* New Line, 1996.

Film Work; Song Performer:
"Alfie," *Alfie,* Paramount, 1966.
Die Kleine Welt, 1977.
"Bad Love," *Foxes,* United Artists, 1980.
"The Beat Goes on," *Dear America: Letters Home from Vietnam,* 1987.
"I Got You Babe," *Buster,* 1988.
"After All," *Chances Are,* TriStar, 1989.
"Trail of Broken Hearts," *Days of Thunder,* Paramount, 1990.
"I Got You Babe," *Look Who's Talking Too,* TriStar, 1990.
"It's in His Kiss (The Shoop Shoop Song)" and "Baby I'm Yours," *Mermaids,* Orion, 1990.

Television Appearances; Series:
Host, *The Sonny and Cher Comedy Hour,* CBS, 1971-74.
Host, *Cher,* CBS, 1975-76.
Host, *The Sonny and Cher Show,* CBS, 1976-77.

Television Appearances; Specials:
Where the Girls Are, NBC, 1968.
Third wife, *The First Nine Months Are the Hardest,* NBC, 1971.
How to Handle a Woman, NBC, 1972.
Host, *Cher,* CBS, 1975.
The Flip Wilson Special, NBC, 1975.
Host, *Cher . . . Special,* ABC, 1978.
Host, *Cher and Other Fantasies,* NBC, 1979.
Tom Snyder's Celebrity Spotlight, NBC, 1980.
Host, *Cher—A Celebration at Caesar's Palace,* Showtime, 1983.
The Barbara Walters Special, ABC, 1985.
Bugs Bunny/Looney Tunes All-Star 50th Anniversary, 1986.
Superstars & Their Moms, ABC, 1987.
Pee-Wee's Playhouse Christmas Special, 1988.
The Barbara Walters Special, ABC, 1988.
Comic Relief III, HBO, 1989.
An Evening with Bette, Cher, Goldie, Meryl, Olivia, Lily, and Robin, 1990.
Cher . . . at the Mirage, CBS, 1991.
Host, *Cher's Video Canteen,* 1991.
Host, *Coca-Cola Pop Music "Backstage Pass to Summer,"* 1991.
Dame Edna's Hollywood, 1991.
Host, *MTV's 10th Anniversary Special,* MTV, 1991.
In a New Light, ABC, 1992.
The Grand Opening of Euro Disney, CBS, 1992.
Tina Turner: Going Home, The Disney Channel, 1993.
What Is This Thing Called Love? (also known as *The Barbara Walters Special*), ABC, 1993.

The American Film Institute Salute to Jack Nicholson, CBS, 1994.
Happy Birthday Elizabeth—A Celebration of Life, ABC, 1997.

Television Work: Specials:
"Love and Understanding," *Cher . . . At The Mirage,* CBS, 1991.

Television Appearances; Episodic:
(With Sonny Bono) *Shindig,* ABC, 1964.
ABC in Concert, ABC, 1991.
London Underground, 1991.
The RuPaul Show, VH1, 1996.

Appeared with Sonny Bono on *Love, American Style,* ABC, and *Hullabaloo,* NBC; performed as voice for "Sonny and Cher," *The New Scooby-Doo Comedy Movies;* also appeared in episodes of *The Man from U.N.C.L.E., Hollywood Palace, Laugh-In,* and *Glen Campbell.*

Television Appearances; Movies:
Dr. Beth Thompson ("1996" segment), *If These Walls Could Talk,* HBO, 1996.

Television Work; Movies:
Director, "1996" segment, and song performer, "One by One," *If These Walls Could Talk,* HBO, 1996.

Television Appearances; Awards Presentations:
Presenter, *The 58th Annual Academy Awards Presentation,* 1986.
MTV's 1988 Video Music Awards, MTV, 1988.
The 60th Annual Academy Awards Presentation, 1988.
MTV's 1989 Video Music Awards, MTV, 1989.
The 61st Annual Academy Awards Presentation, 1989.
Presenter, *MTV's 1991 Video Music Awards,* MTV, 1991.
The 1991 Billboard Music Awards, 1991.

Stage Appearances:
Come Back to the Five and Dime, Jimmy Dean, Jimmy Dean, Martin Beck Theatre, New York City, 1982.

RECORDINGS

Albums; With Sonny Bono, Except Where Indicated:
Look at Us, Atco, 1965.
Baby Don't Go, Reprise, 1965.
Wondrous World, Atco, 1966.

In Case You're in Love, Atlantic, 1967.
Good Times, Atlantic, 1967.
The Best of Sonny and Cher, Atlantic, 1968.
Sonny & Cher Live, Kapp, 1969, re-released, MCA, 1972.
All I Ever Need Is You, Kapp, 1971, re-released, MCA, 1975.
Live in Las Vegas, MCA, 1974.
Greatest Hits, MCA, 1975.
The Beat Goes On, Atco, 1975.
(With Black Rose) *Black Rose,* Casablanca, 1980.
(Contributor) *For Our Children Too!,* 1996.

Singles with Sonny Bono include "I Got You Babe" and "You Better Sit Down Kids"; also recorded single "After All" (theme song from the film *Chances Are*), with Peter Cetera, 1989.

Solo Albums:
All I Really Want to Do, Imperial, 1965.
Sonny Side of Cher, Imperial, 1966.
With Love, Imperial, 1966.
Cher, Imperial, 1967.
Backstage, Imperial, 1968.
Golden Greats, 1968.
3614 Jackson Highway, Atco, 1969.
Cher, Kapp, 1972.
Foxy Lady, MCA, 1972.
Hits of Cher, United Artists, 1972.
Bittersweet White Light, MCA, 1973.
Dark Lady, MCA, 1974.
Half Breed, MCA, 1974.
Stars, Warner Bros., 1975.
Greatest Hits, MCA, 1975.
I'd Rather Believe in You, Warner Bros., 1977.
Cherished, Warner Bros., 1977.
Take Me Home, Casablanca, 1978.
Prisoner, Casablanca, 1979.
The Best of Cher, EMI America, 1987.
Cher, Geffen, 1988.
Heart of Stone, Geffen, 1989.
Love Hurts, Geffen, 1991.
Bang Bang and Other Hits, Capitol, 1992.
It's a Man's World, 1996.
Cher: The Casablanca Years, 1996.

Also recorded *This Is Cher,* Sunset; *Cher Sings the Hits,* Springboard; *Greatest Hits,* Springboard; *Live; The Two of Us; Allman and Woman;* and *You Better Sit Down Kids.* Singles include "Gypsies, Tramps and Thieves," "Dark Lady," "Take Me Home," "Half Breed," "I Found Someone," and "It's in His Kiss (The Shoop Shoop Song)."

WRITINGS

(With Robert Haas) *Forever Fit: The Lifetime Plan for Health, Beauty, and Fitness,* Bantam (New York City), 1991.

(With Andrew Ennis and Joan Nielsen) *Cooking for Cher,* Simon and Schuster (New York City), 1997.

OTHER SOURCES

Books:

Goodall, Nigel, *Cher in Her Own Words,* Omnibus Press (London), 1992.

Jacobs, Linda, *Cher: Simply Cher,* EMC Corp. (St. Paul, MN), 1975.

Petrucelli, Rita, *Cher: Singer and Actress,* illustrated by Luciano Lazzarino, Rourke Enterprises (Vero Beach, FL), 1989.

Taraborrelli, J. Randy, *Cher: A Biography,* St. Martin's Press (New York City), 1986.

Periodicals:

Entertainment Weekly, May 31, 1996, p. 22.
Interview, October, 1994, p. 172.
Ladies Home Journal, November, 1996, p. 178.
New York Times, March 20, 1988.
People, January 21, 1991.
Premier, February, 1988.*

CHONG, Thomas
   See CHONG, Tommy

CHONG, Tommy   1938-
   (Thomas Chong)

PERSONAL

Born May 24, 1938, in Edmonton, Alberta, Canada; son of Stanley (a truck driver) and Lorna Jean (a waitress; maiden name, Gilchrist) Chong; married, second wife's name Shelby; children: Rae Dawn and Robbi (actresses), Precious, Paris, Gilbran.

Career: Actor, writer, director, comedian, and musician. Member of the musical groups the Shades and Bobby Taylor and the Vancouvers; City Works (improvisational comedy troupe), founder and performer; with Richard "Cheech" Marin, member of comedy duo Cheech and Chong, 1969-85.

Awards, Honors: Grammy Award, best comedy album, National Academy of Recording Arts and Sciences, 1973, for *Los Cochinos.*

CREDITS

Film Appearances:

Man Stoner, *Up in Smoke,* Paramount, 1978.

Chong, *Cheech and Chong's Next Movie* (also known as *High Encounters of the Ultimate Kind*), Universal, 1980.

Chong, *Cheech and Chong's Nice Dreams,* Columbia, 1981.

Chong, Prince Habib, *Things Are Tough All Over,* Columbia, 1982.

Chong, *Still Smokin'* (also known as *Cheech and Chong's Still Smokin'*), Paramount, 1983.

El Nebuloso, *Yellowbeard,* Orion, 1983.

It Came From Hollywood, Paramount, 1983.

Corsican Brother, *The Corsican Brothers* (also known as *Cheech and Chong's The Corsican Brothers*), Orion, 1984.

Pepe, *After Hours,* Warner Bros., 1985.

The Canadian Conspiracy, 1986.

The Tommy Chong Roast (also known as *Playboy Comedy Roast—Tommy Chong*), 1986.

Title role, *Far Out Man* (also known as *Soul Man II*), CineTel, 1990.

Merle Shine, *Tripwire,* Columbia Home Video, 1990.

Stoner, *The Spirit of '76,* SVS/Triumph Home Video, 1991.

Life after Sex, 1991.

Voice of Root, *Ferngully: The Last Rainforest* (animated), Twentieth Century-Fox, 1992.

Red, *National Lampoon's Senior Trip,* New Line, 1995.

Armando/Ernesto, *McHale's Navy,* Universal, 1997.

Squirrel Master, *Half Baked,* Universal, 1998.

Film Work; Director:

Cheech and Chong's Next Movie (also known as *High Encounters of the Ultimate Kind*), Universal, 1980.

Cheech and Chong's Nice Dreams, Columbia, 1981.

Still Smokin' (also known as *Cheech and Chong's Still Smokin'*), Paramount, 1983.

The Corsican Brothers (also known as *Cheech and Chong's The Corsican Brothers*), Orion, 1984.

Far Out Man (also known as *Soul Man II*), CineTel, 1990.

Television Appearances; Specials:

Cheech and Chong: Get out of My Room, 1985.

Baloney, CBC, 1989.

Television Appearances; Episodic:
"Trust Fund Pirates," *Miami Vice,* NBC, 1986.
Van Elsinger, "Stoker," *Sliders,* Fox, 1997.
Barry Chen, "Wild Cards," *Nash Bridges,* CBS, 1997.

Television Work; Specials:
Executive producer, *The Family Martinez,* 1986.

Television Work; Series:
Executive producer, *Trial and Error,* CBS, 1988.

WRITINGS

Screenplays:
(With Richard "Cheech" Marin) *Up in Smoke,* Paramount, 1978.
(With Marin) *Cheech and Chong's Next Movie* (also known as *High Encounters of the Ultimate Kind*), Universal, 1980.
(With Marin) *Cheech and Chong's Nice Dreams,* Columbia, 1981.
(As Thomas Chong; with Marin) *Things Are Tough All Over,* Columbia, 1982.
(With Marin) *Still Smokin'* (also known as *Cheech and Chong's Still Smokin'*), Paramount, 1983.
(With Marin) *The Corsican Brothers* (also known as *Cheech and Chong's The Corsican Brothers*), Orion, 1984.
(And songwriter) *Far Out Man* (also known as *Soul Man II*), CineTel, 1990.

Television Specials:
The Family Martinez, 1986.

Other:
Songwriter, "Up in Smoke," 1978.

RECORDINGS

Albums; with Cheech and Chong:
Big Bambu, Warner Bros. Records, 1972.
Cheech and Chong, Ode Records, 1972.
Los Cochinos, Reprise, 1973.
The Wedding Album, Reprise, 1974.
Sleeping Beauty, Warner Bros. Records, 1976.
Let's Make a New Dope Deal, Warner Bros. Records, 1987.
Get Out of My Room, MCA Records, 1987.
Cheech and Chong's Greatest Hit, Reprise, 1991.

OTHER SOURCES

Books:
Contemporary Authors, Volume 112, Gale, 1985.

Periodicals:
People Weekly, December 23, 1996, p. 57.*

CHUNG, Connie   1946-

PERSONAL

Full name, Constance Yu-Hwa Chung; born August 20, 1946, in Washington, DC; daughter of William Ling (a financial manager and former diplomat) and Margaret (Ma) Chung; married Maury Povich (a talk show host), December 2, 1984; children: Matthew Jay. *Education:* University of Maryland, B.S. (journalism), 1969.

Addresses: *Home*—New York City. *Manager*—Geller Media Management, 250 West 57th St., Suite 213, New York, NY 10019.

Career: Broadcast journalist and writer. WTTG-TV, Washington, DC, department news secretary, then editor and news reporter, 1969-71; Columbia Broadcasting System (CBS-TV), CBS News, Washington, DC, radio and television news correspondent, 1971-76; KNXT-TV (became KCBS-TV), Los Angeles, CA, news anchor, reporter, and substitute anchor for *CBS Morning News,* 1976-83; National Broadcasting Company (NBC-TV), New York City, news anchor and reporter, 1983-89, co-host of television news magazines, 1985-86; CBS News, New York City, news anchor, reporter, and host of television news magazines, 1989-95; Shorenstein Center on the Press, Politics and Public Policy, John F. Kennedy School of Government, Harvard University, Cambridge, MA, fellow, 1997; American Broadcasting Corporation (ABC-TV), correspondent, reporter, substitute anchor, 1997—.

Awards, Honors: Certificate of Achievement, United States Humane Society, 1969, for series of broadcasts that enhanced public awareness of cruelty in seal hunting; Metro Area Mass Media Award, Association of American University Women, 1971; National Association of Media Women Award, Atlanta Chapter, 1973; Outstanding Excellence in News Reporting and Public Service Award, Chinese-American Citizens Alliance, 1973; honorary doctorate in journalism, Norwich University, 1974; Woman of Distinction Award, Golden Slipper Club (Philadelphia, PA), 1975; nominated for Woman of the Year, *Ladies Home Journal,* 1975; Outstanding Young Woman of the Year, *Ladies Home Journal,* 1975; Best

Television Reporting Award, KNXT-TV and L.A. Press Club, 1977; Outstanding Television Broadcasting Award, Valley Press Club, 1977; Golden Mike award, 1978, for best documentary; Emmy Awards for individual achievement, 1978, 1980, and 1987; Best News Broadcast, Women in Communications Award, California State University, Los Angeles, CA, 1979; Mark Twain trophy, California Associated Press, Television, and Radio Association, 1979; George Foster Peabody Award, 1980, for *Terra Our World;* Newscaster of the Year Award, Temple Emanuel Brotherhood, 1981; Portraits of Excellence Award, B'nai B'rith, Pacific Southwest Region, 1981; First Amendment Award, Anti-Defamation League of B'nai B'rith, 1981; Best Newscast (6:00 p.m.), Associated Press and California Associated Press, Television, and Radio Association, both 1981; Golden Mike award, 1981, best news broadcast.

Mr. Blackwell's Fashion Independents, 1983; Women in Business award, 1983; Los Angeles Press Club award, 1983, for 4:30 p.m. news broadcast; Honorary doctorate of humanities, Brown University, 1987; Emmy Award, 1987, for "Shot in Hollywood," *1986;* honorary doctorate in journalism, Providence College, 1988; honorary doctorate of laws, Wheaton College, 1989; Emmy Award, outstanding interview, 1989; Emmy Award, outstanding interview, 1990; Silver Gavel Award, American Bar Association, 1991; Ohio State of Achievement of Merit Award, 1991; National Headliner Award, National Conference of Christians and Jews, 1991; Clarion Award, Women in Communications, 1991; first female co-anchor of *CBS Evening News,* 1993.

CREDITS

Television Appearances; News Reporter:
Anchor and reporter, *NBC Nightly News,* NBC, 1983-89.
Anchor and reporter, *Today Show,* NBC, 1983-89.
Anchor and reporter, *News Digest,* NBC, 1983-89.
Anchor and reporter, *NBC News at Sunrise,* NBC, 1983-89.
Chief correspondent, *American Almanac,* NBC, 1985.
Co-host, *1986* (news magazine), NBC, 1986.
Reporter, *CBS Evening News,* CBS, 1989-93.
Host, *Saturday Night with Connie Chung* (series; originally *West 57th Street*), CBS, 1989-90.
Host, *Face to Face with Connie Chung,* CBS, 1990.
Anchor, *Eye to Eye with Connie Chung,* CBS, 1993-95.
Co-anchor, *CBS Evening News,* CBS, 1993-95.

Correspondent, *PrimeTime Live,* ABC, 1997—.
Correspondent, *20/20,* ABC, 1997—.

Also occasional anchor for ABC news programs, including *ABC World News Tonight* (also known as *ABC World News Tonight with Peter Jennings*).

Television Appearances; Specials:
Terra Our World, Maryland Center for Public Broadcasting, 1980.
Herself, *NBC's 60th Anniversary Celebration,* NBC, 1986.
Correspondent, *The Baby Business,* NBC, 1987.
Correspondent, *Scared Sexless,* NBC, 1987.
David Letterman's Old Fashioned Christmas, NBC, 1987.
Men, Women, Sex and AIDS, NBC, 1987.
Correspondent, *NBC News Report on America: Life in the Fat Lane,* NBC, 1987.
Anchor, *Summer Showcase,* NBC, 1988.
Correspondent/anchor, *Summer Showcase,* NBC, 1988.
Correspondent, *Campaign Countdown: The California Battleground,* NBC, 1988.
Correspondent, *Campaign Countdown: The Great Lakes Battleground,* NBC, 1988.
Campaign Countdown: Is This Any Way to Elect a President?, NBC, 1988.
Anchor, *Guns, Guns, Guns,* NBC, 1988.
Correspondent, *Everybody's Doing It,* NBC, 1988.
Host, *"Sarafina!" Words of Freedom . . . Songs of Hope,* 1988.
Exit poll reporter, *Decision '88,* NBC, 1988.
Reporter, *NBC News Reports on America: Stressed to Kill,* NBC, 1988.
Anchor and reporter, *Presidential Inauguration,* NBC, 1989.
Anchor, *America on the Line,* CBS, 1992.
Herself, *Donahue: The 25th Anniversary,* NBC, 1992.
Herself, *The 12 Most Fascinating People of 1993,* ABC, 1993.
Anchor, *Space: Last Frontier or Lost Frontier?,* CBS, 1994.
New York anchor, *State of the Union: The President, Congress, and You,* CBS, 1995.
Host and narrator, *Knife to the Heart,* PBS, 1997.

Television Appearances; Episodic:
Herself, "TV or Not TV," *Murphy Brown,* CBS, 1989.

WRITINGS

Television:
NBC News Report on America: Life in the Fat Lane, NBC, 1987.

Everybody's Doing It, NBC, 1988.
Guns, Guns, Guns, NBC, 1988.
Summer Showcase, NBC, 1988.

OTHER SOURCES

Periodicals:
New York Times Biographical Service, December 23, 1992, pp. 1648-1649.
People Weekly, June 5, 1995, pp. 50-52; July 3, 1995, pp. 40-41.*

CIMINO, Michael 1952-

PERSONAL

Born in 1952, in New York, NY; son of a music publisher. *Education:* Yale University, B.F.A. (School of Architecture and Design), 1968, M.F.A. (School of Architecture and Design), 1969; also attended Illinois Institute of Technology.

Addresses: *Home*—New York City, and Los Angeles, CA. *Agent*—Creative Artists Agency, 9830 Wilshire Blvd., Beverly Hills, CA 90212.

Career: Producer, director, and writer. Director of television commercials, 1969-72.

Awards, Honors: Golden Globe Award, best director, Hollywood Foreign Press Association, Academy Awards, best picture and best director, and Directors Guild Award, best director, Directors Guild of America, all 1979, all for *The Deer Hunter;* Golden Palm Award nomination, Cannes International Film Festival, 1996, for *Sunchaser.*

CREDITS

Film Work:
Director, *Thunderbolt and Lightfoot,* United Artists, 1974.
Producer (with Barry Spikings, Michael Deeley, John Peverall, and Joan Carelli) and director, *The Deer Hunter,* Universal, 1979.
Director, *Heaven's Gate* (also known as *Johnson County Wars*), United Artists, 1980.
Producer and director, *Year of the Dragon,* Metro-Goldwyn-Mayer/United Artists, 1985.
Producer (with Joann Carelli) and director, *The Sicilian,* Twentieth Century-Fox, 1987.

Producer (with Dino DeLaurentiis) and director, *Desperate Hours,* Metro-Goldwyn-Mayer/United Artists, 1990.
Producer (with Arnon Milchan, Larry Spiegel, Judy Goldstein, and Joseph M. Vecchio) and director, *Sunchaser,* Warner Bros., 1996.

Film Appearances:
Fifty Years of Action!, 1986.

Television Appearances; Specials:
"Clint Eastwood—The Man from Malpaso," *Crazy about the Movies,* Cinemax, 1993.
Kris Kristofferson: Songwriter, The Disney Channel, 1995.

WRITINGS

Screenplays:
(With Deric Washburn and Steven Bochco) *Silent Running,* Universal, 1972.
(With John Milius) *Magnum Force,* Warner Bros., 1973.
Thunderbolt and Lightfoot, United Artists, 1974.
The Deer Hunter, Universal, 1979.
Heaven's Gate (also known as *Johnson County Wars*), United Artists, 1980.
(With Oliver Stone) *Year of the Dragon,* Metro-Goldwyn-Mayer/United Artists, 1985.

OTHER SOURCES

Books:
Bliss, Michael, *Martin Scorsese and Michael Cimino,* 1985.
Contemporary Authors, Volume 105, Gale (Detroit, MI), 1982.

Periodicals:
Esquire, January 2, 1979.
Film Quarterly, winter, 1984-85.

CLAYBURGH, Jill 1944-

PERSONAL

Born April 30, 1944, in New York, NY; daughter of Albert Henry (a manufacturing executive) and Julia (a former theatrical production secretary; maiden name, Door) Clayburgh; married David Rabe (a playwright), March, 1979; children: Lily. *Education:* Attended the Brearley School; Sarah Lawrence College,

B.A. (philosophy), 1966; studied acting under Uta Hagen and John Lehne. *Avocational interests:* Jogging.

Addresses: *Home*—Connecticut. *Agent*—William Morris Agency, 151 El Camino Dr., Beverly Hills, CA 90212.

Career: Actress. Summer stock at Williamstown Theatre Festival, Williamstown, MA, 1960s; former member of Charles Playhouse, Boston, MA. Co-founder of Ruby Movies Production Company.

Awards, Honors: Emmy Award nomination, 1976, for *Hustling;* Cannes Film Festival Award, best actress, 1978, Academy Award nomination, best actress, 1979, Golden Globe nomination, best actress in a drama, 1979, and Golden Apple Award, all for *An Unmarried Woman;* Academy Award nomination, best actress, and Golden Globe nomination, best actress in a musical or comedy, both 1980, for *Starting Over;* Golden Globe nomination, best actress in a drama, 1980, for *Luna;* Golden Globe nomination, best actress in a musical or comedy, 1982, for *First Monday in October.*

Film Appearances:
Josephine Fish, the bride, *The Wedding Party* (filmed in 1963), Ajay, 1969.
Eyemask, *The Telephone Book,* 1971.
Naomi, *Portnoy's Complaint,* Warner Bros., 1972.
Jackie, *The Thief Who Came to Dinner,* Warner Bros., 1972.
Angela Black, *The Terminal Man,* Warner Bros., 1974.
Carole Lombard, *Gable and Lombard,* Universal, 1976.
Hilly Burns, *Silver Streak,* Twentieth Century-Fox, 1976.
Barbara Jane Bookman, *Semi-Tough,* United Artists, 1977.
Erica Benton, *An Unmarried Woman,* Twentieth Century-Fox, 1978.
Caterina Silveri, *Luna* (also known as *La Luna*), Twentieth Century-Fox, 1979.
Marilyn Holmberg, *Starting Over,* Paramount, 1979.
Mathematician Kate Gunzinger, *It's My Turn,* Columbia, 1980.
Judge Ruth Loomis, *First Monday in October,* Paramount, 1981.
Barbara Gordon, *I'm Dancing as Fast as I Can,* Paramount, 1982.
Hannah Kaufman, *Hannah K.,* Universal, 1983.
Herself, *In Our Hands,* 1984.
Nancy Eldridge, *Where Are the Children?,* Columbia, 1986.

Diana Sullivan, *Shy People,* Cannon, 1987.
Ellen, *Beyond the Ocean,* 1990.
Sally White, *Le Grand Pardon II* (also known as *Day of Atonement*), Vidmark Entertainment, 1992.
Sarah Green, *Whispers in the Dark,* Paramount, 1992.
Helen Odom, *Rich in Love,* Metro-Goldwyn-Mayer, 1993.
Shirley Briggs, *Naked in New York,* Fine Line, 1994.
Nan, *Fools Rush In,* Columbia, 1997.
Alma Burns, *Going All the Way,* Gramercy Pictures, 1997.

Television Appearances; Series:
Appeared as Grace Bolton, *Search for Tomorrow,* CBS.

Television Appearances; Movies:
Mary Nero, *The Snoop Sisters* (also known as *Female Instinct*), NBC, 1972.
Wanda, *Hustling,* ABC, 1975.
Dany, *The Art of Crime* (also known as *Roman Grey: The Fine Art of Crime*), NBC, 1975.
Sarah Phoenix, *Griffin and Phoenix* (also known as *Griffin and Phoenix: A Love Story*), ABC, 1976.
Moira Browning, *Miles to Go . . .* (also known as *Leaving Home*), CBS, 1986.
Vikki Baron, *Who Gets the Friends?,* CBS, 1988.
Ally Maynard, *Fear Stalk,* CBS, 1989.
Dr. Laurie Braga, *Unspeakable Acts,* ABC, 1990.
Jill Ireland, *Reason for Living: The Jill Ireland Story* (also known as *Life Lines*), NBC, 1991.
Anneliese Osborn, *Firestorm: 72 Hours in Oakland* (also known as *Firestorm: A Catastrophe in Oakland*), ABC, 1993.
Sally Walsh, *For the Love of Nancy,* ABC, 1994.
Kitty Menendez, *Honor Thy Father and Mother—The True Story of the Menendez Murders* (also known as *Honor Thy Father and Mother: The Menendez Killings*), Fox, 1994.
Miranda Jessmon, *The Face on the Milk Carton,* CBS, 1995.
Kathy, *Crowned and Dangerous* (also known as *If Looks Could Kill* and *Broken Crown*), ABC, 1997.
Eve Widener, *Sins of the Mind,* USA Network, 1997.
Susan French, *When Innocence Is Lost,* Lifetime, 1997.

Television Appearances; Miniseries:
Judge Louise Parker, *Trial: The Price of Passion* (also known as *Trial*), NBC, 1992.

Television Appearances; Episodic:
Marilyn Polonski, "The Big Ripoff," *The Rockford Files,* NBC, 1974.
Host, *Saturday Night Live,* NBC, 1975.

Television Appearances; Specials:
Gloria, *Going Places,* 1973.
Host, *Ask Me Anything: How to Talk to Kids about Sex,* 1989.
Voice of Emilie Todd Helm, *Lincoln,* ABC, 1992.
Herself, *National Memorial Day Concert 1994,* PBS, 1994.

Stage Appearances:
The Nest, Mercury Theatre, 1970.
(Broadway debut) Hannah Cohen, *The Rothschilds,* Lunt-Fontanne Theatre, New York City, 1970.
Desdemona, *Othello,* Los Angeles, CA, 1971.
Catherine, Pippin's wife, *Pippin,* Imperial Theatre, New York City, 1972.
Jumpers, Billy Rose Theatre, New York City, 1974.
Chrissy, *In the Boom Boom Room,* 1979.
Gilda, *Design for Living,* Circle in the Square, New York City, 1984.

Also appeared with the Charles Street Repertory Company, Boston, MA, 1960s, in *America Hurrah, The Balcony, Love for Love,* and *Dutchman.* Appeared in other plays, including *It's Called the Sugarplum* and *Devil's Disciple.*

OTHER SOURCES

Books:
International Film and Filmmakers, Volume 3, "Actors and Actresses," St. James (Detroit, MI), 1997.

Periodicals:
Films and Filming (London), March, 1988.
New York Times, March, 7, 1982.*

COCA, Imogene   1908-

PERSONAL

Born November 18, 1908, in Philadelphia, PA; daughter of Joseph Fernandez (an orchestra leader under the name Joe Coca) and Sadie (an actress and dancer; maiden name, Brady) Coca; married Robert Burton (an actor), January 7, 1935 (died, 1955); married King Donovan (an actor), 1960 (died, 1987); stepchildren: two sons, one daughter. *Avocational interests:* Dogs and other animals.

Addresses: *Contact*—P.O. Box 5151, Westpoint, CT 06881.

Career: Actress. Singer, Dixie Theatre, Philadelphia, PA, c. 1922. Performer in vaudeville under the names Jill Cameron, Donna Hart, and Helen Gardener.

Awards, Honors: Award of Merit, Women's Division of the Federation of Jewish Philanthropies, 1950; named "Tops in TV," *Saturday Review of Literature* Poll, 1951; Emmy Award, outstanding actress, 1952; George Foster Peabody Broadcasting Award, 1953; Emmy Award, outstanding variety special, 1967, for *The Sid Caesar, Imogene Coca, Carl Reiner, Howard Moss Special;* female lifetime achievement award, American Comedy Awards, 1988; Albert Schweitzer Medal, 1989, for artistry in comedy; Critics Award for *On the Twentieth Century;* and other awards.

CREDITS

Stage Appearances:
Chorus girl, *When You Smile,* National Theatre, New York City, 1925.
Jan, *Bubbling Over,* Werba's Theatre, Brooklyn, NY, 1926.
Dancer, *Snow and Columbus,* Palace Theatre, New York City, 1927.
Ensemble, *Garrick Gaities* (revue), Guild Theatre, New York City, 1930.
Ensemble, *Shoot The Works* (revue), George M. Cohan Theatre, New York City, 1931.
Ensemble, *Flying Colors* (revue), Imperial Theatre, New York City, 1932.
New Faces of 1934 (revue), Fulton Theatre, New York City, 1934.
Ensemble, *Fools Rush In* (revue), Playhouse Theatre, New York City, 1934.
Comique Star, *Up to the Stars,* Lydia Mendelssohn Theatre, Flint, MI, 1935.
Ensemble, *New Faces of 1936* (revue), Vanderbilt Theatre, New York City, 1936.
Spring Dance, Cape Playhouse, MA, 1936.
Priscilla Paine, *Calling All Men,* Cape Playhouse, 1937.
Who's Who, 1938.
Ensemble, *Straw Hat Revue* (revue), Ambassador Theatre, New York City, 1939.
Tonight at 8:30, Community Playhouse, Spring Lake, NJ, 1940.
All in Fun, Majestic Theatre, New York City, 1940.
Ensemble, *Concert Varieties* (revue), Ziegfeld Theatre, New York City, 1945.
Addie, *Happy Birthday,* Music Hall, Clinton, NJ, 1948.
Ruth, *Wonderful Town,* State Fair Music Hall, Dallas, TX, 1954.

Jessica, *Janus,* Plymouth Theatre, New York City, 1956.

Mimsy, *The Girls in 509,* Belasco Theatre, New York City, 1958.

Agnes, *The Fourposter,* Playhouse at Deep Well, Palm Springs, CA, 1960.

The Queen, *Under the Sycamore Tree,* Pasadena Playhouse, Pasadena, CA, 1962.

Mr. Alden and Aunt Veronica, *Why I Went Crazy,* Westport Country Playhouse, Westport, CT, and Falmouth Summer Theatre, Falmouth, MA, 1969.

Penny Moore, *A Girl Could Get Lucky,* Playhouse on the Mall, Paramus, NJ, 1970.

Mrs. Malaprop, *The Rivals,* Philadelphia Drama Guild, Philadelphia, PA, 1972.

Agnes, *The Fourposter,* Showboat Dinner Theatre, St. Petersburg, FL, 1972.

Edna Edison, *The Prisoner of Second Avenue,* Arlington Park, Chicago, IL, 1973.

Letitia Primrose, *On the Twentieth Century,* St. James Theatre, New York City, 1978.

The Gin Game, 1984.

Mrs. Midgit, *Outward Bound,* Apple Corps Theatre, 1984.

Heloise, *My Old Friends,* American Jewish Theatre, New York City, 1985.

Letitia Primrose, *On the Twentieth Century,* Coconut Grove Playhouse, Coconut Grove, FL, 1986.

(With Sid Caesar) *Together Again,* Michael's Pub, New York City, 1990.

Made stage debut as a dancer in vaudeville. Also appeared as Essie Sebastian, *The Sebastians;* in *Double Take,* Arlington Park, IL; in *Send Me No Flowers;* in *The Solid Gold Cadillac;* and in the ensemble, *Hey Look Me Over* (revue), Avery Fisher Hall, New York City. Appeared with Sid Caesar and Anthony Geary in *Your Show of Shows,* Frontier Hall, Las Vegas, NV.

Cabaret Appearances; New York City:
Silver Slipper, 1926.
Rainbow Room, 1937.
La Martinque, 1940.
La Martinque, 1942.
Le Ruban Blew, 1944.
Cafe Society Uptown, 1945.
Blue Angel, 1948.
Le Ruban Blew, 1954.

Also appeared at the Fifth Avenue Club, New Yorker Club, and Jay C. Flippen Club.

Cabaret Performances; Elsewhere:
Sahara Hotel, Las Vegas, NV, 1955.
Trump Plaza, Las Vegas, NV, 1990.
Sands Hotel, Las Vegas, NV, 1991.
Boca Raton, FL, 1991.
Westwood Playhouse, 1991.

Also performed at the Piccadilly Club, Philadelphia, PA; Palmer House, Chicago, IL; and Park Plaza, St. Louis, MO.

Major Tours:
Jan, *Bubbling Over,* U.S. cities, 1926.

Jimmy, the office assistant, *Queen High,* Mayfair, NY, 1928.

A Night at the Folies Bergere, 1940.

Addie, *Happy Birthday,* U.S. cities, 1948.

Essie Sebastian, *The Great Sebastians,* U.S. cities, 1957.

Mimsy, *The Girls in 509,* U.S. cities, 1959.

Princess Winnifred, *Once Upon a Mattress,* U.S. cities, 1960-61.

A Thurber Carnival, U.S. cities, 1961-62.

(With Sid Caesar) *Caesar-Coca Revue,* U.S. cities, 1961-62.

Ella Peterson, *Bells Are Ringing,* U.S. cities, 1962.

Ellen Manville, *Luv,* U.S. cities, 1967.

You Know I Can't Hear You When The Water's Running, 1968-69.

Edna Edison, *The Prisoner of Second Avenue,* U.S. cities, 1973-74.

Letitia Primrose, *On the Twentieth Century,* U.S. cities, 1978.

Letitia Primrose, *On the Twentieth Century,* U.S. cities, 1986-87.

Also toured with George Olsen's orchestra, 1938, and in cabaret tour with Sid Caesar, 1977.

Film Appearances:
(Film debut) *Bashful Ballerina,* 1937.

Herself, *Promises, Promises* (also known as *Promise Her Anything*), NTD, 1963.

Dorkus, *Under the Yum-Yum Tree,* Columbia, 1963.

Ten from Your Show of Shows, Walter Reade, 1973.

Mademoiselle Marie, *Rabbit Test,* Avco-Embassy, 1978.

Aunt Edna, *National Lampoon's Vacation* (also known as *Vacation*), Warner Bros., 1983.

Daisy Schackman, *Nothing Lasts Forever,* Metro-Goldwyn-Mayer/United Artists, 1984.

Buy and Cell, 1989.

Television Appearances; Series:
Host, *Buzzy Wuzzy,* ABC, 1948.
Regular, *Admiral Broadway Revue,* NBC, 1949.
Regular, *Your Show of Shows,* NBC, 1950-54, portions of shows rebroadcast on HA!, 1990.
Betty Crane, *The Imogene Coca Show,* NBC, 1954-55.
Host, *Panorama,* NBC, 1956.
Regular, *Sid Caesar Invites You,* ABC, 1958.
Title role, *Grindl,* NBC, 1963-64.
Shad, *It's about Time,* CBS, 1966-67.
Host, *Hollywood Palace,* ABC, 1967.
Regular, *The Dick Cavett Show,* CBS, 1975.

Appeared as Gladys Mason, *One Life to Live,* ABC.

Television Appearances; Specials:
The Bob Hope Show, NBC, 1951.
"The Funny Heart," *U.S. Steel Hour,* CBS, 1956.
Helpmate, NBC, 1956.
"Made In Heaven," *Playhouse 90,* CBS, 1956.
Effie Floud, *Ruggles of Red Gap,* NBC, 1957.
The Sid Caesar, Imogene Coca, Carl Reiner, Howard Moss Special, CBS, 1967.
The Bob Hope Show, NBC, 1970.
The Bob Hope Show, NBC, 1971.
Broadway Plays Washington! Kennedy Center Tonight, 1982.
Bob Hope Special: Bob Hope's Women I Love—Beautiful but Funny, NBC, 1982.
Hollywood Stars' Screen Tests, NBC, 1984.
The 38th Annual Emmy Awards, 1986.
The 2nd Annual American Comedy Awards, 1988.
More of the Best of the Hollywood Palace, ABC, 1993.
Comic Relief VI, HBO, 1994.
The Second Annual Comedy Hall of Fame (also known as *The 2nd Annual Comedy Hall of Fame*), NBC, 1994.

Television Appearances; Episodic:
Fireside Theatre, NBC, 1957.
Fireside Theatre, NBC, 1958.
Fireside Theatre, ABC, 1963.
The Jackie Gleason Show, CBS, 1968.
The Carol Burnett Show, CBS, 1969.
Love, American Style, ABC, 1969.
"The Good Fairy Strikes Again," *Bewitched,* ABC, 1971.
Wife, "The Merciful," *Night Gallery,* NBC, 1971.
Aunt Jenny, "Jan's Aunt Jenny," *The Brady Bunch,* ABC, 1974.
Gert, *Mama's Family,* NBC, 1983.
Voice, *Garfield and Friends,* 1988.

Also appeared in episodes of *Moonlighting,* ABC; *Kup's Show;* and *Wide World of Mystery.*

Television Appearances; Movies:
Granny's Maw, *Return of the Beverly Hillbillies,* CBS, 1981.
Cook, *Alice in Wonderland,* CBS, 1985.
Missy B, *Papa Was a Preacher,* 1985.

Also appeared in *The Emperor's New Clothes.*

Television Appearances; Pilots:
Emily, *Getting There,* CBS, 1980.

OTHER SOURCES

Books:
Notable Hispanic American Women, first edition, Gale (Detroit, MI), 1994.*

COHENOUR, Patti 1952-

PERSONAL

Full name Patricia Ann Cohenour; born December 17, 1952, in Albuquerque, NM; daughter of William Edward (a physician) and Suzanne (an opera singer; maiden name, Miller) Cohenour; married Thomas Edward Bliss (a film producer). *Education:* Attended University of New Mexico; trained for dance with George Zoritch, Patricia Stander, Suzanne Johnston, Stefan Wenta, Steve Merritt and Joey Sheck. *Avocational interests:* Horseback riding, exercising race horses, guitar playing.

Career: Actress, dancer, and singer. Worked as a backup singer.

Awards, Honors: *Theatre World* Award, 1984, for *La Boheme;* Drama Desk Award nomination and *Theatre World* Award, both 1985, for *Big River;* Antoinette Perry Award nomination, best actress in a featured musical role, 1986, for *The Mystery of Edwin Drood.*

CREDITS

Stage Appearances:
Chava, *Fiddler on the Roof,* Harlequin Dinner Theater, Costa Mesa, CA, 1979.
Let's Call the Whole Thing Gershwin Revue, Westwood Playhouse, Los Angeles, CA, 1980.

Helga and understudy for Nora, *A Doll's Life,* Mark Hellinger Theatre, New York City, 1982.

Julia Finsbury, *The Wrong Box,* Gene Dynarsky Theater, Los Angeles, CA, 1983.

La Boheme, off-Broadway, 1984.

Mary Jane Wilkes, *Big River,* Eugene O'Neill Theatre, New York City, 1985.

Rosa Bud and Deirdre Peregrine, *The Mystery of Edwin Drood,* Delacorte Theatre, New York City, 1985, then Imperial Theatre, New York City, 1985-87.

Christine Daae, *The Phantom of the Opera,* Majestic Theatre, New York City, 1988-89.

Katherine, *The Taming of the Shrew,* Syracuse Stage, Syracuse, NY, 1989-90.

Sweet Adeline, New York City, 1997.

Made stage debut in *A Bluebell,* Krasnoff School of Ballet Recital, Albuquerque Civic Auditorium, Albuquerque, NM.

Major Tours:
The New Christy Minstrels, U.S. and European cities, 1977.

The New Christy Minstrels, U.S. and European cities, 1980.

Also toured in *Pirates of Penzance,* U.S. cities.

Television Appearances; Series:
(Television debut) Singer and dancer, *Music Hall America,* Viacom, 1976-77.

Television Appearances; Episodic:
Appeared in episodes of *Happy Days,* ABC, and *The Powers of Matthew Starr.*

OTHER SOURCES

Periodicals:
New York, December 23-30, 1985, p. 34.*

COLE, Nora 1953-

PERSONAL

Full name Nora Marie Cole; born September 10, 1953, in Louisville, KY; daughter of Lattimore Wallis (a postal supervisor) and Mary Lue (an assembly line worker; maiden name, Bradford) Cole. *Education:* Attended Beloit College; DePaul University,

Goodman School of Drama, B.F.A., 1978; studied acting with Wynn Handman at American Place Theatre, in New York. *Religion:* Christian.

Addresses: *Agent*—Bret Adams Agency, 448 West 44th St., New York, NY 10036.

Career: Actress. Radio City Music Hall, featured soloist, 1980-81.

Member: Actors' Equity Association, American Federation of Television and Radio Artists, Screen Actors Guild, American Guild of Variety Artists.

CREDITS

Stage Appearances:
(Stage debut) Duchess, *Alice in Wonderland,* Louisville Children's Theatre, Louisville, KY, 1965.

Obiah woman, *The Ups and Downs of Theophilus Maitland,* Urban Arts Corporation, New York City, 1976.

Velma, *Movie Buff,* Actors Playhouse, New York City, 1977.

Deidre and understudy for Roby, *Runaways,* New York Shakespeare Festival, New York City, 1978.

Carmen and understudy for Sally Baby, *Inacent Black,* Biltmore Theatre, New York City, 1981.

Singing Mary, *Your Arms Too Short to Box with God,* Alvin Theatre, New York City, 1982.

Mattie, *Joe Turner's Come and Gone,* Studio Arena Theatre, Buffalo, NY, 1989-90.

Shopper, Mrs. Cratchit, and vagrant, *A Christmas Carol,* Studio Arena Theatre, 1990-91.

Cathy, *Birdsend,* Studio Arena Theatre, 1990-91.

Mrs. Willis, *The Good Times Are Killing Me,* Minetta Lane Theatre, New York City, 1991.

Georgette Bergen, *Groundhog,* Stage II, New York City, 1992.

Title role, *Olivia's Opus,* Primary Stages, then Tribeca Performing Arts Center, both New York City, 1993.

Appeared on Broadway in *Jelly's Last Jam;* also appeared in *I'm Laughin' but I Ain't Tickled,* as a widow, *Boogie-Woogie Rumble,* and as Duchess, *Alice in Wonderland,* all at Urban Arts Corporation; in *El Hajj Malik,* Gene Frankel Theatre, New York City; as Mayda, *Cartoons for a Lunch Hour,* Perry Street Theatre, New York City; as Norene, *The Peanut Man,* and as a poet, *Beowulf,* both at AMAS Repertory Theatre, New York City; and as Cassandra, *Trojan Women,* Black Theatre Alliance.

Major Tours:
Addaperle, *The Wiz,* 1980-81.
Singing Mary, *Your Arms Too Short to Box with God,* 1982-83.
Rachael, *When Hell Freezes Over I'll Skate,* 1984.
The All-Night Strut, 1984-85.

Television Appearances; Movies:
Doctor, *The Cosby Mysteries* (also known as *Guy Hanks I*), NBC, 1994.

WRITINGS

Plays:
Olivia's Opus, Primary Stages, then Tribeca Performing Arts Center, both New York City, 1993.*

COLEMAN, Dabney 1932-

PERSONAL

Full name, Dabney W. Coleman; born January 3, 1932, in Austin, TX; son of Melvin Randolph and Mary (Johns) Coleman; married Ann Courtney Harrell, December 21, 1957 (divorced, June 1959); married Carol Jean Hale (an actress), December 11, 1961 (divorced, 1983); children: Kelly Johns, Randolph, Mary. *Education:* Attended Virginia Military Institute, 1949-51; received degree from University of Texas, c. 1954; attended University of Texas Law School until 1957; studied theater at the Neighborhood Playhouse School, 1958-60. *Religion:* Episcopalian.

Career: Actor in New York City, 1960-62, and Los Angeles, CA, 1962—. *Military service:* U.S. Army, 1953-55.

Member: Screen Actors Guild, Phi Delta Theta.

Awards, Honors: Emmy Award nominations, outstanding lead actor in a comedy series, 1983 and 1984, both for *Buffalo Bill;* Emmy Award, outstanding supporting actor in a special, 1987, for *Sworn to Silence;* Golden Globe Award, best actor in a comedy, and Emmy Award nomination, outstanding lead actor in a comedy series, both 1988, both for *The "Slap" Maxwell Story;* Emmy Award nomination, outstanding supporting actor in a special, 1988, for *Baby M;* Emmy Award nomination, outstanding guest actor in a drama series, 1991, for *Columbo.*

CREDITS

Film Appearances:
(Debut) Charlie, *The Slender Thread,* Paramount, 1965.
Salesman, *This Property Is Condemned,* Paramount, 1966.
Jed, *The Scalp Hunters,* United Artists, 1968.
Harrison "Harry" Wilby, *The Trouble with Girls (and How to Get into It)* (also known as *The Chautauqua*), Metro-Goldwyn-Mayer, 1969.
Mayo, *Downhill Racer,* Paramount, 1969.
Frank Donnelly, *I Love My Wife,* Universal, 1970.
Executive officer, *Cinderella Liberty,* Twentieth Century-Fox, 1973.
Charles Huntley, *The Dove,* Paramount, 1974.
Deputy fire chief No. 1, *The Towering Inferno,* Twentieth Century-Fox/Warner Bros., 1974.
Jack Parker, *Bite the Bullet,* Columbia, 1975.
Dave McCoy, *The Other Side of the Mountain* (released in England as *A Window to the Sky*), Universal, 1975.
Bogard, 1975.
The Black Street Fighter (also known as *Black Fist* and *Homeboy*), 1976.
Captain Murray Arnold, *Midway* (released in England as *The Battle of Midway*), Universal, 1976.
Maxwell, *Rolling Thunder,* American International Pictures, 1977.
Ralph Thompson, *Viva Knievel!* (also known as *Seconds to Live*), Warner Bros., 1977.
Emmett, *North Dallas Forty,* Paramount, 1979.
Jack Heintzel, *How to Beat the High Cost of Living,* American International Pictures, 1980.
Judge Keith Hayes, *Melvin and Howard,* Universal, 1980.
Tom Dickerson, *Nothing Personal,* American International/Filmways, 1980.
Franklin Hart, Jr., *Nine to Five,* Twentieth Century-Fox, 1980.
Mark, *Modern Problems,* Twentieth Century-Fox, 1981.
Bill Ray, *On Golden Pond,* Universal, 1981.
Ron, *Tootsie,* Columbia, 1982.
Dr. Joseph Prang, *Young Doctors in Love,* Twentieth Century-Fox, 1982.
McKittrick, *WarGames,* Metro-Goldwyn-Mayer/United Artists, 1983.
Jack Flack/Hal Osborne, *Cloak and Dagger,* Universal, 1984.
Producer (cameo), *The Muppets Take Manhattan,* TriStar, 1984.
Cooper, *The Man with One Red Shoe,* Twentieth Century-Fox, 1985.

Jerry Caesar, *Dragnet,* Universal, 1987.

Walter Sawyer, *Hot to Trot,* Warner Bros., 1988.

Stewart McBain, *Where the Heart Is,* Buena Vista, 1990.

Burt Simpson, *Short Time,* Twentieth Century-Fox, 1990.

Aunt Bea, *Meet the Applegates* (also known as *The Applegates*), Triton Pictures, 1991.

Jeffrey, *There Goes the Neighborhood* (also known as *Paydirt*), 1992.

Chief of Police Cecil Tolliver, *Amos & Andrew,* Columbia, 1993.

Mr. Drysdale, *The Beverly Hillbillies,* Twentieth Century-Fox, 1993.

Gerald Ellis, *Clifford,* Orion, 1994.

Joel, *Witch Way Love* (also known as *Un Amour de sorciere*), TF1 International, 1997.

Television Appearances; Series:

Dr. Leon Bessemer, *That Girl,* ABC, 1966-67.

Dr. Tracy Graham, *Bright Promise,* NBC, 1969-72.

Lt. Lloyd Daggett, *Cannon,* CBS, 1971-76.

Reverend Merle Jeeter, *Mary Hartman, Mary Hartman,* syndicated, 1976-77.

Reverend Merle Jeeter, *Forever Fernwood,* syndicated, 1977.

"Fast" Eddie Barnes, *Apple Pie,* ABC, 1978.

Title role (Bill Bittinger), *Buffalo Bill,* NBC, 1983-84.

Title role ("Slap" Maxwell), *The "Slap" Maxwell Story,* ABC, 1987-88.

Title role (Otis Drexell), *Drexell's Class* (also known as *Oh No, Not Drexell!* and *Shut Up, Kids*), Fox, 1991-92.

Title role (Jack "Madman" Buckner), *Madman of the People,* NBC, 1994-95.

Also appeared on the syndicated series *Fernwood 2-Night.*

Television Appearances; Miniseries:

Tyler Cane, *Fresno,* CBS, 1986.

Television Appearances; Episodic:

Lt. George Webb, "Anybody Here Seen Jeannie?," *I Dream of Jeannie,* NBC, 1965.

"Slow March up a Steep Hill," *The FBI,* ABC, 1965.

Captain Yardley, "The Mod Party," *I Dream of Jeannie,* NBC, 1967.

"The Conspirators," *The FBI,* ABC, 1967.

Captain Mitchell Ross, "The Innocent," *The Invaders,* ABC, 1967.

"The Saucer," *The Invaders,* ABC, 1967.

Clyde, "A Darker Shadow," *Bonanza,* NBC, 1969.

"Incident in the Desert," *The FBI,* ABC, 1970.

Frank Hansen, "Cross and Double Cross," *McMillan and Wife,* NBC, 1971.

George Todd, "Jacob's Boy," *The Streets of San Francisco,* ABC, 1972.

Andrew Horvath, Sr., "The Drop," *The Streets of San Francisco,* ABC, 1972.

Detective Murphy, "Double Shock," *Columbo,* NBC, 1973.

"The Seminar," *Mary Tyler Moore Show,* CBS, 1975.

The Comedy Zone, CBS, 1984.

Hugh Creighton," Columbo and the Murder of a Rock Star," *Columbo,* ABC, 1991.

Voices of William Randolph Hearst and Don Wildmon, *Sex and the Silver Screen,* Showtime, 1996.

Television Appearances; Pilots:

Captain Walter Jones, *Egan,* ABC, 1973.

Captain Logan, *Kiss Me, Kill Me,* ABC, 1976.

Television Appearances; Movies:

The Brotherhood of the Bell, CBS, 1970.

Bob Mitchell, *Dying Room Only,* ABC, 1973.

Senator Burt Haines, *The President's Plane Is Missing,* ABC, 1973.

Ted Seligson, *Savage* (also known as *Watch Dog*), NBC, 1973.

Mr. Wood, *Bad Ronald,* ABC, 1974.

Paul Mathison, *Attack on Terror: The FBI versus the Ku Klux Klan,* CBS, 1975.

Al Stephensen, *Returning Home,* ABC, 1975.

McCallum, *Maneaters Are Loose!,* CBS, 1978.

Josh Harrington, *More Than Friends,* ABC, 1978.

Jack Wilson, *When She Was Bad. . . .* (also known as *A New Life*), ABC, 1979.

Randall Bordeaux, *Callie and Son* (also known as *Rags to Riches*), CBS, 1981.

William S. Paley, *Murrow,* HBO, 1986.

The Return of Mickey Spillane's Mike Hammer, CBS, 1986.

Ed Siegel, *Guilty of Innocence: The Lenell Geter Story* (also known as *Justice Delayed: The Lenell Geter Story*), CBS, 1987.

Jessie Kiplinger, *Plaza Suite,* ABC, 1987.

Hal Gilbert, *Maybe Baby* (also known as *Sooner or Later* and *Baby Makes Three*), NBC, 1988.

William Cox, *Never Forget* (also known as *The Promise*), TNT, 1991.

Charles Mayron, *Judicial Consent* (also known as *My Love, My Honor*), HBO, 1995.

Arthur Milo, *In the Line of Duty: Kidnapped* (also known as *In the Line of Duty: Taxman*), NBC, 1995.

Seymour Kecker, *Devil's Food,* Lifetime, 1996.

Television Appearances; Specials:
The Night of One Hundred Stars Two, ABC, 1985.
Comic Relief Two, HBO, 1987.
Happy Birthday, Hollywood, ABC, 1987.
Marty Costigan, *Sworn to Silence* (also known as *Privileged Information*), ABC, 1987.
Gary N. Skoloff, *Baby M* (also known as *The Baby M Story*), ABC, 1988.
Host, "The Aspen Comedy Festival," *Showtime Presents,* Showtime, 1989.
Voice of Stephen A. Douglas, *Lincoln* (documentary), ABC, 1992.
Richard Williams, *Texan,* Showtime, 1994.
Scribe/Narrator, *Idols of the Game* (also known as *Idols of the Arena;* documentary), TBS, 1995.

Television Work:
Executive consultant, *Drexell's Class,* Fox, 1991-92.

Stage Appearances:
(With Tania Velia) American couple, *A Call on Kuprin,* Broadhurst Theater, New York City, 1961.
The Night of One Hundred Stars Two, Radio City Music Hall, New York City, 1985.

WRITINGS

For Television:
Bright Promise, NBC, 1972.

OTHER SOURCES

Periodicals:
Los Angeles Magazine, February, 1988, p. 16.
Newsweek, July 18, 1983, p. 71.
People, July 11, 1983, p. 71.
Rolling Stone, November 19, 1987, p. 39.
TV Guide, March 2, 1984, p. 36; January 2, 1988, p. 26.*

CONTI, Tom 1941-

PERSONAL

Full name, Thomas Antonio Conti; born November 22, 1941, in Paisley, Scotland; son of Alfonso (a hairdresser) and Mary (a hairdresser; maiden name, McGoldrick) Conti; married Kara Drummond Wilson (an actress), July 2, 1967; children: Nina. *Education:* Attended Royal Scottish Academy of Music and Drama, Glasgow, Scotland; studied acting at Glasgow College of Drama. *Avocational interests:* Playing flamenco guitar.

Addresses: *Agent*—Chatto & Linnit, Prince Wales Theatre, Coventry St., London W1V 7FE, England.

Career: Actor and director. Acted at Citizens' Theatre, Glasgow, Scotland.

Member: Garrick Club (London).

Awards, Honors: Laurence Olivier Award, actor of the year—new play, Society of West End Theatre, and Variety Club of Great Britain Award, both 1978, and Antoinette Perry Award, best actor, 1979, all for *Whose Life Is It Anyway?;* Academy Award nomination and Golden Globe Award nomination, both best actor, 1983, for *Reuben, Reuben;* West End Theatre Managers Award; Royal Television Society Award.

CREDITS

Stage Appearances:
(Stage debut) *The Roving Boy,* Citizens' Theatre, Glasgow, Scotland, 1959.
Harry Vine, *The Black and White Minstrels,* Edinburgh Festival, Edinburgh, Scotland, 1972.
Ben, *Let's Murder Vivaldi,* King's Head Theatre, Islington, England, 1972.
(London debut) Carlos, *Savages,* Royal Court Theatre, then Comedy Theatre, London, both 1973.
Harry Vine, *The Black and White Minstrels,* Hampstead Theatre, London, 1974.
Enrico Zamati, *Other People,* Hampstead Theatre, London, 1974.
Title role, *Don Juan,* Hampstead Theatre, London, 1976.
Dick Dudgeon, *The Devil's Disciple,* Royal Shakespeare Company, Aldwych Theatre, London, 1976.
Ken Harrison, *Whose Life Is It Anyway?,* Mermaid Theatre, then Savoy Theatre, both London, 1978.
(New York debut) Ken Harrison, *Whose Life Is It Anyway?,* Trafalgar Theatre, New York City, 1979.
They're Playing Our Song, 1980.
Romantic Comedy, 1982.
An Italian Straw Hat, Shaftesbury Theatre, London, 1986.
Dave, *Treats,* Hampstead Theatre, London, 1989.

Title role, *Jeffrey Bernard Is Unwell,* Apollo Theatre, London, 1990.
The Ride Down Mount Morgan, Wyndham's Theatre, London, 1991-92.
Present Laughter, Globe Theatre, London, 1993.
Chapter Two, Globe Theatre, London, 1996.

Also appeared in *Two into One.*

Stage Work; Director:
Last Licks, Longacre Theatre, New York City, 1979.
Before the Party, Oxford Playhouse, then Queen's Theatre, London, 1980.
The Housekeeper, Apollo Theatre, London, 1982.
Present Laughter, 1993.
Chapter Two, [London], 1996.

Film Appearances:
(Film debut) Andrea Sarti as a man, *Galileo* (also known as *Galileo Galilei*), American Film Theatre, 1975.
Robert Seymour, *Flame,* VPS/Goodtimes, 1975.
Tom/Geoffrey, *Eclipse,* 1976.
Mark, *Full Circle,* Fester, 1977, released as *The Haunting of Julia,* Discovery, 1981.
Dr. Jacquin, *The Duelists,* Paramount, 1977.
Colonel John Lawrence, *Merry Christmas, Mr. Lawrence,* Universal, 1982.
Gowan McGland, *Reuben, Reuben,* Twentieth Century-Fox, 1983.
Alan McMann, *American Dreamer,* Warner Bros., 1983.
Dr. Roger Briggs, *Miracles,* Orion, 1984.
Pope Leo XIV, *Saving Grace,* Columbia, 1986.
Vic Mathews, *The Gospel According to Vic* (also known as *Heavenly Pursuits*), Skouras, 1986.
Dr. Stuart Framingham, *Beyond Therapy,* New World, 1987.
Moses Bornstein, *Two Brothers Running,* 1988.
Andrija Gavrilovic, *That Summer of White Roses,* 1989.
Daniel, *Blade on the Feather* (also known as *Deep Cover*), 1989.
Costas Caldes, *Shirley Valentine,* Paramount, 1989.
Angelo, *The Siege of Venice,* 1991.
Alonso, *Someone Else's America* (also known as *L'Amerique des autres*), October Films, 1995.
Something to Believe In, 1997.
Out of Control, 1998.

Television Appearances; Series:
The Old Boy Network, 1991.
Charles Wright, *The Wright Verdicts,* CBS, 1995.

Television Appearances; Movies:
Dolek Berson, *The Wall,* CBS, 1982.
Serge Klarsfeld, *Nazi Hunter: The Beate Klarsfeld Story,* ABC, 1986.
David Rose, *Lily,* CBS, 1986.
Duncan McKaskel, *The Quick and the Dead,* HBO, 1987.
Joe Bradley, *Roman Holiday,* NBC, 1987.
Gus, *Basements* (also known as *The Room*), 1987.
Pat Piscitelli, *Fatal Judgment* (also known as *Fatal Dosage*), CBS, 1988.
Dr. "Stanley" Phillips, *Voices Within: The Lives of Truddi Chase* (also known as *When Rabbit Howls*), ABC, 1990.
Henry Hamilton, *Louisa May Alcott's "The Inheritance"* (also known as *The Inheritance*), CBS, 1997.
Harry Reinhardt, *Sub Down* (also known as *Crush Depth*), USA Network, 1997.

Television Appearances; Miniseries:
Charles Bovary, *Madame Bovary,* 1976.

Television Appearances; Specials:
Mother of Men, 1959.
Bruno Varella, "If It's a Man, Hang Up," *Thriller,* ABC, 1975.
Norman, *The Norman Conquests: Living Together,* BBC, 1978.
Gus, *The Dumb Waiter,* ABC, 1987.

Also appeared as Adam Morris, *The Glittering Prizes,* BBC; and in *Treats* and *The Beaux Stratagem.*

Television Appearances; Episodic:
Appeared in "Princess and the Pea," *Faerie Tale Theatre,* Showtime.

OTHER SOURCES

Periodicals:
New York Times, April 22, 1979.

CONWAY, Kevin 1942-

PERSONAL

Born May 29, 1942, in New York, NY; son of James John (a mechanic) and Margaret (a sales representative) Conway; married Mila Quiros (an actress and writer), April 15, 1966. *Education:* Trained for the stage with Uta Hagen and at the Dramatic Workshop, New York City.

Addresses: *Agent*—Innovative Artists, 1999 Avenue of the Stars, Suite 2850, Los Angeles, CA 90067.

Career: Actor and director. Second Stage Company, New York City, member of board of directors; provides voiceovers for television and radio commercials and documentary films. International Business Machines (IBM) Co., worked as sales analyst. *Military service:* U.S. Navy, 1960-62.

Member: Screen Actors Guild (board of directors, 1979-81), National Academy of Television Arts and Sciences, Players Club, Friars Club (New York City).

Awards, Honors: Obie Award, *Village Voice,* and Drama Desk Award, both 1973, for *When You Comin' Back, Red Ryder?;* Outer Critics Circle Award, best actor in a play, 1989, for *Other People's Money.*

CREDITS

Stage Appearances:

(Stage debut) Andy, *The Impossible Years,* Elitch Gardens, Denver, CO, 1967.

Philly Cullen, *Playboy of the Western World,* Long Wharf Theatre, New Haven, CT, 1967.

Leo Davis, *Room Service,* Long Wharf Theatre, 1967.

Tom, *The Knack,* Stage West, Springfield, MA, 1968.

Cliff, *Look Back in Anger,* Charles Playhouse, Boston, MA, 1968.

First messenger, *The Bacchae,* Charles Playhouse, 1968.

(Off-Broadway debut) Number Two, *Muzeeka,* Provincetown Playhouse, 1968.

(Broadway debut) Black Hawk, *Indians,* Brooks Atkinson Theatre, 1969.

Fred, *Saved,* Chelsea Theatre Center, Brooklyn, NY, then Cherry Lane Theatre, New York City, both 1970.

Various roles, *An Evening of Julie Bovasso Plays,* La Mama Experimental Theatre Club, New York City, 1971.

Mike, *Moonchildren,* Arena Stage, Washington, DC, 1971, then Royale Theatre, New York City, 1972.

Covey, *The Plough and the Stars,* Vivian Beaumont Theatre, New York City, 1973.

McMurphy, *One Flew over the Cuckoo's Nest,* Mercer-Hansberry Theatre, then Eastside Playhouse, both New York City, 1973.

Teddy, *When You Comin' Back, Red Ryder?,* Eastside Playhouse, then Berkshire Playhouse, Stockbridge, MA, both 1973.

George, *Of Mice and Men,* Brooks Atkinson Theatre, 1974.

Teddy, *When You Comin' Back, Red Ryder?,* Westwood Playhouse, Los Angeles, 1975.

Allott, *Life Class,* Manhattan Theatre Club, New York City, 1975.

Jamie, *Long Day's Journey into Night,* John F. Kennedy Center for the Performing Arts, Washington, DC, 1975, then Brooklyn Academy of Music, Brooklyn, NY, 1976.

Dr. Frederick Treves and Belgian policeman, *The Elephant Man,* Theatre of St. Peter's Church, then Booth Theatre, both New York City, 1979.

Driver, "Victoria Station," and Nicolas, "One for the Road," in *Other Places,* Manhattan Theatre Club, 1984.

Title role, *King John,* New York Shakespeare Festival, Delacorte Theatre/Central Park, New York City, 1988.

Lawrence Garfinkle, *Other People's Money,* Minetta Lane Theatre, New York City, then Los Angeles, both 1989.

Tom Fearon, *The Man Who Fell in Love with His Wife,* Quaigh Theatre, New York City, 1990.

The Kid, *Ten Below,* Works Progress Administration (WPA) Theatre, New York City, 1993.

Johnny Friendly, *On the Waterfront,* Brooks Atkinson, Theatre, 1995.

Stage Work; Director:

Mecca, Quaigh Theatre, 1980.

"Stops Along the Way" and "Vivian," *The One Act Play Festival,* Mitzi E. Newhouse Theatre, New York City, 1981.

The Elephant Man, Westport Country Playhouse, Westport, CT, 1983.

Short Eyes, Second Stage, New York City, 1984.

The Milk Train Doesn't Stop Here Anymore, WPA Theatre, 1987.

Directed a touring production of *The Elephant Man;* directed *Other People's Money* in Chicago, Los Angeles, and San Francisco productions.

Film Appearances:

Clancy, *Believe in Me,* Metro-Goldwyn-Mayer, 1971.

Weary, *Slaughterhouse Five,* Universal, 1972.

Smolka, *Portnoy's Complaint,* Warner Bros., 1972.

Kid, *Shamus,* Columbia, 1973.

Vince Doyle, *F.I.S.T.,* United Artists, 1978.

Stich Mahon, *Paradise Alley,* Universal, 1978.

Barker, *The Funhouse* (also known as *Carnival of Terror*), Universal, 1981.

Brook, *Flashpoint,* TriStar, 1984.

The Sun and the Moon (also known as *El sol y la luna* and *The Violins Came with the Americans*), Suicide Note Productions, 1987.

Petree, *Funny Farm,* Warner Bros., 1988.

Grazziano, *Homeboy,* Twentieth Century-Fox, 1989.

Dr. Martinson, *Rambling Rose,* Seven Arts, 1991.

Lieutenant Danny Quinn, *One Good Cop,* Buena Vista, 1991.

Citrine, *Jennifer Eight,* Paramount, 1992.

Sergeant "Buster" Kilrain, *Gettysburg,* New Line, 1993.

Eugene Dred, *The Quick and the Dead,* TriStar, 1995.

Jonathan Walker, *Lawnmower Man 2: Beyond Cyberspace* (also known as *Lawnmower Man 2: Jobe's War* and *Lawnmower Man II: Mindfire*), New Line, 1996.

Hastings, *Looking for Richard,* Fox Searchlight Pictures, 1996.

Mercury Rising, Universal, 1998.

The Confession, [independent], 1998.

Film Work:

Co-producer and director, *The Sun and the Moon* (also known as *El sol y la luna* and *The Violins Came with the Americans*), Suicide Note Productions, 1987.

Television Appearances; Series:

Clyde Wheeler, *All My Children,* ABC, 1970.

Television Appearances; Miniseries:

Roger Chillingworth, *The Scarlet Letter,* PBS, 1979.

Mox Mox, *Larry McMurtry's "Streets of Laredo"* (also known as *Streets of Laredo*), CBS, 1995.

Voice, *Lewis and Clark: The Journey of the Corps of Discovery,* 1997.

Television Appearances; Movies:

George Graff, *The Deadliest Season,* CBS, 1977.

David F. Powers, *Johnnie, We Hardly Knew Ye,* NBC, 1977.

Dr. Haber, *The Lathe of Heaven,* PBS, 1980.

Ken Bailey, *Rage of Angels* (also known as *Sidney Sheldon's "Rage of Angels"*), NBC, 1983.

Richard Ofshe, *Attack on Fear,* CBS, 1984.

Dr. Kevin Farley, *Something about Amelia,* ABC, 1984.

Ken Brand, *Jesse,* ABC, 1988.

Jerry Howard, *When Will I Be Loved?,* NBC, 1990.

Jack Hastings, *Breaking the Silence* (also known as *Some Kind of Love*), CBS, 1992.

Hold-Your-Nose-Billy, *The Whipping Boy* (also known as *Prince Brat and the Whipping Boy*), The Disney Channel, 1994.

Kelley, "Calm at Sunset" (also known as "Calm at Sunset, Calm at Dawn"), *Hallmark Hall of Fame,* CBS, 1996.

Television Appearances; Pilots:

Dr. Packer, *RX for the Defense,* ABC, 1973.

Peter Blau, *The Firm,* NBC, 1983.

Television Appearances; Episodic:

Thomas Eakins, "A Motion Portrait," *American Masters,* PBS, 1986.

"Splinters," *The Equalizer,* CBS, 1988.

Kahless the Unforgettable, "Rightful Heir," *Star Trek: The Next Generation,* syndicated, 1993.

Joseph Cardero, "Heartbeat," *Homicide: Life on the Street,* NBC, 1995.

Jim Kowalski, *New York News,* CBS, 1995.

Lieutenant John Flynn, "Corruption," *Law and Order,* NBC, 1996.

Willie, *JAG,* CBS, 1998.

Television Appearances; Specials:

Dr. Frederick Treves, *The Elephant Man,* ABC, 1983.

Stanford White, *Saint Gaudens: Masque of the Golden Bowl,* 1988.

Narrator, *Warning: Medicine May Be Hazardous to Your Health,* 1988.

Also appeared in *Hogan's Goat.*

COOGAN, Keith 1970-
(Keith Mitchell)

PERSONAL

Born January 13, 1970, in Palm Springs, CA; son of Leslie Mitchell (a stand-up comedian and son's business manager); grandson of Jackie Coogan (an actor); companion of Dominique Cole (an actress). *Education:* Attended Santa Monica City College.

Addresses: *Agent*—Harry Gold Agency, 3500 West Olive Ave., Suite 1400, Burbank, CA 91505. *Contact*—1640 South Sepulveda Blvd., No. 218, Los Angeles, CA 90025.

Career: Actor. Appeared in television commercials beginning at age five.

Member: Screen Actors Guild.

CREDITS

Film Appearances:
(As Keith Mitchell) Voice of Young Tod, *The Fox and the Hound* (animated), Buena Vista, 1981.
Brad Anderson, *Adventures in Babysitting*, Buena Vista, 1987.
Patrick Morenski, *Hiding Out*, DEG, 1987.
Ted Johnson, *Cheetah*, Buena Vista, 1989.
Mitch Kozinski, *Cousins*, Paramount, 1989.
Andy, *Under the Boardwalk*, New World, 1989.
Crutch Kane, *Book of Love*, New Line, 1990.
Kenny Crandell, *Don't Tell Mom the Babysitter's Dead* (also known as *The Real World* and *A Night on the Town*), Warner Bros., 1991.
Snuffy Bradberry, *Toy Soldiers*, TriStar, 1991.
Ted Dickson, *Forever*, Triax Entertainment Group, 1993.
Stoner #1, *In the Army Now*, Buena Vista, 1994.
Potto, *A Reason to Believe*, Castle Hill, 1995.
Life 101, Showcase Entertainment, 1995.
Title role, *Downhill Willie*, Overseas Film Group, 1996.

Also appeared as Eric, *The Power Within*, 1995.

Television Appearances; Series:
(As Keith Mitchell) Timothy MacKenzie, *The MacKenzies of Paradise Cove*, ABC, 1979.
(As Keith Mitchell) Jeffrey Burton, *The Waltons*, CBS, 1979-80.
(As Keith Mitchell) Clovis, *Gun Shy*, CBS, 1983.

Television Appearances; Pilots:
Appeared in *Norma Rae*, *Apple Dumpling Gang*, *Wonderland Cove*.

Television Appearances; Episodic:
Waters, "House of Horror," *Tales from the Crypt*, HBO, 1993.
"Things We Said Today," *21 Jump Street*, Fox, 1987.

Also appeared in episodes of *Growing Pains*, *Silver Spoons*, *Fame*, *Mork and Mindy*, *Eight Is Enough*, *Just the Ten of Us*, *Sibs*; appeared as a child in episodes of *CHiPs*, *The Love Boat*, and *Fantasy Island*.

Television Appearances; Movies:
D. G. Reynolds, *Spooner*, The Disney Channel, 1989.

Also appeared in *A Question of Love* (also known as *A Purely Legal Matter*), 1978; Nick McNulty, *The Kid with the Broken Halo*, 1982; *Million Dollar Infield*, *Battered*, and *Memorial Day*.

Television Appearances; Specials:
Erik Nelson, "A Town's Revenge," *ABC Afterschool Special*, ABC, 1989.
Matt Thompson, "Over the Limit," *ABC Afterschool Special*, ABC, 1990.
Jonathan, *The Great O'Grady*, Showtime, 1993.

Also appeared in *All Summer in a Day*, *Wrong Way Kid*, *The Treasure of Alpheus T. Winterborn*, *Rascal*.

Television Appearances; Awards Presentations:
The 61st Annual Academy Awards, ABC, 1989.

WRITINGS

(As Keith Mitchell) *Eddie*, Buena Vista, 1996.

OTHER SOURCES

Periodicals:
People Weekly, July 8, 1991.*

COOPER, Jackie   1922(?)-

PERSONAL

Full name, John Cooper, Jr.; born September 15, 1922 (some sources say 1921), in Los Angeles, CA; son of Jack Cooper (an actor); married June Horne, 1945 (divorced, 1949); married Hildy Parks (an actress), 1950 (divorced, 1951); married Barbara Kraus (an advertising executive), 1954; children: (first marriage) John; (third marriage) Russell, Julie, Christina. *Education:* Attended the University of Notre Dame. *Avocational interests:* Racing sports cars, playing the drums, skeet shooting, piloting, sailing, cooking.

Addresses: *Office*—David Licht Associates, 9171 Wilshire Boulevard, Beverly Hills, CA 90210. *Agent*—Contemporary Artists, 1317 Fifth St., #200, Santa Monica, CA 90401.

Career: Actor, director, and producer. Vice-president in charge of television program production, Columbia Pictures Corporation, 1964-69; founder (with Bob Finkel), producer, and director, Cooper-Finkel Company, 1969-73; also board of directors, Cinema

Circulus, University of Southern California. *Military service:* U.S. Navy, captain, World War II; U.S. Naval Reserve.

Awards, Honors: Academy Award nomination, best actor, 1931, for *Skippy;* Emmy Award, best comedy director, 1974, for *M*A*S*H;* Emmy Award, best dramatic director, 1979, for pilot episode of *The White Shadow;* Film Advisory Board Awards as producer and director, 1982, for *Rosie: The Rosemary Clooney Story;* two Emmy Award nominations as best actor, special citation from the American Medical Association, and Public Service Medal from the United States Navy, all for *Hennessey;* also received awards from the Academy of Motion Picture Arts and Sciences, Directors Guild of America, Writers Guild of America, Caucus for Writers, Producers, and Directors, Hollywood Radio and Television Society, American Center of Films for Children, United Funds and Community Chest, March of Dimes, American Academy of General Practice, Cinema Circulus, University of California at Los Angeles, University of Southern California, Special Olympics, International Motor Sports of America, and the Center for Improvement of Child Caring.

Military honors: Honorary Naval Aviator Wings of Gold award, 1970; Commendation Medal with citation and the Legion of Merit with citation upon retirement from the U.S. Naval Reserve, 1974; also received awards from the Pearl Harbor Survivors Association, U.S. Navy Recruiting Service, Navy League, Association of Naval Aviation, Society of Experimental Test Pilots, and the Combat Pilots Association.

Member: Screen Actors Guild, American Federation of Television and Radio Artists, American Federation of Musicians, Directors Guild of America (council member and member of the national board of directors), Cinema Circulus (board of directors), Naval Aviation Society, Naval Reserve Association, Aircraft Owners and Pilots Association, VIVA to return Missing In Action Prisoners of War from Vietnam (charter member), Sports Car Club of America (former member).

CREDITS

Stage Appearances:
Andy Hamill, *Magnolia Alley,* Mansfield Theatre, New York City, 1949.
Waldo Walton, *Remains to Be Seen,* Morosco Theatre, New York City, 1951.

Ensign Pulver, *Mr. Roberts,* London, 1951.
King of Hearts, Lyceum Theatre, New York City, 1955.

Major Tours:
Ensign Pulver, *Mr. Roberts,* U.S. cities, 1949-50.

Film Appearances:
Himself, *Fox Movietone Follies of '29,* Twentieth Century-Fox, 1929.
Tenement boy, *Sunny Side Up,* Twentieth Century-Fox, 1929.
Dink Purcell, *The Champ,* Metro-Goldwyn-Mayer, 1931.
Skippy Skinner, *Skippy,* Paramount, 1931.
Skippy Skinner, *Sooky,* Paramount, 1931.
Midge Murray, *Young Donovan's Kid* (also known as *Donovan's Kid*), RKO, 1931.
Himself, *Jackie Cooper's Christmas Party* (short film), Metro-Goldwyn-Mayer, 1931.
Himself, *The Voice of Hollywood No. 13,* 1932.
Terry Parker, *Divorce in the Family,* Metro-Goldwyn-Mayer, 1932.
Eddie Randall, *Feller Needs a Friend* (also known as *When a Feller Needs a Friend*), Cosmopolitan, 1932.
Swipes McGurk, *The Bowery,* Twentieth Century-Fox, 1933.
Ted Hackett, Jr. (as a child), *Broadway to Hollywood* (also known as *Ring Up the Curtain*), Metro-Goldwyn-Mayer, 1933.
Scooter O'Neal, *Lone Cowboy,* Paramount, 1934.
Bill Peck, *Peck's Bad Boy,* Twentieth Century-Fox, 1934.
Jim Hawkins, *Treasure Island,* Metro-Goldwyn-Mayer, 1934.
Dinky Daniels, *Dinky,* Warner Bros., 1935.
Stubby O'Shaughnessy, *O'Shaughnessy's Boy,* Metro-Goldwyn-Mayer, 1935.
"Buck" Murphy, *The Devil Is a Sissy* (also known as *The Devil Takes the Count*), Metro-Goldwyn-Mayer, 1936.
Freddie, *Tough Guy,* Metro-Goldwyn-Mayer, 1936.
Chuck, *Boy of the Streets,* Monogram, 1937.
Larry Kelly, *Gangster's Boy,* Monogram, 1938.
Ken, *That Certain Age,* Universal, 1938.
Peter Trimble, *White Banners,* Warner Bros., 1938.
Butch, *Captain Spanky's Show Boat,* 1939.
Timmy Hutchins, *The Big Guy,* Universal, 1939.
Bruce Scott, *Scouts to the Rescue* (twelve part serial), 1939.
"Rifle" Edwards, *Newsboy's Home,* Universal, 1939.
Tom Allen, *The Spirit of Culver* (also known as *Man's Heritage*), Universal, 1939.

Jimmy, *Streets of New York* (also known as *The Abe Lincoln of Ninth Avenue*), Monogram, 1939.
Roy O'Donnell, *Two Bright Boys,* Universal, 1939.
Henry Aldrich, *What a Life,* Paramount, 1939.
Byron "By" Newbold, *Gallant Sons,* Metro-Goldwyn-Mayer, 1940.
Clem (Tom Grayson), *The Return of Frank James,* Twentieth Century-Fox, 1940.
William Sylvanus Baxter, *Seventeen,* Paramount, 1940.
Tiny Barlow, *Glamour Boy* (also known as *Hearts in Springtime*), Paramount, 1941.
Chuck Harris, *Her First Beau,* Columbia, 1941.
Henry Aldrich, *Life with Henry,* Paramount, 1941.
Jerry Regan, *Ziegfeld Girl,* Metro-Goldwyn-Mayer, 1941.
Robert Houston Scott, *Men of Texas* (also known as *Men of Destiny*), Universal, 1942.
Babe, *The Navy Comes Through,* RKO Radio Pictures, 1942.
Johnnie, *Syncopation,* RKO Radio Pictures, 1942.
Danny, *Where Are Your Children?,* Monogram, 1943.
John J. Kilroy, *Kilroy Was Here,* Monogram, 1947.
Ernie, *Stork Bites Man,* Universal, 1947.
Skitch, *French Leave* (also known as *Kilroy on Deck*), Monogram, 1948.
Lieutenant Parnell, *Everything's Ducky,* Columbia, 1961.
Danton Miller, *The Love Machine,* Columbia, 1971.
Raymond Couzins, *Chosen Survivors,* Columbia, 1974.
Eric Hurst, *Journey Into Fear* (also known as *Burn Out*), 1975.
Service repairman, *The Pink Panther Strikes Again,* United Artists, 1976.
Perry White, *Superman* (also known as *Superman: The Movie*), Warner Bros., 1978.
Perry White/Dino, *Superman II,* Warner Bros., 1980.
Perry White, *Superman III,* Warner Bros., 1983.
Perry White, *Superman IV: The Quest for Peace,* Warner Bros., 1987.
Ace Morgan, *Surrender,* Warner Bros., 1987.
Himself, *Going Hollywood: The War Years* (documentary), 1988.

Also appeared in comedies with Bobby Clark and Lloyd Hamilton, beginning c. 1925.

Film Appearances; with Our Gang (also known as the Little Rascals):
Boxing Gloves, Metro-Goldwyn-Mayer, 1929.
Bouncing Babies, Metro-Goldwyn-Mayer, 1929.
Moan and Groan Inc., Metro-Goldwyn-Mayer, 1929.
Shivering Shakespeare, Metro-Goldwyn-Mayer, 1929.
The First Seven Years, Metro-Goldwyn-Mayer, 1930.
When the Wind Blows, Metro-Goldwyn-Mayer, 1930.
Bear Shooters, Metro-Goldwyn-Mayer, 1930.
A Tough Winter, Metro-Goldwyn-Mayer, 1930.
Pups Is Pups, Metro-Goldwyn-Mayer, 1930.
Teacher's Pet, Metro-Goldwyn-Mayer, 1930.
School's Out, Metro-Goldwyn-Mayer, 1930.
Helping Grandma, Metro-Goldwyn-Mayer, 1931.
Love Business, Metro-Goldwyn-Mayer, 1931.
Little Daddy, Metro-Goldwyn-Mayer, 1931.
Bargain Day, Metro-Goldwyn-Mayer, 1931.

Film Work; Director:
Stand Up and Be Counted, Columbia, 1972.
Go for the Gold, LIVE Home Video, 1984.

Television Appearances; Series:
Socrates "Sock" Miller, *The People's Choice,* CBS, 1955-58.
Charles J. "Chick" Hennessey, *Hennessey,* CBS, 1959-62.
Host, *The Dean Martin Comedy World* (also known as *Dean Martin's Comedy World*), NBC, 1974.
Peter Campbell, *Mobile One,* ABC, 1975.
Host, *The Hollywood Chronicles,* 1989.

Television Appearances; Pilots:
Host, *What's Up?,* NBC, 1971.
Widower, "Hot Machine, Cold Machine," *Of Men Of Women,* ABC, 1972.
Father, *Keeping an Eye on Denise,* CBS, 1973.
Dr. Dan Morgan, *Doctor Dan,* CBS, 1974.
Walter Carlson, *The Invisible Man,* NBC, 1975.
Peter Campbell, *Mobile Two,* ABC, 1975.
Admiral, *Operation Petticoat* (also known as *Life in the Pink*), ABC, 1977.

Television Appearances; Episodic:
"The Invisible Killer," *Suspense,* CBS, 1952.
"The Cocoon," *Tales of Tomorrow,* ABC, 1952.
"Life, Liberty, and Orrin Dooley," *Lux Video Theatre,* NBC, 1952.
"A Message for Janice," *Lux Video Theatre,* NBC, 1952.
"The Fall Guy," *Robert Montgomery Presents Your Lucky Strike Theatre,* NBC, 1952.
"Something Old, Something New," *Ford Theatre,* NBC, 1952.
"The Outer Limit," *Robert Montgomery Presents Your Lucky Strike Theatre,* NBC, 1953.
"Birthright" and "Hound Dog Man," *Studio One,* CBS, 1953.

"Big Jim's Boy," *Schlitz Playhouse of Stars,* CBS, 1953.

"The Middle Son" and "Tour of Duty," *Armstrong Circle Theatre,* NBC, 1953.

"A Reputation," *Revlon Mirror Theatre,* CBS, 1953.

"The Diehard," *Kraft Theatre,* NBC, 1953.

"Grand'ma Rebel" and "Twenty-Four Men to a Plane," *Medallion Theatre,* CBS, 1953.

"Westward the Sun," *Motorola TV Hour,* ABC, 1953.

"Towerman," *Danger,* CBS, 1953.

"The 39th Bomb," *Medallion Theatre,* syndicated, 1954.

"Falling Star," *The Elgin Hour,* ABC, 1954.

"A Dreamer of Summer," *Robert Montgomery Presents Your Lucky Strike Theatre,* NBC, 1954.

"Yellow Jack," *Producer's Showcase,* NBC, 1955.

"I Found Sixty Million Dollars," *Armstrong Circle Theatre,* NBC, 1955.

"The Pardon-Me Boy," *Philco Playhouse,* NBC, 1955.

"Yankee Peddler," *General Electric Theatre,* CBS, 1955.

"It Depends on You," *Robert Montgomery Presents Your Lucky Strike Theatre,* NBC, 1955.

"End of Morning" and "Really the Blues," *Robert Montgomery Presents Your Lucky Strike Theatre,* NBC, 1956.

"The Old Lady Shows Her Medals," *The U.S. Steel Hour,* CBS, 1956.

"The Fair-Haired Boy," *Studio One,* CBS, 1958.

"The Hasty Heart," *Dupont Show of the Month,* CBS, 1958.

"Curtain Call," *Goodyear Theatre,* CBS, 1958.

"Mid-Summer," *The U.S. Steel Hour,* CBS, 1958.

Hayes and Henderson, NBC, 1959.

The Revlon Revue, CBS, 1960.

Mrs. G. Goes to College, CBS, 1961.

"Thunder in a Forgotten Town," *The Dick Powell Show,* NBC, 1961.

"Special Assignment," *The Dick Powell Show,* NBC, 1962.

"The Fourposter," *Golden Showcase,* CBS, 1962.

"The Old Lady Shows Her Medals," *The U.S. Steel Hour,* CBS, 1963.

"Thunder in a Forgotten Town," *The Dick Powell Show,* NBC, 1963.

Jonathan West, "Caesar and Me," *The Twilight Zone,* CBS, 1964.

Hawaii Five-O, CBS, 1971.

McCloud, NBC, 1972.

"Cry of the Cat," *Ghost Story,* NBC, 1972.

Ironside, NBC, 1972.

Ironside, NBC, 1973.

"Break-In," *The F.B.I.,* ABC, 1973.

Hec Ramsay, NBC, 1974.

Kojak, CBS, 1974.

Police Story, NBC, 1974.

Police Story, NBC, 1975.

Ironside, NBC, 1975.

Captain Highland, "Claire," *The Rockford Files,* NBC, 1975.

Police Story, NBC, 1976.

"The House on Willis Avenue: Part 1," *The Rockford Files,* NBC, 1977.

"The House on Willis Avenue: Part 2," *The Rockford Files,* NBC, 1977.

Neil Fletcher, *Murder, She Wrote,* CBS, 1986.

Dr. Domedion, "Time Heals: Part 1," *St. Elsewhere,* NBC, 1986.

Dr. Domedion, "Time Heals: Part 2," *St. Elsewhere,* NBC, 1986.

Interviewee, "Judy Garland: Beyond the Rainbow," *Biography,* Arts and Entertainment, 1997.

Also appeared in *Starlight Theatre,* CBS, and "The Hunley," *The Great Adventure,* CBS.

Television Appearances; Movies:

Lieutenant Colonel Andy Davis, *Shadow on the Land,* ABC, 1968.

Ed Miller, *Maybe I'll Come Home in the Spring* (also known as *Deadly Desire* and *Maybe I'll Be Home in the Spring*), ABC, 1971.

Kurt Anderson, *The Astronaut,* ABC, 1972.

Nelson Hayward, *Columbo: Candidate for Crime,* NBC, 1973.

Steve Barker, *The Day the Earth Moved,* ABC, 1974.

Television Appearances; Specials:

Host, *What's Up, America?,* NBC, 1971.

Himself, *The 38th Annual Emmy Awards,* 1986.

Himself, *When We Were Young . . . Growing Up on the Silver Screen,* 1989.

Himself, *MGM: When the Lion Roars* (also known as *The MGM Story*), TNT, 1992.

Himself, *Lucy and Desi: A Home Movie,* NBC, 1993.

Himself, *Inside the Dream Factory* (documentary), Turner Classic Movies, 1995.

Interviewee, *Sports on the Silver Screen,* HBO, 1997.

Television Director; Unless Indicated Elsewhere; Series:

(Also producer) *The People's Choice,* CBS, 1955-58.

(With Hy Averback; also producer with Don McGuire and Dan Cooper) *Hennessey,* CBS, 1959-62.

Television Work; Director (Unless Indicated); Pilots:

Producer, *Charlie Angelo,* CBS, 1962.

Keep the Faith, CBS, 1972.
(Also producer) *Doctor Dan,* CBS, 1974.
The Last Detail, 1975.
Snafu, NBC, 1976.
Having Babies III (also known as *Julie Farr, M.D.*), ABC, 1978.
Paris, CBS, 1979.
The White Shadow, CBS, 1979.
Trapper John, M.D., CBS, 1979.
Family in Blue, CBS, 1982.
(Also producer) *The Ladies,* NBC, 1987.

Television Director; Episodic:
*M*A*S*H* (thirteen episodes), CBS, 1973-74.
The Mary Tyler Moore Show, CBS, 1974.
The Texas Wheelers, ABC, 1974.
The Rockford Files, NBC, 1974-75.
Mobile One, ABC, 1975.
Quincy, M.E. (also known as *Quincy*), NBC, 1976.
(Also producer) *Holmes and YoYo,* ABC, 1976.
McMillan, NBC, 1977.
The Feather and Father Gang, ABC, 1977.
The Black Sheep Squadron (also known as *Baa Baa Black Sheep*), NBC, 1977-78.
Lou Grant, CBS, 1977-82.
The White Shadow, CBS, 1979.
Glitter, ABC, 1984.
Jessie, ABC, 1984.
"The Deacon Street Deer," *Disney Sunday Movie,* ABC, 1986.
Sledge Hammer!, ABC, 1986 and 1987.
The Law and Harry McGraw, CBS, 1987.
Magnum, P.I., CBS, 1987.
Mr. President, Fox, 1987.
Spies, CBS, 1987.
Ohara, ABC, 1987.
Cagney and Lacey, CBS, 1987.
Cagney and Lacey, CBS, 1988.
Simon and Simon, CBS, 1988.
Supercarrier, ABC, 1988.
The Adventures of Superboy (also known as *Superboy*), syndicated, 1988.
Jake and the Fatman, CBS, 1988.

Television Director; Unless Indicated Elsewhere; Movies:
(Also producer) *Perfect Gentlemen,* CBS, 1978.
Rainbow, NBC, 1978.
Sex and the Single Parent, CBS, 1979.
White Mama, CBS, 1980.
Rodeo Girl, CBS, 1980.
Marathon, CBS, 1980.
Leave 'em Laughing, CBS, 1981.

(Also producer) *Rosie: The Rosemary Clooney Story,* CBS, 1982.
The Night They Saved Christmas, ABC, 1984.
Izzy and Moe, CBS, 1985.

Also director of *Uncommon Courage.*

Television Work; Specials:
Director, *The Deacon Street Deer,* 1986.

Also producer (with Bob Finkel) of Bing Crosby and Perry Como specials, 1970, 1971, and 1972.

WRITINGS

Autobiography:
(With Dick Kliener) *Please Don't Shoot My Dog,* William Morrow (New York City), 1981.

OTHER SOURCES

Books:
Contemporary Authors, Volume 133, Gale (Detroit, MI), 1991.
International Dictionary of Film and Filmmakers, Volume 3, "Actors and Actresses," St. James (Detroit, MI), 1997.

Periodicals:
Entertainment Weekly, August 19, 1994, p. 76.*

CORBIN, Barry 1940-

PERSONAL

Born October 16, 1940, in LaMesa, TX; son of Kilmer Blaine and Alma LaMerle (Scott) Corbin; married Marie Elyse Soape, March 15, 1965 (divorced, April, 1972); married Susan James Berger, May 29, 1976 (divorced, 1992); children: James Barry, Christopher Clayton, Shannon Katy Ross, Bernard Weiss. *Education:* Attended Texas Tech University, 1959-64, and University of Colorado, 1964. *Politics:* Democrat. *Avocational interests:* Owning and riding cutting horses.

Addresses: *Agent*—Judy Schoen and Associates, 606 North Larchmont, Hollywood, CA 90048. *Publicist*—Wilkinson/Lipsman, 8170 Beverly Blvd., Suite 205, Los Angeles, CA 90048. *Contact*—c/o Hillard Elkins, 8306 Wilshire Blvd., #438, Beverly Hills, CA 90211-2382.

Career: Actor and writer. American Shakespeare Festival, Stratford, CT, member of company, 1968-69; Actors Theatre of Louisville, Louisville, KY, member of company, 1975-79. North Carolina State University, Raleigh, member of faculty, 1966-67. *Military service:* U.S. Marine Corps Reserve, active duty, 1962-64.

Member: Screen Actors Guild (member of board of directors, 1985, 1987-90), Actors Equity Association, American Federation of Television and Radio Artists, Dramatists Guild, Academy of Motion Picture Arts and Sciences, American Quarter Horse Association, National Cutting Horse Association.

Awards, Honors: Theatre USA Award, 1974, for *Suckerrod Smith and the Cisco Kid;* Emmy Award nomination, outstanding supporting actor in a drama series, 1993, Media Owl Award, and American Television Award nomination, all for *Northern Exposure;* Emmy Award nomination, outstanding informational special, 1995, for *Moon Shot;* Buffalo Bill Cody Award, for quality family entertainment; Western Heritage Award, National Cowboy Hall of Fame, for *Conagher.*

CREDITS

Television Appearances; Series:
Merit Sawyer, *Boone,* NBC, 1983-84.
Maurice Minnifeld, *Northern Exposure,* CBS, 1990-95.
Dylan Montgomery, *Ink,* CBS, 1996-97.
C.D. LeBlanc, *The Big Easy,* USA Network, 1996-98.

Television Appearances; Miniseries:
Pete, *The Thorn Birds,* ABC, 1983.
Roscoe Brown, *Lonesome Dove,* CBS, 1989.

Television Appearances; Pilots:
Vernon Witchard, *Norma Rae,* NBC, 1981.
Sheriff Hack Ames, *Travis McGee,* ABC, 1982.
Governor Howard James, *Camp California* (also known as *Club Fed*), ABC, 1989.

Television Appearances; Episodic:
Ted Lomax, "Murder Is the Key," *Tucker's Witch,* 1983.
"The Way We Weren't," *The Duck Factory,* 1984.
Jenkins, "John Henry," *Shelley Duvall's Tall Tales and Legends,* Showtime, 1987.
Zed Westhymer, "Bobby the Chimp," *The Famous Teddy Z,* 1989.

Zed Westhymer, "A Case of Murder," *The Famous Teddy Z,* 1989.
Richard Cooper, "Bad Company," *Murphy Brown,* 1995.
Narrator/Wilbur Fisk Crafts/Edwin Johnson, *Sex and the Silver Screen,* Showtime, 1996.
Wickes, "Working Girls," *The Magnificent Seven,* CBS, 1998.

Also appeared in *M*A*S*H, Hill Street Blues, Designing Women,* and *Murder, She Wrote.*

Television Appearances; Movies:
Sixth resident, *Rage,* NBC, 1980.
Dr. Agajanian, *Bitter Harvest,* NBC, 1981.
Gus Lobell, *A Few Days in Weasel Creek,* CBS, 1981.
Nick Hanson, *The Killing of Randy Webster,* CBS, 1981.
I. D. McMasters, *Murder in Texas,* NBC, 1981.
Lieutenant Fletcher, *This House Possessed,* ABC, 1981.
Naylor, *Fantasies,* ABC, 1982.
Bob Austin, *Prime Suspect,* CBS, 1982.
Franz Grebner, *Fatal Vision,* NBC, 1984.
Bert Hamilton, *Flight 90: Disaster on the Potomac,* NBC, 1984.
Judge J. Samuel Perry, *The Jesse Owens Story,* syndicated, 1984.
Colonel, *The Ratings Game,* The Movie Channel, 1984.
Assistant D.A. Jim Heusdens, *Death in California,* ABC, 1985.
Floyd Carpenter, *The Defiant Ones,* ABC, 1986.
Captain Johnson, *Firefighter,* CBS, 1986.
The director, *C.A.T. Squad,* NBC, 1986.
Max Ball, *Warm Hearts, Cold Feet* (also known as *Babytalk*), CBS, 1987.
Judge Wirtz, *LBJ: The Early Years,* NBC, 1987.
Elmore, *Young Henry Houdini,* ABC, 1987.
Sheriff Wallace, *Secret Witness* (also known as *No Secrets*), CBS, 1988.
Roy "Big Mac" McCleary, *Man Against the Mob* (also known as *Trouble in the City of Angels*), NBC, 1988.
Malcolm Bryce, *The People across the Lake,* NBC, 1988.
Gil Rosine, *Stranger on My Land,* ABC, 1988.
Bentick, *Red King, White Knight,* HBO, 1989.
I Know My First Name Is Steven, NBC, 1989.
Principal Haskin, *Spooner,* The Disney Channel, 1989.
Captain Bob Berg, *Last Flight Out,* NBC, 1990.
Police Officer Bob Wallis, *The Chase,* NBC, 1991.
Charlie McCloud, *Conagher* (also known as *Louis L'Amour's Conagher*), TNT, 1991.

Earl Buckaloo, *The Keys,* NBC, 1992.
Dolve Potter, *Deadly Family Secrets,* NBC, 1995.
Dr. Jack Clayman, *Robin Cook's Virus* (also known as *Outbreak*), NBC, 1995.
George Reed, *Kiss and Tell* (also known as *Please Forgive Me*), ABC, 1996.
Dan Pendleton, *My Son Is Innocent,* ABC, 1996.
Clifford Calvert, *Columbo: A Trace of Murder,* ABC, 1997.
Mike Hadley, *The Hired Heart,* Lifetime, 1997.

Television Appearances; Specials:
Jimmy Scott Farnsworth, *Maggie,* 1986.
Texas 150: A Celebration Special, 1986.
Thomas Brady, *Spies,* CBS, 1987.
Voice of Wild Bill Hickock, *The Wild West* (documentary), syndicated, 1993.
Narrator, *Moon Shot* (also known as *Giant Step: The Inside Story of the Apollo Mission*), TBS, 1994.
Host/narrator, *Fate of the Plains,* PBS, 1996.
Narrator, *Eyes in the Sky,* Discovery Channel, 1996.

Film Appearances:
Fat Zack, *Any Which Way You Can,* Warner Bros., 1980.
Warden Walter Beatty, *Stir Crazy,* Columbia, 1980.
Uncle Bob, *Urban Cowboy,* Paramount, 1980.
Phil, *Dead and Buried,* Avco Embassy, 1981.
Wimbush, *The Night the Lights Went Out in Georgia,* Avco Embassy, 1981.
Derwood Arnspringer, *Honkytonk Man,* Warner Bros., 1982.
Sheriff, *Six Pack,* Twentieth Century-Fox, 1982.
C. J., *The Best Little Whorehouse in Texas,* Universal, 1982.
B. R. Abernathy, *The Ballad of Gregorio Cortez,* Embassy, 1983.
Roy, *The Man Who Loved Women,* Columbia, 1983.
General Beringer, *WarGames,* Metro-Goldwyn-Mayer/United Artists, 1983.
Attorney Frank Burton, *Hard Traveling,* Shire, 1985.
Lew Harlan, *My Science Project,* Buena Vista, 1985.
Andrew Woolridge, *Nothing in Common,* TriStar, 1986.
Leon, *What Comes Around,* AWO Associates, 1986.
Off the Mark (also known as *Crazy Legs*), Fries Entertainment, 1987.
Sergeant Irwin Lee, *Under Cover,* Cannon, 1987.
Harv, *Critters II: The Main Course,* New Line, 1988.
Jim Sinclair, *Permanent Records,* Paramount, 1988.
George Lawrence, *It Takes Two,* Metro-Goldwyn-Mayer/United Artists, 1988.
P. J. Downing, *Who's Harry Crumb?,* TriStar, 1989.
Captain, *Short Time,* Twentieth Century-Fox, 1990.

Mr. Collins, *Ghost Dad,* Universal, 1990.
Sheriff, *The Hot Spot,* Orion, 1990.
Officer Don, *Career Opportunities,* Universal, 1991.
Siringo, WarnerVision Films, 1995.
Lodger, *Curdled,* Miramax, 1996.
General Clyde Haynes, *Solo,* Triumph Releasing, 1996.

Stage Appearances:
Forester, *As You Like It,* American Shakespeare Festival Theatre, Stratford, CT, 1968.
Mercade, *Love's Labour's Lost,* American Shakespeare Festival Theatre, 1968.
(Broadway debut) Gower, *Henry V,* ANTA Theatre, New York City, 1969.
Othello, American Shakespeare Festival, New York City, 1969.
Sir William Cecil/Lord Burghley/Sir Robert Cecil, *Masquerade,* Theatre Four, New York City, 1971.
Detective, *Crystal and Fox,* McAlpin Rooftop Theatre, 1973.
Bennie, *Getting Out,* Marymount Manhattan Theatre, New York City, 1978.

Also appeared as Judd, *Oklahoma!;* as Falstaff, *Merry Wives of Windsor;* as Henry II, *Beckett;* as Macbeth, *MacBeth;* in *Holy Ghosts;* and in *Suckerrud Smith,* and *The Cisco Kid.*

WRITINGS

Plays:
Suckerrod Smith and the Cisco Kid, 1974.
Throckmorton, Texas 76083, 1983.

Screenplays:

Author of *The Wildcatters,* 1986.*

CORLETT, William 1938-

PERSONAL

Born October 8, 1938, in Darlington, Durham, England; son of Harold and Ida (Allen) Corlett. *Education:* Royal Academy of Dramatic Art, diploma, 1958; attended Fettes College, Edinburgh.

Addresses: *Contact*—Tessa Sayle Agency, 11 Jubilee Place, London SW3 3TE, England.

Career: Writer and actor. Repertory and television actor in England.

Awards, Honors: Pye Television Award, children's writer of the year, 1979; Gold Medal, International Film and Television Festival of New York, 1980, for *Barriers;* Pye Television Award, children's writer of the year, 1981; Gold Medal, International Film and Television Festival of New York, 1983; Dillons First Fiction Award, 1995, for *Now and Then.*

WRITINGS

Television Series:
Emerdale Farm, 1975-77.
The Paper Lads, Tyne Tees Television, 1978-79.
Barriers, Tyne Tees Television, 1980-81.

Television Movies:
"Dreams Lost, Dreams Found" (based on a work by Pamela Wallace), *Harlequin Romance Movie,* Showtime, 1987.

Television Specials:
"The Red Signal" and "The Girl in the Train," *Agatha Christie Stories, Series I,* 1983.
"The Fourth Man" and "In a Glass Darkly," *Agatha Christie Stories, Series II,* 1985.

Other Television Writing:
Dead Set at Dream Boy, 1965.
We Never Went to Cheddar Gorge, 1968.
The Story Teller, 1969.
A Memory of Two Loves, 1972.
Conversations in the Dark, 1972.
Mr. Oddy (from a story by Hugh Walpole), 1975.
The Orsini Emeralds (from a story by G. B. Stern), 1975.
Going Back, Yorkshire Television, 1979.
Kids, London Weekend Television, 1979.
Philip, 1979.
The Gate of Eden (from his novel), YTV, 1980.
The Agatha Christie Hour, Thames Television, 1982.
The Machine Gunners (from a book by Robert Westall), BBC, 1982.
Dearly Beloved, YTV, 1983.
The Christmas Tree (from a novel by Jennifer Johnston), YTV, 1985.
The Watchouse (from a story by Westall), 1988.
The Torch, 1992.
Moonacre, 1994.

Stage Plays:
Another Round, Farnham, England, 1962, published by Samuel French (London), 1963.

The Gentle Avalanche, Farnham, then Royal Court Theatre, London, both 1962, published by Samuel French, 1964.
Return Ticket: A Comedy, Farnham, 1962, then Duchess Theatre, London, 1965, published by English Theatre Guild (London), 1966.
The Scallop Shell, Farnham, 1963.
Flight of a Lone Sparrow, Farnham, 1965.
The Scourging of Mathew Barrow, Leicester, England, 1966.
Tinker's Curse, Nottingham Playhouse, Nottingham, England, 1968, published by Ungar, 1969.
The Illusionist, Perth, Scotland, 1969.
We Never Went to Cheddar Gorge (based on his television script), Perth, 1969.
National Trust, Perth, 1970.
The Deliverance of Fanny Blaydon, Perth, 1971.
Orlando the Marmalade Cat Buys a Cottage (juvenile; from a story by Kathleen Hale), London, 1975.
Orlando's Camping Holiday (juvenile; from a story by Hale), London, 1976.

Books:
(With John H. Moore) *The Question of Religion,* Hamish Hamilton (London), 1978, published in the series "Questions of Human Existence as Answered by Major World Religions," Bradbury (Scarsdale, NY), 1980.
(With Moore) *The Christ Story,* Hamish Hamilton, 1978, published in the series "Questions of Human Existence as Answered by Major World Religions," Bradbury, 1980.
(With Moore), *The Hindu Sound,* Hamish Hamilton, 1978, published in the series "Questions of Human Existence as Answered by Major World Religions," Bradbury, 1980.
(With Moore) *The Judaic Law,* Hamish Hamilton, 1979, published in the series "Questions of Human Existence as Answered by Major World Religions," Bradbury, 1980.
(With Moore) *The Buddha Way,* Hamish Hamilton, 1979, published in the series "Questions of Human Existence as Answered by Major World Religions," Bradbury, 1980.
(With Moore) *The Islamic Space,* Hamish Hamilton, 1979, published in the series "Questions of Human Existence as Answered by Major World Religions," Bradbury, 1980.
Now and Then, Abacus (London), 1996.
Two Gentlemen Sharing, Abacus, 1997.

Children's Books; Fiction, Except Where Indicated:
The Gate of Eden, Hamish Hamilton, 1974, Bradbury, 1975.

The Ideal Tale (poems), Compton Russell (Tisbury, England), 1975.

The Land Beyond, Hamish Hamilton, 1975, Bradbury, 1976.

Return to the Gate, Hamish Hamilton, 1975, Bradbury, 1977.

The Dark Side of the Moon, Hamish Hamilton, 1976, Bradbury, 1977.

(With Moore) *The Once and Forever Christmas* (poems), Compton Russell, 1976.

Barriers, Hamish Hamilton, 1981.

Bloxworth Blue, Julia MacRae Books (London), 1984, Harper (New York City), 1985.

The Secret Line, Walker (London), 1988.

(With Carla Lane) *Mrs. Boswell's Slice of Cake,* BBC Books (London), 1989.

The Steps up the Chimney, Bodley Head (London), 1990.

The Door in the Tree, Bodley Head, 1991.

The Tunnel behind the Waterfall, Bodley Head, 1991.

The Bridge in the Clouds, Bodley Head, 1992.

The Gondolier's Cat, Hodder & Stoughton (London), 1993.

The Summer of the Haunting, Bodley Head, 1993.

OTHER SOURCES

Books:

Contemporary Authors, Volume 103, Gale (Detroit, MI), 1982.

COUSTEAU, Jacques-Yves 1910-1997

PERSONAL

Born June 11, 1910, in St. Andre de Cubzac, France; died of a heart attack, June 25, 1997, in Paris, France; son of Daniel P. (a lawyer) and Elizabeth (Duranthon) Cousteau; married Simone Melchior, July 11, 1937 (died, 1990); married Francine Triplet (a flight attendant), June, 1991; children: (first marriage) Jean-Michel, Philippe (deceased); (second marriage) Diane, Pierre-Yves. *Education:* Stanislas Academy, Paris, B.S., 1927; French Naval Academy, graduated, 1933.

Addresses: *Contact*—Cousteau Society, 777 United Nations Plaza, New York, NY 10017.

Career: Oceanographer, producer, director, and cinematographer. French Oceanography Co., founder and president, beginning in 1950; Center for Marine Studies, Marseille, France, founder and president, beginning in 1952; Oceanographic Museum, director, 1957-88; Institut Oceanographique et Musee, Monaco, director, 1965-88; Cousteau Society, New York City, principal, beginning in 1973; Les Requins Associes (television production company), principal. Calypso Oceanographic Expedition, leader; Conshelf Saturation Dive Program, director, beginning in 1957; conducted numerous oceanographic explorations, in cooperation with National Aeronautic and Space Administration, National Geographic Society, and French Academy of Sciences. International Commission for the Scientific Exploration of the Mediterranean, past general secretary; Eurocean, past chairperson; French Council on the Rights of Future Generations, chairperson, 1992-95. Designer (with Emile Gagnan) of the aqualung for deep-sea diving, 1942, and developer of first underwater television camera equipment; created underwater research group with Commander Philippe Tailliez and Frederic Dumas; acquired the ship *Calypso* in 1950; designer (with Jean Mollard) of diving saucer (submersible), 1959. *Military service:* French Navy, 1930-56, head of Underseas Research Group, 1946; became captaine de corvette. Also served in the French Resistance during World War II.

Awards, Honors: Academy Award, best short documentary, and Golden Palm, Cannes International Film Festival, both 1956, for *The Silent World;* Academy Award, best short subject, 1959, for *The Golden Fish;* Academy Award, best short subject, 1964, and Grand prix du cinema francaise pour la jeunesse, both for *World without Sun;* Bradford Washburn Award, Museum of Science, Boston, MA, 1965; Emmy Award nominations, outstanding achievement in a cultural documentary and "magazine-type" program or series, 1969 and 1970, two Emmy Awards and one Emmy Award nomination, outstanding cultural program, 1972, and Emmy Award, outstanding documentary program achievement, cultural programs category, 1972, all for *The Undersea World of Jacques Cousteau* (in all *The Undersea World of Jacques Cousteau* received forty Emmy Award nominations); Howard N. Potts Medal, Franklin Institute, 1970; Gold Medal, National Geographic Society, 1971; Prix d'oceanographic Albert I, 1971; Grand Medaille d'Or, Societe d'encouragement au progres, 1973; Prix de la Couronne d'Or, 1973; award, New England Aquarium, 1973; International Environmental Prize, United Nations, 1977; Emmy Award nomination, outstanding informational special, 1978, for *Calypso's Search for Atlantis: A Cousteau Odyssey;* Emmy Award nomination, outstanding information program, 1980, for *The Nile: A Cousteau Odyssey;* Lindbergh Award, 1982; prize, Bruno H. Schubert Foundation, 1983.

Emmy Award, outstanding informational special, 1985, for *Cousteau: Mississippi;* Emmy Award nominations, outstanding informational special and outstanding informational series, both 1985, for *Cousteau/Amazon: Snowstorm in the Jungle;* U.S. Presidential Medal of Freedom, 1985; National Academy of Television Arts and Sciences, Founders Award, 1987, inducted into Hall of Fame, 1987; Centennial Award, National Geographic Society, 1988; named to Global 500 Role of Honor for Environmental Achievement, United Nations Environmental Programme, 1988; inducted into Academie Francaise, 1989; Premi Internacional Catalunya, Catalan Institute of Mediterranean Studies, 1991; James Smithson Bicentennial Medal, Smithsonian Institution, 1996; honorary degrees include D.Sc. from University of California, Berkeley, and Brandeis University, 1970, Rensselaer Polytechnic Institute, 1977, Harvard University, 1979, and University of Ghent, 1983; military awards include Croix de Guerre with palm and chevalier, French Legion of Honor.

CREDITS

Film Work:
Cinematographer, *Par Dix-huit Detres de Fond* (short documentary; also known as *Through Eighteen Meters of Water*), 1942.
Cinematographer, *Epaves* (short documentary; also known as *Wrecks*), 1945.
Producer, director, and cinematographer, *The Silent World* (short documentary; also known as *Le Monde du Silence*), Columbia, 1956.
Producer, *The Golden Fish* (short documentary; also known as *Les Requins*), Columbia, 1959.
Producer, *World without Sun* (short documentary; also known as *Le Monde sans Soleil*), Columbia, 1964.
Producer and director, *St. Lawrence: Stairway to the Sea* (also known as *Du Grand Large aux Grand Lacs*), 1982.

Other films include *Voyage to the End of the World* and about twenty short documentaries produced between 1942 and 1956.

Television Appearances; Series:
Host, *The Undersea World of Jacques Cousteau,* ABC, 1968-76.

Television Appearances; Specials:
The World of Jacques-Yves Cousteau, CBS, 1966.
Host, *Cousteau Amazon* (four episodes, including *Cousteau/Amazon: Snowstorm in the Jungle*) TBS, 1984.
Host, *Cousteau: Mississippi,* syndicated, 1984.

Television Appearances; Episodic:
"Undersea Archaeology," *Omnibus,* CBS, 1954.
Monday Night Special, ABC, 1972.
Those Amazing Animals, ABC, 1980.

Television Work; Series:
Co-executive producer, *The Undersea World of Jacques Cousteau,* ABC, 1968-76.
Executive producer, *The Cousteau Odyssey,* PBS, 1977.
Executive producer (with son Philippe Cousteau), *The Nile: A Cousteau Odyssey,* PBS, 1979.

Executive producer of the series *Rediscovery of the World.*

Television Work; Specials:
Producer, *The World of Jacques-Yves Cousteau,* CBS, 1966.
Executive producer (with Philippe Cousteau), *Calypso's Search for Atlantis: A Cousteau Odyssey,* PBS, 1977.
Executive producer (with Jean-Michel Cousteau), *Cousteau Amazon* (four episodes, including *Cousteau/Amazon: Snowstorm in the Jungle*) TBS, 1984.
Executive producer (with Jean-Michel Cousteau), *Cousteau: Mississippi,* syndicated, 1984.

Other Television Work:
Other works include *Oasis in Space.*

WRITINGS

Films:
The Silent World (short documentary; also known as *Le monde du silence*), Columbia, 1956.

Books:
Par Dix-huit Metres de Fond, Durel (Paris), 1946.
(With Frederic Dumas) *La Plongee en Scaphandre,* Laffont (Paris), 1950.
(With Frederic Dumas) *Le Monde du Silence,* Laffont, 1953, published in the U.S. as *The Silent World,* Harper (New York City), 1953.
(With James Dugan) *The Living Sea,* Harper, 1963.

(With J. Polus) *Aldabra, Sanctuaire de Corail,* Hachette (Paris), 1964.

(With Polus) *Le Monde Sans soleil,* Hachette, 1964, published in the U.S. as *World without Sun,* Harper, 1965.

(With Philippe Cousteau) *The Shark: Splendid Savage of the Sea,* Doubleday (New York City), 1970.

(With Philippe Diole) *Vie at Mort des Coraux,* Flammarion (Paris), 1971, published in the U.S. as *Life and Death in the Coral Sea,* Doubleday, 1971.

(With Diole) *Un Tresor Englouti,* Flammarion, 1971.

(With Diole) *Diving for Sunken Treasure,* Doubleday, 1972.

(With Diole) *Nos Amies les Baleines,* Flammarion, 1972, published in the U.S. as *The Whale: Mighty Monarch of the Sea,* Doubleday, 1972.

(With Diole) *Octopus and Squid: The Soft Intelligence,* Doubleday, 1973.

(With Diole) *Trois Aventures de la Calypso,* Flammarion, 1973, published in the U.S. as *Three Adventures: Galapagos, Titicaca, the Blue Hole,* Doubleday, 1973.

Le Monde des Oceans (encyclopedia), twenty volumes, Laffont, 1974.

(With Diole) *Compagnons de Plongee,* Flammarion, 1974, published in the U.S. as *Diving Companions: Sea Lion, Elephant Seal, Walrus,* Doubleday, 1974.

(With Diole) *Les Dauphins at la Libene,* Flammarion-Arthaud, 1975, published in the U.S. as *Dolphins,* Doubleday, 1975.

(With A. Sivirine) *Calypso,* Laffont, 1978.

(With Y. Paccalet) *Saumons, Castors et Loutres,* Flammarion, 1978.

(With Paccalet) *La Vie au Bout du Monde,* Flammarion, 1979.

(With Paccalet) *Les Surprises de la Mer,* Flammarion, 1980.

(With Paccalet) *A la Recherche de l'Atlantide,* Flammarion, 1981.

(With Equipe Cousteau) *Almanach Cousteau de l'Environnement,* Laffont, 1981.

(With H. Jacquier) *Francais, on a Vole ta Mer,* Laffont, 1981.

(With Paccalet) *Le Destin du Nil,* Flammarion, 1982.

Planete Ocean (encyclopedia), twenty-six volumes, Laffont-VPC Liriade, 1983.

(With Paccalet) *Fortunes de Mer,* Flammarion, 1983.

(With M. Richards) *Jacques Cousteau's Amazon Journey* (title in French, *L'Expedition Cousteau en Amazonie*), 1984.

(With Paccalet) *Du Grand Large aux Grands Lacs,* Flammarion, 1985.

(With Paccalet) *La Planete des Baleines,* Laffont, 1986, published in the U.S. as *Jacques Cousteau/ Whales,* 1988.

(With Paccalet) *La Mer Blessee,* Flammarion, 1987.

(With Paccalet) *La Mer de Cortez,* Flammarion, 1988.

(With Paccalet) *Cap Horn a la Turbovoile,* Flammarion, 1989.

(With Paccalet) *Les Grands Fleuves,* Laffont, 1989.

(With Richards) *Papouasie Nouvelle-Guinee,* Laffont, 1989.

(With Paccalet) *La Grande Barriere de Corail,* Flammarion, 1990.

(With Paccalet) *Les Ilesdu Pacifique,* Flammarion, 1990.

(With Paccalet) *Missions Pacifiques,* Laffont, 1990.

(With Richards) *Le Grand Requin Blanc,* Laffont, 1992.

(With Richards) *L'Australie,* Laffont, 1993.

(With F. Sarano) *Madagascar: L'ile des Esprits,* Plon (Paris), 1995.

(With Paccalet) *Le Monde des Dauphins,* Laffont, 1995.

(With D. Ody) *Namibie: Voyages au Sud de l'Afrique,* Laffont, 1996.

(With Paccalet) *Le Monde des Requins: A Paraitre,* Laffont, 1997.

Also published several scientific reports.

Books for Children:

Dauphins, Cousteau Hachette-Jeunesse (Paris), 1991.

Phoques, Cousteau Hachette-Jeunesse, 1991.

Pingouins, Cousteau Hachette-Jeunesse, 1991.

Albatros, Cousteau Hachette-Jeunesse, 1991.

Loutres de Mers, Cousteau Hachette-Jeunesse, 1991.

Le Corail Vivant, Cousteau Hachette-Jeunesse, 1991.

Le Garibaldi, Poisson du Pacifique, Cousteau Hachette-Jeunesse, 1991.

Le Dragon de Mer, Cousteau Hachette-Jeunesse, 1991.

Les Secrets des Antipodes, Cousteau Hachette-Jeunesse, 1991.

Les Secrets de l'Amazonie, Cousteau Hachette-Jeunesse, 1991.

Les Secrets d'une Plongee, Cousteau Hachette-Jeunesse, 1991.

Baleines a Bosse, Cousteau Hachette-Jeunesse, 1992.

Lamantins, Cousteau Hachette-Jeunesse, 1992.

Kangourous, Cousteau Hachette-Jeunesse, 1992.

Elephants de Mer, Cousteau Hachette-Jeunesse, 1992.

Les Crabes, Cousteau Hachette-Jeunesse, 1992.

Les Secrets de Papouasie Nouvelle-Guinee, Cousteau Hachette-Jeunesse, 1992.

Les Secrets de l'Australie, Cousteau Hachette-Jeunesse, 1992.

Les Secrets du Danube, Cousteau Hachette-Jeunesse, 1992.

Les Secrets de Borneo, Cousteau Hachette-Jeunesse, 1992.

Les Secrets de la Calypso et de l'Alcyone, Cousteau Hachette-Jeunesse, 1992.

Planet Terre, La Grande Aventure de la Vie, Cousteau Hachette-Jeunesse, 1993.

Mission en Antarctique, Cousteau Hachette-Jeunesse, 1993.

Mission sur le Mekong, Cousteau Hachette-Jeunesse, 1993.

Mission en Indonesie, Cousteau Hachette-Jeunesse, 1994.

Mission en Alaska, Cousteau Hachette-Jeunesse, 1995.

Adaptations: The film *Cries from the Deep* (also known as *Les Pieges de la Mer*), released in 1981, is based on a story by Cousteau.

OBITUARIES AND OTHER SOURCES

Books:

Contemporary Authors, New Revision Series, Volume 15, Gale (Detroit, MI), 1985.

Notable Twentieth-Century Scientists, Volume 1, Gale (Detroit, MI), 1995.

Periodicals:

E, March-April, 1996, p. 10.
Newsweek, July 7, 1997, p. 56.
New York Times, June 26, 1997, p. A1.
People Weekly, July 7, 1997, p. 112.*

CRAIG, Carl 1954-

PERSONAL

Born August 1, 1954, in Tallahassee, FL; son of Walter O. (a music professor) and Ruth (a secretary; maiden name, Roper) Craig; married Angela E. Fong (an airline worker). *Education:* University of Rochester, B.A., 1976; studied with Stella Adler in New York City. *Religion:* Roman Catholic.

Addresses: *Contact*—244 West 54th St., 8th Floor, New York, NY 10019.

Career: Actor, singer, and producer.

Member: Actors' Equity Association, American Federation of Television and Radio Artists, Screen Actors Guild.

CREDITS

Film Appearances:

Willie, *Tom,* 1973.
Titons gang leader, *Warriors,* Paramount, 1979.
Street punk, *Fort Apache, the Bronx,* Twentieth Century-Fox, 1981.
Junkie, *Prince of the City,* Warner Bros., 1981.
Mental patient, *Endless Love,* Universal, 1981.
Type, reporter, fool, Beaner Gang member, basketball player, and actor in audition, *Hollywood Shuffle,* Goldwyn, 1987.
Man in love, *I'm Gonna Git You Sucka,* Metro-Goldwyn-Mayer/United Artists, 1988.

Film Work:

Executive producer, *Hollywood Shuffle,* Goldwyn, 1987.
Producer (with Peter McCarthy), *I'm Gonna Git You Sucka,* Metro-Goldwyn-Mayer/United Artists, 1988.
Co-producer, *Mo' Money,* Columbia, 1992.
Producer, *House Party 3,* New Line, 1994.

Television Work:

Producer (with Keenen Ivory Wayans), "Robert Townsend and His Partners in Crime" (special), *HBO Comedy Hour,* HBO, 1987.
Associate producer, *Hammer, Slammer, and Slade* (pilot), ABC, 1990.
Producer, "Damon Wayans: The Last Stand?" (special), *HBO Comedy Hour,* HBO, 1991.

Television Appearances:

Hollow Image, 1979.

Appeared as paramedic cop, *As the World Turns,* CBS; as waiter, *All My Children,* ABC; and in "Lead Poisoning," *Black Dimensions,* PBS.

Stage Appearances:

My Fair Lady, Arizona Theatre Company, Phoenix, 1985-86.

Appeared as Shine, *The Great Mac Daddy,* Negro Ensemble Company, New York City; in *The Brownsville Raid,* Negro Ensemble Company; as Bubba, *Second Thoughts,* Afro American Total Theatre, NY; as Universal Man, *Poets from the Inside,* Public Theatre, New York City; as Tony, *Black Sheep,* Billie Holiday Theatre, New York City; as Pierre, *Sister Racher and the Ton Ton Maconte,* La MaMa Experimental Theatre Club, New York City; in *Ceremo-*

nies in *Dark Old Men*, GEVA Theatre, Rochester, NY; and as Catesby, *Richard III*, U.R.S.T., Rochester, NY.*

CROSBY, Mary 1959-

PERSONAL

Full name, Mary Frances Crosby; born September 14, 1959, in Los Angeles, CA; daughter of Harry Lillis ("Bing") (a singer and actor) and Kathryn (Grandstaff) Crosby; married Ebb Lottimer, November, 1978. *Education:* Attended University of Texas at Austin; studied acting at American Conservatory Theatre.

Addresses: *Agent*—Gold/Marshak/Liedtke Talent and Literary Agency, 3500 West Olive Ave., Suite 1400, Burbank, CA 91505.

Career: Actress.

CREDITS

Television Appearances; Series:
Suzi Cooper, *Brothers and Sisters*, NBC, 1979.
Kristin Shepard, *Dallas*, CBS, 1979-81.

Television Appearances; Miniseries:
Patricia North, *Pearl*, ABC, 1978.
Karen Lancaster, *Hollywood Wives*, NBC, 1985.
Isabel Hazard, *North and South, Book II*, ABC, 1986.

Television Appearances; Movies:
Lisa Harris, *With This Ring*, ABC, 1978.
Eloise, *A Guide for the Married Woman*, ABC, 1978.
Cathy Preston, *Midnight Lace*, NBC, 1981.
Ellen Price, *Confessions of a Married Man*, ABC, 1983.
Susan Campbell, *Final Jeopardy*, NBC, 1985.
Lucy Mallory, *Stage Coach*, CBS, 1986.
Adele, *Johann Strauss: The King without a Crown* (also known as *Johann Strauss: Le roi sans couronne* and *Johann Strauss—Der Koenig ohne Krone*), 1987.

Television Appearances; Pilots:
Natalie Kingsley, *Golden Gate*, ABC, 1981.
Cynthia Hughes, *The Big Easy*, NBC, 1982.
Cover Up, CBS, 1984.

Television Appearances; Specials:
Goldilocks, NBC, 1970.
Bing Crosby's Christmas Show, NBC, 1970.

Bing Crosby and the Sounds of Christmas, NBC, 1971.
Christmas with the Bing Crosbys, 1972.
Bing Crosby's Sun Valley Christmas Show, NBC, 1973.
Bing Crosby's White Christmas, CBS, 1976.
Bing! A 50th Anniversary Gala, CBS, 1977.
Bing Crosby's Merrie Olde Christmas, 1977.
Battle of the Network Stars, ABC, 1979.
The 21st Annual Academy of Country Music Awards, 1986.
Bonnie, *Crazy Dan*, NBC, 1986.
Tube Test Two, ABC, 1991.
Jennifer, *Best Sellers: Men Who Hate Women and the Women Who Love Them; The Relationship*, NBC, 1994.

Television Appearances; Episodic:
"Demon under the Bed," *The Danny Thomas Hour*, NBC, 1967.
"Strange Justice," *Starsky and Hutch*, ABC, 1978.
Chris, "Pressure Point," *CHiPs*, NBC, 1979.
"Kristen," *Knots Landing*, CBS, 1980.
Colleen Wilcox, "Ready, Aim . . . Die!," *The Fall Guy*, ABC, 1982.
"The Experiment," *The Love Boat*, ABC, 1982.
"Strange Bedfellows," *The Fall Guy*, ABC, 1983.
"Staying Alive while Running a High Flash Dance Fever," *Automan*, ABC, 1983.
"Yesterday's Child," *Finder of Lost Loves*, ABC, 1984.
"On Your Toes," *Glitter*, ABC, 1984.
"The Wedding," *Hotel*, ABC, 1984.
"Fish out of Water," *The Love Boat*, ABC, 1984.
Kim Donnelly, "Undersea Odyssey," *The Fall Guy*, ABC, 1984.
"Distortions," *Hotel*, ABC, 1985.
"Saving Grace," *Hotel*, ABC, 1985.
"The Matadors," *The Love Boat*, ABC, 1986.
Greta Nordhoff-Roscoe, *Freddy's Nightmares* (also known as *Freddy's Nightmares: A Nightmare on Elm Street; The Series*), syndicated, between 1988 and 1990.
"Sister, Sister," *In the Heat of the Night*, NBC, 1989.
"Hill o' Beans," *The New Adventures of Beans Baxter*, Fox, 1987.
Laura, "Tainted Lady," *Murder, She Wrote*, CBS, 1991.
Monique, *Lois and Clark: The New Adventures of Superman*, ABC, 1993.
Professor Natima Lang, *Star Trek: Deep Space Nine*, syndicated, 1993.
Claudia Van Eyck, *Beverly Hills, 90210*, Fox, 1995.
Heather Bonham, "Who Killed the Tennis Ace?," *Burke's Law*, CBS, 1995.

Heidi, *Platypus Man,* UPN, 1995.
Alya Ransom, *Orleans,* CBS, 1997.

Film Appearances:
Elizabeth Rush, *The Last Plane Out,* 1983.
Child's Play, 1984.
Princess Karina, *The Ice Pirates,* Metro-Goldwyn-
    Mayer/United Artists, 1984.
Samantha Gregory, *Tapeheads,* De Laurentiis Enter-
    tainment Group/Avenue, 1988.
Mary Preston, *Quicker than the Eye* (also known as
    Supertrick), 1988.
Deadly Innocents, 1989.
Marlee Redding, *Body Chemistry,* Concorde, 1990.
Kate, *Eating,* International Rainbow Pictures, 1991.
Jessica Pierce, *Corporate Affairs,* Metro-Goldwyn-
    Mayer/United Artists Home Video, 1991.
Ursula Schneider, *The Berlin Conspiracy,* 1992.
Marcie, *Desperate Motive* (also known as *Distant
    Cousins*), New Line, 1993.
Dana, *Cupid,* Image Organization, 1997.

Stage Appearances:
The Seagull, Los Angeles Theatre Center, Los Ange-
    les, 1988-89.*

CRUTCHLEY, Rosalie 1921-1997

OBITUARY NOTICE—See index for *CTFT* sketch:
Born January 4, 1921, in London, England; died July
28, 1997. Actress. Crutchley is remembered for her
roles on stage, film, and television, particularly her
work in productions involving England's King Henry
VIII. She studied at the Royal Academy of Music and
later found work with the Liverpool Playhouse in
repertory theater in the late 1930s. In 1940 she performed with the H. M. Tennent Players in Scotland,
and from 1940 to 1942 she appeared at the Oxford
Playhouse. She returned to the Liverpool Playhouse
in 1945 with the Old Vic Company. Crutchley made
her stage debut in *Saint Joan* in 1938, followed by
her London debut in *Love for Love* five years later.
Her first performance in the United States was in *The
Heart of the Matter.* Among her other stage performances are roles in *A Midsummer Night's Dream,
Much Ado About Nothing, A Doll's House, Don Juan,*
and *The Crucible.* In 1948 she made her film debut
in *Take My Life* and went on to appear in *Quo Vadis,
The Sword and the Rose, No Time for Tears, A Tale
of Two Cities, The Nun's Story, The Haunting, Who
Slew Auntie Roo?, The Keep, Sons and Lovers,* and
A World Apart. Her television credits included *The

*Six Wives of Henry VIII, Smiley's People, Brother
Cadfael, Poirot, Cold Comfort Farm,* and *Queenie.*
In 1997 she appeared in the mystery *The Killings at
Badger's Drift.* The Guild of Television named her
best actress of the year in 1956 for her performance
in *Black Limelight,* and she received the International
Television Award in 1970 for her work in *The Six
Wives of Henry the VIII.*

OBITUARIES AND OTHER SOURCES

Periodicals:
Times (London; electronic), July 31, 1997.

CRYSTAL, Billy 1947-

PERSONAL

Full name, William Crystal; born March 14, 1947,
in Long Beach, Long Island, NY; son of Jack (a record
store owner, record company executive, and producer of jazz concerts) and Helen Crystal; married
Janice Goldfinger, 1970; children: Jennifer, Lindsay.
Education: Attended Marshall University; graduated
from Nassau Community College; New York University, B.F.A. (television and film direction), 1970.
Avocational interests: Softball, tennis, cooking Japanese food, collecting New York Yankees memorabilia and miniature furniture.

Addresses: *Office*—Rollins, Joffe, Morra, and Brezner,
5555 Melrose Ave., Los Angeles, CA 90038. *Agent*—
Creative Artists Agency, 9830 Wilshire Blvd., Beverly
Hills, CA 90212.

Career: Actor, comedian, producer, director, and
writer. Briefly worked as a substitute teacher at Long
Beach Junior High School; worked with Alumni Theatre Group at Nassau Community College; member
of improvisational comedy troupe variously called
We the People, Comedy Jam, and Three's Company,
1971-75; stand-up comedian, 1975—, performing at
clubs including Catch a Rising Star, Playboy clubs,
and the Comedy Store.

Member: Screen Actors Guild.

Awards, Honors: Emmy Award nomination, best
actor in a variety program, 1985, for *Saturday Night
Live;* Grammy Award nomination, best comedy recording, 1985, for *Mahvelous!;* two ACE awards and
other ACE Award nominations, National Cable Tele-

vision Association, 1986, for *On Location: Billy Crystal—Don't Get Me Started;* Emmy Award nomination, outstanding individual performance in a variety or music program, 1987, for *The 29th Annual Grammy Awards;* Emmy Award nomination, outstanding individual performance in a variety or music program, 1988, for *An All-Star Toast to the Improv;* Emmy Award, outstanding performance in special events, 1989, for *The 31st Annual Grammy Awards;* Golden Apple Award, star of the year, Women's Press Club, 1989; Emmy Award, outstanding writing, and Emmy Award nominations, outstanding individual performance in a variety or music program and outstanding variety, music, or comedy special, all 1989, for *Midnight Train to Moscow;* American Comedy Award, funniest actor in a motion picture, 1989, and Golden Globe Award nomination, best performance by an actor in a motion picture (comedy or musical), 1990, for *When Harry Met Sally . . . .*

Emmy awards for outstanding writing and outstanding individual performance in a variety or music program, both 1991, for *The 63rd Annual Academy Awards;* Golden Globe Award nomination, best actor in a musical or comedy, and American Comedy Award, both 1991, for *City Slickers;* American Comedy Award, 1992, for work on Academy Awards presentation show; Golden Globe Award nomination, best performance by an actor in a motion picture (comedy or musical), 1993, for *Mr. Saturday Night;* Emmy Award nomination, outstanding individual performance in a variety or music program, 1993, for *The 65th Annual Academy Awards.*

CREDITS

Film Appearances:
Lionel, *Rabbit Test,* Avco Embassy, 1978.
Voice, *Animalympics* (animated film), Barber Rose International Films, 1979.
Morty the Mime, *This Is Spinal Tap,* Embassy Pictures, 1984.
Danny Costanzo, *Running Scared,* Metro-Goldwyn-Mayer/United Artists, 1986.
Miracle Max, *The Princess Bride,* Twentieth Century-Fox, 1987.
Larry Donner, *Throw Momma from the Train,* Orion, 1987.
Goodnight Moon, 1987.
Dr. Abbie Polin, *Memories of Me,* Metro-Goldwyn-Mayer/United Artists, 1988.
Harry Burns, *When Harry Met Sally . . .,* Nelson Entertainment, 1989.
Mitch Robbins, *City Slickers,* Columbia, 1991.

Buddy Young Jr., *Mr. Saturday Night,* Columbia, 1992.
Mitch Robbins, *City Slickers II: The Legend of Curly's Gold,* Columbia, 1994.
Mickey, *Forget Paris,* Columbia, 1995.
First gravedigger, *Hamlet,* Columbia, 1996.
Jack Lawrence, *Fathers' Day,* Warner Bros., 1997.
Larry, *Deconstructing Harry,* Fine Line, 1997.
My Giant, 1998.

Film Work:
Producer (with Alan King and Michael Hertzberg), *Memories of Me,* Metro-Goldwyn-Mayer/United Artists, 1988.
Executive producer, *City Slickers,* Columbia, 1991.
Producer and director, *Mr. Saturday Night,* Columbia, 1992.
Producer, *City Slickers II: The Legend of Curly's Gold,* Columbia, 1994.
Producer and director, *Forget Paris,* Columbia, 1995.
Producer, *My Giant,* 1998.

Television Appearances; Series:
Jodie Dallas, *Soap,* ABC, 1977-81.
Host, *The Billy Crystal Comedy Hour,* NBC, 1982.
Saturday Night Live, NBC, 1984-85.

Television Appearances; Episodic:
Guest, *Saturday Night Live with Howard Cosell,* ABC, 1976.
Guest, *Saturday Night Live,* NBC, 1976.
"New Year's Wedding," *All in the Family,* CBS, 1976.
The Kissing Bandit, "The Kissing Bandit," *The Love Boat,* ABC, 1978.
"Make-Up," *Darkroom,* ABC, 1981.
Third Pig, "The Three Little Pigs," *Faerie Tale Theatre,* Showtime, 1984.
Robert Klein Time, USA Network, 1988.
Himself, "Talk Show," *The Larry Sanders Show,* HBO, 1992.
Narrator, "My New Neighbors," *Shelley Duvall's Bedtime Stories,* 1992.
Guest, *The Whoopi Goldberg Show,* syndicated, 1992.
First Person with Maria Shriver, NBC, 1992.
"Addicted to Fame," *First Person with Maria Shriver,* NBC, 1994.
Guest caller Jack, "Leapin' Lizards," *Frasier,* NBC, 1995.
Correspondent, "Extra Point," *Real Sports with Bryant Gumbel,* HBO, 1995.
Himself, *Muppets Tonight!,* ABC, 1996.
Himself, "The One with the Ultimate Fighting Champion," *Friends,* NBC, 1997.

Appeared on numerous talk shows, including *The Tonight Show, That Was the Year That Was, Dinah, The Mike Douglas Show,* and *Later with Bob Costas,* NBC.

Television Appearances; Miniseries:
Baseball, 1994.

Television Appearances; Movies:
David, *SST—Death Flight,* ABC, 1977.
Angel Myles Gordon, *Human Feelings,* NBC, 1978.
Danny Doyle, *Breaking Up Is Hard to Do,* ABC, 1979.
Lieutenant Jake Beser, *Enola Gay: The Men, the Mission, the Atomic Bomb,* NBC, 1980.
Voice of America, *In Search of Dr. Seuss,* TNT, 1994.

Television Appearances; Specials:
ABC team member, *Battle of the Network Stars,* ABC, 1976.
ABC team member, *Battle of the Network Stars,* ABC, 1977.
ABC team member, *Battle of the Network Stars,* ABC, 1978.
Guest, *The 36 Most Beautiful Girls in Texas,* ABC, 1978.
ABC team member, *Battle of the Network Stars,* ABC, 1979.
Host (with Howard Cosell), *Battle of the Network Stars,* ABC, 1979.
Player, *The Celebrity Football Classic,* NBC, 1979.
Regular performer, *The TV Show,* ABC, 1979.
Guest, *Doug Henning's World of Magic,* NBC, 1982.
Host, *Billy Crystal: A Comic's Line,* HBO, 1984.
Host, *A Comedy Salute to Baseball,* NBC, 1985.
Guest, *The Night of 100 Stars II,* ABC, 1985.
Guest performer, *Richard Lewis I'm in Pain Concert,* Showtime, 1985.
Host (with Robin Williams and Whoopi Goldberg), *Comic Relief,* HBO, 1986.
Host, Fernando, Sandy, and Buddy, *On Location: Billy Crystal—Don't Get Me Started,* HBO, 1986.
Guest, *Kraft Salutes the George Burns Ninetieth Birthday Special* (also known as *George Burns' 90th Birthday Special*), CBS, 1986.
Comic Relief: Backstage Pass, 1986.
Host (with Robin Williams and Whoopi Goldberg), *Comic Relief II,* HBO, 1987.
The Lost Minutes of Billy Crystal, HBO, 1987.
An All-Star Celebration: The 1988 Vote, ABC, 1988.
An All-Star Toast to the Improv, HBO, 1988.
Life's Most Embarrassing Moments, syndicated, 1988.
All-Star Tribute to Kareem Abdul-Jabbar, NBC, 1989.
The Barbara Walters Special, ABC, 1989.

Host (with Robin Williams and Whoopi Goldberg), *Comic Relief III,* HBO, 1989.
Grand Slam, syndicated, 1989.
Midnight Train to Moscow, HBO, 1989.
Saturday Night Live Fifteenth Anniversary, NBC, 1989.
Host (with Robin Williams and Whoopi Goldberg), *Comic Relief IV,* HBO, 1990.
Overtime . . . with Pat O'Brien, CBS, 1990.
Guest, *Robert Wuhl's World Tour,* HBO, 1990.
The World of Jewish Humor, PBS, 1990.
Wolf Trap Salutes Victor Borge: An 80th Birthday Celebration, PBS, 1990.
A Comedy Salute to Michael Jordan, NBC, 1991.
Entertainers '91: The Top Twenty of the Year, ABC, 1991.
Voices That Care, Fox, 1991.
HBO's 20th Anniversary—We Hardly Believe It Ourselves, CBS/HBO, 1992.
Muhammad Ali's 50th Birthday Celebration, ABC, 1992.
Host (with Robin Williams and Whoopi Goldberg), *Comic Relief V,* HBO, 1992.
When It Was a Game II, HBO, 1992.
Wax Cracks Hollywood, HBO, 1993.
"What Is This Thing Called Love?," *The Barbara Walters Special,* ABC, 1993.
But . . . Seriously, Showtime, 1994.
Host (with Robin Williams and Whoopi Goldberg), *Comic Relief VI,* HBO, 1994.
20 Years of Comedy on HBO, HBO, 1995.
Interviewee, *Countdown to Comic Relief,* Comedy Central, 1995.
Host (with Robin Williams and Whoopi Goldberg), *Comic Relief VII,* HBO, 1995.
Hollywood Stars: A Century of Cinema, Disney Channel, 1995.
Host, *Caesar's Writers,* PBS, 1996.
Catch a Rising Star 50th Anniversary—Give or Take 26 Years, CBS, 1996.
Host (with Robin Williams and Whoopi Goldberg), *Comic Relief's 10th Anniversary,* HBO, 1996.
I Am Your Child (also known as *From Zero to Three*), ABC, 1997.
Interviewee, *Sports on the Silver Screen,* HBO, 1997.

Television Appearances; Awards Presentations:
The 28th Annual Grammy Awards, CBS, 1986.
Host, *The 29th Annual Grammy Awards,* CBS, 1987.
The 60th Annual Academy Awards, ABC, 1988.
Host, *The 30th Annual Grammy Awards,* CBS, 1988.
The 61st Annual Academy Awards, ABC, 1989.
Host, *The 31st Annual Grammy Awards,* CBS, 1989.
The 4th Annual American Comedy Awards, ABC, 1990.

Host, *The 62nd Annual Academy Awards,* ABC, 1990.
Host, *The 63rd Annual Academy Awards,* ABC, 1991.
Host, *The 64th Annual Academy Awards Presentation,* ABC, 1992.
The 6th Annual American Comedy Awards, ABC, 1992.
Host, *The 65th Annual Academy Awards Presentation,* ABC, 1993.
The 7th Annual American Comedy Awards, ABC, 1993.
The 10th Annual Television Academy Hall of Fame, Disney Channel, 1994.
Presenter, *The Jim Thorpe Pro Sports Awards,* ABC, 1995.
Host, *The 69th Annual Academy Awards,* ABC, 1997.
Host, *The 70th Annual Academy Awards,* ABC, 1998.

Television Work:
Director and producer, *On Location: Billy Crystal—Don't Get Me Started* (special), HBO, 1986.
Executive producer, *Midnight Train to Moscow* (special), HBO, 1989.
Creator and executive producer, *Sessions* (series), HBO, 1991.
Executive producer, *Survival on the Mountain* (movie), NBC, 1997.

Stage Appearances:
Master of Ceremonies in summer stock production of *Cabaret,* Ohio, 1981.

Stage Work:
House manager of production, *You're a Good Man, Charlie Brown,* New York City, 1971.

RECORDINGS

Mahvelous! (comedy album), A & M Records, 1985.

Also recorded song "You Look Mahvelous."

Videos:
Appeared in numerous video releases, including *Your Favorite Laughs from "An Evening at the Improv,"* 1984; and *Big City Comedy,* 1985.

WRITINGS

For Television:
(With others) *The TV Show* (special), ABC, 1979.
(With others) *The Billy Crystal Comedy Hour* (series), NBC, 1982.

(With Rocco Urbisci) *Billy Crystal: A Comic's Line* (special), HBO, 1984.
(With others) *Saturday Night Live* (series), NBC, 1984-85.
A Comedy Salute to Baseball (special), NBC, 1985.
On Location: Billy Crystal—Don't Get Me Started (special), HBO, 1986.
(With others) *Midnight Train to Moscow* (special), HBO, 1989.
(And creator) *Sessions* (series), HBO, 1991.
(Special material) *The 63rd Annual Academy Awards* (awards presentation), ABC, 1991.
(Special material) *The 64th Annual Academy Awards Presentation* (awards presentation), ABC, 1992.
(Special material) *The 65th Annual Academy Awards Presentation* (awards presentation), ABC, 1993.
(Special material) *The 69th Annual Academy Awards* (awards presentation), ABC, 1997.

For Film:
Goodnight Moon, 1987.
(With Eric Roth) *Memories of Me* (screenplay), Metro-Goldwyn-Mayer/United Artists, 1988.
City Slickers (story idea), Columbia, 1991.
Mr. Saturday Night, Columbia, 1992.
City Slickers II: The Legend of Curly's Gold, Columbia, 1994.
Forget Paris, Columbia, 1995.
My Giant, 1998.

Other Writings:
(With Dick Schaap) *Absolutely Mahvelous* (autobiography), Putnam, 1986.

Contributor to periodicals, including *New York Times* and *Playboy.*

OTHER SOURCES

Books:
Crystal, Billy, and Dick Schaap, *Absolutely Mahvelous,* Putnam, 1986.

Periodicals:
American Film, July/August, 1989, pp. 30-33, 48.
Cosmopolitan, June, 1986, p. 80.
Entertainment Weekly, June 17, 1994, pp. 26-29.
Gentlemen's Quarterly, August, 1989, p. 199.
Life, July, 1989, p. 68; April, 1990, p. 90.
McCall's, July, 1991, p. 58.
People, September 30, 1985, p. 40.
Playboy, September, 1985, p. 140; March, 1988, p. 47.
Rolling Stone, October 24, 1985, p. 49.

TV Guide, November 15, 1980, p. 30; March 24, 1990, p. 5.*

CULLIVER, Karen 1959-

PERSONAL

Born December 30, 1959, in Florida; daughter of Robert Eugene (a tax auditor and licensed minister) and Melinda Jane (a reading teacher; maiden name, Jones) Culliver; married Garrett Parks; children: Madison Claire. *Education:* Attended Stetson University, 1978-79, and Orlando School of the Performing Arts; studied voice with Eric Stern and Michael Richardson, dance with Bob Audy, George Koller, and Stanley Kahn.

Career: Actress and singer. Walt Disney World, Orlando, FL, appeared in *Kids of the Kingdom,* 1978-79; voted Miss Orlando of 1980.

Member: Actors' Equity Association, Screen Actors Guild.

CREDITS

Stage Appearances:
(New York debut) Kim, *Showboat,* Gershwin Theatre, New York City, 1983.
Luisa, *The Fantasticks,* Sullivan Street, NY, 1984.
Rosa Bud and Deirdre Peregrine, *The Mystery of Edwin Drood,* Imperial Theatre, New York City, 1986-87.
Fanny, Goodspeed Opera House, East Haddam, CT, 1986-87.
Shirley Vernon, *Lady, Be Good!,* Goodspeed Opera House, 1987-88.
Mary Stewart, *Animal Crackers,* Huntington Theatre Company, Boston, MA, 1987-88.
Animal Crackers: The Marx Brothers Musical, Alliance Theatre Company, Atlanta, GA, 1988-89.
Broadway Jukebox, American Stage Company, Teaneck, NJ, 1988-89.
Lucille Ballard, *Meet Me in St. Louis,* Gershwin Theatre, 1989.
Christine Daae, *The Phantom of the Opera,* Auditorium Theatre, Chicago, IL, 1990, then Majestic Theatre, New York City, 1990-92, then Washington, DC, 1991, then Curran Theatre, San Francisco, CA, 1997.

Made stage debut as Elaine Harper, *Arsenic and Old Lace,* Once Upon a Stage Dinner Theatre; appeared as Linda Christie in *Play It Again, Sam,* Sarah Brown in *Guys and Dolls,* Daisy Mae in *Li'l Abner,* and Laurey in *Oklahoma!,* all at Once Upon a Stage Dinner Theatre; appeared as Pegeen Ryan, *Mame,* Show Boat Dinner Theatre; as Philia, *A Funny Thing Happened on the Way to the Forum,* Country Dinner Playhouse; as Gwendolyn, *Little Mary Sunshine,* Burt Reynolds Theatre, Florida; as Gloria Upson, *Mame,* Coachlight Dinner Theatre; as Mrs. Potiphar, *Joseph and the Amazing Technicolor Dreamcoat,* An Evening Dinner Theatre. Toured in the chorus, *Camelot;* toured as Kim and understudy for Magnolia, *Showboat,* U.S. cities.

Film Appearances:
(Film debut) *Preppies,* Platinum Pictures, 1984.
The Flamingo Kid, Twentieth Century-Fox, 1984.
Falling in Love, Paramount, 1984.
Mayor's aide, *Turk 182!,* Twentieth Century-Fox, 1985.
Whatever It Takes, Aquarius Films, 1986.

RECORDINGS

San Francisco Phantom of the Opera, *Christmas Center Stage,* Cabanna Boy, 1997.*

CURTIN, Valerie 1945(?)-

PERSONAL

Born March 31, c. 1945, in Jackson Heights, NY; daughter of Joseph Curtin (a radio actor); cousin of Jane Curtin (an actress); married Barry Levinson (a director and screenwriter), December 1977 (divorced, 1982); remarried.

Addresses: *Agent*—Writers & Artists Agency, 924 Westwood Blvd., Suite 900, Los Angeles, CA 90024.

Career: Actress and screenwriter.

Member: Authors Guild.

Awards, Honors: Academy Award nomination, best original screenplay, 1979, for *. . .And Justice For All.*

CREDITS

Film Appearances:
Vera, *Alice Doesn't Live Here Anymore,* Warner Bros., 1975.

Naomi Fishbine, *Mother, Jugs, and Speed,* Twentieth Century-Fox, 1976.

Intensive care nurse, *Silent Movie,* Twentieth Century-Fox, 1976.

Plain Jane, *Silver Streak,* Twentieth Century-Fox, 1976.

Miss Milland, *All the President's Men,* Warner Bros., 1976.

Phyllis, *A Different Story,* Avco-Embassy, 1978.

The Great Smokey Roadblock (also known as *The Last of the Cowboys*), Dimension, 1978.

Mrs. Bok, *Why Would I Lie?,* Metro-Goldwyn-Mayer/United Artists, 1980.

Miss Sheffer, *Maxie,* Orion, 1985.

Arlene Hoffman, *Big Trouble,* Columbia, 1986.

Pearl Waxman, *Down and Out in Beverly Hills,* Buena Vista, 1986.

Also appeared in *Elegant John and the Ladies.*

Television Work; Series:

Co-creator, *Square Pegs,* CBS, 1982-83.

Producer, *Good & Evil,* ABC, 1991.

Television Appearances; Series:

Regular, *The Jim Stafford Show,* ABC, 1975.

Judy Bernly, *9 to 5,* ABC, 1982-83, syndicated, 1986-87.

Television Appearances; Pilots:

Sandy Lambert, *The Primary English Class,* ABC, 1977.

Nurse Bob (unaired), NBC, 1988.

Television Appearances; Episodic:

"Dennis' New Love," *The New Dick Van Dyke Show,* CBS, 1974.

"Fear of Flying," *The Bob Newhart Show,* ABC, 1976.

"Sweathogs vs. Phi Beta Kappa," *Welcome Back Kotter,* ABC, 1976.

Barney Miller, ABC, 1976.

"Off to Jail," *Rhoda,* CBS, 1977.

"Quickie Nirvana," *Rockford Files,* NBC, 1977.

Mrs. Warren, *Frasier,* NBC, 1993.

Also appeared on *Happy Days.*

Television Appearances; Movies:

Miss Goldfarb, *The Greatest Thing That Almost Happened,* CBS, 1977.

Kitty, *A Love Affair: The Eleanor and Lou Gehrig Story,* NBC, 1978.

Chief Warden Stelina Shell, *Brave New World,* NBC, 1980.

Muriel, *A Christmas without Snow,* CBS, 1980.

Stage Appearances:

Edna Klein, *Children of a Lesser God,* Center Theatre Group, Ahmanson Theatre, Los Angeles, CA, 1979.

Also appeared in productions with New Theatre for Now, Center Theatre Group, Mark Taper Forum, Los Angeles, 1983.

WRITINGS

Film:

(With Barry Levinson) *. . . And Justice for All,* Columbia, 1979.

(With Levinson) *Inside Moves* (adapted from the Todd Walton novel of the same title), Associated, 1980.

(With Levinson) *Best Friends,* Warner Bros., 1982.

(With Levinson and Robert Klane) *Unfaithfully Yours* (adapted from the 1948 Preston Sturges film of the same title), Twentieth Century-Fox, 1984.

(With Levinson) *Toys,* Twentieth Century-Fox, 1992.

Television Series:

The Mary Tyler Moore Show, CBS, 1970.

Other Television:

"Mary's Delinquent," *The Mary Tyler Moore Show* (episodic), CBS, 1975.

Phyllis (episodic), CBS, 1975-77.

"Dusk Before Fireworks," *Women & Men: Stories of Seduction* (movie), HBO, 1990.*

CUSACK, Sinead   1948-

PERSONAL

Given name is pronounced *Shin*-ed; full name, Sinead Moira Cusack; born February 18, 1948, in Dalkey, Ireland; daughter of Cyril James (an actor) and Maureen (an actress) Cusack; married Jeremy Irons (an actor), March 28, 1978; children: Samuel James Brefni, Maximilian Paul Diarmiud; sister of Sorcha Cusack, Niamh Cusack, and Catherine Cusack. *Education:* Attended Holy Child Convent, Killiney, Ireland, and Dublin University.

Career: Actress.

Awards, Honors: Antoinette Perry Award nomination, best dramatic actress, 1985, for *Much Ado about Nothing.*

CREDITS

Stage Appearances:
(Stage debut) Phoebe, *The Importance of Mr. O,* Olympia Theatre, Dublin, Ireland, 1960.
Beatrice and Joanna, *The Changeling,* Gardner Centre, Brighton, England, 1971.
Mirandolina, 1971.
The Silence of St. Just, 1971.
Juliet, *Romeo and Juliet,* Shaw Theatre, London, 1972.
Grace Harkaway, *London Assurance,* New Theatre, London, 1972.
Laura Wingfield, *The Glass Menagerie,* Gardner Centre, 1973.
Desdemona, *Othello,* Ludlow Festival, 1974.
Raina Petkoff, *Arms and the Man,* Oxford Festival, Oxford, England, 1976.
Lady Amaranth, *Wild Oats,* Piccadilly Theatre, London, 1977, then Royal Shakespeare Company, Aldwych Theatre, London, 1979.
Lisa, *Children of the Sun,* Royal Shakespeare Company, Aldwych Theatre, 1979.
Isabella, *Measure for Measure,* Royal Shakespeare Company, Aldwych Theatre, 1979.
Celia, *As You Like It,* Memorial Theatre, Stratford-upon-Avon, England, 1980.
Evadne, *The Maid's Tragedy,* Memorial Theatre, 1980.
Roxanne, *Cyrano de Bergerac,* London, then Gershwin Theatre, New York City, 1984.
Beatrice, *Much Ado about Nothing,* London, then Gershwin Theatre, 1984.
Lady Macbeth, *Macbeth,* Barbican Theatre, London, 1987.
Alice, *Aristocrats,* Hampstead Theatre, London, 1988.
Masha, *Three Sisters,* Royal Court Theatre, London, 1990.
Ruth Steadman, *Map of the Heart,* Globe Theatre, London, 1991.
Grace, *Faith Healer,* Royal Court Theatre, 1992.
Marguerite De Bourgogne, *The Tower,* Almeida Theatre, London, 1995-96.

Appeared at Abbey Theater, Dublin, Ireland. Toured as Raina Petkoff, *Arms and the Man,* British cities, 1976.

Film Appearances:
Edith, *Alfred the Great,* Metro-Goldwyn-Mayer, 1969.
Janet Smith, *Hoffman,* Levitt/Pickman, 1970.
Rose, *Terror from under the House* (also known as *Inn of the Frightened People, After Jenny Died,* *Behind the Cellar Door,* and *Revenge*), Hemisphere, 1971.
Rose, *Tam Lin* (also known as *The Ballad of Tam-Lin, The Devil's Widow,* and *The Devil's Woman*), AIP, 1971.
Isabel Geste, *The Last Remake of Beau Geste,* Universal, 1977.
Amanda "Billi" Rockwell, *Rocket Gibraltar,* Columbia, 1988.
Dublin Murders, 1988.
Miss Balsilbie, *Venus Peter,* 1989.
Mary Crick, *Waterland,* Fine Line, 1992.
The mother, *The Cement Garden,* October Films, 1992.
Ellie McAllister, *Bad Behavior,* October Films, 1993.
Matilde, *Sparrow* (also known as *Storia di una capinera*), 1993.
Menchu, *Uncovered,* CiBy 2000, 1994.
Diana Grayson, *Stealing Beauty* (also known as *I'll Dance Alone, I Dance Alone,* and *Dancing by Myself*), Fox Searchlight Pictures, 1996.
The Nephew, 1998.

Television Appearances; Specials:
Sally, *The Eyes Have It,* 1974.
Olivia, *Twelfth Night,* BBC, then PBS, 1980.
Nelly Mann, "Tales from Hollywood," *American Playhouse,* PBS, 1992.
Roxanne, *Cyrano de Bergerac,* Bravo, 1994.
Diane Priest, "Oliver's Travels," *Mystery!,* PBS, 1996.

Television Appearances; Movies:
Emily, *David Copperfield,* NBC, 1970.
Rosalind, *Quiller: Night of the Father,* 1975.
Rosalind, *Quiller: Price of Violence,* 1975.

Television Appearances; Episodic:
Jenny Lindley, "Take Seven," *The Persuaders,* ABC, 1971.
Marie Dorval, "Notorious Woman," *Masterpiece Theatre,* PBS, 1975.

Television Appearances; Miniseries:
Herself, *Playing Shakespeare,* 1984.
Charlotte Dawson, *Have Your Cake and Eat It,* 1997.

Other Television Appearances:
Ermine, *The Black Knight,* 1977.
Ellie Marsh, *God on the Rocks,* 1990.

Appeared in *The Shadow of a Gunman* and *Trilby.**

D

DANCE, Charles 1946-

PERSONAL

Born October 10, 1946, in Rednal (some sources say Birmingham, one source says Plymouth), England; son of Walter (an engineer) and Eleanor (a cook; maiden name, Perks) Dance; married Joanna Haythorn (an artist), July 18, 1970; children: Oliver, Rebecca. *Education:* Attended Plymouth College of Art; Leicester College of Art, diploma, graphic design; studied privately with Leonard Bennett and Martin St. John Burchardt.

Addresses: Agent—William Morris Agency, 151 El Camino Dr., Beverly Hills, CA 90212.

Career: Actor. Worked as a stagehand at theaters in London's West End.

Member: Screen Actors Guild, British Actors Equity Association.

Awards, Honors: Scottish Academy Award, best actor, Scottish Academy of Television Arts, 1984, for *The Secret Servant;* Scottish Academy Award, best actor, and British Academy Award nomination, best actor, British Academy of Film and Television Arts, both 1984, for *The Jewel in the Crown.*

CREDITS

Film Appearances:
Claus, *For Your Eyes Only,* United Artists, 1981.
Paul Hatcher, *The McGuffin,* BBC Films, 1985.
Raymond Brock, *Plenty,* Twentieth Century-Fox, 1985.
Sardo Numspa, *The Golden Child,* Paramount, 1986.
D. W. Griffiths, *Good Morning, Babylon* (also known as *Good Morning Babilonia*), Vestron, 1987.
James Richards, *Hidden City,* Hidden City, 1987.
Josslyn Hay, Earl of Erroll, *White Mischief,* Columbia, 1987.
Television panel guest, *A Cry in the Dark,* Warner Bros., 1988.
Anthony Bowles, *Pascali's Island,* Avenue, 1988.
Gallery stuffed shirt, *Rikky and Pete,* Metro-Goldwyn-Mayer/United Artists, 1988.
Clemens, *Alien 3,* Twentieth Century-Fox, 1992.
Surveyor, *Kalkstein* (also known as *La valle di pietra* and *The Valley of Stone*), 1992.
Professor Mandry, *Century,* 1993.
Benedict, *The Last Action Hero,* Columbia, 1993.
Rupert Munro, *China Moon* (also known as *Lune Rouge*), Orion, 1994.
Robert Flaherty, *Kabloonak* (also known as *Nanook*), 1994.
Quinn, *Shortcut to Paradise* (also known as *Desvio al Paraiso*), 1994.
Dr. Mittlesbay, *Exquisite Tenderness* (also known as *The Surgeon, Intensive Care,* and *Dr. Death*), A-PIX Entertainment, 1995.
Soames, *Michael Collins,* Warner Bros., 1996.
Nabel/Macanudo, *Space Truckers* (also known as *Star Truckers*), Goldcrest Films International, 1996.
Cyril, *The Blood Oranges,* 1997.
Us Begins with You, 1998.

Television Appearances; Miniseries:
Guy Perron, *The Jewel in the Crown,* Granada, 1984.
Edward Hartford Jones, *Nancy Astor,* BBC, 1984.
James Latimer, *This Lightning Always Strikes Twice,* Granada, 1984.
Aircraft company manager, *The Lancaster Miller Affair,* 1990.

Television Appearances; Movies:
Gerry Stamford, *Out on a Limb,* ABC, 1987.

Dr. Edward Forester, *First Born,* Arts and Entertainment, 1989.

Ian Fleming, *Goldeneye: The Secret Life of Ian Fleming,* syndicated, 1990.

Erik (title role), *Phantom of the Opera,* NBC, 1990.

Lyle Yates, *Undertow,* Showtime, 1996.

Captain Richter, *In the Presence of Mine Enemies,* Showtime, 1997.

Television Appearances; Episodic:

"Skeleton in the Cupboard," *Roald Dahl's Tales of the Unexpected,* syndicated, 1979.

Parker, "The Ojuka Situation," *The Professionals,* London Weekend Television, 1982.

Michael Hayden, "Out of the Shadows," *Harlequin Romance Movie,* Showtime, 1988.

Television Appearances; Specials:

Maxim deWinter, "Rebecca," *Mobil Masterpiece Theatre,* PBS, 1997.

Host, *Ira Gershwin: A Centenary Celebration—Who Could Ask for Anything More?,* Arts and Entertainment, 1997.

Other Television Appearances:

The Secret Servant, BBC, c. 1984.

Michael St. Dennis, *Darlings of the Gods,* 1991.

Appeared as Duke of Clarence, *Edward VIII,* ATV; as Siegfried Sassoon, *The Fatal Spring,* BBC; as Alan, *Saigon: The Last Day,* BBC; as Reynaed Callaghan, *Frost in May,* BBC; as Borghejm, *Little Eyolf,* BBC; as Captain Truman, *Rainy Day Woman,* BBC; as Charleston, *Thunder Rock,* BBC; as O'Brien, *Father Brown;* and as Teddy, *Raffles.* Also appeared in *Dreams of Loving,* BBC, and in *Very Like a Whale* and *The McGuffin.*

Stage Appearances:

(London debut) Reynaldo and Fortinbras, *Hamlet,* Royal Shakespeare Company, 1975.

Title role, *Henry V,* Royal Shakespeare Company, Brooklyn Academy of Music, Brooklyn, NY, 1975.

Title role, *Coriolanus,* Odeon Nationale, Paris, 1979.

Nestor, *Irma la Douce,* West End production, 1980.

Frank, *Turning Over,* Bush Theatre, London, 1983.

Title role, *Coriolanus,* Barbican Theatre, London, 1990.

Appeared as Badger, *Toad of Toad Hall,* Swindon, England; as Beaudricort, *St. Joan,* Oxford, England; as Henry Carr, *Travesties,* Leeds, England; as Soliony, *The Three Sisters,* Greenwich, England; as hotel manager, *Born Yesterday,* Greenwich; as understudy for Macheath, *The Beggar's Opera,* Chichester Festival, Chichester, England; and as Morris Townsend, *The Heiress,* Nottingham Playhouse, Nottingham, England. Also appeared in Royal Shakespeare Company productions as Lancaster, *Henry IV, Parts I and II;* as Catesby, *Richard III;* as Spanish envoy, *Perkin Warbeck;* as Williams and Scroop, *Henry V;* as Oliver, *As You Like It;* as Tomazo, *The Changeling;* as Freeman, *The Jail Diary of Albie Sachs;* and as Tullus, *Aufidius.*

Major Tours:

It's a Two-Foot Six-Inch above the Ground World, British cities, 1970.

OTHER SOURCES

Periodicals:

Saturday Review, January 2, 1986, p. 35.

Sunday Times (London), April 22, 1990, p. G3.*

D'ANGELO, Beverly   1953(?)-

PERSONAL

Born November 15, 1953 (some sources say 1954), in Columbus, OH; daughter of a bass player and a violinist.

Addresses: *Agent*—International Creative Management, 8942 Wilshire Blvd., Beverly Hills, CA 90211.

Career: Actress. Hanna-Barbera Studios, Hollywood, CA, cartoonist; formerly a singer with the music group Elephant and with Rompin' Ronnie Hawkins.

Awards, Honors: Golden Globe Award nomination, best supporting actress, Hollywood Foreign Press Association, 1981, for *Coal Miner's Daughter;* Country Music Association Award, 1981; Golden Reel Award, 1981; Emmy Award nomination, 1985; *Theatre World* Award, 1995, for *Simpatico.*

CREDITS

Film Appearances:

Sandra, *The Sentinel,* Universal, 1977.

Actress in Rob's television show, *Annie Hall* (also known as *Anhedonia*), United Artists, 1977.

Shelley, *First Love,* 1977.

Echo, *Every Which Way But Loose,* Warner Bros., 1978.

Sheila, *Hair,* United Artists, 1979.

Patsy Cline, *Coal Miner's Daughter,* Universal, 1980.

Carmen Odessa Shelby, *Honky Tonk Freeway,* Universal, 1981.

Maggie, *Paternity* Paramount, 1981.

Ellen Griswold, *National Lampoon's Vacation,* Warner Bros., 1983.

Standish Logan, *Finders Keepers,* Warner Bros., 1984.

Lise Hatcher, *High Point,* New World, 1984.

Ellen Griswold, *National Lampoon's European Vacation,* Warner Bros., 1985.

Blanche Rickey, *Big Trouble,* Columbia, 1986.

Gilda, "Rigoletto," *Aria,* RVP/Virgin Vision, 1987.

Stella, *Maid to Order,* New Century/Vista, 1987.

Francine Glatt, *In the Mood* (also known as *The Woo Woo Kid*), Lorimar, 1987.

Donna Nottingham, *Trading Hearts* (also known as *Tweeners*), Cineworld, 1988.

Sharon, *High Spirits,* TriStar, 1988.

Ellen Griswold, *National Lampoon's Christmas Vacation,* Warner Bros., 1989.

Amanda O'Rourke, *Cold Front,* 1989.

Carter's lover, Anne, *Pacific Heights,* Twentieth Century-Fox, 1990.

Evalita, *Daddy's Dyin' . . . Who's Got the Will?,* Metro-Goldwyn-Mayer/United Artists, 1990.

Renee Barker, *The Miracle,* Miramax, 1991.

Veronica Dante, *The Pope Must Diet!* (also known as *The Pope Must Die!*), Miramax, 1992.

Andy Ellerman, *Man Trouble,* Twentieth Century-Fox, 1992.

Alma Bates, *Lonely Hearts,* LIVE Home Video, 1992.

Lana, *Lightning Jack,* Savoy Pictures, 1994.

Miranda, *Love Always* (also known as *All Points Between*), Legacy Releasing, 1995.

Edie, *The Crazysitter* (also known as *Two Much Trouble* and *How Much Are Those Children in the Window?*), Saban Entertainment, 1995.

Dolly Green, *Fye for an Eye,* Paramount, 1996.

Pixie Chandler, *Pterodactyl Woman from Beverly Hills,* PFG Entertainment, 1996.

Darkman's mom, *Nowhere,* Fine Line Features, 1997.

Ellen Griswold, *National Lampoon's Las Vegas Vacation* (also known as *Vegas Vacation*), Warner Bros., 1997.

Mom's on the Roof, 1997.

Mrs. Dollart, *Die Story von Monty Spinnerratz,* 1997.

American History X, 1998.

Film Work; Song Performer:

"Back in My Baby's Arms," "Walking After Midnight," "Crazy," "Sweet Dreams," *Coal Miner's Daughter,* Universal, 1980.

"You Find Your Way," "Daddy You Can't Blame Me," "Harder Than Your Husband," "Hungry for Love," "Dark Side of Life," "Still Tryin'," "I'll Fly Away," and "Rock of Ages," *Daddy's Dyin' . . . Who's Got the Will?,* Metro-Goldwyn-Mayer/United Artists, 1990.

"Lovin' You," *National Lampoon's Las Vegas Vacation* (also known as *Vegas Vacation*), Warner Bros., 1997.

Film Work:

Associate producer, *Pterodactyl Woman from Beverly Hills,* PFG Entertainment, 1996.

Television Appearances; Miniseries:

Miss Emmy, *Captains and the Kings,* NBC, 1976.

Caroline Wallace, *Doubletake,* CBS, 1985.

Johnnie Faye Boudreau, *Trial: The Price of Passion,* NBC, 1992.

Kitty Menendez, *Menendez: A Killing in Beverly Hills* (also known as *Deadly Games* and *The Menendez Murders*), CBS, 1994.

Television Appearances; Movies:

Stella Kowalski, *A Streetcar Named Desire,* ABC, 1984.

Lainie Fleischer, *Slow Burn,* 1986.

Mary Hearn, *Hands of a Stranger,* CBS, 1987.

Eva Milton, *The Man Who Fell to Earth,* 1987.

Jerry Sherwood, *A Child Lost Forever* (also known as *The Jerry Sherwood Story*), NBC, 1992.

Helen List, *Judgment Day: The John List Story* (also known as *Deliver Them from Evil: The John List Story* and *To Save Their Souls*), CBS, 1993.

Dee Fine, *The Switch,* CBS, 1993.

Annie Hayes, *Jonathan Stone: Threat of Innocence* (also known as *Frame-Up*), NBC, 1994.

Barlady, *Edie and Pen,* HBO, 1996.

Jesse Larson, *Sweet Temptation* (also known as *Sweet Mouthful*), CBS, 1996.

Vivian Fairchild, *Widow's Kiss,* HBO, 1996.

Television Appearances; Specials:

Ringmaster, *Circus of the Stars,* 1983.

Cheech and Chong Get Out of My Room, 1985.

Katrina, *The Legend of Sleepy Hollow,* 1986.

Joyce, "The Parallax Garden," *General Motors Playwrights Theatre,* Arts and Entertainment, 1993.

Alain, "Marks" in "Talking With," *Great Performances,* PBS, 1995.

Television Appearances; Episodic:

Henbane, "Sleeping Beauty," *Faerie Tale Theatre,* Showtime, 1982.

Voice of Lurleen, "Colonel Homer," *The Simpsons* (animated), Fox, 1991.
Nitecap, 1992.
Janice Baird, "Werewolf Concerto," *Tales from the Crypt,* HBO, 1992.

Other Television Appearances:
1996, 1986.

Stage Appearances:
Rosie, *Simpatico,* New York Shakespeare Festival, Public/Newman Theatre, New York City, 1994.

Made New York debut as Ophelia, *Rockabye Hamlet;* appeared as Marilyn, *Hey, Marilyn,* Charlottetown Festival Repertory Company; also appeared in an off-Broadway production, *The Zinger.*

OTHER SOURCES

Periodicals:
Gentlemen's Quarterly, November, 1996, p. 113.*

DAVID, Lolita
   See DAVIDOVICH, Lolita

DAVIDOVICH, Lolita   1961(?)-
   (Lolita David)

PERSONAL

Born c. 1961, in Ontario, Canada.

Addresses: *Agent*—International Creative Management, 8942 Wilshire Blvd., Beverly Hills, CA 90211.

Career: Actress.

Awards, Honors: CableACE Award nomination, best actress in a movie or miniseries, 1991, for "Parole Board," *Prison Stories: Women on the Inside.*

CREDITS

Film Appearances:
Blaze Starr, *Blaze,* Buena Vista, 1989.
Joan, *The Object of Beauty,* Avenue Entertainment, 1991.
Anastasia Sanshin, *The Inner Circle,* Columbia, 1991.
Vikki, *Boiling Point,* Warner Bros., 1993.

Penelope Younger, *Younger and Younger,* Academy Entertainment, 1993.
Ramona, *Cobb,* Warner Bros., 1994.
Olivia Marshak, *Intersection,* Paramount, 1994.
Valerie, *For Better or Worse,* Columbia, 1995.
Mrs. Albertson, *Now and Then,* New Line Cinema, 1995.
Charlotte, *Jungle2Jungle,* (also known as *Un Indien Dans la Ville*), Buena Vista, 1997.
Eleanor, *Santa Fe,* Nu Image, 1997.
Antoinette Baker, *Touch,* Metro-Goldwyn-Mayer/ United Artists, 1997.

Also appeared as first motel girl, *Class,* 1983; (as Lolita David) Susan, *Recruits,* 1986; (as Lolita David) blonde, *Adventures in Babysitting,* 1987; (as Lolita David) Adele, *Blindside,* 1987; (as Lolita David) black lace stripper, *The Big Town;* (as Lolita David) groupie, *Circleman,* 1988; Marva, *Leap of Faith,* 1992; Jenny, *Raising Cain,* 1992; *Gods and Monsters,* 1998.

Television Appearances; Episodic:
Loretta, "Parole Board," *Prison Stories: Women on the Inside* (also known as *Women in Prison* and *Doing Time: Women in Prison*), HBO, 1991.
Voiceover, "About Face," *Duckman* (animated), USA Network, 1994.

Also appeared as Christy, "Wedding Bell Blues," *Friday the 13th,* 1987.

Television Appearances; Movies:
Uncut Gem, TBS, 1990.
Ellen Overstreet Kelton, *Keep the Change,* TNT, 1992.
Kee MacFarlane, *Indictment: The McMartin Trial* (also known as *The Naked Movie Star Games* and *Nothing But the Truth: The McMartin Story*), HBO, 1995.
Sharon Foster, *Dead Silence* (also known as *A Maiden's Grave*), HBO, 1996.
Sally Russell, *Harvest of Fire,* CBS, 1996.
Sheila, *Neil Simon's Jake's Women,* CBS, 1996.
Eva, *Salt Water Moose,* Showtime, 1996.
Gina Antonelli, *Trial at Fortitude Bay,* Lifetime, 1996.

Also appeared in *Two Fathers' Justice,* 1985.*

DAVIS, Geena   1957-

PERSONAL

Born Virginia Elizabeth Davis, January 21, 1957, in Wareham, MA; father, an engineer; mother, Lucille

Davis (a teacher's aide); married Richard Emmolo, 1981 (divorced, 1983); married Jeff Goldblum (an actor), November 1, 1987 (divorced, 1990); married Renny Harlin (a director), September 18, 1993 (divorced, 1997). *Education:* Attended New England College; Boston University, B.F.A. (acting), 1979; studied flute, piano, and organ.

Addresses: *Agent*—Creative Artists Agency, 9830 Wilshire Blvd., Beverly Hills, CA 90212-1804. *Publicist*—Susan Geller and Associates, 335 North Maple Dr., Suite 254, Beverly Hills, CA 90210.

Career: Actress. Actress with Mount Washington Repertory Theatre Company, North Conway, NH; model for Zoli Agency, New York City; appeared in television commercials. Founder of Genial Pictures.

Awards, Honors: Academy Award, best supporting actress, 1988, for *The Accidental Tourist;* Academy Award nomination, best actress, British Academy of Film and Television Arts Award nomination, best actress in a leading role, and Golden Globe Award nomination, best actress in a motion picture (drama), all 1991, for *Thelma and Louise;* Golden Globe Award nomination, best actress in a musical or comedy, 1995, for *Speechless.*

CREDITS

Film Appearances:
April, *Tootsie,* Columbia, 1982.
Larry, *Fletch,* Universal, 1985.
Odette, *Transylvania 6-5000,* New World, 1985.
Veronica "Ronnie" Quaife, *The Fly,* Twentieth Century-Fox, 1986.
Barbara Maitland, *Beetlejuice,* Warner Bros., 1988.
Muriel Pritchett, *The Accidental Tourist,* Warner Bros., 1988.
Valerie Dale, *Earth Girls Are Easy,* Vestron, 1989.
Phyllis, *Quick Change,* Warner Bros., 1990.
Thelma Dickinson, *Thelma and Louise,* Metro-Goldwyn-Mayer, 1991.
Gale Gayley, *Hero,* Columbia, 1992.
Dottie Hinson, *A League of Their Own,* Columbia, 1992.
Julia Mann, *Speechless,* Metro-Goldwyn-Mayer/United Artists, 1994.
Angie Scacciapensieri, *Angie,* Buena Vista, 1994.
Morgan Adams, *Cutthroat Island,* Metro-Goldwyn-Mayer/United Artists, 1995.
Samantha Caine/Charly, *The Long Kiss Goodnight,* New Line Cinema, 1996.

Film Work:
Producer, *Speechless,* Metro-Goldwyn-Mayer/United Artists, 1994.

Television Appearances; Series:
Wendy Killian, *Buffalo Bill,* NBC, 1983-84.
Sara McKenna, *Sara,* NBC, 1985.

Television Appearances; Episodic:
Grace Farron, "Kitt the Cat," *Knight Rider,* NBC, 1983.
Housekeeper, "Help Wanted," *Family Ties,* NBC, 1984.
Karen Nicholson, "Karen 2, Alex 0," *Family Ties,* NBC, 1984.
"Don Juan's Last Affair," *Fantasy Island,* ABC, 1984.
Melba Bozinski, "Raiders of the Lost Sub," *Riptide,* NBC, 1984.
"Dream, Dream, Dream," *George Burns Comedy Week,* CBS, 1985.
"Steele in the Chips," *Remington Steele,* NBC, 1985.
Guest, *Late Night with David Letterman,* NBC, 1988.
Guest, *The Today Show,* NBC, 1988.
Guest, *CBS in the Morning,* CBS, 1989.
Host, *Saturday Evening Live,* NBC, 1989.
Hollywood Insider, USA Network, 1989.
Narrator, "Princess Scargo and the Birthday Pumpkin," *American Heroes and Legends,* 1992.
Storytime, 1994.

Television Appearances; Movies:
Tamara Reshevsky, *Secret Weapons* (also known as *Secrets of the Red Bedroom*), NBC, 1985.

Television Appearances; Specials:
Day to Day Affairs, HBO, 1985.
Daphne, *Hit List* (also known as *Trying Times*), PBS, 1989.
Time Warner Presents the Earth Day Special, ABC, 1990.
Big Bird's Birthday or, Let Me Eat Cake, PBS, 1991.
Fox/MTV Guide to Summer '92, Fox, 1992.
Host, *Breaking Through: Women Behind the Wheel,* Lifetime, 1997.

Television Appearances; Awards Presentations:
The 61st Annual Academy Awards Presentation, ABC, 1989.
Presenter, *The 62nd Annual Academy Awards Presentation,* ABC, 1990.
Presenter, *The 63rd Annual Academy Awards Presentation,* ABC, 1991.
Presenter, *The 64th Annual Academy Awards Presentation,* ABC, 1992.

Presenter, *The 65th Annual Academy Awards Presentation*, ABC, 1993.
Presenter, *The 66th Annual Academy Awards Presentation*, ABC, 1994.
The 67th Annual Academy Awards Presentation, ABC, 1995.
The 68th Annual Academy Awards Presentation, ABC, 1996.

Television Work; Movies:
Executive producer, *Mistrial*, HBO, 1996.

Stage Appearances:
Appeared in *One Flew Over the Cuckoo's Nest*, *Harvey*, and *Play It Again, Sam*, all Mount Washington Repertory Theatre, North Conway, NH.

WRITINGS

Television Series:
(With others) *Buffalo Bill*, NBC, 1983-84.

OTHER SOURCES

Periodicals:
American Premiere, May-June, 1991, p. 17.
Esquire, August, 1989, p. 86.
Gentlemen's Quarterly, June, 1989, p. 222.*

DAVIS, Ossie   1917-

PERSONAL

Born December 18, 1917, in Cogdell, GA; son of Kince Charles (a railway construction engineer) and Laura (Cooper) Davis; married Ruby Ann Wallace (an actress and writer known as Ruby Dee), December 9, 1948; children: Nora, Guy, LaVerne. *Education:* Attended Howard University, 1935-38, and Columbia University, 1948; trained for the stage with Paul Mann and Lloyd Richards.

Addresses: *Office*—Emmalyn II Productions, P.O. Box 1318, New Rochelle, NY 10802. *Agent*—Artists Agency, 10000 Santa Monica Blvd, Suite 305, Los Angeles, CA 90067. *Manager*—Marian Searchinger Associates Inc., 327 Central Park W., New York, NY 10025.

Career: Actor, playwright, and director. Worked as janitor, shipping clerk, and stock clerk in New York

City, 1938-41; began acting career with Rose McClendon Players; chairman of the board for Institute for New Cinema Artists; founder with wife, Ruby Dee, of Emmalyn II Productions; served on the advisory board of CORE, supports the NAACP, the Urban League, SCLC and is involved in the Civil Rights Movement. *Military service:* U.S. Army, Medical Corps and Special Services, 1942-45.

Member: Actors' Equity Association, Screen Actors Guild, American Federation of Radio and Television Artists, Director's Guild of America, National Association for the Advancement of Colored People (advisory board), Southern Christian Leadership Conference (advisory board), Congress of Racial Equality, Masons.

Awards, Honors: First Mississippi Freedom Democratic Party Citation, 1965; Emmy Award nomination, best actor in a special, 1969, for "Teacher, Teacher," *Hallmark Hall of Fame*; Emmy Award nomination, c. 1978, for *King*; Antoinette Perry Award nomination, best musical, 1970, for *Purlie*; Frederick Douglass Award from New York Urban League, for "distinguished leadership toward equal opportunity," 1970; Paul Robeson Citation from Actors' Equity Association, 1975, for "outstanding creative contributions in the performing arts and in society at large"; Coretta Scott King Book Award from American Library Association and Jane Addams Children's Book Award from Jane Addams Peace Association, both 1979, for *Escape to Freedom*; Jury Award from Neil Simon Awards, 1983, for "For Us the Living," *American Playhouse*; National Association for the Advancement of Colored People (NAACP) Image Award, best performance by a supporting actor, 1989, for *Do the Right Thing*; Hall of Fame Award for outstanding artistic achievement, 1989; Lifetime Achievement Award (with Ruby Dee), Multicultural Motion Picture Association, 1995; National Medal of the Arts (with Dee), 1995.

CREDITS

Stage Appearances:
Joy Exceeding Glory, Rose McClendon Players, Harlem, NY, 1941.
(Broadway debut) Jeb Turner, *Jeb*, Martin Beck Theatre, New York City, 1946.
Rudolph, *Anna Lucasta*, American Negro Theatre Playhouse, New York City, 1948.
Trem, *The Leading Lady*, National Theatre, New York City, 1948.

John Hay, *The Washington Years,* National Theatre, 1948.

Stewart, *The Smile of the World,* Lyceum Theatre, New York City, 1949.

Lonnie Thompson, *Stevedore,* Equity Library Theatre, New York City, 1949.

Jacques, *The Wisteria Trees,* Martin Beck Theatre, 1950.

Jo, *The Royal Family,* City Center Theatre, New York City, 1951.

Gabriel, *The Green Pastures,* Broadway Theatre, New York City, 1951.

Al, *Remains to Be Seen,* Morosco Theatre, New York City, 1951.

Dr. Joseph Clay, *Touchstone,* Music Box Theatre, New York City, 1953.

A lieutenant, *No Time for Sergeants,* Alvin Theatre, New York City, 1955.

Jacques, *The Wisteria Trees,* City Center Theatre, 1955.

Cicero, *Jamaica,* Imperial Theatre, New York City, 1957.

Walter Lee Younger, *A Raisin in the Sun,* Ethel Barrymore Theatre, New York City, 1959.

Title role, *Purlie Victorious,* Cort Theatre, New York City, 1961.

Sir Radio, *Ballad for Bimshire,* Mayfair Theatre, New York City, 1963.

The Talking Skull, White Barn Theatre, Westport, CT, 1965.

Johannes, *The Zulu and the Zayda,* Cort Theatre, 1965.

Take It from the Top, New Federal Theatre, New York City, 1979.

Midge, *I'm Not Rappaport,* Booth Theatre, New York City, 1986.

(And writer with Dee) *Two Hah Hahs and a Homeboy,* Crossroads Theatre Company, 1995.

Also appeared in *Zora Is My Name!,* Howard University, Washington, DC, and *Ain't Supposed to Die a Natural Death,* New York City.

Major Tours:

Rudolf, *Anna Lucasta,* U.S. cities, 1947.

Walter Lee Younger, *A Raisin in the Sun,* U.S. cities, 1959.

A Treasury of Negro World Writing, U.S. cities, 1964.

Stage Work:

Stage manager, *The World of Sholom Aleichem,* City Center Theatre, 1955.

Producer (with Bernard Waltzer and Page Productions), *Ballad for Bimshire,* Mayfair Theatre, 1963.

Director, *The Talking Skull,* White Barn Theatre, 1965.

Director, *Bingo,* AMAS Repertory Theatre, New York City, 1985.

Also director of *Goldbrickers of 1944,* Liberia, 1944, and *Take It from the Top,* 1979.

Film Appearances:

(Film debut) John, *No Way Out,* Twentieth Century-Fox, 1950.

Cab driver, *Fourteen Hours,* Twentieth Century-Fox, 1951.

The Joe Louis Story, United Artists, 1953.

Reverend Purlie, *Gone Are the Days* (also known as *The Man from C.O.T.T.O.N.* and *Purlie Victorious*), Hammer Bros., 1963.

Father Gillis, *The Cardinal,* Columbia, 1963.

Capshaw, *Shock Treatment,* Arcola/Fox, 1964.

Jacko King, *The Hill,* Seven Arts/Metro-Goldwyn-Mayer, 1965.

Nelson Davis, *A Man Called Adam,* Trace-Mark/Embassy Pictures Corporation, 1966.

Joseph Winfield Lee, *The Scalphunters,* Bristol-Norlan/United Artists, 1968.

Jedidiah Hooker, *Sam Whiskey,* Brighton Pictures/United Artists, 1969.

Luke, *Slaves,* Theatre Guild-Walter Reade/Continental, 1969.

Elder Johnson, *Let's Do It Again,* First Artists/Warner Bros., 1975.

Ernest Motapo, *Countdown at Kusini,* Columbia, 1976.

Captain Geibarger, *Hot Stuff,* Rastar-Mort Engelberg/Columbia, 1979.

Raymond, *Harry and Son,* Orion, 1984.

Dr. Sanders, *The House of God,* United Artists, 1984.

Captain Moradian, *Avenging Angel,* Republic Entertainment International/New World, 1985.

Coach Odom, *School Daze,* Columbia, 1988.

Da Mayor, *Do the Right Thing,* Universal, 1989.

Reverend Purify, *Jungle Fever,* Universal, 1991.

Noah, *Gladiator,* Columbia, 1992.

Eulogy performer, *Malcolm X,* Warner Bros., 1992.

Chuck, *Grumpy Old Men,* Warner Bros., 1993.

Judge Harry Roosevelt, *The Client,* Warner Bros., 1994.

Jeremiah, *Get on the Bus,* Columbia TriStar, 1996.

Midge, *I'm Not Rappaport,* Gramercy Pictures, 1996.

Himself, *Four Little Girls,* Green Valley Films, 1997.

Also appeared in *Nothing Personal,* 1979; as himself, *Making of "Do the Right Thing,"* 1989; Himself,

Route One/U.S.A., 1989; Marshall, *Joe Versus the Volcano,* 1990; *Love Supreme.*

Film Work; Director:
Cotton Comes to Harlem, United Artists, 1970.
Kongi's Harvest, Calpenny Films Nigeria, 1971.
Black Girl, Cinerama, 1972.
Gordon's War, Twentieth Century-Fox, 1973.
(And producer) *Countdown at Kusini,* Columbia, 1976.

Television Appearances; Series:
Host, *The Negro People,* PBS, 1965-67.
Ponder Blue, *Evening Shade,* CBS, 1990-1994.
Judge Harry Roosevelt, *John Grisham's The Client* (also known as *The Client*), CBS, 1995-96.
Erasmus Jones (recurring), *Promised Land,* CBS, 1996.

Also appeared as co-host, *With Ossie and Ruby* (series), PBS.

Television Appearances; Movies:
James Lucas, *The Sheriff,* ABC, 1971.
Narrator, *Freedom Road,* NBC, 1979.
Blane Whitfield, *All God's Children,* ABC, 1980.
Chuffy Russell, *Don't Look Back,* ABC, 1981.
Boxer Oz Jackson, *B. L. Stryker: The Dancer's Touch,* ABC, 1989.
Grandfather, *The Ernest Green Story,* The Disney Channel, 1993.
Uncle Phil, *Ray Alexander: A Taste for Justice,* NBC, 1994.
Dr. Winston, *The Android Affair* (also known as *The Human Touch* and *Teach 905*), USA Network, 1995.
Uncle Phil, *Ray Alexander: A Menu for Murder,* NBC, 1995.
Mr. Evers, *Miss Evers' Boys,* HBO, 1997.

Also appeared as Oz, *Auntie Sue, Blind Chess, The King of Jazz,* and *Royal Gambit,* all 1989; and as Oz, *Night Train, Plates, Grand Theft Hotel,* and *High Rise,* all 1990. Appeared as narrator in *The Red Shoes,* 1990; appeared as Juror number two, *12 Angry Men,* 1997.

Television Appearances; Specials:
The Green Pastures, Showtime USA, 1951.
Title role, "The Emperor Jones," *Kraft Television Theatre,* NBC, 1955.
Tell It on the Mountain, CBS, 1965.
Charles Carter, "Teacher, Teacher," *Hallmark Hall of Fame,* NBC, 1969.
Today Is Ours, CBS, 1974.

Dr. Fredericks, *Billy: Portrait of a Street Kid,* NBC, 1977.
Mr. Eolin, *A Piece of Cake,* NBC, 1977.
"For Us the Living," *American Playhouse,* PBS, 1983.
Host, *Martin Luther King: The Dream and the Drum,* PBS, 1986.
Eyes on the Prize II, PBS, 1990.
Zora Is My Name, PBS, 1990.
Narrator, *Haiti: Killing the Dream,* PBS, 1992.
Voice of Frederick Douglass, *Lincoln,* ABC, 1992.
Narrator, *Goin' Back to T-Town,* PBS, 1993.
Narrator, *Arthur Ashe: Citizen of the World,* HBO, 1994.
Malcolm X: Make It Plain, PBS, 1994.
Host, *National Memorial Day Concert,* PBS, 1994.
African-American Summit: Coming Home, PBS, 1995.
Narrator, *Arlington National Cemetery: A Mirror of America,* The Disney Channel, 1995.
Host, *National Memorial Day Concert,* PBS, 1995.
Celebrate the Dream: 50 Years of Ebony, ABC, 1996.
Lena Horne: In Her Own Voice, PBS, 1996.
Narrator (with Dee), *Mississippi, America,* PBS, 1996.
Host, *National Memorial Day Concert,* PBS, 1996.
Host, *National Memorial Day Concert,* PBS, 1997.
Narrator, *Thomas Jefferson,* PBS, 1997.

Also appeared as narrator, *And Every Man Is Free: A Tribute to Langston Hughes,* 1984; narrator, *Treemonisha,* 1986; Dred Scott, *The Blessings of Liberty,* 1987; Jay, Bruce Castleberry, and Reggie Bates, *Alice in Wonder,* 1987; host with Robert Terrell, *A Letter to Booker T.,* 1987; *The Twenty-Second Annual NAACP Image Awards,* 1990; *The 24th Annual NAACP Image Awards,* 1992; Voice of Frederick Douglass, *Smithsonian's Great Battles of the Civil War,* 1994; and *The 48th annual Tony Awards,* 1994.

Television Appearances; Episodic:
The Creative Person, PBS, 1965.
The Great Depression, PBS, 1993.
Erasmus, *Touched by an Angel,* CBS, 1996.
Voice, *The West,* PBS, 1996.

Also appeared in *The Sheriff, N.Y.P.D., The Fugitive,* and *12 O'Clock High,* all ABC; *The Defenders, Look Up and Live, Slattery's People, Hawaii Five-O, Doctors/Nurses,* and *Car 54, Where Are You?,* all CBS; and *Night Gallery, The Name of the Game, The Outsider, Run for Your Life, Eternal Light,* and *Bonanza,* all NBC.

Television Appearances; Miniseries:
Martin Luther King Sr., *King,* NBC, 1978.

Dad Jones, *Roots: The Next Generation*, ABC, 1979.
Parson Dick, *Queen* (also known as *Alex Haley's Queen*), CBS, 1993.
Judge Farris, *Stephen King's The Stand* (also known as *The Stand*), ABC, 1994.
Voice, *Baseball*, (also known as *The History of Baseball*), PBS, 1994.

Television Appearances; Other:
"Seven Times Monday," *Play of the Week*, WNTA, 1960.
Lieutenant Wagner, *The Outsider* (pilot), NBC, 1967.
Osmond Portifoy, *Night Gallery* (pilot), NBC, 1969.

Television Work; Specials:
Director and producer, *Today Is Ours*, CBS, 1974.
Executive producer, *Martin Luther King: The Dream and the Drum*, PBS, 1986.

Executive producer and director of *Crown Dick*, 1987; producer and director of *A Letter to Booker T.* and *My Man Bovanne*, both 1987; producer of *The 85-Year-Old Swinger, Alice in Wonder, Crazy Hattie Enters the Ice Age, Mama,* and *Refrigerator*, all 1987, and *A Walk through the Twentieth Century with Bill Moyers.*

Radio Appearances:
Host (with Ruby Dee), *The Ossie Davis and Ruby Dee Story Hour*, National Black Network, 1974-75.

RECORDINGS

The Poetry of Langston Hughes, Caedmon, 1969.
The Best Poems of Countee Cullen, Caedmon, 1972.
The Black Cinema: Foremost Representatives of the Black Film World Air Their Views, Center for Cassette Studies, 1975.

Also participated in recording *Simple Stories*, Caedmon.

WRITINGS

Stage:
Goldbrickers of 1944, produced in Liberia, 1944.
Alice in Wonder (one-act), produced in New York City, 1952, revised and expanded version produced as *The Big Deal* in New York City, 1953.
Purlie Victorious, Cort Theatre, New York City, 1961.
Curtain Call, Mr. Aldredge, Sir (produced in Santa Barbara, CA, 1968), published in *The Black Teacher and the Dramatic Arts: A Dialogue, Bibliography and Anthology*, edited by William R.

Reardon and Thomas D. Pawley, Negro Universities Press, 1970.
(With Philip Rose, Peter Udell, and Gary Geld) *Purlie* (musical; produced on Broadway, 1970), Samuel French, 1971.
Escape to Freedom: A Play about Young Frederick Douglass (produced in New York City, 1976), Viking, 1978.
Langston: A Play, produced in New York City, 1982.
(With Hy Gilbert) *Bingo*, produced at AMAS Repertory Theatre, 1985.
(With Dee) *Two Hah Hahs and a Homeboy*, Crossroads Theatre Company, 1995.

Also author of *Last Dance for Sybil.*

Film:
Gone Are the Days (adapted from Davis's *Purlie Victorious*; also known as *Purlie Victorious* and *The Man from C.O.T.T.O.N.*), Hammer Bros., 1963.
(With Arnold Perl) *Cotton Comes to Harlem* (based on a novel by Chester Himes), United Artists, 1970.

Television:
"School Teacher," *East Side/West Side* (episode), CBS, 1963.
"Slavery," *The Negro People* (episode), PBS, 1965.
Today Is Ours (special), CBS, 1974.
(With Ladi Ladebo and Al Freeman, Jr.) *Countdown at Kusini* (based on a story by John Storm Roberts), CBS, 1976.

Also writer for episodes of *Just Say the Word*, 1969; *The Eleventh Hour* and *Bonanza*, both NBC; *N.Y.P.D.*; and for special *Alice in Wonder*, 1987.

Other:
(Contributor) *Anger, and Beyond: The Negro Writer in the United States*, Harper, 1966.
(Contributor) *Soon, One Morning: New Writing by American Negroes, 1940-1962*, Knopf, 1968.
"Ain't Now But It's Going to Be" (song), *Cotton Comes to Harlem*, United Artists, 1970.
(With Ruby Dee) *Glowchild, and Other Poems*, Third Press, 1972.
(With others) *The Black Cinema: Foremost Representatives of the Black Film World Air Their Views*, Center for Cassette Studies, 1975.
Escape to Freedom, Viking, 1979.
Just Like Martin, Simon & Schuster, 1992.

Contributor to periodicals and journals, including *Negro History Bulletin, Negro Digest,* and *Freedomways.*

OTHER SOURCES

Books:
Dictionary of Literary Biography, Gale, Volume 7: *Twentieth-Century American Dramatists,* 1981, Volume 38: *Afro-American Writers after 1955: Dramatists and Prose Writers,* 1985.
Funke, Lewis, *The Curtain Rises: The Story of Ossie Davis,* Grosset & Dunlap, 1971.

Periodicals:
American Theatre, July/August, 1995, pp. 12-13.
Essence, December, 1994, pp. 76-80.
Jet, December 18, 1995, p. 20.
Modern Maturity, July/August, 1994, pp. 64-70.
Parade, October 20, 1996, p. 24. *

DAVIS, William B.   1938-

PERSONAL

Full name, William Bruce Davis; born January, 1938, in Toronto, Ontario, Canada; father, an attorney; mother, a psychologist; married (divorced); children: two. *Education:* University of Toronto, B.A. (philosophy), 1959; attended the London Academy of Music and Dramatic Art. *Avocational interests:* Waterskiing, downhill skiing.

Addresses: *Agent*—c/o 100 West Pender, Ninth Floor, Vancouver, British Columbia V6B 1R8, Canada.

Career: Actor. Owner, director, and teacher, William Davis Centre for Actors' Study, Vancouver, British Columbia, Canada; member of the National Theatre, London, England, 1965-66; former artistic director of the national Theatre School of Canada, English acting program. Also a Canadian national waterskiing champion.

CREDITS

Television Appearances; Series:
Cigarette smoking man (also known as Smoking man and Cancer man) *The X-Files,* Fox, 1993—.

Television Appearances; Miniseries:
Mr. Gedreau, *Stephen King's It* (also known as *It*), ABC, 1990.

Television Appearances; Movies:
Ted, *The Cuckoo Bird,* CBC, 1985.
Heath Harris, *Matinee* (also known as *Midnight Matinee*), 1988.
Dr. Reynolds, *Anything to Survive,* ABC, 1990.
Marvin Parkins, *Diagnosis of Murder,* CBS, 1992.
Vern, *Heart of a Child,* NBC, 1994.
Huddleston, *Don't Talk to Strangers,* 1994.
Gene Reuschel, *Circumstances Unknown,* USA Network, 1995.
Group leader, *Dangerous Intentions,* CBS, 1995.
Dr. Alexander, *When the Vows Break,* Lifetime, 1995.

Television Appearances; Episodic:
High school teacher, "Mean Streets and Pastel Houses," *21 Jump Street,* Fox, 1987.
Doctor, "Sanctuary for a Child," *Nightmare Cafe,* NBC, 1992.
Ed, "The Conversion," *The Outer Limits,* Showtime, 1995.
Professor Myman, "Eggheads," *Sliders,* Fox, 1995.
John Wymer, "Out of Body," *The Outer Limits,* Showtime, 1996.

Also appeared on *North of 60,* CBC; *Captain Power; Wiseguy,* CBS; *Airwolf,* CBS; *Street Justice,* syndicated; and *MacGyver,* ABC.

Film Appearances:
Beyond Obsession, Facets Multimedia, 1982.
Ambulance driver, *Dead Zone,* Paramount, 1983.
University dean, *Head Office,* TriStar, 1986.
Beyond the Stars, LIVE Home Video, 1989.
Drug doctor, *Look Who's Talking,* TriStar, 1989.
Doctor Atkins, *Hitman,* Cannon, 1991.
Omen IV: The Awakening, Fox Video, 1991.
Dr. Smoot, *Unforgettable,* Metro-Goldwyn-Mayer/United Artists, 1996.
Cigarette smoking man, *X-Files: The Movie,* 1998.

Stage Appearances:
Appeared as Wilson, *Back to Beulah;* Harry, *On the Job;* Jefry, *Two for the See Saw;* Puppet Master, *The Puppet Master;* George, *Chapter Two;* and as Tony Orr, *Emma Orr.*

OTHER SOURCES

Periodicals:
Entertainment Weekly, February 9, 1996, p. 22.
People Weekly, November 25, 1996, p. 67.*

DELANY, Dana   1956-

PERSONAL

Born March 13, 1956, in New York, NY. *Education:* Phillips Andover Academy, graduated, 1974; graduated from Wesleyan University, Middletown, CT.

Addresses: *Agent*—c/o International Creative Management, 8942 Wilshire Blvd., Beverly Hills, CA 90211.

Career: Actress.

Awards, Honors: Emmy Awards, outstanding lead actress in a drama series, 1988 and 1991, Women at Work Commissioners Award, National Commission on Working Women, and Quality Award, best actress in a drama series, Viewers for Quality Television, all 1989, and Emmy Award nomination, outstanding lead actress in a drama series, 1990, all for *China Beach.*

CREDITS

Television Appearances; Series:
Amy Russell, *Love of Life,* CBS, 1979-80.
Hayley Wilson, *As the World Turns,* CBS, 1981.
Georgia Holden, *Sweet Surrender,* NBC, 1986-87.
Colleen McMurphy, *China Beach,* ABC, 1987-91.
Voice of Lois Lane, *Superman* (animated), The WB, 1996-98.

Also appeared as voice of Gwen "Archer" Bowman, *Wing Commander Academy,* 1996.

Television Appearances; Miniseries:
Grace Wyckoff, *Wild Palms,* ABC, 1993.
Sarah Ashby McClure, *True Women,* CBS, 1997.

Television Appearances; Pilots:
Jeannie, *The Streets* (also known as *Street Heat*), NBC, 1984.
May Thayer, *The City,* ABC, 1986.

Television Appearances; Episodic:
Jillian Armstrong, "Knowing Her," *Moonlighting,* ABC, 1985.
Cynthia Farrell, "L.A.," *Magnum, P.I.,* CBS, 1986.
Cynthia Farrell, "Out of Sync," *Magnum, P.I.,* CBS, 1987.
Eve, "South by Southwest," *thirtysomething,* ABC, 1987.

"The Promise," *The Larry Sanders Show,* HBO, 1992.
"The Breakdown: Part 2," *The Larry Sanders Show,* HBO, 1993.
Helen Fiske, "Good Housekeeping," *Fallen Angels,* Showtime, 1995.
Honey Trapp, "Dead and Gone, Honey," *Spy Game,* ABC, 1997.

Television Appearances; Movies:
Laura Shaper, *Threesome,* CBS, 1984.
Moya Trevor, *Liberty,* NBC, 1986.
Nora, *A Winner Never Quits,* ABC, 1986.
Jane Goodrich, *A Promise to Keep* (also known as *Angels without Wings*), NBC, 1990.
Dina Donato, *Donato and Daughter,* CBS, 1993.
Chief of Staff Betsy Corcoran, *The Enemy Within,* HBO, 1994.
Margaret Sanger, *Choice of the Heart: The Margaret Sanger Story* (also known as *Crusaders*), Lifetime, 1995.
Hope Robbins, *For Hope,* ABC, 1996.
Grace, *The Patron Saint of Liars,* CBS, 1998.

Television Appearances; Specials:
Time Warner Presents the Earth Day Special, ABC, 1990.
Voice of Libby Custer, *The Wild West* (documentary), syndicated, 1993.
Anne Williams, *Texan,* Showtime, 1994.
Host, *Earth Day at Walt Disney World,* The Disney Channel, 1996.

Television Appearances; Awards Presentations:
The 41st Annual Emmy Awards, Fox, 1989.
The 47th Annual Golden Globe Awards, TBS, 1990.
The 42nd Annual Primetime Emmy Awards Presentation, Fox, 1990.
Host, *The 48th Annual Golden Globe Awards,* TBS, 1991.
The 43rd Annual Primetime Emmy Awards Presentation, Fox, 1991.
The 44th Annual Primetime Emmy Awards, Fox, 1992.
Fourth Annual Environmental Media Awards, TBS, 1994.
The Screen Actors Guild Awards, NBC, 1997.

Film Appearances:
Linda, *The Fan,* Paramount, 1981.
Susan McCall, *Almost You,* Twentieth Century-Fox/TLC, 1984.
Sister Ana, *Where the River Runs Black,* Metro-Goldwyn-Mayer/United Artists, 1986.
Jenny, *Moon over Parador,* Universal, 1988.

Celina, *Patty Hearst,* Atlantic-Zenith, 1988.
Anne Briscoe, *Masquerade,* Metro-Goldwyn-Mayer/
United Artists, 1988.
Marianne, *Light Sleeper,* New Line Cinema, 1992.
Becky Metcalf, *Housesitter,* Universal, 1992.
Voice of Andrea Beaumont, *Batman: The Animated
Movie* (also known as *Batman: Mask of the Phantasm;* animated), Warner Bros., 1993.
Josephine Earp, *Tombstone,* Buena Vista, 1993.
Lisa Emerson, *Exit to Eden,* Savoy Pictures, 1994.
Jill, *Live Nude Girls,* Republic Pictures, 1995.
Susan Barnes, *Fly Away Home,* Columbia Pictures,
1996.
Joshua's mother, *Wide Awake,* Miramax, 1998.
Dr. Ashley, *Dead Man's Curve,* Click Productions/
Mount Royal Entertainment, 1998.
Cat Bonfairn, *The Outfitters,* 1998.

Stage Appearances:
The Resistible Rise of Arturo Ui, Hartman Theatre
Company, Stamford, CT, 1979-80.
Dorothy, *A Life,* Morosco Theatre, New York City,
1980-81.
Manya, *Blood Moon,* Production Company Theatre,
then Actors and Directors Theatre, both New
York City, 1983.
Rocket to the Moon, Hartman Theatre, 1984.
Beloved Friend, Hartman Theatre, 1984-85.
Translations, Plymouth Theatre, New York City,
1995.

---

del TORO, Benicio   1967-

PERSONAL

Born February 19, 1967, in Santurce, Puerto Rico;
raised in Puerto Rico and Pennsylvania. *Education:*
Studied business at the University of California, San
Diego.

Addresses: *Agent*—c/o IFA Talent Agency, 8730 Sunset Blvd., Suite 490, Los Angeles, CA 90069. *Manager*—c/o Addis-Wechsler and Associates, 955 South
Carillo Dr., Suite 300, Los Angeles, CA 90048.

Career: Actor, producer, and writer.

Awards, Honors: Independent Spirit Awards, best
supporting male, 1996, for *The Usual Suspects,* and
1997, for *Basquiat.*

CREDITS

Film Appearances:
Duke, the dog-faced boy, *Big Top Pee-Wee,* Paramount, 1988.
Dario, *License to Kill* (also known as *License Revoked*), Metro-Goldwyn-Mayer/United Artists,
1989.
Miguel, *The Indian Runner,* Metro-Goldwyn-Mayer/
Pathe, 1991.
Alvaro Harana, *Christopher Columbus: The Discovery,* Warner Bros., 1992.
Dino Palladino, *Money for Nothing,* Buena Vista,
1993.
Bon, the friend from Miami, *Huevos de Oro* (also
known as *Golden Balls* and *Macho*), Lola Films,
1993.
Manny Rodrigo, *Fearless,* Warner Bros., 1993.
Lamar Dickey, *China Moon* (also known as *Lune
Rouge*), Orion, 1994.
Rex, *Swimming with Sharks* (also known as *The
Boss* and *The Buddy Factor*), Trimark Pictures,
1995.
Fred Fenster, *The Usual Suspects,* Gramercy Pictures,
1995.
Himself, *Cannes Man,* Rocket Pictures Home Video,
1996.
Benny Dalmau, *Basquiat* (also known as *Build a Fort,
Set It on Fire*), Miramax, 1996.
Juan Primo, *The Fan,* Sony Pictures Entertainment,
1996.
Gaspare Spoglia, *The Funeral,* October Films, 1996.
Detective Lopez, *Joyride,* Live Entertainment/Showcase Entertainment, 1997.
Vincent Roche, *Excess Baggage,* Sony Pictures Entertainment, 1997.
Oscar Zeta Acosta, *Fear and Loathing in Las Vegas,*
MCA/Universal, 1998.

Film Director and Producer:
Submission, 1995.

Television Appearances; Miniseries:
Rafael Caro Quintero, *Drug Wars: The Camarena
Story,* NBC, 1990.

Television Appearances; Episodic:
Ohara, ABC, 1987.
"Everybody's in Showbiz," *Miami Vice,* NBC, 1987.
"The Bribe," *Tales from the Crypt,* HBO, 1994.
Paco, "Good Housekeeping," *Fallen Angels,*
Showtime, 1995.

WRITINGS

Screenplays:
Submission, 1995.

OTHER SOURCES

Periodicals:
Newsweek, January 15, 1996, pp. 60-63.*

DeLUISE, Dom 1933-

PERSONAL

Full name, Dominick DeLuise; born August 1, 1933, in Brooklyn, NY; son of John (a civil servant) and Vicenza "Jennie" (DeStefano) DeLuise; married Carol Arata (an actress; professional name, Carol Arthur), November 23, 1965; children: Peter John (an actor), Michael Robert (an actor), David Dominick. *Education:* Attended Tufts College. *Avocational interests:* Furniture refinishing, herb gardening.

Addresses: *Agent*—Artists Group, 10100 Santa Monica Blvd., Suite 2490, Los Angeles, CA 90067.

Career: Actor, director, and commercial spokesperson.

CREDITS

Film Appearances:
(Film debut) Sergeant Collins, *Fail Safe,* Columbia, 1964.
Marvin Rollins, *Diary of a Bachelor,* American International Pictures, 1964.
Julius Pritter, *The Glass Bottom Boat* (also known as *The Spy in Lace Panties*), Metro-Goldwyn-Mayer, 1966.
Kurt Brock, *The Busybody,* Paramount, 1967.
J. Gardner Monroe, *What's So Bad about Feeling Good?,* Universal, 1968.
Father Fyodor, *The Twelve Chairs,* UMC, 1969.
Bill Bird, *Norwood,* Paramount, 1970.
Irwin, *Who Is Harry Kellerman and Why Is He Saying Those Terrible Things about Me?,* National General, 1971.
Azzecca, *Every Little Crook and Nanny,* Metro-Goldwyn-Mayer, 1972.
Buddy Bizarre, *Blazing Saddles,* Warner Bros., 1974.
Eduardo Gambetti, *The Adventures of Sherlock Holmes's Smarter Brother,* Twentieth Century-Fox, 1975.

Dom Bell, *Silent Movie,* Twentieth Century-Fox, 1976.
Zitz, *The World's Greatest Lover,* Twentieth Century-Fox, 1977.
Diary of a Young Comic, 1977.
Pepe Domascus, *The Cheap Detective,* Columbia, 1978.
Dan Turner, *Sexette,* Crown International, 1978.
Marlon Borunki, *The End,* United Artists, 1978.
Ernie Fortunato, *Hot Stuff,* Columbia, 1979.
Bernie (the Hollywood agent), *The Muppet Movie,* Associated Film Distribution, 1979.
Dominick DiNapoli, *Fatso,* Twentieth Century-Fox, 1980.
Walter Holmes, *The Last Married Couple in America,* Universal, 1980.
Doc, *Smokey and the Bandit II* (also known as *Smokey and the Bandit Ride Again*), Columbia, 1980.
Shadrach, *Wholly Moses,* Columbia, 1980.
Victor/Captain Chaos, *The Cannonball Run,* Twentieth Century-Fox, 1981.
Emperor Nero, *History of the World, Part One,* Twentieth Century-Fox, 1981.
Melvin P. Thorpe, *The Best Little Whorehouse in Texas,* Universal, 1982.
Voice of Jeremy, *The Secret of NIMH* (animated; also known as *Mrs. Brisby and the Rats of NIMH*), Metro-Goldwyn-Mayer/United Artists, 1982.
Victor/Captain Chaos, *Cannonball Run II,* Warner Bros., 1984.
The Pope, *Johnny Dangerously,* Twentieth Century-Fox, 1984.
Voice of Tiger, *An American Tail* (animated), Universal, 1986.
Aunt Kate, *Haunted Honeymoon,* Orion, 1986.
Voice of Pizza the Hutt, *Space Balls,* Metro-Goldwyn-Mayer/United Artists, 1987.
Police Chief, *Un Tassinaro, a New York* (also known as *A Taxi Driver in New York*), Italian International Film, 1987.
Big Bad Joe, *Going Bananas* (also known as *My African Adventure*), Cannon, 1987.
Voice of Fagin, *Oliver and Company* (animated), Buena Vista, 1988.
Gutterman, *Loose Cannons,* TriStar, 1989.
Voice of Itchy, *All Dogs Go to Heaven* (animated), United Artists, 1989.
Mr. B., *Driving Me Crazy* (also known as *Trabbi Goes to Hollywood*), 1991.
Voice of Tiger, *An American Tail: Fievel Goes West,* 1991.
Voice of Munchie, *Munchie,* Concorde, 1992.
Dr. Beckhard, *Almost Pregnant,* Columbia TriStar Home Video, 1992.

Voice of Christopher Columbus, *The Magic Voyage,* 1992.

Voice of Rip, *The Skateboard Kid,* Concorde-New Horizons, 1993.

Don Giovanni, *Robin Hood: Men in Tights,* Twentieth Century-Fox, 1993.

Voice of Looking Glass, *Happily Ever After* (animated), First National Film Corp., 1993.

Voice of Stanley, *A Troll in Central Park* (animated), Warner Bros., 1994.

Munchie Strikes Back, 1994.

Dr. Animal Cannibal Pizza, *Silence of the Hams* (also known as *Il Silenzio dei Prosciutti*), 1994.

Voice of Ichy Itchiford, *All Dogs Go to Heaven 2* (animated), Metro-Goldwyn-Mayer/United Artists, 1996.

"Fingers" the cashier, *Toonstruck,* 1996.

Jerry, *Red Line,* Mondofin/Triboro, 1996.

Judge, *The Good Bad Guy* (also known as *Killer per caso*), Medusa (Italy), 1997.

Also appeared in *Benito.*

Film Work:

Director, *Hot Stuff,* Columbia, 1979.

Television Appearances; Series:

Regular, *The Entertainers,* CBS, 1964-65.

Regular, *The Dean Martin Summer Show,* NBC, 1966.

Host, *The Dom DeLuise Show,* CBS, 1968.

Regular, *The Glen Campbell Goodtime Hour,* CBS, 1971-72.

Regular, *The Dean Martin Show* (also known as *The Dean Martin Comedy Hour*), NBC, 1972-73.

Voice of Mr. Evictus, *The Roman Holidays* (animated), NBC, 1972-73.

Stanley Belmont, *Lotsa Luck!,* NBC, 1973-74.

Dominick DeLuca, *The Dom DeLuise Show,* syndicated, 1987.

Host, *Candid Camera,* syndicated, 1991.

Voice of Tiger, *Fievel's American Tails* (documentary), CBS, 1992.

Vinnie Piatte, *Burke's Law,* CBS, 1994-95.

Also appeared as Dominick the Great on *The Garry Moore Show,* CBS.

Television Appearances; Episodic:

Dr. Edward Dudley, "Just Another Pretty Face," *The Munsters,* CBS, 1966.

Please Don't Eat the Daisies, NBC, 1966.

The Girl from U.N.C.L.E., NBC, 1966.

"This Is Sholom Aleichem," *Experiment in Television,* NBC, 1969.

The Ghost and Mrs. Muir, ABC, 1969.

Guest host, *The Golddiggers,* syndicated, 1971.

Medical Center, CBS, 1974.

Himself, *The Muppet Show,* syndicated, 1977.

Guilt, "Guilt Trip," *Amazing Stories,* NBC, 1985.

Vito, *Easy Street,* NBC, 1987.

Win, Lose, or Draw, syndicated, 1987.

Uncle Dominic, "Woolly Bullies," *21 Jump Street,* Fox, 1989.

Toby Beaumont, "Die Laughing," *B. L. Stryker,* ABC, 1989.

A Conversation with Dinah, 1989.

Buddy Blake, *Diagnosis Murder,* CBS, 1993.

Voice of Floyd the dog, "Change for a Buck," *Married . . . with Children,* Fox, 1993.

Nick Piccolo, "Vapors," *SeaQuest DSV,* NBC, 1994.

Voice, *The Magic School Bus,* PBS, 1994.

Himself, *Murphy Brown,* CBS, 1995.

Interviewee, "Dean Martin: Everybody Loves Somebody," *Biography,* A&E, 1995.

Magic Morton, "I Only Have Eyes for You," *Beverly Hills 90210,* Fox, 1996.

Duck, *Cybill,* CBS, 1996.

Voice of the governor, "A Star Is Abhorred," *Duckman* (animated), USA Network, 1997.

Television Appearances; Specials:

The Bar-rump Bump Show, 1964.

The Arthur Godfrey Special, NBC, 1972.

The Arthur Godfrey Portable Electric Medicine Show, NBC, 1972.

Dean Martin's Red Hot Scandals of 1926, NBC, 1976.

Dean Martin's Red Hot Scandals, Part 2, NBC, 1977.

Dean Martin Celebrity Roast: Frank Sinatra, NBC, 1978.

Dean Martin Celebrity Roast: George Burns, NBC, 1978.

Ann-Margret's Hollywood Movie Girls, ABC, 1980.

Dean Martin's Comedy Classics, NBC, 1981.

Baryshnikov in Hollywood, CBS, 1982.

The Best Little Special in Texas, CBS, 1982.

Dean Martin at the Wild Animal Park, NBC, 1982.

Magic with the Stars, NBC, 1982.

Hollywood: The Gift of Laughter, 1982.

Host, *Dom DeLuise and Friends,* ABC, 1983.

Dean Martin Celebrity Roast: Joan Collins, NBC, 1984.

Host, *Dom DeLuise and Friends, Part II,* ABC, 1984.

The Funniest Joke I Ever Heard, ABC, 1984.

Host, *Dom DeLuise and Friends, Part III,* ABC, 1985.

Host, *Dom DeLuise and Friends, Part IV,* ABC, 1986.

Narrator and voice, *Henry's Cat,* 1986.

NBC News Report on America: Life in the Fat Lane, NBC, 1987.

The 59th Annual Academy Awards Presentation, 1987.

Friday Night Surprise!, 1988.

Host, *Superstars and Their Moms,* 1989.

Dinah Comes Home Again, TNN, 1990.

Voice of Nicodemus the pig, *A Precious Christmas Moment,* 1991.

The 43rd Annual Primetime Emmy Awards Presentation, 1991.

Host, *Laurel and Hardy: A Tribute to the Boys,* The Disney Channel, 1992.

Presenter, *The 19th Annual Daytime Emmy Awards,* 1992.

Hal Roach: Hollywood's King of Laughter (documentary), The Disney Channel, 1994.

Shari's Passover Surprise, PBS, 1997.

Television Appearances; Movies:

Roger Hanover, *Happy,* CBS, 1983.

Father Drobney, *Don't Drink the Water,* ABC, 1994.

Mr. Fallon, *The Tin Soldier,* Showtime, 1995.

Television Appearances; Pilots:

Logan Delp, *Evil Roy Slade,* NBC, 1972.

Murray West, *Only with Married Men,* ABC, 1974.

Television Work; Movies:

Executive producer, *Happy,* CBS, 1983.

Stage Appearances; Plays:

(Off-Broadway debut) Struthion, *The Jackass,* Barbizon-Plaza Theatre, 1960.

Corporal Billy Jester, *Little Mary Sunshine,* Orpheum Theatre, then Players Theatre, both New York City, 1961.

Ensemble, *Another Evening with Harry Stoones* (revue), Gramercy Arts Theatre, New York City, 1961.

Bob Acres, *All in Love,* Martinique Theatre, New York City, 1961.

The King, *Half-Past Wednesday,* Orpheum Theatre, 1962.

(Broadway debut) Muffin T. Ragamuffin, *The Student Gypsy; or, The Prince of Liederkrantz,* 54th Street Theatre, 1963.

Mr. Faddish, *Too Much Johnson,* Phoenix Theatre, New York City, 1964.

Mr. Psawyer, *Here's Love,* Shubert Theatre, New York City, 1964.

Barney Cashman, *Last of the Red Hot Lovers,* Eugene O'Neill Theatre, New York City, 1971.

Also appeared in *The School for Scandal, Hamlet,* and *Stalag 17,* all Cleveland Playhouse, Cleveland, OH; *Mixed Company,* Provincetown, MA; *Little Shop of Horrors;* and *Peter and the Wolf;* starred in the cabaret act *An Evening with Dom DeLuise* in Las Vegas, NV, and Atlantic City, NJ.

Stage Appearances; Operas:

Public opinion, *Orpheus in the Underworld,* Los Angeles Opera Company, 1989.

Froesch, *Die Fledermaus,* Metropolitan Opera of New York, 1990 and 1991.

Major Tours:

Appeared in *Luv,* U.S. cities.

Stage Work; Director:

Same Time Next Year Burt Reynolds Theatre, Jupiter, FL, 1980.

Butterflies Are Free, Burt Reynolds Theatre, 1980.

Brighton Beach Memoirs, Burt Reynolds Theatre, 1986.

WRITINGS

Teleplays:

Dom DeLuise and Friends, Part III, ABC, 1985.

Dom DeLuise and Friends, Part IV, ABC, 1986.

Other:

Eat This . . . It Will Make You Feel Better: Mama's Italian Home Cooking and Other Favorites of Family and Friends (cookbook), Simon & Schuster (New York City), 1988.

Charlie the Caterpillar (children's book), Simon & Schuster, 1990.

Also coauthor of the film *Benito.*

OTHER SOURCES

Periodicals:

Jersey Journal, April 28, 1988.*

De MORNAY, Rebecca   1961-

PERSONAL

Original name, Rebecca George; born August 29, 1961, in Santa Rosa, CA; raised in Europe; daughter of Wally (a disc jockey and talk show host) and Julia (an actress) George; married Bruce Wagner, 1989 (divorced, 1990). *Education:* Attended high school in Kitzbuehel, Austria; studied acting at Lee Strasberg Theatre Institute, Los Angeles, CA, and with Sandra Seacat and Geraldine Page; apprentice at Francis Ford Coppola's Zoetrope Studio, 1981.

Addresses: *Agent*—Steve Dontanzille, International Creative Management, 8942 Wilshire Blvd., Beverly Hills, CA 90211.

Career: Actress, director, and producer.

CREDITS

Film Appearances:
(Film debut) *One from the Heart,* Columbia, 1982.
Lana, *Risky Business,* Warner Bros., 1983.
Cathy Pitkin, *Testament,* Paramount, 1983.
Debby Palmer, *Neil Simon's "The Slugger's Wife"* (also known as *The Slugger's Wife*), Columbia, 1985.
Thelma, *The Trip to Bountiful,* Island Alive, 1985.
Sara, *Runaway Train,* Cannon, 1985.
Beauty, *Beauty and the Beast,* Cannon, 1987.
Robin Shay, *And God Created Woman,* Vestron, 1988.
Elizabeth "Ellie" DeWitt, *Feds,* Warner Bros., 1988.
Anna Schuman, *Dealers,* J. Arthur Rank, 1989.
Helen McCaffrey, *Backdraft,* Universal, 1991.
Peyton Flanders, *The Hand That Rocks the Cradle,* Buena Vista, 1992.
Milady DeWinter, *The Three Musketeers,* Buena Vista, 1993.
Jennifer Haines, *Guilty as Sin,* Buena Vista, 1993.
Dr. Sarah Taylor, *Never Talk to Strangers,* TriStar, 1995.
Louise, *The Winner,* LIVE Entertainment, 1996.

Film Work; Executive Producer:
Never Talk to Strangers, TriStar, 1995.
The Winner, LIVE Entertainment, 1996.

Television Appearances; Miniseries:
Wendy Torrance, *Stephen King's The Shining* (also known as *The Shining*), ABC, 1997.

Television Appearances; Movies:
Claire Dupin, *The Murders in the Rue Morgue,* 1986.
Moreau, *By Dawn's Early Light* (also known as *The Grand Tour*), HBO, 1990.
Flo March, *An Inconvenient Woman,* ABC, 1991.
Lynn Kaines, *Blind Side,* HBO, 1993.
Arlene Holsclaw, *Getting Out,* ABC, 1994.
Barbara/Nancy, *Pascagoula,* 1997.

Television Appearances; Episodic:
Rose Peasley, "Pecos Bill, King of the Cowboys," *Shelley Duvall's Tall Tales and Legends,* Showtime, 1986.
Mysterious woman, "The Conversion," *The Outer Limits,* Showtime, 1995.

Television Work; Episodic:
Director, "The Conversion," *The Outer Limits,* Showtime, 1995.

Television Appearances; Specials:
Presenter, *The 58th Annual Academy Awards Presentation,* ABC, 1986.
Rock the Vote, Fox, 1992.
The 49th Annual Golden Globe Awards, TBS, 1992.
Presenter, *The MTV Movie Awards,* MTV, 1992.
Presenter, *The 64th Annual Academy Awards Presentation,* ABC, 1992.
Presenter, *The Blockbuster Entertainment Awards,* 1995.

Stage Appearances:
Born Yesterday, 1988.
Marat/Sade, 1990.

OTHER SOURCES

Periodicals:
American Film, April, 1986, p. 37.
Entertainment Weekly, March 15, 1996, p. 71.
People Weekly, October 3, 1983, p. 100; February 27, 1984, p. 28.
Premiere, February, 1992, p. 88.
Saturday Review, January-February, 1986, p. 30.
TV Guide, April 23, 1994, p. 24.*

De NIRO, Robert   1943-

PERSONAL

Born August 17, 1943, in New York, NY; son of Robert (an artist) and Virginia (a painter; maiden name, Admiral) De Niro; married Diahnne Abbott (an actress), 1976 (divorced, 1988); married Grace Hightower (a former flight attendant), June 17, 1997; children: (first marriage) Drena, Raphael Eugene; (with Toukie Smith) Aaron Kendrick and Julian Henry (twins). *Education:* Studied with Stella Adler and Lee Strasberg at the Actors Studio.

Addresses: *Office*—Tribeca Productions, 375 Greenwich St., New York, NY 10013. *Agent*—Creative

Artists Agency, 9830 Wilshire Blvd., Beverly Hills, CA 90212-1804.

Career: Actor. Founder of Tribeca Productions and Tribeca Film Center, New York City, 1989.

Member: Screen Actors Guild, Actors' Equity Association.

Awards, Honors: New York Film Critics Award, best supporting actor, 1973, for *Bang the Drum Slowly;* New York Film Critics Award, best supporting actor, 1973, for *Mean Streets;* Academy Award, best supporting actor, 1974, for *The Godfather, Part II;* Academy Award nomination, best actor, and Golden Globe Award nomination, best actor in a motion picture (drama), Hollywood Foreign Press Association, both 1977, for *Taxi Driver;* Golden Globe Award nomination, best actor in a motion picture (musical or comedy), 1978, for *New York, New York;* Academy Award nomination, best actor, and Golden Globe Award nomination, best actor in a motion picture (drama), both 1979, for *The Deer Hunter;* Hasty Pudding Man of the Year Award, Harvard University, 1979; Academy Award, best actor, 1980, and Golden Globe Award, best actor in a film or drama, 1981, for *Raging Bull;* Golden Globe Award nomination, best performance by an actor in a motion picture, 1989, for *Midnight Run;* D. W. Griffith Award, best actor, 1990; Academy Award nomination, best performance by an actor in a leading role, and Golden Globe Award nomination, best performance by an actor in a motion picture (drama), both 1991, for *Awakenings;* Academy Award nomination, best actor, and Golden Globe Award nomination, best actor in a drama, both 1991, for *Cape Fear;* MTV Movie Award nominee, best villain, 1997, for *The Fan; Theatre World* Award, for *Cuba and His Teddy Bear.*

CREDITS

Film Appearances:
Bit, *Trois Chambres a Manhattan,* 1965.
Cecil, *The Wedding Party,* Ajay, 1967.
Jon Rubin, *Greetings,* Sigma III, 1968.
Sam, *Sam's Song* (also known as *The Swap*), Cannon, 1969.
Lloyd Barker, *Bloody Mama,* American International Pictures, 1970.
Jon Rubin, *Hi, Mom* (also known as *Confessions of a Peeping John*), Sigma III, 1970.
Gypsy cab driver, *Jennifer on My Mind,* United Artists, 1971.

Danny, *Born to Win,* United Artists, 1971.
Mario, *The Gang That Couldn't Shoot Straight,* Metro-Goldwyn-Mayer, 1971.
Bruce Pearson, *Bang the Drum Slowly,* Paramount, 1973.
Johnny Boy, *Mean Streets,* Warner Bros., 1973.
Vito Corleone, *The Godfather, Part II,* Paramount, 1974.
America at the Movies, 1976.
Travis Bickle, *Taxi Driver,* Columbia, 1976.
Monroe Stahr, *The Last Tycoon,* Paramount, 1977.
Jimmy Doyle, *New York, New York,* United Artists, 1977.
Alfredo Berlinghieri, *1900* (also known as *Novecento*), Paramount, 1977.
Michael Vronsky, *The Deer Hunter,* Warner Bros., 1978.
Jake LaMotta, *Raging Bull,* United Artists, 1980.
Des Spellacy, *True Confessions,* United Artists, 1981.
Himself, *Acting: Lee Strasberg and the Actors Studio,* 1981.
Rupert Pupkin, *The King of Comedy,* Twentieth Century-Fox, 1983.
David "Noodles" Aaronson, *Once upon a Time in America,* Warner Bros., 1984.
Frank Raftis, *Falling in Love,* Paramount, 1984.
Archibald "Harry" Tuttle, *Brazil,* Universal, 1985.
Captain Rodrigo Mendoza, *The Mission,* Warner Bros., 1986.
Louis Cypher, *Angel Heart,* TriStar, 1987.
Al Capone, *The Untouchables,* Paramount, 1987.
Himself, *Hello Actors Studio,* 1987.
Jack Walsh, *Midnight Run,* Universal, 1988.
Joseph "Megs" Megessey, *Jacknife,* Cineplex Odeon, 1989.
Ned, *We're No Angels,* Paramount, 1989.
Stanley Cox, *Stanley and Iris,* Metro-Goldwyn-Mayer/United Artists, 1990.
James Conway, *GoodFellas,* Warner Bros., 1990.
Leonard Lowe, *Awakenings,* Columbia, 1990.
Himself, *Hollywood Mavericks,* Roxie Releasing, 1990.
Max Cady, *Cape Fear,* Universal, 1991.
Donald Rimgale, *Backdraft,* Universal, 1991.
David Merrill, *Guilty by Suspicion,* Warner Bros., 1991.
Evan M. Wright, *Mistress,* Rainbow Releasing/Tribeca Productions, 1992.
Harry Fabian, *Night and the City,* Twentieth Century-Fox, 1992.
Dwight Hansen, *This Boy's Life,* Warner Bros., 1993.
Wayne "Mad Dog" Dobie, *Mad Dog and Glory,* Universal, 1993.
Lorenzo Anello, *A Bronx Tale,* Savoy Pictures, 1993.

The Creature/Sharp featured man, *Mary Shelley's Frankenstein,* TriStar, 1994.

Neil McCauley, *Heat,* Warner Bros., 1995.

Sam "Ace" Rothstein, *Casino,* Universal, 1995.

Actor for a day, *One Hundred and One Nights* (also known as *Les Cent et Une Nuits*), Twentieth Century-Fox, 1995.

Gil Renard, *The Fan,* TriStar, 1996.

Father Bobby, *Sleepers,* Warner Bros., 1996.

Dr. Wally, *Marvin's Room,* Miramax, 1996.

Mo Tilden, *Copland,* Miramax, 1997.

Louis Gara, *Jackie Brown,* Miramax, 1997.

Conrad Brean, *Wag the Dog,* New Line Cinema, 1998.

Lustig, *Great Expectations,* Twentieth Century-Fox, 1998.

Ronin, 1998.

Film Work:

Executive producer, *We're No Angels,* Paramount, 1989.

Producer, *Thunderheart,* TriStar, 1992.

Producer, *Mistress,* Rainbow Releasing/Tribeca Productions, 1992.

Producer and director, *A Bronx Tale,* Savoy Pictures, 1993.

Associate producer, *Mary Shelley's Frankenstein,* TriStar, 1994.

Producer, *Marvin's Room,* Miramax, 1996.

Producer, *Faithful,* New Line Cinema/Savoy Pictures, 1996.

Producer, *Wag the Dog,* New Line Cinema, 1998.

Stage Appearances:

(Off-Broadway debut) Boy, *One Night Stands of a Noisy Passenger,* Actors Playhouse, New York City, 1970.

Douglas One and Fatboy, *Kool Aid,* Forum Theatre, Repertory Theatre of Lincoln Center, New York City, 1971.

Strange Show, 1982.

Night of 100 Stars, Radio City Music Hall, New York City, 1982.

Cuba, *Cuba and His Teddy Bear,* New York Shakespeare Festival, Public Theatre, New York City, 1986.

Television Appearances; Specials:

The Night of 100 Stars II, ABC, 1985.

Narrator, *Dear America: Letters Home from Vietnam,* 1987.

Martin Scorsese Directs, PBS, 1990.

The New Hollywood, NBC, 1990.

Himself, *The Godfather Family: A Look Inside,* HBO, 1990.

Aretha Franklin: Duets, Fox, 1993.

The 25th American Film Institute Achievement Award: A Salute to Martin Scorsese, CBS, 1997.

Television Appearances; Awards Presentations:

Presenter, *The 62nd Annual Academy Awards Presentation,* ABC, 1990.

Presenter, *The 67th Annual Academy Awards,* ABC, 1995.

Television Appearances; Episodic:

Saturday Night Live, NBC, 1997.

Television Work; Series:

Executive producer, *Tribeca,* Fox, 1993.

OTHER SOURCES

Periodicals:

New York Times, March, 1977.

Sunday Times (London), April 22, 1990, p. G1.*

DEPP, Johnny   1963-

PERSONAL

Full name, John Christopher Depp; born June 9, 1963, in Owensboro, KY; son of John (an engineer) and Betty Sue (a homemaker) Depp; married Lori Anne Allison (divorced).

Addresses: *Agent*—Tracey Jacobs, International Creative Management, 8942 Wilshire Blvd., Beverly Hills, CA 90211.

Career: Actor. Guitarist in the rock 'n' roll bands The Flames, The Kids, and Rock City Angels; owner of the Viper Room, a rock 'n' roll club.

Awards, Honors: Male Star of Tomorrow Award, NATO/ShoWest, 1990; Golden Globe Award nomination, best actor in a musical or comedy, 1994, for *Benny & Joon;* Golden Globe Award nomination, best actor in a musical or comedy, 1995, for *Ed Wood.*

CREDITS

Film Appearances:

Glen Lantz, *A Nightmare on Elm Street,* New Line Cinema, 1984.

Jack Marshall, *Private Resort,* TriStar, 1985.

Lerner, *Platoon,* Orion, 1986.

Wade "Cry-Baby" Walker, *Cry-Baby,* Universal, 1990.

Title role, *Edward Scissorhands,* Twentieth Century-Fox, 1990.

(Cameo appearance) *Freddy's Dead: The Final Nightmare,* New Line Cinema, 1991.

Sam, *Benny & Joon,* Metro-Goldwyn-Mayer, 1993.

Gilbert Grape, *What's Eating Gilbert Grape,* Paramount, 1993.

Title role, *Ed Wood,* Buena Vista, 1994.

William Blake, *Dead Man,* Miramax, 1995.

Title role, *Don Juan DeMarco,* New Line Cinema, 1995.

Gene Watson, *Nick of Time* (also known as *Counted Moments*), Paramount, 1995.

(Cameo appearance) *Cannes Man,* Vine International, 1996.

Title role, *Donnie Brasco,* TriStar, 1997.

Also appeared as Axel Blackmar, *Arizona Dream,* 1992; Raphael, *The Brave,* 1998; Raoul Duke, *Fear and Loathing in Las Vegas,* 1998.

Film Work:
Director, *The Brave,* 1998.

Television Appearances; Series:
Officer Tom Hanson, *21 Jump Street,* Fox, 1987-89.

Television Appearances; Episodic:
ABC in Concert, ABC, 1991.

Also appeared in *Hotel,* ABC.

Television Appearances; Movies:
Donnie Fleischer, *Slow Burn,* Showtime, 1986.

Television Appearances; Specials:
Idols, Fox, 1991.

Television Appearances; Awards Presentations:
The 41st Annual Emmy Awards, Fox, 1989.
The 66th Annual Academy Awards Presentation, ABC, 1994.

WRITINGS

Screenplays:
Author of *The Brave,* 1998.

OTHER SOURCES

Periodicals:
Interview, April, 1990, p. 84.*

DERN, Bruce   1936-

PERSONAL

Full name, Bruce MacLeish Dern; born June 4, 1936, in Chicago (some sources say Winnetka), IL; son of John and Jean (MacLeish) Dern; married Marie Dean (divorced); married Diane Ladd (an actress; divorced, 1969); married Andrea Beckett, October 20, 1969; children: (second marriage) Laura Elizabeth (an actress). *Education:* Attended University of Pennsylvania; studied for the theater with Gordon Phillips and at American Foundation of Dramatic Art.

Addresses: *Agent*—Creative Artists Agency, 9830 Wilshire Blvd., Beverly Hills, CA 90212-1825.

Career: Actor. Actors Studio, member, 1959—.

Member: Actors' Equity Association, Screen Actors Guild, Santa Monica Track Club.

Awards, Honors: National Society of Film Critics Award, 1971, for *Drive, He Said;* Pacific Archives Award, actor of the year, Berkeley, CA, 1972; Golden Globe Award nomination, best supporting actor, Hollywood Foreign Press Association, 1974, for *The Great Gatsby;* Academy Award nomination, best supporting actor, Golden Globe Award nomination, best supporting actor, and People's Choice Award, all 1978, for *Coming Home;* Genie Award, 1980, for *Middle Age Crazy;* Silver Bear Award, best actor, Berlin International Film Festival, 1982, for *That Championship Season.*

CREDITS

Film Appearances:
(Film debut) Jack Roper, *Wild River,* Twentieth Century-Fox, 1960.

Joe Krajac, *The Crimebusters,* 1961.

Bedtime Story, Universal, 1963.

John Mayhew, *Hush . . . Hush, Sweet Charlotte* (also known as *Cross of Iron* and *What Ever Happened to Cousin Charlotte?*), Twentieth Century-Fox, 1964.

Sailor, *Marnie,* Universal, 1964.

Loser, *The Wild Angels,* American International Pictures, 1966.

John, *The Trip,* American International Pictures, 1967.

Hammond, *The War Wagon,* Universal, 1967.

Deputy, *Waterhole No. 3,* Paramount, 1967.

John May, *The St. Valentine's Day Massacre,* Twentieth Century-Fox, 1967.

Steve, *Psych-Out* (also known as *Love Children*), American International Pictures, 1968.

Miller, *Hang 'em High,* United Artists, 1968.

Rafe Quint, *Will Penny,* Paramount, 1968.

Richie Fowler, *Number One,* United Artists, 1969.

Joe Danby, *Support Your Local Sheriff,* United Artists, 1969.

Billy Bix, *Castle Keep,* Columbia, 1969.

Keeg, *The Cycle Savages,* American International Pictures, 1969.

Kevin Dirkman, *Bloody Mama,* American International Pictures, 1970.

James, *They Shoot Horses, Don't They?,* Cinerama, 1970.

J. J. Weston, *Rebel Rousers* (also known as *Limbo*), Four Star, 1970.

Bullian, *Drive, He Said,* Columbia, 1971.

Dr. Roger Girard, *The Incredible Two-Headed Transplant* (also known as *The Incredible Transplant*), American International Pictures, 1971.

Rustler, *The Cowboys,* Warner Bros., 1972.

Lowell Freeman, *Silent Running* (also known as *Running Silent*), Universal, 1972.

Jason Staebler, *The King of Marvin Gardens,* Columbia, 1972.

Smitty, *Thumb Tripping,* Avco-Embassy, 1972.

Leo Larsen, *The Laughing Policeman* (also known as *An Investigation of Murder*), Twentieth Century-Fox, 1973.

Tom Buchanan, *The Great Gatsby,* Paramount, 1974.

"Big Bob" Freelander, *Smile,* United Artists, 1975.

Jack Strawhorn, *Posse,* Paramount, 1975.

Lumley, *Family Plot,* Universal, 1976.

Grayson Potchuck, *Won Ton Ton, the Dog Who Saved Hollywood,* Paramount, 1976.

William Brandels, *Folies Bourgeoises* (also known as *The Twist* and *Die Verrueckten Reichen*), UGC/Parafrance, 1976.

Michael Lander, *Black Sunday,* Paramount, 1977.

Captain Bob Hyde, *Coming Home,* United Artists, 1978.

Detective, *The Driver,* Twentieth Century-Fox, 1978.

Bobby Lee, *Middle Age Crazy* (also known as *Heartfarm*), Twentieth Century-Fox, 1980.

Karl Kinsky, *Tattoo,* Twentieth Century-Fox, 1981.

George Sitkowski, *That Championship Season,* Cannon Films, 1982.

Title role, *Harry Tracy—Desperado,* Quartet, 1982.

Wes Holman, *On the Edge,* New Front Films, 1986.

Mr. Edwards, *The Big Town* (also known as *The Arm*), Columbia, 1987.

Ethan, *World Gone Wild,* Lorimar, 1988.

Cliff, *1969,* Atlantic, 1988.

Mark Rumsfield, *The 'Burbs,* Universal, 1989.

Uncle Bud, *After Dark, My Sweet,* Avenue Entertainment, 1990.

John Gillon, *Diggstown* (also known as *Midnight Sting*), Metro-Goldwyn-Mayer, 1992.

Will Plummer, *Wild Bill* (also known as *Wild Bill Hickok* and *Deadwood*), Metro-Goldwyn-Mayer/United Artists, 1995.

Rear Admiral Yancy Graham, *Down Periscope,* Twentieth Century-Fox, 1996.

Sheriff Ed Galt, *Last Man Standing* (also known as *Welcome to Jericho, Gangster!, Gundown,* and *The Bodyguard*), New Line Cinema, 1996.

The chief, *Mulholland Falls,* Metro-Goldwyn-Mayer/United Artists, 1996.

Television Appearances; Episodic:

"The Man on the Monkey Board," *Route 66,* CBS, 1960.

Sea Hunt, syndicated, 1961.

"Bullets Cost Too Much," *Naked City,* ABC, 1961.

"The Fault in Our Stars," *Naked City,* ABC, 1961.

"Daphne, Girl Detective," *Surfside 6,* ABC, 1961.

"Dark Night for Bill Harris," *Ben Casey,* ABC, 1961.

"The Remarkable Mrs. Hawk," *Thriller,* NBC, 1961.

"Act of God," *The Detectives,* ABC, 1961.

"Poor Eddie's Dad," *The Law and Mr. Jones,* ABC, 1962.

"Old Man and the City," *The Dick Powell Show,* NBC, 1962.

"The Other Side of the Mountain," *The Fugitive,* ABC, 1963.

"The Eli Bancroft Story," *Wagon Train,* ABC, 1963.

"The Hunt," *Kraft Suspense Theatre,* NBC, 1963.

Ben Garth, "The Zanti Misfits," *The Outer Limits,* ABC, 1963.

"Lover's Lane," *77 Sunset Strip,* ABC, 1964.

"Come Watch Me Die," *The Fugitive,* ABC, 1964.

"Night Caller," *Alfred Hitchcock Hour,* CBS, 1964.

"First to Thy Own Self," *The Virginian,* NBC, 1964.

"The Last of the Strongmen," *The Greatest Show on Earth,* ABC, 1964.

"Those Who Stay Behind," *Wagon Train,* ABC, 1964.

"Lonely Place," *Alfred Hitchcock Hour,* NBC, 1964.

"The Payment," *The Virginian,* NBC, 1964.

"The Lorelei," *12 O'Clock High,* ABC, 1965.

"Corner of Hell," *The Fugitive,* ABC, 1965.

"The Mission," *12 O'Clock High,* ABC, 1965.

"The Indian Girl Story," *Wagon Train,* ABC, 1965.

"Walk into Terror," *Rawhide,* CBS, 1965.

"Rendezvous at Arillo," *Laredo,* CBS, 1965.

"Ten Little Indians," *Gunsmoke,* CBS, 1965.

"The Verdict," *A Man Called Shenandoah,* ABC, 1965.

"South Wind," *Gunsmoke,* CBS, 1965.

"The Jones Boys," *12 O'Clock High,* ABC, 1965.

"The Good Guys and the Bad Guys," *The Fugitive,* ABC, 1965.

"Pound of Flesh," *The F.B.I.,* ABC, 1965.

"The Wolfers," *Branded,* NBC, 1966.

"Under a Dark Star," *The Big Valley,* ABC, 1966.

"To Hang a Dead Man," *The Loner,* CBS, 1966.

Dixon, "By Force of Violence," *The Big Valley,* ABC, 1966.

"The Lost Treasure," *The Big Valley,* ABC, 1966.

Lou Stone, "The Jailer," *Gunsmoke,* CBS, 1966.

"Gallagher Goes West," *The World of Disney,* NBC, 1966.

"The Treasure Seekers," *Run for Your Life,* NBC, 1966.

"The Devil's Disciples," *The Fugitive,* ABC, 1966.

"Trip to the Far Side," *Run for Your Life,* NBC, 1967.

"At the End of the Rainbow There's Another Rainbow," *Run for Your Life,* NBC, 1967.

Abe Skeels, "Four Days to Furnace Hill," *The Big Valley,* ABC, 1967.

Cully Maco, "The Trackers," *Bonanza,* NBC, 1968.

Thorg, "Wild Journey," *Land of the Giants,* ABC, 1968.

"Julie," *Lancer,* CBS, 1968.

"The Nightmare," *The F.B.I.,* ABC, 1968.

"The Prize," *The Big Valley,* ABC, 1968.

"The Long Night," *Gunsmoke,* CBS, 1969.

"Amid Splinters of the Thunderbolt," *Then Came Bronson,* NBC, 1969.

"A Person Unknown," *Lancer,* CBS, 1969.

"Wild Journey," *Land of the Giants,* ABC, 1970.

"The Gold Mine," *Bonanza,* NBC, 1970.

"Only the Bad Come to Sonora," *High Chaparral,* NBC, 1970.

"To the Gods Alone," *The Immortal,* ABC, 1970.

Also appeared on *Saturday Night Live,* NBC, and *Fallen Angels,* Showtime.

Television Appearances; Movies:

Deputy Doyle Pickett, *Sam Hill: Who Killed the Mysterious Mr. Foster?* (also known as *Sam Hill: Who Killed Mr. Foster?*), ABC, 1971.

Rob Charles, *Toughlove* (also known as *Tough Love*), ABC, 1985.

Augustine St. Clare, *Uncle Tom's Cabin,* Showtime, 1987.

Douglas Osborne, *Roses Are for the Rich,* CBS, 1987.

John Hollander, *Trenchcoat in Paradise,* CBS, 1989.

Scout Ed Higgins, *The Court-Martial of Jackie Robinson,* TNT, 1990.

T. L. Barston, *Into the Badlands,* USA Network, 1991.

Junior Stoker, *Carolina Skeletons,* NBC, 1991.

Billy Archer, *It's Nothing Personal,* NBC, 1993.

Payton McCay, *Dead Man's Revenge* (also known as *You Only Die Once*), USA Network, 1994.

George Putnam, *Amelia Earhart: The Final Flight,* TNT, 1994.

John Walker, *A Mother's Prayer,* USA Network, 1995.

Patrick Leary, *Mrs. Munck,* Showtime, 1996.

Comfort, Texas (also known as *The Untitled Brian Benben Project*), 1997.

Television Appearances; Series:

E. J. Stocker, *Stoney Burke,* ABC, 1962-63.

Television Appearances; Miniseries:

Stanley Mott, *James Michener's Space* (also known as *Space*), CBS, 1985.

Television Appearances; Specials

Interviewee, *Big Gun Talk: The Story of the Western* (documentary), TNT, 1997.

Voice of Mojave Max, *Mojave Adventure,* TBS, 1997.

Stage Appearances:

(New York debut) *Shadow of a Gunman,* New York City, 1959.

F. Scott Fitzgerald, *Strangers,* New York City, 1979.

Appeared as Chance Wayne, *Sweet Bird of Youth;* also appeared in *Orpheus Descending.*

OTHER SOURCES

Films in Review, October, 1980.

People Weekly, March, 1994, p. 210.

Take One (Montreal, Quebec, Canada), July, 1973.*

DERN, Laura 1967-

PERSONAL

Full name, Laura Elizabeth Dern; born February 10, 1967, in Santa Monica, CA; daughter of Bruce Dern (an actor) and Diane Ladd (an actress). *Education:* Attended University of California, Los Angeles; studied acting at Lee Strasberg Theatre Institute and Royal Academy of Dramatic Art.

Addresses: *Agent*—United Talent Agency, 9560 Wilshire Blvd., Fifth Floor, Beverly Hills, CA 90212. *Contact*—760 North La Cienega Blvd., Los Angeles, CA 90069.

Career: Actress.

Awards, Honors: New Generation Award, Los Angeles Film Critics, 1985, for *Smooth Talk* and *Mask;* Academy Award nomination, best actress, 1991, for *Rambling Rose;* Golden Globe Award, best performance by an actress in a miniseries or motion picture made for television, 1993, for *Afterburn;* Emmy Award nomination, best actress in a drama, 1994, for *Fallen Angels.*

CREDITS

Film Appearances:
Debbie, *Foxes,* United Artists, 1980.
Jessica McNeil, *Ladies and Gentlemen: The Fabulous Stains,* Paramount, 1982.
Diane, *Teachers,* Metro-Goldwyn-Mayer/United Artists, 1984.
Diana, *Mask,* Universal, 1985.
Connie, *Smooth Talk,* Spectrafilm, 1985.
Sandy Williams, *Blue Velvet,* DiLaurentiis, 1986.
Kathleen Robinson, *Fat Man and Little Boy,* Paramount, 1988.
Lula Pace Fortune, *Wild at Heart,* Samuel Goldwyn, 1990.
Rose, *Rambling Rose,* New Line Cinema, 1991.
Sally Gerber, *A Perfect World,* Warner Bros., 1993.
Dr. Ellie Sattler, *Jurassic Park,* Universal, 1993.
Ruth Stoops, *Citizen Ruth,* Miramax, 1996.

Also appeared in *White Lightning,* 1973; *Alice Doesn't Live Here Anymore,* 1975; Claire Clairmont, *Haunted Summer,* 1988.

Television Appearances; Episodic:
Rebecca Laymon, "The Strange Case of Dr. Jekyll and Mr. Hyde," *Nightmare Classics,* Showtime, 1989.
Annie, "Murder, Obliquely," *Sydney Pollack's Fallen Angels* (also known as *Fallen Angels*), Showtime, 1993.
Storytime, PBS, 1994.
Guest caller June, "Sleeping with the Enemy," *Frasier,* NBC, 1996.
Susan, "The Puppy Episode," *Ellen,* ABC, 1997.

Also appeared as narrator, "The Song of Sacajawea," *American Heroes & Legends,* 1992; *Secret Storm.*

Television Appearances; Miniseries:
Vicki Weaver, *Ruby Ridge: An American Tragedy* (also known as *Every Knee Shall Bow: The Siege at Ruby Ridge*), CBS, 1996.

Television Appearances; Movies:
Audrey Constantine, *Happy Endings,* NBC, 1983.
Mrs. Harduvel, *Afterburn,* HBO, 1992.
Helen McNulty, *Down Came a Blackbird,* Showtime, 1995.
Voice of adult Bone, *Bastard Out of Carolina,* Showtime, 1996.

Also appeared as Crissy, *The Three Wishes of Billy Grier,* 1984.

Television Appearances; Specials:
Voice of Amelia Earhart, *A Century of Women* (also known as *A Family of Women;* documentary), TBS, 1994.
The American Film Institute Salute to Steven Spielberg, NBC, 1995.

Also appeared in *Rock the Vote,* 1992.

Television Appearances; Awards Presentations:
Fourth Annual Environmental Media Awards, TBS, 1994.
The 51st Annual Golden Globe Awards, TBS, 1994.
The 66th Annual Academy Awards Presentation, ABC, 1994.
Family Film Awards, CBS, 1996.
The 54th Annual Golden Globe Awards, NBC, 1997.
The Blockbuster Entertainment Awards, UPN, 1997.

Also appeared in *The 18th Annual People's Choice Awards,* 1992.

Television Work:
Director, *The Gift* (special), Showtime, 1994.
Executive producer, *Down Came a Blackbird* (movie), Showtime, 1995.

Stage Appearances:
Charlene Loody, *The Palace of Amateurs,* Minetta Lane Theatre, New York City, 1988.

Also appeared in *Brooklyn Laundry,* 1988; *Hamlet,* and *A Midsummer Night's Dream.*

OTHER SOURCES

Periodicals:
American Film, October, 1989, p. 46.
Interview, March, 1986, p. 146; September, 1990, p. 118.
New York Times, May 4, 1986.

People, April 29, 1985, p. 107; October 8, 1990, p. 59.
Premiere, September, 1990, p. 86.*

DERRICKS, Cleavant 1953-

PERSONAL

Born 1953, in Knoxville, TN.

Addresses: *Home*—Agoura Hills, CA. *Agent*—c/o Susan Smith & Associates, 121 North San Vincente Blvd., Beverly Hills, CA 90211-2303.

Career: Actor.

Awards, Honors: Antoinette Perry Award, best actor in a featured musical role, 1982, for *Dreamgirls;* Antoinette Perry Award nomination, best actor in a musical, 1986, for *Big Deal.*

CREDITS

Stage Appearances:
Hud, *Hair,* Biltmore Theatre, New York City, 1977.
Caterpillar, Cook, Tweedledee, and Seven of Spades, *But Never Jam Today,* Longacre Theatre, New York City, 1979.
Your Arms Too Short to Box with God, Ambassador Theatre, New York City, 1980.
James Thuder Early, *Dreamgirls,* Imperial Theatre, New York City, 1981.
Charley, *Big Deal,* Broadway Theatre, New York City, 1986.
Boris, *Romance in Hard Times,* Public/Newman Theatre, New York City, 1989.

Also appeared in *I Have a Dream* and *Jesus Christ Superstar,* both on Broadway.

Stage Work:
Choral arrangements and vocal preparation, *But Never Jam Today,* Longacre Theatre, New York City, 1979.
Vocal arrangements, *Dreamgirls,* Imperial Theatre, New York City, 1981.

Television Appearances; Series:
Jeff Mussberger, *Good Sports,* CBS, 1991.
George Foster, *Drexell's Class* (also known as *Oh No, Not Drexell* and *Shut Up, Kids*), Fox, 1991-92.
Dr. Frederick Ross, *Woops!,* Fox, 1992.

Charles, *Thea,* ABC, 1993-94.
Caleb, *Something Wilder,* NBC, 1994-95.
Reverend Michaels, *Cleghorne!,* 1995-96.
Rembrandt "Crying Man" Brown, *Sliders,* Fox, 1995-97.

Television Appearances; Movies:
Michael Simpson, *Cindy,* ABC, 1978.
The Ambush Murders, CBS, 1982.
Cal, *Bluffing It,* ABC, 1987.
Marvin, *Mickey and Nora,* CBS, 1987.

Television Appearances; Episodic:
And performer of song "Love Is for Sale," "The Dutch Oven," *Miami Vice,* NBC, 1985.
"Joyride," *The Equalizer,* CBS, 1986.
"Father Knows Last," *Moonlighting,* ABC, 1987.
Mac Dickerson, "My Enemy, My Friend," *Spenser: For Hire,* ABC, 1987.
Tommy Greene, "Five of a Kind," *Roseanne,* ABC, 1989.
"There Goes the Judge," *L.A. Law,* NBC, 1991.

Also appeared in *A Different World,* NBC.

Television Appearances; Pilots:
Charles Slater, *The Bakery,* CBS, 1990.
Wally, *Piece of Cake,* CBS, 1990.

Film Appearances:
Suspect number four, *Fort Apache, The Bronx,* Twentieth Century-Fox, 1981.
Lionel Witherspoon, *Moscow on the Hudson,* Columbia, 1984.
Manny Alvarado, *The Slugger's Wife* (also known as *Neil Simon's The Slugger's Wife*), Columbia, 1984.
Abe Washington, *Off Beat,* Buena Vista, 1985.*

DE VARONA, Joanna
See Kerns, Joanna

DEVLIN, Dean 1962-

PERSONAL

Born August 27, 1962, in New York, NY; son of a producer and an actress. *Education:* Graduated from North Hollywood High School, CA.

Addresses: *Agent*—Creative Artists Agency, 9830 Wilshire Blvd., Beverly Hills, CA 90212.

Career: Screenwriter, actor, and producer. Former member of Nervous Service (a rock band).

Awards, Honors: Best Film Maker Award, California Super Eight-Millimeter Film Festival.

CREDITS

Film Work; Producer:
Stargate, Metro-Goldwyn-Mayer, 1994.
Independence Day (also known as *ID4*), Twentieth Century-Fox, 1996.
Godzilla, forthcoming.

Film Work; Other:
Production assistant, *My Bodyguard,* Twentieth Century-Fox, 1980.
Second unit director, *Independence Day* (also known as *ID4*), Twentieth Century-Fox, 1996.

Film Appearances:
Boy, *My Bodyguard,* Twentieth Century-Fox, 1980.
Liquor store clerk, *The Wild Life,* Universal, 1984.
Milton, *Real Genius,* TriStar, 1985.
Ernie, *City Limits,* Atlantic, 1985.
Gum chewer, *3:15—The Moment of Truth,* Dakota, 1986.
Tyler, *Moon 44* (also known as *Intruder*), LIVE Home Video, 1989.
Joe Fledermaus, *Martians Go Home,* Taurus Entertainment, 1990.
Adult bookstore manager, *Total Exposure,* Republic Pictures, 1991.

Television Work; Executive Producer and Creator:
The Visitor, Fox, 1997.

Television Appearances; Series:
Jeffrey Sullivan, *L.A. Law,* NBC, 1986.
David Del Valle, *Hard Copy,* CBS, 1987.
Chris Mendoza, *Generations,* NBC, 1989.

Television Appearances; Episodic:
Appeared on *Too Close for Comfort,* ABC; *Hill Street Blues,* NBC; *Misfits of Science,* NBC; and *Insiders,* ABC.

Television Appearances; Movies:
Pedro Sanchez, *North Beach and Rawhide,* CBS, 1985.

Television Appearances; Specials:
Himself, *Star Wars: The Magic and the Mystery,* Fox, 1997.

Stage Appearances:
Appeared in *Comedies by Shakespeare,* Los Angeles, CA, and *There Must Be a Pony,* New York City.

WRITINGS

Screenplays:
Universal Soldier, TriStar, 1992.
Stargate, Metro-Goldwyn-Mayer, 1994.
Independence Day (also known as *ID4*), Twentieth Century-Fox, 1996.
Godzilla, forthcoming.

Adaptations: The film *Stargate* was adapted as a television series, *Stargate SG-1,* Showtime, based on the original film.

OTHER SOURCES

Periodicals:
Time, July 8, 1996, pp. 58-64.

Other:
www.centropolis.com (web page)*

DEWS, Peter   1929-1997

OBITUARY NOTICE—See index for *CTFT* sketch: Born September 26, 1929, in Wakefield, England; died of a heart attack, August 25, 1997. Educator, actor, director, producer. Dews is best remembered for his work with the London theater and for his adaptations of William Shakespeare's plays for BBC Television. Deciding he wanted to be an actor at the age of four, Dews first began his career as a schoolmaster in Barnsley, England. Then, he pursued his interest in the theater at the Civic Playhouse in Bradford as an actor and also as a director. In 1952 he directed *Crime Passionel* at the Playhouse. Next he set up shop at BBC-Radio and produced 300 plays while in its employ. Dews then began work in television. From 1954 to 1964 he served as drama director for the BBC's Midland region. In 1960 he achieved celebrity when he serialized Shakespeare's histories—including *Richard II* and *Richard III*—for the BBC in a series titled *An Age of Kings.* The series, which included stars such as Sean Connery, earned Dews the Guild of Television Producers and Directors

Award for best drama production that year. He engaged in other series for television called *The Spread of the Eagle* in 1963. Other television shows he directed for the BBC included *A Man for All Seasons, The Alchemist,* and *The Cruel Necessity.*

In addition to his television pursuits, Dews still maintained a love of the theater and later worked as director of the Birmingham Repertory Theatre from 1966 to 1972. While at Birmingham, he directed productions such as *1066 and All That, Peer Gynt, Equus, Twelfth Night, A Crack in the Ice,* and *Hadrian VII.* The latter work was also performed on Broadway and earned Dews an Antoinette Perry Award as best director. In 1978 he began two years with the Chichester Festival Theatre, where he directed *Othello, Julius Caesar, Much Ado about Nothing,* and *The Importance of Being Earnest* among others. His later career included productions of *King Lear, An Inspector Calls,* and *She Stoops to Conquer.* Named Midland Man of the Year in 1972, he also received honorary degrees from De Paul University and Bradford.

OBITUARIES AND OTHER SOURCES

Books:
Who's Who, St. Martin's Press, 1996.

Periodicals:
Times (London; electronic), September 3, 1997.

DILLMAN, Bradford   1930-

PERSONAL

Born April 14, 1930, in San Francisco, CA; son of Dean (a stockbroker) and Josephine (Moore) Dillman; married Frieda Harding, June 16, 1956 (divorced, April 4, 1962); married Suzy Parker (an actress and model), April 20, 1963; children: (first marriage) Jeffrey, Pamela; (second marriage) Diana, Christopher, Georgina Belle LaSalle (stepdaughter). *Education:* Yale University, B.A. (English literature), 1951; studied with Lee Strasberg at Actors Studio, New York City, beginning in 1955, and with John Lehne, beginning in 1962.

Addresses: *Agent*—Agency for the Performing Arts, 9000 Sunset Blvd., Suite 1200, Los Angeles, CA 90069.

Career: Actor. *Military service:* U.S. Marine Corps, became first lieutenant, 1952-53.

Member: Actors' Equity Association, American Federation of Television and Radio Artists, Screen Actors Guild, Players Club.

Awards, Honors: Blum Award, outstanding new person in the theater, 1957; *Theatre World* Award, 1957, for *Long Day's Journey into Night;* Golden Globe Award, new male star of the year, Hollywood Foreign Press Association, 1959; Best Actor Award, Cannes International Film Festival, 1959, for *Compulsion;* Emmy Award nomination, outstanding single performance by an actor in a leading role, 1962, for "The Voice of Charlie Pont," *Premiere, Presented by Fred Astaire;* Emmy Award, outstanding actor in a daytime drama special, 1975, for "The Last Bride of Salem," *ABC Afternoon Playbreak.*

CREDITS

Film Appearances:
Bertrand Griot, *A Certain Smile,* Twentieth Century-Fox, 1958.

Alan Newcombe, *In Love and War,* Twentieth Century-Fox, 1958.

Artie Straus, *Compulsion,* Twentieth Century-Fox, 1959.

Larnier/Claude, *Crack in the Mirror,* Twentieth Century-Fox, 1960.

Paul Raine, *Circle of Deception,* Twentieth Century-Fox, 1961.

Francis Bernardone, *Francis of Assisi,* Twentieth Century-Fox, 1961.

Gowan Stevens, *Sanctuary,* Twentieth Century-Fox, 1961.

Captain David Young, *Sergeant Ryker,* Universal, 1963.

Sidney Tate, *A Rage to Live,* United Artists, 1965.

Lieutenant Stiles, *The Plainsman,* Universal, 1966.

Luther Sebastian, *The Helicopter Spies,* Metro-Goldwyn-Mayer, 1968.

Jonathan Fields, *Jigsaw,* Universal, 1968.

Captain David Young, *Sergeant Ryker,* Universal, 1968.

Major Barnes, *The Bridge at Remagen,* United Artists, 1969.

Captain Myerson, *Suppose They Gave a War and Nobody Came?* (also known as *War Games*), Cinerama, 1970.

Lloyd Thomas, *Brother John,* Columbia, 1971.

Dr. Lewis Dixon, *Escape from the Planet of the Apes,* Twentieth Century-Fox, 1971.

Bill Delancey, *The Mephisto Waltz,* Twentieth Century-Fox, 1971.

Senator Zachary Wheeler, *The Resurrection of Zachary Wheeler,* Vidtronics, 1971.

Willie Oban, *The Iceman Cometh,* American Film Theatre, 1973.

J. J., *The Way We Were,* Columbia, 1973.

Peter Macomber, *Chosen Survivors,* Columbia, 1974.

Manfred Steyner, *Gold,* Allied Artists, 1974.

Big Eddie, *99 and 44/100 Percent Dead* (also known as *Call Harry Crown*), Twentieth Century-Fox, 1974.

Professor James Parmiter, *Bug,* Paramount, 1975.

Captain McKay, *The Enforcer,* Warner Bros., 1976.

John Wilkes Booth, *The Lincoln Conspiracy,* Sunn Classic, 1977.

Jabez Link, *Mastermind,* Goldstone, 1977.

Odums, *The Amsterdam Kill,* Columbia, 1978.

Paul Grogan, *Piranha,* World, 1978.

Major Baker, *The Swarm,* Warner Bros., 1978.

Brickman, *Love and Bullets,* Associated Film Distribution, 1979.

Dr. Gary Shaw, *Guyana, Cult of the Damned* (also known as *Guyana, Crime of the Century*), Universal, 1980.

Arthur Jaeger, *Running Scared,* 1980.

Captain Briggs, *Sudden Impact,* Warner Bros., 1983.

Clark, *The Treasure of the Amazon* (also known as *El Tesoro del Amazours*), Videocine-S.A., 1985.

Frank Simmons, *Man Outside,* Virgin Vision, 1987.

Hot Pursuit, Paramount, 1987.

Dobler, *Lords of the Deep,* Concorde, 1989.

Walt Simmons, *Heroes Stand Alone,* Metro-Goldwyn-Mayer Home Entertainment, 1989.

Also appeared in *Black Ribbon for Deborah.*

Television Appearances; Series:
Captain David Young, *Court-Martial,* ABC, 1966.
Paul Hollister, *King's Crossing,* ABC, 1982.
Darryl Clayton, *Falcon Crest,* CBS, 1982-83.

Television Appearances; Pilots:
Duke Paige, *Longstreet,* ABC, 1971.
Randy Jamison, *The Delphi Bureau,* ABC, 1972.
Jeffrey Winslow, *The Eyes of Charles Sand,* ABC, 1972.
Avery Stanton, *Kingston: The Power Play,* NBC, 1976.
Howard Bronstein, *Street Killing,* ABC, 1976.
Donald Prince, *Jennifer: A Woman's Story,* NBC, 1979.
Harry Flemington, *Tourist,* syndicated, 1980.

Television Appearances; Episodic:
Kraft Television Theater, NBC, 1953.

Eric Valkay, "There Shall Be No Night," *Hallmark Hall of Fame,* NBC, 1957.

The Eleventh Hour, NBC, 1962.

Charlie Pont, "The Voice of Charlie Pont," *Premiere, Presented by Fred Astaire,* ABC, c. 1962.

Naked City, ABC, 1963.

Espionage, NBC, 1963.

The Virginian, NBC, 1963.

"The Kitty Pryer Story," *Wagon Train,* NBC, 1963.

Captain David Young, "The Case against Paul Ryker," *Kraft Suspense Theater,* NBC, 1963.

"To Catch a Butterfly," *Alfred Hitchcock Theater,* CBS, 1963.

"Chain Reaction," *Alcoa Premiere,* ABC, 1963.

Vito Fortunato, *The Greatest Show on Earth,* ABC, 1963-64.

The Nurses, CBS, 1964.

Ben Casey, ABC, 1964.

Dr. Kildare, NBC, 1964.

Profiles in Courage, NBC, 1965.

Dr. Kildare, NBC, 1966.

12 O'Clock High, ABC, 1966.

"The Divided Man," *The F.B.I.,* ABC, 1966.

Eric Mercer, "Day of the Comet," *The Big Valley,* ABC, 1966.

Bob Hope Presents the Chrysler Theater, NBC, 1966.

Bob Hope Presents the Chrysler Theater, NBC, 1967.

"Sky on Fire," *The F.B.I.,* ABC, 1967.

The Man from U.N.C.L.E., NBC, 1967.

James Beldon, "A Noose Is Waiting," *The Big Valley,* ABC, 1967.

"Southwind," *The F.B.I.,* ABC, 1968.

Judd for the Defense, ABC, 1968.

Paul Shepherd, "Recover," *Mission: Impossible,* CBS, 1968.

Fear No Evil, NBC, 1969.

Marcus Welby, M.D., ABC, 1969.

"The Traitor," *The F.B.I.,* ABC, 1970.

Matt, "You Certainly Are a Big Boy," *The Mary Tyler Moore Show,* CBS, 1971.

"Face of Fear," *Bonanza,* NBC, 1971.

Richard Upton Pickman, "Pickman's Model," *Night Gallery,* NBC, 1971.

"The Mastermind: Part I," *The F.B.I.,* ABC, 1971.

"The Mastermind: Part II," *The F.B.I.,* ABC, 1971.

Tom Fitz, "Murder by Proxy," *The Streets of San Francisco,* ABC, 1972.

Tony Goodland, "The Greenhouse Jungle," *Columbo,* NBC, 1972.

Richard Alexander, "Cain's Mark," *Cannon,* CBS, 1972.

Larry Edison, "Stone Pillow," *Mission: Impossible,* CBS, 1972.

"The McCreedy Bust—Going, Going, Gone," *Alias Smith and Jones,* ABC, 1972.

Douglas McGee, "Missing at FL307," *Cannon*, CBS, 1975.

"The Last Bride of Salem," *ABC Afternoon Playbreak*, ABC, 1975.

Gary Stevens, "Death in Deep Water," *Thriller*, ABC, 1975.

Sam Kay, "Look Back in Darkness" (also known as "The Next Voice You See"), *Thriller*, ABC, 1975.

Tony Kramer, "Angels of the Deep," *Charlie's Angels*, ABC, 1980.

Victor Modrian, *Hot Pursuit*, NBC, 1984.

Lieutenant Kershaw, "Murder to a Jazz Beat," *Murder, She Wrote*, CBS, 1985.

Dennis McConnell, "Death Takes a Dive," *Murder, She Wrote*, CBS, 1987.

Avery Stone, "Steal Me a Story," *Murder, She Wrote*, CBS, 1987.

Also appeared on *Wide World of Mystery*.

Television Appearances; Movies:

Paul Varney, *Fear No Evil*, NBC, 1969.

Lyle Fawcett, *Black Water Gold*, ABC, 1970.

Jim Meeker, *Five Desperate Women*, ABC, 1971.

Frank Klaner, *Revenge* (also known as *There Once Was a Woman*), ABC, 1971.

Andrew Rodanthe, *Moon of the Wolf*, ABC, 1972.

Steven Dennis, *Deliver Us from Evil*, ABC, 1973.

Major Mike Dunning, *The Disappearance of Flight 412*, NBC, 1974.

Sam Champion, *Murder or Mercy*, ABC, 1974.

Martin Reed, *Adventures of the Queen*, CBS, 1975.

Michael Dominick, *Force Five*, CBS, 1975.

Arthur Deal III, *Wonder Woman Meets Baroness Von Gunther*, 1976.

Richard, *Widow*, NBC, 1976.

Dr. Eric Lake, *The Hostage Heart*, CBS, 1977.

Jack Mathews, *Before and After*, ABC, 1979.

Jason Eddington, *The Memory of Eva Ryker*, CBS, 1980.

Singer, *The Legend of Walks Far Woman*, NBC, 1982.

Eric Noble, *Covenant*, NBC, 1985.

Peter Merkin, *Easy Come, Easy Go* (also known as *Christine Cromwell*), ABC, 1989.

Mr. Burgess, *The Heart of Justice*, TNT, 1993.

Stage Appearances:

Richard, *The Scarecrow*, Theatre de Lys, New York City, 1953.

Freddie, *Pygmalion*, Sharon Playhouse, Sharon, CT, 1953.

Marchbanks, *Candida*, Sharon Playhouse, 1953.

Hadrian, *You Touched Me*, Sharon Playhouse, 1953.

Understudy, *End as a Man*, Theatre de Lys, 1953.

Pierre, *The Madwoman of Chaillot*, Sharon Playhouse, 1954.

Happy, *Death of a Salesman*, Sharon Playhouse, 1954.

Young teacher, *The Browning Version*, Sharon Playhouse, 1954.

Danny, *Night Must Fall*, Sharon Playhouse, 1954.

Kip Ames, *Third Person*, President Theatre, New York City, 1955.

Extra, *Inherit the Wind*, National Theatre, New York City, 1955.

Morgan, *The Corn Is Green*, Sharon Playhouse, 1955.

Octavius, *The Barretts of Wimpole Street*, Sharon Playhouse, 1955.

Frederic and Hugo, *Ring 'round the Moon*, Sharon Playhouse, 1955.

The radical, *Counsellor-at-Law*, Sharon Playhouse, 1955.

Black Chiffon, University of Michigan, Ann Arbor, 1955.

Jimmy, *The Rainmaker*, Sharon Playhouse, 1956.

Edmund Tyrone, *Long Day's Journey into Night*, Helen Hayes Theatre, New York City, 1956-58.

Gil Stanford, *The Fun Couple*, Lyceum Theatre, New York City, 1962.

WRITINGS

Books:

Inside the New York Giants, Third Story Books (Bridgeport, CT), 1994.

Are You Anybody?: An Actor's Life (autobiography), Fithian Press (Santa Barbara, CA), 1997.*

DOOHAN, James 1920-

PERSONAL

Full name, James Montgomery Doohan; born March 3, 1920, in Vancouver, British Columbia, Canada; son of William (a pharmacist, veterinarian, and dentist) and Sarah (a homemaker) Doohan; married Judy, 1948 (divorced, 1965); married Anita Yagel (a television production secretary), November 22, 1967 (divorced); married Wende Braunberger, 1974; children: (first marriage) Larkin, Deirdre, Montgomery, Christopher; (second marriage) two; (third marriage) Eric and Thomas. *Education:* Studied acting at the Neighborhood Playhouse, 1946. *Avocational interests:* Carpentry, woodcarving.

Addresses: *Home*—Washington state. *Agent*—DMG Management, 4470 Sunset Blvd., Suite 792, Los Angeles, CA 90027.

Career: Actor. Performed in 400 live television shows and 4,000 radio shows for the Canadian Broadcasting Corporation; actor in approximately 120 stage productions; acting teacher, Neighborhood Playhouse, New York City; speaker, college tour circuit; appeared in television commercials, including advertisements for Frosted Cheerios cereal, 1996. Writer. *Military service:* Royal Canadian Army, became captain of artillery.

CREDITS

Film Appearances:
The Wheeler Dealers (also known as *Separate Beds*), Metro-Goldwyn-Mayer, 1963.
Les, *Bus Riley's Back in Town,* Universal, 1965.
Bit, *The Satan Bug,* United Artists, 1965.
Bishop, *36 Hours,* Metro-Goldwyn-Mayer, 1965.
Phillip Bainbridge, *One of Our Spies Is Missing,* Metro-Goldwyn-Mayer, 1966.
Building superintendent, *Jigsaw,* Universal, 1968.
Benoit, *Man in the Wilderness,* Warner Bros., 1971.
Follo, *Pretty Maids All in a Row,* Metro-Goldwyn-Mayer, 1971.
Danny, Monterey Home Video, 1979.
Chief O'Brien, *Double Trouble,* Motion Picture Corporation of America, 1992.
Dr. Landon, *Amore!,* 1993.
Scotty, *National Lampoon's Loaded Weapon I,* New Line Cinema, 1993.
New York Skyride, 1994.
Uncle Monty, *Storybook,* Republic Pictures Home Video, 1995.
William Shatner's Star Trek Memories!, Paramount Home Video, 1995.

Film Appearances as Lieutenant Commander Montgomery "Scotty" Scott, Chief Engineer of the USS *Enterprise*:
Star Trek: The Motion Picture, Paramount, 1979.
Star Trek II: The Wrath of Khan (also known as *Star Trek II: The Vengeance of Khan* and *Star Trek: The Wrath of Khan*), Paramount, 1982.
Star Trek III: The Search for Spock, Paramount, 1984.
Star Trek IV: The Voyage Home, Paramount, 1986.
Star Trek V: The Final Frontier, Paramount, 1989.
Star Trek VI: The Undiscovered Country, Paramount, 1991.
Star Trek: Generations (also known as *Star Trek VII*), Paramount, 1994.

Television Appearances; Series;
Space Command, 1953.

Lieutenant Commander Montgomery "Scotty" Scott, Chief Engineer of the USS *Enterprise, Star Trek,* NBC, 1966-69.
Voice of Lieutenant Commander Montgomery "Scotty" Scott, Lieutenant Arex, Ensign Pavel Chekov, and others, *Star Trek* (animated), NBC, 1973-75.
Commander Carnarvin, *Jason of Star Command,* CBS, 1979-81.
Damon Warwick, *The Bold and the Beautiful* (also known as *Glamour* and *Top Models*), CBS, 1993-94, 1996-97.
Pippen, *Homeboys in Outer Space,* UPN, 1996-97.

Television Appearances; Episodic:
(Television debut) Detective, *Martin Kane, Private Eye,* NBC, 1949.
Davit, "Quint Asper Comes Home," *Gunsmoke,* CBS, 1962.
"Hazel's Highland Fling," *Hazel,* NBC, 1962.
Father, "Valley of the Shadow," *The Twilight Zone,* CBS, 1963.
Officer, "The Shark Affair," *The Man from U.N.C.L.E.,* NBC, 1964.
Lieutenant Branch, "Expanding Human," *The Outer Limits,* ABC, 1964.
"I, Robot," *The Outer Limits,* ABC, 1964.
Presidential assistant, "Hot Line," *Voyage to the Bottom of the Sea,* ABC, 1964.
Lawrence Tobin, "Hail to the Chief," *Voyage to the Bottom of the Sea,* ABC, 1964.
"Fringe Benefits," *The Rogues,* NBC, 1964.
"The Man Who Couldn't Die," *The Virginian,* NBC, 1964.
"A Strange Little Visitor," *Bewitched,* ABC, 1965.
Blue Light, ABC, 1966.
Professor, "The Bridge of Lions," *The Man from U.N.C.L.E.,* NBC, 1966.
Professor, "One of Our Spies Is Missing," *The Man from U.N.C.L.E.,* NBC, 1966.
Archie MacPherson, "The Big Blow," *Magnum, P.I.,* CBS, 1983.
Lieutenant Commander Montgomery "Scotty" Scott, Chief Engineer of the USS *Enterprise,* "Relics," *Star Trek: The Next Generation,* syndicated, 1987.
"Harry's Will," *MacGyver,* ABC, 1990.
Himself, *The Ben Stiller Show,* Fox, 1992.
Chief Engineer Montgomery "Scotty" Scott, "Trials and Tribble-ations," *Star Trek: Deep Space Nine,* syndicated, 1996.

Also appeared in *Ben Casey,* ABC; *Bonanza,* NBC; *Daniel Boone,* NBC; *Fantasy Island,* ABC; *The F.B.I.,*

ABC; *The Fugitive,* ABC; *The Gallant Men,* ABC; *The Iron Horse,* ABC; *Marcus Welby, M.D.,* ABC; *Peyton Place,* ABC; *Return to Peyton Place,* NBC; *Shenandoah; Suspense,* CBS; *Tales of Tomorrow,* ABC; *Then Came Bronson,* NBC; and *Thriller,* NBC.

Television Appearances; Specials:
53rd Annual King Orange Jamboree Parade, NBC, 1986.
Star Trek: A Captain's Log, CBS, 1994.
It's Hot in Here: UPN Fall Preview, UPN, 1996.

Television Appearances; Pilots:
Scrimp, "Scalplock," *ABC Sunday Night Movie,* ABC, 1966.
Lieutenant Commander Montgomery "Scotty" Scott, Chief Engineer of the USS *Enterprise, Star Trek—Where No Man Has Gone Before* (also known as *Where No Man Has Gone Before*), NBC, 1966.

Television Appearances; Movies:
1996, [France], 1986.
Himself, *Knight Rider 2000,* NBC, 1991.

WRITINGS

Memoirs:
(With Peter David) *Beam Me Up, Scotty,* Pocket Books (New York City), 1996.

Fiction:
(With S. M. Stirling) *Rising: Volume One of The Flight Engineer,* Baen (Riverdale, NY), 1996.

OTHER SOURCES

Periodicals:
Omni, December, 1994, pp. 54-55.
People Weekly, December 19, 1994, pp. 73-74.
Publishers Weekly, October 28, 1996, p. 62; November 11, 1996, p. 70; October 25, 1993, pp. 25-26.*

DOOLEY, Paul 1928-

PERSONAL

Original name, Paul Brown; born February 22, 1928, in Parkersburg, WV; son of Peter James (a factory worker) and Ruth Irene (a homemaker; maiden name, Barringer) Brown; married Donna Lee Wasser, September 19, 1958 (divorced); married Winifred

Holzman (a writer and actress), November 18, 1984; children: (first marriage) Robin, Adam, Peter; (second marriage) Savannah. *Education:* West Virginia University, B.A. (speech and drama), 1952.

Addresses: *Agent*—Agency for the Performing Arts, 9000 Sunset Blvd., Suite 1200, Los Angeles, CA 90069.

Career: Actor and writer. All over Creation, owner. Once worked as a cartoonist for a newspaper in Parkersburg, WV; also worked as magician and clown. *Military service:* U.S. Navy, 1946-48.

Member: Actors' Equity Association, Screen Actors Guild, American Federation of Television and Radio Artists.

Awards, Honors: Named D. W. Griffith Best Supporting Actor, 1979, for *Breaking Away.*

CREDITS

Film Appearances:
(Film debut) Television reporter, *What's So Bad About Feeling Good,* Universal, 1968.
Day porter, *The Out of Towners,* Paramount, 1970.
Up the Sandbox, National General, 1972.
Gravy Train, Columbia, 1974.
Death Wish, Paramount, 1974.
Hyannisport announcer, *Slap Shot,* Universal, 1977.
Voice, *Raggedy Ann and Andy* (animated), Twentieth Century-Fox, 1977.
Snooks Brenner, *A Wedding,* Twentieth Century-Fox, 1978.
Alex Theodopoulos, *A Perfect Couple,* Twentieth Century-Fox, 1979.
Simon Peterfreund, *Rich Kids,* United Artists, 1979.
Ray Stohler, *Breaking Away* (also known as *Bambino*), Twentieth Century-Fox, 1979.
Wimpy, *Popeye,* Paramount, 1980.
Kurt, *Paternity,* Paramount, 1981.
Joe Hiatt, *Endangered Species,* Metro-Goldwyn-Mayer/United Artists, 1982.
Hugh Kendall, *Kiss Me Goodbye,* Twentieth Century-Fox, 1982.
Dr. Gil Gainey, *Health,* Twentieth Century-Fox, 1982.
Claude Elsinore, *Strange Brew* (also known as *The Adventures of Bob and Doug McKenzie*), Metro-Goldwyn-Mayer/United Artists, 1983.
Dr. Ted, *Going Berserk,* Universal, 1983.
Jim Baker, *Sixteen Candles,* Universal, 1984.
Little Shop of Horrors, Universal, 1986.

Noozel, *Big Trouble,* Columbia, 1986.

Roy Crane, *Monster in the Closet,* Troma, 1987.

Father Freddie, *Last Rites,* Metro-Goldwyn-Mayer/ United Artists, 1988.

Randall Schwab, *O. C. and Stiggs,* Metro-Goldwyn-Mayer, 1988.

FBI director Donald R. Stark, *Flashback,* Paramount, 1990.

Owen Chase, *Shakes the Clown,* IRS Releasing, 1992.

As himself, *The Player,* Fine Line, 1992.

Big Chuck, *My Boyfriend's Back* (also known as *Johnny Zombie*), Buena Vista, 1993.

Tupperware salesman, *A Dangerous Woman,* Gramercy Pictures, 1993.

Peebo, *The Traveling Poet,* 1993.

Ed Dutton, *The Underneath* (also known as *Present Tense*), Gramercy Pictures, 1995.

Pollo, *God's Lonely Man,* Cinequanon Pictures International, 1996.

UFO abductee, *Waiting for Guffman,* SONY Pictures Classics, 1996.

Bud Chapman, *Clockwatchers,* BMG Independents, 1997.

Leo, *Loved,* MDP Worldwide, 1997.

Father Norton, *Telling Lies in America,* Banner Entertainment, 1997.

Television Appearances; Series:

Dick Hale, *Coming of Age,* CBS, 1988-89.

John Shirley, *Grace under Fire,* ABC, 1994-97.

Enabran Tain, *Star Trek: Deep Space Nine,* 1994-97.

Television Appearances; Miniseries:

William Burns, *The Murder of Mary Phagan* (also known as *The Ballad of Mary Phagan*), NBC, 1988.

Robert "Bud" McFarlane, *Guts and Glory: The Rise and Fall of Oliver North,* CBS, 1989.

Herb Tolliver, "Armistead Maupin's Tales of the City," *American Playhouse,* PBS, 1994.

Television Appearances; Movies:

Ben McKenna, *When He's Not a Stranger* (also known as *Someone You Know*), CBS, 1989.

Doc, *Guess Who's Coming for Christmas?* (also known as *UFO Cafe* and *George Walters Will Be Away for the Holidays*), NBC, 1990.

Willy Bailey, *The Court-Martial of Jackie Robinson,* TNT, 1990.

Hal Roach, *White Hot: The Mysterious Murder of Thelma Todd* (also known as *Hot Toddy*), NBC, 1991.

Twittenham, "Frogs!," *WonderWorks Family Movie,* PBS, 1992.

Assistant District Attorney Robert Norell, *Perry Mason: The Case of the Heartbroken Bride* (also known as *Perry Mason: The Case of the Bad Blood Wedding*), NBC, 1992.

Sid Wiggins, "Cooperstown," *TNT Screenworks,* TNT, 1993.

Richard Becker, *Mother of the Bride,* CBS, 1993.

Jim Anderson, "State of Emergency" (also known as "Slow Bleed"), *HBO Showcase,* HBO, 1994.

Emmett David, *Out There,* Showtime, 1995.

Senator Thatch, "The Computer Wore Tennis Shoes," *Disney Family Films* (also known as *The ABC Family Movie*), ABC, 1995.

Jerry Briggs, *Evolver,* Sci-Fi Channel, 1996.

Angels in the Endzone, ABC, 1997.

Television Appearances; Specials:

Let's Celebrate, 1972.

Ames Prescott, *Momma the Detective,* 1981.

Detective, *The Shady Hill Kidnapping,* 1982.

Dick Albright, *The Firm,* 1983.

Don Liddle, *Steel Collar Man,* 1985.

Dr. Womer, *The Day the Senior Class Got Married,* 1985.

Detroit host, *The CBS All-American Thanksgiving Day Parade,* 1988.

Gil Hutchinson, "Lip Service," *HBO Showcase,* HBO, 1988.

Superman's 50th Birthday: A Celebration of the Man of Steel, CBS, 1988.

Casey Bengal, *Mathnet: The Case of the Unnatural,* PBS, 1992.

"Forever Ambergris," *Tales from the Crypt,* HBO, 1993.

Andy Milligan, "Traveler's Rest," *Showtime 30-Minute Movie,* Showtime, 1993.

Television Appearances; Episodic:

The Dom DeLuise Show, CBS, 1968.

Father, "Hansel and Gretel," *Faerie Tale Theatre,* Showtime, 1982.

Horace Van Dam, *Coach,* ABC, 1990.

Mickey Tupper, "May Divorce Be with You," *Dream On,* HBO, 1990.

Mickey Tupper, "Pop Secret," *Dream On,* HBO, 1990.

Mickey Tupper, "The Taking of Pablum 1-2-3," *Dream On,* HBO, 1990.

Mickey Tupper, "Steinway to Heaven," *Dream On,* HBO, 1990.

Mickey Tupper, "The Courtship of Martin's Father," *Dream On,* HBO, 1990.

Mad about You (also known as *Loved by You*), NBC, 1992.

Mr. Adult, *The Ben Stiller Show* (also known as *The Best Man*), Fox, 1992.

Walter McTeague, *Chicago Hope*, CBS, 1994.

Voice, "Dammit Hollywood," *Duckman* (animated), USA Network, 1994.

Sisters, NBC, 1994.

Storytime, PBS, 1994.

Chuck Wood, *My So-Called Life*, ABC, 1994.

Mr. Lewis, *ER*, NBC, 1995.

Thomas Kelsey, *Ellen*, ABC, 1995.

Joe Bangs, "The Well-Worn Lock," *Millennium*, Fox, 1996.

Also appeared in episodes of *Alf*, NBC; *The Golden Girls*, NBC; *thirtysomething*, ABC; *Evening Shade*, CBS; *Wonder Years*, ABC; *The Boys*, CBS; *L.A. Law*, NBC; and *The Mommies*, NBC.

Stage Appearances:

(Stage debut) The Butler, *Holiday*, Mt. Gretna, PA, 1951.

Elwood P. Dowd, *Harvey*, Jackson, WY, 1954.

Sills and Company, Lamb's Theatre, New York City, 1986.

Made New York debut as Walt Dreary, *The Threepenny Opera*, off-Broadway production; appeared in Second City Revue; appeared in *The Odd Couple*, Broadway production; also appeared in *Fallout*, *Adaptation/Next*, *The White House Murder Case*, *Hold Me*, *'Toinette*, *Dr. Willy Nilly*, and *The Amazin' Casey Stengel*, all off-Broadway productions.

WRITINGS

Teleplays; Series:

(Head writer) *Take Five* (series), 1976-77.

Writer for the series *The Electric Company*, PBS.

Screenplays:

(With Robert Altman and Frank Barhyte) *Health*, Twentieth Century-Fox, 1982.*

DOW, Tony 1945-

PERSONAL

Full name, Anthony Lee Dow; born April 13, 1945, in Hollywood, CA; son of John Stevens (a designer and general contractor) and Muriel Virginia (Montrose) Dow; married, 1969 (divorced, 1978); married second wife, Laura Shulkind, June 16, 1980; children: (first marriage) Christopher T. *Education:* Attended University of California, Los Angeles, Columbia College, and Sherwood Oaks Experimental College; trained at Film Industry Workshop.

Addresses: *Manager*—Phil Gittelman, Phillip B. Gittelman Management, 1221 North Kings Rd., Los Angeles, CA 90019.

Career: Actor, producer, and director. Owner of a construction firm; also professional painter. *Military service:* Served in National Guard, beginning in 1965.

CREDITS

Television Appearances; Series:

Wally Cleaver, *Leave It to Beaver*, CBS, 1957-58, then ABC, 1958-63.

Chet, *Never Too Young*, 1965.

Wally Cleaver, *Still the Beaver*, The Disney Channel, 1985-86, retitled *The New Leave It to Beaver*, TBS, 1986-89.

Television Appearances; Movies:

Johnny, *A Great American Tragedy* (also known as *A New American Tragedy*), 1972.

Joey, *Death Scream* (also known as *Streetkill* and *The Woman Who Cried Murder*), 1975.

Dr. Russell, *The Ordeal of Bill Carney*, 1981.

Pete Kinney, *High School, U.S.A.*, 1983.

Wally Cleaver, *Still the Beaver*, The Disney Channel, 1983.

The producer, *The Adventures of Captain Zoom in Outer Space*, Starz!, 1995.

Television Work; Movies:

Producer (with Peter V. Ware), *The Adventures of Captain Zoom in Outer Space*, Starz!, 1995.

Visual effects producer, *Doctor Who* (also known as *Doctor Who and the Enemy Within*), Fox, 1996.

Producer (with Roger Duchowny), *It Came from Outer Space II*, Sci-Fi Channel, 1996.

Television Appearances; Episodic:

Ed Greene, "A Child's Christmas in Weemawee," Parts 1 and 2, *Square Pegs*, CBS, 1982.

Mickey Spillane's Mike Hammer, CBS, 1984.

Freddy's Nightmares, syndicated, between 1989 and 1990.

Appeared in episodes of *Mod Squad*, ABC; *Knight Rider*, NBC; *The Love Boat*, ABC; *Quincy, M.E.*, NBC;

General Hospital, ABC; *Merv Griffin Show,* CBS; *Today,* NBC; and *Good Morning America,* ABC.

Television Work; Episodic:
Director, *Coach,* ABC, between 1989 and 1996.
Director, *Lassie,* 1989.
Director, *Babylon 5* (also known as *B5*), syndicated, 1993.
Producer, *The High Life,* 1994.
Director, *Blue Heaven,* 1994.
Producer, *Ain't Misbehavin',* 1994.

Also directed an episode of *Get a Life.*

Other Television Appearances:
The 12th Annual Circus of the Stars (special), 1987.

Host, *Weekday Heroes;* also appeared in *Four Feet in the Morning.*

Other Television Work:
Contributing director, *The Coach Retrospective: Mary Hart Goes One-on-One with "Coach"* (special), ABC, 1994.
Director, *Over Here,* 1996.

Film Appearances:
Wally, *The Kentucky Fried Movie,* United Film, 1977.
Judge number one, *Back to the Beach,* Paramount, 1987.
Kill Crazy, Media Home Entertainment, 1990.

Film Work:
Director, *U.F.O.,* PolyGram, 1993.

Stage Appearances:
Appeared in *Lovers and Other Strangers, Barefoot in the Park,* and *Come Blow Your Horn.* Toured in *So Long, Stanley.*

WRITINGS

Television Episodes:
"Slumber Party," *Still the Beaver,* The Disney Channel, c. 1984.

OTHER SOURCES

Periodicals:
People Weekly, May 20, 1996, p. 17.
TV Guide, August 23, 1997, p. 32.*

DUGAN, Dennis   1946-

PERSONAL

Born September 5, 1946, in Wheaton, IL; married Joyce Van Patten (an actress). *Education:* Studied acting at the Goodman Theatre School; attended Wheaton Central High School, Wheaton, IL.

Career: Actor and director. International Arts Relations Theatre, New York City, lighting designer, 1979-80.

CREDITS

Film Appearances:
Night Call Nurses, New World, 1974.
Apprentice, *The Day of the Locust,* Paramount, 1975.
Young man, *Night Moves,* Warner Bros., 1975.
Logan, *Smile,* United Artists, 1975.
Lewis, *Harry and Walter Go to New York,* Columbia, 1976.
Garson Hobart, *Norman . . . Is That You?,* Metro-Goldwyn-Mayer/United Artists, 1976.
Tom Trimble, *Unidentified Flying Oddball* (also known as *The Spaceman and King Arthur, A Spaceman in King Arthur's Court, U.F.O.,* and *The Unidentified Flying Oddball*), Buena Vista, 1979.
Chris, *The Howling,* Avco-Embassy, 1981.
Rob, *Water,* Rank, 1985.
David Miller, *Can't Buy Me Love* (also known as *Boy Rents Girl*), Buena Vista, 1987.
Mr. Settigren, *The New Adventures of Pippi Longstocking,* Columbia, 1988.
Bill, *She's Having a Baby,* Paramount, 1988.
David Brodsky, *Parenthood,* Universal, 1989.
All-American dad, *Problem Child,* Universal, 1990.
Stage hand, *Brain Donors* (also known as *Lame Ducks*), Paramount, 1992.
Doug Thompson, *Happy Gilmore,* Universal, 1996.

Film Director:
Problem Child, Universal, 1990.
Brain Donors (also known as *Lame Ducks*), Paramount, 1992.
Happy Gilmore, Universal, 1996.
Beverly Hills Ninja, Sony Pictures, 1997.

Television Appearances; Series:
Title role, *Richie Brockelman, Private Eye,* NBC, 1978.
Ben Christian, *Empire,* CBS, 1984.

Edgar "Benny" Benedek, *Shadow Chasers,* ABC, 1985-86.

Television Appearances; Miniseries:
Claude Tinker, *Rich Man, Poor Man* (also known as *Rich Man, Poor Man—Book 1*), ABC, 1976.

Television Appearances; Pilots:
Joel Snedeger, *Alice,* CBS, 1976.
Father Morgan, *Father, O Father,* ABC, 1977.
Josh Fowler, *Did You Hear About Josh and Kelly?!,* CBS, 1980.
Ivan Travalian, *Full House,* CBS, 1983.
Edgar "Benny" Benedek, *Shadow Chasers,* ABC, 1985.
Marty Kessler, *Channel 99,* NBC, 1988.

Television Appearances; Episodic:
"Love and the Lie," *Love, American Style,* ABC, 1973.
"Love and Marriage," *M*A*S*H,* CBS, 1975.
"Last Salute to the Commodore," *Columbo,* NBC, 1976.
"The Fatal Weakness," *Hollywood Television Theater,* PBS, 1976.
"The Broken Badge," *Police Story,* NBC, 1978.
Richie Brockelman, "The House on Willis Avenue," *The Rockford Files,* NBC, 1977.
Richie Brockelman, "The Return of Richie Brockelman" (also known as "Never Send a Boy King to Do a Man's Job"), *The Rockford Files,* NBC, 1979.
Captain Freedom, "The World According to Freedom," *Hill Street Blues,* NBC, 1982.
Captain Freedom, "Pestolozzi's Revenge," *Hill Street Blues,* NBC, 1982.
Captain Freedom, "The Spy Who Came in from Delgado," *Hill Street Blues,* NBC, 1982.
Captain Freedom, "Freedom's Last Stand," *Hill Street Blues,* NBC, 1982.
Lloyd Hoffmeyer, *Making a Living,* ABC, 1982.
"Strange Bedfellows," *M*A*S*H,* CBS, 1983.
Scene of the Crime, NBC, 1985.
Shadow, "The Snitch," *Hooperman,* ABC, 1988.
"Tracks of My Tears," *Moonlighting,* ABC, 1988.
"Eek! A Spouse!," *Moonlighting,* ABC, 1988.
"Maddie Hayes Got Married," *Moonlighting,* ABC, 1988.
"And the Flesh Was Made Word," *Moonlighting,* ABC, 1988.

Voice characterization, *These Are the Days* (animated), ABC.

Television Appearances; Movies:
Private Becker, *Death Race,* ABC, 1973.

Charlie Elliott, *The Girl Most Likely To . . . . ,* ABC, 1973.
Richie Brockelman, *Richie Brockelman: The Missing 24 Hours* (also known as *The Missing 24 Hours*), NBC, 1976.
Richie Brockelman, *Diary of Richie Brockelman,* syndicated, 1978.
Officer Johnny Lucas, *Last of the Good Guys,* CBS, 1978.
Darryl, *Country Gold,* CBS, 1982.
Dick, *The Toughest Man in the World,* CBS, 1984.

Television Appearances; Specials:
Andy Martin, "The Girl Who Couldn't Lose," *ABC Afternoon Playbreak,* ABC, 1975.
NBC team member, *Battle of the Network Stars* (also known as *Battle of the Network Stars IV*), ABC, 1978.
Officer Needham, *Leadfoot,* syndicated, 1982.

Television Director; Episodic:
Hunter, NBC, 1987.
Sonny Spoon, NBC, 1988.
"Phantom Pain," *Wiseguy,* CBS, 1988.
"Between a Yuk and a Hard Place," *Moonlighting,* ABC, 1988.
"Lunar Eclipse," *Moonlighting,* ABC, 1989.
"Take My Wife, For Example," *Moonlighting,* ABC, 1989.
"Those Lips, Those Lies," *Moonlighting,* ABC, 1989.
"When Girls Collide," *Moonlighting,* ABC, 1989.
NYPD Blue, ABC, 1993.
Picket Fences, CBS, 1993.
"Who Killed Nick Hazard?," *Burke's Law,* CBS, 1994.
"Who Killed the Starlet?," *Burke's Law,* CBS, 1994.
Chicago Hope, CBS, 1994.
"The Final Adjustment," *NYPD Blue,* ABC, 1994.
"Frosted Flakes," *Picket Fences,* CBS, 1994.
"Who Killed the Gadget Man?," *Burke's Law,* CBS, 1995.
"Who Killed the King of the Country Club?," *Burke's Law,* CBS, 1995.
"Freeze Cuts," *Chicago Hope,* CBS, 1995.
"Mr. Seed Goes to Town," *Picket Fences,* CBS, 1995.

Television Director; Movies:
Columbo: Butterflies in Shades of Grey, ABC, 1994.
The Shaggy Dog (also known as *The ABC Family Movie* and *The Disney Family Movie*), ABC, 1994.

Television Director; Pilots:
Marker, UPN, 1995.

Stage Appearances:

(Off-Broadway debut) *The House of Blue Leaves,* Truck and Warehouse Theatre, New York City, 1971.

Rainbows for Sale, Center Theatre Group, New Theatre for Now, Music Center of Los Angeles, Los Angeles, CA, 1972.

Stage Work:

Stage manager, *Rice and Beans,* International Arts Relations Theatre, New York City, 1979.*

DUKES, David   1945-

PERSONAL

Born June 6, 1945, in San Francisco, CA; son of a California highway patrolman; married first wife, 1965 (divorced, 1975); married Carol Muske; children: (first marriage) Shawn. *Education:* Attended College of Marin; trained for the stage at the American Conservatory Theatre, San Francisco, CA.

Addresses: *Agent*—International Creative Management, 8942 Wilshire Blvd., Beverly Hills, CA 90211.

Career: Actor. Company member, American Conservatory Theatre, San Francisco, CA, 1966-69; company member, Alley Theatre, Houston, TX, 1969-70; company member, National Shakespeare Festival, San Diego, CA, 1970; company member, Philadelphia Drama Guild, Philadelphia, PA, 1971-72. Fencing instructor, Juilliard School, New York City.

Awards, Honors: Los Angeles Drama Critics Award, outstanding actor, for *Design for Living;* Antoinette Perry Award nomination, best featured actor in a play, 1980, for *Bent;* Emmy Award nomination, outstanding supporting actor in a miniseries or special, and CableAce Award nomination, both 1991, for *The Josephine Baker Story.*

CREDITS

Stage Appearances:

Murderous Angels, Center Theatre Group, Mark Taper Forum, Los Angeles, CA, 1969.

In 3 Zones, Charles Playhouse, Boston, MA, 1970.

(Broadway debut) Horace, *The School for Wives,* Lyceum Theatre, New York City, 1971.

Aubrey Beardsley, *The Neophyte,* Center Theatre Group, New Theatre for Now, Los Angeles, CA, 1971.

Don Carlos, *Don Juan,* New Phoenix Repertory Company, Lyceum Theatre, 1972.

Committee member, *The Great God Brown,* New Phoenix Repertory Company, Lyceum Theatre, 1972.

Albert Adam, *The Play's the Thing,* Bijou Theatre, New York City, 1973.

The judge, *The Government Inspector,* New Phoenix Repertory Company, Edison Theatre, New York City, 1973.

Husbands number seven, eight, and nine, *The Visit,* New Phoenix Repertory Company, Ethel Barrymore Theatre, New York City, 1973.

Coustouillu, *Chemin de fer,* New Phoenix Repertory Theatre, Ethel Barrymore Theatre, 1973.

Nick Potter, *Holiday,* New Phoenix Repertory Company, Ethel Barrymore Theatre, New York City, 1973.

The Death and Life of Jesse James, New Theatre for Now, Ahmanson Theatre, Los Angeles, CA, 1974.

Scandal, *Love for Love,* New Phoenix Repertory Theatre, Helen Hayes Theatre, New York City, 1974.

Guido Venanzi, *The Rules of the Game,* New Phoenix Repertory Company, Helen Hayes Theatre, 1974.

Billy, *The Salty Dog Saga,* New Dramatists, New York City, 1975.

Henry, *Travesties,* Ethel Barrymore Theatre, 1975.

Design for Living, Goodman Theatre, Chicago, IL, 1976, and at the National Shakespeare Festival, Old Globe Theatre, San Diego, CA, 1981.

Harold, *The Man Who Drew Circles,* New Dramatists, 1976.

General William Tecumseh Sherman, *Rebel Women,* New York Shakespeare Festival, Public Theatre, New York City, 1976.

Henry, *Travesties,* Center Theatre Group, Mark Taper Forum, Los Angeles, 1977.

Horst, *Bent,* New Apollo Theatre, New York City, 1979.

Victor Frankenstein, *Frankenstein,* Palace Theatre, New York City, 1981.

Benjamin, *Another Part of the Forest,* Center Theatre Group, Ahmanson Theatre, 1982.

Antonio Salieri, *Amadeus,* Broadhurst Theatre, New York City, 1982.

Charles and Harold, *Light Comedies,* Center Theatre Group, Ahmanson Theatre, 1984.

Rene Gallimard, *M. Butterfly,* Eugene O'Neill Theatre, New York City, 1988.

Andrew Makepeace Ladd III, *Love Letters,* Edison Theatre, 1989-90.

Narrator, *Shipwreck,* Getty Museum, 1990.

Edward, *Someone Who'll Watch Over Me,* Booth Theatre, New York City, 1992.

Dr. Harry Hyman, *Broken Glass,* Booth Theatre, 1994.

Also appeared as Dr. Harry Hyman, *Broken Glass,* Long Wharf Theatre, New Haven, CT.

Stage Work:
Choreographer of sword fights, *Macbeth,* New York Shakespeare Festival, Mitzi E. Newhouse Theatre, New York City, 1974.

Major Tours:
Horace, *The School for Wives,* Canadian cities, 1971-72.

Title role, *Dracula,* U.S. cities, 1979.

Film Appearances:
Guard, *The Strawberry Statement,* Metro-Goldwyn-Mayer, 1970.

James Morrison, *The Wild Party,* American International Pictures, 1975.

George de Marco, *A Little Romance,* Orion, 1979.

Daniel Blank, *The First Deadly Sin,* Filmways, 1980.

David, *Only When I Laugh* (also known as *It Hurts Only When I Laugh* and *Neil Simon's Only When I Laugh*), Columbia, 1981.

Graham Selky, *Without a Trace,* Twentieth Century-Fox, 1983.

Phillip, *The Men's Club,* Atlantic, 1986.

Waldo Tarr, *Catch the Heat* (also known as *Feel the Heat*), Trans World, 1987.

Ed Winston, *Date with an Angel,* De Laurentiis Group, 1987.

Howard Hellenbeck, *Rawhead Rex* (also known as *RawHeadRex*), Empire, 1987.

Myron Weston, *Deadly Intent,* Fries Distribution, 1988.

Peter Goodwin, *See You in the Morning,* Warner Bros., 1989.

Doctor, *The Handmaid's Tale,* Cinecom, 1990.

Bo Peterson, *The Rutanga Tapes,* Shapiro Glickenhaus Home Video, 1991.

Under Surveillance, 1991.

Victor Feldman, *Me and the Kid,* Orion, 1993.

Chris Paine, *Fled,* Metro-Goldwyn-Mayer/United Artists, 1996.

Television Appearances; Series:
Robert Lassiter, *Beacon Hill,* CBS, 1975.

Dr. Wade Halsey, *Sisters,* NBC, 1991-92.

Jack Larson, *The Mommies* (also known as *Mommies*), NBC, 1993-95.

Edward Sherman, *Pauly* (also known as *Mommy and Me*), Fox, 1996-97.

Television Appearances; Miniseries:
Mike Koshko, *Harold Robbins' 79 Park Avenue* (also known as *79 Park Avenue*), NBC, 1977.

Leslie Slote, *The Winds of War,* ABC, 1983.

George William Fairfax, *George Washington,* CBS, 1984.

Leopold Strabismus, *James A. Michener's Space* (also known as *Space*), CBS, 1985.

David Osborne, *Kane and Abel,* CBS, 1985.

Leslie Slote, *War and Remembrance,* ABC, 1988.

Television Appearances; Pilots:
Dr. Chase, *The Many Loves of Arthur,* NBC, 1978.

Mike Kelly, *The Bakery,* CBS, 1990.

Television Appearances; Episodic:
"Corporation," *Barney Miller,* ABC, 1977.

All That Glitters, syndicated, 1977.

Jim Walsh, "Jack's Navy Pal," *Three's Company,* ABC, 1978.

The man who tried to rape Edith, *All in the Family,* CBS, 1978.

Ted Miller, "Remembering Melody," *The Hitchhiker,* HBO, 1984.

Todd Ettinger, "Ye Gods," *The Twilight Zone,* CBS, 1985.

Barry Worthy, *Diagnosis Murder,* CBS, 1996.

Also appeared in *Family,* ABC.

Television Appearances; Movies:
David Allen, *A Fire in the Sky,* NBC, 1978.

Reverend Crane, *Go West, Young Girl!,* ABC, 1978.

Miles Standish, *Mayflower: The Pilgrim's Adventures,* CBS, 1979.

Joe Dine, *Some Kind of Miracle,* CBS, 1979.

Lou Ribin, *The Triangle Factory Fire Scandal,* NBC, 1979.

Bill Sanger, *Portrait of a Rebel: Margaret Sanger* (also known as *Portrait of a Rebel: The Remarkable Mrs. Sanger*), CBS, 1980.

Avery McPherson, *Miss All-American Beauty,* CBS, 1982.

Bill Gardner, *Sentimental Journey,* CBS, 1984.

Barney Powers, *Turn Back the Clock* (also known as *Repeat Performance*), NBC, 1989.

Murdoch, *Snow Kill* (also known as *Over the Edge*), USA Network, 1990.

Jo Bouillon, *The Josephine Baker Story,* HBO, 1991.

Jerry Levin, *Held Hostage: The Sis and Jerry Levin Story* (also known as *Beirut* and *Forgotten: The Sis and Jerry Levin Story*), ABC, 1991.

Joe Hubbard, *Wife, Mother, Murderer—The Marie Hilley Story* (also known as *Black Widow—The Marie Hilley Story, The Marie Hilley Story,* and *Wife, Mother, Murderer*), ABC, 1991.

Sloane, *She Woke Up,* ABC, 1992.

Dr. Mervyn Silverman, *And the Band Played On,* HBO, 1993.

Tim Curtiz, *Look at It This Way,* Arts and Entertainment, 1993.

Robert, *Spies,* The Disney Channel, 1993.

Stuart Quinn, *The Surrogate,* ABC, 1995.

Arthur Miller, *Norman Jean and Marilyn* (also known as *Norma Jean & Marilyn*), HBO, 1996.

Edward Janroe, *Last Stand at Saber River,* TNT, 1997.

Television Appearances; Specials:

Guido, *Rules of the Game,* 1975.

Cutting, *Valley Forge,* NBC, 1975.

Dr. O'Brien, *Handle with Care,* CBS, 1977.

Gooper, "Cat on a Hot Tin Roof," *American Playhouse,* PBS, 1984.

Levi Strauss, "My Darlin' Clementine," *American Tall Tales and Legends,* Showtime, 1987.

Dr. Ned Darrell, "Strange Interlude," *American Playhouse,* PBS, 1988.

Narrator, *Gabriel Garcia Marquez—Magic and Reality,* PBS, 1990.

RECORDINGS

Taped Readings:

Michel Foucault, "A Question of Place," *A Sound Portrait of Michel Foucault,* National Public Radio (Washington, DC), 1980.

Narrator, *Breakfast at Tiffany's,* Caedmon (New York City), 1983.

Best of Science Fiction and Fantasy, Dove Audio (Beverly Hills, CA), 1991.

Deadly Allies, Dove Audio, 1992.

My Other Life, Dove Audio, 1996.

Dr. Neruda's Cure for Evil, Dove Audio, 1996.*

DUVALL, Shelley 1949-

PERSONAL

Born July 7, 1949, in Houston, TX; daughter of Robert and Bobby (Crawford) Duvall.

Addresses: *Agent*—The Gersh Agency, 232 North Canon Dr., Beverly Hills, CA 90210.

Career: Actress and producer. Think Entertainment (television production company), founder, 1988; Amarillo Productions, founder; narrator of sound and video recordings. International Children's Film Festival, guest of honor, 1997.

Member: Screen Actors Guild, National Academy of Cable Programming (member of board of governors).

Awards, Honors: Cannes Film Festival Award, best actress, 1977, for *Three Women;* Emmy Award nomination, best children's program, 1988, for *Shelley Duvall's Tall Tales and Legends;* Peabody Award for *Faerie Tale Theatre.*

CREDITS

Film Appearances:

(Film debut) Suzanne, *Brewster McCloud,* Metro-Goldwyn-Mayer, 1970.

Ida Coyle, *McCabe and Mrs. Miller,* Warner Bros., 1971.

Leechie Mobley, *Thieves Like Us,* United Artists, 1974.

Voice, *Un homme qui dort,* 1974.

L. A. Joan, *Nashville,* Paramount, 1975.

Mrs. Cleveland, *Buffalo Bill and the Indians, or Sitting Bull's History Lesson,* United Artists, 1976.

Millie Lammoreaux, *Three Women,* Twentieth Century-Fox, 1977.

Pam, *Annie Hall* (also known as *Anhedonia*), United Artists, 1977.

Olive Oyl, *Popeye,* Paramount, 1979.

Wendy Torrance, *The Shining,* Warner Bros., 1980.

Pansy, *Time Bandits,* Embassy, 1981.

Susan Frankenstein, *Frankenweenie,* 1984.

Dixie, *Roxanne,* Columbia, 1987.

Jenny Wilcox, *Suburban Commando,* New Line Cinema, 1991.

Night nurse, *The Underneath* (also known as *Present Tense*), Gramercy Pictures, 1995.

Countess Gemini, *The Portrait of a Lady,* Gramercy Pictures, 1996.

Sister Agatha, *Changing Habits,* A-pix Entertainment, 1996.

Amelia, *Twilight of the Ice Nymphs,* Alliance International, 1997.

Mrs. Randall, *Rocket Man,* Buena Vista, 1997.

Russell Mulcahy's "Talos the Mummy" (also known as *Talos the Mummy*), Buena Vista, 1998.

Home Fries, Warner Bros., 1998.

Television Appearances; Series:
Host, *Faerie Tale Theatre,* Showtime, 1982-87.
Host, *Nightmare Classics,* Showtime, beginning in 1989.
Host, *Shelley Duvall's Bedtime Stories,* Showtime, 1991-96.

Television Series; Executive Producer:
Faerie Tale Theatre, Showtime, 1982-87.
Shelley Duvall's Tall Tales and Legends, Showtime, 1985-87.
Nick Jr. Rocks, Nickelodeon, 1991.
Shelley Duvall's Bedtime Stories, Showtime, 1991-96.
Mrs. Piggle-Wiggle, Showtime, 1993-95.

Television Appearances; Episodic:
Liz Christie, "The Seventh Grave," *Cannon,* CBS, 1973.
"The Prisoners," *Cannon,* CBS, 1973.
"Love and Mr. and Mrs. Love," *Love, American Style,* ABC, 1973.
"Aggie," *Baretta,* ABC, 1976.
"Bernice Bobs Her Hair," *American Short Story,* PBS, 1977.
Title role, "Rapunzel," *Faerie Tale Theatre,* Showtime, 1982.
The miller's daughter, "Rumpelstiltskin," *Faerie Tale Theatre,* Showtime, 1982.
"Snow White and the Seven Dwarfs," *Faerie Tale Theatre,* Showtime, 1984.
Margaret, "Saucer of Loneliness," *The Twilight Zone,* CBS, 1986.
Title role, "Darlin' Clementine," *Shelley Duvall's Tall Tales and Legends,* Showtime, 1987.
Narrator, *Shelley Duvall's Bedtime Stories,* Showtime, 1991-96.
"The Tombstone," *The Ray Bradbury Theatre,* USA Network, 1992.
Voice of Caroline, "Dark Victory," *Frasier,* NBC, 1994.
Potsi Piggle-Wiggle, "There's Something in My Attic," *Mrs. Piggle-Wiggle,* Showtime, 1994.
Potsi Piggle-Wiggle, "The Little Rabbit Who Wanted Red Wings," *Mrs. Piggle-Wiggle,* Showtime, 1994.
Alice Flitt, *The Adventures of Shirley Holmes,* 1997.

Television Episodes; Executive Producer:
"Carmilla," *Nightmare Classics,* Showtime, 1989.
"The Eyes of the Panther," *Nightmare Classics,* Showtime, 1989.
"The Strange Case of Dr. Jekyll and Mr. Hyde," *Nightmare Classics,* Showtime, 1989.
"The Turn of the Screw," *Nightmare Classics,* Showtime, 1989.

Television Appearances; Movies:
Little Bo Peep, *Mother Goose Rock 'n' Rhyme,* The Disney Channel, 1990.

Television Movies; Executive Producer:
Dinner at Eight, TNT, 1989.
Mother Goose Rock 'n' Rhyme, The Disney Channel, 1990.
Backfield in Motion, ABC, 1991.

Television Appearances; Specials:
"Booker," *WonderWorks,* PBS, 1984.
Secret World of the Very Young, CBS, 1984.
Annie, "Frog," *WonderWorks,* PBS, 1988.
The Chipmunks Rockin' through the Decades (animated), NBC, 1990.
Together for Our Children—M.U.S.I.C., syndicated, 1993.
The American Film Institute Salute to Jack Nicholson, CBS, 1994.
Ms. Hastings, "Aliens for Breakfast," *McDonald's Family Theatre,* ABC, 1995.

Television Specials; Executive Producer:
Mr. Bill's Real Life Adventures, Showtime, 1986.
"Frog," *WonderWorks,* PBS, 1988.
Stories from Growing Up, 1991.
(With Thomas F. Frank) "Aliens for Breakfast," *McDonald's Family Theatre,* ABC, 1995.

Television Appearances; Pilots:
Title role, *Lily,* CBS, 1986.
An American Saturday Night, ABC, 1991.

Television Pilots; Executive Producer:
(With Andy Borowitz; also creator) *Lily,* CBS, 1986.

Television Appearances; Awards Presentations:
The 19th Annual NAACP Image Awards, 1987.
The 9th Annual ACE Awards, 1988.
Presenter, *The 11th Annual ACE Awards,* 1990.
Presenter, *The 20th International Emmy Awards,* 1992.

RECORDINGS

Taped Readings:
Hello, I'm Shelley Duvall: Merry Christmas, 1992.
Hello, I'm Shelley Duvall: Sweet Dreams, 1992.
The Animal Express, 1992.

CD-ROMs:
Narrator, *Digby's Adventures,* Sanctuary Woods (San Mateo, CA), 1994.

WRITINGS

Television:
Live action sequences, and composer of "Humpty's Theme," *Shelley Duvall's Bedtime Stories,* Showtime, 1991-96.

CD-ROMs:
Digby's Adventures, Sanctuary Woods (San Mateo, CA), 1994.

SIDELIGHTS

Duvall was named after *Frankenstein* author Mary Shelley.

OTHER SOURCES

Periodicals:
American Film, July-August, 1989, p. 56.
Entertainment Weekly, May 15, 1992.
Savvy Woman, November, 1990, p. 34.*

DYKSTRA, John 1947-
(John C. Dykstra)

PERSONAL

Born June 3, 1947, in Long Beach, CA. *Education:* Attended design school.

Addresses: *Office*—Apogee Productions, 6842 Valjean Avenue, Van Nuys, CA 91406. *Agent*—International Creative Management, 8942 Wilshire Blvd., Beverly Hills, CA 90211.

Career: Special effects designer and producer. Founder and supervisor of special effects, Apogee Productions, Van Nuys, CA; cinematographer, National Science Foundation; special effects designer, "Voyage to the Outer Planets," Ruben H. Fleet Space Theatre, San Diego, CA; (with Douglas Trumbull) producer and creator of amusement park rides and aircraft simulator films; inventor, Dykstraflex camera. Also worked at the Institute of Urban Development, Berkeley, CA; and as head of Industrial Light and Magic.

Awards, Honors: Academy Awards, best visual effects and best development of facility oriented toward visual effects photography, both 1977, for *Star Wars;* Academy Award nomination, best visual effects, 1979, for *Star Trek: The Motion Picture;* Emmy Award, outstanding individual achievement (creative technical crafts division), 1979, for *Battlestar Galactica.*

CREDITS

Film Work; Special Effects Designer (Except As Noted):
Silent Running, Universal, 1972.
(And special effects cinematographer), *Star Wars,* Twentieth Century-Fox, 1977.
(Also producer and supervisor, effects unit), *Battlestar Galactica,* Universal, 1978.
Avalanche Express, Twentieth Century-Fox, 1979.
Special photographic effects supervisor, *Star Trek: The Motion Picture,* Paramount, 1979.
Caddyshack, Warner Bros., 1980.
(With Robert Shepherd, Roger Dorney, and Al Miller) *Firefox,* Warner Bros., 1982.
(With John Grant) *Lifeforce,* TriStar, 1985.
(And second unit director) *Invaders from Mars,* Cannon, 1986.
Mac and Me, Orion, 1988.
Special effects supervisor, *My Stepmother Is an Alien,* Columbia, 1988.
Special effects director, *The Unholy,* Vestron, 1988.
Special creative consultant, *Spontaneous Combustion,* Taurus, 1989.
Visual effects head supervisor, *Batman Forever,* Warner Bros., 1995.
Visual effects, *Batman & Robin,* Warner Bros., 1997.
Visual effects, *Contact,* Warner Bros., 1997.

Television Work; Special Effects Designer (Except As Noted):
(Also producer) *Battlestar Galactica* (series), ABC, 1978-80.
Return of the Six Million Dollar Man and the Bionic Woman II (pilot), NBC, 1989.
Starflight One: The Plane That Couldn't Land (movie), ABC, 1983.
Special visual effects, *Alice in Wonderland* (miniseries), 1985.
Effects supervisor (Canada), *Amerika* (miniseries), 1987.
Effects supervisor, *Out On a Limb* (miniseries), 1987.
Special effects, *Something Is Out There* (series), 1988.
Special effects, *Shivers* (special), 1989.
Assistance, *The Astronomer* (also known as *Triple Play II;* special), PBS, 1991.

Television Appearances:

Masters of Fantasy: Joel Schumacher (special), Sci-Fi
    Channel, 1997.*

DYKSTRA, John C.
    See DYKSTRA, John

E-F

EBERT, Joyce 1933-1997

OBITUARY NOTICE—See index for *CTFT* sketch: Born Joyce Anne Womack, June 26, 1933, in Munhall (one source says Homestead), PA; died of cancer, August 28, 1997, in Southport, CT. Actress. Ebert is remembered for her performances on the stage, notably her work in more than eighty plays at the Long Wharf Theatre in New Haven, CT. Long Wharf artistic director Arvin Brown, who also was married to Ebert, directed her in many of the plays. She made her stage debut in 1953 in *White Sheep of the Family* in Pittsburgh, and she made her off-Broadway debut as Julie in *Liliom* in 1956. Among her performances during her prolific stage career were roles in *The Merchant of Venice, Hamlet, Pygmalion, King Lear, Romeo and Juliet, Love's Labour's Lost, The Iceman Cometh, The Miracle Worker, The Cherry Orchard,* and *Requiem for a Heavyweight.* She first performed at the Long Wharf in 1966 in *Misalliance,* followed by *The Glass Menagerie* in 1967. Later performances included roles in *She Stoops to Conquer, A Streetcar Named Desire, The Lion in Winter, Tobacco Road, Song at Twilight,* and *The Show Off.* She also appeared on television, first on *Frontiers of Faith* for NBC in 1956. She also appeared in television movies such as *Ah! Wilderness* and *The Widowing of Mrs. Holyroyd.* Among the awards she received are the San Diego Shakespeare Festival's Atlas Award in 1959, the Clarence Derwent Award and the Obie Award, both in 1964, a Drama Desk nomination in 1977, and the Connecticut Critics Circle's special achievement award in 1996.

OBITUARIES AND OTHER SOURCES

Periodicals:
New York Times, August 30, 1997, p. 52.

EISNER, Michael D. 1942-

PERSONAL

Full name, Michael Dammann Eisner; born March 7, 1942, in Mount Kisco, NY; son of Lester Jr., and Margaret (Dammann) Eisner; married Jane Breckenridge; children: Michael, Eric, Anders. *Education:* Denison University, B.A., 1964.

Addresses: *Office*—Walt Disney Company, 500 South Buena Vista St., Burbank, CA 91521-0001.

Career: Executive producer. CBS, worked in programming department; ABC-TV, manager of talent and specials, 1966, director of program development, director of program planning and executive assistant to the vice president in charge of programming, vice president of daytime television programming, and vice president of children's programs, 1966-75, ABC Entertainment, senior vice president of prime time production and development, 1976; Paramount Pictures, president and chief operating officer with creative responsibilities for all divisions, 1976-84; Walt Disney Company, chairman and chief executive officer, 1984—. Board of directors, Denison University, California Institute of Arts, American Film Institute, the Performing Arts Council of the Los Angeles Music Center, and Sega Enterprises, Inc. (amusement game manufacturer).

CREDITS

Television Appearances; Series:
Host, *Disney Sunday Movie,* ABC, 1986-88.
Host, *The Magical World of Disney,* NBC, 1988-90.
American Cinema, PBS, 1994-95.

Television Appearances; Specials:
The Wonderful World of Disney: 40 Years of Television Magic, ABC, 1994.

Also appeared in *The Best of Disney: 50 Years of Magic,* 1991; host, *The Dream Is Alive: The 20th Anniversary Celebration of Walt Disney World,* 1991.

Television Appearances; Awards Presentations:
Fourth Annual Environmental Media Awards, TBS, 1994.
The 10th Annual Television Academy Hall of Fame, The Disney Channel, 1994.

Also appeared in *The Television Academy Hall of Fame,* 1987.

OTHER SOURCES

Periodicals:
Parade Magazine, November 15, 1987.*

EKBERG, Anita 1931-

PERSONAL

Born September 29, 1931, in Malmo, Sweden; came to the United States in 1951; married Anthony Steele, 1956 (divorced, 1959); married Rick Van Nutter, 1963 (divorced, 1975).

Career: Actress; former model; Miss Sweden, 1951.

CREDITS

Film Appearances:
Venusian woman, *Abbott and Costello Go to Mars,* Universal, 1953.
Handmaiden, *The Golden Blade,* Universal, 1953.
Bridesmaid, *The Mississippi Gambler,* Universal, 1953.
Dance hall girl (uncredited), *Take Me to Town,* Universal, 1953.
Anita, *Artists and Models,* Paramount, 1955.
Wei Long, *Blood Alley,* Warner Bros., 1955.
I'll Cry Tomorrow, 1955.
Rena, *Back from Eternity,* RKO, 1956.
Herself, *Hollywood or Bust,* Paramount, 1956.
Flo Randall, *Man in the Vault,* RKO, 1956.
Helene, *War and Peace,* Paramount, 1956.
Salma, *Zarak,* Columbia, 1956.
Gina Broger, *Pickup Alley* (also known as *Interpol* and *International Police*), Columbia, 1957.

Title role, *Valerie,* United Artists, 1957.
Trudie Hall, *The Man Inside,* Columbia, 1958.
Zara, *Paris Holiday,* United Artists, 1958.
Virginia Wilson, *Screaming Mimi,* Columbia, 1958.
Zenobia, Queen of Palmyra, *Sign of the Gladiator* (also known as *Nel Segno Di Roma, Sign of Rome,* and *Sheba and the Gladiator*), American International, 1959.
Olga Dubovich, *Behind Locked Doors,* 1960.
Sylvia, *La Dolce Vita* (also known as *The Sweet Life*), Astor/American International, 1961.
Anita, "The Temptation of Dr. Antonio," *Boccaccio '70,* Gray, 1962.
Luba, *Call Me Bwana,* United Artists, 1963.
Elya Carlson, *Four for Texas,* Warner Bros., 1963.
Who Wants to Sleep?, 1965.
How I Learned to Love Women, 1966.
Amanda Beatrice Cross, *The Alphabet Murders* (also known as *The ABC Murders*), Metro-Goldwyn-Mayer, 1966.
Huluna, *The Mongols* (also known as *I Mongoli*), Colorama, 1966.
Anna Soblova, *Way . . . Way Out,* Twentieth Century-Fox, 1966.
Aberchiaria, "The Unkindest Cut," *White, Red, Yellow, Pink* (also known as *Love Factory*), Seymour Borde, 1966.
Claudie ("Snow"), *Women Times Seven,* 1967.
Lou, *The Cobra,* American International, 1968.
Paulette, *The Glass Sphinx,* American International, 1968.
Title role, *Malenka, the Vampire* (also known as *La Nipole del Vampiro, Fangs of the Living Dead, The Vampire's Niece, Bloody Girl,* and *The Niece of the Vampire*), Europix, 1968.
Nightclub performer, *If It's Tuesday, This Must Be Belgium,* United Artists, 1969.
Death Knocks Twice, 1969.
Herself, *I Clowns* (also known as *The Clowns* and *Les Clowns*), Levitt-Pickman, 1970.
Madame Colette, *Murder in Paris* (also known as *The Paris Sex Murders*), 1973.
Valley of the Widows (also known as *Das Tal der Witwen*), 1974.
Northeast to Seoul, 1974.
Killer Nun (also known as *Suor Omicidi*), 1979.
Daisy Chain, 1981.
Cicciambomba, 1983.
Dolce Pella Di Angela (also known as *Angela's Sweet Skin* and *The Seduction of Angela*), Cineglobo, 1987.
Herself, *Federico Fillini's Intervista* (also known as *Intervista* and *The Interview*), Aljosta/RAI-TV/Cinecitta/Ferlyn, 1987.

Marika, *Il Conte Max* (also known as *Count Max*), 1991.

Clarice, *Ambrogio,* 1992.

Mama Greta, *Bambola,* Union Generale du Cinematographique Droites Audiovisual (UGC-DA), 1996.

Also appeared in *The Dam on the Yellow River* (also known as *Last Train to Shanghai*), *Little Girls and High Finance, The Last Judgment,* and *L'Incastro.*

Television Appearances; Pilots:
Dr. Else Biebling, *S*H*E,* CBS, 1980.

Television Appearances; Miniseries:
Ilsa Lund Laszlo, "Casablanca," *Warner Brothers Presents,* ABC, 1955-56.

Television Appearances; Movies:
Queen Na-Eela, *Gold of the Amazon Women,* NBC, 1979.

Television Appearances; Specials:
The Bob Hope Show, NBC, 1955.
The Bob Hope Show, NBC, 1958.
The Bob Hope Show, NBC, 1966.

Television Appearances; Episodic:
"The Hubby Killer," *Private Secretary,* CBS, 1953.
Person to Person, CBS, 1956.

OTHER SOURCES

Periodicals:
Vanity Fair, January 1994, pp. 88-95.*

EKLAND, Britt 1942-

PERSONAL

Born Britt-Marie Eklund, October 6 (one source says September 29), 1942, in Stockholm, Sweden; married Peter Sellers (an actor), 1963 (divorced, 1968); companion of Rod Stewart (a singer); married Jim McDonnell (aka "Slim" Jim Phantom, a drummer with the band the Stray Cats; divorced 1992); children: Victoria (with Sellers), Nikolai (with Lou Adler, a restauranteur), and Thomas Jefferson (with McDonnell).

Addresses: *Home*—West Hollywood, CA, and London, England. *Manager*—Paul Cohen Management, P.O. Box 241609, Los Angeles, CA 90024.

Career: Actress; former model.

CREDITS

Film Appearances:
(Debut) *Short Is the Summer,* [Sweden/Norway], 1962.

Mrs. Pickett, *The Happy Thieves* (also known as *Once a Thief*), United Artists, 1962.

Il Commandante, [Italy], 1963.

Greta, *Advance to the Rear* (also known as *Company of Cowards*), Metro-Goldwyn-Mayer, 1964.

Gina Romantica, *After the Fox,* United Artists, 1966.

Olimpia Segura, *The Bobo,* Warner Bros., 1967.

Gina, *The Double Man,* Warner Bros., 1967.

Rachel Schpitendavel, *The Night They Raided Minsky's* (also known as *The Night They Invented Striptease*), United Artists, 1968.

Too Many Thieves, Metro-Goldwyn-Mayer, 1968.

Illeana, *Stiletto,* Avco-Embassy, 1969.

Antigone, *The Cannibals,* Doria/San Marco, 1970.

Irene Tucker, *Machine Gun McCann* (also known as *Gli Intoccabili*), Columbia, 1970.

Greta, *Endless Night* (also known as *Agatha Christie's Endless Night*), British Lion, 1971.

Anna Fletcher, *Get Carter,* Metro-Goldwyn-Mayer, 1971.

Elise, *Night Hair Child* (also known as *Child of the Night* and *What the Peeper Saw*), Towers, 1971.

Dorothy Chiltern-Barlow, *Percy,* Metro-Goldwyn-Mayer, 1971.

A Time for Loving (also known as *Paris Was Made for Lovers*), London Screen Plays, 1971.

Lucy, *Asylum* (also known as *House of Crazies*), Cinerama, 1972.

Chris Bentley, *Baxter,* National General, 1973.

Mary Goodnight, *The Man with the Golden Gun,* United Artists, 1974.

Michelle, *The Ultimate Thrill* (also known as *The Ultimate Chase*), General Cinema, 1974.

Willow MacGregor, *The Wicker Man* (also known as *Anthony Shaffer's "The Wicker Man"*), British Lion/Warner Bros., 1974.

People Who Own the Dark, Sean Cunningham, 1975.

Duchess Irma, *Royal Flash,* Twentieth Century-Fox, 1975.

Mrs. Anderson, *High Velocity,* First Asian Films of California, 1977.

Anna Von Erken, *Slavers,* ITM, 1977.

Nypeptha, *King Solomon's Treasures,* Canafox/Towers, 1978.

Countess Trivulzi, *Some Like It Cool* (also known as *The Rise and Rise of Casanova* and *Casanova and Co.*), Pro International, 1979.

Lintom's mother, "The Vampire Story," *The Monster Club,* ITC, 1981.

Anne-Marie, *Satan's Mistress* (also known as *Fury of the Succubus, Demon Rage,* and *Dark Eyes*), Motion Pictures Marketing, 1982.

Priscilla Lancaster/Penny, *Dead Wrong* (also known as *Death Fighter* and *The Columbia Connection*), Comworld, 1983.

Annie, *Love Scenes* (also known as *Ecstacy*), Starways, 1985.

Marbella (also known as *Hot Spot*), 1985.

Evette, *Fraternity Vacation,* New World, 1985.

Linda, *Moon in Scorpio,* Trans World, 1987.

Madame Cassandra, *Beverly Hills Vamp,* [USA], 1989.

Jackie Mallon, *Cold Heat,* 1989.

Mariella Novotny, *Scandal,* Miramax, 1989.

Lady Wrench, *The Children,* Hemdale Home Video, 1990.

Az Aldozat (also known as *The Victim*), 1994.

Also appeared in *At Any Price, Tintomara, Triple Cross,* and *Hellhole.*

Television Appearances; Series:

Host, *Britt Ekland's Juke Box,* syndicated, 1979.

Also host of talk show in Sweden.

Television Appearances; Pilots:

Katrina Volana, "Wine, Women and War," *The Six Million Dollar Man,* ABC, 1973.

Television Appearances; Episodic:

"The Greatest Game," *The Trials of O'Brien,* CBS, 1966.

"The Barefoot Stewardess Caper," *McCloud,* NBC, 1972.

"The Moscow Connection," *McCloud,* NBC, 1977.

Tenna, "The Gun on Ice Planet Zero" (two episodes), *Battlestar Galactica,* ABC, 1979.

"Aphrodite," *Fantasy Island,* ABC, 1980.

"Accident Prone," *The Love Boat,* ABC, 1980.

"The Proxy Billionaire," *Fantasy Island,* ABC, 1981.

"Safety Last," *The Love Boat,* ABC, 1982.

"Wuthering Heights," *Fantasy Island,* ABC, 1982.

"Deadly Fashion," *Matt Houston,* ABC, 1982.

"The Sisters," *Fantasy Island,* ABC, 1983.

"Always Say Always," *The Fall Guy,* ABC, 1984.

"Love and/or Marriage," *Simon and Simon,* CBS, 1985.

"Abandon Earth," *Superboy,* syndicated, c. 1989.

Herself, "New Best Friend," *Absolutely Fabulous,* [England], 1994.

Television Appearances; Movies:

Jenny Wallenda, *The Great Wallendas,* NBC, 1978.

Anny Ondra Schmelling, *Ring of Passion* (also known as *Countdown to the Big One*), NBC, 1978.

Leah, *The Hostage Tower,* CBS, 1980.

Francoise, *Jacqueline Susann's "Valley of the Dolls"* (also known as *Valley of the Dolls*), CBS, 1981.

Television Appearances; Specials:

Mother, *Carol for Another Christmas,* ABC, 1964.

US against the World II, ABC, 1978.

Circus of the Stars, CBS, 1981 and 1986.

Women Who Rate a "10," NBC, 1981.

Also appeared in *A Cold Peace* [England].

Stage Appearances:

Olivia, *Mate!,* Comedy Theatre, London, England, 1978.

Run for Your Wife, 1996.

RECORDINGS

Videos:

Host, *Electric Blue #3,* 1981.

Britt Fit (fitness video), 1993.

WRITINGS

Books:

True Britt (autobiography), 1980.

OTHER SOURCES

Periodicals:

Entertainment Weekly, March 5, 1993, p. 68.

People Weekly, December 4, 1995, pp. 40-47.*

ELFMAN, Danny 1953-

PERSONAL

Born May 29, 1953, in Amarillo, TX; raised in Los Angeles, CA; son of Milton (a teacher) and Blossom (a teacher and writer; maiden name, Bernstein) Elfman; married (separated); children: Lola, Mali.

Addresses: *Agent*—Kraft-Benjamin Agency, 19668 Grandview Dr., Topanga, CA 90290. *Manager*—L.A. Personal Development, 1201 Larrabee, Penthouse 302, West Hollywood, CA 90069, or P.O. Box 10815, Beverly Hills, CA 90213.

Career: Composer and musician. Member of the Mystic Knights of the Oingo Boingo theatre ensemble, 1971-89; singer, songwriter and guitarist with the band Oingo Boingo (also known as Boingo), 1979—; also has composed music for television commercials.

Awards, Honors: Grammy Award, best instrumental composition, 1989, for "The Batman Theme," from the movie *Batman;* Grammy Award nomination, best score, 1989, for *Batman;* Emmy Award nomination, outstanding achievement in main title theme music, 1990, for *The Simpsons;* Grammy Award nomination, best score, 1991, for *Dick Tracy;* Golden Globe Award nomination, outstanding original score, 1994, for *The Nightmare Before Christmas;* Grammy Award nomination, best instrumental composition written for a motion picture or television, 1998, for the main theme from *Men in Black.*

CREDITS

Film Appearances:
Singer, *Hot Tomorrows,* American Film Institute, 1978.
Satan, *Forbidden Zone,* Borack, 1980.
Oingo Boingo band member, *Back to School,* Orion, 1986.
The Magical World of Chuck Jones, 1992.
Voice of Clown with the Tear Away Face, voice of Barrel, and singing voice of Jack Skellington, *The Nightmare Before Christmas* (animated; also known as *Tim Burton's The Nightmare Before Christmas*), Buena Vista, 1993.

Film Work:
Associate producer, *The Nightmare Before Christmas* (animated; also known as *Tim Burton's The Nightmare Before Christmas*), Buena Vista, 1993.

Television Appearances:
The Hollywood Soundtrack Story (special), AMC, 1995.

RECORDINGS

Albums; with Oingo Boingo:
Oingo Boingo (EP), IRS, 1980.
Only A Lad, A&M Records, 1981.
Nothing to Fear, A&M Records, 1982.
Good for Your Soul, A&M Records, 1984.
Dead Man's Party, MCA, 1986.
BOI-NGO, MCA, 1987.
Boingo Alive, MCA, 1988.

Skeletons in the Closet (compilation), A&M Records, 1988.
Dark at the End of the Tunnel (compilation), MCA, 1990.
Best O'Boingo, MCA, 1991.
Farewell, A&M Records, 1996.

Solo Albums:
So-lo (also known as *So Lo*), MCA, 1985.
Music for a Darkened Theatre: Music from Television and Movies (compilation), MCA, 1990.
Music for A Darkened Theatre: Film and Television Music (compilation), MCA, 1996.

WRITINGS

Film Music:
Forbidden Zone, Borack, 1980.
Pee-Wee's Big Adventure, Warner Bros., 1985.
Back to School, Orion, 1986.
Wisdom, Twentieth Century-Fox, 1986.
Summer School, Paramount, 1987.
Beetlejuice, Warner Bros., 1988.
Big Top Pee-Wee, Paramount, 1988.
Hot to Trot, Warner Bros., 1988.
Midnight Run, Universal, 1988.
Scrooged, Paramount, 1988.
Batman, Warner Bros., 1989.
Darkman, Universal, 1990.
Dick Tracy, Touchstone-Buena Vista, 1990.
Edward Scissorhands, Twentieth Century-Fox, 1990.
Nightbreed, Twentieth Century-Fox, 1990.
Article 99, Orion, 1992.
Batman Returns, Warner Bros., 1992.
Sommersby, Warner Bros., 1993.
The Nightmare Before Christmas (animated; also known as *Tim Burton's The Nightmare Before Christmas*), Buena Vista, 1993.
Black Beauty, Warner Bros., 1994.
Darkman II: The Return of Durant, 1994.
Dead Presidents, Buena Vista, 1995.
Dolores Claiborne, Columbia, 1995.
To Die For, Columbia, 1995.
Extreme Measures, Columbia, 1996.
Mars Attacks!, Warner Bros., 1996.
Mission: Impossible, Paramount, 1996.
The Frighteners, Universal, 1996.
Men in Black, Columbia TriStar, 1997.
Good Will Hunting, Miramax, 1997.
Flubber, Buena Vista, 1997.
(Additional score) *Scream 2,* Dimension Films, 1997.
Superman Lives (also known as *Superman Reborn*), 1998.

Also composer for two short films, *Oh No, Not Them!* and *Face Like a Frog.*

Songs Used in Films:
"Ain't This the Life," *Urgh! A Music War,* 1981.
"Little Girls," *Tempest,* Columbia, 1982.
"Goodbye, Goodbye," *Fast Times at Ridgemont High,* Universal, 1982.
"Who Do You Want to Be Today," "Something Isn't Right," and "Bachelor Party Theme," *Bachelor Party,* Twentieth Century-Fox, 1983.
"Hold Me Back" and "Only a Lad," *Surf II,* Music Video Distributors, 1984.
"Weird Science," *Weird Science,* Universal, 1985.
"Not My Slave," *Something Wild,* Orion, 1986.
"No One Lives Forever," *The Texas Chainsaw Massacre Part 2,* Media Home Entertainment, 1986.
"Tears Run Down" and "Rock Me Baby," *Wisdom,* Twentieth Century-Fox, 1986.
"Same Man I Was Before," *My Best Friend Is a Vampire* (also known as *I Was a Teenage Vampire*), Kings Road Entertainment, 1988.
"Flesh 'n' Blood," *Ghostbusters II,* Columbia, 1989.
"Winning Side," *She's Out of Control,* Columbia, 1989.
"Skin," *Nightbreed,* Twentieth Century-Fox, 1990.
Main title theme and "Mariachi Parade," *Pure Luck,* Universal, 1991.
Main title theme from *Big Top Pee-Wee,* Dutch, Twentieth Century-Fox, 1991.
"Face to Face," *Batman Returns,* Warner Bros., 1992.
"We Close Our Eyes," *Buffy the Vampire Slayer,* Twentieth Century-Fox, 1992.
"March of the Dead" theme, *Army of Darkness* (also known as *Captain Supermarket* and *The Medieval Dead*), Universal, 1993.
Main title theme, *Shrunken Heads,* Full Moon Entertainment, 1994.
Main title theme, *Tales from the Crypt Presents Demon Knight,* Universal, 1995.
"Tales from the Crypt" theme, *Tales from the Crypt Presents: Bordello of Blood,* Universal, 1996.

Television Themes; Series:
Sledge Hammer!, ABC, 1986-88.
Beetlejuice (animated), ABC, Fox, 1989-93.
The Flash, CBS, 1990.
The Simpsons, Fox, 1990—.
Tales from the Crypt, HBO, 1990—.
The Adventures of Batman and Robin (animated; also known as *Batman: The Animated Series*), 1992—.
Family Dog, CBS, 1993.

Television Music: Episodic:
"The Jar," *Alfred Hitchcock Presents,* NBC, 1985.

"Mummy Dearest," *Amazing Stories,* NBC, 1985.
"Family Dog," *Amazing Stories,* NBC, 1985.
"Fast Times," *Fast Times,* CBS, 1986.
Pee-Wee's Playhouse, CBS, 1986.

Television Music; Movies:
Freeway, HBO, 1996.

Television Music; Specials:
A Special Evening of Pee-Wee's Playhouse, CBS, 1987.
Theme song, *Simpsons Roasting on an Open Fire* (also known as *The Simpsons Christmas Special*), Fox, 1989.
"Batman," *Cincinnati Pops Holiday: Erich Kunzel's Halloween Spooktacular,* PBS, 1996.

OTHER SOURCES

Books:
Contemporary Authors, volume 148, Gale (Detroit, MI), 1996.
Contemporary Musicians, volume 9, Gale, 1993.

Periodicals:
American Film, February, 1991, p. 42.
Movieline, November, 1993, pp. 54-58, 86-87.
Rolling Stone, November 11, 1993, pp. 80-81.
Time, October 11, 1993, pp. 80-81.*

ERMAN, John 1935-
(Bill Sampson)

PERSONAL

Born August 3, 1935, in Chicago, IL; son of Milton G. (in sales) and Lucille Arlie (Straus) Erman. *Education:* University of California, Los Angeles, B.A. (applied arts), 1957. *Politics:* Democrat. *Religion:* Jewish.

Addresses: *Agent*—Steve Glick, William Morris Agency, 151 El Camino Dr., Beverly Hills, CA 90210.

Career: Director. Freelance actor, 1959-63; Twentieth Century-Fox, casting director, 1959-63, head of television casting, 1960-61; Faculty Acting School, Los Angeles, CA, founder.

Member: Directors Guild of America.

Awards, Honors: Emmy Award nomination (with David Greene, Marvin J. Chomsky, and Gilbert

Moses), outstanding directing in a drama series, 1977, for *Roots;* Humanitas Prize, 1977, for *Green Eyes;* Directors Guild of America Award and Christopher Award, both 1979, for *Roots: The Next Generations;* Emmy Award nomination, outstanding directing in a limited series or special, 1980, for *Moviola: The Scarlett O'Hara War;* Emmy Award, outstanding directing of a limited series or special, 1983, for *Who Will Love My Children?;* Directors Guild of America Award, outstanding directorial achievement for television, 1985, for *An Early Frost;* Emmy Award nomination, outstanding drama or miniseries, 1987, for *The Two Mrs. Grenvilles;* Emmy Award nominations, outstanding drama or comedy special and outstanding directing in a miniseries or special, 1988, for "The Attic: The Hiding of Anne Frank," *General Foods Golden Showcase;* Emmy Award nomination, outstanding drama or comedy special, 1988, for *David.*

CREDITS

Television Director; Series:
(With Philip Leacock) *The New Land,* ABC, 1974.

Television Director; Miniseries:
(With David Greene, Marvin J. Chomsky, and Gilbert Moses) *Roots,* ABC, 1977.
(With Charles S. Dubin, Georg Stanford Brown, and Lloyd Richards) *Roots: The Next Generations,* ABC, 1979.
(And coproducer) *Alex Haley's Queen,* CBS, 1993.
(And producer) *Scarlett,* CBS, 1994.

Television Director; Pilots:
Letters from Three Lovers, ABC, 1973.

Television Director; Episodic:
The Outer Limits, ABC, 1963-65.
My Favorite Martian, CBS, 1963-66.
Please Don't Eat the Daisies, NBC, 1965-67.
That Girl, ABC, 1966-71.
"The Empath," *Star Trek,* NBC, 1968.
The Ghost and Mrs. Muir, NBC, 1968-69, ABC, 1969-70.
Bracken's World, NBC, 1969-71.
Karen, ABC, 1975.
Good Heavens, ABC, 1976.
Family, ABC, 1976-80.
(And supervising producer) "The Attic: The Hiding of Anne Frank," *General Foods Golden Showcase,* CBS, 1988.

Directed an episode of *Stoney Burke,* 1962.

Television Director, Except Where Indicated; Movies:
Alexander: The Other Side of Dawn, NBC, 1977.
(And producer) *Green Eyes,* ABC, 1977.
Just Me and You, NBC, 1978.
My Old Man, CBS, 1979.
Moviola: This Year's Blonde (also known as *The Secret Love of Marilyn Monroe*), NBC, 1980.
Moviola: The Scarlett O'Hara War, NBC, 1980.
Moviola: The Silent Lovers, NBC, 1980.
The Letter, ABC, 1982.
Eleanor: First Lady of the World, CBS, 1982.
Another Woman's Child (also known as *The Far Shore*), CBS, 1983.
Who Will Love My Children?, ABC, 1983.
A Streetcar Named Desire, ABC, 1984.
The Atlanta Child Murders, CBS, 1985.
An Early Frost, NBC, 1985.
Right to Kill?, ABC, 1985.
(And producer) *The Two Mrs. Grenvilles,* ABC, 1987.
(And producer) *When the Time Comes,* ABC, 1987.
(And producer) *David,* ABC, 1988.
(And supervising producer) *The Last Best Year* (also known as *The Last Best Year of My Life*), ABC, 1990.
(And supervising producer) *Carolina Skeletons,* NBC, 1991.
(And producer) *The Last to Go,* ABC, 1991.
(And supervising producer) *Our Sons,* ABC, 1991.
(And producer) *Breathing Lessons,* CBS, 1994.
(And producer) *The Boys Next Door,* CBS, 1996.
(And producer) *Ellen Foster,* CBS, 1997.

Also directed *Child of Glass,* 1978; (and producer) *The Sunshine Boys,* 1995.

Film Director:
Making It, Twentieth Century-Fox, 1971.
(As Bill Sampson) *Ace Eli and Rodger of the Skies,* Twentieth Century-Fox, 1973.
Stella, Buena Vista, 1990.

FAHEY, Jeff   1956-

PERSONAL

Born November 29, 1956, in Olean, NY; raised in Buffalo, NY.

Addresses: *Agent*—International Creative Management, 8942 Wilshire Blvd., Beverly Hills, CA 90211.

Career: Actor. Danced with the Joffrey Ballet for three years.

Awards, Honors: Gemini Award nominee, best performance by a lead actor in a single dramatic program, 1986, for *The Execution of Raymond Graham.*

CREDITS

Film Appearances:
Tyree, *Silverado,* Columbia, 1985.
Duane Duke, *Psycho III,* Universal, 1986.
Donnie, *Backfire,* Vidmark, 1987.
Riot on 42nd Street, 1987.
Ray McGuinn, *Split Decisions,* New Century-Vista, 1988.
Jake Bonner, *Alexander's Treasures* (also known as *Out of Time*), Motion Picture International, 1989.
Ricky Rodriguez, *The Last of the Finest* (also known as *Blue Heat* and *Last of the Finest*), Orion, 1989.
Ben Creed, *Outback* (also known as *The Fighting Creed, Minnamurra,* and *Wrangler*), Samuel Goldwyn Company, 1989.
Jake Bonner, *The Serpent of Death* (also known as *In Search of the Serpent of Death*), Paramount Home Video/Prism, 1989.
Raymond "Ray" Trueblood, *True Blood,* Fries, 1989.
Stan Harris, *Impulse,* Warner Bros., 1990.
Pete Verrill, *White Hunter, Black Heart,* Warner Bros., 1990.
Dr. Bill Chrushank, *Body Parts,* Paramount, 1991.
Barry Mikowski, *Iron Maze,* Castle Hill, 1991.
Jobe Smith, *The Lawnmower Man* (also known as *Stephen King's The Lawnmower Man*), New Line Cinema, 1992.
Dex Dellum, *Freefall* (also known as *Firefall*), October Films, 1994.
Muncie, *Quick,* Academy Entertainment, 1994.
Eddie Lanarsky, *Temptation,* LIVE Home Video, 1994.
Jack Lynch, *Woman of Desire,* Trimark Pictures, 1994.
Ike Clanton, *Wyatt Earp,* Warner Bros., 1994.
Paul Weyman, *Eye of the Wolf,* Vidmark Entertainment, 1995.
Tom Bennett, *Serpent's Lair,* Republic Pictures Home Video, 1995.
Dale Goddard, *The Sweeper,* PM Entertainment, 1995.
Peter Rooker, *Darkman III: Die Darkman Die,* Universal Home Video, 1996.
The Dutchman, *Small Time* (also known as *Smalltime*), British Film Institute, 1996.
When Justice Fails, 1997.
Lang, *Operation Delta Force,* Nu World/Live Entertainment, 1997.
Catherine's Grove (also known as *Crossover*), 1997.

David Chase, *Lethal Tender,* Deadly Current Productions/Le Monde Entertainment, 1997.

Film Work:
Associate producer, *The Sweeper,* PM Entertainment, 1995.

Television Appearances; Series:
Gary Corelli, *One Life to Live,* ABC, 1982-85.
Deputy Marshal Winston MacBride, *The Marshal,* ABC, 1995.

Television Appearances; Movies:
Raymond Graham, *The Execution of Raymond Graham,* ABC, 1985.
Michael Manus, *Curiosity Kills* (also known as *Curiosity Kills the Cat*), USA Network, 1990.
Title role, *Parker Kane,* NBC, 1990.
Hamilton Jordan, *Iran: Days of Crisis* (also known as *444 Days* and *L'Amerique en Otage*), TNT, 1991.
Jack, *Sketch Artist,* Showtime, 1992.
Will McCaid, *In the Company of Darkness,* CBS, 1993.
Charlie Pike, *The Hit List,* Showtime, 1993.
Frank McKenna, *Blindsided,* USA Network, 1993.
Paul Weyman, *Baree: The Wolf Dog* (also known as *Baree* and *Northern Passage*), 1994.
Liam Bass, *Virtual Seduction* (also known as *Addicted to Love*), 1995.
Jack Whitfield, *Sketch Artist II: Hands That See* (also known as *A Feel for Murder* and *Sketch Artist II*), Showtime, 1995.
Mitch Parker, *Every Woman's Dream,* CBS, 1996.

Television Appearances; Episodic:
"When Irish Eyes Are Crying," *Miami Vice,* NBC, 1986.
Ray Lee, "Enough Rope for Two," *Alfred Hitchcock Presents,* NBC, 1986.

Stage Appearances:
Brigadoon, New York City, 1980.
John, *Pastorale,* The Second Stage Theatre, New York City, 1982.

Also appeared in *West Side Story* in Paris, France, and in *Orphans,* in London, England.

Major Tours:
Curly, *Oklahoma!,* U.S. cities, 1981.

OTHER SOURCES

Periodicals:
Cosmopolitan, June, 1990, p. 88.*

FARENTINO, James 1938-

PERSONAL

Born James Ferrantino, February 24, 1938, in Brooklyn, NY; son of Anthony (a clothing designer) and Helen (a homemaker; maiden name, Enrico) Ferrantino; married Elizabeth Ashley (an actress), 1961 (divorced); married Michele Lee Dusick (an actress and singer; professional name, Michele Lee), February 20, 1966 (divorced, c. 1981); married Deborah Mullowney (an actress; professional name, Debrah Farentino), June, 1985 (divorced); married; wife's name, Stella, 1994; children: (second marriage) David Michael (an actor). *Education:* Trained for the stage at the American Academy of Dramatic Arts.

Addresses: Agent—c/o William Morris Agency, 151 El Camino Drive, Beverly Hills, CA 90212. *Office*— 1340 Londonderry Pier, Los Angeles, CA, 90069.

Career: Actor. Illinois Association of Retarded Citizens, honorary chair.

Awards, Honors: Golden Globe Award, most promising newcomer—male, 1966, for *The Pad . . . And How to Use It;* Best Actor Award, Chicago, IL, 1973; Theatre World Award, 1973, for *A Streetcar Named Desire;* Charles MacArthur Award, Chicago Drama League, 1974; Emmy Award nomination, outstanding supporting actor in a drama, 1977, for *Jesus of Nazareth.*

CREDITS

Film Appearances:
Insigna, *Ensign Pulver,* Warner Bros., 1964.
Charlie Perone, *Psychomania* (also known as *Violent Midnight*), Victoria-Emerson, 1964.
Marc, *The War Lord,* Universal, 1965.
Ted Veasey, *The Pad . . . And How to Use It* (also known as *The Pad*), Universal, 1966.
Chris Patton, *Banning,* Universal, 1967.
Matt Stone, *The Ride to Hangman's Tree* (also known as *The Ride to Hangman's Tree*), Universal, 1967.
David Wheelwright, *Rosie,* Universal, 1967.
David Harris, *Me, Natalie,* National General, 1969.
Bruno Cardini, *Story of a Woman* (also known as *Storia di una Donna*), Universal, 1970.
Commander Richard Owens and Mr. Tideman, *The Final Countdown,* United Artists, 1980.
Sheriff Dan Gillis, *Dead and Buried,* Avco-Embassy, 1981.

Frank Polito, *Her Alibi,* Warner Bros., 1989.
Joey, *Deep Down,* 1994.
The Spy Within (also known as *Flight of the Dove*), New Horizons Home Video, 1995.
Captain Will Jensen, *Bulletproof,* Universal, 1996.

Television Appearances; Series:
Neil Darrell, *The Bold Ones: The Lawyers* (also known as *The Bold Ones* and *The Lawyers*), NBC, 1969-72.
Jefferson Keyes, *Cool Million,* NBC, 1972-73.
Dr. Nick Toscanni, *Dynasty,* ABC, 1981-82.
Frank Chaney, *Blue Thunder,* ABC, 1984.
Frank DeMarco, *Mary,* CBS, 1985-86.
Sam McGuire, *Julie,* ABC, 1992.
Ray Ross, Doug's father, *ER,* NBC, 1995-96.

Television Appearances; Miniseries:
Gene Culligan, *Vanished,* NBC, 1971.
Simon Peter, *Jesus of Nazareth* (also known as *Gesu di Nazareth*), NBC, 1977.
Juan Peron, *Evita Peron,* NBC, 1981.
David Westfield, *Sins,* CBS, 1986.
The Secrets of the Sahara, 1987.
Jimmy Rosemont, *Dazzle* (also known as *Judith Krantz's Dazzle*), CBS, 1995.

Television Appearances; Episodic:
"Let Me Die Before I Wake," *Naked City,* ABC, 1962.
"Black Curtain," *The Alfred Hitchcock Hour,* CBS, 1962.
"The Illusion," *The Defenders,* ABC, 1963.
"Bonus Baby," *77 Sunset Strip,* ABC, 1963.
"Cries of Persons Close to One," *Route 66,* CBS, 1964.
"Super Star," *The Reporter,* CBS, 1964.
"Death Scene," *The Alfred Hitchcock Hour,* NBC, 1965.
"P.O.W.," *Twelve O'Clock High* (also known as *12 O'Clock High*), ABC, 1965.
"O' the Big Wheel Turns by Faith," *Ben Casey,* ABC, 1965.
"I See by Your Outfit," *Laredo,* NBC, 1965.
"All the Streets Are Silent," *The FBI,* ABC, 1965.
"The Wolves up Front, the Jackals behind," *The Virginian,* NBC, 1966.
"The Sister and the Savage," *Bob Hope Presents the Chrysler Theatre,* NBC, 1966.
"Reap the Whirlwind," *The Road West,* NBC, 1967.
"Passage to Helena," *The Fugitive,* ABC, 1967.
"Cry Hard, Cry Fast," *Run for Your Life,* NBC, 1967.
"Something for Nothing," *Ironside,* NBC, 1968.
"Brave on a Mountain Top," *Marcus Welby, M.D.,* ABC, 1970.

"Love and the Neighbor," *Love, American Style,* ABC, 1971.

"Since Aunt Ada Came to Stay," *Night Gallery,* NBC, 1971.

"Birdbath," *Hollywood Television Theatre,* PBS, 1971.

"The Girl with the Hungry Eyes," *Night Gallery,* NBC, 1972.

"Dangerous Games," *Police Story,* NBC, 1973.

"The Soft, Kind Brush," *Love Story,* NBC, 1973.

"Requiem for C. Z. Smith," *Police Story,* NBC, 1974.

"Incident in the Kill Zone," *Police Story,* NBC, 1975.

"No Margin for Error," *Police Story,* NBC, 1978.

"Plus Time Served," *Insight,* syndicated, 1979.

"Resurrection," *Insight,* syndicated, 1980.

"God's Guerilla's," *Insight,* syndicated, 1981.

"Rendezvous," *Insight,* syndicated, 1981.

Television Appearances; Movies:

Taff Malloy, *Wings of Fire* (also known as *Cloudburst*), NBC, 1967.

Gino Rico, *The Family Rico* (also known as *The Brothers Rico*), CBS, 1972.

John Danbury, *The Longest Night,* ABC, 1972.

Eddie Holcomb, *The Elevator,* ABC, 1974.

Joe Crane, "Emily, Emily," *Hallmark Hall of Fame,* NBC, 1977.

Kevin Leahy, *The Possessed,* NBC, 1977.

Duffy Hambleton, *Silent Victory: The Kitty O'Neill Story* (also known as *The Kitty O'Neill Story* and *Silent Victory*), CBS, 1979.

Arnie Potts, *Something So Right,* CBS, 1982.

Dr. Edgar Highley, *The Cradle Will Fall,* CBS, 1983.

John Peterson, *License to Kill,* CBS, 1984.

Dan Hagan, *Picking Up the Pieces,* CBS, 1985.

Tom Wyler, *A Summer to Remember,* CBS, 1985.

Voice of Jesus, *The Fourth Wise Man,* 1985.

Gerald Remson, *That Secret Sunday,* CBS, 1986.

Gordon Williams, *Family Sins,* CBS, 1987.

Lt. Daniel B. Malone, *The Red Spider,* CBS, 1988.

Buddy Baron, *Who Gets the Friends?,* CBS, 1988.

Jonathan Morris, *Naked Lie* (also known as *Inadmissible Evidence*), CBS, 1989.

Mayor Kevin White, *Common Ground,* NBC, 1990.

Ray Wiltern, *In the Line of Duty: A Cop for the Killing* (also known as *A Cop for the Killing* and *In the Line of Duty: The Dallas Drug Murders*), NBC, 1990.

John Reilly, *Miles from Nowhere,* 1992.

Gary Cochran, *When No One Would Listen* (also known as *My Husband Is Going to Kill Me*), CBS, 1992.

Jose Menendez, *Honor Thy Father and Mother: The True Story of the Menendez Murders* (also known as *Honor Thy Father and Mother: The Menendez Killings*), Fox, 1994.

Lieutenant Bill Lawson, *One Woman's Courage* (also known as *Saving Grace*), NBC, 1994.

Also appeared in *Undercover Cop.*

Television Appearances; Specials:

Happy Loman, *Death of a Salesman,* CBS, 1966.

Husband, *The First Nine Months Are the Hardest,* NBC, 1971.

John Dos Passos: U.S.A., 1971.

Mitzi and a Hundred Guys, CBS, 1975.

Male team member, *Celebrity Challenge of the Sexes,* CBS, 1977.

Barry Kaufman, "Son Rise: A Miracle of Love" (also known as "Son Rise: A Story of Love" and "Son Rise"), *NBC Theatre,* NBC, 1979.

The Television Academy Hall of Fame, 1986.

Mickey Dunne, "American Nuclear," *CBS Summer Playhouse,* CBS, 1989.

Robin Leach's Private Files: The Price of Fame, syndicated, 1993.

Host, *Crimes of the Century,* NBC, 1996.

Narrator, *Outlaws and Lawmen,* The Discovery Channel, 1996.

Television Appearances; Pilots:

Neil Darrell, *The Sound of Anger,* NBC, 1968.

The Singers, CBS, 1969.

Neil Darrell, *The Whole World Is Watching,* NBC, 1969.

Jefferson Keyes, *Cool Million* (also known as *The Mask of Marcella*), NBC, 1972.

Vince Rossi, *Crossfire,* NBC, 1975.

George Bassett, *My Wife Next Door,* NBC, 1975.

Stage Appearances:

Pedro, *The Night of the Iguana,* Royale Theatre, New York City, 1961.

The Days and Nights of BeeBee Fenstermaker, Sheridan Square Playhouse, New York City, 1963.

Mr. Solares, *In the Summer House,* Little Fox Theatre, New York City, 1964.

Stanley Kowalski, *A Streetcar Named Desire,* Vivian Beaumont Theatre, New York City, 1973.

Randall Patrick McMurphy, *One Flew Over the Cuckoo's Nest,* Chicago, IL, 1973.

The Best Man, Chicago, IL, 1974.

Biff Loman, *Death of a Salesman,* Circle in the Square Theatre, New York City, 1975.

The Big Knife, Arlington Park Theatre, Chicago, IL, 1976.

Also appeared in *The Best Man; Goodbye Charlie;* and *A Thousand Clowns.*

Major Tours:
California Suite, U.S. cities, 1978.

OTHER SOURCES

Periodicals:
People Weekly, November 16, 1992, pp. 59, 61-62; April 18, 1994, p. 63.*

FENN, Sherilyn   1965-

PERSONAL

Born February 1, 1965, in Detroit, MI; niece of Suzi Quatro (a singer and actress); married Toulouse Holliday (a musician); children: Myles. *Education:* Attended West Bloomfield High School, West Bloomfield, MI.

Addresses: *Agent*—The Agency, 10351 Santa Monica Blvd., Suite 211, Los Angeles, CA 90069. *Contact*—Creative Artists Agency, 9830 Wilshire Blvd., Beverly Hills, CA 90212.

Career: Actress.

Awards, Honors: Emmy Award nomination, best supporting actress in a drama series, 1990, for *Twin Peaks.*

CREDITS

Television Appearances; Series:
Audrey Horne, *Twin Peaks,* ABC, 1990-91.

Television Appearances; Miniseries:
Kitt, *A Season in Purgatory,* CBS, 1996.

Television Appearances; Episodic:
Gabrielle, "The Groom Wore Clearasil," *Cheers,* NBC, 1985.
Diane Nelson, "Blindsided," *21 Jump Street,* Fox, 1987.
Erika, "You, Murderer," *Tales from the Crypt,* HBO, 1995.
Ginger, "The One with Phoebe's Ex-Partner," *Friends,* NBC, 1997.

Also appeared in *Heart of the City,* ABC.

Television Appearances; Movies:
Monica, *Silence of the Heart* (also known as *Death of a Sibling*), CBS, 1984.
Billie Frechette, *Dillinger* (also known as *The Last Days of John Dillinger*), ABC, 1991.
"Spring Awakening," *CBS Sunday Afternoon Movie,* CBS, 1994.
Title role, *Liz: The Elizabeth Taylor Story,* NBC, 1995.
Zulaikah, Potiphar's wife, *Slave of Dreams,* Showtime, 1996.
Lauren Jacobs, *The Assassination File* (also known as *Out in the Cold*), Starz!, 1996.

Television Appearances; Specials:
Betty, "A Table at Ciros," (also known as "Tales from the Hollywood Hills") *Great Performances,* PBS, 1987.
Lorraine, *Divided We Stand,* ABC, 1988.
Beth, "A Family Again," *ABC Family Theater,* ABC, 1988.

Television Appearances; Awards Presentations:
MTV's 1990 Video Music Awards, MTV, 1990.
Presenter, *The 42nd Annual Primetime Emmy Awards Presentation* (also known as *The 42nd Annual Emmy Awards* and *The Emmy Awards*), Fox, 1990.

Film Appearances:
Ups and Downs (also known as *Prep School*), Astral Films, 1983.
Penny Harlin, *The Wild Life,* Universal, 1984.
Sandy, *Just One of the Guys,* Columbia, 1985.
Katie Toland, *Out of Control,* New World, 1985.
Velvet, *Thrashin',* Fries Entertainment, 1986.
Keri Johnson, *The Wraith,* New Century-Vista, 1986.
Suzi, *Zombie High* (also known as *The School That Ate My Brain*), Cinema Group, 1987.
April Delongpre, *Two Moon Junction,* Lorimar, 1988.
Helen, *Crime Zone,* Concorde, 1988.
Jennifer Scott, *True Blood,* Fries Entertainment, 1989.
Girl in accident, *Wild at Heart,* Samuel Goldwyn, 1990.
Catherine Bomarzini, *Meridian: Kiss of the Beast* (also known as *Kiss of the Beast, Meridian,* and *Phantoms*), Paramount Home Video, 1990.
Lucy Costello, *Backstreet Dreams* (also known as *Backstreet Strays* and *Back Street Strays*), Vidmark, 1990.
Candy Cane, *Ruby,* Triumph Releasing, 1992.
Bridey DeSoto, *Desire and Hell at Sunset Motel,* Two Moon Releasing, 1992.
Jain, *Diary of a Hitman,* Vision International, 1992.
Curley's wife, *Of Mice and Men,* Metro-Goldwyn-Mayer, 1992.

Audrey Horne, *Twin Peaks: Fire Walk with Me,* New Line Cinema, 1992.

Ellen, *Three of Hearts,* New Line Cinema, 1993.

Laura Lincolnberry, *Fatal Instinct,* Metro-Goldwyn-Mayer, 1993.

Helena, *Boxing Helena,* Orion Classics, 1993.

Molly, *Lovelife,* Skyline Entertainment, 1997.

Just Write, Curb Entertainment, 1997.

OTHER SOURCES

Periodicals:

Cosmopolitan, May, 1992.

Details, December, 1991.

Playboy, December, 1990.

Rolling Stone, October 14, 1990.*

FIELD, Sally 1946-

PERSONAL

Full name, Sally Margaret Field; born November 6, 1946, in Pasadena, CA; daughter of Maggie Field O'Mahoney (one source says Mahoney; an actress); stepdaughter of Jock Mahoney (an actor); married Steve Craig, September, 1968 (divorced, 1975); married Alan Greisman (a film producer), December, 1984 (divorced, 1994); children: (first marriage) Peter, Eli; (second marriage) Samuel. *Education:* Attended Actors Studio, 1968, 1973-75; studied acting with David Craig.

Addresses: *Agent*—Creative Artists Agency, 9830 Wilshire Blvd., Beverly Hills, CA 90212. *Contact*—P.O. Box 492417, Los Angeles, CA 90049.

Career: Actress. Fogwood Films Ltd., producer, beginning in 1984.

Member: Screen Actors Guild, American Federation of Television and Radio Artists.

Awards, Honors: Emmy Award, outstanding lead actress in a drama or comedy special, 1976, for *Sybil;* Golden Globe Award nomination, best motion picture actress in a comedy or musical, 1978, for *Smokey and the Bandit;* best actress award, Cannes International Film Festival, Academy Award, best actress, New York Film Critics Award, and National Society of Film Critics Award, all 1979, and Golden Globe Award, best actress in a dramatic film, Hollywood Foreign Press Association, 1980, all for *Norma Rae;* NATO Star of the Year Award, National Association of Theatre Owners, 1981; People's Choice Award (with Jane Fonda), best motion picture actress, Proctor and Gamble Productions, 1982; Golden Globe Award nomination, best motion picture actress in a drama, 1982, for *Absence of Malice;* Golden Globe Award nomination, best motion picture actress in a comedy or musical, 1983, for *Kiss Me Goodbye;* Golden Apple Award (with John Forsythe), star of the year, Hollywood Women's Press Club, 1984; Academy Award, best actress, 1984, and Golden Globe Award, best actress in a dramatic film, 1985, both for *Places in the Heart;* Hasty Pudding Woman of the Year Award, Hasty Pudding Theatricals, 1986; Golden Globe Award nomination, best motion picture actress in a comedy or musical, 1986, for *Murphy's Romance;* Golden Globe Award nomination, best motion picture actress in a drama, 1990, for *Steel Magnolias;* Screen Actors Guild Award nomination, outstanding performance by a female actor in a supporting role, 1995, for *Forrest Gump;* Emmy Award nomination, outstanding lead actress in a miniseries or a special, and outstanding miniseries, both 1995, and Golden Globe Award nomination, best performance by an actress in a miniseries or motion picture made for television, 1996, all for *A Woman of Independent Means;* Berinale Camera, Berlin International Film Festival, 1996.

CREDITS

Film Appearances:

(Film debut) Mercy McBee, *The Way West,* United Artists, 1967.

Mary Tate Farnsworth, *Stay Hungry,* United Artists, 1976.

Carol Bell, *Heroes,* Universal, 1977.

Carrie, *Smokey and the Bandit,* Universal, 1977.

Gwen, *Hooper,* Warner Bros., 1978.

Mary Ellen, *The End,* United Artists, 1978.

Title role, *Norma Rae,* Twentieth Century-Fox, 1979.

Celeste Whitman, *Beyond the Poseidon Adventure,* Warner Bros., 1979.

Carrie, *Smokey and the Bandit II* (also known as *Smokey and the Bandit Ride Again*), Universal, 1980.

Amy Post, *Back Roads,* Warner Bros., 1981.

Megan Carter, *Absence of Malice,* Columbia, 1981.

Kay Villano, *Kiss Me Goodbye,* Twentieth Century-Fox, 1982.

Edna Spalding, *Places in the Heart,* TriStar, 1984.

Emma Moriarty, *Murphy's Romance,* Columbia, 1985.

Daisy Morgan, *Surrender,* Warner Bros., 1987.

Lilah Krytsick, *Punchline,* Columbia, 1988.

M'Lynn Eatenton, *Steel Magnolias,* TriStar, 1989.

Betty Mahmoody, *Not without My Daughter,* Metro-Goldwyn-Mayer/Pathe, 1991.

Celeste Talbert, *Soapdish,* Paramount, 1991.

Voice of Sassy, *Homeward Bound: The Incredible Journey,* Buena Vista, 1993.

Miranda Hillard, *Mrs. Doubtfire,* Twentieth Century-Fox, 1993.

Herself, *A Century of Cinema,* 1994.

Mrs. Gump, *Forrest Gump,* Paramount, 1994.

Karen McCann, *Eye for an Eye,* Paramount, 1996.

Voice of Sassy, *Homeward Bound II: Lost in San Francisco,* Buena Vista, 1996.

Film Work:

Executive producer, *Murphy's Romance,* Columbia, 1985.

Producer, *Punchline,* Columbia, 1988.

Producer, *Dying Young* (also known as *Choice of Love*), Twentieth Century-Fox, 1991.

Television Appearances; Series:

Frances "Gidget" Lawrence, *Gidget,* ABC, 1965-66.

Sister Bertrille, *The Flying Nun,* ABC, 1967-70.

Sally Burton, *The Girl with Something Extra,* NBC, 1973-74.

Television Appearances; Miniseries:

Bess Steed Garner, *A Woman of Independent Means,* NBC, 1995.

Television Appearances; Episodic:

Bonnie Banner, "Woody, Can You Spare a Sister?," *Hey, Landlord,* NBC, 1967.

Bonnie Banner, "Sharin Sharon," *Hey, Landlord,* NBC, 1967.

Bonnie Banner, "Big Brother Is Watching You," *Hey, Landlord,* NBC, 1967.

Bonnie Banner, "A Little Off the Top," *Hey, Landlord,* NBC, 1967.

"Jenny, Who Bombs Buildings," *Bracken's World,* NBC, 1970.

"I Can Hardly Tell You Apart," *Marcus Welby, M.D.,* ABC, 1971.

Clementine Hale, "Dreadful Sorry Clementine," *Alias Smith and Jones,* ABC, 1971.

Clementine Hale, "The Clementine Incident," *Alias Smith and Jones,* ABC, 1972.

Irene, "Whisper," *Night Gallery,* NBC, 1973.

Molly Follett, "All the Way Home," *NBC Live Theater,* NBC, 1981.

First Person with Maria Shriver, NBC, 1990.

Herself, *The Larry Sanders Show,* HBO, 1992.

"Addicted to Fame," *First Person with Maria Shriver,* NBC, 1994.

Inside the Actors Studio, Bravo, 1995.

Interviewee, "Arnold Schwarzenegger: Flex Appeal," *Biography,* Arts and Entertainment, 1996.

Narrator, "New York Society for the Prevention of Cruelty to Children/Committee Praying," *Sex and the Silver Screen,* Showtime, 1996.

Voice of Junie Harper, "Hilloween," *King of the Hill* (animated), Fox, 1997.

Television Appearances; Movies:

Denise Miller, *Maybe I'll Come Home in the Spring,* ABC, 1971.

Jane Duden, *Marriage: Year One,* NBC, 1971.

Vicki, *Mongo's Back in Town,* CBS, 1971.

Christine Morgan, *Home for the Holidays,* ABC, 1972.

Roselle Bridgeman, *Hitched* (also known as *Westward the Wagon*), NBC, 1973.

Jennifer Melford, *Bridges,* ABC, 1976.

Sybil Dorsett, *Sybil,* NBC, 1976.

Narrator/Mrs. Bailey, *Merry Christmas, George Bailey,* PBS, 1997.

Television Appearances; Specials:

Narrator, *California Girl* (documentary), ABC, 1968.

Beth Barber, *Lily for President,* CBS, 1982.

American Film Institute Salute to Lillian Gish, 1984.

American Film Institute Salute to Billy Wilder, 1986.

Jimmy Stewart: A Wonderful Life, 1987.

Punchline Party (also known as *Sally Field and Tom Hank's Punchline Party*), HBO, 1988.

The New Hollywood, NBC, 1990.

Host/narrator, *Barbara Stanwyck: Fire and Desire,* TNT, 1991.

Voices That Care, Fox, 1991.

The Kennedy Center Honors: A Celebration of the Performing Arts, 1992.

An American Reunion: The 52nd Presidential Inaugural Gala, CBS, 1993.

Voice of Elizabeth Gurley Flynn, *A Century of Women* (documentary; also known as *A Family of Women*), TBS, 1994.

Inside the Academy Awards, TNT, 1995.

The American Film Institute Salute to Steven Spielberg, NBC, 1995.

The Good, the Bad and the Beautiful (also known as *Popcorn Venus*), TBS, 1996.

Television Appearances; Awards Presentations:

Presenter, *The 58th Annual Academy Awards Presentation,* 1986.

Presenter, *The 64th Annual Academy Awards Presentation*, 1992.
The 65th Annual Academy Awards Presentation, ABC, 1993.
Presenter, *The 67th Annual Academy Awards*, ABC, 1995.

Television Work:
Executive producer, *A Woman of Independent Means* (miniseries), NBC, 1995.
Executive producer and director, *The Christmas Tree* (movie), ABC, 1996.

WRITINGS

For Television:
The Christmas Tree (movie), ABC, 1996.

OTHER SOURCES

Books:
The International Dictionary of Film and Filmmakers, Volume III: *Actors and Actresses,* St. James Press (Detroit, MI), 1992.

Periodicals:
American Film, October, 1982, p. 58.
New York Times, September 16, 1984.
People, October 15, 1984, p. 112; October 15, 1988, p. 90.*

FOLLOWS, Megan   1968-

PERSONAL

First name pronounced "*Mee-gan*"; born March 14, 1968, in Toronto, Ontario, Canada; daughter of Ted Follows (an actor) and Dawn Greenhalgh (an actress); sister of Samantha (an actress); sister of Edwina (a producer and writer); sister of Laurence (a producer); married Christopher Porter (a gaffer), April 21, 1991 (separated); children: one son, one daughter.

Addresses: *Agent*—Brian Mann, International Creative Management, 8942 Wilshire Blvd., Beverly Hills, CA 90211; Lisa Loosemore, International Creative Management, 40 West 57th Street, New York, NY 10019. *Publicist*—Karen Williams, 268 Poplar Plains Road, Suite 901, Toronto, Ontario, Canada M4V 2P2.

Career: Actress; also appeared in television commercials.

Member: Actors' Equity Association, Canadian Actors' Equity Association, Screen Actors Guild, American Federation of Television and Radio Artists, Association of Canadian Television and Radio Artists.

Awards, Honors: Gemini Award, best actress in a drama miniseries, Canadian Academy of Television Arts and Sciences, 1986, for *Anne of Green Gables;* CableACE Award nomination, best actress, 1987, and Gemini Award, best actress in a drama miniseries, Canadian Academy of Television Arts and Sciences, 1988, both for *Anne of Avonlea;* Association of Canadian Television and Radio Artists Award nomination, best actress, 1988, for *Hockey Night.*

CREDITS

Stage Appearances:
The Effect of Gamma Rays on Man-in-the-Moon Marigolds, Young People's Theatre, Toronto, Ontario, Canada, 1988.
Cecile de Volanges, *Les Liaisons Dangereuses,* Williamstown Theatre Festival, Williamstown, MA, 1988.
A Doll's House, Guthrie Theatre, Minneapolis, MN, 1996.

Film Appearances:
Claire's Wish (short film), 1978.
Margaret, *Boys and Girls,* Atlantis Films, 1982.
Jane Coslaw, *Silver Bullet* (also known as *Stephen King's Silver Bullet*) De Laurentiis Entertainment Group/Paramount, 1985.
Irene, *A Time of Destiny,* Columbia, 1988.
Micheline Dushane, *Termini Station,* 1989.
Voice of Clara, *The Nutcracker Prince,* 1990.
Shelley McBride, *Deep Sleep,* 1990.

Television Appearances; Series:
A Gift to Last, 1978.
Jenny, *Matt and Jenny on the Wilderness Trail* (also known as *Matt and Jenny*), Canadian television, 1979, later The Disney Channel, 1988.
Lucy Baxter, *The Baxters,* syndicated, 1979-80.
Didi Crane, *Domestic Life,* CBS, 1984.
Anne Shirley, *Anne of Green Gables,* CBC, 1985, then *WonderWorks,* PBS, 1986.
Anne Shirley, *Anne of Avonlea,* CBC, then The Disney Channel, 1987.

Anne of Avonlea: The Sequel (re-edited material from *Anne of Avonlea*), CBC, then *WonderWorks*, PBS, 1988.
Kate Benedict, *Second Chances*, 1993.

Television Appearances; Miniseries:
Louise, *Champagne Charlie*, CTV, then syndicated in the United States, both 1989.

Television Appearances; Pilots:
Tina Jackson, *The Faculty*, ABC, 1986.

Television Appearances; Episodic:
"Jo's Cousins," *The Facts of Life*, NBC, 1982.
Aimee, "The Dwarf," *The Ray Bradbury Theater*, USA Network, 1989.
"Happily Ever After," *The Hidden Room*, 1991.
Karen Ross, "The Choice," *The Outer Limits*, Showtime, 1995.

Television Appearances; Movies:
Laura McClain, *The Mating Season*, CBS, 1980.
Sal, *The Olden Day Coat*, 1982.
Cathy Yarrow, *Hockey Night*, CBC, then HBO, 1985.
Jenny Colleran, *Sin of Innocence* (also known as *Two Young People*), CBS, 1986.
Rachel Brown, *Inherit the Wind*, NBC, 1988.
Peggy Ann Bradnick, *Cry in the Wild: The Taking of Peggy Ann*, 1990.
Becky, *Back to Hannibal: The Return of Tom Sawyer and Huckleberry Finn*, 1990.
Gloria, *The Chase*, 1991.
Rosetta Basilio, *Under the Piano*, 1995.

Television Appearances; Specials:
Jennifer, *Jen's Place*, CBC, then *WonderWorks*, PBS, both 1982.
The Making of Anne of Green Gables, PBS, 1986.
Dana Sherman, "Seasonal Differences," *ABC Afterschool Special*, ABC, 1987.
Anna Mae Morgan, "Stacking" (also known as "Season of Dreams"), *American Playhouse*, 1989.

RECORDINGS

Taped Readings:
A Monstrous Regiment of Women, 1996.
My Gal Sunday, 1996.
The Beekeeper's Apprentice, 1997.

Recorded *Anne of Green Gables*, *Anne of Avonlea*, and *Anne of the Island.* *

FONDA, Bridget   1964-

PERSONAL

Born January 27, 1964, in Los Angeles, CA; raised in Los Angeles, CA, and Montana; daughter of Peter (an actor, director, producer, and writer) and Susan (maiden name, Brewer) Fonda; granddaughter of Henry Fonda (an actor); niece of Jane Fonda (an actress). *Education:* Attended New York University; studied at the Lee Strasberg Theatre Institute.

Addresses: *Publicist*—c/o Nancy Seltzer & Associates, Inc., 6220 Del Valle Dr., Los Angeles, CA 90048.

Career: Actress.

Awards, Honors: Golden Globe Award nomination, best supporting actress, 1990, for *Scandal*; Emmy Award nomination, outstanding supporting actress in a miniseries or a special, 1997, for *In the Gloaming*.

Member: Screen Actors Guild.

CREDITS

Film Appearances:
Partners, 1982.
(Film debut) Young lover, "Tristan und Isolde," *Aria*, Warner Bros., 1987.
Voice of historian/head, *Light Years* (animated), Miramax, 1988.
Peggy Kellogg, *You Can't Hurry Love*, Lightning, 1988.
Melaina Buller, *Shag: The Movie* (also known as *Shag*), TriStar, 1988.
Mandy Rice-Davies, *Scandal*, Miramax, 1989.
Amy Hempel, *Strapless*, Atlantic Releasing, 1989.
Mary Godwin Shelley, *Frankenstein Unbound* (also known as *Roger Corman's Frankenstein Unbound*), Twentieth Century-Fox, 1990.
Grace Hamilton, *The Godfather, Part III* (also known as *Mario Puzo's The Godfather: Part III*), Paramount, 1990.
Claudi, *Leather Jackets*, Triumph Releasing, 1991.
Nancy Lee, *Doc Hollywood*, Warner Bros., 1991.
Annabelle, *Drop Dead Fred*, New Line Cinema, 1991.
Chris Sugita, *Iron Maze*, Castle Hill, 1991.
Jo, *Out of the Rain* (also known as *End of Innocence* and *Remains*), Vision International, 1991.
Janet Livermore, *Singles*, Warner Bros., 1992.
Allison Jones, *Single White Female*, Columbia, 1992.

Maggie, *Point of No Return* (also known as *The Assassin, La Femme Nikita, Nikita,* and *The Specialist*), Warner Bros., 1993.

Lisa Conrad, *Little Buddha,* Miramax, 1993.

Beth, *Bodies, Rest and Motion* (also known as *Bodies, Rest & Motion*), Fine Line Features, 1993.

Linda, *Army of Darkness* (also known as *Army of Darkness: Evil Dead 3, Captain Supermarket, Evil Dead 3,* and *The Medieval Dead*), Universal, 1993.

Yvonne Biasi, *It Could Happen to You* (also known as *Cop Gives Waitress 2 Million Dollar Tip*), TriStar, 1994.

Freda Lopez, *Camilla,* Miramax, 1994.

Eleanor Lightbody, *The Road to Wellville,* Columbia, 1994.

Myra Shumway, *Rough Magic,* Samuel Goldwyn, 1995.

Voice of Jenna, *Balto* (animated; also known as *Snowballs*), Universal, 1995.

Kelly Porter, *Grace of My Heart,* Gramercy Pictures, 1996.

Marybeth Cogan, *City Hall,* Columbia, 1996.

Lynn Faulkner, *Touch,* Metro-Goldwyn-Mayer/United Artists, 1997.

Melanie Ralston, *Jackie Brown* (also known as *Rum Punch*), Miramax, 1997.

Ashley, *The Road to Graceland,* 1997.

The Breakup, Millenium Films, forthcoming.

Also appeared in student film *PPT.*

Television Appearances; Movies:
Anne, *In the Gloaming,* HBO, 1997.

Television Appearances; Episodic:
"Blinded by the Thousand Points of Light," *21 Jump Street,* Fox, 1989.

Louise Bradshaw, "Jacob Have I Loved," *WonderWorks,* PBS, 1989.

Dorite, "Professional Man," *The Edge,* HBO, 1989.

Herself, *The Late Show with David Letterman,* CBS, 1997.

Television Appearances; Specials:
Host, *Dolphins in Danger: On Location with Bridget Fonda* (also known as *TOPX, Wild! Life Adventures,* and *A World with Dolphins*), TBS, 1996.

Stage Appearances:
Sissy, *Class 1 Acts,* Nat Horne Theatre, New York City, 1988.

Also appeared in *Confession,* Warren Robertson Workshop, and *Pastels,* Lee Strasberg Theatre Institute.

OTHER SOURCES

Periodicals:
InStyle, March, 1996, pp. 94-99.
Interview, June, 1989, p. 86.
Rolling Stone, April 20, 1989, p. 40.
TV Guide, issue 951, 1997, p. 84.
US, May 29, 1989.

FORREST, Frederic   1936-

PERSONAL

Born December 23, 1936, in Waxahachie, TX. *Education:* Attended Texas Christian University and the University of Oklahoma; studied acting with Sanford Mesner and Lee Strasberg at the Actors Studio, New York City.

Addresses: *Agent*—c/o Camden, 822 South Robertson, Suite 200, Los Angeles, CA 90035.

Career: Actor. Performed in off-Broadway productions and in New York City cafes.

Member: Actors' Equity Association, Screen Actors Guild, American Federation of Television and Radio Artists.

Awards, Honors: Golden Globe Award nomination, most promising newcomer—male, 1972, for *When the Legends Die;* Academy Award nomination and Golden Globe nomination, both best supporting actor, 1979, for *The Rose.*

CREDITS

Stage Appearances:
Silhouettes, Los Angeles, CA, 1970.

Appeared in *Futz, Massachusetts Trust, Tom Paine,* and *Viet Rock,* all with the La MaMa Experimental Theatre Club, New York City, 1965-69. Also appeared with the Fort Worth Community Theatre, Fort Worth, TX; the Alley Theatre, Houston, TX; and with the Center Stage, Baltimore, MD.

Film Appearances:
Futz, Commonwealth United, 1969.

Tom Black Bull, *When the Legends Die,* Twentieth Century-Fox, 1972.

Tony, *The Don Is Dead* (also known as *Beautiful but Deadly* and *The Deadly Kiss*), Universal, 1973.

Rut, *The Gravy Train* (also known as *The Dion Brothers*), Columbia, 1974.

Mark, *The Conversation,* Paramount, 1974.

Scott Alexander, *Permission to Kill* (also known as *Vollmacht zum Mord*), Avco-Embassy, 1975.

Cary, *The Missouri Breaks,* United Artists, 1976.

Eugene Scott, *It Lives Again* (also known as *It's Alive II* and *It's Alive 2*), Warner Bros., 1978.

Dyer, *The Rose,* Twentieth Century-Fox, 1979.

Hicks, the "chef," *Apocalypse Now,* United Artists, 1979.

Hank, *One from the Heart,* Columbia, 1982.

Dashiell Hammett, *Hammett,* Orion/Warner Bros., 1982.

Steve Richman, *Valley Girl* (also known as *Bad Boyz*), Atlantic Releasing, 1983.

Andy Jansen, *The Stone Boy,* TLC Films/Twentieth Century-Fox, 1984.

Brian Stoving, *Return* (also known *Return: A Case of Possession*), Silver Productions, 1986.

Courtney Parrish, *Where Are the Children?,* Columbia, 1986.

Buster McGuire, *Stacking* (also known as *Season of Dreams*), Spectrafilm, 1987.

Petronius, *Quo Vadis,* 1988.

Eddie Dean, *Tucker: The Man and His Dream,* Paramount, 1988.

Sonny Gibbs, *Valentino Returns,* Skouras, 1989.

Jack Burke, *Music Box,* TriStar, 1989.

Chuck Newty, *The Two Jakes,* Paramount, 1990.

The Game, Shapiro Glickenhaus Entertainment, 1991.

Nolan Tyner, *Cat Chaser,* LIVE Home Video, 1991.

Steve Delvaux, *Twin Sisters,* Vidmark Entertainment, 1992.

Walker Point warden, *Rain without Thunder,* Orion Classics, 1992.

Surplus store owner, *Falling Down,* Warner Bros., 1993.

Dr. Judd, *Dario Argento's Trauma* (also known as *Trauma*), Worldvision Home Video, 1994.

Sam Garland, *Lassie,* Paramount, 1994.

Mike Witherspoon, *Hidden Fears,* Prism Entertainment, 1994.

Dr. Paul Harkness, *Double Obsession,* Columbia TriStar Home Video, 1994.

Duane, *Chasers,* Warner Bros., 1994.

Michael Joslyn, *One Night Stand* (also known as *Before the Night*), New Horizons Home Video, 1995.

Edsel Dundee, *Boogie Boy,* 1997.

Lou Sr., *The Brave,* 1997.

Ranger MacDermot, *The End of Violence,* 1997.

Television Appearances; Series:

Captain Richard Jenko, *21 Jump Street,* Fox, 1987.

Lomax, "Die Kinder," *Mystery!,* PBS, 1991.

Television Appearances; Movies:

Larry Herman, *Larry,* CBS, 1974.

Paul Hunter, *Promise Him Anything . . . ,* ABC, 1975.

Lee Harvey Oswald, *Ruby and Oswald* (also known as *Four Days in Dallas*), CBS, 1978.

Bob Chesneau, *Saigon—Year of the Cat,* Thames Television, 1983.

Ivan Fray, *Who Will Love My Children?,* ABC, 1983.

Blaise Dietz, *Best Kept Secrets,* ABC, 1984.

Wild Bill Hickock, *Calamity Jane,* CBS, 1984.

Matt Kirby, *The Parade* (also known as *The Hit Parade*), 1984.

Richard Jahnke Sr., *Right to Kill?,* ABC, 1985.

Quo Vadis, Italian television, 1985.

Pap Finn, *The Adventures of Huckleberry Finn,* PBS, 1986.

Tim Brady, *Little Girl Lost,* ABC, 1988.

Raoul Schumacher, *Beryl Markham: A Shadow on the Sun* (also known as *Shadow on the Sun*), CBS, 1988.

Father George, *Gotham* (also known as *The Dead Can't Lie*), Showtime, 1988.

Erskine Caldwell, *Margaret Bourke-White* (also known as *Double Exposure* and *Double Exposure: The Story of Margaret Bourke-White*), TNT, 1989.

Dashiell Hammett, *Citizen Cohn* (also known as *Rules of Misconduct: The Roy Cohn Story*), HBO, 1992.

Leonard Tolliver, "The Habitation of Dragons," *TNT Screenworks,* TNT, 1992.

Sheriff Frank Yocom, *Precious Victims,* 1993.

Lieutenant Weisbad, *Against the Wall* (also known as *Attica! Attica!* and *Attica: Line of Fire*), HBO, 1994.

Jack Neuland, *Double Jeopardy,* CBS, 1996.

Admiral Pendelton, *Crash Dive* (also known as *Crash Dive: The Chase is On*), HBO, 1997.

Reasonable Force, 1997.

Television Appearances; Miniseries:

Detective Bob Keppel, *The Deliberate Stranger,* NBC, 1986.

Blue Duck, *Lonesome Dove,* CBS, 1989.

Sergeant James McSpadden, *Andersonville,* TNT, 1996.

Television Appearances; Specials:

Hearts of Darkness: A Filmmaker's Apocalypse (documentary), Showtime, 1991.

OTHER SOURCES

Periodicals:
TV Guia, issue 951, 1997, p. 84.*

FOSTER, Frances   1924-1997

OBITUARY NOTICE—See index for *CTFT* sketch: Born Frances Helen Brown, June 11, 1924, in Yonkers, NY; died of a cerebral hemorrhage, June 17, 1997, in Fairfax, VA. Actress and director. Foster was a character actress who is remembered for her work on the stage, film, and television. From 1967 to 1986, she performed with the Negro Ensemble Company in New York City. A founding member of the company, she appeared in productions such as *Brotherhood, First Breeze of Summer, Henrietta,* and *House of Shadows.* She also appeared in stage productions of *Do Lord Remember Me, A Raisin in the Sun, The Crucible, God Is a (Guess What?), Ground People,* and *Having Our Say,* among many others. Foster was the director of *Hospice* in 1983 at the New Federal Theatre in New York City. She also appeared in various films. Among them are *Cops and Robbers, Streets of Gold, The Distinguished Gentleman, The Juror, James Baldwin: The Price of the Ticket,* and *Tammy and the Doctor.* She made several films with director Spike Lee, including *Crooklyn, Malcolm X,* and *Clockers.*

Foster also appeared on many daytime dramas, including *All My Children, Ryan's Hope, One Life to Live, Search for Tomorrow, The Guiding Light,* and *Love of Life. Sesame Street* and the miniseries *North and South* are also among her credits. In addition, she served as artist in resident at the City College of New York in the mid-1970s. She also served the Actors' Equity Association as a member of its council from 1953 to 1967. Among her numerous honors are two Audelco Awards (for *Do Lord Remember Me* and *Hospice*), an Obie Award for sustained excellence performance, an Adolph Caesar Performing Arts Award, and a Black Women in the Theatre Lifetime Achievement Award.

Books:
Who's Who in America, Marquis Who's Who, 1996.

Periodicals:
Los Angeles Times, June 24, 1997, p. B8.
New York Times, June 23, 1997, p. D9.

FULLER, Sam
   See FULLER, Samuel

FULLER, Samuel   1912-1997
  (Sam Fuller)

OBITUARY NOTICE—See index for *CTFT* sketch: Born August 12, 1912, in Worcester, MA; died of natural causes, October 30, 1997, in Hollywood Hills, CA. Journalist, director, producer, writer. Fuller, who gained more popularity in Europe than he did in the United States, was an acclaimed director of low-budget films. In movies such as *I Shot Jesse James, Fixed Bayonets, Shock Corridor, White Dog,* and *The Big Red One,* Fuller penned the screenplays as well as directed. *The Big Red One,* released in 1980, was a semi-autobiographical account of his experiences during World War II. He had recorded his experiences with the combat infantry in diaries, which he later used to script the film. Fuller mainly used black and white photography for his tales and filmed them fast on a shoe-string budget. Fuller began his career as a journalist, first working as a copyboy for Arthur Brisbane of the *New York Evening Journal.* His later reporting pursuits took him to the *New York Evening Graphic* and the *San Diego Sun.* His first motion picture screenplays were *Hats Off* and *It Happened in Hollywood,* both released in 1937. After writing and directing a few films in the 1940s, with time out for service in the U.S. Army, he began filmmaking in earnest in the 1950s with productions such as *The Baron of Arizona, Scandal Sheet, Pickup on South Street, Forty Guns,* and *China Gate.* In the 1960s he remade *Pickup on South Street* as *Capetown Affair,* and created films such as *Merrill's Marauders* and *The Naked Kiss.* His later films included *The Big Red One, Street of No Return,* and *White Dog.* He appeared in numerous films, including *All Night Long* and *Hammett.* According to the *New York Times,* "Fuller objected to his films being called B-movies. He said that to him, a B-movie was 'a $20 million film with no content,' adding 'I always thought that "A" and "B" should stand for content, not how much a picture costs.'" In addition to his film career, he appeared in the television production of *The Blood of Others* and directed and wrote episodes of *The Virginian* and *The Iron Horse.* Fuller also established himself as a writer of fiction with *Burn, Baby, Burn!, The Dark Page, Dead Pigeon on Beethoven Street,* and *Pecos Bill and the Soho Kid.*

OBITUARIES AND OTHER SOURCES

Books:

Who's Who in America, Marquis Who's Who, 1997.

Periodicals:

Los Angeles Times, October 31, 1997, p. B10.
New York Times, November 1, 1997, p. D16.
Washington Post, November 1, 1997, p. B6.

G

GALLAGHER, Megan   1960-
(Meg Gallagher)

PERSONAL

Born February 6, 1960, in Reading, PA. *Education:* Juilliard School of Music, B.A. (drama division).

Addresses: *Agent*—c/o The Gersh Agency Inc., 232 N. Canon Dr., Beverly Hills, CA 90210.

Career: Actress. Performer with John Houseman's Acting Company.

Awards, Honors: Theatre World Award, 1990, and Outer Critics Circle Award, outstanding debut, both for *A Few Good Men.*

CREDITS

Television Appearances; Series:
Louella, *Dallas,* CBS, 1979-81.
Detective Tina Russo, *Hill Street Blues,* NBC, 1986-87.
Judy Ralston, *The "Slap" Maxwell Story,* ABC, 1987-88.
Wayloo Marie Holmes, *China Beach,* ABC, 1988-89.
Detective Sandy Calloway, *Pacific Station,* NBC, 1991-92.
Jeannie Sanders, *The Larry Sanders Show,* HBO, 1992-93.
Alyson Veil, *Nowhere Man,* UPN, 1995-96.
Catherine Black, *Millennium,* Fox, 1996-97.

Television Appearances; Movies:
Ellen Easton, *Sins of the Past,* ABC, 1984.
Laura McKillin, . . .*And Then She Was Gone* (also known as *And Then She Was Gone, In a Stranger's Hand, Lost and Found,* and *Trouble-shooter*), NBC, 1991.
Shannon, *Justice in a Small Town* (also known as *Ordinary Heroes: The Sandra Prine Story* and *The Sandra Prine Story*), NBC, 1994.
Joanna Hocken, *The Birds II: Land's End,* Showtime, 1994.
Annie Sobel, *Breaking Free,* The Disney Channel, 1995.
Karen Hughes, *Trade-Off* (also known as *Trade Off*), Showtime, 1995.
Veronica, *Abducted: A Father's Love* (also known as *Father: Fugitive from Justice*), NBC, 1996.

Television Appearances; Miniseries:
Peggy Shippen, *George Washington,* CBS, 1984.
Pauline, *Champagne Charlie,* syndicated, 1989.

Television Appearances; Episodic:
Reporter, "The Violence of Summer," *Law & Order,* NBC, 1991.
Mareel, "Invasive Procedures," *Star Trek: Deep Space Nine,* syndicated, 1993.
Sydney Hall, "Dairy Queen," *Picket Fences,* CBS, 1993.
Nurse Garland, "Little Green Men," *Star Trek: Deep Space Nine,* syndicated, 1995.
Alyson Veil, "Absolute Zero," *Nowhere Man,* UPN, 1995.
Cathy Snyder, *ER,* NBC, 1996.
Alyson Veil, "Zero Minus Ten," *Nowhere Man,* UPN, 1996.

Television Appearances; Pilots:
Audrey Ritter, *At Your Service,* NBC, 1984.

Stage Appearances:

Elmire, *Tartuffe,* Acting Company, American Place Theatre, New York City, 1983.

W2, "Play," and Ru, "Krapp's Last Tape," in *"Play" and Other Plays,* Acting Company, American Place Theatre, 1983.

Title role, *Miss Julie,* Theatre of the Open Eye, New York City, 1985.

All's Well That Ends Well, Colorado Shakespeare Festival, Boulder, CO, 1981.

Oliver, Oliver, Long Wharf Theatre, New Haven, CT, 1984.

Lieutenant Commander Joanne Galloway, *A Few Good Men,* Music Box Theatre, New York City, 1989-90.

Harper Pitt, *Angels in America: Perestroika,* Walter Kerr Theatre, New York City, 1993-94.

Harper Pitt and Martin Heller, *Angels in America: Millennium Approaches,* Walter Kerr Theatre, 1993-94.

Appeared as Ann, *Man and Superman,* and in *Major Barbara,* both Baltimore, MD; also appeared in *Come and Go.*

Major Tours:

Roxanne, *Cyrano de Bergerac,* U.S. cities, 1985-86.

Also appeared in *Twelfth Night* and *The Country Wife,* both Acting Company, U.S. cities.

Film Appearances:

(As Meg Gallagher) *Fyre,* 1978.

Sandra Molloy, *The Ambulance,* Triumph Releasing, 1993.

Anna Hennessey, *Crosscut,* A-pix Entertainment, 1996.

RECORDINGS

Taped Readings:

Recorded *Remember Me* and *Moonlight Becomes You* by Mary Higgins Clark and *Range of Motion* by Elizabeth Berg.*

GARR, Teri   1949(?)-
(Terry Garr)

PERSONAL

Full name, Teri Ann Garr; born December 11, 1949 (some sources say 1952), in Los Angeles, CA (some sources say Lakewood, OH); daughter of Eddie (a vaudeville performer) and Phyllis (a dancer and model; maiden name, Lind) Garr; married John O'Neil (a contractor), November, 1993; children: Molly. *Education:* Graduated from California State University, Northridge, with a degree in speech and drama; studied under Stella Adler and Lee Strasberg.

Addresses: *Agent*—Brillstein/Grey, 9150 Wilshire Blvd., Suite 350, Beverly Hills, CA 90212-3430. *Publicist*— Pat Kingsley, PMK Public Relations, Inc., 955 South Camillo Dr., No. 200, Los Angeles, CA 90048.

Career: Actress. Former dancer with the San Francisco Ballet.

Member: Screen Actors Guild, American Federation of Television and Radio Artists.

Awards, Honors: Academy Award nomination, best supporting actress, 1982, for *Tootsie.*

CREDITS

Film Appearances:

For Pete's Sake!, Worldwide, 1966.

(Uncredited) Showgirl, *Viva Las Vegas,* 1968.

Testy True, *Head,* Columbia, 1968.

Terri, *Maryjane,* American International, 1968.

Changes, Cinerama, 1969.

Tourist's wife, *The Moonshine War,* Metro-Goldwyn-Mayer, 1970.

Amy, *The Conversation,* Paramount, 1974.

Inga, *Young Frankenstein,* Twentieth Century-Fox, 1974.

Fluffy Peters, *Won Ton Ton, the Dog Who Saved Hollywood,* Paramount, 1976.

Ronnie Neary, *Close Encounters of the Third Kind,* Columbia, 1977.

Robbie Landers, *Oh, God!,* Warner Bros., 1977.

Margaret Lightman, *Witches' Brew,* 1978.

Alec's mother, *The Black Stallion,* United Artists, 1979.

Ericka Kramer, *Honky Tonk Freeway,* Universal/Anchor, 1981.

Arlene, *The Escape Artist,* Orion/Warner Bros., 1982.

Frannie, *One from the Heart,* Columbia, 1982.

Sandy, *Tootsie,* Columbia, 1982.

Alec's mother, *The Black Stallion Returns,* Metro-Goldwyn-Mayer/United Artists, 1983.

Caroline Butler, *Mr. Mom,* Twentieth Century-Fox, 1983.

Veronica, *The Sting II,* Universal, 1983.

Wendy, *Firstborn,* Paramount, 1984.

Julie, *After Hours,* Warner Bros., 1985.

Jean Briggs, *Miracles,* Orion, 1987.

Louise, *Full Moon in Blue Water,* Trans World, 1988.

Sunny Cannald, *Out Cold,* Hemdale, 1988.

Stiffs, 1988.

Pam Trotter, *Let It Ride,* Paramount, 1989.

Carolyn Simpson, *Short Time,* Twentieth Century-Fox, 1990.

Kay Harris, *Waiting for the Light,* Columbia TriStar Home Video, 1990.

Herself, *The Player,* Fine Line, 1992.

Marge Nelson, *Mom and Dad Save the World,* Warner Bros., 1992.

Save the Rabbits (short), 1994.

Louise Hamilton, *Ready to Wear* (also known as *Pret-a-Porter*), Miramax, 1994.

Helen Swanson, *Dumb and Dumber,* New Line Cinema, 1994.

Laney Tolbert, *Perfect Alibi,* WarnerVision Films, 1995.

Judge Esther Newberg, *Michael,* New Line Cinema, 1996.

Connie, *Changing Habits,* Initial Entertainment Group, 1996.

Rena, *A Simple Wish,* Universal, 1997.

Also appeared in *Lies.*

Television Appearances; Series:

Dancer, *Shindig,* ABC, 1965-66.

The Ken Berry "Wow" Show, ABC, 1972.

Mabel, *Banyon,* NBC, 1972-73.

The Burns and Schreiber Comedy Hour, ABC, 1973.

Amber, *The Girl with Something Extra,* NBC, 1973-74.

The Sonny and Cher Comedy Hour, CBS, 1973-74.

The Sonny Comedy Review, ABC, 1974.

Cher, 1975-76.

Paige Turner, *Good Advice,* CBS, 1993-94.

Sissy Emerson, *Women of the House,* CBS, 1995.

Television Appearances; Episodic:

Girl, "Instant Freeze," *Batman,* CBS, 1966.

(As Terry Garr) Roberta Lincoln, "Assignment: Earth," *Star Trek,* NBC, 1968.

(As Terry Garr) Maggie Philbin, "Guess Who's Coming to Rio?," *It Takes a Thief,* ABC, 1969.

(As Terry Garr) "The Beautiful People," *It Takes a Thief,* ABC, 1969.

Airline employee, "Felix Flies," *The Odd Couple,* ABC, 1972.

Miss Brennan, "Confessions of an Orthodontist," *The Bob Newhart Show,* CBS, 1973.

Miss Brennan, "Emily in for Carol," *The Bob Newhart Show,* CBS, 1973.

Helen Schaefer, "Pack of Lies," *Hallmark Hall of Fame,* CBS, 1987.

Robin Stone, "Drive, She Said," *Trying Times,* PBS, 1987.

Helen Eagles, "Teri Garr in Flapjack Floozie," *Cinemax Comedy Experiment,* Cinemax, 1988.

"The Trap" (also known as "Loved to Death" and "Carrion Death"), *Tales from the Crypt,* HBO, 1991.

Marsha Pegler, "A Quiet Little Neighborhood, a Perfect Little Murder" (also known as "Honey, Let's Kill the Neighbors"), *The Don and Judy Show,* NBC, 1991.

Voiceover, *The Legend of Prince Valiant,* 1991.

The Duchess, *Adventures in Wonderland,* 1992.

Sandra McCadden, "And Bimbo Was His Name-O," *Dream On,* HBO, 1992.

"Bump in the Night," *Murphy Brown,* CBS, 1993.

"The Breakdown: Part 2," *The Larry Sanders Show,* HBO, 1993.

Nancy (guest caller), "She's the Boss," *Frasier,* NBC, 1993.

"It's the Thing of the Principal," *Duckman* (animated), USA Network, 1994.

American Cinema, PBS, 1995.

Carol, "Christmas," *Men Behaving Badly,* NBC, 1996.

Herself, "Time Machine," *The Weird Al Show,* CBS, 1997.

Phoebe Abbot, "The One at the Beach," *Friends,* NBC, 1997.

Phoebe Abbot, "The One with Phoebe's Uterus," *Friends,* NBC, 1998.

Also appeared as the Princess, "The Tale of the Frog Prince," *Faerie Tale Theatre,* Showtime, and on *McCloud.*

Television Appearances; Miniseries:

Talon Kensington, *Fresno,* CBS, 1986.

Television Appearances; Movies:

Rita Wusinski, *Law and Order,* NBC, 1976.

Kelli Fisher, *Doctor Franken* (also known as *The Franken Project*), NBC, 1980.

Amy McCleary, *Prime Suspect* (also known as *Cry of Innocence*), CBS, 1982.

Mary Hawley, *John Steinbeck's The Winter of Our Discontent* (also known as *The Winter of Our Discontent*), CBS, 1983.

Hannah Winter, *To Catch a King,* HBO, 1984.

The History of White People in America, Part I, 1985.

Sally Bierston, *Intimate Strangers,* CBS, 1986.

Jill, *Mother Goose Rock 'n' Rhyme,* The Disney Channel, 1990.

Randi Thompson, *Stranger in the Family* (also known as *My Son's Memories*), ABC, 1991.

Susan Woolley, *Deliver Them from Evil: The Taking of Alta View,* CBS, 1992.

Brenda Burrows, *Fugitive Nights: Danger in the Desert,* NBC, 1993.

Storytime, PBS, 1994.

Cindy Dubroski, *Double Jeopardy,* CBS, 1996.

Elizabeth Monroe, *Ronnie and Julie,* Showtime, 1997.

Julie Ordwell, *Nightscream,* NBC, 1997.

Joanna McGrath, *Murder Live!,* NBC, 1997.

Television Appearances; Specials:

"Death at Dinner," *The Booth,* PBS, 1985.

Guest, *Deja Vu,* syndicated, 1985.

The Night of 100 Stars II, ABC, 1985.

David Letterman's 2nd Annual Holiday Film Festival, NBC, 1986.

David Letterman's Old-Fashioned Christmas, NBC, 1987.

"Martin Mull Live! From North Ridgeville," *HBO Comedy Hour,* HBO, 1987.

"Paul Reiser: Out on a Whim," *On Location,* HBO, 1987.

Host, *Jackie Gleason: The Great One* (also known as *How Sweet It Is: A Wake for Jackie Gleason*), CBS, 1988.

Memories Then and Now, CBS, 1988.

Host, *Celebration of Country,* ABC, 1991.

Host, *Love Laughs,* Lifetime, 1991.

An American Saturday Night, ABC, 1991.

The Best of Disney: Fifty Years of Magic, ABC, 1991.

Math: Who Needs It?, PBS, 1991.

TGIF Comedy Preview, ABC, 1991.

David Steinberg's Biased and Insensitive Review of the Year, Arts and Entertainment, 1992.

The Full Wax, 1992.

Host, *Growing Up Scared: Giving Childhood Back to Our Kids,* NBC, 1994.

Edna Doe, *The Whole Shebang,* Arts and Entertainment, 1993.

Edna Time, Fox, 1993.

The NFL at 75: An All-Star Celebration, ABC, 1995.

The American Film Institute Salute to Steven Spielberg, NBC, 1995.

Shining Time Station Family Special: One of the Family, PBS, 1995.

Celebrity First Loves, Fox, 1995.

Mrs. Bickerstaff, *Aliens for Breakfast,* ABC, 1995.

Host, "Pacific Coast Highway," *Great Drives,* 1996.

Television Appearances; Awards Presentations:

The 58th Annual Academy Awards Presentation, ABC, 1986.

The Movie Awards, CBS, 1991.

The 7th Annual American Comedy Awards, ABC, 1993.

Presenter, *The 50th Annual Golden Globe Awards,* TBS, 1993.

Television Appearances; Pilots:

Denise, *Good and Evil,* ABC, 1991.

Death and Taxes, 1993.

Stage Appearances:

Helen, *One Crack Out,* Marymount Manhattan Theatre, New York City, 1978.

Billie Moore, *Broadway,* Wilbur Theatre, Boston, MA, 1978.

"The Good Parts," *Second Annual New Plays Festival,* Actors Studio, New York City, 1979.

Ladyhouse Blues, Queens Theatre, New York City, 1979.

Night of 100 Stars II, Radio City Music Hall, New York City, 1985.

"Play," and Mommy, "The American Dream," *50/60 Vision: Plays and Playwrights That Changed the Theatre! Thirteen Plays in Repertory,* Center Theatre Group, Mark Taper Forum, Los Angeles, CA, 1989-90.

Major Tours:

Toured as a dancer in *West Side Story,* U.S. cities; also danced with the San Francisco Ballet and the Los Angeles Ballet.

Videos:

Appeared on *Mr. Mike's Mondo Video,* 1979.

OTHER SOURCES

Periodicals:

Cosmopolitan, July, 1983, p. 72.

Entertainment Weekly, February 17, 1995, p. 49.

Glamour, September, 1983, p. 346.

Interview, May, 1990, p. 32.

People, February 21, 1983, p. 43; October 28, 1991, p. 89.

Playboy, May, 1988, p. 114.

Redbook, August, 1990, p. 66.*

GARR, Terry
    See GARR, Teri

GEARY, Anthony 1947-

PERSONAL

Born May 29, 1947, in Coalville, UT; son of a contractor and a homemaker. *Education:* Attended the University of Utah. *Avocational interests:* Traveling, scuba diving, in-line skating, swimming, hip hop dancing, riding horses.

Addresses: *Manager*—Raymond Katz Enterprises, 3455 North Maple, Suite 297, Beverly Hills, CA 90210.

Career: Actor. Worked as a nightclub entertainer and a teacher of improvisation and theatrical techniques. Also worked as a toy salesperson.

Awards, Honors: Cindy Award, Information Film Producers of America, 1979, for *The 9 P.M. Turn-On;* Daytime Emmy Award, outstanding actor in a daytime drama, 1981, for *General Hospital;* and Cindy Award, Information Film Producers of America, for *Sound of Sunshine, Sound of Rain.*

CREDITS

Stage Appearances:
Tom, *The Glass Menagerie,* Los Angeles Theatre Center, Los Angeles, CA, 1987.
The Wild Duck, Los Angeles Theatre Center, 1990-91.

Also appeared in *The Inspector General, The Cat's Paw, The Glass Menagerie,* and *Barabbas,* all at the Los Angeles Theatre Center. Appeared with Sid Caesar and Imogene Coca in *Your Show of Shows,* Frontier Hall, Las Vegas, NV.

Major Tours:
The Subject Was Roses, U.S. cities, 1967.

Also toured as the title role, *Jesus Christ Superstar.*

Film Appearances:
Blood Sabbath, 1969.
Redhead, *Johnny Got His Gun,* Cinemation, 1971.
Bork, *The Amazing Captain Nemo,* 1978.
Stonewall, *Pass the Ammo,* New Century/Vista, 1987.
Larry, *Private Investigations,* Metro-Goldwyn-Mayer/United Artists, 1987.
Winslow Lowry, *Disorderlies,* Warner Bros., 1987.
Serenghetti, *Penitentiary III,* Cannon, 1987.

Tony, *You Can't Hurry Love* (also known as *Greetings from L.A.* and *Lovestruck*), Vestron, 1987.
Mickey, *Dangerous Love,* 1988.
Wheel, *It Takes Two,* 1988.
Dockett, *Crack House,* 21st Century, 1989.
Philo, *UHF* (also known as *The Vidiot from UHF*), Orion, 1989.
Night Life, RCA/Columbia Pictures Home Video, 1991.
Lynch, *Night of the Warrior,* Trimark Pictures, 1991.
Preacher, *Scorchers,* FoxVideo, 1992.

Television Appearances; Series:
George Curtis, *The Young and the Restless,* CBS, 1976.
Luke Spencer, *General Hospital,* ABC, 1978-83.
Luke Spencer and Bill Eckert, *General Hospital,* ABC, 1991—.

Also appeared as David Lockhart, *Bright Promise,* NBC.

Television Appearances; Episodic:
Lieutenant Alexandrov, "From Russia . . . With Blood," *Murder, She Wrote,* CBS, 1989.
Eric Grant, "Hannigan's Wake," *Murder, She Wrote,* CBS, 1990.
Clayton Cole, "Who Killed the Centerfold?," *Burke's Law,* CBS, 1995.

Also appeared as Greg Houser, *The Partridge Family,* ABC; and as Gary Jelinek, "The Thrill Killers," *The Streets of San Francisco,* ABC; also appeared in *All in the Family,* CBS; *Hotel,* ABC; *Mannix,* CBS; *Room 222,* ABC; *The Six Million Dollar Man,* ABC; and *Star Search,* syndicated.

Television Appearances; Movies:
Dr. Kyle Richardson, *Intimate Agony,* ABC, 1983.
Cade Malloy, *The Imposter,* ABC, 1984.
Lieutenant Andy Malovich, *Sins of the Past,* ABC, 1984.
Martin Cheever, *Kicks,* ABC, 1985.
Steve Reynolds, *Perry Mason: The Case of the Murdered Madam,* NBC, 1987.
Stephen Pugliotti, *Do You Know the Muffin Man?,* CBS, 1989.
Dr. Jim Cole, *High Desert Kill* (also known as *Desert Kill* and *The Hunters*), USA Network, 1989.

Also appeared in *Sorority Kill,* ABC.

Television Appearances; Specials:
The Osmond Family Thanksgiving Special, NBC, 1981.

I Love Liberty, ABC, 1982.

Octavius Caesar, *Antony and Cleopatra,* PBS and BBC, 1983.

Celebrity Daredevils, ABC, 1983.

Hollywood's Private Home Movies II, ABC, 1983.

The Funniest Joke I Ever Heard, ABC, 1984.

Sam Billings, *You Are the Jury,* 1986.

Host (with Ellen DeGeneres, Genie Francis, Joey Lawrence, and Jerry Van Dyke), *Before They Were Stars,* ABC, 1994.

Fifty Years of Soaps: An All-Star Celebration (also known as *50 Years of Soaps: An All-Star Celebration*), CBS, 1994.

Television Appearances; Awards Presentations:

The 18th Annual Daytime Emmy Awards, 1991.

Presenter, *The 20th Annual Daytime Emmy Awards,* ABC, 1993.

Presenter, *The 22nd Annual Daytime Emmy Awards,* NBC, 1995.

Luke Spencer, *General Hospital: Twist of Fate,* ABC, 1996.

Radio Producer; Series:

Produced *The 9 P.M. Turn-On.*

Radio Producer; Specials:

Produced *Sound of Sunshine, Sound of Rain,* Public Radio.

OTHER SOURCES

Periodicals:

Entertainment Weekly, November 5, 1993, p. 15; November, 22, 1996, p. 154.

People Weekly, June 14, 1993, pp. 83-84.

TV Guide, October 16, 1993, pp. 12-15; October 26, 1996, p. 79; December 28, 1996, p. 49; May 17, 1997, pp. 42-45.*

GEORGE, Colin   1929-

PERSONAL

Born September 20, 1929, in Pembroke Dock, Wales; son of Edward Thomas and Helen Mary (Sandercock) George; married Dorothy Vernon. *Education:* Surrey and University College, Oxford, M.A.

Addresses: *Office*—Hong Kong Academy for the Performing Arts, G.P.O. Box 12288, Hong Kong.

Career: Director and actor. Elizabethan Theatre Company, cofounder and actor, 1953; Nottingham Playhouse, director, 1957; Sheffield Playhouse, Sheffield, England, associate director, 1962-64; Ludlow Festival, artistic director, 1964-66; Sheffield Playhouse and Crucible Theatre, Sheffield, England, director, 1965-74; Theatre Vanguard, founder, 1967; Crucible Theatre, Sheffield, England, advisor and director, 1971; University of New England, New South Wales, Australia, founder of department of drama, 1975; State Theatre Company, Adelaide, Australia, artistic director, 1977-80; Haymarket Theatre, Leicester, England, director, 1980-81; Hong Kong Academy for the Performing Arts, Hong Kong, head of acting, stage movement, English production, 1984—; Coventry and Birmingham Repertory, actor; and Royal Shakespeare Company, member.

CREDITS

Stage Appearances:

Jack Lucas, *Celebration,* Duchess Theatre, London, England, 1961.

First senator, *Coriolanus,* Barbican Theatre, London, England, 1995.

Friar, *Measure For Measure,* Barbican Theatre, 1995.

Begriffenfeldt and strange passenger, *Peer Gynt,* Young Vic Theatre, London, England, 1995.

Second barker, Palau, and stage manager, *Les Enfants du Paradis,* Barbican Theatre, 1996.

Stage Work; Director:

Romeo and Juliet, National Children's Theatre, Belgrade, Yugoslavia, 1959.

Richard III, Old Vic Theatre, London, England, 1962.

The Duchess of Malfi, Warsaw, Poland, 1967.

Vatslav, Stratford, Ontario, Canada, 1968.

The Hostage, N.A.C., Ottawa, Ontario, Canada, 1968.

Playboy of the Western World, Abbey Theatre, Dublin, Ireland, 1969.

Strip Jack Naked, Royal Court Theatre, London, England, 1969.

Oedipus Rex, 1978.

Elisir D'Amore, State Opera S.A., Australia, 1979.

Just Ruth, Australia, 1979.

Last Day in Wooloomooloo, Australia, 1979.

A Manual of Trench Warfare, Australia, 1979.

Marx, Australia, 1979.

Too Early to Say, Australia, 1979.

Mystery Plays of Wakefield, Adelaide Festival, Adelaide, Australia, 1980.

Whale Music, Haymarket Theatre, Leicester, England, 1980.

Falstaff, Haymarket Theatre, 1981.

Servant of Two Masters, Chung Ying Theater Company, Hong Kong, 1981.

The Pearl Fishers, Chung Ying Theater Company, 1981.

The Magic Flute, Chung Ying Theater Company, 1981.

Royal Hunt of the Sun, Hong Kong Academy for the Performing Arts, Hong Kong, 1984.

Fidelio, Academy for the Performing Arts, 1984.

Major Tours:

Toured as an actor, Elizabethan Theatre Company, British cities, 1953.

Film Appearances:

Burke, *Shadow of China,* 1990.

OTHER SOURCES

Theatre Record (London), June 4-17, 1995, p. 745; July 30-August 12, 1995, p. 1071; August 27-September 9, 1995, p. 1210; January 29-February 11, 1996, p. 117.*

GILBERT, Ronnie   1926-

PERSONAL

Born September 7, 1926, in New York, NY; daughter of Charles (a factory worker) and Sarah (a dressmaker) Gilbert; married Martin Weg (divorced, 1959); children: Lisa. *Education:* Lone Mountain College, M.A. (clinical psychology), 1974. *Politics:* Progressive.

Addresses: *Office*—Redwood Records, 476 W. MacArthur Blvd., Oakland, CA 94609.

Career: Singer and actress. Member of various singing groups, including the Priority Ramblers, c. 1942, the Weavers, 1948-52 and 1955-63; and HARP (Holly Near, Arlo Guthrie, Ronnie Gilbert, and Pete Seeger), toured in 1984. Toured as a solo singer in 1962-64 and 1985; toured with Holly Near, 1983-84. Also acted with the Open Theatre.

CREDITS

Stage Appearances:

The Man in the Glass Booth, Royale Theatre, New York City, 1968.

Is This Real?, Terrace Theater, John F. Kennedy Center for the Performing Arts, Washington, DC, 1985.

Title role, *Mother Jones,* Stackner Cabaret, Milwaukee Repertory Theatre, Milwaukee, WI, 1991-92, then Berkeley Repertory Theatre, Berkeley, CA, 1993.

Also appeared in *Antigone* and *Specimen Days,* both Public Theatre, New York City; *Re-Arrangements, Tourists and Refugees,* and *Trespassing,* all Theatre La MaMa, New York City; *Medea* and *Tongues & Savage Love,* both St. Louis Repertory Theatre, St. Louis, MO; *Houdini,* Lamb's Theatre, New York City; *America Hurrah,* Royal Court Theatre, London, England; *Happy Days,* Waterfront Theatre, Vancouver, British Columbia, Canada; *Playgrounds (Dance Play),* Vancouver Playhouse, Toronto, Ontario, Canada; *Tourists and Refugees II,* Venezuela Festival, Caracas, Venezuela; *A Christmas Carol,* Ford's Theatre, Washington, DC; and *The Roundhouse* and *The Tempest,* both London, England.

Stage Work; Director:

(With Dianne Houston) *Is This Real?,* Terrace Theater, John F. Kennedy Center for the Performing Arts, 1985.

Major Tours:

Appeared in *Trio* (also known as *Lies and Secrets*), New York City; London, England; Edinburgh, Scotland; and Paris, France. Also appeared in *Three Journeys of Aladdin,* New York City, Rennes, France; Angers, France; Orleans, France; Paris, France; London, England; and Glasgow, Scotland.

Film Appearances:

Reporter, *Danger Woman,* Universal, 1946.

Herself, *Festival* (documentary) Patchke Productions, 1967.

Miss Chase, *Isadora* (also known as *The Loves of Isadora*), Universal, 1968.

Mother, *Windflowers* (also known as *The Story of a Draft Dodger*), Film-Makers, 1968.

Herself, *The Weavers: Wasn't That a Time* (documentary), 1981.

Hard Travelin', 1985.

Herself, *Women of Summer,* 1985.

Mace, *Club Life,* Troma, 1987.

Second Mugger, *Crossing Delancey,* Warner Bros., 1988.

Mrs. Taylor, *Running on Empty,* Warner Bros., 1988.

Narrator, *Forever Activists* (documentary), Tara Releasing, 1991.

Also appeared in *Going On, The Hopi: Songs from the Fourth World,* and *Loin de Vietnam.*

Television Appearances; Specials:
Song performer, *Sing Out America! With Judy Collins,* 1989.
"Peter, Paul & Mary: Lifelines," *Great Performances,* PBS, 1996.

Television Appearances; Miniseries:
Voice, *The Civil War,* PBS, 1990.

RECORDINGS

The Spirit Is Free, Redwood, 1985.

Recorded extensively with the Weavers, 1950-81, for Decca, Vanguard and Loom Records, including: *Folk Songs Around the World; Carnegie Hall, Vols. I and II; Fifteenth Reunion; American Folk Singers and Balladeers; Reunion at Carnegie Hall; The Weavers: Together Again;* others. Also *Legend of Bessie Smith,* RCA Victor; *Alone with Ronnie Gilbert,* Mercury; others.

WRITINGS

Plays; Unless Indicated Otherwise:
Is This Real?, Terrace Theatre, John F. Kennedy Center for the Performing Arts, 1985.
Author of book for musical, *Mother Jones,* Stackner Cabaret, Milwaukee Repertory Theatre, 1991-92, then Berkeley Repertory Theatre, Berkeley, CA, 1993.

Nonfiction:
Ronnie Gilbert on Mother Jones, Conari Press (Berkeley, CA), 1993.

OTHER SOURCES

Periodicals:
American Theatre, July-August, 1993, pp. 47-48.*

GILL, Peter　1939-

PERSONAL

Born September 7, 1939, in Cardiff, Wales; son of George John and Margaret Mary (Browne) Gill. *Education:* Attended secondary school in Cardiff.

Addresses: *Agent*—Casarotto Ramsey Ltd., 60-66 Wardour St., London W1V 3HP, England.

Career: Director, writer, and actor. Worked as an actor, 1957-67; Royal Court Theatre, London, associate director, 1970-72; Riverside Studios, Hammersmith, England, director, 1976-80, associate director, 1980; National Theatre, London, associate director, 1980-84, director of National Theatre Studio, 1984-90.

Awards, Honors: First prize for a play, Belgrade International Theatre Festival, 1968, for *The Daughter-in-Law;* George Devine Award, 1968; member, Order of the British Empire, 1980.

CREDITS

Stage Work; Director:
A Collier's Friday Night, Royal Court Theatre, London, 1965.
The Local Stigmatic, Royal Court Theatre, 1966.
The Ruffian on the Stair, Royal Court Theatre, 1966.
A Provincial Life, Royal Court Theatre, 1966.
The Local Stigmatic, Traverse Theatre, London, 1966.
The Dwarfs, Traverse Theatre, 1966.
O'Flaherty VC, Mermaid Theatre, London, 1966.
A Soldier's Fortune, Royal Court Theatre, 1967.
The Daughter-in-Law, Royal Court Theatre, 1967.
Crimes of Passion, Royal Court Theatre, 1967.
The Widowing of Mrs. Holroyd, Royal Court Theatre, 1968.
Life Price, Royal Court Theatre, 1969.
Over Gardens Out, Royal Court Theatre, 1969.
The Sleeper's Den, Royal Court Theatre, 1969.
Much Ado about Nothing, Stratford, Ontario, Canada, 1969.
Landscape and Silence, Lincoln Center, New York City, 1970.
Hedda Gabler, Stratford, Ontario, Canada, 1970.
The Duchess of Malfi, Royal Court Theatre, 1971.
Macbeth, Stratford, Ontario, Canada, 1971.
Crete and Sergeant Pepper, Royal Court Theatre, 1972.
A Midsummer Night's Dream, Zurich Schauspielhaus, Zurich, Switzerland, 1972.
The Daughter-in-Law, Bochum Schauspielhaus, 1972.
The Merry-Go-Round, Royal Court Theatre, 1973.
Twelfth Night, Stratford-upon-Avon, England, 1974.
Fishing, New York Shakespeare Festival, 1975.
As You Like It, Nottingham Playhouse, Nottingham, England, then Edinburgh Festival, Edinburgh, Scotland, both 1975, later Riverside Studios, Hammersmith, England, 1976.

The Fool, Royal Court Theatre, 1976.
As You Like It, Riverside Studios, 1976.
Small Change, Royal Court Theatre, 1976, then Riverside Studios, 1977.
The Cherry Orchard, Riverside Studios, 1978.
The Changeling, Riverside Studios, 1978.
Measure for Measure, Riverside Studios, 1978.
Julius Caesar, Riverside Studios, 1980.
Scrape off the Black, Riverside Studios, 1980.
Don Juan, National Theatre, London, 1981.
Scrape Off the Black, National Theatre, 1981.
Much Ado about Nothing, National Theatre, 1981.
A Month in the Country, National Theatre, 1981.
Danton's Death, National Theatre, 1983.
Major Barbara, National Theatre, 1983.
Small Change, National Theatre, 1983.
Kick for Touch, National Theatre, 1983.
Tales from Hollywood, National Theatre, 1983.
(Codirector) *Antigone,* National Theatre, 1983.
Venice Preserv'd, National Theatre, 1984.
Fool for Love, National Theatre, 1984.
As I Lay Dying, National Theatre, 1984.
The Garden of England, National Theatre, 1984.
Up for None, National Theatre, 1984.
The Murderers, National Theatre, 1985.
Twist of Lemon, National Theatre Studio, London, 1985.
In the Blue, National Theatre Studio, 1985.
Fool for Love, Lyric Theatre, London, 1985.
Bouncing, National Theatre, 1985.
(Codirector) *The Garden of England,* National Theatre, 1985.
(Codirector) *Down by the Green Wood Side,* Queen Elizabeth Hall, 1987.
(Codirector) *Bow Down,* Queen Elizabeth Hall, 1987.
Mean Tears, Cottesloe Theatre, 1987.
Marriage of Figaro, Opera North, 1987.
Mrs. Klein, Cottesloe Theatre, then Apollo Theatre, both London, 1988.
Juno and the Paycock, Lyttelton Theatre, London, 1989.
The Way of the World, Lyric Hammersmith Theatre, London, 1992.
New England, The Pit, London, 1994.
Uncle Vanya, Tricycle Theatre, London, 1995.
A Patriot for Me, Barbican Theatre, London, 1995.

Television Work; Director:
Grace, BBC, 1972.
Girl, BBC, 1973.
A Matter of Taste, BBC, 1974.
Fugitive, BBC, 1974.
Hitting Town, Thames TV, 1976.

Film Appearances:
Lieutenant D'Arblay, *Damn the Defiant!* (also known as *H.M.S. Defiant*), 1962.
Private G12 Williams, *Zulu,* 1964.

WRITINGS

Plays:
A Provincial Life (based on *My Life,* by Anton Chekhov), Royal Court Theatre, 1966.
The Sleeper's Den, Royal Court Theatre, 1969, published with *Over Gardens Out,* Calder & Boyars (London), 1970.
Over Gardens Out, Royal Court Theatre, 1969, published with *The Sleeper's Den,* Calder & Boyars, 1970.
The Merry-Go-Round (based on a play by D. H. Lawrence), Royal Court Theatre, 1973.
Small Change, Royal Court Theatre, 1976, then Riverside Studios, 1977, published with *Kick for Touch,* Marion Boyars, 1985.
Touch and Go (based on a play by Lawrence), 1980.
Kick for Touch, National Theatre, 1983, published by Samuel French (New York City), 1979, published with *Small Change,* Marion Boyars, 1985.
As I Lay Dying (based on the novel by William Faulkner), National Theatre, 1984.
In the Blue, National Theater Studio, 1985, published, 1987.
Mean Tears, Cottesloe Theatre, 1987, published, 1987.
Certain Young Men, published, 1992.
The Cherry Orchard (adaptation of a play by Chekhov), Albery Theatre, London, 1996.
Cardiff East, published by Faber and Faber (London), 1997.

OTHER SOURCES

Periodicals:
Times (London), February 17, 1983; February 25, 1983.*

GILPIN, Peri

PERSONAL

Born May 27, in Waco, TX; daughter of Jim O'Brien (a nationally known broadcaster). *Education:* Attended University of Texas at Austin; attended the British-American Academy, London.

Addresses: *Agent*—Steven Huvane, 8383 Wilshire Blvd., Suite 444, Beverly Hills, CA 90211.

Career: Actress. Began acting in commercials at age nine; worked as a makeup artist.

CREDITS

Television Appearances; Series:
Irene, *Flesh 'n' Blood,* NBC, 1991.
Roz Doyle, *Frasier,* NBC, 1993—.

Television Appearances; Episodic:
Rebecca Warfield, "Out of Body," *The Outer Limits,* Showtime, 1995.
"Etherically Yours," *The Outer Limits,* Showtime, 1996.

Also appeared in episodes of *Cheers, Wings, Designing Women, 21 Jump Street, Max Monroe: Loose Cannon,* and *Matlock.*

Television Appearances; Movies:
Charlotte, *Fight for Justice: The Nancy Conn Story* (also known as *Fighting Back: The Nancy Conn Story*), NBC, 1995.
Ellen Hayward, *The Secret She Carried* (also known as *Cradle Song*), NBC, 1996.

Television Appearances; Specials:
Host, *Christmas in Washington,* NBC, 1995.
Star Trek: 30 Years and Beyond, UPN, 1996.

Stage Appearances:
Appeared in productions at Stagewest, Springfield, MA, 1986-87; also appeared in *Lucky Lucy and the Fortune Man, The Crucible, Hawthorne County, A Midsummer Night's Dream,* and *The Maderati.*

Stage Work:
Associate producer, *The Maderati.**

GINTY, Robert 1948-

PERSONAL

Born November 14, 1948, in Brooklyn, NY; son of Michael Joseph (a construction worker) and Elsie M. (a government worker; maiden name, O'Hara) Ginty; married Francine Tacker, May, 1980 (divorced, 1983); married Lorna Patterson (an actress), November 26, 1983; children: (first marriage) James F. *Edu-*

cation: Attended Harvard University, Yale University, City University of New York, Princeton University, 1966-1970; studied acting with Sanford Meisner at the Neighborhood Playhouse, Lee Strasberg at the Actors Studio, and Herbert Berghof at Berghof Studios.

Addresses: *Agent*—International Creative Management, 8942 Wilshire Blvd., Beverly Hills, CA 90211.

Career: Actor, writer, producer, and director. Founder of Fairfax Irish Theatre Arts Foundation.

Member: Actors' Equity Association, Screen Actors Guild.

CREDITS

Stage Appearances:
(Broadway debut) *Three in One,* New York City, 1970.
Silent Partner, Actors Studio, 1971.
More Stately Mansions, Provincetown Playhouse, New York City, 1971.
Orpheus Descending, Provincetown Playhouse, 1971.
Bring It All Back Home, Provincetown Playhouse, 1971.
Great God Brown, New York City, 1972.

Appeared in *Don Juan* and *The Government Inspector,* New York City; appeared in *The Indian Wants the Bronx, The Lion in Winter, Once in a Lifetime, Cat on a Hot Tin Roof, Henry IV, Part I, A Midsummer's Night Dream, Macbeth, As You Like It,* all at the New Hampshire Shakespeare Festival.

Film Appearances:
To Have Your Cake and Eat It, 1971.
Incident of October 20th, 1971.
Children Come Back, 1971.
Dr. Khuri, *And Baby Makes Three,* 1972.
Bound for Glory, United Artists, 1976.
Vendor, *Two-Minute Warning,* Universal, 1976.
Sergeant Dink Mobley, *Coming Home,* United Artists, 1978.
John Eastland, *The Exterminator,* Avco-Embassy, 1980.
Aaron McCallum, *The Alchemist,* LIVE Home Video, 1981.
Don Tucker, *The Act* (also known as *Bless 'Em All*), Film Ventures, 1982.
Murphy, *Escarabajos Asesinos* (also known as *Scarab*), Tesauro and Alloi, 1982.

Gold Raiders, Media Home Entertainment, 1983.

Johnny Eastland, *Exterminator II,* Cannon, 1984.

Beau Donnelly, *Vivre pour Survivre* (also known as *White Fire*), Trans World Entertainment, 1984.

Cooper, *Mission Kill,* Goldfarb, 1985.

Warrior, *Warrior of the Lost World,* 1985.

Eric Matthews, *Programmed to Kill* (also known as *Retaliator*), Trans World Entertainment, 1987.

Elliot Cromwell, *Three Kinds of Heat,* Warner Home Video, 1987.

Mania, 1988.

Duke Evans, *The Bounty Hunter* (also known as *Bounty Hunters*), American International Pictures, 1989.

Monroe Bieler, *Code Name Vengeance* (also known as *Codename: Vengeance*), Action, 1989.

Joe Bodek, *Loverboy,* TriStar, 1989.

John Dee, *Out on Bail,* Trans World, 1989.

Cop Target, 1990.

Dale, *Madhouse,* Orion, 1990.

Thomas McCain, *Vietnam, Texas,* Vision/Columbia, 1990.

Thom, *Harley Davidson and the Marlboro Man,* Metro-Goldwyn-Mayer/Pathe, 1991.

Shootfighter, A.N.A. Productions, 1992.

Gibson, *Lady Dragon,* Imperial Entertainment, 1992.

Woman of Desire, Nu Image, 1994.

Robert Boyd, *Taken Alive,* DKMC, 1995.

Also appeared in *Covenant.*

Film Work; Director, Except Where Indicated:

My Father's House (short film), 1979.

Perfect Master (short film), 1979.

The Bounty Hunter, American International Pictures, 1989.

(And producer) *Vietnam, Texas,* Vision/Columbia, 1990.

Woman of Desire, Nu Image, 1994.

Television Appearances; Series:

Lieutenant T. J. Wiley, *Baa Baa Black Sheep,* NBC, 1976-78.

Thomas Anderson, *The Paper Chase,* CBS, 1978-79.

Detective Mac Riley and narrator, *Hawaiian Heat,* ABC, 1984.

Walker Daniels, *Falcon Crest,* CBS, 1989-90.

Television Appearances; Episodic:

Sacks, *Baywatch Nights,* syndicated, 1995.

Raymond Reegun, *Baywatch Nights,* syndicated, 1996.

Also appeared in *Police Story, The Rookies, Gibbsville, Griffin and Phoenix,* 1974.

Television Appearances; Movies:

Arthur Pond, *The Turning Point of Jim Malloy* (also known as *John O'Hara's Gibbsville* and *Gibbsville: The Turning Point of Jim Malloy*), NBC, 1975.

Airman Donald Berkle, *The Courage and the Passion,* NBC, 1978.

Henry Graham, *I Want to Live,* ABC, 1983.

Warren Cates, *The Big One: The Great Los Angeles Earthquake* (also known as *Earthquake Los Angeles: The Big One*), NBC, 1990.

Television Appearances; Specials:

Mr. Pearson, *The Big Stuffed Dog,* 1980.

Jack Keenan, *Hardesty House,* 1986.

The Hollywood Christmas Parade, 1989.

Television Work; Director; Episodic:

"Flight of the Pedalbee," *Dream On,* HBO, 1990.

Television Work; Director; Movies:

Here Come The Munsters, Fox, 1995.

Television Work; Director; Series:

Campus Cops, USA Network, 1996.

Nash Bridges, CBS, 1996.

Lois & Clark: The New Adventures of Superman, ABC, 1996-97.

Television Work; Executive Producer:

Hardesty House (special), 1986.

Day of Reckoning (movie; also known as *The Wisdom Keeper*), NBC, 1994.

WRITINGS

Screenplays:

The Bounty Hunter, American International Pictures, 1989.

Woman of Desire, Nu Image, 1994.

OTHER SOURCES

Periodicals:

Back Stage West, March 31, 1994, p. 3.*

GIVENS, Robin   1964(?)-

PERSONAL

Born November 27, 1964 (some sources say 1965), in New York, NY; daughter of Ruth Roper; married Mike Tyson (a boxer), February 7, 1988 (divorced,

1988). *Education:* Graduated from Sarah Lawrence College; postgraduate studies at Harvard University; attended American Academy of Dramatic Arts. *Avocational interests:* Swimming, working out, watching movies.

Addresses: *Agent*—Innovative Artists, 1999 Avenue of the Stars, Los Angeles, CA 90067.

Career: Actress; worked as a model. Never Blue Productions, New York City, founder, 1990, director, 1990—.

CREDITS

Television Appearances; Series:
Darlene Merriman, *Head of the Class,* ABC, 1986-91.
Detective Anita King, *Angel Street,* CBS, 1992-93.
Suzanne Graham, *Courthouse* (also known as *Courtroom*), CBS, 1995-96.
Wilma Cuthbert, *Sparks* (also known as *Sparks, Sparks and Sparks*), UPN, 1996—.

Also appeared in *The Guiding Light,* CBS; *Loving,* ABC; and *Philip Marlowe: Private Eye.*

Television Appearances; Episodic:
"Theo and the Older Woman," *The Cosby Show,* NBC, 1985.
"The Big Bribe," *Diff'rent Strokes,* ABC, 1986.
People Magazine on TV, CBS, 1988.
"Crime below the Waist," *Sonny Spoon,* NBC, 1988.
20/20, ABC, 1988.
"Picking up the Pieces," *People Magazine on TV,* CBS, 1989.
Denise, *The Fresh Prince of Bel-Air,* NBC, 1990.
Alex, *In the House,* NBC, 1995.

Also appeared in *Me and the Boys,* ABC.

Television Appearances; Movies:
April Baxter, *Beverly Hills Madam,* NBC, 1986.
Dinah St. Clair, *The Penthouse,* ABC, 1989.
Kiswana Browne, *The Women of Brewster Place,* NBC, 1989.
Kaye Ferrar, *Dangerous Intentions* (also known as *Nowhere to Hide* and *On Wings of Fear*), CBS, 1995.
Claudia, *A Face to Die For,* NBC, 1996.

Television Appearances; Specials:
Fallen Champ: The Untold Story of Mike Tyson (documentary), NBC, 1993.
It's Hot in Here: UPN Fall Preview, UPN, 1996.

Television Appearances; Awards Presentations:
The 15th Annual People's Choice Awards, 1989.
Blockbuster Entertainment Awards, UPN, 1997.

Film Appearances:
The Wiz, Universal, 1978.
Fort Apache, The Bronx, Twentieth Century-Fox, 1981.
Imabelle, *A Rage in Harlem,* Miramax, 1991.
Jacqueline, *Boomerang,* Paramount, 1992.
April, *Foreign Student* (also known as *L'Etudiant Etranger*), Gramercy Pictures, 1994.
Kimberly Jonz, *Blankman* (also known as *Blank Man*), Columbia, 1994.

OTHER SOURCES

Periodicals:
Interview, July, 1987, p. 68; March, 1991, p. 38.
Jet, August 15, 1994, pp. 58-61; February 27, 1995, p. 32; September 18, 1995, pp. 60-63.
People Weekly, May 11, 1987, p. 127; February 22, 1988, p. 32; October 17, 1988, p. 60; October 24, 1988, pp. 56-58.
Time, October 17, 1988, p. 65.*

GOETZ, Peter Michael 1941-

PERSONAL

Born December 10, 1941, in Buffalo, NY; son of Irving A. (a construction engineer) and Esther L. Goetz; married Constance Fleurat, June 11, 1966; children: Michael, Kevin. *Education:* Attended University of Miami, Coral Gables, FL; State University of New York College at Fredonia, B.A. (speech and theatre); Southern Illinois University, Carbondale, M.A. (playwrighting and theatre); University of Minnesota, Ph.D (theatre).

Addresses: *Agent*—Silver Massetti and Associates, 8730 Sunset Blvd., Suite 480, Los Angeles, CA 90069.

Career: Actor. Actors Theatre of Louisville, Louisville, KY, guest artist, 1989-90.

CREDITS

Stage Appearances:
Typist and the Tiger, 1968.
The Alchemist, Cricket Theatre, Minneapolis, MN, 1968.

Troilus and Cressida, University of Minnesota—Twin Cities, Minneapolis, 1968.

Malloy, *A Touch of the Poet,* Tyrone Guthrie Theatre, Minneapolis, 1969.

Mrs. Young's husband, *The Beauty Part,* Tyrone Guthrie Theatre, 1969.

Sebastian, *The Tempest,* Tyrone Guthrie Theatre, 1970.

Polly, *A Man's a Man,* Tyrone Guthrie Theatre, 1970.

Love Girl and the Innocent, Tyrone Guthrie Theatre, 1970.

Julius Caesar, Tyrone Guthrie Theatre, 1970.

Cyrano de Bergerac, Tyrone Guthrie Theatre, 1970.

Biondello, *The Taming of the Shrew,* Tyrone Guthrie Theatre, 1970.

The Relapse, Tyrone Guthrie Theatre, 1970.

Ferdinand, *The Italian Straw Hat,* Tyrone Guthrie Theatre, 1970.

Lenny, *Of Mice and Men,* Tyrone Guthrie Theatre, 1971.

Snug, *A Midsummer Night's Dream,* Tyrone Guthrie Theatre, 1971.

Pozzo, *Waiting for Godot,* Tyrone Guthrie Theatre, 1971.

Tevye, *Fiddler on the Roof,* Chanhassen Dinner Theatre, Minneapolis, 1972.

Ghost Dancer, Tyrone Guthrie Theatre, 1973.

Ekhart, *Baal,* Tyrone Guthrie Theatre, 1973.

Title role, *Becket,* Tyrone Guthrie Theatre, 1973.

Bobchinski, *The Government Inspector,* Tyrone Guthrie Theatre, 1973.

Jerry Devine, *Juno and the Paycock,* Tyrone Guthrie Theatre, 1973.

Richard, *Richard III,* St. Mary's College, Winona, MN, 1974.

Ash, *The National Health,* Tyrone Guthrie Theatre, 1974.

Ferdinand, *Love's Labour's Lost,* Tyrone Guthrie Theatre, 1974.

Cleante, *Tartuffe,* Tyrone Guthrie Theatre, 1974.

Milo Tindle, *Sleuth,* Chanhassen Dinner Theatre, 1974.

Fedot, *Chemin de Fer,* Chanhassen Dinner Theatre, 1974.

Mortimer, *Arsenic and Old Lace,* Tyrone Guthrie Theatre, 1975.

Mitch, *A Streetcar Named Desire,* Tyrone Guthrie Theatre, 1975.

Elif, *Mother Courage,* Tyrone Guthrie Theatre, 1975.

Narrator One, *Under Milkwood,* Tyrone Guthrie Theatre, 1975.

Provost, *Measure for Measure,* Tyrone Guthrie Theatre, 1975.

The Merchant of Venice, Tyrone Guthrie Theatre, 1975.

Elder One, *Oedipus,* Tyrone Guthrie Theatre, 1975.

Cornelius Hackle, *The Matchmaker,* Tyrone Guthrie Theatre, 1976.

Gooper, *Cat on a Hot Tin Roof,* Tyrone Guthrie Theatre, 1976.

Hovstad, *An Enemy of the People,* Tyrone Guthrie Theatre, 1976.

Polixines, *The Winter's Tale,* Tyrone Guthrie Theatre, 1976.

Charles Dickens, *A Christmas Carol,* Tyrone Guthrie Theatre, 1976.

Creep, *Pantagleize,* Tyrone Guthrie Theatre, 1977.

Young Marlow, *She Stoops to Conquer,* Tyrone Guthrie Theatre, 1977.

Bracciano, *The White Devil,* Tyrone Guthrie Theatre, 1977.

Fledis and King Skule, *The Pretenders,* Tyrone Guthrie Theatre, 1978.

Tyrone, *A Moon for the Misbegotten,* Tyrone Guthrie Theatre, 1978.

Benson, *Boy Meets Girl,* Tyrone Guthrie Theatre, 1979.

Podkolyossin, *Marriage,* Tyrone Guthrie Theatre, 1979.

Six roles, *Eugene O'Neill Playwrights Conference of New Plays,* Waterbury, CT, 1979 and 1980.

(New York debut) *Jail Diary of Albie Sachs,* Manhattan Theatre Club, 1980.

Balthazer, *Solomon's Child,* Long Wharf Theatre, New Haven, CT, 1980.

Rudge, *Jerusalem,* Minneapolis Children's Theatre, Minneapolis, 1980.

Jack (John Barrymore), *Ned and Jack,* Hudson Guild Theatre, then Helen Hayes Theatre, both New York City, 1981.

Ben, *The Little Foxes,* Berkshire Theatre Festival, Stockbridge, MA, 1981.

Maiden Stakes, Circle in the Square, New York City, then White Barn, CT, both 1982.

Dr. Framingham, *Beyond Therapy,* Brooks Atkinson Theatre, New York City, 1982.

Amos, *The Queen and the Rebels,* Purchase, NY, then Plymouth Theatre, New York City, 1982.

Jack Jerome, *Brighton Beach Memoirs,* Neil Simon Theatre, New York City, 1983-84.

Miss Lulu Bett, Berkshire Theatre Festival, 1984.

Starkman, *Before the Dawn,* American Place Theatre, New York City, 1985.

An Evening with Colleen Dewhurst and Peter Michael Goetz, Vistaford Lines, at sea, 1985.

Caught, Berkshire Theatre Festival, 1985.

Anton Skvoznik-Dmuchanovsky, *The Government Inspector,* Lyceum Theatre, New York City, 1994.

Made stage debut as Joey, *The Homecoming,* Tyrone Guthrie Theatre; appeared as Jack Jerome, *Brighton Beach Memoirs,* pre-Broadway tour.

Film Appearances:
(Film debut) *Just Be There,* 1973.
Jackpot, 1974.
The Director, 1975.
Selden Ross, *Wolfen,* Warner Bros., 1981.
Charles Delehuth, attorney, *Prince of the City,* Warner Bros., 1981.
John Wolfe, Jenny's publisher, *The World According to Garp,* Warner Bros., 1982.
Joyner, *Best Defense,* Paramount, 1984.
Gramps, *C.H.U.D.,* New World, 1984.
Dr. Ingersoll, *King Kong Lives,* DeLaurentiis Entertainment Group, 1986.
Mr. Page, *Jumpin' Jack Flash,* Twentieth Century-Fox, 1986.
Harley Feemer, *Beer* (also known as *The Selling of America*), Orion, 1986.
Norman Bettinger, *My Little Girl,* Hemdale Releasing, 1988.
Francis Shaw, *Glory,* TriStar, 1989.
Dr. Ethridge, *Dad,* Universal, 1989.
Dr. Welty, *My Girl,* Columbia, 1991.
John MacKenzie, *Father of the Bride,* Buena Vista, 1991.
Therapist, *Another You,* TriStar, 1991.
Judge, *Above Suspicion* (also known as *The Rhinehart Theory*), 1994.
John MacKenzie, *Father of the Bride, Part II* (also known as *Father's Little Dividend*), Buena Vista, 1995.
Dr. Hellman, *Infinity,* First Look Pictures, 1996.
Sigmund Freud, *The Empty Mirror,* Walden Woods Films, 1996.

Television Appearances; Series:
Ben Hecht, PBS, 1981.
George Shields, *One of the Boys,* NBC, 1982.
Wally Wainwright, *After M*A*S*H,* CBS, 1984.
Charles "Chuck" Cavanaugh, *The Cavanaughs,* CBS, 1986-89.
Ken Kazurinsky, *Room for Two,* ABC, 1992-93.
Principal Herbert Adams, *The Faculty,* ABC, 1996.

Television Appearances; Miniseries:
Pat Hallford, *I Know My First Name Is Steven* (also known as *The Missing Years*), NBC, 1989.
Colonel St. George, "The Buccaneers," *Masterpiece Theatre,* PBS, 1995.

Television Appearances; Movies:
Dr. Warren Fitzpatrick, *Act of Love,* NBC, 1979.

Gerald Diems, prosecuting attorney, *An Invasion of Privacy,* ABC, 1980.
Stuart, "Promise," *Hallmark Hall of Fame,* CBS, 1986.
Woodie Harris, *Right to Die,* NBC, 1987.
Chapin, *A Father's Homecoming* (also known as *The Oakmont Stories, Town and Gown,* and *Oakmont*), NBC, 1988.
Homer Keller, *A Stoning in Fulham County* (also known as *The Stoning, The Amish Story,* and *Incident at Tile Mill Road*), NBC, 1988.
Mayor Maneri, *Maybe Baby* (also known as *And Baby Makes Three* and *Sooner or Later*), NBC, 1988.
Harold Carpenter, *The Karen Carpenter Story* (also known as *A Song for You*), CBS, 1989.
Everett Madison, *The Outside Woman,* CBS, 1989.
Danielle Steel's Fine Things (also known as *Fine Things*), NBC, 1990.
Alexander Howell, *Tagget* (also known as *Dragonfire*), USA Network, 1991.
First soapbox speaker, "The Water Engine," *TNT Screenworks,* TNT, 1992.
Josh Tabor, *My Brother's Keeper,* CBS, 1995.

Television Appearances; Pilots:
Walt Parker, *All Together Now,* 1984.
Captain Joyce, *Braker: Chief of Police* (also known as *Braker*), ABC, 1985.
Dad, *What's Alan Watching?* (also known as *Outrageous*), CBS, 1989.

Appeared in pilot for *In Trouble Dad.*

Television Appearances; Episodic:
"The Count," *St. Elsewhere,* NBC, 1983.
Dr. Messina, *The Bronx Zoo,* NBC, 1987.
Jared, "Invitation to Love," *Twin Peaks,* ABC, 1990.
Dr. Aaron Haber, "Cross Examination," *Picket Fences,* CBS, 1993.
Sisters, NBC, 1995.
Dr. Hendricks, "Pilot," *The Pretender,* NBC, 1996.
Jordan DuBois, *Touched by an Angel,* CBS, 1996.
Dr. Haddassi, "Makin' Whoopie," *Ellen,* ABC, 1997.

Appeared in episodes of *Lou Grant, The Phoenix,* and *Nurse.*

Television Appearances; Specials:
Salesman, *Carl Sandburg: Echoes and Silences,* 1982.
The Day My Parents Ran Away (also known as *Missing Parents*), Fox, 1993.*

GOLDWYN, Samuel Jr. 1926-

PERSONAL

Full name, Samuel John Goldwyn Jr.; born September 7, 1926, in Los Angeles, CA; son of Samuel John (a film producer) and Frances (Howard) Goldwyn; married Peggy Elliott, August 23, 1969; children: Catherine, Francis, John, Anthony (an actor; also known as Tony), Elizabeth, Peter. *Education:* Attended the University of Virginia.

Addresses: *Office*—The Samuel Goldwyn Company, 10203 Santa Monica Boulevard, Los Angeles, CA 90067-6403.

Career: Producer, director, writer, and distributor. J. Arthur Rank Organization, writer and associate producer; Universal Studios, Universal City, CA, associate producer; The Samuel Goldwyn Company, Los Angeles, CA, president, 1955—, owner and chief executive officer, 1978—; American Film Institute, trustee; Centre Theatre Group, Los Angeles, CA, board of directors; Samuel Goldwyn Foundation, president; Fountain Valley School, CO, president of the board of trustees. *Military service:* U.S. Army, 1944-46 and 1951-52.

Awards, Honors: Emmy Award, outstanding variety/music events programming, 1988, for *The 60th Annual Academy Awards Presentation;* Edinburgh Film Festival Prize for *Alliance for Peace.*

CREDITS

Film Work; Producer; Unless Indicated Otherwise:
Associate producer, *Good Time Girl,* 1950.
Man with the Gun (also known as *Deadly Peacemaker, Man without a Gun,* and *The Trouble Shooter*), United Artists, 1955.
The Sharkfighters, United Artists, 1956.
The Proud Rebel, Buena Vista, 1958.
The Adventures of Huckleberry Finn (also known as *Huckleberry Finn*), Metro-Goldwyn-Mayer, 1960.
And director, *The Young Lovers,* Metro-Goldwyn-Mayer, 1964.
Cotton Comes to Harlem, United Artists, 1970.
Come Back, Charleston Blue, Warner Bros., 1972.
The Golden Seal, The Samuel Goldwyn Company/New Realm, 1983.

Executive producer, *Once Bitten,* The Samuel Goldwyn Company, 1985.
Executive producer, *A Prayer for the Dying,* The Samuel Goldwyn Company, 1987.
Mr. North, The Samuel Goldwyn Company, 1988.
Executive producer, *Mystic Pizza,* The Samuel Goldwyn Company, 1988.
Minnamurra (also known as *The Fighting Creed, Outback,* and *Wrangler*), Burrowes Film Group, 1989.
Stella, Buena Vista, 1990.
The Program, Buena Vista, 1993.
The Preacher's Wife, Buena Vista, 1996.

Also director of *Alliance for Peace* and other documentaries for the U.S. Army.

Television Producer; Unless Indicated Otherwise; Series:
Adventure, CBS, 1952-53.
The Unexpected, 1954.
Executive producer, *Flipper* (also known as *The Adventures of Flipper*), syndicated, 1995-97.

Television Producer; Unless Indicated Otherwise; Specials:
The 59th Annual Academy Awards Presentation, ABC, 1987.
The 60th Annual Academy Awards Presentation, ABC, 1988.
(With others) Executive producer, "April Morning," *Hallmark Hall of Fame,* CBS, 1988.

Television Producer; Pilots:
The Unexplained, NBC, 1956.

Stage Work; Producer:
Producer, *Gathering Storm,* London, England.

OTHER SOURCES

Periodicals:
Forbes, October 28, 1991, pp. 174, 176.*

GORMAN, Cliff 1936-

PERSONAL

Born October 13, 1936, in New York, NY; son of Samuel and Ethel (Kaplan) Gorman; married Gayle Stevens, May 31, 1963. *Education:* University of New Mexico, 1954-55; University of California, Los Angeles, 1955-56; New York University, B.S. (education), 1959.

Addresses: *Agent*—Paradigm, 10100 Santa Monica Blvd., Los Angeles, CA 90067-4003.

Career: Actor. Jerome Robbins's American Theatre Lab, member, 1966-67. Also worked variously as a probationary officer, truck driver, ambulance driver, and at a collection agency.

Member: Honor Legion of the New York City Police Department, Friends of George Spelvin.

Awards, Honors: Obie Award, 1968, for *Ergo;* Antoinette Perry Award, La Guardia Memorial Award, Show Business Award, and Drama Desk Award, all 1972, for *Lenny.*

CREDITS

Film Appearances:
Devil's Canyon, RKO, 1953.
Toto, *Justine,* Twentieth Century-Fox, 1969.
Emory, *The Boys in the Band,* National General/Cinema Center, 1970.
Tom, *Cops and Robbers,* United Artists, 1973.
Yafet Hamlekh, *Rosebud,* United Artists, 1975.
Charlie, *An Unmarried Woman,* Twentieth Century-Fox, 1978.
David Newman, *All That Jazz,* Twentieth Century-Fox, 1979.
Gus Soltic, *Night of the Juggler,* Columbia, 1979.
Lieutenant Andrews, *Angel,* New World, 1983.
Solly Stein, *Hoffa,* Twentieth Century-Fox, 1992.
Phil, *Night and the City,* Twentieth Century-Fox, 1992.

Television Appearances; Movies:
The Trial of the Chicago Seven, 1970.
Mickey Swerner, *Class of '63,* ABC, 1973.
Detective Joey Gentry, *Strike Force,* NBC, 1975.
Stanley Greenberg, *The Silence,* NBC, 1975.
Danny Conforti, *Brink's: The Great Robbery,* CBS, 1976.
Arthur Magee, *Having Babies II* (also known as *Having Babies*), ABC, 1977.
Joseph Goebbels, *The Bunker,* CBS, 1981.
Rikki Anatole, *Cocaine and Blue Eyes,* NBC, 1983.
Dick Bernstein, *Howard Beach: Making the Case For Murder* (also known as *Howard Beach* and *Skin*), NBC, 1989.
Detective Aaron Greenberg, *Murder Times Seven* (also known as *End Run* and *Murder x 7*), CBS, 1990.

Detective Aaron Greenberg, *Murder in Black and White* (also known as *Janek: Cause of Death* and *Murder in Black & White*), CBS, 1990.
Sanderson, *Vestige of Honor,* CBS, 1990.
Detective Sergeant Aaron Greenberg, *Terror on Track 9* (also known as *Janek: The Grand Central Murders*), CBS, 1992.
Joe McManus, *The Return of Ironside,* NBC, 1993.
Detective Sergeant Aaron Greenberg, *A Silent Betrayal* (also known as *Janek: The Brownstone Murders, Janek: The Silent Betrayal,* and *Silent Betrayal*), CBS, 1994.
Detective Sergeant Aaron Greenberg, *The Forget-Me-Not Murders* (also known as *Forget-Me-Not Murders* and *Janek: Forget-Me-Not Murders*), CBS, 1994.
Nick the Greek, *Down Came a Blackbird* (also known as *Ramirez*), Showtime, 1995.

Television Appearances; Miniseries:
Detective Sergeant Aaron Greenberg, *Doubletake,* CBS, 1985.
Detective Sergeant Aaron Greenberg, *Internal Affairs,* CBS, 1988.

Television Appearances; Episodic:
"Naked in the Streets," *N.Y.P.D.,* ABC, 1968.
"Paradise Lost," *NET Playhouse,* PBS, 1971.
Sergeant Earl Eddie Mack, California Department of Corrections, "Time Out," *The Streets of San Francisco,* ABC, 1972.
"The Wyatt Earp Syndrome, *Police Story,* NBC, 1974.
"The Chicago Conspiracy Trial," *Hollywood Television Theater,* PBS, 1975.
"Officer Needs Help," *Police Story,* NBC, 1975.
"An Air Full of Death," *Medical Story,* NBC, 1975.
"Tour de Force—Man Abroad," *Hawaii Five-O,* CBS, 1976.

Also appeared in *Cagney and Lacey,* CBS; *Friday the 13th* (also known as *Friday the 13th—The Series*), syndicated; *Murder, She Wrote,* CBS; *Spenser: For Hire,* ABC; and *Trapper John, M.D.,* CBS.

Stage Appearances:
Peter Boyle, *Hogan's Goat,* American Place Theatre, New York City, 1965.
Arnulf, *Ergo,* Anspacher Theatre, New York City, 1968.
Emory, *The Boys in the Band,* Theatre Four, New York City, 1968, then Huntington Hartford Theatre, Los Angeles, CA, 1969.
Lenny Bruce, *Lenny,* Brooks Atkinson Theatre, New York City, 1971.

Leo Schneider, *Chapter Two,* Ahmanson Theatre Center, Los Angeles, CA, then Imperial Theatre, New York City, 1977.
Doubles, New York City, 1985.
Social Security, 1986.

Major Tours:
Emory, *The Boys in the Band,* U.S. cities, 1970.*

GOULD, Harold 1923-

PERSONAL

Born Harold V. Goldstein, December 10, 1923, in Schenectady, NY; son of Louis Glen (a post office clerk) and Lillian (a clerk for the New York State Department of Health) Goldstein; married Lea Shampanier (an actress; professional name, Lea Vernon), August 20, 1950; children: Deborah, Joshua David, Lowell Seth. *Education:* New York State College for Teachers (now State University of New York at Albany), B.A., 1947; Cornell University, M.A., 1948, Ph.D. (theater), 1953. *Avocational interests:* Reading, jogging, and swimming.

Addresses: *Manager*—Starstruck Films, 100 Universal City Plaza, Bldg. 507, #30, Universal City, CA 91608. *Agent*—Writers and Artists Agency, 924 Westwood Blvd., Suite 900, Los Angeles, CA 90024.

Career: Actor and teacher. Randolph Macon Women's College, Lynchburg, VA, assistant professor of drama and speech, 1953-56; University of California at Riverside, assistant professor of drama, 1956-60. *Military service*—U.S. Army, 1943-45.

Member: Academy of Motion Picture Arts and Sciences.

Awards, Honors: Obie Award, *Village Voice,* best performance, 1969, for *The Increased Difficulty of Concentration;* Emmy Award nomination, 1974, for *Police Story;* Emmy Award nomination, 1977, for *Rhoda;* Emmy Award nomination, 1979, for *Moviola: The Scarlett O'Hara War;* Emmy Award nomination, 1986, for *Mrs. Delafield Wants to Marry;* Centennial Alumnus Award, State University of New York at Albany, National Association of State Universities and Land-Grant Colleges, 1987; CableACE Award, best actor in a dramatic series, and Emmy Award nomination, 1990, both for *The Ray Bradbury Theatre;* Los Angeles Drama Critics Award, 1994, for *Incommunicado.*

CREDITS

Stage Appearances:
Thomas Jefferson, *The Common Glory,* Amphitheatre, Williamsburg, VA, 1955.
Edmund, *King Lear,* Oregon Shakespeare Festival, Ashland, OR, 1958.
Troilus and Cressida, Oregon Shakespeare Festival, 1958.
Benedict, *Much Ado about Nothing,* Oregon Shakespeare Festival, 1958.
Rhinoceros, Los Angeles, CA, 1962.
Old man, *The World of Ray Bradbury,* Coronet Theatre, Los Angeles, 1964.
Seidman and Son, Los Angeles, 1964.
Merchant of Venice, Los Angeles, 1964.
Goldberg, *The Birthday Party,* University of California at Los Angeles Theatre Group, Los Angeles, 1966.
The Devils, Center Theatre Group, Mark Taper Forum, Los Angeles, 1967.
Anselme and Harpagon, *The Miser,* Center Theatre Group, Mark Taper Forum, 1968.
Dr. Edward Huml, *The Increased Difficulty of Concentration,* Repertory Theatre of Lincoln Center, Forum Theatre, 1969.
Sosias, *Amphitryon,* Repertory Theatre of Lincoln Center, Forum Theatre, New York City, 1970.
Artie Shaughnessy, *The House of Blue Leaves,* Truck and Warehouse Theatre, New York City, 1971.
Buying Out, Studio Arena Theatre, Buffalo, NY, 1971.
Glogauer, *Once in a Lifetime,* Center Theatre Group, Mark Taper Forum, 1975.
Touching Bottom, American Place Theatre, New York City, 1978.
Dr. Zubritsky, *Fools,* Eugene O'Neill Theatre, New York City, 1981.
Life with Father, 1982.
Jack, *Grownups,* Lyceum Theatre, New York City, 1981, then Center Theatre Group, Mark Taper Forum, 1982.
Mr. Antrobus, *The Skin of Our Teeth,* Old Globe Theatre, San Diego, CA, 1983.
Nat, *I'm Not Rappaport,* Seattle Repertory Theatre, Seattle, WA, 1984.
Goldberg, *The Birthday Party,* Los Angeles Theatre Center, Los Angeles, 1986.
Through Roses, New Rochelle, NY, 1987.
Tom Garrison, *I Never Sang for My Father,* Eisenhower Theatre, Kennedy Center for the Performing Arts, Washington, DC, then Center Theatre Group, Ahmanson Theatre, Los Angeles, both 1987.
Beauchamp, *Artist Descending a Staircase,* Helen Hayes Theatre, New York City, 1989.

Freud (one man show), 1988-90.
Love Letters, Old Globe Theatre, 1990.
Herman Lewis, *Mixed Emotions,* Golden Theatre, New York City, 1993.
King Lear, Utah Shakespeare Festival, Cedar City, UT, 1992.
Incommunicado, Odyssey Theater, Los Angeles, 1993.
Old Business, 1995.
The Tempest, Utah Shakespeare Festival, 1995.

Film Appearances:
The Couch, Warner Bros., 1962.
Two for the Seesaw, United Artists, 1962.
Ponelli, *The Yellow Canary,* Twentieth Century-Fox, 1963.
Arnie Tomkins, *Ready for the People,* Warner Bros., 1964.
Marnie, Universal, 1964.
Cop, *Inside Daisy Clover,* Warner Bros., 1965.
Dr. Ostrer, *The Satan Bug,* United Artists, 1965.
Ganucci's lawyer, *An American Dream* (also known as *See You in Hell, Darling*), Warner Bros., 1966.
Sheriff Spanner, *Harper* (also known as *The Moving Target*), Warner Bros., 1966.
Doctor, *The Spy with My Face,* Metro-Goldwyn-Mayer, 1966.
Colonel Holt, *Project X,* Paramount, 1968.
Dr. Liebman, *The Arrangement,* Warner Bros., 1969.
Eric P. Scott, *The Lawyer,* Paramount, 1970.
Colonel Nexdhet, *Mrs. Pollifax: Spy,* United Artists, 1971.
Dr. Zerny, *Where Does It Hurt?,* Cinerama, 1972.
Kid Twist, *The Sting,* Universal, 1973.
Mayor, *The Front Page,* Universal, 1974.
Count Anton Ivanovich, *Love and Death,* United Artists, 1975.
Dietz, *The Strongest Man in the World,* Buena Vista, 1975.
Professor Baxter, *The Big Bus,* Paramount, 1976.
Charles Gwynn, *Gus,* Buena Vista, 1976.
Engulf, *Silent Movie,* Twentieth Century-Fox, 1976.
Hector Moses, *The One and Only,* Paramount, 1978.
Judge, *Seems Like Old Times* (also known as *Neil Simon's Seems Like Old Times*), Columbia, 1980.
Rockerfeller, *Playing for Keeps,* Universal, 1986.
Francisco Galedo, *Romero,* August Entertainment/Four Seasons Entertainment, 1989.
Sidewalk Motel, 1990.
Jack, *Birch Street Gym* (short film), 1991.
Tate, *Flesh Suitcase,* Kushner-Locke International, 1995.
Alan Smithee, *Lover's Knot,* Cabin Fever Entertainment, 1995.

Old Henry Lesser, *Killer: A Journal of Murder,* Spelling Films, 1996.
My Giant, 1998.

Television Appearances; Series:
Hong Kong, *To Catch a Star,* 1960.
Chamberlain, *The Long, Hot Summer,* ABC, 1965-66.
Norman Nugent, *He and She,* CBS, 1967-68.
Martin Morgenstern, *Rhoda,* CBS, 1974-78.
Harry Danton, *The Feather and Father Gang,* ABC, 1977.
Attorney David Ross, *Park Place,* CBS, 1981.
Jonah Foot, *Foot in the Door,* CBS, 1983.
Ben Sprague, *Under One Roof* (also known as *Spencer*), NBC, 1985.
Miles Webber (recurring role), *The Golden Girls,* NBC, 1989-92.
Nathan Singer, *Singer and Sons,* NBC, 1990.
Velvil, *The Sunset Gang,* 1991.

Television Appearances; Miniseries:
Carl Tessler, *Washington: Behind Closed Doors,* ABC, 1977.

Television Appearances; Pilots:
Mr. Hunnicutt, *Under the Yum Yum Tree,* ABC, 1969.
Howard Cunningham, *Love and the Happy Days* (broadcast as an episode of *Love, American Style*), ABC, 1972.
Dave Ryker, *Murdock's Gang,* CBS, 1973.
Matthew Brandon, *Bachelor at Law,* CBS, 1973.
Samuel Quilt, *Flannery and Quilt,* CBS, 1976.
Harry Danton, *Never Con a Killer,* ABC, 1976.
Sergeant T. K. Yu, NBC, 1979.
Jack Waine, *No Complaints!,* NBC, 1985.

Television Appearances; Episodic:
"Markdown on a Man," *Cain's Hundred,* ABC, 1961.
"Another Part of the Jungle," *Follow the Sun,* ABC, 1961.
"Go Read the River," *Route 66,* CBS, 1962.
"Rebel with a Cause," *The Donna Reed Show,* ABC, 1962.
"The Long Short Cut," *It's a Man's World,* NBC, 1962.
"The Accomplice," *The Virginian,* NBC, 1962.
"Stopover on the Way to the Moon," *Empire,* ABC, 1963.
"Jack Fires Don," *The Jack Benny Program,* CBS, 1963.
"The Three R's," *Dennis the Menace,* CBS, 1963.
"The Two-Star Giant," *Lieutenant,* NBC, 1963.
"The Stone Guest," *Route 66,* CBS, 1963.

General Larrabee, "Probe Seven, Over and Out," *The Twilight Zone,* CBS, 1963.

Radio announcer, "The Bewitchin' Pool," *The Twilight Zone,* CBS, 1964.

"The Income Tax Show," *The Jack Benny Program,* NBC, 1964.

"The Brazos Kid," *The Virginian,* NBC, 1964.

Mr. Boake, "Doctor's Wife," *Gunsmoke,* CBS, 1964.

"The Double Affair," *The Man from U.N.C.L.E.,* NBC, 1964.

"All Nice and Legal," *The Virginian,* NBC, 1964.

Kentucky Jones, NBC, 1964.

"Please Let My Baby Live," *Dr. Kildare,* NBC, 1965.

"The Oscar Hummingbird Story," *The Farmer's Daughter,* ABC, 1965.

"Jack Joins the Acrobats," *The Jack Benny Program,* NBC, 1965.

"George's Man Friday," *Hazel,* NBC, 1965.

"The Threat," *12 O'Clock High,* ABC, 1965.

"Farewell to Honesty," *The Virginian,* NBC, 1965.

"Wings of an Angel," *The Fugitive,* ABC, 1965.

"Day of the Scorpion," *The Virginian,* NBC, 1965.

"Slow March Up a Steep Hill," *The FBI,* ABC, 1965.

The Farmer's Daughter, ABC, 1965.

"No More Souvenirs," *Convoy,* NBC, 1965.

"The Man Who Went Mad by Mistake," *The FBI,* ABC, 1966.

"The Chinchilla Rag," *Love on a Rooftop,* ABC, 1966.

Get Smart, NBC, 1966.

General Von Lintzer, "Klink's Rocket," *Hogan's Heroes,* CBS, 1966.

"May the Best Man Lose," *The Green Hornet,* ABC, 1966.

"The Courier," *The FBI,* ABC, 1967.

"The Experiment," *The Invaders,* ABC, 1967.

"Concrete Evidence," *The Fugitive,* ABC, 1967.

"The Assassin," *Run for Your Life,* NBC, 1967.

"The Savage Streets," *The Felony Squad,* ABC, 1967.

Wilson, "Cage of Eagles," *The Big Valley,* ABC, 1967.

"The Night of the Bubbling Death," *The Wild Wild West,* CBS, 1967.

"Shadow of a Killer," *Judd, for the Defense,* ABC, 1967.

"The Trial," *The Invaders,* ABC, 1967.

The Flying Nun, ABC, 1967.

Colonel Enzio, "Friendly Enemies," *Garrison's Gorillas,* ABC, 1967.

General von Scheider, "D-Day at Stalag 13," *Hogan's Heroes,* CBS, 1967.

"Watts Made Out of Thread," *Insight,* syndicated, 1968.

"The Daughter," *The FBI,* ABC, 1968.

"The Imposter," *Daniel Boone,* NBC, 1968.

"The Challenge," *The Big Valley,* ABC, 1968.

The Flying Nun, ABC, 1968.

"Weep the Hunter Home," *Judd, for the Defense,* ABC, 1968.

"The Last Train for Charlie Poe," *Lancer,* CBS, 1968.

"The Night of the Avaricious Actuary," *The Wild Wild West,* CBS, 1968.

"The Butcher," *The FBI,* ABC, 1968.

Mr. Winkler, "Invisible House for Sale," *I Dream of Jeannie,* NBC, 1969.

"The Royal Road," *The Big Valley,* ABC, 1969.

"Here's Debbie," *The Debbie Reynold's Show,* NBC, 1969.

Vincente Bravo, "The Code," *Mission: Impossible,* CBS, 1969.

"Break the Bank of Tacoma," *Here Come the Brides,* ABC, 1970.

"Dream of Falcons," *Lancer,* CBS, 1970.

"Lady Chitterly's Lover: Part 1," *Hogan's Heroes,* CBS, 1970.

"Lady Chitterly's Lover: Part 2," *Hogan's Heroes,* CBS, 1970.

"A Good Sound Profit," *The High Chaparral,* NBC, 1970.

General Wetherby, "Jeannie's Beauty Cream," *I Dream of Jeannie,* NBC, 1970.

"The Stalking Horse," *The FBI,* ABC, 1971.

Nicholas Troas, "A Lonely Place to Die," *Cannon,* CBS, 1971.

"The Loser," *The Mob Squad,* ABC, 1971.

"The Test," *The FBI,* ABC, 1972.

Howard Cunningham, "Love and the Happy Days," *Love, American Style,* ABC, 1972.

Martin Morgenstern, "Enter Rhoda's Parents," *The Mary Tyler Moore Show,* CBS, 1972.

"The Man Upstairs/The Man Downstairs Project," *Delphi Bureau,* ABC, 1972.

"One Step to Midnight," *Mannix,* CBS, 1972.

"V for Vashon" (three episodes), *Hawaii Five-O,* CBS, 1972.

"The Takers," *The Streets of San Francisco,* ABC, 1972.

"Happy Birthday, Marvin," *Insight,* syndicated, 1973.

Robert L. Jardine, "The Prisoners," *Cannon,* CBS, 1973.

Martin Morgenstern, "Rhoda's Sister Gets Married," *The Mary Tyler Moore Show,* CBS, 1973.

"Beethoven, Brahms, and Partridge," *The Partridge Family,* ABC, 1973.

"The Free Trip," *The New Dick Van Dyke Show,* CBS, 1973.

"The Armageddon Gang," *Ironside,* NBC, 1973.

Lotsa Luck, NBC, 1973.

"John Doe Bucks," *Chase,* NBC, 1974.

"Double Solitaire," *Conflicts,* PBS, 1974.

"Death and The Favored Few," *The Streets of San Francisco,* ABC, 1974.

"The Guns of Cibola Blanca," *Gunsmoke,* CBS, 1974.

"Fathers and Sons," *Police Story,* NBC, 1974.

"Death in High Places," *Petrocelli,* NBC, 1974.

"Mirror Mirror on the Wall," *Petrocelli,* NBC, 1974.

"But I Love My Wife," *The Bob Crane Show,* NBC, 1975.

Mirza, "Tomorrow Ends at Noon," *Cannon,* CBS, 1975.

"The Case Against McGarrett," *Hawaii Five-O,* CBS, 1975.

"Measure of Mercy," *The Rookies,* ABC, 1975.

"For the Love of Annie," *Insight,* syndicated, 1976.

"The Quality of Mercy," *Medical Story,* NBC, 1976.

"Eamon Kinsella Royce," *Police Story,* NBC, 1976.

"The Blue Frog," *Police Story,* NBC, 1977.

"Acts of Love" (three episodes), *Family,* ABC, 1977.

Soap, ABC, 1977.

"The Caper," *The Love Boat,* ABC, 1978.

Grandpa Goes to Washington, NBC, 1978.

"Never Send a Boy King to Do a Man's Job: Part 1," *The Rockford Files,* NBC, 1978.

"Never Send a Boy King to Do a Man's Job: Part 2," *The Rockford Files,* NBC, 1978.

"Holy Moses," *Insight,* syndicated, 1979.

"The Man Who Mugged God," *Insight,* syndicated, 1979.

"The Return of Richie Brockelman," *The Rockford Files,* NBC, 1979.

The Misadventures of Sheriff Lobo, NBC, 1979.

Lou Grant, CBS, 1979.

"The Long Road Home," *Insight,* syndicated, 1980.

"He Married an Angel," *Charlie's Angels,* ABC, 1981.

"Up On the Roof," *St. Elsewhere,* NBC, 1984.

"Girls Just Want to Have Fun," *St. Elsewhere,* NBC, 1984.

"The Great Walnutto," *Webster,* ABC, 1984.

"Echoes," *Finder of Lost Loves,* ABC, 1984.

Arnie Peterson, "Rose the Prude," *The Golden Girls,* NBC, 1985.

Dr. Victor Kosciusko, "Just Around the Corner," *Trapper John, M.D.,* CBS, 1985.

Andrei Zernov, "One Bear Dances, One Bear Doesn't," *Scarecrow and Mrs. King,* CBS, 1986.

"New Year's Leave," *Night Court,* NBC, 1986.

Harry Finneman, "Simian Chanted Evening," *L.A. Law,* NBC, 1986.

Walter Wise, *Night Court,* NBC, 1986.

Charlie Drexel, *Midnight Caller,* NBC, 1989.

Old man, "To the Chicago Abyss," *The Ray Bradbury Theatre,* USA Network, 1989.

"Colonel Stonesteel and the Desperate Empties," *The Ray Bradbury Theatre,* USA Network, 1992.

Edwin Griffen, "The Prankster," *Lois and Clark: The Adventures of Superman,* ABC, 1994.

Edwin Griffen, "The Return of the Prankster," *Lois and Clark: The New Adventures of Superman,* ABC, 1995.

Gerry, "Paradise," *The Outer Limits,* Showtime, 1996.

Sam, *Touched by an Angel,* CBS, 1996.

Television Appearances; Movies:

Carlson, *Ransom for a Dead Man,* NBC, 1971.

Alexander Weisberg, *A Death of Innocence,* CBS, 1971.

Judgment: The Trial of Ethel and Julius Rosenberg, ABC, 1974.

Doctor Federicci, *Medical Story,* NBC, 1975.

Mr. Henshaw, *How to Break Up a Happy Divorce,* NBC, 1976.

Benny Barnet, *The Eleventh Victim* (also known as *11th Victim*), CBS, 1979.

Dr. Hoxley, *Aunt Mary,* CBS, 1979.

Harry Landers, *Better Late than Never,* NBC, 1979.

Dickie Dayton, *The Man in the Santa Claus Suit,* NBC, 1979.

Arthur Stowbridge, *Kenny Rogers as The Gambler* (also known as *The Gambler*), CBS, 1980.

Louis B. Mayer, *Moviola: The Scarlett O'Hara War,* NBC, 1980.

Louis B. Mayer, *Moviola: The Silent Lovers,* NBC, 1980.

Mr. Campana, *King Crab,* ABC, 1980.

Robert Westfield, *Born To Be Sold,* NBC, 1981.

Eliot Bingham, *Help Wanted: Male,* CBS, 1982.

Arthur Stowbridge, *Kenny Rogers as The Gambler: The Adventure Continues,* CBS, 1983.

Oliver Sully, *The Red Light Sting,* CBS, 1984.

Dr. Marvin Elias, *Mrs. Delafield Wants to Marry,* CBS, 1986.

Jack Traynor, "Tickets, Please," *CBS Summer Playhouse,* CBS, 1988.

Nicholas Dimente, *Get Smart, Again!,* ABC, 1989.

Dave, *For Hope,* ABC, 1996.

The Love Bug, ABC, 1997.

Television Appearances; Specials:

Leo Silver, "Have I Got a Christmas for You," *The Hallmark Hall of Fame,* NBC, 1977.

Sol Wurtzel, *Actor,* PBS, 1978.

George Antrobus, "The Skin of Our Teeth," *American Playhouse,* PBS, 1983.

Rabbi, *The Fourth Wise Man,* ABC, 1985.

B. J., "Tales from the Hollywood Hills: The Closed Set" (also known as "The Closed Set"), *Great Performances,* PBS, 1988.

Tom Garrison, "I Never Sang for My Father," *American Playhouse*, PBS, 1988.
Hanukkah: Let There Be Lights, 1989.
The Sunset Gang, *Yiddish,* PBS, 1990.
Mr. Goldberg, *The Writing on the Wall,* 1994.

GRANT, Lee   1931-

PERSONAL

Born Lyova Haskell Rosenthal, October 31, 1931, in New York, NY; daughter of A. W. (an educator and realtor) and Witia (a teacher; maiden name, Haskell) Rosenthal; married Arnold Manoff (a playwright; died, 1965); married Joseph Feury (a producer), 1967; children: (first marriage) Dinah, (second marriage) Belinda. *Education:* Attended the Art Student League and the High School of Music and Art; studied voice, violin, and dance at the Juilliard School of Music; attended the Metropolitan Opera Ballet School; studied acting at the Neighborhood Playhouse with Sanford Meisner and at the Actors' Studio.

Addresses: *Contact*—21243 Ventura Blvd., Suite 101, Woodland Hills, CA 91364.

Career: Actress and director. Ballet dancer, Metropolitan Opera Company, New York City; company member, American Ballet Theatre, New York City; painter and acting teacher. Blacklisted in Hollywood for refusing to state names of suspected communists for the House Un-American Activities Committee, 1952-1964.

Member: Actors' Equity Association, American Federation of Television and Radio Artists, Screen Actors Guild, Directors Guild of America.

Awards, Honors: New York Drama Critics Circle Award, 1949, for *Detective Story;* Academy Award nomination, best supporting actress, 1951, and Best Actress Award, Cannes Film Festival, 1952, both for *Detective Story;* Obie Award, *Village Voice,* 1964, for *The Maids;* Emmy Award, outstanding performance by an actress in a supporting role in a drama, 1966, for *Peyton Place;* Academy Award nomination, best supporting actress, 1970, for *The Landlord;* Emmy Award, outstanding single performance by an actress in a lead role, 1971, for *The Neon Ceiling;* Emmy Award nomination, 1971, for *Ransom for a Dead Man;* Academy Award, best supporting actress, and Golden Globe nomination, best supporting ac-

tress, 1975, for *Shampoo;* Academy Award nomination, best supporting actress, and Golden Globe nomination, best supporting actress, both 1976, for *Voyage of the Damned;* Congressional Arts Caucus Award, outstanding achievement in acting and independent filmmaking, 1983, for *Tell Me a Riddle;* Academy Award, best documentary feature, 1986, for *Down and Out in America;* Directors Guild Award, best dramatic television special, 1987, for *Nobody's Child;* Crystal Award, Women in Film, 1988; Emmy Award nomination for *Bob Hope Presents the Chrysler Theatre;* Lifetime Achievement Award, Women in Film, 1989.

CREDITS

Stage Appearances:
Princess Ho Chee, *L'Oracolo* (opera), Metropolitan Opera House, New York City, 1933.
Liliom, Green Mansions Theatre, Warrensburg, NY, 1947.
This Property Is Condemned, Green Mansions Theatre, 1947.
Mildred, *Joy to the World,* Plymouth Theatre, New York City, 1948.
Shoplifter, *Detective Story,* Hudson Theatre, New York City, 1949.
Diane, *All You Need Is One Good Break,* Mansfield Theatre, New York City, 1950.
Raina Petkoff, *Arms and the Man,* Arena Theatre, New York City, 1950.
Daisy Durole, *Lo and Behold!,* Booth Theatre, New York City, 1951.
Sally, *I Am a Camera,* Mount Kisco Playhouse, Mt. Kisco, NY, 1952.
Amy, *They Knew What They Wanted,* Mount Kisco Playhouse, 1953.
Title role, *Gigi,* Mount Kisco Playhouse, 1954.
Stella, *Wedding Breakfast,* 48th Street Theatre, New York City, 1954.
Eliza, *Pygmalion,* Mount Kisco Playhouse, 1956.
Lizzie, *The Rainmaker,* Mount Kisco Playhouse, 1957.
Mrs. Rogers, *A Hole in the Head,* Plymouth Theatre, 1957.
Gittel Mosca, *Two for the Seesaw,* Booth Theatre, 1959.
Rose Collins, *Captains and the Kings,* Playhouse Theatre, New York City, 1962.
Solange, *The Maids,* One Sheridan Square Theatre, New York City, 1963.
Title role, *Electra,* New York Shakespeare Festival, Delacorte Theatre, New York City, 1964.

Title role, *Saint Joan,* Moorestown Theatre, Moorestown, NJ, 1966.

Edna Edison, *The Prisoner of Second Avenue,* Eugene O'Neill Theatre, New York City, 1971.

Regina, *The Little Foxes,* 1975.

Also appeared in a series of one-act plays with Henry Fonda, American National Theatre and Academy Theatre, New York City, 1949.

Stage Work; Director:

The Adventures of Jack and Max, Actors' Studio West, Los Angeles, CA, 1968.

A Private View, New York Shakespeare Festival, Public Theatre, New York City, 1983.

The Lay of the Land, Pittsburgh Public Theatre, Pittsburgh, PA, 1990.

Major Tours:

Oklahoma, U.S. cities, 1948.

The Tender Trap, U.S. cities, 1962.

Ninotchka, *Silk Stockings,* U.S. cities, 1963.

Karen Nash, "Visitor from Mamaroneck," Muriel Tate, "Visitor from Hollywood," and Norma Hubley, "Visitor from Forest Hills," in *Plaza Suite,* U.S. cities, 1968.

Film Appearances:

Don "Red" Barry, *The Man from the Rio Grande,* Republic, 1943.

Shoplifter, *Detective Story,* Paramount, 1951.

Edna, *Storm Fear,* United Artists, 1956.

Run of the Arrow, Universal, 1957.

The Blue Angel, Twentieth Century-Fox, 1959.

Marilyn, *Middle of the Night,* Columbia, 1959.

From Russia With Love, United Artists, 1963.

Carmen, *The Balcony,* Continental, 1963.

Katherine McCleod, *An Affair of the Skin* (also known as *Love as a Disorder*), Zenith, 1964.

Suzy, *Pie in the Sky* (also known as *Terror in the City*), Allied Artists, 1964.

Dede Murphy, *Divorce American Style,* Columbia, 1967.

Mrs. Leslie Colbert, *In the Heat of the Night,* United Artists, 1967.

Miriam Polar, *Valley of the Dolls,* Twentieth Century-Fox, 1967.

Fritzie Braddock, *Buona Sera, Mrs. Campbell,* United Artists, 1968.

Joanne, motel resident, *The Big Bounce,* Warner Brothers/Seven Arts, 1969.

Celia Pruett, *Marooned* (also known as *Space Travelers*), Columbia, 1969.

Mrs. Enders, *The Landlord,* United Artists, 1970.

Mrs. Bullard, *There Was a Crooked Man,* Warner Bros., 1970.

Norma Hubley, *Plaza Suite,* Paramount, 1971.

Sophie Portnoy, *Portnoy's Complaint,* Warner Bros., 1972.

Jean Robertson, *The Internecine Project,* Allied Artists, 1974.

Felicia Carr, *Shampoo,* Columbia, 1975.

The Prisoner of Second Avenue, Warner Bros., 1975.

Lillian Rosen, *Voyage of the Damned,* Avco-Embassy, 1976.

Karen Wallace, *Airport '77,* Universal, 1977.

Ann Thorn, *Damien—Omen II,* Twentieth Century-Fox, 1978.

Ellen, *The Mafu Cage* (also known as *My Sister, My Love, The Cage,* and *Deviation*), Clouds, 1978.

Anne MacGregor, *The Swarm,* Warner Bros., 1978.

Clarisse Ethridge, *When You Comin' Back Red Ryder?,* Columbia, 1979.

Judge, *Little Miss Marker,* Universal, 1980.

Mrs. Lupowitz, *Charlie Chan and the Curse of the Dragon Queen,* American Cinema, 1981.

Deborah Ballin, *Visiting Hours* (also known as *The Fright* and *Get Well Soon*), Twentieth Century-Fox, 1981.

Narrator, *The Wilmar Eight* (documentary), California Newsreel, 1981.

I Ought To Be in Pictures, Twentieth Century-Fox, 1982.

Narrator, *What Sex Am I?* (documentary), Joseph Feury Productions, 1984.

Mrs. Barr, *Constance,* Mirage/New Zealand Film Commission/Miramax/Enterprise, 1984.

Mrs. Jones, *Trial Run,* Miracle Films/New Zealand Film Commission, 1984.

Dr. Burke, *Teachers,* Metro-Goldwyn-Mayer/United Artists, 1984.

Herself, *Sanford Meisner—The Theatre's Best Kept Secret* (documentary), Columbia, 1984.

Narrator, *Down and Out in America* (documentary), Joseph Feury Productions, 1986.

Arriving Tuesday, Cinepro/New Zealand Film Commission/Walker, 1986.

Herself, *Hello Actors' Studio* (documentary), Actors' Studio, 1987.

Ferguson Edwards, *The Big Town,* Columbia, 1987.

Calling the Shots (documentary), World Artists Releasing, 1988.

Lena Foster, *Defending Your Life,* Warner Bros., 1991.

Voice, *Earth and the American Dream,* 1993.

Jane, *Under Heat,* 1994.

Amalia Stark, *It's My Party,* Metro-Goldwyn-Mayer/United Artists, 1995.

Cora Cahn, *The Substance of Fire,* Miramax, 1996.

Film Work; Director:
The Stronger (short film), American Film Institute, 1976.
Tell Me a Riddle, Filmways, 1980.
The Wilmar Eight (documentary), California Newsreel, 1981.
What Sex Am I? (documentary), Joseph Feury Productions, 1984.
Down and Out in America (documentary), Joseph Feury Productions, 1986.
Staying Together, Hemdale, 1989.
Women on Trial (documentary), 1992.

Television Appearances; Series:
Rose Peabody, *Search for Tomorrow,* CBS, 1953-54.
Stella Chernak, *Peyton Place,* ABC, 1965-66.
Fay Stewart, *Fay,* NBC, 1975-76.

Television Appearances; Miniseries:
Grace Coolidge, *Backstairs at the White House,* NBC, 1979.
Ava Marshall, *Bare Essence,* CBS, 1982.
Rachele Mussolini, *Mussolini: The Untold Story,* NBC, 1985.

Television Appearances; Pilots:
Wife, *Justice* (broadcast as an episode of *Plymouth Playhouse*), ABC, 1953.
Leslie Williams, *Ransom for a Dead Man,* NBC, 1971.
Diane Harper, *The Ted Bessell Show,* CBS, 1973.
Meredith Leland, *Partners in Crime,* NBC, 1973.
Maxine Lochman, *Thou Shalt Not Kill,* NBC, 1981.
Evalyna, *The Million Dollar Face,* NBC, 1981.

Television Appearances; Episodic:
"Screwball," *The Play's the Thing,* CBS, 1950.
"Zone of Quiet," *Comedy Theatre,* CBS, 1950.
"Dark as Night," *Danger,* CBS, 1952.
"Death to the Lonely," *Danger,* CBS, 1952.
"The Face of Fear," *Danger,* CBS, 1952.
"Justice," *ABC Album,* ABC, 1953.
"The Noose," *Broadway Television Theatre,* syndicated, 1953.
"The Blonde Comes First," *Summer Theatre,* CBS, 1953.
"Death Is a Spanish Dancer," *Ponds Theatre,* ABC, 1955.
"Shadow of the Champ," *Philco Television Playhouse,* NBC, 1955.
"Keyhole," *Playwrights '56,* NBC, 1956.
"Even the Weariest River," *Alcoa Hour,* NBC, 1956.
"Moony's Kids Don't Cry," *Kraft Theatre,* NBC, 1958.

"Three Plays by Tennessee Williams," *Kraft Theatre,* NBC, 1958.
"Look What's Going On," *Kraft Theatre,* NBC, 1958.
"Man in the Middle," *Brenner,* CBS, 1959.
Martirio, "The House of Bernarda Alba," *Play of the Week,* syndicated, 1960.
"Lucy," *Great Ghost Tales,* NBC, 1961.
"Saturday's Children," *Breck Golden Showcase,* CBS, 1962.
Avenging Angel, "The World of Sholem Aleichem," *Play of the Week,* syndicated, 1962.
"To Spend, to Give, to Want," *The Nurses,* CBS, 1963.
"The Gift," *The Nurses,* CBS, 1963.
"Not Bad for Openers," *East Side/West Side,* CBS, 1963.
"The Empty Heart," *The Defenders,* CBS, 1963.
"Question: Where Vanished the Tragic Piper?," *Slattery's People,* CBS, 1964.
"Taps For a Dead War," *The Fugitive,* ABC, 1964.
"For Just a Man Falleth Seven Times," *Ben Casey,* ABC, 1964.
"For Jimmy, the Best of Everything," *Ben Casey,* ABC, 1964.
"With Intent to Influence," *For the People,* CBS, 1965.
"A Couple of Dozen Tiny Pills," *Doctors and the Nurses,* CBS, 1965.
"Nobody Asks What Side You're On," *The Defenders,* CBS, 1965.
"The Diplomat," *Mission: Impossible,* CBS, 1965.
"The People Trap," *ABC Stage '67,* ABC, 1966.
Laura, "The Love Song of Barney Kempinski," *ABC Stage '67,* ABC, 1966.
"The Lady from Mesa," *The Big Valley,* ABC, 1967.
"Deadlock," *Bob Hope Presents the Chrysler Theatre,* NBC, 1967.
"Eat, Drink, and Be Buried," *Ironside,* NBC, 1967.
"The Gates of Cerberus," *Judd, for the Defense,* ABC, 1968.
Susan Buchanan, "The Diplomat," *Mission: Impossible,* CBS, 1968.
"The Loner," *Medical Center,* CBS, 1969.
"Mother of Sorrow," *The Mod Squad,* ABC, 1970.
"Tarot," *Name of the Game,* NBC, 1970.
"Whatever Happened to Happy Endings?," *Bracken's World,* NBC, 1970.
"A Love to Remember," *Name of the Game,* NBC, 1970.
"Yesterday Is But a Dream," *Men at Law,* CBS, 1971.
"The Seagull," *Theatre in America,* PBS, 1975.
"The Good Doctor," *Great Performances,* PBS, 1978.
One Day at a Time, CBS, 1984.
Guest, *At Rona's,* NBC, 1989.
Mrs. Rogers, "The Handler," *The Ray Bradbury Theatre,* USA Network, 1992.

Television Appearances; Movies:
Lizzie, *The Respectful Prostitute,* BBC, 1964.
Marjorie Howard, *Night Slaves,* ABC, 1970.
Carrie Miller, *The Neon Ceiling,* NBC, 1971.
Leslie Williams, *Ransom for a Dead Man* (also known as *Columbo: Ransom for a Dead Man*), NBC, 1971.
Ellie Schuster, *Lieutenant Schuster's Wife,* ABC, 1972.
Adele Ross, *What Are Best Friends For?,* ABC, 1973.
Partners in Crime, NBC, 1973.
Virginia Monroe, *Perilous Voyage,* NBC, 1976.
Marion Matchett, *The Spell,* NBC, 1977.
Esther Jack, *You Can't Go Home Again,* CBS, 1979.
The Million Dollar Face, NBC, 1981.
Anne Holt, *For Ladies Only,* NBC, 1981.
Thou Shalt Not Kill, NBC, 1982.
Bare Essence, CBS, 1982.
Lillian Farmer, *Will There Really Be a Morning?,* CBS, 1983.
Marilyn Klinghoffer, *The Hijacking of the Achille Lauro* (also known as *Sea of Terror, The Last Voyage,* and *Achille Lauro: Terror at Sea*), NBC, 1989.
District Attorney Doris Cantore, *She Said No,* NBC, 1990.
Carol Gertz, *Something to Live For: The Alison Gertz Story* (also known as *Fatal Love*), ABC, 1992.
Maureen Leeds, *In My Daughter's Name,* CBS, 1992.
Dora, *Citizen Cohn,* HBO, 1992.

Television Appearances; Specials:
"Where is Thy Brother?," *Jewish Appeal Special,* NBC, 1958.
Florrie Sands, *Saturday's Children,* CBS, 1962.
The Wonderful World of Aggravation, ABC, 1972.
Robert Young and the Family, CBS, 1973.
Wife, "Raincheck," *Three for the Girls,* CBS, 1973.
The Shape of Things, CBS, 1973.
Irina Arkadina, "The Seagull," *Great Performances,* PBS, 1975.
Narrator, *Why Me?,* syndicated, 1975.
Host, *Once Upon a Time . . . Is Now: The Story of Princess Grace* (documentary), NBC, 1977.
Karen Nash, "Visitor from Mamaroneck," Muriel Tate, "Visitor from Hollywood," and Claire Hubley, "Visitor from Forest Hills," *Plaza Suite,* HBO, 1982.
Narrator, "When Women Kill" (documentary), *America Undercover,* HBO, 1984.
Harry Belafonte: Don't Stop the Carnival, HBO, 1985.
Host, *Battered,* HBO, 1989.
Herself, *Blacklist: Hollywood on Trial,* American Movie Classics, 1996.

Television Work; Episodic; Director:
"For the Use of the Hall," *Hollywood Television Theater,* PBS, 1975.

Television Work; Movies; Director:
A Matter of Sex, NBC, 1984.
Nobody's Child, CBS, 1986.
Battered, HBO, 1989.
No Place Like Home, CBS, 1989.
Seasons of the Heart (also known as *The Winter Garden*), NBC, 1994.
Following Her Heart (also known as *Sing Me the Blues, Lena*), NBC, 1994.
Reunion, CBS, 1994.

Television Work; Specials; Director:
(With Carolyn Raskin) *The Shape of Things,* CBS, 1973.
"When Women Kill" (documentary), *America Undercover,* HBO, 1984.
"Cindy Eller: A Modern Fairy Tale," *ABC Afterschool Specials,* ABC, 1985.

WRITINGS

Television Specials:
(Cowriter) *The Shape of Things,* CBS, 1973.

OTHER SOURCES

Periodicals:
American Film, February, 1990, pp. 16-19.
People Weekly, February 26, 1996, p. 14.*

———————

GRAY, Simon   1936-
   (Hamish Reade)

PERSONAL

Full name, Simon James Holliday Gray; born October 21, 1936, in Hayling Island, Hampshire, England; son of James Davidson (a pathologist) and Barbara Cecelia Mary (Holliday) Gray; married Beryl Mary Kevern (a picture researcher), August 20, 1964; children: Benjamin, Lucy. *Education:* Dalhousie University, B.A. (English, with honors), 1958; Trinity College, Cambridge University, M.A. (English, with honors), 1962.

Addresses: *Agent*—c/o Judy Daish Associates, Ltd., 2 St. Charles Place, London W10 6EG, England.

Career: Playwright, screenwriter, and director. University of British Columbia, Vancouver, British Columbia, Canada, lecturer, 1963-64; Trinity College, Cambridge University, England, supervisor in English, 1964-66; Queen Mary College, University of London, England, lecturer in drama and literature, 1966-86; also worked as an editor for *Delta* (magazine) and taught in France, 1960-61, and Spain, 1962-63.

Member: Dramatists Guild, Societe des Auteurs (France).

Awards, Honors: Writers Guild Award, best play, 1967, for *Death of a Teddy Bear; Evening Standard* Award, best play, 1972, for *Butley; Evening Standard* Award, *Plays and Players* Award, and New York Drama Critics Circle Award, all best play, 1976, for *Otherwise Engaged;* Cheltenham Prize for Literature, 1981, for *Quartermaine's Terms;* British Academy of Film and Television Arts Awards, The Writers Award, British Academy of Film and Television Arts, 1990.

CREDITS

Stage Work; Director:
Dog Days, Hudson Guild Theatre, New York City, 1985.
(With Michael McGuire) *The Common Pursuit,* Promenade Theatre, New York City, 1986, then Phoenix Theatre, London, 1988.
Hidden Laughter, Vaudeville Theatre, London, 1990.
The Holy Terror, Tucson and Phoenix, AZ, 1991.
Cell Mates, Aldbery Theatre, London, 1995.

Stage Work; Other:
Lighting, *Gary,* Warehouse, Croydon, England, 1989.
Musical director, *Treasure Island,* Mermaid Theatre, London, 1995-96.
Lighting, *Sympathy for the Devil,* Oval House, then Tricycle, both 1996.

WRITINGS

Stage:
Wise Child, Wyndham's Theatre, London, 1967, then Helen Hayes Theatre, New York City, 1972, published by Faber and Faber (London), 1968, then Samuel French (New York City), 1974.
Dutch Uncle, Theatre Royal, Brighton, England, National Theatre, London, and Aldwych Theatre, London, all 1969, published by Faber and Faber, 1969.

(Adapted from the novel by Fyodor Dostoevsky) *The Idiot,* National Theatre, 1970, published by Methuen, 1971.
Spoiled, Close Theatre Club, Glasgow, Scotland, 1970, then Royal Haymarket Theatre, London, 1971, later Morosco Theatre, New York City, 1972, published by Methuen, 1971.
Butley, Oxford Playhouse, Oxford, England, then Criterion Theatre, London, both 1971, then Morosco Theatre, 1972, later Duke's Head, 1991, published by Methuen, 1971, then Viking, 1972.
Otherwise Engaged, Queen's Theatre, London, 1975, then Plymouth Theatre, New York City, 1977, published by Samuel French, 1976, and in *Otherwise Engaged and Other Plays,* Methuen, then Viking, both 1976.
Dog Days, Oxford Playhouse, 1976, later Hudson Guild Theatre, New York City, 1985, published by Methuen, 1977.
Molly, Palace Theatre, Watford, England, 1977, then Comedy Theatre, London, 1978, then Hudson Guild Theatre, 1978, published by Samuel French, 1979, and in *The Rear Column and Other Plays,* Methuen, 1978, then Viking, 1979.
The Rear Column, Globe Theatre, London, 1978, then Manhattan Theatre Club, New York City, 1978, published in *The Rear Column and Other Plays,* Methuen, 1978, then Viking, 1979.
Close of Play, Lyttleton Theatre, 1979, then Manhattan Theatre Club, 1981, published by Faber and Faber, 1979, and in *Close of Play and Pig in a Poke,* Methuen, 1979.
Stage Struck, Vaudeville Theatre, London, 1979, then Wayside Theatre, Middletown, VA, 1992, published by Methuen, 1979.
Quartermaine's Terms, Queen's Theatre, 1981, then Long Wharf Theatre, New Haven, CT, 1982, later Playhouse 91, New York City, 1983, and Actors Theatre of Louisville, Louisville, KY, 1991, published by Methuen, 1981.
(Adaptor) *Tartuffe,* Kennedy Center, Washington, DC, 1982.
The Common Pursuit, Lyric Hammersmith Theatre, London, 1984, then Long Wharf Theatre, 1985, then Matrix Theatre, Los Angeles, CA, and Promenade Theatre, New York City, both 1986, then Phoenix Theatre, London, 1988; published by Methuen, 1984, Samuel French, 1990.
Melon, Royal Haymarket Theatre, 1987, published by Methuen, 1987.
Hidden Laughter, Vaudeville Theatre, 1990, then Hartford Stage Company, Hartford, CT, 1991, published by Faber and Faber, 1990, Samuel French, 1992.

The Holy Terror, Tucson and Phoenix, AZ, 1991, then Promenade Theatre, New York City, 1992, published by Faber and Faber, 1990, Samuel French, 1993.

Cell Mates, Aldbery Theatre, 1995, published by Faber and Faber, 1995.

Simply Disconnected, 1996, published by Faber and Faber, 1996.

Life Support, Aldwych Theatre, 1997.

Film:

Butley, American Film Theatre, 1974.
A Month in the Country, Orion Classics, 1988.
Old Flames, 1989.
They Never Slept, 1990.
Femme Fatale, 1993.
Running Late, 1993.

Television; Movies:

After Pilkington, BBC, 1987, published by Methuen, 1987.
Unnatural Pursuits, Arts and Entertainment, 1994.

Television; Specials:

Quartermaine's Terms, 1987.
"The Common Pursuit," *Great Performances,* PBS, 1992.

Television; Plays:

The Caramel Crisis, BBC, 1966.
A Way with the Ladies, BBC, 1967.
Sleeping Dog, BBC, 1967, published by Faber and Faber, 1968.
Death of a Teddy Bear, BBC, 1967.
Spoiled, BBC, 1968.
The Dirt on Lucy Lane, BBC, 1969.
Pig in a Poke, London Weekend Television, 1969, published in *Close of Play and Pig in a Poke,* Methuen, 1979.
Style of the Countess, BBC, 1970.
The Princess, BBC, 1970.
Man in a Side-Car, BBC, 1971, published in *The Rear Column and Other Plays,* Methuen, 1978, Viking, 1979.
Two Sundays, BBC, 1975, published in *Otherwise Engaged and Other Plays,* Methuen and Viking, both 1976.
Plaintiffs and Defendants, BBC, 1975, published in *Otherwise Engaged and Other Plays,* Methuen and Viking, both 1976.

Radio Plays:

The Rector's Daughter, 1992.

Suffer the Little Children, 1993.
With a Nod and a Bow, 1993.

Other:

Colmain (novel), Faber and Faber, 1963.
Simple People (novel), Faber and Faber, 1965.
(Editor with Keith Walker) *Selected English Prose,* Faber and Faber, 1967.
Little Portia (novel), Faber and Faber, 1967.
(As Hamish Reade) *A Comeback for Stark,* Faber and Faber, 1969.
An Unnatural Pursuit and Other Pieces (journal), Faber and Faber, 1985, St. Martin's (New York City), 1986.
Plays, One (compilation), Metheun, 1986.
How's That for Telling 'em, Fat Lady? (journal), Faber and Faber, 1988.
Old Flames and A Month in the Country (screenplay), Faber and Faber, 1990.
Fat Chance (memoir), Faber and Faber, 1995.

OTHER SOURCES

Books:

Burkman, Katherine H., editor, *Simon Gray: A Casebook,* Garland Publishing, 1992.
Contemporary Authors, New Revision Series, Volume 32, Gale (Detroit, MI), 1991.
Contemporary Dramatists, fourth edition, St. James Press (Detroit, MI), 1988.
Contemporary Literary Criticism, Volume 36, Gale, 1986.
Dictionary of Literary Biography, Volume 13, *British Dramatists since World War II,* Gale, 1982.

Periodicals:

Independent, May 8, 1996, p. S8-S9; August 5, 1997, pp. S6-S7.
New Statesman and Society, August 11, 1995, p. 40.
Time, March 27, 1995, p. 75.
Times (London), February 5, 1993, p. 13; May 17, 1996, p. 19.*

GREENE, Lyn   1954(?)-
   (Lynnie Greene)

PERSONAL

Born May 21, 1954 (some sources say 1955), in Newton (some sources say Boston), MA; daughter of Kermit (a businessman) and Elinore A. (a teacher and author; maiden name, Ziff) Greene. *Education:* Attended Drama Division, Juilliard School, 1972-75; New York University, B.A., 1976.

Addresses: *Contact—c/o* Actors' Equity Association, Actors' Equity Association, 165 West 46th St., New York, NY 10036.

Career: Actress, sometimes under the name Lynnie Greene.

Member: Actors' Equity Association, American Federation of Television and Radio Artists, Screen Actors Guild.

CREDITS

Stage Appearances:
(Stage debut) Lead singer, *Earthlight,* Charles Playhouse, Boston, MA, 1972.
Michelle Schwartz, *Kid Purple,* Roundabout Theatre II, New York City, 1984.
Painting Churches, Cincinnati Playhouse in the Park, Cincinnati, OH, 1985-86.
Jane, *Villa Serena,* American Stage Company, Teaneck, NJ, 1986-87.
Charlotte, *Flora, the Red Menace,* Vineyard Theatre, New York City, 1987-88.
Aldrich, *Freeze Tag,* Henry Street Settlement Theatre, New York City, 1989.
Edna Edison, *The Prisoner of Second Avenue,* American Jewish Theatre, New York City, 1989.
Emma Goldman, *Assassins,* Playwrights Horizons Theatre, New York City, 1990-91.
Josie, *A Moon for the Misbegotten,* Missouri Repertory Theatre, Kansas City, MO, 1990-91.
Working One Acts '91, Theatre Row Theatre, New York City, 1991.
A Christmas Carol, McCarter Theatre, Princeton, NJ, 1991-92.

Appeared in *Quirks,* Edison, NY; *Say Goodnight Gracie,* Actors Playhouse, New York City; *Hi Low,* a solo show staged in New York; appeared as Hope, *Amateurs,* Michael Bennet Studios, New York City; as Nancy, *Oliver,* the Leader, *Zorba,* and Sally Bowles, *Cabaret,* all at Colorado Center for the Performing Arts; as Mary Warren, *The Crucible,* and Anne Rutledge, *Spoon River Anthology,* both at Meadowbrook Summer Theatre; as Susie La Reve, *The Gang's All Here,* Ralph Freud Playhouse, Los Angeles, CA; as Sister Ralph, *Ready or Not,* Pennsyl-

vania Stage Company; as Lina, *Misalliance,* and Rosalind, *As You Like It,* both Arizona Theatre Company; in the lead roles, *Sprechen Sie Brecht,* White Barn, Westport, CT, and *Brecht on Brecht,* St. Louis Repertory Company, Loretto-Hilton Hotel, St. Louis, MO; as Jenny, *The Threepenny Opera,* Portland Stage Company, Portland, OR; as Lucy Brown, *The Threepenny Opera,* St. Louis Repertory Company, Loretto-Hilton Hotel; as Lenny, *Crimes of the Heart,* Portland Stage Company; and as Helena, *A Midsummer Night's Dream,* Denver Center Theatre, Denver, CO. Toured as Rotonde, *The Love Cure,* with Lincoln Center tour.

Stage Work:
Director of *Hi Low,* a solo show, produced off-Broadway.

Film Appearances:
(As Lynnie Greene) Cynthia, *Over the Brooklyn Bridge,* United Artists, 1983.

Television Appearances; Series:
(As Lynnie Greene) Maria Teresa Bonino, *On Our Own,* CBS, 1977-78.

Television Appearances; Episodic:
Young Dorothy, "A Piece of Cake," *The Golden Girls,* NBC, 1987.
Young Dorothy, "One for the Money," *The Golden Girls,* NBC, 1987.
Young Dorothy, "Dateline—Miami," *The Golden Girls,* NBC, 1991.
Mercedes Macomber, "Alex, Then and Now," *The Five Mrs. Buchanans,* 1994.

Also appeared on various talk shows.

Television Work; Series:
Executive story editor (with Richard Levine), *Lush Life,* Fox, 1996.

WRITINGS

(With others) *Lush Life* (television series), Fox, 1996.

Adapted the stage play *Sprechen sie Brecht,* with Swen Swenson, produced at White Barn.*

GREENE, Lynnie
   See GREENE, Lyn

GROSBARD, Ulu 1929-

PERSONAL

Born January 9, 1929, in Antwerp, Belgium; immigrated to the United States in 1948; naturalized citizen, 1954; son of Morris (in business) and Rose (Tennenbaum) Grosbard; married Rose Gregorio (an actress), February 25, 1965. *Education:* University of Chicago, B.A. (with honors), 1950, M.A. (with honors), 1952; trained at the Yale School of Drama, 1952-53. *Avocational interests:* Chess, swimming.

Addresses: *Agent*—International Creative Management, 8942 Wilshire Blvd., Beverly Hills, CA 90211.

Career: Director, producer, and writer. *Military service:* U.S. Army Intelligence, 1953-55.

Member: Directors Guild of America, Society of Stage Directors and Choreographers, Dramatists Guild of the Authors League of America.

Awards, Honors: Drama Desk-Vernon Rice Award and Obie Award, *Village Voice,* both for direction, 1965, for *A View from the Bridge;* Antoinette Perry Award nomination, best dramatic director, 1965, for *The Subject Was Roses;* Antoinette Perry Award nomination, best director, 1977, for *American Buffalo.*

CREDITS

Stage Work; Director:
A View from the Bridge, Gateway Playhouse, Belleport, Long Island, NY, 1957.
Director, *The Days and Nights of Beebee Fenstermaker,* Sheridan Square Playhouse, 1962.
The Subject Was Roses, 1964.
A View from the Bridge, 1965.
The Investigation, 1966.
That Summer—That Fall, 1967.
The Price, 1968.
American Buffalo, 1977.
The Woods, 1979.
The Floating Light Bulb, 1981.
The Wake of Jamie Foster, 1982.
Weekends Like Other People, 1982.
The Tenth Man, Lincoln Center Theater Company, Vivian Beaumont Theater, New York City, 1989.

Film Work; Director:
The Subject Was Roses, Metro-Goldwyn-Mayer, 1968.

Who Is Harry Kellerman and Why Is He Saying Those Terrible Things About Me?, National General, 1971.
Straight Time, Warner Bros., 1978.
True Confessions, United Artists, 1981.
Falling in Love, Paramount, 1984.
(And producer) *Georgia,* Miramax, 1995.
The Deep End of the Ocean, 1998.

Film Work; Other:
Assistant director, *Splendor in the Grass,* Warner Bros., 1961.
Assistant director, *West Side Story,* United Artists, 1961.
Assistant director, *The Hustler,* Twentieth Century-Fox, 1961.
Assistant director, *The Miracle Worker,* United Artists, 1962.
Unit manager, *The Pawnbroker,* Allied Artists/Landau, 1965.

Television Work:
Production manager, *Deadline,* syndicated, 1959-60.
Production manager, *The Investigation,* 1967.

WRITINGS

Plays:
(Translator with Jan Swan) Peter Weiss, *The Investigation,* Atheneum, 1966.

Screenplays:
Who Is Harry Kellerman and Why Is He Saying Those Terrible Things About Me?, National General, 1971.

OTHER SOURCES

Books:
Contemporary Authors, Volumes 25-28, first revision, Gale (Detroit, MI), 1977.*

GROVER, Stanley 1926-1997

OBITUARY NOTICE—See index for *CTFT* sketch: Born Stanley Grover Nienstedt, March 28, 1926, in Woodstock, IL; died August 24, 1997, in Los Angeles, CA. Actor. Grover is best remembered for his stage work in supporting roles on Broadway. Early in his career he worked as a page boy for NBC in Chicago. His first television appearance was as a contestant on *Arthur Godfrey's Talent Scouts* in 1950.

The next year he made his New York stage debut as a chorus member in *Seventeen.* Many other stage productions followed, including roles in *Finian's Rainbow, Kismet, Plain and Fancy, South Pacific, Fanny, Wish You Were Here, West Side Story, The King and I, Desert Song, Brigadoon, Oklahoma,* and *Gentlemen Prefer Blondes.* His work in a tour of *South Pacific* took him to more than seventy-five cities. Grover also appeared in other popular musicals, including playing the title role in the 1956 production of *Candide.* He also ventured into other entertainment mediums. His work on television included appearances in the series *That Was the Week That Was, The Edge of Night, Somerset, Married: The First Year,* and *L.A. Law.* He also was featured in television movies such as *Enola Gay, Shannon's Deal,* and *Nutcracker: Money, Madness, and Murder.* His film work included *Network, The Onion Field, The Falcon and the Snowman, Being There,* and *Ghostbusters.* In addition to his work on the stage, in film, and on television, he also performed in nightclubs in the United States, Canada, and Puerto Rico.

OBITUARIES AND OTHER SOURCES

Periodicals:
New York Times, September 22, 1997, p. D15.

GUBER, Peter 1942-

PERSONAL

Full name, Howard Peter Guber; born March 1, 1942, in Boston, MA (some sources say Syracuse, NY); son of Samuel and Ruth Guber; married Lynda Gellis (a film producer); children: Jodie, Elizabeth. *Education:* Syracuse University, B.A.; New York University, M.B.A., J.D., and L.L.M.; University of Florence, S.S.P.

Addresses: *Office*—Mandalay Entertainment, Astaire Building, 10202 West Washington Blvd., Culver City, CA 90232.

Career: Producer. Columbia Pictures, production executive, 1968-76; Casablanca Record and Film Works, chairperson of board of directors, 1976-80; Polygram Pictures, chairperson, 1980-83; Guber-Peters Entertainment Company, cochairperson and coowner, 1983-88; Guber-Peters-Barris Entertainment Co., cochairperson and managing director, 1988-89, chairperson, 1989; Columbia Pictures, studio chief and cochairperson, 1989-94. Sony Pictures Entertainment, chairperson and chief executive officer, 1989-94; Peter Guber's Filmworks, principal. University of California, Los Angeles, adjunct professor and chairperson of producer's department, School of Theatre Arts. Bel Air Savings and Loan Association, founder and director.

Awards, Honors: Named NATO Producer of the Year, National Association of Theatre Owners, 1971 and 1979; Academy Award nomination and Golden Globe Award nomination, both c. 1977, for *The Deep;* six Golden Globe Awards, Hollywood Foreign Press Association, two Academy Awards, three British Academy Awards, British Academy of Film and Television Arts, and Los Angeles Film Critics Award, all c. 1978, for *Midnight Express;* Academy Award, c. 1981, for *An American Werewolf in London;* Palm D'Or Award, Cannes International Film Festival, five Golden Globe Award nominations, four Academy Awards, seven British Academy Awards, Christopher Award, best picture of the year, all c. 1982, for *Missing.*

Academy Award, two Golden Globe Awards, and four Grammy Award nominations, National Academy of Recording Arts and Sciences, all c. 1983, for *Flashdance;* Emmy Award nomination, best information, cultural, or historical program, 1984, for *Television and the Presidency;* Academy Award nomination, best picture, 1985, for *The Color Purple;* Academy Award, best picture, 1988, for *Rain Man;* Academy Award and Double Platinum Award, for *Thank God It's Friday;* Emmy award, documentary category, for *Mysteries of the Sea;* Albert Gallatin fellow, New York University; Ardent Award, Syracuse University.

CREDITS

Film Work; Executive Producer, Except Where Indicated:
Producer, *The Deep,* Columbia, 1977.
Midnight Express, Columbia, 1978.
Producer, *Thank God It's Friday,* Columbia, 1978.
Producer, *An American Werewolf in London,* Universal, 1981.
Producer, *Missing,* Universal, 1982.
Producer, *Six Weeks,* Universal, 1982.
Flashdance, Paramount, 1983.
D.C. Cab, Universal, 1983.
Producer, *Vision Quest* (also known as *Crazy for You*), Warner Bros., 1985.
The Legend of Billie Jean (also known as *Fair Is Fair*), TriStar, 1985.

The Color Purple, Warner Bros., 1985.

(With Jon Peters, George Folsey Jr., and John Landis) *Clue,* Paramount, 1985.

(With Peters) *Youngblood,* Metro-Goldwyn-Mayer/ United Artists, 1986.

(With Peters) *Head Office,* TriStar, 1986.

(With Peters, Mark Damon, and John W. Hyde) *The Clan of the Cave Bear,* Warner Bros., 1986.

Producer (with Peters and Neil Canton), *The Witches of Eastwick,* Warner Bros., 1987.

(With Peters and Roger Birnbaum) *Who's That Girl?,* Warner Bros., 1987.

(With Peters and Steven Spielberg) *Innerspace,* Warner Bros., 1987.

(With Peters) *Rain Man,* Metro-Goldwyn-Mayer/ United Artists, 1988.

(With Peters) *Gorillas in the Mist,* Universal, 1988.

Producer (with Peters and Canton), *Caddyshack II,* Warner Bros., 1988.

Producer (with Peters), *Tango and Cash,* Warner Bros., 1989.

Producer (with Peters and Chris Kenny), *Batman,* Warner Bros., 1989.

(With Peters, Benjamin Melniker, and Michael Uslan) *Batman Returns,* Warner Bros., 1992.

(With Peters) *This Boy's Life,* Warner Bros., 1993.

(With Peters) *With Honors,* Warner Bros., 1994.

Producer, *Endless Love;* other films include *Johnny Handsome.*

Television Series; Executive Producer:

Dreams, CBS, 1984.

Oceanquest, NBC, 1985.

Television Movies; Executive Producer:

(With Peters) *Brotherhood of Justice,* ABC, 1986.

The Toughest Man in the World, CBS, 1984.

Bay Coven (also known as *Strangers in Town* and *Eye of the Demon*), NBC, 1987.

Nightmare at Bitter Creek (also known as *Bitter Creek*), CBS, 1988.

Other Television Work:

Producer, *Stand by Your Man,* 1981.

Executive producer (with Peters), *Television and the Presidency,* syndicated, 1983.

Producer, *The Selling of the President,* 1984.

Executive producer, *Clue: Movies, Murder, and Mystery* (special), CBS, 1986.

Executive producer, *Finish Line,* 1989.

Producer of *Mysteries of the Sea, The Donna Summer Special, Double Platinum,* and *David Steinberg's Hollywood Stars.*

WRITINGS

Author of *Inside the Deep* and *Above the Title.*

OTHER SOURCES

Periodicals:

New York Times, October 22, 1989.*

GUDEGAST, Hans
   See BRAEDEN, Eric

H

HACK, Shelley 1952-

PERSONAL

Born July 6, 1952, in Greenwich, CT. *Education:* Attended Smith College and University of Sydney (Australia); studied acting at the Herbert Berghof Studio.

Addresses: *Agent*—c/o Metropolitan Talent, 4526 Wilshire Blvd., Los Angeles, CA 90010-3801.

Career: Actress and model. Appeared in television commercials as a Charlie Girl for Revlon. Member, BeatBob political organization, California, 1993-96; supporter, Brad Sherman's political campaign for Congressional representative, California, 1996.

CREDITS

Television Appearances; Series:
Tiffany Welles, *Charlie's Angels,* ABC, 1979-80.
Dr. Beth Gilbert, *Cutter to Houston,* CBS, 1983.
Jackie Shea, *Jack and Mike,* ABC, 1986-87.

Television Appearances; Movies:
Janette Clausen, *Death Car on the Freeway* (also known as *Death on the Freeway*), CBS, 1979.
Leslie Phillips, *Found Money* (also known as *My Secret Angel*), NBC, 1983.
Logan Gay, *Trackdown: Finding the Goodbar Killer,* CBS, 1983.
Frankie, *Single Bars, Single Women,* ABC, 1984.
Maggie, *Kicks,* ABC, 1985.
Kimberly Bradstreet, *Bridesmaids,* CBS, 1989.
Monica Browne, "A Casualty of War" (also known as "Casualty of War"), *Frederick Forsyth Presents,* USA Network, 1990.
Nan Horvat, *Taking Back My Life: The Nancy Ziegenmeyer Story* (also known as *The Rape of Nancy Ziegenmeyer* and *Taking Back My Life*), CBS, 1992.
Abby Walters Morrison, "A Perry Mason Mystery: The Case of the Wicked Wives" (also known as "The Case of the Wicked Wives" and "Perry Mason: The Case of the Wicked Wives"), *NBC Friday Night Mystery,* NBC, 1993.
Becky Worth, *Not in My Family* (also known as *Breaking the Silence* and *Shattering the Silence*), ABC, 1993.
Lynn Brown, *Falling From the Sky: Flight 174* (also known as *Freefall* and *Freefall: Flight 174*), ABC, 1995.
Jobeth Rawlings, *Frequent Flyer,* ABC, 1996.

Television Appearances; Specials:
Mary, *Vanities,* HBO, 1981.
Anna, *Close Ties,* The Entertainment Channel, 1983.

Television Appearances; Episodic:
"Dumb Luck," *The Love Boat,* ABC, 1980.
Janet McKay, "The Assassin," *Tales from the Crypt,* HBO, 1989.
Stark, "To Be or Not to Be," *seaQuest DSV* (also known as *seaQuest 2032*), NBC, 1993.
"Whose San Andreas Fault Is It, Anyway?," *L.A. Law,* NBC, 1994.

Television Appearances; Pilots:
Dr. Beth Gilbert, *Cutter to Houston,* CBS, 1983.
Jackie Shea, *Jack and Mike,* ABC, 1986.

Film Appearances:
Street stranger, *Annie Hall,* United Artists, 1977.
Jennifer Corly, *If Ever I See You Again,* Columbia, 1978.
Docent, *Time After Time,* Warner Bros./Orion, 1979.

Cathy Long, *The King of Comedy,* Twentieth Century-Fox, 1983.

Anne Potter, *Troll,* Empire, 1986.

Susan Blake, *The Stepfather* (also known as *Stepfather I*), New Century-Vista, 1987.

Erika Breen, *Blind Fear,* 1989.

Hannah Stone, *The Finishing Touch,* Columbia TriStar Home Video, 1992.

Jennifer, *Me, Myself, and I,* 1992.

Self-help author, *House Arrest,* Metro-Goldwyn-Mayer/United Artists, 1996.

Stage Appearances:

Billie Dawn, *Born Yesterday,* Pennsylvania Stage Company, Allentown, PA, 1982.

RECORDINGS

Taped Readings:

Lord of Hawkfell Island, The Publishing Mill, 1993.

OTHER SOURCES

Other:

http://www.bulmash.com/washed/archive/wu-angl2.html (web page), December 15, 1997.

http://www.charliesangels.com/shelley.html (web page), December 15, 1997.*

HALL, Peter   1930-
    (Peter J. Hall, Sir Peter Hall)

PERSONAL

Full name, Peter Reginald Frederick Hall; born November 22, 1930, in Bury St. Edmunds, Suffolk, England; son of Reginald Edward Arthur (a stationmaster) and Grace (Pamment) Hall; married Leslie Caron (a ballet dancer and actress), August 6, 1956 (divorced, 1965); married Jacqueline Taylor, 1965 (divorced, 1981); married Maria Ewing (an opera singer), 1982 (divorced, 1990); married Nicola Frei, 1990; children: six. *Education:* Attended Perse School, Cambridge; St. Catharine's College, Cambridge, B.A. (with honours), 1953, M.A., 1958. *Avocational interests:* Music.

Addresses: *Office*—Peter Hall Company, Ltd., 18 Exeter St., London WC2E 7DU, England.

Career: Director and television host. Director with Cambridge Amateur Dramatic Club, Marlowe Soci-

ety, and University Actors; Theatre Royal, Windsor, England, director, 1953; Elizabethan Theatre Company, artistic director, 1953; Oxford Playhouse, Oxford, England, and Worthing Repertory Theatre, director, 1954-55; Arts Theatre, London, assistant director, 1954, director, 1955-56; International Playwrights Theatre, founder, 1957, artistic director, 1957-60; Aldwych Theatre, London, England, director, 1960; Shakespeare Memorial Theatre, Stratford-upon-Avon, England, director, 1960; Royal Shakespeare Company, director, 1960-68, codirector, 1968-73; Warwick University, associate professor of drama, 1966—; National Theatre of Great Britain, director, 1972-88; Glyndebourne Festival Opera, Glyndebourne, England, artistic director, 1984-90; Peter Hall Company, Ltd., London, England, founder, 1988; Old Vic Theatre, London, England, artistic director, 1996-97; Royal Opera at Covent Garden, London, England, codirector. Billed sometimes as Peter J. Hall. *Military service:* Royal Air Force, 1948-50, served in education corps.

Member: Theatre Directors' Guild of Great Britain (founding member), Garrick Club, Athenaeum Club.

Awards, Honors: Antoinette Perry Award nomination, outstanding direction, 1958, for *The Rope Dancers;* London Theatre Critics Award, best director, 1963, for *The Wars of the Roses;* Order of Commander of the British Empire, 1963; honorary fellow, St. Catharine's College, Cambridge, 1964; London Theatre Critics Awards, best director, 1965, for *The Homecoming* and *Hamlet;* Chevalier de l'Ordre des Arts et des Lettres, 1965; honorary doctorates, University of York, 1966, University of Reading, 1973, University of Liverpool, 1974, University of Leicester, 1977, and Cornell University, 1980; Hamburg University Shakespeare Prize, 1967; Antoinette Perry Award, best director of a dramatic play, 1967, for *The Homecoming;* Emmy Award nomination, outstanding dramatic program, 1969, for *A Midsummer Night's Dream;* Drama Desk Award, outstanding director, and Antoinette Perry Award, best director of a dramatic play, both 1972, for *Old Times;* Knight of the British Empire, 1977; London *Standard* Special Award, 1979, for twenty-five years of service to the theatre; Antoinette Perry Award nomination (with Alan Ayckbourn), best director of a dramatic play, 1979, for *Bedroom Farce;* Antoinette Perry Award nomination, best director of a dramatic play, 1980, for *Betrayal;* London *Standard* awards, best director and outstanding achievement in opera, both 1981, for *A Midsummer Night's Dream;* Antoinette Perry Award, best director of a dramatic play, and

Drama Desk Award, best director of a play, both 1981, for *Amadeus;* London *Standard* Award, best director, 1987; Antoinette Perry Award nominations, best director of a dramatic play and best revival of a play or musical, both 1990, for *The Merchant of Venice.*

CREDITS

Stage Work; Director:

The Letter, Theatre Royal, Windsor, England, 1953.

Blood Wedding, Arts Theatre, London, England, 1954.

The Immoralist, Arts Theatre, 1954.

The Lesson, Arts Theatre, 1954.

South, Arts Theatre, 1954.

Mourning Becomes Electra, Arts Theatre, 1955.

Waiting for Godot, Arts Theatre, 1955.

Burnt Flower-Bed, Arts Theatre, 1955.

Listen to the Wind, Arts Theatre, 1955.

Summertime, Apollo Theatre, London, England, 1955.

The Waltz of the Toreadors, Arts Theatre, 1955.

Gigi, New Theatre, London, 1956.

Love's Labour's Lost, Shakespeare Memorial Theatre, Stratford-upon-Avon, England, 1956.

Camino Real, Phoenix Theatre, London, England, 1957.

The Moon and Sixpence, Sadler's Wells Theatre, London, England, 1957.

Cymbeline, Shakespeare Memorial Theatre, 1957.

The Rope Dancers, Cort Theatre, New York City, 1957.

Cat on a Hot Tin Roof, Comedy Theatre, London, England, 1958.

Twelfth Night, Shakespeare Memorial Theatre, 1958.

Brouhaha, Aldwych Theatre, London, England, 1958.

Shadow of Heroes, Piccadilly Theatre, London, England, 1958.

Madame De, Arts Theatre, then Statford-upon-Avon, England, 1959.

A Traveler without Luggage, Arts Theatre, 1959, then Stratford-upon-England, 1959.

A Midsummer Night's Dream, Shakespeare Memorial Theatre, 1959.

Coriolanus, Shakespeare Memorial Theatre, 1959.

The Wrong Side of the Park, Stratford-upon-Avon, England, 1959, then Cambridge Theatre, London, England, 1960.

The Two Gentleman of Verona, Shakespeare Memorial Theatre, 1960.

Twelfth Night, Shakespeare Memorial Theatre, then Aldwych Theatre, both 1960.

(With John Barton) *Troilus and Cressida,* Shakespeare Memorial Theatre, 1960.

The Taming of the Shrew, Shakespeare Memorial Theatre, 1960.

The Merchant of Venice, Shakespeare Memorial Theatre, 1960.

The Winter's Tale, Shakespeare Memorial Theatre, 1960.

The Duchess of Malfi, Aldwych Theatre, 1960.

The Hollow Crown, Shakespeare Memorial Theatre, 1960, then Aldwych Theatre, 1961, later Henry Miller's Theatre, New York City, 1963.

Ondine, Royal Shakespeare Company, Aldwych Theatre, 1961.

Becket, Royal Shakespeare Company, Aldwych Theatre, 1961.

Romeo and Juliet, Royal Shakespeare Company, Royal Shakespeare Theatre, 1961.

A Midsummer Night's Dream, Royal Shakespeare Company, Royal Shakespeare Theatre, 1961.

The Collection, Royal Shakespeare Company, Aldwych Theatre, 1961.

Troilus and Cressida, Royal Shakespeare Company, Aldwych Theatre, 1961.

A Midsummer Night's Dream, Royal Shakespeare Company, Royal Shakespeare Theatre, 1963.

The War of the Roses (adapted from Shakespeare's *Henry VI, Parts I, II,* and *III,* and *Richard III*), Royal Shakespeare Company, Royal Shakespeare Theatre, 1963-64.

A Cycle of Seven History Plays (includes *Richard II, Henry IV Parts I* and *II, Henry V, Henry VI, Part I, Edward IV,* and *Richard III*), Royal Shakespeare Company, Royal Shakespeare Theatre, 1963, then Aldwych Theatre, 1964.

Eh?, Royal Shakespeare Company, 1964.

The Homecoming, Royal Shakespeare Company, Aldwych Theatre, 1965, then Music Box Theatre, New York City, 1967.

Hamlet, Royal Shakespeare Company, Royal Shakespeare Theatre, 1965.

The Government Inspector, Royal Shakespeare Company, Aldwych Theatre, 1965.

Staircase, 1966.

Macbeth, 1967.

A Midsummer Night's Dream, Royal Shakespeare Company, Royal Shakespeare Theatre, 1967.

A Delicate Balance, Aldwych Theatre, 1969.

Dutch Uncle, 1969.

Landscape, Aldwych Theatre, 1969.

Silence, Aldwych Theatre, 1969.

The Battle of Shrivings, Lyric Theatre, London, England, 1970.

Old Times, Royal Shakespeare Company, Aldwych Theatre, 1971, then New York City, 1971-72.

Via Galactica, Uris Theatre, New York City, 1972.

All Over, Royal Shakespeare Company, Aldwych Theatre, 1972.

Alte Zeiten (Austrian production of *Old Times*), Burgtheatre, Vienna, Austria, 1972.

The Tempest, National Theatre Company, Old Vic Theatre, London, England, 1973.

John Gabriel Borkman, National Theatre Company, 1974.

Happy Days, National Theatre Company, 1974.

No Man's Land, National Theatre Company, 1975.

Hamlet, National Theatre Company, 1975.

Judgement, National Theatre Company, 1975.

Tamburlaine the Great, National Theatre Company, 1977.

(With Alan Ayckbourn) *Bedroom Farce*, National Theatre Company, 1977.

Volpone, National Theatre Company, 1978.

The Country Wife, National Theatre Company, 1978.

The Cherry Orchard, National Theatre Company, 1978.

Macbeth, National Theatre Company, 1978.

Betrayal, National Theatre Company, 1978.

Amadeus, National Theatre Company, 1979.

(With Alan Ayckbourn) *Bedroom Farce*, Brooks Atkinson Theatre, New York City, 1979.

Betrayal, Trafalgar Theatre, New York City, 1980.

Amadeus, Broadhurst Theatre, New York City, 1980-83.

Othello, 1980.

Family Voices, National Theatre Company, Lyttelton Theatre, London, England, 1981.

Amadeus, National Theatre Company, Her Majesty's Theatre, London, England, 1981.

The Oresteia, National Theatre Company, Olivier Theatre, London, England, 1981.

The Importance of Being Earnest, National Theatre Company, Lyttelton Theatre, 1982.

Other Places: Family Voices, Victoria Station, and a Kind of Alaska, National Theatre Company, Cottesloe Theatre, London, England, 1982.

Jean Seberg, National Theatre Company, 1983.

Animal Farm, National Theatre Company, 1984.

Coriolanus, National Theatre Company, Olivier Theatre, 1984.

Martine, National Theatre Company, Lyttelton Theatre, 1985.

Yonadab, National Theatre Company, Olivier Theatre, 1985.

The Oresteia, National Theatre Company, 1986.

The Petition, National Theatre Company, Lyttelton Theatre, then Wyndham's Theatre, London, England, then John Golden Theatre, New York City, all 1986.

Coming into Land, National Theatre Company, Lyttelton Theatre, 1987.

Antony and Cleopatra, National Theatre Company, Olivier Theatre, 1987.

Entertaining Strangers, National Theatre Company, Cottesloe Theatre, 1987.

The Winter's Tale, National Theatre Company, Cottesloe Theatre, then Olivier Theatre, both 1988.

The Tempest, National Theatre Company, Cottesloe Theatre, then Olivier Theatre, both 1988.

Cymbeline, National Theatre Company, Cottesloe Theatre, then Olivier Theatre, both 1988.

Orpheus Descending, Peter Hall Company, Theatre Royal, Haymarket, London, England 1988-89, then Neil Simon Theatre, New York City, 1989.

Merchant of Venice, Peter Hall Company, Phoenix Theatre, 1989, then 46th Street Theatre, New York City, 1989-90.

The Wild Duck, Peter Hall Company, Phoenix Theatre, 1990.

The Homecoming, Peter Hall Company, Comedy Theatre, 1991.

Twelfth Night, Peter Hall Company, Playhouse Theatre, London, England, 1991.

The Rose Tattoo, Peter Hall Company, Playhouse Theatre, 1991.

Tartuffe, Peter Hall Company, Playhouse Theatre, 1991.

An Ideal Husband, Globe Theatre, London, England, 1992.

All's Well that Ends Well, Royal Shakespeare Company, 1992.

Four Baboons Adoring the Sun, New York City, 1992.

Sienna Red, 1992.

The Gift of the Gorgon, Wyndham's Theatre, 1993.

An Absolute Turkey, Globe Theatre, 1994.

The Master Builder, Royal Alexandra Theatre, Toronto, Ontario, Canada, 1995-96.

An Ideal Husband, Ethel Barrymore Theatre, New York City, 1996.

The Oedipus Plays, Olivier Theatre, Royal National Theatre, 1996.

Also directed *An Impresario from Smyrna*, Arts Theatre.

Stage Director; Major Tours:
The Gates of Summer, English cities, 1956.
King Lear, Royal Shakespeare Company, 1964.
The Comedy of Errors, Royal Shakespeare Company, 1964.

Stage Director; Operas:
Moses and Aaron, Royal Opera House, Covent Garden, London, England 1965.

The Magic Flute, Royal Opera House, 1966.

The Knot Garden, Royal Opera House, 1970.

La Calisto, Glyndebourne Festival Opera, Glyndebourne, England, 1970.

Eugene Onegin, Royal Opera House, 1971.

Tristan and Isolde, Royal Opera House, 1971.

Il Ritorno d'Ulisse in Patria, Glyndebourne Festival Opera, 1972.

The Marriage of Figaro, Glyndebourne Festival Opera, 1973.

Don Giovanni, Glyndebourne Festival Opera, 1978.

Cosi Fan Tutte, Glyndebourne Festival Opera, 1978.

Fidelio, Glyndebourne Festival Opera, 1979.

A Midsummer Night's Dream, Glyndebourne Festival Opera, 1982.

Orfeo ed Euridice, Glyndebourne Festival Opera, 1982.

Macbeth, Glyndebourne Festival Opera, then Metropolitan Opera, New York City, 1982.

Der Ring des Nibelungen, Bayreuth, West Germany, 1983.

The Marriage of Figaro, Geneva, Switzerland, 1983.

Don Giovanni, Glyndebourne Festival Opera, 1984.

Cosi Fan Tutte, Glyndebourne Festival Opera, 1984.

L'Incoronazione di Poppea, Glyndebourne Festival Opera, 1984.

Carmen, Glyndebourne Festival Opera, 1985.

Albert Herring, Glyndebourne Festival Opera, 1985-86.

L'Incoronazione di Poppea, Glyndebourne Festival Opera, 1986.

Simon Boccanegra, Glyndebourne Festival Opera, 1986.

Carmen, Metropolitan Opera, 1986.

Salome, Los Angeles, CA, 1986.

The Marriage of Figaro, Chicago, IL, 1987.

La Traviata, Glyndebourne Festival Opera, 1987-88.

Cosi Fan Tutte, Los Angeles, CA, 1988.

Falstaff, Glyndebourne Festival Opera, 1988.

Salome, Covent Garden, then Chicago, IL, both 1988.

Albert Herring, Covent Garden, 1989.

The Marriage of Figaro, Glyndebourne Festival Opera, 1989.

A Midsummer Night's Dream, Glyndebourne Festival Opera, 1989.

New Year, Houston, TX, 1989.

The Magic Flute, Los Angeles, CA, 1992.

Carmen, Metropolitan Opera, 1996.

Film Director; Unless Otherwise Indicated:

Work Is a Four Letter Word (also known as *Work Is a 4-Letter Word*), Universal, 1968.

A Midsummer Night's Dream, Eagle, 1969.

Three into Two Won't Go, Universal, 1969.

Perfect Friday, Chevron, 1970.

The Homecoming, American Film Theatre Distributing, 1973.

Landscape, 1974.

(And producer) *Akenfield,* Angle Films, 1974.

She's Been Away, BBC Films, 1989.

Dialogue editor, *Dallas Doll*, 1994.

(And producer) *Delinquent*, 1994.

Never Talk to Strangers, TriStar, 1995.

Also directed *All Over* and *Old Times*.

Film Appearances:

Rudolf Hartmann, *The Pedestrian*, 1974.

She's Been Away, BBC Films, 1989.

Television Appearances; Specials:

Living Shakespeare: A Year with the RSC, Arts and Entertainment, 1992.

Television Director, Unless Otherwise Indicated; Specials:

The War of the Roses, BBC, 1964.

A Midsummer Night's Dream, CBS, 1969.

(As Sir Peter Hall) *Fidelio*, Arts and Entertainment, 1985.

Albert Herring, 1986.

L'Incoronazione di Poppea, 1986.

Oresteia, Channel Four, 1986.

La Traviata, 1987.

"*Carmen*," *Live from the Met*, PBS, 1987.

Production manager, *ABC Presents a Royal Gala*, ABC, 1988.

The Marriage of Figaro, 1989.

Television Director; Movies:

Orpheus Descending, TNT, 1991.

Jacob: A TNT Bible Story (also known as *Jacob*), TNT, 1994.

Television Director; Miniseries:

The Camomile Lawn, Channel Four, 1992.

Television Appearances; Series:

Host, *Aquarius*, London Weekend Television, 1975-77.

Radio Director:

Family Voices, BBC, 1981.

WRITINGS

Screenplays:

Delinquent, 1994.

Teleplays; Movies:
Orpheus Descending, TNT, 1991.

Translations:
(With Inga-Stina Ewbank) Henrik Ibsen, *John Gabriel Borkman: An English Version,* Athlone Press (London, England), 1975.
(With Nicola Frei) Georges Feydeau, *An Absolute Turkey,* Globe Theatre, 1994.

Nonfiction:
(Author of foreword) David Addenbrooke, *The Royal Shakespeare Company: The Peter Hall Years,* afterword by Trevor Nunn, Kimber (London, England), 1974.
(Preparer with John Russell Brown) Christopher Marlowe, *Tamburlaine the Great, Parts I and II,* R. Collins (London, England), 1976.
(Edited by John Goodwin) *Peter Hall's Diaries: The Story of a Dramatic Battle,* Hamish Hamilton (London, England), 1983, Harper (New York City), 1984.
Making an Exhibition of Myself, Sinclair-Stevenson (London, England), 1993.

Adapted Plays:
(With John Barton) *The War of the Roses* (from Shakespeare's *Henry VI, Parts I, II, and III* and *Richard III*), Royal Shakespeare Company, published by the British Broadcasting Corporation, 1970.
George Orwell's Animal Farm, with lyrics by Adrian Mitchell and music by Richard Peaslee, Methuen (London, England), 1985.
(With Inga-Stina Ewbank) *The Wild Duck: An English Adaptation,* 1990.

RECORDINGS

Contributor to albums, including *Das Rheingold, Gotterdaemmerung, Purcell: Music for Westminster Abbey, Stravinksy: The Flood, Abraham and Isaac, Variations, Requiem, Canticles;* and *Wuorinen: A Reliquary for Igor Stravinsky.*

OTHER SOURCES

Books:
Fay, Stephen, *Power Play: The Life and Times of Peter Hall,* Hodder and Stoughton (London, England), 1995.
Hall, Peter, *Peter Hall's Diaries: The Story of a Dramatic Battle,* edited by John Goodwin, Hamish Hamilton, 1983, Harper, 1984.

Periodicals:
American Record Guide, March-April, 1996, p. 168; September-October, 1996, pp. 34-36.
MacLean's, January 29, 1996, p. 61.
New Statesman, September 20, 1996, p. 39.
Stereo Review, April, 1996, p. 101.
Variety, May 6, 1996, p. 210; July 29, 1996, pp. 63-64.
Wall Street Journal, November 18, 1996, p. A10.*

HALL, Peter J.
　　See HALL, Peter

HALL, Sir Peter
　　See HALL, Peter

HAMEL, Veronica　1945(?)-

PERSONAL

Born November 20, 1945 (some sources say 1943), in Philadelphia, PA; father, a carpenter. *Education:* Attended Temple University.

Addresses: *Agent*—c/o International Creative Management, 8942 Wilshire Blvd., Beverly Hills, CA 90211.

Career: Actress and producer. Model with the Eileen Ford Agency.

Awards, Honors: Q Award, Viewers for Quality Television Awards, best supporting actress in a quality drama series, 1985, and Emmy Award nominations, 1981, 1982, and 1983, all for *Hill Street Blues.*

CREDITS

Stage Appearances:
Annie Sullivan, *The Miracle Worker,* St. Louis, MO, 1982.

Also appeared on Broadway in *Rumors,* New York City; off-Broadway in *The Ballad of Boris K.;* and off-off-Broadway in *The Big Knife,* New York City; also appeared in dinner theatre productions.

Major Tours:

Appeared in *Cactus Flower,* U.S. cities.

Film Appearances:

Apple Pie, Aumont Productions, 1976.

Linda, *Cannonball* (also known as *Carquake*), New World, 1976.

Suzanne Constantine, *Beyond the Poseidon Adventure,* Warner Bros., 1979.

Nikki, *When Time Ran Out* (also known as *Earth's Final Fury*), Warner Bros., 1980.

Kay Hutton, *A New Life,* Paramount, 1988.

Elizabeth Barnes, *Taking Care of Business* (also known as *Filofax*), Buena Vista, 1990.

Television Appearances; Series:

Joyce Davenport, *Hill Street Blues,* NBC, 1981-87.

Television Appearances; Miniseries:

Laura DeWitt Koshko, *Harold Robbins' 79 Park Avenue* (also known as *79 Park Avenue*), NBC, 1977.

Kate Kane, *Kane and Abel,* CBS, 1985.

Deborah, *Twist of Fate,* NBC, 1989.

Television Appearances; Episodic:

"Fashion Mart," *Joe Forrester,* NBC, 1975.

"A House of Prayer, a Den of Thieves," *Kojak,* CBS, 1975.

"Peeper-Two," *The Bob Newhart Show,* CBS, 1976.

Sandy Lederer, "A Bad Deal in the Valley," *The Rockford Files,* NBC, 1976.

"Round Up the Usual Suspects," *Switch,* CBS, 1976.

Thelma, "The Castle of Dreams," *City of Angels,* NBC, 1976.

"Tap Dancing Their Way Back into Your Hearts," *Starsky and Hutch,* ABC, 1976.

Marcy, "Return to the 38th Parallel" (also known as "Return to the Thirty-eighth Parallel"), *The Rockford Files,* NBC, 1976.

"Change of Heart," *Family,* ABC, 1977.

"The Intimate Friends of Jenny Wilde," *The Eddie Capra Mysteries,* NBC, 1978.

"Blackmail," *Dallas,* CBS, 1979.

"Judgment Call," *Doctors' Private Lives,* ABC, 1979.

"Powder Burn," *Eischied,* NBC, 1980.

"Lupe Anguiano," *An American Portrait,* CBS, 1985.

Herself, "The Annies," *The Duck Factory,* NBC, 1985.

Television Appearances; Movies:

Helen Thornton, *The Gathering,* ABC, 1977.

Andrea Mason, *Ski Lift to Death* (also known as *Snowblind*), CBS, 1978.

Helen Thornton, *The Gathering, Part II* (also known as *The Gathering II*), NBC, 1979.

Sheila Dodge, *The Hustler of Muscle Beach,* ABC, 1980.

Jennifer North, *Jacqueline Susann's Valley of the Dolls 1981* (also known as *Valley of the Dolls*), CBS, 1981.

Leigh Churchill and Randy Churchill, *Sessions,* ABC, 1983.

Brotherhood of the Rose, 1989.

Elizabeth Early, *She Said No,* NBC, 1990.

Dr. Kathy Holland, *Deadly Medicine,* NBC, 1991.

Stop at Nothing, Lifetime, 1991.

Bianca Hudson, *Baby Snatcher,* CBS, 1992.

Kitty Dodds, *The Conviction of Kitty Dodds* (also known as *Conviction: The Kitty Dodds Story*), CBS, 1993.

Nora Freemont, *The Disappearance of Nora* (also known as *The Stranger in the Mirror*), CBS, 1993.

Dr. Paula Spencer, *A Child's Cry For Help* (also known as *Intensive Care*), NBC, 1994.

Rebecca Kendall, *Shadow of Obsession* (also known as *Unwanted Attentions*), NBC, 1994.

Lily Munster, *Here Come the Munsters,* Fox, 1995.

Etta Berter, *Secrets,* ABC, 1995.

Micki Dickoff, *In the Blink of an Eye* (also known as *Blink of an Eye*), ABC, 1996.

Sadie Frost, *Talk to Me,* ABC, 1996.

Georgia Patchett, *Home Invasion,* NBC, 1997.

Jenifer Richmond, *Stranger in My Home* (also known as *Brother's Keeper*), CBS, 1997.

Television Appearances; Specials:

Host, *Breast Cancer: What You Don't Know Can Hurt You,* 1990.

Television Work; Coexecutive Producer; Movies:

Deadly Medicine, NBC, 1991.

Baby Snatcher, CBS, 1992.*

HAMILTON, George   1939-

PERSONAL

Born George Stevens Hamilton IV, August 12, 1939, in Memphis, TN; married Alana Collins (an actress), 1972 (divorced, 1976); children: Ashley Steven. *Education:* Attended Hackley Prep School, New York, and Palm Beach High School, Palm Beach, FL.

Addresses: *Agent*—Agency for the Performing Arts, 9000 Sunset Blvd., Suite 1200, Los Angeles, CA 90069.

Career: Actor, producer, talk show host, and writer.

Awards, Honors: Golden Globe, most promising male newcomer (with Barry Coe, Troy Donahue, and James Shigeta), 1960; Saturn Award, best actor, Academy of Science Fiction and Fantasy Films, USA, and Golden Globe nomination, best actor in a musical or comedy, both 1980, for *Love At First Bite;* Showman star of the year, ShoWest Convention, USA, 1981; Golden Globe nomination, best actor in a musical or comedy, 1982, for *Zorro, the Gay Blade.*

CREDITS

Film Appearances:
Robert Cole, *Crime and Punishment, USA,* Allied Artists, 1959.

Theron Hunnicutt, *Home from the Hill,* Metro-Goldwyn-Mayer, 1960.

Tony McDowall, *All the Fine Young Cannibals,* Metro-Goldwyn-Mayer, 1960.

Ryder Smith, *Where the Boys Are,* Metro-Goldwyn-Mayer, 1960.

Paul Strand, *Angel Baby,* Allied Artists, 1961.

Warren Winner, *By Love Possessed,* United Artists, 1961.

Lieutenant Curtis McQuade, *A Thunder of Drums,* Metro-Goldwyn-Mayer, 1961.

Fabrizio Naccarelli, *Light in the Piazza,* Metro-Goldwyn-Mayer, 1962.

Davie Drew, *Two Weeks in Another Town,* Metro-Goldwyn-Mayer, 1962.

Moss Hart, *Act One,* Warner Bros., 1963.

Corporal Trower, *The Victors,* Columbia, 1963.

Himself, *Looking for Love,* Metro-Goldwyn-Mayer, 1965.

Hank Williams, *Your Cheatin' Heart,* Metro-Goldwyn-Mayer, 1965.

Flores, *Viva Maria* (also known as *Viva Maria!*), United Artists, 1966.

George, *That Man George* (also known as *Our Man in Marrakesh, El Hombre de Marrakech, L'Homme de Marrakech, Los Saqueadores del Domingo,* and *L'Uomo di Casablanca*), Allied Artists, 1967.

Harlan Wycliff, *Doctor, You've Got to Be Kidding!,* Metro-Goldwyn-Mayer, 1967.

Jeff Hill, *Jack of Diamonds* (also known as *Der Diamantenprinz*), Metro-Goldwyn-Mayer, 1967.

Captain Bentley, *A Time for Killing* (also known as *The Long Ride Home*), Columbia, 1967.

Jim Tanner, *The Power,* Metro-Goldwyn-Mayer, 1968.

Togetherness, 1970.

Title role, *Evel Knievel,* Fanfare, 1972.

Medusa (also known as *The Rhodes Incident* and *Twisted*), 1973.

Crocker, *The Man Who Loved Cat Dancing,* Metro-Goldwyn-Mayer, 1973.

David Milford, *Once Is Not Enough* (also known as *Jacqueline Susann's Once Is Not Enough*), Paramount, 1975.

Ward Thompson, *The Happy Hooker Goes to Washington,* Cannon, 1977.

Vance, *Sextette,* Crown International, 1978.

Count Vladimir Dracula, *Love at First Bite,* American International, 1979.

Express to Terror, 1979.

Maurice, *From Hell to Victory* (also known as *Da Dunkerque alla Vittoria, De Dunkerque a la Victoria,* and *De L'Enfer a la Victoire*), New Film, 1979.

Don Diego Vega/Bunny Wigglesworth, *Zorro, the Gay Blade,* Twentieth Century-Fox, 1981.

B. J. Harrison, *The Godfather, Part III* (also known as *Mario Puzo's The Godfather, Part III*), Paramount, 1990.

Doctor Halberstrom, *Doc Hollywood,* Warner Bros., 1991.

Alfonso de la Pena, *Once Upon a Crime,* Metro-Goldwyn-Mayer, 1992.

Rudolfo Carbonera, *Amore!,* 1993.

Himself, *Double Dragon* (also known as *Double Dragon: The Movie*), Gramercy Pictures, 1994.

Gil Braman, *Playback,* Paramount Home Video, 1995.

Dick Bennett, *8 Heads in a Duffel Bag* (also known as *Eight Heads in a Duffel Bag*), Orion Pictures, 1997.

Himself, *Meet Wally Sparks,* Trimark, 1997.

Film Work:
Producer, *Evel Knievel,* Fanfare, 1972.

Producer, *Medusa* (also known as *The Rhodes Incident* and *Twisted*), 1973.

Executive coproducer, *Love at First Bite,* American International, 1979.

(With C. O. Erickson) Coproducer, *Zorro, the Gay Blade,* Twentieth Century-Fox, 1981.

Television Appearances; Series:
Duncan Carlyle, *The Survivors* (also known as *Harold Robbins's The Survivors*), ABC, 1969.

Jack Brennan, *Paris 7000,* ABC, 1970.

Joel Abrigore, *Dynasty,* ABC, 1985-86.

Ian Stone, *Spies,* CBS, 1987.

Sonny Stone, *The Bold and the Beautiful* (also known as *Glamour, Top Models,* and *Belleza y Poder*), CBS, 1987.

Host (with Alana Stewart), *The George & Alana Show,* syndicated, 1995-96.
Alan Van Buren, *The Guilt,* 1996.
Guy Hathaway, *Jenny,* NBC, 1997—.

Television Work; Series:
Coproducer, *The George & Alana Show,* syndicated, 1995-96.

Television Appearances; Episodic:
"Two of a Kind," *The Rogues,* 1964.
Dan McCadden, "And Bimbo Was His Name-O," *Dream On,* HBO, 1990.
Himself, *Cybill,* CBS, 1995.
Himself, *Dave's World,* CBS, 1995.
Craig Wohlman, *Diagnosis Murder,* CBS, 1995.
Himself, "Cosmetic Perjury," *The John Larroquette Show,* NBC, 1995.
Himself, "Woman Who Rises in World Falls on Face," *The Naked Truth* (also known as *Pix* and *Wilde Again*), ABC, 1995.
Don Green *NewsRadio* (also known *News Radio*), NBC, 1995.
Dirk Lawson, "Up All Night," *The Bonnie Hunt Show* (also known as *Bonnie*), CBS, 1996.

Also appeared on *The Adventures of Rin Tin Tin,* ABC, and *The Donna Reed Show,* ABC.

Television Appearances; Miniseries:
Stephen Bennett, *Roots,* ABC, 1977.
Lieutenant Hamilton Stovall, *The Seekers,* 1979.
Jay Pomerantz, *Malibu,* 1983.
Harry Price, *Monte Carlo,* CBS, 1986.
William Randolph Hearst, *Rough Riders* (also known as *Teddy Roosevelt and the Rough Riders*), TNT, 1997.

Television Work; Miniseries:
Producer, *Roots,* ABC, 1977.

Television Appearances; Movies:
Dr. Mark Collier, *Columbo: A Deadly State of Mind,* ABC, 1975.
Don Drake, *The Dead Don't Die,* 1975.
Glenn Lyle, *Killer on Board,* 1977.
Greg Oliver, *The Strange Possession of Mrs. Oliver,* 1977.
Adam Baker, *The Users,* 1978.
Ray Jeffries, *Death Car on the Freeway* (also known as *Death on the Freeway*), CBS, 1979.
Alan Roberto, *Institute for Revenge,* 1979.
Hightower, *The Great Cash Giveaway Getaway,* 1980.

Bradley, *Two Fathers' Justice,* NBC, 1985.
Cousin John, *Poker Alice,* CBS, 1987.
Wade Anders, *Caution: Murder Can Be Hazardous to Your Health* (also known as *Columbo*), ABC, 1991.
J. D. Gantry, *The House on Sycamore Street* (also known as *Murder on Sycamore Street* and *Remedy For Murder*), CBS, 1992.
Henry von Hohenlodern, *Das Paradies am Ende der Berge,* 1993.
Bradley, *Two Fathers: Justice For the Innocent* (also known as *Two Fathers Return*), NBC, 1994.
Malcolm Patterson, *Danielle Steel's Vanished* (also known as *Vanished*), NBC, 1995.
Karl Von Ostenberg, *Hart to Hart: Till Death Do Us Hart* (also known as *Hart to Hart: Double Trouble*), The Family Channel, 1996.

Television Appearances; Specials:
Ringmaster, *Circus of the Stars,* 1977.
The Fantastic Miss Piggy Show, 1982.
Richard Manning III, *Poor Richard,* 1984.
Cohost, *Super Model Search: Look of the Year,* 1988.
Host, *Dracula: Live From Transylvania,* 1989.
The Golden Globe Awards, 1989.
The 75th Anniversary of Beverly Hills, 1989.
Host, *The Lords of Hollywood,* 1990.
(With Dr. Ruth Westheimer) Host, *Comedy Battle of the Sexes,* Lifetime, 1992.
Dame Edna's Hollywood, NBC, 1992.
Host, *Heartstoppers . . . Horror at the Movies,* syndicated, 1992.
Host, *The Soap Opera Digest Awards* (also known as *The 8th Annual Soap Opera Digest Awards*), NBC, 1992.
Host, *Canned Ham: 8 Heads in a Duffel Bag,* Comedy Central, 1997.
(With Marla Maples) Host, *The 1997 Miss Universe Pageant,* CBS, 1997.
(With Marla Maples) Host, *The 1997 Miss USA Pageant,* CBS, 1997.

Producer, *The Veil.*

OTHER SOURCES

Periodicals:
People Weekly, August 8, 1994, p. 88; November 6, 1995, pp. 77-80; October 13, 1997, pp. 15-16.
TV Guide, September 30, 1995, pp. 26-31.
Vanity Fair, August, 1994, pp. 106-114.*

HANCOCK, Herbert
  See HANCOCK, Herbie

HANCOCK, Herbie   1940-
  (Herbert Hancock)

PERSONAL

Full name, Herbert Jeffrey Hancock; born April 12, 1940, in Chicago, IL; son of Wayman Edward (a government meat inspector) and Winnie Belle (Griffin) Hancock; married Gudrun Meixner (a decorator and art collector), August 31, 1968; children: Jessica Dru. *Education:* Grinnell College, B.A., 1960; graduate work, Roosevelt University, 1960; also studied at the Manhattan School of Music, 1962, and at the New School for Social Research, 1967. *Religion:* Nichiren Shoshu Buddhist. *Avocational interests:* Computers and international travel.

Addresses: *Publicist*—c/o Bobbi Marcus, Bobbi Marcus Public Relations, 1616 Butler Avenue, West Los Angeles, CA 90025.

Career: Composer, musician, music director, and actor. Keyboardist with Coleman Hawkins, 1960, Donald Byrd, 1960-63, Miles Davis, 1963-68, and with the Herbie Hancock Sextet, V.S.O.P. Quintet, Chick Corea, Oscar Peterson, and various other projects, 1968—; Hancock Music Company, Los Angeles, CA, founder, 1962, owner and publisher, 1962—; Hancock and Joe Productions, Los Angeles, founder, 1989, owner, 1989—; Harlem Jazz Music Center, New York City, president; as a jazz musician, has appeared in concerts throughout the world, including a limited engagement with Natalie Cole and the Manhattans, Winter Garden Theatre, New York City, 1976.

Member: National Academy of Recording Arts and Sciences, American Federation of Musicians, Screen Actors Guild, American Federation of Television and Radio Artists, Pioneer Club (Grinnell College).

Awards, Honors: Citation of Achievement, Broadcast Music Inc., 1963; Jay Award, *Jazz* magazine, 1964; *Downbeat* magazine Critics' Poll Award, talent deserving wider recognition, 1967; *Record World* magazine award, best new artist—all-star band, 1968, for the Herbie Hancock Sextet; *Downbeat* magazine Critics' Poll Award, keyboard player of the year, 1968, 1969, and 1970; *Downbeat* magazine Critics' Poll Award, composer of the year, 1971; Gold Record Award, Recording Industry Association of America, 1973, for *Headhunters; Black Music* magazine Award, top jazz artist, 1974; Grammy Award, best r&b instrumental performance, 1983, for "Rockit" from *Future Shock; Rolling Stone* magazine Critics' Poll Award, jazz artist of the year, and *Rolling Stone* magazine Readers' Poll Award, jazz artist of the year, both 1984; Grammy Award, best r&b instrumental performance, 1984, for *Sound-System;* Academy Award, best original score, and Golden Globe nomination, best music—original score, 1987, both for *'Round Midnight;* Grammy Award, best jazz instrumental composition, 1987, for "Call Street Blues" from *'Round Midnight.* Also awarded honorary degrees from Grinnell College and Berklee College of Music.

CREDITS

Film Appearances:
Eddie Wayne, *'Round Midnight* (also known as *Autour de Minuit*), Warner Bros., 1986.
Himself, *Listen Up: The Lives of Quincy Jones* (also known as *Listen Up*), 1991.
Himself, *Indecent Proposal,* Paramount, 1993.

Film Work; Music Director:
'Round Midnight (also known as *Autour de Minuit*), Warner Bros., 1986.

Television Appearances; Series:
Host, *Rock-School,* PBS.

Television Appearances; Episodic:
Gideon, *Concrete Cowboys,* CBS, 1981.
Himself, "Firestorm," *Mickey Spillane's Mike Hammer* (also known as *The New Mike Hammer*), CBS, 1985.
Performer, *Birdland,* 1992.

Also appeared on *Late Night with David Letterman,* NBC; *The Mike Douglas Show,* CBS; *Phil Donahue,* syndicated; *Saturday Night Live,* NBC; and *Sesame Street,* PBS.

Television Appearances; Specials:
Sun City, MTV, 1985.
"Miles Ahead: The Music of Miles Davis," *Great Performances,* PBS, 1986.
Host, *Showtime Coast to Coast,* Showtime, 1987.
A Jazz Session—Sass and Brass, Cinemax, 1987.

Late Night with David Letterman Fifth Anniversary Show, NBC, 1987.

Performer, *Celebrating a Jazz Master: Thelonious Sphere Monk,* PBS, 1987.

Host, *The New Orleans Jazz and Heritage Festival,* Showtime, 1988.

"A Duke Named Ellington," *American Masters,* PBS, 1988.

Performer, *Newport Jazz '88,* PBS, 1988.

All-Star Tribute to Kareem Abdul-Jabbar, NBC, 1989.

Grammy Living Legends, CBS, 1989.

Our Common Future, syndicated, then Arts and Entertainment, 1989.

Performer, *The Neville Brothers: Tell It Like It Is,* Cinemax, 1989.

Host, *Showtime Coast to Coast: American Music,* Showtime, 1990.

Host, *Showtime Coast to Coast: The London Sessions,* Showtime, 1990.

Performer, *The Best of Cinemax Sessions,* Cinemax, 1990.

Miles and Friends, Bravo, 1992.

The Kennedy Center Honors: A Celebration of the Performing Arts, CBS, 1992.

Performer, "A Salute to the Newport Jazz Festival," *In Performance at the White House,* PBS, 1993.

An American Reunion: The 52nd Presidential Inaugural Gala, CBS, 1993.

"Miles Davis: A Tribute" (also known as "Miles at Montreux"), *Great Performances,* PBS, 1993.

Host, "Carnegie Hall Salutes the Jazz Masters," *Great Performances,* PBS, 1994.

Performer, "Partners," *Directed By,* Showtime, 1994.

Nissan Presents a Celebration of America's Music, ABC, 1996.

Television Music Director; Specials:

The Neville Brothers: Tell It Like It Is, Cinemax, 1989.

Showtime Coast to Coast: American Music, Showtime, 1990.

Showtime Coast to Coast: The London Sessions, Showtime, 1990.

Television Appearances; Awards Presentations:

Presenter, *American Video Awards,* 1985.

The 28th Annual Grammy Awards, 1986.

Performer, *The 29th Annual Grammy Awards,* 1987.

The American Music Awards, 1987.

The 30th Annual Grammy Awards, 1988.

The American Music Awards, 1988.

The 22nd Annual NAACP Image Awards, 1990.

The 32nd Annual Grammy Awards, 1990.

Presenter, *The American Music Awards,* 1992.

Presenter, *The 35th Annual Grammy Awards,* 1993.

Presenter and performer, *Cybermania '94: The Ultimate Gamer Awards,* 1994.

The 39th Annual Grammy Awards, 1997.

WRITINGS

Film; Composer:

Herbie (student film), 1966.

(As Herbert Hancock) *Blow-Up* (also known as *Blowup*), Premier Productions, 1966.

The Spook Who Sat By the Door, United Artists, 1973.

Death Wish, Paramount, 1974.

A Soldier's Story, Columbia, 1984.

(And arranger) *'Round Midnight* (also known as *Autour de Minuit*), Warner Bros., 1986.

Jo Jo Dancer, Your Life Is Calling, Columbia, 1986.

(With Michael Kamen) *Action Jackson,* Lorimar, 1988.

Colors, Orion, 1988.

Harlem Nights, Paramount, 1989.

Songs Used in Films:

"You Bet Your Love," *Sunburn,* 1979.

"I Thought It Was You," *The Bitch,* 1979.

"Cantaloupe Island," *American Pop,* 1981.

L'Homme aux Yeux d'Argent, 1985.

"Hardrock," *Fast Forward,* 1985.

"Watermelon Man," "Chan's Song," "I Love a Party," "Call Street Blues," *'Round Midnight* (also known as *Autour de Minuit*), Warner Bros., 1986.

"Wipe Out," *Back to the Beach,* 1987.

"Livin' Large," *Livin' Large,* 1991.

"Cantaloop," *Super Mario Bros.,* 1993.

"Cantaloop," *Jimmy Hollywood,* Paramount, 1994.

"Cantaloop (Flip Fantasia)," *Renaissance Man,* Buena Vista, 1997.

"Just Around the Corner," *Donnie Brasco,* Columbia/TriStar, 1997.

Television Composer; Series:

Hey, Hey, Hey, It's Fat Albert, CBS, 1969.

Television Composer; Movies:

The George McKenna Story, CBS, 1986.

Television Composer; Episodic:

"Koi and the Kola Nuts," *We All Have Tales,* Showtime, 1992.

RECORDINGS

Albums:

My Point of View, Blue Note, 1963.

Inventions and Dimensions, Blue Note, 1963.
Takin' Off, Blue Note, 1963.
Empyrean Isles, Blue Note, 1964.
(With Ron Carter, Freddie Hubbard, Elvin Jones, and Wayne Shorter) *Speak No Evil,* 1964.
Succotash, Pausa, 1964.
Maiden Voyage, Blue Note, 1965.
Speak Like a Child, Blue Note, 1968.
The Prisoner, Blue Note, 1969.
Fat Albert Rotunda, Warner Bros., 1970.
Mwandishi, Warner Bros., 1971.
Crossings, Warner Bros., 1972.
Sextant, Columbia, 1972.
Headhunters (also known as *Head Hunters*), Columbia, 1973.
Thrust, Columbia, 1974.
Death Wish (original soundtrack), Columbia, 1974.
The Best of Herbie Hancock, Blue Note, 1974.
Flood, 1975.
Man-Child, Columbia, 1975.
Secrets, Columbia, 1976.
(With Ron Carter, Freddie Hubbard, Wayne Shorter, and Tony Williams) *V.S.O.P.: The Quintet,* Columbia, 1977.
V.S.O.P., Columbia, 1977.
(With Ron Carter and Tony Williams) *The Herbie Hancock Trio,* 1977.
(With Chick Corea) *In Concert, 1978,* Polydor, 1978.
Sunlight, Columbia, 1978.
(With Chick Corea) *An Evening with Herbie Hancock and Chick Corea in Concert,* Columbia, 1979.
Direct Step, 1979.
Feets Don't Fail Me Now, Columbia, 1979.
Mr. Hands, Columbia, 1980.
Monster, Columbia, 1980.
Greatest Hits, Columbia, 1980.
(With Ron Carter and Tony Williams) *The Herbie Hancock Trio with Ron Carter and Tony Williams,* 1981.
(With Ron Carter, Wynton Marsalis, and Tony Williams) *The Herbie Hancock Quartet,* Columbia, 1982.
Lite Me Up, Columbia, 1982.
Future Shock, Columbia, 1983.
Sound-System, Columbia, 1984.
(With Foday Musa Suso) *Village Life,* Columbia, 1985.
'Round Midnight (original soundtrack; also known as *Autour de Minuit*), Columbia, 1986.
Jo Jo Dancer, Your Life Is Calling (original soundtrack), Warner Bros., 1986.
(With Dexter Gordon) *The Other Side of 'Round Midnight,* Blue Note, 1987.
Perfect Machine, Columbia, 1988.
Vibe Alive, CBS Records, 1988.

The Best of Herbie Hancock: The Blue Note Years, Blue Note, 1988.
Herbie Hancock: A Jazz Collection, Columbia, 1991.
Herbie Hancock: The Collection, Castle Communications, 1991.
The Very Best of Herbie Hancock, Sony Music, 1991.
(With Whoopi Goldberg and Bill Summers) *Koi and the Kola Nuts,* Rabbit Ears, 1991.
The Best of Herbie Hancock, Volume II, Sony Music, 1992.
Dis Is Da Drum, Mercury, 1994.
(With Michael Brecker, Al Foster, Greg Osby, Buster Williams, and vocalist Bobby McFerrin) *The Herbie Hancock Quintet Live,* Jazz Door, 1994.
(With Gene Jackson and Jeff Littleton) *The Herbie Hancock Trio: Live in New York,* Jazz Door, 1994.
Cantaloupe Island, Blue Note, 1994.
Mwandishi Herbie Hancock: The Complete Warner Bros. Recordings, Warner Archives, 1994.
Herbie Hancock: Dance Singles, Sony Records, 1995.
The New Standard, Verve, 1996.

Also recorded *Herbie Hancock,* Blue Note; *Magic Windows,* Columbia; *Corea/Hancock,* Polydor; (with V.S.O.P.) *Live Under the Sky,* Columbia; and *Hot and Heavy.*

Albums; Contributor:
Miles Davis, *Nefertiti,* Columbia, 1967.
Miles Davis, *Filles de Kilimanjaro,* 1968.
Miles Davis, *In a Silent Way,* Columbia, 1969.
Joe Zawinul, *Zawinul,* Atlantic, 1971.
Bobby Womack, *Safety Zone,* United Artists, 1975.
Miles Davis, *Circle in the Round,* 1979.
George Benson, *Give Me the Night,* 1980.
Alphonse Mouzon, *By All Means,* Pausa, 1981.
Alphonse Mouzon, *Morning Sun,* Pausa, 1981.
Quincy Jones, *The Dude,* A&M, 1981.
(And producer) Wynton Marsalis, *Wynton Marsalis,* 1982.
Manu Dibango, *Electric Africa,* Celluloid, 1985.
Mandingo *Watto Sitta,* 1987.
Quincy Jones, *Back on the Block,* Qwest, 1989.
George Clinton, *Hey Man . . . Smell My Finger,* 1993.
Manifestation: Axiom Collection II, Axiom, 1993.
(And producer) *A Tribute to Miles,* Qwest, 1994.
Axiom Funk, *Funkcronomicon,* Axiom, 1995.
Quincy Jones, *Q's Jook Joint,* Warner Bros., 1995.
Tony Williams, *Wilderness,* 1996.

OTHER SOURCES

Periodicals:
Down Beat, January, 1990, pp. 16-21, 56-57.
Entertainment Weekly, March 8, 1996, p. 63.*

HANNA, William 1910-

PERSONAL

Full name, William Denby Hanna; born July 14, 1910, in Melrose, NM; son of William John and Avice Joyce (Denby) Hanna; married Violet Blanch Wogatzke, August 7, 1936; children: David William, Bonnie Jean. *Education:* Studied engineering and journalism at Compton Junior College, 1929-30.

Addresses: *Office*—Hanna-Barbera Productions, 3400 West Cahuenga Blvd., Hollywood, CA 90068.

Career: Animator, producer, director, and writer. Warner Bros., Burbank, CA, animator, scriptwriter, and story editor, 1931-33; Harman-Ising Animation Studios, Hollywood, CA, animator, scriptwriter, lyricist, and composer, 1933-37; Metro-Goldwyn-Mayer, Hollywood, CA, animator, director, producer, and story editor, 1937-57, head of animation department (with Joseph Barbera), 1955-57; Hanna-Barbera Productions, Hollywood, CA, founder (with Joseph Barbera) and senior vice president, 1957—. Also worked as a structural engineer.

Awards, Honors: (All with Joseph Barbera) Academy Award nominations, best animated short subject, 1940, for *Puss Gets the Boot,* and 1941, for *The Night before Christmas;* Academy Awards, best animated short subject, 1943, for *Yankee Doodle Mouse,* 1944, for *Mouse Trouble,* 1945, for *Quiet, Please!,* and 1946, for *The Cat Concerto;* Academy Award nomination, best animated short subject, 1947, for *Dr. Jekyll and Mr. Mouse;* Academy Award, best animated short subject, 1948, for *The Little Orphan;* Academy Award nominations, best animated short subject, 1949, for *Hatch Up Your Troubles,* and 1950, for *Jerry's Cousin;* Academy Awards, best animated short subject, 1951, for *The Two Mouseketeers,* and 1952, for *Johann Mouse;* Academy Award nominations, best animated short subject, 1954, for *Touche, Pussy Cat,* 1955, for *Good Will to Men,* and 1957, for *One Droopy Knight;* Emmy Award, outstanding achievement in the field of children's programming, 1960, for *The Huckleberry Hound Show;* Golden Globe Award, outstanding achievement in international television cartoons, Hollywood Foreign Press Association, 1965, for *The Flintstones;* Emmy Award, outstanding children's special, 1966, for *Jack and the Beanstalk;* Emmy Award, outstanding achievement in children's programming (informational/factual), 1973, for *The Last of the Curlews;* Emmy Award,

outstanding informational children's series, 1974, for *The Runaways;* Annie Award, 1977, for *Charlotte's Web;* Christopher Award and Emmy Award, outstanding special—drama or comedy, both 1978, for *The Gathering;* Emmy Award, outstanding children's entertainment series, 1982, for *The Smurfs;* Golden Reel Award, animation sound editing, and Bronze Award, best children's special, both from International Film and Television Festival of New York, 1982, for *The Smurfs' Springtime Special;* Emmy Award, outstanding children's entertainment series, 1983, for *The Smurfs;* Bronze Award, best children's special, 1984, for *The Smurfic Games;* Men of the Year Award, National Center for Hyperactive Children, 1986; Gold Angel Award, Religion in Media, 1986, for excellence in media; Distinguished Service Award, National Religious Broadcasters, and Award of Excellence, Film Advisory Board, both 1987, for *The Greatest Adventure: Stories from the Bible;* Humanitas Prize, 1987, for "Lure of the Orb" episode of *The Smurfs;* Governor's Award, National Academy of Television Arts and Sciences, 1988; inducted into Television Academy Hall of Fame, 1994.

CREDITS

Film Work; With Joseph Barbera, Except Where Indicated:

Animation director, *Anchors Aweigh,* Metro-Goldwyn-Mayer, 1945.

Animation director, *Holiday in Mexico,* Metro-Goldwyn-Mayer, 1946.

Animation director, *Neptune's Daughter,* Metro-Goldwyn-Mayer, 1949.

Animation director (also with Fred Quimby), *Dangerous When Wet,* Metro-Goldwyn-Mayer, 1953.

Animation director (also with Quimby), *Invitation to the Dance,* Metro-Goldwyn-Mayer, 1956.

Producer and director, *Hey There, It's Yogi Bear* (animated), Columbia, 1964.

Producer and director, *The Man Called Flintstone* (animated; also known as *That Man Flintstone*), Columbia, 1966.

Producer and animation director, *Project X,* Paramount, 1968.

Producer, *Charlotte's Web* (animated), Paramount, 1973.

Producer, *C.H.O.M.P.S.,* AID, 1979.

Executive producer, *Liar's Moon,* Crown International, 1982.

Producer, *Heidi's Song* (animated), Paramount, 1982.

Director, *Escape from Grumble Gulch,* 1983.

Director, *Les Dalton en Cavale* (also known as *Les Dalton en Balade*), 1983.

Executive producer, *GoBots: Battle of the Rock Lords* (animated), Atlantic Releasing, 1986.

Executive producer, *The Greatest Adventure: Stories from the Bible* (home video release), 1986.

Producer and director, *Jetsons: The Movie* (animated), Universal, 1990.

Executive producer (with Paul Gertz), *Once upon a Forest* (animated), Twentieth Century-Fox, 1993.

Executive producer (with Barbera and others), *The Flintstones*, Universal, 1994.

Producer of the film *Forever Like a Rose.*

Director of Short Animated Films; With Barbera, Except Where Indicated:

To Spring, 1936.

Sole director, *Blue Monday,* Metro-Goldwyn-Mayer, 1938.

Sole director, *What a Lion,* Metro-Goldwyn-Mayer, 1938.

Sole director, *Old Smokey,* Metro-Goldwyn-Mayer, 1938.

Gallopin' Gals, Metro-Goldwyn-Mayer, 1940.

Swing Social, Metro-Goldwyn-Mayer, 1940.

Puss Gets the Boot, Metro-Goldwyn-Mayer, 1940.

Romeo in Rhythm, Metro-Goldwyn-Mayer, 1940.

The Goose Goes South, Metro-Goldwyn-Mayer, 1941.

Midnight Snack, Metro-Goldwyn-Mayer, 1941.

The Night before Christmas, Metro-Goldwyn-Mayer, 1941.

Officer Pooch, Metro-Goldwyn-Mayer, 1941.

The Bowling-Alley Cat, Metro-Goldwyn-Mayer, 1942.

Dog Trouble, Metro-Goldwyn-Mayer, 1942.

Fine Feathered Friend, Metro-Goldwyn-Mayer, 1942.

Fraidy Cat, Metro-Goldwyn-Mayer, 1942.

Puss 'n' Toots, Metro-Goldwyn-Mayer, 1942.

Baby Puss, Metro-Goldwyn-Mayer, 1943.

Yankee Doodle Mouse, Metro-Goldwyn-Mayer, 1943.

Lonesome Mouse, Metro-Goldwyn-Mayer, 1943.

Sufferin' Cats, Metro-Goldwyn-Mayer, 1943.

War Dogs, Metro-Goldwyn-Mayer, 1943.

The Bodyguard, Metro-Goldwyn-Mayer, 1944.

The Million Dollar Cat, Metro-Goldwyn-Mayer, 1944.

The Zoot Cat, Metro-Goldwyn-Mayer, 1944.

Puttin' on the Dog, Metro-Goldwyn-Mayer, 1944.

Mouse Trouble (also known as *Cat Nipped* and *Kitty Foiled*), Metro-Goldwyn-Mayer, 1944.

The Mouse Comes to Dinner (also known as *Mouse to Dinner*), Metro-Goldwyn-Mayer, 1945.

Flirty Birdy (also known as *Love Boids*), Metro-Goldwyn-Mayer, 1945.

Mouse in Manhattan (also known as *Manhattan Serenade*), Metro-Goldwyn-Mayer, 1945.

Quiet, Please!, Metro-Goldwyn-Mayer, 1945.

Tee for Two, Metro-Goldwyn-Mayer, 1945.

The Milky Waif, Metro-Goldwyn-Mayer, 1946.

Solid Serenade, Metro-Goldwyn-Mayer, 1946.

The Cat Concerto, Metro-Goldwyn-Mayer, 1946.

Springtime for Thomas, Metro-Goldwyn-Mayer, 1946.

Trap Happy, Metro-Goldwyn-Mayer, 1946.

The Invisible Mouse, Metro-Goldwyn-Mayer, 1947.

Part-Time Pal (also known as *Fair Weathered Friend*), Metro-Goldwyn-Mayer, 1947.

Cat Fishin', Metro-Goldwyn-Mayer, 1947.

A Mouse in the House, Metro-Goldwyn-Mayer, 1947.

Dr. Jekyll and Mr. Mouse, Metro-Goldwyn-Mayer, 1947.

Salt Water Tabby, Metro-Goldwyn-Mayer, 1947.

Kitty Foiled, Metro-Goldwyn-Mayer, 1948.

Old Rockin' Chair Tom, Metro-Goldwyn-Mayer, 1948.

The Little Orphan, Metro-Goldwyn-Mayer, 1948.

Professor Tom, Metro-Goldwyn-Mayer, 1948.

Make Mine Freedom, Metro-Goldwyn-Mayer, 1948.

Mouse Cleaning, Metro-Goldwyn-Mayer, 1948.

The Truce Hurts, Metro-Goldwyn-Mayer, 1948.

Polka Dot Puss, Metro-Goldwyn-Mayer, 1949.

Hatch Up Your Troubles, Metro-Goldwyn-Mayer, 1949.

The Cat and the Mermouse, Metro-Goldwyn-Mayer, 1949.

Heavenly Puss, Metro-Goldwyn-Mayer, 1949.

Jerry's Diary, Metro-Goldwyn-Mayer, 1949.

Love That Pup, Metro-Goldwyn-Mayer, 1949.

Tennis Chumps, Metro-Goldwyn-Mayer, 1949.

Framed Cat, Metro-Goldwyn-Mayer, 1950.

Tom and Jerry in the Hollywood Bowl, Metro-Goldwyn-Mayer, 1950.

Jerry and the Lion (also known as *Hold That Lion*), Metro-Goldwyn-Mayer, 1950.

Little Quacker, Metro-Goldwyn-Mayer, 1950.

Saturday Evening Puss (also known as *Party Cat*), Metro-Goldwyn-Mayer, 1950.

Jerry's Cousin (also known as *City Cousin* and *Muscles Mouse*), Metro-Goldwyn-Mayer, 1950.

Texas Tom, Metro-Goldwyn-Mayer, 1950.

Cue Ball Cat, Metro-Goldwyn-Mayer, 1950.

Safety Second (also known as *F'r Safety Sake*), Metro-Goldwyn-Mayer, 1950.

Casanova Cat, Metro-Goldwyn-Mayer, 1951.

Cat Napping, Metro-Goldwyn-Mayer, 1951.

His Mouse Friday, Metro-Goldwyn-Mayer, 1951.

Jerry and the Goldfish, Metro-Goldwyn-Mayer, 1951.

The Two Mouseketeers, Metro-Goldwyn-Mayer, 1951.

Nit-Witty Kitty, Metro-Goldwyn-Mayer, 1951.

Sleepy-Time Tom, Metro-Goldwyn-Mayer, 1951.

Slicked-Up Pup, Metro-Goldwyn-Mayer, 1951.

The Flying Cat, Metro-Goldwyn-Mayer, 1952.

Cruise Cat, Metro-Goldwyn-Mayer, 1952.

The Dog House, Metro-Goldwyn-Mayer, 1952.

The Duck Doctor, Metro-Goldwyn-Mayer, 1952.

Fit to Be Tied, Metro-Goldwyn-Mayer, 1952.

Johann Mouse, Metro-Goldwyn-Mayer, 1952.

Little Runaway, Metro-Goldwyn-Mayer, 1952.

Push-Button Kitty, Metro-Goldwyn-Mayer, 1952.

Smitten Kitten, Metro-Goldwyn-Mayer, 1952.

Triplet Trouble, Metro-Goldwyn-Mayer, 1952.

The Missing Mouse, Metro-Goldwyn-Mayer, 1953.

Jerry and Jumbo, Metro-Goldwyn-Mayer, 1953.

That's My Pup, Metro-Goldwyn-Mayer, 1953.

Just Ducky, Metro-Goldwyn-Mayer, 1953.

Two Little Indians, Metro-Goldwyn-Mayer, 1953.

Life with Tom, Metro-Goldwyn-Mayer, 1953.

Pet Peeve, Metro-Goldwyn-Mayer, 1954.

Little School Mouse, Metro-Goldwyn-Mayer, 1954.

Baby Butch, Metro-Goldwyn-Mayer, 1954.

Mice Follies, Metro-Goldwyn-Mayer, 1954.

Neapolitan Mouse, Metro-Goldwyn-Mayer, 1954.

Downhearted Duckling, Metro-Goldwyn-Mayer, 1954.

Posse Cat, Metro-Goldwyn-Mayer, 1954.

Hic-Cup Pup (also known as *Tyke Takes a Nap*), Metro-Goldwyn-Mayer, 1954.

Puppy Tale, Metro-Goldwyn-Mayer, 1954.

Touche, Pussy Cat, Metro-Goldwyn-Mayer, 1954.

(Also with Quimby) *Good Will to Men,* Metro-Goldwyn-Mayer, 1955.

Pup on a Picnic, Metro-Goldwyn-Mayer, 1955.

Designs on Jerry, Metro-Goldwyn-Mayer, 1955.

Southbound Duckling, Metro-Goldwyn-Mayer, 1955.

Pecos Pest, Metro-Goldwyn-Mayer, 1955.

Smarty Cat, Metro-Goldwyn-Mayer, 1955.

That's My Mommie, Metro-Goldwyn-Mayer, 1955.

Mouse for Sale, Metro-Goldwyn-Mayer, 1955.

Tom and Cherie, Metro-Goldwyn-Mayer, 1955.

Barbeque Brawl, Metro-Goldwyn-Mayer, 1956.

The Flying Sorceress, Metro-Goldwyn-Mayer, 1956.

Blue Cat Blues, Metro-Goldwyn-Mayer, 1956.

Give and Take, Metro-Goldwyn-Mayer, 1956.

Busy Buddies, Metro-Goldwyn-Mayer, 1956.

The Egg and Jerry, Metro-Goldwyn-Mayer, 1956.

Scat Cats, Metro-Goldwyn-Mayer, 1956.

Down Beat Bear, Metro-Goldwyn-Mayer, 1956.

Muscle Beach Tom, Metro-Goldwyn-Mayer, 1956.

One Droopy Knight, Metro-Goldwyn-Mayer, 1957.

Feedin' the Kiddie, Metro-Goldwyn-Mayer, 1957.

Mucho Mouse, Metro-Goldwyn-Mayer, 1957.

Timid Tabby, Metro-Goldwyn-Mayer, 1957.

Tom's Photo Finish, Metro-Goldwyn-Mayer, 1957.

Tops with Pops, Metro-Goldwyn-Mayer, 1957.

Happy Go Ducky (also known as *One Quack Mind*), Metro-Goldwyn-Mayer, 1958.

Royal Cat Nap, Metro-Goldwyn-Mayer, 1958.

Robin Hoodwinked, Metro-Goldwyn-Mayer, 1958.

Tot Watchers, Metro-Goldwyn-Mayer, 1958.

The Vanishing Duck, Metro-Goldwyn-Mayer, 1958.

Little Bo Bopped, Metro-Goldwyn-Mayer, 1958.

Wolf Hounded, Metro-Goldwyn-Mayer, 1958.

Creepy Time Pal, Columbia, 1960.

Tale of a Wolf, Columbia, 1960.

The Do-Good Wolf, Columbia, 1960.

Life with Loopy, Columbia, 1960.

Snoopy Loopy, Columbia, 1960.

No Biz Like Shoe Biz, Columbia, 1960.

Here Kiddie, Kiddie, Columbia, 1960.

Count Down Clown, Columbia, 1961.

Happy Go Loopy, Columbia, 1961.

Two-Faced Wolf, Columbia, 1961.

Catch Meow, Columbia, 1961.

Child Sock-Cology, Columbia, 1961.

Fee Fie Foes, Columbia, 1961.

Kooky Loopy, Columbia, 1961.

Loopy's Hare-Do, Columbia, 1961.

This Is My Ducky Day, Columbia, 1961.

Zoo Is Company, Columbia, 1961.

Bungle Uncle, Columbia, 1962.

Bearly Able, Columbia, 1962.

Beef-for and After, Columbia, 1962.

Bunnies Abundant, Columbia, 1962.

Chicken Fracas-see, Columbia, 1962.

Common Scents, Columbia, 1962.

Rancid Ransom, Columbia, 1962.

Slippery Slippers, Columbia, 1962.

Swash Buckled, Columbia, 1962.

Just a Wolf at Heart, Columbia, 1963.

Chicken-Hearted Wolf, Columbia, 1963.

Whatcha Watchin, Columbia, 1963.

A Fallible Fable, Columbia, 1963.

Drum-Sticked, Columbia, 1963.

Bear Up!, Columbia, 1963.

The Crook That Cried Wolf, Columbia, 1963.

Habit Rabbit, Columbia, 1963.

Not in Nottingham, Columbia, 1963.

Sheep Stealers Anonymous, Columbia, 1963.

Wolf in Sheepdog's Clothing, Columbia, 1963.

Elephantastic, 1964.

Bear Hug, 1964.

Bear Knuckles, 1964.

Trouble Bruin, 1964.

Raggedy Rug, 1964.
Habit Troubles, 1964.
Big Mouse-Take, Columbia, 1965.
Pork Chop Phooey, Columbia, 1965.
Crow's Fete, Columbia, 1965.
Horse Shoo, Columbia, 1965.

Film Appearances:
Tire salesman, *Roadie,* United Artists, 1980.

Television Series with Barbera; Executive Producer; Animated:
Producer (with Bob Cottle), *The Ruff and Reddy Show,* NBC, 1957-64.
Producer and director, *The Huckleberry Hound Show* (also featuring *Pixie and Dixie, Hokey Wolf,* and *Yogi Bear*), syndicated, 1958-62.
Producer and director, *Yogi Bear* (also featuring *Snagglepuss* and *Yakky Doodle Duck*), syndicated, 1958-62.
Producer, *The Quick Draw McGraw Show* (also featuring *Snooper and Blabber* and *Augie Doggie and Doggie Daddy*), syndicated, 1959-62.
Producer and director, *The Flintstones,* ABC, 1960-66.
Producer and director, *Top Cat,* ABC, 1961-62.
Producer and director, *Lippy the Lion,* syndicated, 1962.
Producer and director, *Touche Turtle,* syndicated, 1962.
Producer and director, *Wally Gator,* syndicated, 1962.
(Also director) *The Jetsons,* ABC, 1962-63.
(Also director) *The Adventures of Jonny Quest* (also known as *Jonny Quest*), ABC, 1964-65.
Producer and director, *The Magilla Gorilla Show* (also featuring *Ricochet Rabbit* and *Punkin Puss and Mush Mouse*), syndicated, 1964-67.
Producer and director, *The Peter Potamus Show* (also featuring *Yippie, Yappie, and Yahooey* and *Breezly and Sneezly*), syndicated, 1964-67.
Producer and director, *The Atom Ant/Secret Squirrel Show* (also featuring *The Hillbilly Bears, Squiddly Diddly,* and *Precious the Dog*), NBC, 1965-68.
Producer, *Sinbad, Jr., the Sailor* (also known as *The Adventures of Sinbad, Jr.*), syndicated, 1966.
Producer and director, *The Abbott and Costello Cartoon Show,* syndicated, 1966.
Producer (also with Larry Harmon), *Laurel and Hardy,* syndicated, 1966-67.
Producer and director, *Space Kiddettes,* NBC, 1966-67.
Producer and director, *Space Ghost* (also featuring *Dino Boy*), CBS, 1966-68.

Producer and director, *Frankenstein, Jr. and the Impossibles,* CBS, 1966-68.
Producer, *Samson and Goliath,* NBC, 1967-68.
Producer and director, *Birdman and the Galaxy Trio,* NBC, 1967-68.
Producer and director, *The Herculoids,* CBS, 1967-69.
Producer, *Moby Dick and the Mighty Mightor,* CBS, 1967-69.
Producer and director, *Shazzan!,* CBS, 1967-69.
(Also director) *The Fantastic Four,* ABC, 1967-70.
Here Come the Stars (live-action), syndicated, 1968.
Producer, *The New Adventures of Huck Finn* (live-action and animated), NBC, 1968-69.
Producer and director, *The Wacky Races,* CBS, 1968-70.
Producer, *The Banana Splits Adventure Hour* (live-action and animated; also featuring *The Micro Venture, Danger Island, The Three Musketeers, The Hillbilly Bears,* and *The Arabian Knights*), NBC, 1968-70.
(Also director) *The Adventures of Gulliver* (also known as *The Adventures of Young Gulliver*), ABC, 1969-70.
Producer and director, *The Perils of Penelope Pitstop,* CBS, 1969-71.
(Also director) *The Cattanooga Cats* (also featuring *It's the Wolf, Around the World in 79 Days,* and *Auto Cat and Motor Mouse*), ABC, 1969-71.
(Also director) *Dastardly and Muttley in Their Flying Machines,* CBS, 1969-71.
(Also director with Charles A. Nichols) *Scooby-Doo, Where Are You?,* CBS, 1969-74.
(Also director) *Motor Mouse,* 1970.
(Also director) *Where's Huddles?,* CBS, 1970-71.
(Also director) *The Harlem Globetrotters,* CBS, 1970-73.
(Also director) *Josie and the Pussycats,* CBS, 1970-72, 1974-76.
Pebbles and Bamm Bamm, CBS, 1971-72.
(Also director) *Help! It's the Hair Bear Bunch,* CBS, 1971-72.
(Also director) *The Funky Phantom,* ABC, 1971-72.
Producer and director, *Wait 'til Your Father Gets Home,* syndicated, 1972.
Sealab 2020, NBC, 1972-73.
The Roman Holidays, NBC, 1972-73.
(Also director) *The Amazing Chan and the Chan Clan,* CBS, 1972-74.
(Also director) *The Flintstone Comedy Hour,* CBS, 1972-74.
(Also director with Nichols) *Josie and the Pussycats in Outer Space,* CBS, 1972-74.
The New Scooby-Doo Movies, CBS, 1972-74.

Speed Buggy, CBS, 1973-74.

(Also director) *Butch Cassidy and the Sundance Kids,* NBC, 1973-74.

Producer, *Peter Puck,* NBC, 1973-74.

Inch High, Private Eye, NBC, 1973-74.

Yogi's Gang, ABC, 1973-75.

Jeannie, CBS, 1973-75.

Goober and the Ghost Chasers, ABC, 1973-75.

The Addams Family, NBC, 1973-75.

Super Friends, ABC, 1973-83.

Wheelie and the Chopper Bunch, NBC, 1974-75.

The Partridge Family: 2200 A.D., CBS, 1974-75.

Korg: 70,000 B.C. (live-action), ABC, 1974-75.

Hong Kong Phooey, ABC, 1974-76.

These Are the Days, ABC, 1974-76.

Devlin, ABC, 1974-76.

Valley of the Dinosaurs, CBS, 1974-76.

(Also director) *The Scooby-Doo/Dynomutt Hour,* ABC, 1976-77.

Mumbly, ABC, 1976-77.

The Clue Club, CBS, 1976-77.

Jabberjaw, ABC, 1976-78.

The Skatebirds (also featuring *The Robonic Stooges, Wonder Wheels, Woofer and Wimper,* and *Mystery Island*), CBS, 1977-78.

The Tom and Jerry/Great Grape Ape Show, ABC, 1977-78.

(Also director) *The New Super Friends Hour,* ABC, 1977-78.

Scooby's All-Star Laff-a-Lympics, ABC, 1977-78.

Fred Flintstone and Friends, syndicated, 1977-78.

The C.B. Bears (also featuring *Blast Off Buzzard and Crazy Legs, Posse Impossible, Undercover Elephant, Shake, Rattle, and Roll,* and *Heyyyyyy, It's the King*), CBS, 1977-78.

The Hanna-Barbera Happiness Hour (live-action), NBC, 1978.

Yogi's Space Race, NBC, 1978-79.

The Galaxy Goofups, NBC, 1978-79.

Scooby's All Stars, ABC, 1978-79.

Challenge of the Super Friends, ABC, 1978-79.

(Also director) *The World's Greatest Super Heroes,* ABC, 1978-80.

Godzilla (also known as *Godzilla and the Super 90* and *The Godzilla Power Hour;* also featuring *Jana of the Jungle*), NBC, 1978-81.

Producer, *The Three Robonic Stooges,* CBS, 1978-81.

The All-New Popeye Hour, CBS, 1978-81.

The New Shmoo, NBC, 1979.

Fred and Barney Meet the Thing, NBC, 1979.

Buford and the Ghost, NBC, 1979.

Scooby-Doo and Scrappy-Doo, ABC, 1979.

The Super Globetrotters, NBC, 1979.

The New Fred and Barney Show, NBC, 1979.

Casper and the Angels, NBC, 1979-80.

Fred and Barney Meet the Shmoo, NBC, 1979-80.

Captain Caveman and the Teen Angels, ABC, 1980.

Flintstone Family Adventures (also featuring *The Frankenstones* and *Captain Caveman*), NBC, 1980-81.

The Scooby-Doo and Scrappy-Doo Show, ABC, 1980-82.

The Drak Pack, CBS, 1980-82.

Fonz and the Happy Days Gang, ABC, 1980-82.

The Richie Rich Show, ABC, 1980-82.

The Flintstones, NBC, 1981.

Space Stars (featuring *Space Ghost, Teen Force, The Herculoids,* and *Astro and the Space Mutts*), NBC, 1981-82.

The Kwicky Koala Show (also featuring *Dirty Dawg, Crazy Claws,* and *The Bungle Brothers*), CBS, 1981-82.

Trollkins, CBS, 1981-82.

Private Olive Oyl, CBS, 1981-82.

Laverne and Shirley in the Army, ABC, 1981-82.

The Flintstone Funnies, NBC, 1981-84.

The Smurfs, NBC, 1981-88.

Laverne and Shirley with the Fonz, ABC, 1982-83.

(Also director) *Jokebook,* NBC, 1982.

Mork and Mindy, ABC, 1982-83.

Scooby, Scrappy, and Yabba Doo, ABC, 1982-83.

The Gary Coleman Show, NBC, 1982-83.

The Little Rascals, ABC, 1982-84.

The Shirt Tales, NBC, 1982-84.

Pac-Man, ABC, 1983-84.

The Biskitts, CBS, 1983-84.

Monchhichis, ABC, 1983-84.

The Dukes, CBS, 1983-84.

Scooby and Scrappy-Doo, ABC, 1983-84.

The Pink Panther and Sons, NBC, 1984-85.

The New Scooby-Doo Mysteries, ABC, 1984-85.

Super Friends: The Legendary Super Powers Show, ABC, 1984-85.

(Also with Freddy Monnickendam) *Snorks,* NBC, 1984-86.

Challenge of the GoBots, syndicated, 1984-86.

Scooby's Mystery Funhouse, ABC, 1985.

The Thirteen Ghosts of Scooby-Doo, ABC, 1985-86.

The Super Powers Team: Galactic Guardians, ABC, 1985-86.

The New Jetsons, syndicated, 1985-88.

The Funtastic World of Hanna-Barbera (featuring *Yogi's Treasure Hunt, Paw Paws, Goltar and the Golden Lance,* and *The New Adventures of Jonny Quest*), syndicated, 1986-87.

The Flintstone Kids, ABC, 1986-87.

Pound Puppies, ABC, 1986-87.

Wildfire, CBS, 1986-87.

Foofur, NBC, 1986-87.

The Funtastic World of Hanna-Barbera (featuring *Yogi's Treasure Hunt, Sky Commanders, The New Adventures of the Snorks,* and *The New Adventures of Jonny Quest*), syndicated, 1987-88.

Popeye and Son, CBS, 1987-88.

A Pup Named Scooby Doo, 1988.

Fantastic Max, 1988.

(Also with Jay Wolpert) *Skedaddle* (live-action), syndicated, 1988—.

The Completely Mental Misadventures of Ed Grimley, NBC, 1988-89.

The Yogi Bear Show, 1988.

(Also with Paul Sabella) *The Adventures of Don Coyote and Sancho Panda,* syndicated, 1990.

Timeless Tales from Hallmark, USA Network, 1990.

(Also with Sabella) *The Tom and Jerry Kids Show,* Fox, 1990.

Yo! Yogi, NBC, 1991.

Television Pilots with Barbera; Executive Producer:

The Beach Girls (live-action), syndicated, 1977.

The Funny World of Fred and Bunni (live-action and animated), CBS, 1978.

Sergeant T. K. Yu (live-action), NBC, 1979.

Television Movies with Barbera; Executive Producer; Live-Action, Except Where Indicated:

Hardcase, ABC, 1972.

Shootout in a One-Dog Town, ABC, 1974.

The Gathering, ABC, 1977.

The Beasts Are on the Streets, NBC, 1978.

The Gathering, Part II, NBC, 1979.

Lucky Luke (animated), syndicated, 1987.

Stone Fox, NBC, 1987.

Scooby-Doo Meets the Boo Brothers (animated), 1987.

The Jetsons Meet the Flintstones (animated), 1987.

Rockin' with Judy Jetson (animated), 1988.

Yogi's Great Escape (animated), 1988.

(Also director) *Hollyrock-a-Bye Baby* (animated), ABC, 1993.

(Also director) *I Yabba-Dabba Do!* (animated), ABC, 1993.

Jonny's Golden Quest (animated), TNT, 1993.

(Also with Buzz Potamkin) *Jonny Quest versus the Cyber Insects* (animated), TNT, 1995.

Television Appearances; Movies:

Voice, *I Yabba-Dabba Do!* (animated), ABC, 1993.

Television Specials with Barbera; Executive Producer, Except Where Indicated; Animated, Except Where Indicated:

Alice in Wonderland, ABC, 1966.

Jack and the Beanstalk (live-action and animated), NBC, 1967.

The Thanksgiving That Almost Wasn't, syndicated, 1971.

A Christmas Story, syndicated, 1971.

Producer, *The Last of the Curlews,* ABC, 1972.

Yogi's Ark Lark, ABC, 1972.

Robin Hoodnik, ABC, 1972.

Oliver and the Artful Dodger, ABC, 1972.

Here Come the Clowns, ABC, 1972.

The Banana Splits in Hocus Pocus Park, ABC, 1972.

Gidget Makes the Wrong Connection, ABC, 1973.

Lost in Space, ABC, 1973.

20,000 Leagues under the Sea, syndicated, 1973.

(Also director) *The Three Musketeers,* syndicated, 1973.

The Count of Monte Cristo, syndicated, 1973.

The Crazy Comedy Concert (live-action and animated), ABC, 1974.

The Runaways (live-action), ABC, 1974.

Cyrano de Bergerac, ABC, 1974.

The Last of the Mohicans, syndicated, 1975.

Phantom Rebel (live-action), NBC, 1976.

"Davy Crockett on the Mississippi," *Famous Classic Tales,* CBS, 1976.

Taggart's Treasure (live-action), ABC, 1976.

Five Weeks in a Balloon, CBS, 1977.

Yabba Dabba Doo! The Happy World of Hanna-Barbera (live-action and animated), CBS, 1977.

Energy: A National Issue, 1977.

A Flintstones' Christmas, NBC, 1977.

The Flintstones' Little Big League, NBC, 1978.

Hanna-Barbera's All Star Comedy Ice Revue (live-action and animated), CBS, 1978.

"It Isn't Easy Being a Teenage Millionaire" (live-action), *ABC Afterschool Specials,* ABC, 1978.

Yabba Dabba Doo II, CBS, 1978.

Black Beauty, CBS, 1978.

Yogi's Space Race, 1978.

Super Heroes Roast, NBC, 1979.

Challenge of the Super Heroes, NBC, 1979.

America vs. the World (live-action), NBC, 1979.

Scooby Goes Hollywood, ABC, 1979.

Casper's First Christmas, NBC, 1979.

Popeye Valentine Special: The Sweethearts at Sea, CBS, 1979.

Gulliver's Travels, CBS, 1979.

Casper's Halloween Special: He Ain't Scary, He's Our Brother, NBC, 1979.

The Gymnast (live-action), ABC, 1980.

The Hanna-Barbera Arena Show (live-action), NBC, 1981.

Jogging Fever, NBC, 1981.

The Great Gilly Hopkins (live-action), CBS, 1981.

Daniel Boone, CBS, 1981.

Yabba Dabba Doo (live-action and animated), CBS, 1982.

The Smurfs' Springtime Special, NBC, 1982.

The Smurfs' Christmas Special, NBC, 1982.

Christmas Comes to Pac-Land, ABC, 1982.

Yogi Bear's All-Star Christmas Caper, CBS, 1982.

My Smurfy Valentine, NBC, 1983.

The Secret World of Og, ABC, 1983.

The Amazing Bunjee Venture, CBS, 1984.

The Smurfic Games, NBC, 1984.

Smurfily-Ever After, NBC, 1985.

Star Fairies, syndicated, 1985.

The Smurfs Christmas Special, 1986.

The Flintstones' 25th Anniversary Celebration (live-action and animated), CBS, 1986.

Ultraman! The Adventure Begins, syndicated, 1987.

Yogi and the Magical Flight of the Spruce Goose, syndicated, 1987.

Scooby and the Reluctant Werewolf, syndicated, 1987.

The Jetsons Meet the Flintstones, syndicated, 1987.

Top Cat and the Beverly Hills Cats, syndicated, 1987.

Rockin' with Judy Jetson (also known as *Judy Jetson and the Rockers*), syndicated, 1987.

Yogi's Great Escape, syndicated, 1987.

Scooby-Doo and the Ghoul School, syndicated, 1987.

Tis the Season to Be Smurfy, NBC, 1987.

The Good, the Bad, and the Huckleberry Hound, syndicated, 1987.

Scooby-Doo Meets the Boo Brothers, syndicated, 1987.

Yogi and the Invasion of the Space Bears, syndicated, 1987.

The Flintstone Kids "Just Say No" Special, ABC, 1988.

Hanna-Barbera's 50th: A Yabba Dabba Doo Celebration (live-action and animated), TNT, 1989.

Hagar the Horrible, 1989.

"Fender Bender 500," Wake, Rattle, and Roll, syndicated, 1990.

Animation supervisor, *The Last Halloween,* CBS, 1991.

A Flintstone Family Christmas, ABC, 1993.

(Also with Potamkin) *A Flintstones Christmas Carol,* syndicated, 1994.

(Also with Potamkin) *Arabian Nights,* syndicated, 1994.

Producer of *Rock Odyssey.*

Television Appearances; Specials:

The 40th Annual Emmy Awards, Fox, 1988.

Hanna-Barbera's 50th: A Yabba Dabba Doo Celebration, TNT, 1989.

Narrator, *The Last Halloween* (animated), CBS, 1991.

MGM: When the Lion Roars (documentary), TNT, 1992.

The 10th Annual Television Academy Hall of Fame, The Disney Channel, 1994.

Television Work; Episodic:

Director, *Love, American Style,* ABC, 1969.

WRITINGS

Screenplays:

(With Joseph Barbera and Warren Foster) *Hey There, It's Yogi Bear* (animated), Columbia, 1964.

Songs:

Songwriter, "(Meet) the Flintstones," *Bring on the Night,* 1985.

Songwriter, "(Meet) the Flintstones," *St. Elmo's Fire,* Columbia, 1985.

Songwriter, "(Meet) the Flintstones," *Planes, Trains, and Automobiles,* Paramount, 1987.

Co-author of title song, *Jetsons: The Movie* (animated), Universal, 1990.

Songwriter, "Snagglepuss Song," *Crooklyn,* Universal, 1994.

Songwriter, "(Meet) the Flintstones" and "The Bedrock Twist," *The Flintstones,* Universal, 1994.

Television Series:

(With Barbera and Douglas Widley) *The Adventures of Jonny Quest* (animated; also known as *Jonny Quest*), ABC, 1964-65.

Television Specials:

Composer, *The Three Musketeers* (animated), syndicated, 1973.

Television Movies; Animated:

Composer of title music, *Scooby-Doo Meets the Boo Brothers,* 1987.

Songwriter, "Bedrock Rock," *The Jetsons Meet the Flintstones,* 1987.

Songwriter, "(Meet) the Flintstones," *Hollyrock-a-Bye Baby,* ABC, 1993.

Songwriter, "(Meet) the Flintstones," *I Yabba-Dabba Do!,* ABC, 1993.

Songwriter, "Jonny Quest," *Jonny's Golden Quest,* TNT, 1993.

Songwriter, "Jonny Quest," *Jonny Quest versus the Cyber Insects,* TNT, 1995.

Songwriter, "Jonny Quest," *The Real Adventures of Jonny Quest* (also known as *The New Adventures of Jonny Quest*), TBS/TNT/Cartoon Network, 1996—.

Other:

(With Tom Ito) *A Cast of Friends,* foreword by Joseph Barbera, Taylor Publishing (Dallas, TX), 1996.

Adaptations: Hanna's work has been collected and recorded on the albums *The Flintstones: Modern Stone-Age Melodies* and *The Flintstone Story,* both released by Rhino Records in 1994.

OTHER SOURCES

Books:

International Dictionary of Films and Filmmakers, Volume 4, Gale (Detroit, MI), 1993.

Sennett, Ted, *Art of Hanna-Barbera: 50 Years of Creativity,* Viking (New York City), 1989.*

HARPER, Tess   1950(?)-

PERSONAL

Born Tessie Jean Washam, August 15, 1950 (some sources say 1952), in Mammoth Springs, AR. *Education:* Southwest Missouri State College, B.S. (education and theatre).

Addresses: *Agent*—c/o William Morris Agency, 151 El Camino Drive, Beverly Hills, CA 90212.

Career: Actress. Performed in dinner theatre, children's theatre, and television commercials in Houston, TX, and Dallas, TX. Performed at the theme parks Dogpatch USA in Jasper, AR and Silver Dollar City in Branson, MO, both 1960s.

Member: Screen Actors Guild, American Federation of Television and Radio Artists.

Awards, Honors: Golden Globe nomination, best supporting actress, 1984, for *Tender Mercies;* Academy Award nomination, best supporting actress, 1987, for *Crimes of the Heart.*

CREDITS

Film Appearances:

Rosa Lee Wadsworth, *Tender Mercies,* EMI, 1983.

Nancy Baxter, *Amityville 3-D* (also known as *Amityville: The Demon* and *Amityville III: The Demon*), Orion, 1983.

Linda Dawson, *Silkwood,* Twentieth Century-Fox, 1983.

Ellen, *Flashpoint,* TriStar, 1984.

Chick Boyle, *Crimes of the Heart,* De Laurentiis Entertainment Group, 1986.

Willa, *Ishtar,* Columbia, 1987.

Rita, *Far North,* Alive, 1988.

Detective Stillwell, *Criminal Law,* TriStar, 1989.

Sally Blackwood, *Her Alibi,* Warner Bros., 1989.

Sara Lee, *Daddy's Dyin'. . . Who's Got the Will?,* Metro-Goldwyn-Mayer/United Artists, 1990.

Cheryl Hornby, *My Heroes Have Always Been Cowboys,* Samuel Goldwyn, 1991.

Abigail Trant, *The Man in the Moon* (also known as *Man in the Moon*), Metro-Goldwyn-Mayer/Pathe, 1991.

Kimmy Hayes, *My New Gun,* IRS Releasing, 1992.

The Colors of Love, 1992.

Martha Harnish, *The Turning* (also known as *Home Fires Burning* and *Pocahontas, Virginia*), 1992.

Beth Greene, *Dirty Laundry,* Hollywood Productions/Rogue Features, 1996.

The first lady, *The Jackal* (also known as *The Day of the Jackal*), Universal, 1997.

Television Appearances; Series:

Fairlight Spencer, *Christy,* CBS, 1994-95.

Television Appearances; Miniseries:

Carrie Lee, *Chiefs,* CBS, 1983.

Susan French, *Celebrity,* NBC, 1984.

Television Appearances; Episodic:

Sarah, "Welcome to Winfield," *The Twilight Zone,* CBS, 1985.

"The Smiths," *George Burns Comedy Week,* CBS, 1985.

"Quarantine," *The Twilight Zone,* CBS, 1986.

"Simon Says Color Me Dead," *Murder, She Wrote,* CBS, 1987.

"Sparky Brackman, R.I.P.," *L.A. Law,* NBC, 1987.

Virginia, *Gun,* ABC, 1997.

Also appeared in "After the Crash," *The Hidden Room,* Lifetime.

Television Appearances; Movies:

Lorna Whateley, *Kentucky Woman,* CBS, 1983.

Janet Briggs, *Starflight: The Plane That Couldn't Land* (also known as *Starflight One*), ABC, 1983.

Gwen Palmer, *Promises to Keep,* CBS, 1985.

Meredith Craig, *Reckless Disregard,* Showtime, 1985.
Jeannie Wyler, *A Summer to Remember,* CBS, 1985.
Ann Burnette, *Daddy,* ABC, 1987.
Clara Brady, *Little Girl Lost,* ABC, 1988.
Mary Flowers, *Unconquered* (also known as *Invictus*), CBS, 1989.
Betty McFall, *Incident at Dark River* (also known as *Dark River—A Father's Revenge* and *The Smell of Money*), TNT, 1989.
Vicky Singer, *In the Line of Duty: Siege at Marion* (also known as *Children of Fury, In the Line of Duty: The Hostage Murders, In the Line of Duty: Standoff at Marion,* and *Siege at Marion*), NBC, 1992.
Verna Heath, *Willing to Kill: The Texas Cheerleader Story* (also known as *Pom Pom Mom* and *Willing to Kill*), ABC, 1992.
Assistant District Attorney Jerri Sims, *Death in Small Doses,* ABC, 1995.
Linda Grant, *A Stranger to Love* (also known as *Journey Home*), CBS, 1996.
Julia Archer, *The Road to Galveston,* USA Network, 1996.
Joanne Chandler, *A Child's Wish,* CBS, 1997.
Tina DeCapprio, *Whatever Happened to Angel?* (also known as *The Secret*), NBC, 1997.
Katie Malloy, *Walker, Texas Ranger: Sons of Thunder* (also known as *Sons of Thunder*), CBS, 1997.

Stage Appearances:
Macon Hill, *Abundance,* Manhattan Theatre Club, New York City, 1990.*

HARRIS, Julie 1925-

PERSONAL

Full name, Julia Ann Harris; born December 2, 1925, in Grosse Pointe Park, MI; daughter of William Pickett (an investment banker) and Elsie (a nurse; maiden name, Smith) Harris; married Jay I. Julien (an attorney and film producer), August 16, 1946 (divorced, July, 1954); married Manning Gurian (a stage manager), October 21, 1954 (divorced, 1967); married Walter Erwin Carroll (a writer), April 27, 1977 (divorced, 1982); children: (second marriage) Peter Alston. *Education:* Attended Yale University School of Drama, 1944-45; trained for the stage at Perry-Mansfield School of the Dance and Theatre, 1941-43, and at Actors' Studio. *Avocational interests:* Tennis, reading, gardening, knitting, cooking.

Addresses: *Agent*—William Morris Agency, 151 El Camino Dr., Beverly Hills, CA 90210.

Career: Actress. Actors' Studio, New York City, member.

Member: Actors' Equity Association, Screen Actors Guild, American Federation of Television and Radio Artists, American Guild of Variety Artists.

Awards, Honors: *Theatre World* Award, 1949, for *Sundown Beach;* Donaldson Award, best supporting actress, 1950, and Academy Award nomination, best actress, 1952, both for *The Member of the Wedding;* Antoinette Perry Award, Donaldson Award, and *Variety*-New York Drama Critics' Poll, all best actress, 1952, for *I Am a Camera;* Sylvania Award, 1955, for "A Wind from the South," *U.S. Steel Hour;* Antoinette Perry Award, best dramatic actress, 1956, for *The Lark;* Emmy Award, best single performance by an actress, 1959, for "Little Moon of Alban," *Hallmark Hall of Fame;* Emmy Award, outstanding single performance by an actress in a leading role, 1962, for "Victoria Regina," *Hallmark Hall of Fame;* Antoinette Perry Award nomination, best dramatic actress, 1964, for *Marathon '33;* Antoinette Perry Award nomination, best actress in a musical, 1966, for *Skyscraper;* Antoinette Perry Award, best dramatic actress, 1969, for *Forty Carats;* Antoinette Perry Award, best dramatic actress, Drama Desk Award, and Outer Critics' Circle Award, all 1973, for *The Last of Mrs. Lincoln;* Antoinette Perry Award nomination, best dramatic actress, 1974, for *The Au Pair Man;* Grammy Award, best spoken word recording, National Academy of Recording Arts and Sciences, and Antoinette Perry Award, best actress in a play, both 1977, for *The Belle of Amherst;* National Medal of the Arts, 1994; also inducted into Theatre Hall of Fame; honorary degrees include D.F.A., Mount Holyoke College, 1976, and degrees from Smith College, LaSalle College, Ithaca College, and Wayne State University.

CREDITS

Stage Appearances:
(Broadway debut) Atlanta, *It's a Gift,* Playhouse Theatre, 1945.
Nelly, *The Playboy of the Western World,* Booth Theatre, New York City, 1946.
Henry IV, Part Two, Old Vic Company, Century Theatre, New York City, 1946.
Oedipus, Old Vic Company, Century Theatre, 1946.

White Rabbit, *Alice in Wonderland,* International Theatre, then Majestic Theatre, both New York City, 1947.

Arianne, *We Love a Lassie,* Shubert Theatre, Boston, MA, then National Theatre, Washington, DC, both 1947.

Weird sister, *Macbeth,* National Theatre, New York City, 1948.

Ida Mae, *Sundown Beach,* Belasco Theatre, New York City, 1948.

Nancy Gear, *The Young and Fair,* Fulton Theatre, New York City, 1948.

Angel Tuttle, *Magnolia Alley,* Mansfield Theatre, New York City, 1949.

Felisa, *Montserrat,* Fulton Theatre, 1949.

Frankie Addams, *The Member of the Wedding,* Empire Theatre, New York City, 1950.

Sally Bowles, *I Am a Camera,* Empire Theatre, 1951.

Title role, *Mademoiselle Colombe,* Longacre Theatre, New York City, 1954.

Jeanne d'Arc, *The Lark,* Longacre Theatre, 1955.

Mrs. Margery Pinchwife, *The Country Wife,* Adelphi Theatre, New York City, 1957.

Ruth Arnold, *The Warm Peninsula,* Helen Hayes Theatre, New York City, 1959.

Brigid Mary Mangan, *Little Moon of Alban,* Longacre Theatre, 1960.

Juliet, *Romeo and Juliet,* Stratford Shakespeare Festival, Stratford, Ontario, Canada, 1960.

Blanche of Spain, *King John,* Stratford Shakespeare Festival, 1960.

Josefa Lantenay, *A Shot in the Dark,* Booth Theatre, 1961.

June, *Marathon '33,* American National Theatre and Academy (ANTA) Theatre, New York City, 1963.

Ophelia, *Hamlet,* New York Shakespeare Festival, Delacorte Theatre, New York City, then Playhouse in the Park, Philadelphia, PA, both 1964.

Annie, *Ready When You Are, C.B.!,* Brooks Atkinson Theatre, New York City, 1964.

Teresa, *The Hostage,* Bucks County Playhouse, New Hope, PA, 1965.

Georgina, *Skyscraper,* Lunt-Fontanne Theatre, New York City, 1965.

Blanche Dubois, *A Streetcar Named Desire,* Falmouth Playhouse, Falmouth, MA, then Tappan Zee Playhouse, Nyack, NY, 1967.

Ann Stanley, *Forty Carats,* Morosco Theatre, New York City, 1968.

The Women, Repertory Theatre of New Orleans, New Orleans, LA, 1970.

Anna Reardon, *And Miss Reardon Drinks a Little,* Morosco Theatre, 1971.

Claire, *Voices,* Ethel Barrymore Theatre, New York City, 1972.

Mary Lincoln, *The Last of Mrs. Lincoln,* ANTA Theatre, 1972.

Mrs. Rogers, *The Au Pair Man,* New York Shakespeare Festival, Vivian Beaumont Theatre, New York City, 1973.

Lydia Cruttwell, *In Praise of Love,* Morosco Theatre, 1974.

Emily Dickinson, *The Belle of Amherst* (solo show), Longacre Theatre, 1976, then (London debut) Phoenix Theatre, 1977.

Gertie Kessel, *Break a Leg,* Palace Theatre, New York City, 1979.

Ethel Thayer, *On Golden Pond,* Center Theatre Group, Ahmanson Theatre, Los Angeles, 1980.

Clarice, *Mixed Couples,* Brooks Atkinson Theatre, 1980.

Under the Ilex, Repertory Theatre of St. Louis, St. Louis, MO, 1983, then Long Wharf Theatre, New Haven, CT, 1984.

The Night of 100 Stars II, Radio City Music Hall, New York City, 1985.

Melissa Gardner, *Love Letters,* Promenade Theatre, New York City, 1989.

Girl, Scrooge's niece, and fan, *A Christmas Carol,* Hudson Theatre, New York City, 1990.

Is He Still Dead?, Long Wharf Theatre, 1990.

Isak Dinesen, Baroness Karen Blixen, *Lucifer's Child* (solo show), Eisenhower Theatre, Washington, DC, then Music Box Theatre, New York City, 1991.

Lettice and Lovage, Shubert Theater, Boston, MA, 1992.

Eunice, *The Fiery Furnace,* Lucille Lortel Theatre, New York City, 1993.

Amanda, *The Glass Menagerie,* Roundabout Theatre, Criterion Center/Stage Right, New York City, 1994-95.

Sonya, Phoenix Theatre, Purchase, NY, 1996.

The Gin Game, Lyceum Theatre, New York City, 1997.

The Road to Mecca, New Haven, CT, 1997.

Also appeared in *Currer Bell* (solo show).

Stage Appearances; Major Tours:

Sally Bowles, *I Am a Camera,* U.S. and Canadian cities, 1952-53.

Jeanne d'Arc, *The Lark,* U.S. cities, 1956.

Anna Reardon, *And Miss Reardon Drinks a Little,* U.S. cities, 1971-72.

Emily Dickinson, *The Belle of Amherst* (solo show), international cities, 1976-77.

Daisy Werthan, *Driving Miss Daisy,* U.S. cities, 1988.

Lettice Doufflet, *Lettice and Lovage,* U.S. cities, 1992.

Film Appearances:

Frankie Addams, *The Member of the Wedding,* Columbia, 1952.

Abra, *East of Eden,* Warner Bros., 1955.

Sally Bowles, *I Am a Camera,* Distributors Corporation of America, 1955.

Helen Cooper, *The Truth about Women,* Continental Distributing, 1958.

Sally Hamil, *The Poacher's Daughter* (also known as *Sally's Irish Rogue*), Show Corporation of America, 1960.

Grace Miller, *Requiem for a Heavyweight* (also known as *Blood Money*), Columbia, 1962.

Eleanor Vance, *The Haunting,* Metro-Goldwyn-Mayer, 1963.

Miss Thing, *You're a Big Boy Now,* Seven Arts, 1966.

Beth Fraley, *Harper* (also known as *The Moving Target*), Warner Bros., 1966.

Allison Landon, *Reflections in a Golden Eye,* Warner Bros., 1967.

Gladys, *The Split,* Metro-Goldwyn-Mayer, 1968.

Journey into Midnight, Twentieth Century-Fox, 1968.

Gerrie Mason, *The People Next Door,* Avco-Embassy, 1970.

Betsie ten Boom, *The Hiding Place,* Worldwide, 1975.

Alice Feinchild, *Voyage of the Damned,* Avco-Embassy, 1976.

Mrs. Greenwood, *The Bell Jar,* Avco-Embassy, 1979.

Prostitute, Connaught International, 1980.

Charlotte Bronte, *Bronte,* Charlotte Ltd./Radio Telefis Eireann, 1983.

Voice of Claire, *Nutcracker: The Motion Picture,* 1986.

Narrator, *Isadora Duncan: Movement from the Soul* (documentary), Geller/Goldfine, 1988.

Roz Carr, *Gorillas in the Mist,* Universal, 1988.

Edna Davis, *Housesitter,* Universal, 1992.

Reggie Delesseps, *The Dark Half,* Orion, 1993.

Narrator, *Ruth Orkin: Frames of Life* (short), 1995.

Joseph's mother, *Carried Away* (also known as *Acts of Love*), Fine Line, 1996.

Marta, *Gentle into the Night* (also known as *Lift to Heaven* and *Passaggio per il Paradiso*), In Pictures, 1996.

Dr. Harper, *Bad Manners,* Davis Entertainment Classics/Skyline Entertainment Partners/Wavecrest, 1997.

Television Appearances; Series:

Nellie Paine, *Thicker Than Water,* ABC, 1973.

Elizabeth Holvak, *The Family Holvak,* NBC, 1975.

Lilimae Clements, *Knots Landing,* CBS, 1981-87.

Voice of Mary Chesnut, *The Civil War,* PBS, 1990.

Television Appearances; Miniseries:

Helen "Nellie" Taft, *Backstairs at the White House,* NBC, 1979.

Hostess, *The Prime of Miss Jean Brodie,* PBS, 1979.

Alice Hearn, *When Love Kills: The Seduction of John Hearn* (also known as *Soldiers of Misfortune*), CBS, 1993.

Eleanor Butler, *Scarlett,* CBS, 1994.

Voice, *Baseball* (also known as *The History of Baseball*), PBS, 1994.

Voice, *The West* (documentary), PBS, 1996.

Television Appearances; Movies:

Katherine Colleigh, *How Awful about Allan,* ABC, 1970.

Elizabeth Hall Morgan, *Home for the Holidays* (also known as *Deadly Desires*), ABC, 1972.

Anne Devlin, *The Gift,* CBS, 1979.

Irene Culver, *The Love Boat: Who Killed Maxwell Thorn?,* 1986.

Alice Warfield, *The Woman He Loved,* CBS, 1988.

Margaret Berent, *Too Good to Be True* (also known as *Leave Her to Heaven*), NBC, 1988.

Iris, *The Christmas Wife,* HBO, 1988.

Lucille Frankel, *Single Women, Married Men,* CBS, 1989.

Odessa Ray, *They've Taken Our Children: The Chowchilla Kidnapping Story* (also known as *Buried Alive: The Chowchilla Kidnapping* and *Vanished without a Trace*), ABC, 1993.

Sook, *One Christmas* (also known as *Truman Capote's "One Christmas"*), NBC, 1994.

Mrs. Phelan, *Secrets,* ABC, 1995.

Sister Anthony, *The Christmas Tree,* ABC, 1996.

Ellen Foster, CBS, 1997.

Television Appearances; Specials:

Lu, "The Good Fairy," *Hallmark Hall of Fame,* NBC, 1956.

Jeanne d'Arc, "The Lark," *Hallmark Hall of Fame,* NBC, 1957.

Belinda McDonald, "Johnny Belinda," *Hallmark Hall of Fame,* NBC, 1958.

Brigid Mary Mangan, "Little Moon of Alban," *Hallmark Hall of Fame,* NBC, 1958.

Nora Helmer, "A Doll's House," *Hallmark Hall of Fame,* NBC, 1959.

Title role, "Victoria Regina," *Hallmark Hall of Fame,* NBC, 1961.

Maria, *The Power and the Glory,* NBC, 1961.

Eliza Doolittle, "Pygmalion," *Hallmark Hall of Fame*, NBC, 1963.

Brigid Mary Mangan, "Little Moon of Alban," *Hallmark Hall of Fame*, NBC, 1964.

Ophelia, *Hamlet*, CBS, 1964.

Florence Nightingale, "The Holy Terror," *Hallmark Hall of Fame*, NBC, 1965.

Title role, "Anastasia," *Hallmark Hall of Fame*, NBC, 1967.

Ed Sullivan's Broadway, CBS, 1973.

Emily Dickinson, *The Belle of Amherst*, PBS, 1976.

Jolene Henderson, "Stubby Pringle's Christmas," *Hallmark Hall of Fame*, NBC, 1978.

Voice of Emily Roebling, *Brooklyn Bridge*, PBS, 1982.

Actors on Acting, PBS, 1984.

The 39th Annual Tony Awards, 1985.

The Night of 100 Stars II, 1985.

Voice, *The Shakers: Hands to Work, Hearts to God*, 1985.

NBC's 60th Anniversary Celebration, NBC, 1986.

"Forever James Dean," *Crazy about the Movies*, Cinemax, 1988.

Iris, "The Christmas Wife," *HBO Showcase*, HBO, 1988.

Voice, *The Congress*, PBS, 1989.

"Harold Clurman: A Life of Theatre," *American Masters*, PBS, 1989.

"Anthony Quinn" (documentary), *Crazy about the Movies*, Cinemax, 1990.

The 47th Annual Tony Awards, 1993.

Knots Landing Block Party, CBS, 1993.

Isak Dinesen, "Lucifer's Child," *A & E Stage*, Arts and Entertainment, 1995.

Mrs. Ethel Sanford, *Little Surprises* (short; also known as *The Best Night* and *The Red Eye*), Showtime, 1996.

Voice of Mary Todd Lincoln, "Mary Lincoln's Insanity File" (documentary), *Discovery Sunday*, The Discovery Channel, 1996.

Voice, *Thomas Jefferson* (documentary), PBS, 1997.

Television Appearances; Pilots:

Leona Miller, *The House on Greenapple Road*, ABC, 1970.

Elizabeth Holvak, *The Greatest Gift*, NBC, 1974.

Television Appearances; Episodic:

(Television debut) *Actors' Studio*, ABC, 1948.

Philco Television Playhouse, NBC, between 1948 and 1955.

"A Trip to Czardis," *Actors' Studio*, CBS, 1949.

"Dead Man," *Actors' Studio*, CBS, 1949.

"Spreading the News," *Actors' Studio*, CBS, 1949.

"Bernice Bobs Her Hair," *Starlight Theatre*, CBS, 1951.

"October Story," *Goodyear Television Playhouse*, NBC, 1951.

"The Happy Rest," *Goodyear Television Playhouse*, NBC, 1953.

"A Wind from the South," *U.S. Steel Hour*, CBS, 1955.

"Ethan Frome," *Dupont Show of the Month*, CBS, 1960.

"Turn the Key Softly," *Sunday Showcase*, NBC, 1960.

"Night of the Storm," *Dupont Show of the Month*, CBS, 1961.

"He Who Gets Slapped," *Play of the Week*, WNTA, 1961.

Catherine Sloper, "The Heiress," *Family Classics*, CBS, 1961.

Ben Casey, ABC, 1964.

"The Robrioz Ring," *Kraft Suspense Theatre*, NBC, 1964.

"The Calf Woman," *Rawhide*, CBS, 1965.

"Rendezvous at Arillo," *Laredo*, NBC, 1965.

"Nightmare," *Bob Hope Presents the Chrysler Theatre*, NBC, 1966.

The Bell Telephone Hour, NBC, 1966.

Charity Jones, "The Perils of Charity Jones," *Tarzan*, NBC, 1967.

Therese, "Run from Death," *Garrison's Gorillas*, ABC, 1968.

"The Rape of Lucrece," *Run for Your Life*, NBC, 1968.

"A Stranger Everywhere," *The Big Valley*, ABC, 1968.

Faith, "Faith's Way," *Daniel Boone*, NBC, 1968.

Charity Jones, "The Four o'Clock Army," *Tarzan*, NBC, 1968.

"Dream to Dream," *Bonanza*, NBC, 1968.

"Jane Brown's Body," *Journey to the Unknown*, ABC, 1968.

"The Bobby Currier Story," *Name of the Game*, NBC, 1969.

"So Long, Baby, and Amen," *Name of the Game*, NBC, 1970.

"Wolf Track," *Men from Shiloh*, NBC, 1971.

"The Upper Hand," *The Evil Touch*, syndicated, 1972.

"The Guilty," *Medical Center*, CBS, 1973.

"Die, Darling, Die," *Hawkins*, CBS, 1973.

The Bob Newhart Show, CBS, 1973.

Karen Fielding, "Any Old Port in a Storm," *Columbo*, NBC, 1974.

Harry O, ABC, 1975.

"The Last of Mrs. Lincoln," *Hollywood Television Theater*, PBS, 1976.

"Mrs. Bixby and the Colonel's Coat," *Tales of the Unexpected*, syndicated, 1979.

Margaret Hollings, "The Freshman and the Senior," *Family Ties,* NBC, 1986.

Irene Culver, *The Love Boat,* ABC, 1987.

Radio Appearances; Episodic:

"The Queen of Darkness," *WOR Mystery Theatre,* WOR (New York City), 1975.

WRITINGS

(With Barry Tarshis) *Julie Harris Talks to Young Actors* (nonfiction), Lothrop (New York City), 1971.

RECORDINGS

Albums:

The Hostage, Columbia, 1965.

The Glass Menagerie, Caedmon, 1965.

Heroes, Gods, and Monsters of the Greek Myths, Spoken Arts, 1968.

The Belle of Amherst, Credo, 1976.

Stuart Little, 1991.

West with the Night, 1992.

Anne Frank: The Diary of a Young Girl, 1993.

Great American Poetry: Three Centuries of Classics, 1993.

Curious George, 1994.

Victoria and Albert, 1996.

Enchanted Tales, 1996.

Other recordings include *Little House in the Big Woods.* *

HARROLD, Kathryn 1950-

PERSONAL

Born August 2, 1950, in Tazewell, VA. *Education:* Attended Mills College; studied acting at Neighborhood Playhouse and with Uta Hagan in New York City.

Addresses: *Agent*—The Gersh Agency, 232 North Canon Dr., Beverly Hills, CA 90210.

Career: Actress. Section Ten (experimental theatre group), teacher and performer at Connecticut College and New York University.

Member: Actors' Equity Association, Screen Actors Guild, American Federation of Television and Radio Artists.

CREDITS

Film Appearances:

(Film debut) Anne Dillon, *Nightwing,* Columbia, 1979.

Dotty, *The Hunter,* Paramount, 1980.

Hannah, *The Pursuit of D. B. Cooper* (also known as *Pursuit*), Universal, 1981.

Mary Harvard, *Modern Romance,* Columbia, 1981.

Pamela Taylor, *Yes, Giorgio,* Metro-Goldwyn-Mayer/United Artists, 1982.

Gail Farmer, *The Sender,* Paramount, 1982.

Cyd Mills, *Heartbreakers,* Orion, 1984.

Christie, *Into the Night,* Universal, 1985.

Monique, *Raw Deal* (also known as *Triple Identity*), De Laurentiis Entertainment Group, 1986.

Someone to Love, International Rainbow, 1987.

Television Appearances; Series:

Detective Jenny Loud, *MacGruder and Loud,* NBC, 1985.

Sara Newhouse, *The Bronx Zoo,* NBC, 1987-88.

Christina LeKatzis, *I'll Fly Away,* NBC, 1991-93.

Francine, *The Larry Sanders Show,* HBO, beginning in 1992.

Karen Wilder, *Chicago Hope,* CBS, beginning in 1996.

Also appeared as Nora Aldrich, *The Doctors,* NBC.

Television Appearances; Movies:

Leslie Rawlins, *Vampire,* ABC, 1979.

Dr. Jill Bates, *Women in White,* NBC, 1979.

Suzie Kaufman, *Son-Rise: A Miracle of Love,* NBC, 1979.

Bliss, *The Women's Room,* ABC, 1980.

Lauren Bacall, *Bogie,* CBS, 1980.

Cynthia Malcolm, *An Uncommon Love,* CBS, 1983.

Marilyn Butler, *Man against the Mob,* NBC, 1988.

Beverly T. Lee, *Dead Solid Perfect,* HBO, 1988.

Christine, *Rainbow Drive* (also known as *City of Angels*), Showtime, 1990.

Angela Menteer, *Deadly Desire,* USA Network, 1991.

Gillian Tanner, *The Companion,* USA Network, 1994.

Megan Dougherty Adams, *The Rockford Files: Punishment and Crime* (also known as *The Rockford Files: Night Fishing*), CBS, 1996.

Hillary Waugh, *Tell Me No Secrets,* ABC, 1997.

Television Appearances; Episodic:

Megan Dougherty, "Black Mirror" (also known as "Love Is the Word"), *The Rockford Files,* NBC, 1978.

Veronica Sheridan, "To Have and Have and Have and Have Not," *Dream On,* HBO, 1990.

Also appeared on an episode of *Starsky and Hutch,* ABC.

Other Television Appearances:
Leslie Applegate, *The Best Legs in the Eighth Grade* (special), HBO, 1984.
Mary Ward, *Capital News* (pilot), ABC, 1990.

Stage Appearances:
Rebecca West, *Rosmersholm,* Classic Theatre, New York City, 1977.*

HARRY, Debbie
　　See HARRY, Deborah

HARRY, Deborah　1945-
　　(Debbie Harry)

PERSONAL

Full name, Deborah Ann Harry; born July 1, 1945, in Miami, FL; raised in Hawthorne, NJ; adopted daughter of Richard Smith and Catherine (Peters) Harry. *Education:* Centenary College, A.A., 1965.

Addresses: *Agent*—Creative Artists Agency, 9830 Wilshire Blvd., Beverly Hills, CA 90212.

Career: Singer, actress, and songwriter. Singer and songwriter with the rock group Blondie, 1974-82; began solo career, 1981; also member of the folk-rock group Wind in the Willows, beginning in 1968, and the group The Stilletoes; performer with Jazz Passengers and Elvis Costello, c. 1995. Gives poetry readings. Worked as a Playboy bunny and waitressed at Max's Kansas City. Appears in television commercials for products such as Revlon and Sara Lee.

Member: American Federation of Television and Radio Artists, Screen Actors Guild, American Society of Composers, Artists, and Publishers.

Awards, Honors: Award from American Society of Composers, Artists, and Publishers, 1979, for "Heart of Glass"; National Jewish Book Award for Fiction, 1979, for *Ten Cents a Dance with a Nickel Change!;* also recipient (with Blondie) of silver, gold, and plati-

num records, Recording Industries Association of America.

CREDITS

Film Appearances:
Dee Trick, *The Foreigner,* Visions, 1978.
Herself, *Mr. Mike's Mondo Video,* New Line Cinema, 1979.
Herself, *Roadie,* United Artists, 1980.
Lillian, *Union City,* Kinesis, 1980.
Unmade Beds, 1980.
Herself, *A New Face of Debbie Harry,* 1982.
Nicki Brand, *Videodrome,* Universal, 1983.
Voice of Angel, *Rock and Rule* (animated; also known as *Rock 'n' Rule* and *Ring of Power*), Metro-Goldwyn-Mayer Home Entertainment, 1983.
Lulu, *Forever, Lulu* (also known as *Crazy Streets*), TriStar, 1987.
Velma Von Tussle, *Hairspray* (also known as *White Lipstick*), New Line Cinema, 1988.
Tina, *Satisfaction* (also known as *Girls of Summer*), Twentieth Century-Fox, 1988.
Girl at Blind Alley, "Life Lessons" in *New York Stories,* Buena Vista, 1989.
Betty, "Wraparound Story," *Tales from the Darkside: The Movie,* Paramount, 1990.
Mrs. Kurtz, *Dead Beat* (also known as *The Phony Perfector*), Northern Arts Entertainment, 1994.
Delores, *Heavy,* CFP Distribution, 1995.
Herself, *Wigstock: The Movie,* Hallmark Home Entertainment, 1995.
Thor Thorvalsen (some sources say Spazz-O), *Drop Dead Rock,* 1996.
Kate Odum, *Six Ways to Sunday,* Prosperity Electric, 1997.
Delores, *Copland* (also known as *Cop Land*), Miramax, 1997.

Film Work; Song Performer:
"Angel's Song," "Send Love Through," and "Invocation Song," *Rock and Rule* (animated; also known as *Rock 'n' Rule* and *Ring of Power*), 1983.
"Rush Rush," *Scarface,* Universal, 1983.
"Rush Rush," *The Money Pit,* Universal, 1986.
"Prelude to a Kiss," *Prelude to a Kiss,* Twentieth Century-Fox, 1992.
"Communion," *Coneheads,* Paramount, 1993.
"Summertime Blues," *That Night,* Warner Bros., 1993.

Television Appearances; Episodic:
Musical guest and host (with Blondie), *The Midnight Special,* NBC, 1979.

Musical guest (with Blondie), *The Old Grey Whistle Test* [United Kingdom], 1979.

Musical guest (with Blondie), *Saturday Night Live,* NBC, 1979.

Host, *The Muppet Show,* syndicated, 1980.

Musical guest and host, *Saturday Night Live,* NBC, 1981.

Host, *Solid Gold,* syndicated, 1981.

Musical guest, *Saturday Night Live,* NBC, 1986.

"The Moth," *Tales from the Darkside,* syndicated, 1987.

Bambi, *Crime Story,* NBC, 1987.

"Desirable Alien," *Monsters,* syndicated, 1988.

Diana Price, "Dead Dog Lives," *Wiseguy,* CBS, 1989.

Diana Price, "And It Comes Out Here," *Wiseguy,* CBS, 1989.

Diana Price, "The Rip-Off Stick," *Wiseguy,* CBS, 1989.

New Visions, VH1, 1989.

Musical guest, *RollerGames,* syndicated, 1989.

Musical guest, *Night Music,* syndicated, 1989.

Musical guest and interviewee, *The Arsenio Hall Show,* syndicated, 1989.

The Old Woman Who Lived in a Shoe, "The Old Woman Who Lived in a Shoe," *Mother Goose Rock 'n' Rhyme,* 1990.

Voice of Vaingloria, *Phantom 2040: The Ghost Who Walks* (animated), syndicated, 1994.

Performer, *Live from the House of Blues,* TBS, 1995.

Interviewee, *Lauren Hutton and . . .,* syndicated, 1995.

Interviewee, *Rock and Roll,* PBS, 1995.

Cassandra, "Pilot," *Sabrina, the Teenage Witch,* ABC, 1996.

Guest, *The RuPaul Show,* VH1, 1996.

Television Appearances; Specials:

Blondie, HBO, 1983.

Rapido, BBC-2, 1989.

Co-host, *120 Minutes New Year's Countdown,* MTV, 1989.

Homemaker, *The Adventures of Pete and Pete: New Year's Pete,* Nickelodeon, 1993.

The State's Halloween Special, CBS, 1995.

MTV's Fashionably Loud, MTV, 1996.

Television Appearances; Movies:

Cory Wheeler, *Intimate Stranger* (also known as *After Midnight*), Showtime, 1991.

Nurse, "Hair," in *John Carpenter Presents Body Bags* (also known as *Body Bags* and *Mind Games*), Showtime, 1993.

Madam Jacqueline, *L.A. Johns* (also known as *Johns* and *Confessions*), Fox, 1997.

Television Appearances; Pilots:

Music Central, syndicated, 1981.

Stage Appearances:

Title role, *Teaneck Tanzi: The Venus Flytrap,* Nederlander Theatre, New York City, 1983.

RECORDINGS

Albums:

Koo Koo, Chrysalis, 1981.

Rockbird, Geffen, 1986.

Once More into the Bleach, Chrysalis, 1988.

Def, Dumb, and Blonde, Sire, 1989.

Debravation, Sire/Reprise, 1993.

Singles include "Backfired," Chrysalis, 1981; "The Jam Was Moving," Chrysalis, 1981; "Rush Rush," Chrysalis, 1983; "Feel the Spin," Geffen, 1985; "French Kissin," Geffen, 1986; "In Love with Love," Geffen, 1987; "Sweet and Low," Atlantic, 1989; "I Want that Man," Atlantic, 1989; (with Iggy Pop) "Well, Did You Evah!," Chrysalis, 1990; and "I Can See Clearly," Sire/Reprise, 1993;

Albums with Blondie:

Blondie, Chrysalis, 1977.

Plastic Letters, Chrysalis, 1978.

Parallel Lines, Chrysalis, 1979.

Eat to the Beat, Chrysalis, 1979.

Autoamerican, Chrysalis, 1980.

Best of Blondie (compilation), Chrysalis, 1981.

The Hunter, Chrysalis, 1982.

Live!, MCA, 1988.

Once More into the Bleach, Chrysalis, 1988.

Blonde and Beyond, Chrysalis, 1993.

Platinum Collection (boxed set), Chrysalis, 1994.

Remixed, Remade and Remodeled, Chrysalis, 1995.

Back to Back Hits, Capitol/Specia, 1996.

Picture This Live, EMD/Capitol, 1997.

Essential Collection (compilation), EMI Gold, 1997.

Singles include "Heart of Glass," Chrysalis, 1978 and 1979; "Hanging on the Telephone," Chrysalis, 1978; "The Hardest Part," Chrysalis, 1979; "One Way or Another," Chrysalis, 1979; "Dreaming," Chrysalis, 1979; "Call Me," Chrysalis, 1980; "Atomic," Chrysalis, 1980; "The Tide Is High," Chrysalis, 1980; "Rapture," Chrysalis, 1981; and "Island of Lost Souls," Chrysalis, 1982.

Albums with Jazz Passengers:

In Love, High Street Records, 1994.

Individually Twisted, 32 Records, 1997.

Albums with Wind in the Willows:
Wind in the Willows, 1968, re-released on compact disc by Dropout France, 1985.

Videos with Blondie:
Best of Blondie: The Videos, Pacific Arts, 1981.
Live in Concert (also known as *Blondie: Live*), MCA, 1987.

WRITINGS

Songwriter; Films:
"Heart of Glass," *Just before Dawn,* Oakland, 1980.
"One Way or Another," *Little Darlings,* Paramount, 1980.
"Heart of Glass," *Endless Love,* Universal, 1981.
"Polyester," "Be My Daddy Baby (Lu-Lu's Theme)," and "The Best Thing (Love Song)," *Polyester,* New Line, 1981.
"Call Me," *Partners,* Paramount, 1982.
"Heart of Glass," *Party, Party,* Twentieth Century-Fox, 1982.
"In the Flesh," *The Last American Virgin,* Metro-Goldwyn-Mayer Home Entertainment, 1982.
"Pretty Baby" and "Rapture," *Wild Style,* Facets Multimedia, 1982.
Rock and Rule (animated; also known as *Rock 'n' Rule* and *Ring of Power*), Metro-Goldwyn-Mayer Home Entertainment, 1983.
Scarface, Universal, 1983.
The Money Pit, Universal, 1986.
"In the Flesh," *A Nightmare on Elm Street 4: The Dream Master,* New Line, 1988.
"One Way or Another," *My Best Friend Is a Vampire,* HBO Home Video, 1988.
Coneheads (also known as *Coneheads—The Movie*), Paramount, 1993.
"One Way or Another," *Carpool,* Warner Bros., 1996.
"Atomic," *Trainspotting,* Miramax, 1996.
"One Way or Another," *Beverly Hills Ninja,* Sony Pictures, 1997.
"One Way or Another" and "Heart of Glass," *Donnie Brasco,* Columbia/TriStar, 1997.

Songs Featured in Television Episodes:
"Heart of Glass," *Due South,* CBS, 1995.

"Call Me" also featured in *Homicide: Life on the Street.*

Other:
(With Blondie) *Making Tracks: The Rise of Blondie,* Horizon Book Promotions, 1982.

Author of *Ten Cents a Dance with a Nickel Change!* (fiction).

OTHER SOURCES

Periodicals:
Interview, June, 1990, p. 110.
People Weekly, February 18, 1997, p. 30.*

HART, Melissa Joan   1976-

PERSONAL

Born April 18, 1976, in Smithtown, NY; daughter of William (an entrepreneur) and Paula (an executive producer) Hart. *Education:* Attended New York University. *Avocational interests:* Snowboarding, skiing, collecting Shirley Temple memorabilia.

Addresses: *Contact*—VIACOM Productions, 100 Universal City Plaza, Building 506, Suite E, Universal City, CA 91608.

Career: Actress. Began appearing in commercials at the age of four.

Awards, Honors: Youth in Film Awards, best actress in a cable show, 1992 and 1993, and CableAce Award nomination, best actress in a comedy series, all for *Clarissa Explains It All.*

CREDITS

Television Appearances; Series:
Clarissa Darling, *Clarissa Explains It All,* Nickelodeon, 1991-94.
Title role, *Sabrina the Teenage Witch,* ABC, 1996—.

Television Appearances; Miniseries:
(As Melissa Hart) Florentyna Rosnovski, age seven, *Kane & Abel,* CBS, 1985.

Television Appearances; Episodic:
The Lucie Arnaz Show, CBS, 1985.
Where in the World Is Carmen Sandiego?, PBS, 1991.
Storytime, PBS, 1994.

Also appeared in *Another World,* NBC; *Are You Afraid of the Dark?,* Nickelodeon; *The Equalizer,* CBS; *Saturday Night Live,* NBC; and *Touched By an Angel,* CBS.

Television Appearances; Movies:
Samantha, *Family Reunion: A Relative Nightmare*, ABC, 1995.
Title role, *Sabrina the Teenage Witch*, Showtime, 1996.
Jennifer Stanton, *Twisted Desire*, NBC, 1996.
Mary, *Silencing Mary*, NBC, 1997.
Susan, *Two Came Back*, ABC, 1997.
Melanie, *Right Connections*, Showtime, 1997.

Also appeared in *Christmas Snow*.

Television Appearances; Specials:
"The Adventures of Con Sawyer and Hucklemary Finn," *ABC Afterschool Specials*, ABC, 1985.
NBA All-Star Stay in School Jam, syndicated, 1992.
Cohost, *Nickelodeon's Big Helpathon*, Nickelodeon, 1994.
Cohost, *Nickelodeon's Big Helpathon*, Nickelodeon, 1995.
Host, *ABC Saturday Morning Preview Party*, ABC, 1996.
Host, *Halloween Jam V*, ABC, 1996.
Cohost, *Nickelodeon's Big Helpathon*, Nickelodeon, 1996.
Host, *Walt Disney World's 25th Anniversary Party*, ABC, 1997.
Cohost, *Nickelodeon's Big Helpathon*, Nickelodeon, 1997.
Host, *Walt Disney World's Christmas Parade*, ABC, 1997.

Television Appearances; Awards Presentations:
The 7th Annual Nickelodeon Kids' Choice Awards, Nickelodeon, 1994.
The 8th Annual Kids' Choice Awards, Nickelodeon, 1995.
The 18th Annual CableAce Awards, TNT, 1996.
The 9th Annual Kids' Choice Awards, Nickelodeon, 1996.
The 24th Annual American Music Awards, ABC, 1997.
The 10th Annual Kids' Choice Awards, Nickelodeon, 1997.

Stage Appearances:
Alexandra, *Beside Herself*, Circle Repertory Theatre, New York City, 1989.
Valerie, *Imagining Brad*, Players Theatre, New York City, 1990.
Understudy, *The Crucible*, Belasco Theatre, New York City, 1991-92.

RECORDINGS

Clarissa and the Straightjackets, 1994.

Narrator, *Britten: Young Person's Guide to the Orchestra—Prokofiev: Peter and the Wolf*, 1994.

HASKINS, Dennis

PERSONAL

Born November 18, in Chattanooga, TN.

Addresses: *Contact*—NBC Burbank, 3000 West Alameda Ave., Burbank, CA 91523.

Career: Actor. Worked as a manager, agent, and promoter in the music industry.

CREDITS

Television Appearances; Series:
Principal Richard Belding, *Good Morning, Miss Bliss*, NBC, 1988-89.
Mr. Richard Belding, *Saved By the Bell*, 1989-93.
Mr. Richard Belding, *Saved By the Bell: The New Class*, NBC, 1993—.

Television Appearances; Pilots:
Biker (guest), *One Night Band*, CBS, 1983.

Television Appearances; Episodic:
Moss, "One Armed Bandits," *The Dukes of Hazzard*, CBS, 1979.
Elmo, "Cale Yarborough Comes to Hazzard," *The Dukes of Hazzard*, CBS, 1984.
Hal Latimer, "Hiroshima Maiden," *WonderWorks*, PBS, 1988.
Dr. Stan, "No Free Lunch," *Doctor Doctor*, CBS, 1990.
Bayside principal Richard Belding, "A Thanksgiving Story," *Saved By the Bell: The College Years*, 1993.

Also appeared in episodes of *Storytime*, 1994; *Frank's Place*, *Amazing Stories*, *Magnum P.I.*, *The Twilight Zone*, and *Ohara*.

Television Appearances; Movies:
Airline attendant, *Deadly Intentions*, ABC, 1985.
Steven Fish, *The Image*, HBO, 1990.
Mr. Richard Belding, *Saved By the Bell—Hawaiian Style*, NBC, 1992.
Mr. Richard Belding, *Saved By the Bell—Wedding in Las Vegas*, NBC, 1994.

Television Appearances; Specials:
Mr. Richard Belding, *Saved By the Bell Graduation Special*, NBC, 1993.

Film Appearances:
Dr. Baldwin, *Eyewitness to Murder*, New Horizons Home Video, 1991.

Stage Appearances:
The Taming of the Shrew, Alliance Theatre Company, Atlanta, GA, 1978.
Look Homeward, Angel, Pasadena Playhouse, Pasadena, CA, 1986.
Angry Housewives, The Odyssey Theatre, Los Angeles, CA, 1988.

WRITINGS

Author of *Rating the Agents* (nonfiction), vols. 1 and 2.

HAUSER, Cole

PERSONAL

Born March 22, in Santa Barbara, CA.

Addresses: *Contact*—DreamWorks Television, 100 Universal City Plaza, Building 477, Universal City, CA 91608.

Career: Actor.

CREDITS

Film Appearances:
Jack Connors, *School Ties*, Paramount, 1992.
Benny, *Dazed and Confused*, Gramercy Pictures, 1993.
Scott Moss, *Higher Learning*, Columbia, 1995.
Skins, Sunset Films International, 1995.
Mark, *All Over Me*, Fine Line Features, 1996.

Television Appearances; Series:
Randy Willitz, *High Incident*, ABC, 1996-97.

Television Appearances; Miniseries:
Rocky Jackson, *A Matter of Justice* (also known as *Final Justice*), NBC, 1993.*

HAYDEN, Michael   1963-

PERSONAL

Born July 28, 1963, in St. Paul, MN; married, wife's name, Elizabeth; children: one daughter. *Education:* Graduated from St. John's University and from the Julliard School.

Addresses: *Contact*—Steve Bochco, c/o 20th Century Fox, 10201 West Pico Blvd., Los Angeles, CA 90035.

Career: Actor.

Awards, Honors: *Theatre World* Award, Laurence Olivier Award nomination, and Drama Desk Award nomination, all c. 1994, for *Carousel*.

CREDITS

Stage Appearances:
Ambrose/August, *The Matchmaker*, Roundabout Theatre, New York City, 1991.
Dean Swift, *Nebraska*, Theatre Row Theatre, New York City, 1992.
Billy Bigelow, *Carousel*, London and New York City, c. 1994.
Easter Bonnet Competition: A Salute to 100 Years of Broadway, Minskoff Theatre, New York City, 1994.

Also appeared in *Hello Again, Off-Key, End of the Day*, and *All My Sons*.

Television Appearances; Series:
Chris Docknovich, *Murder One*, ABC, 1995-97.

Also appeared in *Another World* and *As the World Turns*.

Television Appearances; Movies:
Luke Constable, *In the Name of Love: A Texas Tragedy* (also known as *After Laurette* and *Texas Heat: Love and Murder*), Fox, 1995.*

HEALD, Anthony   1944-

PERSONAL

Born August 25, 1944, in New Rochelle, NY. *Education:* Graduated from Michigan State University.

Addresses: *Agent*—J. Michael Bloom Ltd., 233 Park Ave. S., 10th Floor, New York, NY 10017.

Career: Actor. Asolo State Theatre, Sarasota, FL, member of company, 1968-69; Hartford Stage Company, Hartford, CT, member of company, 1968-69 and 1970-71; Milwaukee Repertory Company, Milwaukee, WI, member of company, 1969-70 and 1977-78; Actors Theatre of Louisville, Louisville, KY, member of company, 1979-80; appeared at Oregon Shakespeare Festival, Ashland, 1997.

Awards, Honors: *Theatre World* Award, 1982, for *Misalliance;* Antoinette Perry Award nomination, best featured actor in a play, 1995, for *Love! Valour! Compassion!*

CREDITS

Stage Appearances:
J.B., Asolo Theatre Festival, Saratoga, FL, 1968.
Look Back in Anger, Asolo Theatre Festival, 1968.
The Rose Tattoo, Hartford Stage Company, Hartford, CT, 1968.
Bonjour la Bonjour, Hartord Stage Company, 1979.
The Matchmaker, Hartford Stage Company, 1979.
Orestes, *The Electra Myth,* Equity Library Theatre, Lincoln Center Library and Museum, New York City, 1979.
(Off-Broadway debut) Tom Wingfield, *The Glass Menagerie,* Lion Theatre, 1980.
Fables for Friends, Playwrights Horizons, New York City, 1980.
Jones, *Inadmissable Evidence,* Roundabout Theatre, New York City, 1981.
Gunner, *Misalliance,* Roundabout Theatre, 1981.
(Broadway debut) Wayne Foster, *The Wake of Jamey Foster,* Eugene O'Neill Theatre, New York City, 1982.
Aston, *The Caretaker,* Roundabout Theatre, 1982.
Henry Grenfel, *The Fox,* Roundabout Theatre, 1982.
Derek Meadle, *Quartermaine's Terms,* Long Wharf Theatre, New Haven, CT, 1982, then Playhouse 91, New York City, 1983.
Donald, *The Philanthropist,* Manhattan Theatre Club, New York City, 1983.
Fluellen, *Henry V,* New York Shakespeare Festival, Delacorte Theatre, New York City, 1984.
Charlie Baker, *The Foreigner,* Astor Place Theatre, New York City, 1984.
Figaro, *The Marriage of Figaro,* Circle in the Square Theatre, New York City, 1985.
Digby Merton, *Digby,* City Center Theatre, New York City, 1985.

Bill Howell, *Principia Scriptoriae,* Manhattan Theatre Club, City Center Theatre, 1986.
Stephen, *The Lisbon Traviata,* Manhattan Theatre Club, 1989, then Promenade Theatre, New York City, 1989-90.
Elliot Loves, Promenade Theatre, 1990.
Henry Higgins, *Pygmalion,* Christian C. Yegen Theatre, New York City, then Roundabout Theatre, both 1991.
John Haddock, *Lips Together, Teeth Apart,* Manhattan Theatre Club, 1991-92, then Lucille Lortel Theatre, New York City, 1992.
Benedict Hough, *A Small Family Business,* Music Box Theatre, New York City, 1992.
A Cheever Evening (staged reading), Playwrights Horizons, 1993.
Later Life, Playwrights Horizons, 1993, then Westside Arts Theatre/Upstairs, New York City, 1993-94.
Perry Sellars, *Love! Valour! Compassion!,* Walter Kerr Theatre, New York City, 1995, then Manhattan Theater Club, NYC, 1995.
Inherit the Wind, Royale Theatre, New York City, 1996.

Also appeared in *Anything Goes.*

Film Appearances:
Doctor, *Silkwood,* Twentieth Century-Fox, 1983.
Narcotics officer, *Teachers,* United Artists, 1984.
Weldon, *Outrageous Fortune,* Buena Vista, 1987.
Man in the park, *Orphans,* Lorimar, 1987.
Dinner guest, *Happy New Year,* Columbia, 1987.
George Lazan, *Postcards from the Edge,* Columbia, 1990.
Dr. Frederick Chilton, *The Silence of the Lambs,* Orion, 1991.
Ron Nessim, *The Super,* Twentieth Century-Fox, 1991.
Paul, *Whispers in the Dark,* Paramount, 1992.
Fighting patient, *Searching for Bobby Fischer* (also known as *Innocent Moves*), Paramount, 1993.
Mr. Henry Grey, *The Ballad of Little Jo,* Fine Line Features, 1993.
Marty Velmano, *The Pelican Brief,* Warner Bros., 1993.
Trumann, *The Client,* Warner Bros., 1994.
Bragdon, *Bushwhacked* (also known as *The Tenderfoot*), Twentieth Century-Fox, 1995.
Jack Gold, *Kiss of Death,* Twentieth Century-Fox, 1995.
Dr. Wilbert Rodeheaver, *A Time to Kill,* Warner Bros., 1996.
Deep Rising (also known as *Tentacle*), 1996.

Television Appearances; Miniseries:
Kevin Kensington, *Fresno,* CBS, 1986.

Television Appearances; Episodic:
"One for the Road," *Cheers,* NBC, 1982.
Reverend Robert Morgan, *Hard Copy,* CBS, 1987.
Roger Jankowski, *Crime Story,* NBC, 1987.
"Troubles," *Law and Order,* NBC, 1991.
Councilman, *Law and Order,* NBC, 1994.
Matthew Tenzer, *New York News,* CBS, 1995.
Damon Ballard, "Sins of the Father," *Poltergeist: The Legacy,* Showtime, 1996.

Other Television Appearances:
Dr. Uldrich, *The Beniker Gang* (movie; also known as *Dear Lola; or, How to Start Your Own Family*), 1985.
Dave O'Brien, *A Case of Deadly Force* (movie), CBS, 1986.
Nick, *After Midnight* (pilot), ABC, 1988.
Dr. Gil Morris, "Abby, My Love" (special), *CBS Schoolbreak Specials,* CBS, 1991.

RECORDINGS

Taped Readings:
The Things They Carried, 1991.
The Cat Who Went to Paris, 1992.
The Gemini Contenders, 1993.
The Lost World, 1995.
Midnight in the Garden of Good and Evil, 1995.
Dark Debts, 1996.
Where the Red Fern Grows, 1996.*

HECHT, Paul   1941-

PERSONAL

Born August 16, 1941, in London, England; married Ingeberg Uta; children: one daughter. *Education:* Attended McGill University; trained for the stage at the National Theatre School of Canada, 1963.

Addresses: *Agent*—Susan Smith, 850 Seventh Ave., New York, NY 10036.

Career: Actor. Commercial voiceover performer; also provided voices for productions by puppeteer Bil Baird.

Awards, Honors: Antoinette Perry Award nomination, best supporting or featured actor in a drama, 1967, for *Rosencrantz and Guildenstern Are Dead.*

CREDITS

Stage Appearances:
Look After Lu Lu, Equity Library Theatre, New York City, 1965.
(Off-Broadway debut) The Pugnacious Collier, *Sergeant Musgrave's Dance,* Theatre De Lys, 1966.
Jacques Dumaine, *All's Well That Ends Well,* New York Shakespeare Festival, Delacorte Theatre, New York City, 1966.
Friar Peter, *Measure for Measure,* New York Shakespeare Festival, Delacorte Theatre, 1966.
George, Duke of Clarence, *Richard III,* New York Shakespeare Festival, Delacorte Theatre, 1966.
(Broadway debut) The Player, *Rosencrantz and Guildenstern Are Dead,* Alvin Theatre, New York City, 1967.
John Ken O'Dunc and Wayne of Morse, *MacBird!,* Village Gate Theatre, New York City, 1967.
Voltore, *Volpone,* New York Shakespeare Festival, Mobile Theatre, New York City, 1967.
John Dickinson, *1776,* 46th Street Theatre, New York City, 1969.
Nathan Rothschild, *The Rothschilds,* Lunt-Fontanne Theatre, New York City, 1970.
Title role, *Cyrano de Bergerac,* Tyrone Guthrie Theatre, Minneapolis, MN, 1971.
Marcus Antonius, *Julius Caesar,* American Shakespeare Festival, Stratford, CT, 1972.
Antony and Cleopatra, American Shakespeare Festival, 1972.
Mr. Brown, *The Great God Brown,* New Phoenix Repertory Company, Lyceum Theatre, New York City, 1972.
Title role, *Don Juan,* New Phoenix Repertory Company, Lyceum Theatre, 1972.
The Ride across Lake Constance, Repertory Theatre of Lincoln Center, Forum Theatre, New York City, 1972.
Baron Tito Belcredi, *Emperor Henry IV,* Ethel Barrymore Theatre, New York City, 1973.
Theodor Herzl, *Herzl,* Palace Theatre, New York City, 1976.
Oronte, *The Misanthrope,* New York Shakespeare Festival, Public Theatre, New York City, 1977.
Rufio, *Caesar and Cleopatra,* Palace Theatre, 1977.
Rakityin, *A Month in the Country,* McCarter Theatre, Princeton, NJ, 1978.
Dick Wagner, *Night and Day,* American National Theatre and Academy Theatre, New York City, 1979.
Lloyd Dallas, *Noises Off,* Brooks Atkinson Theatre, New York City, 1985.

The Three Sisters, Hartman Theatre, Stamford, CT, 1986.

Menenius Agrippa, *Coriolanus,* New York Shakespeare Festival, Public Theatre, 1988.

Title role, *Enrico IV,* Roundabout Theatre, New York City, 1989.

Billy, Sidney, and Dr. McMerlin, *London Suite,* Union Square Theatre, New York City, 1995.

Moonlight, Laura Pels Theatre, New York City, then Roundabout Theatre, both 1995.

Also appeared as Dick Dudgeon, *The Devil's Disciple,* Shaw Festival, Niagara-on-the Lake, Ontario, Canada; and as Macduff, *Macbeth,* New York Shakespeare Festival; appeared off-Broadway in *Phaedra, The Cherry Orchard, Androcles and the Lion,* and *Too Clever by Half.*

Tours:

Made stage debut on tour in *Henry IV, Part One* and *An Enemy of the People,* both with Canadian Players Touring Company, U.S. and Canadian cities, 1963-64.

Film Appearances:

Rabbi Isaac Sherman, *Only God Knows,* Canart and Queensbury, 1974.

Dr. Samuel Goodman, *The Reincarnation of Peter Proud,* American International, 1975.

Voice, *Poets on Film, No. 1,* 1977.

Khalid, *Rollover,* Warner Bros., 1981.

Paul, *Tempest,* Columbia, 1982.

Fallaci, *Threshold,* Twentieth Century-Fox, 1983.

Narrator, *Ezra Pound/American Odyssey* (documentary), NYC for Visual History, 1984.

Eli Seligson, *Joshua Then and Now,* Twentieth Century-Fox, 1985.

Barry, *A New Life,* Paramount, 1988.

Walking the Dog, 1991.

Tom, *Jack and His Friends,* 1992.

Martin, *Ride for Your Life,* Interfilm, 1995.

Member of "A Certain Age" cast, *The First Wives Club,* Paramount, 1996.

Ross Buckingham, *Private Parts* (also known as *Howard Stern's "Private Parts"*), Paramount, 1997.

Voice, *Young Hercules,* 1997.

Television Appearances; Series:

Charles Lowell, *Kate and Allie,* CBS, 1984-86.

Cohost, *Witness to Survival,* syndicated, 1990.

Dr. Duvall, *Law and Order,* NBC, 1996.

Television Appearances; Miniseries:

Jay Gould, *The Adams Chronicles,* PBS, 1976.

Television Appearances; Movies:

Paul, *Fear on Trial,* CBS, 1975.

Dr. Rufus Carter, *The Savage Bees,* NBC, 1976.

Joachim, *Mary and Joseph: A Story of Faith,* NBC, 1979.

Thomas Eichen, *Ohms,* CBS, 1980.

Vernon Markham, *Family Reunion,* NBC, 1981.

Michel Genet, *Running Out,* CBS, 1983.

Pavka Meyer, *I'll Take Manhattan,* CBS, 1987.

Chief Darnell, *With Hostile Intent* (also known as *Two Cops: The Long Beach Sexual Harassment Case* and *With Hostile Intent: Sisters in Black and Blue*), CBS, 1993.

Van Dorn, *A Silent Betrayal* (also known as *Janek: The Brownstone Murders*), CBS, 1994.

Television Appearances; Specials:

Lieutenant F. R. Harris, "Pueblo," *ABC Theatre,* ABC, 1973.

Narrator, *The Selfish Giant,* CBS, 1973.

Mr. Wilson, *The Haunted Mansion Mystery,* ABC, 1983.

Host, *Journey into Sleep,* PBS, 1989.

Renaissance, 1993.

Tobacco executive, *Smoke Alarm: The Unfiltered Truth about Cigarettes* (documentary), HBO, 1996.

Television Appearances; Episodic:

Stefan Kubler, "Psych-Out," *Tucker's Witch,* CBS, 1982.

"Life Choice," *Law and Order,* NBC, 1991.

"Helpless," *Law and Order,* NBC, 1992.

Appeared as Fielding, *Remington Steele,* NBC; also appeared in episodes of *All My Children,* ABC; *The Guiding Light,* CBS; *Another World,* NBC; and *Starsky and Hutch,* ABC.

Television Appearances; Pilots:

Joe Tyler, *The Imposter,* NBC, 1975.

Carelli, *Street Killing,* ABC, 1976.

Radio Appearances; Series:

Made regular appearances on *Hi Brown's Radio Mystery Theatre,* CBS.

RECORDINGS

The Shipping News, 1996.

Time and Again, 1996.

The Lost World, 1996.
Ironman (abridged), 1996.*

HEDISON, Al
See HEDISON, David

HEDISON, David 1928(?)-
(Al Hedison)

PERSONAL

Original name, Albert David Heditsian Jr.; born May 20, 1928 (some sources say 1930), in Providence, RI; son of Albert David and Rose (Boghosian) Heditsian; married Bridget Mori, June 29, 1968; children: Alexandra Mary, Serena Rose. *Education:* Attended Brown University, 1949-51; studied acting at the Neighborhood Playhouse School of Theatre, 1953.

Addresses: *Agent*—The Artists Group, Ltd., 10100 Santa Monica Blvd., Suite 2490, Los Angeles, CA 90067-4045.

Career: Actor.

Member: Actors' Studio.

Awards, Honors: *Theatre World* Award, 1956, for *A Month in the Country;* Barter Theatre Award for *Summer and Smoke.*

CREDITS

Television Appearances; Series:
Victor Sebastian, *Five Fingers,* NBC, 1959-60.
Spencer Harrison, *Another World,* NBC, 1964.
Commander/Captain Lee Crane, *Voyage to the Bottom of the Sea,* ABC, 1964-68.
Sir Roger Langdon, *Dynasty II: The Colbys,* ABC, 1986.

Television Appearances; Miniseries:
Porcius Festus, *A.D.* (also known as *A.D.—Anno Domini*), NBC, 1985.

Television Appearances; Movies:
Roger Edmonds, *The Cat Creature,* ABC, 1973.
Dr. Peter Brooks, *Adventures of the Queen,* CBS, 1975.

Steven Cord, *Murder in Peyton Place,* NBC, 1977.
Power Man, ABC, 1979.
Carson, *Kenny Rogers as "The Gambler"—The Adventure Continues,* CBS, 1983.

Television Appearances; Pilots:
Nick Kelton, *Crime Club,* CBS, 1973.
Parker Sharon, *The Art of Crime* (also known as *Roman Grey: The Fine Art of Crime*), NBC, 1975.
Wes Dolan, *The Lives of Jenny Dolan,* NBC, 1975.
David Royce, *Colorado C.I.,* CBS, 1978.
Danton, *The Power Within,* ABC, 1979.
John Taylor, *Benson,* ABC, 1979.
T. J. Hooker, ABC, 1982.

Television Appearances; Episodic:
"Eleven o'Clock Flight," *Kraft Television Theatre,* NBC, 1955.
"Follow the Leader," *The Big Story,* NBC, 1956.
"A Lesson in Fear," *Hong Kong,* ABC, 1961.
"Call Back Yesterday," *Bus Stop,* ABC, 1961.
"The Case of the Dodging Domino," *Perry Mason,* CBS, 1962.
"The Mink Machine," *Farmer's Daughter,* ABC, 1964.
"Louella," *The Saint,* NBC, 1966.
"Somewhere in a Crown," *Journey to the Unknown,* ABC, 1968.
Rob, "Love and the Other Love," *Love, American Style,* ABC, 1969.
"The Buyer," *The F.B.I.,* ABC, 1972.
Bell, "The Dead Samaritan," *Cannon,* CBS, 1972.
"A Gathering of Sharks," *The FBI,* ABC, 1973.
John Sandler, "Night Flight to Murder," *Cannon,* CBS, 1973.
"The Case of the Frenzied Feminist," *The New Adventures of Perry Mason,* CBS, 1973.
"The Capricorn Murders," *Shaft,* CBS, 1974.
"Dark Warning," *Medical Center,* CBS, 1974.
"Murder Impossible," *Wide World of Mystery,* ABC, 1974.
"The Man Who Thought He Was Dillinger," *Manhunter,* CBS, 1974.
"For the Use of the Hall," *Hollywood Television Theater,* PBS, 1975.
"Betrayal," *Bronk,* CBS, 1975.
David Farnum, "The Star," *Cannon,* CBS, 1975.
"The Adventure of the Eccentric Engineer," *Ellery Queen,* NBC, 1976.
"Coming Apart," *Family,* ABC, 1976.
Paul Nugent, "The Deadly Charade," *Barnaby Jones,* CBS, 1977.
Evan Robley, "The Queen and the Thief," *Wonder Woman,* CBS, 1977.

Buddy Stanfield, "Julia's Old Flame," *The Love Boat,* ABC, 1977.

Steve Darnell, "It Didn't Happen One Night," *The Bob Newhart Show,* CBS, 1978.

"Sighting 4011: The Doll House Incident," *Project UFO,* NBC, 1978.

"High Rollers," *Flying High,* CBS, 1978.

Carter Gillis, "Angels in the Stretch," *Charlie's Angels,* ABC, 1978.

Carlyle Cranston, "Family Reunion," *Fantasy Island,* ABC, 1978.

Sherman, "Tug of War," *The Love Boat,* ABC, 1979.

John Thornwood, "He Married an Angel," *Charlie's Angels,* ABC, 1981.

Karl Dixon/Claude Duncan, "The Chateau," *Fantasy Island,* ABC, 1981.

Allan Christenson, "Eye of the Beholder," *The Love Boat,* ABC, 1981.

"Murder by the Book," *Nero Wolfe,* NBC, 1981.

David Tabori, "Man Beast," *Fantasy Island,* ABC, 1981.

"Daniel and King Nebuchadnezzar," *Greatest Heroes of the Bible,* NBC, 1981.

Captain John Day, "Show Me a Hero," *Fantasy Island,* ABC, 1981.

Milo Hendricks, "Undersea Odyssey," *The Fall Guy,* ABC, 1981.

Miles Wiatt, "Hart of Diamonds," *Hart to Hart,* ABC, 1982.

Jordan Stevens, "Snow Job," *The Fall Guy,* ABC, 1982.

Bradford York, "April in Boston," *The Love Boat,* ABC, 1982.

"Receipt for Murder," *Matt Houston,* ABC, 1982.

Pierre Cerdan, "Murder in Aspic," *Matt Houston,* ABC, 1982.

Cliff Jacobs, "The Role Model," *The Love Boat,* ABC, 1982.

Phillip Camden, "Face of Fire," *Fantasy Island,* ABC, 1982.

Erix Saxon, "The Protectors," *T. J. Hooker,* ABC, 1982.

"Amanda's by the Sea," *Amanda's,* ABC, 1983.

Sam Dexter, "The Downstairs Bride," *Dynasty,* ABC, 1983.

Sam Dexter, "The Vote," *Dynasty,* ABC, 1983.

Daniel Garman, "Final Adieu," *Fantasy Island,* ABC, 1984.

"Fantasyland," *Partners in Crime,* NBC, 1984.

David Burke, *Double Trouble,* NBC, 1984.

Monte Sorrenson, "Her Bodyguard," *The Fall Guy,* ABC, 1985.

Austin Tyler, "Simon without Simon," *Simon and Simon,* CBS, 1985.

Barry Singer, "Her Honor, the Mayor," *The Love Boat,* ABC, 1985.

Jack Fitzpatrick, "Distortions," *Hotel,* ABC, 1985.

Ted Cooper, "Knight in Retreat," *Knight Rider,* NBC, 1985.

Ed Galbin, "Eye in the Sky," *Crazy like a Fox,* CBS, 1985.

Miles Warner, "The Second Best Man," *Trapper John, M.D.,* CBS, 1985.

Vaughn, "Mind Games," *The A-Team,* NBC, 1985.

Mitch Payne, "The Perfect Foil," *Murder, She Wrote,* CBS, 1986.

Howard Bentley, *Hotel,* ABC, 1987.

Mr. Ratcliff, "Mona," *Who's the Boss?,* ABC, 1987.

"Mr. Chapman, I Presume," *The Law and Harry McGraw,* CBS, 1987.

Victor Caspar, *Murder, She Wrote,* CBS, 1989.

Television Appearances; Specials:

Clay Hollinger, "Can I Save My Children?" *ABC Afternoon Playbreak,* ABC, 1974.

ABC's Silver Anniversary Special—25 and Still the One, ABC, 1978.

For the Use of the Hall, Arts and Entertainment, 1986.

TV Guide Looks at Science Fiction, USA Network, 1997.

Also appeared in *Summer and Smoke,* BBC.

Film Appearances:

(As Al Hedison) Lieutenant Ware, *The Enemy Below,* Twentieth Century-Fox, 1957.

(As Al Hedison) Andre, *The Fly,* Twentieth Century-Fox, 1958.

(As Al Hedison) Jamie, *Son of Robin Hood,* Twentieth Century-Fox, 1959.

Ed Malone, *The Lost World,* Twentieth Century-Fox, 1960.

David Chatfield, *Marines, Let's Go,* Twentieth Century-Fox, 1961.

Philip, *The Greatest Story Ever Told,* United Artists, 1965.

Nick, *Kemek,* GHM, 1970.

Felix Leiter, *Live and Let Die,* United Artists, 1973.

King, *Ffolkes* (also known as *North Sea Hijack* and *Assault Force*), Universal, 1980.

Dr. Hadley, *The Naked Face,* Cannon, 1984.

Frank Wheeler, *Smart Alec* (also known as *The Movie Maker*), American Twist/Boulevard, 1986.

Felix Leiter, *License to Kill* (also known as *License Revoked*), United Artists, 1989.

The Undeclared War, 1992.

Stage Appearances:

Beliaev, *A Month in the Country,* Phoenix Theatre, New York City, 1956.

Are You Now or Have You Ever Been?, 1985.
Forty Deuce, 1985.
The Abduction from the Seraglio, Music Hall, Cincinnati, OH, 1992.

Also appeared in *Clash By Night,* New York City; *Bad Bad Jo Jo,* London; and *Return Engagement.* Toured U.S. cities in *Chapter II* and *Come into My Parlor.* *

HEIKIN, Nancy 1948-
  (Nancy Heikin-Pepin)

PERSONAL

Born November 28, 1948, in Philadelphia, PA; daughter of Abraham (in the clothing business) and Judith (Kaplan) Heikin. *Education:* Sarah Lawrence, B.A. (dance and theatre), 1970; attended the Juilliard School of Music, 1981-82; studied for the stage with Stella Adler and Peter Flood; studied dance and choreography with Bessie Schoenberg; studied voice with Marge Rivington and Tony Franco; studied music composition with Heiner Stadler and Ben Johnston; and studied playwriting with Wilford Leach, John Braswell, and Crispin Larengiero. *Avocational interests:* Playing piano and the balalaika, speaking French.

Addresses: *Agent*—Howard Rosenstock, Rosenstock/Wender, 3 East Fourth Street, New York, NY 10003.

Career: Actress, composer, and writer. Involved with Dance for Children at Sarah Lawrence College, Bronxville, NY and the Head Start program with the Philadelphia Board of Education, Philadelphia, PA; La MaMa, New York City, instructor; Metropolitan Museum of Art, New York City, instructor of master classes in arts awareness; University of Illinois, Champaign-Urbana, vocal coach, opera division; St. Ann's School, NY, teacher of musical theatre; *Native American Theatre Ensemble,* guest director for two years and taught music, dance and western acting and developed, with the members of the company, a piece on Nez Perce Coyote legends entitled *Coyote Tracks,* which has since been performed worldwide. Performed at the Theatre Gerard-Phillipe and Centre Americain Theatre, both Paris, France; also performed at various clubs in New York City and with Frank Zappa and the Mothers of Invention, New York City.

Member: Actors' Equity Association, American Federation of Television and Radio Artists, Screen Actors Guild, Dramatists Guild, American Society of Composers, Authors, and Publishers.

Awards, Honors: American Society of Composers, Authors and Publishers Award; women's fund award, for *Warsaw Opera;* National Endowment for the Arts grant, for choreography; Samuel Rubin Foundation grant for composers and playwrights; Theatre Communications Group grant, special travel grant to native American reservations.

CREDITS

Stage Appearances:
The Carrot, *Peter Rabbit,* Children's Theatre, Playhouse in the Park, Philadelphia, PA, 1963.
Title role, *Carmilla,* La MaMa, New York City, 1970.
Edith, *The Pirates of Penzance,* Uris Theatre, New York City, 1981.
Edna Burge, *Mrs. Farmer's Daughter,* American Music Theatre Festival, Philadelphia, PA, 1984.

Also appeared as Marlowe, *Forget Him,* New York City; Weaver, a suicide, *A Trilogy,* New York City; Debby Specialist, *C.O.R.F.A.X. (Don't Ask),* New York City; Rosemary, *Rat's Mass,* New York City; Creusa, *Medea,* New York City; the singer and understudy for the role of Madonna Sostrada, *The Mandrake,* Violenta, *All's Well That Ends Well,* and the understudy for the role of Mabel, *The Pirates of Penzance,* all at New York Shakespeare Festival, New York City; *La Boheme,* New York Shakespeare Festival; Maria, *West Side Story;* Anna I, *The Seven Deadly Sins;* title role, *Miss Julie;* and Serafina, *The Rose Tattoo.*

Major Tours:
Made several tours of Europe for La MaMa with Wilford Leach's ETC company and Andrei Serban's company.

Television Appearances; Specials:
Appeared in *That's the Trouble with Water* (documentary), WCAU-TV, Philadelphia, PA.

Television Appearances; Episodic:
Appeared on *Saturday Night Live,* NBC and *The Today Show,* NBC.

WRITINGS

Stage Plays:
Trio for Two Feet and a Bag, La MaMa, later European and American cities, 1970.
Humonic Symphony, La MaMa, later Spoleto Festival, Italy, 1972.
Crumbs, La MaMa, 1973.
Frame, Washington Square Methodist Church, New York City, 1974.
Serenade, La MaMa, 1974-75.
Weeks, Cubiculo, New York City, 1976.
Cloud 9, Thirteenth Street Theatre, New York City, 1976.

Also wrote *T.K.O/Arena,* La MaMa, later Theatre Gerard-Phillipe, Paris, France.

Musical Works:
Warsaw Opera (music-drama), workshop at Actors Studio, New York City, 1981-82.
(With Anthony Giles) *Non Pasquale* (musical; an adaptation of *Don Pasquale*), Delacorte Theatre, New York City, 1983.
Carmen Monoxide (unproduced), commissioned by the New York Shakespeare Festival, 1983, completed 1984.
No Kidding (unproduced), optioned by the New York Shakespeare Festival, spring, 1985.
America Needs a Mom (unproduced), 1985.
Fountain Heads (unproduced), 1985.

Also composed *Juana* (opera; unproduced), libretto by Crispin Larangeira.

Screenplays; Billed as Nancy Heikin-Pepin:
Screenplay adaptor, *Les Epoux Ripoux,* 1991.
(With Grant Morris) *Does This Mean We're Married?,* New Line Home Video, 1992.

Also wrote *About Face* (unproduced); with Ellen Kesend, wrote *C'est Cheese* (unproduced).

SIDELIGHTS

Nancy Heikin earlier remarked to *CTFT*, "I love to travel and have been fortunate to have spent a lot of time in Europe, particularly France. In 1968, I toured Russia (Leningrad, Moscow and Kiev) with the Sarah Lawrence touring chorus. One of my main musical influences is the melodious folk music of eastern European and Russian Jews. I used to sing and dance with Frank Zappa and the Mothers of Invention at the Fillmore East (a long time ago)."*

HEIKIN-PEPIN, Nancy
    See HEIKIN, Nancy

HENDERSON, Florence 1934-

PERSONAL

Born February 14, 1934, in Dale, IN; raised in Owensboro, KY; daughter of Joseph (a tobacco sharecropper) and Elizabeth (Elder) Henderson; married Ira Bernstein, January 9, 1956 (divorced), married John Kappas, August 4, 1987; children (with Bernstein): Barbara, Joey, Robert Norman, Elizabeth. *Education:* Attended St. Francis Academy, Owensboro, KY; studied acting with Christine Johnson and at the American Academy of Dramatic Arts.

Addresses: *Agent*—c/o The Blake Agency, 415 North Camden Dr., Suite 111, Beverly Hills, CA 90210.

Career: Actress, television host, singer, and writer. Appeared in television commercials for Wesson cooking oil. Worker with charitable organizations, including City of Hope and House Ear Institute.

Awards, Honors: Sarah Siddons Award, for *The Sound of Music.*

CREDITS

Stage Appearances:
New girl, *Wish You Were Here,* Imperial Theatre, New York City, 1952.
Laurey, *Oklahoma!,* City Center, New York City, 1953.
Resi, *The Great Waltz,* Los Angeles Civic Light Opera, Los Angeles, CA, later Curran Theatre, San Francisco, CA, both 1953.
Title role, *Fanny,* Majestic Theatre, New York City, 1954.
Mary Morgan, *The Girl Who Came to Supper,* New York City, 1963.
Nellie Forbush, *South Pacific,* New York State Theatre, later Lincoln Center, New York City, 1967.
The Sound of Music, Los Angeles Civic Light Opera, 1978.
Bells Are Ringing, Los Angeles Civic Light Opera, 1979.

Also appeared in *The King and I,* Los Angeles Music Center, Los Angeles, CA.

Major Tours:
Laurey, *Oklahoma!*, 1952-53.
Maria, *The Sound of Music*, 1961.
Annie Oakley, *Annie Get Your Gun*, 1974.

Film Appearances:
Nina Grieg, *The Song of Norway*, Cinerama, 1970.
The unknown woman, *Shakes the Clown*, IRS Releasing, 1992.
Herself, *Naked Gun 33 1/3: The Final Insult*, Paramount, 1994.
Grandma, *The Brady Bunch Movie*, Paramount, 1995.

Television Appearances; Series:
Regular, *Sing Along*, CBS, 1958.
(With Bill Hayes) Host, *Oldsmobile Music Theatre* (also known as *Oldsmobile Presents* and *Oldsmobile Theatre*), NBC, 1959.
Today girl, *The Today Show*, NBC, 1959-60.
Carol Brady, *The Brady Bunch*, ABC, 1969-74.
Carol Brady, *The Brady Bunch Hour*, ABC, 1976-77.
Carol Brady, *The Brady Brides* (also known as *The Brady Girls Get Married*), NBC, 1980-81.
Host, *Country Kitchen* (also known as *Florence Henderson's Home Cooking*), TNN, 1985-92.
Carol Brady, *The Bradys*, CBS, 1989-90.
Maggie Colby, *Dave's World*, CBS, 1993-94.

Television Appearances; Episodic:
"Huck Finn," *The U.S. Steel Hour*, CBS, 1957.
"A Family Alliance," *The U.S. Steel Hour*, CBS, 1958.
Alice, CBS, 1976.
Herself, *The Muppet Show*, syndicated, 1976.
Fantasy Island, ABC, 1981.
Hart to Hart, ABC, 1981.
"Rendezvous at Big Gulch," *Police Squad!*, ABC, 1982.
The Love Boat, ABC, 1983.
The New Love, American Style, ABC, 1985.
Host, "A Team Show," *Musical Encounter*, part one, KLCS, 1985.
Host, "A Record Show," *Musical Encounter*, part three, KLCS, 1985.
Host, "Musical Families," *Musical Encounter*, part five, KLCS, 1985.
Margaret Flanagan, *L.A. Law*, NBC, 1986.
Carol Brady, "Brady Dimension," *Day by Day*, NBC, 1989.
Everyday with Joan Lunden, 1989.
Florence Anderson, *Roseanne*, ABC, 1993.
Flo, "Suck Up or Shut Up," *Roseanne*, ABC, 1994.
"Mommies Day," *The Mommies*, NBC, 1994.
Herself, *Caroline in the City*, NBC, 1995.

Herself, *Night Stand*, 1995.
Madeline, *Ellen*, ABC, 1996.
Guest Host, *The Vicki Lawrence Show* (also known as *Fox After Breakfast*), Fox, 1996.
Voice, *Nightmare Ned*, ABC, 1997.
The Late, Late Show, CBS, 1997.

Also appeared in *Burke's Law*, CBS; *Hollywood Squares*, NBC; *Murder, She Wrote*, CBS; *It's Garry Shandling's Show*, Showtime and Fox; *The Tonight Show*, NBC; and *The Wil Shriner Show*.

Television Appearances; Specials:
Oscar Hammerstein II—An Appreciation (also known as *Tribute to Oscar Hammerstein*), NBC, 1960.
A World of Love, 1970.
City vs. Country, 1971.
A Salute to Television's 25th Anniversary, 1972.
The Paul Lynde Halloween Special, 1976.
Bob Hop Special: Bob Hope's All-Star Comedy Special From Australia, 1978.
Bob Hope Special: Bob Hope's Women I Love—Beautiful But Funny, 1982.
The Night of 100 Stars II, 1985.
Sylvia Fine Kaye's Musical Comedy Tonight III, 1985.
Host, *Star Tour Australia*, 1986.
Candid Camera Christmas Special, 1987.
Happy Birthday, Hollywood!, 1987.
Jay Leno's Family Comedy Hour, 1987.
Ellen Casio, *Just a Regular Kid: An AIDS Story*, 1987.
Host, *The Mrs. America Pageant*, 1987.
Today at 35, 1987.
Host, *The Fourth Annual Mrs. of the World Pageant*, 1988.
Host, *Still a Family*, 1989.
There Really Is a Santa Claus, 1989.
Bob Hope Lampoons Show Business, 1990.
Stand-Up Comics Take a Stand!, 1990.
Starathon '90, 1990.
Host, *The Mrs. America Pageant*, 1990.
The Tube Test, 1990.
Funny Business With Charlie Chase, 1991.
New York Host, *Starathon '91*, 1991.
Mom Knows Best (also known as *Sitcom Moms*), CBS, 1992.
Host, *Starathon '92: A Weekend With the Stars*, syndicated, 1992.
Segment Host, *A 70s Celebration: The Beat is Back*, NBC, 1993.
Bob Hope: The First Ninety Years, NBC, 1993.
Host, *Bradymania: A Very Brady Special* (also known as *Bradymania*), ABC, 1993.
A Capitol Fourth, PBS, 1994.
Brady Bunch Home Movies, CBS, 1995.

Gail Sheehy's New Passages, ABC, 1996.
Host, *Mom USA,* syndicated, 1996.
Host, *A Capitol Fourth,* PBS, 1997.
Fifty Years of Television: A Celebration of the Academy of Television Arts & Sciences Golden Anniversary, HBO, 1997.

Also appeared in *An Evening with Richard Rodgers* and *Little Women.*

Television Appearances; Awards Presentations:
The 41st Annual Emmy Awards, 1989.
MTV Movie Awards, MTV, 1993.

Television Appearances; Movies:
Carol Brady, *A Very Brady Christmas,* CBS, 1988.
Muriel, *Fudge-A-Mania,* ABC, 1995.

Television Appearances; Pilots:
Monica Richardson, *The Love Boat,* ABC, 1976.

RECORDINGS

Albums:
With One More Look at You, Manhattan Records, 1979.

Taped Readings:
(With Linda Lavin and Marcia Rodd) *The Performances of John Vliet Lindsay,* 1970.

WRITINGS

Cookbooks:
A Little Cooking, A Little Talking and a Whole Lotta Fun, edited by Elyssa A. Harte, Panorama Publishing (Van Nuys, CA), 1988.

Other:
(Adaptor with Shari Lewis) *One-Minute Bible Stories, New Testament,* researched by Gerry Matthews, illustrated by C. S. Ewing, Doubleday (Garden City, NY), 1986.

OTHER SOURCES

Periodicals:
The Advocate, August, 1993, pp. 54-55.
Entertainment Weekly, May 29, 1992, pp. 43-44.
People Weekly, July 26, 1993, pp. 60-64.*

HENNESSY, Jill
    See HENNESSY, Jillian

HENNESSY, Jillian   1969-
    (Jill Hennessy)

PERSONAL

Born November 25, 1969, in Edmonton, Alberta, Canada; raised in various Canadian cities, including Kitchener, Ontario, Canada; daughter of John (a sales and marketing executive) and Maxine (a secretary) Hennessy; twin sister of Jacqueline Hennessy (an actress); companion of Paolo Mastropietro (an attorney and actor). *Avocational interests:* Playing the guitar.

Addresses: *Agent*—c/o William Morris Agency, 151 El Camino Dr., Beverly Hills, CA 90212.

Career: Actress; guitarist for the New Originals, an alternative and folk band; also worked as a model.

CREDITS

Television Appearances; Series:
(As Jill Hennessy) Assistant district attorney Claire Kincaid, *Law and Order,* NBC, 1993-96.

Television Appearances; Episodic:
Patty, "Goliath Is My Name," *War of the Worlds* (also known as *War of the Worlds: The Second Invasion*), syndicated, 1988.
Marla, "Striptease," *The Hitchhiker,* USA Network, 1989.
Elisabeth, "Pawns," *The Hitchhiker,* USA Network, 1989.
Secretary, "Year of the Monkey," *Friday the 13th* (also known as *Friday the 13th: The Series*), syndicated, 1990.
(As Jill Hennessy) Lauren Benjamin, "Crazy for You . . . And You," *Flying Blind,* Fox, 1992.
Assistant district attorney Claire Kincaid, "For God and Country," *Homicide: Life on the Street* (also known as *Homicide* and *Homicide: LOTS*), NBC, 1996.

Film Appearances:
Mimsy, *Dead Ringers* (also known as *Gemini* and *Twins*), Twentieth Century-Fox, 1988.
Dr. Marie Lazarus, *Robocop 3,* Orion, 1993.

Deanne White, *The Paper,* Universal, 1994.

Laura, *I Shot Andy Warhol,* The Samuel Goldwyn Company, 1996.

Lindsay Hamilton, *A Smile Like Yours,* Paramount, 1997.

Dr. Victoria Constantini, *Most Wanted,* New Line Cinema, 1997.

Dead Broke, 1998.

Stage Appearances:

Maria Elena, *Buddy: The Buddy Holly Story,* Shubert Theatre, New York City, 1990-91.

OTHER SOURCES

Periodicals:

People Weekly, November 27, 1995, p. 113.

TV Guide, May 4, 1996, pp. 36-37.*

HENRITZE, Bette
(Bette Howe)

PERSONAL

Surname is pronounced "hen-rit-*see*"; born May 23, in Betsy Layne, KY. *Education:* Graduated from the University of Tennessee; studied at the American Academy of Dramatic Arts.

Addresses: *Agent*—c/o Writers and Artists Agency, 924 Westwood Blvd., Suite 900, Los Angeles, CA 90024.

Career: Actress. Arena Stage, Washington, DC, guest artist, 1988-89.

Awards, Honors: Obie Award, *Village Voice,* 1967, for *Measure for Measure, Thorton Wilder's Triple Bill, The Displaced Person,* and *The Rimers of Eldritch.*

CREDITS

Stage Appearances:

(As Bette Howe) Mary Delaney, *Jenny Kissed Me,* Hudson Theatre, New York City, 1948.

Cloyne, *Purple Dust,* Cherry Lane Theatre, New York City, 1956.

Various roles, *Pictures in the Hallway,* Playhouse Theatre, New York City, 1956.

Peasant woman, *The Power and the Glory,* Phoenix Theatre, New York City, 1958.

Nirodyke, *Lysistrata,* Phoenix Theatre, 1959.

Peer Gynt, Phoenix Theatre, 1960.

Pimple, *She Stoops to Conquer,* Phoenix Theatre, 1960.

Bessie Burgess, *The Plough and the Stars,* Phoenix Theatre, 1960.

Mrs. Peyton, *The Octoroon,* Phoenix Theatre, 1961.

Margaret, *Much Ado about Nothing,* New York Shakespeare Festival, Wollman Memorial Skating Rink, New York City, 1961.

Duchess of York, *King Richard II,* New York Shakespeare Festival, Wollman Memorial Skating Rink, 1961.

Mrs. Gensup, *Giants, Sons of Giants,* Alvin Theatre, New York City, 1962.

Nerissa, *The Merchant of Venice,* New York Shakespeare Festival, New York City, 1962.

Goneril, *King Lear,* New York Shakespeare Festival, 1962.

Mary Todd, *Abe Lincoln in Illinois,* Anderson Theatre, New York City, 1963.

Cross-Lane Nora, *The Lion in Love,* One Sheridan Square Theatre, New York City, 1963.

Charmian, *Antony and Cleopatra,* New York Shakespeare Festival, Delacorte Theatre, New York City, 1963.

Paulina, *The Winter's Tale,* New York Shakespeare Festival, Delacorte Theatre, 1963.

Mrs. Hasty Malone, *The Ballad of the Sad Cafe,* Martin Beck Theatre, New York City, 1963.

Various roles, *The White House,* Henry Miller's Theatre, New York City, 1964.

Emilia, *Othello,* New York Shakespeare Festival, Delacorte Theatre, then Martinique Theatre, New York City, 1964.

Louise, Maja, landlady, and young lady, *Baal,* Martinique Theatre, 1965.

Mariana, *All's Well That Ends Well,* New York Shakespeare Festival, Delacorte Theatre, 1966.

Mariana, *Measure for Measure,* New York Shakespeare Festival, Delacorte Theatre, 1966.

Ermengarde, "A Long Christmas Dinner," and Mademoiselle Pointevin, "Queens of France," *Thornton Wilder's Triple Bill,* Cherry Lane Theatre, 1966.

Mrs. Shortley, *The Displaced Person,* St. Clements Church, New York City, 1966.

Mary Windrod, *The Rimers of Eldritch,* Cherry Lane Theatre, 1967.

Bea Schmidt, *Dr. Cook's Garden,* Belasco Theatre, New York City, 1967.

Mrs. Bacon, *Here's Where I Belong,* Billy Rose Theatre, New York City, 1968.

Edna, "The Acquisition," *Trainer, Dean,* and *Liepolt and Co.* (triple-bill), American Place Theatre, New York City, 1968-69.

Jessie Mason, *Crime of Passion,* Astor Place Theatre, New York City, 1969.

Understudy, *Hello and Goodbye,* Sheridan Square Playhouse, New York City, 1969.

Margaret Jourdain, *Henry VI, Part I,* New York Shakespeare Festival, Delacorte Theatre, 1970.

The Duchess of York, *Henry VI, Part II,* New York Shakespeare Festival, Delacorte Theatre, 1970.

The Duchess of York, *Richard III,* New York Shakespeare Fesitval, Delacorte Theatre, 1970.

Anna Ames, *The Happiness Cage,* Estelle Newman Theatre, New York City, 1970.

Fay, Clarice, Wendy, and the woman, *Older People,* Public/Anspacher Theatre, New York City, 1972.

Ursula, *Much Ado about Nothing,* Delacorte Theatre, 1972, then Winter Garden Theatre, New York City, 1972-73.

Trixie, *Lotta; or, The Best Thing Evolution's Come Up With,* Public/Anspacher Theatre, 1973.

Mother, *Over Here* (also known as *Over Here!*), Sam S. Shubert Theatre, New York City, 1974.

Margaret, *Richard III,* Mitzi E. Newhouse Theatre, New York City, 1974.

Mrs. Soames, *Our Town,* American Shakespeare Theatre, Stratford, CT, 1975.

Pauline, *The Winter's Tale,* American Shakespeare Theatre, 1975.

Elizabeth, *Angel Street,* Lyceum Theatre, New York City, 1975-76.

Nora, *Home,* Long Wharf Theatre, New Haven, CT, 1976.

Mrs. Mihaly Almasi, *Catsplay,* Manhattan Theatre Club, then Promenade Theatre, both New York City, 1978.

Susan Ramsden, *Man and Superman,* Circle in the Square Theatre, New York City, 1978-79.

Anna, *A Month in the Country,* Roundabout Theatre, New York City, 1979-80.

Understudy for Margie, *One Night Stand,* Nederlander Theatre, New York City, 1980.

Essie, *Ah! Wilderness,* Indiana Repertory Theatre, Indianapolis, IN, 1981.

Mother Superior, *Agnes of God,* GeVa Theatre, Rochester, NY, 1981.

Second witch, *Macbeth,* Circle in the Square Theatre, 1981.

Miss Ericson and Monica Reed, *Present Laughter,* Circle in the Square Theatre, 1982-83.

Emily Stilson, *Wings,* Center Stage Theatre, Baltimore, MD, 1983.

Rabbi's wife, *The Golem,* New York Shakespeare Festival, Delacorte Theatre, 1984.

Mary Margaret Donovan, *The Octette Bridge Club,* Music Box Theatre, New York City, 1985.

Mom, *Daughters,* Westside Arts Theatre, New York City, 1986.

Nurse Guinness, *Heartbreak House,* Yale Repertory Theatre, New Haven, CT, 1986.

Grace Tanner, *Amazing Grace,* Alliance Theatre, Atlanta, GA, 1987.

Ouiser, *Steel Magnolias,* WPA Theatre, New York City, 1987, then Lucille Lortel Theatre, New York City, 1987-89.

Mrs. Hedges, *Born Yesterday,* Philadelphia Drama Guild, Philadelphia, PA, 1987-88.

Eva Temple, *Orpheus Descending,* Neil Simon Theatre, New York City, 1989.

Miss Framer, *Lettice and Lovage,* Ethel Barrymore Theatre, New York City, 1990.

Demetria Riffle, *On Borrowed Time,* Circle in the Square Theatre, 1991.

Rinalda, *All's Well That Ends Well,* Central Park/ Delacorte Theatre, New York City, 1993.

Berte, *Hedda Gabler,* Criterion Center Stage Right, 1994.

Maryina (Nanny), *Uncle Vanya,* Circle in the Square Uptown Theatre, New York City, 1995.

Appeared at the Manasquan Theatre, NJ, 1951.

Major Tours:

Paulina, *The Winter's Tale,* New Jersey and Connecticut cities, 1976.

Mrs. Putnam, *The Crucible,* New Jersey and Connecticut cities, 1976.

Anna, *A Month in the Country,* New Jersey and Pennsylvania cities, 1976.

Jenny, *The Torch-Bearers,* New Jersey and Pennsylvania cities, 1976.

Helga Ten Dorp, *Deathtrap,* U.S. cities, summers of 1979 and 1980.

Also toured Virginia cities with the Barter Theatre Company, 1950.

Film Appearances:

Mrs. Kimball, an operating room nurse, *The Hospital,* United Artists, 1971.

Anna Kraus, *The Happiness Cage* (also known as *The Mind Snatchers*), Cinerama, 1972.

Sarah Parker, *Rage,* Warner Bros., 1972.

All That Jazz, Twentieth Century-Fox, 1979.

Sally Devlin, a female candidate, *The World According to Garp,* Warner Bros., 1982.

Mrs. Murphy, *Brighton Beach Memoirs* (also known as *Neil Simon's Brighton Beach Memoirs*), Universal, 1986.

Emma, *Other People's Money,* Warner Bros., 1991.

Tina Boyer, *Souvenir,* Showtime, 1988.
Angela Berk, *Spy,* USA Network, 1989.
Laura Whittaker, *Running against Time,* USA Network, 1990.
Carol Stadler, *Hi Honey, I'm Dead,* Fox, 1991.
Julia Riordan, "Redwood Curtain," *Hallmark Hall of Fame,* ABC, 1995.

Television Appearances; Episodic:
Late Night with David Letterman, NBC, 1988.
The Tonight Show, NBC, 1989.
Lauren Ridgeway, *Diagnosis Murder,* CBS, 1993.
Pamela Crawford, *Burke's Law,* CBS, 1995.

Other Television Appearances:
(As Cathy Hicks) Valerie, *Sparrow* (pilot), CBS, 1978.
Allison Ploutzer, *Up to No Good* (special), ABC, 1992.
Nancy, *The Circle Game* (special), ABC, 1993.

Stage Appearances:
Sally Haines, *Tribute,* Brooks Atkinson Theatre, New York City, 1978.

Also appeared on Broadway in *Present Laughter.**

HICKS, Cathy
   See HICKS, Catherine

HILLERMAN, John   1932-

PERSONAL

Full name, John Benedict Hillerman; born December 20, 1932, in Denison, TX; son of Christopher Benedict and Lenora JoAnn (Medinger) Hillerman. *Education:* Attended University of Texas, 1949-52; studied acting at American Theatre Wing, 1958-59.

Addresses: *Agent*—Borinstein, Oreck, Bogart, 8271 Melrose Ave., Suite 110, Los Angeles, CA 90046.

Career: Actor. Theatre Club, Washington, DC, member of company, 1965-69. *Military service:* U.S. Air Force, 1953-57.

Member: Actors' Equity Association, Academy of Motion Picture Arts and Sciences, Academy of Television Arts and Sciences, Screen Actors Guild, American Federation of Television and Radio Artists.

Awards, Honors: Golden Globe Award, best supporting actor in a television series, Hollywood Foreign Press Association, 1982, and Emmy Award, outstanding supporting actor in a drama series, 1987, both for *Magnum, P.I.*

CREDITS

Film Appearances:
Teacher, *The Last Picture Show,* Columbia, 1971.
Totts, *Lawman,* United Artists, 1971.
Honky, 1971.
Jenkins, *The Carey Treatment,* Metro-Goldwyn-Mayer, 1972.
Walter Brandt, *Skyjacked* (also known as *Sky Terror*), Metro-Goldwyn-Mayer, 1972.
Mr. Kaltenborn, *What's Up Doc?,* Warner Bros., 1972.
Bootmaker, *High Plains Drifter,* Universal, 1973.
Department store manager, *The Outside Man* (also known as *Un Homme est mort* and *Funerale a Los Angeles*), United Artists, 1973.
Sheriff Hardin and Jess Hardin, *Paper Moon,* Paramount, 1973.
Laxker, *The Thief Who Came to Dinner,* Warner Bros., 1973.
The Naked Ape, 1973.
Howard Johnson, *Blazing Saddles,* Warner Bros., 1974.
Yelburton, *Chinatown,* Paramount, 1974.
Carl, *The Nickel Ride,* Twentieth Century-Fox, 1974.
Rodney James, *At Long Last Love,* Twentieth Century-Fox, 1975.
Ned Grote, *The Day of the Locust,* Paramount, 1975.
Christy McTeague, *Lucky Lady,* Twentieth Century-Fox, 1975.
Scott Velie, *Audrey Rose,* United Artists, 1977.
Webb, *Sunburn,* Paramount, 1979.
Rich man, *History of the World, Part I,* Twentieth Century-Fox, 1981.
Dean Burch, *Up the Creek,* Orion, 1984.
Pfarrer, *Gummibarchen Kusst Man Nicht* (also known as *Real Men Don't Eat Gummi Bears*), Tivoli Filmverleih, 1989.
Dr. Whitehead, *A Very Brady Sequel* (also known as *Very Brady* and *Brady Bunch 2*), Paramount, 1996.

Television Appearances; Series:
Simon Brimmer, *The Adventures of Ellery Queen,* NBC, 1975-76.
John Elliot, *The Betty White Show,* CBS, 1977-78.
Jonathan Quale Higgins III and Father Paddy MacGuinnes, *Magnum, P.I.,* CBS, 1980-88.

Lloyd Hogan, *The Hogan Family* (also known as *The Hogans, Valerie,* and *Valerie's Family*), NBC, 1990-91.

Television Appearances; Miniseries:
Sir Francis Commarty, *Around the World in 80 Days,* NBC, 1989.

Television Appearances; Movies:
Medical examiner, *Sweet, Sweet Rachel,* ABC, 1971.
Major Underwood, *The Great Man's Whiskers,* NBC, 1973.
Thomas Q. Rachel, *The Law,* NBC, 1974.
Major Walcott, *The Invasion of Johnson County,* NBC, 1976.
Major Leo Hargit, *Relentless,* CBS, 1977.
George Davis, *Kill Me If You Can,* NBC, 1977.
Marvin, *A Guide for the Married Woman,* ABC, 1978.
Victor Slavin, *Betrayal,* NBC, 1978.
Greg Previn, *Marathon,* CBS, 1980.
Maury Paul, *Little Gloria . . . Happy at Last,* NBC, 1982.
Cyril Combs, *Assault and Matrimony,* NBC, 1987.
Raymond Kepler, *Street of Dreams,* CBS, 1988.
Dr. John Watson, *Hands of a Murderer* (also known as *Sherlock Holmes and the Prince of Crime* and *The Napoleon of Crime*), CBS, 1990.

Television Appearances; Pilots:
Tree inspector, *The Last Angry Man,* ABC, 1974.
Simon Brimmer, *Ellery Queen: Too Many Suspects,* NBC, 1975.
John Peacock, *Beane's of Boston,* CBS, 1979.
Mr. Dempster, *Gossip,* NBC, 1979.
Voice of IFR 7000, *Institute for Revenge,* NBC, 1979.
Tales of the Gold Monkey, ABC, 1982.
Paul Harrison, *Battles: The Murder That Wouldn't Die,* NBC, 1980.

Television Appearances; Episodic:
"Play It Again, Samuelson," *The Sandy Duncan Show,* CBS, 1972.
"Silent Target," *Mannix,* CBS, 1973.
"The Only Way Out," *Kojak,* CBS, 1974.
"Search for a Dead Man," *Mannix,* CBS, 1975.
Donald Blair, "Man on Fire," *Hawaii Five-0,* CBS, 1976.
"Raped Fire," *Serpico,* NBC, 1976.
"Wonder Woman vs. Gargantua," *The New, Original Wonder Woman,* ABC, 1976.
"Licensed to Kill," *Delvecchio,* CBS, 1977.
"Fear of Cheesecake," *Flying High,* CBS, 1978.
"Harriet's Happenings," *Little House on the Prairie,* NBC, 1978.

The Love Boat, ABC, 1979.
"Makin' Tracks," *Young Maverick,* CBS, 1980.
Soap, ABC, 1980.
William Whitney, "Diamonds Aren't Forever," *Tenspeed and Brown Shoe,* ABC, 1980.
Claude "Al" Connors, *One Day at a Time,* CBS, 1980.
"Cruise at Your Own Risk," *Hart to Hart,* ABC, 1980.
Nobody's Perfect, ABC, 1980.
"Pack," *Lou Grant,* CBS, 1980.
One Day at a Time, CBS, 1980.
"Emeralds Are Not a Girl's Best Friend," *Simon and Simon,* CBS, 1982.
"The Last Case," *The Love Boat,* ABC, 1983.
"Mary Kawena Pukui," *An American Portrait,* CBS, 1984.
"Magnum on Ice," *Murder, She Wrote,* CBS, 1986.
Mac MacKenzie, *Berlin Break,* 1992.

Also appeared in episodes of *Comedy Break,* syndicated; *The F.B.I.,* ABC; and *Maude,* CBS.

Television Appearances; Specials:
The Dean Martin Celebrity Roast: Betty White, NBC, 1978.
The Funniest Joke I Ever Heard, ABC, 1984.
Host, *CBS All-American Thanksgiving Day Parade,* CBS, annually, 1983-87.
Texas 150: A Celebration Special, ABC, 1986.
Sea World's All-Star Lone Star Celebration, CBS, 1988.
Stop the Madness, CBS, 1989.

Stage Appearances:
Lady of the Camellias, Winter Garden Theatre, New York City, 1963.

Also appeared in *The Great God Brown,* a Broadway production, and in productions of *Death of a Salesman, The Lion in Winter, The Little Foxes, Come Blow Your Horn, Caligula, Rhinoceros, The Fourposter, The Lark,* and *The Devil's Disciple.**

HINDMAN, Earl   1942-

PERSONAL

Born October 20, 1942, in Bisbee, AZ; married, wife's name Molly (an Episcopal priest).

Addresses: *Home*—Connecticut. *Agent*—The Tischerman Agency, 6767 Forest Lawn Dr., Suite 101, Los Angeles, CA 90068.

Career: Actor. Member of company at Syracuse Repertory Theatre, Syracuse, NY, 1967, Contemporary Theatre, Seattle, WA, 1974-75, and New Jersey Shakespeare Festival at Drew University, Madison, NJ, 1976.

CREDITS

Television Appearances; Series:
Detective Bob Reid, *Ryan's Hope,* ABC, 1975-84.
Wilson Wilson, *Home Improvement,* ABC, 1991—.

Television Appearances; Miniseries:
Lieutenant Commander Wade McClusky, *War and Remembrance,* ABC, 1988.
Mike Kettmann Sr., *Stay the Night,* ABC, 1992.

Television Appearances; Movies:
J. H. Potts, *Murder in Coweta County,* CBS, 1983.
Detective Jake Stern, *One Police Plaza,* CBS, 1986.
Danny Keeler, *Kojak: The Price of Justice,* CBS, 1987.
Stern, *The Red Spider,* CBS, 1988.
Donleavy, "It's Always Something" (also known as "Kojak"), *The ABC Saturday Mystery,* ABC, 1990.
Victor, *Rising Son,* TNT, 1990.

Television Appearances; Specials:
D. Law, "Pueblo," *ABC Theatre,* ABC, 1974.
William, "A Memory of Two Mondays," *Great Performances,* PBS, 1974.
FBI agent Lombardo, *Concealed Enemies,* 1984.
Walt Disney World Very Merry Christmas Parade, 1992.
Behind Closed Doors with Joan Lunden, ABC, 1995.
Segment host, *The 11th Annual Soap Opera Awards,* 1995.

Television Appearances; Episodic:
Clayton, *Spenser: For Hire,* ABC, 1985.
Findlay, "Coal Black Soul," *The Equalizer,* CBS, 1986.
Lieutenant Elmer, *The Equalizer* (three episodes), CBS, 1986 and 1987.
Max Ordella, *Spenser: For Hire,* ABC, 1987.

Television Appearances; Pilots:
Rick, *Key West,* NBC, 1973.

Film Appearances:
Three into Two Won't Go, 1969.
Whitey, *Who Killed Mary What's 'er Name?* (also known as *Death of a Hooker*), Cannon, 1971.
Brown, *The Taking of Pelham One, Two, Three,* United Artists, 1974.

Deputy Red, *The Parallax View,* Paramount, 1974.
Garrity, *Shoot It: Black, Shoot It: Blue,* Levitt/Pickman, 1974.
Beau Welles, *Greased Lightning,* Warner Bros., 1977.
FBI agent, *The Brinks Job* (also known as *Big Stickup at Brinks*), Universal, 1978.
Lieutenant Hanson, *Taps,* Twentieth Century-Fox, 1981.
J. T., *Silverado,* Columbia, 1985.
Satch, *Three Men and a Baby,* Buena Vista, 1987.
Voices of Chet, Black John, and Jerry, *Talk Radio,* Universal, 1988.
Henry Macy, *Ballad of the Sad Cafe,* Angelika, 1991.
Sergeant, *Fires Within,* 1991.

Stage Appearances:
Marvin Hudgins, *Dark of the Moon,* Mercer-Shaw Arena Theatre, New York City, 1970.
The Rivalry, Mummers Theatre, Oklahoma City, OK, 1970.
Kress, *The Basic Training of Pavlo Hummel,* New York Shakespeare Festival, Public Theatre, New York City, 1971.
Captain Martin, *The Love Suicide at the Schofield Barracks,* American National Theatre and Academy Theatre, New York City, 1972.
Asa Trenchard, *The Lincoln Mask,* Plymouth Theatre, New York City, 1972.
Henry IV, Part One, Folger Theatre Group, Washington, DC, 1974.
Rubin Flood, *The Dark at the Top of the Stairs,* Roundabout Theatre, New York City, 1979.
The Magnificent Cuckold, Yale Repertory Theatre, New Haven, CT, 1981.
Red, *Red and Blue,* New York Shakespeare Festival, Public Theatre, 1982.
Exeter, *Henry V,* New York Shakespeare Festival, Delacorte Theatre/Central Park, New York City, 1984.
Owen Musser, *The Foreigner,* Studio Arena Theatre, Buffalo, NY, 1986.
Gaspard Caderousse, *The Count of Monte Cristo,* Kennedy Center for the Performing Arts, Washington, DC, 1986.
Flint and Roses, Alliance Theatre Company, Atlanta, GA, 1986.
Big Albert Connor, *The Stick Wife,* Hartford Stage Company, Hartford, CT, 1987.
Melons, Yale Repertory Theatre, 1987-88.
Phaedra and Hippolytus, Yale Repertory Theatre, 1988-89.
Caius Lucius, *Cymbeline,* New York Shakespeare Festival, Public/Newman Theatre, New York City, 1989.

Sheriff Royce Landon Jr., *The Night Hank Williams Died,* Orpheum Theatre, New York City, 1989.
T. John Blessington, *The Solid Gold Cadillac,* Yale Repertory Theatre, 1989.

Major Tours:
The Great White Hope, U.S. cities, 1969-70.

OTHER SOURCES

Periodicals:
Entertainment Weekly, July 24, 1992, p. 12.*

HOGESTYN, Drake

PERSONAL

Born Donald Drake Hogestyn, in Fort Wayne, IN; son of Bill (a manufacturing executive) and Shug (a homemaker) Hogestyn; married Victoria Post, 1984; children: Whitney, Alexandra. *Education:* Graduated from University of South Florida, 1976.

Addresses: *Contact*—NBC Burbank, 3000 West Alameda Ave., Burbank, CA 91523.

Career: Actor. Played baseball on minor league teams for the New York Yankees.

Awards, Honors: *Soap Opera Digest* Award, hottest male star, 1994; *Daytime TV* Award, best actor, for *Days of Our Lives; Soap Opera Update* Award, best of the best.

CREDITS

Television Appearances; Series:
Brian McFadden, *Seven Brides for Seven Brothers,* CBS, 1982-83.
John Black, *Days of Our Lives,* NBC, 1986—.

Television Appearances; Movies:
Rod, *Beverly Hills Cowgirl Blues,* CBS, 1985.

Also appeared as Jack Breed, *Generation,* 1985.

Television Appearances; Specials:
The 12th Annual Circus of the Stars, CBS, 1987.
John Black, *Days of Our Lives: One Stormy Night,* NBC, 1992.

John Black, *Days of Our Lives: Night Sins,* NBC, 1993.
Superstar American Gladiators, ABC, 1995.

Television Appearances; Awards Presentations:
The 13th Annual Daytime Emmy Awards, NBC, 1986.
Host, *Soap Opera Digest Awards,* NBC, 1988.
Soap Opera Digest Awards, NBC, 1992.
The 19th Annual Daytime Emmy Awards, NBC, 1992.
The 20th Annual Daytime Emmy Awards, ABC, 1993.
The 9th Annual Soap Opera Awards, NBC, 1993.
The 21st Annual Daytime Emmy Awards, ABC, 1994.
The 11th Annual Soap Opera Awards, NBC, 1995.
Host, *The 12th Annual Soap Opera Awards,* NBC, 1996.*

HOLBROOK, Anna (Kathryn)

PERSONAL

Born April 18, in Fairbanks, AK; raised in Tucson, AZ; father, in the military; mother, Johanna Stephens, a professional photographer; married, husband's name, Bruce Holbrook (an airline pilot); children: Johanna, Henry. *Education:* Studied nursing at University of Arizona; studied broadcast journalism and film at Trinity University.

Addresses: *Agent*—Nancy Texbehi, Paradigm, 200 West 57th St., New York, NY 10019.

Career: Actress. In college, toured with Up with People; involved with charities, including The Covenant House and The Huntington Hospice. Appeared in commercials for Fruit and Fibre.

Awards, Honors: Emmy Award, outstanding supporting actress, 1996, and *Soap Opera Digest* Award nomination, outstanding supporting actress, 1997, both for *Another World.*

CREDITS

Television Appearances; Series:
Darah, *Benji, Zax and the Alien Prince,* CBS, 1983-84.
Sharlene Frame, Sharly Watts, and Kate Baker, *Another World,* NBC, 1988-91, 1993-97.

Television Appearances; Episodic:
Janet Silver, "Extended Family," *Law and Order,* NBC, 1993.

Christine Whitburn, "Family Values," *Law and Order*, NBC, 1994.
Heidi Longley, "Bone Free," *Spin City*, ABC, 1997.
Velma Darcy, "Matrimony," *Law and Order*, NBC, 1997.

Appeared in episodes of *Dallas*, CBS; *Gunsmoke*, CBS; *Petrocelli*, NBC; *The High Chaparral*, NBC; and *One Life to Live*, ABC.

Television Appearances; Awards Presentations:
Soap Opera Awards, NBC, 1990.

Television Appearances; Movies:
Vera Marquel, *Pep Devlin, Private Eye*, USA Network, 1997.

Stage Appearances:
Susie/Martha/Jili Gerard, *St. Hugo of Central Park*, Lamb's Theatre, New York City, 1988.
Woman, *The Dolphin Position*, Primary Stages, New York City, 1992.

Also appeared in *The Great Nebula in Orion*, *Blue Plains*, *Mr. Parnell*.

Film Appearances:
Woman in sportscar, *I Love Trouble*, Buena Vista, 1994.*

HORTON, Peter   1953-

PERSONAL

Born August 20, 1953, in Bellevue, WA; father, in the shipping business; married Michelle Pfeiffer (an actress), 1981 (divorced, 1988); married. *Education:* University of California, Santa Barbara, degree in music composition; also attended Principia College. *Avocational interests:* Playing classical piano.

Addresses: *Agent*—Bauer/Benedek Agency, 9255 Sunset Blvd., Suite 710, Los Angeles, CA 90069.

Career: Actor, director, producer, and composer. Performed on stage with Lobero Repertory Theatre in Santa Barbara, CA.

CREDITS

Film Appearances:
Joey Madona, *Fade to Black*, American Cinema, 1980.

Cult member, *Serial*, Paramount, 1980.
Jacob, *Split Image*, Orion, 1982.
Dr. Burt Stanton, *Stephen King's Children of the Corn* (also known as *Children of the Corn*), New World, 1984.
Father Mahoney, *Where the River Runs Black*, Metro-Goldwyn-Mayer/United Artists, 1986.
Harry, "Hospital," *Amazon Women on the Moon* (also known as *Cheeseburger Film Sandwich*), Universal, 1987.
Zack Barnes, *Side Out*, TriStar, 1990.
Jamie, *Singles*, Warner Bros., 1992.
Patrick Brewer, *The Baby-Sitter's Club*, Columbia, 1995.
Roy Foxx, *Two Days in the Valley*, Metro-Goldwyn-Mayer/United Artists, 1996.
Brian, *The End of Violence*, 1997.

Film Work; Director:
"Two I.D.s" in *Amazon Women on the Moon* (also known as *Cheeseburger Film Sandwich*), Universal, 1987.
The Cure, Universal, 1995.
Powers That Be, 1997.

Television Appearances; Series:
Crane McFadden, *Seven Brides for Seven Brothers*, CBS, 1982-83.
Professor Gary Shepherd, *thirtysomething*, ABC, 1987-91.

Television Appearances; Movies:
Tony Smith, *She's Dressed to Kill*, NBC, 1979.
Jack O'Callahan, *Miracle on Ice*, ABC, 1981.
Bill, *Freedom*, ABC, 1981.
Doug, *Choices of the Heart* (also known as *In December the Roses Will Bloom Again*), NBC, 1983.
Jim Harrison, *Children of the Dark*, CBS, 1994.
General George Armstrong Custer, *Crazy Horse*, TNT, 1996.
Steven Keeney, *Death Benefit*, USA Network, 1996.
Lieutenant Clay Maloney, *Murder Live!*, NBC, 1997.
Scott Fischer, *Into Thin Air: Death on Everest*, ABC, 1997.

Television Work; Movies:
Director, *Extreme Close-Up* (also known as *Home Video*), NBC, 1990.
Executive producer, *Murder Live!*, NBC, 1997.

Television Appearances; Episodic:
"Lust et Veritas," *St. Elsewhere*, NBC, 1983.
Jack, *Gun*, ABC, 1997.

Television Director; Episodic:
thirtysomething, ABC, 1988.
"Whose Woods Are These?," *The Wonder Years,* ABC, 1988.
thirtysomething, ABC, 1989.
The Wonder Years, ABC, 1989.
Gun, ABC, 1997.

Television Appearances; Pilots:
Tom Sawyer, *Sawyer and Finn,* NBC, 1983.

Television Director; Pilots:
(And series consultant) *Class of '96,* Fox, 1993.
Birdland, ABC, 1994.

Television Appearances; Specials:
Host, *Dolphins, Whales, and Us* (documentary), CBS, 1990.
Times Warner Presents the Earth Day Special, ABC, 1990.
Host, *Marine Life Miracles* (documentary), PBS, 1992.
Joe, "The Gift," *Directed By,* Showtime, 1994.

Television Work; Specials:
Director, "One Too Many," *ABC Afterschool Specials,* ABC, 1985.

Stage Appearances:
Appeared in *Butterflies Are Free,* Masquers Theatre, Los Angeles, CA; also appeared with the Lobero Repertory Company Theatre, Santa Barbara, CA.

Adaptations: The television movie *Murder Live!* is based on a story by Horton.

OTHER SOURCES

TV Guide, November 8, 1997, pp. 30-33, 51.*

HOWARD, Shawn Michael

PERSONAL

Born July 31, in Newark, NJ. *Education:* Graduated from New York University.

Addresses: *Contact*—4024 Redford Ave., Building 6, Studio City, CA 91604.

Career: Actor. Began career in an AT&T commercial directed by and starring Spike Lee. Writes songs for and sings lead vocals with the band Invisible Culture.

CREDITS

Film Appearances:
Bobby, *Above the Rim,* New Line Cinema, 1994.
Kurt, *Sunset Park* (also known as *Coach*), TriStar, 1996.

Also appeared as Spike Lee, *Plump Fiction;* appeared in *The Cable Guy* and *Flirting with Disaster.*

Television Appearances; Series:
Russell, *The Single Guy,* NBC, 1996-97.
Warren Cruickshank, *The Practice,* ABC, 1997—.

Television Appearances; Episodic:
Appeared in episodes of *Nash Bridges,* CBS; *Married . . . with Children,* Fox; and *Law & Order,* NBC.*

HOWE, Bette
See HENRITZE, Bette

HUBERT, Janet
See HUBERT-WHITTEN, Janet

HUBERT-WHITTEN, Janet
(Janet Hubert)

PERSONAL

Born January 13, in Momence, IL; married; husband's name, James Whitten; children: Elijah Isaac Whitten. *Education:* Attended the Juilliard School of Drama; studied acting with Peggy Freeman, Gene Lesser, and Stephen Aaron; studied voice with Edith Skinner, Liz Smith, and Robert Williams; and studied dance with Douglas Wassell, Phil Black, Luigi, and Miguel Gidrioux.

Addresses: *Agent*—c/o Actors Group Agency, 157 West 57th St., Suite 604, New York, NY 10019.

Career: Actress, dancer, and singer. Alvin Ailey Dance Theatre, dancer, 1977-79.

Member: Actors' Equity Association, American Federation of Television and Radio Artists, Screen Actors Guild.

CREDITS

Stage Appearances; Billed as Janet Hubert:
Opal, *The First,* Martin Beck Theatre, New York City, 1981.
Joy, *Anteroom,* Playwrights Horizons, New York City, 1985.
Irina, *Lost in the Stars,* Long Wharf Theatre, New Haven, CT, 1985-86.
Sophie, *Camille,* Long Wharf Theatre, 1986-87.

Also appeared as Tantomile, *Cats,* Winter Garden Theatre, New York City; Carameen, *Sleeping Beauty,* Municipal Opera House, St. Louis, MO; woman number one, *Home,* Indiana Repertory Theatre, Indianapolis, IN; as a member of the company, *Sophisticated Ladies,* Lunt-Fontanne Theatre, New York City; and in *Joseph and the Amazing Technicolor Dreamcoat,* Golden Theatre, New York City.

Major Tours; Billed as Janet Hubert:
Appeared as Afrique, *Sophisticated Ladies,* International tour, including Tokyo, Japan and Paris, France; also appeared as a principal dancer, *Dancin',* U.S. cities.

Film Appearances; Billed as Janet Hubert:
Looking for Mr. Goodbar, Paramount, 1977.
The Fury, Twentieth Century-Fox, 1978.
A Piece of the Action, 1985.
Lola, *Agent on Ice,* 1985.
Dinner guest, *White Man's Burden,* Savoy Pictures, 1995.

Television Appearances; Series:
Vivian Banks, *The Fresh Prince of Bel-Air,* NBC, 1990-93.
Karen Williams, *Coach,* ABC, 1993-94.
Esther Hayes, *Lawless,* Fox, 1996-97.

Television Appearances; Movies:
Ashtarte, *New Eden,* 1994.

Television Appearances; Specials:
Song performer, *The All Night Strut!,* 1988.
Elaine Baham, *What About Your Friends?,* CBS, 1995.

Television Appearances; Episodic; Billed as Janet Hubert:
"Fun with Animals," *21 Jump Street,* Fox, 1989.
Storytime, PBS, 1994.
Dr. Pamela Fordham, *Goode Behavior,* UPN, 1996.
Edwina Dubois, *The Jamie Foxx Show* (also known as *Good to Go*), The WB, 1996.
Anette Freeman, *The Faculty,* ABC, 1996.

OTHER SOURCES

Periodicals:
Ebony, June, 1993, pp. 30-32.
Jet, August 9, 1993, pp. 17-18.*

HUTTON, Lauren   1944(?)-

PERSONAL

Born Mary Laurence Hutton, November 17, 1944 (some sources say 1943), in Charleston, SC; daughter of Laurence Hutton (a writer). *Education:* Attended University of Florida and Sophia Newcombe College.

Addresses: *Office*—PMK, 955 South Carrillo Drive, Suite 200, Los Angeles, CA 90048.

Career: Actress and model. Hutton was one of the top fashion models from the 1960s through the 1980s.

CREDITS

Film Appearances:
Kate, *Paper Lion,* United Artists, 1968.
Rita Nebraska, *Little Fauss and Big Halsey,* Paramount, 1970.
Pamela Gibson, *Pieces of Dreams,* United Artists, 1970.
Jenny, *Excuse Me, My Name Is Rocco Papaleo* (also known as *Permette? Rocco Papaleo* and *Rocco Papaleo*), Rumson, 1972.
Billie, *The Gambler,* Paramount, 1974.
Nashville, Paramount, 1975.
Aggie Maybank, *Gator,* United Artists, 1976.
Kate Morgan, *Viva Knieval!* (also known as *Seconds to Live*), Warner Bros., 1977.
Nona Bruce, *Welcome to L.A.,* Lion's Gate, 1977.
Florence "Flo" Farmer, *A Wedding,* Twentieth Century-Fox, 1978.
Michelle Stratton, *American Gigolo,* Paramount, 1980.
Charlotte Taylor Wilson, *Zorro, the Gay Blade,* Twentieth Century-Fox, 1981.
Jenny Loften, *Paternity,* Paramount, 1981.
Clothilde de Watteville, *Hecate,* 1981.
Jane, *All Fired Up* (also known as *Tout Feu, Tout Flamme*), 1981.
Herself, *Burroughs,* 1983.
Kari, *Lassiter,* Warner Bros., 1984.
Countess, *Once Bitten,* Samuel Goldwyn, 1985.

Marlene Belle-Ferguson, *A Certain Desire* (also known as *Flagrant Desir*), Worldwide Entertainment Corp., 1986.

Jamie, *Malone* (also known as *Blue Blood*), Orion, 1987.

Scandalous, Anchor Bay, 1988.

Gap-Toothed Women, 1988.

Francine Lake, *Forbidden Sun,* Filmscreen, 1989.

Jennifer, *Missing Pieces,* Orion, 1991.

Cristina, *Miliardi* (also known as *Millions*), 1991.

Liz Stanford, *Guilty as Charged,* IRS Releasing, 1991.

Megan, *My Father, the Hero,* Buena Vista, 1994.

Evelyn Jellybelly, *Die Story von Monty Spinnerratz,* 1997.

54, 1998.

Television Appearances; Movies:

Leigh Michaels, *Someone's Watching Me,* NBC, 1978.

Lilah, *Institute For Revenge,* NBC, 1979.

Marathon, CBS, 1980.

Cocaine: One Man's Seduction, NBC, 1983.

Kathy DeMaio, *The Cradle Will Fall,* CBS, 1983.

Erika Hansen, *Starflight: The Plane That Couldn't Land* (also known as *Starflight One*), ABC, 1983.

Meg North, *Scandal Sheet,* ABC, 1985.

Joanna Lake, *Return of Mickey Spillane's Mike Hammer,* CBS, 1986.

Georgia Crawford, *Timestalkers,* CBS, 1987.

Barbara Caldwell, *Perfect People,* ABC, 1988.

Jessica Moreau, *Fear,* Showtime, 1990.

Wynne Atwood, *We the Jury,* USA Network, 1996.

Television Appearance; Series:

Liz McDowell, *Falcon Crest,* 1981.

Colette Ferrier, *Paper Dolls,* ABC, 1984.

Linda Fairchild Rush, *Central Park West* (also known as *CPW*), CBS, 1995-96.

Host, *Lauren Hutton and. . .,* syndicated, 1995—.

Television Appearances; Specials:

Steve Martin's Best Show Ever, 1981.

From Here to Maternity, 1986.

People's 20th Birthday, ABC, 1994.

Host, *The World of Audubon 10th Anniversary Special,* TBS, 1994.

To the Ends of the Earth, USA Network, 1994.

Herself, *Richard Avedon: Darkness and Light,* PBS, 1995.

Narration, *Intimate Portrait: Marilyn Monroe,* Lifetime, 1996.

Narration, *Intimate Portrait: Bette Davis,* Lifetime, 1996.

The Late Show With David Letterman Video Special 2, CBS, 1996.

Presenter, *The VH1 Fashion Awards,* VH1, 1996.

Hollywood Diaries, American Movie Classics, 1997.

Little Warriors: On Location With Lauren Hutton, TBS, 1997.

Television Appearances; Miniseries:

Leslie Jenner Hawkewood, *The Rhinemann Exchange,* NBC, 1977.

Evelyn MacIntyre, *Monte Carlo,* CBS, 1986.

Z. Z. Bryant, *Sins,* CBS, 1986.

Television Appearances; Episodic:

"Riding the Nightmare," *The Hitchhiker,* HBO, 1986.

Television Work:

Creator and executive producer, *Lauren Hutton and . . .* (series), syndicated, 1995—.

Producer, *Little Warriors: On Location With Lauren Hutton* (special), TBS, 1997.

Stage Appearances:

Appeared in *Extremities,* Los Angeles Public Theatre.

OTHER SOURCES

Cosmopolitan, May, 1995, p. 270.

Ladies Home Journal, November, 1995, p. 62.

Vanity Fair, July, 1995, p. 144.

WWD, January 9, 1997, p. S2.*

I-J

ITALIANO, Anne
See BANCROFT, Anne

ITO, Robert 1931-

PERSONAL

Born July 2, 1931, in Vancouver, British Columbia, Canada.

Addresses: *Agent*—Chateau Billings Talent Agency, 5657 Wilshire Blvd., Suite 340, Los Angeles, CA 90036.

Career: Actor. National Ballet of Canada, member of company for ten years.

CREDITS

Film Appearances:

Sato, *Dimension 5,* Feature Films, 1966.

Tang, *Women of the Prehistoric Planet* (also known as *Prehistoric Planet Women*), Real Art, 1966.

George Toyota, *Some Kind of a Nut,* United Artists, 1969.

The Naked Ape, Universal, 1973.

Anesthetist, *The Terminal Man,* Warner Bros., 1974.

Asian instructor, *Rollerball,* United Artists, 1975.

Butler, *Peeper* (also known as *Fat Chance*), Twentieth Century-Fox, 1975.

Mr. Chu, *Special Delivery* (also known as *Dangerous Break*), American International, 1976.

Midway (also known as *Battle of Midway*), Universal, 1976.

Professor Hikita, *The Adventures of Buckaroo Banzai: Across the Eighth Dimension,* Twentieth Century-Fox, 1984.

Koga, *Pray for Death,* Transworld Entertainment/American Distribution Group, 1986.

Kim, *P.I. Private Investigations,* Metro-Goldwyn-Mayer/United Artists, 1987.

Ted Tanaka, *Aloha Summer,* 1988.

Auctioneer, *The Vineyard,* 1989.

Yamashita's aide, *Crazy People,* 1990.

Television Appearances; Series:

Regular, *The Burns and Schreiber Comedy Hour,* ABC, 1973.

Voice of Henry Chan, *The Amazing Chan and the Chan Clan* (animated), CBS, 1974.

Sam Fujiyama, *Quincy, M.E.* (also known as *Quincy*), NBC, 1976-83.

Voice characterization, *Rambo* (animated), syndicated, 1986.

Voice of Dr. Sato, "Deadly Force" (animated), *Gargoyles,* syndicated, 1994—.

Television Appearances; Movies:

Masai Ikeda, *Fer de Lance* (also known as *Death Dive* and *Operation Serpent*), CBS, 1974.

Arnold, *Aloha Means Goodbye,* CBS, 1974.

Intern, *Death Scream* (also known as *The Woman Who Cried Murder*), ABC, 1975.

Drees Darrin, *Helter Skelter,* CBS, 1976.

Roy Nakamura, *SST—Death Flight* (also known as *SST: Disaster in the Sky*), ABC, 1977.

Mr. Hashimoto, *American Geisha,* CBS, 1986.

Hasamu Mochadomi, *The Great Pretender* (also known as *Dead End Brattigan*), NBC, 1991.

Voice, *Jonny Quest versus the Cyber Insects* (animated), TNT, 1995.

Mr. Tawashima, *The War between Us,* Lifetime, 1995.

Shin Chan, *Hollow Point* (also known as *Rysk Roulette*), HBO, 1996.

Voice of priest and Benjamin, "The Magic Pearl" (animated; also known as "Po Po and the Magic

Pearl" and "Mystery of the Magic Pearl"), *ABC Kids Movie Matinee,* ABC, 1996.

Methusala, *Trial at Fortitude Bay,* Lifetime, 1996.

Television Appearances; Episodic:

"The Way of Violence Has No Name," *Kung Fu,* ABC, 1973.

"The Assassin," *Kung Fu,* ABC, 1973.

"Jororo Farewell," *Magnum, P.I.,* CBS, 1983.

Sato, "WGOD," *The Hitchhiker,* HBO, 1985.

Tran Van Hieu, *Airwolf,* CBS, 1986.

Yoshio Shinno, *Knots Landing,* CBS, 1986.

Vang Pau, *Supercarrier,* ABC, 1988.

Kazu, *Ohara,* ABC, 1988.

Joe Matsumuro, *Tour of Duty,* CBS, 1988.

Lawrence Mishima, *Falcon Crest,* CBS, 1988.

Tac Officer Chang, "Coming of Age," *Star Trek: The Next Generation,* syndicated, 1988.

"Children of Light," *MacGyver,* ABC, 1989.

Books, "Murder Maybe," *Mom P.I.,* CBC, 1990.

Books, "Undue Influence," *Mom P.I.,* CBC, 1990.

Tanaka, "Year of the Monkey," *Friday the 13th,* syndicated, 1990.

Voice, *ProStars* (animated and live-action), NBC, 1991.

The Ninja/Kyodai Ken, *Batman: The Animated Series,* Fox, 1992.

Mr. Kato, *Animaniacs,* 1993.

Johnny Leong, "Revenge of the Sword," *Highlander,* syndicated, 1993.

Voice of Mandarin, "Distant Boundaries" (animated), *Iron Man* (also known as *Marvel Action Hour* and *Marvel Action Universe*), syndicated, 1994.

Kenji Yoshimida, "Before the Axe," *E.N.G.,* CBC and Lifetime, 1994.

Hideo Koto, "The Samurai," *Highlander,* syndicated, 1994.

Dr. Ishimaru, "Nisei," *The X-Files,* Fox, 1995.

Dr. Ishimaru, "731," *The X-Files,* Fox, 1995.

Hiro Miyamoto, *Chicago Hope,* CBS, 1996.

Colonel Raymond, "Worlds Apart," *The Outer Limits,* Showtime, 1996.

Television Appearances; Pilots:

Fong, *Kung Fu,* ABC, 1972.

Li-Teh, *Men of the Dragon,* ABC, 1974.

Dr. Sam Fujiyama, *The Eyes of Texas II,* NBC, 1980.

The godfather, *John Woo's "Once a Thief"* (also known as *Once a Thief*), Fox, 1996.

Television Appearances; Specials:

North Korean negotiator, "Pueblo," *ABC Theatre,* ABC, 1973.

Mr. Sumida, "The War between the Classes," *CBS Schoolbreak Special,* CBS, 1985.

Voice of the old man, "The Magic Paintbrush" (animated), *McDonald's Family Theatre,* CBS, 1993.

Stage Appearances:

Flower Drum Song, St. James Theatre, New York City, 1958.

Our Town, Circle in the Square Theatre, New York City, 1959.*

IVES, Burl 1909-1995

OBITUARY NOTICE—See index for *CTFT* sketch: Born June 14, 1909, in Hunt City Township, IL; died of cancer, April 14, 1995, in Anacortes, WA. Actor, singer, and writer. An Academy Award-winning actor, Ives was also a popular folk singer who was particularly known for children's recordings, including "I Know an Old Lady (Who Swallowed a Fly)" and "On Top of Old Smoky." Ives began singing professionally at an early age and during the 1930s traveled widely throughout North America collecting material to add to his act. He settled in New York City, where he made his stage debut in 1938 in *I Married an Angel.* He appeared in several Broadway productions, including *The Boys from Syracuse, This Is the Army,* and *Sing Out, Sweet Land,* before making his film debut in *Smoky* in 1946. In the 1950s and 1960s Ives appeared in such films as *East of Eden, Desire under the Elms, Our Man in Havana,* and *Ensign Pulver* in addition to the two roles for which he remains best known: his performance as Big Daddy in *Cat on a Hot Tin Roof,* a role that he had originated on Broadway; and his Academy Award-winning performance as Rufus Hannassey in *The Big Country* in 1958. He occasionally acted in television series and was seen in the miniseries *Roots* in 1977. Ives's recording career spanned several decades beginning with "The Wayfaring Stranger" in 1949 and included such notable hits as "Foggy, Foggy Dew," "The Big Rock Candy Mountain," "Frosty the Snowman," "Holly Jolly Christmas," and "Blue Tail Fly." Ives's writings include the memoir *Wayfaring Stranger,* 1948, and several song books.

OBITUARIES AND OTHER SOURCES

Books:

International Who's Who, Europa, 1993, p. 782.

Periodicals:

Chicago Tribune, April 16, 1995, section 2, p. 6.

Los Angeles Times, April 15, 1995, pp. A1, A18.

New York Times, April 15, 1995, p. 10.
Times (London), April 15, 1995, p. 19.

IVEY, Dana   1942-

PERSONAL

Full name, Dana Robins Ivey; born August 12 (some sources say August 14), 1942, in Atlanta, GA; daughter of Hugh Daugherty (a physicist and professor) and Mary Nell (an actress and teacher; maiden name, McKoin) Ivey. *Education:* Rollins College, B.A. (theatre), 1963; trained for the stage at the London Academy of Music and Dramatic Art. *Avocational interests:* Classical music, reading (historical fiction and mysteries), traveling, supporting animal rights groups.

Addresses: *Agent*—c/o Paradigm, 10100 Santa Monica Blvd, 25th floor, Los Angeles, CA, 90067.

Career: Actress and teacher. Georgia Institute of Technology, director of Drama Tech, 1974-77; WGKA-AM, Atlanta, GA, disc jockey, interviewer, and classical music programmer, 1974-76; Atlanta, GA, teacher, 1974-77; South Coast Repertory Company, Costa Mesa, CA, guest artist, 1989-90; teacher at the Circle in the Square Theatre School, the National Theatre School of Canada, and the Academy Theatre School.

Member: Actors' Equity Association, American Federation of Television and Radio Artists, Screen Actors Guild, Canadian Actors' Equity Association, Association of Canadian Television and Radio Artists.

Awards, Honors: Fulbright grant to study at the London Academy of Dramatic Arts, 1964; best actress, Atlanta Circle of Drama Critics, 1977, for *Come Back to the Five and Dime, Jimmy Dean, Jimmy Dean;* Dramalogue Award, 1979, for *Romeo and Juliet;* Drama League Award, California Shakespeare Festival, 1979; Clarence Derwent Award, 1983; Drama Desk nomination, 1983, for *Present Laughter;* Obie Award from the *Village Voice,* and Drama Desk nomination, both 1983, for *Quartermaine's Terms;* Antoinette Perry Award nominations, all for best supporting actress, 1984, for *Heartbreak House* and *Sunday in the Park with George,* and 1997, for *The Last Night of Ballyhoo;* Obie Award, 1987, Circle Award, 1988, and Drama Desk nomination, 1988, all for *Driving Miss Daisy;* Circle Award, 1988, for *Wenceslas Square.*

CREDITS

Stage Appearances:
Hermia, *A Midsummer Night's Dream,* Front Street Theatre, Memphis, TN, 1964-65.
Sara, *Major Barbara,* Front Street Theatre, 1964-65.
Marian's mother, *The Music Man,* Front Street Theatre, 1964-65.
Mrs. Teale, *Roberta,* Front Street Theatre, 1964-65.
Madame Rosepettle, *Oh Dad, Poor Dad, Mama's Hung You in the Closet and I'm Feeling So Sad,* Front Street Theatre, 1964-65.
Wife and mother, *Ah! Wilderness,* Front Street Theatre, 1964-65.
Wife, *The Seven Year Itch,* Front Street Theatre, 1964-65.
Mrs. Higgins, *My Fair Lady,* Front Street Theatre, 1964-65.
Mrs. Mullins, *Carousel,* Theatre of the Stars, Atlanta, GA, 1965.
Member of the chorus, *Murder in the Cathedral,* Canadian Players, Toronto, Ontario, Canada, 1965-66.
Anna, *The Firebugs,* Canadian Players, 1965-66.
Sara Tansey, *The Playboy of the Western World,* Canadian Players, 1965-66.
Mrs. Sowerberry, *Oliver!,* Theatre of the Stars, 1966.
Margaret, *Galileo,* Manitoba Theatre Centre, Winnipeg, Manitoba, Canada, 1966.
Solange, *The Maids,* Manitoba Theatre Centre, 1966.
Kitty, *Charley's Aunt,* Manitoba Theatre Center, 1966.
Title role, *Antigone,* Hartford Stage Company, Hartford, CT, 1968.
Lucy Brown, *The Threepenny Opera,* Hartford Stage Company, 1968.
Baroness and Clea, *White Liars/Black Comedy,* Theatre Calgary, Calgary, Alberta, Canada, 1969-70.
Mia, *The Three Desks,* Theatre Calgary, 1969-70.
Amanda, *Private Lives,* Theatre Calgary, 1969-70.
Pioneer woman and singer, *You Two Stay Here, the Rest Come with Me,* Theatre Calgary, 1969-70.
Gillian, *Bell, Book, and Candle,* Theatre Calgary, 1969-70.
Gwendolyn, *The Importance of Being Earnest,* Theatre Calgary, 1969-70.
Mrs. Gargary, *Great Expectations,* Theatre Calgary, 1969-70.
Fay, *Loot,* Theatre Calgary, 1969-70.
Lill, *Revenge,* Centaur Theatre, Montreal, Quebec, Canada, 1970-71.
Ruth, *The Homecoming,* Centaur Theatre, 1970-71.
Nurse, *The Death of Bessie Smith,* Centaur Theatre, 1970-71.

Miss Moscowitz, *The Electronic Nigger,* Centaur Theatre, 1970-71.

Sonya, *Uncle Vanya,* Centaur Theatre, 1970-71.

Emilia, *Othello,* Centaur Theatre, 1970-71.

Mrs. Harford, *A Touch of the Poet,* Centaur Theatre, 1970-71.

Title role, *Electra,* Centaur Theatre, 1971-72.

Jean, *The Entertainer,* Centaur Theatre, 1971-72.

Narrator, *At the Hawk's Well,* Centaur Theatre, 1971-72.

Queen, *Full Moon in March,* Centaur Theatre, 1971-72.

Woman, *The Exception and the Rule,* Centaur Theatre, 1971-72.

Claire, *The Maids,* Centaur Theatre, 1971-72.

Isabelle, *Total Eclipse,* Centaur Theatre, 1971-72.

Gwendolyn Pidgeon, *The Odd Couple,* Theatre of the Stars, 1972.

Helene, *En Pieces Detachees,* Manitoba Theatre Centre, 1973.

Woman, *Thurber Carnival,* Manitoba Theatre Centre, 1973.

Stella, *A Streetcar Named Desire,* Manitoba Theatre Centre, 1973.

Shen-Te, *The Good Woman of Setzuan,* Theatre London, London, Ontario, Canada, 1973.

Sara, *A Touch of the Poet,* St. Lawrence Center, National Arts Centre, Ottawa, Ontario, Canada, 1973.

Sara, *Sunrise on Sara,* Festival Lennoxville, Lennoxville, Quebec, Canada, 1973.

Nurse, *Romeo and Juliet,* Alliance Theatre, Atlanta, GA, 1974.

Sister Woman, *Cat on a Hot Tin Roof,* Alliance Theatre, 1974.

Jenny, *Everything in the Garden,* Druid Cellar Dinner Theatre, 1974.

Elizabeth Proctor, *The Crucible,* Alliance Theatre, 1975.

Annie Sullivan, *The Miracle Worker,* Alliance Theatre, 1976.

Mistress Quickly, *Henry IV, Part I,* Alliance Theatre, 1977.

Mary, *All the Way Home,* Alliance Theatre, 1977.

Lina, *Misalliance,* Alliance Theatre, 1977.

Mona, *Come Back to the Five and Dime, Jimmy Dean, Jimmy Dean,* Alliance Theatre, 1977.

Title role, *Hedda Gabler,* Alliance Theatre, 1977.

Catherine, *Great Catherine,* Shaw Festival, Niagara-on-the-Lake, Ontario, Canada, 1977.

Alma, *Eccentricities of a Nightingale,* Alaska Repertory Theatre, Anchorage, AK, 1978.

Miss Casewell, *The Mousetrap,* Newport Actors Company, Newport, RI, 1978.

Elaine, *The Last of the Red Hot Lovers,* Newport Actors Company, 1978.

Mrs. Linde, *A Doll's House,* Manitoba Theatre Centre, 1978.

Pearl and Dot, *Patio/Porch,* Dallas, TX, 1978.

Regina, *The Little Foxes,* Alliance Theatre, 1979.

Claire, *The Taking Away of Little Willie,* Mark Taper Forum, Los Angeles, CA, 1979.

Katherine, *The Taming of the Shrew,* California Shakespearean Festival, Visalia, CA, 1979.

Lady Capulet, *Romeo and Juliet,* California Shakespearean Festival, 1979.

Miss Giddens, *The Innocents,* Vancouver Playhouse, Vancouver, British Columbia, Canada, 1979.

Elvira, *Blithe Spirit,* Vancouver Playhouse, 1979.

Julia, *The Philanderer,* Shaw Festival, 1980.

Lucienne, *A Flea in Her Ear,* Shaw Festival, 1980.

Gentlewoman and witch, *Macbeth,* Vivian Beaumont Theatre, New York City, 1980.

Isabel, *A Call from the East,* Manhattan Theatre Club, New York City, 1981.

Madwoman, *The Hunchback of Notre Dame,* New York Shakespeare Festival, Public Theatre, 1981.

Miss Prism, *The Importance of Being Earnest,* Peterborough Players, Peterborough, NH, 1981.

Ellie, *Bing and Walker,* Peterborough Players, 1981.

Hilda, *Am I Blue?,* Hartford Stage Company, 1981.

Renata, *Forbidden Copy,* Hartford Stage Company, 1981.

Andrea, *Twinkle, Twinkle,* Hartford Stage Company, 1981.

Lizzie Borden and actress, *Blood Relations,* Centaur Theatre, 1981.

Miss Tendesco, *Vivien,* Arc Theatre, New York City, 1982.

Monica Reed, *Present Laughter,* Circle in the Square Theatre, New York City, 1982.

Melanie Garth, *Quartermaine's Terms,* Long Wharf Theatre, New Haven, CT, 1982, then Playhouse 91, New York City, 1983.

Nanny, Kate, Principal, *Baby with the Bathwater* (also known as *Baby with the Bath Water*), Playwrights Horizons, New York City, 1983.

Lady Ariadne Utterwod, *Heartbreak House,* Circle in the Square Theatre, 1983.

Naomi Eisen and Yvonne, *Sunday in the Park with George,* Booth Theatre, New York City, 1984.

Helen Kroger, *Pack of Lies,* Royale Theatre, New York City, 1984.

Countess, *The Marriage of Figaro,* Circle in the Square Theatre, 1985.

Daisy Werthan, *Driving Miss Daisy,* Playwrights Horizons, 1987, then John Houseman Theatre, 1987-89.

The women, *Wenceslas Square,* New York Shakespeare Festival, Public Theatre/Martinsen Hall, New York City, 1988.

Melissa, *Love Letters,* Promenade Theatre, New York City, 1989.

Gertrude, *Hamlet,* New York Shakespeare Festival, Public Theatre/Anspacher Theatre, New York City, 1990.

Nettie Cleary, *The Subject Was Roses,* Roundabout Theatre Company, New York City, 1991.

Ma-Noreen, *Beggars in the House of Plenty,* Manhattan Theatre Club, City Center Stage II, New York City, 1991.

Julia Budder, *It's Only a Play,* Center Theatre Group, James A. Doolittle Theatre, Los Angeles, CA, 1992.

Evelyn, *Kindertransport,* Manhattan Theatre Club, City Center Stage I, New York City, 1994.

Sonia, *It Changes Every Year,* and *Sons and Fathers* (two one-act plays), Malaparte Theatre Company, New York City, 1994.

Naomi Eisen and Yvonne, *Sunday in the Park With George,* St. James Theatre, New York City, 1994.

Leonie (also known as Leo), *Indiscretions (Les Parents Terribles),* Ethel Barrymore Theatre, New York City, 1995.

Bridget McCrea, *Sex and Longing,* Cort Theatre, New York City, 1996.

Boo, *The Last Night of Ballyhoo,* Helen Hayes Theatre, New York City, 1997—.

Also appeared as seventh fairy and palace guard, *Sleeping Beauty,* Children's Civic Theatre, Atlanta, GA; also appeared in *Candida in Concert* and *Major Barbara in Concert.*

Major Tours:

Member of chorus, *Murder in the Cathedral,* Canadian Players, Canadian cities, 1966.

Anna, *The Firebugs,* Canadian Players, Canadian cities, 1966.

Sara Tansey, *Playboy of the Western World,* Canadian Players, Canadian cities, 1966.

Lady-in-waiting, *Twelfth Night,* Stratford Shakespearean Festival Centennial tour, Canadian cities, 1967.

Avdotya, *The Government Inspector,* Stratford Shakespearean Festival Centennial tour, Canadian cities, 1967.

Androgyne, *Volpone,* National Shakespeare Company, U.S. cities, 1967.

Viola, *Twelfth Night,* National Shakespeare Company, U.S. cities, 1967.

Juliet, *Romeo and Juliet,* National Shakespeare Company, U.S. cities, 1967.

Miss McCormack and Mimsey, *Plaza Suite,* U.S. cities, 1969.

Performer in scenes from *The Taming of the Shrew,* Canadian schools, 1970.

Television Appearances; Series:

Dr. Maria Thompson, *Search for Tomorrow,* CBS, 1978.

Eleanor Standard, *Easy Street,* NBC, 1986.

Ms. Langer, *Frasier,* NBC, 1996.

Television Appearances; Movies:

Gabrielle Harwood, *Die Laughing,* ABC, 1989.

Lois Jurgens, *A Child Lost Forever,* NBC, 1992.

Mrs. Julia Peyton, *Class of '61,* ABC, 1993.

Television Appearances; Specials:

Lady Utterwod, *Heartbreak House,* PBS and Showtime, 1984.

Naomi Eisen and Yvonne, *Sunday in the Park with George,* PBS and Showtime, 1985.

Gertrude, *Hamlet,* 1990.

Television Appearances; Miniseries:

Little Gloria . . . Happy at Last, NBC, 1982.

Television Appearances; Episodic:

"Die Laughing," *B.L. Stryker* (also known as *The ABC Saturday Mystery*), ABC, 1989.

Margie Bolander, "Law and Disorder," *Homicide: Life on the Street* (also known as *Homicide* and *Homicide: LOTS*), NBC, 1995.

Margie Bolander, "End Game," *Homicide: Life on the Street* (also known as *Homicide* and *Homicide: LOTS*), NBC, 1995.

Margie Bolander, "Dead End," *Homicide: Life on the Street* (also known as *Homicide* and *Homicide: LOTS*), NBC, 1995.

Shore, "Girlfriends," *Law and Order* (also known as *Law & Order*), NBC, 1996.

Film Appearances:

Mrs. Mueller, *The Explorers* (also known as *Explorers*), Paramount, 1984.

Miss Millie, *The Color Purple,* Warner Bros., 1985.

Wedding speaker, *Heartburn,* Paramount, 1986.

Mrs. Reed, *Dirty Rotten Scoundrels,* Orion, 1988.

Engagement party guest, *Another Woman,* 1988.

Wardrobe mistress, *Postcards From the Edge,* Columbia, 1990.

Margaret Alford, *The Addams Family,* Paramount, 1991.

Mrs. Stone, the desk clerk, *Home Alone 2: Lost in New York,* Twentieth Century-Fox, 1992.

The widow Douglas, *The Adventures of Huck Finn,* Buena Vista, 1993.

Judge Tompkins, *Guilty as Sin,* Buena Vista, 1993.

Claire, *Sleepless in Seattle,* TriStar, 1993.

Margaret, *Addams Family Values,* Paramount, 1993.

Meredith Stonehall, *The Scarlet Letter,* Buena Vista, 1995.

Mack, Linus's secretary, *Sabrina,* Paramount, 1995.

Ship of Fools, 1998.

RECORDINGS

Taped Readings:

Composing a Life, Penguin-HighBridge, 1992.

The Evening Star, Simon and Schuster (New York City), 1992.

For My Daughters, Harper, 1994.

Cheaper by the Dozen, Bantam Doubleday Dell Audio, 1995.

SIDELIGHTS

On an earlier occasion, Dana Ivey told *CTFT* that her favorite roles include Annie Sullivan in *The Miracle Worker.*

OTHER SOURCES

Periodicals:

American Theatre, April, 1997, pp. 24-29.*

JACKSON, Anne   1926-

PERSONAL

Full name, Anna June Jackson; born September 3, 1926, in Allegheny (some sources say Millvale), PA; daughter of John Ivan (a beautician) and Stella Germaine (Murray) Jackson; married Eli Wallach (an actor), March 5, 1948; children: Peter, Roberta, Katherine. *Education:* Attended New School for Social Research, 1943; trained for the stage with Sanford Meisner at the Neighborhood Playhouse, 1943-44, and with Herbert Berghof and Lee Strasberg at the Actors Studio, 1948. *Avocational interests:* Writing.

Addresses: *Agent*—International Creative Management, 8942 Wilshire Blvd., Beverly Hills, CA 90211.

Career: Actress.

Member: Actors' Equity Association, American Federation of Television and Radio Artists, Screen Actors Guild.

Awards, Honors: Obie Award, *Village Voice,* 1962, for *"The Typists"* and *"The Tiger";* Lions of the Performing Arts Award, New York Public Library, 1987.

CREDITS

Stage Appearances:

(Stage debut) Anya, *The Cherry Orchard,* Wilmington, DE, 1944.

(Broadway debut) Guest, *The Cherry Orchard,* City Center Theatre, New York City, 1945.

Alice Stewart, *Signature,* Forrest Theatre, Philadelphia, PA, 1945.

Frida Foldal, *John Gabriel Borkman,* American Repertory Company, International Theatre, New York City, 1946.

A Christian, *Androcles and the Lion,* American Repertory Company, International Theatre, 1946.

What Every Woman Knows, American Repertory Company, International Theatre, 1946.

Henry VIII, American Repertory Company, International Theatre, 1946.

Miss Blake, *Yellow Jack,* American Repertory Company, International Theatre, 1947.

Judith, *The Last Dance,* Belasco Theatre, New York City, 1948.

Pat, *The Young and Fair,* Falmouth Playhouse, Falmouth, MA, 1948.

Nellie Ewell, *Summer and Smoke,* Music Box Theatre, New York City, 1948.

Nita, *Magnolia Alley,* Mansfield Theatre, New York City, 1949.

Margaret Anderson, *Love Me Long,* 48th Street Theatre, New York City, 1949.

Hilda, *The Lady from the Sea,* Fulton Theatre, New York City, 1950.

Louka, *Arms and the Man,* Hotel Edison Theatre, New York City, 1950.

Coralie Jones, *Never Say Never,* Booth Theatre, New York City, 1951.

Mildred Turner, *Oh Men! Oh Women!,* Henry Miller's Theatre, New York City, 1953.

The Daughter, *The Middle of the Night,* American National Theatre and Academy Theatre, New York City, 1956.

Title role, *Major Barbara,* Martin Beck Theatre, New York City, 1956.

Laura, *The Glass Menagerie,* Westport Country Playhouse, Westport, CT, then John Drew Theatre, Easthampton, NY, both 1959.

Daisy, *Rhinoceros,* Longacre Theatre, New York City, 1961.

Brecht on Brecht (staged reading), Theatre De Lys, New York City, 1962.

Sylvia, "The Typists," and Gloria, "The Tiger," in *"The Typists" and "The Tiger"* (double-bill), Orpheum Theatre, New York City, 1963, then (London debut) Globe Theatre, London, England, 1964.

Ellen Manville, *Luv,* Booth Theatre, 1964.

The actress, *The Exercise,* Berkshire Festival, Stockbridge, MA, 1967, then John Golden Theatre, New York City, 1968.

Molly Malloy, *The Front Page,* Ethel Barrymore Theatre, New York City, 1969.

Ethel Rosenberg, *The Inquest,* Music Box Theatre, 1970.

Mother H., Doris, and Joan J., *Promenade, All!,* Alvin Theatre, New York City, 1972.

Madame St. Pe, *Waltz of the Toreadors,* Eisenhower Theatre, Kennedy Center for the Performing Arts, Washington, DC, then Circle in the Square Theatre, New York City, both 1973.

Madame Ranevskaya, *The Cherry Orchard,* Hartford Stage Company, Hartford, CT, 1974.

Mrs. McBride, *Marco Polo Sings a Solo,* New York Shakespeare Festival, Public Theatre, New York City, 1977.

Diana, *Absent Friends,* Long Wharf Theatre, New Haven, CT, 1977.

Mrs. Frank, *The Diary of Anne Frank,* Theatre Four, New York City, 1978.

Margaret Heinz, "A Need for Brussels Sprouts," and Edie Frazier, "A Need for Less Expertise," *Twice Around the Park* (double-bill), Syracuse Stage Theatre, Syracuse, NY, 1981, then Cort Theatre, New York City, 1982, later Edinburgh Theatre Festival, Edinburgh, Scotland, 1984.

Natalya Gavrilovna, *The Nest of the Wood Grouse,* New York Shakespeare Festival, Public Theatre, 1984.

Title role, *The Madwoman of Chaillot,* Mirror Repertory Company, New York City, 1985.

Company F, Mirror Repertory Company, Theatre at St. Peter's Church, New York City, 1985-86.

Odile, *Opera Comique,* Eisenhower Theatre, Kennedy Center for the Performing Arts, 1987.

Waitin' in the Wings: The Night the Understudies Take Center Stage, Triplex Theatre, New York City, 1988.

Anna Cole, *Cafe Crown,* New York Shakespeare Festival, Public Theatre, 1988, then Brooks Atkinson Theatre, New York City, 1989.

Lost in Yonkers, Richard Rodgers Theatre, New York City, between 1991 and 1993.

The Flowering Peach, Lyceum Theatre, New York City, 1994.

Also appeared in a poetry reading at John Drew Playhouse, 1960; appeared in *Just an Evening with Anne Jackson and Eli Wallach* and *In Persons.* Performed with the Arena Stage, Washington, DC, 1977-78. Also appeared at Bucks County Playhouse, New Hope, PA; Clinton Playhouse, Clinton, NJ; Equity Library Theatre, New York City; and Actors Studio, New York City.

Major Tours:

Zelda Rainier, *Donnigan's Daughter,* U.S. cities, 1945.

Bella, *The Barretts of Wimpole Street,* U.S. cities, 1947.

Mildred Turner, *Oh Men! Oh Women!,* U.S. cities, 1955.

Ellen Manville, *Luv,* U.S. cities, 1964.

Sylvia, "The Typists," and Gloria, "The Tiger," in *"The Typists" and "The Tiger"* (double-bill), U.S. cities, 1966.

Mother H., Doris, and Joan J., *Promenade, All!,* U.S. cities, 1971.

Madame St. Pe, *Waltz of the Toreadors,* U.S. cities, 1973.

Diana, *Absent Friends,* U.S. and Canadian cities, 1977.

Film Appearances:

(Film debut) Jackie, *So Young, So Bad,* United Artists, 1950.

Mrs. Margie Rhinelander, *The Journey,* Metro-Goldwyn-Mayer, 1959.

Myra Sullivan, *Tall Story,* Warner Bros., 1960.

Gloria Fiske, *The Tiger Makes Out,* Columbia, 1967.

Muriel Laszlo, *How to Save a Marriage—and Ruin Your Life* (also known as *Band of Gold*), Columbia, 1968.

Victoria Layton, *The Secret Life of an American Wife,* Twentieth Century-Fox, 1968.

Belle, *Dirty Dingus Magee,* Metro-Goldwyn-Mayer, 1970.

Lady in the store, *The Angel Levine,* United Artists, 1970.

Cathy, *Lovers and Other Strangers,* Cinerama, 1970.

Jean Cameron, *Zigzag* (also known as *False Witness*), Metro-Goldwyn-Mayer, 1970.

Abigail Adams, *Independence,* Twentieth Century-Fox, 1975.

Sub-Prioress Mildred (Mistress of Novices), *Nasty Habits* (also known as *The Habit*), Brut, 1976.

Dr. Nolan, *The Bell Jar,* Avco-Embassy, 1979.

Doctor, *The Shining,* Warner Bros., 1980.

As herself, *Sanford Meisner—The Theatre's Best Kept Secret* (documentary), Columbia, 1984.

Harriet Orowitz, *Sam's Son,* Invictus, 1984.

A View to Kill, Metro-Goldwyn-Mayer/United Artists, 1984.

Narrator, *Are We Winning, Mommy? America and the Cold War* (documentary), Cine Information/National Film Board of Canada/Channel Four/Svenges TV2, 1986.

"The Sahara Forest," "Sons of Bees," and "The Gorilla Safari," *Funny,* 1988.

Adele Bergman, *Funny about Love* (also known as *New York Times*), Paramount, 1990.

Mildred Aldrich, *Folks!,* Twentieth Century-Fox, 1992.

Television Appearances; Series:

Rae Matthews, *Everything's Relative,* CBS, 1987.

Also appeared in *Love of Life,* CBS.

Television Appearances; Movies:

Maggie Madden, *The Family Man,* CBS, 1979.

Frances Bowers, *Blinded by the Light,* CBS, 1980.

Kathryn Morgan Ryan, *A Private Battle,* CBS, 1980.

Shirlee Thum, *Leave 'em Laughing,* CBS, 1981.

Lou Kaddar and narrator, *A Woman Called Golda,* syndicated, 1982.

Television Appearances; Miniseries:

Bella Abzug, *Out on a Limb,* ABC, 1987.

Lorraine Abraham, *Baby M,* ABC, 1988.

Television Appearances; Episodic:

"Zone of Quiet," *Actor's Studio,* CBS, 1949.

"Greasy Luck," *Actor's Studio,* CBS, 1949.

"In the Shadow of the Glen," *Academy Theatre,* NBC, 1949.

"Johnny Pickup," *The Armstrong Circle Theatre,* NBC, 1951.

"Happy Birthday George," *Robert Montgomery Presents,* NBC, 1952.

"Promotion," *Lux Video Theatre,* CBS, 1952.

"The Man in Half Moon Street," *Kraft Television Theatre,* NBC, 1952.

"The Vanished Hours," *Lux Video Theatre,* CBS, 1952.

"Call from a Killer," *Suspense,* CBS, 1952.

"Marti," *The Doctor* (also known as *The Visitor*), NBC, 1952.

"Night Riders in Apartment A," *The Doctor* (also known as *The Visitor*), NBC, 1952.

"The Decision," *The Doctor* (also known as *The Visitor*), NBC, 1953.

"No Rap Charlie," *The Doctor* (also known as *The Visitor*), NBC, 1953.

"The Big Deal," *Philco Television Playhouse,* NBC, 1953.

"Statute of Limitations," *Philco Television Playhouse,* NBC, 1954.

"The Merry-Go-Round," *Goodyear Playhouse,* NBC, 1955.

"O'Hoolihan and the Leprechaun," *General Electric Theatre,* CBS, 1956.

"Hostages to Fortune," *Alcoa Hour,* NBC, 1957.

"Lullaby," *Play of the Week,* WNTA, 1960.

"Cooker in the Sky," *The Untouchables,* ABC, 1962.

"Acres and Pains," *General Electric Theatre,* CBS, 1962.

"Moment of Truth," *The Defenders,* CBS, 1964.

"Dear Friends," *CBS Playhouse,* CBS, 1967.

"The Typists," *Hollywood Television Theatre,* 1971.

"Blind Man's Bluff," *Gunsmoke,* CBS, 1972.

"A Taste of Salt," *Marcus Welby, M.D.,* ABC, 1972.

"Come into My Parlour," *Orson Welles' Great Mysteries,* syndicated, 1973.

"Twenty Shades of Pink," *General Electric Theatre,* CBS, 1976.

Maude, CBS, 1976.

Rhoda, CBS, 1977.

Gwen Schaeffer, "We Get Letters," *The Facts of Life,* NBC, 1985.

"Rachel Carson," *An American Portrait,* CBS, 1985.

Mrs. Fields, "The Confrontation Day," *The Equalizer,* CBS, 1985.

Marge Malloy, "A Father's Faith," *Highway to Heaven,* NBC, 1987.

"My Brother's Keeper," *Everything's Relative,* CBS, 1988.

Appeared in episodes of *Danger,* CBS; and *The Web,* CBS.

Television Appearances; Specials:

Sticks and Bones, CBS, 1973.

Helene Hanff, *84 Charing Cross Road,* British television, then syndicated, 1976.

"Sanford Meisner: The Theatre's Best Kept Secret" (documentary), *American Masters,* PBS, 1990.

"Helen Hayes: First Lady of the American Theatre" (documentary), *American Masters,* PBS, 1991.

"Miracle on 44th Street: A Portrait of the Actors Studio" (documentary), *American Masters,* PBS, 1991.

Narrator, *River of Steel* (documentary), PBS, 1994.

Voice of Ada Lichtman, *The Trial of Adolf Eichmann* (documentary), PBS, 1997.

Television Appearances; Pilots:
Jenny Dutton, *Acres and Pains,* CBS, 1965.

WRITINGS

Early Stages (autobiography), Little, Brown (Boston, MA), 1979.

OTHER SOURCES

Charlotte, Susan, and others, *Creativity: Conversations with Twenty-Eight Who Excel,* Momentum Books, 1993.*

JAECKEL, Richard   1926-1997

OBITUARY NOTICE—See index for *CTFT* sketch: Full name, Richard Hanley Jaeckel; born October 10, 1926, in Long Beach, NY; died of cancer, June 14, 1997, in Woodland Hills, CA. Actor. Jaeckel was a character actor who made his mark in film as well as television productions. Remembered for work in some seventy films, including *The Dirty Dozen, Pat Garrett and Billy the Kid,* and *Sands of Iwo Jima,* he later appeared in television series such as *Baywatch* and *Spencer: For Hire.* Early in his career, Jaeckel worked in the mailroom of Twentieth Century-Fox until a studio executive insisted he take a screentest in 1943. Despite protests from the future actor, he took the test and was cast in *Guadalcanal Diary* that same year.

He then served in the U.S. Navy during World War II. Later, Jaeckel appeared in varied roles in films such as *King of the Kickboxers, Come Back Little Sheba, Starman, Delta Force II, The Drowning Pool,* and *Part II: Walking Tall.* He also appeared in the 1970s television series *Banyon, Firehouse,* and *Salvage I.* In the 1980s he appeared as Major Hawkins in the series *At Ease.* He also reprised his film role from *The Dirty Dozen* for a television sequel *The Dirty Dozen: The Next Mission.* Among the honors he received during his career was a 1971 Academy Award nomination for best supporting actor. The nomination acknowledged his work in the film *Sometimes a Great Notion.* He also found time to coach Little League in West Los Angeles.

OBITUARIES AND OTHER SOURCES

Books:
Who's Who in Entertainment, Marquis Who's Who, 1992.

Periodicals:
Chicago Tribune, June 17, 1997, section 3, p. 12.
Los Angeles Times, June 18, 1997, p. A16.
New York Times, June 17, 1997, p. A19.
Times (London; electronic), July 8, 1997.
Washington Post, June 18, 1997, p. B4.

JOHNSON, Chas. Floyd

PERSONAL

Original name Charles Johnson; born February 12, in Camden, NJ; son of Orange Maull (a real property officer) and Bertha Ellen (a school principal; maiden name, Seagers) Johnson; married Sandra Brashears, June 5, 1967 (divorced, 1971); married Anne Burford (a television production executive), June 18, 1983; children: Kristin Suzanne. *Education:* Attended University of Delaware, 1960-61; Howard University, B.A. (political science), 1962; Howard University, J.D., 1965. *Politics:* Democrat. *Religion:* Methodist.

Addresses: *Office*—Universal Television, Ren-Mar Studios, 846 North Cahuenga Blvd., Building D, Los Angeles, CA 90038.

Career: Actor, producer, and writer. Universal Television, production coordinator, 1971-74, associate producer, 1974-76, producer, 1976-82, supervising producer, 1982—, executive producer, 1985-87; Communications Bridge (media organization for minority-training in video technology), Los Angeles, vice president; Media Forum, founding member and vice president, vice chairperson, 1978-82; Crossroads Theatre Arts Academy, member, 1990. Howard Berg Law Offices, Wilmington, DE, attorney, 1965; U.S. Copyright Office, Washington, DC, attorney, 1967-70; UNESCO International Copyright Conference, Paris, France, member of U.S. delegation, 1970; Swedish Ministry of Justice, Stockholm, Sweden, attorney, 1970. Kwanza Foundation, member of board of directors, 1985. *Military service:* U.S. Army, defense counsel, Judge Advocate General's Corps, 1965-67; became specialist fifth class; received Army Commendation Medal.

Member: Screen Actors Guild; Producers Guild of America (member of board of directors); Writers Guild of America—West; American Federation of Television and Radio Artists; National Academy of Television Arts and Sciences; American Film Institute; Caucus for Producers, Directors, and Writers; American Independent Video Filmmakers (member of board of directors, 1985-90); Omega Psi Phi.

Awards, Honors: Emmy Award, outstanding drama series, 1978, and Emmy Award nominations, outstanding drama series, 1979 and 1980, all for *The Rockford Files;* Alumni Achievement Award, Stony Brook College Preparatory School, 1979; Los Angeles Area Emmy Award, best entertainment special, 1981, for *Voices of Our People . . . In Celebration of Black Poetry;* Outstanding Alumnus Award, Howard University Alumni Club of Southern California, 1982; commendations from California State Legislature, California State Senate, City of Los Angeles, and Hawaii State Senate, all 1982; Emmy Award nominations, 1983 and 1984, for *Magnum, P.I.;* Outstanding Alumnus Award, Howard University, 1985; commendations from Hawaii House of Representatives and City of Honolulu, 1988, and City of Los Angeles, 1993.

CREDITS

Television Work; Series:
Associate producer, then producer, later coexecutive producer, *The Rockford Files,* NBC, 1974-80.
Producer, *Magnum, P.I.,* CBS, 1980-84, then supervising producer, 1985-86, later coexecutive producer, 1987-88.
Producer (with Geoffrey Fischer), *Bret Maverick* (also known as *Bret Maverick: The Lazy Ace*), NBC, 1981-82.
Producer (with Richard Chapman), *Simon and Simon,* CBS, 1982-83.
Coexecutive producer, *B. L. Stryker,* ABC, 1989-90.
Coexecutive producer, *Quantum Leap,* NBC, 1992-93.
Executive producer (with Stephen Zito), *JAG,* CBS, 1996—.

Television Work; Pilots:
Producer, *Baa Baa Black Sheep,* NBC, 1975.
Producer, *Hellinger's Law,* CBS, 1981.
Producer (with Nick Thiel and Reuben Leder), *The Return of Luther Gillis,* CBS, 1984.
Executive producer (with Tom Selleck and Chris Abbott) and cocreator, *Silver Fox* (also known as *Our Man James* and *Double Old 7*), ABC, 1991.

Television Work; Movies:
Coexecutive producer, *Auntie Sue,* 1989.
Coexecutive producer, *Die Laughing,* 1989.
Coexecutive producer, *Royal Gambit,* 1989.
Coexecutive producer, *The Dancer's Touch,* 1989.
Coexecutive producer, *The King of Jazz,* 1989.
Coexecutive producer (with Chris Abbott and Burt Reynolds), *Grand Theft Hotel* (also known as *B. L. Stryker: Grand Theft Hotel*), ABC, 1990.
Coexecutive producer (with Abbott and Reynolds) *High Rise* (also known as *B. L. Stryker: High Rise*), ABC, 1990.
Coexecutive producer (with Abbott and Reynolds) *Night Train* (also known as *B. L. Stryker: Night Train*), ABC, 1990.
Coexecutive producer (with Abbott and Reynolds) *Plates* (also known as *B. L. Stryker: Plates*) ABC, 1990.
Executive producer (with Tom Selleck and Abbott), *Revealing Evidence: Stalking the Honolulu Strangler* (pilot), NBC, 1990.
Coexecutive producer (with Abbott and Reynolds) *Winner Takes All* (also known as *B. L. Stryker: Winner Takes All*), ABC, 1990.
Executive producer (with James Garner and Juanita Bartlett) *The Rockford Files: I Still Love L.A.* (also known as *The Rockford Files: I Love L.A.*), CBS, 1994.
Executive producer (with Garner and Bartlett) *The Rockford Files: A Blessing in Disguise* (also known as *The Rockford Files: Little Ezekial*), CBS, 1995.
Executive producer (with Garner and Bartlett) *Rockford Files: If the Frame Fits* (also known as *Rockford Files: Suitable for Framing*), CBS, 1996.
Executive producer (with Garner and Bartlett) *The Rockford Files: Friends and Foul Play,* CBS, 1996.
Executive producer (with Garner and Bartlett) *The Rockford Files: Godfather Knows Best,* CBS, 1996.
Executive producer (with Garner and Bartlett) *The Rockford Files: Punishment and Crime* (also known as *The Rockford Files: Night Fishing*), CBS, 1996.
Executive producer (with Garner) *The Rockford Files: Murder and Misdemeanor,* CBS, 1997.

Television Work; Specials:
Producer, *Voices of Our People . . . In Celebration of Black Poetry,* PBS, 1982.

Television Appearances; Specials:
Voices of Our People . . . In Celebration of Black Poetry, PBS, 1982.

Television Appearances; Episodic:
(Television debut) Leroy, *Toma*, ABC, 1973.
Corporal, *The Six Million Dollar Man*, ABC, 1973.
Police officer, *Kojak*, CBS, 1974.

Stage Appearances:
(Stage debut) *Focus on Blacks in American Theatre*, Back Alley Theatre, Washington, DC, 1967.
Alton Scales, *The Sign in Sidney Brustein's Window*, Theatre Lobby, Washington, DC, 1967.
Bernard, *The Boys in the Band*, Morgan Theatre, Santa Monica, CA, 1972.
Lieutenant, *The Drumhead*, Merle Oberon Theatre, Los Angeles, 1974.

WRITINGS

Television Episodes:
"The Deep Blue Sleep," *The Rockford Files*, NBC, 1975.
"The Prisoner of Rosemont Avenue," *The Rockford Files*, NBC, 1976.
"Paradise Blues," *Magnum, P.I.*, CBS, 1984.
"Photoplay," *Magnum, P.I.*, CBS, 1985.

Television Specials:
Voices of Our People . . . In Celebration of Black Poetry, PBS, 1982.

Other:
The Origins of the Stockholm Protocol, U.S. Copyright Society, 1970.
(With George Hill and Lorraine Raglin) *Black Women in Television: An Illustrated History and Bibliography*, Garland Publishing (New York City), 1990.

Adaptations: The television pilot *Silver Fox* was adapted from a story by Johnson, Tom Selleck, and Chris Abbott.*

JOHNSTON, Kristen   1967-

PERSONAL

Born September 20, 1967, in Washington, DC; raised in Milwaukee, WI; daughter of a state senator (later a realtor). *Education:* New York University, B.F.A.

Addresses: *Contact*—YBLY Productions, CBS Studio Center, Building 2, 2nd Floor, 4024 Redford Ave., Studio City, CA 91604.

Career: Actress; member of Atlantic Theatre Company, mid-1980s.

Awards, Honors: Drama Desk Award nomination, best supporting actress, for *The Lights;* Screen Actors Guild nomination, Golden Globe nomination, and Emmy Award, outstanding supporting actress in a comedy series, 1997, all for *Third Rock from the Sun.*

CREDITS

Television Appearances; Series:
Sally Solomon, *3rd Rock from the Sun*, NBC, 1996—.

Television Appearances; Episodic:
Dr. Wendy Smythe, *Chicago Hope*, CBS, 1994.

Appeared in episodes of *Hearts Afire* and *The Five Mrs. Buchanans.*

Television Appearances; Movies:
Grace Chapman, *Neil Simon's "London Suite,"* NBC, 1996.

Television Appearances; Specials:
Host, *Christmas in Washington*, NBC, 1996.

Television Appearances; Awards Presentations:
The 22nd Annual People's Choice Awards, CBS, 1996.
The Screen Actors Guild Awards, NBC, 1997.
The 1997 Emmy Awards, CBS, 1997.

Film Appearances:
Appeared in *The Debt* and *Grosse Pointe Blank.*

Stage Appearances:
Tina, "Wonderful Party," *Five Very Live*, Atlantic Theatre, New York City, 1992.
Sue, *Vox Pop*, Atlantic Theatre, New York City, 1992.
Rose, *The Lights*, Lincoln Center Theatre, New York City, 1993.
Mary Kay Paterson, *Baby Anger*, Playwrights Horizons, New York City, 1997.

Also appeared in several productions for the Atlantic Theatre Company, Atlantic Theatre, New York City, including *Overruled, As You Like It, Girl's Talk, Stage Door, Author's Voice, Portrait of a Woman, Boy's Life*, and *Rosemary for Remembrance.* Also appeared in *The Stand In*, Naked Angels Theatre Company; *Hot Keys*, Naked Angels Theatre Company; and *Kim's Sister*, New York Stage and Film.*

JONES, Renee

PERSONAL

Born in Opalacka, FL.

Addresses: *Contact*—NBC Burbank, 3000 West Alameda Ave., Burbank, CA 91523.

Career: Actress.

CREDITS

Television Appearances; Series:
Ellie, *Jessie*, ABC, 1984.
Diane Moses, *L.A. Law*, NBC, 1989-90.
Nikki Wade, then Lexie Carver, *Days of Our Lives*, NBC, 1982-83, 1993—.

Television Appearances; Pilots:
Jolie, *Isabel Sanford's Honeymoon Hotel*, syndicated, 1987.
Brenda Kincaid, *Heart and Soul* (also known as *It Will Stand*), ABC, 1989.

Television Appearances; Episodic:
"Deadly Bidding," *Murder, She Wrote*, CBS, 1995.

Appeared in episodes of *The White Shadow, Star Trek, In the Heat of the Night, Night Court, Sunset Beat: American Dreams, 21 Jump Street, Insiders, Highway to Heaven, Marblehead Manor, What's Happening Now, T.J. Hooker, Bodies of Evidence, Fresh Prince of Bel Air, The Jeffersons, Different Strokes,* and *Trapper John, M.D.*

Television Appearances; Movies:
Michelle, *Forbidden Love*, CBS, 1982.
Cally, *Deadly Lessons*, ABC, 1983.
Lilah, *The Liberators*, ABC, 1987.
Daisy Morris Taylor, *Tracks of Glory: The Major Taylor Story*, The Disney Channel, 1992.

Television Appearances; Specials:
Cynthia Beale, *The Hero Who Couldn't Read*, 1984.

Film Appearances:
Sissy, *Friday the 13th, Part VI: Jason Lives*, Paramount, 1986.
The Terror Within II, LIVE Home Video, 1991.

Also appeared as Kimmie, *Talkin' Dirty after Dark*, 1991; *Three of a Kind*, 1994.

JONES, Tamala

PERSONAL

Born November 12, in Los Angeles, CA.

Addresses: *Contact*—Walt Disney Studios, 500 South Buena Vista Blvd., Burbank, CA 91521-0668.

Career: Actress.

CREDITS

Television Appearances; Series:
Callie Timmons, *Dangerous Minds*, ABC, 1996-97.

Television Appearances; Episodic:
Joanie, *ER*, NBC, 1994.
Nia, *JAG*, NBC, 1995.

Also appeared in episodes of *California Dreams* and *The Fresh Prince of Bel-Air*; appeared in episodes of *Parent 'Hood, On Our Own,* and *The Wayans Brothers*, all WB.

Film Appearances:
Anna's great grandmother, *How to Make an American Quilt*, Universal, 1995.
Nikki, *Booty Call*, Columbia, 1997.*

JONES, Terry 1942-

PERSONAL

Born February 1, 1942, in Colwyn Bay, North Wales; son of Alick George Parry (a bank clerk) and Dilys Louisa (Newnes) Jones; married Alison Telfer (a botanist), 1970; children: Sally, Bill. *Education:* Attended St. Edmund Hall, Oxford, 1961-64.

Addresses: *Office*—Python Productions, 68-A Delancey St., London NW1 7RY, England; also Prominent Features.

Career: Actor, director, and writer. Monty Python (a comedy troupe), member of company, beginning in 1969; British Broadcasting Corp., worked in script department; actor in repertory, early in his career.

Awards, Honors: Press Critics of Great Britain Award, best comedy show, 1977, for *Ripping Yarns*; shared

Golden Palm Award, Cannes International Film Festival, 1983, for *Monty Python's The Meaning of Life.*

CREDITS

Film Appearances:
Various roles, *And Now for Something Completely Different,* Columbia, 1972.
Sir Bedevere, not-quite-dead corpse, Dennis's wife, head of the Three-Headed Knight, Knight Who Says "Ni," and Herbert, *Monty Python and the Holy Grail,* Cinema V, 1975.
Pleasure at Her Majesty's (also known as *Monty Python Meets Beyond the Fringe*), Roger Graef, 1976.
Poacher, *Jabberwocky,* Cinema V, 1977.
Mother of Brian, Colin, Simon the Holy Man, Bob Hoskins, Mandy, and saintly passerby, *Monty Python's Life of Brian* (also known as *The Life of Brian*), Warner Bros./Orion, 1979.
The Secret Policeman's Ball, Tigon/Amnesty International, 1979.
Various roles, *Monty Python Live at the Hollywood Bowl,* Columbia, 1982.
The Secret Policeman's Other Ball, Amnesty International, 1982.
Various roles, *Monty Python's The Meaning of Life,* Celandine/Monty Python Partnership/Universal, 1983.
The Secret Policeman's Private Parts, Independent, 1984.
King Arnulf, *Erik the Viking,* Orion, 1989.
Voice of Sara's mother (uncredited), *L.A. Story,* TriStar, 1991.
Toad, *The Wind in the Willows* (also known as *Mr. Toad's Wild Ride*), Buena Vista Home Video/Columbia/Sony Pictures, 1996.
Voice of Parot, *Starship Titanic* [video], 1998.

Film Work; Director:
(With Terry Gilliam) *Monty Python and the Holy Grail,* Cinema V, 1975.
Monty Python's Life of Brian (also known as *The Life of Brian*), Warner Bros./Orion, 1979.
Monty Python's The Meaning of Life, Celandine/Monty Python Partnership/Universal, 1983.
Personal Services, VIP/Vestron, 1987.
Erik the Viking, Orion, 1989.
The Wind in the Willows (also known as *Mr. Toad's Wild Ride*), Buena Vista Home Video/Columbia/Sony Pictures, 1996.

Television Appearances; Series:
Twice a Fortnight, 1967.

Do Not Adjust Your Set, BBC, 1968.
Complete and Utter History of Britain, BBC, 1969.
Monty Python's Flying Circus, BBC, 1969-74, then PBS, 1974-82.
Ripping Yarns, BBC, 1976-77, then PBS, 1979.

Television Appearances; Specials:
Life of Python (documentary), Showtime, 1990.
Twenty Years of Monty Python (Parrot Sketch Not Included) (documentary), Showtime, 1990.
Narrator, *Crusades* (documentary), The History Channel and Arts and Entertainment, both 1995.

Television Appearances; Episodic:
Broaden Your Mind, 1968.
Drunk vicar, "Nasty," *The Young Ones,* 1984.
"Explode," *Space Ghost Coast to Coast,* Cartoon Network, 1994.
Ruby, 1997.

Also appeared in episodes of *Late Night Lineup, The Late Show,* and *A Series of Birds.*

Television Work; Episodic:
Director, *The Young Indiana Jones Chronicles,* ABC, 1992.

Other Television Appearances:
Pythons in Deutschland (movie), Bavaria Atelier, 1971.
Presenter, *So This Is Progress,* 1991.

Stage Appearances:
Various roles, *Monty Python's First Farewell Tour,* Drury Lane Theatre, London, 1974.
Various roles, *Monty Python Live!,* City Center Theatre, New York City, 1976.
Various roles, *Monty Python Live at the Hollywood Bowl,* Hollywood Bowl, Los Angeles, CA, 1980.

As a member of the comedy troupe Monty Python, appeared in concert tours in U.S., British, and Canadian cities, during the 1970s.

RECORDINGS

Albums; All with Monty Python:
Monty Python's Flying Circus, BBC Records, 1969.
Another Monty Python Record, Charisma, 1970.
Monty Python's Previous Record, Charisma, 1972.
Monty Python's Matching Tie and Handkerchief, Charisma, 1973, Arista, 1975.
Monty Python Live at Drury Lane, Charisma, 1974.

The Album of the Soundtrack of the Trailer of the Film "Monty Python and the Holy Grail," Arista, 1975.

Monty Python Live at City Center, Arista, 1976.

Monty Python's Instant Record Collection, Charisma, 1977.

Monty Python's Life of Brian, Warner Bros., 1979.

Monty Python's Contractual Obligation Album, Arista, 1980.

Monty Python's The Meaning of Life, Columbia Records, 1983.

With Monty Python, released a box set of albums.

Computer Software:

(With Monty Python) *Monty Python's Complete Waste of Time,* 7th Level, 1994.

WRITINGS

Screenplays:

(With Monty Python members Graham Chapman, John Cleese, Terry Gilliam, Michael Palin, and Eric Idle) *And Now for Something Completely Different,* Columbia, 1972.

(With Monty Python members) *Monty Python and the Holy Grail,* Cinema V, 1975, published by Methuen, 1977, published as *Monty Python's Second Film: A First Draft,* Methuen, 1977.

(With Monty Python members) *Monty Python's Life of Brian* (also known as *The Life of Brian*), Warner Bros./Orion, 1979, published in *Monty Python's Life of Brian (of Nazareth) [and] Montypythonscrapbook,* Grosset, 1979.

The Secret Policeman's Ball, Tigon-Amnesty International, 1979.

(With Monty Python members) *Monty Python Live at the Hollywood Bowl,* Columbia, 1982.

(With Monty Python members; also songwriter) *Monty Python's The Meaning of Life,* Celandine/Monty Python Partnership/Universal, 1983, published by Methuen, 1983.

(With Laura Phillips) *Labyrinth,* TriStar, 1986.

Erik the Viking, Orion, 1989, published by Applause Theatre Book Publishers (New York City), 1990.

Film Songs:

"Christmas in Heaven" and "Every Sperm Is Sacred," *Monty Python's The Meaning of Life,* Celandine/Monty Python Partnership/Universal, 1983.

Television Series:

The Frost Report, BBC, 1965-67.

Twice a Fortnight, 1967.

Do Not Adjust Your Set, BBC, 1968.

Complete and Utter History of Britain, BBC, 1969.

(With Monty Python members) *Monty Python's Flying Circus,* BBC, 1969-74, then PBS, 1974-82.

(With Michael Palin) *Ripping Yarns,* PBS, 1979.

The Wind in the Willows (also known as *Mr. Toad's Wild Ride*), 1996.

Television Specials:

(With Michael Palin) *Secrets* (play), BBC, 1973.

(With Monty Python members) *Life of Python,* Showtime, 1990.

(With Monty Python members) *Twenty Years of Monty Python (Parrot Sketch Not Included),* Showtime, 1990.

(With Alan Ereira) *Crusades,* The History Channel and Arts and Entertainment, both 1995.

Other Television:

(With Monty Python members) *Pythons in Deutschland* (movie), Bavaria Atelier, 1971.

So This Is Progress, 1991.

Story Ideas:

(With Michael Palin) *Fierce Creatures* (also known as *Death Fish II*), Universal, 1997.

Other:

(With Monty Python members) *Monty Python's Big Red Book,* edited by Monty Python member Eric Idle, Methuen, 1972, Warner Books (New York City), 1975, published in *The Complete Works of Shakespeare and Monty Python,* Methuen, 1981.

(With Monty Python members) *The Brand New Monty Python Book,* edited by Idle, Eyre Methuen, 1973, published as *The Brand New Monty Python Papperbok,* Methuen, 1974, published in *The Complete Works of Shakespeare and Monty Python,* 1981.

(With Michael Palin) *Bert Fegg's Nasty Book for Boys and Girls,* Methuen, 1974, published as *Dr. Fegg's Nasty Book of Knowledge,* Peter Bedrick Books (New York City), 1985.

(With Michael Palin) *Ripping Yarns,* Methuen, 1978, Pantheon, 1979.

(With Monty Python members) *Monty Python's Life of Brian (of Nazareth) [and] Montypython-scrapbook,* Grosset, 1979.

(With Michael Palin) *More Ripping Yarns,* Methuen, 1980.

Janice Neiman, *Picket Fences*, CBS, 1994.
Maureen Cutler, "Police Story," *Frasier*, NBC, 1995.
Bonnie Bell, *Touched by an Angel*, CBS, 1995.
Martin's date, *Frasier*, NBC, 1996.
Pamela Bourge, *The Practice*, ABC, 1997.

Television Appearances; Specials:
Joanna Brady, *The Last Leaf*, syndicated, 1984.
Mary Reed, "Boys Will Be Boys," *ABC Afterschool Specials*, ABC, 1994.
Nancy Gallagher, "Educating Mom," *ABC Afterschool Specials*, ABC, 1996.

Television Appearances; Pilots:
Margie Spoleto, *For Lovers Only*, ABC, 1982.
Crazy like a Fox, CBS, 1984.

Stage Appearances:
Timon of Athens, Yale Repertory Theatre, New Haven, CT, 1980.
The Suicide, Yale Repertory Theatre, 1980.
Rip Van Winkle or "The Works," Yale Repertory Theatre, 1981-82.
The Man Who Could See through Time, Yale Repertory Theatre, 1981-82.
Love's Labour's Lost, Yale Repertory Theatre, 1981-82.
Lizzy Bennet, *Pride and Prejudice*, Long Wharf Theatre, New Haven, CT, 1985.
Diane Newbury, *The Hands of Its Enemy*, Manhattan Theatre Club, City Center Theatre, New York City, 1986.
Eve's Diary [and] *The Story of a Tiger* (double-bill), New York Theatre Workshop, New York City, 1991.
Bella, *Lost in Yonkers*, Richard Rodgers Theatre, New York City, 1991.
Helga, *Kindertransport*, Manhattan Theatre Club/Stage 1, 1994.

Appeared in *Loose Ends*, Second Stage Theatre, New York City; and *Ice Cream/Hot Fudge*, Public Theatre, New York City; also appeared in productions at Williamstown Theatre Festival, Berkshire Theatre Festival, O'Neill Playwriting Conference, and Sundance Institute.*

KATIMS, Robert   1927-

PERSONAL

Born April 22, 1927, in Brooklyn, NY; children: Jason (a creator and executive producer for television,

and a playwright). *Education:* Attended Brooklyn College.

Addresses: *Contact*—8660 Hayden Place, Culver City, CA 90232.

Career: Actor. Worked for 30 years selling law books.

CREDITS

Television Appearances; Series:
Hal Roth, *Relativity*, ABC, 1996-97.

Television Appearances; Pilots:
Sergeant Polsky, *Ladies on Sweet Street*, ABC, 1990.

Television Appearances; Episodic:
Appeared as Arnold Deansfrei, *Seinfeld*, NBC; Jacob Bloom, *Law and Order*; appeared in episodes of *My So-Called Life*, *L.A. Law*, *Civil Wars*, and *Divorce Court*.

Television Appearances; Movies:
Moscowitz, *Double Exposure: The Story of Margaret Bourke-White*, TNT, 1989.
Detective Goldman, *The Bride in Black* (also known as *The Bride Wore Black*), ABC, 1990.

Television Appearances; Specials:
Voiceover, *Lincoln* (documentary), ABC, 1992.

Film Appearances:
Martin Klein, *Broadcast News*, Twentieth Century-Fox, 1987.
Cody, *Presumed Innocent*, Warner Bros., 1990.
Minister, *The Pallbearer*, Miramax, 1996.

Also appeared in *Histoires d'Amerique*, 1988.

Stage Appearances:
Troilus and Cressida, Globe Playhouse, Los Angeles, CA, 1985.
Colonel, *The Invasion of Aratooga*, CSC Theatre, New York City, 1987.
Uncle Umbi, *Bricklayers*, Winterfest 11, Yale Repertory Company, 1990.
Father, *Shmulnik's Waltz*, Jewish Repertory Theatre, then Houseman Theatre, both New York City, 1991.
No Conductor, Threshold Theatre, New York City, 1992.
In Shadow, Threshold Theatre, 1992.
Rabbi, *Teible and Her Demon*, Jewish Repertory Theatre, New York City, 1994.

Also appeared as Ben, *Broadway Bound,* South Jersey Regional Theatre; appeared in *A Dybbuk,* Denver Center Theatre Conservatory; *The Penguin, On the Wing,* and *Men in Pits.* *

KEITH, Brian 1921-1997

OBITUARY NOTICE—See index for *CTFT* sketch: Full name, Brian Michael Keith; born November 14, 1921, in Bayonne, NJ; died of a self-inflicted gunshot wound, June 24, 1997, in Malibu, CA. Actor and executive. Keith charmed audiences in film, stage, and television productions in roles that cast him as President Theodore Roosevelt (*The Wind and the Lion*), retired judge Milton C. Hardcastle (*Hardcastle and McCormick*), and bachelor turned guardian Uncle Bill (*Family Affair*). Although he is best remembered for his work in film and television, Keith began his adult acting career on the stage in productions such as *Heyday, Mister Roberts, Darkness at Noon, Out West of Eighth.* He served in the U.S. Marine Corps during World War II as an aerial gunner, then turned to work on films. He made his adult debut in *Arrowhead* and followed it with roles in movies such as *Nightfall, The Young Philadelphians, The Pleasure Seekers, The Hallelujah Trail, The Yakuza, Moonraker, Sharky's Machine,* and *Young Guns.* (Keith had actually made an earlier film, the silent picture *Piper Malone,* at the age of three.) He also appeared in humorous films such as *The Parent Trap, The Russians Are Coming, The Russians Are Coming,* and *With Six You Get Eggroll.* One of his most memorable roles was in the television series *Family Affair,* in which he played "Uncle Bill" Davis, a bachelor who takes in three young orphans and tries to raise them with the help of his butler, Mr. French. The series aired from 1966 to 1971 and earned the actor three Emmy Award nominations. He also appeared on series such as *The Brian Keith Show, Archer,* and *How the West Was Won.* In *Hardcastle and McCormick* (1983 to 1986), he portrayed retired Judge Milton C. Hardcastle, a man who again took in an orphan of sorts. This time it was Mark McCormick, an ex-con that Hardcastle helps. Together the duo bring justice to criminals who somehow have managed to evade the law.

Keith also appeared in television movies such as *The Quest, In the Matter of Karen Ann Quinlan, The Seekers,* and *The Alamo: Thirteen Days to Glory,* and he portrayed Axel Dumire in the lengthy miniseries *Centennial.* He returned to the stage in 1978 for a run in the production *Da.* Despite suffering from cancer, Keith, who had appeared as President Theodore Roosevelt in the film *The Wind and the Lion,* worked on the TNT miniseries *The Rough Riders* in 1997. The television production focused on the life of Roosevelt and American involvement in the Spanish American War in 1898.

As noted in the *Washington Post:* "'I never made a career move in my life,' [Keith] said in a 1991 interview. . . . 'I just took what came along. I never looked for stepping stones to becoming a star. . . . I never gave a hoot.'"

OBITUARIES AND OTHER SOURCES

Books:
Who's Who in America, Marquis Who's Who, 1996.

Periodicals:
Chicago Tribune, June 25, 1997, section 1, p. 10.
New York Times, June 25, 1997, p. D20.
Washington Post, June 25, 1997, p. B4.

KELKER-KELLY, Robert 1965(?)-

PERSONAL

Born April 18, c. 1965, in Cleveland, OH; son of Robert Kelly (a pathologist) and Jonetta Kelker (a nurse); married Linda Rattner (a production assistant), 1988 (divorced, 1992).

Addresses: *Contact*—30 Rockefeller Plaza, New York, NY 10112.

Career: Actor.

Awards, Honors: Soap Opera Award, outstanding lead actor, 1994, for *Days of Our Lives.*

CREDITS

Television Appearances; Series:
Sam Fowler, *Another World,* NBC, 1987-89.
Bo Brady, *Days of Our Lives,* NBC, 1992-95.
Bobby Reno, *Another World,* NBC, 1996—.

Television Appearances; Episodic:
Appeared in episodes of *Touched by an Angel,* CBS; *Miami Vice; Saturday's;* and *Maybe This Time.*

Television Appearances; Movies:
Munson, *Hart to Hart: Crimes of the Hart* (also known as *Hart to Hart: Hart Throb*), NBC, 1994.

Television Appearances; Specials:
Bo Brady, *Days of Our Lives: Night Sins,* NBC, 1993.
50 Years of Soaps: An All-Star Celebration, CBS, 1994.
Bo Brady, *Days of Our Lives: Winter Heat,* NBC, 1994.

Television Appearances; Awards Presentations:
The 9th Annual Soap Opera Awards, NBC, 1993.
Host, *The 22nd Annual Daytime Emmy Awards,* NBC, 1995.

Film Appearances:
Man in phone booth, *Mr. Write,* Shapiro Glickenhaus Entertainment, 1994.
Trent, *Dream for an Insomniac,* Tritone Productions, 1996.

Stage Appearances:
Appeared in *Measure for Measure, The Taming of the Shrew, The Tempest, Normal Heart, Our Town,* and *A Slice of Buffalo, a Piece of Paris.**

KELLER, Micheline   1948-
    (Micheline H. Keller)

PERSONAL

Full name, Micheline Herskovic Keller; born December 19, 1948, in Brussels, Belgium; daughter of William (a business executive) and Maria (a business executive) Herskovic; married Max A. Keller (an attorney and film executive), October 31, 1971; children: Nicole, David. *Education:* University of California at Los Angeles, B.A. (political science), 1971; Southwestern University, J.D., 1974. *Religion:* Jewish.

Addresses: *Office*—Inter Planetary Productions, 14225 Ventura Blvd., Sherman Oaks, CA 91423.

Career: Producer, film company executive, and lawyer. Admitted to the California bar, 1974; Keller and Keller (law firm), Beverly Hills, CA, partner, 1974-76; Inter Planetary Pictures, Inc., Sherman Oaks, CA, president, 1976—; Inter Planetary Productions Corporation, Sherman Oaks, CA, president, 1978—.

Member: Academy of Television Arts and Sciences, Women in Film, United Jewish Welfare, Southwestern Themis.

Awards, Honors: Emmy Award and the Themis Society Gold Medal from the New York Film Festival, both 1981, for *Kent State;* Image Award from the National Association for the Advancement of Colored People, 1981, Golden Halo Award, 1981, and Gold Medal from the New York Film Festival, 1982, all for *Grambling's White Tiger;* California Governors Media Access Award, best movie, 1985, for *A Summer to Remember;* Chicago Film Festival Award, 1986, for *Betrayed by Innocence.*

CREDITS

Television Work; Movies; Producer, Unless Indicated Otherwise:
Summer of Fear, 1978.
Executive producer, *Kent State,* 1980.
Grambling's White Tiger, 1981.
Voyage of the Rock Aliens, 1984.
A Summer to Remember, 1985.
Supervising producer, *Dreams of Gold: The Mel Fisher Story,* CBS, 1986.
Betrayed by Innocence, CBS, 1986.
Executive producer, *Swimsuit,* 1989.
Executive producer, *Tarzan's Return,* syndicated, 1996.

Television Work; Series:
Developer, *Tarzan,* syndicated, 1991-92.
Developer and executive producer, *Acapulco H.E.A.T.,* syndicated, 1993-96.
Executive producer, *Tarzan: The Epic Adventures,* syndicated, 1996—.
Developer and executive producer, *Conan,* syndicated, 1997—.

Film Work; Producer:
Deadly Blessing, United Artists, 1981.*

KELLER, Micheline H.
    See KELLER, Micheline

KELLMAN, Barnet   1947-

PERSONAL

Full name, Barnet Kramer Kellman; born November 9, 1947, in New York, NY; son of Joseph A. G. (an attorney) and Verona D. (Kramer) Kellman; married Nancy Mette (an actress), June 26, 1982; children: Katherine Mette, Eliza Mette. *Education:* Colgate University, B.A., 1969; Yale School of Drama, 1970; Union Graduate School, Ph.D., 1972. *Religion:* Jewish.

Addresses: *Agent*—c/o Creative Artists Agency, 9300 Beverly Hills, CA. *Office*—Warner Bros. Bld. 140, Rm. 212, 300 Television Plaza, Burbank, CA, 91505.

Career: Director and instructor. North Carolina School of the Arts, instructor and guest director, 1973-80; City College of New York, instructor and guest director, 1975-76; Columbia University School of the Arts, graduate film division, Ithaca, NY, instructor and guest director, 1984-87; also an instructor at the Leonard Davis Center for the Arts, the Circle in the Square Acting School, and the Corner Loft Studio.

Member: Society of Stage Directors and Choreographers (member of the board of directors, 1984-86 and member of the executive board, 1985), Directors Guild of America, Actors' Equity Association, Screen Actors Guild, New Dramatists (member of the board of directors).

Awards, Honors: Thomas J. Watson fellow, 1969-71; Danforth fellow, 1969-72; Emmy Awards, outstanding comedy series, 1989, 1990, and 1992, outstanding individual achievement in directing a comedy series (for single episode "Birth 101"), 1992, all for *Murphy Brown;* outstanding directional achievement award for television, Directors Guild of America, 1989, for "Brown Like Me," *Murphy Brown;* Emmy Award nomination, for *Another World.*

CREDITS

Stage Work; Director:
Key Exchange, WPA Theatre, New York City, then Orpheum Theatre, New York City, both 1981.
Breakfast with Les and Bess, Hudson Guild, Lambs Theatre, New York City, 1982.
The Good Parts, Astor Place Theatre, New York City, 1982.
Danny and the Deep Blue Sea, Actors' Theatre of Louisville, Louisville, KY, later Circle in the Square Theatre, New York City, 1984.
The Loman Family Picnic, Stage II, Manhattan Theatre Club, 1989.

Also directed *Eden Court,* Promenade Theatre, New York City; *Friends,* Manhattan Theatre Club, New York City; also directed productions at the American Place Theatre, New York City; Public Theatre, New York City; Eugene O'Neill Theatre Center, CT; Yale Repertory Theatre, New Haven, CT; Folger Theatre, Washington, DC; and the Williamstown Theatre Festival, Williamstown, MA.

Film Work; Director:
Key Exchange, Twentieth Century-Fox, 1985.
Straight Talk, Buena Vista, 1992.
Stinkers (also known as *Slappy and the Stinkers*), 1997.

Film Appearances:
Director, *Straight Talk,* Buena Vista, 1992.

Television Work; Series:
Director, *Gemini,* Showtime, 1981.
Director, *All Is Forgiven,* NBC, 1986.
Take Five, CBS, 1987.
Director, *The Robert Guillaume Show,* ABC, 1988.
Director, *Murphy Brown,* CBS, 1988-92, and 1993-94.
Producer, *Murphy Brown,* CBS, 1989-91.
Director and coexecutive producer, *Mad About You,* NBC, 1992-93.
Coexecutive producer, *Good Advice,* CBS, 1993-94.
Creator, director, and executive producer, *Something Wilder,* NBC, 1994.

Television Producer; Episodic:
My Sister Sam, CBS, 1987.
Designing Women, CBS, 1987.
ER, NBC, 1995.
Hope and Gloria, NBC, 1995.
If Not For You (also known as *One of Those Things*), CBS, 1995.
Ink, CBS, 1996.
Life With Roger, The WB, 1996.
Suddenly Susan, NBC, 1996.

Television Director; Specials:
Sons of Gunz, 1987.
Cowboy Joe, 1988.
The Designing Women Special: Their Finest Hour, CBS, 1990.

Television Director; Pilots:
Good Advice, CBS, 1993.
The Second Half, NBC, 1993.
Daddy's Girls, CBS, 1994.
Thunder Alley, ABC, 1994.
Bless This House, CBS, 1995.

Also directed *Another World,* NBC; *Hometown,* CBS; and *Orphans, Waifs, and Wards,* CBS.

WRITINGS

Teleplays; Story Ideas; Pilots:
Something Wilder, NBC, 1994.*

KENNEDY, Mimi   1948(?)-

PERSONAL

Born September 25, 1948 (some sources say 1949), in Rochester, NY; daughter of Daniel Gerald and Nancy Helen (Colgan) Kennedy; married Lawrence Edwin Dilg, May 27, 1978; children: John Francisco, Mary Jacinta. *Education:* Smith College, graduated, 1970.

Addresses: *Agent*—Agency for the Performing Arts, 9000 Sunset Blvd., Suite 1200, Los Angeles, CA 90069.

Career: Actress.

CREDITS

Television Appearances; Series:
Regular, *Three Girls Three,* NBC, 1977.
Victoria Chasen, *Stockard Channing in Just Friends,* CBS, 1979.
Regular, *The Big Show,* NBC, 1980.
Nan Gallagher, *The Two of Us,* CBS, 1981-82.
Doris Winger, *Spencer* (also known as *Under One Roof*), NBC, 1984-85.
Andrea Tobin, *Family Man,* ABC, 1988.
Ruth Sloan, *Homefront,* ABC, 1991.
Barbara Gennaro, *Joe's Life,* ABC, 1993.
Abby, *Dharma and Greg,* ABC, 1997—.

Television Appearances; Miniseries:
Pat Kennedy, *Robert Kennedy and His Times,* CBS, 1985.

Television Appearances; Movies:
Jenny, *Getting Married,* CBS, 1978.
Arlene Gilbert, *Thin Ice,* CBS, 1981.
Eloise Davis, *Bride of Boogedy,* ABC, 1987.
Jane, *Baby Girl Scott,* CBS, 1987.
Annie Willis, *A Promise to Keep* (also known as *Promises to Keep* and *Angels without Wings*), NBC, 1990.

Karen Turner, *Sins of the Mother,* CBS, 1991.
Kate Cantrell, *Flashfire,* HBO, 1994.
Connie, *Once You Meet a Stranger* (also known as *Don't Talk to Strangers*), CBS, 1996.
Celia Barton, *Reasons of the Heart* (also known as *Lover's Leap*), USA Network, 1996.

Television Appearances; Episodic:
"Going Straight," *Family,* ABC, 1979.
"Homecoming," *St. Elsewhere,* NBC, 1982.
"The Children's Hour," *St. Elsewhere,* NBC, 1982.
"Popular Neurotics," *American Playhouse,* PBS, 1984.
"Married Alive," *Night Court,* NBC, 1985.
Kristi Carruthers, "Aqua Vita," *The Twilight Zone,* CBS, 1986.
Mrs. Parker, "Davy Crockett," *Shelley Duvall's Tall Tales and Legends,* Showtime, 1987.
Miss Wagner, *Homeroom,* ABC, 1989.
"The Man Who Was Death," *Tales from the Crypt,* HBO, 1989.
"Second Time Aground," *Dream On,* HBO, 1990.
Voice of Glenda Molehill, *Dinosaurs,* ABC, 1991.
Baywatch Nights, syndicated, 1995.
Homicide: Life on the Street, NBC, 1995.
Shana, *Partners,* Fox, 1995.
Realtor, *The Single Guy,* NBC, 1995.
Gretchen, *Cybill,* CBS, 1996.
Eleanor Buton Alexander, *Savannah,* The WB, 1996.
Pacific Palisades (also known as *Brentwood*), Fox, 1997.

Television Appearances; Specials:
Battle of the Network Stars, ABC, 1981.
I've Had It Up to Here, NBC, 1981.
Eloise Davis, *Mr. Boogedy,* ABC, 1986.
Voice of Mrs. Gridley, "The Mouse and the Motorcycle" (animated), *ABC Weekend Specials,* ABC, 1986.
Voice of Mrs. Gridley, "Ralph S. Mouse" (animated), *ABC Weekend Specials,* ABC, 1991.
Elaine Marshall, "Fast Forward," *ABC Afterschool Specials,* ABC, 1995.

Film Appearances:
Sally, *Chances Are,* TriStar, 1989.
Eli's mom, *Immediate Family* (also known as *Parental Guidance*), Columbia, 1989.
Martha Hunter, *Pump up the Volume,* New Line, 1990.
Second woman, *Death Becomes Her,* Universal, 1992.
Mrs. Bowman, *Buddy,* Columbia, 1997.

Stage Appearances:
Last of the Red Hot Lovers, 1972.
(Broadway debut) Jan, *Grease,* Broadhurst Theatre, New York City, 1975.
(Off-Broadway debut) Anne Bonney, *Hot Grog,* Marymount Manhattan Theatre, New York City, 1977.
Marilyn, *Grownups,* Center Theatre Group, Mark Taper Forum, Los Angeles, CA, 1982.

WRITINGS

Plays:
(Contributor) *Hard Sell,* New York Shakespeare Festival, Public Theatre, New York City, 1980.

Books:
Taken to the Stage: The Education of an Actress, Smith & Kraus (Lyme, NH), 1996.*

KENZLE, Leila   1961-

PERSONAL

Born July 16, 1961, in Patchogue, Long Island, NY; daughter of Kurt (an electrical supply salesman) and Lee (an antiques dealer) Kenzle; married Neil Monaco (a writer and director), 1994. *Education:* Mason Gross School of the Arts, Rutgers University, B.F.A., 1984.

Addresses: *Agent*—William Morris Agency, 151 El Camino Dr., Beverly Hills, CA 90212. *Manager*—Fenton Management, 427 North Canon Dr., Suite 108, Beverly Hills, CA 90210. *Publicist*—Colleen Schlatter or Lori Williams, Baker, Winokur, and Ryder, 405 South Beverly Dr., Fifth Floor, Beverly Hills, CA 90212. *Contact*—TriStar Productions, Montrose Productions, 9336 West Washington Blvd., Culver City, CA 90232.

Career: Actress. Worked as a hotel telephone operator.

CREDITS

Television Appearances; Series:
Debra Kirshner-Kleckner, *Princesses,* CBS, 1991.
Fran Devanow, *Mad About You,* NBC, 1992—.

Television Appearances; Pilots:
Gina DeSalvo, *The World According to Straw,* Fox, 1990.

Stand By Your Man, 1992.
Speed of Life, 1997.

Television Appearances; Episodic:
Fran Devanow, "The One with the Two Parts, Part I," *Friends,* NBC, 1995.
Fran Devanow, "The One with the Two Parts, Part II," *Friends,* NBC, 1995.

Appeared in episodes of *The Golden Girls, thirtysomething,* and *The Cosby Show.*

Television Appearances; Movies:
Jessie Frank, *All She Ever Wanted* (also known as *The Ties That Bind* and *Mother's Day*), ABC, 1996.

Also appeared in *The Charmer.*

Television Appearances; Specials:
The 17th Annual All New Circus of the Stars and Side Show, CBS, 1992.

Film Appearances:
Marcia, *Other People's Money,* Warner Bros., 1991.
Bigger Fish (short film), Second Hand Smoke, 1996.

Film Work; Producer:
Bigger Fish (short film), Second Hand Smoke, 1996.

Stage Appearances:
Madeline Monroe, *Tony 'n' Tina's Wedding,* Washington Square Church & Carmelita's, then St. John's Church, then Vinnie Black's Coliseum, all New York City, 1988-89; then in Los Angeles, CA, 1989.

KERNS, Joanna   1953-
(Joanna de Varona)

PERSONAL

Born Joanna de Varona, February 12, 1955, in San Francisco, CA; daughter of David Thomas and Martha Louise (Smith) de Varona; married Richard Martin Kerns (a producer and director), December 11, 1976 (divorced, December, 1986); children: Ashley Cooper. *Education:* Attended University of California at Los Angeles, 1970-71. *Politics:* Democrat.

Addresses: *Agent*—Creative Artists Agency, 9830 Wilshire Blvd., Beverly Hills, CA 90212-1825.

Career: Actress and writer. Appeared in television commercials. Gymnast. Appeared in the music video (as a member of the choir) for the song "Voices That Care."

CREDITS

Television Appearances; Series:
Pat Devon, *The Four Seasons*, CBS, 1984.
Maggie Seaver, *Growing Pains*, ABC, 1985-92.
Cohost, *Home*, ABC, 1989.

Television Appearances; Miniseries:
Marjorie Donovan, *V*, NBC, 1983.
Maria Marshall, *Blind Faith* (also known as *The Toms River Case*), NBC, 1990.
Dr. Clare Winslow, *The Big One: The Great Los Angeles Earthquake* (also known as *The Great Los Angeles Earthquake*), NBC, 1990.

Television Appearances; Pilots:
"Hunter," *Hunter*, NBC, 1984.

Television Appearances; Movies:
Meg, *Marriage Is Alive and Well*, NBC, 1980.
Doris Marshall, *Mother's Day on Walton's Mountain*, NBC, 1982.
Doris Marshall, *A Wedding on Walton's Mountain*, NBC, 1982.
Doris Marshall, *A Day of Thanks on Walton's Mountain*, NBC, 1982.
Pamela Saletta, *The Return of Marcus Welby, M.D.*, ABC, 1984.
Andrea, *A Bunny's Tale*, ABC, 1985.
Anita Parrish, *The Rape of Richard Beck* (also known as *The Broken Badge*), ABC, 1985.
Lana Singer, *Stormin' Home*, CBS, 1985.
Stephanie Blume, *Mistress*, CBS, 1987.
Diane Pappas, *Those She Left Behind*, NBC, 1989.
Linda Fairstein, *The Preppie Murder*, ABC, 1989.
Sally Raynor, *Deadly Intentions . . . Again?*, ABC, 1991.
Kathy Plunk, *Captive* (also known *Season of Fear*), ABC, 1991.
Eve Rhodes, *The Nightman* (also known as *The Watchman*), NBC, 1992.
Mary Ellen "Mel" Robbins, *Desperate Choices: To Save My Child* (also known as *The Final Choice* and *Solomon's Choice*), NBC, 1992.
Veronica Ricci, *Not in My Family* (also known as *Shattering the Silence* and *Breaking the Silence*), ABC, 1993.
Katy, *The Man with Three Wives*, CBS, 1993.

Maryanne Walker-Tate, *Shameful Secrets* (also known as *Going Underground*), ABC, 1993.
Dr. Jennifer Kessler, *Robin Cook's Mortal Fear* (also known as *Mortal Fear*), NBC, 1994.
Laura Eagerton, *Whose Daughter Is She?* (also known as *Semi-Precious, Moms*, and *For the Love of My Daughter*), CBS, 1995.
Jane Ravenson, *See Jane Run*, ABC, 1995.
Jessica Rayner, *No One Could Protect Her*, ABC, 1996.
Cynthia, the mother, *Terror in the Family*, Fox, 1996.
Celeste Cooper, *Mother Knows Best*, ABC, 1997.
Gail Connelly, *Sisters and Other Strangers* (also known as *Suspicion of Innocence*), CBS, 1997.

Television Appearances; Episodic:
"Officer Luca, You're Dead," *S.W.A.T.*, ABC, 1976.
"Romance Roulette," *The Love Boat*, ABC, 1977.
"Playoff," *Switch*, CBS, 1978.
Bobby Trilling, *Three's Company*, ABC, 1981.
Colleen, "Dead Man's Riddle," *CHiPs*, NBC, 1981.
"Difficult Lesson," *Fitz and Bones*, NBC, 1981.
"The Last Page," *Magnum, P.I.*, CBS, 1982.
"Spring Is in the Air," *Star of the Family*, ABC, 1982.
"The Fashion Show," *Laverne and Shirley*, ABC, 1982.
"Birds of a Feather," *Magnum, P.I.*, CBS, 1983.
"Fatal Error," *Whiz Kids*, CBS, 1983.
Trish, "A Nice Place to Visit," *The A-Team*, NBC, 1983.
Ryan's 4, ABC, 1983.
"Jack Be Quick," *Three's Company*, ABC, 1983.
"Hair Apparent," *Hill Street Blues*, NBC, 1984.
"Hot Target," *Street Hawk*, ABC, 1985.
Cheryl Blaste, "Blaste from the Past," *Hooperman*, ABC, 1988.
"Love Struck," *Short Stories*, Arts and Entertainment, 1988.
Animal Crack-Ups, ABC, 1988.
Herself, *Hope and Gloria*, NBC, 1995.
Voiceover, *Aliens in the Family*, ABC, 1996.

Also appeared on *The Associates*, ABC.

Television Appearances; Specials:
Are You a Missing Heir?, ABC, 1978.
Lifetime Salutes Mom, Lifetime, 1987.
The Regis Philbin Show, Lifetime, 1987.
Host, *The National Love and Sex Test*, ABC, 1988.
Host, *Second Annual Star-Spangled Celebration*, ABC, 1988.
Like Mother, Like Daughter, Lifetime, 1988.
Host, *Sea World's Miracle Babies and Friends* (also known as *The Miracle Babies of Sea World*), ABC, 1989.

Herself, *The 15th Annual People's Choice Awards,* 1989.
Herself, *The Hollywood Christmas Parade,* 1989.
Herself, *Starathon '90,* syndicated, 1990.
The 16th Annual People's Choice Awards, 1990.
Herself, *The Television Academy Hall of Fame* (also known as *The 6th Annual Television Academy Hall of Fame*), Fox, 1990.
Herself, *The Tube Test,* ABC, 1990.
Host, *Fantasies,* ABC, 1991.
Host, *Starathon '91,* syndicated, 1991.
Herself, *Welcome Home, America!—A USO Salute to America's Sons and Daughters,* ABC, 1991.
Herself, *Voices That Care,* Fox, 1991.
The 53rd Annual Golden Globe Awards, 1996.

Television Work:
Coexecutive producer, *The Nightman* (also known as *The Watchman*), NBC, 1992.
Director, *Hope and Gloria* (episodic), NBC, 1995.

Film Appearances:
Marilyn Baker, *A*P*E* (also known as *Ape, Attack of the Giant Horny Gorilla, Hideous Mutant, The New King Kong,* and *Super Kong*), New World Entertainment, 1976.
Diana, *Coma,* United Artists, 1978.
Nancy, *Cross My Heart,* Universal, 1987.
Cameo appearance, *She's Having A Baby,* Paramount, 1988.
Katharine Watson, *Street Justice,* Lorimar, 1989.
Aunt Sunny, *An American Summer,* Castle Hill, 1991.
No Dessert Dad, Til You Mow the Lawn, New Horizons Home Video, 1994.

Stage Appearances:
(As Joanna de Varona) Zoe, blushing bride, nymph, pygmy, and Yew, *Ulysses in Nighttown,* Winter Garden Theatre, New York City, 1974.

Stage Work:
Director, *What Every Woman Knows,* West Coast Ensemble Theatre, Los Angeles, CA, 1989.

Major Tours:
(As Joanna de Varona) *Two Gentlemen of Verona,* New York Shakespeare Festival, U.S. and Canadian cities, 1973.

WRITINGS

For Television; Episodic:
"Guess Who's Coming to Dinner," *Growing Pains,* ABC, 1989.*

KHALI, Simbi

PERSONAL

Born April 28, in Jackson, MS. *Education:* California Institute of Arts, B.F.A.

Addresses: *Contact*—YBLY Productions, CBS Studio Center, Building 2, 2nd Floor, 4024 Radford Ave., Studio City, CA 91604.

Career: Actress.

CREDITS

Television Appearances; Series:
She TV, ABC, 1994.
Nina Campbell, *3rd Rock from the Sun,* NBC, 1996—.

Television Appearances; Episodic:
Appeared in episodes of *Martin,* Fox; and *Sinbad.*

Film Appearances:
Nikki, *A Vampire in Brooklyn,* Paramount, 1995.
Adrienne, *A Thin Line between Love & Hate,* New Line Cinema/Savoy Pictures, 1996.

Stage Appearances:
Appeared in *The Colored Museum, For Colored Girls Who Have Considered Suicide When the Rainbow Is Enuf, A Midsummer Night's Dream,* and *Troilus and Cressida.**

KOPACHE, Thomas   1945-

PERSONAL

Born October 17, 1945, in Manchester, NH; son of Dorothy E. (maiden name, Sterling) Kopache. *Education:* San Diego State University, B.A. (theatre), 1971; California Institute of the Arts, M.F.A. (acting), 1973; studied acting with Sam Schact.

Addresses: *Agent*—ADM Associates Inc., 165 West 46th Street, Suite 1109, New York, NY 10036.

Career: Actor. Founding member of Camera Obscura, based in Amsterdam and touring throughout Europe, 1973-76; University of California at La Jolla and San Diego City College, teacher of movement for actors, 1975; Cleveland Playhouse, Cleveland, OH, guest artist, 1986-87. *Military service:* U.S. Navy, 1963-66; served in Vietnam, receiving the Armed Forces Expedition Army Medal for landing at Chu Lai.

Member: Actors Equity Association, Screen Actors Guild, American Federation of Television and Radio Artists.

CREDITS

Stage Appearances:

Conrade, *Much Ado About Nothing,* San Diego Shakespeare Festival, San Diego, CA, 1970.

The Emperor, *The Architect and Emperor of Assyria,* La MaMa Etc. Theatre, New York City, 1976.

Macbeth, *Macbeth,* La MaMa Etc. Theatre, 1977.

Scipio, *Caligulia,* La MaMa Etc. Theatre, 1978.

Buthcer, the actor, *Arturo Ui,* La MaMa Etc. Theatre, 1978.

Wagner, *Faust,* La MaMa Etc. Theatre, 1978.

Prospero, *The Tempest,* La MaMa Etc. Theatre, 1978.

Morris, *The Bloodknot,* Syracuse Stage, Syracuse, NY, then Walnut Street Theatre, Philadelphia, PA, both 1979.

Recruiting officer, *Mother Courage,* Center Stage, 1980.

Rover, *Hurrah for the Bridge,* La MaMa Etc. Theatre, 1981.

Harry Roat, *Wait Until Dark,* Wye Mills Theatre, 1981.

George, *Hunting Scenes from Lower Bavaria,* Manhattan Theatre Club, New York City, 1981.

First presser, *The Workroom,* Center Stage, Baltimore, MD, 1982.

Macduff, *Macbeth,* Shakespeare and Company, 1982.

Ioga, *The Extravagant Triumph. . .,* INTAR Hispanic American Theatre, New York City, 1982.

Pedro, *The Seniorita from Tacna,* INTAR Hispanic American Theatre, 1982.

Kevin Morrow, *Friends Too Numerous to Mention,* Jewish Repertory Theatre, New York City, 1982.

Morris, *The Bloodknot,* New Stage, 1983.

Westmoreland, *Henry IV, Parts I and II,* Indiana Repertory Company, 1983.

Bob Cratchit, *A Christmas Carol,* Indiana Repertory Company, 1983.

Deeley, *Old Times,* Indiana Repertory Company, 1983.

The Dark Man, *The Woman,* Center Stage, 1983.

Jack, *Plainsong,* Ensemble Studio Theatre, New York City, 1984.

The waiter and the doctor, *The Danube,* American Place Theatre, New York City, 1984.

Coach, *Baseball Play,* Ensemble Studio Theatre, 1984.

Jimmy, *Cayuses,* Ensemble Studio Theatre, 1985.

Polixenes, *The Winter's Tale,* Lincoln Center Symphony Space, New York City, 1985.

Dr. Bailey/Buford Bullough/Griswold Plankman, *Laughing Stock,* Long Wharf Theatre, New Haven, CT, 1987.

Titus Lartius, *Coriolanus,* New York Shakespeare Festival, Delacorte Theater, New York City, 1988.

Smith, *The Last Temptation of Joe Hill,* INTAR Stage 2, New York City, 1988.

Understudy for the roles of Prof. Willard/Constable Warren/Farmer McCarty, *Our Town,* Lyceum Theatre, New York City, 1988-89.

First man, *Orpheus Descending,* Neil Simon Theatre, New York City, 1989.

Julian, *The Encanto File,* Judith Anderson Theatre, New York City, 1991.

Karl Streber, *Temporary Help,* Long Wharf Theatre, 1991.

Major Tours:

With Camera Obscura, productions throughout Europe, 1973-76.

The Emperor, *The Architect and Emperor of Assyria,* European tour, La MaMa, 1976.

Film Appearances:

Police officer, *Without a Trace,* Twentieth Century-Fox, 1982.

Highway patrolman, *Strange Invaders,* Orion, 1983.

Truck driver, *Home Free All,* Almi, 1983.

Cory, *And Then You Die,* Trimark Home Video, 1988.

TV station man, *Loose Cannons,* TriStar, 1990.

Doctor Parker, *Liebestraum,* Metro-Goldwyn-Mayer/Pathe, 1991.

Mr. Wilson, *Mr. Jones,* TriStar, 1993.

Geiger Counter Vendor, *This Boy's Life,* Warner Bros., 1993.

Com Officer, *Star Trek: Generations,* Paramount, 1994.

Mr. Simpson, *Leaving Las Vegas,* United Artists, 1995.

Thorn McIntyre, *Ghosts of Mississippi,* Columbia, 1996.

Calhoun, *Breakdown* (also known as *The Breakdown Mile*), Paramount, 1997.

Merv, *One Night Stand,* New Horizons Home Video, 1997.

Television Appearances; Miniseries:
Mike O'Rourke, *People Like Us,* NBC, 1990.

Television Appearances; Specials:
Mr. Carter, "Our Town," *Great Performances,* PBS, 1989.
Dr. Darrold Treffert, *On Trial,* NBC, 1994.

Television Appearances; Movies:
Carl Fitzpatrick, *A Woman Scorned: The Betty Broderick Story* (also known as *Till Murder Do Us Part*), CBS, 1992.
Janos, "Miss Rose White," *Hallmark Hall of Fame,* NBC, 1992.
Steve Dahlberg, *A Case for Murder,* USA Network, 1993.
Blood Bank Executive, *And the Band Played On,* HBO, 1993.
Mason, *Hart to Hart Returns,* NBC, 1993.
Jed, "Journey," *Hallmark Hall of Fame,* CBS, 1995.
Ray Keyes, *Breaking Through* (also known as *Breaking Free*), ABC, 1996.

Television Appearances; Episodic:
Cab driver, *Another World,* NBC, 1983.
Carl, *Guiding Light,* CBS, 1985.
Mirok, "The Next Phase," *Star Trek: The Next Generation,* syndicated, 1992.
Donald Bobeck, "Looking for Loans in All the Wrong Places," *Roseanne,* ABC, 1992.
Chief, "Dead-End for Delia," *Fallen Angels,* Showtime, 1993.
Sal DalBazzo, "Dirty Deeds," *The John Larroquette Show,* NBC, 1994.
Tu'Pari, "The Parliament of Dreams," *Babylon 5,* syndicated, 1994.
"Family Values," *Law and Order,* NBC, 1994.
Engineer, "Emergence," *Star Trek: The Next Generation,* syndicated, 1994.
Dr. Stevens, *Melrose Place,* Fox, 1994.
Dr. Leland O'Conner, *Murder One,* ABC, 1995.
General Thomas Callahan, "The Walk," *The X-Files,* Fox, 1995.
Kaplinger, *The Burning Zone,* UPN, 1996.
Viorsa, "The Thaw," *Star Trek: Voyager,* UPN, 1996.
Kira Taban, "Ties of Blood and Water," *Star Trek: Deep Space Nine,* syndicated, 1997.*

KURALT, Charles   1934-1997

OBITUARY NOTICE—See index for *CTFT* sketch: Born September 10, 1934, in Wilmington, NC; died of complications from lupus, July 4, 1997, in New York, NY. Television news reporter, producer, writer. Kuralt is remembered as the television anchor who shun-piked his way across the backroads of the United States, searching for unique stories about ordinary people. His "On the Road" segments for the *CBS Evening News with Walter Cronkite,* aired from 1967 to 1980, and eventually led to a position as anchor for *CBS News Sunday Morning.* Broadcasting and reporting were a way of life for Kuralt. At the age of fourteen he announced minor-league baseball games and edited the student newspaper while in college. In 1955 he joined the staff of the *Charlotte News* as a reporter. In 1957 he went to work for the Columbia Broadcasting System (CBS) in New York as a writer; by 1959 he was the host of *Eyewitness to History.* For the next eight years Kuralt covered hard news stories in Latin America and Vietnam. His career changed in 1967 when he began covering human interest stories. Traveling more than 50,000 miles each year in a motorhome from 1967 to 1980, Kuralt and his camera crew set off in search of the real America. According to Arthur Unger of the *Christian Science Monitor,* Kuralt convinced CBS into sponsoring his "On the Road" segment by explaining: "I got the idea . . . one night in an airplane as I looked down at the lights in the countryside and wondered . . . what was going on down there. There are a lot of Americans who don't live in cities and don't make headlines. I was interested in finding out about them."

His forty-year career afforded Kuralt three George Foster Peabody Awards, thirteen Emmy Awards, and a 1985 broadcaster of the year award from the International Radio and Television Society. His television credits are numerous and include *Dateline America, America Tonight, 60 Minutes . . . 25 Years* (also known as *60 Minutes Turns 25*), *On the Road with Charles Kuralt,* and *An American Moment.* His written works include *Charles Kuralt's America, To the Top of the World: The Adventures and Misadventures of the Plaisted Polar Expedition, March 28-May 4, 1967, Southerners: Portrait of a People,* and *A Life on the Road.* He also wrote two companion pieces for his television shows: *Dateline America* and *On the Road with Charles Kuralt.*

OBITUARIES AND OTHER SOURCES

Books:
Who's Who in America, Marquis Who's Who, 1996.

Periodicals:
Chicago Tribune, July 5, 1997, section 1, p. 4.

Christian Science Monitor, July 24, 1974.
CNN Interactive (electronic), July 4, 1997.
Los Angeles Times, July 5, 1997, p. A1.
MSNBC (electronic), July 5, 1997.
New York Times, July 5, 1997, p. 24.
USA Today (electronic), July 4, 1997.
Washington Post, July 5, 1997, p. B4.

LADD, Cheryl 1951-
(Cherie Moore, Cheryl Stoppelmoor, Cheryl Jean Stoppelmoor)

PERSONAL

Born Cheryl Jean Stoppelmoor, July 12 (some sources say July 2), 1951, in Huron, SD; daughter of Marion and Dolores (Katz) Stoppelmoor; married second husband, David Ladd (an actor and producer), May, 1973, (divorced, September, 1980); married Brian Russell (a producer), January 3, 1981; children: (first marriage) Jordan Elizabeth (an actress); stepchildren: Lindsay. *Education:* Studied at the Milton Katselas Acting Workshop. *Politics:* Republican. *Avocational interests:* Golf.

Addresses: *Agent*—c/o International Creative Management, 8942 Wilshire Boulevard, Beverly Hills, CA, 90211. *Publicist*—c/o Richard Grant & Associates, 8500 Wilshire Boulevard, Suite 520, Beverly Hills, CA 90211.

Career: Actress, singer, dancer, and writer. Member of touring musical group named the Music Shop Band, 1968-70; Childhelp USA, goodwill ambassador, 1979—; Buick Motor Division, golf ambassador, 1997—; actress in television commercials, including advertisements for Dento-Med Hydron Plus Hand and Body Moisturizer, Max Factor, Prell, ShapeMate; Retinitis Pigmentosa International, spokesperson.

Member: American Federation of Television and Radio Artists, Screen Actors Guild, American Guild of Variety Artists.

Awards, Honors: Photoplay Award, 1978; Woman of the World Award, Childhelp USA, 1987; Child Caring Award, Center for the Improvement of Child Care, for *When She Was Bad . . .*; received four gold singles from the albums *Cheryl Ladd,* 1978 and *Dance Forever,* 1979.

CREDITS

Stage Appearances:
Reno Sweeney, *Anything Goes,* Santa Barbara Theatre Festival, Santa Barbara, CA, 1986.

Also appeared in *The Hasty Heart* (also known as *Hasty Heart*).

Film Appearances:
Zabby, *The Treasure of Jamaica Reef* (also known as *Evil in the Deep* and *Treasure of the Jamaica Deep*), Golden-Selected (unreleased), 1976.
Jessie Clark, *Now and Forever,* Inter Planetary, 1983.
Deborah Solomon, *Purple Hearts,* Warner Bros., 1984.
Louise Baltimore, *Millennium,* Twentieth Century-Fox, 1989.
Katherine, *Lisa* (also known as *Candlelight Killer*), Metro-Goldwyn-Mayer/United Artists, 1990.
Georgie Cooper, *Poison Ivy,* New Line Cinema, 1992.

Also appeared in *Marriage of a Young Stockbroker.*

Television Appearances; Series:
(As Cherie Moore) Singing voice of Melody, *Josie and the Pussycats* (animated), CBS, 1970-72, and 1974-75, then NBC, 1975-76.
(As Cherie Moore) Singing voice of Melody, *Josie and the Pussycats in Outer Space* (animated), CBS, 1972-74.
(As Cheryl Jean Stoppelmoor) Regular, *The Ken Berry Wow Show* (also known as *Ken Berry's Wow*), ABC, 1972.
(As Cheryl Stoppelmoor) Amy, a Probe control agent, *Search,* NBC, 1972-73.
Kris Monroe, *Charlie's Angels,* ABC, 1977-81.
Dr. Dawn "Holli" Holliday, *One West Waikiki,* CBS, 1994.

Television Appearances; Miniseries:
Black Beauty, 1978.
Hope Masters, *A Death in California,* ABC, 1985.
Liane De Villiers, *Crossings,* ABC, 1986.
Maude Sage Breen, *Bluegrass,* CBS, 1988.

Television Appearances; Episodic:
"Double Trouble," *The Partridge Family,* ABC, 1973.
Cindy Shea, *Happy Days,* ABC, 1974.
Buffy, "Prime Rib," *Police Story,* NBC, 1976.
"The Innocent Prey," *The Fantastic Journey,* NBC, 1977.
Herself, *Donny and Marie,* ABC, 1977.

Herself, *The Muppet Show,* syndicated, 1978.

Herself, *Donny and Marie,* ABC, 1978.

Mercedes Haverset, "The Black Book," *Ink,* CBS, 1997.

Appeared as a teenage girl, "Such Dust as Dreams Are Made on," *Harry O,* ABC; as Susan Ellen Morley, "Blockade," *The Streets of San Francisco,* ABC; and in "Angels and Bums," *The San Pedro Beach Bums,* ABC; also appeared in *Ironside,* NBC; *Police Woman,* NBC; *The Rookies,* ABC; *Switch,* CBS; and *The Tonight Show,* NBC.

Television Appearances; Movies:

The Devil's Daughter, 1972.

(As Cheryl Jean Stoppelmoor) Jody Keller, *Satan's School for Girls,* ABC, 1973.

Thaddeus Rose and Eddie, 1978.

Betina "Teeny" Morgan, *When She Was Bad . . . ,* ABC, 1979.

Willa, 1979.

Guyana Tragedy: The Story of Jim Jones (also known as *The Mad Messiah*), 1980.

Title role, *Grace Kelly* (also known as *The Grace Kelly Story*), ABC, 1983.

Maggie Telford, *Kentucky Woman,* CBS, 1983.

The Hasty Heart, 1983.

Lily Conrad, *Romance on the Orient Express,* NBC, 1985.

Crime of Innocence, 1985.

Anne Halloran, *Deadly Care,* CBS, 1987.

Mary Gray, *The Fulfillment of Mary Gray* (also known as *Fulfillment* and *The Fulfillment*), CBS, 1989.

The Lookalike, 1990.

Diane Halstead, *Crash: The Mystery of Flight 1501* (also known as *Aftermath* and *Aftermath: The Fate of Flight 1501*), 1990.

Sara Crawford, *Jekyll and Hyde* (also known as *Dr. Jekyll and Mr. Hyde* and *Jekyll & Hyde*), ABC, 1990.

Laura Huntoon, *The Girl Who Came Between Them* (also known as *Face of Love* and *Victim of Innocence*), NBC, 1990.

Melanie Adams, *Danielle Steel's Changes* (also known as *Changes*), NBC, 1991.

Annie Gallagher, *Locked Up: A Mother's Rage* (also known as *The Delores Donovan Story, Other Side of Love,* and *They're Doing My Time*), CBS, 1991.

Pam Cheney, *Broken Promises: Taking Emily Back* (also known as *Broken Promises*), CBS, 1993.

Linda DeSilva Edelman, *Dead Before Dawn,* ABC, 1993.

Mary Dannon, *Dancing with Danger* (also known as *The Last Dance*), USA Network, 1994.

The Lady, 1995.

Vows of Deception, 1996.

Lucinda Michaels, *A Tangled Web* (also known as *Tangled Web*), CBS, 1996.

Jean McAvoy, *Kiss and Tell* (also known as *Please Forgive Me*), ABC, 1996.

Ellen Downey, *The Haunting of Lisa,* Lifetime, 1996.

Television Appearances; Specials:

ABC team member, *Battle of the Network Stars III,* 1977.

Ben Vereen . . . His Roots, 1978.

General Electric's All-Star Anniversary, NBC, 1978.

That Thing on ABC, ABC, 1978.

John Denver and the Ladies, 1978.

Host, *The Cheryl Ladd Special* (also known as *Cheryl Ladd*), ABC, 1979.

Host, *Cheryl Ladd . . . Looking Back—Souvenirs* (also known as *Cheryl Ladd—Souvenirs* and *Looking Back: Souvenirs*), ABC, 1980.

Perry Como's Spring in San Francisco, 1981.

Host, *Cheryl Ladd: Scenes from a Special* (also known as *Scenes from a Special*), ABC, 1982.

Fascinated, syndicated, 1983.

The Presidential Inaugural Gala, 1989.

Host, *Your Skin and How to Save It,* CNBC and WGN, 1995.

50 Years of Television: A Celebration of the Academy of Television Arts and Sciences Golden Anniversary, HBO, 1997.

Television Work; Executive Producer; Specials:

Cheryl Ladd . . . Looking Back—Souvenirs (also known as *Cheryl Ladd—Souvenirs* and *Looking Back: Souvenirs*), ABC, 1980.

Television Appearances; Awards Presentations:

The Twelfth Annual People's Choice Awards (also known as *The People's Choice Awards* and *The 12th Annual People's Choice Awards*), 1986.

Host, *The 44th Annual Golden Globe Awards,* 1987.

Presenter, *The 48th Annual Golden Globe Awards,* 1991.

Presenter, *The 18th Annual People's Choice Awards* (also known as *The People's Choice Awards*), CBS, 1992.

Presenter, *The 18th Annual CableACE Awards,* TNT, 1996.

Television Appearances; Pilots:

Dr. Dawn "Holli" Holliday, *One West Waikiki,* CBS, 1994.

RECORDINGS

Albums:
Cheryl Ladd, Capitol, 1978.
Dance Forever, Capitol, 1979.

WRITINGS

Juvenile Fiction:
(With Brian Russell) *The Adventures of Little Nettie Windship,* illustrated by Ezra Tucker and Nancy Krause, Penguin USA, 1996.

OTHER SOURCES

Periodicals:
Barron's, February 1, 1993, p. 62.
Drug Topics, April 10, 1995, p. 34.
Entertainment Weekly, August 5, 1994, pp. 42-43; August 19, 1994, p. 50.
People Weekly, June 9, 1997, pp. 67-68.
Redbook, July, 1994, pp. 70-74.*

LAGERFELT, Caroline

PERSONAL

Born September 23, in Paris, France; daughter of Baron Karl-Gustav Israel (an ambassador) and Mary Charmian Sara Chapion (maiden name, de Crespigny) Lagerfelt. *Education:* Sigtuna Stiftelsens Humanistiska Larouerket, Sigtuna, Sweden; studied acting at the American Academy of Dramatic Arts.

Addresses: *Agent*-Schiffman, Ekman, Morrision, Marx, Inc., 22 West 19th St., 8th Floor, New York, NY 10011.

Career: Actress. The Guthrie Theater, member of acting company, Minneapolis, MN, 1987-88; volunteer, Children's Village, Dobbs Ferry, NY.

Member: Actors' Equity Association (council), American Academy of Dramatic Arts Alumni Association (president).

Awards, Honors: Villager Downtown Award, 1982, for *The Sea Anchor;* Obie Award, *Village Voice,* 1983, for *Quartermaine's Terms.*

CREDITS

Stage Appearances:
Anita, *Quartermaine's Terms,* Playhouse 91, New York City, 1983.
The Wall of Water (part of *Winterfest 8: Four New Plays in Repertory*), Yale Repertory Theatre, New Haven, CT, 1988.
Governor's wife, *Phaedre Britannica,* CSC Repertory, New York City, 1988-89.
Diana, *Lend Me a Tenor,* Royale Theatre, New York City, 1989-90.
Izz, *Swim Visit,* Primary Stages, New York City, 1990.
Anita, *A Small Family Business,* Music Box Theatre, New York City, 1992.
Tekla, *Creditors,* CSC Theater, New York City, 1992.
Suzanne, *Don't Dress for Dinner,* Paper Mill Playhouse, Millburn, NJ, 1992.
The Misanthrope, Long Wharf Theatre, New Haven, CT, 1993.
Simone, *The Workroom,* American Jewish Theatre, New York City, 1993.
Death Takes a Holiday, Lobero Theater, Santa Barbara, CA, 1997.

Also appeared as Liz, *The Philanthropist,* New York City; *Four on a Garden,* New York City; Lady Ursula Itchin, *The Jockey Club Stakes,* New York City; Marie-Louise, *The Constant Wife,* New York City; Beth, *Otherwise Engaged,* New York City; Emma, *Betrayal,* New York City; Annie, *The Real Thing,* New York City; Gila/Pauline, *Other Places,* Manhattan Theatre Club, New York City; Edward/Victoria, *Cloud 9,* Manhattan Theatre Club; Jean, *The Sea Anchor,* Open Space, New York City; Margaret, *Close of Play,* Manhattan Theatre Club; Alison, *Look Back in Anger,* Manhattan Theatre Club; Ruth Carson, *Night and Day,* Huntington Theatre, Boston, MA; Monika Stettler, *The Physicists,* Kennedy Center for the Performing Arts, Washington, DC; Mary, *Vanities,* George Street Playhouse, New Brunswick, NJ; Gwendolyn, *The Importance of Being Earnest,* Pittsburgh Public Theatre, Pittsburgh, PA; Judith, *The Devil's Disciple,* Meadow Brook Theatre, Rochester, MI; Anita, *Quartermaine's Terms,* Long Wharf Theatre; and Clarissa, *Spider's Web,* Nassau Repertory.

Major Tours:
Appeared in as Sally Boothroyd, *Lloyd George Knew My Father;* Beatrice, *To Grandmother's House We Go;* Sister Margaret, *The Hasty Heart;* and Nia, *The Right Honorable Gentleman.*

Film Appearances:
Elizabeth Masters, *The Iron Eagle*, TriStar, 1986.
Sidewalk Motel, 1990.
Mother at McDonald's, *Bye Bye, Love*, Twentieth Century-Fox, 1995.
Check-in nurse, *Father of the Bride Part II* (also known as *Father of the Bride 2*), Buena Vista, 1995.

Television Appearances; Movies:
Liz Shaw, *Do You Remember Love*, CBS, 1985.
Emily Fukes, *No Way Back*, 1996.

Television Appearances; Specials:
Christina, "Home at Last," *WonderWorks*, PBS, 1988.

Television Appearances; Series:
Sheila Silver, *Beverly Hills, 90210*, Fox, 1994-95.
Inger Dominguez, *Nash Bridges*, CBS, 1996-97.

Television Appearances; Episodic:
Governess, "Haunting," *Spenser: For Hire*, ABC, 1987.
"Eighteen with a Bullet," *The Equalizer*, CBS, 1988.
Mary Ann Miller, "But Now a Word from Our Sponsor," *Murphy Brown*, CBS, 1990.
"Black Tie," *Law and Order*, NBC, 1993.
Kitty Lear, "Good Time Charlie," *NYPD Blue*, ABC, 1994.
Nurse Holder, *Chicago Hope*, CBS, 1994.
Andrea, *ER*, NBC, 1994.
Mary Beiler, *Picket Fences*, CBS, 1995.
Makbar, "Tribunal," *Star Trek: Deep Space Nine*, syndicated, 1995.
Mrs. Hoyt, "Atomic Cat Fight," *The Drew Carey Show*, ABC, 1996.

Also appeared in *Archie Bunker's Place*, *The Twilight Zone*, *T.J. Hooker*, *The Guiding Light*, and *The Edge of Night*.*

LAUER, Andy

PERSONAL

Born June 19, in Los Angeles, CA. *Education:* Attended San Diego State University; attended University of New Hampshire.

Addresses: *Contact*—CBS Entertainment, 4024 Radford Ave., Bungalow 3, Studio City, CA 91604.

Career: Actor. Worked as a busboy at the Friar's Club; worked with the improvisational group, The Groundlings, and with L.A. Connection.

Awards, Honors: Emmy Award nomination, 1989, for *21 Jump Street*.

CREDITS

Television Appearances; Series:
Charlie Moran, *Going to Extremes*, ABC, 1992-93.
Charlie, *Caroline in the City*, NBC, 1995—.

Television Appearances; Episodic:
Appeared in episodes of *21 Jump Street*, *Gabby*, *Matlock*, *Grand*, *thirtysomething*, and *Murder, She Wrote*.

Film Appearances:
Corpsman on battlefield, *For the Boys*, Twentieth Century-Fox, 1991.
Ace, *Screamers*, Triumph, 1996.

Also appeared in *Never on Tuesday*, *The Doors*, *Born on the Fourth of July*, and *Necessary Roughness*.*

LAWRENCE, Sharon   1961(?)-

PERSONAL

Born June 29, 1961 (some sources say 1962), in Charlotte, NC; daughter of Tom (a television news reporter) and Earlyn (a Head Start supervisor) Lawrence; *Education:* University of North Carolina, Chapel Hill, B.A. (journalism), 1983. *Avocational interests:* Singing.

Addresses: *Agent*—c/o Joel Shire, International Creative Management, 8942 Wilshire Blvd., Beverly Hills, CA 90211. *Manager*—c/o Hyler Management, 25 Sea Colony Dr., Santa Monica, CA 90405. *Publicist*—c/o 1888 Century Park East, fifth floor, Los Angeles, CA 90067.

Career: Actress and producer.

Member: Belongs to an investment group for women.

Awards, Honors: Emmy Award nominations, outstanding supporting actress in a drama series, 1995 and 1996, and Screen Actors Guild Award nomination, outstanding performance by a female actor in a drama series, 1996, all for *N.Y.P.D. Blue*. Named Junior Miss in Raleigh, NC.

CREDITS

Stage Appearances:
Panache, off-Broadway, 1984.
Member of kissing couple and member of ensemble, *Cabaret,* Imperial Theatre, New York City, 1987, later Minskoff Theatre, New York City, 1988.
Tzeitel, *Fiddler on the Roof,* San Francisco, CA, 1989, later Gershwin Theatre, New York City, 1990.

Also appeared in *Berlin in Light.*

Major Tours:
Katina and cafe prostitute, *Zorba,* U.S. cities, including John F. Kennedy Center for the Performing Arts, Washington, DC, 1984, and Westbury Music Fair, Westbury, NY, 1986.
Member of kissing couple and member of ensemble, *Cabaret,* U.S. cities, including Playhouse Theatre, Wilmington, DE, 1987.

Television Appearances; Series:
Assistant district attorney Sylvia Costas, *N.Y.P.D. Blue,* ABC, 1994-97.
Gwen Leonard, *Fired Up* (also known as *Fired*), NBC, 1997—.

Television Appearances; Episodic:
Beverly Hills, 90210, Fox, 1991.
Civil Wars, ABC, 1992.
Rachel, "The Guy Can't Help It," *Cheers,* NBC, 1993.
Amelia Earhart, "The 37s," *Star Trek: Voyager,* UPN, 1995.
Employment counselor, *Caroline in the City,* NBC, 1996.
Contestant, "Celebrity Tournament," *Jeopardy!,* syndicated, 1997.

Television Appearances; Movies:
In the Line of Duty: The Price of Vengeance, 1994.
Sharon, *Someone She Knows,* 1994.
Beth, *The Shaggy Dog,* 1994.
Jill, *The Heidi Chronicles,* TNT, 1995.
Sada Sands, *The Face on the Milk Carton,* 1995.
Nina, *A Friend's Betrayal* (also known as *Stolen Youth*), 1996.
Clair Ballard, *Five Desperate Hours,* 1997.

Television Appearances; Miniseries:
Mary Carelli, *Degree of Guilt,* 1995.

Film Appearances:
Joleen Quillet, *The Only Thrill* (also known as *Tennessee Valley*), 1997.

OTHER SOURCES

Periodicals:
Entertainment Weekly, April 11, 1997, p. 69.
People Weekly, October 17, 1994, pp. 67-68.
TV Guide, May 20-26, 1995, pp. 18-20.*

LeBLANC, Matt

PERSONAL

Born July 25.

Addresses: *Contact*—11766 Wilshire Blvd., No. 1470, Los Angeles, CA 90025.

Career: Actor. Began his career acting in commercials.

CREDITS

Television Appearances; Series:
Chuck Bender, *TV 101,* CBS, 1988-89.
Vinnie Verducci, *Top of the Heap,* Fox, 1991.
Vinnie Verducci, *Vinnie & Bobby,* Fox, 1992.
Joey Tribbiani, *Friends,* NBC, 1994—.

Television Appearances; Episodic:
"Just Like That," *Red Shoe Diaries,* Showtime, 1992.

Television Appearances; Movies:
Motorcycle Gang, Showtime, 1994.
Vince, *Reform School Girl,* Showtime, 1994.

Television Appearances; Specials:
Comic Relief VII, HBO, 1995.

Television Appearances; Awards Presentations:
The 47th Annual Primetime Emmy Awards, Fox, 1995.
The 22nd Annual People's Choice Awards, CBS, 1996.

Film Appearances:
Cooper, *Ed* (also known as *Ed and Me, Mickey's Monkey,* and *You Should See Them Play*), Universal, 1996.

Also appeared in *The Ghost Brigade,* 1993; Anthony Manetti, *Lookin' Italian,* 1994; and *Anything to Survive.* *

LEE, William
    See BURROUGHS, William S.

LEE, Willy
    See BURROUGHS, William S.

LEEVES, Jane   1962-

PERSONAL

Born April 18, 1962, in London, England; daughter of Colin (an engineer) and Ruth (a nurse) Leeves.

Addresses: *Contact*—9560 Wilshire Blvd., No. 516, Beverly Hills, CA 90212.

Career: Actress. Began career as a ballet dancer; also worked as a model and as a dancer in commercials and music videos.

Awards, Honors: Golden Globe Award nomination, best supporting actress in a series, miniseries, or motion picture made for television, 1995, for *Frasier.*

CREDITS

Television Appearances; Series:
Blue (Prudence Anne Bartlett), *Throb,* syndicated, 1986-88.
Daphne Moon, *Frasier,* NBC, 1993—.

Also appeared as Audrey Cohen, *Murphy Brown,* CBS; appeared in *The Benny Hill Show.*

Television Appearances; Miniseries:
Narrator, and voice of Adrienne Corri, *Sex and the Silver Screen* (documentary), Showtime, 1996.
Rachel Sherwood, *Pandora's Clock,* NBC, 1996.
Voice of Caroline Webb, *The Great War and the Shaping of the 20th Century* (documentary), PBS, 1996.

Television Appearances; Pilots:
Annie Ballin, *The Gregory Harrison Show,* CBS, 1989.
Amy, *Just Deserts,* ABC, 1992.

Television Appearances; Episodic:
Marla, *Seinfeld,* NBC, 1992.
Daphne, *Caroline in the City,* NBC, 1995.

Television Appearances; Specials:
The Golden Globe's 50th Anniversary Celebration, NBC, 1994.
Host, *Christmas in Washington,* NBC, 1995.
Star Trek: 30 Years and Beyond, UPN, 1996.

Television Appearances; Awards Presentations:
Host, *The 12th Annual Soap Opera Awards,* NBC, 1996.
The 48th Annual Primetime Emmy Awards, ABC, 1996.
The 53rd Annual Golden Globe Awards, NBC, 1996.

Film Appearances:
Alberta Leonard, *Miracle on 34th Street,* Twentieth Century-Fox, 1994.
Wylie, *Mr. Write,* Shapiro Glickenhaus Entertainment, 1994.
Voice of Ladybug, *James and the Giant Peach,* Buena Vista, 1996.

Also appeared as Serena, *To Live and Die in L.A.,* 1985; appeared in *The Meaning of Life* and *The Hunger.* *

LEITCH, Ione Skye
    See SKYE, Ione

LEWIS, Geoffrey   1935-

PERSONAL

Born January 1, 1935, in San Diego, CA; children: Deirdre (an actress), Lightfield (an actor), Juliette (an actress), Peter (an actor). *Religion:* Church of Scientology.

Addresses: *Agent*—William Morris Agency, 151 El Camino Dr., Beverly Hills, CA, 90212. *Manager*—Joel Stevens Entertainment, 1325 6th Ave., New York, NY, 10019.

Career: Actor. Member of Celestial Navigations, a group performing spoken-word pieces.

CREDITS

Television Appearances; Series:
Earl Tucker, *Flo,* CBS, 1979-80.

Barney Broomick, *Bret Maverick,* NBC, 1981-82.

Amos, *Gun Shy,* CBS, 1983.

Frank Murphy, *Maximum Security,* 1984-85.

Harry, *The Oldest Rookie,* CBS, 1987-88.

Cast, *The Smothers Brothers Comedy Hour,* CBS, 1988-89.

Beau Langley, *Walker, Texas Ranger,* CBS, 1994-95.

Willis P. Dunleevy, *Land's End,* syndicated, 1995-96.

Television Appearances; Miniseries:

Bishop Fisher, *The Six Wives of Henry VIII,* 1971.

Ed Duncan, *Attack on Terror: The FBI versus the Ku Klux Klan* (also known as *Attack on Terror: The FBI vs. the Ku Klux Klan*), 1975.

Sheriff Bogardus, *Centennial,* 1978.

Mike Ryerson, *Salem's Lot* (also known as *Blood Thirst, Salem's Lot: The Miniseries,* and *Salem's Lot: The Movie*), 1979.

Lynch, *The Gambler V: Playing For Keeps* (also known as *The Gambler 5: Playing for Keeps*), CBS, 1994.

Eli, *Rough Riders* (also known as *Teddy Roosevelt and the Rough Riders*), TNT, 1997.

Television Appearances; Specials:

Koup, *Skyward Christmas,* 1981.

Rudy Hopper, *Poor Richard,* 1984.

Bill, *NBC Presents the AFI Comedy Special,* NBC, 1987.

Andy Johnson, *The Johnsons Are Home,* 1988.

Pirate story teller, *Disney's Greatest Hits on Ice,* CBS, 1994.

Television Appearances; Movies:

Lawrence Burrifors, *Moon of the Wolf,* 1972.

Roper, *Honky Tonk,* 1974.

Archie, *The Great Ice Rip-Off,* 1974.

The Gun and the Pulpit, 1974.

Dr. Crandon, *The Great Houdinis* (also known as *The Great Houdini*), 1976.

Dutton, *The New Daughters of Joshua Cabe,* 1976.

Red Bayliss, *The Deadly Triangle,* 1977.

Mr. Eckert, *The Hunted Lady,* 1977.

Albert Cavanaugh, *When Every Day Was the Fourth of July,* 1978.

Harold Tigner, *Samurai,* 1979.

Dr. Bill Janowski, *The Jericho Mile,* 1979.

Reverend Meeks, *Belle Starr,* 1980.

Captain Charley Rawlins, *Life of the Party: The Story of Beatrice,* 1982.

Major Ashbury, *Louis L'Amour's The Shadow Riders* (also known as *The Shadow Riders*), 1982.

Sheriff Bill Johnson, *September Gun,* 1983.

Janus, *The Return of the Man From U.N.C.L.E.,* 1983.

John Tuckerman, *Travis McGee* (also known as *Travis McGee: The Empty Copper Sea*), 1983.

Scooter Lee, *Stormin' Home,* 1985.

Ed Porter, *Dallas: The Early Years* (also known as *The Early Years*), CBS, 1986.

Professor Alan Jeffries, *The Annihilator,* NBC, 1986.

Dirty Jerry, *Spot Marks the X,* 1986.

Del Rains, *Desert Rats,* NBC, 1988.

Ben Catlin, *Pancho Barnes* (also known as *The Happy Bottom Riding Club* and *The Pancho Barnes Story*), CBS, 1988.

Oliver Ostrow, *Desperado: The Outlaw Wars,* NBC, 1989.

Bodine, *Gunsmoke: The Last Apache* (also known as *Gunsmoke II: The Last Apache*), CBS, 1990.

Frank Harper, *Matters of the Heart,* USA Network, 1990.

Matt Corman, *Day of Reckoning* (also known as *The Wisdom Keeper*), NBC, 1994.

J. D., *Kansas,* ABC, 1995.

Parmenter, *When the Dark Man Calls,* USA Network, 1995.

Draper Jewett, *An Occasional Hell,* HBO, 1996.

Stubbs, *Trilogy of Terror II,* USA Network, 1996.

Television Appearances; Episodic:

Rogers, "A Matter of Faith," *Bonanza,* NBC, 1959.

"The Russell Incident," *The Young Lawyers,* ABC, 1970.

"The Bounty Hunter," *Alias Smith and Jones,* ABC, 1971.

George, "To Kill a Guinea Pig," *Cannon,* CBS, 1972.

Harris, "School of Fear," *The Streets of San Francisco,* ABC, 1972.

"What Happened at the XST?," *Alias Smith and Jones,* ABC, 1972.

"Chains," *Kung Fu,* ABC, 1972.

Kaye Lusk, "Committed," *Mission: Impossible,* CBS, 1972.

Proctor, "Kidnap," *Mission: Impossible,* CBS, 1972.

James Bancroft, "Nobody Beats the House," *Cannon,* CBS, 1972.

Senator John Elton, "Mayday," *Harry O,* ABC, 1975.

"The Killing Ground," *S.W.A.T.,* ABC, 1975.

"Mirror Image," *Hunter,* CBS, 1977.

"Hallie," *Bret Maverick,* NBC, 1981.

"A Clear and Present Danger," *Blue Thunder,* ABC, 1984.

Lloyd DeWitt, "The Return of Luther Gillis," *Magnum, P.I.,* CBS, 1984.

Kale Sykes, "Semi-Friendly Persuasion," *The A Team,* NBC, 1984.

Cooper, "The Middle of Somewhere," *Shadow Chasers,* ABC, 1985.

Peter Sacker, "Utopia Now," *Scarecrow and Mrs. King,* CBS, 1985.

Gus Zimmer, "I Never Wanted to Go to France, Anyway," *Magnum, P.I.,* CBS, 1985.

Stoddard, "The Doctor is Out," *The A Team,* NBC, 1985.

"Until The Fat Lady Sings," *Wildside,* ABC, 1985.

"Silent World," *MacGyver,* ABC, 1986.

Kenny Oats, "Who Threw the Barbitals in Mrs. Fletcher's Chowder?," *Murder, She Wrote,* CBS, 1987.

Lester Grinshaw, "No Accounting for Murder," *Murder, She Wrote,* CBS, 1987.

Film Appearances:

Motel owner, *Welcome Home, Soldier Boys,* 1971.

Hobbs, a gang member, *Bad Company,* 1972.

Russ Sterve, *The Culpepper Cattle Company* (also known as *The Culpepper Cattle Co.*), Twentieth Century-Fox, 1972.

Harry Pierpoint, *Dillinger,* 1973.

Stacey Bridges, *High Plains Drifter,* Universal, 1973.

My Name is Nobody (also known as *Il Mio Nome e Nessuno*), 1973.

Goody, *Thunderbolt and Lightfoot,* 1974.

Hamp, *Macon County Line,* 1974.

Damion Gummere, *The Wind and the Lion,* United Artists, 1975.

Captain Aaron Mosely, *Lucky Lady,* 1975.

Wilson Shears, *Smile,* 1975.

Newt, *The Great Waldo Pepper,* Universal, 1975.

Zenas Morro, *The Return of a Man Called Horse,* United Artists, 1976.

Orville Boggs, *Every Which Way but Loose,* Warner Bros., 1978.

Doubletten-Snake, *Sella d'argento,* 1978.

Truck driver, *Tilt,* 1979.

Walter Stoll, *Tom Horn,* 1980.

Dr. Kline, *Human Experiments* (also known as *Beyond the Gate*), Crown, 1980.

Trapper, *Heaven's Gate* (also known as *Johnson County Wars*), United Artists, 1980.

John Arlington, *Bronco Billy,* 1980.

Orville Boggs, *Any Which Way You Can,* Warner Bros., 1980.

Shoot the Sun Down, 1981.

Joe Butler, *I, the Jury,* 1982.

Dave Dante, *Ten to Midnight* (also known as *10 to Midnight*), Cannon, 1983.

Carter, *Night of the Comet,* 1984.

Hard Case Williams, *Lust in the Dust,* 1985.

Ralph Rizzo, *Stitches,* 1985.

Smith, *Time Out,* 1987.

Mr. Johnson, *Catch Me If You Can,* 1989.

Ku Klux Klan leader, *Fletch Lives,* Universal, 1989.

Dennis, *Out of the Dark,* 1989.

Ricky Z, *Pink Cadillac,* Warner Bros., 1989.

Captain Schroeder, *Tango & Cash,* Warner Bros., 1989.

Paint It Black, 1990.

Michael Kahn, *Disturbed,* LIVE Home Video, 1991.

Frank Avery, *Double Impact,* Columbia, 1991.

Terry McKeen, *The Lawnmower Man* (also known as *Stephen King's the Lawnmower Man*), New Line Cinema, 1992.

Hitchcock, *Wishman,* 1992.

Drugstore owner, *Point of No Return* (also known as *The Assassin, La Femme Nikita, Nikita,* and *The Specialist*), Warner Bros., 1993.

Chief Stark, *The Man Without a Face,* Warner Bros., 1993.

Matthew Wicker, *Maverick,* Warner Bros., 1994.

Uncle Rex, *National Lampoon's Last Resort* (also known as *National Lampoon's Scuba School*), Rose & Ruby, 1994.

The Dragon Gate, 1994.

Heath, *White Fang II: Myth of the White Wolf* (also known as *White Fang 2: Myth of the White Wolf*), Buena Vista, 1994.

Cyclops Baby, 1996.

Willy, *American Perfekt,* American Perfekt Productions, Inc., 1997.

Luther Driggers, *Midnight in the Garden of Good and Evil,* Warner Bros., 1997.

Stage Appearances:

Celestial Navigations, Matrix Theatre, Los Angeles, CA, 1984.

RECORDINGS

Albums; With Celestial Navigations:

Chapter II, K-tel International, 1989.

WRITINGS

Screenplays:

The Janitor, 1993.*

LIPNICKI, Jonathan William   1990-

PERSONAL

Born October 22, 1990, in Westlake Village, CA; son of Joe Lipnicki.

Addresses: *Contact*—Brillstein-Grey, 9150 Wilshire Blvd., Suite 350, Beverly Hills, CA 90212.

Career: Actor. Began career acting in commercials.

CREDITS

Film Appearances:
Ray Boyd, *Jerry Maguire,* TriStar, 1996.

Television Appearances; Series:
Justin Foxworthy, *The Jeff Foxworthy Show,* NBC, 1996-97.
Alex Parker, *Meego,* CBS, 1997.

Television Appearances; Awards Presentations:
The 11th Annual American Comedy Awards, ABC, 1997.*

M-N

MARNO, Anne
    See BANCROFT, Anne

MITCHELL, Keith
    See COOGAN, Keith

MITCHUM, Robert   1917-1997

OBITUARY NOTICE—See index for *CTFT* sketch: Full name, Robert Charles Duran Mitchum; born August 6, 1917, in Bridgeport, CT; died of emphysema and lung cancer, July 1, 1997, in Santa Barbara, CA. Actor, director, writer. During his lengthy show business career, Mitchum was a major star who was cast in more than 125 films, often in tough-guy roles. A writer for *CNN Interactive* called him "a rugged leading man and sometime bad boy who defined cool before Hollywood knew what it was." Mitchum's talents allowed him to take on a variety of roles, from villains and heroic soldiers to Old West lawmen and psychotic killers. According to the *Washington Post*, "Mitchum, known for his self-deprecating humor, described himself as a 'poet with an ax.' He said that 'when producers have a part that's hard to cast, they say "Send for Mitchum; he'll do anything."' He seemed to agree, saying 'I don't care what I play; I'll play Polish gays, women, midgets, anything.'"

Born in Connecticut, Mitchum lived for a time in New York City before he left home at the age of twelve. In performed a variety of odd jobs, including work in a local theater as a stagehand, director, and actor, as well as work as a aircraft assembler, deckhand, ditch digger, nightclub bouncer, shoe salesman, coal miner, boxer, and radio script writer.

He was also arrested for vagrancy in Georgia at age sixteen and was sentenced to time on a chain gang.

His first film work began in the 1940s as he was signed to appear in westerns featuring Hopalong Cassidy. In 1943 alone he made more than a dozen films. The decade also saw Mitchum in movies such as *Thirty Seconds Over Toyko, Holiday Affair,* and *The Story of G.I. Joe.* He was nominated for an Academy Award for best supporting actor for the last film. The decade also ended with Mitchum in trouble again with the law. He was arrested on charges of marijuana possession and served two months on a prison honor farm. "The drug charge could have destroyed some careers, but at the time it enhanced his image as a rebel," reported the *New York Times.* In the 1950s he starred in motion pictures such as *Heaven Knows, Mr. Allison, Fire Down Below,* and *The Wonderful Country.* In 1962 he appeared as a psychotic killer in *Cape Fear,* and he later made a cameo appearance in the 1991 remake starring Robert De Niro. Other 1960s appearances included roles in *The Sundowners, What a Way to Go!, El Dorado,* and *Five Card Stud.* In the 1970s and 1980s he worked in movies such as *Ryan's Daughter, The Friends of Eddie Coyle, The Last Tycoon, Scrooged,* and *That Championship Season.* His later work included the opening narration in the western *Tombstone,* starring Kurt Russell and Val Kilmer, and a role in *Dead Man.* Mitchum also made television appearances in the miniseries *The Winds of War, War and Remembrance,* and *North and South,* and he appeared on the series *A Family for Joe* and *Family Man.* "Mitchum's trademarks were his athletic 6-foot-1 frame, heavy-lidded eyes and a casual attitude that could unerringly convey either stoic heroism or devious sadism," explained a *Chicago Tribune* writer. "He parlayed these qualities, plus his instinctive gifts and unflappability, into a career playing movie tough guys of all varieties." The London *Times* surmised:

"A gift for impressionists, Mitchum was a big man with sleepy eyes, a laconic voice and drooping shoulders whose world-weary cynicism was often laced with dry humour. He could be menacing or charming and was sometimes both at once." He received a lifetime achievement award from American Theatre Arts in 1983 and a Golden Globe Lifetime Achievement Award in 1992, but never was honored with an Academy Award.

OBITUARIES AND OTHER SOURCES

Books:
Who's Who in America, Marquis Who's Who, 1995.

Periodicals:
Chicago Tribune, July 2, 1997, section 1, p. 10; July 4, 1997, section 2, p. 10.
CNN Interactive (electronic), July 1, 1997.
E! Online (electronic), July 1, 1997.
Hollywood Online (electronic), July 2, 1997.
Los Angeles Times, July 2, 1997, p. A1.
People Weekly (electronic), July 1, 1997.
New York Times (electronic), July 2, 1997.
Times (London; electronic), July 3, 1997.
USA Today, July 2, 1997, p. D1.
Washington Post, July 2, 1997, pp. B4, C1, C2.

MOORE, Cherie
    See LADD, Cheryl

MUMY, Bill 1954-

PERSONAL

Surname is pronounced "Moo-my"; born Charles William Mumy Jr., February 1, 1954, in San Gabriel, CA; son of Charles William (a cattle rancher) and Muriel Gertrude (Gould) Mumy; married Eileen Joy Davis, October 9, 1986; children: Seth, Liliana. *Education:* Attended Santa Monica City College, CA, 1972-73. *Politics:* Democrat. *Avocational interests:* Comic book collecting, racquetball, swimming, sketching.

Addresses: *Agent*—Richard Sindell and Associates, 8271 Melrose Avenue, Suite 202, Los Angeles, CA 90046.

Career: Actor, writer, and recording artist. Actor since age 6; played with America (rock band) in 1970s, also with bands Bill Mumy & The Igloos and The Jenerators; recording artist with Rhino Records, CBS Records, and Barnes & Barnes since 1980; creator and writer (with Miguel Ferrer) of comic books.

Member: Academy Motion Picture Arts and Sciences, American Society of Composers, Authors, and Publishers, Screen Actors Guild, American Federation of Musicians, American Federation of Television and Radio Artists.

Awards, Honors: Emmy Award nomination, outstanding music composition, 1992, for *Disney's Adventures in Wonderland.*

CREDITS

Film Appearances:
Neil Bateman, *Tammy, Tell Me True,* Universal, 1961.
Petey Loomis, *Sammy the Way Out Seal,* 1962.
Boom-Boom, *Palm Springs Weekend,* Warner Bros., 1963.
Alex Martin, *A Ticklish Affair,* Metro-Goldwyn-Mayer, 1963.
Child, *A Child Is Waiting,* United Artists, 1963.
Erasmus Leaf, *Dear Brigitte,* Twentieth Century-Fox, 1965.
Sterling North, *Rascal,* Buena Vista, 1969.
Teft, *Bless the Beasts and Children,* Columbia, 1971.
Lariot, *Papillon,* Allied Artists, 1973.
Weaver, *Sunshine Part II,* 1976.
Tim, "It's a Good Life" in *Twilight Zone—The Movie,* Warner Bros., 1983.
Keyboardist of the James Roberts Band, *Hard to Hold,* Universal, 1983.
Young General Fleming, *Captain America,* Columbia TriStar, 1992.
Bob, *Double Trouble,* Motion Picture Corporation of America, 1992.
Neighbor, *Three Wishes,* Savoy Pictures, 1995.

Also appeared in *The Wizard of Bagdad.*

Film Work:
Artist, writer, producer, *Zabagabee* (video), 1987.

Television Appearances; Series:
Voice of Matty Matel, *Matty's Funday Funnies* (animated), ABC, 1959-61.
Will Robinson, *Lost in Space,* CBS, 1965-68.
Weaver, *Sunshine,* NBC, 1974-75.
Host, *Inside Space,* 1992-97.
Lennier, *Babylon 5,* syndicated, 1994—.

Television Appearances; Pilots:
Chris Williams, *The Two of Us,* CBS, 1966.
Nick Butler, *The Rockford Files,* NBC, 1974.
Larry, *Archie,* ABC, 1976.

Also appeared as Will Robinson, *Space Family Robinson.*

Television Appearances; Episodic:
Anthony Fremont, "It's a Good Life," *The Twilight Zone,* CBS, 1960.
Billy Bayles, "Long Distance Call," *The Twilight Zone,* CBS, 1961.
Jackie Chester, "Bang! You're Dead," *Alfred Hitchcock Presents,* NBC, 1961.
Mickey Hollins, "The Door without a Key," *Alfred Hitchcock Presents,* CBS, 1962.
"The Sam Darland Story," *Wagon Train,* NBC, 1962.
Pip, "In Praise of Pip," *The Twilight Zone,* CBS, 1963.
Michael, "A Vision of Sugar Plums," *Bewitched,* ABC, 1964.
The Virginian, NBC, 1964.
Custer, "Whatever Became of Baby Custer?," *I Dream of Jeannie,* NBC, 1965.
Darrin as a boy, "Junior Executive," *Bewitched,* ABC, 1965.
Googie, "Come Back, Little Googie," *The Munsters,* CBS, 1965.
Trask, "Aura Lee, Farewell," *The Rockford Files,* NBC, 1975.
Clerk, "Bang! You're Dead," *Alfred Hitchcock Presents,* NBC, 1985.
Dr. Irwin Bruckner, "The Genius," *Matlock,* NBC, 1986.
Doctor Irwin Bruckner, *Matlock,* NBC, 1988.
Roger Braintree, "Goodnight, Central City," *The Flash,* CBS, 1991.
Voice of farmer, *Animaniacs,* Fox, 1993.
Interviewee, *Space Ghost Coast to Coast,* Cartoon Network, 1994.
A Fernaherna, "A Day in the Life," *Space Cases,* Nickelodeon, 1996.
Delivery guy, "Back to School," *The Weird Al Show,* CBS, 1997.

Appeared in his debut on *Romper Room,* syndicated; also on *Lancer,* CBS; *Here Come the Brides,* ABC; *Riverboat,* NBC; *Have Gun, Will Travel,* CBS; *The Adventures of Ozzie and Harriet,* ABC; *Ben Casey,* ABC; *Playhouse 90,* CBS; *The Red Skelton Show; The Tennessee Ernie Ford Show; The Loretta Young Show; Dr. Kildare; Me and Mom;* and *Superboy.*

Television Appearances; Movies:
Weaver, *Sunshine,* CBS, 1973.
Weaver, *Sunshine Christmas,* NBC, 1977.

Television Work:
Additional music, *Disney's Adventures in Wonderland,* Disney Channel, 1992.
Creator (with Peter David), *Space Cases,* Nickelodeon, 1996-97.

RECORDINGS

Albums:
Bill Mumy, 'BB,' 1980.
Dying to be Heard, Renaissance, 1997.

Songs recorded include, "Fish Heads," "Love Tap," "Soak It Up," and "Pizza Face."

Albums; With America (rock Band); as Musician:
View from the Ground, Capitol, 1982.
Encore: More Greatest Hits, Warner Bros., 1991.

Albums; Other:
Choir, *Which One of Us Is Me,* by Jay Gruska, Rhino, 1984.
Musician, *Loozanteen,* with Barnes & Barnes (rock group), Rhino, 1991.

WRITINGS

(With Miguel Ferrer) *Comet Man* (comic book), Marvel Comics, 1986.

Also wrote (with Miguel Ferrer) *Trip to the Acid Dog; Star Trek* (3 issues); *Lost In Space* (4 issues), Innovation; *The Hulk;* and *Spiderman.*

OTHER SOURCES

Periodicals:
People Weekly, July 17, 1995, pp. 46-47.*

NEILL, Jeffery K. 1938-

PERSONAL

Born John Neal Phillips, April 26, 1938, in Indianapolis, IN; son of Audrian Neal (a farmer) and Chloe Zora (a model; maiden name, Jones) Phillips.

Addresses: *Home*—57 West 75th Street, New York, NY 10023.

Career: Director and choreographer.

Member: Actors' Equity Association, Society of Stage Directors and Choreographers.

CREDITS

Stage Work; Director and choreographer:
All My Sons, New York City, 1958.
Countdown, New York City, 1959.
Finian's Rainbow, New York City, 1962.
Can-Can, Enchanted Hills, Syracuse, IN, 1962.
Girl Crazy, Enchanted Hills, 1962.
The Music Man, Enchanted Hills, 1962.
Silk Stockings, Enchanted Hills, 1962.
Will the Mail Train Run Tonight?, Enchanted Hills, 1962.
Fiorello, New York City, 1964.
Pajama Game, New York City, 1965.
Sabrina Fair, New York City, 1966.
Bells Are Ringing, New York City, 1966.
Archy and Mehitabel, New York City, 1967.
Once Upon a Mattress, New York City, 1968.
Gentlemen Prefer Blondes, New York City, 1969.
Love and Marriage, New York City, 1969.
Eat Your Spinach, Baby, Cookes Tavern, CT, 1970.
Say It with Music, Cookes Tavern, 1970.
Darling Eileen, Cookes Tavern, 1970.
Judy Garland Story, Pig 'n Whistle, NY, 1970.
Kiss Me Kate, Pig 'n Whistle, 1970.
Pajama Game, Pig 'n Whistle, 1970.
Goldilocks, New York City, 1971.
Hello, Dolly!, Club Bene, NJ, 1971.
Ernest in Love, New York City, 1971.
Camelot, Camelback Summer Theater, Tannersville, PA, 1971-72.
Charlie Brown, Camelback Summer Theater, 1971-72.
Fantasticks, Camelback Summer Theater, 1971-72.
Fiddler on the Roof, Camelback Summer Theater, 1971-72.
Guys and Dolls, Camelback Summer Theater, 1971-72.
I Do! I Do!, Camelback Summer Theater, 1971-72.
Kiss Me Kate, Camelback Summer Theater, 1971-72.
Little Mary Sunshine, Camelback Summer Theater, 1971-72.
Man of La Mancha, Camelback Summer Theater, 1971-72.

First Impressions, New York City, 1972.
Gypsy, New York City, 1972.
One for the Money, New York City, 1972.
Antiques, New York City, 1973.
Company, New York City, 1973.
Mame, New York City, 1973.
Only an Orphan Girl, New York City, 1973.
Plaza Suite, Amber Lantern, NY, 1973.
Kiss Me Kate, New York City, 1974 and 1983.
Judy: A Garland of Songs, New York City, 1974.
The Pirate, New York City, 1974.
Can-Can, New York City, 1975.
Ape Over Broadway, New York City, 1975.
Let's Face It, New York City, 1977.
Happy Hunting, New York City, 1977.
Tune the Grand Up, Lincoln Center, New York City, 1978.
Reunion, New York City, 1978.
Judy: A Garland of Songs, New York City, 1978.
Say It with Music, New York City, 1978-79.
Unsinkable Molly Brown, Canal Fulton, Carousel, OH, 1978.
No, No, Nanette, Carousel, OH, 1979.
Funny Girl, Carousel, OH, 1979.
The Constant Wife, New York City, 1979.
Anything Goes, New York City, 1979.
Anything Goes, Bakersfield Community Theater, CA, 1979.
Side by Side by Sondheim, Bakersfield Community Theater, 1980.
Gypsy, Starlight Theater of Kern, Bakersfield, CA, 1980.
Irma La Douce, New York City, 1980.
The Mousetrap, Chatham Players, 1981.
Applause, Chatham Players, 1981.
Carnival, New York City, 1981.
Guys and Dolls, Resorts International Hotel, Atlantic City, NJ, 1981.
Oklahoma!, Naples Dinner Theater, FL, 1981.
Love and Marriage, Donnell Library, New York City, 1982.
The Women, New York City, 1982.
West Side Story, Three Little Bakers Dinner Theatre, 1982.
The King and I, Three Little Bakers Dinner Theatre, 1982.
Babes in Arms, Three Little Bakers Dinner Theatre, 1982.
Do I Hear a Waltz?, Three Little Bakers Dinner Theatre, 1982.
Once Upon a Mattress, Three Little Bakers Dinner Theatre, 1983.
Fiddler on the Roof, Three Little Bakers Dinner Theatre, 1983.

Fabulous 40s Radio Show, Three Little Bakers Dinner Theatre, 1983.

Annie, Three Little Bakers Dinner Theatre, 1983.

Side by Side by Sondheim, MHB Repertory, Glen Cove, NY, 1983.

She Loves Me, New York City, 1983.

Merman: Who Could Ask for Anything More, Donnell Library, New York City, 1983.

Gypsy, Three Little Bakers Dinner Theatre, 1984.

Judy: A Garland of Songs, New York City, then San Francisco, CA, both 1984.

Roberta, New York City, 1985.

Silk Stockings, All Souls Church, New York City, 1986.

A Connecticut Yankee, All Souls Fellowship Hall, New York City, 1986.

Company, Unitarian Church of All Souls, New York City, 1988.

Spider's Web, All Souls Fellowship Hall, New York City, 1989.

Out of This World, All Souls Church, New York City, 1989.

Let It Ride, All Souls Players, New York City, 1991.

Dear World, All Souls Theatre, New York City 1992.

Ernest in Love, All Souls Theatre, New York City, 1994.

Also, all at Tibbits Opera House, Coldwater, MI, 1966-71, 1973-80, and 1984: *Annie Get Your Gun; Anything Goes; Any Wednesday; Babes in Arms; Barefoot in the Park; Bells Are Ringing; Brigadoon; Butterflies Are Free; Cabaret; Carousel; Camelot; Can-Can; Champagne Complex; Dames at Sea; Desert Song; Fantasticks; Fiorello; Funny Girl; George M!; Gigi; Godspell; God's Favorite; Guys and Dolls; Gypsy; H.M.S. Pinafore; Hello, Dolly!; How to Succeed; I Do! I Do!; Jesus Christ Superstar; Joseph and the Amazing Technicolor Dreamcoat; Jubilee; Kiss Me Kate; Luv; Mame; Merry Widow; Mikado; No, No, Nanette; No Sex Please, We're British; Nude with Violin; The Odd Couple; Oklahoma!; Oliver!; The Owl and the Pussycat; Play It Again, Sam; Promises, Promises; Same Time, Next Year; Showboat; 6 Rms Riv Vu; 1776; Sleuth; The Sound of Music; South Pacific; Stop the World I Want to Get Off; Student Prince; Sweet Charity; The Bat; The King and I; The Mousetrap; Three Men on a Horse; Under the Gaslight; The Unsinkable Molly Brown; West Side Story; Write Me a Murder; Wonderful Town;* and *Vanities.*

Major Tours:

Gypsy, U.S. cities, 1985.*

NICASTRO, Michelle   1960-

PERSONAL

Born March 31, 1960, in Washington, DC; daughter of Norman Joseph (an ophthalmologist) and Carole Rose (Guarino) Nicastro. *Education:* Northwestern University, B.F.A., 1982; studied acting with Bud Beyer and Alice Spivak. *Avocational interests:* Foreign travel, French, singing.

Addresses: *Agent*—David Shapira and Associates, 15301 Ventura Blvd., Suite 345, Sherman Oaks, CA 91403.

Career: Actress and singer.

Awards, Honors: Sarah Siddons, 1978, for vocal competition.

CREDITS

Stage Appearances:

Ariadne, *Merlin,* Mark Hellinger, New York City, 1982-83.

Anne Egerman, *A Little Night Music,* Center Theatre Group, Ahmanson Theatre, Los Angeles, CA, 1990.

Barry Manilow's Show Stoppers, Paramount Theatre, New York City, 1992.

Unsung Musicals, Sylvia and Danny Kaye Playhouse, New York City, 1994.

Appeared in her debut as Chava, *Fiddler on the Roof,* Candlelight Dinner Playhouse, Chicago, IL.

Film Appearances:

Darlene, *Body Rock,* New World Pictures, 1984.

Janice Edwards, *Bad Guys,* InterPictures, 1986.

Amanda, *When Harry Met Sally,* Columbia, 1989.

Voice of Princess Odette, *The Swan Princess* (animated), New Line, 1994.

Voice of Princess Odette, *The Swan Princess: Escape from Castle Mountain* (animated), Legacy Releasing/Nest Entertainment, 1997.

Television Appearances; Series:

Diana Barstow, *Maggie Briggs* (also known as *Suzanne Pleshette Is Maggie Briggs*), CBS, 1984.

Sasha Roberts, *Days of Our Lives,* NBC, 1987.

Sasha Schmidt, *Santa Barbara,* NBC, 1989-90.

Television Appearances; Episodic:
Nurse Susan, *Airwolf,* CBS, 1984.
Terry Major, "Circus Knights," *Knight Rider,* NBC, 1985.
Lois Scranton, "Double Date," *Who's the Boss?,* 1985.
Vanessa, "Christopher Bundy Died on Sunday," *Murder, She Wrote,* CBS, 1986.
Roxanne, "Sea Cruise," *Full House,* 1987.

Beverly Hills, 90210, Fox, 1991.
Ariel Reed, "The Lady Vanishes," *Wings,* 1996.
Mary Beth, *Coach,* 1996.

Television Appearances; Movies:
Dori Maitlin, *Hart to Hart: Crimes of the Heart,* NBC, 1994.*

O-P

O'BRIEN, Timothy 1929-

PERSONAL

Born Timothy Brian O'Brien, March 8, 1929, in Shillong, Assam, India; son of Brian Palliser Tiegue and Elinor Laura (Mackenzie) O'Brien. *Education:* Attended Wellington College, Crowthome, Berkshire, England, 1942-47; attended Corpus Christi College, Cambridge, MA, 1952; studied stage design under Donald Oenslager at Yale University, 1952-53. *Avocational interests:* Sailing.

Addresses: *Office*—33 Lansdowne Gardens, London SW8 2EQ, England.

Career: British stage and exhibition designer. BBC-TV, London, design assistant, 1954-55; Associated Rediffusion Television, London, designer, 1955-56; ABC Television, London, head of design, 1956-66; partnership in stage design with Tazeena Firth, 1961-79; Royal Shakespeare Company, Stratford-upon-Avon, Warwickshire, England, associate designer, 1966-88, honorable associate artist, 1988—; National Theatre, London, designer, 1974-77; Lecturer, Royal College of Art, London, 1966-67. *Military service:* Sergeant in the British Army Intelligence Corps, served in Austria, 1948-49.

Member: Society of British Theatre Designers (chairperson, 1984-91).

Awards, Honors: Prague Quadriennale, Gold Medal Award, best set design, 1975; Golden Triga, best national exhibit, 1991; Royal Designer for Industry, 1991.

CREDITS

Stage Work; Scenic Designer:
The Bald Primadonna, London, 1956.
The New Tenant, London, 1956.
Hunter's Moon, London, 1958.
Five Finger Exercise, London, 1958.
The Daring Buds of May, London, 1959.
Don't Shoot, We're English, London, 1960.
Henry IV, Part I, London, 1961.
Progress to the Park, London, 1961.
The Bartered Bride, 1962.
The Girl of the Golden West, 1962.
Next Time I'll Sing to You, London, 1963.
Licence to Murder, London, 1963.
Luv, London, 1963.
Poor Bitos, London, 1963, later New York City, 1964.
Hedda Gabler, London, 1964.
Entertaining Mr. Sloane, London, 1964.
A Scent of Flowers, London, 1964.
Waiting for Godot, London, 1964.
Traveling Light, London, 1965.
A Scent of Flowers, Stuttgart, Germany, 1965.
Tango, Royal Shakespeare Company, London, and Trafalgar at Madame Tussaud's, both 1966.
Days in the Trees, Royal Shakespeare Company, and Trafalgar at Madame Tussaud's, both 1966.
Joey Joey, Royal Shakespeare Company, and Trafalgar at Madame Tussaud's, both 1966.
Staircase, Royal Shakespeare Company, and Trafalgar at Madame Tussaud's, both 1966.
All's Well That Ends Well, Royal Shakespeare Company, 1967.
As You Like It, Royal Shakespeare Company, 1967.
Romeo and Juliet, Royal Shakespeare Company, 1967.
The Merry Wives of Windsor, Royal Shakespeare Company, 1968.
Troilus and Cressida, Royal Shakespeare Company, 1968.

The Latent Heterosexual, Royal Shakespeare Company, 1968.

Pericles, Royal Shakespeare Company, 1969.

Women Beware Women, Royal Shakespeare Company, 1969.

Bartholomew Fair, Royal Shakespeare Company, 1969.

The Knot Garden, Royal Opera, 1970.

Measure for Measure, Royal Shakespeare Company, and Madame Tussaud's, both 1970.

The Merchant of Venice, Royal Shakespeare Company, 1971.

Enemies, Royal Shakespeare Company, 1971.

The Man of Mode (with Tazeena Firth), Royal Shakespeare Company, 1971.

La Cenerentola, Oslo, Norway, 1972.

Lower Depths, The Island of the Mighty, Royal Shakespeare Company, 1972.

As You Like It, OC Shakespeare Company, 1972.

Richard II, Royal Shakespeare Company, 1973.

Love's Labour's Lost, Royal Shakespeare Company, 1973.

Next of Kin, National Theater of Great Britain, London, 1974.

The Bassarids, English National Opera, 1974.

Summerfolk, Royal Shakespeare Company, 1974.

Pericles, Comedie Francaise, Paris, 1974.

The Merry Wives of Windsor, Royal Shakespeare Company, 1975.

The Marrying of Ann Leete, Royal Shakespeare Company, 1975.

Peter Grimes, Royal Opera, London, later Goteborg, Sweden and Paris, France, all 1975.

John Gabriel Borkman, National Theater of Great Britain, 1975.

The Bassarids, Frankfurt, 1975.

Wozzeck, Adelaide Festival, 1976.

The Zykovs, Royal Shakespeare Company, 1976.

Troilus and Cressida, National Theater of Great Britain, 1976.

The Force of Habit, National Theater of Great Britain, 1976.

Falstaff, Berlin Opera, 1977.

Tales from the Vienna Woods, National Theater of Great Britain, 1977.

Bedroom Farce, National Theater of Great Britain, 1977.

The Cunning Little Vixen, Goteborg, Sweden, 1978.

A Midsummer Night's Dream, Sydney Opera House, Australia, 1978.

Evita, National Theater of Great Britain, later in Australia, Austria, both 1978, then New York, 1979.

The Rake's Progress, Royal Opera, London, 1979.

Peter Grimes, Goteborg, Sweden, 1979.

Lulu, Royal Opera, London, 1981.

La Ronde, Royal Shakespeare Company, 1982.

A Doll's Life, New York City, 1982.

Le Grand Macabre, English National Opera, London, 1982.

Turandot, Vienna State Opera, 1983.

Tannhauser, Royal Opera, London, 1984.

The Mastersingers of Nuremberg, English National Opera, 1984.

Tramway Road, Lyric Theatre-Hammersmith, London, 1984.

Samson, Royal Opera, 1985.

Sicilian Vespers, Grande Theatre, Geneva, 1985.

Old Times, Theatre Royal, Haymarket, London, 1985.

Lucia di Lammermoor, Koln Opera, 1985.

The Threepenny Opera, National Theatre Company, London, 1986.

Die Meistersinger von Nurnberg, Netherlands Opera, 1986.

The American Clock, National Theatre Company, 1986.

Otello, Royal Opera, 1987, revived 1990.

Die Entfuhrung aus dem Serail, Royal Opera, 1987.

Three Sisters, Royal Shakespeare Company, Barbican Center Theatre, London, 1988.

Cymbeline, Royal Shakespeare Company, 1989.

Exclusive, Strand Theatre, London, 1989.

King, Piccadilly Theatre, London, 1990.

Love's Labour's Lost, Royal Shakespeare Company, Barbican Center Theatre, 1991.

Twelfth Night, Playhouse, 1991.

Tartuffe, Playhouse, 1991.

War and Peace, Kirov, Leningrad, Russia, 1991.

Beauty and the Beast, City of Birmingham Touring Opera, 1991.

Columbus and the Discovery of Japan, Royal Shakespeare Company, Barbican Center Theatre, 1992.

Eugene Onegin, Royal Opera, 1993.

Misha's Party, Royal Shakespeare Company, Pit, London, 1993.

On Approval, Playhouse, 1994.

The Clandestine Marriage, Queen's Theatre, London, 1994.

The Merry Wives of Windsor, National Theatre Company, Olivier Theatre, London, then Oslo, Norway, both 1995.

The Master Builder, Theatre Royal Haymarket, London, 1995.

Film Work; Scenic Designer:
Night Must Fall, 1964.

Television Work; Scenic Designer:
The Flying Dutchman, ABC, 1958.

Exhibitions:
British Theatre Design '83-87, Riverside Studios, London, 1988.

WRITINGS

(With David Fingleton) *British Theatre Design '83-87,* London, 1988.

OTHER SOURCES

Contemporary Designers, third edition, St. James (Detroit, MI), 1990.*

OLIVER, Rochelle   1937-

PERSONAL

Born Rochelle Olshever, April 15, 1937, in New York, NY; daughter of Sol and Bess (Goldsmith) Olshever; married James Patterson, October 15, 1959 (died, 1972); children: John. *Education:* Attended Brooklyn College; trained for the stage at the Henry Street Playhouse and the Herbert Berghof Studio with Uta Hagen. *Religion:* Jewish.

Addresses: *Agent*—International Creative Management, 8942 Wilshire Blvd., Beverly Hills, CA 90211.

Career: Actress. Teacher, Herbert Berghof Studio, New York City, 1976–.

Awards, Honors: Clarence Derwent Award, 1960, for *Toys in the Attic.*

CREDITS

Stage Appearances:
Fenya, *The Brothers Karamazov,* Village Gate, New York City, 1956-57.
The Cave Dwellers, Olney Playhouse, MD, 1957.
The Diary of Anne Frank, Olney Playhouse, 1958.
Lolly, *Jackknife,* Village Gate, 1958.
Vincent, Cricket, New York City, 1959.
Lily, *Toys in the Attic,* Hudson, New York City, 1960.
Summer and Smoke, John Drew Theatre, 1961.
The Lady's Not for Burning, John Drew Theatre, 1961.
The Bald Soprano, John Drew Theatre, 1961.
The Maids, Playwrights at Second City, Chicago, IL, 1961-62.
Iris, *Harold,* Cort Theatre, New York City, 1962.
Honey, *Who's Afraid of Virginia Woolf?,* Billy Rose Theatre, New York City, 1963.

Mary, *Happily Ever After,* Eugene O'Neill Theatre, New York City, 1966.
Hunger and Thirst, Stockbridge, MA, 1969.
The Enclave, Theatre Four, New York City, 1973.
Stella, *A Streetcar Named Desire,* Ivanhoe Theatre, Chicago, IL, 1973.
Bits and Pieces, Manhattan Theatre Club, New York City, 1975.
Solomon's Child, Long Wharf Theatre, New Haven, CT, 1980-81.
Vonnie Hayhurst, *The Roads to Home,* Manhattan Punch Line, New York City, 1982.
Bananas, *House of Blue Leaves,* Adelphi Festival, 1982.
Goodbye Moscow, Philadelphia Festival of New Plays, PA, 1983.
Standby, *Driving Miss Daisy,* John Houseman Theatre, New York City, 1987-88.
Love Letters, Promenade Theatre, New York City, 1989.
Fayebird, American Jewish Theatre, New York City, 1991.
Vonnie Hayhurst, *The Roads to Home,* Lamb's Little Theatre, New York City, 1992.
Emily Paine, *After-Play,* Manhattan Theatre Club, Stage II, then Theatre Four, both New York City, 1995.
Mrs. Loman, *Death of a Salesman,* Manitoba Theatre Center, Winnipeg, Manitoba, Canada, 1997.

Also appeared as Lonesome Sally, *Terrible Jim Fitch,* Stage 73, New York City; and as a standby, *Same Time Next Year,* New York City.

Film Appearances:
Norma, *The Happy Hooker,* Cannon, 1975.
Dr. Marsha, *Next Stop, Greenwich Village,* Twentieth Century-Fox, 1976.
Betty, *Lianna,* United Artists, 1982.
Mrs. Vaughn, *1918,* Cinecom, 1985.
Mrs. Vaughn, *On Valentine's Day,* Cinecom, 1986.
An Unremarkable Life, SVS, 1989.
Narrator, *American Dreaming: Atlantic City's Casino Gamble,* 1989.
Gretchen, *Scent of a Woman,* Universal, 1992.

Television Appearances; Movies:
Mrs. Giankanis, *In Defense of Kids,* CBS, 1983.

Television Appearances; Specials:
Mrs. Vaughn, *Story of a Marriage,* 1987.
Steven Wright in the Appointments of Dennis Jennings, 1989.
Tales of the Days of Awe, 1991.

Television Appearances; Series:
Judge Grace Larkin (recurring), *Law and Order,* NBC, 1992-96.

Television Appearances; Episodic:
"Saw My Baby There," *Naked City,* ABC, 1959.

Also appeared in *Defenders, Nurses,* and *U.S. Steel Hour.*

OTHER SOURCES

Periodicals:
Maclean's, January 27, 1997, p. 63.
New Leader, October 5, 1992, p. 22; September 11, 1995, p. 23.*

PARKER, Ursula
   See ANDRESS, Ursula

PROETT, Daniel (M.) 1953-

PERSONAL

Born December 27, 1953, in Wakefield, NE; son of Maurice (a baker) and Joann (a florist; maiden name, Powers) Proett. *Education:* University of Nebraska at Lincoln, B.F.A.; studied at the Polakov Studios in New York City.

Addresses: *Home*—Sunland, CA. *Contact*—c/o General Hospital, ABC-TV, ABC Television Center, 4151 Prospect Ave., Los Angeles, CA 90027.

Career: Scenic designer. Nebraska Repertory Company, Lincoln, NE, resident designer, 1976-77; South Carolina Repertory Company, Columbia, SC, resident designer, 1978; George Street Playhouse, New Brunswick, NJ, resident designer, 1979-85; Lamb's Club, New York City, resident designer, 1980-81; Crossroads Theatre Company, New Brunswick, NJ, resident designer, 1981-84. Rutgers University, New Brunswick, NJ, associate professor, 1980-84, resident designer for university theatre company, 1981-84.

Member: United Scenic Artists (Local 829).

Awards, Honors: New Jersey Drama Critics Circle Award, outstanding design, for *Tobacco Road* and *Talley's Folly;* Daytime Emmy Award, outstanding

set decoration/scenic design, 1995-96, for *General Hospital.*

CREDITS

Stage Work; Scenic Designer:
The Night of the Iguana, Nebraska Repertory Company, Lincoln, NE, 1976-77.
Loot, Nebraska Repertory Company, 1976-77.
Cabaret, Nebraska Repertory Company, 1976-77.
The Matchmaker, Nebraska Repertory Company, 1976-77.
When You Coming' Back Red Ryder?, South Carolina Repertory Company, Columbia, SC, 1978.
The Importance of Being Earnest, South Carolina Repertory Company, 1978.
Prisoner of Second Avenue, South Carolina Repertory Company, 1978.
Master Harold . . . and the Boys, George Street Playhouse, New Brunswick, NJ, between 1979 and 1985.
A Little Night Music, George Street Playhouse, between 1979 and 1985.
Tobacco Road, George Street Playhouse, between 1979 and 1985.
Death of a Salesman, George Street Playhouse, between 1979 and 1985.
A Streetcar Named Desire, George Street Playhouse, between 1979 and 1985.
Long Day's Journey into Night, George Street Playhouse, between 1979 and 1985.
Petticoat Lane, Anneberg Center Theatre, Philadelphia, PA, 1980.
Comedy of Errors, Lamb's Club, New York City, 1980-81.
Simple Stuff, Lamb's Club, 1980-81.
Somersaults, Lamb's Club, 1980-81.
Christmas Almost Passed Us By, Lamb's Club, 1980-81.
Raisin, Crossroads Theatre Company, New Brunswick, NJ, between 1981 and 1984.
A Lovesong for Miss Lydia, Crossroads Theatre Company, between 1981 and 1984.
The Amen Corner, Crossroads Theatre Company, between 1981 and 1984.
The Bloodknot, Crossroads Theatre Company, between 1981 and 1984.
American Buffalo, Crossroads Theatre Company, between 1981 and 1984.
Purlie, Crossroads Theatre Company, between 1981 and 1984.
Talley's Folly, Rutgers Theatre Company, Rutgers University, New Brunswick, NJ, between 1981 and 1984.

A Coupla White Chicks, Sitting and Talking, Rutgers Theatre Company, Rutgers University, between 1981 and 1984.

On the Razzle, Rutgers Theatre Company, Rutgers University, between 1981 and 1984.

Cap and Bells, Rutgers Theatre Company, Rutgers University, between 1981 and 1984.

West Side Story, Plays in the Park, Edison, NJ, 1982.

The Truth, Wonder Horse Theatre, New York City, 1983.

Porch Sole, Saturday Night. . ., 18th Street Playhouse, New York City, 1983.

Children of a Lesser God, Queens Theatre in the Park, New York City, 1983.

Knucklebones, Nat Horne Musical Theatre, New York City, 1983.

Family and Friend, Ensemble Studio Theatre, New York City, 1983.

Burden's Pie, Theatre 55, New York City, 1984.

Ties That Bind, Amistad World Theatre/INTAR II, New York City, 1984.

Running Time, Circle Repertory Theatre, New York City, 1984.

American Dreams, Negro Ensemble Theatre, New York City, 1984.

Split Second, Theatre Four, New York City, 1984.

Latin Festival, New York Shakespeare Festival, 1984.

Show Girls, White Barn Theatre, Westport, CT, 1984.

Snow Leopards, Actor's Outlet Theatre, New York City, 1985.

Outside Waco, Hudson Guild Theatre, New York City, 1985.

Nzinga's Children, National Black Theatre, New York City, 1985.

Little Me, Ford's Theatre, Washington, DC, 1985-86.

Hot Mikado, Ford's Theatre, 1985-86.

One Mo' Time, Crossroads Theatre Company, 1985-86.

Tamer of Horses, Crossroads Theatre Company, 1985-86.

Roads of the Mountaintop, Crossroads Theatre Company, 1985-86.

House of Shadows, Negro Ensemble Company, Theatre Four, 1986.

National Lampoon's Class of '86, Village Gate Theatre Downstairs, New York City, 1986.

Marathon '86, Ensemble Studio Theatre, 1986.

The Late Great Ladies of Blues and Jazz, John Houseman Theatre, New York City, 1987.

The Misanthrope, Pelican Studio Theatre, New York City, 1987.

Princess Grace and the Fazzaris, George Street Playhouse, 1987-88.

Spell Number 7, Crossroads Theatre Company, 1987-88.

Grandma, Pray for Me, Shakespeare Center, New York City, 1988.

Like Them That Dream, Negro Ensemble Theatre Company, Theatre Four, 1988.

Scenic designer, *Hello, Dolly!,* Harlequin Dinner Theatre, Atlanta, GA; and *Slow Dance on the Killing Ground.*

Film Work:
Assistant designer, *The Flyer,* Smithsonian, 1981.

Television Work; Scenic Designer:
General Hospital, ABC, 1995—.

Designer for episodes of *Another World,* NBC; *Late Night with David Letterman,* NBC; and several episodes of *Twin Peaks,* ABC.*

R

RACHINS, Alan 1947-

PERSONAL

Born October 10, 1947, in Cambridge, MA; married Joanna Frank (an actress); children: Robby. *Education:* Attended Wharton School of Finance, University of Pennsylvania; trained for the stage with William Ball, Warren Robertson, Kim Stanley, and Harvey Lembeck in New York City; studied film directing and writing with the American Film Institute, 1972.

Addresses: *Manager*—Black & Lawrence Management, 10350 Santa Monica Blvd., Suite 295, Los Angeles, CA 90025.

Career: Actor, director, and screenwriter. Worked as a studio script reader for two years. Operator of an ice cream topping and cake decorating business, Boston, MA.

CREDITS

Television Appearances; Series:
Paris, CBS, 1979.
Douglas Brackman Jr., *L.A. Law,* NBC, 1986-94.
Voice of Temple Fugate, the clock king, *The Adventures of Batman and Robin* (also known as *Batman: The Animated Series*), 1992.
Dr. Frank Donati, *Diagnosis Murder,* CBS, 1996.
Larry Finkelstein, *Dharma and Greg,* ABC, 1997—.

Television Appearances; Miniseries:
Mickey Stoner, *Jackie Collins's "Lady Boss"* (also known as *Lady Boss*),NBC, 1992.

Television Appearances; Movies:
Fear on Trial, CBS, 1975.
Ben Washburn, *Mistress,* CBS, 1987.
Dr. Jerry Zimmer, *Single Women, Married Men* (also known as *Single Men and Married Lovers*), CBS, 1989.
Sean Lassiter, *Perry Mason: The Case of the Silenced Singer,* NBC, 1990.
Matthew, *She Says She's Innocent* (also known as *A Violation of Trust* and *Reason to Believe*), NBC, 1991.
David Kramer, *Hart to Hart: Crimes of the Hart* (also known as *Hart to Hart: Hart Throb*), NBC, 1994.
Jammad, *Star Quest,* Sci-Fi Channel, 1996.
Derek Canfield, *The Stepsister,* USA Network, 1997.

Television Appearances; Episodic:
Pasban Bapu, "Enlightened," *J. J. Starbuck,* NBC, 1988.
D.C. Follies, syndicated, 1988.
Ferris Bueller, NBC, 1990.
Host, "Sex, Lies, and Toupee Tape," *Nova,* PBS, 1991.
Husband, "Spoiled," *Tales from the Crypt,* HBO, 1991.
Mr. Maculhaney, "Afterlife," *The Outer Limits,* Showtime, 1995.
Professor Jefferson Cole, "The People v. Lois Lane," *Lois and Clark: The New Adventures of Superman,* ABC, 1996.
Professor Jefferson Cole, "Dead Lois Walking," *Lois and Clark: The New Adventures of Superman,* ABC, 1996.
Arkady, "The Bones of St. Anthony," *Poltergeist: The Legacy,* Showtime, 1996.

Television Work; Episodic:
Director, *Paris,* CBS, 1979.

Television Appearances; Specials:
Macy's Thanksgiving Day Parade, 1989.
The 14th Annual Circus of the Stars, CBS, 1989.
The "L.A. Law" 100th Episode Special, NBC, 1991.
Super Bloopers and New Practical Jokes, 1992.

Film Appearances:

Jeweler, *Time Walker* (also known as *Being from Another Planet*), 1982.

Eddie, *Always (But Not Forever)*, Samuel Goldwyn, 1985.

Carlos, *Thunder Run*, Cannon, 1986.

Dr. Posner, *Heart Condition*, New Line, 1990.

Defense attorney, *North*, Columbia, 1994.

Tony Moss, *Showgirls*, Metro-Goldwyn-Mayer/United Artists, 1995.

Judge Randel Williams, *Meet Wally Sparks*, Trimark, 1997.

Fred Rutherford, *Leave It to Beaver*, Universal, 1997.

Stage Appearances:

After the Rain, John Golden Theatre, New York City, 1967.

Hadrian the Seventh, Helen Hayes Theatre, New York City, 1969.

Oh, Calcutta!, Eden Theatre, New York City, 1969.

Also appeared in *The Trojan Women*, New York City.

WRITINGS

Television Episodes:

Writer for *Hill Street Blues*, NBC; *The Fall Guy*, ABC; *Hart to Hart*, ABC; *Knight Rider*, NBC; and *Quincy, M.E.*, NBC.

OTHER SOURCES

People Weekly, November 28, 1988, p. 111.
TV Guide, July 23, 1988, p. 12.*

RAINEY, Ford   1908-

PERSONAL

Born August 8, 1908, in Mountain Home, ID; son of Archie Coleman (a jack of all trades) and Vyrna (a teacher; maiden name, Kinkade) Rainey; married Sheila Mary Hayden (an actress and artist), February 4, 1954; children: Robert, James, Kathleen. *Education:* Attended Centralia College, 1929-30, Cornish Institute, 1931-34, and Santa Monica College, 1983-85; studied acting with Michael Chekhov. *Avocational interests:* Beekeeping, golfing.

Addresses: *Home*—Malibu, CA. *Agent*—Amsel, Eisenstadt and Frazier, 6310 San Vicente Blvd., Suite 401, Los Angeles, CA 90048.

Career: Actor. South Coast Repertory Company, Costa Mesa, CA, member of company, 1987-88. *Military service:* U.S. Coast Guard, boatswain's mate, 1942-45; served in Pacific theatre of World War II.

Awards, Honors: Los Angeles Drama Critics Award, 1978, for *Home;* Dramalogue Awards, 1980, for *In Celebration,* and 1982, for *Long Day's Journey into Night.*

CREDITS

Film Appearances:

(Film debut) Zuckie Hommell, *White Heat*, Warner Bros., 1949.

Ernest Craig, *Perfect Strangers* (also known as *Too Dangerous to Love*), Warner Bros., 1950.

Ship's Captain, *The Robe*, Twentieth Century-Fox, 1953.

Marshal, *3:10 to Yuma*, Columbia, 1957.

Warden, *The Badlanders*, Metro-Goldwyn-Mayer, 1958.

Convict "Red" Kirby, *The Last Mile*, United Artists, 1959.

Lieutenant Simpson, *John Paul Jones*, Warner Bros., 1959.

Doc Phillips, *Flaming Star*, Twentieth Century-Fox, 1960.

Henry Clay, *Two Rode Together*, Columbia, 1961.

John Donati, *Parrish*, Columbia, 1961.

Congressman Keach, *Dead to the World*, United Artists, 1961.

Reverend Armstrong, *Claudelle Inglish* (also known as *Young and Eager*), 1961.

Speaker, *Ada*, Metro-Goldwyn-Mayer, 1961.

Judge, *Forty Pounds of Trouble*, Universal, 1962.

The chief, *Kings of the Sun*, United Artists, 1963.

Harris, *The Sand Pebbles*, Twentieth Century-Fox, 1966.

Sam Tiger, *Johnny Tiger*, Universal, 1966.

Emerson, *Gunpoint*, Universal, 1966.

Captain Robert R. Foster, *Chuka*, Paramount, 1967.

Stand owner, *The Gypsy Moths*, Metro-Goldwyn-Mayer, 1969.

Stanley Mae, *The Traveling Executioner*, Metro-Goldwyn-Mayer, 1970.

Mr. Golden, *The Naked Zoo* (also known as *The Grove* and *The Hallucinators*), R and S, 1970.

Sheriff Coleman, *Glory Boy* (also known as *My Old Man's Place*), Cinerama, 1971.

The Andromeda Strain, Universal, 1971.

Like a Crow on a June Bug (also known as *Sixteen*), Futurama, 1972.

Commission spokesman, *The Parallax View*, Paramount, 1974.

Abraham Lincoln, *Guardian of the Wilderness* (also known as *Mountain Men*), Sunn Classic, 1977.

Dr. Mixer, *Halloween II*, Universal, 1981.

The Cellar, Hemdale Home Video, 1989.

Amos, *Bed and Breakfast*, Hemdale Releasing, 1992.

Television Appearances; Series:

Lloyd Ramsey, *Window on Main Street*, CBS, 1961.

The Richard Boone Show, NBC, 1963.

Dr. Barnett, *Search* (also known as *Probe*), NBC, 1972.

Police Chief Vernon, *Tenafly*, NBC, 1973.

James Barrett, *Manhunter*, CBS, 1974.

Jim Elgin, *The Bionic Woman*, ABC, 1976.

Frank Evans, *Days of Our Lives*, NBC, 1977-78.

Television Appearances; Miniseries:

Abraham Lincoln, *Captains and the Kings*, NBC, 1976.

Secretary of the Navy, *Backstairs at the White House*, NBC, 1979.

Will Milford, *Amerika* (also known as *Topeka, Kansas . . . U.S.S.R.*), ABC, 1987.

Cross of Fire, NBC, 1989.

Television Appearances; Movies:

Treadwell, *My Sweet Charlie*, NBC, 1970.

Bud Henshaw, *A Howling in the Woods*, NBC, 1971.

Prescott Webb, *Key West*, NBC, 1973.

Chief Vernon, *Linda*, ABC, 1973.

Dr. Tatum, *Babe*, CBS, 1974.

Mr. Suggs, *The Story of Pretty Boy Floyd*, ABC, 1974.

Mr. Gilbert, *The Stranger Who Looks Like Me*, ABC, 1974.

Dr. Patterson, *Medical Story*, NBC, 1975.

Sirus, *Strange New World*, ABC, 1975.

The judge, *The New Daughters of Joshua Cabe*, 1976.

Charlie Case, *A Family Upside Down*, NBC, 1978.

Hamilton, *Friendly Fire*, ABC, 1979.

Mr. Meecham, *Strangers: The Story of a Mother and Daughter*, CBS, 1979.

Second Supreme Court justice, *Gideon's Trumpet*, CBS, 1980.

Beatrice's father, *Life of the Party: The Story of Beatrice*, CBS, 1982.

The commentator, *Who Is Julia?*, CBS, 1986.

Harlan Fisk-Stone, *J. Edgar Hoover* (also known as *Hoover*), Showtime, 1987.

Father Ramirezti, *There Was a Little Boy*, CBS, 1993.

Oldtimer, *Marshal Law* (also known as *After Shock* and *Block Party*), Showtime, 1996.

Television Appearances; Episodic:

Sheriff, "Incident of the Wager on Payday," *Rawhide*, CBS, 1961.

Tate Gifford, "Cale," *Gunsmoke*, CBS, 1962.

Tate, "The Search," *Gunsmoke*, CBS, 1962.

Julius Chavis, "Come and Kill Me," *The Untouchables*, ABC, 1962.

Captain Roy Gunther, "Line of Fire," *The Untouchables*, ABC, 1963.

U.S. president, "Hot Line," *Voyage to the Bottom of the Sea*, ABC, 1964.

District Attorney Thomas Coyle, "I, Robot," *The Outer Limits*, ABC, 1964.

President, "Doomsday," *Voyage to the Bottom of the Sea*, ABC, 1965.

Lincoln, "The Death Trap," *The Time Tunnel*, ABC, 1966.

"The Legend of John Rim," *The F.B.I.*, ABC, 1967.

"Passage into Fear," *The F.B.I.*, ABC, 1967.

Gabriel Bingham, "Check Rein," *Bonanza*, NBC, 1967.

Captain Arnholt, "The Deserter," *Bonanza*, NBC, 1968.

"The Swindler," *The F.B.I.*, ABC, 1969.

"The Alienation Kick," *The Young Lawyers*, ABC, 1970.

"Legal Maneuver," *The Young Lawyers*, ABC, 1971.

Judge Taylor, "A Home for Jamie," *Bonanza*, NBC, 1971.

Judge Simms, "Fallen Woman," *Bonanza*, NBC, 1971.

Sheriff, "The Phantom Farmhouse," *Night Gallery*, NBC, 1971.

"The Man Who Broke the Bank at Red Gap," *Alias Smith and Jones*, ABC, 1972.

"The Biggest Game in the West," *Alias Smith and Jones*, ABC, 1972.

Haggard Mellon, "Trail of Terror," *The Streets of San Francisco*, ABC, 1972.

Manny Tolan, "Counter Gambit," *The Rockford Files*, NBC, 1975.

Dr. Rainey, "Mary Midwife," *The Mary Tyler Moore Show*, CBS, 1976.

Mr. Harkins, "Angels on the Street," *Charlie's Angels*, ABC, 1979.

Vance Pooley, *Wiseguy*, CBS, 1987.

Lesley, *Picket Fences*, CBS, 1995.

Nate, *Ned and Stacey*, Fox, 1996.

Appeared in episodes of *Rawhide, The Virginian, The Tall Man, The Six Million Dollar Man, St. Elsewhere, Remington Steele, The Bob Newhart Show, General Hospital, M*A*S*H, Perry Mason,* and *Quincy, M.E.*

Other Television Appearances:
(Television debut) Title role, "Abraham Lincoln" (special), *Hallmark Hall of Fame,* NBC, 1953.
James Barrett, *Manhunter* (pilot), 1974.

Also in *Our Town* and *The Last of Mrs. Lincoln.*

Stage Appearances:
Toby Belch, *Twelfth Night,* Michael Chekhov Theatre, Ridgefield, CT, 1941-42.
Title role, *King Lear,* Michael Chekhov Theatre, 1941-42.
Macbeth, Las Palmas Theatre, Hollywood, CA, 1948.
Danforth, *The Crucible,* Martinque Theatre, New York City, 1958.
Title role, *J.B.,* American National Theatre and Academy, New York City, 1959.
Naked, University of California, Los Angeles, 1961.
Home, Theatre of Angels, Los Angeles, 1978.
Old Dodge, *Buried Child,* Yale Repertory Theatre, New Haven, CT, 1979.
Willie Loman, *Death of a Salesman,* Trinity Square Repertory Company, Providence, RI, between 1979 and 1982.
Old Dodge, *Buried Child,* Trinity Square Repertory Company, between 1979 and 1982.
Norman, *On Golden Pond,* Trinity Square Repertory Company, between 1979 and 1982.
Arsenic and Old Lace, Trinity Square Repertory Company, between 1979 and 1982.
In Celebration, Theatre of Angels, 1980.
Long Day's Journey into Night, 1982.
Richard III, Mark Taper Forum, Los Angeles, CA, 1983.
A Month in the Country, Mark Taper Forum, 1983.
Aslaksen, *An Enemy of the People,* Los Angeles Actors Theatre, Los Angeles, CA, 1984.
Hamlet, Los Angeles Actors Theatre, 1985.
King Lear, *Exploring King Lear,* Sound Studio, Hollywood, CA, 1985.
Painting Churches, South Coast Repertory Theater, Costa Mesa, CA, 1985-86.
Alpha, Los Angeles Theatre Center, Los Angeles, CA, 1986-87.
Piotr, *Nothing Sacred,* Center Theatre Group, Mark Taper Forum, 1988-89.
Uncle George and father, *Aristocrats,* Center Theatre Group, Mark Taper Forum, 1989-90.
Underground, Winterfest 11 Festival, off-Broadway, 1990-91.

Made New York debut as reporter, *The Possessed,* Lyceum Theatre; also appeared in *Playboy of the Western World.*

Major Tours:
Old Dodge, *Buried Child,* Indian cities, 1982.
Of Mice and Men, Indian cities, 1982.
John Tarleton, *Misalliance,* U.S. cities, 1984-85.*

READ, James   1952(?)-

PERSONAL

Full name is James Christopher Read; born July 31, 1952 (some sources say 1953 or 1954), in Buffalo, NY; married Wendy Kilbourne (an actress).

Addresses: *Agent*—Pakula/King and Associates, 9229 Sunset Blvd., Suite 315, Los Angeles, CA 90069.

Career: Actor. Denver Center Theatre Company, Denver, CO, member of company, 1980-81.

CREDITS

Television Appearances; Series:
Murphy Michaels, *Remington Steele,* NBC, 1982-83.
Riley/John Reid, *Shell Game,* CBS, 1987.

Television Appearances; Miniseries:
Ted Kennedy, *Robert Kennedy and His Times,* CBS, 1985.
George Hazard, *North and South,* ABC, 1985.
George Hazard, *North and South, Book II,* ABC, 1986.
Cary Grant, *Poor Little Rich Girl: The Barbara Hutton Story,* NBC, 1987.
George Hazard, *John Jakes's "Heaven and Hell: North and South, Part III"* (also known as *North and South, Part III*), ABC, 1994.

Television Appearances; Movies:
Daryl Webster, *Lace II,* ABC, 1985.
James Marston, *Celebration Family,* ABC, 1987.
"Back to Hannibal: The Return of Tom Sawyer and Huckleberry Finn," *The Magical World of Disney,* The Disney Channel, 1990.
Dr. Wesley Corman, "Uneasy Lies the Crown" (also known as "Columbo"), *The ABC Saturday Mystery,* ABC, 1990.
Paul Evanston, *Web of Deceit* (also known as *Conspiracy to Kill*), USA Network, 1990.
Senator James Guthrie, *The President's Child,* CBS, 1992.
Michael Bryan, *The Other Woman* (also known as *Mothers and Daughters*), CBS, 1995.

Detective Michael Lieberman, *When the Dark Man Calls,* USA Network, 1995.

Judge Russell Carver, *Danielle Steel's "Full Circle"* (also known as *Full Circle*), NBC, 1996.

Scot, "Harvest of Fire," *Hallmark Hall of Fame,* CBS, 1996.

Television Appearances; Episodic:

H. W. Sawyer, "Friends, Romans, Accountants," *Cheers,* NBC, 1982.

"The Agony of d'Feet," *Trapper John, M.D.,* CBS, 1983.

Boyd Venton, "Death 'n' Denial," *Murder, She Wrote,* CBS, 1984.

Jack Olsen, "The Dad Who Came in from the Cold," *Lois and Clark: The New Adventures of Superman,* ABC, 1995.

Captain Jenkins, *Home Improvement,* ABC, 1996.

Bill Sanders, *Seventh Heaven,* The WB, 1996.

Television Appearances; Pilots:

Josh Landau, *Midas Valley,* ABC, 1985.

Peter Baltic, *Lola* (also known as *Escape from 212*), CBS, 1990.

Film Appearances:

Bridge policeman, *Blue Thunder,* Columbia, 1983.

Peter, *The Initiation,* New World, 1984.

Lefty Williams, *Eight Men Out,* Orion, 1988.

Michael Essex, *Beaches,* Buena Vista, 1988.

Stanton Gray, *Love Crimes,* Millimeter Films, 1992.*

READE, Hamish
    See GRAY, Simon

RECHT, Ray   1947-

PERSONAL

Born August 9, 1947, in New York, NY; son of Morton (a certified public accountant) and Lillian F. (an accountant; maiden name, Dembner) Recht; married Claire Des Becker (a ceramic designer), June 27, 1982. *Education:* Carnegie-Mellon University, B.F.A., 1969; Yale University, M.F.A. (drama), 1972; prepared for career as assistant to Ming Cho Lee and Tony Walton. *Religion:* Jewish.

Addresses: *Office*—267 West 89th St., New York, NY 10024-1725.

Career: Scenic (set) designer. Goucher College, Baltimore, MD, lecturer, 1973-76; Queensborough Community College of the City University of New York, Bayside, NY, guest artist, 1977-84; Long Island University, C. W. Post College, New York City, adjunct faculty member, 1981; Albright College, Reading, PA, guest artist, 1983-84; Marymount Manhattan College, resident designer. Work represented in exhibitions, including "Contemporary Stage Design, U.S.A.," at International Theatre Institute, and "200 Years of America Onstage," presented by Kennedy Center and Mobil Corp.

Member: United Scenic Artists (Local 829).

CREDITS

Stage Work; Set Designer, Except Where Indicated:

(And media and lighting designer) *Happy End,* Yale Repertory Theatre, New Haven, CT, 1972.

Medal of Honor Rag, Theatre de Lys, New York City, 1975.

(Associate designer) *Woman of the Year,* Palace Theatre, New York City, 1981.

Anyone Can Whistle, Berkshire Theatre Festival, Stockbridge, MA, 1981.

(Associate designer) *The First,* Martin Beck Theatre, New York City, 1982.

Trick, Broadway production, 1982.

Slab Boys, Playhouse, New York City, 1983.

The Babe, Broadway production, 1984.

A . . . My Name Is Alice, Top of the Gate, Village Gate Theatre, New York City, 1984.

Planet Fires, GeVa Theatre, 1985.

Lies My Father Told Me, Jewish Repertory Theatre, New York City, 1985-86.

The Real Thing, Pittsburgh Public Theatre, Pittsburgh, PA, 1985-86.

Gardenia, Pittsburgh Public Theatre, 1985-86.

Our Own Family, Jewish Repertory Theatre, 1986-87.

Joe Egg, Theatre by the Sea, Portsmouth, NH, 1986-87.

Isle of Swans, Westside Arts Theatre Upstairs, New York City, 1987.

Half a World Away, Jewish Repertory Theatre, 1987-88.

Yard Sale, Jewish Repertory Theatre, 1987-88.

Like Them That Dream, Capital Repertory Company, Albany, NY, 1987-88.

Thursday's Child, Capital Repertory Company, 1987-88.

Isolate, Westbeth Theatre Center, New York City, 1988.

The Sunshine Boys, Jewish Repertory Theatre, 1988-89.

Double Blessing, Jewish Repertory Theatre, 1988-89.

(And lighting designer) *Laughing Matters,* Arts Common Theatre at St. Peter's Church, New York City, 1989.

George Washington Slept Here, Pittsburgh Public Theatre, 1989-90.

Reckless, Pittsburgh Public Theatre, 1989-90.

Noises Off, Pennsylvania Stage Company, Allentown, 1989-90.

The Witch, Jewish Repertory Theatre, 1989-90.

Dividends, Jewish Repertory Theatre, 1989-90.

What's Wrong with This Picture?, Jewish Repertory Theatre, 1990-91.

Taking Stock, Jewish Repertory Theatre, 1990-91.

A Fierce Attachment, Jewish Repertory Theatre, 1990-91.

Lusting after Pipino's Wife, Primary Stages, New York City, 1990, 1991.

Better Days, Primary Stages, 1991.

Don Quixote (ballet), Vienna Staatsoper Ballet Company, Vienna, Austria, 1991.

I Do! I Do!, Pittsburgh Public Theatre, 1991-92.

Shmulnik's Waltz, Jewish Repertory Theatre, 1991-92.

The Sunset Gang, Jewish Repertory Theatre, 1991-92.

Twelfth Night, Hudson Guild Theatre, 1992.

The Dolphin Position, Primary Stages, 1992.

Them . . . within Us, Theatre Row Theatre, New York City, 1992.

The Old Lady's Guide to Survival, Pittsburgh Public Theatre, 1992-93.

The King of Carpets, Jewish Repertory Theatre, 1993.

Tangents, George Street Playhouse, New Brunswick, NJ, 1993-94.

The Flowering Peach, Lyceum Theatre, New York City, 1994.

Set designer for *The Offering* and *Black Body Blues,* both Negro Ensemble Company; *A Backer's Audition* and *Mensch Meier,* both Manhattan Theatre Club; *Judgement,* Theatre at St. Peter's, Citicorp Center; *Upstairs at O'Neals,* O'Neals Theatre at 43rd Street; *A Hell of a Town,* West Side Arts Theatre; and many regional theatre productions at Actor's Theatre of Louisville, Louisville, KY, Barter Theatre, Capitol Repertory Theatre, Center Stage, Folger Theatre, Washington, DC, Indiana Repertory Theatre, Manitoba Theatre Centre, and McCarter Theatre, Princeton, NJ. Opera work includes set design assistant to David Mitchell, *The Italian Straw Hat,* Santa Fe Opera, NM; and set designer for *One Christmas*

Long Ago, Manhattan School of Music, New York City; *The Impressario* and *Aunt Caroline's Will,* both Mannes College of Music, New York City; *Werther,* Opera Ensemble of New York; *Song of Norway,* Pittsburgh Civic Light Opera, Pittsburgh; and *Peter Grimes,* Yale Symphony, New Haven, CT. Designer for touring production of *Sarafina!,* 1990.

Film Work; Art Director, Except Where Indicated:

(Assistant) *All That Jazz,* Columbia, 1978.

(Assistant art director) *Just Tell Me What You Want,* Warner Bros., 1980.

(Assistant production designer) *The First Deadly Sin,* Filmways, 1980.

Amityville II: The Possession, Orion, 1982.

Exposed, Metro-Goldwyn-Mayer/United Artists, 1983.

Mortal Sins, Academy Entertainment, 1989.

Missing Pieces (also known as *Auf der Sonnenseite des Lebens*), Orion/HBO Home Video, 1990.

Dangerous Obsession, Panorama Entertainment, 1991.

The Search for One-Eye Jimmy, Northern Arts Entertainment, 1996.

Television Specials; Set Designer:

Almost Partners, CBS, 1987.

All That Glitters, 1990.

The Story behind the Story, 1990.

Other Television Work:

Art director, *French-American Perspective,* Telefrance, cable, 1982.

Set designer, *Another World* (series), NBC, 1984.

Art director, *Way Cool,* 1991.

Also art director for the cable presentation *The Babe,* Corniche Productions.*

REYNOLDS, Bill
  See REYNOLDS, William

REYNOLDS, William   1910-1997
  (Bill Reynolds, William H. Reynolds)

OBITUARY NOTICE—See index for *CTFT* sketch: Full name William Henry Reynolds; born June 14, 1910, in Elmira, NY; died of cancer, July 16, 1997, in South Pasadena, CA. Editor and producer. Reynolds was a prolific film editor, working as a freelance editor since

1962. His work on *The Sound of Music* and *The Sting* earned him Academy Awards, while his editing on *Fanny, The Sand Pebbles, Hello, Dolly, The Godfather,* and *The Turning Point* earned him Oscar nominations. Early in his career, he worked for the Fox Film Corporation as a swing gang laborer beginning in 1934. He joined Paramount in 1936 as an assistant editor becoming an editor a year later. During World War II, he served in the U.S. Army and was involved in making training films. After the war, he resumed work as an editor at Twentieth Century-Fox and remained in its employ from 1947 until he went to freelance status in 1962. His early films as an assistant editor include *The Farmer Takes a Wife, Palm Springs,* and *Honeymoon in Bali.* His films as an editor include *Mother Is a Freshman, Give My Regards to Broadway, The Day the Earth Stood Still, The Outcasts of Poker Flat, Three Coins in the Fountain, Daddy Long Legs, Love Is a Many-Splendored Thing, Carousel, Our Man Flint, The Great Waldo Pepper, Heaven's Gate, The Lonely Guy, Ishtar, Taking Care of Business,* and *Newsies.* He was also the producer of *Time Limit,* with actor Richard Widmark.

OBITUARIES AND OTHER SOURCES

Books:
Who's Who in America, Marquis Who's Who, 1995.

Periodicals:
Chicago Tribune, July 22, 1997, section 1, p. 10.
New York Times, July 22, 1997, p. A17.
Washington Post, July 20, 1997, p. B7.

REYNOLDS, William H.
    See REYNOLDS, William

ROBERTS, Doris 1930-

PERSONAL

Born November 4, 1930, in St. Louis, MO; daughter of Larry and Ann (Meltzer) Roberts; married Michael E. Cannata (marriage ended); married William Goyen (a novelist), November 10, 1963 (deceased); children: Michael Robert Cannata. *Education:* Attended New York University, 1950-51; trained for the stage at Neighborhood Playhouse with Stanford Meisner, 1952-53, and at Actors Studio with Lee Strasberg, 1956. *Avocational interests:* Painting, re-doing old furniture, needlepoint.

Addresses: *Agent*—Innovative Artists, 1999 Avenue of the Stars, Suite 2850, Los Angeles, CA 90067.

Career: Actress.

Member: Actors' Equity Association, Screen Actors Guild, American Federation of Television and Radio Artists, Directors Guild of America.

Awards, Honors: Outer Critics Circle Award, 1974, for *Bad Habits;* Emmy Award, best supporting actress, 1984, for "Cora and Arnie," *St. Elsewhere;* Emmy Award nomination, best supporting actress, 1985, for *Remington Steele;* Emmy Award nomination, best guest actress, *Perfect Strangers;* Emmy Award nomination, best supporting actress, 1992; *Los Angeles* Weekly Award.

CREDITS

Television Appearances; Series:
Mary Hartman, *Mary Hartman, Mary Hartman,* syndicated, 1977.
Theresa Falco, *Angie,* ABC, 1979-80.
Mildred Krebs, *Remington Steele,* NBC, 1983-86.
Doris Greenblatt, *The Boys,* CBS, 1993.
Mrs. Shenker, *The John Larroquette Show,* NBC, 1993.
Aunt Edna, *Step by Step,* CBS, 1994.
Elaine Portugal, *Walker, Texas Ranger,* CBS, 1994.
Marie Barone, *Everybody Loves Raymond,* CBS, 1996—.

Television Appearances; Miniseries:
Tessie McBride, *Blind Faith* (also known as *The Toms River Case*), NBC, 1990.

Television Appearances; Movies:
Marion Davidson, *The Storyteller,* NBC, 1977.
Mrs. Bailey, *It Happened One Christmas,* ABC, 1977.
Eva, *Ruby and Oswald* (also known as *Four Days in Dallas*), CBS, 1978.
Kay, *Jennifer: A Woman's Story,* NBC, 1979.
Mrs. Van Daan, *Diary of Anne Frank,* NBC, 1980.
Myrna, *Another Woman's Child,* CBS, 1983.
Sadie Finney, *A Letter to Three Wives,* NBC, 1985.
Mama, *California Girls,* ABC, 1985.
Edith Bernside, *Ordinary Heroes,* ABC, 1986.
Dottie Wilson, *If It's Tuesday It Still Must Be Belgium,* NBC, 1987.
Philomena, *A Mom for Christmas,* NBC, 1990.
Maddy, *A Time to Heal* (also known as *Jenny's Story* and *Out of the Darkness*), NBC, 1994.

Television Appearances; Episodic:

"Jane Eyre," *Studio One,* CBS, 1952.

"One of the Most Important Men in the Whole World," *Naked City,* ABC, 1962.

"Mad Man," *The Defenders,* CBS, 1962.

"Father Was an Intern," *Ben Casey,* ABC, 1963.

"Claire Cheval Died in Boston," *The Defenders,* CBS, 1963.

"Phyllis Whips Inflation," *The Mary Tyler Moore Show,* CBS, 1975.

Joe and Sons, CBS, 1975.

"Two against Death," *Medical Center,* CBS, 1975.

"Sharper Than a Serpent's Truth," *Baretta,* ABC, 1975.

"Edith's Night Out," *All in the Family,* CBS, 1976.

"The Nurse's Pipes," *Viva Valdez,* ABC, 1976.

Mrs. Strauss, "The Thrill Killers," *The Streets of San Francisco,* ABC, 1976.

"Meet the Levys," *Rhoda,* CBS, 1976.

"Such Sweet Sorrow," *Family,* ABC, 1976.

Mona Spevack, *Alice,* CBS, 1976.

"Sex Surrogate," *Barney Miller,* ABC, 1977.

Blansky's Beauties, ABC, 1977.

"The Sighting," *Barney Miller,* ABC, 1978.

Mrs. Floski, "Episode 30," *Soap,* ABC, 1978.

"Wojo's Girl," *Barney Miller,* ABC, 1979.

"Goose for the Gander," *Fantasy Island,* ABC, 1979.

Crystal, *The Mary Tyler Moore Comedy Hour,* CBS, 1979.

"Sergeant Bull," *The Love Boat,* ABC, 1980.

"Agent Orange," *Barney Miller,* ABC, 1980.

Fantasy Island, ABC, 1981.

"Alice's Big Four-Oh!," *Alice,* CBS, 1981.

Loretta Davenport, *Maggie,* ABC, 1982.

"Cora and Arnie," *St. Elsewhere,* NBC, 1982.

"Our Son, the Lawyer," *The Love Boat,* ABC, 1983.

Cagney and Lacey, CBS, 1983.

"The Perils of Pauline," *The New Odd Couple,* ABC, 1983.

"The Night Stalker," *The New Odd Couple,* ABC, 1983.

"Call Me a Doctor," *The Love Boat,* ABC, 1984.

Mom, "The Three Little Pigs," *Faerie Tale Theatre,* Showtime, 1985.

"Deportation," *Mr. Belvedere,* ABC, 1986.

Michele Loring, "The State of Oregon vs. Stanley Manning," *You Are the Jury,* NBC, 1987.

Great Aunt Eliza, "The Fig Tree," *WonderWorks,* PBS, 1987.

"School Daze," *Cagney and Lacey,* CBS, 1988.

"Maid to Order," *Perfect Strangers,* ABC, 1989.

Helen Owens, *Murder, She Wrote,* CBS, 1990.

"Toby's Choice," *Dream On,* HBO, 1990.

Mimi, "Yiddish," a segment of "The Sunset Gang," *American Playhouse,* PBS, 1991.

Mrs. Colfax, *Murder, She Wrote,* CBS, 1994.

Betsy Meadows, "Who Killed Cock-a-Doodle Dooley?," *Burke's Law,* CBS, 1995.

Television Appearances; Pilots:

Irma DeGroot, *In Trouble,* ABC, 1981.

Ethel Connelly, *Me and Mrs. C.,* NBC, 1984.

Cecile Rickwald, *The Gregory Harrison Show,* CBS, 1989.

Bea, *The Ladies on Sweet Street,* ABC, 1990.

Television Appearances; Specials:

Waitress, *The Trouble with People,* NBC, 1972.

The Lily Tomlin Special, 1975.

Aunt Enid, *Bell, Book, and Candle,* 1976.

Paula Handy, *The Oath: Thirty-Three Hours in the Life of God,* 1976.

NBC's 60th Anniversary Celebration, NBC, 1986.

Doris, *Alvin Goes Back to School,* 1986.

Marie, *Sea World and Busch Gardens Adventures: Alien Vacation!,* CBS, 1997.

Film Appearances:

Girl in 5 and 10, *Something Wild,* United Artists, 1961.

Barefoot in the Park, Paramount, 1968.

Sylvia Poppie, *No Way to Treat a Lady,* Paramount, 1968.

Feeney, *A Lovely Way to Die,* Universal, 1968.

Bunny, *The Honeymoon Killers* (also known as *The Lonely Hearts Killers*), Cinerama, 1970.

Mrs. Gold, *Such Good Friends,* Paramount, 1971.

Mrs. Chamberlain, *Little Murders,* Twentieth Century-Fox, 1971.

Mrs. Traggert, *A New Leaf,* Paramount, 1971.

Mrs. Cantrow, *The Heartbreak Kid,* Twentieth Century-Fox, 1972.

The mayor's wife, *The Taking of Pelham 1-2-3,* United Artists, 1974.

Mrs. Kavarsky, *Hester Street,* Midwest, 1975.

Mrs. Carpenter, *Rabbit Test,* Avco-Embassy, 1978.

Lars Brady's ex-wife, *Once in Paris,* Leigh McLaughlin, 1978.

Rose's mother, *The Rose,* Twentieth Century-Fox, 1979.

Rene, *Good Luck Miss Wykoff* (also known as *Secret Yearnings, The Shaming,* and *The Sin*), 1979.

Mrs. Berzak, *Number One with a Bullet,* Cannon, 1986.

Francis, *National Lampoon's Christmas Vacation,* Warner Bros., 1989.

Anna DiLorenzo, *Simple Justice* [USA], 1989.

Mrs. Nelson, *Honeymoon Academy* (also known as *For Better or for Worse*), Triumph Releasing, 1990.

Aunt Lonnie, *Used People,* Twentieth Century-Fox, 1992.
Neighbor, *The Night We Never Met,* Miramax, 1993.
Mrs. Richards, *The Grass Harp,* Fine Line Features, 1995.
A Fish in the Bathtub, 1998.
My Giant, Castle Rock, 1998.

Stage Appearances:
(Broadway debut) Prostitute, *The Time of Your Life,* City Center, New York City, 1955.
Miss Rumple, *The Desk Set,* Broadhurst Theatre, New York City, 1955.
Nurse, *The Death of Bessie Smith,* York Playhouse, New York City, 1961.
Mommy, *The American Dream,* York Playhouse, 1961, revived at Cherry Lane Theatre, New York City, 1971.
Color of Darkness, Writers Stage Theatre, New York City, 1963.
Cracks, Writers Stage Theatre, 1963.
Rae Wilson, *Marathon '33,* American National Theatre and Academy (ANTA) Theatre, New York City, 1963.
Understudy for Madame Girard and Eloisa, *Malcolm,* Shubert Theatre, New York City, 1966.
Miss Punk, *The Office,* Henry Miller's Theatre, New York City, 1966.
Edna, *The Natural Look,* Longacre Theatre, New York City, 1967.
Jeanette Fisher, *Last of the Red Hot Lovers,* Eugene O'Neill Theatre, New York City, 1969.
May, *Felix,* Actors Studio, New York City, 1972.
Miss Manley, *The Secret Affairs of Mildred Wild,* Ambassador Theatre, New York City, 1972.
Dolly Scupp, "Ravenswood," and Becky Hedges, "Dunelawn" in *Bad Habits* (double-bill), Astor Place Theatre, then Booth Theatre, New York City, 1974.

Dede, *Ladies at the Alamo,* Actors Studio, 1975.
Grace, *Cheaters,* Biltmore Theatre, New York City, 1978.
Emma, *It's Only a Play,* Center Theatre Group, James A. Doolittle Theatre, Los Angeles, 1991-92.

Made professional stage debut in Ann Arbor, MI, 1953; performed in summer stock, Chatham, MA, 1955.

Major Tours:
Claudia, *The Opening,* U.S. cities, 1972.
Mornings at Seven, U.S. cities, 1976.

SIDELIGHTS

Doris Roberts told *CTFT:* "I wanted to be an actress since I was five. In kindergarten, in a little project, I was given the line 'I am Patrick Potato and this is my cousin, Mrs. Tomato,' and I heard laughter after I heard that line, and that was the bug that bit. When I was a young student, I went to the Museum of Modern Art and saw a film of Eleonora Duse and she took my breath away, and I knew then that's what I had to do in my lifetime—to try to be as great as she was in her lifetime.

"Often young people ask me what they can do to get ahead in this business, and I ask them one question which is 'Do you want to be an actor or a celebrity?' If it's an actor, I can help you. If you want to be a celebrity, I cannot. It requires not only diligence and perseverance but passion and talent, and although a difficult profession, wonderfully rewarding."

ROBIN
See ANA-ALICIA

S

SADLER, Bill
See SADLER, William

SADLER, William 1950-
(Bill Sadler)

PERSONAL

Born April 13, 1950, in Buffalo, NY. *Education:* Graduated from State University of New York College at Geneseo; also attended Cornell University.

Addresses: *Agent*—J. Michael Bloom and Associates, 233 Park Avenue S., New York, NY 10003.

Career: Actor, often under name William Sadler.

Awards, Honors: Obie Award, *Village Voice,* and Villager Award, both 1981, for *Limbo Tales.*

CREDITS

Stage Appearances:
(Off-Broadway debut) Title role, *Ivanov,* City Playworks, 1975.

Ensemble, *Henry V,* New York Shakespeare Festival, Delacorte Theatre, New York City, 1977.

Ensemble, *Measure for Measure,* New York Shakespeare Festival, Delacorte Theatre, 1977.

Ramblings, Playwrights Horizons, New York City, 1977.

Cracks, Playwrights Horizons, 1977.

Dial M for Murder, Playwrights Horizons, 1978.

Journey's End, Long Wharf Theatre, New Haven, CT, 1978.

Editor, bellboy, janitor, body guard, Harry the Horse, priest, soundman, and pirate, *New Jerusalem,* New York Shakespeare Festival, Public Theatre, New York City, 1979.

Jimmy, *A History of the American Film,* Seattle Repertory Theatre, Seattle, WA, 1979.

Time Steps, Playwrights Horizons, 1980.

Ladies in Retirement, Royal Poinciana Playhouse, Palm Beach, FL, 1981.

Len Jenkins, *Limbo Tales,* off-Broadway production, New York City, 1981.

Jeweler, *Dark Ride,* Soho Repertory Theatre, New York City, 1981.

Betty and Gerry, *Cloud 9,* Theatre De Lys (renamed Lucille Lortel Theatre), New York City, 1981.

Hector, *The Chinese Viewing Pavilion,* The Production Company, Actors and Directors Theatre, New York City, 1982.

Jasper, boyfriend of Ginger, and friend of Burt, *Necessary Ends,* New York Shakespeare Festival, Public Theatre, 1982.

Pete Shotton, Alan Williams, Victor Spinetti, Arthur Janov, and Andy Peebles, *Lennon,* Entermedia Theatre, New York City, 1982.

Night Must Fall, Hartman Theatre, Stamford, CT, 1982.

Much Ado about Nothing, Yale Repertory Theatre, New Haven, CT, 1982.

Sergeant Merwin J. Toomey, *Biloxi Blues,* Center Theatre Group, Ahmanson Theatre, Los Angeles, CA, 1984, then (Broadway debut) Neil Simon Theatre, New York City, 1985-86.

Made stage debut in title role, *Hamlet,* Colorado Shakespeare Festival. Also appeared as Bill Sprightly, *A Mad World, My Masters,* La Jolla Playhouse, La Jolla, CA; Charley, *Charley's Aunt,* Academy Festival Theatre; Hamm, *Endgame,* Florida Studio Theatre; in *Hannah,* off-Broadway production, New York City; and with the Trinity Square Repertory Company, Providence, RI, 1975-76.

Film Appearances:

(Film debut; as Bill Sadler) Hotel clerk, *Hanky-Panky,* Columbia, 1982.

(As Bill Sadler) Dickson, *Off Beat,* Touchstone Pictures, 1986.

(As Bill Sadler) Dr. Lynnard Carroll, *Project X,* Twentieth Century-Fox, 1987.

(As Bill Sadler) Salesman Don, *K-9,* Universal, 1989.

Frank Sutton, *The Hot Spot,* Orion, 1990.

(As Bill Sadler) Vernon Trent, *Hard to Kill* (also known as *Seven Year Storm*), Warner Bros., 1990.

Colonel Stuart, *Die Hard 2: Die Harder,* Twentieth Century-Fox, 1990.

Monroe, *Rush,* Metro-Goldwyn-Mayer, 1991.

Grim reaper, *Bill and Ted's Bogus Journey* (also known as *Bill and Ted Go to Hell*), Orion, 1991.

Don, *Trespass* (also known as *Looters*), Universal, 1992.

Dick Brian, *Freaked* (also known as *Hideous Mutant Freekz*), 1994.

Heywood, *The Shawshank Redemption,* Columbia, 1994.

Brayker, *Tales from the Crypt Presents: Demon Knight* (also known as *Demon Keeper* and *Demon Knight*), Universal, 1995.

Colonel Madden, *Solo,* Triumph, 1996.

The mummy, *Tales from the Crypt Presents: Bordello of Blood* (also known as *Bordello of Blood*), Universal, 1996.

Reach the Rock, Universal, 1997.

Mission commander Captain "Wild Bill" Overbeck, *Rocket Man* (also known as *Space Cadets*),Buena Vista, 1997.

Also appeared in *By the Rivers of Babylon,* produced by Wolf Films/Crescendo Productions/Logo Productions.

Film Work:

Song performer, "The Reaper Rap," *Bill and Ted's Bogus Journey* (also known as *Bill and Ted Go to Hell*), Orion, 1991.

Television Appearances; Series:

(As Bill Sadler) Lieutenant Charlie Fontana, *Private Eye,* NBC, 1987-88.

Television Appearances; Episodic:

Rick Dillon, *The Equalizer,* CBS, 1986.

Richie Epson, *In the Heat of the Night* (two episodes), NBC, 1988.

Ken, *Dear John,* NBC, 1988.

"The Abby Singer Show," *St. Elsewhere,* NBC, 1988.

(As Bill Sadler) Colonel Fitzpatrick, *Murphy Brown,* CBS, 1989.

(As Bill Sadler) Dwight Hooper, *Roseanne* (two episodes), ABC, 1989.

Larry Harbin, "Look Homeward Dirtbag," *Hooperman,* ABC, 1989.

(As Bill Sadler) Niles Talbot, "The Man Who Was Death," *Tales from the Crypt,* HBO, 1989.

The grim reaper, "The Assassin," *Tales from the Crypt,* HBO, 1989.

Frank Hellner, "Valerie 23," *The Outer Limits,* Showtime, 1995.

Shamus Bloom, "The Fifth Sepulchre," *Poltergeist: The Legacy,* Showtime, 1996.

Appeared on *AfterM*A*S*H* and *Newhart,* both CBS.

Television Appearances; Movies:

Dieter Schmidt, *The Great Wallendas,* NBC, 1978.

Joey, *Charlie and the Great Balloon Race* (also known as *Charlie's Balloon*), NBC, 1981.

(As Bill Sadler) Coach Dickey, *Unconquered* (also known as *Invictus*), CBS, 1989.

Anthony Prine, *The Face of Fear,* CBS, 1990.

Uri Chelenkoff, *Tagget* (also known as *Dragonfire*), USA Network, 1991.

Treat, *The Last to Go,* ABC, 1991.

Detective Sam Grace, *Bermuda Grace,* NBC, 1993.

David Anatole, *Jack Reed: Badge of Honor* (also known as *Jack Reed: An Honest Cop*), NBC, 1993.

Sarge, *Roadracers* (also known as *Rebel Highway*), Showtime, 1994.

Television Appearances; Specials:

Henry Winkler Meets William Shakespeare, CBS, 1977.

Mr. Rush, *Two-Fisted Tales,* Fox, 1992.

Eddy, *Night Driving* (also known as *Showtime 30-Minute Movie*), Showtime, 1993.

Appeared in *Assaulted Nuts,* Cinemax, and *The Other Side of Victory* and *The Rocking Chair Rebellion.*

Television Appearances; Pilots:

The Neighborhood, NBC, 1982.

(As Bill Sadler) Colonel Tom Sturdivant, *Cadets* (also known as *Rotten to the Corps*), ABC, 1988.

Dr. Linus, *The Omen,* NBC, 1995.

WRITINGS

For Film:

Additional lyrics, "The Reaper Rap," *Bill and Ted's Bogus Journey* (also known as *Bill and Ted Go to Hell*), Orion, 1991.*

SAGET, Bob 1956-

PERSONAL

Full name, Robert Saget; born May 17, 1956, in Philadelphia, PA (some sources say Norfolk, VA); son of Benjamin M. (a supermarket executive) and Rosalyn C. (a hospital administrator) Saget; married Sherri K. Kramer (an attorney), May 16, 1983 (separated, 1997); children: three daughters, including Aubrey Michelle and Lara. *Education:* Temple University, B.A. (film), 1978; graduate work, University of Southern California; trained for the stage with Darryl Hickman, Harvey Lembeck, and Vincent Chase.

Addresses: *Agent*—International Creative Management, 8942 Wilshire Blvd., Beverly Hills, CA 90211.

Career: Comedian, actor, producer, and writer. Groundlings (improvisational comedy troupe), member; as a comedian has appeared in nightclubs and concert halls throughout the United States and Canada, 1979—.

Member: Screen Actors Guild, American Federation of Television and Radio Artists, Directors Guild of America, American Society of Composers, Authors, and Publishers.

Awards, Honors: Student Academy Award, 1978, for *Through Adam's Eyes;* CableACE Award nomination, best direction, 1991, for "Bob Saget—In the Dream State," *HBO Comedy Hour.*

CREDITS

Television Appearances; Series:
Cohost, *The Morning Program,* CBS, 1987.
Danny Tanner, *Full House,* ABC, 1987-95.
Host, *America's Funniest Home Videos,* ABC, 1990-97.

Television Work; Series:
Producer and director of video segments, *The Morning Program,* CBS, 1987.

Television Appearances; Specials:
The Fact, 1982.
Rodney Dangerfield Hosts the 9th Annual Young Comedians Special, HBO, 1985.
HBO Young Comedians Special, HBO, 1986.

A Comedy Celebration: The Comedy and Magic Club's 10th Anniversary Special, Showtime, 1989.
Host, *America's Funniest Home Videos: An Inside Look,* ABC, 1990.
"Bob Saget—In the Dream State," *HBO Comedy Hour,* HBO, 1990.
Comic Relief IV, HBO, 1990.
Funny You Should Ask, CBS, 1990.
The MDA Jerry Lewis Telethon (also known as *The 25th Anniversary MDA Jerry Lewis Labor Day Telethon*), syndicated, 1990.
A User's Guide to Planet Earth: The American Environmental Test, ABC, 1991.
George Burns's 95th Birthday Party, CBS, 1991.
HBO's 20th Anniversary—We Hardly Believe It Ourselves (also known as *HBO's 20th Anniversary Special—We Don't Believe It Ourselves*), CBS and HBO, 1992.
Inside America's Totally Unsolved Lifestyles, ABC, 1992.
The Comedy Store's 20th Birthday, NBC, 1992.
What about Me? I'm Only 3!, CBS, 1992.
Game show host, *To Grandmother's House We Go,* 1992.
Segment host, *ABC's 40th Anniversary Special,* ABC, 1994.
Comic Relief VI, HBO, 1994.
Host, *A Comedy Salute to Andy Kaufman,* NBC, 1995.
Host, *America's Funniest Home Videos Guide to Parenting,* ABC, 1995.
Comic Relief VII, HBO, 1995.
Host, *America's Funniest Home Videos Salute to Boneheads,* ABC, 1996.
Host, *America's Funniest Home Videos: Kids and Animals,* ABC, 1996.
Catch a Rising Star 50th Anniversary—Give or Take 26 Years, CBS, 1996.
"Rodney Dangerfield's 75th Birthday Toast," *HBO Comedy Hour,* HBO, 1997.

Also appeared on *Comedy Tonight,* PBS; *Evening at the Improv,* syndicated; *Comic of the Month,* Showtime; and *Comedy Break,* syndicated.

Television Work; Specials:
Director, "Bob Saget—In the Dream State," *HBO Comedy Hour,* HBO, 1990.

Television Appearances; Episodic:
Contestant, *The Dating Game,* ABC, 1979.
Himself, *Make Me Laugh,* syndicated, 1980.

"The Show Must Go On," *Bosom Buddies,* ABC, 1981.
The Greatest American Hero, ABC, 1984.
It's a Living, ABC, 1985.
Late Night with David Letterman, NBC, 1988.
Macklyn MacKay, "Stand-Up," *Quantum Leap,* NBC, 1989.
Himself, "Hey Now," *The Larry Sanders Show,* HBO, 1992.
Himself, "Office Romance," *The Larry Sanders Show,* HBO, 1994.
Himself, *Ellen,* ABC, 1994.
Grace under Fire, ABC, 1995.
Himself, *The Jeff Foxworthy Show* (also known as *Somewhere in America*), ABC, 1995.
Himself, *The Naked Truth* (also known as *Pix* and *Wilde Again*), ABC, 1995.

Appeared in episodes of *At Ease,* ABC; *The Merv Griffin Show,* syndicated; and *The Tonight Show,* NBC. Also hosted *Saturday Night Live,* NBC.

Television Appearances; Awards Presentations:
The 16th Annual People's Choice Awards, 1990.
The 43rd Annual Primetime Emmy Awards Presentation, 1991.
Master of ceremonies, *Jim Thorpe Pro Sports Awards,* ABC, 1992.

Other Television Appearances:
Spenser Paley, "Father and Scout" (movie), *The ABC Family Movie,* ABC, 1994.

Appeared on the pilot *Love, American Style '85,* ABC; cohost of the pilots *Knock-Knock,* syndicated, and *Surprise,* CBS; also appeared in the pilot *Good News/ Bad News.*

Television Work; Movies:
Executive producer, "Father and Scout," *The ABC Family Movie,* ABC, 1994.
Executive producer and director, *For Hope,* ABC, 1996.
Director, *Jitters,* Lifetime, 1997.

Film Appearances:
(Film debut) Student and sportscaster, *Full Moon High,* Orion, 1979.
Therapy patient, *Devices,* 1980.
Computer voice, *Spaced Out,* Miramax, 1981.
Moving (also known as *Apartment Hunting*), 1981.
Dr. Joffe, *Critical Condition,* Paramount, 1987.
Cameo appearance as reporter, *Meet Wally Sparks,* Trimark, 1997.

Film Work:
Producer, director, and editor, *Through Adam's Eyes* (documentary), 1978.
Director (with Alan Bloom), *Moving* (also known as *Apartment Hunting*), 1981.
Director, *Dirty Work,* Metro-Goldwyn-Mayer, scheduled for release in 1998.

Stage Appearances:
(Stage debut) Douglas, *Audience,* Fig Tree Theatre, Hollywood, CA, 1986.

Stage Work:
Producer, *Audience,* Fig Tree Theatre, Hollywood, CA, 1986.

WRITINGS

Screenplays:
Through Adam's Eyes (documentary), 1978.
(Additional dialogue) *Spaced Out,* Miramax, 1981.
Stepbrothers, 1985.
Two Orphans (short film), 1985.
Coffee Shop (short film), 1986.
Temporary Asylum, 1988.

Teleplays:
The Morning Program (series), CBS, 1987.
America's Funniest Home Videos (series), ABC, 1990-97.
America's Funniest Home Videos: An Inside Look (special), ABC, 1990.
"Bob Saget—In the Dream State" (special), *HBO Comedy Hour,* HBO, 1990.
Jim Thorpe Pro Sports Awards (awards presentation), ABC, 1992.
America's Funniest Home Videos: Kids and Animals (special), ABC, 1996.

Other:
(With Tony Hendra) *Bob Saget's Tales from the Crib,* Perigee (New York City), 1991.

SIDELIGHTS

Bob Saget's *For Hope* is a semi-biographical account of his sister Gay Saget's fight with scleroderma, an autoimmune disease. Gay died at the age of forty-seven from the disease.

OTHER SOURCES

Periodicals:
Entertainment Weekly, May 19, 1995, pp. 38-39.

Los Angeles Magazine, November, 1990, p. 174.
People Weekly, March 26, 1990, p. 38.
Redbook, September, 1990, p. 80.
TV Guide, March 31, 1990, p. 2.*

SAHL, Mort 1927-

PERSONAL

Full name, Morton Lyon Sahl; born May 11, 1927, in Montreal, Quebec, Canada; son of Harry Sahl (a court reporter; later, an administrator for the Federal Bureau of Investigation); married Sue Babior, June 25, 1955 (divorced, 1957); married China Lee; children: Morton Jr. *Education:* Attended Compton Junior College; University of Southern California, B.S. (city management and engineering), 1950.

Addresses: *Agent*—Irving Arthur Associates, 9363 Wilshire Blvd., Suite 212, Beverly Hills, CA 90210.

Career: Comedian, actor, and writer. As a comedian, has appeared in nightclubs and concert halls throughout the United States, including the Hungry i; also editor of the military periodical *Poop from the Group;* actor in experimental theatre productions. *Military service:* U.S. Army Air Forces; served during World War II.

CREDITS

Television Appearances; Specials:
The Mort Sahl Special, NBC, 1960.
A Last Laugh at the Sixties, 1970.
Comedy News, 1972.
Dick Clark's Good Old Days: From Bobby Sox to Bikinis, NBC, 1977.
All Star Party for Clint Eastwood, CBS, 1986.
Jonathan Winters: On the Ledge, Showtime, 1987.
Humor and the Presidency, HBO, 1987.
"Mort Sahl: The Loyal Opposition" (documentary), *American Masters,* PBS, 1989.
Laughing Matters (documentary; also known as *Funny Business*), Showtime, 1993.
Sam Peckinpah: Man of Iron, Arts and Entertainment, 1993.
But. . .Seriously, Showtime, 1994.

Appeared on *Wide Wide World.*

Television Appearances; Episodic:
"Kiss Me Again, Stranger," *Pursuit,* CBS, 1958.

The Big Party, CBS, 1959.
"The Sport," *Richard Diamond, Private Detective,* CBS, 1959.
The Jerry Lewis Show, ABC, 1963.
That Was the Week That Was, NBC, 1964.
Guest host, *Evening at the Improv,* syndicated, 1981.
"JFK: A Personal Story" (documentary), *Biography,* Arts and Entertainment, 1996.

Appeared on episodes of *The Steve Allen Show,* NBC; *The Jack Paar Show,* NBC; *The Eddie Fisher Show,* NBC; *The Tonight Show,* NBC; *Nightline,* ABC; *Thriller,* NBC; and *Emergency,* NBC.

Other Television Appearances:
Comedy News II (pilot), ABC, 1973.
Werner Fink, *Inside the Third Reich* (miniseries), ABC, 1982.

Film Appearances:
(Film debut) Danny Krieger, *In Love and War,* Twentieth Century-Fox, 1958.
Crane, *All the Young Men,* Columbia, 1960.
Ben Morro, *Johnny Cool,* United Artists, 1963.
Dan Ruskin, *Doctor, You've Got to Be Kidding,* Metro-Goldwyn-Mayer, 1967.
Sam Lingonberry, *Don't Make Waves,* Metro-Goldwyn-Mayer, 1967.
Lenny Bruce without Tears, 1971.
The Hungry i Reunion (documentary), 1981.
Uncle Mort, *Nothing Lasts Forever,* Metro-Goldwyn-Mayer/United Artists, 1984.

Stage Appearances:
The Next President (revue), Bijou Theatre, New York City, 1958.
Mort Sahl on Broadway (solo show), Neil Simon Theatre, New York City, 1987.
Comedy Tonight (revue), Lunt-Fontanne Theatre, New York City, 1994.
Mort Sahl's America (solo show), Theatre Four, New York City, 1994, then Boston, MA, 1997.

Radio Appearances; Series:
Talk show host on WRC-Radio, Washington, DC, 1978.

WRITINGS

Heartland (autobiography), Harcourt (San Diego, CA), 1976.
Mort Sahl's America (solo stage show), Theatre Four, New York City, 1994.

Contributor to magazines in Los Angeles, CA, and San Francisco, CA.

RECORDINGS

Albums:
Albums include *The Future Lies Ahead, Mort Sahl 1960, A Way of Life, At the Hungry i, The Next President,* and *Great Moments in Comedy,* all Verve Records; *The New Frontier* and *On Relationships,* both Reprise; *Anyway Onward,* Mercury; *Mort Sahl at Sunset,* Fantasy; and *Sing a Song of Watergate: Apocryphal of Lie,* GNP Crescendo.

Videos:
Videos include *Hungry i Reunion Concert* and *Laughing Room Only.**

SAINT JAMES, Susan 1946-

PERSONAL

Born Susan Jane Miller, August 14, 1946, in Los Angeles, CA; raised in Rockford, IL; daughter of Charles Daniel (in business) and Constance (a teacher; maiden name, Geiger) Miller; married Richard Newbert (a writer), 1967 (divorced, c. 1968); married Tom Lucas, 1971 (divorced, c. 1975); married Dick Ebersol (a television executive), 1981; children: (second marriage) Sunshine, Harmony; (third marriage) Charles, William James, Edward Bright. *Education:* Graduated from Woodlands Academy of the Sacred Heart; studied theater at Rockford College; attended Connecticut College for Women.

Addresses: *Home*—Litchfield, CT, and Telluride, CO. *Agent*—Creative Artists Agency, 9830 Wilshire Blvd., Beverly Hills, CA 90212.

Career: Actress. Professional model in Paris, France; stagehand, Olympia Theatre, Paris, France; assistant to Charles Aznavour; Radio talk show host, WZBG-FM, 1992—. Vice president and national chairperson, Connecticut Special Olympics, Inc.; member, Board of the International Special Olympics, 1994—.

Awards, Honors: Emmy Award, outstanding continued performance by an actress in a supporting role in a series, 1969, and two additional Emmy Award nominations, all for *The Name of the Game;* also three Emmy Award nominations for *McMillan and Wife;* two Emmy Award nominations for *Kate and* *Allie;* Caritas Society Saint Coletta Award, 1981, for work in the field of mental retardation; Gold Key Award, Connecticut Sport Writer's Alliance; Walter Camp Football Foundation Award (first female recipient); honorary doctorates from Albertus Manus College, University of New Haven, University of Connecticut, Southern Connecticut State University, and University of Bridgeport.

CREDITS

Television Appearances; Movies:
Timothea Lamb, *Magic Carpet,* ABC, 1972.
Esther Winters, *Desperate Women,* NBC, 1978.
Jeannie Haskins, *Night Cries,* ABC, 1978.
Rita Massaro, *The Girls in the Office,* ABC, 1979.
Sally Bass, *Sex and the Single Parent,* CBS, 1979.
Leigh Goodwin, *S.O.S. Titanic,* ABC, 1979.
Samantha Kandal, *The Kid from Nowhere,* NBC, 1982.
Carol Sherwood, *I Take These Men,* CBS, 1983.

Television Appearances; Series:
Peggy Maxwell, *The Name of the Game,* NBC, 1968-71.
Sally McMillan, *McMillan and Wife,* NBC, 1971-76.
Kate McArdle, *Kate and Allie,* CBS, 1984-89.

Television Appearances; Pilots:
Peggy Maxwell, *Fame Is the Name of the Game,* NBC, 1966.
Miss Porter, *Alias Smith and Jones,* ABC, 1971.
Sally McMillan, *Once Upon a Dead Man,* NBC, 1971.
Julia Prescott, *Ready and Willing,* CBS, 1974.
Holly, *Scott Free,* NBC, 1976.
Susan Roberts, *After George,* CBS, 1983.

Television Appearances; Episodic:
"Girl in the Night," *Ironside,* NBC, 1967.
"Something for Nothing," *Ironside,* NBC, 1968.
Stewardess, "A Thief Is a Thief," *It Takes a Thief,* ABC, 1968.
Charlene "Charlie" Brown, "It Takes One To Know One," *It Takes a Thief,* ABC, 1968.
Charlene "Charlie" Brown, "When Thieves Fall In," *It Takes a Thief,* ABC, 1968.
Charlene 'Charlie' Brown, "Payoff at the Piazza," *It Takes a Thief,* ABC, 1969.
"Walk in the Dark," *McCloud,* NBC, 1970.
Charlene "Charlie" Brown, "The Suzie Simone Caper," *It Takes a Thief,* ABC, 1970.
Aggie O'Shea, "War Co-Respondent," *M*A*S*H,* CBS, 1980.

Guest host, *Saturday Night Live*, NBC, 1981.
Host and narrator, "Eunice Kennedy Shriver," *An American Portrait*, CBS, 1986.
Interviewee, *Later with Bob Costas*, NBC, 1988-94.
Host, *Friday Night Videos*, NBC, 1985.
"Broken Windows," *Tattingers*, NBC, 1988.
Lynn O'Brien, *The Drew Carey Show*, ABC, 1996.

Also appeared on *Saturday Night Live*, NBC, and *Love, American Style*, ABC.

Television Appearances; Specials:
Celebrity Challenge of the Sexes, CBS, 1977.
Circus of the Stars, CBS, 1977.
John Denver in Australia, ABC, 1978.
Life's Most Embarrassing Moments, syndicated, 1985.
The 37th Annual Prime Time Emmy Awards, 1985.
The Flintstones 25th Anniversary Celebration, CBS, 1986.
The Special Olympics Opening Ceremonies, 1987.
A Very Special Christmas Party (also known as *Special Olympics Christmas Party*), ABC, 1988.
Rock Hudson: Tall, Dark and Handsome, 1989.
Saturday Night Live 15th Anniversary, NBC, 1989.
Woodstock: Return to the Planet of the '60s, 1989.
The Opening Ceremonies of the 1995 Special Olympics World Games, NBC, 1995.

Film Appearances:
Linette Orbison, *P.J.* (also known as *New Face in Hell*), Universal, 1968.
Ida, *Jigsaw*, Universal, 1968.
Aida, *What's So Bad About Feeling Good?*, Universal, 1968.
Rosabelle, *Where Angels Go . . . Trouble Follows*, Columbia, 1968.
Tina Waters, *Outlaw Blues*, Warner Bros., 1977.
Cindy Sondheim, *Love at First Bite*, American International, 1979.
Jane Mahoney, *How to Beat the High Cost of Living*, American International, 1980.
Vivian Whitney, *Carbon Copy*, Avco-Embassy, 1981.
Katherine, *Don't Cry, It's Only Thunder*, Sanrio Communications, 1982.

Principal Stage Appearances:
Ready When You Are, C.B.!, Marriott's Lincolnshire Theatre, Lincolnshire, IL, 1978.

OTHER SOURCES

Periodicals:
Sports Illustrated, December 25, 1995, p. 52.
Time, June 25, 1990, p. 53.*

SAMPSON, Bill
See ERMAN, John

SANDERS, Richard 1940-

PERSONAL

Born Richard Kinard Sanders, August 23, 1940, in Harrisburg, PA; son of Henry Irvine and Thelma S. Sanders. *Education:* Leavenworth High School, diploma (valedictorian), 1958; Carnegie Institute of Technology, B.F.A., 1962; trained for the stage at the London Academy of Music and Dramatic Art on a Fulbright grant.

Addresses: *Office*—c/o Blood Star, Inc., P.O. Box 1644, Woodinville, WA 98072-1644.

Career: Actor and writer. President, Blood Star, Inc. Peace Corps volunteer in Brazil, 1966-69, where he served as director of acting and stage movement for the State Theatre of Paraiba, Brazil, 1966-68.

Member: Actors' Equity Association, Screen Actors Guild, American Federation of Television and Radio Artists, Writers Guild of America.

Awards, Honors: Buckeye Newshawk Award, 1974-79.

CREDITS

Television Appearances; Series:
Les Nessman, *WKRP in Cincinnati*, CBS, 1978-82.
Benjamin Beanley, *Spencer* (also known as *Under One Roof*), NBC, 1984-85.
Frank Chapman (recurring), *Berrenger's*, NBC, 1984-85.
Voice, *The Inhumanoids* (animated), 1986-87.
Paul Sycamore, *You Can't Take it with You*, syndicated, 1987-88.
Les Nessman, *The New WKRP in Cincinnati*, syndicated, 1991-93.

Television Appearances; Episodic:
Mr. Beach, *Newhart*, CBS, 1982.
Bob Wormser, "It Happened One Summer," *Who's the Boss?*, ABC, 1985.
Mr. Conner, "Sixteen Years and What Do You Get," *Married With Children*, Fox, 1987.
Warren Graustrak, *Coach*, ABC, 1990.
Mr. Peabody, *Unhappily Ever After*, The WB, 1998.

"Rendezvous with Terror," *Barnaby Jones,* CBS, 1974.

"Rampage," *The Streets of San Francisco,* ABC, 1974.

"Robbery: 48 Hours," *Police Story,* NBC, 1974.

"A Lamb to the Slaughter," *Kung Fu,* ABC, 1975.

"The Secret of Terry Lake," *Baretta,* ABC, 1975.

"Spanish Class," *Police Story,* NBC, 1976.

"A Game of Love," *Joe Forrester,* NBC, 1976.

"Two Frogs on a Mongoose," *Police Story,* NBC, 1976.

"Monster Manor," *Police Story,* NBC, 1976.

"Trial Board," *Police Story,* NBC, 1977.

"Barrio," *Lou Grant,* CBS, 1977.

"River of Promises," *Police Story,* NBC, 1978.

"The Show Must Go On—Sometimes," *The Black Sheep Squadron,* NBC, 1978.

"Running the Hill," *David Cassidy—Man Undercover,* NBC, 1978.

"Spanish Eight," *Eischied,* NBC, 1979.

"Fritz's Boys," *Paris,* CBS, 1980.

"Hair Apparent," *Hill Street Blues,* NBC, 1981.

"Space Ranger," *The Greatest American Hero,* ABC, 1983.

"Five Days," *Masquerade,* ABC, 1984.

"Lucky Ducks," *Hill Street Blues,* NBC, 1984.

"Eva's Brawn," *Hill Street Blues,* NBC, 1984.

Rudy Garcia, "Trouble on Wheels," *The A-Team,* NBC, 1984.

"Let's Steele a Plot," *Remington Steele,* NBC, 1984.

"The Bribe," *T. J. Hooker,* ABC, 1985.

Doug Kelleher, "The Library," *The Twilight Zone,* CBS, 1986.

Jimmy "The Eraser" Kendall, "The Eraser," *MacGyver,* ABC, 1986.

Lieutenant Nolan Page, "Death and Taxes," *Magnum, P.I.,* CBS, 1986.

Ben Mohammed, "Speed of Light," *Adderly,* CBS, 1987.

Joe Rinaldi, "The Bottom Line Is Murder," *Murder, She Wrote,* CBS, 1987.

Jimmy "The Eraser" Kendall, "Back from the Dead," *MacGyver,* ABC, 1987.

Lieutenant Nolan Page, "Laura," *Magnum, P.I.,* CBS, 1987.

Lieutenant Nolan Page, "Tigers Fan," *Magnum, P.I.,* CBS, 1987.

Lieutenant Alfano, *Murder, She Wrote,* CBS, 1988.

Oscar Carrera, *Miami Vice,* NBC, 1988.

Lieutenant Nolan Page, "Resolutions," *Magnum, P.I.,* CBS, 1988.

Angelo Marino, "Pilot," *NYPD Blue,* ABC, 1993.

Angelo Marino, "4B or Not 4B," *NYPD Blue,* ABC, 1993.

Bakersfield P.D., Fox, 1994.

Also appeared on *The Doctors,* NBC.*

SAWYER, Diane 1945(?)-

PERSONAL

Born December 22, 1945 (some sources say 1946), in Glasgow, KY; raised in Louisville, KY; daughter of E. P. (a county judge) and Jean W. (an elementary school teacher; maiden name, Dunagan) Sawyer; married Mike Nichols (a producer and director), April 29, 1988. *Education:* Wellesley College, B.A. (journalism), 1967; studied law at University of Louisville. *Avocational interests:* Reading (especially nineteenth-century novels), watching films, singing.

Addresses: *Home*—New York, NY. *Office*—*Prime-Time Live,* ABC News, 147 Columbus Ave., New York, NY 10023-5900.

Career: Broadcast journalist. WLKY-TV, Louisville, KY, weather reporter and general reporter, 1967-70; assistant to White House Deputy Press Secretary Jerry Warren, White House Press Secretary Ron Ziegler, and President Richard M. Nixon, Washington, DC, 1970-74; researcher for Nixon's memoirs, San Clemente, CA, 1974-78; CBS-News, New York City, general assignment reporter and State Department correspondent, 1978-81, coanchor for various programs, 1981-84, correspondent and coeditor, 1984-89, ABC News, New York City, coanchor and correspondent for various news programs and occasional anchor for other programs, 1989—.

Member: Council on Foreign Relations.

Awards, Honors: Selected America's Young Woman of the Year (also known as America's Junior Miss), 1963; Emmy Award nominations, outstanding news and documentary program segment, 1979, for "Hostages—300 Days," and outstanding interview segment, 1981, for "Richard Nixon," both *CBS Morning News;* Emmy Award nomination, outstanding interview segment, 1983, for "Admiral Rickover," *60 Minutes;* Matrix Award, New York chapter of Women in Communications, 1984; Emmy Award nominations, outstanding interview segments, 1986, for "Dancing on Her Grave," and 1987, for "The City of Garbage—Sister Emanuelle," both *60 Minutes;* Peabody Award for public service, 1989; Emmy Award nominations, outstanding investigative journalism segment, for "The Second Battlefield," outstanding interview segment, for "Katherine the Great," and outstanding coverage of a continuing news story, for "Murder in Beverly Hills," all 1991, *PrimeTime*

Live; Robert F. Kennedy Journalism Award (Grand Prize), c. 1991-92, for investigative report about racism; National Headliner Award, Ohio State University Award, and Sigma Delta Chi Award, c. 1991-92, for investigative report about childcare centers; Crowning Glory Award, Role Models on the Web, 1997, "for having conquered her shyness" and thus serving as a role model. Also received nine Emmy Awards, a du Pont Award; an International Radio and Television Society Lifetime Achievement Award, a Broadcast Hall of Fame Award, a University of Southern California Distinguished Achievement in Journalism Award, and another Peabody Award for public service.

CREDITS

Television Appearances; Series:
Coanchor, *Morning with Charles Kuralt and Diane Sawyer,* CBS, 1981-82.
Coanchor, *CBS Morning News,* CBS, 1982-84.
Correspondent, *60 Minutes,* CBS, 1984-89.
Coanchor, *PrimeTime Live,* ABC, 1989—.
The Class of the 20th Century, 1992.
Correspondent, *Day One,* ABC, 1993-95, coanchor, 1995.
Coanchor and correspondent, *Turning Point* (also known as *Moment of Crisis*), ABC, 1994—.

Also occasional anchor for *ABC News Nightline,* ABC Nightly News, and *ABC World News Tonight* (also known as *ABC World News Tonight with Peter Jennings*).

Television Appearances; Specials:
David Letterman's Second Annual Holiday Film Festival (also known as *David Letterman's 2nd Annual Holiday Film Festival*), NBC, 1986.
Correspondent, *48 Hours on Crack Street,* CBS, 1986.
The Television Academy Hall of Fame, 1986.
Correspondent, *The Soviet Union—Seven Days in May,* CBS, 1987.
Correspondent, *Campaign '88: The Democratic Convention,* CBS, 1988.
Correspondent, *Campaign '88: The Republican Convention,* CBS, 1988.
Reporter, *Campaign '88: Election Night,* CBS, 1988.
The Television Academy Hall of Fame, Fox, 1990.
Edward R. Murrow: This Reporter, PBS, 1990.
Donahue: The 25th Anniversary, 1992.
60 Minutes . . . 25 Years (also known as *60 Minutes Turns 25*), CBS, 1993.
Host, *James Reston: The Man Millions Read* (documentary), PBS, 1993.

Kathie Lee Gifford's Celebration of Motherhood, ABC, 1993.
Anchor, *Murder in Beverly Hills: The Menendez Trial,* 1993.
Barbara Walters Presents "The Ten Most Fascinating People of 1994," ABC, 1994.
Correspondent, "Baby, Oh Baby: The Six Pack Turns Two," *Turning Point,* ABC, 1995.
The NFL at 75: An All-Star Celebration (also known as *NFL 75th Anniversary Special*), ABC, 1995.
"The Rosemary Clooney Golden Anniversary Celebration," *A & E Stage,* Arts and Entertainment, 1995.
Correspondent, "Baby, Oh Baby: The Six Pack Is Back," *Turning Point,* ABC, 1996.
Host, "Deadly Game: The Mark and Delia Owens Story," *Turning Point,* ABC, 1996.
Host, *Domestic Violence: Faces of Fear,* PBS, 1996.
Anchor, "Heroin: The New High School High," *Turning Point,* ABC, 1997.
Hollywood and the News, 1997.
Correspondent, "Baby, Oh Baby: The Six Pack Talks Back," *Turning Point,* ABC, 1997.

Television Appearances; Episodic:
Occasional correspondent, *The American Parade* (also known as *Crossroads*), 1984.

Occasional correspondent, *Walter Cronkite's Universe.* Appeared in *Murphy Brown,* CBS, and *Live with Regis and Kathie Lee,* syndicated.

OTHER SOURCES

Books:
Contemporary Authors, Volume 115, Gale (Detroit, MI), 1985.
Newsmakers 1994 Cumulation, Gale, 1994, pp. 438-441.

Periodicals:
Entertainment Weekly, March 4, 1994, p. 9; July 28, 1995, pp. 50-51; November 8, 1996, pp. 34-38.
Esquire, January, 1995, pp. 76-83.
Harper's Bazaar, November, 1984, p. 232.
Interview, September, 1984, p. 100.
Life, August, 1989, p. 72.
New Leader, March 14, 1994, pp. 20-21.
Newsweek, February 28, 1994, p. 58.
New Yorker, February 14, 1994, pp. 61-63.
New York Times, September 30, 1981; April 1, 1997, p. B3.
People Weekly, November 5, 1984, p. 78.
Time, February 28, 1994, p. 69; September 26, 1994, p. 10.

TV Guide, March 26, 1994, pp. 8-14; November 5, 1994, p. 43.
Variety, February 21, 1994, pp. 171-172.
Wall Street Journal, April 1, 1997, p. B7.

Other:
http://www.newsltr.com/rolemodel/sawyer/dsawyer.htm (web page), November 24, 1997.*

SCALIA, Jack   1951(?)-

PERSONAL

Born November 10, 1951 (some sources say 1950), in Brooklyn, NY; son of a baseball player; married Joan Rankin (a model; divorced); married Karen Baldwin; children: Olivia. *Ethnicity:* Irish-Italian American. *Education:* Attended Ottawa University, Ottawa, KS. *Religion:* Roman Catholic.

Addresses: *Agent*—William Morris Agency, 151 El Camino Dr., Beverly Hills, CA 90212.

Career: Actor, producer, and director. Montreal Expos, professional baseball player; worked as a professional model, construction worker, and food packager. Child Health USA (child abuse prevention organization), national ambassador, 1990.

Member: Mothers Against Drunk Driving (MADD), Celebrities Against Drunk Driving.

CREDITS

Television Appearances; Series:
Nick Corsello, *The Devlin Connection,* NBC, 1982.
Blue Stratton, *High Performance,* ABC, 1983.
Danny Krucek, *Berrengers,* NBC, 1985.
Detective Nick McCarren, *Hollywood Beat,* ABC, 1985.
Tony Roselli, *Remington Steele,* 1986-87.
Nicholas Pearce, *Dallas,* CBS, 1987-88.
Title role (Tony Wolf) *Wolf,* CBS, 1989-91.
Cohost, *Stuntmasters* (documentary), syndicated, 1991-92.
Detective Nico Bonetti, *Tequila and Bonetti,* CBS, 1992.
Constantine "Connie" Harper, *Pointman,* syndicated, 1994-95.

Television Appearances; Miniseries:
Rocco Cipriani, *I'll Take Manhattan,* CBS, 1987.

Lennie Golden, *Jackie Collins's "Lady Boss"* (also known as *Lady Boss*), NBC, 1992.

Television Appearances; Movies:
Vince Martino, *The Star Maker,* NBC, 1981.
Lieutenant Tony Monaco, *Amazons,* ABC, 1984.
Jack Hollander, *The Other Lover,* CBS, 1985.
O'Shea, *Club Med,* ABC, 1986.
Jack Thompson, *After the Shock* (also known as *To the Heroes: The San Francisco Earthquake, October 17, 1989*), USA Network, 1990.
Dr. Eugene Kesselman, *Donor,* CBS, 1990.
Frank Decker, *Deadly Desire,* USA Network, 1991.
Tommy Griffin, *Runaway Father,* CBS, 1991.
Mike Barcetti, *With a Vengeance,* CBS, 1992.
Joey Buttafuoco, *Casualties of Love: The "Long Island Lolita" Story* (also known as *Casualty of Love* and *The Buttafuoco Story*), CBS, 1993.
Mike, *Judith Krantz's "Torch Song"* (also known as *Torch Song*), ABC, 1993.
Michael Carvella, *Shadow of Obsession* (also known as *Unwanted Attentions*), NBC, 1994.
Brian Dillon, *Shattered Image,* USA Network, 1994.
Roy Calvin, *Tall, Dark, and Deadly* (also known as *The Charmer*), USA Network, 1995.
Michael DeMarco, *Barbara Taylor Bradford's "Everything to Gain"* (also known as *Everything to Gain*), CBS, 1996.

Television Appearances; Specials:
Battle of the Network Stars, 1988.
The Hollywood Christmas Parade, 1988.
New York parade host, *The CBS All-American Thanksgiving Day Parade,* CBS, 1989.
The Hollywood Christmas Parade, 1989.
The 61st Annual Hollywood Christmas Parade, 1992.

Television Appearances; Episodic:
Max Chamberlain, *Touched by an Angel,* CBS, 1995.

Other Television Appearances:
Nick Corsello, *The Devlin Connection* (pilot), 1982.
Richard Devereaux, *The Ring of Scorpio,* 1990.
Constantine "Connie" Harper, *Pointman* (pilot), syndicated, 1994.
The Art of the Cigar, 1996.

Film Appearances:
Nicky Piacenza, *Fear City* (also known as *Border* and *Ripper*), Chevy Chase Distribution, 1984.
Wick Hayes, *La Grieta* (also known as *Endless Descent* and *The Rift*), LIVE Home Video, 1989.
Mike Yarnell, *Illicit Behavior,* Prism Pictures, 1992.
Saul Schwartz, *Amore!,* 1993.

Detective Sergeant Vince Morgan, *Beyond Suspicion,* Libra Home Entertainment, 1994.

Brandon's dad, *Storybook,* Republic Pictures Home Video, 1995.

Jack Floyd, *T-Force,* PM Home Video, 1995.

Chuck Rafferty, *The Silencers,* PM Entertainment, 1995.

Nick Saxon, *Dark Breed,* PM Entertainment, 1996.

Scott Thompson, *Follow Your Heart,* Republic, 1997.

Urban Justice (also known as *Blood Money* and *Under Oath*), Concorde-New Horizons, 1997.

Everything to Gain, 1997.

Film Work; Associate Producer:

T-Force, PM Home Video, 1995.

The Silencers, PM Entertainment, 1995.

Dark Breed, PM Entertainment, 1996.

Stage Appearances:

Red River Rats, Burbage Theatre, Los Angeles, 1994.

OTHER SOURCES

Periodicals:

Good Housekeeping, April, 1990, pp. 56, 58.*

SCHAEFER, George   1920-1997

PERSONAL

Born George Louis Schaefer, December 16, 1920, in Wallingford, CT; died September 10, 1997, in Los Angeles, CA; son of Louis (in sales) and Elsie (Otterbein) Schaefer; married Mildred Trares (an actress), February 5, 1954. *Education:* Lafayette College, B.A. (English), 1941; graduate work at the Yale University School of Drama, 1942. *Avocational Interests:* Contract bridge, travel, theater, and film going.

Career: Director and producer. Central Pacific Base Command, U.S. Army Special Services, Honolulu, HI, director of over fifty productions, 1942-45; City Center Theatre, New York City, executive producer and artistic director, 1949-52; Compass Productions Inc., president, 1959-86; Schaefer/Karpf Productions, founder with Merrill H. Karpf, 1982; National Council of the Arts, 1983-88; Department of theatre, film, and television, University of California, Los Angeles, associate dean, 1986-91, emeritus professor, 1991-97. *Military service:* U.S. Army, Special Services, sergeant, 1942-45.

Member: Directors Guild of America (national board of directors, 1960-75, vice president, 1961-79, president, 1979-81), Academy of Motion Picture Arts and Sciences, Academy of Television Arts and Sciences, Caucus for Producers, Writers, and Directors, American National Theatre and Academy—West (board of directors), Variety Clubs International, Players Club, Phi Beta Kappa.

Awards, Honors: Antoinette Perry Award (with Maurice Evans), best producer of a play, 1954, for *The Teahouse of the August Moon;* Sylvania Award, outstanding dramatic series, and Peabody Award, outstanding television entertainment, both 1958, for *Hallmark Hall of Fame; Look* (magazine) Award, and *Radio-Television Daily* Award, both 1957, for "The Green Pastures," *Hallmark Hall of Fame; Radio-Television Daily* Award, director of the year, 1957; *Radio-Television Daily* Award, 1959, for "Johnny Belinda," *Hallmark Hall of Fame;* Sylvania Award, Peabody Award, and Emmy Awards, best special dramatic program and best direction of a single dramatic program, all 1959, for "Little Moon of Alban," *Hallmark Hall of Fame;* Outstanding Achievement Award, Directors Guild of America, 1960, *TV Guide* Award, best single dramatic program on television, *Radio-Television Daily* Award, dramatic show of the year, and Emmy Awards, program of the year, outstanding program achievement in the field of drama, and outstanding directorial achievement in drama, 1961, all for "Macbeth," *Hallmark Hall of Fame; Radio-Television Daily* Award, director of the year, 1961; *Saturday Review* Special Commendation for Notable Production, and Emmy Award, program of the year, both 1962, for "Victoria Regina," *Hallmark Hall of Fame; Radio-Television Daily* All-American Award, producer of the year and director of the year, 1963; Honorary doctor of literature, Lafayette College, 1963; Outstanding Achievement Award, Directors Guild of America, best television director, 1963, for "Pygmalion," *Hallmark Hall of Fame; Radio-Television Daily* Award, director of the year, 1964; Dineen Award, National Catholic Theatre Conference, 1964; Emmy Award, outstanding program achievement in entertainment, 1965, for "The Magnificent Yankee," *Hallmark Hall of Fame; Radio-Television Daily* Award, director of the year, 1965; Emmy Award, outstanding dramatic program, 1968, for "Elizabeth the Queen," *Hallmark Hall of Fame;* Outstanding Achievement Award, Directors Guild of America, best television director, 1967, for "Do Not Go Gentle into That Good Night," *CBS Playhouse;* Outstanding Achievement Award, Directors Guild of America, best television director, 1968, for "My

Father and My Mother," *Hallmark Hall of Fame;* Emmy Award, outstanding single program—drama or comedy, 1973, for *A War of Children;* Honorary degree, Coker College, L.H.D., 1973; Member of the Year Award, Caucus for Producers, Writers and Directors, 1983; Emmy Award nomination, 1983, for *The Best Christmas Pageant Ever;* received more than 30 Emmy Award nominations and 17 Directors Guild of America Award nominations; first person to win four Directors Guild America Awards.

CREDITS

Stage Work; Director, Except Where Indicated:
Leave It to Smith, Pastime Players, Oak Park, IL, 1937.
Hamlet (also known as *G.I. Hamlet*), City Center Theatre, New York City, 1946.
(And producer with Maurice Evans) *The Teahouse of the August Moon,* Her Majesty's Theatre, London, 1954.
Hamlet (also known as *G.I. Hamlet*), Columbus Circle Theatre, New York City, 1945.
(With Maurice Evans) *Man and Superman,* Alvin Theatre, New York City, 1947.
The Linden Tree, Music Box Theatre, New York City, 1948.
(And producer) *Man and Superman,* City Center Theatre, 1949.
(And producer) *She Stoops to Conquer,* City Center Theatre, 1949.
(And producer) *The Corn Is Green,* City Center Theatre, 1950.
(And producer) *The Heiress,* City Center Theatre, 1950.
(And producer) *The Devil's Disciple,* City Center Theatre, 1950.
(And producer) *Captain Brassbound's Conversion,* City Center Theatre, 1950.
(And producer) *The Royal Family, Richard II,* City Center Theatre, 1951.
(And producer) *The Taming of the Shrew,* City Center Theatre, 1951.
(And producer) *Dream Girl,* City Center Theatre, 1951.
(And producer) *Idiot's Delight,* City Center Theatre, 1951.
(And producer) *The Wild Duck,* City Center Theatre, 1951.
(And producer) *Anna Christie,* City Center Theatre, 1952.
(And producer) *Come of Age,* City Center Theatre, 1952.
(And producer) *The Male Animal,* City Center Theatre, 1952.

(And producer) *Tovarich,* City Center Theatre, 1952.
(And producer) *First Lady,* City Center Theatre, 1952.
Producer with Maurice Evans, *The Teahouse of the August Moon,* Martin Beck Theatre, New York City, 1953.
Kiss Me Kate, City Center Theatre, 1955.
The Southwest Corner, Holiday Theatre, New York City, 1955.
The Apple Cart, Plymouth Theatre, New York City, 1956.
The Body Beautiful, Broadway Theatre, New York City, 1958.
(And producer) *Write Me a Murder,* Belasco Theatre, New York City, 1961, then Lyric Theatre, London, 1962.
Producer, *To Broadway with Love,* Texas Pavilion, New York World's Fair, Flushing, NY, 1964.
The Great Indoors, Eugene O'Neill Theatre, New York City, 1966.
The Last of Mrs. Lincoln, Kennedy Center for the Performing Arts, Opera House, Washington, DC, then American National Theatre and Academy Theatre, New York City, both 1972.
On Golden Pond, Center Theatre Group, Ahmanson Theatre, Los Angeles, 1980.
Mixed Couples, Brooks Atkinson Theatre, New York City, 1980.
Another Part of the Forest, Center Theatre Group, Ahmanson Theatre, 1981.
Lyndon, Wilmington Playhouse, Wilmington, DE, 1984.
Leave It to Jane, Los Angeles, 1987.

Also director of productions at the State Fair Music Hall, Dallas, TX, 1952-56 and 1958.

Major Tours; Director:
Hamlet, U.S. cities, 1946-47.
Darling, Darling, Darling, U.S. cities, 1947.
(With Maurice Evans) *Man and Superman,* U.S. cities, 1948-49.
The Teahouse of the August Moon, U.S. cities, 1954, then 1956.
The Apple Cart, U.S. cities, 1957.
Zenda, U.S. cities, 1963.
The Student Prince, U.S. cities, 1973.
Ah! Wilderness, U.S. cities, 1975.
Lyndon, U.S. cities, 1984.

Film Work; Director, Except Where Indicated:
Macbeth, Prominent, 1963.
Pendulum, Columbia, 1969.
Generation, Avco-Embassy, 1969.
Doctors' Wives, Columbia, 1971.

Once Upon a Scoundrel, Carlyle, 1973.
(And producer) *An Enemy of the People,* Warner Bros., 1978.

Television Appearances; Specials:
The Television Makers, PBS, 1987.

Television Work; "Hallmark Hall of Fame"
Specials; Director, Except Where Indicated:
"Hamlet," *Hallmark Hall of Fame,* NBC, 1953.
"Richard II," *Hallmark Hall of Fame,* NBC, 1954.
"Macbeth," *Hallmark Hall of Fame,* NBC, 1954.
"Alice in Wonderland," *Hallmark Hall of Fame,* NBC, 1955.
"Dream Girl," *Hallmark Hall of Fame,* NBC, 1955.
"The Devil's Disciple," *Hallmark Hall of Fame,* NBC, 1955.
"Taming of the Shrew," *Hallmark Hall of Fame,* NBC, 1956.
"The Good Fairy," *Hallmark Hall of Fame,* NBC, 1956.
"The Corn Is Green," *Hallmark Hall of Fame,* NBC, 1956.
(And producer) "Man and Superman," *Hallmark Hall of Fame,* NBC, 1956.
(And producer) "The Little Foxes," *Hallmark Hall of Fame,* NBC, 1956.
(And producer) "The Cradle Song," *Hallmark Hall of Fame,* NBC, 1956.
(And producer) "Born Yesterday," *Hallmark Hall of Fame,* NBC, 1956.
(And producer) "The Lark," *Hallmark Hall of Fame,* NBC, 1957.
(And producer) "The Green Pastures," *Hallmark Hall of Fame,* NBC, 1957.
(And producer) "On Borrowed Time," *Hallmark Hall of Fame,* NBC, 1957.
(And producer) "Twelfth Night," *Hallmark Hall of Fame,* NBC, 1957.
(And producer) "There Shall Be No Night," *Hallmark Hall of Fame,* NBC, 1957.
(And producer) "The Yeomen of the Guard," *Hallmark Hall of Fame,* NBC, 1957.
(And producer) "Dial 'M' for Murder," *Hallmark Hall of Fame,* NBC, 1958.
(And producer) "Little Moon of Alban," *Hallmark Hall of Fame,* NBC, 1958.
(And producer) "Kiss Me Kate," *Hallmark Hall of Fame,* NBC, 1958.
(And producer) "Johnny Belinda," *Hallmark Hall of Fame,* NBC, 1958.
(And producer) "Hans Brinker, or The Silver Skates," *Hallmark Hall of Fame,* NBC, 1958.

(And producer) "A Doll's House," *Hallmark Hall of Fame,* NBC, 1959.
(And producer) "Berkeley Square," *Hallmark Hall of Fame,* NBC, 1959.
(And producer) "Ah! Wilderness," *Hallmark Hall of Fame,* NBC, 1959.
(And producer) "Winterset," *Hallmark Hall of Fame,* NBC, 1959.
(And producer) "Captain Brassbound's Conversion," *Hallmark Hall of Fame,* NBC, 1960.
(And producer) "Macbeth," *Hallmark Hall of Fame,* NBC, 1960.
(And producer) "The Tempest," *Hallmark Hall of Fame,* NBC, 1960.
(And producer) "Shangri-La," *Hallmark Hall of Fame,* NBC, 1960.
(And producer) "Golden Child," *Hallmark Hall of Fame,* NBC, 1960.
(And producer) "Give Us Barabbas!," *Hallmark Hall of Fame,* NBC, 1961.
(And producer) "The Joke and the Valley," *Hallmark Hall of Fame,* NBC, 1961.
(And producer) "Time Remembered," *Hallmark Hall of Fame,* NBC, 1961.
(And producer) "Victoria Regina," *Hallmark Hall of Fame,* NBC, 1961.
(And producer) "Arsenic and Old Lace," *Hallmark Hall of Fame,* NBC, 1962.
(And producer) "The Invincible Mr. Disraeli," *Hallmark Hall of Fame,* NBC, 1962.
(And producer) "Cyrano de Bergerac," *Hallmark Hall of Fame,* NBC, 1962.
(And producer) "Pygmalion," *Hallmark Hall of Fame,* NBC, 1963.
(And producer) "The Patriots," *Hallmark Hall of Fame,* NBC, 1963.
(And producer) "A Cry of Angels," *Hallmark Hall of Fame,* NBC, 1963.
(And producer) "Abe Lincoln in Illinois," *Hallmark Hall of Fame,* NBC, 1964.
(And producer) "The Fantasticks," *Hallmark Hall of Fame,* NBC, 1964.
(And producer) "Little Moon of Alban," *Hallmark Hall of Fame,* NBC, 1964.
(And producer) "The Magnificent Yankee," *Hallmark Hall of Fame,* NBC, 1965.
(And producer) "Inherit the Wind," *Hallmark Hall of Fame,* NBC, 1965.
(And producer) "The Holy Terror," *Hallmark Hall of Fame,* NBC, 1965.
(And producer) "Eagle in a Cage," *Hallmark Hall of Fame,* NBC, 1965.
(And producer) "Blithe Spirit," *Hallmark Hall of Fame,* NBC, 1966.

(And producer) "Barefoot in Athens," *Hallmark Hall of Fame*, NBC, 1966.

(And producer) "Lamp at Midnight," *Hallmark Hall of Fame*, NBC, 1966.

(And producer) "Anastasia," *Hallmark Hall of Fame*, NBC, 1967.

(And producer) "Soldier in Love," *Hallmark Hall of Fame*, NBC, 1967.

(And producer) "Saint Joan," *Hallmark Hall of Fame*, NBC, 1967.

(And producer) "The Admirable Crichton," *Hallmark Hall of Fame*, NBC, 1968.

(And producer) "My Father and My Mother," *Hallmark Hall of Fame*, NBC, 1968.

(And producer) "Elizabeth the Queen," *Hallmark Hall of Fame*, NBC, 1968.

(And producer) "The File on Devlin," *Hallmark Hall of Fame*, NBC, 1969.

Producer, "Hamlet," *Hallmark Hall of Fame*, NBC, 1970.

(And producer) "Gideon," *Hallmark Hall of Fame*, NBC, 1971.

"Truman at Potsdam," *Hallmark Hall of Fame*, NBC, 1976.

Television Work; Series:

Executive producer, *Love Story*, NBC, 1973-74.

Television Director; Pilots:

Land of Hope, CBS, 1976.

Television Director; Episodic:

"Hour of the Bath," *Alcoa Theatre*, NBC, 1962.

"The Hands of Donofrio," *Alcoa Premiere*, ABC, 1962.

Love Story, NBC, 1973.

Love Story, NBC, 1974.

"Jimmy Stewart: Hometown Hero," *Biography*, Arts and Entertainment, 1993.

Television Work; Movies; Director, Except Where Indicated:

(And producer) *A War of Children*, CBS, 1972.

F. Scott Fitzgerald and The Last of the Belles, ABC, 1974.

(And producer) *In This House of Brede*, CBS, 1975.

Amelia Earhart, NBC, 1976.

(And producer) *The Girl Called Hatter Fox*, CBS, 1977.

First You Cry, CBS, 1978.

(And producer) *Who'll Save Our Children?*, CBS, 1978.

(And producer) with Renee Valente, *Blind Ambition*, CBS, 1979.

Mayflower: The Pilgrims' Adventure, CBS, 1979.

(And producer) *People vs. Jean Harris*, NBC, 1981.

(And producer with Aida Young) *The Bunker*, CBS, 1981.

(And producer) *A Piano for Mrs. Cimino*, CBS, 1982.

(And producer) *Right of Way*, HBO, 1983.

(And producer with Frank Prendergast and Charles Haid) *Children in the Crossfire*, NBC, 1984.

(And producer) *Stone Pillow*, CBS, 1985.

(And producer) *Mrs. Delafield Wants to Marry*, CBS, 1986.

(And coproducer) *Laura Lansing Slept Here*, NBC, 1988.

(And producer) *The Man Upstairs*, CBS, 1992.

Television Work; Specials; Director, Except Where Indicated:

One Touch of Venus, NBC, 1955.

Harvey, CBS, 1958.

(And producer) *Gift of the Magi*, CBS, 1958.

Meet Me in St. Louis, CBS, 1959.

(And producer) *Hallmark Hall of Fame Christmas Festival*, NBC, 1959.

(And producer) *The Teahouse of the August Moon*, NBC, 1962.

"Do Not Go Gentle into That Good Night," *CBS Playhouse*, CBS, 1967.

U.S.A., PBS, 1971.

(And producer) *Sandburg's Lincoln* (a series of six specials), NBC, 1974-76.

(And producer) *Our Town*, NBC, 1977.

The Second Barry Manilow Special, ABC, 1978.

Barry Manilow—One Voice, ABC, 1980.

(And producer) *Answers*, NBC, 1982.

The Deadly Game, HBO, 1982.

(And producer) *The Best Christmas Pageant Ever*, ABC, 1983.

(And producer) *The Booth*, PBS, 1985.

Let Me Hear You Whisper, 1990.

WRITINGS

Television Specials:

(With James Prideaux, Israel Horovitz, and Rose Leiman Goldemberg) *The Booth*, PBS, 1985.

Nonfiction:

From Live to Tape to Film: Sixty Years of Inconspicuous Directing (autobiography), Directors Guild of America (Hollywood, CA), 1996.

OTHER SOURCES

Periodicals:

Entertainment Weekly, September 26, 1997, p. 14.

Los Angeles Times, September 12, 1997, p. A20.
New York Times, September 12, 1997, p. B8.*

SCHELL, Maximilian   1930-

PERSONAL

Born December 8, 1930, in Vienna, Austria; raised in Switzerland; son of Hermann Ferdinand (a writer and poet) and Margarethe (an actress; maiden name, Noe von Nordberg) Schell; married Natasha Andreichenko (an actress), 1985; children: one daughter. *Education:* Attended the universities of Zurich, Basel, and Munich. *Avocational interests:* Playing piano, conducting.

Addresses: *Home*—Zurich, Switzerland. *Office*—2 Keplerstrasse, 8000 Munich 80, Germany. *Agent*—ITG Talent Agency, 822 South Robertson Blvd., Suite 200, Los Angeles, CA 90035.

Career: Actor, director, producer, and writer. Director, Volkstheater, Munich, West Germany, 1981—. *Military service:* Swiss Army, 1948-49, became Corporal.

Awards, Honors: New York Critics Circle Award, best actor, 1961, Academy Award, best actor, 1961, Golden Globe, best actor, 1962, all for *Judgment at Nuremberg;* San Sebastian Film Festival Silver Medal, best picture, 1970, Filmband in Gold (Germany), best picture, 1971, Swiss Film Award, best picture, 1971, Academy Award nomination, best foreign film, 1971, Panama Film Festival, best director, 1971, Cartagena Film Festival, special award of the jury, 1971, all for *First Love;* Sorrento and Naples Film Festival Silver Sirene, best picture, 1973, Chicago Film Critics Award, best foreign film, 1973, Golden Cup (Germany), best picture, 1974, Academy Award nomination, best foreign film, 1974, Golden Globe, best foreign film, 1974, and forty-six other international awards, all for *The Pedestrian;* Academy Award nomination, best actor, 1975, for *The Man in the Glass Booth;* San Sebastian Film Festival Silver Medal, best picture, 1975, Filmband in Silver (Germany), best picture, 1979, both for *The End of the Game;* New York Critics Circle Award, best supporting actor, 1978, Academy Award nomination, best supporting actor, 1978, both for *Julia;* Chicago Film Festival Golden Hugo Award, best foreign film, 1979, Filmband in Silver (Germany), best picture, 1980, Oxford Film Festival, best screenplay, 1980, all for

Tales from the Vienna Woods; Berlin Festival Silver Bear Award, best picture, 1984, Golden Federation Award (Germany), best actor, 1984, both for *Morgen in Alabama;* Academy Award nomination, best documentary, New York Film Critics Award, and National Board of Review award, all 1984, for *Marlene;* honorary doctorate degree, University of Chicago, 1992; Emmy Award nomination, best supporting actor, Golden Globe award, best supporting actor, and CableACE Award, best supporting actor, all 1992, for his portrayal of Lenin, *Stalin;* Emmy Award nomination, 1993, for "Miss Rose White"; Silver Lion, Venice Film Festival, 1994, for *Little Odessa.*

CREDITS

Film Appearances:
Der 20. Juli, 1955.
Reifende Jugend, 1955.
Kinder, Muetter und ein General, 1955.
Ein Madchen aus Flandern (also known as *The Girl from Flanders*), 1956, released in United States in 1963.
Die Ehe des Dr. Med. Danwitz, 1956.
Ein Herz Kehrt Heim, 1956.
Die Letzten Werden Die Ersten Sein, 1957.
Toni Schellenberg, *Taxichauffeur Banz,* 1957.
Der Meisterdieb, 1957.
Ein Wunderbarer Sommer, 1958.
Die Bernauerin, 1958.
Die Sechste Frau, 1958.
Child of Our Time, 1958.
Captain Hardenberg, *The Young Lions,* Twentieth Century-Fox, 1958.
Perilous, 1959.
Eine Dummheit macht Auch Der Gescheiteste, 1959.
The Observer, 1960.
The Three Musketeers, 1960.
Hans Rolfe, *Judgment at Nuremberg,* United Artists, 1961.
Walter, *Five Finger Exercise,* Columbia, 1961.
Title role, *Hamlet,* Dmytryk-Weiler/Bavaria Atelier Besellschaft, 1962.
Giuseppe, *The Reluctant Saint,* Columbia, 1962.
Franz, *The Condemned of Altona,* Twentieth Century-Fox, 1963.
Walter Harper, *Topkapi,* United Artists, 1964.
Letters of Mozart, 1964.
John F. Kennedy, 1964.
Stanislaus Pilgrin, *Return from the Ashes,* United Artists, 1965.
Der Seidene Schuh, 1965.
A Time to Love, 1966.
Dieter Freey, *The Deadly Affair,* Columbia, 1967.

General Schiller, *Counterpoint,* Universal, 1967.
Heide Kehrt Heim, 1967.
Captain Chris Hanson, *Krakatoa, East of Java* (also known as *Volcano*), Cinerama, 1969.
Marek, *The Desperate Ones* (also known as *Beyond the Mountains*), Commonwealth United, 1969.
Simon Bolivar, 1969.
"K," *The Castle* (also known as *Das Schloss*), Continental, 1969.
Father, *First Love* (also known as *Erste Liebe*), UMC Pictures, 1970.
Brother Adrian, *Pope Joan* (also known as *The Devil's Imposter*), Columbia, 1972.
Count Cantarini, *Paulina 1880,* 1972.
Trotta, 1972.
Andreas Giese, *The Pedestrian* (also known as *Der Fubgaenger*), Cinerama, 1973.
The Rehearsal, 1974.
Eduard Roschmann, *The Odessa File,* Columbia, 1975.
Arthur Goldman, *The Man in the Glass Booth,* American Film Theatre, 1975.
Dr. John Constable, *St. Ives,* Warner Bros., 1976.
Lieutenant General Bittrich, *A Bridge Too Far,* United Artists, 1977.
Captain Stransky, *Cross of Iron,* Avco-Embassy, 1977.
Johann, *Julia,* Twentieth Century-Fox, 1977.
Djuro Sarac, *The Day that Shook the World* (also known as *Assassination in Sarajevo* and *Sarajevsky Atentat*), 1977.
Amo non Amo, 1978.
Nikolai Bunin, *Avalanche Express,* Twentieth Century-Fox, 1978.
Gesprache mit Jedermann, 1978.
Marco, *Players,* Paramount, 1979.
Together?, New Line, 1979.
Tales from the Vienna Woods (also known as *Geschichten aus dem Wienerwald*), 1979.
Dr. Hans Reinhardt, *The Black Hole,* Buena Vista, 1979.
Professor David Malter, *The Chosen,* Twentieth Century-Fox, 1982.
Les Iles, 1982.
The Great Hamlets, 1983.
Landau, *Morgen in Alabama* (also known as *Man under Suspicion* and *Tomorrow in Alabama*), 1983.
Colonel Mueller, *The Assisi Underground,* Metro-Goldwyn-Mayer/United Artists, 1985.
Aaron Reichenbach, *The Rose Garden* (also known as *Der Rosengarten*), Cannon, 1989.
Larry London, *The Freshman,* TriStar, 1990.
Himself, *Labyrinth,* 1992.
Isaak Kohler, *Justiz* (also known as *Justice*), 1993.

Colonel Mopani Theron, *A Far Off Place,* Buena Vista, 1993.
Pharaoh, *Abraham,* Malofilm Distribution, 1994.
Arkady Shapira, *Little Odessa,* Fine Line, 1995.
Father Chaja, *Left Luggage,* 1997.
The Eighteenth Angel, Rysher Entertainment, 1997.
Dr. Jonas, *Telling Lies in America,* 1997.
Vampires, forthcoming.
Deep Impact, forthcoming.

Film Work; Producer:
(With Rudolf Noelte) Coproducer, *The Castle* (also known as *Das Schloss*), Continental, 1969.
Coproducer, *First Love* (also known as *Erste Liebe*), UMC Pictures, 1970.
The Pedestrian (also known as *Der Fubgaenger*), Cinerama, 1973.
The Clown (also known as *Ansichten eines Clowns*), 1975.
Murder on the Bridge, 1975.
(With Arlene Sellers) *The End of the Game* (also known as *Getting Away with Murder* and *Der Richter und sein Henker*), Twentieth-Century Fox, 1976.
Tales from the Vienna Woods (also known as *Geschichten aus dem Wienerwald*),1978.
Marlene, 1983.
Morgen in Alabama (also known as *Man under Suspicion* and *Tomorrow in Alabama*), 1983.

Film Work; Director:
First Love (also known as *Erste Liebe*), UMC Pictures, 1970.
The Pedestrian (also known as *Der Fubgaenger*), Cinerama, 1973.
The End of the Game (also known as *Getting Away with Murder* and *Der Richter und sein Henker*), Twentieth Century-Fox, 1976.
The Clown (also known as *Ansichten eines Clowns*), 1975.
Murder on the Bridge, 1975.
Tales from the Vienna Woods (also known as *Geschichten aus dem Wienerwald*), 1978.
Marlene, 1983.

Stage Appearances:
Philotas, Berlin Theatre am Kurfurstendamn, 1957.
Leonce, Berlin Theatre am Kurfurstendamn, 1957.
Interlock, American National Theatre Academy Playhouse, 1958.
Der Turn, Salzburg Festival, Austria, 1959.
Sappho, Hamburg, West Germany, 1959.
Hamlet, 1961.

A Patriot for Me, Royal Court Theatre, London, 1965, then Bremen, West Germany, 1966, later New York City, 1969.

The Venetian Twins, Josefstadt, Vienna, 1966.

Herostrat, Bochum, West Germany, 1966.

Title role, *Hamlet,* Munich, West Germany, 1968.

Old Times, Vienna, Austria, 1973.

Poor Murderer, Berlin, West Germany, 1982.

Der Seidene Schuh, 1982.

Appeared annually in *Everyman,* Salzburg Festival, 1978-82; also appeared in *The Prince of Homburg, Mannerhouse,* and *Don Carlos.*

Stage Work; Director:

Tales from the Vienna Woods, National Theatre, London, 1977.

The Undiscovered Country, Salzburg Festival, 1979 and 1980.

Coronet, Deutsche Opera, Berlin, 1985.

All the Best, Bremen, then Vienna, both 1966.

Hamlet, Munich, 1968.

Pygmalion, Dusseldorf, West Germany, 1970.

La Traviata, 1975.

Der Seidene Schuh, Salzburg Festival, 1985.

Television Appearances; Specials:

50th Annual Golden Globe Awards, 1993.

51st Annual Golden Globe Awards, 1994.

Television Appearances; Episodic:

"Judgment at Nuremberg," *Playhouse 90,* CBS, 1959.

Television Appearances; Miniseries:

Commentator, *Bernstein/Beethoven,* 1981.

Title role, *Peter the Great,* NBC, 1986.

Lenin, *Stalin,* HBO, 1992.

Cardinal Vittorio, *The Thornbirds: The Missing Years,* CBS, 1996.

Television Appearances; Movies:

The Fifth Column, 1959.

Turn the Key Deftly, 1960.

Title role, *Hamlet,* German television, 1960.

The Diary of Anne Frank, 1980.

The Phantom of the Opera, 1982.

Frederick the Great, *Young Catherine,* 1991.

Father, "Miss Rose White," *Hallmark Hall of Fame,* NBC, 1992.

Colonel Arkush, *Candles in the Dark,* 1993.

Pharaoh, *Abraham* (also known as *The Bible: Abraham*), TNT, 1994.

Television Appearances; Series:

Amado Guzman, *Wiseguy,* CBS, 1990.

Television Work; Director:

Candles in the Dark, 1993.

WRITINGS

Screenplays:

(With John Gould) *First Love* (also known as *Erste Liebe*), UMC Pictures, 1970.

Trotta, 1972.

The Pedestrian (also known as *Der Fubgaenger*), Cinerama, 1973.

(With Friedrich Durrenmatt) *The End of the Game* (also known as *Getting Away with Murder* and *Der Richter und sein Henker*), Twentieth Century-Fox, 1976.

Tales from the Vienna Woods (also known as *Geschichten aus dem Wienerwald*), 1979.

Marlene, 1983.

Stage:

Murder on the Bridge, 1975.

(With Christopher Hampton) *Tales from the Vienna Woods,* 1978.

OTHER SOURCES

Books:

Contemporary Authors, Volume 116, Gale (Detroit, MI), 1986.*

SCHICKEL, Richard　1933-

PERSONAL

Full name, Richard Warren Schickel; born February 10, 1933, in Milwaukee, WI; son of Edward John and Helen (Hendricks) Schickel; married Julia Carroll Whedon, March 11, 1960 (divorced); married Carol Rubinstein, December 27, 1985 (deceased); children: (first marriage) Erika, Jessica. *Education:* University of Wisconsin at Madison, B.S., 1956, graduate study, 1956-57.

Addresses: *Home*—Los Angeles, CA. *Contact*—Lorac Productions, Inc., 1551 South Robertson Blvd., Los Angeles, CA 90069.

Career: Writer, producer, and director. *Sports Illustrated,* New York City, reporter, 1956-57; *Look,* New

York City, senior editor, 1957-60; *Show,* New York City, senior editor, 1960-62, book columnist, 1963-64; NBC-TV, New York City, book critic for *Sunday,* 1963-64; Rockefeller Brothers Fund, New York City, consultant, 1965; *Life,* New York City, film reviewer, 1965-72; *Film,* coeditor, 1967-68; Yale University, New Haven, CT, lecturer in art history, 1972 and 1976; *Time,* New York City, film reviewer, 1972—; Lorac Productions, president, 1986—. University of Southern California, Los Angeles, CA, instructor.

Member: National Society of Film Critics, Writers Guild of America, Directors Guild of America, New York Film Critics.

Awards, Honors: Young Writer Award, *New Republic,* 1959; Guggenheim fellowship, 1964-65; Emmy Award nomination, outstanding documentary program achievement, 1973, for *The Men Who Made the Movies;* Emmy Award nomination, outstanding program achievement, 1976, for *Life Goes to the Movies: The Big Event;* Book Prize, British Film Institute, 1985, and Theatre Library Association Award, 1987, both for *D. W. Griffith: An American Life;* Emmy Award nomination, outstanding informational special, 1987, for *Minnelli on Minnelli: Liza Remembers Vincente.*

CREDITS

Television Work; Specials; Producer, Except Where Indicated:
Hollywood: You Must Remember This, PBS, 1972.
And director, *The Men Who Made the Movies* (eight parts, includes *Alfred Hitchcock, Frank Capra, George Cukor, Howard Hawks, King Vidor, Raoul Walsh, Vincente Minnelli,* and *William A. Wellman*), PBS, 1973.
Life Goes to the Movies: The Big Event, NBC, 1976.
The Making of "Star Wars," ABC, 1976.
And director, *Into the Morning: Willa Cather's America,* PBS, 1978.
And director, *Funny Business,* CBS, 1978.
And director, *The Horror Show,* CBS, 1979.
SPFX: The Making of "The Empire Strikes Back," CBS, 1980.
And director, *James Cagney: That Yankee Doodle Dandy,* PBS, 1981.
From Star Wars to Jedi: The Making of a Saga, CBS, 1983.
And director, *Minnelli on Minnelli: Liza Remembers Vincente,* PBS, 1987.

Cary Grant: A Celebration, ABC, 1988.
And director, *Gary Cooper: American Life, American Legend,* TNT, 1989.
And director, *Myrna Loy: So Nice to Come Home To,* TNT, 1990.
"Akira Kurosawa" segment, *The 62nd Annual Academy Awards Presentation,* ABC, 1990.
"Myrna Loy and Zanuck/Brown Tribute Films" segment, *The 63rd Annual Academy Awards Presentation,* ABC, 1991.
And director, *Barbara Stanwyck: Fire and Desire,* TNT, 1991.
"Satyajit Ray" segment, *The 64th Annual Academy Awards Presentation,* ABC, 1992.
And director, *Eastwood & Co. Making "Unforgiven,"* 1992.
And director, *Hollywood on Hollywood,* American Movie Classics, 1993.
Director only, *Elia Kazan: A Director's Journey,* American Movie Classics, 1995.
And director, *The Moviemakers: Arthur Penn* (also known as *Arthur Penn*), PBS, 1996.
And director, *The Moviemakers: Robert Wise* (also known as *Robert Wise*), PBS, 1996.
And director, *The Moviemakers: Stanley Donen* (also known as *Stanley Donen*), PBS, 1996.
And director, *Eastwood on Eastwood,* TNT, 1997.

Film Director; Documentaries:
Alfred Hitchcock, 1973.
Frank Capra, 1973.
George Cukor, 1973.
Howard Hawks, 1973.
King Vidor, 1973.
Raoul Walsh, 1973.
Vincente Minnelli, 1973.
William A. Wellman, 1973.

WRITINGS

Books:
The World of Carnegie Hall, Messner (New York City), 1960.
The Stars, Dial (New York City), 1962.
Movies: The History of an Art and an Institution, Basic Books (New York City), 1964.
The Gentle Knight (juvenile), Abelard (New York City), 1964.
(With Lena Horne) *Lena,* Doubleday (Garden City, NY), 1965.
A Special Report on the Rockefeller Foundation's Program Toward Equal Opportunities for All, photographs by Arthur Rickerby, Heinz

Kluetmeier, and Sol Libsohn, Rockefeller Foundation (New York City), 1965.

The Disney Version: The Life, Times, Art, and Commerce of Walt Disney, Simon and Schuster, 1968, published in England as *Disney Version,* Weidenfeld and Nicolson (London, England), 1968, revised edition, Touchstone (New York City), 1985, published with new introduction, Ivan R. Dee (Chicago, IL), 1997.

The World of Goya, 1746-1828, Time-Life Books (New York City), 1968.

(Editor with John Simon) *Film 67/68,* Simon and Schuster (New York City), 1968.

The Museum, photographs by Dan Budnik, Museum of Modern Art (New York City), 1970.

Second Sight: Notes on Some Movies, 1965-1970, Simon and Schuster, 1972.

His Pictures in the Papers; a Speculation on Celebrity in America Based on the Life of Douglas Fairbanks, Charterhouse (New York), 1973, published in England as *Douglas Fairbanks: The First Celebrity,* Elm Tree Books (London, England), 1976.

The World of Carnegie Hall, Greenwood Press (Westport, CT), 1973.

Harold Lloyd: The Shape of Laughter, New York Graphic Society (New York City), 1974.

(With Bob Willoughby) *The Platinum Years,* Random House (New York City), 1974.

The Men Who Made the Movies: Interviews with Frank Capra, George Cukor, Howard Hawks, Raoul Walsh, and William A. Wellman, Atheneum (New York City), 1975.

The World of Tennis, Random House, 1975.

(With Douglas Fairbanks Jr.) *The Fairbanks Album,* New York Graphic Society, 1976.

Another I, Another You: A Love Story for the Once Married (novel), Harper (New York City), 1978.

Singled Out: A Civilized Guide to Sex and Sensibility for the Suddenly Single Man—Or Woman, Viking (New York City), 1981.

Cary Grant: A Celebration, Little, Brown (Boston, MA), 1983.

D. W. Griffith: An American Life, Simon and Schuster, 1984.

Intimate Strangers: The Culture of Celebrity, Doubleday, 1985, published as *Common Fame: The Culture of Celebrity,* Pavilion (London, England), 1985.

James Cagney: A Celebration, Little, Brown, 1985.

Gary Cooper, Little, Brown, 1985.

(With Michael Walsh) *Carnegie Hall: The First One Hundred Years,* Abrams (New York City), 1987.

Striking Poses, Workman Publishing (New York City), 1987.

Schickel on Film: Encounters—Critical and Personal—With Movie Immortals, Morrow (New York City), 1989.

(Author of essay) *Clint Eastwood Directs,* Walker Art Center (Minneapolis, MN), 1990.

(With Sid Avery) *Hollywood at Home: A Family Album, 1950-1965,* Crown (New York City), 1990.

Brando: A Life in Our Times, Atheneum, 1991.

Double Indemnity, British Film Institute (London, England), 1992.

Clint Eastwood: A Biography, Knopf (New York City), 1996.

Also contributor to periodicals.

Teleplays; Specials, Except Where Indicated:
The Film Generation, PBS, 1969.

The Movie-Crazy Years, PBS, 1971.

Hollywood: You Must Remember This, PBS, 1972.

The Men Who Made the Movies (eight parts, includes *Alfred Hitchcock, Frank Capra, George Cukor, Howard Hawks, King Vidor, Raoul Walsh, Vincente Minnelli,* and *William A. Wellman*), PBS, 1973.

Life Goes to the Movies: The Big Event, NBC, 1976.

The Making of "Star Wars," ABC, 1976.

The Coral Jungle (series), syndicated, 1976.

Into the Morning: Willa Cather's America, PBS, 1978.

Funny Business, CBS, 1978.

The Horror Show, CBS, 1979.

SPFX: The Making of "The Empire Strikes Back," CBS, 1980.

James Cagney: That Yankee Doodle Dandy, PBS, 1981.

From Star Wars to Jedi: The Making of a Saga, CBS, 1983.

Happy Anniversary 007—25 Years of James Bond, 1987.

Minnelli on Minnelli: Liza Remembers Vincente, PBS, 1987.

Cary Grant: A Celebration, ABC, 1988.

Gary Cooper: American Life, American Legend, TNT, 1989.

Myrna Loy: So Nice to Come Home To, TNT, 1990.

Barbara Stanwyck: Fire and Desire, TNT, 1991.

Eastwood & Co. Making "Unforgiven," 1992.

1968: 25th Anniversary, Fox, 1993.

Hollywood on Hollywood, American Movie Classics, 1993.

Elia Kazan: A Director's Journey, American Movie Classics, 1995.

The Moviemakers: Arthur Penn (also known as *Arthur Penn*), PBS, 1996.

The Moviemakers: Robert Wise (also known as *Robert Wise*), PBS, 1996.

The Moviemakers: Stanley Donen (also known as *Stanley Donen*), PBS, 1996.

Eastwood on Eastwood, TNT, 1997.

The Harry Lawsen Chronicles, AMC, 1998.

OTHER SOURCES

Books:

Contemporary Authors New Revision Series, Volume 34, Gale (Detroit, MI), 1991.

Other:

http://pathfinder.com/time/bios/richardschickel.html (web page), November 24, 1997.

http://www.randomhouse.com/releases/9612/0-679-42974-3.html (web page), November 24, 1997.

SCHILLER, Lawrence 1936-

PERSONAL

Born Lawrence Julian Schiller, born December 28, 1936, in New York, NY; son of Isidore (a merchant) and Jean (Liebowitz) Schiller; married Judith Holtzer, 1961 (divorced, 1975); married Stephanie Wolf, November 5, 1977; children: (first marriage) Suzanne, Marc, Howard; (second marriage) Anthony, Cameron. *Education:* Pepperdine College, B.A.; special training as a photojournalist with Time-Life. *Politics:* Democrat. *Religion:* Jewish.

Addresses: *Agent*—c/o Chasin Agency, 8899 Beverly Blvd., Suite 716, Los Angeles, CA 90048.

Career: Director, producer, photographer, cinematographer, film editor, and actor. Photojournalist with *Sport*, 1956-60, *Sports Illustrated*, 1956-64, *Life*, 1958-70, *Saturday Evening Post*, 1958-70, *Paris Match*, 1960-69, *London Sun Times*, 1960-69, *Stern*, 1960-69, and *Look*, 1963-65. Moscow International Forum on Peace, American delegate, 1987; American-Soviet Film Initiative, chair of the board of directors, 1988; U.S.S.R.-USA Bi-Lateral Talks, member, 1988.

Member: Directors Guild of America, Academy of Motion Picture Arts and Sciences, National Press Photographers Association, California Press Photographers Association.

Awards, Honors: National Press Photographers Association Award, 1975; Pulitzer Prize, 1980, for *The Executioner's Song;* Emmy Award, outstanding miniseries, 1986, for *Peter the Great;* Emmy Award, for *The Executioner's Song;* numerous awards in photojournalism.

CREDITS

Television Work; Miniseries:

Associate producer, *The Trial of Lee Harvey Oswald*, 1977.

Producer and director, *The Executioner's Song*, 1982.

(With Marvin J. Chomsky) Director, *Peter the Great*, NBC, 1985.

Television Work; Movies:

(With L. M. Kit Carson) Director, *Hey, I'm Alive!*, 1975.

Producer, *The Winds of Kitty Hawk*, 1978.

Producer and creator of montages and flying sequences, *The Winds of Kitty Hawk*, 1978.

Producer and director of special sequence, *Marilyn: The Untold Story*, 1980.

Executive producer, *An Act of Love: The Patricia Neal Story*, 1981.

Producer, *Raid on Short Creek* (also known as *Child Bride of Short Creek*), 1981.

Executive producer, *Her Life As a Man*, 1984.

Producer, *Murder: By Reason of Insanity* (also known as *My Sweet Victim*), 1985.

Producer and director, *Margaret Bourke-White* (also known as *Double Exposure* and *Double Exposure: The Story of Margaret Bourke-White*), TNT, 1989.

Director, *The Plot to Kill Hitler*, CBS, 1990.

Producer and director, *Double Jeopardy*, Showtime, 1992.

Television Work; Specials:

Producer and director, *Come with Me—Lainie Kazan*, 1971.

Film Producer and Director, Except Where Indicated:

Creator of special still montages and titles, *Butch Cassidy and the Sundance Kid*, Twentieth Century-Fox, 1969.

And cinematographer, *The Lexington Experience*, Corda, 1971.

And editor, *The American Dreamer*, EYR, 1971.

Creator of special still montages and titles, *Lady Sings the Blues*, Paramount, 1972.

The Man Who Skied Down Everest, 1975.

Co-producer, *Quiet Days in Clichy*, 1990.

WRITINGS

Nonfiction:
Author of foreword and photographer, Richard Alpert and Sidney Cohen, *LSD,* New American Library (New York City), 1966.

Nonfiction; As Investigator, Compiler, and Interviewer:
Richard Warren Lewis, *The Scavengers and Critics of the Warren Report: The Endless Paradox,* Delacorte (New York City), 1967.

Norman Mailer, *Marilyn, a Biography,* Grosset and Dunlap (New York City), 1973.

Norman Mailer, *The Faith of Graffiti,* Praeger (New York City), 1974.

Albert Goldman, *Ladies and Gentlemen—Lenny Bruce!,* Random House (New York City), 1975.

Wilfrid Sheed, *Muhammad Ali: A Portrait in Words and Photographs,* Crowell (New York City), 1975.

W. Eugene Smith and Aileen M. Smith, *Minamata: Words and Photographs,* 1976.

Norman Mailer, *The Executioner's Song,* Little, Brown (Boston, MA), 1979.

O. J. Simpson, *I Want to Tell You: My Response to Your Letters, Your Messages, Your Questions* (also known as *I Want to Tell You*), Little, Brown, 1995.

Norman Mailer, *Oswald's Tale: An American Mystery,* Random House, 1995.

James Willwerth, *American Tragedy: The Uncensored Story of the Simpson Defense,* Random House, 1996.

Charles Brennan, *Boulder: JonBenet and the West,* HarperCollins, forthcoming.

Screenplays:
The Lexington Experience, Corda, 1971.
The American Dreamer, EYR, 1971.

OTHER SOURCES

Periodicals:
Business Wire, October 17, 1997.
Playboy, February, 1997, p. 47.*

SEAGAL, Steve
    See SEAGAL, Steven

SEAGAL, Steven   1952(?)-
    (Steve Seagal)

PERSONAL

Born April 10, 1952 (some sources say 1951), in Lansing, MI; raised in Lansing, MI, and Fullerton, CA; son of a high school math teacher and a medical technician; married Miyako Fujitani (a dojo owner; divorced); married Adrienne La Russa (divorced); married Kelly LeBrock (an actress and model; divorced); companion of Arissa Wolfe; children: (first marriage) Justice (also known as Kentaro), Ayako; (third marriage) Annaliza; Dominic San Rocco, Arissa; (with Arissa Wolfe) Savannah. *Education:* Studied martial arts under masters in Japan.

Career: Actor, writer, producer, and martial arts expert. Earned black belt in numerous martial arts disciplines, including karate and aikido; became first non-Asian to open a martial arts academy in Japan; worked as fight scene choreographer for motion pictures; worked in international security and personal protection; opened Aikido Ten Shin Dojo, a martial arts academy in Los Angeles, CA, and a martial arts academy in Taos, NM. Owner of Arroyo Perdido Winery in Los Olivos, CA. With Chuck Norris, investor in restaurants in Russia.

Addresses: *Contact*—1021 Stone Canyon Rd., Los Angeles, CA 90077; 2282 Mandeville Canyon, Los Angeles, CA 90049.

Member: Screen Actors Guild.

CREDITS

Film Appearances:
(Film debut) Nico Toscani, *Above the Law* (also known as *Nico*), Warner Bros., 1988.

Mason Storm, *Hard to Kill* (also known as *Seven Year Storm*), Warner Bros., 1990.

John Hatcher, *Marked for Death* (also known as *Screwface*), Twentieth Century-Fox, 1990.

Gino Felino, *Out for Justice* (also known as *The Night* and *The Price of Our Blood*), Warner Bros., 1991.

Casey Ryback, *Under Siege,* Warner Bros., 1992.

Forrest Taft, *On Deadly Ground* (also known as *Rainbow Warrior* and *Spirit Warrior*), Warner Bros., 1994.

Casey Ryback, *Under Siege 2: Dark Territory* (also known as *Dark Territory, End of the Line, Under Siege 2,* and *Under Siege II*), Warner Bros., 1995.

Lieutenant Colonel Austin Travis, *Executive Decision* (also known as *Critical Decision*), Warner Bros., 1996.

Jack Cole, *The Glimmer Man* (also known as *Glimmerman*), Warner Bros., 1996.

Universal Cops, Unia Films, 1996.

Jack Taggart, *Fire Down Below,* Warner Bros., 1997.

My Giant, Castle Rock Entertainment, forthcoming.

The Patriot, forthcoming.

Film Work; Producer, Except Where Indicated:

(With Andrew Davis) *Above the Law* (also known as *Nico*), Warner Bros., 1988.

(With Michael Grais and Mark Victor) *Marked for Death* (also known as *Screwface*), Twentieth Century-Fox, 1990.

(With Arnold Kopelson) *Out for Justice* (also known as *The Night* and *The Price of Our Blood*), Warner Bros., 1991.

Under Siege, Warner Bros., 1992.

And director, *On Deadly Ground* (also known as *Rainbow Warrior* and *Spirit Warrior*), Warner Bros., 1994.

Under Siege 2: Dark Territory (also known as *Dark Territory, End of the Line, Under Siege 2,* and *Under Siege II*), Warner Bros., 1995.

And song producer (with Todd Smallwood), *The Glimmer Man* (also known as *Glimmerman*), Warner Bros., 1996.

Film Work; Martial Arts Choreographer/Coordinator:

(As Steve Seagal) *The Challenge* (also known as *Sword of the Ninja*), Rank Film Distributors, 1982.

Above the Law (also known as *Nico*), Warner Bros., 1988.

Hard to Kill (also known as *Seven Year Storm*), Warner Bros., 1990.

Marked for Death (also known as *Screwface*), Twentieth Century-Fox, 1990.

Television Appearances; Specials:

"Naked Hollywood," *A & E Premieres,* Arts and Entertainment, 1991.

Presenter, *The 67th Annual Academy Awards,* ABC, 1995.

Happy Birthday Elizabeth—A Celebration of Life, ABC, 1997.

Television Appearances; Episodic:

Guest host, *Saturday Night Live,* NBC, 1991.

Himself, "Roseambo," *Roseanne,* ABC, 1996.

WRITINGS

Screenplays:

Hard to Kill (also known as *Seven Year Storm*), Warner Bros., 1990.

Out for Justice (also known as *The Night* and *The Price of Our Blood*), Warner Bros., 1991.

Story Ideas; Films:

(With Andrew Davis) *Above the Law* (also known as *Nico*), Warner Bros., 1988.

OTHER SOURCES

Periodicals:

Entertainment Weekly, February 10, 1995, pp. 6-7; April 5, 1996, p. 14; May 17, 1996, p. 13; October 11, 1996, p. 19; November 15, 1996, p. 16.

Esquire, July, 1995, pp. 124-125.

Gentleman's Quarterly, March, 1991, p. 231.

People Weekly, November 19, 1990, p. 163.

Time, November 14, 1994, p. 39; March 18, 1996, p. 101.

Vanity Fair, February, 1993, p. 100.*

SEINFELD, Jerry   1954(?)-

PERSONAL

Born April 29, 1954 (some sources say 1955), in Brooklyn, NY; raised in Massapequa, NY; son of Kalman (owner of a sign company) and Betty Seinfeld. *Education:* Queens College of the City University of New York, B.A. in theatre arts and mass communications, 1976.

Addresses: *Contact*—147 El Camino Dr., #205, Beverly Hills, CA 90212. *Agent*—c/o Creative Artists Agency, 9830 Wilshire Blvd., Beverly Hills, CA 90212-1825.

Career: Comedian, actor, and screenwriter. Toured regularly as a stand-up comic. Appeared in television commercials for American Express credit cards. Worked as a light bulb salesman, waiter, and street vendor of jewelry.

Awards, Honors: American Comedy Award, funniest male comedy club stand-up, 1988; Clio Award, best announcer of a radio commercial, 1988; American Comedy Award, funniest actor in a television series, 1992, Emmy Award, outstanding comedy series, 1993, Golden Globe Awards, best television series, comedy or musical, 1994, best actor in a television musical or comedy, 1994, Emmy Award nominations, outstanding writing in a comedy series, 1991, outstanding comedy series, 1992, 1994, 1995, 1996, and 1997, outstanding lead actor in a comedy series, 1993, 1995, and 1996, and Golden Globe Award nominations, best television series, comedy or musical, 1995, 1996, and 1997, best actor in a television musical or comedy, 1995 and 1996, all for *Seinfeld;* honorary doctorate, Queens College of the City University of New York, 1994.

CREDITS

Television Appearances; Series:
Title role, *Seinfeld,* NBC, 1990—.

Television Appearances; Pilots:
Title role, *Seinfeld* (also known as *The Seinfeld Chronicles*), NBC, 1989.

Television Appearances; Specials:
The Tonight Show Starring Johnny Carson 19th Anniversary Special, NBC, 1981.
The Tonight Show Starring Johnny Carson 24th Anniversary Special, NBC, 1986.
Disneyland's Summer Vacation Party, NBC, 1986.
"Rodney Dangerfield—It's Not Easy Bein' Me," *On Location,* HBO, 1986.
"Jerry Seinfeld—Stand-Up Confidential," *On Location,* HBO, 1987.
An All-Star Celebration: The '88 Vote, ABC, 1988.
Late Night with David Letterman Seventh Anniversary Show, NBC, 1989.
"Montreal International Comedy Festival," *HBO Comedy Hour,* HBO, 1989.
The 2nd Annual Valvoline National Driving Test, CBS, 1990.
Night of 100 Stars III, NBC, 1990.
Funny Business with Charlie Chase III, TNN, 1990.
Host, *Spy Magazine Presents How to Be Famous,* NBC, 1990.
Host, *The Second Annual Aspen Comedy Festival,* Showtime, 1990.
Today at 40, NBC, 1992.
Back to School '92, 1992.
Carol Leifer: Gaudy, Bawdy, and Blue, 1992.
Free to Laugh: A Comedy and Music Special for Amnesty International, 1992.
HBO's 20th Anniversary—We Hardly Believe It Ourselves, HBO, 1992.
The Barbara Walters Special, ABC, 1992.

Baseball Relief: An All-Star Comedy Salute, Fox, 1993.
Laughing Matters (also known as *Funny Business*), Showtime, 1993.
What Is This Thing Called Love? (also known as *The Barbara Walters Special*), ABC, 1993.
The NBC Super Special All-Star Comedy Hour, NBC, 1993.
Rolling Stone '93: The Year in Review, Fox, 1993.
The Barbara Walters Special with Kathie Lee and Frank Gifford, Al Pacino, Jerry Seinfeld, and Clint Eastwood, ABC, 1993.
Host, *Abbott and Costello Meet Jerry Seinfeld,* NBC, 1994.
Twenty Years of Comedy on HBO, HBO, 1995.
Comedy Club Superstars (also known as *Comedy Club All-Stars*), ABC, 1996.
The Late Show with David Letterman Video Special 2 (also known as *The Late Show with David Letterman Primetime Video Special 2*), CBS, 1996.

Also appeared in a tribute to Brandon Tartikoff, 1997.

Television appearances; Episodic:
Frankie, the governor's joke writer, *Benson,* ABC, 1980.
The Tonight Show Starring Johnny Carson, NBC, 1981.
Alan King: Inside the Comedy Mind, 1991.
Himself, "The Grand Opening," *The Larry Sanders Show,* HBO, 1993.
Himself, "The Raw Deal," *NewsRadio* (also known as *News Radio*), NBC, 1996.

Also appeared on *Dennis Miller Live,* HBO; *Late Night with David Letterman,* NBC; *The Late Show with David Letterman,* CBS; and *The New WKRP in Cincinnati,* syndicated.

Television Appearances; Awards Presentations:
The 4th Annual American Comedy Awards, ABC, 1990.
The 42nd Annual Primetime Emmy Awards Presentation (also known as *The 42nd Annual Emmy Awards* and *The Emmys*), Fox, 1990.
The 43rd Annual Primetime Emmy Awards Presentation (also known as *The 43rd Annual Emmy Awards* and *The Emmys*), Fox, 1991.
Presenter, *The 44th Annual Primetime Emmy Awards* (also known as *The 44th Annual Emmy Awards* and *The Emmys*), 1992.
The 6th Annual American Comedy Awards, 1992.

Presenter, *The 45th Annual Primetime Emmy Awards* (also known as *The 45th Annual Emmy Awards* and *The Emmys*), 1993.
The 7th Annual American Comedy Awards, 1993.
The American Television Awards, 1993.
Presenter, *The 46th Annual Primetime Emmy Awards* (also known as *The 46th Annual Emmy Awards* and *The Emmys*), 1994.
Presenter, *The 47th Annual Primetime Emmy Awards* (also known as *The 47th Annual Emmy Awards* and *The Emmys*), 1995.
Presenter, *The 9th Annual American Comedy Awards,* 1995.
Presenter, *The Second Annual Screen Actors Guild Awards,* 1996.
Presenter, *The 49th Annual Primetime Emmy Awards* (also known as *The 49th Annual Emmy Awards* and *The Emmys*), CBS, 1997.

Television Appearances; Movies:
Network representative, *The Rating Game* (also known as *The Mogul*), The Movie Channel, 1984.

Television Work; Pilots:
(With Larry David) Creator, *Seinfeld* (also known as *The Seinfeld Chronicles*), NBC, 1989.

Television Work; Series:
Producer, *Seinfeld,* NBC, 1991-96.
Executive producer, *Seinfeld,* NBC, 1996—.

Film Appearances:
Himself, *Good Money,* Pfquad Group, 1995.

Stage Appearances:
Night of 100 Stars III, Radio City Music Hall, New York City, 1990.

RECORDINGS

Videos:
The Tommy Chong Roast (also known as *Playboy Comedy Roast—Tommy Chong*), Playboy Entertainment Group, Inc., 1986.
Johnny Carson: The Comedians—"Good Stuff"—Stand-Up Debuts from "The Tonight Show Starring Johnny Carson," Buena Vista Home Video, 1996.

Other:
Appears on *The Seinfeld CD-ROM* (based on the television show *Seinfeld*), Arts and Commerce.

WRITINGS

Teleplays; Series:
Seinfeld (series), NBC, 1990—.

Teleplays; Pilots:
Seinfeld (also known as *The Seinfeld Chronicles*), NBC, 1989.

Teleplays; Specials:
"Jerry Seinfeld—Stand-up Confidential," *On Location,* HBO, 1987.

Humor:
SeinLanguage, Bantam (New York City), 1993.

OTHER SOURCES

Books:
Authors and Artists for Young Adults, Volume 11, Gale (Detroit, MI), 1993.
Contemporary Authors, Volume 140, Gale, 1993.
Newsmakers 1992 Cumulation, Gale, 1992.

Periodicals:
Entertainment Weekly, March 1, 1991, pp. 29-30; September 11, 1992, p. 35.
New York, February 20, 1995, p. 45.
New York Times, September 29, 1991, pp. H33-H34.
People Weekly, June 4, 1990, p. 14; December 2, 1991, pp. 87-88.
Rolling Stone, September 22, 1994, pp. 47-50, 112-114.
TV Guide, May 23, 1992, pp. 11-15.
US, April 4, 1991, pp. 16-19.
USA Today, October 2, 1991, p. D1.*

SENN, Herbert 1924-

PERSONAL

Born October 9, 1924, in Ilion, NY; son of Robert Charles (a farmer) and Elizabeth Amelia (a teacher; maiden name, Deutsch) Senn. *Education:* Columbia University, 1953-57.

Career: Production designer for theater, television, and film. Associated with the Cape Playhouse, Dennis, MA, 1952-c. 1996; substantial work with Helen Pond. *Military service:* U.S. Army, 1949-50.

CREDITS

Stage Work; Production Designer, Except Where Indicated:

Decor designer, *House of Connelly,* Equity Library Theatre, New York City, 1955.

Liliom, 1956.

The Beaver Coat, 1956.

Idiot's Delight, 1957.

Right You Are (If You Think You Are), 1957.

The Brothers Karamazov, 1957.

Oklahoma!, 1958.

Ardele, 1958.

Hamlet of Stepney Green, 1958.

She Shall Have Music, 1959.

Time of Vengeance, 1959.

The Gay Divorcee, 1960.

La Ronde, 1960.

The Idiot, 1960.

Man and Superman, 1960.

Emanuel, 1960.

Montserrat, 1961.

Five Posts in the Market Place, 1961.

Smiling the Boy Fell Dead, 1961.

Lighting Designer, *O Marry Me,* 1961.

The Merchant of Venice, 1962.

I Got Shoes, 1963.

Set design, *The Boys from Syracuse,* Theatre Royal Drury Lane, 1963.

Lighting Designer, *Double Dublin,* 1963.

Lighting Designer, *What Makes Sammy Run?,* 1964.

Roar Like a Dove, 1964.

Great Scot! 1965.

Hippolyte, Boston Opera Company, 1966.

By Jupiter, 1967.

The Dodo Bird, 1967.

The Peddler, 1967.

Private Lives, 1968.

Little Boxes, a double bill of *Trevor, The Coffee Lace,* 1969.

The Divorce of Judy and Jane, 1971.

Berlin to Broadway with Kurt Weill, 1972.

Oh, Coward!, 1972.

The Trojans, Boston Opera Company, 1972.

No Sex Please, We're British, 1973.

A Community of Two, U. S. Cities, 1974.

War and Peace, Boston Opera Company, 1974.

Benvenuto Cellini, Boston Opera Company, 1975.

A Musical Jubilee, 1975.

Oh, Coward!, London, 1975.

Ariadne and Naxos, New York City Opera, 1975.

Montezuma, Boston Opera Company, 1976.

Russlan and Ludmilla, Boston Opera Company, 1977.

The Ice Break, Boston Opera Company, 1979.

Merry Widow, New York City Opera, 1983.

Showboat, Houston Grand Opera tour, then Gershwin, NY, 1984.

Oh, Coward!, Helen Hayes Theatre, New York City, 1986.

The Magic Flute, Opera Company of Boston, The Opera House, Boston, MA, 1990.

Driving Miss Daisy, Bushnell Theatre, Hartford, CT, 1994.

Definitely Doris!, 57 Theatre, Boston, MA, 1996.

The Nutcracker, Boston Ballet, Wang Center, Boston, MA, 1997-98.

Also has done production design over 40 seasons at the Cape Playhouse, Dennis, MA.

Television Work:
Scenic Designer, *The Barber of Seville* (special), 1976.

Film Work:
Production Designer, *Macbeth,* 1982.*

SERBAN, Andrei   1943-

PERSONAL

Full name, Andrei George Serban; born June 21, 1943, in Bucharest, Romania; immigrated to the United States in 1969; son of Gheorghe and Elpis (Lichardopu) Serban; married; two children. *Education:* Attended the Theatre Institute of Bucharest, 1963-68; also attended the University of Bucharest; has studied Asian theatre.

Addresses: *Office*—Columbia University, School of Arts, 601C Dodge Hall, 2960 Broadway, New York, NY 10027-6902.

Career: Director. International Theatre Institute, Paris, France, assistant to Peter Brook, 1970-71; La MaMa Experimental Theatre Club, New York City, director, 1970-77; Carnegie Institute of Technology, Pittsburgh, PA, and Sarah Lawrence College, Bronxville, NY, professor of drama, both 1974; Paris Conservatory (also known as La Conservatoire de Paris), Paris, France, professor of drama, 1975; Yale University, New Haven, CT, guest professor of drama, 1977; Yale Repertory Theatre, New Haven, CT, associate director, 1977-78; American Repertory Theatre, Cambridge, MA, resident director, 1986-87; National Theatre of Romania, general manager, 1990; Oscar

Hammerstein II Center for Theatre Studies, Columbia University, director, School of Arts, professor, New York, 1997—; founder of Great Jones Repertory Company and American Repertory Theatre (1979); also taught at University of California at San Diego.

Awards, Honors: Ford Foundation fellowship, 1969-70; European Festival Awards, 1972, 1973, and 1975; Obie Award, *Village Voice*, 1975, for distinguished direction of Greek tragedy; Drama Desk Award, outstanding director, 1975, for *Medea*; Guggenheim fellowship, 1976-77; Outer Critics Circle Award, 1977, for his direction of *The Cherry Orchard*; Rockefeller Foundation fellowship, 1980; Lifetime Achievement Award, Government of Romania.

CREDITS

Stage Work; Director, Except Where Indicated:
Arden of Faversham, Romania, 1965.
Ubu Roi, Romania, 1966.
Julius Caesar, Romania, 1968.
The Good Woman of Setzuan, Young People's Theatre of Piatra Neampt, Bucharest, Romania, 1968.
Jonah, Bucharest's Little Theatre, Romania, 1969.
Arden of Faversham, La MaMa Experimental Theatre Club, New York City, 1970.
Ubu Roi, La MaMa Experimental Theatre Club, 1970.
The Fragments of a Trilogy, (composed of three plays: *The Trojan Women, Medea,* and *Elektra*), La MaMa Experimental Theatre Club, 1974-76.
The Good Woman of Setzuan, La MaMa Experimental Theatre Club, 1975.
As You Like It, La MaMa Experimental Theatre Club, 1976.
The Cherry Orchard, New York Shakespeare Festival, Vivian Beaumont Theatre, New York City, 1977.
Agamemnon, New York Shakespeare Festival, Vivian Beaumont Theatre, then Delacorte Theatre, New York City, both 1977.
The Ghost Sonata, Yale Repertory Theatre, New Haven, CT, 1977.
Sganarelle: An Evening of Moliere Farces, Yale Repertory Theatre, then New York Shakespeare Festival, Public Theatre, New York City, both 1978.
(And set designer) *The Master and Margarita,* New York Shakespeare Festival, Public Theatre, 1978.
The Umbrellas of Cherbourg New York Shakespeare Festival, Public Theatre, 1979, then Phoenix Theatre, London, England, 1980.
Happy Days, New York Shakespeare Festival, Public Theatre, 1979.

The Seagull, New York Shakespeare Festival, Public Theatre, 1980.
Eugene Onegin, Welsh National Opera, Cardiff, Wales, 1980.
Sganarelle, American Repertory Theatre, Cambridge, MA, 1981.
I Puritani, Welsh National Opera, 1981.
Norma, Welsh National Opera, 1981, and 1985.
La Traviata, Julliard American Opera Centre, New York City, 1981.
The Marriage of Figaro, Tyrone Guthrie Theatre, Minneapolis, MN, 1982.
Zastrozzi, New York Shakespeare Festival, Public Theatre, 1982.
The Three Sisters, American Repertory Theatre, 1982.
Uncle Vanya, La MaMa Annex, New York City, 1983.
Alcina, New York City Opera, State Theatre, New York City, 1983.
Orpheus Descending, Circle in the Square Theatre, New York City, 1984.
The King Stag American Repertory Theatre, 1984.
Turandot, Royal Opera House, London, England, 1984.
The Love of Three Oranges, American Repertory Theatre, 1984.
The Juniper Tree, American Repertory Theatre, 1985.
The Marriage of Figaro, Circle in the Square Theatre, 1985.
Fidelio, Covent Garden Theatre, London, England, 1986.
Sweet Table at the Richelieu, American Repertory Theatre, 1986.
The Good Woman of Setzuan, American Repertory Theatre, 1986.
I Puritani, Paris Opera, Paris, France, 1987.
Fragments of a Greek Trilogy (also known as *Fragments of a Trilogy;* composed of three plays, *Medea, Elektra,* and *The Trojan Women*), La MaMa Experimental Theatre Club, 1987.
The Miser, 1988.
Twelfth Night, American Repertory Theatre, 1989.
An Ancient Trilogy (composed of three plays: *Medea, The Trojan Women,* and *Elektra*), National Theatre, Bucharest, Romania, 1990.
Lucia di Lammermoor, Civic Opera House, Chicago, IL, 1992, then Los Angeles, CA, and Paris, France.
Elektra, War Memorial Opera House, San Francisco, CA, 1992.
The Fiery Angel, Opera Bastille, Paris, France, 1992.
Les Contes d'Hoffman, Vienna State Opera, Vienna, Austria, 1994.
I Puritani, War Memorial Opera House, San Francisco, CA, 1994.
Lucia di Lammermoor, Opera Bastille, Paris, France, 1995.

The Taming of the Shrew, American Repertory Theatre, Loeb Drama Center, 1997-98.

Also directed *The Magic Flute,* Paris Opera; *The Serpent Woman; Rodelinda* and *The Merry Widow,* National Welsh Opera; *Don Carlos, Caballera Rusticana I Pagliacci,* and *The Fiery Angel,* in Geneva, Switzerland; *Oedipe,* Romanian National Opera; *Prince Igor* and *I Puritani,* Covent Garden Theatre; *Eugene Onegin,* Lisbon, Portugal; *Rigoletto,* Venice, Italy; *Don Giovanni* and *Les Contes,* Vienna, Austria; *Adriana Lecouvreur,* Zurich, Switzerland; and *Elektra* and *Thaie,* Nice, France.

Film Work:

Workshop sequence supervisor, *Jane Austen in Manhattan,* Contemporary/Cinecom International/ New Yorker, 1980.

Adaptations: (With Elizabeth Swados) *Agamemnon,* produced by New York Shakespeare Festival, Vivian Beaumont Theatre, then Delacorte Theatre, New York City, both 1977; *The Master and Margarita,* produced by New York Shakespeare Festival, Public Theatre, New York City, 1978; *Fragments of a Greek Trilogy,* produced by La MaMa Experimental Theatre Club, New York City, 1987.

OTHER SOURCES

Books:

Menta, Ed, *The Magic World Behind the Curtain: Andrei Serban in the American Theatre,* Lang Publishing.
International Dictionary of Theatre, Volume 3, "Actors, Directors and Designers," St. James Press (Detroit, MI), 1996.

Periodicals:

Yale Theatre, spring, 1977.

___

SHALLO, Karen

PERSONAL

Born in Philadelphia, PA; daughter of Andrew Anthony (an artist) and Blanche Ruth (a government worker; maiden name, Walunas) Shallo. *Education:* Pennsylvania State University, B.S. (English and speech education), 1968, M.F.A. (acting), 1975.

Addresses: *Agent*—Henderson Hogan Agency, 850 Seventh Ave., #1003, New York, NY 10019-5230.

Career: Actress.

Member: Actors' Equity Association, American Federation of Television and Radio Artists, Screen Actors Guild.

CREDITS

Stage Appearances:

Lady Macbeth, *Macbeth,* Arts Company Repertory, 1969-71.
Velma, *Birdbath,* Actors Theatre of Louisville, Louisville, KY, 1970.
Elizabeth, *The Crucible,* Arts Company Repertory, 1970.
Mary Tyrone, *Long Days Journey into Night,* Studio Theatre, 1970.
Mrs. Crowe, *Hadrian VII,* Alley Theatre, 1971-72.
Madame Dubonnet, *The Boyfriend,* Clark Arts Center, 1971.
Masha, *The Three Sisters,* Pavilion Theatre, 1971.
Stella and Eunice, *A Streetcar Named Desire,* Pavilion Theatre, 1973.
Luce, *The Boys from Syracuse,* Washington Theatre Club, Washington, DC, 1973.
Laetitia, *Children of Darkness,* Greenwich Mews Theatre, 1973.
Doll Tearsheet, *Henry VI, Parts I and II,* Goodman Theatre, Chicago, IL, 1974.
Multiple roles, *Scenes from American Life,* Washington Theatre Club, 1974.
Patsy, *Little Murders,* Pavilion Theatre, 1975.
Olivia, *Twelfth Night,* Festival, Royal Shakespeare Company, 1975.
Vicky, *My Fat Friend,* New York City, 1975.
Mrs. Malaprop, *The Rivals,* Festival, Royal Shakespeare Company, 1975.
Clarisse, *When You Coming Home, Red Ryder?,* Cincinnati Playhouse in the Park, Cincinnati, OH, 1976.
Ernesta, *Sacraments,* Theatre Off Park, New York City, 1976.
Madeleine, *Moliere in Spite of Himself,* Colonnades, New York City, 1978-80.
Rita, *Ballroom in St. Pat's Cathedral,* Colonnades Theatre, 1978-80.
Martha, *Who's Afraid of Virginia Woolf,* Magus Theatre Centre, 1979.
Maggie, *The Shadow Box,* Williamstown Theatre and Boston, MA, 1979.
Valerie, *Carnival Dreams,* Promenade Theatre, New York City, 1979.
Gertrude, *The Sea Horse,* Stage West, 1980.

Antonia, *We Won't Pay! We Won't Pay!,* Chelsea Theatre Centre, 1981.

Josie, *Moon for the Misbegotten,* Stage West, 1981.

Anastasia, *The Overcoat,* Westside Mainstage, New York City, 1981.

Dionyza, *Pericles,* New York City, 1982.

Tina, *Raggedy Ann and Andy,* New York City, 1983.

The Rose Tattoo, Broadway, New York City, 1985.

Marriage, Yale Repertory Theatre, New Haven, CT, 1985-86.

Rosa, *About Face,* off-Broadway, New York City, 1985-86.

Maria, *Two into One,* Paper Mill Playhouse, Millburn, NJ, 1987-88.

Honorine, *Fanny,* Paper Mill Playhouse, 1989-90

Also appeared as Monika, *The Physicists,* Pavilion Theatre, and in *Standby.*

Major Tours:
Appeared in *My Fat Friend,* U.S. cities.

Film Appearances:
Landlady, *Dana's Time,* Hornbein-Wood, 1970.

Mrs. Aiello, *Once Upon a Time in America,* Regency, 1983.

Marlena, *Over the Brooklyn Bridge,* Cannon, 1983.

Lina, *The Word Processor,* Laurel, 1984.

Harriet, *Garbo Talks,* Metro-Goldwyn-Mayer/United Artists, 1984.

Psychic, *Hannah and Her Sisters,* Orion, 1985.

Wig-pulling woman, *Hello Again,* Buena Vista, 1987.

Blondie, *Spike of Bensonhurst,* 1988.

Singing secretary, *Me and Him,* Columbia, 1990.

Gloria Urbanski, *Mortal Thoughts,* Columbia, 1991.

Edie, *School Ties,* Paramount, 1992.

Woman in red, *Two Bits* (also known as *A Day to Remember*), Miramax, 1995.

Chubby's wife, *Big Night* (also known as *The Big Night, Pasta e Fagioli,* and *Pasta e Fasule*), The Samuel Goldwyn Company, 1996.

Lifebreath, 1997.

Television Appearances; Specials:
Frosine, *The Miser,* PBS, 1970.

Mrs. Alving, *Ghosts,* PBS, 1970.

Wife, *Play,* PBS, 1970.

Maggie Green, *The Burgher Family,* PBS, 1981.

Woman with necklace, "Road Show" (also known as "Travellin'" and "O'Malley"), *CBS Summer Playhouse,* CBS, 1989.

Television Appearances; Series:
Louise Adams, *As the World Turns,* CBS, 1982-83.

Television Appearances; Episodic:
Another World, NBC, 1984.

Saturday Night Live, NBC, 1984.

Marie Greevey, *Law & Order* (also known as *Law and Order*), NBC, 1991.

Hester Blight, *Law & Order* (also known as *Law and Order*), NBC, 1994.

Nurse Bullrumple, *Cosby,* CBS, 1996.

Television Appearances; Movies:
Betty Vehon, *A Time to Live,* NBC, 1985.

Marie Sarantopolous, *A Case of Deadly Force,* CBS, 1986.

Jean Gabrielson, *Trapped in Silence* (also known as *Silent Rage*), CBS, 1986.*

SHELTON, Reid   1924-1997

OBITUARY NOTICE—See index for *CTFT* sketch: Born October 7, 1924, in Salem, OR; died of a stroke, June 8, 1997, in Portland, OR. Actor. Shelton is remembered for being the first to play the role of the bald, businessman Daddy Warbucks in the stage musical *Annie.* Although Shelton had hair when he began his *Annie* run at Connecticut's Goodspeed Opera House, he opted to shave his head for later performances. Many others who have performed the role have followed his lead. Shelton's stint as Daddy Warbucks ran for three years on Broadway and included more than 2,300 performances.

Early in his career, he worked as a singer at Radio City Music Hall. He made his New York stage debut in *Wish You Were Here* and his London debut in *Phedre.* His other appearances include *1600 Pennsylvania Avenue, My Fair Lady, Oh, What a Lovely War!, The Saint of Beeker Street, By the Beautiful Sea,* and *Carousel.* He toured in various productions, including *Annie, The Rothschilds, 1776, My Fair Lady,* and *Phedre.* His work in *Annie* earned him an Antoinette Perry Award nomination. His work in *Man with a Load of Mischief* also earned him recognition as best actor in a musical and a Drama Desk Award nomination. Shelton also appeared on television as well in shows such as *Tales of the Gold Monkey, Merv Griffin Show, St. Elsewhere, Remington Steele, Golden Girls, Cheers, Knight Rider, Family Ties, L.A. Law, Three's Company, Webster, Hunter, Amen,* and *The Scarecrow and Mrs. King.* He also appeared in the HBO series *First and Ten.*

OBITUARIES AND OTHER SOURCES

Books:
Who's Who in Entertainment, Marquis Who's Who, 1992.

Periodicals:
Los Angeles Times, June 10, 1997, p. A25.
New York Times, June 10, 1997, p. D27.
Washington Post, June 10, 1997, p. E4.

SHELTON, Ron   1945-

PERSONAL

Full name, Ronald W. Shelton; born September 15, 1945, in Whittier, CA; children: two daughters. *Education:* Graduated from Westmont College, 1967; University of Arizona, Tucson, M.F.A. (sculpture), 1974.

Addresses: *Office*—Raleigh Studios, 650 North Bronson, Los Angeles, CA 90004. *Agent*—Sanford, Gross, and Associates, 1015 Gayley Ave., Suite 301, Los Angeles, CA 90024.

Career: Screenwriter, director, and producer. Played for several minor league baseball teams, including the Baltimore Orioles farm team for five years, before attending graduate school; worked at odd jobs during the 1970s, including work in landscaping, carpentry, and substitute teaching; after receiving his master's degree, exhibited his sculpture, including a one-man exhibition at the Space Gallery.

Awards, Honors: Writers Guild of America award, New York Film Critics Award, Los Angeles Film Critics Award, National Film Critics Award, and Academy Award nominee, all for best original screenplay, all 1988, for *Bull Durham.*

CREDITS

Film Work; Director:
Bull Durham, Orion, 1988.
Blaze, Buena Vista, 1990.
White Men Can't Jump, Twentieth Century-Fox, 1992.
Cobb, Warner Bros., 1994.
Tin Cup, Warner Bros., 1996.

Film Work:
Associate producer, *The Pursuit of D.B. Cooper* (also known as *Pursuit*), Universal, 1981.
Executive producer, *Blue Chips,* Paramount, 1994.
Executive producer, *Open Season,* Legacy Releasing, 1996.

Film Work; Other:
Second unit action director, *Under Fire,* Orion, 1983.
Second unit director, *The Best of Times,* Universal, 1986.

Television Appearances; Specials:
Himself, *Diamonds on the Silverscreen,* American Movie Classics, 1992.
Interviewee, *Sports on the Silverscreen,* HBO, 1997.

WRITINGS

Screenplays:
Under Fire, Orion, 1983.
The Best of Times, Universal, 1986.
Bull Durham, Orion, 1988.
Blaze, Buena Vista, 1990.
White Men Can't Jump, Twentieth Century-Fox, 1992.
Blue Chips, Paramount, 1994.
Cobb, Warner Bros., 1994.
The Great White Hype, Twentieth Century-Fox, 1996.
Tin Cup, Warner Bros., 1996.

OTHER SOURCES

Periodicals:
Saturday Night (part of *Toronto Life and Saturday Night Golf Series '96*), June, 1996, p. S12.
Sport, December, 1994, p. 66.
Sporting News, January 30, 1995, p. 8.
Sports Illustrated, November 28, 1994, p. 7.

Other:
E-mail interview, www.wga.org/craft/interviews/shelton.html*

SHEPHERD, Cybill   1950-

PERSONAL

Born Cybill Lynne Shepherd, February 18, 1950, in Memphis, TN; daughter of William Jennings Shepherd (manager of the family home appliance business) and Patty (a homemaker; maiden name, Shobe)

Micci; married David Ford (an auto parts manager, then musician and Shepherd's manager), November 19, 1978 (divorced); married Bruce Oppenheim (a chiropractor), March 1, 1987 (divorced, 1989); engaged to Robert Martin (a musician); children: (first marriage) Clementine; (second marriage) Molly Ariel and Cyrus Zachariah (twins). *Education:* Attended Hunter College of the City University of New York, 1969, College of New Rochelle, 1970, New York University, 1971 and 1973, and University of Southern California, 1972.

Addresses: *Home*—Los Angeles, CA. *Manager*—Hofflund/Polone Management, 9615 Brighton Way, Suite 320, Beverly Hills, CA 90210.

Career: Actress, producer, singer, and writer. Worked as a fashion model for Stewart Model Agency and appeared on numerous magazine covers, including *Glamour* and *Harper's Bazaar*. Performed with the Memphis All Stars.

Member: Voters for Choice (national spokesperson, 1990).

Awards, Honors: Model of the Year Award, c. 1968; Golden Globe award nomination, most promising female newcomer, Hollywood Foreign Press Association, 1971, for *The Last Picture Show;* Golden Globe Award, best actress in a comedy series, 1987, for *Moonlighting;* Emmy Award nominations, outstanding lead actress in a comedy, 1995, 1996, and 1997, Golden Globe Award, best television comedy or musical actress, 1996, Golden Globe Award, best comedy series, 1996, and Golden Globe Award nomination, best television comedy or musical actress, 1997, all for *Cybill;* honored with star on Hollywood's Walk of Fame.

CREDITS

Television Appearances; Series:
Colleen Champion, *The Yellow Rose,* NBC, 1983-84.
Maddie Hayes, *Moonlighting,* ABC, 1985-89.
Title role (Cybill Sheridan), *Cybill,* CBS, 1995—.

Television Work; Series:
Executive producer, *Cybill,* CBS, 1995—.

Television Appearances; Movies:
Julie, *A Guide for the Married Woman,* ABC, 1978.
Elaine, *Secrets of a Married Man,* NBC, 1984.
Vicki Orloff, *Seduced,* CBS, 1985.

Karen Parsons, *Which Way Home,* TNT, 1991.
Reeny Perdew, *Memphis,* TNT, 1992.
Samantha "Sam" Weathers, *Stormy Weathers,* ABC, 1992.
Julie Warner, *There Was a Little Boy,* CBS, 1993.
Debbie Freeman, *Baby Brokers* (also known as *Stolen Hearts*), NBC, 1994.
Jody Stokes, *While Justice Sleeps* (also known as *For the Love of My Daughter*), NBC, 1994.
Janice Johnson, *Journey of the Heart,* CBS, 1997.

Television Work; Movies:
Executive producer (with Larry McMurtry), *Memphis,* TNT, 1992.
Executive producer, *Stormy Weathers,* ABC, 1992.
Coexecutive producer, *Journey of the Heart,* CBS, 1997.

Television Appearances; Specials:
Herself, *Miss Teenage America,* CBS, 1968.
Elvis Memories, syndicated, 1985.
ABC All-Star Spectacular, ABC, 1985.
Herself, *The Barbara Walters Special,* ABC, 1985.
Herself, *Superstars and Their Moms,* ABC, 1987.
Herself, *Face to Face with Connie Chung,* 1990.
A Party for Richard Pryor, CBS, 1991.
Picture This: The Times of Peter Bogdanovich in Archer City, Texas (also known as *The Making of Texasville*), Showtime, 1991.
Segment host, *ABC's 40th Anniversary Special,* ABC, 1994.
Out There II, Comedy Central, 1994.
People's 20th Birthday, ABC, 1994.
CBS Sneak Peak '95, CBS, 1995.

Television Appearances; Episodic:
"No Friends like Old Friends," *Fantasy Island,* ABC, 1983.
"Love Is. . .," *The New Love, American Style,* ABC, 1986.
Ariel, *Cybill,* CBS, 1997.

Also appeared on *Late Night with David Letter* and *The Tonight Show Starring Johnny Carson.*

Television Appearances; Awards Presentations:
The 37th Annual Prime Time Emmy Awards, 1985.
The 38th Annual Emmy Awards, 1986.
The 39th Annual Emmy Awards, 1987.
The 61st Annual Academy Awards Presentation, 1989.
The 16th Annual People's Choice Awards, 1990.
Host, *The 47th Annual Golden Globe Awards,* 1990.
The 17th Annual People's Choice Awards, 1991.
Presenter, *The 48th Annual Golden Globe Awards,* 1991.

Host, *The 13th Annual ACE Awards,* 1992.

Presenter, *The 44th Annual Prime Time Emmy Awards,* 1992.

Presenter, *The 50th Annual Golden Globe Awards,* 1993.

The 28th Academy of Country Music Awards, 1993.

Host, *The 47th Annual Prime Time Emmy Awards,* 1995.

Presenter, *The 30th Annual Academy of Country Music Awards,* 1995.

Presenter, *The 52nd Annual Golden Globe Awards,* 1995.

Presenter, *The 1996 Emmy Awards,* 1996.

Presenter, *The 54th Annual Golden Globe Awards,* 1997.

Other Television Appearances:

Masquerade (pilot), ABC, 1983.

Eula Varner, *The Long Hot Summer* (miniseries), NBC, 1985.

Faith Kelsey, *Telling Secrets* (miniseries; also known as *Contract for Murder*), ABC, 1993.

Film Appearances:

(Film debut) Jacy Farrow, *The Last Picture Show,* Columbia, 1971.

Kelly Corcoran, *The Heartbreak Kid,* Twentieth Century-Fox, 1972.

Title role (Annie P. "Daisy" Miller), *Daisy Miller,* Paramount, 1974.

Brooke Carter, *At Long Last Love,* Twentieth Century-Fox, 1975.

Mary Jane, *Special Delivery* (also known as *Dangerous Break*), American International, 1976.

Betsy, *Taxi Driver,* Columbia, 1976.

Debbie Luckman, *Silver Bears,* Columbia, 1978.

Amanda Kelly, *The Lady Vanishes,* Rank/Group 1, 1980.

Jennifer, *The Return* (also known as *The Alien's Return* and *Earthright*), Greydon Clark, 1980.

Corinne Jeffries, *Chances Are,* TriStar, 1989.

Jacy Farrow, *Texasville,* Columbia, 1990.

Returning Napoleon, Universal, 1991.

Nancy Brill, *Alice,* Orion, 1990.

Marilyn Schwary, *Once upon a Crime,* Metro-Goldwyn-Mayer, 1992.

Claire Laurent, *Married to It,* Orion, 1993.

Stage Appearances:

A Shot in the Dark, 1977.

Picnic, 1980.

Vanities, 1982.

Also appeared in *Lunch Power.*

RECORDINGS

Albums:

Cybill Does It . . . to Cole Porter, Paramount, 1974.

Cybill and Stan Getz, 1977.

Mad about the Boy, Inner City, 1977.

Vanilla with Phineas Newborn, Jr., Gold Coast/ Peabody, 1978.

Talk to Me Memphis, Drive, 1997.

Also recorded *At Long Last Love,* RCA; *The Heartbreak Kid,* Columbia; *Moonlighting,* MCA; and *Somewhere down the Road.*

WRITINGS

(With Larry McMurtry) *Memphis* (television movie; also known as *September*), TNT, 1992.

OTHER SOURCES

Periodicals:

Entertainment Weekly, January 20, 1995, pp. 22-25.

Good Housekeeping, April, 1995, p. 116.

McCalls, November, 1995, p. 112.

People Weekly, August 1, 1994, pp. 82-84.

TV Guide, January 7, 1995, p. 24; April 20, 1996, pp. 18-21, 24.*

SHORT, Robert
  See ARKIN, Alan

SHORT, Sylvia   1927-

PERSONAL

Born October 22, 1927, in Concord, MA; daughter of Seabury Tuttle (a sugar refiner) and Eleanor (Ballou) Short; married Fritz Weaver (an actor), February 7, 1953 (divorced, 1979); children: Lydia, Tony. *Education:* Smith College, B.A., 1949; New York University, Ph.D. (marine biology), 1974; studied at the Old Vic Theatre School in London.

Addresses: *Office*—c/o Judy Schoen & Associates, 606 North Larchmont Ave., Suite 509, Los Angeles, CA 90004.

Career: Actress. Teacher and director, Juilliard School Drama Division; reader, *Talking Books,* American Foundation for the Blind.

Member: Actors' Equity Association, Screen Actors Guild, American Federation of Television and Radio Artists.

Awards, Honors: Fulbright Fellowship to the Old Vic Theatre School, 1949-51; Barter Theatre Award, 1952.

CREDITS

Stage Appearances:

Portia, *The Merchant of Venice*, Barter Theatre, Abingdon, VA, 1952.

Regan, *King Lear*, City Center, New York City, 1956.

'84 Shorts, Actors Theatre of Louisville, Louisville, KY, 1984.

Mother Miriam Ruth, *Agnes of God*, Theatre Virginia, Richmond, VA, 1985-86.

The Importance of Being Earnest, GeVa Theatre, Rochester, NY, 1985-86.

Sarah, *Quilters*, Studio Arena Theatre, Buffalo, NY, 1986-87.

Whispers, The American Stage Company, Fairleigh-Dickinson University, Teaneck, NJ, 1987-88.

Starting Monday, Yale Repertory Theatre, New Haven, CT, 1988-89.

Also appeared as Martha Turner, *Hide and Seek*, Broadway; Mary, Dolly, and standby, *A Life*, Broadway; mother and Mrs. Prynne, *Da*, Broadway; Alicia, *After You've Gone*, New York City; Nina, *Stay Where You Are*, New York City; Martha, *The Broken Pitcher*, New York City; Mother Miriam Ruth, *Agnes of God*, Theatre by the Sea, Portsmouth, NH; Lady Bracknell, *The Importance of Being Earnest*, Guthrie Theatre, Minneapolis, MN; Anna, the pig woman, *What I Did Last Summer*, Buffalo Studio Arena, Buffalo, NY; Gertrude, *Hamlet*, and Mistress Quickly, *Henry IV*, both American Shakespeare Theatre, Stratford, CT; and Lady Alice, *A Man for All Seasons*, Baltimore Center Stage, Baltimore, MD.

Also appeared in *Milk of Paradise*, American Place Theatre, New York City; *Just a Little Bit Less Than Normal*, Manhattan Theatre Club, New York City; *Nasty Rumours and Final Remarks*, New York Shakespeare Festival, Public Theatre, New York City; *Says I, Says He* Phoenix Theatre, New York City; *The Smile of the Cardboard Man*, Herbert Berghof Studio, New York City; *The Golden Apple*, New York City; *The Passion of Gross*, New York City; *The Clandestine Marriage*, New York City; *Desire Caught by the Tail*, New York City; and *Chopin in Space*, Ark Theatre.

Film Appearances:

Head nurse, *Endless Love*, Universal, 1981.

Miss Lalor, *Broken Vows*, Brademan-Self Productions/Robert Halmi Productions, 1987.

Nun, *Newsies* (also known as *Newsboys*), Buena Vista, 1992.

Fergus Groupie, *Ruby Cairo* (also known as *Deception* and *The Missing Link: Ruby Cairo*), Miramax, 1993.

Doctor Travis, *S.F.W.*, Gramercy Pictures, 1994.

Matron, *The Birdcage* (also known as *Bird Cage, Birds of a Feather*, and *La Cage aux Folles*), Metro-Goldwyn-Mayer/United Artists, 1996.

Also appeared as a psychiatrist, *The Firm*.

Television Appearances; Movies:

Rose, *The Whereabouts of Jenny*, 1991.

Nice lady, *Absolute Strangers*, 1991.

Donato and Daughter (also known as *Dead to Rights*), 1993.

Dr. Millichope, *Silent Cries* (also known as *Guests of the Emperor*), 1993.

Television Appearances; Specials:

Appeared in "Man and Superman," *Hallmark Hall of Fame*.

Television Appearances; Episodic:

Appeared in episodes of *All My Children*, ABC; *Another World*, NBC; *As the World Turns*, CBS; *The Nurses*, CBS; *One Life to Live*, ABC; and *The U.S. Steel Hour*, ABC/CBS. Also appeared in *The Doctors, The Edge of Night*, and *Texas*.*

SIERRA, Gregory

PERSONAL

Born January 25, in New York, NY.

Addresses: *Contact*—532 Vista Del Mar, Aptos, CA 95003.

Career: Actor.

CREDITS

Television Appearances; Series:

Julio Fuentes, *Sanford and Son*, NBC, 1972-75.

Detective Sergeant Chano Amenguale, *Barney Miller* (also known as *The Life and Times of Captain Barney Miller*), ABC, 1975-76.

Dr. Antonio "Tony" Menzies, *A.E.S. Hudson Street*, ABC, 1978.
Carlos "El Puerco" Valdez, *Soap*, ABC, 1980-81.
Commandante Paco Pico, *Zorro and Son*, CBS, 1983.
Captain Victor Maldonado, *Something Is Out There*, NBC, 1988-89.
Hector, *The Fresh Prince of Bel-Air*, NBC, 1992.
Ely Parker, *Dr. Quinn, Medicine Woman*, CBS, 1994.
Rafael Mendoza, *Walker, Texas Ranger*, CBS, 1994.
Luis Alvarez, *Common Law*, ABC, 1996.

Television Appearances; Movies:
Police sergeant, *Weekend of Terror*, ABC, 1970.
Slade, *Honky Tonk*, NBC, 1974.
Mayor Acambarros, *Antonio and the Mayor*, CBS, 1975.
Omar Welk, *The Night They Took Miss Beautiful*, NBC, 1977.
Fabricio, *Evening in Byzantium*, syndicated, 1978.
Dr. Galfas, *Three Hundred Miles for Stephanie*, NBC, 1981.
Silvera, *Kenny Rogers as the Gambler—The Legend Continues*, CBS, 1983.
Diego Ramirez, *The Night the Bridge Fell Down*, NBC, 1983.
Vic "The Dancer" Reva, *Her Secret Life* (also known as *Code Name: Dancer* and *One for the Dancer*), ABC, 1987.
General, *Where the Hell's That Gold?!* (also known as *Dynamite and Gold*), 1988.
Jesus Gutierrez, *Desperado: Badlands Justice*, NBC, 1989.
Hector Aliosa, *Donor*, CBS, 1990.
Frank Fuster, *Unspeakable Acts*, ABC, 1990.

Television Appearances; Pilots:
First deputy, *McCloud: Who Killed Miss U.S.A.?* (also known as *Portrait of a Dead Girl*), NBC, 1970.
Renaldo, *Where's the Fire?*, ABC, 1975.
Officer Mike Rodriguez, *Farrell: For the People* (also known as *Farrell for the People*), NBC, 1982.
George Callender, *Uncommon Valor*, CBS, 1983.
Lieutenant Lou Rodriguez, *Miami Vice*, NBC, 1984.
Delgado, *Command 5*, ABC, 1985.
Tony Mendosa, *Stingray*, NBC, 1985.
Captain Victor Maldonado, *Something Is Out There*, NBC, 1988.

Television Appearances; Episodic:
"Rock Bye-Bye," *It Takes a Thief*, ABC, 1969.
"A Ticket for Bertrille," *The Flying Nun*, ABC, 1969.
"The Somnaviatrix," *The Flying Nun*, ABC, 1970.
"The Long Shadow," *High Chaparral*, NBC, 1970.
Butler, "The Crane" (also known as "Chico"), *Mission: Impossible*, CBS, 1970.

"A Town Called Sincere," *The Mod Squad*, CBS, 1970.
Gomal, "Phantoms," *Mission: Impossible*, CBS, 1970.
"Papa Carlos," *The Flying Nun*, ABC, 1970.
"A Gift for El Charro," *The Flying Nun*, ABC, 1970.
Patrolman Cross, *McCloud*, 1970.
"Journey from San Juan," *Alias Smith and Jones*, ABC, 1971.
Fernando Laroca, "Cocaine," *Mission: Impossible*, CBS, 1972.
Young Doctor Kildare, syndicated, 1972.
"The Murder Game," *Banyon*, NBC, 1972.
"Hey, Janitor," *Insight*, syndicated, 1973.
"The Gypsies," *The Waltons*, CBS, 1973.
"Love Me in December," *Ironside*, NBC, 1973.
"The Two Million Clams of Cap'n Jack," *Banacek*, NBC, 1973.
"Archie Is Branded," *All in the Family*, CBS, 1973.
"The Stone," *Kung Fu*, ABC, 1973.
"Women for Sale," *Gunsmoke*, CBS, 1973.
"A Wrongful Death," *The Streets of San Francisco*, ABC, 1973.
"Tricks Are No Treats," *Hawaii Five-0*, CBS, 1973.
"Publish or Perish," *Columbo*, NBC, 1974.
"This Must Be the Alamo," *McCloud*, NBC, 1974.
"Death in High Places," *Petrocelli*, NBC, 1974.
"Hard Labor," *Gunsmoke*, CBS, 1975.
"The Malflores," *Police Story*, NBC, 1977.
"The K-Group," *Hunter*, CBS, 1977.
"River of Promises," *Police Story*, NBC, 1978.
"Plus Time Served," *Insight*, syndicated, 1979.
"Decision to Love," *Insight*, syndicated, 1981.
"A Couple of Harts," *Hart to Hart*, ABC, 1981.
"Hog Wild," *The Greatest American Hero*, ABC, 1981.
"Immigrants," *Lou Grant*, CBS, 1982.
Gloria, CBS, 1982.
"The Last Hero," *McClain's Law*, NBC, 1982.
"Anything for a Friend," *Cassie and Company*, NBC, 1982.
"Baby Rattlesnakes," *Quincy, M.E.*, NBC, 1982.
"To Kill a Princess," *Bring 'em Back Alive*, CBS, 1983.
"The Club Murder Vacation," *Simon and Simon*, ABC, 1983.
Untitled episode, *Hill Street Blues*, NBC, 1983.
"The Belles of St. Mary's," *Hill Street Blues*, NBC, 1983.
"Life in the Minors," *Hill Street Blues*, NBC, 1983.
"Eugene's Comedy Empire Strikes Back," *Hill Street Blues*, NBC, 1983.
"Ice on the Road," *High Performance*, ABC, 1983.
"Max's Waltz," *Hart to Hart*, ABC, 1984.
"Oil," *Masquerade*, ABC, 1984.
"The Long Flight," *Blue Thunder*, ABC, 1984.

"Heart of Darkness," *Miami Vice,* NBC, 1984.

"Cool Runnin'," *Miami Vice,* NBC, 1984.

"Hit List," *Miami Vice,* NBC, 1984.

"Broadway Malady," *Murder, She Wrote,* CBS, 1985.

"The Assassin," *Cover Up,* CBS, 1985.

Cagney and Lacey, CBS, 1985.

"The Gauntlet," *MacGyver,* ABC, 1985.

"The Enchilada Express," *Simon and Simon,* CBS, 1985.

"Forced Landing," *Blacke's Magic,* NBC, 1986.

"Jack of Lies," *MacGyver,* ABC, 1986.

You Again, NBC, 1986.

"Ahead of the Game," *Cagney and Lacey,* CBS, 1987.

"A Rumor with a View," *Hard Copy,* CBS, 1987.

Miguel Torres, "Pleasure Principle," *Magnum, P.I.,* CBS, 1987.

"Flashpoint," *Hunter,* NBC, 1987.

Sanchez, "Murder through a Looking Glass," *Murder, She Wrote,* CBS, 1988.

Captain Diaz, "The Treasure of Manco," *MacGyver,* ABC, 1990.

Lieutenant Orly, *P.S. I Luv U,* CBS, 1991.

"Sun and Shadow," *The Ray Bradbury Theater,* USA Network, 1992.

Dr. Diamond, "The Jersey Devil," *The X-Files,* Fox, 1993.

General Colon, *Ellen,* ABC, 1995.

Entek, "Second Skin," *Star Trek: Deep Space Nine,* syndicated, 1995.

Dr. Arturo Navarro, *Kirk* (also known as *Life Happens*), The WB, 1996.

Television Appearances; Specials:

Loser Take All, HBO, 1979.

Film Appearances:

Gorilla sergeant, *Beneath the Planet of the Apes,* Twentieth Century-Fox, 1970.

Garcia, *Getting Straight,* Columbia, 1970.

Chamaco, *Red Sky at Morning,* Universal, 1971.

Verger, *Believe in Me,* 1971.

One-eyed thief, *The Culpepper Cattle Company,* Twentieth Century-Fox, 1972.

Jurado, *The Wrath of God,* Metro-Goldwyn-Mayer, 1972.

Chavarin, *Pocket Money,* National General, 1972.

Antonio, *Papillon,* Allied Artists, 1973.

Dynamite, *The Thief Who Came to Dinner,* Warner Bros., 1973.

The Clones, Filmmakers International, 1973.

The Laughing Policeman, Twentieth Century-Fox, 1973.

Carlos, *The Towering Inferno,* Twentieth Century-Fox/Warner Bros., 1974.

Marrujo, *The Castaway Cowboy,* 1974.

Jesus Gonzales, *Mean Dog Blues,* American International, 1978.

Gilles, the Count, *The Prisoner of Zenda,* Universal, 1979.

Alphonso, *Let's Get Harry* (also known as *The Rescue*), TriStar, 1987.

Captain Sanchez, *The Trouble with Spies,* DeLaurentiis Entertainment Group/HBO Productions, 1987.

Felix Barbosa, *Deep Cover,* New Line Cinema, 1992.

Terence Wheeler, *Honey, I Blew Up the Kid,* Buena Vista, 1992.

The captain, *Hot Shots! Part Deux* (also known as *Hot Shots! 2*), Twentieth Century-Fox, 1993.

Captain Nunez, *A Low Down Dirty Shame* (also known as *Mister Cool*), Buena Vista, 1994.*

SILLIMAN, Maureen 1949-

PERSONAL

Born December 3, 1949, in New York, NY; daughter of Russell James (an airline executive) and Eleanor Mathilda (maiden name, Manzitti) Silliman; married Craig Carnelia (a composer and lyricist), March 8, 1969. *Education:* Attended State University of New York at Geneseo, and Hofstra University. *Religion:* Catholic.

Addresses: *Agent*—Bret Adams, Ltd., 448 West 44th St., New York, NY 10036.

Career: Actress. South Coast Repertory, Costa Mesa, CA, member, 1986-87.

Awards, Honors: New Jersey Drama Critics, best supporting actress, *The Effect of Gamma Rays on Man-in-the-Moon Marigolds;* best supporting actress, *The Umbrellas of Cherbourg.*

CREDITS

Stage Appearances:

(Debut) Polly, *The Gingerbread Lady,* Huntington Hartford, Los Angeles, CA, 1971.

Jenny, *Shenandoah,* Alvin, 1975.

Little Jane, *Three Postcards,* Playwrights Horizons, New York, NY, 1987.

Hannah, *We,* Negro Ensemble Company, Theater Four, New York, NY, 1989.

Laura Durand, *A Fine and Private Place,* The Norma Terris Theatre, Goodspeed-at-Chester, East Haddam, CT, 1989.

Emma/Rainbow Woman, *Blanco!,* Norman Terris Theatre, Goodspeed Opera House, 1990.

Celebration of Cabaret, Eighty Eights, New York, NY, 1990.

Luisa Weiss Pechenik, *A Shayna Maidel,* Delaware Theatre Company, Wilmington, DE, 1991.

Frankie/Francis/Susie, *Voice of the Prairie,* Holy Trinity, New York, NY, 1991.

Julie Grant, *Democracy and Esther,* Triangle Theatre Company, Holy Trinity, New York, NY, 1992.

A Christmas Carol, Huntington Theatre Company, Boston, MA, 1992.

Picking Up the Pieces, Eighty Eights, New York, NY, 1992.

Nina, *The Cocktail Hour,* Delaware Theatre Company, Wilmington, DE, 1993.

Juliet Bonetti, *Marathon Dancing,* En Garde Theatre, Masonic Grand Lodge, New York, NY, 1994.

Also appeared as Homecoming Queen, *Is There Life After High School?,* Barrymore, NY; Katrin, *I Remember Mama,* Majestic, NY; and Emily, *Blue Window,* Production Company, NY; *Notes,* Manhattan Theatre Club; Kathy, *Leaving Home,* Theatre of Riverside Church, NY; Nel, *One Wedding, Two Rooms, Three Friends,* Manhattan Theatre Club; Pooty, *Reckless,* Production Company, NY; Madeleine, *The Umbrellas of Cherbourg,* New York Shakespeare Festival, Public Theatre, NY; Terese, *Amerika,* Musical Theatre Lab, Kennedy Center, Washington, DC; Sophie, *Semmelweiss,* Kennedy Center, Washington, DC; Katherine, *A View from the Bridge,* Baltimore Center Stage; Nancy, *The Knack,* Baltimore Center Stage; Homecoming Queen, *Is There Life After High School?,* Hartford Stage Company; Becky, *Hubba Hubba,* Goodspeed Opera House, East Haddam, CT; Stock: Tillie, *The Effect of Gamma Rays on Man-in-the-Moon Marigolds;* Laurie, *New Mt. Olive Motel;* and Alexandra, *The Little Foxes.*

Television Appearances:

Beth, *Sanctuary of Fear,* NBC, 1979.
Dixie: *Changing Habits,* CBS, 1983.

Also appeared in *The Andros Targets,* CBS; *Six Rms Riv Vu;* and *The Guiding Light.*

Film Appearances:

Shelter reporter, *Reckless,* Samuel Goldwyn, 1995.
Mrs. Meyer, *Childhood's End,* Monarch Films, 1996.*

SKELTON, Red 1913-1997
(Richard Skelton)

OBITUARY NOTICE—See index for *CTFT* sketch: Born Richard Bernard Skelton, July 18, 1913, in Vincennes, IN; died of pneumonia, September 17, 1997, in Rancho Mirage, CA. Comedian, actor, artist, writer. Skelton was known to millions as an affable performer who used pantomime and humorous dialogue to bring delight to audiences around the globe. A professional clown, Skelton drew from a stock of memorable characters such as bumpkin Clem Kadiddlehopper, hobo Freddie the Freeloader, Old West lawman Sheriff Deadeye, drunkard Willie Lump-Lump, seagulls Gertrude and Heathcliffe, and the Mean Widdle Kid who often confessed "I Dood It." "His innate flexibility combined with a rubber face and superb comic timing virtually guaranteed that audiences would dissolve into laughter during his routines," noted the London *Times.* "What was surprising was that Skelton, often amused by his own antics, would stop his own act to join them in their mirth." The clowning profession came naturally to Skelton, who was nicknamed "Red" in his youth because of his hair color. His father, Joseph, had been a circus clown. Skelton never knew his father, as the elder Skelton died two months before his son's birth. The future comic was raised in poverty as his mother struggled to make money by scrubbing floors. Skelton himself began work at the age of seven, selling newspapers.

By age ten he had joined a medicine show. He began to learn about comic timing during his first day on the job when he accidentally fell off the stage and knocked over some bottles, bringing laughter from the crowd. Thereafter the "accident" became part of the act. Skelton, who dropped out of school in the seventh grade, went on to jobs performing in a minstrel show, on the Cotton Blossom showboat, and with the Hagenbeck & Wallace Circus—the same company that had earlier employed his father. He later worked the burlesque circuit. According to the *Los Angeles Times* Skelton recalled: "It was real burlesque—not the sex show that it became in later years, but comedy parody of well-known Broadway shows and top vaudeville acts." Eventually Skelton worked at various clubs in the United States and Canada. In 1937 he made his debut on Broadway and was invited to appear on Rudy Vallee's radio show and later at the White House for Franklin and Eleanor Roosevelt. Although he had failed a screen test in 1932, Skelton found success in motion pictures in the 1940s. Among his film appearances during his career were roles in *Having a Wonderful Time, Around the World in 80 Days, The People vs. Dr. Kildare, Whistling in the Dark, I Dood It, The Fuller Brush Man, Ziegfeld Follies, Ocean's Eleven,* and *Those Magnificent Men in Their Flying Machines.* He also established a presence on radio with *Red Skelton's Scrapbook of Satire,* a weekly show. During World War II he joined the U.S. Army and ultimately began performing in fifteen shows a day. Trying to maintain that schedule, he suffered from exhaustion and was hospitalized; he was later discharged. Unlike other comedians of the vaudeville era, Skelton was able to overcome the difficulties of adapting to new media, such as television. In 1951 he began a twenty-year stint on network television as the star of his own series. *The Red Skelton Show* was a success with audiences, young and old. Although the comic's popularity continued into the 1970s, and his show continued to draw significant ratings, his show was canceled by network executives who felt his squeaky-clean comedy wouldn't continue to reach their target audience.

Nevertheless, Skelton didn't veer from his brand of comedy. As quoted in the *New York Times,* Skelton said: "I'd rather have people say, 'Boy, he's hokey, isn't he?' . . . rather than, 'Who was the guy who told all those dirty jokes?'" His attitude on profanity was summed up simply: "I don't think anybody should have to pay money at the box office to hear what they can read on restroom walls." Skelton continued to perform into the 1990s drawing huge crowds in college concert halls and in other venues. He used to joke, as cited in the *New York Times,* that "I can't retire. . . I've got a government to support." In addition to his theatrical pursuits he also painted more than 1,000 pictures of clowns—some earned him $80,000 per painting. Skelton, who had begun his life in poverty, reported that he earned $2.5 million a year from lithographs alone. He never forgot those less fortunate and supported charities such as the Shriners' Crippled Children's Hospital. He also was a major benefactor of the Red Skelton Foundation in Vincennes. During his lifetime he received many honors, including three Emmy Awards, the Screen Actors Guild Achievement Award, a Golden Globe Award, the Governor's Award from the Academy of Television Arts and Sciences, and various honorary degrees. He was inducted into the Television Hall of Fame in 1988. Skelton wrote some of his own material, including compositions for *Red Skelton in Concert,* dialogue for his television series, and comic pieces for other television shows such as *The Red*

Skelton Timex Special, Red Skelton's Christmas Dinner, Red Skelton's Funny Faces, and *Red Skelton: A Royal Performance.* The three latter specials aired on HBO. He also penned *Clown Alley,* a story coloring book; *I'll Tell All,* an autobiography; and *Red Skelton's Gertrude and Healthcliffe.* He also edited *A Red Skelton in Your Closet: Ghost Stories Gay and Grim.* As reported on *CNN Interactive* he once remarked: "I don't want to be called 'the greatest' or 'one of the greatest' . . . let other guys claim to be the best. I just want to be known as a clown because to me, that's the height of my profession. It means you can do everything—sing, dance and above all, make people laugh." His one regret was "that I didn't meet one particular guy, a clown named Joe Skelton," as explained in the *Los Angeles Times.* "You know, he sure picked the right profession. I mean, a clown's got it all. He never has to hold back: He can do as he pleases. The mouth and the eyes are painted on. So, if you wanta cry, you can go right ahead. The makeup won't smear. You'll still be smiling." His classic signoff for his performances was always "Good night, and God bless."

OBITUARIES AND OTHER SOURCES

Books:
Who's Who in America, Marquis Who's Who, 1995.

Periodicals:
Chicago Tribune, September 18, 1997, section 1, p. 1.
CNN Interactive (electronic), September 17, 1997.
Detroit Free Press, September 18, 1997, pp. A1, A7.
Los Angeles Times, September 18, 1997, p. A1.
New York Times, September 18, 1997, p. B11.
Times (London; electronic), September 19, 1997.
Washington Post, September 18, 1997, p. D6.

SKELTON, Richard
 See SKELTON, Red

SKYE, Ione 1971-
 (Ione Skye Leitch)

PERSONAL

Full name, Ione Skye Leitch; born September 4, 1971, in London, England; raised in Los Angeles, San Francisco, and Connecticut; daughter of Donovan Leitch (a singer and songwriter) and Enid Karl (a model); married Adam Horovitz (a member of the music group Beastie Boys and an actor), July, 1992. *Education:* Graduated from Hollywood High School.

Addresses: *Agent*—Jason Weinberg and Associates, 122-124 East 25th St., 2nd Floor, New York, NY 10010.

Career: Actress.

CREDITS

Film Appearances:
(As Ione Skye Leitch) Clarissa, *River's Edge,* Hemdale Releasing Corporation, 1987.
Deirdre Clark, *Stranded,* New Line, 1987.
Denise Hunter, *A Night in the Life of Jimmy Reardon,* Twentieth Century-Fox, 1988.
Diane Court, *Say Anything,* Twentieth Century-Fox, 1990.
Rachel Seth-Smith, *The Rachel Papers,* United Artists, 1990.
Kit Hoffman, *Mindwalk,* Overseas Filmgroup, 1990.
Trudi, *Gas, Food and Lodging,* IRS Releasing, 1992.
Elaine, *Samantha,* Academy Entertainment, 1992.
Elyse, *Wayne's World,* Paramount, 1992.
The Color of Evening (filmed 1991), York Home Video, 1995.
Eva, "Strange Brew," *Four Rooms,* Miramax, 1995.
Young woman, *CITYSCRAPES los angeles,* High Octane Productions/Centre Films/FilmTribe Moving Pictures, 1996.
Frankie, *Dream for an Insomniac,* Tritone Productions, 1996.
Maggie, *The Size of Watermelons* (also known as *Chicken Blood and Other Fables*), Norstar Entertainment, 1996.
Gabby, *Went to Coney Island on a Mission from God . . . Be Back By Five,* Evenmore Entertainment, 1996.
Charlie's friend, *One Night Stand,* New Line, 1997.

Film Work; Director:
Bed, Bath and Beyond, Hi-8 Productions, 1996.

Television Appearances; Series:
Eleanor Gray, *Covington Cross* (also known as *Charing Cross*), ABC, 1992.

Television Appearances; Miniseries:
Pauline, *Napoleon and Josephine: A Love Story,* ABC, 1987.

Television Appearances; Specials:
Marie, "Carmilla," *Nightmare Classics,* Showtime, 1989.
Joanna Dibble, "It's Called the Sugar Plum" (one-act play), *General Motors Playwrights Theatre,* Arts and Entertainment, 1991.

Television Appearances; Movies:
Joy, *Guncrazy,* Showtime, 1992.
Carol Madison, *Girls in Prison* (also known as *Rebel Highway*), Showtime, 1994.
Kathryn Mitrou, *The Perfect Mother* (also known as *Kathryn Alexandra*), CBS, 1997.

WRITINGS

Screenplays:
Bed, Bath and Beyond, Hi-8 Productions, 1996.

OTHER SOURCES

Periodicals:
People Weekly, August 3, 1987.
Premiere, December, 1987.
US, October 2, 1989.*

SOMMER, Josef　1934-
(M. Josef Sommer)

PERSONAL

Full name, Maximilian Josef Sommer; born June 26, 1934, in Greifswald, Germany; raised in North Carolina; son of Clemons (a professor) and Elisebeth Sommer; children: Maria. *Education:* Carnegie-Mellon University, B.F.A., 1957; also studied at the American Shakespeare Festival, Stratford, CT, 1962-64.

Career: Actor. *Military service:* U.S. Army, 1958-60.

Awards, Honors: Fulbright grant to study professional theatre in Germany, 1960-61; Obie Award, *Village Voice,* 1982, for *Lydie Breeze.*

CREDITS

Stage Appearances:
(Debut) Bodo, *Watch on the Rhine,* Carolina Playmakers, Chapel Hill, NC, 1943.
Lord Ross, *Richard II,* American Shakespeare Festival, Stratford, CT, 1962.

Edward Millerton, *Hidden in America,* Showtime, 1996.

Nick Mirsky, *Mistrial,* HBO, 1996.

Television Appearances; Specials:

Nikolai Skrobotov, *Enemies,* 1974.

Varnum, *Valley Forge,* 1975.

Nathaniel Hawthorne, host and narrator, *The Scarlet Letter,* 1979.

Jim Neal, *The Execution of Raymond Graham,* 1985.

Narrator, *Fires of the Mind* (also known as *The Infinite Voyage*), PBS, 1988.

Sam Turner, *The Last Ferry Home,* 1992.

Also appeared in the special, *Mourning Becomes Electra.*

Television Appearances; Episodic:

Raoul Nesbitt, "Need to Know," *Scarecrow and Mrs. King,* CBS, 1986.

Doc, "The Wide Net," *American Playhouse,* PBS, 1987.

"Endgame," *The Equalizer,* CBS, 1988.

Polonius, "Hamlet," *Great Performances,* PBS, 1990.

Woodrow Wilson, "Paris," *The Young Indiana Jones Chronicles,* ABC, 1993.

Judge Lawrence Sullivan, "Corruption," *Law and Order,* NBC, 1996.

Television Appearances; Series:

The Doctors, NBC, 1963.

The Adams Chronicles, PBS, 1976.

Dr. Sam Garrison, *Hothouse* (also known as *The Clinic*), ABC, 1988.

Dobbs, *Early Edition,* CBS, 1996.

RECORDINGS

Taped Readings:

Pope John Paul II, by Tad Szulc, Simon and Schuster, 1995.*

SOMMER, M. Josef
    See SOMMER, Josef

STARR, Ringo 1940-

PERSONAL

Born Richard Starkey, July 7, 1940, in Dingle, near Liverpool, England; son of Richard (a bakery worker and housepainter) and Elsie (a bakery worker and barmaid; maiden name, Cleave) Starkey; married Mary (Maureen) Cox (an artist and hairdresser), February 11, 1965 (divorced, 1975); married Barbara Bach (an actress), April 27, 1981; children: (first marriage) Zak (a musician), Jason, Lee Parkin (a retailer and actress); stepchildren: (second marriage) two. *Avocational interests:* Painting.

Addresses: *Home*—Monte Carlo, Monaco. *Office*—2 Glynde Mews, London SW3 1SB, England. *Agent*—c/o Creative Artists Agency, 9830 Wilshire Blvd., Beverly Hills, CA 90212.

Career: Musician, singer, composer, actor, producer, and director. Musician with the Darktown Skiffle group, c. late-1950s, Rory Storme's Hurricanes, 1959-62, and the Beatles, 1962-69; solo performer, 1970—. Ringo or Robin Ltd. (design firm), founder (with Robin Cruikshank), 1971, designer (with Robin Cruikshank, 1971-76. Wobble Music Ltd. (music publishing company), founder, 1973; Reckongrade Ltd. (production company), founder, 1974; Ring O Records, founder, 1975, owner and executive, 1975-78. Co-owner of cable television company, Liverpool, England, beginning in 1981. The Brasserie, Atlanta, GA, partner, 1986-89. Toured with All-Starr Band, 1989, 1992, 1995, 1997, and 1998.

Appeared in concerts, including concerts in Washington, DC (with the Beach Boys), and in Miami, FL, both 1984, at the John Lennon Scholarship Concert, 1990, at Radio City Music Hall, New York City, 1992, and at the Earth Day Concert (with Paul McCartney), 1993. Host, concert and celebrity golf tournament for the Sierra Tucson clinic, 1992. Designer of ProMark signature series drumsticks, 1995. Appeared in television commercials for Oldsmobile, Pizza Hut, Sun Country Classic wine coolers, the Discover card, and Ringo Suttar (a Japanese brand of apple juice). Contributor of paintings to Image Makers Rock N Roll (an art show) and to a Make-A-Wish Foundation auction. Also worked as a messenger with the British railroad, a barman on a boat, and an apprentice joiner at an engineering firm.

Awards, Honors: Named to the Order of the British Empire, 1966; as a member of the Beatles, received several Grammy awards and was inducted into Rock and Roll Hall of Fame, 1988; Daytime Emmy Award nomination, 1989, for *Shining Time Station;* award from BMI, 1991, for one million broadcasts of the song "It Don't Come Easy."

CREDITS

Film Appearances:
(Film debut) Himself, *A Hard Day's Night,* United
    Artists, 1964.
Himself, *Help!,* United Artists, 1965.
The Beatles at Shea Stadium, 1965.
Himself, *Yellow Submarine,* United Artists, 1968.
Emmanuel, *Candy,* Cinerama, 1968.
Youngman Grand, *The Magic Christian,* Common-
    wealth, 1970.
Himself, *Let It Be,* United Artists, 1970.
Frank Zappa and Larry the Dwarf, *200 Motels,* United
    Artists, 1971.
Candy, *Blindman* (also known as *Il Cieco* and *Il
    Pistolero Cieco*), Twentieth Century-Fox, 1972.
Himself, *Born to Boogie,* 1972.
Himself and song performer, *The Concert for
    Bangladesh,* 1972.
Himself, *Weekend of a Champion,* 1973.
Ziggy Stardust and the Spiders from Mars, 1973.
Merlin the Magician, *Son of Dracula* (also known as
    Young Dracula), Apple, 1974.
Harry and Ringo's Night Out [never released], 1974.
Mike, *That'll Be the Day,* EMI, 1974.
The pope, *Lisztomania,* Warner Bros., 1975.
Ringo Stars, 1976.
Laslo Karolny, *Sextette,* Crown International, 1978.
Himself and performer of song "I Shall Be Released,"
    The Last Waltz (concert film), United Artists,
    1978.
Tonight, 1978.
I Wanna Hold Your Hand, Universal, 1978.
Himself, *The Kids Are Alright,* New World, 1979.
Atouk, *Caveman,* United Artists, 1981.
Prisoner, *The Cooler* (short film), 1982.
The Compleat Beatles, 1982.
Himself and drummer on songs, *Give My Regards to
    Broad Street,* Twentieth Century-Fox, 1984.
Singing rebel band member, *Water,* Rank, 1985.
Walking after Midnight, Kay Film, 1988.
Himself, *Imagine: John Lennon,* 1988.
The True Story of Frank Zappa's 200 Motels, 1988.
Performer of song "You Never Know," *Curly Sue,*
    Warner Bros., 1991.

Film Work:
Executive producer, *Let It Be,* United Artists, 1970.
Producer and director, *Born to Boogie,* 1972.
Producer, *Son of Dracula* (also known as *Young
    Dracula*), Apple, 1974.
(With Nancy Andrews) Producer, *Tonight,* 1978.

Television Appearances; Series:
Narrator, *Thomas: The Tank Engine and Friends,* ITV,
    1984-87.
Mr. Conductor, *Shining Time Station,* PBS, 1988-91.

Television Appearances; Miniseries:
Robin Valerian, *Princess Daisy,* NBC, 1983.

Television Appearances; Episodic:
Himself and song performer with the Beatles,
    Parnell's Sunday Night at the London Palladium,
    1963.
Himself and song performer with the Beatles, *The
    Morecambe and Wise Show,* 1963.
Himself and song performer with the Beatles, *The
    Jack Paar Show,* NBC, 1964.
Himself and song performer with the Beatles, *The Ed
    Sullivan Show,* CBS, 1964.
Himself and song performer with the Beatles, *The Ed
    Sullivan Show,* CBS, 1965.
Himself and song performer, *The David Frost Show,*
    syndicated, 1968.
Himself and song performer, *The Morecambe and
    Wise Show,* 1969.
Host, *Saturday Night Live,* NBC, 1984.
Himself and song performer with the Beatles, *Ready,
    Steady, Go!* (rebroadcast of 1960s series), The
    Disney Channel, 1989.
Himself and song performer with the Beatles, *Ready,
    Steady, Go!* (rebroadcast of 1960s series), The
    Disney Channel, 1990.
Voice of himself and Ognir Rrats, "Brush with Great-
    ness," *The Simpsons* (animated), Fox, 1990.
Narrator, "Elbert's Bad Word," *Shelley Duvall's Bed-
    time Stories,* Showtime, 1992.

Also appeared and performed with the Beatles,
Ready, Steady, Go!, 1960s.

Television Appearances; Movies:
Himself, *Magical Mystery Tour,* BBC, 1967.
Voice of Dad/narrator, *The Point* (animated), ABC,
    1971.
Mock Turtle, *Alice in Wonderland,* CBS, 1985.

Television Work; Movies:
Producer and director, *Magical Mystery Tour,* BBC,
    1967.

Television Appearances; Specials:
Himself and song performer with the Beatles, *1963
    Royal Command Performance* (also known as
    Royal Variety Show), ITV, 1963.

Himself and song performer with the Beatles, *Around the Beatles,* ITV, 1964.

Voice of Scouse the Mouse, *Scouse the Mouse,* 1977.

As himself and Ognir Rrats, *Ringo,* NBC, 1978.

A Rockabilly Session: Carl Perkins and Friends (also known as *Blue Suede Shoes: Carl Perkins and Friends*), 1986.

The Prince's Trust All-Star Rock Concert, 1987.

The Return of Bruno, 1987.

Late Night with David Letterman 8th Anniversary Special, NBC, 1990.

Mr. Conductor, *Shining Time Station Holiday Special: 'Tis a Gift,* PBS, 1990.

The Best of Cinemax Sessions, Cinemax, 1990.

Tribute to John Lennon, syndicated, 1990.

Dame Edna's Hollywood, NBC, 1992.

The Jerry Lewis MDA Labor Day Telethon, 1992.

The Making of Sergeant Pepper (documentary), The Disney Channel, 1992.

Ringo Starr: Going Home, The Disney Channel, 1993.

Farm Aid VI, The Nashville Network, 1993.

Together for Our Children—M.U.S.I.C., syndicated, 1993.

The Beatles Anthology (documentary), ABC, 1995.

The Beatles on E!, E! Entertainment Television, 1995.

The Band (documentary), Arts and Entertainment, 1996.

Host, *Classic Albums* (documentary), VH1, 1997.

Concert with All-Star Band from Budokan Hall, Tokyo, Japan aired on Japanese television, 1995.

Television Appearances; Awards Presentations:

Presenter, *The 34th Annual Grammy Awards,* 1992.

Presenter, *The 1994 World Music Awards,* 1994.

The American Music Awards, 1994.

Presenter, *The 1995 World Music Awards,* 1995.

Television Appearances; Music Videos:

(With Paul McCartney) Drummer, "Take It Away," 1982.

(With Bill Wyman) "Willie and the Poor Boys," 1985.

(With George Harrison) "When We Was Fab," 1987.

"Spirit of the Forest," 1989.

(With Tom Petty) "I Won't Back Down," 1989.

(With Buck Owens) "Act Naturally," 1989.

(With Nils Loffgren and Bruce Springsteen) "Valentine," 1991.

"Weight of the World," VH1, 1992.

(With the Beatles) "Free as a Bird," 1995.

(With the Beatles) "Real Love," 1995.

Other Television Appearances:

What's Happening! The Beatles in the U.S.A., 1964.

Radio Appearances; Series:

Himself and song performer with the Beatles, *Pop Go the Beatles,* BBC, 1963.

Host, *Ringo's Yellow Submarine,* 1983.

Radio Appearances; Specials:

Himself and song performer with the Beatles, *The Beatles, Popgrupp fran Liverpool pa Besoek i Stockholm* (title means *The Beatles, Pop Group from Liverpool Visiting Stockholm*), Sveriges Radio, 1963.

Himself and song performer with the Beatles, *1963 Royal Command Performance* (also known as *Royal Variety Show;* highlights from the television special), BBC, 1963.

RECORDINGS

Albums:

Sentimental Journey, Apple, 1969.

Beaucoups of Blues, Apple, 1970.

Ringo, Apple, 1973.

Goodnight Vienna, Apple, 1975.

Blast from Your Past, Capitol, 1975.

Starrstruck: Ringo's Best, 1976.

Ringo's Rotogravure (also known as *Rotogravure*), Atlantic, 1976.

Ringo the 4th (also known as *Ringo the Fourth*), Atlantic, 1977.

Scouse the Mouse, Atlantic, 1977.

Bad Boy, Portrait Records, 1978.

Stop and Smell the Roses, Boardwalk, 1981.

Old Wave, RCA, 1985.

Stay Awake, 1988.

Starr Struck, 1989.

Ringo Starr and His All-Star Band, 1990.

Trouble for Thomas and Other Stories, 1991.

Starr Time for Ringo, 1992.

Time Takes Time, Private Music, 1992.

Ringo Starr and the All-Starr Band, Volume Two: Live from Montreux (also known as *Live from Montreux*), 1993.

Old Wave, 1994.

Ringo and His Third All-Starr Band (Volume 1), Blockbuster Music, 1997.

Released another album, 1998. Also appeared on John Lennon's album *Plastic Ono Band,* the George Harrison albums *All Things Must Pass, Living in the Material World, Dark Horse,* and *Cloud Nine,* and the Paul McCartney albums *Tug of War* and *Pipes of Peace;* also appeared on Harry Nilsson's *Pussy Cats;* appeared on *Sun City.*

Singles:
"Beaucoups of Blues"/"Coochy Coochy," Apple, 1970.
"It Don't Come Easy"/"Early 1971," Apple, 1971.
"Back off Boogaloo," Apple, 1972.
"Photograph," Apple, 1973.
"You're Sixteen," Apple, 1974.
"Oh My My"/"Step Lightly," Apple, 1974.
"Only You," Apple, 1974.
"The No No Song"/"Snookeroo," Apple, 1975.
"Goodnight Vienna"/"Oo-Wee," Apple, 1975.
"A Dose of Rock 'n' Roll"/"Crying," Atlantic, 1976.
"Hey Baby"/"Lady Gaye," Atlantic, 1977.
"Wings"/"Just A Dream," Atlantic, 1977.
"Drowning in a Sea of Love," Atlantic, 1977.
"Lipstick Traces"/"Old Time Relovin'," Portrait Records, 1978.
"Heart on My Sleeve"/"Who Needs a Heart," Portrait Records, 1978.
"Wrack My Brain"/"Drumming Is My Madness," Boardwalk, 1981.
"Private Property"/"Stop and Take the Time to Smell the Roses," Boardwalk, 1982.
(Contributor) "When You Wish upon a Star," *Stay Awake,* 1988.
"Spirit of the Forest," 1989.
(With Buck Owens) "Act Naturally," 1989.
(Contributor) "A Little Help from My Friends" (live version), *Nobody's Child,* 1989.
"You Never Know," Private Music, 1991.
"Weight of the World," Private Music, 1992.
(With Paul McCartney) "Drive My Car," 1994.
(With Stevie Nicks) "Lay Down Your Arms," *For the Love of Harry, Everybody Sings Nilsson,* 1995.

Albums with the Beatles:
Please, Please Me, EMI, 1963.
With the Beatles, EMI, 1963.
A Hard Day's Night, EMI, 1964.
The Beatles for Sale, EMI, 1965.
Help!, EMI, 1965.
Rubber Soul, EMI, 1966.
Revolver, EMI, 1966.
Sergeant Pepper's Lonely Hearts Club Band, EMI, 1967.
Magical Mystery Tour, EMI, 1967.
Yellow Submarine, Apple, 1968.
The Beatles (also known as *The White Album*), Apple, 1968.
Abbey Road, Apple, 1969.
Let It Be, Apple, 1970.

Singles with the Beatles:
"I Want to Hold Your Hand"/"I Saw Her Standing There," Capitol, 1964.

"Can't Buy Me Love"/"You Can't Do That," Capitol, 1964.
"A Hard Day's Night"/"I Should Have Known Better," Capitol, 1964.
"I'll Cry Instead"/"I'm Happy Just to Dance with You," Capitol, 1964.
"And I Love Her"/"If I Fell," Capitol, 1964.
"Matchbox"/"Slow Down," Capitol, 1964.
"I Feel Fine"/"She's a Woman," Capitol, 1964.
"Eight Days a Week"/"I Don't Want to Spoil the Party," Capitol, 1965.
"Ticket to Ride"/"Yes It Is," Capitol, 1965.
"Help"/"I'm Down," Capitol, 1965.
"Yesterday"/"Act Naturally," Capitol, 1965.
"Twist and Shout"/"There's a Place," Capitol Starline, 1965.
"Love Me Do"/"P.S. I Love You," Capitol Starline, 1965.
"Please Please Me"/"From Me to You," Capitol Starline, 1965.
"Do You Want to Know a Secret"/"Thank You Girl," Capitol Starline, 1965.
"Roll Over Beethoven"/"Misery," Capitol Starline, 1965.
"Boys"/"Kansas City"-"Hey Hey Hey Hey," Capitol Starline, 1965.
"We Can Work It Out"/"Day Tripper," Capitol, 1965.
"Nowhere Man"/"What Goes On," Capitol, 1966.
"Paperback Writer"/"Rain," Capitol, 1966.
"Yellow Submarine"/"Eleanor Rigby," Capitol, 1967.
"Penny Lane"/"Strawberry Fields Forever," Capitol, 1967.
"All You Need Is Love"/"Baby You're a Rich Man," Capitol, 1967.
"Hello Goodbye"/"I Am the Walrus," Capitol, 1967.
"Lady Madonna"/"The Inner Light," Capitol, 1968.
"Hey Jude"/"Revolution," Apple, 1968.
"Get Back"/"Don't Let Me Down," Apple, 1969.
"The Ballad of John and Yoko"/"Old Brown Shoe," Apple, 1969.
"Something"/"Come Together," Apple, 1969.
"Let It Be"/"You Know My Name (Look Up the Number)," Apple, 1970.
"The Long and Winding Road"/"For You Blue," Apple, 1970.
"Got to Get You into My Life"/"Helter Skelter," Capitol, 1976.
"Ob-La-Di Ob-La-Da"/"Julia," Capitol, 1976.
"Sergeant Pepper's Lonely Hearts Club Band"/"With a Little Help from My Friends"/"A Day in the Life," Capitol, 1978.
"The Beatles' Movie Medley"/"I'm Happy Just to Dance with You," Capitol, 1982.
"Love Me Do"/"P.S. I Love You," Capitol, 1982.

"Free as a Bird"/"Christmastime Is Here Again,"
    Apple, 1995.
"Real Love," Apple, 1996.

Videos:

*Ringo Starr and the All-Starr Band, Volume Two: Live
    from Montreux* (also known as *Live from
    Montreux*), 1993.
The Beatles Live at the BBC, 1994.
The Beatles Anthology (expanded version of the ABC
    television special), 1995.

Video of 1989 concert tour with the All-Star band,
1990. Video of 1997 concert tour with the All-Star
Band, MPI Home Video, 1998.

WRITINGS

Composer for Films:

Help!, United Artists, 1965.
Let It Be, United Artists, 1970.
I Wanna Hold Your Hand, Universal, 1978.

Composer for Television:

Magical Mystery Tour, BBC, 1967.

OTHER SOURCES

Periodicals:

Entertainment Weekly, April 22, 1994, p. 35; Sep-
    tember 30, 1994, p. 62.
Interview, June, 1992, pp. 78-79.
Life, June, 1981, pp. 137-142.
Los Angeles Magazine, August, 1991, p. 24.
People Weekly, February 23, 1981, pp. 32-36; May
    11, 1981, p. 44; October 14, 1985, pp. 136-137;
    August 28, 1989, pp. 66-69; July 1, 1991, pp.
    66-67; January 16, 1995, p. 50; September 16,
    1996, p. 51.
Redbook, May, 1981, pp. 14-15.
Rolling Stone, July 9, 1992, pp. 87-89.
Time, November 20, 1995, pp. 104-107.
TV Guide, March 11, 1989, pp. 18-20.

Other:

http://web2.airmail.net/gshultz/bio1.html, http://
    web2.airmail.net/gshultz/bio2.html, http://
    web2.airmail.net/gshultz/bio3.html (web pages),
    December 12, 1997.
http:///www.sci.fi/~mike/beatles/beasingleus.htm
    (web page), December 15, 1997.*

STEIGER, Rod   1925-

PERSONAL

Full name, Rodney Stephen Steiger; born April 14,
1925, in Westhampton, Long Island, NY; son of
Frederick (an entertainer) and Lorraine (an entertainer;
maiden name, Driver) Steiger; married Sally Gracie
(an actress), 1952 (divorced, 1958); married Claire
Bloom (an actress), September 19, 1959 (divorced,
1969); married Sherry Nelson, April, 1973 (divorced,
1979); married Paula Ellis, 1986; children: (second
marriage) Anna Justine. *Education:* Studied acting at
New School for Social Research, 1946-47; studied
at American Theatre Wing, Dramatic Workshop, and
at Actors Studio, New York City. *Avocational interests:* Swimming, tennis, painting, composing music,
writing poetry, collecting modern art.

Addresses: *Agent*—c/o Martin Baum, Creative Artists Agency, 1888 Century Park East, 14th Floor, Los
Angeles, CA 90067.

Career: Actor. Veteran's Administration, Office of
Dependents and Beneficiaries, office assistant, c.
1945. Member of Civil Service Little Theatre Group.
Military service: U.S. Naval Reserve, 1942-45.

Member: Screen Actors Guild, Metropolitan Museum
of Art (lifetime member).

Awards, Honors: Sylvania Award, one of five best
dramatic television performers of the year, 1953, for
Marty and *You Are There;* Academy Award nomination, best supporting actor, 1954, for *On the Waterfront;* Berlin Film Festival Award, best actor, 1964,
Academy Award nomination, best actor, 1965, and
British Film Academy Award, best foreign actor,
1966, all for *The Pawnbroker;* Emmy Award, best
actor, 1958, for "The Lonely Wizard," *Schlitz Playhouse of the Stars;* Emmy nomination, outstanding
single performance by an actor in a lead role, 1964,
for *Bob Hope Presents the Chrysler Theatre.*

Academy Award, best performance by an actor in a
leading role, 1967, New York Film Critics Award,
best actor, 1967, British Film Academy Award, best
foreign actor in a leading role, 1967, and Golden
Globe Award, best actor, 1968, all for *In the Heat of
the Night;* Genie Award nomination, best performance by a foreign actor, 1980, for *Jack London's
Klondike Fever;* Genie Award nomination, best performance by a foreign actor, 1981, for *The Lucky*

Star; Montreal World Film Festival Award, best actor, 1981, for *The Chosen.*

CREDITS

Film Appearances:
Radio Operator, *My Brother's Keeper* [England], Eagle-Lion, 1949.

Frank, *Teresa,* Metro-Goldwyn-Mayer, 1951.

Charley Malloy, *On the Waterfront,* Columbia, 1954.

Stanley Hoff, *The Big Knife,* United Artists, 1955.

Major Allan Guillion, *The Court Martial of Billy Mitchell* (also known as *One-Man Mutiny*), Warner Bros., 1955.

Jud Fry, *Oklahoma!,* Magna Theatres, 1955.

Nick Benko, *The Harder They Fall,* Columbia, 1956.

Vasquez, *Back from Eternity,* RKO, 1956.

Pinky, *Jubal,* Columbia, 1956.

O'Meara, *Run of the Arrow* (also known as *Hot Lead*), Universal, 1957.

Paul Hochen, *The Unholy Wife,* Universal, 1957.

Carl Schaffer, *Across the Bridge,* Rank, 1957.

Paul Hoplin, *Cry Terror,* Metro-Goldwyn-Mayer, 1958.

Title role, *Al Capone,* Allied Artists, 1959.

Paul Mason, *Seven Thieves,* Twentieth Century-Fox, 1960.

Dr. Edmund McNally, *The Mark,* Twentieth Century-Fox, 1960.

Frank Morgan, *The World in My Pocket* (also known as *Vendredi 13 Heures, Pas de Mentalite, Il Mondo Nella Mia Tasca, An Einem Freitag um Halb Zwolf,* and *On Friday at 11*), Metro-Goldwyn-Mayer, 1960.

Detective Sergeant Koleski, *Thirteen West Street* (also known as *The Tiger Among Us*), Columbia, 1961.

Destroyer Commander, *The Longest Day,* Twentieth Century-Fox, 1962.

Tiptoes, *Convicts Four* (also known as *Reprieve*), Allied Artists, 1962.

Dante DiPinto, *Hands Across the City* (originally released as *La Mani Sulla Cite,* 1962), Galatea Films, 1963.

Sol Nazerman, *The Pawnbroker,* Allied Artists/Landau/American International, 1964.

Leo, *Time of Indifference* (originally released as *Gli Indifferenti* and *Les Deux Rivales*), Continental Distributing, 1965.

Victor Komarovsky, *Doctor Zhivago,* Metro-Goldwyn-Mayer, 1965.

Mr. Joyboy, *The Loved One,* Metro-Goldwyn-Mayer, 1965.

The Movie Maker, 1967.

Bill Gillespie, *In the Heat of the Night,* United Artists, 1967.

The General, *The Girl and the General* (also known as *La Ragazza e il Generale*), Metro-Goldwyn-Mayer, 1967.

Christopher Gill, *No Way to Treat a Lady,* Paramount, 1968.

Pope John XIII, *And There Came a Man* (also known as *E Venne un Uomo*), Brandon, 1968.

Master Sergeant Albert Callan, *The Sergeant,* Warner Bros., 1968.

Carl, *The Illustrated Man,* Warner Bros., 1969.

Steve Howard, *Three Into Two Won't Go,* Universal, 1969.

Napoleon Bonaparte, *Waterloo,* Paramount, 1970.

Harold Ryan, *Happy Birthday, Wanda June,* Columbia, 1971.

Juan Miranda, *Duck! You Sucker* (originally released as *Giu la Testa;* also known as *Fist Full of Dynamite*), United Artists, 1972.

Guenther von Lutz, *Eroi, Gli* (also known as *The Heroes* and *Los Heroes Millonarios*), 1972.

Laban Feather, *The Lolly-Madonna War* (also known as *Lolly-Madonna XXX*), Metro-Goldwyn-Mayer, 1973.

Benito Mussolini, *The Last Days of Mussolini* (originally released as *Mussolini: Ultimo Atto;* also known as *The Last Four Days* and *The Last Tyrant*), Paramount, 1974.

Gene Giannini, *Re: Lucky Luciano* (originally released as *A Proposito Luciano;* also known as *Lucky Luciano*), Avco Embassy, 1975.

Niall Hennessy, *Hennessy,* American International, 1975.

W.C. Fields, *W.C. Fields and Me,* Universal, 1976.

General Webster, *Breakthrough* (also known as *Sergeant Steiner*), Maverick, 1978.

Senator Andrew Madison, *F.I.S.T.,* United Artists, 1978.

Charlie, *Wolf Lake* (also known as *The Honor Guard*), released on video by Prism Entertainment, 1978.

Louis Wormser, *Dirty Hands* (originally released as *Les Innocents aux Mains Sales,* 1975), New Line, 1978.

Father Delaney, *The Amityville Horror,* American International, 1979.

Soapy Smith, *Jack London's Klondike Fever* (also known as *Klondike Fever*), CFI Investments, 1979.

Colonel Webster, *Teil Steiner: Das Eiserne Kreuz 2,* 1979.

Joe Bomposa, *Love and Bullets,* Associated Film Distribution, 1979.

Colonel Gluck, *The Lucky Star,* Tele Metropole Internationale, 1980.

Benito Mussolini, *Lion of the Desert* (also known as *Omar Mukhtar*), United Film Distributors, 1980.

U.S. Marshall Bill Tilghman, *Cattle Annie and Little Britches,* Universal, 1981.

Reb Saunders, *The Chosen,* Twentieth Century-Fox, 1982.

The Magic Mountain (also known as *Der Zauberberg*), 1982.

Max Andreotti, *Portrait of a Hitman* (also known as *Jim Buck* and *The Last Contract*), 1977.

Lieutenant McGreavy, *The Naked Face,* Cannon, 1985.

Dr. Phillip Lloyd, *The Kindred,* F/M Entertainment, 1987.

Pa, *American Gothic,* Vidmark, 1987.

Jason Hannibal, *Feel the Heat* (also known as *Catch the Heat*), Trans World, 1987.

Himself, *Hello Actors Studio* (documentary), 1987.

Mayor Eamon Flynn, *The January Man,* Metro-Goldwyn-Mayer/United Artists, 1988.

Sauf Votre Respect (also known as *Try This One on for Size*), 1989.

Martin, *That Summer of White Roses,* 1989.

Himself, *Exiles,* 1989.

Reverend Willin, *Ballad of the Sad Cafe,* Angelika Films, 1991.

Charlie D'Amico, *Men of Respect,* Columbia, 1991.

Ben Kallin, *Guilty as Charged,* IRS Releasing, 1992.

Himself, *The Player,* Fine Line, 1992.

Myron Hatch, *The Neighbour* [Canada], Allegro, 1993.

Benjamin, *Seven Sundays,* CiBy Sales, 1994.

Judge Prescott, *Black Water* (also known as *Tennessee Nights*), Icarus Films, 1994.

Major General Frank Zane, *The Last Tattoo* (also known as *Taking Liberties*), Capella International, 1994.

Joe Leon, *The Specialist,* Warner Bros., 1994.

Victor, *Livers Ain't Cheap,* Windy City, 1995.

Joe, *Little Surprises,* Showtime, 1995.

The President, *Captain Nuke and the Bomber Boys* (also known as *Demolition Day*), New Horizons, 1995.

Mr. Hammerman, *Carpool,* Warner Bros., 1996.

General Decker, *Mars Attacks!,* Warner Bros., 1996.

Doc Wallace, *Shiloh,* Legacy, 1997.

Tony Vago, *Truth or Consequences, N.M.,* Triumph, 1997.

Icognito, forthcoming.

Revenant, forthcoming.

Television Appearances; Movies:

Robert E. Peary, *Cook and Peary: The Race to the Pole,* CBS, 1983.

Mordechai Samuels, *Sword of Gideon,* HBO, 1986.

Silas Slaten, *Desperado: Avalanche at Devil's Ridge,* NBC, 1988.

Gordon Kahl, *In the Line of Duty: Manhunt in the Dakotas* (also known as *The Twilight Murders*), NBC, 1991.

Sam (Salvatore) 'Momo' Giancana, *Sinatra,* 1992.

Anthony Comstock, *Choices of the Heart: The Margaret Sanger Story* (also known as *Crusaders*), Lifetime, 1995.

Vincenzo Fortelli, *Columbo: Strange Bedfellows,* ABC, 1995.

Colonel Owen Stuart, *In Pursuit of Honor* (also known as *Fiddler's Green*), HBO, 1995.

Colonel Buck Gunner, *Out There,* Showtime, 1995.

Grandfather, *Dalva,* ABC, 1996.

Oskar Rothman, *The Commish: Redemption,* ABC, 1996.

Television Appearances; Miniseries:

Pontius Pilate, *Jesus of Nazareth,* NBC, 1977.

Oliver Easterne, *Hollywood Wives,* ABC, 1985.

Sir Harry Oakes, *Passion and Paradise,* ABC, 1989.

Bookstore owner, *Tales of the City* (also known as *Armistead Maupin's Tales of the City*), PBS, 1993.

Boroda, *Tom Clancy's OP Center,* NBC, 1995.

Television Appearances; Episodic:

"The Window," *Tales of Tomorrow,* ABC, 1952.

"Raymond Schindler, Case One," *Goodyear Television Playhouse,* NBC, 1952.

"The Dutch Schultz Story," *Suspense,* CBS, 1953.

Marty Poletti, "Marty," *Goodyear Television Playhouse,* NBC, 1953.

Andrei Vishinsky, "Rudolph Hess," *You Are There,* CBS, 1953.

Charles Steinmetz, "The Lonely Wizard," *Schlitz Playhouse of Stars,* CBS, 1957.

Sheriff, "A Town Has Turned to Dust," *Playhouse 90,* CBS, 1958.

"Welcome to the Wedding," *Route 66,* NBC, 1963.

"Simpson Tide," *The Simpsons,* Fox, 1989.

Guest appearance, *Reflections on the Silver Screen with Professor Richard Brown,* AMC, 1990.

Miracle on 44th Street, A Portrait of the Actors Studio (documentary, part of the *American Masters* series), PBS, 1991.

Appeared in over 250 live television dramas from 1948-53, including *Kraft Television Theatre,* NBC; *Philco Television Playhouse,* NBC; and *Bob Hope Presents the Chrysler Theater,* NBC; also appeared in other shows, including *Danger,* CBS, and *Sure as Fate,* CBS.

Television Appearances; Specials:
I Love Liberty, 1982.
The 12th Annual People's Choice Awards, CBS, 1986.
AFI Salute to Sidney Poitier, NBC, 1992.
Voice of General Ulysses S. Grant, *Lincoln,* 1992.
Listen Up! Voices in Celebration of Education, 1992.
Street Scenes: New York on Film, 1992.
Voice of General George Marshall, *The Year of the Generals,* CBS, 1992.
Voice, *Earth and the American Dream,* HBO, 1993.
Doctor Zhivago: The Making of a Russian Epic, PBS, 1995.
Narration, *The Forbidden City: The Great Within,* Discovery, 1995.
Mr. Sanford, *Little Surprises,* Showtime, 1996.
Narration, *Ray Bradbury: An American Icon,* Sci-Fi Channel, 1996.
Presenter, *The 54th Annual Golden Globe Awards,* NBC, 1997.

Television Appearances; Series:
Francis Quinn, *EZ Streets,* CBS, 1996-97.

Stage Appearances:
Detective, *Night Music,* Equity Library Theatre, New York City, 1951.
Bandit, *Rashomon,* Music Box Theatre, New York City, 1959.
Harry Davis, *A Short Happy Life,* Moore Theatre, Seattle, WA, then Harford Theatre, Los Angeles, 1961.
Actor-manager, Father Mapple, and Captain Ahab, *Moby Dick,* New York City, 1962.
Voice of Poisedon, *The Trojan Women,* Circle in the Square Theatre, New York City, 1963.

Also performed in *Seagulls over Sorento,* 1953, and *An Enemy of the People,* 1953; performed in the Actor's Studio touring production of *The Trial of Mary Dugan.*

WRITINGS

Screenplays:
Writer of *In Time of War.**

STEVENS, Shadoe   1947-

PERSONAL

Born Terry Ingstad, November 3, 1947, in Jamestown, ND; married; wife's name, Beverly; children: Amber Dawn, Chyna Rose.

Addresses: *Agent*—Don Buchwald and Associates, 9229 Sunset Blvd., Los Angeles, CA 90069.

Career: Actor, announcer, comedian, producer, and writer. Worked as radio personality and television show host. Six Flags Hurricane Harbor water park, Los Angeles, CA, participant in ceremonies, 1997.

Member: Sigma Nu.

CREDITS

Television Appearances; Series:
Cohost, *Hot City Disco,* syndicated, 1978.
Announcer and participant, *The New Hollywood Squares,* NBC, 1986-89.
Title role, *Max Monroe: Loose Cannon,* CBS, 1990.
Kenny Becket, *Dave's World,* CBS, 1993-97.
Voice of Doc Samson, *The Incredible Hulk* (animated), 1996.

Television Appearances; Specials:
Djony Dakota, "Shadoevision," *Cinemax Comedy Experiment,* Cinemax, 1986.
The 41st Annual Emmy Awards, Fox, 1989.
Comic Relief IV, HBO, 1990.
Happy Birthday, Bugs: 50 Looney Years (also known as *Hollywood Celebrates Bugs Bunny's 50th Birthday*), CBS, 1990.
Host, *The Miss Hawaiian Tropic Beauty Pageant,* syndicated, 1990.
Announcer, *Wake, Rattle, and Roll* (animated; also known as *Monster Tails* and *Fender Bender 500*), syndicated, 1990.
Announcer, *HBO's 20th Anniversary—We Hardly Believe It Ourselves* (also known as *HBO's 20th Anniversary Special—We Don't Believe It Ourselves*), HBO, 1992.
Host from Hawaii, *The All-American Thanksgiving Day Parade,* CBS, 1994.
Comic Relief VI, HBO, 1994.
Announcer, *Fifty Years of Soaps: An All-Star Celebration,* CBS, 1994.
Comic Relief VII, HBO, 1995.
Competitor, *Superstar American Gladiators,* ABC, 1995.
Harry Anderson: The Tricks of His Trade, CBS, 1996.
Host, *The 107th Tournament of Roses Parade,* CBS, 1996.
Host, *The 108th Tournament of Roses Parade,* NBC, 1997.

Television Appearances; Episodic:
As himself, "Hank's Night in the Sun," *The Larry Sanders Show,* HBO, 1994.

Charlie Stone, "Who Killed the World's Greatest Chef?," *Burke's Law,* CBS, 1995.

Weird TV, syndicated, 1995.

As himself, *Caroline in the City,* NBC, 1997.

Television Appearances; Movies:

Maxwell, *Bucket of Blood* (also known as *Dark Secrets* and *The Death Artist*), 1995.

Television Work; Specials:

Creator and executive producer, "Shadoevision," *Cinemax Comedy Experiment,* Cinemax, 1986.

Film Appearances:

Voiceover, *The Kentucky Fried Movie,* United Film, 1977.

Title role, *Traxx,* DeLaurentiis Entertainment Group, 1988.

Fred, *Mr. Saturday Night,* Columbia, 1992.

WRITINGS

Young Adults:

Wrote *Doc and the Button-Sided Hooeys.*

Teleplays:

"Shadoevision" (television special), *Cinemax Comedy Experiment,* Cinemax, 1986.*

STING 1951-
(Gordon Matthew Sumner)

PERSONAL

Full name, Gordon Matthew Sumner; born October 2, 1951, in Newcastle upon Tyne (some sources say Wallsend), England; son of Ernest Matthew (an engineer and milkman) and Audrey (a hairdresser; maiden name, Cowell) Sumner; married Frances Eleanor Tomelty, May 1, 1976 (divorced, March, 1984); married Trudie Styler (a film producer, actress, and model), August 22, 1992; children: (first marriage) Joseph, Katherine; (second marriage) Brigette Michael, Jake, Eliot Pauline. *Education:* Graduated from University of Warwick.

Addresses: *Home*—Wiltshire, England. *Office*—c/o A&M Records, Inc., P.O. Box 118, Hollywood, CA 90078; c/o Polygram International, 1416 North La Brea Ave., Los Angeles, CA 90028.

Career: Singer, bass player, actor, and songwriter. The Police, singer, bass player, and songwriter, 1977-83; solo performer, 1985—; Blue Turtles (jazz group), founder; affiliated with Strontium Ninety (a rock band); actor in British television commercials. School teacher, Newcastle upon Tyne, England, 1975-77; Kaleidoscope Cameras, London, England, managing director, beginning in 1982; also worked as a soccer coach, a musical performer on a cruise ship, an income tax clerk, and a construction worker. Rainforest Foundation International, cofounder with wife Trudie Styler and member of board of trustees, 1989—; also affiliated with Amnesty International.

Member: Performing Rights Society.

Awards, Honors: (With the Police) Named best new artist, *Rolling Stone,* 1979; (with the Police) Grammy Award, National Academy of Recording Arts and Sciences, best rock instrumental performance, 1980, for "Regatta de Blanc"; (with the Police) named best band, *Rolling Stone,* 1981; named best male singer, *Rolling Stone,* 1981; (with the Police) Grammy Award, best rock instrumental performance, 1981, for "Behind My Camel"; (with the Police) Grammy Award, best rock vocal performance, duo or group, 1981, for "Don't Stand So Close To Me"; (with the Police) Grammy Awards, pop song of the year, and best vocal performance, duo or group, 1983, for "Every Breath You Take"; (with the Police) best single, *Rolling Stone,* 1983, for "Every Breath You Take"; (with the Police) Grammy Award, best rock vocal performance, duo or group, 1983, for "Synchronicity"; Grammy Award, best long form music video, 1986, for *Bring on the Night;* Grammy Award, best pop vocal performance, male, 1987, for *Bring on the Night;* Readers' Poll awards, pop/rock musician of the year and best pop/rock group, *Downbeat,* 1989; honorary D.Mus. degrees from University of Northumbria, 1992, and Berklee College of Music, 1994; Grammy Award, best long form music video, 1994, for *Ten Summoner's Tales.*

CREDITS

Film Appearances:

Ace Face, *Quadrophenia,* World Northal, 1979.

Just Like Eddie, *Radio On,* Unifilm, 1980.

Himself, *Urgh! A Music War* (concert film), 1981.

Martin Taylor, *Brimstone and Treacle,* United Artists, 1982.

Himself, *The Secret Policeman's Other Ball,* Metro-Goldwyn-Mayer Home Video, 1982.

Feyd-Rautha, *Dune,* Universal, 1984.

Victor Frankenstein, *The Bride,* Columbia, 1985.

Himself, *Bring on the Night* (concert film), Goldwyn/A&M, 1985.

Mick, *Plenty*, Twentieth Century-Fox, 1985.

Daniel Osler, *Julia and Julia* (also known as *Giulia e Giulia*), Cinecom, 1987.

Finney, *Stormy Monday*, Atlantic, 1988.

Heroic officer, *The Adventures of Baron Munchausen*, TriStar/Columbia, 1988.

Himself, *Resident Alien* (documentary; also known as *Resident Alien: Quentin Crisp in America*), Greycat Films, 1991.

Himself, *Dance of Hope* (documentary), Baker and Taylor Video, 1991.

Himself, *Branford Marsalis: The Music Tells You* (documentary), 1992.

Reader of Pablo Neruda's sonnet, "Morning," *Il Postino* (also known as *The Postman*), Miramax, 1994.

Fledge, *Gentlemen Don't Eat Poets* (also known as *The Grotesque* and *Grave Indiscretion*), LIVE Entertainment/Ster-Kinekor Pictures, 1995.

Also appeared in *The Police: Synchronicity Concert Film*, Polygram Pictures.

Film Work:

Music producer, *Bring on the Night* (concert film), Goldwyn/A&M, 1985.

Television Appearances; Specials:

Helith, *Artemus 81*, BBC, 1981.

The Prince's Trust All-Star Rock Concert, HBO, 1986.

The Flintstones 25th Anniversary Celebration, 1986.

Rolling Stone Magazine's 20 Years of Rock 'n' Roll, ABC, 1987.

Top of the Pops: A Very Special Christmas, CBS, 1987.

"Human Rights Now Tour," *HBO World Stage*, HBO, 1988.

Freedomfest: Nelson Mandela's 70th Birthday Celebration, 1988.

"Sting in Tokyo," *HBO World Stage*, HBO, 1989.

Our Common Future, Arts and Entertainment, 1989.

Late Night with David Letterman Eighth Anniversary Special, NBC, 1990.

Coca-Cola Pop Music Backstage Pass to Summer, Fox, 1991.

Hard Rock Cafe New Year's Eve Special, CBS, 1991.

Spaceship Earth: Our Global Environment, The Disney Channel, 1991.

"Two Rooms: Tribute to Elton John and Bernie Taupin," *ABC in Concert '91*, ABC, 1991.

Rolling Stone 25: The MTV Special, MTV, 1992.

Sting at the Hollywood Bowl: A Birthday Celebration, The Disney Channel, 1992.

The 25th Montreux Music Festival, 1992.

Music in Movies '93, ABC, 1993.

Pavarotti and Friends, PBS, 1993.

"Sting: Summoner's Travels" (also known as "Sting: A Musical Voyage"), *In the Spotlight*, PBS, 1993.

Narrator, "Peter and the Wolf: A Prokofiev Fantasy," *A & E Stage*, Arts and Entertainment, 1994.

Sounds of Summer Preview '96, ABC, 1996.

"Sting," *The South Bank Show*, Bravo, 1996.

Independence Day Concert from the Glastonbury Festival, ABC, 1997.

Television Appearances; Episodic:

Musical guest, *Saturday Night Live*, NBC, 1987.

Host and musical guest, *Saturday Night Live*, NBC, 1991.

Voice, "Radio Bart," *The Simpsons*, Fox, 1991.

Musical guest, *Saturday Night Live*, NBC, 1995.

Himself, *On Tour*, 1997.

Host, *Saturday Night Live*, NBC, 1997.

Also appeared on *MTV Unplugged*, MTV.

Television Appearances; Awards Presentations:

The 28th Annual Grammy Awards, 1986.

Grammy Lifetime Achievement Award Show, 1987.

The 32nd Annual Grammy Awards, 1990.

The 33rd Annual Grammy Awards, 1991.

The 3rd Annual International Rock Awards, 1991.

The 1993 MTV Music Video Awards, MTV, 1993.

The 36th Annual Grammy Awards, 1994.

The 1995 BRIT Awards, 1995.

The BRIT Awards '96, 1996.

The 39th Grammy Awards, 1997.

Performer, *The MTV Video Music Awards*, MTV, 1997.

Other Television Appearances:

Ligmalion [England], 1985.

Voice of Zarm, *The New Adventures of Captain Planet* (animated series; also known as *Captain Planet and the Planeteers* and *Captain Planet's Mission to Save Earth*), TBS, 1990.

Stage Appearances:

Macheath, *Threepenny Opera*, Lunt-Fontanne Theatre, New York City, 1989.

RECORDINGS

Albums:

Brimstone and Treacle (original soundtrack), A&M Records (Hollywood, CA), 1982.

The Dream of The Blue Turtles, A&M Records, 1985.
Bring on the Night, A&M Records, 1986.
Nothing Like the Sun, A&M Records, 1987, five songs translated into Spanish and released as *Nada Como el Sol. . .,* A&M Records, 1988.
The Soul Cages, A&M Records, 1991.
Live in Newcastle, Alex, 1991.
Ten Summoner's Tales, A&M Records, 1993.
Fields of Gold: The Best of Sting, 1984-1994 (compilation), A&M Records, 1994.
Mercury Falling, A&M Records, 1996.
Sting at the Movies (compilation), A&M Records, 1997.
The Very Best of Sting and the Police (compilation), A&M Records, 1997.

Singles:
Spread a Little Happiness, A&M Records, 1982.
I Burn for You, A&M Records, 1982.
(With Band Aid) *Do They Know It's Christmas,* 1984.
Russians, A&M Records, 1985.
Fortress Around Your Heart, A&M Records, 1985.
If You Love Somebody Set Them Free, A&M Records, 1985.
Love Is the Seventh Wave, A&M Records, 1985.
We'll Be Together, A&M Records, 1987.
Be Still My Beating Heart, A&M Records, 1987.
Fragile, A&M Records, 1987.
Englishman in New York, A&M Records, 1987.
They Dance Alone, A&M Records, 1987.
All This Time, A&M Records, 1991.
Why Should I Cry for You, A&M Records, 1991.
If I Ever Lose My Faith in You, A&M Records, 1993.
Demolition Man, A&M Records, 1993.
Fields of Gold, A&M Records, 1993.
(With Bryan Adams and Rod Stewart) *All for Love,* A&M Records, 1993.
Fortress, Angel, 1994.
This Cowboy Song, Phantom, 1994.
When We Dance, A&M Records, 1994.
(With Pato Banton) *Spirits in the Material World,* MCA, 1995.
You Still Touch Me, A&M Records, 1996.
I'm So Happy I Can't Stop Crying, A&M Records, 1996.
Let Your Soul Be Your Pilot, A&M Records, 1996.
(With Puff Daddy) *Roxanne '97: Puff Daddy Remix,* A&M Records, 1997.

Albums; with the Police:
Outlandos d'Amour, A&M Records, 1978.
Reggatta de Blanc, A&M Records, 1979.
Zenyatta Mondatta, A&M Records, 1980.
Ghost in the Machine, A&M Records, 1981.

Synchronicity, A&M Records, 1983.
Police: Live, A&M Records, 1985.
Every Breath You Take: The Singles (compilation), A&M Records, 1986.
Message in a Box: Complete Recordings (compilation, boxed set of four compact discs), A&M Records, 1993.
Every Breath You Take: The Classics (compilation), A&M Records, 1995.

Albums; with Strontium Ninety:
Police Academy (recordings from 1970s), Ark 21/ Pangea, 1997.

Albums; Contributing Vocals:
Eberhard Schoener, *Video Flashback,* Harvest, 1979.
Eberhard Schoener, *Video Magic,* Harvest, 1981.
Phil Collins, *Hello, I Must Be Going,* Atlantic, 1982.
Phil Collins, *No Jacket Required,* Virgin, 1985.
Dire Straits, *Brothers in Arms,* Warner Bros., 1985.
Various artists, *Tribute to Kurt Weill: Lost in the Stars,* A&M Records, 1985.
Red Hot & Rio, *Red Hot & Rio,* Antilles/Verve, 1986.
Dire Straits, *Money for Nothing,* Warner Bros., 1988.
Kip Hanrahan, *Tenderness,* American Clave, 1990.
Vinx, *Rooms in My Fatha's House,* IRS, 1991.
Lucianno Pavarotti, *Pavarotti and Friends,* London, 1993.
Plus from Us, *Plus from Us,* Realworld, 1993.
Julio Iglesias, *Crazy,* Columbia, 1994.
Tammy Wynette, *Without Walls,* Epic, 1994.
Chieftains, *Long Black Veil,* RCA, 1995.
Vanessa Williams, *Sweetest Days,* Mercury, 1995.
Tina Turner, *Wildest Dreams,* Virgin, 1996.
Various artists, *Carnival: Rainforest Foundation Concert,* RCA, 1997.
Joe Henderson, *Porgy & Bess,* Polygram, 1997.
James Taylor, *Hour Glass,* Sony, 1997.

Albums; Bass Player:
Eberhard Schoener, *Video Flashback,* Harvest, 1979.
Eberhard Schoener, *Video Magic,* Harvest, 1981.
Kip Hanrahan, *Tenderness,* American Clave, 1990.
Andy Summers, *Charming Snakes,* Private Music, 1990.
Vinx, *Rooms in My Fatha's House,* IRS, 1991.
Vinnie Colaiuta, *Vinnie Colaiuta,* Stretch, 1994.
John McLaughlin, *Promise,* Verve, 1995.

Albums; Contributor of Songs:
"Love Is the Seventh Wave," *Green Peace: Rainbow Warriors,* Geffen, 1989.
"Gabriel's Message," *A Very Special Christmas,* A&M Records, 1989.

"Cushie Butterfield," *For Our Children,* Disney, 1991.

"The Wind Cries Mary," by Jimi Hendrix, *In from the Storm: A Tribute to Jimi Hendrix,* BMG, 1995.

Albums; Producer:

Various artists, *Green Peace: Rainbow Warriors,* Geffen, 1989.

Various artists, *Very Special Christmas,* A&M Records, 1989.

Vinx, *Rooms in My Fatha's House,* IRS, 1991.

Various artists, *Four Weddings and a Funeral* (soundtrack), Polygram, 1994.

Various artists, *The Truth about Cats and Dogs* (soundtrack), A&M Records, 1996.

Albums; Sound Engineer:

Various Artists, *Tan-Yah Presents Mission,* Tan-Yah Records, 1992.

Various artists, *Mission,* Tan-Yah Records, 1995.

Red Fox, *Face the Fox,* VP Records, 1996.

Videos:

(With the Police) *Police: Around the World,* Polygram, 1981.

(With the Police) *Synchronicity,* Polygram, 1983.

(With the Police) *The Police: Every Breath You Take,* Polygram, 1986.

Nothing Like the Sun: The Videos, 1987.

(With Branford Marsalis) *Steep,* Sony Music Video, 1988.

Soul Cages Videos, Polygram, 1991.

Soul Cages Concert, Polygram, 1991.

Ten Summoner's Tales (music videos), Polygram, 1993.

Sting: Fields of Gold, Polygram, 1995.

The Police: Outlandos to Synchronicities, Polygram, 1995.

Also appeared in other videos, including *Do They Know It's Christmas* (documentary), 1984.

WRITINGS

Composer for Films:

Radio On, Unifilm, 1980.

Brimstone and Treacle, United Artists, 1982.

Title song, *Demolition Man,* Warner Bros., 1993.

The Living Sea (documentary), A&M Records, 1995.

Kingdom of the Sun (animated), Walt Disney Pictures, forthcoming.

Songs in Films:

"Walking on the Moon" and "Deathwish," *Riding High,* 1980.

"Demolition Man," *Ils Appellent ca un Accident,* 1981.

"Roxanne," *Remembrance,* Mainline, 1981.

"Driven to Tears," "Roxanne," and "So Lonely," *Urgh! A Music War* (concert film), 1981.

Party, Party, Twentieth Century-Fox, 1982.

"Roxanne," *48 Hours,* Paramount, 1982.

"De Do Do Do, De Da Da Da," *The Last American Virgin,* Cannon, 1982.

"Roxanne" and "Message in a Bottle," *The Secret Policeman's Other Ball,* Metro-Goldwyn-Mayer Home Video, 1982.

"Every Breath You Take," *Risky Business,* Warner Bros., 1983.

"Rehumanize Yourself," *Bachelor Party,* Twentieth Century-Fox, 1984.

"Every Breath You Take," *Cat's Eye,* Metro-Goldwyn-Mayer,/United Artists, 1985.

"Someone to Watch Over Me," *Someone to Watch Over Me,* Columbia, 1987.

"If You Love Somebody, Set Them Free," *Dudes,* New Century/Vista, 1987.

"Englishman in New York," *Stars and Bars,* Columbia, 1988.

"Money for Nothing," *UHF,* Orion, 1989.

"Roxanne," *Another 48 Hours,* Paramount, 1990.

"Englishman in New York," *Resident Alien* (documentary; also known as *Resident Alien: Quentin Crisp in New York*), Greycat Films, 1991.

Dance of Hope, Baker and Taylor Video, 1991.

"Walking on the Moon," *Regarding Henry,* Paramount, 1991.

"It's Probably Me," *Lethal Weapon 3,* Warner Bros., 1992.

"Every Breath You Take," *Man Trouble,* Twentieth Century-Fox, 1992.

"Every Breath You Take," *The Gun in Betty Lou's Handbag,* Buena Vista, 1992.

The Panama Deception, Empowerment Project, 1992.

"Shape of My Heart," *Three of Hearts,* New Line Cinema, 1993.

(With Bryan Adams and Rod Stewart) "All for Love," *The Three Musketeers,* Buena Vista, 1993.

"This Cowboy Song," *Terminal Velocity,* Buena Vista, 1994.

"Shape of My Heart," *The Professional* (also known as *Leon*), Columbia, 1994.

"The Secret Marriage," *Four Weddings and a Funeral,* Gramercy, 1994.

The Living Sea (short documentary), MacGillivray Freeman Films Productions, 1995.

"Angel Eyes," "It's a Lonesome Town," and "My One and Only Love," *Leaving Las Vegas,* Metro-Goldwyn-Mayer/United Artists, 1995.

"Moonlight," *Sabrina,* Paramount, 1995.

"Spirits in the Material World," *Ace Ventura: When Nature Calls,* Warner Bros., 1995.

"Murder by Numbers," *Copycat,* Warner Bros., 1995.

"This Was Never Meant To Be," *Gentleman Don't Eat Poets* (also known as *The Grotesque* and *Grave Indiscretion*), LIVE Entertainment/Ster-Kinekor Pictures, 1995.

"Valparaiso," *White Squall,* Buena Vista, 1996.

"This Bed's Too Big Without You," *The Truth about Cats and Dogs,* Twentieth Century-Fox, 1996.

"Every Breath You Take," *Speed 2: Cruise Control,* Twentieth Century-Fox, 1997.

Nonfiction:

(With Jean-Pierre Dutilleux) *Jungle Stories: The Fight for the Amazon,* Barrien and Jenkins (London), 1989, republished by St. Martin's (New York City), 1996.

Adaptations: Ten of Sting's songs were adapted by Darryl Way for performance by the London Symphony Orchestra, released as *Fortress: The London Symphony Orchestra Performs the Music of Sting,* Capitol, 1995.

OTHER SOURCES

Books:

Clarkson, Wensley, *Sting, the Secret Life of Gordon Sumner,* Blake, 1996.

Contemporary Literary Criticism, Volume 26, (Detroit, MI), 1983.

Contemporary Musicians, Volume 2, Gale, 1990.

Miles, *The Police,* Omnibus Press, 1981.

Sellers, Robert, *Sting: A Biography,* Omnibus Press, 1988.

Sutcliffe, Phil, and Hugh Fielder, *L'Historia Bandido,* Proteus, 1981.

Periodicals:

Details, February, 1994, p. 114.

Entertainment Weekly, August 9, 1996, p. 30.

Interview, July, 1996, p. 90.

Spin, July, 1985.

Other:

All-Music Guide, http://205.186.189.2/root/amg/music_root.html*

STOPPELMOOR, Cheryl
    See LADD, Cheryl

STOPPELMOOR, Cheryl Jean
    See LADD, Cheryl

STRASSMAN, Marcia 1948-

PERSONAL

Born April 28, 1948, in New York, NY (some sources say New Jersey).

Addresses: *Contact*—520 18th St., Santa Monica, CA 90402.

Career: Actress.

CREDITS

Film Appearances:

Kristine, *Changes,* Cinerama, 1969.

Maria, *Soup for One,* Warner Bros., 1982.

Rose Stiller, *The Aviator,* Metro-Goldwyn-Mayer/United Artists, 1984.

Diane Szalinski, *Honey, I Shrunk the Kids,* Buena Vista, 1989.

Sarah Carson, *And You Thought Your Parents Were Weird* (also known as *Robodad*), Trimark Pictures, 1991.

Lorraine, *Fast Getaway,* RCA/Columbia Pictures Home Video, 1991.

Diane Szalinski, *Honey, I Blew Up the Kid,* Buena Vista, 1992.

Pam O'Hara, *Another Stakeout* (also known as *The Lookout* and *Stakeout 2*), Buena Vista, 1993.

Diane Szalinski, *Honey, I Shrunk the Audience,* Buena Vista, 1995.

Television Appearances; Series:

Julie Kotter, *Welcome Back, Kotter,* ABC, 1975-79.

Carol Younger, *Good Time Harry,* CBS, 1980.

Alicia Rudd, *Booker* (also known as *Booker, P.I.*), Fox, 1989-90.

Althea "Bunny" McClure, *Sweet Justice,* NBC, 1994-95.

Andrea Farrell, *Charlie Grace,* ABC, 1995.

Lisa Patcherik, *Touched by an Angel,* CBS, 1995.

Television Appearances; Movies:

Nancy, *Journey from Darkness,* NBC, 1975.

Lenina Disney, *Brave New World,* NBC, 1980.

Pam Ferguson, *Once Upon a Family,* CBS, 1980.

Rita Kamen, *Haunted by Her Past,* NBC, 1987.

Merry Chase, *Mastergate*, Showtime, 1992.
Margaret, "Family Reunion: A Relative Nightmare," *The ABC Family Movie*, ABC, 1995.
Dr. Trish George, *The Rockford Files: Friends and Foul Play*, CBS, 1996.

Television Appearances; Pilots:
Sandy Goldberg, *Wednesday Night Out*, NBC, 1972.
Kentucky Smith, *Brenda Starr*, NBC, 1976.
Pat MacFarland, *The Love Boat II*, ABC, 1977.
Officer Jenny Palermo, *The Nightingales*, NBC, 1979.
Dr. Eve Sheridan, *E/R*, CBS, 1984.
Stella Pence, *Shadow Chasers*, ABC, 1985.

Television Appearances; Episodic:
"The Perfect Teenager," *The Patty Duke Show*, ABC, 1964.
"How to Succeed in Romance," *The Patty Duke Show*, ABC, 1964.
"The Raffle," *The Patty Duke Show*, ABC, 1965.
"The Man Who Believed," *Ironside*, NBC, 1967.
Nurse Margie Cutler, "Requiem for a Lightweight," *M*A*S*H*, CBS, 1972.
"No More Mr. Nice Guy," *The Paul Lynde Show*, ABC, 1972.
Nurse Margie Cutler, "Edwina," *M*A*S*H*, CBS, 1973.
"Mirabelle's Summer," *Love Story*, NBC, 1973.
"The Ripper," *Police Story*, NBC, 1974.
"The Latch-Key Child," *Marcus Welby, M.D.*, ABC, 1974.
"Million Dollar Man," *The Love Boat*, ABC, 1978.
Fantasy Island, ABC, 1978.
Whitney Cox, "Only Rock and Roll Will Never Die," *The Rockford Files*, NBC, 1979.
"Heal Thyself," *Magnum, P.I.*, CBS, 1982.
"Love Sick," *At Ease*, ABC, 1983.
"Gemini," *Stingray*, NBC, 1987.
"Such Interesting Neighbors," *Amazing Stories*, NBC, 1987.
"A Matter of Moulding," *I Married Dora*, ABC, 1987.
"First Love," *TV 101*, CBS, 1989.
Tracy Takes On. . ., HBO, 1996.
Betsy Fields, "Glory Days," *Highlander*, syndicated, 1996.

Television Appearances; Specials:
Julie Kotter, *Sweathog Back-to-School Special*, ABC, 1977.
ABC's Silver Anniversary Celebration—25 and Still the One, ABC, 1978.
Mary Watson, "Daddy Can't Read," *ABC Afterschool Special*, ABC, 1988.
Elaine, *Tickets, Please*, CBS, 1988.

Candace Crawford, *Julie Brown: The Show*, CBS, 1989.
Host, *Miss Teen USA*, CBS, 1989.

RECORDINGS

Taped Readings:
Trust Me, 1995.*

STRODE, Woodrow
  See STRODE, Woody

STRODE, Woody   1914-1994
  (Woodrow Strode)

PERSONAL

Born Woodrow Wilson Woolwine Strode, July 28, 1914, in Los Angeles, CA; died December 31, 1994, in Glendora, CA; married Luukialuana Kalaeloa (a Hawaiian princess), 1941 (died, 1980); married; wife's name, Tina, May 10, 1982. *Education:* Attended the University of California at Los Angeles.

Career: Actor. Also played college football at University of California at Los Angeles and professionally with the Cleveland Rams (now the St. Louis Rams) and the Calgary Stampeders (in the Canadian Football League); also worked as a professional wrestler.

CREDITS

Film Appearances:
Tribal policeman, *Sundown*, United Artists, 1941.
"Smart as a Tack" number, *Star Spangled Rhythm*, Paramount, 1942.
Sandhog, *No Time for Love*, Paramount, 1943.
Policeman, *Bride of the Gorilla*, Real Art, 1951.
Walu, *The Lion Hunters* (also known as *Bomba and the Lion*), Monogram, 1951.
Esau, *Caribbean* (also known as *Caribbean Gold*), Paramount, 1952.
The Lion, *Androcles and the Lion*, RKO Pictures, 1952.
Native mail boy, *African Treasure* (also known as *Bomba and the African Treasure*), Monogram, 1952.
Djion, *City Beneath the Sea* (also known as *One Hour to Doom's Day*), Universal, 1953.
Malaka, *Jungle Gents*, Allied Artists, 1954.

Josh, *The Gambler from Natchez,* Twentieth Century-Fox, 1954.

Gladiator, *Demetrius and the Gladiators,* Twentieth Century-Fox, 1954.

Guard, *Son of Sinbad* (also known as *Nights in a Harem*), RKO Pictures, 1955.

King of Ethiopa, *The Ten Commandments,* Paramount, 1956.

Ramo, *Tarzan's Fight for Life,* Metro-Goldwyn-Mayer, 1958.

Soldier, *The Buccaneer,* Paramount, 1958.

Franklin, *Pork Chop Hill,* United Artists, 1959.

Hank Lawson, *The Last Voyage,* Metro-Goldwyn-Mayer, 1960.

First Sergeant Braxton Rutledge, *Sergeant Rutledge* (also known as *The Trial of Sergeant Rutledge*), Warner Bros., 1960.

Draba, *Spartacus,* Universal, 1960.

Muwango, *The Sins of Rachel Cade* (also known as *Rachel Cade*), Warner Bros., 1961.

Stone Calf, *Two Rode Together,* Columbia, 1961.

Pompey, *The Man Who Shot Liberty Valance,* Paramount, 1962.

Khan/Tarim, *Tarzan's Three Challenges,* Metro-Goldwyn-Mayer, 1963.

Sengal, *Genghis Khan* (also known as *Dzingis-Kan* and *Dschingis Khan*), Columbia, 1965.

Lean Warrior, *7 Women,* Metro-Goldwyn-Mayer, 1966.

Jacob Sharp, *The Professionals,* Columbia, 1966.

Maurice Lalubi, *Seated at His Right* (also known as *Black Jesus, Out of Darkness, Seduta Alla Sua Destra,* and *Super Brother*), Castoro, 1968.

Chato, *Shalako,* Cinerama, 1968.

Thomas, *Boot Hill* (also known as *La Collina Degli Stivali* and *Trinity Rides Again*), Film Ventures, 1969.

Guillermo, *Che!,* Twentieth Century-Fox, 1969.

Stony, *Once Upon a Time in the West* (also known as *C'era una Volta Il West*), Paramount, 1969.

Marshak, *Tarzan's Deadly Silence* (also known as *The Deadly Silence*), National General, 1970.

The Unholy Four (also known as *L'uomo della Vendetta*), Atlas, 1970.

Duncan, *The Last Rebel,* Columbia, 1971.

Jackson, *The Deserter* (also known as *Ride to Glory* and *La Spina Dorsale del Diavolo*), Paramount, 1971.

Narrator, *Black Rodeo* (documentary), 1972.

Job, *The Revengers,* National General, 1972.

Runner, *The Gatling Gun* (also known as *King Gun*), Ellman, 1972.

Frank, *The Italian Connection* (also known as *Hired to Kill, La Mala Ordina, Manhunt,* and *Manhunt in Milan*), AIP, 1973.

Silvera, *Loaded Guns* (also known as *Colpo in Canna* and *Stick 'em Up, Darlings*), Live Home Video, 1975.

Black Bill, *Noi non Siamo Angeli* (also known as *We Are No Angels*), 1975.

Big Rude, *Winterhawk,* Howco, 1976.

Oil, Video Communications Inc., 1977.

Walter Colby, *Kingdom of the Spiders,* Dimension Pictures, 1977.

Brown, *Ravagers,* Columbia, 1979.

Sensei, *Jaguar Lives!* (also known as *El Felino*), American International Pictures, 1979.

Titi, *Cuba Crossing* (also known as *Assignment: Kill Castro, Kill Castro, The Mercenaries, Sweet Dirty Tony,* and *Sweet Violent Tony*), Key West, 1980.

Woody, *Angkor: Cambodia Express,* Monarex, 1981, released in the U.S., 1985.

Rake, *Vigilante* (also known as *Street Gang*), Film Ventures, 1983.

Charlie Winters, *Scream* (also known as *The Outing*), LIVE Home Video/Vestron, 1983.

Sam, *The Final Executioner* (also known as *The Last Warrior* and *L'Ultimo Guerriero*), Cannon, 1983.

Meslar, *The Black Stallion Returns,* United Artists, 1983.

Luther, *Jungle Warriors,* Aquarius, 1984.

Holmes, *The Cotton Club,* Orion, 1984.

Blackman, *Lust in the Dust,* New World, 1985.

The Bronx Executioner, Cannon Video, 1986.

Paolo, *The Violent Breed* (also known as *Razza Violenta*), Metro-Goldwyn-Mayer/United Artists, 1986.

Yank, *Murder on the Bayou* (also known as *A Gathering of Old Men*), Vidmark Entertainment, 1991.

Charlie Sumpter, *Storyville,* Twentieth Century-Fox, 1992.

Storyteller, *Posse,* Gramercy Pictures, 1993.

Charlie Moonlight, *The Quick and the Dead,* TriStar, 1995.

Television Appearances; Movies:
Breakout, 1970.
Key West, 1973.
On Fire, 1987.
Yank, *A Gathering of Old Men,* 1987.

Television Appearances; Episodic:
Soldiers of Fortune, syndicated, 1955.
Jungle Jim, 1955.
The Man from Blackhawk, ABC, 1960.
Binnaburra, "Incident of the Boomerang," *Rawhide,* CBS, 1961.
The Lieutenant, NBC, 1964.
The Farmer's Daughter, ABC, 1964.

Tarzan, NBC, 1966.
Daniel Boone, NBC, 1966.
Tarzan, NBC, 1967.
Tarzan, NBC, 1968.
The Manhunter, CBS, 1973.
"The Longest Drive," *The Quest,* NBC, 1976.
Arapaho Chief, *How the West Was Won,* ABC, 1978.
"Return of the Fighting 69th," *Buck Rogers in the 25th Century,* NBC, 1979.

WRITINGS

(With Sam Young) *Goal Dust: An Autobiography,* Madison Books (Lanham, MD), 1990.

OBITUARIES AND OTHER SOURCES

Periodicals:
Time ("Milestones" column), January 16, 1995.*

SULLIVAN, Susan 1944-

PERSONAL

Full name, Susan Michaelin Sullivan; born November 18, 1944, in New York, NY; daughter of Brendan and Helen (Rockett) Sullivan; partner, Connell Cowan (a psychologist and author). *Education:* Hofstra University, B.A. (theatre and psychology), 1966; studied at the American Academy of Dramatic Arts, New York, NY. *Avocational interests:* Literature, travel, music, skiing, analyzing her friends, and collecting art.

Addresses: *Agent*—Paradigm, 200 West 57th St., Suite 900, New York, NY 10019.

Career: Actress. Cleveland Playhouse, Cleveland, OH, member of company, 1966-68; later affiliated with Hartford Stage Company, National Repertory Theatre, and Channel 13 Repertory Company. Spokeswoman for Tylenol for eleven years. Volunteer with Adult Children of Alcoholics; sponsor of Save the Children and founder of Save the Children Champions; founding member of Celebrity Action Council, Los Angeles Mission; affiliated with the Arthritis Foundation; boardmember of the Felice; boardmember of the Museum of Natural History.

Member: Actors Equity Association, Screen Actors Guild, American Federation of Television and Radio Artists, National Hospice Organization, Women in Film Association, Muscular Dystrophy Association (vice president, 1983-84).

Awards, Honors: Emmy Award nomination, best supporting actress in a special, 1977, for *Rich Man, Poor Man—Book II;* Emmy Award nomination, best actress—drama series, 1978, for *Julie Farr, M.D.;* George M. Esterbrook Distinguished Alumni Award, Hofstra University, 1982; fellowship from Cleveland Playhouse.

CREDITS

Television Appearances; Series:
Nancy Condon, *A World Apart,* ABC, 1970-71.
Lenore Moore, *Another World,* NBC, 1971-76.
Dr. Julie Farr, *Julie Farr, M.D.* (also known as *Having Babies*), ABC, 1978-79.
Lois Adams, *It's a Living,* ABC, 1980-81.
Maggie Gioberti Channing, *Falcon Crest,* CBS, 1981-89.
Kathleen Rachowski (recurring role), *The George Carlin Show,* Fox, 1994-95.
Kathryn Monroe, *The Monroes,* ABC, 1995.
Kitty Montgomery, *Dharma and Greg,* ABC, 1997—.

Television Appearances; Movies:
Girl on bus, *No Place to Run,* ABC, 1972.
Midway, 1976.
Cindy St. Claire, *Roger and Harry: The Mitera Target* (also known as *Love for Ransom*), ABC, 1977.
C. B. Macauley, *The Magnificent Magical Magnet of Santa Mesa* (also known as *The Magnificent Magnet of Santa Mesa* and *The Adventures of Freddy*), NBC, 1977.
Dr. Elaina Marks, *The Incredible Hulk,* CBS, 1977.
Carol Carter, *The City,* NBC, 1977.
Dr. Julie Farr, *Having Babies II,* ABC, 1977.
Linda Greg, *The Comedy Company,* CBS, 1978.
Dr. Julie Farr, *Having Babies III,* ABC, 1978.
Rainbow, *Deadman's Curve,* CBS, 1978.
Poker Alice, *The New Maverick,* ABC, 1978.
Diane Sealey, *Breaking Up Is Hard to Do,* ABC, 1979.
Panic on Page One, ABC, 1979.
Francis Mudd, *The Ordeal of Dr. Mudd,* CBS, 1980.
Madelaine Crawford, *City in Fear,* ABC, 1980.
Sara Fish, *Marriage Is Alive and Well,* NBC, 1980.
Senator Kate Lassiter, *Cave-in!,* NBC, 1983.
Mary Beth Warner, *Rage of Angels: The Story Continues,* NBC, 1986.
Twyla Cooper, *Perry Mason: The Case of the Ruthless Reporter,* NBC, 1991.

Kaye, *Danielle Steel's A Perfect Stranger* (also known as *A Perfect Stranger*), NBC, 1994.
Patricia Clarkson, *Two Come Back*, ABC, 1997.

Also appeared in *Twelfth Night, Macbeth,* and *The Winter's Tale,* all for PBS.

Television Appearances; Miniseries:
Maggie Porter, *Rich Man, Poor Man—Book II,* ABC, 1977-78.

Television Appearances; Episodic:
"Macbeth," *Actors Company,* syndicated, 1969.
"No Hiding Place," *Medical Center,* CBS, 1975.
"The Vendetta," *S.W.A.T.,* ABC, 1975.
"Requiem for a Bride," *Macmillan and Wife,* NBC, 1975.
"Too Many Alibis," *Petrocelli,* NBC, 1975.
"The House on Orange Grove Avenue," *City of Angels,* NBC, 1976.
"Deadline for Dying," *Barnaby Jones,* CBS, 1976.
"Both Sides of the Law," *Kojak,* CBS, 1976.
"When You Hear the Beep, Drop Dead," *Kojak,* CBS, 1977.
"Yesterday's Woman," *Dog and Cat,* ABC, 1977.
Elaine Marks, *The Incredible Hulk,* CBS, 1978.
"The Final Judgment," *Barnaby Jones,* CBS, 1978.
The Love Boat, ABC, 1979.
Nora, "What Price Bobby," *Taxi,* ABC, 1980.
"The Perfect Husband," *Fantasy Island,* ABC, 1981.
"Nellie Blye," *An American Portrait,* CBS, 1986.
Guest, *At Rona's,* NBC, 1989.
Laura, *Doctor, Doctor,* CBS, 1990.

Television Appearances; Pilots:
Our Man Flint: Dead on Target, ABC, 1976.
Rosemary, *Bell, Book, and Candle,* NBC, 1976.

Also appeared in *Ruth Harper* and *Satellite News.*

Television Appearances; Specials:
Host, *CBS Tournament of Roses Parade,* CBS, 1984.
Host (Hawaii), *CBS All-American Thanksgiving Day Parade,* CBS, 1984.
An All-Star Party for "Dutch" Reagan, CBS, 1985.
Host (New York), *First Annual CBS Easter Parade,* CBS, 1985.
Host (New York), *CBS All-American Thanksgiving Day Parade,* CBS, 1986.
Happy Birthday, Hollywood!, ABC, 1987.
Drug Free Kids: A Parents Guide, PBS, 1988.
Diet America Challenge, CBS, 1989.
Valvoline National Driving Test, CBS, 1989.
The Television Academy Hall of Fame, Fox, 1990.

Film Appearances:
Woman, *Star Trek: The Motion Picture,* Paramount, 1979.
Isabelle Wallace, *My Best Friend's Wedding,* TriStar, 1997.
Show and Tell, 1997.

Stage Appearances:
Elizabeth (Broadway debut), *Jimmy Shine,* 1968.
The Beauty Part, American Place Theatre, New York City, 1974.
The Fifth of July, Mark Taper Forum Theatre, Los Angeles, 1979.
Last Summer at Blue Fish Cove, Theatre-on-the-Square, San Francisco, CA, 1983.
Dangerous Corner, Matrix Theater, 1997.

Also appeared in *She Stoops to Conquer,* National Repertory Theatre Company, Ford's Theatre, Washington, DC; and in *Uncle Vanya, The Three Sisters,* and *Mourning Becomes Electra,* National Touring Company.

OTHER SOURCES

Periodicals:
People, April 18, 1988, p. 107.*

───────────

SUMNER, Gordon Matthew
See STING

───────────

SUNDE, Karen   1942-

PERSONAL

Born July 18, 1942, in Wausau, WI; daughter of John E. (a retail manager) and B. Marie (Schoen) Sunde; children: John, Paul. *Education:* Iowa State University, B.S. (English and speech), 1963; Kansas State University, M.A. (dramatic literature), 1965.

Addresses: *Home*—New York, NY. *Agent*—Michael Imison, 28 Almeida Street, London N1, England.

Career: Director, actress, and writer. Colorado Shakespeare Festival, Boulder, CO, actress, 1967; The New Shakespeare Company, San Francisco, CA, actress, 1967-68; Arrow Rock Lyceum, Arrow Rock, MO, actress, 1969-70; CSC Repertory, New York City, actress, 1971-85; associate director, 1975-85;

Actors Theatre of St. Paul, St. Paul, MN, playwright, 1987-88.

Member: Actors' Equity Association, Screen Actors Guild, New Jersey State Council on the Arts (theatre panel).

Awards, Honors: Bob Hope Award, 1963, for *The Sound of Sand;* Scandinavian Foundation Finnish Literature Center, 1981; Finnish Literature Center Production grant, 1982; Outer Critic's Circle Award nomination, Villager Award, 1983, for *Balloon;* McKnight Fellowship, 1986; Aide de la Creation grant, 1987.

CREDITS

Stage Appearances:
Helena, *A Midsummer Night's Dream,* New Shakespeare Company, San Francisco, 1967.
Artist, *Portrait of the Artist,* Playbox, 1970.
Ruth, *The Homecoming,* 1972-76.
Celimene, *The Misanthrope,* 1973-74.
Viola, *Twelfth Night,* 1973-74.
Hedda, *Hedda Gabler,* CSC Repertory Theatre, New York City, 1974-77.
Antigone, *Antigone,* CSC Repertory Theatre, 1975-77.
Isabella, *Measure for Measure,* CSC Repertory Theatre, 1975.
Hesione, *Heartbreak House,* CSC Repertory Company, 1976-77.
Rebecca West, *Rosmersholm,* 1977-78.
Countess Aurelie, *The Madwoman of Chaillot,* CSC Repertory Theatre, 1978.
Portia, *The Merchant of Venice,* CSC Repertory Theatre, 1980.
Jocasta and Antigone, *Oedipus Cycle* (composed of *Oedipus Rex, Antigone,* and *Oedipus at Colonus*), 1980-81.
Aase, *Peer Gynt I/II,* CSC Repertory Theatre, 1981-82.
Lotte, *Big and Little,* CSC Repertory Theatre, 1983-84.
Alice, *Dance of Death,* CSC Repertory Theatre, 1984.
Clytemnestra, *The Orestia,* 1984-85.

Also appeared in the following with the CSC Repertory Company: *The Cherry Orchard,* as Mother Aase and Ruth, *The Homecoming,* and as Celestina, *La Celestina;* created and performed *Poems from Finland,* New York and Minneapolis; performed for the Circle Repertory Company's playwright's workshop, McCarter Theatre; staged readings program at the

Colorado Shakespeare Festival, and at the Arrow Rock Lyceum Theatre.

Stage Work; Director:
Exit the King, Jean Cocteau Repertory Theatre, New York City, 1978.
Philoctetes, Jean Cocteau Repertory Theatre, 1983.

Director of *Balloon* and *Leonice and Lena,* and codirector, *Ghost Sonata,* all CSC Repertory.

Television Appearances; Movies:
Mary Brewster, *Mayflower: The Pilgrim's Adventure* (also known as *The Mayflower*), CBS, 1979.

Film Appearances:
Narrator, *Image Before My Eyes,* 1981.

WRITINGS

Stage:
Day Before Noon, New York City, 1970.
The Running of the Deer, CSC Repertory Theatre, 1978.
Balloon, produced in New York City, 1983, published by Broadway Play Publishing (New York City), 1983.
(Adapted from the play by Sophocles) *Philoctetes,* Jean Cocteau Repertory Theatre, 1983.
Dark Lady, produced in Santa Maria, CA, 1986, then Dublin, 1988, and Requested-Jeu de Lumiere, Avignon, published by Dramatic Publishing Company (Wilton, CT), 1985.
Kabuki Othello, produced in Philadelphia, PA, 1986.
To Moscow, produced in Minneapolis, MN, 1986, then New York City, 1991, later One Dream Theatre, New York City, 1996.
(With Christopher Martin; adapted from *The Hunchback of Notre Dame* by Victor Hugo) *Quasimodo* (musical), produced in Woodstock, NY, 1987.
(Edited by Michael Bigelow Dixon) *Anton, Himself,* Actor's Theatre of Louisville, Louisville, KY, 1988.
Kabuki Macbeth, The Acting Company, Davis, CA, 1988.
Haiti: A Dream, produced in Atlanta, GA, 1990.
Masha, Too, produced in Philadelphia, PA, 1991.
Achilles, produced in Kourion, Cyprus, and Philadelphia, PA, 1991.
In a Kingdom by the Sea, produced in Madison, NJ, and New York City, both 1992.

Manuscript collection at Lincoln Center Library for the Performing Arts, New York City.

Radio Plays:
The Sound of Sand, Iowa State University Players, 1963.
Balloon, workshop, 1980, CSC Repertory, 1983, published by Broadway Play Publishing, 1983.
Haiti: A Dream, 1991.

Also wrote D'Eon, a libretto for Andrew Thomas.

Teleplays:
Wrote Deborah: The Adventures of a Soldier, (unproduced).

OTHER SOURCES

Periodicals:
Back Stage, October 11, 1996, p. 43.*

SWERLING, Jo Jr. 1931-

PERSONAL

Born June 18, 1931, in Los Angeles, CA; son of Jo (a writer) and Florence (Manson) Swerling; children: Timothy David, Tanya Manson. Education: Attended University of California, Los Angeles, 1948-51, and California Maritime Academy, 1951-54.

Addresses: Office—The Cannell Studios, 7083 Hollywood Blvd., Hollywood, CA 90028.

Career: Producer and screenwriter. Revue Productions/Universal Television, began as production coordinator, became associate producer, producer, associate executive producer, executive producer, director, and writer, 1957-81; Stephen J. Cannell Productions, Hollywood, CA, senior vice-president; University of Southern California, Los Angeles, member of industry advisory committee for screenwriting department. Community of Hidden Hills, CA, member of Planning Commission, 1973-80. Military service: U.S. Navy, 1954-56; served in far East; became lieutenant junior grade.

Member: Writers Guild of America, Directors Guild of America, Screen Actors Guild, Academy of Television Arts and Sciences.

Awards, Honors: Emmy Award nomination, best dramatic series, 1976, for Baretta; Emmy Award nomination and Golden Globe Award nomination, Hollywood Foreign Press Association, both best limited series, both 1977, for Captains and the Kings; also two Emmy Award nominations, both best dramatic series, for Run for Your Life.

CREDITS

Television Work; Series:
Producer (with Paul Freeman), Run For Your Life, NBC, 1965-68.
Producer (with Roy Huggins), The Outsider, NBC, 1968-69.
Producer (with Steve Helpern), The Lawyers, NBC, 1969-72.
Executive producer (with Huggins), Alias Smith and Jones, ABC, 1971-73.
Producer (with David J. O'Connell), Cool Million, NBC, 1972-73.
Associate executive producer (with Stephen J. Cannell), Toma, ABC, 1973-74.
Supervising producer, The Rockford Files, NBC, 1974-80.
Producer, Baretta, ABC, 1975-78.
Supervising producer and executive producer, City of Angels, NBC, 1976.
Supervising producer, Lobo, NBC, 1980-81.
Executive producer (with Frank Lupo) and supervising producer, The Greatest American Hero, ABC, 1981-83.
Supervising producer (with John Ashley and Lupo), The Quest, ABC, 1982.
Supervising producer, The A Team, NBC, 1983-87.
Supervising producer, Hardcastle and McCormick, ABC, 1983.
Supervising producer, The Rousters, NBC, 1983-84.
Supervising producer (with Cannell and Lupo) and executive producer, Riptide, NBC, 1983-86.
Supervising producer, Hunter, NBC, 1984-91.
Supervising producer, Stingray, NBC, 1985.
Supervising producer, J. J. Starbuck, NBC, 1987-88.
Supervising producer, 21 Jump Street, Fox, 1987-88.
Supervising producer, Wiseguy, CBS, 1987-91.
Supervising producer, Sonny Spoon, NBC, 1988.
Supervising producer, UNSUB, NBC, 1989.
Supervising producer, Booker, Fox, 1989.
Supervising producer, Top of the Hill, CBS, 1989.
Supervising producer, Broken Badges, CBS, 1990.
Supervising producer (with Jack Bernstein), Disney Presents the 100 Lives of Black Jack Savage (also known as Black Jack Savage), NBC, 1991.
Supervising producer, The Commish, ABC, 1991-92.
Supervising producer, The Hat Squad, CBS, 1992.
Supervising producer, Traps, CBS, 1994.
Supervising producer (with N. John Smith), Profit, Fox, 1996.

Also associate producer, then producer, *Kraft Suspense Theatre*, NBC. Production coordinator of the series *The Restless Gun*, NBC; *Markham*, CBS; *M Squad*, NBC; *Cimarron City*, NBC; *Suspicion*, NBC; *Thriller*, NBC; *The 87th Precinct*, NBC; *Alcoa Premiere*, ABC; and *Wagon Train*.

Television Work; Miniseries:
Producer, *Captains and the Kings*, NBC, 1976.
Producer, *Aspen*, NBC, 1977.
Executive producer and director (with Sidney Hayers and Gus Trikonis), *The Last Convertible*, NBC, 1979.

Television Work; Pilots:
Producer, *The Green Felt Jungle*, NBC, 1965.
Producer, *Rapture at Two-Forty* (broadcast as an episode of *Kraft Suspense Theater*), NBC, 1965.
Producer (with Huggins), *The Outsider*, NBC, 1967.
Producer, *The Sound of Anger*, NBC, 1968.
Producer, *The Lonely Profession*, NBC, 1969.
Producer, *The Whole World Is Watching*, NBC, 1969.
Producer, *Sam Hill: Who Killed the Mysterious Mr. Foster?*, NBC, 1971.
Producer, *Jigsaw* (also known as *Man on the Move*), ABC, 1972.
Producer, *Toma*, ABC, 1973.
Associate executive producer, *The Rockford Files*, NBC, 1974.
Executive producer, *Target Risk*, NBC, 1975.
Executive producer, *Hazard's People*, CBS, 1976.
Producer, *The 3000 Mile Chase*, NBC, 1977.
Producer, *The Jordan Chance*, CBS, 1978.
Producer, *Pirate's Key*, CBS, 1979.
Supervising producer, *The A Team*, NBC, 1983.
Supervising producer, *Hardcastle and McCormick*, ABC, 1983.
Supervising producer, *The Rousters*, NBC, 1983.
Supervising producer (with Cannell and Lupo), *Riptide*, NBC, 1983.
Supervising producer, *Hunter*, NBC, 1984.
Supervising producer, *Stingray*, NBC, 1985.
Supervising producer, *Brothers-in-Law*, ABC, 1985.

Supervising producer, *The Last Precinct*, NBC, 1986.
Supervising producer, *21 Jump Street*, Fox, 1987.
Supervising producer, *Wiseguy*, CBS, 1987.
Supervising producer, *J. J. Starbuck*, NBC, 1987.
Supervising producer, *Sonny Spoon*, NBC, 1988.

Television Work; Movies:
Producer, *Do You Take This Stranger?*, NBC, 1971.
Producer, *How to Steal an Airplane*, NBC, 1972.
Producer, *Drive Hard, Drive Fast*, NBC, 1973.
Producer, *The Story of Pretty Boy Floyd*, ABC, 1974.
Producer, *This Is the West That Was*, NBC, 1974.
Executive producer, *The Invasion of Johnson County*, NBC, 1976.
Supervising producer, *Destination: America*, 1987.
Supervising producer (with Stuart Segall), *Thunder Boat Row*, ABC, 1989.
Supervising producer (with Stuart Segall), *Greyhounds*, CBS, 1994.
Supervising producer, *The Commish: Father Image*, ABC, 1995.
Supervising producer, *The Commish: In the Shadow of the Gallows*, ABC, 1995.
Supervising producer, *The Commish: Redemption*, ABC, 1996.

Television Work; Episodic:
Producer for *Bob Hope Presents the Chrysler Theater*, NBC.

WRITINGS

Television Pilots:
(With Heywood Gould and Roy Huggins) *Hazard's People*, CBS, 1976.

Television Episodes:
The A Team, NBC, 1983.
Sonny Spoon, NBC, 1988.

Author of scripts for episodes of *Run for Your Life*, NBC; *The Lawyers*, NBC; and *The Rockford Files*, NBC.

T-V

TARTIKOFF, Brandon   1949-1997

OBITUARY NOTICE—See index for *CTFT* sketch: Born January 13, 1949, in Freeport, Long Island, NY; died from complications from Hodgkin's disease, August 27, 1997, in Los Angeles, CA. Television network, film, and Internet executive. The youngest man to become president of a major television network's entertainment division, Tartikoff had a keen understanding of what the American viewing audience wanted in its programs and was responsible for popular shows such as *The Cosby Show, Miami Vice, The A-Team, Cheers, Hill Street Blues, St. Elsewhere, L.A. Law, The Golden Girls, Family Ties,* and *Seinfeld.* Tartikoff developed his interest in television programming as a child, and he even displayed evidence of his future occupation when he told his parents at age ten that the *Dennis the Menace* lead was miscast. He eventually attended Yale University and received his B.A. in 1970. While at Yale, he coedited the school's humor magazine with Garry Trudeau, who later rose to fame as the creator of the *Doonesbury* cartoon strip.

Early in his television career, Tartikoff joined WYNH-TV, an ABC-affiliate station in New Haven, Connecticut, as director of advertising and promotion. After two years with WYNH-TV, he went to Chicago in 1973 for three years with WLS-TV, another ABC affiliate. Again the director of advertising and promotion, he rose to the challenge of finding creative ways to promote movies that the station aired. He was so successful, in fact, that he landed a job at ABC-TV in New York City as director of dramatic programs in 1976. A year later, however, he left New York and ABC-TV for California and NBC-TV. From 1977 to 1978 he worked as director of comedy programs before becoming vice president of programs in 1978.

In 1980 he was promoted to president of NBC-TV Entertainment, a moved which shocked the industry due to Tartikoff's youthful age, thirty-one. When he took over as president, NBC-TV was last in ratings and faltering. During Tartikoff's tenure at the network, NBC eventually began to win the ratings battle. According to the *New York Times:* "No other television programmer was so closely identified with a network's success as Mr. Tartikoff was in the 1980s. NBC, which had been widely regarded as the laughing stock of the television industry when he began, ended the decade with the longest laugh in network history: a streak of dominance never equaled, as NBC finished first in the Nielsen ratings 68 weeks in a row."

While at NBC, Tartikoff was responsible for programming some of the most popular shows of the 1980s, including *Hill Street Blues, Cheers,* and *Miami Vice.* The initial idea for the last show, a gritty drama about undercover detectives in fashionable Miami, came from Tartikoff himself. During a meeting with producer Anthony Yerkovich, he jotted down an idea on a napkin. The idea, "MTV cops," was eventually developed into the highly stylized police drama. He was also responsible for bringing Bill Cosby and Jerry Seinfeld to the network. In addition to all these popular shows, there were a few less successful ventures such as *Bay City Blues, Manimal,* and *Beverly Hills Buntz.*

Tartikoff became chairman of NBC Entertainment in 1990, but left the network to become chairman of Paramount Pictures in 1991. According to industry sources, Tartikoff was not as successful in the film industry, although he was responsible for popular motions pictures such as *Wayne's World, A Clear and Present Danger, The Firm,* and *Patriot Games.* He left Paramount in 1992 when both he and his daughter, Calla Lianne, were hurt in a car accident. As noted in MSNBC, "Since [his daughter] needed rehabilitation services in New Orleans, he chucked his seven-figure salary and moved to New Orleans to be with his daughter and wife. After his daughter's condition slowly improved, he returned to the business."

Later, established a production company called H. Beale & Co., which created independent productions. He named the company after fictional character Howard Beale, a television news anchorman in the movie *Network* who goes mad. In 1992 he issued an autobiography called *The Last Great Ride.* Toward the end of his life, he became acting chairman of Entertainment Asylum, which is part of America Online's Greenhouse Network.

His work with the Internet powerhouse was in developing original content, specifically an online site devoted to entertainment. According to MSNBC: "And through his H. Beale & Co. production house, he had been developing a feature called *Beggars and Choosers,* intended for both the Internet and television."

In addition to waging various ratings wars during his career, Tartikoff had a personal battle he fought as well. At age 23, he was diagnosed with Hodgkin's disease, a cancer which affects the lymph nodes. Despite chemotherapy and other treatments, he reportedly never missed a day of work in his first bout with cancer, which went into remission. However, the cancer returned in 1981 and ultimately claimed his life. Earlier in 1997 the disease forced him to take a sabbatical, which ended after only a month. According to the *Chicago Tribune,* he joked about his return to work: "Tartikoff quoted George Burns: 'I can't die now. I'm already booked.'"

OBITUARIES AND OTHER SOURCES

Periodicals:
Chicago Tribune (electronic), August 28, 1997.
CNN Interactive (electronic), August 27, 1997.
Detroit Free Press (electronic), August 28, 1997.
Los Angeles Times, August 28, 1997, p. A1.
MSNBC (electronic), August 28, 1997.
New York Times, August 28, 1997, p. B8.
Times (London; electronic), August 30, 1997.
USA Today (electronic), August 27, 1997.
Washington Post, August 28, 1997, p. B6.

TAYLOR, Elizabeth 1932-
(Liz Taylor)

PERSONAL

Full name, Elizabeth Rosemond Taylor; born February 27, 1932, in London, England; daughter of Francis (an art dealer and historian) and Sara (an actress; maiden name, Southern) Taylor; married Conrad Nicholas Hilton Jr., May 6, 1950 (divorced, 1951); married Michael Wilding (an actor), 1952 (divorced, 1957); married Michael Todd (a producer), February 2, 1957 (died, March, 1958); married Eddie Fisher (a singer and actor), 1959 (divorced, 1964); married Richard Burton (an actor), March 15, 1964 (divorced, 1974); remarried Richard Burton, October 10, 1975 (divorced, 1976); married William John Warner (a politician), 1976 (divorced, 1982); married Larry Fortensky (a construction worker), 1991 (divorced, 1996); children: (second marriage) Michael Wilding Jr., Christopher Wilding; (third marriage) Elizabeth Frances (Liza Todd Tivey); (with Burton) Maria Burton Carson.

Addresses: *Agent*—Chen Sam and Associates, Inc., 315 East 72nd St., New York, NY 10021. *Contact*—700 Nimes Rd., Los Angeles, CA 90077.

Career: Actress and producer. Elizabeth Group (theatrical production company), founder and producer (with Zev Bufman). Creator of perfumes, including Passion, Passion for Men, Diamonds and Rubies, Diamonds and Sapphires, White Diamonds, and Black Pearls; creator of a jewelry line for Avon, The Elizabeth Taylor Fashion Jewelry Collection. Chaim Sheba Hospital, contributor and fundraiser, Israel War Victims' Fund, 1976; Ben Gurion University-Elizabeth Taylor Fund for Children of the Negev, founder, 1982; American Foundation for AIDS Research, founder and national chairperson, 1985—, founder of international fund, 1985; AIDS Project, Los Angeles, CA, supporter, 1985; Elizabeth Taylor AIDS Foundation, founder, 1991; Variety Clubs International, fundraiser for hospital children's wings; Botswana Clinics, Africa, fundraiser and contributor. Also known as Liz Taylor.

Awards, Honors: Golden Globe Special Award, Hollywood Foreign Press Association, 1957; Academy Award nominations, best actress, 1957, for *Raintree County,* and 1958, for *Cat on a Hot Tin Roof;* Academy Award nomination, best actress, 1959, and Golden Globe Award, best motion picture actress in a drama, 1960, both for *Suddenly, Last Summer;* Academy Award, best actress, 1960, for *Butterfield 8;* Academy Award and British Academy Award, British Academy of Film and Television Arts, both best actress, 1966, for *Who's Afraid of Virginia Woolf?* Silver Bear Award, best actress, Berlin Film Festival, 1972, for *Hammersmith Is Out;* Golden Globe Award nomination, best actress in a drama, 1974, for *Ash Wednesday;* Golden Globe Award, female world film favorite, 1974; Hasty Pudding Woman of the Year Award, Harvard Hasty Pudding Theatricals, 1977; *Theatre World* Special Award and Antoinette Perry Award nomination, best actress in a play, both 1981, for *The Little Foxes;* Cecil B. De Mille Award, Hollywood Foreign Press Association, 1985; Golden Apple Star of the Year Award, Hollywood Women's Press Club, 1985; Commander des arts et des lettres (France), 1985; French Legion of Honor, 1987, for work with American Foundation for AIDS Research; Onassis Prize for Man and Science, Aristotle S. Onassis Foundation, 1988, for work against AIDS; Life Achievement Award, American Film Institute, 1993; Jean Hersholt Humanitarian Award, Academy Awards, 1993; the Elizabeth Taylor Medical Center was dedicated in her honor at Whitman-Walker Clinic in Washington, 1993.

CREDITS

Film Appearances:
(Film debut) Gloria Twine, *There's One Born Every Minute,* Universal, 1942.
Priscilla, *Lassie, Come Home,* Metro-Goldwyn-Mayer, 1943.
Helen Burns, *Jane Eyre,* Twentieth Century-Fox, 1944.
Velvet Brown, *National Velvet,* Metro-Goldwyn-Mayer, 1944.
Betsy at age ten, *The White Cliffs of Dover,* Metro-Goldwyn-Mayer, 1944.
Kathie Merrick, *Courage of Lassie* (also known as *Blue Sierra*), Metro-Goldwyn-Mayer, 1946.
Cynthia Bishop, *Cynthia* (also known as *The Rich, Full Life*), Metro-Goldwyn-Mayer, 1947.
Mary Skinner, *Life with Father,* Warner Bros., 1947.
Carol Pringle, *A Date with Judy,* Metro-Goldwyn-Mayer, 1948.
Susan Packett, *Julia Misbehaves,* Metro-Goldwyn-Mayer, 1948.
Melinda Greyton, *Conspirator,* Metro-Goldwyn-Mayer, 1949.
Amy March, *Little Women,* Metro-Goldwyn-Mayer, 1949.
Mary Belney, *The Big Hangover,* Metro-Goldwyn-Mayer, 1950.

Kay Banks, *Father of the Bride,* Metro-Goldwyn-Mayer, 1950.
Kay Banks Dunstan, *Father's Little Dividend,* Metro-Goldwyn-Mayer, 1951.
As herself, *Callaway Went Thataway* (also known as *The Star Said No*), Metro-Goldwyn-Mayer, 1951.
Woman in crowd, *Quo Vadis,* Metro-Goldwyn-Mayer, 1951.
Angela Vickers, *A Place in the Sun,* Paramount, 1951.
Rebecca, *Ivanhoe,* Metro-Goldwyn-Mayer, 1952.
Anastacia Macaboy, *Love Is Better Than Ever* (also known as *The Light Fantastic*), Metro-Goldwyn-Mayer, 1952.
Jean Latimer, *The Girl Who Had Everything,* Metro-Goldwyn-Mayer, 1953.
Lady Patricia, *Beau Brummell,* Metro-Goldwyn-Mayer, 1954.
Ruth Wiley, *Elephant Walk,* Paramount, 1954.
Helen Ellswirth, *The Last Time I Saw Paris,* Metro-Goldwyn-Mayer, 1954.
Louise Durant, *Rhapsody,* Metro-Goldwyn-Mayer, 1954.
Leslie Lynnton Benedict, *Giant,* Warner Bros., 1956.
Susanna Drake, *Raintree County,* Metro-Goldwyn-Mayer, 1957.
Maggie Pollitt, *Cat on a Hot Tin Roof,* Metro-Goldwyn-Mayer, 1958.
Catherine Holly, *Suddenly, Last Summer,* Columbia, 1959.
Gloria Wandrous, *Butterfield 8,* Metro-Goldwyn-Mayer, 1960.
Sally Kennedy, *Scent of Mystery* (also known as *Holiday in Spain*), Michael Todd Jr., 1960.
Title role, *Cleopatra,* Twentieth Century-Fox, 1963.
Frances Andros, *The V.I.P.s* (also known as *International Hotel*), Metro-Goldwyn-Mayer, 1963.
Laura Reynolds, *The Sandpiper,* Metro-Goldwyn-Mayer, 1965.
Martha, *Who's Afraid of Virginia Woolf?,* Warner Bros., 1966.
Martha Pineda, *The Comedians,* Metro-Goldwyn-Mayer, 1967.
Helen of Troy, *Doctor Faustus,* Columbia, 1967.
Leonora Penderton, *Reflections in a Golden Eye,* Warner Bros., 1967.
Katharina, *The Taming of the Shrew,* Columbia, 1967.
Flora "Sissy" Goforth, *Boom!,* Universal, 1968.
Leonora, *Secret Ceremony,* Universal, 1968.
Masked courtesan, *Anne of the Thousand Days,* Universal, 1969.
Fran Walker, *The Only Game in Town,* Twentieth Century-Fox, 1970.
Jimmie Jean Jackson, *Hammersmith Is Out,* Cinerama, 1972.

Zee Blakeley, *X, Y, and Zee* (also known as *Zee & Co.*), Columbia, 1972.

Ellen Wheeler, *Night Watch*, Avco-Embassy, 1973.

Rosie Probert, *Under Milkwood*, Altura Films International, 1973.

Narrator, *That's Entertainment*, Metro-Goldwyn-Mayer, 1974.

Barbara Sawyer, *Ash Wednesday*, Paramount, 1974.

Lise, *The Driver's Seat* (also known as *Identikit* and *Psychotic*), Avco-Embassy, 1975.

It's Showtime (documentary), United Artists, 1975.

Mother, Light, Witch, and Maternal Love, *The Blue Bird*, Twentieth Century-Fox, 1976.

Desiree Armfeldt, *A Little Night Music*, New World Cinema, 1977.

Lola Comante, *Winter Kills*, Avco-Embassy, 1979.

Marina Rudd, *The Mirror Crack'd*, Associated Film Distribution, 1980.

Narrator, *Genocide* (documentary), Simon Wiesenthal Center, 1981.

As herself, *George Stevens: A Filmmaker's Journey* (documentary), Castle Hill, 1984.

Nadia Bulichoff, *Il Giovane Toscanini* (also known as *Young Toscanini* and *Toscanini*), Italian International/Union Generale Cinematographique/Carthago, 1988.

Pearl Slaghoople, *The Flintstones*, Universal, 1994.

Film Work:

Executive producer, *Number 13* (also known as *Fragments of a Fate Forgotten*, *The Magic Mushroom People of Oz*, *The Oz*, and *The Tin Woodman's Dream*), 1962.

Producer (with Richard Burton and Franco Zeffirelli), *The Taming of the Shrew*, Columbia, 1967.

Television Appearances; Miniseries:

Madame Conti, *North and South*, ABC, 1985.

Television Appearances; Movies:

Jane Reynolds, *Divorce His/Divorce Hers*, ABC, 1973.

Edra Vilnofsky, *Victory at Entebbe*, ABC, 1976.

Deborah Shapiro, *Between Friends* (also known as *Nobody Makes Me Cry*), HBO, 1983.

Louella Parsons, *Malice in Wonderland* (also known as *The Rumor Mill*), CBS, 1985.

Marguerite Sydney, *There Must Be a Pony*, ABC, 1986.

Title role (Alice Moffett), *Poker Alice*, CBS, 1987.

Alexandra Del Lago, *Tennessee Williams's "Sweet Bird of Youth"* (also known as *Sweet Bird of Youth*), NBC, 1989.

Television Appearances; Specials:

Host, *Elizabeth Taylor in London*, CBS, 1963.

The Barbara Walters Special, ABC, 1977.

Dr. Emily Loomis, "Return Engagement," *The Hallmark Hall of Fame*, NBC, 1978.

General Electric's All-Star Anniversary, ABC, 1978.

Happy Birthday, Bob, NBC, 1978.

Bob Hope's Stand Up and Cheer for the National Football League's 60th Year, NBC, 1981.

Bob Hope's Women I Love—Beautiful but Funny, NBC, 1982.

Bob Hope's Star-Studded Spoof of the New TV Season—G-Rated—With Glamour, Glitter, and Gags, NBC, 1982.

The 50th Presidential Inaugural Gala, ABC, 1985.

An All-Star Celebration Honoring Martin Luther King Jr., NBC, 1986.

Bob Hope's High-Flying Birthday, NBC, 1986.

Liberty Weekend, ABC, 1986.

The Spencer Tracy Legacy: A Tribute by Katharine Hepburn, PBS, 1986.

The Barbara Walters Special, ABC, 1987.

"Natalie Wood," *Crazy about the Movies*, Cinemax, 1987.

AIDS: The Global Explosion, syndicated, 1988.

Michael Jackson, 1988.

"Richard Burton: In from the Cold," *Great Performances*, PBS, 1989.

America's All-Star Tribute to Elizabeth Taylor (also known as *The 2nd Annual America's Hope Award*), ABC, 1989.

Miss Hollywood Talent Search, syndicated, 1989.

Entertainers '91: The Top 20 of the Year, 1991.

In a New Light, ABC, 1992.

Michael Jackson. . .The Legend Continues, CBS, 1992.

In a New Light '93, ABC, 1993.

Larry King TNT Extra, TNT, 1993.

Michael Jackson Talks . . . to Oprah—90 Primetime Minutes with the King of Pop (also known as *Oprah Live with Michael Jackson—90 Minutes with the King of Pop* and *Live and Dangerous*), ABC, 1993.

The American Film Institute Salute to Elizabeth Taylor, ABC, 1993.

The Jackson Family Honors, NBC, 1994.

How to Be Absolutely Fabulous, Comedy Central, 1995.

Happy Birthday Elizabeth—A Celebration of Life, ABC, 1997.

Television Appearances; Episodic:

What's My Line?, CBS, 1954.

Person to Person, CBS, 1957.

The Sammy Davis Jr. Show, NBC, 1966.
"Lucy Meets the Burtons," *Here's Lucy,* CBS, 1970.
The Lucy Show, CBS, 1971.
Helena Cassadine, *General Hospital,* ABC, 1981.
Charwoman, *All My Children,* ABC, 1983.
"Intimate Strangers," *Hotel,* ABC, 1984.
Fame, Fortune, and Romance, 1986.
Hour Magazine, syndicated, 1986.
Lifestyles of the Rich and Famous, syndicated, 1988.
Voice, *The New Adventures of Captain Planet* (also known as *Captain Planet and the Planeteers*), TBS, 1990.
Voice of Maggie, "Itchy and Scratchy: The Movie," *The Simpsons* (animated), Fox, 1992.
The Whoopie Goldberg Show, syndicated, 1992.
"Elizabeth Taylor," *Biography,* Arts and Entertainment, 1993.
As herself, "Krusty Gets Kancelled," *The Simpsons* (animated), Fox, 1993.
As herself, *Can't Hurry Love,* CBS, 1995.
As herself, *Murphy Brown,* CBS, 1995.
As herself, *The Nanny,* CBS, 1995.
As herself, *High Society,* CBS, 1996.
As herself, *Roseanne,* ABC, 1996.

Appeared on episodes of *Hollywood and the Stars,* NBC; and *The David Frost Show,* syndicated.

Television Appearances; Awards Presentations:
The 59th Annual Academy Awards Presentation, 1987.
Presenter, *The 64th Annual Academy Awards Presentation,* 1992.
The 65th Annual Academy Awards Presentation, 1993.
The American Music Awards, 1993.

Other Television Appearances:
On Top All over the World (pilot), syndicated, 1985.

Stage Appearances:
Regina Giddens, *The Little Foxes,* Center Theatre Group, Ahmanson Theatre, Los Angeles, CA, 1981, then (Broadway debut) Martin Beck Theatre, New York City, 1981, later London, England, 1982.
Amanda Prynne, *Private Lives,* Lunt-Fontanne Theatre, New York City, 1983.

Stage Work:
Producer (with Zev Bufman as the Elizabeth Group), *Private Lives,* Lunt-Fontanne Theatre, New York City, 1983.

Producer (with Bufman as Elizabeth Group), *The Corn Is Green,* Lunt-Fontanne Theatre, 1983.

WRITINGS

World Enough and Time (poetry), 1964.
Elizabeth Taylor—Her Own Story (memoirs), 1965.
Elizabeth Taylor Takes Off on Weight Gain, Weight Loss, Self-Esteem, and Self-Image, Putnam Publishing Group (New York City), 1988.

Author (with Richard Burton) of *Nibbles and Me.*

Adaptations: Elizabeth Taylor's life formed the basis for a television movie, *Liz: The Elizabeth Taylor Story,* 1995.

OTHER SOURCES

Books:
Adler, Bill, *Elizabeth Taylor: Triumphs and Tragedies,* Ace Books (New York City), 1982.
Allan, John B., *Elizabeth Taylor: A Fascinating Story of America's Most Talented Actress and the World's Most Beautiful Woman,* Monarch (Derby, CT), 1961.
D'Arcy, Susan, *The Films of Elizabeth Taylor,* BCW Publishing (Bembridge), 1977.
Heymann, C. David, *Liz: An Intimate Biography of Elizabeth Taylor,* Carol Publishing Group (New York City), 1995.
Kelley, Kitty, *Elizabeth Taylor: The Last Star,* Simon and Schuster (New York City), 1981.
Latham, Caroline, and Jeannie Sakol, *All About Elizabeth Taylor: Elizabeth Taylor, Public and Private,* Onyx (New York), 1991.
Nickens, Christopher, *Elizabeth Taylor: A Biography in Photos,* Doubleday (Garden City, NY), 1984.
Robin-Tani, Marianne, *The New Elizabeth,* St. Martin's (New York City), 1988.
Sheppard, Dick, *Elizabeth: The Life and Career of Elizabeth Taylor,* Doubleday (Garden City, NY), 1974.
Spoto, Donald, *A Passion for Life: The Biography of Elizabeth Taylor,* HarperCollins (New York), 1995.
Vermilye, Jerry, and Mark Ricci, *The Films of Elizabeth Taylor,* Carol Publishing Group (New York City), 1989.
Walker, Alexander, *Elizabeth: The Life of Elizabeth Taylor,* G. Weidenfeld (New York), 1991.

Periodicals:
Advocate, October 15, 1996.

Choices for Retirement Living, June, 1995, p. 26.
Good Housekeeping, March, 1995, pp. 96-98.
People Weekly, March 4, 1996, p. 70.
TV Guide, June 4, 1994, p. 8.
Vanity Fair, May, 1995, p. 90.*

TAYLOR, Liz
   See TAYLOR, Elizabeth

TAYLOR, Meshach

PERSONAL

Born April 11, in Boston, MA; son of a sociology professor and a college professor; married second wife, Bianca Fergerson (an actress); children: (first marriage) Tamar; (second marriage) Yasmine, Esme Alana. *Education:* Studied theater at Florida A & M University. *Avocational interests:* Travel, foreign languages.

Addresses: *Contact*—William Morris Agency, 151 El Camino Dr., Beverly Hills, CA 90212.

Career: Actor. Organic Theatre Group, Chicago, IL, member. Political reporter for a radio station in Indianapolis, IN; head of privately funded program for rehabilitating street gang members, Indianapolis, IN; also worked as an accountant and security guard.

Awards, Honors: Joseph Jefferson Award for *Sizwe Banzi Is Dead*; Chicago Emmy Award for *Huckleberry Finn.*

CREDITS

Film Appearances:
Dr. Kane, *Damien—Omen II,* Twentieth Century-Fox, 1978.
Shantz, *The Howling,* Avco-Embassy, 1981.
Deputy Herbert, *The Beast Within,* Metro-Goldwyn-Mayer/United Artists, 1982.
The Haircut (short film), 1982.
Gordon Miller, *Explorers,* Paramount, 1985.
Video technician, *Warning Sign,* Twentieth Century-Fox, 1985.
Bill Neal, *One More Saturday Night* (also known as *Datenight*), Columbia, 1986.
Philip, *The Allnighter,* Universal, 1987.
Mr. Dean, *House of Games,* Orion, 1987.

Hollywood Montrose, *Mannequin,* Twentieth Century-Fox, 1987.
From the Hip, De Laurentiis Entertainment Group, 1987.
Elijah, *Welcome to Oblivion* (also known as *Ultra Warrior*), Concorde, 1990.
Doorman and Hollywood Montrose, *Mannequin Two: On the Move,* Twentieth Century-Fox, 1991.
Duncan's dad, *Class Act,* Warner Bros., 1992.

Television Appearances; Series:
Tony, *Buffalo Bill,* NBC, 1983-84.
Anthony Bouvier, *Designing Women,* CBS, 1986-93.
Sheldon Baylor, *Dave's World,* CBS, 1993—.
Mr. Winsproggle, *Mrs. Piggle-Wiggle,* Showtime, 1994.
James, *Caroline in the City,* NBC, 1995.
Host, *The Urban Gardener with Meshach Taylor,* HGTV, 1996.

Host of *Black Life,* WMAQ-TV (Chicago, IL).

Television Appearances; Miniseries:
Gus Venable, *Sidney Sheldon's "Nothing Lasts Forever"* (also known as *Nothing Lasts Forever*),CBS, 1995.

Television Appearances; Movies:
Crosby, *The Last Innocent Man,* HBO, 1987.
Danny, *How to Murder a Millionaire* (also known as *The Beverly Hills Get Rich Quick Caper, Bad Times in Beverly Hills, Your Money or Your Wife,* and *The Couch Potato Murders*), CBS, 1990.
Mr. "N" Nofziger, *Double, Double, Toil and Trouble* (also known as *The Twins Halloween Caper*), ABC, 1993.
Anderson, *"Virtual Seduction"* (also known as *"Addicted to Love"*), *Roger Corman Presents,* Showtime, 1995.

Television Appearances; Specials:
Virgil, *"The Rec Room," NBC Presents the AFI Comedy Special,* NBC, 1987.
The 41st Annual Emmy Awards, 1989.
Toronto host, *The CBS All-American Thanksgiving Day Parade,* CBS, 1990.
Motown 30: What's Goin' On!, CBS, 1990.
Anthony Bouvier, *The Designing Women Special: Their Finest Hour,* CBS, 1990.
The 43rd Annual Primetime Emmy Awards Presentation, 1991.
Laughing Back: Comedy Takes a Stand, Lifetime, 1992.

The 61st Annual Hollywood Christmas Parade, 1992.
Side show barker, *The All New Circus of the Stars and Side Show XVII* (also known as *The 17th Annual Circus of the Stars and Side Show*), CBS, 1992.
Voice of the rat, "Jirimpimbira: An African Folktale" (animated), *ABC Weekend Specials,* ABC, 1995.
Harry Anderson: The Tricks of His Trade, CBS, 1996.

Appeared in the special *Huckleberry Finn,* PBS.

Television Appearances; Episodic:
Barney Miller, ABC, 1982.
Cop, "Pilot," *The Golden Girls,* NBC, 1985.
Rick, *Melba,* CBS, 1986.
"Brother's Keeper," *In the Heat of the Night,* NBC, 1988.
Storytime, PBS, 1994.
Anthony Bouvier, "Dear Diary," *Women of the House,* CBS, 1995.

Appeared in episodes of *Lou Grant,* CBS; *The White Shadow,* CBS; *ALF,* NBC; and *M*A*S*H,* CBS.

Other Television Appearances:
Blue collar man, *I'd Rather Be Calm* (pilot), CBS, 1982.
Lionel Clark, *The Right Connections,* 1997.

Stage Appearances:
Streamers, Goodman Theatre, Chicago, IL, 1976.
Sizwe Banzi Is Dead, Goodman Theatre, 1976.
Native Son, Goodman Theatre, 1978.
The Island, Goodman Theatre, Annenberg Center, Philadelphia, PA, 1979.

Also appeared in *Sizwe Banzi Is Dead,* Westwood Playhouse, Los Angeles, CA, and in *The Wonderful Ice Cream Suit, Bloody Bess, The Sirens of Titan, Night Feast,* and *Cops.* Toured U.S. cities in *Hair.**

TESICH, Steve 1942-1996

OBITUARY NOTICE—See index for *CTFT* sketch: Born Stoyan Tesich, September 29, 1942, in Uzice, Yugoslavia; died following a heart attack, July 1, 1996, in Sydney, Nova Scotia, Canada. Screenwriter and playwright. Steve Tesich is best remembered for his Academy Award-winning screenplay *Breaking Away* (1979). Tesich was born in war-torn Yugoslavia and immigrated to the United States with his family around 1955. *Breaking Away* was based on Tesich's own experience growing up in Bloomington, IN, home of Indiana University, and tells of the ri-

valry between the college students and the "townies" of Bloomington. "The film's idyllic portrayal of a middle-American town, its lovable, idiosyncratic American characters and its sense of a dream being achieved," wrote Bruce Weber in the *New York Times,* "were very much the product of a grateful writer who felt himself to be a welcomed outsider."

Tesich attended Indiana University (his tuition was covered by a wrestling scholarship), majored in Russian literature, and moved on to Columbia University to obtain his master's in 1967. He began playwrighting while living in New York, and the first of his dramas, "The Carpenters," was produced in 1970. During the 1980s he turned largely to writing for films and produced the scripts for *Eyewitness* (1981), *The World According to Garp* (1982), and *Eleni* (1985). Many of his films reflect his belief in the basic decency of American society and in the strength of American values. He also wrote a novel, *Summer Crossing* (1982).

Tesich's plays after 1989, however, were less optimistic than his scripts of the 1980s. "The Speed of Darkness" (1989), "Square One" (1990) and "On the Open Road" (1992) all reflect a much darker vision of America than had been characteristic of Tesich's early work. "The American failure to intervene in the Yugoslav conflict affected him deeply," declared a writer for the London *Times;* "it was as though the fractured world of his childhood had come full circle." His most recent work, "Arts and Leisure," closed in New York in June, 1996.

OBITUARIES AND OTHER SOURCES

Books:
Who's Who in America, 51st edition, Marquis, 1996.

Periodicals:
Chicago Tribune, July 2, 1996, section 3, p. 11; July 7, 1996, section 4, p. 4.
Los Angeles Times, July 3, 1996, p. B10.
New York Times, July 2, 1996, p. A12.
Times (London), July 12, 1996, p. 21.
Washington Post, July 4, 1996, p. B5.

TUCCI, Michael 1950(?)-

PERSONAL

Born April 15, 1950 (some sources say 1946), in New York, NY; son of Nicholas (a business executive) and

Minerva D. (LaRosa) Tucci; married Kathleen Mary Gately (a network executive), April 30, 1983; children: one. *Education:* C. W. Post College, Long Island University, B.A., 1968; Brooklyn Law School, J.D., 1971; studied acting at the American Place Theatre with Mira Rostova, Wynn Handman, and Howard Fine; studied voice with Lee and Sally Sweetland.

Addresses: *Contact*—c/o 9229 Sunset Blvd., Suite 710, Los Angeles, CA 90069.

Career: Actor and lawyer. Also works at a Christian church in Kentucky.

Awards, Honors: *Dramalogue* Awards for acting, 1978, for *Kid Twist,* 1987, for *The Boys from Syracuse,* and 1988, for *The Wizard of Oz.*

CREDITS

Television Appearances; Series:
Dr. Charlie Nichols, *Trapper John, M.D.,* CBS, 1980-84.
Gerald Golden, *The Paper Chase: The Second Year,* Showtime, 1983.
Pete Schumaker, *It's Gary Shandling's Show,* Fox, 1988-90.
Jeremy Barash, *Flying Blind,* Fox, 1992-93.
Norman Briggs, *Diagnosis Murder,* CBS, 1993—.

Television Appearances; Movies:
Captain Claude Eatherly, *Enola Gay: The Men, the Mission, and the Atomic Bomb,* NBC, 1980.
Randall, *Change of a Lifetime* (also known as *A Change of Heart* and *Heather's Journey*), NBC, 1991.
Harvey Bell, "MacShayne: Final Roll of the Dice" (also known as "MacShayne's Big Score"), *NBC Friday Night Mystery,* NBC, 1994.
Danny, *The Man Who Captured Eichmann,* TNT, 1996.

Television Appearances; Episodic:
"Hash," *Barney Miller,* ABC, 1975.
Barney Miller, ABC, 1976 and 1978.
Phil Goldenstein, *On Our Own,* CBS, 1977.
People's Court, ABC, 1980.
"Honest Abe," *MacGyver,* ABC, 1991.
Principal Blair, "Harrassment," *Life's Work,* ABC, 1997.

Other Television Appearances:
Teddy Serrano, *Friends* (pilot), CBS, 1978.

Armando, *The Rainbow Girl* (pilot), NBC, 1982.
Lionel, *The Princess Who Had Never Laughed* (special), 1986.

Appeared as Chico Marx in the special *Groucho in Revue,* HBO.

Film Appearances:
Lou, *The Night They Robbed Big Bertha's,* Scotia American, 1975.
Sonny, *Grease,* Paramount, 1978.
Harry Cimoli, *Sunnyside,* American International Pictures, 1979.
Arnie, *Lunch Wagon* (also known as *Lunch Wagon Girls* and *Come 'n Get It*), Bordeaux, 1981.
Frank Turner, *Just Like Dad,* Leucadia Film Corp., 1995.

Stage Appearances:
(Off-Broadway debut) Herbie, *Godspell,* 1973.
(Broadway debut) Sonny, *Grease,* Royale Theatre, New York City, 1975.
Theatre Songs by Maltby and Shire, Manhattan Theatre Club, New York City, 1976.
Hold Me!, American Place Theatre, New York City, 1977.
Kid Twist, Mark Taper Forum, Los Angeles, CA, 1978.
The Boys from Syracuse, Los Angeles, CA, 1987.
The Wizard of Oz, Los Angeles, CA, 1988.
Cockian, *Philemon,* York Theatre Company, 1991.
Tales of Tinseltown, Coconut Grove Playhouse, Miami, FL, between 1991 and 1992.

Appeared in *American Mosaic,* Mark Taper Forum. Toured as Chico Marx, *Minnie's Boys,* U.S. cities; also toured U.S. cities in *Grease, Godspell,* and *Turn to the Right.*

WRITINGS

Author (with actor Joe Mantegna) of the stage play *Leonardo.**

VAN ARK, Joan   1948(?)-

PERSONAL

Born June 16, 1948 (some sources say 1943 or 1946), in New York, NY; daughter of Carroll (in public relations) and Dorothy Jean (a writer; maiden name, Hemenway) Van Ark; married John Marsillo (a news reporter), February 1, 1966; children: Vanessa Jean

Marshall. *Education:* Attended Yale University School of Drama. *Religion:* Presbyterian.

Addresses: *Contact*—10950 Alta View Dr., Studio City, CA 91604; 1325 Avenue of the Americas, New York, NY 10019-4702. *Agent*—c/o William Morris Agency, 151 El Camino Dr., Beverly Hills, CA 90212.

Career: Actress, producer, and director. Appeared in a television commercial for Betty Crocker products, 1971, and occasional spokesperson in Estee Lauder commercials. Advocate for the Humane Society.

Member: Actors' Equity Association, Screen Actors Guild, American Federation of Television and Radio Artists, San Fernando Valley Track Club.

Awards, Honors: *Theatre World* Award, 1971, for *The School for Wives;* Los Angeles Drama Critics Award, 1973; *Soap Opera Digest* Awards, outstanding actress, 1986 and 1989; best young adult programming nomination, New York Festivals, 1995, for *Boys Will Be Boys.*

CREDITS

Television Appearances; Series:
Janine Whitney, *Days of Our Lives,* NBC, 1970.
Nurse Ann "Annie" Carlisle, *Temperatures Rising* (also known as *The New Temperatures Rising Show*), ABC, 1972-73.
Dee Dee Baldwin, *We've Got Each Other,* CBS, 1977-78.
Voice of Manta, "Manta and Moray, Monarchs of the Deep," *Tarzan and the Super Seven* (animated), CBS, 1978-80.
Valene Clements Ewing, *Dallas,* CBS, 1978-81.
Voices of Jessica Drew and Spider-Woman, *Spider-Woman* (animated), ABC, 1979-80.
Valene Ewing Gibson Waleska, *Knots Landing,* CBS, 1979-92.
Voice of Moray, "Manta and Moray, Monarchs of the Deep," *Batman and the Super Seven* (animated), NBC, 1980-81.
Voice characterizations, *Thundarr the Barbarian* (animated), ABC, 1980-82.
Voice characterizations, *Heathcliff and Dingbat* (animated), 1980-81.
Voices of Amelia and fly number two, *Santo Bugito,* 1996.

Also appeared as the voice of Queen Esther, *Adventures from the Book of Virtues,* PBS.

Television Appearances; Miniseries:
Jane Robson, *Testimony of Two Men,* syndicated, 1977.
Valene Ewing, *Knots Landing: Back to the Cul-de-Sac,* CBS, 1997.

Television Appearances; Movies:
Frankie Banks, *The Last Dinosaur,* ABC, 1977.
Marie Rivers, *Red Flag: The Ultimate Game,* CBS, 1981.
Brenda Allen, *Shakedown on the Sunset Strip,* CBS, 1988.
Claire Thomas, *My First Love,* ABC, 1988.
Martha Mendham, *Always Remember I Love You* (also known as *To Cast a Shadow*), CBS, 1990.
Julia Alberts, *Menu for Murder* (also known as *Murder at the PTA Luncheon*), CBS, 1990.
Leslie Renner, *Terror on Track 9* (also known as *Janek: The Grand Central Murders*), CBS, 1992.
Cinnie Merritt, *In the Shadows, Someone's Watching* (also known as *Someone's Watching*), NBC, 1993.
Mrs. Drew, *Tainted Blood,* USA Network, 1993.
With Harmful Intent, 1993.
Nora McGill, *Moment of Truth: A Mother's Deception* (also known as *Moment of Truth: Cult Rescue*), NBC, 1994.
Julie Kaiser, *When the Dark Man Calls,* USA Network, 1995.

Television Work; Movies:
Executive producer, *In the Shadows, Someone's Watching* (also known as *Someone's Watching*), NBC, 1993.

Television Appearances; Pilots:
Alicia Dodd, *The Judge and Jake Wyler,* NBC, 1972.
Nina, *Big Rose: Double Trouble* (also known as *Big Rose* and *Double Trouble*), CBS, 1974.
Shirley, *Shell Game,* CBS, 1975.
Glitter, ABC, 1984.

Television Appearances; Episodic:
"Cry Hard, Cry Fast," *Run for Your Life,* NBC, 1967.
"A Fashion for Dying," *The Felony Squad,* ABC, 1968.
"Twinkle, Twinkle, Little Starlet," *Mod Squad,* ABC, 1968.
Title role, "Sweet Annie Laurie," *Bonanza,* NBC, 1969.
"The Maze," *The FBI,* ABC, 1969.
"The Man Who Killed Jim Sonnett," *Guns of Will Sonnett,* ABC, 1969.
"Stryker," *Gunsmoke,* CBS, 1969.
"Love and the Proposal," *Love, American Style,* ABC, 1970.

"The Condemned," *The FBI,* ABC, 1970.
"A Deadly Game of Love," *The Silent Force,* ABC, 1970.
"Nick," *Matt Lincoln,* ABC, 1970.
"The Double Wall," *Hawaii Five-0,* CBS, 1970.
"The Deadly Gift," *The FBI,* ABC, 1971.
"Country Blues," *Cannon,* CBS, 1971.
"Close-Up," *Bold Ones: The Doctors,* NBC, 1971.
"The Break-Up," *The FBI,* ABC, 1972.
"A Night to Dismember," *The Odd Couple,* ABC, 1972.
"Love and the Triple Threat," *Love, American Style,* ABC, 1972.
Sandra Blanco, "The Ring with the Red Velvet Ropes," *Night Gallery,* NBC, 1972.
"The Girl in the Polka Dot Dress," *Mannix,* CBS, 1973.
"Radar's Report," *M*A*S*H,* CBS, 1973.
"Duel in the Desert," *Cannon,* CBS, 1974.
"A Zicorn in the Rough," *The Girl with Something Extra,* NBC, 1974.
Marian Gerard, *Rhoda,* CBS, 1974.
"Vendetta," *The FBI,* ABC, 1974.
"Adults Only," *Medical Center,* CBS, 1974.
"The Challenge," *Barnaby Jones,* CBS, 1974.
"Trial of Terror," *Ironside,* NBC, 1974.
"The Deadly Brothers," *Manhunter,* CBS, 1974.
Barbara Kelbaker/Florence Baker, "Find Me If You Can," *The Rockford Files,* NBC, 1974.
"The Seven Million Dollar Man," *The Six Million Dollar Man,* ABC, 1974.
"The Man Who Couldn't Forget," *Cannon,* CBS, 1974.
Marian Gerard, "Joe's Ex," *Rhoda,* CBS, 1975.
"Guns for a Queen," *Barbary Coast,* ABC, 1975.
"Too Late for Tomorrow," *Medical Center,* CBS, 1975.
Susan Alexander, "Resurrection in Black and White," *The Rockford Files,* NBC, 1975.
"Woman in White," *Medical Story,* NBC, 1975.
"The Night Visitor," *Petrocelli,* NBC, 1976.
"Girl on a String," *Joe Forrester,* NBC, 1976.
"The Bionic Boy," *The Six Million Dollar Man,* ABC, 1976.
Christina Marks, "There's One in Every Port," *The Rockford Files,* NBC, 1977.
"Lady in the Squadroom," *Kojak,* CBS, 1977.
"Have You Heard about Vanessa?," *McMillan,* NBC, 1977.
"Gone but Not Forgotten," *Quincy, M.E.,* NBC, 1978.
Having Babies, ABC, 1978.
"All the Emperor's Quasi-Norms," *Quark,* NBC, 1978.
"Time Bomb," *The New Adventures of Wonder Woman,* CBS, 1978.
Haven Grant, "Death Mountain," *Vega$,* ABC, 1979.

The Love Boat, ABC, 1979.
"She Stole His Heart," *The Love Boat,* ABC, 1980.
"Jewels and Jim," *The Love Boat,* ABC, 1981.
"Seems Like Old Times," *The Love Boat,* ABC, 1984.
The Pat Sajak Show, CBS, 1989.
Jewel Pemberton, *The Fresh Prince of Bel-Air,* NBC, 1995.
Kim, *Touched by an Angel,* CBS, 1995.
Herself, "Women in Film," *Women of the House,* CBS, 1995.
Herself, *Cybill,* CBS, 1997.

Television Work; Episodic:
Director of episodes "Letting Go" and "Hints and Evasions," both *Knots Landing,* CBS.

Television Appearances; Specials:
Voice of Roxanne, "Cyrano," *ABC Afterschool Specials,* ABC, 1974.
Silia Gala, "Rules of the Game," *Theatre in America,* PBS, 1975.
Ladies and Gentlemen . . . Bob Newhart, 1980.
Celebrity Challenge of the Sexes, CBS, 1980.
Battle of the Network Stars VIII, ABC, 1980.
Battle of the Network Stars IX, ABC, 1980.
Battle of the Network Stars XII, ABC, 1982.
Battle of the Network Stars XIII, ABC, 1982.
Battle of the Network Stars XV, ABC, 1983.
Host, *The CBS Tournament of Roses Parade,* CBS, 1984.
Host, *The 1984 Miss USA Pageant,* 1984.
Host, *The 1984 Miss Universe Pageant,* 1984.
Host, *Battle of the Network Stars XVIII,* ABC, 1985.
Bob Hope's Comedy Salute to the Soaps, NBC, 1985.
Host, *The CBS Tournament of Roses Parade,* CBS, 1985.
Host, *The 1985 Miss USA Pageant,* 1985.
Host, *The 1985 Miss Universe Pageant,* 1985.
The Night of 100 Stars II, 1985.
Host, *The CBS Tournament of Roses Parade,* CBS, 1986.
Dom DeLuise and Friends, Part 4, 1986.
Fit for a Lifetime, 1986.
Happy Birthday, Hollywood!, ABC, 1987.
The Hollywood Christmas Parade, 1988.
Host, *Women of Seoul,* 1988.
All-Star Tribute to Kareem Abdul-Jabbar, NBC, 1989.
Host, *The CBS All-American Thanksgiving Day Parade,* CBS, 1989.
Host, *The CBS Tournament of Roses Parade,* CBS, 1989.
Bob Hope's 1990 Christmas Show from Bermuda (also known as *Bob Hope's Christmas Special from Bermuda*), NBC, 1990.

Anchor, *The CBS All-American Thanksgiving Day Parade,* CBS, 1990.

Ringmaster, *The 15th Annual Circus of the Stars,* 1990.

Night of 100 Stars III (also known as *Night of One Hundred Stars*), NBC, 1990.

The 61st Annual Hollywood Christmas Parade, 1992.

Host, *The Tournament of Roses Parade,* CBS, 1992.

Knots Landing Block Party, CBS, 1993.

Judge, *The Miss America Pageant,* 1993.

Susan Cooper, "Boys Will Be Boys," *ABC Afterschool Specials,* ABC, 1994.

Television Work; Specials:

Director, "Boys Will Be Boys," *ABC Afterschool Specials,* ABC, 1994.

Television Appearances; Awards Presentations:

The 37th Annual Prime Time Emmy Awards, 1985.

The Stuntman Awards, 1986.

Presenter, *The 13th Annual People's Choice Awards,* 1987.

Host, *The 9th Annual Emmy Awards for Sports,* 1988.

The 14th Annual People's Choice Awards, 1988.

The 47th Annual Golden Globe Awards, 1990.

Presenter, *The 18th Annual Daytime Emmy Awards,* 1991.

Other Television Appearances:

Appeared in "Baseball Boogie" music video with the Los Angeles Dodgers.

Stage Appearances:

Corie Bratter, *Barefoot in the Park,* Biltmore Theatre, New York City, 1965.

Chemin de Fer, New Theatre for Now, Los Angeles, CA, 1969.

In a Fine Castle, New Theatre for Now, 1971.

Agnes, *The School for Wives,* Lyceum Theatre, New York City, 1971.

Silia Gala, *The Rules of the Game,* New Phoenix Repertory Company, Helen Hayes Theatre, New York City, 1974.

Night of 100 Stars II, Radio City Music Hall, New York City, 1985.

Melissa, *Love Letters,* Promenade Theatre, New York City, 1989.

Night of 100 Stars III, Radio City Music Hall, 1990.

A Little Night Music, 1994.

Three Tall Women, New York City, 1995.

Stardust, Los Angeles, CA, 1997.

Appeared in productions of *Cyrano de Bergerac* and *Ring Round the Moon;* appeared at Tyrone Guthrie Theatre, Minneapolis, MN, and Arena Stage, Washington, DC.

Major Tours:

Corie Bratter, *Barefoot in the Park,* U.S. cities, 1965.

Film Appearances:

Karen Crockett, *Frogs,* American International Pictures, 1972.*

VAN PEEBLES, Melvin   1932-

PERSONAL

Born August 21, 1932, in Chicago, IL; children: Mario (an actor and producer), Megan, Melvin. *Education:* Ohio Wesleyan University, B.A., 1953; also attended West Virginia State College.

Addresses: *Office*—353 West 56th St., Apt. 10F, New York, NY 10019.

Career: Writer, composer, producer, director, and actor. Appeared in a cabaret production, Bottom Line, New York City, 1974; appeared in nightclubs and cabarets in France; journalist and avant-garde filmmaker in France. Director of the music video *Funky Beat.* Also worked as a cable car grip operator, San Francisco, CA, a floor trader for the American Stock Exchange, and a portrait painter in Mexico. *Military service:* U.S. Air Force, navigator and bombardier.

Member: Directors Guild of America, Writers Guild of America, Screen Actors Guild, Actors' Equity Association, American Federation of Television and Radio Artists, French Directors Guild.

Awards, Honors: Honorary doctorate, Hofstra University, 1995; first prize from Belgian Festival for *Don't Play Us Cheap.*

CREDITS

Film Appearances:

Sweetback, *Sweet Sweetback's Baadasssss Song,* Cinemation, 1971.

America (also known as *Moonbeam*), ASA, 1986.

Jake Witherspoon, *Jaws: The Revenge,* Universal, 1987.

Wino Bob, *O. C. and Stiggs,* Metro-Goldwyn-Mayer/United Artists, 1987.

Himself, *Making "Do the Right Thing,"* 1989.

Taxi driver, *True Identity*, Buena Vista, 1991.
The editor, *Boomerang*, Paramount, 1992.
Himself, *Last Action Hero*, 1993.
Papa Joe, *Posse*, Gramercy Pictures, 1993.
Noble, *Terminal Velocity*, Buena Vista, 1994.
Cynical jailbird, *Panther*, Gramercy Pictures, 1995.

Film Work:
Producer and director, *Sunlight* (short film) Cinema 16, 1958.
Producer and director, *Three Pick Up Men for Herrick* (short film) Cinema 16, 1958.
Director, *The Story of a Three Day Pass* (also known as *La Permission*), Sigma III, 1968.
Director and music director, *Watermelon Man*, Columbia, 1970.
Producer, director, and editor, *Sweet Sweetback's Baadasssss Song*, Cinemation, 1971.
Producer, director, and editor, *Don't Play Us Cheap*, 1973.
Producer, director, and editor, *Identity Crisis*, Academy, 1989.
Producer, director, and editor, "Vrooom, Vrooom, Vrooom" (short film; also known as "Vroom Vroom Vroom!"), in *Tales of Erotica* (also known as *Erotic Tales*), Mercure Distribution, 1994.
Producer (with Mario Van Peebles), *Panther*, Gramercy Pictures, 1995.

Television Appearances; Series:
Mel Spoon, *Sonny Spoon*, NBC, 1988.

Television Appearances; Episodic:
Hawk, "Taking Care of Terrific," *WonderWorks*, PBS, 1988.
Norman Green, "Steinway to Heaven," *Dream On*, HBO, 1990.
Warner Devant, *Living Single*, Fox, 1995.
Bennett Jackson, "The Documentary," *Homicide: Life on the Street* (also known as *Homicide* and *Homicide: LOTS*), NBC, 1997.

Television Work; Episodic:
Director, *The Big Room*, 1990.

Television Appearances; Movies:
Walter Moon and Silkie Porter, *The Sophisticated Gents*, NBC, 1981.
Vernon, "Homecoming Day," *Riot* (also known as *Riot in the Streets*), Showtime, 1995.
Asher, *Fist of the North Star* (also known as *Fist of the Northstar*), HBO, 1995.
Andre Speier, *Gang in Blue* (also known as *The Phantom*), Showtime, 1996.

Television Work; Movies:
Associate producer, *The Sophisticated Gents*, NBC, 1981.
Producer (with Robert Lawrence, Mario Van Peebles, David Fuller, and Rick Natkin) and director (with Mario Van Peebles), *Gang in Blue* (also known as *The Phantom*), Showtime, 1996.

Television Appearances; Specials:
Voice of Louis Armstrong, "Satchmo: The Life of Louis Armstrong," *American Masters*, PBS, 1989.
Bucket, "Calm at Sunset" (also known as "Calm at Sunset, Calm at Dawn"), *Hallmark Hall of Fame*, CBS, 1996.

Television Appearances; Miniseries:
Dick Halloran, *Stephen King's The Shining* (also known as *The Shining*), ABC, 1997.

Stage Appearances:
Out There by Your Lonesome (solo show), Philharmonic Hall, New York City, 1973.
Don't Play Us Cheap, Shubert Theatre, Chicago, IL, 1975.
Waltz of the Stork, Century Theatre, New York City, 1982.
Kickin' the Science, Ensemble Studio Theatre, 1992.

Also appeared in *The Hostage* with the Dutch National Theatre.

Major Tours:
Out There by Your Lonesome (solo show), U.S. cities, 1973.

Stage Work:
Director, *Ain't Supposed to Die a Natural Death*, Ethel Barrymore Theatre, New York City, 1971.
Producer and director, *Don't Play Us Cheap*, Ethel Barrymore Theatre, 1972.
Producer and director, *Waltz of the Stork*, Century Theatre, New York City, 1982.
Director, *Champeeen!*, New Federal Theatre, Harry DeJur Playhouse, New York City, 1983.

RECORDINGS

Albums:
Br'er Soul, 1969.
As Serious as a Heart Attack, A&M, 1971.
What the . . . You Mean I Can't Sing, A&M, 1974.

Also recorded *Ain't Supposed to Die a Natural Death* and *Ghetto Gothic*.

WRITINGS

Stage Plays; Also Composer and Lyricist, Except Where Indicated:

Harlem Party, produced in Belgium, 1964, produced as *Don't Play Us Cheap,* Ethel Barrymore Theatre, 1972, and Shubert Theatre, Chicago, IL, 1975.

Ain't Supposed to Die a Natural Death, Ethel Barrymore Theatre, 1971, published by Bantam (New York City), 1973.

Out There by Your Lonesome (solo show), Philharmonic Hall, and U.S. cities, 1973.

(Book only) *Reggae,* Biltmore Theatre, New York City, 1980.

Waltz of the Stork, Century Theatre, 1982.

Champeeen!, New Federal Theatre, Harry DeJur Playhouse, 1983.

Also wrote music and comedy material for cabaret productions.

Screenplays:

Sunlight (short film), Cinema 16, 1958.

Three Pick Up Men for Herrick (short film), Cinema 16, 1958.

And composer (with Mickey Baker), *The Story of a Three Day Pass* (also known as *La Permission*), Sigma III, 1968.

Composer, *Watermelon Man,* Columbia, 1970.

And composer, *Sweet Sweetback's Baadasssss Song,* Cinemation, 1971, published by Lancer Books, 1971.

And composer and lyricist, *Don't Play Us Cheap,* 1973.

(With Kenneth Vose, Lawrence Dukore, and Leon Capetanos) *Greased Lightning,* Warner Bros., 1977, published by Yeah, 1976.

Identity Crisis, Academy, 1989.

And composer, "Vrooom, Vrooom, Vrooom" (short film; also known as "Vroom Vroom Vroom!"), in *Tales of Erotica* (also known as *Erotic Tales*), Mercure Distribution, 1994.

Panther, Gramercy Pictures, 1995.

Teleplays; Pilots:

And composer of title song, *Just an Old Sweet Song,* CBS, 1976, published by Ballantine (New York City), 1976.

Down Home, CBS, 1978.

Teleplays; Movies:

And composer of the song "Greased Lightning," *The*

Sophisticated Gents (based on *The Junior Bachelor Society* by John A. Williams), NBC, 1981.

Teleplays; Specials:

"The Day They Came to Arrest the Book," *CBS Schoolbreak Specials,* CBS, 1987.

Novels:

Un Ours pour le F.B.I., Buchet-Chastel (Paris, France), 1964, translation published as *A Bear for the F.B.I.,* Trident, 1968.

Un Americain en Enfer, Editions Denoel (Paris, France), 1965, translation published as *The True American: A Folk Fable,* Doubleday (New York City), 1976.

La Fete a Harlem (adapted from his play *Harlem Party*), J. Martineau, 1967, translation published as *Don't Play Us Cheap: A Harlem Party,* Bantam (New York City), 1973.

Panther, Thunder's Mouth Press (New York City), 1995.

Short Fiction:

Le Chinois du XIV, Le Gadenet, 1966.

Nonfiction:

The Making of Sweet Sweetback's Baadasssss Song, Lancer Books, 1972.

Bold Money: A New Way to Play the Options Market, Warner Books (New York City), 1986.

Bold Money: A New Way to Get Rich in the Options Market, Warner Books, 1987.

(With Mario Van Peebles) *No Identity Crisis: A Father and Son's Own Story of Working Together,* Simon & Schuster (New York City), 1990.

Photography:

The Big Heart (photo essay), 1967.

Other:

La Permission, J. Martineau, 1967.

OTHER SOURCES

Books:

Contemporary Authors, New Revision Series, Volume 27, Gale (Detroit, MI), 1989.

Contemporary Literary Criticism, Gale, Volume 2, 1974; Volume 20, 1982.

Periodicals:

Jet, May 22, 1995, p. 32.

VAUGHN, Robert 1932-

PERSONAL

Born Robert Francis Vaughn, November 22, 1932, in New York, NY; son of Gerald Walter (an actor) and Marcella Frances (an actress; maiden name, Gaudel) Vaughn; married Linda Staab (an actress), 1974; children: Caitlin, Cassidy. *Education:* Studied journalism at the University of Minnesota, 1950-51; Los Angeles State College of Applied Arts and Sciences (now California State University), B.S. (theatre arts), 1956; University of Southern California, M.A. (theatre arts), 1960, Ph.D. (communications), 1970. *Politics:* Democrat. *Religion:* Roman Catholic.

Addresses: *Agent*—c/o Agency for the Performing Arts, 9000 Sunset Boulevard, Suite 1200, Los Angeles, CA 90069, and 888 Seventh Avenue, Suite 520, Nashville, TN, 37203.

Career: Actor and writer. Began as a child actor on radio in the 1940s; sports reporter for the Minneapolis Star Journal, Minneapolis, MN, early 1950s; full-time actor on television, in film and on stage since the late 1950s. *Military service:* U.S. Army, 1956-57.

Member: Screen Actors Guild, American Federation of Television and Radio Artists, American Academy of Political and Social Scientists, California Democratic Committee.

Awards, Honors: Photoplay Gold Medal Award, most popular actor, 1956; Academy Award nomination, best supporting actor, 1959, for *The Young Philadelphians;* British Academy Award nomination, best supporting actor, 1968, for *Bullitt;* Emmy Award, outstanding continuing performance by a supporting actor in a drama series, 1978, for *Washington: Behind Closed Doors.*

CREDITS

Television Appearances; Series:
Captain Ray Rambridge, *The Lieutenant,* NBC, 1963-64.
Napoleon Solo, *The Man from U.N.C.L.E.,* NBC, 1964-68.
Harry Rule, *The Protectors,* syndicated, 1972-74.
Harlan Adams, *Emerald Point, N.A.S.,* CBS, 1983-84.

Retired General Hunt Stockwell, *The A-Team,* NBC, 1986-87.
Host/Narrator, *Reaching for the Skies,* 1988-89.
Narration, *America at War,* 1990.
Host/Narrator, *Danger Theatre,* Fox, 1993.
Rick Hamlin, a lawyer, *As the World Turns,* CBS, 1995.

Television Appearances; Miniseries:
Charles Desmond, *Captains and the Kings,* NBC, 1976.
Frank Flaherty, *Washington: Behind Closed Doors,* ABC, 1977.
Morgan Wendell, *Centennial,* NBC, 1978.
Seth McLean, *The Rebels,* Operation Prime Time, 1979.
President Woodrow Wilson, *Backstairs at the White House,* NBC, 1979.
Senator Reynolds, *The Blue and the Gray,* CBS, 1982.
Field Marshall Erhard Milch, *Inside the Third Reich,* ABC, 1982.
John Bradford, *Evergreen,* NBC, 1985.

Television Appearances; Movies:
Jerry Hunter, *The Woman Hunter,* CBS, 1972.
Edward Fuller, *Kiss Me . . . Kill Me,* ABC, 1976.
Michael Jacoby, *Mirror Mirror,* 1979.
Dr. Arno Franken, *Doctor Franken* (also known as *The Franken Project*), NBC, 1980.
Mark Case, *The Gossip Columnist,* Operation Prime Time, 1980.
Harrison Crawford III, *City in Fear* (also known as *Panic on Page One*), ABC, 1980.
Girard, *Fantasies,* ABC, 1982.
Richard Whitney, *The Day the Bubble Burst,* NBC, 1982.
Frederick Walker, *A Question of Honor,* CBS, 1982.
Napoleon Solo, *The Return of the Man from U.N.C.L.E.,* CBS, 1983.
Dave Fairmont, *Intimate Agony,* ABC, 1983.
Captain Powell, *International Airport,* ABC, 1985.
Oliver Coles, *Private Sessions,* NBC, 1985.
President Franklin Delano Roosevelt, *Murrow,* HBO, 1986.
Stanley Auerbach, *The Prince of Bel Air,* ABC, 1986.
Sheriff John Whaley, *Desperado,* NBC, 1987.
Jay Corelli, *Perry Mason: The Case of the Defiant Daughter,* NBC, 1990.
Commissioner Peter Kinghorn, *Dark Avenger,* CBS, 1990.
Mr. Morris, *Tracks of Glory: The Major Taylor Story* (also known as *The Major Taylor Story*), Disney Channel, 1992.
Dennis Forbes, *Dancing in the Dark,* Lifetime, 1995.

Witch Academy (also known as *Little Devils*), USA Network, 1995.
Edward Bolt, "Escape to Witch Mountain,"*ABC Family Movie,* ABC, 1995.

Television Appearances; Specials:
The 37th Annual Prime Time Emmy Awards, 1985.
Macy's Thanksgiving Day Parade, 1986.
NBC's 60th Anniversary Special, 1986.
Host and Charles Hemming, defense attorney, *You Are the Jury,* 1986.
Host, *Manhunt . . . Update!,* syndicated, 1989.
Macy's Thanksgiving Day Parade, 1989.
Host, *Dangerous Game of Fame,* syndicated, 1992.
Voice of Isaac Arnold, *Lincoln,* ABC, 1992.
Host, *Classic Spy Movies,* TNT, 1996.

Television Appearances; Pilots:
The Boston Terrier, 1963.
Senator Gerald Stratton, *The Islander,* CBS, 1978.

Television Director; Series:
Police Woman, NBC, 1974.

Television Appearances; Episodic:
"Black Friday," *Medic,* NBC, 1955.
"Cooter," *Gunsmoke,* CBS, 1956.
"The Marine Story," *Big Town,* NBC, 1956.
"Fake SOS," *Big Town,* NBC, 1956.
"Bitter Waters," *Screen Directors Playhouse,* NBC, 1956.
"The Operator and the Martinet," *West Point,* CBS, 1956.
Jay Powers, "The Story of Jay Powers," *The Millionaire,* CBS, 1956.
"Betty Goes Steady," *Father Knows Best,* NBC, 1956.
"Courage Is a Gun," *Zane Grey Theatre,* CBS, 1956.
"The Twisted Road," *Frontier Doctor,* syndicated, 1957.
"The Consort," *Telephone Time,* CBS, 1957.
"A Gun Is for Killing," *Zane Grey Theatre,* CBS, 1957.
"Billy the Kid," *Tales of Wells Fargo* (also known as *Wells Fargo*), NBC, 1957.
Andy Bowers, "Romeo," *Gunsmoke,* CBS, 1957.
"File #35," *Walter Winchell File,* ABC, 1958.
"The Big Rat Pack," *Dragnet,* NBC, 1958.
"The John Wilbot Story," *Wagon Train,* NBC, 1958.
"Return," *Jefferson Drum,* NBC, 1958.
Dan Willard, "The Apprentice Sheriff," *The Rifleman,* ABC, 1958.
Miguel Roverto, "Spark of Revenge," *Zorro,* ABC, 1959.
"Borrowed Glory," *Bronco,* ABC, 1959.
"Made in Japan," *Playhouse 90,* CBS, 1959.

"About Roger Mowbray," *Riverboat,* NBC, 1959.
"Prelude to Violence," *The Lineup,* CBS, 1959.
Art, "Dry Run," *Alfred Hitchcock Presents,* CBS, 1959.
"Passage to the Enemy," *Wichita Town,* NBC, 1959.
"The Dude," *Law of the Plainsman,* NBC, 1959.
"The Innocent," *Law of the Plainsman,* NBC, 1959.
"The Last Flight," *Alcoa Theater,* NBC, 1960.
"Noblesse Oblige," *The Rebel,* ABC, 1960.
"Mooncloud," *Men into Space,* CBS, 1960.
"Interrupted Honeymoon," *Checkmate,* CBS, 1960.
"The Dark Trail," *Laramie,* NBC, 1960.
"The Awakening," *The Garlund Touch* (also known as *Mr. Garlund*), CBS, 1960.
"Emergency," *The June Allyson Show,* CBS, 1960.
Roger Bigelow, "The Roger Bigelow Show," *Wagon Train,* NBC, 1960.
"Object," *Stagecoach West,* ABC, 1961.
Dr. Frank Cordell, "The Ordeal of Dr. Cordell," *Thriller,* NBC, 1961.
"The Landslide Adventure," *Malibu Run,* CBS, 1961.
"The Scott Machine," *The Asphalt Jungle,* ABC, 1961.
"A Rage for Justice," *Follow the Sun,* ABC, 1961.
"Treasure Coach," *Tales of Wells Fargo* (also known as *Wells Fargo*), NBC, 1961.
"To Wear a Badge," *Target: The Corruptors,* ABC, 1961.
"The Far Side of Nowhere," *Follow the Sun,* ABC, 1961.
"The Heckler," *87th Precinct,* NBC, 1961.
"The Debasers," *Cain's Hundred,* NBC, 1962.
"The Boston Terrier," *The Dick Powell Show,* NBC, 1962.
"Death of a Dream," *Kraft Mystery Theater,* NBC, 1962.
Luke Martin, "The Way Station," *Bonanza,* NBC, 1962.
"The Blues My Baby Gave Me," *The Eleventh Hour,* NBC, 1962.
"Defendant," *G.E. True,* CBS, 1963.
"No Small Wars," *Empire,* NBC, 1963.
"If You Have Tears," *The Virginian,* NBC, 1963.
Charlie Argos, "The Charlie Argos Story," *The Untouchables,* ABC, 1963.
Jim Darling, "It's a Shame She Married Me," *The Dick Van Dyke Show,* CBS, 1963.
"Your Fortune for a Penny," *77 Sunset Strip,* ABC, 1963.
"The Silence of Good Men," *The Eleventh Hour,* NBC, 1963.
"Say Uncle," *Please Don't Eat the Daisies,* NBC, 1966.
"The Mother Muffin Affair," *The Girl from U.N.C.L.E.,* NBC, 1966.

"Blast," *Police Woman,* NBC, 1975.

Hayden Danziger, "Troubled Waters," *Columbo,* NBC, 1975.

"Generation of Evil," *Police Woman,* NBC, 1976.

Charles Clay, "Last Salute to the Commodore," *Columbo,* NBC, 1976.

"Murder at F-Stop 11," *The Feather and Father Gang,* ABC, 1977.

"Who Killed Charles Pendragon?," *Eddie Capra Mysteries,* NBC, 1978.

"The Story of Daniel in the Lion's Den," *Greatest Heroes of the Bible,* 1978.

Hawaii Five-O, CBS, 1979.

"The Spirit is Willie," *Centennial* (also known as *The Big Event*), NBC, 1979.

"The Scream of Eagles," *Trapper John, M.D.,* CBS, 1980.

"Girl Under Glass," *The Love Boat,* ABC, 1981.

Hotel, ABC, 1983.

Deputy Chief Curtis Moorehead, "City Under Siege," *Hunter,* NBC, 1984.

"Face to Face," *The Hitchhiker,* HBO, 1984.

Gideon Armstrong, "Murder Digs Deep," *Murder, She Wrote,* CBS, 1985.

You Are the Jury, 1986.

"Abnormal Psych," *Stingray,* NBC, 1986.

Huxley, "Fruit at the Bottom of the Bowl," *The Ray Bradbury Theater,* HBO, 1987.

Edwin Chancellor, "The Grand Old Lady," *Murder, She Wrote,* CBS, 1989.

Charles Winthrop, "The Witch's Curse," *Murder, She Wrote,* CBS, 1992.

Walker Texas Ranger, CBS, 1993.

Rykker, "Dragonswing," *Kung Fu: The Legend Continues,* syndicated, 1993.

Rykker, "Dragonswing II," *Kung Fu: The Legend Continues,* syndicated, 1994.

Bill Stratton, *Diagnosis Murder,* CBS, 1995.

William Shane, "Who Killed the Movie Mogul?," *Burke's Law,* CBS, 1995.

James Sheffield, "Me and Mrs. Jones," *The Nanny,* CBS, 1996.

Dr. Stewart Rizor, "The Plague," *Walker, Texas Ranger,* CBS, 1996.

Alexander Drake, "Discard," *Diagnosis Murder,* CBS, 1997.

Carl Anderton, "Burned," *Law and Order* (also known as *Law & Order*), NBC, 1997.

Judge, "One Day Out West," *The Magnificent Seven,* CBS, 1998.

Also appeared in *Telephone Time,* CBS, and *General Electric True,* CBS.

Film Appearances:

Photographer (bit part), *I'll Cry Tomorrow,* Metro-Goldwyn-Mayer, 1955.

Spearman and Hebrew at Golden Calf, *The Ten Commandments,* Paramount, 1956.

Bob Ford, *Hell's Crossroads,* Republic, 1957.

Buddy Root, *No Time to Be Young* (also known as *Teenage Delinquents*), Columbia, 1957.

Boy, *Teenage Caveman* (also known as *Prehistoric World* and *Out of the Darkness*), American International Pictures, 1958.

Don Bigelow, *Unwed Mother,* Allied Artists, 1958.

Edward "The Kid" Campbell, *Good Day for a Hanging,* Columbia, 1959.

Chester "Chet" Gwynn, *The Young Philadelphians,* Warner Bros., 1959.

Lee, *The Magnificent Seven,* United Artists, 1960.

Klaus Everard, *The Big Show,* Twentieth Century-Fox, 1961.

Jim Melford, *The Caretakers* (also known as *Borderlines*), United Artists, 1963.

Cameo as Napoleon Solo, *The Glass Bottom Boat,* Metro-Goldwyn-Mayer, 1966.

Napoleon Solo, *To Trap a Spy,* Metro-Goldwyn-Mayer, 1966.

Napoleon Solo, *The Spy with My Face,* Metro-Goldwyn-Mayer, 1966.

Napoleon Solo, *The Spy in the Green Hat,* Metro-Goldwyn-Mayer, 1966.

Napoleon Solo, *One Spy Too Many,* Metro-Goldwyn-Mayer, 1966.

Napoleon Solo, *One of Our Spies Is Missing,* Metro-Goldwyn-Mayer, 1966.

Bill Fenner, *The Venetian Affair,* Metro-Goldwyn-Mayer, 1967.

Napoleon Solo, *The Karate Killers,* Metro-Goldwyn-Mayer, 1967.

Napoleon Solo, *The Helicopter Spies,* Metro-Goldwyn-Mayer, 1968.

Napoleon Solo, *How to Steal the World,* Metro-Goldwyn-Mayer, 1968.

Walter Chalmers, *Bullitt,* Warner Bros., 1968.

Major Paul Kreuger, *The Bridge at Remagen,* United Artists, 1969.

Street photographer, *If It's Tuesday, This Must Be Belgium,* United Artists, 1969.

Casca, *Julius Caesar,* American International Pictures, 1970.

Dr. Michael Bergen, *The Mind of Mr. Soames,* Columbia, 1970.

Ray, *The Statue,* Cinerama, 1971.

Neilson, *The Clay Pigeon,* Metro-Goldwyn-Mayer, 1971.

Senator Gary Parker, *The Towering Inferno*, Twentieth Century-Fox, 1974.

Stuart "Star" Chase, *Wanted: Babysitter* (also known as *Un Maledetto Pasticio, La Babysitter, Jeune Fille Libre le Soir*, and *The Babysitter*), SNC, 1975.

Atraco en la Jungla, 1976.

Voice of Proteus IV, *Demon Seed*, United Artists, 1977.

Professor Duncan, *Starship Invasions*, Warner Bros., 1978.

Lucifer Complex, VCI Home Video, 1978.

Colonel Donald Rogers, *Brass Target*, United Artists, 1979.

Dr. Neal, *Good Luck, Miss Wyckoff* (also known as *The Sin*), Bel-Air/Gradison, 1979.

Hudd, *Cuba Crossing* (also known as *Assignment: Kill Castro, Kill Castro, Key West Crossing, The Mercenaries, Sweet Dirty Tony*, and *Sweet Violent Tony*), Key West, 1980.

Barkley, *Virus* (also known as *Fukkatsu no hi* and *Day of Ressurection*), Media, 1980.

Gelt, *Battle Beyond the Stars*, Orion, 1980.

Gordon Cain, *Hanger 18*, Sunn Classic, 1980.

David Blackman, *S.O.B.*, Paramount, 1981.

Ross Webster, *Superman III*, Warner Bros., 1983.

Veliki Transport (also known as *Heroes*), 1983.

The Last Bastion, Academy Entertainment, 1984.

Ryland, *Black Moon Rising*, New World, 1986.

General Woodbridge, *The Delta Force*, Cannon, 1986.

Max, *Brutal Glory*, 1987.

Sam Merrick, CIA agent, *Hour of the Assassin*, Concorde, 1987.

Ray Melton, *Nightstick*, Columbia TriStar Home Video, 1987.

Another Way (also known as *D Kikan Joho*), 1988.

Edward Delacorte, *Captive Rage*, The Movie Group, 1988.

Lawson, *Renegade*, 1988.

Ambassador MacKay, *The Emissary*, 1989.

Colonel Schneider, *Skeleton Coast*, Silvertree, 1989.

Masters, *C.H.U.D. II: Bud the C.H.U.D.*, Vestron, 1989.

Lord Byron Orlock, *Transylvania Twist*, Concorde Pictures, 1989.

Dr. Gary, *Buried Alive* (also known as *Edgar Allen Poe's Buried Alive*), Columbia TriStar Home Video, 1989.

Adolf Hitler, *That's Adequate*, Hemdale Home Video, 1990.

Wolfgang Manteuffil, *River of Death* (also known as *Alistair MacLean's River of Death*), Cannon, 1990.

Dr. Duncan, *Nobody's Perfect*, Moviestore, 1990.

Wedgewood, *Going Under*, Warner Home Video, 1991.

Mr. X, *Blind Vision*, Worldvision Home Video, 1992.

Senator Dougherty, *Joe's Apartment*, Warner Bros., 1996.

Senator Powell, *Menno's Mind*, 1996.

Baxter, *Vulcan*, Premiere Entertainment, 1997.

Motel Blue, DeMartini/Anderson Productions, 1997.

Milk and Money, 1997.

Walter Denkins, *McCinsey's Island*, 1997.

Professor Michaels, *An American Affair*, TSC, 1997.

Also appeared in *The City Jungle, Twilight Blue, Dive!, Fair Trade*, and *Rampage*.

Stage Appearances:

Title role, *Hamlet*, Pasadena Playhouse, Pasadena, CA, 1964.

Title role, *F.D.R.* (one-man play), 1978.

Henry Drummond, *Inherit the Wind*, Paper Mill Playhouse, Millburn, NJ, 1984-85.

I Hate Hamlet, Jupiter Theatre, Jupiter, FL, 1992.

WRITINGS

Only Victims: A Study of Show Business Blacklisting, Putnam, 1972, republished by Limelight Editions, 1996.

OTHER SOURCES

Books:

Contemporary Authors, Volumes 61-64, Gale (Detroit, MI), 1976.*

VENNERA, Chick 1952-

PERSONAL

Original name, Francis Vennera; born March 27, 1952, in Herkimer, NY; son of Frank (a musician) and Victoria (Guido) Vennera; married Suzanne Messbauer (a clothing designer), April 9, 1983; children: Nicole. *Education:* Trained for the stage at Pasadena Playhouse and with Milton Katselas at Actors Lab. *Avocational interests:* Golf.

Addresses: *Agent*—c/o Premiere Artists Agency, 8899 Beverly Blvd., Suite 510, Los Angeles, CA 90048.

Career: Actor, screenwriter, and composer. Saxophone player and singer in a nightclub band, New

York City; appeared as Goofy, *Disney on Parade;* commercial voiceover performer. Also worked as a telephone salesperson and delivered flowers. *Military service:* U.S. Army, Signal Corps, Special Services.

Member: Academy of Motion Picture Arts and Sciences, Nosotros.

Awards, Honors: *Theatre World* Award, 1977, for *Jockeys.*

CREDITS

Film Appearances:
(Film debut) Marv Gomez, *Thank God It's Friday,* Columbia, 1978.
Sergeant Danny Ruffelo, *Yanks,* Universal, 1979.
Tony, *High Risk,* American Cinema, 1981.
Pepper Zombie, *Hysterical,* American Cinema, 1981.
Ness, *Boarding School,* Trankis, 1985.
Tony Leonard, *Kidnapped,* Hickmar, 1986.
Edgar Ness, *Free Ride,* 1986.
Joe Mondragon, *The Milagro Beanfield War,* Universal, 1988.
Nuzo, *Last Rites,* Metro-Goldwyn-Mayer, 1988.
Shapiro, *Night Eyes* (also known as *Hidden View* and *Hidden Vision*), Paramount/Prism Entertainment, 1990.
Santos, *McBain,* Shapiro/Glickenhaus Entertainment, 1991.
Kyle, *The Terror Within II,* Concorde, 1991.
Stephen Ross, *Double Threat,* American International Pictures, 1992.
Freddie Summers, *Body Chemistry 3* (also known as *Body Chemistry III: Point of Seduction*), New Horizons Home Video, 1994.
Alex Stein, *Night Eyes 4* (also known as *Night Eyes . . . Fatal Passion*), 1995.
Freddie Summers, *Body Chemistry 4: Full Exposure* (also known as *Body Chemistry IV*), 1995.
Raul Solo, *Kissing Miranda,* Cinequanon Pictures International, 1995.
Perry, *Alone in the Woods,* 1996.

Television Appearances; Series:
Luis, *Baretta,* ABC, 1976.
Raoul, *Hail to the Chief,* ABC, 1985.
Voice of Sammy the Rat, *Foofer* (animated), NBC, 1986.
Johnny, *Mad about You,* NBC, 1995.
Voice of Pesto, *Steven Spielberg Presents Pinky and the Brain,* The WB, 1995.

Voice, *The Real Adventures of Jonny Quest* (animated; also known as *Jonny Quest: The Real Adventures*), TNT, TBS, and The Cartoon Network, 1996.

Television Appearances; Miniseries:
Arthur Hailey's "The Moneychangers" (also known as *The Moneychangers*), NBC, 1976.
Once an Eagle, NBC, 1976.

Television Appearances; Pilots:
Mitch Costigan, *Vega$,* ABC, 1978.
Private Joseph Battaglia, *G.I.'s,* CBS, 1980.

Television Appearances; Episodic:
Mitch Costigan, "Comeback" (also known as "Casualty of War"), *Vega$,* ABC, 1980.
Mitch Costigan, "Magic Sister Slayings," *Vega$,* ABC, 1980.
Stack, *Hollywood Beat,* ABC, 1985.
Hector Rivera, *Night Court,* NBC, 1986.
Spider, *Diff'rent Strokes,* ABC, 1986.
Voice of Joe P. (Pesto Pigeon), *Animaniacs,* Fox, 1993.

Made television debut as a ruffian, *Lucas Tanner,* NBC; also appeared in *T.J. Hooker,* ABC.

Television Appearances; Movies:
Luis, *Billy: Portrait of Street Kid* (also known as *Ghetto Child*), CBS, 1977.
Frankie, *A Bunny's Tale,* ABC, 1985.

Television Appearances; Specials:
Coach Pingatore, *A Mother's Courage: The Mary Thomas Story,* 1989.
Frank de la Grana, *Runaway Father,* 1991.

Stage Appearances:
(Broadway debut) Sonny, *Grease,* Royale Theatre, New York City, 1976.
(Off-Broadway debut) Angel Quiton, *Jockeys,* Promenade Theatre, New York City, 1977.

Appeared in productions of *The Tigers, Dark of the Moon,* and *The Rose Tattoo,* all in Los Angeles, CA.

Major Tours:
Sonny, *Grease,* U.S. and Canadian cities, 1973-75.

WRITINGS

Story Ideas for Teleplays:
"Comeback" (also known as "Casualty of War"), *Vega$*, ABC, 1980.
"Magic Sister Slayings," *Vega$*, ABC, 1980.

Composer for an episode of *Vega$*, ABC.*

W-Z

WALLACH, Eli 1915-

PERSONAL

Born December 7, 1915, in Brooklyn, NY; son of Abraham and Bertha (Schorr) Wallach; married Anne Jackson (an actress), March 5, 1948; children: Peter Douglas, Roberta Lee, and Katherine Beatrice. *Education:* University of Texas at Austin, B.A., 1936; City College (now the City University of New York), M.S., education, 1938; trained for the stage at Neighborhood Playhouse, 1938-40, and with Lee Strasberg at Actors Studio. *Avocational interests:* Woodworking, collecting antiques, collecting clocks, tennis, baseball, architecture, photography, watercoloring, swimming.

Addresses: *Agent*—c/o Paradigm, 200 West 57th St., Suite 900, New York, NY 10019. *Contact*—90 Riverside Dr., New York, NY 10024.

Career: Actor. WLID-Radio, Brooklyn, NY, actor in radio plays, 1936-38; Actors Studio, New York City, original member, 1947—, vice-president, 1980-81, and teacher; Jewish Repertory Theatre, New York City, member of advisory board, 1991-92; Neighborhood Playhouse School Theatre, member and director; Arena Stage, Washington, DC, guest artist. Also worked as playground director, camp counselor, and hospital registrar. *Military service:* U.S. Army, Medical Corps, served during World War II; became captain.

Member: Actors' Equity Association, Screen Actors Guild, American Federation of Television and Radio Artists.

Awards, Honors: Antoinette Perry Award, *Variety* New York Drama Critics Poll, Donaldson Award, and *Theatre World* Award, all 1951, for *The Rose Tattoo;* British Academy Award, most outstanding newcomer to film, British Academy of Film and Television Arts, 1956, for *Baby Doll;* Emmy Award, 1966, for *The Poppy Is Also a Flower;* inducted into Theatre Hall of Fame, 1988; honorary doctorate, School for the Visual Arts, 1991; honorary degree from Emerson College.

CREDITS

Stage Appearances:
Title role, *Liliom,* Curtain Club, University of Texas, Austin, TX, 1936.

The Bo Tree, Locust Valley, NY, 1939.

(Broadway debut) Crew chief, *Skydrift,* Belasco Theatre, New York City, 1945.

Cromwell, *Henry VIII,* American Repertory Theatre, International Theatre, New York City, 1946.

Busch, *Yellow Jack,* American Repertory Theatre, International Theatre, 1947.

Two of Spades and Leg of Mutton, *Alice in Wonderland,* American Repertory Theatre, International Theatre, 1947.

Diomedes, *Antony and Cleopatra,* Martin Beck Theatre, New York City, 1947.

Androcles and the Lion, American Repertory Theatre, International Theatre, 1947.

Stefanowski, *Mister Roberts,* Alvin Theatre, New York City, 1949.

Alvarro Mangiacavallo, *The Rose Tattoo,* Martin Beck Theatre, 1951.

Kilroy, *Camino Real,* National Theatre, New York City, 1953.

Dickson, *Scarecrow,* Theatre De Lys, New York City, 1953.

Julien, *Mademoiselle Colombe,* Longacre Theatre, New York City, 1954.

(London debut) Sakini, *The Teahouse of the August Moon,* Her Majesty's Theatre, London, 1954, then Martin Beck Theatre, 1955.

Bill Walker, *Major Barbara*, Martin Beck Theatre, 1956.

Old Man, "The Chairs" in *The Chairs [and] The Lesson* (double-bill), Phoenix Theatre, New York City, 1958.

Willie, *The Cold Wind and the Warm*, Morosco Theatre, New York City, 1958.

Berenger, *Rhinoceros*, Longacre Theatre, 1961.

Ben, "The Tiger," and Paul XXX, "The Typists," in *The Tiger [and] The Typists* (double-bill), Orpheum Theatre, New York City, 1963, then Globe Theatre, London, 1964.

Milt Manville, *Luv*, Booth Theatre, New York City, 1964.

Charles Dyer, *Staircase*, Biltmore Theatre, New York City, 1968.

Ollie H. and Wesley, *Promenade All!*, Alvin Theatre, 1972.

General St. Pe, *The Waltz of the Toreadors*, Circle in the Square, New York City, then Eisenhower Theatre, Kennedy Center for the Performing Arts, Washington, DC, 1973.

Peppino, *Saturday, Sunday, Monday*, Martin Beck Theatre, 1974.

Arthur Canfield, *The Sponsor*, Peachtree Playhouse, Atlanta, GA, 1975.

Colin, *Absent Friends*, Long Wharf Theatre, New Haven, CT, then Eisenhower Theatre, Kennedy Center for the Performing Arts, later Royal Alexandra Theatre, Toronto, Ontario, all 1977.

Mr. Frank, *The Diary of Anne Frank*, Theatre Four, New York City, 1978.

The Neighborhood Playhouse at Fifty: A Celebration, Shubert Theatre, New York City, 1978.

Alexander, *Every Good Boy Deserves Favour*, Metropolitan Opera House, New York City, then Concert Hall, Kennedy Center for the Performing Arts, both 1979.

Leon Rose, "A Need for Brussels Sprouts," and Gus Frazier, "A Need for Less Expertise," in *Twice around the Park* (double-bill), Syracuse Stage, Syracuse, NY, 1981, then Cort Theatre, New York City, 1982, later Edinburgh Festival, Edinburgh, Scotland, 1984.

Stephan, *The Nest of the Woodgrouse*, New York Shakespeare Festival, Public Theatre, New York City, 1984.

The Flowering Peach, Coconut Grove Playhouse, Coconut Grove, FL, 1986.

Monsieur Paul Vigneron, *Opera Comique*, Eisenhower Theatre, Kennedy Center for the Performing Arts, 1987.

Waitin' in the Wings: The Night the Understudies Take Center Stage, Triplex International Theatre Festival, Triplex Theatre, New York City, 1988.

David Cole, *Cafe Crown*, New York Shakespeare Festival, Newman/Public Theatre, 1988, then Brooks Atkinson Theatre, New York City, 1989.

The Players Club Centennial Salute, Shubert Theatre, 1989.

Marley's ghost and Fezziwig, *A Christmas Carol*, Hudson Theatre, New York City, 1990.

Gregory Solomon, *The Price*, Criterion Theatre/Center Stage Right, New York City, 1992.

In Persons, Kaufman Theatre, New York City, 1993.

Noah, *The Flowering Peach*, Lyceum Theatre, New York City, 1994.

Also appeared in *This Property Is Condemned*, Equity Library Theatre, New York City; *Lady from the Sea* and *What Every Woman Knows*, both in New York City.

Stage Appearances; Major Tours:

Alvarro Mangiacavallo, *The Rose Tattoo*, U.S. cities, 1951.

Sakini, *The Teahouse of the August Moon*, U.S. cities, 1956.

Ben, "The Tiger," and Paul XXX, "The Typists," in *The Tiger [and] The Typists* (double-bill), U.S. cities, 1966.

Ollie H. and Wesley, *Promenade All!*, U.S. cities, 1971.

General St. Pe, *Waltz of the Toreadors*, U.S. cities, 1973-74.

Colin, *Absent Friends*, U.S. cities, 1977.

Alexander, *Every Good Boy Deserves Favour*, U.S. cities, 1979.

Film Appearances:

Danger, 1952.

Silva Vacarro, *Baby Doll*, Warner Bros., 1956.

Dancer, *The Lineup*, Columbia, 1958.

Calvera, *The Magnificent Seven*, United Artists, 1960.

Poncho, *Seven Thieves*, Twentieth Century-Fox, 1960.

Guido, *The Misfits*, United Artists, 1961.

John, *Adventures of a Young Man* (also known as *Hemingway's Adventures of a Young Man*), Twentieth Century-Fox, 1962.

Charlie Gant, *How the West Was Won*, Cinerama, 1962.

Sergeant Craig, *The Victors*, Columbia, 1963.

Warren Stone, *Act One*, Warner Bros., 1964.

Rodriguez Valdez, *Kisses for My President* (also known as *Kisses for the President*), Warner Bros., 1964.

Stratos, *The Moon-Spinners*, Buena Vista, 1964.

Shah of Khwarezm, *Genghis Khan* (also known as *Dschingis Khan* and *Dzingis-Kan*), Columbia, 1965.

The General, *Lord Jim,* Columbia, 1965.

David Leland, *How to Steal a Million* (also known as *How to Steal a Million and Live Happily Ever After*), Twentieth Century-Fox, 1966.

Locarno, *The Poppy Is Also a Flower* (also known as *Danger Grows Wild, The Opium Connection,* and *Poppies Are Also Flowers*), Comet, 1966.

Tuco, *The Good, the Bad, and the Ugly* (also known as *Il Buono, il Brutto, il Cattivo*), United Artists, 1967.

Ben Harris, *The Tiger Makes Out,* Columbia, 1967.

Harry Hunter, *How to Save a Marriage (and Ruin Your Life)* (also known as *Band of Gold*), Columbia, 1968.

Tennessee Fredericks, *A Lovely Way to Die* (also known as *A Lovely Way to Go*), Universal, 1968.

Cab driver, *New York City—The Most* (documentary), 1968.

Cacopoulos, *Revenge at El Paso* (also known as *Ace High, Four Gunmen of Ave Maria, Revenge in El Paso,* and *Il Quattro dell'ave Maria*), Paramount, 1969.

Scannapieco, *The Brain* (also known as *Le Cerveau*), Paramount, 1969.

Ben Baker, *MacKenna's Gold,* Columbia, 1969.

Napoleon Bonaparte, *The Adventures of Gerard* (also known as *Adventures of Brigadier Gerard*), United Artists, 1970.

Store clerk, *The Angel Levine,* United Artists, 1970.

Arthur Mason, *The People Next Door,* Avco-Embassy, 1970.

Mario Gambretti, *Zigzag* (also known as *False Witness* and *Zig-Zag*), Metro-Goldwyn-Mayer, 1970.

Kifke, *Romance of a Horse Thief,* Allied Artists, 1971.

Sotto a Chi Tocca! (also known as *Besos para Ella, Punetazos para Todos* and *Vier Froehliche Rabauken*), 1972.

Lynn Forshay, *Cinderella Liberty,* Twentieth Century-Fox, 1973.

Don Vittorio, *Crazy Joe,* Columbia, 1974.

Don't Turn the Other Cheek (also known as *The Killer from Yuma, Long Live Your Death,* and *Viva la Muerte . . . Tua*), International Amusement Corporation, 1974.

Narrator, *L'Chaim—To Life!,* 1974.

Black, *Il Bianco, il Giallo, il Nero* (also known as *Samurai, White, Yellow, Black,* and *El Blanco, el Amarillo, y el Negro*), CIDIF, 1975.

Ras, *Attenti al Buffone!* (also known as *Eye of the Cat*), Medusa Distribuzione, 1975.

Monsignor, *Nasty Habits* (also known as *The Abbess*), Brut, 1976.

Benjamin Franklin, *Independence* (short film), Twentieth Century-Fox, 1976.

Stateline Motel (also known *Last Chance, Last Chance for a Born Loser, Last Chance Motel,* and *L'ultima Chance*), International Cinefilm-NMD, 1976.

Detective, *E Tanta Paura,* 1976.

Adam Coffin, *The Deep,* Columbia, 1977.

General Tom Reser, *The Domino Principle* (also known as *The Domino Killings*), Avco-Embassy, 1977.

Detective Gatz, *The Sentinel,* Universal, 1977.

Rabbi Gold, *Girlfriends,* Warner Bros., 1978.

Vince Marlowe, "Dynamite Hands," and Pop, "Baxter's Beauties of 1933," *Movie Movie,* Warner Bros., 1978.

Gerolamo Giarra, *Squadra Antimafia* (also known as *Little Italy*), 1978.

Man in oil, *Circle of Iron* (also known as *The Silent Flute*), Avco-Embassy, 1979.

Sal Hyman, *Firepower,* Associated Film Distribution, 1979.

Joe Diamond, *Winter Kills,* Avco-Embassy, 1979.

Ritchie Blumenthal, *The Hunter,* Paramount, 1980.

Himself, *Acting: Lee Strasberg and the Actors Studio* (documentary), Davada Enterprises, 1981.

Lieutenant General Leporello, *The Salamander,* ITC, 1983.

Sam Orowitz, *Sam's Son,* Invictus, 1984.

Himself, *Sanford Meisner—The Theatre's Best Kept Secret* (documentary), Columbia, 1984.

Leon B. Little, *Tough Guys,* Buena Vista, 1986.

Himself, *Hello Actors Studio* , Actors Studio, 1987.

Dr. Herbert A. Morrison, *Nuts,* Warner Bros., 1987.

"The Sahara Forest" and "Climbed up the Ladder and Had Her" in *Funny,* Associates and Ferren, 1988.

Narrator, *Terezin Diary,* 1989.

Rosengarten (also known as *The Rose Garden*), 1989.

Smoke, 1990.

Cotton Weinberger, *The Two Jakes,* Paramount, 1990.

Don Altobello, *Mario Puzo's The Godfather, Part III* (also known as *The Godfather, Part III*), Paramount, 1990.

Sam Abrams, *Article 99,* Orion, 1992.

George Lieberhoff, *Mistress,* Rainbow Releasing/Tribeca Productions, 1992.

Peck, *Night and the City,* Twentieth Century-Fox, 1992.

Miele, Dolce Amore, 1993.

Don Siro, *Honey Sweet Love,* 1994.

Sheldon, *Two Much* (also known as *Loco de Amor*), Buena Vista, 1995.

Fallon, *The Associate,* Buena Vista, 1996.

Television Appearances; Series:

Vincent Danzig, *Our Family Honor,* ABC, 1985-86.

Narrator, *Sex and the Silver Screen,* Showtime, 1996.

Television Appearances; Miniseries:

Gus Farber, *Seventh Avenue*, NBC, 1977.

Ben Ezra, *Harold Robbins' The Pirate* (also known as *The Pirate*), CBS, 1978.

Hernando DeTalavera, *Christopher Columbus*, CBS, 1985.

Latella, *Vendetta: Secrets of a Mafia Bride* (also known as *A Bride of Violence, A Family Matter, A Woman of Honor*, and *Dona d'onore,*), syndicated, 1991.

Frank Latella, *Vendetta II: The New Mafia* (also known as *Bride of Violence 2, Vendetta 2*, and *Dona d'onore 2*), syndicated, 1993.

Voice, *Baseball* (also known as *The History of Baseball*), PBS, 1994.

Television Appearances; Movies:

Dr. Frank Enari, *A Cold Night's Death* (also known as *The Chill Factor*), ABC, 1973.

DeWitt Foster, *Indict and Convict*, ABC, 1974.

Olan Vacio, *Fugitive Family*, CBS, 1980.

Sal Galucci, *The Pride of Jesse Hallam*, CBS, 1981.

Bert Silverman, *Skokie*, CBS, 1981.

Mauritzi Apt, *The Wall*, CBS, 1982.

Uncle Vern Damico, *The Executioner's Song*, NBC, 1982.

Dr. William Hitzig, *Anatomy of an Illness*, CBS, 1984.

Dr. Huffman, *Murder: By Reason of Insanity* (also known as *My Sweet Victim*), CBS, 1985.

Norman Voss, *Something in Common*, CBS, 1986.

Yacov, *The Impossible Spy*, HBO, 1987.

Moses Zelnick, *Legacy of Lies*, USA Network, 1992.

Bill Presser, *Teamster Boss: The Jackie Presser Story* (also known as *Life on the High Wire* and *Teamster Boss*), HBO, 1992.

Television Appearances; Episodic:

"The Beautiful Bequest," *Philco Television Playhouse*, NBC, 1949.

"Rappaccini's Daughter," *Lights Out*, NBC, 1951.

"The System," *Danger*, CBS, 1952.

"Stan, the Killer," *Summer Studio One*, CBS, 1952.

"Deadlock," *The Web*, CBS, 1952.

"The Baby," *Philco Television Playhouse*, NBC, 1953.

"The Brownstone," *Goodyear Playhouse*, NBC, 1954.

"Shadow of the Champ," *Philco Television Playhouse*, NBC, 1955.

"Mr. Blue Ocean," *General Electric Theatre*, CBS, 1955.

"The Outsiders," *Philco Television Playhouse*, NBC, 1955.

"A Fragile Affair," *The Kaiser Aluminum Hour*, NBC, 1956.

"The Man Who Wasn't Himself," *Studio One*, CBS, 1957.

"The World of Nick Adams," *The Seven Lively Arts*, CBS, 1957.

"Albert Anastasia," *Climax!*, CBS, 1958.

"The Plot to Kill Stalin," *Playhouse 90*, CBS, 1958.

"My Father the Fool," *Desilu Playhouse*, CBS, 1958.

"The Emperor's New Clothes," *Shirley Temple's Storybook*, NBC, 1958.

"For Whom the Bell Tolls," *Playhouse 90*, CBS, 1959.

"The Margaret Bourke-White Story," *Sunday Showcase*, NBC, 1960.

"Birthright," *Goodyear Theatre*, NBC, 1960.

"Lullaby," *Play of the Week*, syndicated, 1960.

"Hope Is the Thing with Feathers," *Robert Herridge Theatre*, CBS, 1960.

"A Death of Princes," *Naked City*, ABC, 1960.

"A Bit of Glory," *Outlaws*, NBC, 1962.

"A Run for the Money," *Naked City*, ABC, 1962.

"Tomorrow the Man," *Dick Powell Show*, NBC, 1962.

Mr. Freeze number three, "Ice Spy," *Batman*, ABC, 1967.

Mr. Freeze number three, "The Duo Defy," *Batman*, ABC, 1967.

"Dear Friends," *CBS Playhouse*, CBS, 1967.

"Legal Maneuver," *The Young Lawyers*, ABC, 1971.

"Paradise Lost," *N.E.T. Playhouse*, PBS, 1971.

"The Typists," *Hollywood Television Theater*, PBS, 1971.

"Compliments of the Season," *Orson Welles' Great Mysteries*, syndicated, 1973.

"A Question of Answers," *Kojak*, CBS, 1975.

Tales of the Unexpected, syndicated, 1981.

"Tommy Howell," *An American Portrait*, CBS, 1985.

"The Silver Maiden," *Shortstories*, Arts and Entertainment, 1986.

Tim Charles, "To Bind the Wounds," *Highway to Heaven*, NBC, 1986.

Gene Malloy, "A Father's Faith," *Highway to Heaven*, NBC, 1987.

Salvatore Gambino, "A Very Good Year for Murder," *Murder, She Wrote*, CBS, 1988.

Yosef Kandinsky, "Kandinsky's Vault," *Alfred Hitchcock Presents*, USA Network, 1988.

Union worker, *Law and Order*, NBC, 1991.

Simon Valaness, "The Working Stiff," *Law and Order*, NBC, 1992.

Narrator, "The Western," *American Cinema*, PBS, 1995.

"Yul Brynner: The Man Who Was King," *Biography*, Arts and Entertainment, 1995.

"Marilyn Monroe: The Mortal Goddess," *Biography*, Arts and Entertainment, 1996.

Appeared in episodes of *Alcoa/Goodyear Theater*, NBC; *Dupont Show of the Month*; CBS; and *Suspicion*, NBC.

Television Appearances; Specials:
Dauphin, "The Lark," *Hallmark Hall of Fame*, NBC, 1957.

"Where Is Thy Brother?," *Jewish Appeals Special*, NBC, 1958.

Happy Locarno, *The Poppy Is Also a Flower* (also known as *Poppies Are Also Flowers*), ABC, 1966.

"Paradise Lost," *Great Performances*, PBS, 1974.

"Twenty Shades of Pink," *General Electric Theatre*, CBS, 1976.

The Kennedy Center Honors: A Celebration of the Performing Arts, CBS, 1984.

The ABC All-Star Spectacular, ABC, 1985.

Mr. Prince, "Rocket to the Moon," *American Playhouse*, PBS, 1986.

We the People 200: The Constitutional Gala, CBS, 1987.

Host and narrator, *Hollywood's Favorite Heavy: Businessmen on Primetime TV*, PBS, 1987.

The Typists, Arts and Entertainment, 1987.

Narrator, *It's Up to Us: The Giraffe Project* (documentary), PBS, 1988.

Ira Abrams, "A Matter of Conscience" (also known as "Silent Witness"), *CBS Schoolbreak Specials*, CBS, 1989.

"Sanford Meisner: The Theatre's Best Kept Secret," *American Masters*, PBS, 1990.

Himself, *The Godfather Family: A Look Inside*, HBO, 1990.

Voice, "Coney Island," *The American Experience*, PBS, 1991.

"Helen Hayes: First Lady of the American Theatre," *American Masters*, PBS, 1991.

Michael Landon: Memories with Laughter and Love, NBC, 1991.

"Miracle on 44th Street: A Portrait of the Actors Studio," *American Masters*, PBS, 1991.

World War II: A Personal Journey, The Disney Channel, 1991.

Voice of William H. Crook, *Lincoln*, ABC, 1992.

Street Scenes: New York on Film, American Movie Classics, 1992.

Voice, "The Donner Party," *The American Experience*, PBS, 1992.

Narrator, *Elia Kazan: A Director's Journey*, American Movie Classics, 1995.

Voice of Horace Greeley and Henry Bergh, *P. T. Barnum: America's Greatest Showman*, The Discovery Channel, 1995.

Voice, "The Way West" (also known as "The West"), *The American Experience*, PBS, 1995.

Clark Gable: Tall, Dark, and Handsome, TNT, 1996.

Cronkite Remembers (also known as *Walter Cronkite Remembers*), CBS, 1996.

The 50th Annual Tony Awards, 1996.

Narrator, *The Man Who Drew Bug-Eyed Monsters*, PBS, 1996.

Narrator, *The Moviemakers: Arthur Penn* (also known as *Arthur Penn*), PBS, 1996.

Narrator, *The Moviemakers: Robert Wise* (also known as *Robert Wise*), PBS, 1996.

Narrator, *The Moviemakers: Stanley Donen* (also known as *Stanley Donen*), PBS, 1996.

Himself, *James Dean: A Portrait*, 1996.

Voice of Pinchas Freudiger and David Ben-Gurion, *The Trial of Adolf Eichmann*, PBS, 1997.

Television Appearances; Pilots:
Joe Verga, *Embassy*, ABC, 1985.

Television Appearances; Other:
Worlds Beyond: The Black Tombs, 1987.

WRITINGS

Contributor to periodicals, including *Films and Filming*.

SIDELIGHTS

Wallach's favorite roles include Kilroy in *Camino Real* and Alvarro Mangiacavallo in *The Rose Tattoo*.

OTHER SOURCES

Books:
Thomas, Nicholas, editor, *The International Dictionary of Films and Filmmakers*, Volume 3: *Actors and Actresses*, second edition, St. James Press (Detroit, MI), 1992.

Periodicals:
Films in Review, August-September, 1983.*

WALTER, Jessica 1944(?)-

PERSONAL

Born January 31, 1944 (some sources say 1940), in New York, NY; daughter of David (a musician) and Esther (a teacher; maiden name, Groisser) Walter;

married Ross Bowman, March 27, 1966 (divorced, 1978); married Ron Leibman (an actor), June 26, 1983; children: (first marriage) Brooke. *Education:* Trained for the stage at Neighborhood Playhouse and Bucks County Playhouse.

Addresses: *Agent*—Bob Gersh, The Gersh Agency, 222 North Canon Drive, Beverly Hills, CA 90210.

Career: Actress.

Member: Screen Actors Guild (member of board of directors, 1973—; vice-president, 1975-83), American Federation of Television and Radio Artists, Actors' Equity Association.

Awards, Honors: Clarence Derwent Award, 1963, for *Photofinish;* Golden Globe Award nomination, best actress in a drama, Hollywood Foreign Press Association, 1971, for *Play Misty for Me;* Emmy Award, outstanding lead actress, 1975, for *Amy Prentiss;* Emmy Award nominations, 1976, for *The Streets of San Francisco,* and 1980, for *Trapper John, M.D.*

CREDITS

Television Appearances; Series:
Julie Morano, *Love of Life,* CBS, 1962-65.
Phyllis Koster, *For the People,* CBS, 1965.
Title role, *Amy Prentiss,* NBC, 1974-75.
Joan Hamlyn, *All That Glitters,* syndicated, 1977.
Melanie McIntyre, *Trapper John, M.D.,* CBS, 1979-84.
Ava Marshall, *Bare Essence,* NBC, 1983.
Voice of Diabolyn, *Wildfire* (animated), CBS, 1986-87.
Connie Lo Verde, *Aaron's Way,* NBC, 1988.
Voice of Fran Sinclair, *Dinosaurs,* ABC, 1991-94.
Anne, *The Round Table,* NBC, 1992.
Eleanor Armitage, *One Life to Live,* ABC, 1996-97.

Television Appearances; Miniseries:
Ursula, *Arthur Hailey's "Wheels"* (also known as *Wheels*), NBC, 1978.
Maggie McGregor, *Scruples,* ABC, 1981.

Television Appearances; Movies:
Jessica Carson, *Three's a Crowd,* ABC, 1969.
Dee Dee, *Women in Chains,* ABC, 1972.
Fredrica Morgan, *Home for the Holidays* (also known as *Deadly Desires*), ABC, 1972.
Louise Damon, *Hurricane* (also known as *Hurricane Hunters*), ABC, 1974.

Nomi Haroun, *Victory at Entebbe,* ABC, 1976.
Louise Carmino, *Black Market Baby* (also known as *A Dangerous Love* and *Don't Steal My Baby*), ABC, 1977.
Christina Wood, *Secrets of Three Hungry Wives,* NBC, 1978.
Megan, *Wild and Wooly,* ABC, 1978.
Nicole DeCamp, *Vampire,* ABC, 1979.
Irene Barton, *She's Dressed to Kill* (also known as *Someone's Killing the World's Greatest Models*), NBC, 1979.
Pat Brooks, *Miracle on Ice,* ABC, 1981.
Roz Richardson, *Thursday's Child,* CBS, 1983.
Gertrude Simon, *The Execution,* NBC, 1985.
Francesca DeLorca, *Killer in the Mirror,* NBC, 1986.
Ms. Peggy Shields, *Jenny's Song,* syndicated, 1988.
Bess Kaufman, *Leave of Absence,* NBC, 1994.
Joan, *Mother Knows Best,* ABC, 1997.

Television Appearances; Pilots:
Vivien Scott, *Pursue and Destroy,* ABC, 1966.
Janet Braddock, *The Immortal,* ABC, 1969.
Jane Antrim, *They Call It Murder,* NBC, 1971.
Sally McNamara, *Having Babies,* ABC, 1976.
Morgan LeFay, *Dr. Strange,* CBS, 1978.
Astrid Carlisle, *The Return of Marcus Welby, M.D.,* ABC, 1984.
Jessica Craigmont, *T.L.C.,* NBC, 1984.
Connie Lo Verde, *Aaron's Way* (also known as *Aaron's Way: The Harvest*), NBC, 1988.
Bonnie Balian, *Dad's a Dog,* ABC, 1990.

Television Appearances; Episodic:
"Curse of the Gypsy," *Diagnosis: Unknown,* CBS, 1960.
"Hold for Gloria Christmas," *Naked City,* ABC, 1962.
"A Long Way from St. Louis," *Route 66,* CBS, 1963.
"Take Sides with the Sun," *East Side/West Side,* CBS, 1964.
"The Ordeal of Mrs. Snow," *The Alfred Hitchcock Hour,* CBS, 1964.
"The Fine Line," *The Defenders,* CBS, 1964.
"August Is the Month before Christmas," *Ben Casey,* ABC, 1964.
Flipper, NBC, 1964.
"The Suspect," *The Doctors and the Nurses,* CBS, 1964.
"House of Cards," *The Rogues,* NBC, 1964.
"The Unwritten Law," *The Defenders,* CBS, 1965.
"Act of Violence," *The Doctors and the Nurses,* CBS, 1965.
"Picture Me a Murder," *Trials of O'Brien,* CBS, 1965.
"Flight to Harbin," *The FBI,* ABC, 1966.
"The White Knight," *The Fugitive,* ABC, 1966.

"Rope of Gold," *The FBI*, ABC, 1967.

"Counter-Stroke," *The FBI*, ABC, 1967.

"Moving Target," *Mannix*, CBS, 1967.

"Death of a Fixer," *The FBI*, ABC, 1968.

"The Ordeal," *Name of the Game*, NBC, 1968.

"The Baranoff Time Table," *It Takes a Thief*, ABC, 1969.

"Where Will the Trumpets Be?," *Then Came Bronson*, NBC, 1969.

Love, American Style, ABC, 1969.

"Who Is Sylvia?," *Mannix*, CBS, 1970.

Valerie, "Orpheus," *Mission: Impossible*, CBS, 1970.

"Breakdown," *The Most Deadly Game*, ABC, 1970.

"Love and the Kidnapper," *Love, American Style*, ABC, 1971.

"Let the Dier Beware," *Medical Center*, CBS, 1971.

"The Showdown," *Name of the Game*, NBC, 1971.

"Montserrat," *Hollywood Television Theatre*, PBS, 1971.

"The House of Alquist," *Marcus Welby, M.D.*, ABC, 1971.

"Circle of Power," *Medical Center*, CBS, 1971.

"Love and the Big Leap," *Love, American Style*, ABC, 1971.

Louise Carson, "Everything Else You Can Steal," *Alias Smith and Jones*, ABC, 1971.

"The Recruiter," *The FBI*, ABC, 1971.

"Moving Target," *Mannix*, CBS, 1972.

"The Heart That Wouldn't Stay Buried," *The Sixth Sense*, ABC, 1972.

"The Old College Try," *Banyon*, NBC, 1972.

Jane Butler, "That Was No Lady," *Cannon*, CBS, 1972.

"A Game for One Player," *Medical Center*, CBS, 1972.

"A More Exciting Game," *Marcus Welby, M.D.*, ABC, 1973.

"A Gathering of Sharks," *The FBI*, ABC, 1973.

Love, American Style, ABC, 1973.

"The Two Million Clams of Cap'n Jack," *Banacek*, NBC, 1973.

"Kiss the Dream Goodbye," *Jigsaw*, ABC, 1973.

"The Danford File," *Mannix*, CBS, 1973.

"The Stamp of Death," *Streets of San Francisco*, ABC, 1973.

"The Cash and Carry Caper," *Tenafly*, NBC, 1973.

"Woman for Hire," *Medical Center*, CBS, 1973.

"Venus—As in Flytrap," *Barnaby Jones*, CBS, 1974.

Margaret Nicholson, "Mind over Mayhem," *Columbo*, NBC, 1974.

"The Illusion of Evil Spikes," *The Magician*, NBC, 1974.

"The Chief" (pilot for *Amy Prentiss*), *Ironside*, NBC, 1974.

"Dead Man's Run," *Barnaby Jones*, CBS, 1974.

Carla, "The Two-Faced Corpse," *Hawaii Five-0*, CBS, 1974.

"The Park Avenue Pirates," *McCloud*, NBC, 1975.

Maggie Jarris/Mrs. Reston/Mrs. McCluskey, "Till Death Do Us Part," *Streets of San Francisco*, ABC, 1976.

"All Bets Off," *McMillan*, NBC, 1976.

"The Return of Wonder Woman," *The New Adventures of Wonder Woman*, CBS, 1977.

"The Girl Nobody Knew," *What Really Happened to the Class of '65?*, NBC, 1977.

"Crash Diet Course," *The Love Boat*, ABC, 1978.

Jessica Ross, "Images," *Quincy, M.E.*, NBC, 1978.

"Doc's 'Ex' Change," *The Love Boat*, ABC, 1979.

"Doc's Dismissal," *The Love Boat*, ABC, 1981.

Aloha Paradise, ABC, 1981.

Victoria Hill, "Reunion," *Knots Landing*, CBS, 1982.

"Everybody Loves Aunt Vanessa," *Joanie Loves Chachi*, ABC, 1982.

"Joey's Here," *Matt Houston*, ABC, 1982.

Claudia Bradford, "The Maternal Triangle," *Three's a Crowd*, ABC, 1984.

"Jack's Problem," *Three's a Crowd*, ABC, 1984.

"A Foreign Affair," *Three's a Crowd*, ABC, 1984.

"Father Knows Nothing," *Three's a Crowd*, ABC, 1985.

"Deeds of Trust," *Three's a Crowd*, ABC, 1985.

"The New Mr. Bradford," *Three's a Crowd*, ABC, 1985.

"King for a Day," *Three's a Crowd*, ABC, 1985.

"Hits and Missus," *The Love Boat*, ABC, 1985.

Joyce Holleran, "Murder in the Afternoon," *Murder, She Wrote*, CBS, 1985.

Irene Fitzgerald, "Child's Play," *Hotel*, ABC, 1986.

Joan Fulton, "Magnum on Ice," *Murder, She Wrote*, CBS, 1986.

Joan Fulton, "Novel Connection," *Magnum, P.I.*, CBS, 1986.

Interior design editor, "Murder by Design," *J. J. Starbuck*, NBC, 1988.

Jane Dawson, "Unauthorized Obituary," *Murder, She Wrote*, CBS, 1991.

Susan Miller, *Coach*, ABC, 1994.

Ann Kopell, "House Counsel," *Law and Order*, NBC, 1994.

Voice of Ashley Walker-Club-Dupree, *The Magic School Bus*, PBS, 1994.

Senator Elise Voudreau, "A Spider in the Web," *Babylon 5*, syndicated, 1994.

Gwen Noble, "Murder in the Afternoon," *Murder, She Wrote*, CBS, 1994.

Television Appearances; Specials:

Lois Lane, *Kiss Me, Kate*, ABC, 1968.

Anna II, "The Prison Game," *Visions,* PBS, 1977.
Day-to-Day Affairs, HBO, 1985.
Dr. Stein, "Just a Regular Kid: An AIDS Story," ABC *Afterschool Specials,* ABC, 1987.
"Clint Eastwood—The Man from Malpaso," *Crazy about the Movies,* Cinemax, 1993.
Presenter, *The 7th Annual Genesis Awards,* 1993.
Presenter, *The 9th Annual Genesis Awards,* 1995.

Other Television Appearances:
Secretary, *Doomsday Rock,* 1997.

Film Appearances:
(Film debut) Laura, *Lilith,* Columbia, 1964.
Pat Stoddard, *Grand Prix,* Metro-Goldwyn-Mayer, 1966.
Libby MacAusland, *The Group,* United Artists, 1966.
Inez Braverman, *Bye Bye Braverman,* Warner Bros., 1968.
Julie Catlan, *Number One* (also known as *The Pro*), United Artists, 1969.
Evelyn Draper, *Play Misty for Me,* Universal, 1971.
Goldengirl, 1979.
Fiona, *Going Ape!,* Paramount, 1981.
Celia Berryman, *Spring Fever* (also known as *Sneakers*), Com-World, 1983.
Phyllis Brody, *The Flamingo Kid,* Twentieth Century-Fox, 1984.
First girl in art room, *Secret Places,* 1984.
Kay Mart, *Tapeheads,* De Laurentiis Entertainment Group, 1988.
Elaine, *Ghost in the Machine* (also known as *Deadly Terror*), Twentieth Century-Fox, 1993.
President Garcia-Thompson, *PCU* (also known as *PCU Pit Party*), Twentieth Century-Fox, 1994.
Dr. Phyllis Evergreen, *Temptress* (also known as *Dark Goddess*), Paramount Home Video, 1995.

Stage Appearances:
(Stage debut) Kid sister, *Middle of the Night,* Bucks County Playhouse, New Hope, PA, 1958.
(Broadway debut) Liz, *Advise and Consent,* Cort Theatre, 1961.
Cigarette girl, *Nightlife,* Brooks Atkinson Theatre, New York City, 1962.
Clarice and Ada, *Photofinish,* Brooks Atkinson Theatre, 1963.
Mistress, *A Severed Head,* Royale Theatre, New York City, 1964.
The Women, Repertory Theatre of New Orleans, New Orleans, LA, 1970.
Rosalind Gambol, *Fighting International Fat,* Playwrights Horizons, New York City, 1985.

Tartuffe, Los Angeles Theatre Center, Los Angeles, CA, 1986.
Claire Ganz, *Rumors,* Broadhurst Theatre, New York City, 1988.
Claire, *Rumors,* Centre Theatre Group, James A. Doolittle Theatre, Los Angeles, 1989-90.

Major Tours:
Tartuffe, U.S. cities, 1986.

Also appeared in *The Murder of Me,* New York City.

WARREN, Michael 1946-
(Mike Warren)

PERSONAL

Born March 5, 1946, in South Bend, IN; married, wife's name Susie; children: Koa, Cash. *Education:* University of California, Los Angeles, B.A., theatre arts.

Addresses: *Contact*—189 Greenfield Ave., Los Angeles, CA 90049.

Career: Actor, producer, and writer. Basketball technical adviser for the film *Drive, He Said,* Columbia, 1971; All-American basketball player with the Bruins while attending college.

Awards, Honors: Emmy Award nomination for *Hill Street Blues.*

CREDITS

Television Appearances; Series:
Ranger P. J. Lewis, *Sierra,* NBC, 1974.
Detective Marshall, *Joe Forrester,* NBC, 1975.
Sergeant Willie Miller, *Paris,* CBS, 1979-80.
Officer Bobby Hill, *Hill Street Blues,* NBC, 1981-87.
Michael "T-Dog" Turner, *Sweet Justice,* NBC, 1994-95.

Television Work; Series:
Producer, *What's Happening!,* ABC, 1976.
Creator and executive producer, *Family Matters,* ABC, 1989—.
Creator and executive producer, *The Family Man,* ABC, 1990.
Creator and executive producer, *Step by Step,* ABC, 1991—.
Creator and executive producer, *Getting By,* ABC, 1993.

Executive producer, *Hangin' with Mr. Cooper,* ABC, 1994-97.

Co-executive producer, *Kirk* (also known as *Life Happens*), The WB, 1995-96.

Television Appearances; Miniseries:
Dr. McCoy, *Robin Cook's "Invasion"* (also known as *Robin Cook's Lethal Invasion* and *Robin Cook's Alien Infestation*), NBC, 1997.

Television Appearances; Movies:
Rennie Stuart, *The Child Saver,* NBC, 1988.
Tony Parks, *The Kid Who Loved Christmas* (also known as *The Boy Who Loved Christmas*), syndicated, 1990.
Calvin Hunter, *Stompin' at the Savoy,* CBS, 1992.
Cpl. Eddie Tockes, *Buffalo Soldiers,* TNT, 1997.
The Wedding, ABC, 1998.

Television Appearances; Pilots:
Most Wanted, ABC, 1976.
Michael Davis, *Home Free,* NBC, 1988.
Ben Masters, *A Little Bit Strange,* NBC, 1989.

Television Work; Pilots:
Producer (with Kevin Inch), *Home Free,* NBC, 1988.

Television Appearances; Episodic:
Wyatt, "Death Score," *S.W.A.T.,* ABC, 1975.
"The Satanic Piano," *Tales from the Darkside,* syndicated, 1984.
Mitchell Evans, *227,* NBC, 1987.
Matthew Pogue, "The Hammer and the Glove," *In the Heat of the Night,* NBC, 1988.
Widower, *L.A. Law,* NBC, 1989.
"The Taking of Pablum 1-2-3," *Dream On,* HBO, 1990.
Walt Nestor, *Against the Grain,* NBC, 1993.
Time Trax, syndicated, 1993.
Milton, *In the House,* NBC, 1995.
Murder One, ABC, 1995.
Connie Hooks, *Early Edition,* CBS, 1996.
Ron, *High Incident,* ABC, 1996.
Eddie, *Living Single,* Fox, 1996.
Swaboda, *Murder One,* ABC, 1996.

Also guest host, *Friday Night Videos,* NBC; appeared in episodes of *Adam-12,* NBC; *Marcus Welby, M.D.,* ABC; *The Mod Squad,* ABC; *The White Shadow,* CBS; *Police Story,* NBC; and *Days of Our Lives,* NBC.

Television Work; Episodic:
Director, *Sanford and Son,* NBC, 1972.
Director, *The Diahann Carroll Show,* CBS, 1976.
Director, *Fish,* ABC, 1977.

Television Appearances; Specials:
Battle of the Network Stars X, ABC, 1981.
Battle of the Network Stars XIII, ABC, 1982.
Just a Little More Love, NBC, 1984.
Dr. Garcia, "Private Affairs" (also known as "Student Affairs"), *ABC Afterschool Specials,* ABC, 1989.
Judge, *The 1989 Miss Universe Pageant,* 1989.
Magic Johnson's All-Star Slam 'n Jam, syndicated, 1992.
Andre Dyson, "Crosses on the Lawn," *CBS Schoolbreak Specials,* CBS, 1993.

Television Work; Specials:
Creator, "Family Matters," *The ABC Saturday Morning Preview,* ABC, 1990.
Creator, "Step by Step," *The Saturday Morning Preview Special,* ABC, 1992.

Film Appearances:
(As Mike Warren) Easly, *Drive, He Said,* Columbia, 1971.
Roy, *Butterflies Are Free,* Columbia, 1972.
Andy, *Cleopatra Jones,* Warner Bros., 1973.
Norman Chambers, *Norman . . . Is That You?,* Metro-Goldwyn-Mayer/United Artists, 1976.
Preacher, *Fast Break,* Columbia, 1979.
Ace, *Dreamaniac* (video), Infinity, 1987.
Eddie, *Cold Steel,* 1987.
Byron, *Heaven Is a Playground,* Columbia TriStar Home Video, 1991.
Nathan LeFleur, *Storyville,* Twentieth Century-Fox, 1992.
Martindale, *A Passion to Kill* (also known as *Rules of Obsession*), A-Pix Entertainment, 1994.
Chase, *The Hunted,* Universal, 1995.

Stage Appearances:
A Flea in Her Ear, Meadow Brook Theatre, Rochester, MI, 1986.

WRITINGS

Television Episodes:
Laverne and Shirley, ABC, 1976.
Family Matters, ABC, 1989.
The Family Man, ABC, 1990.
Step by Step, ABC, 1991.
Getting By, ABC, 1993.
Kirk (also known as *Life Happens*), The WB, 1995.*

WARREN, Mike
    See WARREN, Michael

WASS, Ted 1952-

PERSONAL

Born October 27, 1952, in Lakewood, OH; married Janet Margolin (an actress), 1979 (died, 1993); children: two, including Julian. *Education:* Studied acting at the Goodman School, Chicago, IL.

Addresses: *Contact*—7667 Seattle Place, Los Angeles, CA 90046.

Career: Actor and director.

CREDITS

Television Appearances; Series:
Danny Dallas, *Soap,* ABC, 1977-81.
Steven Ratajkowski, *Men,* ABC, 1989.
Nick Russo, *Blossom,* NBC, 1991-95.

Television Work; Series:
Co-director, *Local Heroes* (also known as *Glory Days*), Fox, 1996.
Co-director, *Mr. Rhodes,* NBC, 1996.
Director, *My Guys,* CBS, 1996.
Co-director, *The Jeff Foxworthy Show,* NBC, 1996.

Television Appearances; Movies:
Vinnie, *The Triangle Factory Fire Scandal,* NBC, 1979.
Robert Fitzgerald, *I Was a Mail Order Bride,* CBS, 1982.
David Mitchell, *Baby Sister,* ABC, 1983.
Gregory Scott Murchison, *Sins of the Father,* NBC, 1985.
Elliot Taffle, *Triplecross,* ABC, 1986.
Paul Sheridan, *Sunday Drive,* ABC, 1986.
Harry, *The Canterville Ghost,* syndicated, 1986.
Mickey, *Mickey and Nora,* CBS, 1987.
Frank Clarke, *Pancho Barnes,* (also known as *The Pancho Barnes Story* and *The Happy Bottom Riding Club*), CBS, 1988.
Andre, *Fine Gold,* syndicated, 1990.
Steve Warner, *Sparks: The Price of Passion,* CBS, 1990.
Nick Russo, *Blossom in Paris* (also known as *Blossom in France*), NBC, 1993.
Ernie, *Danielle Steel's "Star"* (also known as *Star*), NBC, 1993.
Bryan Norcross, *Triumph over Disaster: The Hurricane Andrew Story,* NBC, 1993.

Television Appearances; Pilots:
Corporal Tillingham, *Handle with Care,* CBS, 1977.
Simon, *The 13th Day: The Story of Esther,* ABC, 1979.

Television Appearances; Specials:
ABC's Silver Anniversary Celebration—25 and Still the One, ABC, 1978.
Mike Maclaren, *Camp California* (also known as *Camp Fed*), ABC, 1989.

Film Appearances:
Clifton Sleigh, *Curse of the Pink Panther,* Metro-Goldwyn-Mayer/United Artists, 1983.
Bobby Shelton, *Oh God! You Devil,* Warner Bros., 1984.
Vic Casey, *Sheena,* Columbia, 1984.
Stump, *The Longshot,* Orion, 1986.

Stage Appearances:
(Off-Broadway debut) *Columbus,* 1975.
(Broadway debut) *Grease,* Royale Theatre, 1976.
Vernon Gersch, *They're Playing Our Song,* Imperial Theatre, New York City, 1981.*

WEITZ, Bruce 1943-

PERSONAL

Full name, Bruce Peter Weitz; born May 27, 1943, in Norwalk, CT; son of Alvin Weitz (a liquor store owner) and Sybil Weitz Rubel; married second wife, Cecilia Hart (an actress), 1973 (divorced, 1980). *Education:* Carnegie Institute of Technology (now Carnegie-Mellon University), B.A., 1964, M.F.A., 1966. *Avocational interests:* Golf, racquetball, weaving, cooking, reading.

Addresses: *Contact*—5030 Arundel Drive, Woodland Hills, CA 91364. *Agent*—William Morris Agency, 151 El Camino Boulevard, Beverly Hills, CA 90212.

Career: Actor. Restaurant manager on the Spanish island Formentera, 1966.

Awards, Honors: Emmy Award nominations, outstanding supporting actor in a drama series, 1981, 1982, and 1983, and Emmy Award, outstanding supporting actor in a drama series, 1984, all for *Hill Street Blues.*

CREDITS

Television Appearances; Series:
Ryan's Hope, ABC, 1975.
Detective Mick Belker, *Hill Street Blues,* NBC, 1981-87.
Jake McCasky, *Mama's Boy,* NBC, 1987.
Mike Urbanek, *Anything But Love,* ABC, 1991-92.
Dr. Murray Rubenstein, *The Byrds of Paradise,* ABC, 1994.

Television Appearances; Movies:
Paul Snider, *Death of a Centerfold: The Dorothy Stratten Story,* NBC, 1981.
Bob Cousins, *A Reason to Live,* NBC, 1985.
Martini, *If It's Tuesday, It Still Must Be Belgium,* NBC, 1987.
Rick Whitehead, *Baby M,* ABC, 1988.
Burton Weinstein, *A Cry for Help: The Tracy Thurman Story* (also known as *Under the Law: The Tracy Thurman Story*), NBC, 1989.
Detective James McCready, *A Deadly Silence,* ABC, 1989.
Joe Lubin, *Leona Helmsley: The Queen of Mean,* CBS, 1990.
Dan Crawford, *Rainbow Drive* (also known as *City of Angels*), Showtime, 1990.
Miller Huggins, *Babe Ruth* (also known as *The Sultan of Swat*), NBC, 1991.
Coach Woodhouse, *Windrunner,* The Disney Channel, 1994.
Dr. Alex Johnson, *Danielle Steel's "Mixed Blessings"* (also known as *Mixed Blessings*), NBC, 1995.
Lieutenant Levine, *Her Hidden Truth* (also known as *When Summer Comes*), NBC, 1995.
Robert Shapiro, *The O. J. Simpson Story,* Fox, 1995.
Detective Steve McAdams, *Justice for Annie: A Moment of Truth Movie,* NBC, 1996.
Bill McLean, *Legend of the Ruby Silver* (also known as *Ruby Silver*), ABC, 1996.
Lieutenant Dominick Caroselli, *Sudden Terror: The Hijacking of School Bus No. 17* (also known as *The Miami School Bus Hijacking*), ABC, 1996.
Ron O'Brien, *Breaking the Surface: The Greg Louganis Story,* USA Network, 1997.

Television Appearances; Pilots:
Sergeant Mike Pirelli, *Every Stray Dog and Kid,* NBC, 1981.
Mick Belker, *Hill Street Blues,* NBC, 1981.
Dr. Matt Jennings, *Catalina C-Lab,* NBC, 1982.
Joe Maples, *Fair Game,* NBC, 1989.

Television Appearances; Episodic:
Robert Clark, "Kid Stuff," *Happy Days,* ABC, 1978.
The White Shadow, CBS, 1979.
"Burnout," *Paris,* CBS, 1979.
"The Gambler," *Matlock,* NBC, 1987.
Simon Foster, "The Mind of Simon Foster," *The Twilight Zone,* syndicated, 1988.
"Hit and Run," *The Hitchhiker,* HBO, 1988.
"The Murderer," *The Ray Bradbury Theatre,* USA Network, 1990.
"The Taking of Pablum 1-2-3," *Dream On,* HBO, 1990.
"Lock-Up," *Batman: The Animated Series,* Fox, 1992.
Bernard Ryman, *Civil Wars,* ABC, 1993.
Voice, *Duckman* (animated), USA Network, 1994.
Martin Snell, "Church of Metropolis," *Lois and Clark: The New Adventures of Superman,* ABC, 1994.
"The Fighter," *Highlander,* syndicated, 1994.
Agent Moe Bocks, *The X-Files,* Fox, 1994.
Officer Bert Coleman, *Cybill,* CBS, 1995.
Pug Finnigan, *Sisters,* NBC, 1995.
Lawrence Curry, "Yes, Sir, That's My Baby," *NYPD Blue,* ABC, 1996.
Voice of Bruno Manheim, *Superman,* (animated) Warner Bros., 1996.
Paul Bauwer, *JAG,* CBS, 1997.

Appeared in episodes of *Quincy, M.E.,* NBC; *Lou Grant,* CBS; and *The Rockford Files,* NBC.

Television Appearances; Specials:
"Henry Winkler Meets William Shakespeare," *CBS Festival of Lively Arts for Young People,* CBS, 1977.
Battle of the Network Stars, ABC, 1980, 1982, and 1983.
Celebrity Daredevils, ABC, 1983.
The Chemical People (documentary), PBS, 1983.
The Stuntman Awards, syndicated, 1986.
Host, *Man and the Animals* (documentary), PBS, 1987.
Macy's Thanksgiving Day Parade, NBC, 1987.
Time Warner Presents the Earth Day Special, ABC, 1990.

Stage Appearances:
Oh, What a Lovely War!, Long Wharf Theatre, New Haven, CT, 1966.
Polo Pope, *A Hatful of Rain,* Equity Library Theatre, Master Theatre, New York City, 1970.
In the Matter of J. Robert Oppenheimer, Goodman Theatre Center, Chicago, IL, 1972.
Roland, *The Conditioning of Charlie One,* Playwrights Horizons, New York City, 1973.

Sam, *Creeps,* Playhouse Two Theatre, New York City, 1973.

Johnny, *Frankie and Johnny in the Claire de Lune,* Westside Arts Theatre, New York City, 1988.

Sidney Black, *Light Up the Sky,* Roundabout Theatre, New York City, 1990.

Also appeared in *Death of a Salesman, The Basic Training of Pavlo Hummel,* and *Norman, Is That You?,* all in New York City. Appeared with Long Wharf Repertory Theatre, 1967; Tyrone Guthrie Theatre, Minneapolis, MN, 1967-69; Arena Stage, Washington, DC, 1971-72; Actors Theatre of Louisville, Louisville, KY, 1971-73; and in thirteen New York Shakespeare Festival productions, Delacorte Theatre, New York City, 1976-80.

Film Appearances:

The Private Files of J. Edgar Hoover, 1977.

Ultra-Stereo consultant, *Mr. North,* Samuel Goldwyn, 1988.

Captain Nelson Silva, *No Place to Hide,* Cannon, 1993.

Jack, *The Liar's Club,* New Horizons Home Video, 1993.

Paymer, *Molly and Gina,* A-Pix Entertainment, 1994.

Uncle Hal MacGregor, *Prehisteria! 3,* Paramount Home Video, 1995.

Snapper, *Coyote Summer,* Warner Home Video, 1996.

Stuart Caley, *Deep Impact,* 1998.*

WELD, Tuesday 1943-

PERSONAL

Original name, Susan Ker Weld; born August 27, 1943, in New York, NY; daughter of Lathrop Motley and Aileen (Ker) Weld; married Claude Harz, October, 1965 (divorced, 1971); married Dudley Moore (an actor), September 20, 1975 (divorced, 1980); married Pinchas Zuckerman (a violinist), 1985; children: (first marriage) Natasha; (second marriage) Patrick. *Education:* Attended Hollywood Professional School.

Addresses: *Home*—Sante Fe, NM, and Manhattan, NY. *Contact*—P.O. Box 367, Valley Stream, NY 11582.

Career: Actress. Worked as a fashion model.

Awards, Honors: Golden Globe Award, most promising female newcomer, Hollywood Foreign Press Association, 1960; Golden Globe Award nomination, best actress in a drama, 1973, for *Play It as It Lays;* Academy Award nomination, best supporting actress, 1978, for *Looking for Mr. Goodbar.*

CREDITS

Film Appearances:

(Film debut) Dori, *Rock, Rock, Rock,* Vanguard Productions, 1956.

Giggly girl, *The Wrong Man,* Warner Bros., 1956.

Comfort Goodpasture, *Rally Round the Flag Boys!,* Twentieth Century-Fox, 1959.

Dorothy Nichols (age 12-14), *The Five Pennies,* Columbia, 1959.

Vangie Harper, *The Private Lives of Adam and Eve,* Universal, 1960.

Anne, *Because They're Young,* Columbia, 1960.

Joy Elder, *High Time,* Twentieth Century-Fox, 1960.

Jody, *Sex Kittens Go to College* (also known as *The Beauty and the Robot*), Allied Artists, 1960.

Selena Cross, *Return to Peyton Place,* Twentieth Century-Fox, 1961.

Noreen, *Wild in the Country,* Twentieth Century-Fox, 1961.

Libby Bushmill, *Bachelor Flat,* Twentieth Century-Fox, 1961.

Bobby Jo Pepperdine, *Soldier in the Rain,* Allied Artists, 1963.

Christian, *The Cincinnati Kid,* Metro-Goldwyn-Mayer, 1965.

Jojo Holcombe, *I'll Take Sweden,* United Artists, 1965.

Barbara Ann Greene, *Lord Love a Duck,* United Artists, 1966.

Sue Ann Stepanek, *Pretty Poison,* Twentieth Century-Fox, 1968.

Alma McCain, *I Walk the Line,* Columbia, 1970.

Susan/Noah, *A Safe Place,* Columbia, 1971.

Maria Wyeth, *Play It as It Lays,* Universal, 1972.

Katherine Dunn, *Looking for Mr. Goodbar,* Paramount, 1977.

Marge Converse, *Who'll Stop the Rain?* (also known as *Dog Soldiers*), United Artists, 1978.

Kate, *Serial,* Paramount, 1980.

Jessie, *Thief* (also known as *Violent Street*), United Artists, 1981.

Gloria Travalian, *Author! Author!,* Twentieth Century-Fox, 1982.

Carol, *Once Upon a Time in America,* Warner Bros., 1984.

Marie Wolfe, *Heartbreak Hotel,* Buena Vista, 1988.

Mrs. Amanda Prendergast, *Falling Down,* Warner Bros., 1993.

Nora Clayton, *Feeling Minnesota,* Fine Line, 1996.

Television Appearances; Series:

Thalia Menninger, *The Many Loves of Dobie Gillis,* CBS, 1959-60.

Television Appearances; Movies:

Vicky, *Reflections of a Murder,* ABC, 1974.

Zelda Fitzgerald, *F. Scott Fitzgerald in Hollywood,* ABC, 1976.

Doris Winters, *A Question of Guilt,* CBS, 1978.

Lillie Lloyd McCann, *Mother and Daughter: The Loving War,* ABC, 1980.

Holly Richardson, *Madame X,* NBC, 1981.

Margie Young-Hunt, *John Steinbeck's "The Winter of Our Discontent"* (also known as *The Winter of Our Discontent*), CBS, 1983.

Sharon Clark, *Scorned and Swindled,* CBS, 1984.

Georgia Benfield, *Circle of Violence: A Family Drama* (also known as *A Family of Strangers*), CBS, 1986.

Shelly Grant, *Something in Common* (also known as *Love 40*), CBS, 1986.

Television Appearances; Episodic:

"Backwoods Cinderella," *Goodyear Theatre,* NBC, 1957.

"The Other Guy's Girl," *The Adventures of Ozzie and Harriet,* ABC, 1959.

"Secret Island," *77 Sunset Strip,* ABC, 1959.

"Rick Gets Even," *The Adventures of Ozzie and Harriet,* ABC, 1959.

"Condor's Lair," *77 Sunset Strip,* ABC, 1960.

"Millionaire Katherine Boland," *The Millionaire,* CBS, 1960.

"The Doll in the Bathing Suit," *The Tab Hunter Show,* NBC, 1960.

"The Mormons," *Zane Grey Theatre,* CBS, 1960.

"The Highest Wall," *Follow the Sun,* ABC, 1961.

"Cherie," *Bus Stop,* ABC, 1961.

"A Time to Die," *The Dick Powell Show,* NBC, 1962.

"The Velvet Trap," *Adventures in Paradise,* ABC, 1962.

"A Case Study of Two Savages," *Naked City,* ABC, 1962.

"Birth of a Salesman," *Dobie Gillis,* CBS, 1962.

"Love Is a Skinny Kid," *Route 66,* CBS, 1962.

"When You See an Evil Man," *Ben Casey,* ABC, 1962.

"Run Till It's Dark," *The Dick Powell Show,* NBC, 1962.

"Something Crazy's Going on in the Back Room," *Eleventh Hour,* NBC, 1963.

"The Legend of Lylah Claire," *DuPont Show of the Month,* NBC, 1963.

"Silent Love, Secret Love," *The Greatest Show on Earth,* ABC, 1963.

"Keep an Eye on Emily," *Mr. Broadway,* CBS, 1964.

"Dark Corner," *The Fugitive,* ABC, 1964.

"Heller," *Cimarron Strip,* CBS, 1968.

Also appeared in episodes of *Playhouse 90,* CBS; *Kraft Theatre,* NBC; *Alcoa Theatre,* ABC; and *Climax,* CBS.

Television Appearances; Specials:

The Bob Hope Show, NBC, 1961.

The Bob Hope Show, NBC, 1963.

The Crucible, CBS, 1967.

Bob Hope Special: Bob Hope's Women I Love—Beautiful but Funny, 1982.

Lizzie Curry, *The Rainmaker,* HBO, 1982.

OTHER SOURCES

Books:

International Directory of Films and Filmmakers, St. James Press, 1997, pp. 1029-1031.

Periodicals:

People Weekly, September 30, 1996, p. 18.*

WENDT, George   1948-

PERSONAL

Full name, George Robert Wendt; born October 17, 1948, in Chicago, IL; married Bernadette Birkett (an actress), 1978; children: Joshua, Andrew, Hilary, and two stepchildren. *Education:* Rockhurst College, B.A. (economics), 1971. *Avocational interests:* Baseball, football, basketball.

Addresses: *Home*—Los Angeles, CA. *Agent*—c/o Sutton, Barth, and Vennari, 145 South Fairfax Ave., Suite 310, Los Angeles, CA 90036.

Career: Actor. Second City (improvisational comedy troupe), Chicago, IL, member of company, 1974-81; actor in television commercials. Also worked in construction.

Awards, Honors: Emmy Award nominations, outstanding supporting actor in a comedy series, 1984, 1985, 1986, 1987, 1988, and 1989, all for his portrayal of Norm Peterson, *Cheers;* Award for Excellence in the Arts, Goodman School of Drama, DePaul University.

CREDITS

Television Appearances; Series:
Gus Bertoia, *Making the Grade,* CBS, 1982.
Norm Peterson, *Cheers,* NBC, 1982-93.
George Coleman, *The George Wendt Show* (also known as *Under the Hood*), CBS, 1995.
Les Polonsky, *The Naked Truth* (also known as *Wilde Again*), NBC, 1997.

Also appeared as Bob Swerski, "Bears/Bulls Fans," *Saturday Night Live,* NBC.

Television Appearances; Movies:
Mr. Sweeney, *The Ratings Game* (also known as *The Mogul*), The Movie Channel, 1984.
Oblomov, *Oblomov,* BBC, 1989.
Warren Kooey, *Hostage for a Day,* Fox, 1994.
Mr. MacAfee, *Bye Bye Birdie,* ABC, 1995.
Graham McVeigh, *Columbo: Strange Bedfellows,* ABC, 1995.
Mac, *Shame II: The Secret,* Lifetime, 1995.
Charlie, "Alien Avengers" (also known as "Welcome to Planet Earth"), *Roger Corman Presents,* Showtime, 1996.
Charlie, "Alien Avengers II" (also known as "Welcome to Planet Earth II"), *Roger Corman Presents,* Showtime, 1997.
Sam, *The Price of Heaven,* 1997.

Television Appearances; Specials:
Voice of Raoul, *Garfield on the Town* (animated), CBS, 1983.
Voice of second ranger, *Garfield in the Rough* (animated), CBS, 1984.
Voice of Johnnie Throat, *The Romance of Betty Boop* (animated), CBS, 1985.
The Second City 25th Anniversary Special, HBO, 1985.
Comic Relief, HBO, 1986.
The 55th Annual King Orange Jamboree Parade, NBC, 1988.
Improv Tonight, syndicated, 1988.
"Mickey's 60th Birthday Special," *The Magical World of Disney,* NBC, 1988.
Cheers: Special 200th Episode Celebration, NBC, 1990.
"Disneyland's 35th Anniversary Celebration," *The Magical World of Disney,* NBC, 1990.
Super Bloopers and New Practical Jokes, 1990.
Time Warner Presents the Earth Day Special, ABC, 1990.

A Comedy Salute to Michael Jordan (also known as *Los Angeles and Chicago Salute to Michael Jordan*), NBC, 1991.
Dangerous (also known as *Black or White*), Fox, 1991.
"The Reluctant Vampire," *Tales from the Crypt,* HBO, 1991.
Comic Relief V, HBO, 1992.
Last Call! A Cheers' Celebration, NBC, 1993.
Comic Relief American Comedy Festival, ABC, 1996.

Television Appearances; Episodic:
The exterminator, "Latka the Playboy," *Taxi,* ABC, 1981.
American Dream, ABC, 1981.
Sergeant Tate (Hardy), "Murder Is a Drag," *Hart to Hart,* ABC, 1981.
Private La Roche, "Trick or Treatment," *M*A*S*H,* CBS, 1982.
Monty, "Monty Falls for Alice," *Alice,* CBS, 1982.
Barney Slessinger, "The World Next Door," *The Twilight Zone,* CBS, 1985.
George, "Behind Every Great Man," *Cheers,* NBC, 1985.
Norm, "Cheers," *St. Elsewhere,* NBC, 1985.
Host, *Saturday Night Live,* NBC, 1986.
Norm Peterson, *The Tortellis,* NBC, 1987.
Stan, *Day by Day,* NBC, 1989.
Norm, "The Story of Joe," *Wings,* NBC, 1990.
Host, *Saturday Night Live,* NBC, 1991.
Himself, "The Trip, Part I," *Seinfeld,* NBC, 1992.
Himself, "Hank's Night in the Sun," *The Larry Sanders Show,* HBO, 1994.
Voice of Norm Peterson, "Fear of Flying," *The Simpsons* (animated), Fox, 1994.
Himself, *Good Company* (also known as *The Cube*), CBS, 1996.
Dan Donaldson, *Spin City* (also known as *Spin*), ABC, 1996.

Appeared in episodes of *Soap,* ABC.

Television Appearances; Awards Presentations:
The 16th Annual People's Choice Awards, 1990.
The 44th Annual Primetime Emmy Awards, 1992.
The 45th Annual Primetime Emmy Awards, 1993.
The 10th Annual American Comedy Awards, 1996.

Television Appearances; Pilots:
Toonces, the Cat Who Could Drive a Car (pilot; also known as *Toonces and Friends*), NBC, 1992.

Appeared in the pilot *Nothing but Comedy,* NBC.

Film Appearances:

Student, *Somewhere in Time,* Universal, 1980.

Engineer, *My Bodyguard,* Twentieth Century-Fox, 1980.

Agent at counter, *Airplane II: The Sequel* (also known as *Flying High II*), Paramount, 1982.

Injured man, *Jekyll and Hyde . . . Together Again,* Paramount, 1982.

The Woman in Red, Orion, 1984.

Charlie Prince, *Dreamscape,* Twentieth Century-Fox, 1984.

Fat Sam, *Fletch,* Universal, 1984.

Jake, *No Small Affair,* Columbia, 1984.

Marty Morrison, *Thief of Hearts,* Paramount, 1984.

Buster, *Gung Ho* (also known as *Working Class Man*), Paramount, 1986.

Harold Gorton, *House,* New World, 1986.

Witten, *Never Say Die,* Kings Road International, 1988.

Chet Butler, *Plain Clothes* (also known as *Glory Day*), Paramount, 1988.

Bunny Baxter, *Guilty by Suspicion,* Warner Bros., 1991.

Cameo, *Masters of Menace,* RCA/Columbia Pictures Home Video, 1991.

Harry, *Forever Young,* Warner Bros., 1992.

Lumberyard clerk, *The Little Rascals,* Universal, 1994.

Chet Bronski, *The Man of the House* (also known as *Man 2 Man* and *Pals Forever*), Buena Vista, 1995.

Mr. Keller, *Space Truckers* (also known as *Star Truckers*), Goldcrest Films International, 1996.

Therapist, *The Lovemaster,* 1996.

Outside Providence, forthcoming.

Stage Appearances:

Super Sunday, Williamstown Theatre Festival, Williamstown, MA, 1988.

Tom Jones, Williamstown Theatre Festival, 1988.

Ken Finnerty, *Wild Men!,* Westside Theatre/Downstairs, New York City, 1993.

Also appeared in *Lakeboat.*

RECORDINGS

Videos:

Appeared in music videos, including Soul Asylum's *Black Gold,* 1992, Michael Jackson's *Black or White,* and Ray Parker, Jr.'s *Ghostbusters.*

OTHER SOURCES

Periodicals:

Entertainment Weekly, March 10, 1995, p. 28.*

WILLARD, Fred   1939-

PERSONAL

Born September 18, 1939, in Shaker Heights, OH. *Education:* Graduated from Virginia Military Institute.

Addresses: *Agent*—Cunningham, Escott, Dipene and Associates, 257 Park Avenue South, Suite 900, New York, NY 10010.

Career: Actor. Second City (improvisational comedy troupe), Chicago, IL, member of company; Ace Trucking Company (improvisational comedy troupe), San Francisco, CA, member; and former member of The Committee (improvisational comedy troupe).

CREDITS

Television Appearances; Series:

Regular, *The Burns and Schreiber Comedy Hour,* ABC, 1973.

Assistant District Attorney H. R. "Bud" Nugent, *Sirota's Court,* NBC, 1976-77.

Jerry Hubbard, *Forever Fernwood,* syndicated, 1977.

Jerry Hubbard, *Fernwood 2-Night,* syndicated, 1977, renamed *America 2-Night,* syndicated, 1977-78.

Host, *Real People,* NBC, 1979, then 1981-83.

Host, *What's Hot, What's Not,* 1985.

Fred, the bartender, *D.C. Follies,* syndicated, 1987-89.

Host, *Access America,* 1990.

Vice Principal Mallet, *Family Matters,* ABC, 1994-96.

President Garner, *Lois and Clark: The New Adventures of Superman,* ABC, 1995.

Television Appearances; Movies:

Lance Colson, *How to Break Up a Happy Divorce,* NBC, 1976.

Pearson, *Escape from Bogen County,* CBS, 1977.

Larry Crockett, *Salem's Lot* (also known as *Blood Thirst, Salem's Lot: The Miniseries,* and *Salem's Lot: The Movie*), CBS, 1979.

A. J. Foley, *Lots of Luck,* The Disney Channel, 1985.

Hal Harrison, *Martin Mull in Portrait of a White Marriage* (also known as *Scenes from a White Marriage*), Cinemax, 1988.

Master of ceremonies Georgie Porgie, *Mother Goose Rock 'n' Rhyme,* The Disney Channel, 1990.

"Hart to Hart: Old Friends Never Die" (also known as "Hart to Hart: Hart Attack"), *NBC Friday Night Mystery,* NBC, 1994.

Clarence Gentry, *Sodbusters,* Showtime, 1994.
Loan officer, *Back to Back: American Yakusa II* (also known as *Back to Back*), HBO, 1996.

Television Appearances; Pilots:
Bower, *Operation Greasepaint,* CBS, 1968.
Captain Thomas Woods, *Space Force,* NBC, 1978.
Jack LaRosa, *Flatbed Annie and Sweetiepie: Lady Truckers,* CBS, 1979.
Ralph, *Pen 'n' Inc.,* CBS, 1981.

Television Appearances; Episodic:
John Emil Tobin, "Tobin's Back in Town," *The Bob Newhart Show,* CBS, 1975.
"The Bonanza," *We've Got Each Other,* CBS, 1977.
Himself, *Thicke of the Night,* syndicated, 1983 and 1984.
"No More Alimony," *The Love Boat,* ABC, 1984.
Larry, "The Three Little Pigs," *Faerie Tale Theatre,* Showtime, 1985.
"Couples," *The Love Boat,* ABC, 1985.
"Home for Dinner," *George Burns Comedy Week,* CBS, 1985.
"A Friendly Christmas," *The New Love, American Style,* ABC, 1985.
"Love and the Lambergenni," *The New Love, American Style,* ABC, 1986.
"CPR," *Punky Brewster,* NBC, 1986.
"Secret Romance," *Fast Times,* CBS, 1986.
"The Box Is Missing," *Out of This World,* syndicated, 1988.
"For Old Time's Sake," *My Secret Identity,* syndicated, 1988.
Life's Most Embarrassing Moments, 1988.
Himself, *Comics Only,* 1991.
Scott, "The Wedding," *Roseanne,* ABC, 1991.
Stan, "Dinner with Anthrax," *Married . . . with Children,* Fox, 1992.
Guest performer, *The Ben Stiller Show,* Fox, 1992.
Fenton Harley, "Up All Night," *Dream On,* HBO, 1992.
Hatfield Walker, "Stand up for Bastards," *The Jackie Thomas Show,* 1993.
Bud Long, *Dave's World,* CBS, 1993.
Dick, "Dick and Dottie," *Murphy Brown,* CBS, 1995.
Scott, "December Bride," *Roseanne,* ABC, 1995.
Mr. Mitushka, *Sister, Sister,* The WB, 1995.
President Garner, "I Now Pronounce You. . .," *Lois and Clark: The New Adventures of Superman,* ABC, 1996.
Mr. Lipson, "The One after the Superbowl, Part I," *Friends,* NBC, 1996.
Scott, "Out of the Past," *Roseanne,* ABC, 1996.
Joe Pasadine, *Clueless,* ABC, 1996.

Award show host, "The Competition," *The Weird Al Show,* CBS, 1997.

Also appeared on *SCTV Network 90,* NBC.

Television Appearances; Specials:
Madhouse 90, 1972.
The Paul Lynde Comedy Hour, 1975.
Gabriel Kaplan Presents the Small Event, ABC, 1977.
NBC team member, *Battle of the Network Stars,* ABC, 1981.
Host, *Getting the Last Laugh,* 1985.
The Second City 25th Anniversary Special, HBO, 1985.
Martin Mull Live! from North Ridgeville, Ohio, HBO, 1987.
This Week Indoors, 1987.
Merrill Markoe's Guide to Glamorous Living, Cinemax, 1988.
Superman's 50th Anniversary: A Celebration of the Man of Steel, 1988.
The 14th Annual Circus of the Stars, CBS, 1989.
The 3rd Annual American Comedy Awards, 1989.
Candid Camera . . . Funny Money, CBS, 1990.
Candid Camera . . . Smile, You're on Vacation!, CBS, 1990.
Louise DuArt: The Secret Life of Barry's Wife, Showtime, 1991.
Host, *Real People Reunion Special,* NBC, 1991.
"Rodney Dangerfield's The Really Big Show," *HBO Comedy Hour,* HBO, 1991.
Tom Arnold: The Naked Truth, HBO, 1991.
The 5th Annual American Comedy Awards, 1991.
A Spinal Tap Reunion, NBC, 1992.
Subaru Presents Fair Enough: Martin Mull at the Iowa State Fair, Comedy Central, 1994.
steve.oedekerk.com (comedy special), NBC, 1997.

Other Television Appearances:
The History of White People in America: Volume I, Cinemax, 1985.
The History of White People in America: Volume II, Cinemax, 1986.

Film Appearances:
Jenny (also known as *And Jenny Makes Three*), Cinerama, 1969.
Gas station attendant, *The Model Shop,* Columbia, 1969.
Member of the Ace Trucking Company, *The Harrad Experiment,* Cinerama, 1973.
Harrad Summer (also known as *Student Union*), Cinerama, 1974.
Interrogator, *Hustle,* Paramount, 1975.

Jerry Jarvis, *Silver Streak,* Twentieth Century-Fox, 1976.
FBI agent Peter, *Chesty Anderson, U.S. Navy* (also known as *Anderson's Angels* and *Chesty Anderson, U.S.N.*), Atlas, 1976.
Bob, *Fun with Dick and Jane,* Columbia, 1977.
Cracking Up, American International, 1977.
Vanderhoff, *Americathon,* United Artists, 1979.
Presidential Assistant Feebleman, *First Family,* Warner Bros., 1980.
Robert, *How to Beat the High Cost of Living,* American International, 1980.
President Fogarty, "Success Wanters," *National Lampoon Goes to the Movies* (also known as *National Lampoon's Movie Madness*), Movies Unlimited, 1981.
Himself, *Second City Insanity,* Lorimar Home Video, 1981.
Lieutenant Hookstratten, *This Is Spinal Tap* (also known as *Spinal Tap*), Embassy, 1984.
Terrence "Doc" Williams, *Moving Violations,* Twentieth Century-Fox, 1985.
Himself, *Big City Comedy,* LIVE Home Video, 1986.
Mayor Deebs, *Roxanne,* Columbia, 1987.
Tom Osborne, *Ray's Male Heterosexual Dance Hall,* Chanticleer Films, 1987.
Insurance salesman, *High Strung,* Rocket Pictures, 1991.
Thomas MacGregor, *Prehistoria! 3* (also known as *Prehysteria 3*), Paramount Home Video, 1995.
Ron Albertson, *Waiting for Guffman* (also known as *The Christopher Guest Project*), Sony Pictures Classics, 1996.

Stage Appearances:
The Return of the Second City in "20,000 Frozen Grenadiers," Square East Theatre, New York City, 1966.
Arf, Stage 73, New York City, 1969.
Little Murders, Circle in the Square, New York City, 1969.
Elvis and Juliet, Theatre at the Improv, Los Angeles, 1994.

WRITINGS

Television Specials:
Getting the Last Laugh, 1985.*

WILLIAMSON, Fred 1937(?)-

PERSONAL

Born March 5, 1937 (some sources say 1938), in Gary, IN; married, wife's name, Linda. *Education:*

Northwestern University, B.A. (architectural engineering), 1960.

Addresses: *Agent*—10880 Wilshire Blvd., Suite 1101, Los Angeles, CA 90024.

Career: Actor, director, producer, and screenwriter. Professional football player, with San Francisco Forty-Niners, 1962-64, Kansas City Chiefs, 1964-67, and Oakland Raiders, 1967-71. Architect.

CREDITS

Film Appearances:
(Film debut) Captain Oliver Harmon "Spearchucker" Jones, *M*A*S*H,* Twentieth Century-Fox, 1970.
Beach boy, *Tell Me That You Love Me, Junie Moon,* Paramount, 1970.
B. J. Hammer, *Hammer,* United Artists, 1972.
Nigger Charley, *The Legend of Nigger Charley,* Paramount, 1972.
Tommy Gibbs, *Black Caesar* (also known as *The Godfather of Harlem*), American International, 1973.
Tommy Gibbs, *Hell Up in Harlem,* American International, 1973.
Charley, *The Soul of Nigger Charley,* Paramount, 1973.
Jefferson Bolt, *That Man Bolt* (also known as *To Kill a Dragon* and *Thunderbolt*), Universal, 1973.
Stone, *Black Eye,* Warner Bros., 1974.
Boss Nigger, *Boss Nigger* (also known as *Boss, The Black Bounty Hunter,* and *The Black Bounty Killer*), Dimension, 1974.
Willy, *Crazy Joe,* Columbia, 1974.
Jagger Daniels, *Three the Hard Way,* Allied Artists, 1974.
Joe Snake, *Three Tough Guys* (also known as *Uomini Duri*), Paramount, 1974.
Ben, *Adios Amigo,* Atlas, 1975.
Duke, *Bucktown,* American International, 1975.
Tyree, *Take a Hard Ride* (also known as *La Lunga Cavalcata*), Twentieth Century-Fox, 1975.
Darktown, 1975.
Johnny Barrows, *Mean Johnny Barrows,* Atlas, 1976.
Jess Crowder, *No Way Back,* Atlas, 1976.
Joshua, *Joshua* (also known as *Black Rider* and *Joshua the Black Rider*), Lone Star, 1976.
Jess Crowder, *Death Journey,* Unicorn Video, 1976.
Mr. Mean, *Mr. Mean,* 1977.
Jesse Crowder, *Blind Rage,* Metro-Goldwyn-Mayer Home Video, 1978.
Express to Terror, Prism Entertainment, 1979.

Himself, *Fist of Fear, Touch of Death* (documentary), Aquarius, 1980.

Fred, *Counterfeit Commandoes* (also known as *Deadly Mission, Hell's Heroes, Quel Maledetto Treno Blindato,* and *Inglorious Bastards*), Aquarius, 1981.

Cal, *One Down, Two to Go,* Almi, 1982.

Frank Hooks, *The Big Score,* Almi, 1983.

Jesse Crowder, *The Last Fight,* Best Film and Video, 1983.

Nick Coleman, *Vigilante* (also known as *Street Gang*), Film Ventures, 1983.

The Ogre, *1990: The Bronx Warriors* (also known as *1990: I Guerrieri del Bronx* and *Bronx Warriors*), United Film Distribution, 1983.

Nadir, *The New Barbarians* (also known as *Metropolis 2000, I Nuovi Barbari* and *Warriors of the Wasteland*), Deaf International, 1983.

Lou, *Deadly Impact* (also known as *Impatto Mortale* and *Giant Killer*), LIVE Home Video, 1983.

Rome, *2072 A.D.—The New Gladiators* (also known as *Warriors of the Year 2072, The New Gladiators, Fighting Centurions,* and *I Guerrieri dell Anno 2072*), Media Home Entertainment, 1983.

Noah, *Vivre pour Survivre* (also known as *White Fire*), Trans-World Entertainment, 1984.

Henchman, *Warrior of the Lost World,* Visto International/ADI, 1985.

Thomas Fox, *Foxtrap,* Snizzlefritz, 1986.

Jake Sebastian Turner, *The Messenger,* Snizzlefritz, 1987.

The Black Cobra, Trans-World Entertainment, 1987.

Curt Slate, *Deadly Intent,* Fries Distribution, 1988.

Captain Beck, *Delta Force Commando,* Vestron Video, 1989.

The Black Cobra 2, Hemdale Home Video, 1989.

Robert Malone, *Black Cobra III: The Manila Connection* (also known as *Cobra nero*), Hemdale Home Video, 1990.

Sergeant Soda Cracker, *The Kill Reflex,* Columbia TriStar Home Video, 1990.

Detective Malone, 1990.

Captain Sam Beck, *Delta Force Commando 2: Priority Red One,* LIVE Home Video, 1991.

John Steele, *Steele's Law,* Academy, 1991.

Calvin Sims, *Three Days to a Kill,* HBO Home Video, 1992.

Mack Derringer, *South Beach,* Prism Entertainment, 1993.

Sheriff Mantee, *Silent Hunter,* New Line Home Video, 1995.

Frost, *From Dusk till Dawn,* Dimension, 1996.

John Bookman, *Original Gangstas* (also known as *Hot City*), Orion, 1996.

Himself, *Full Tilt Boogie,* Miramax, 1997.

Paulie Solano, *Whatever It Takes,* Full Moon Entertainment, 1998.

Sheriff Skaggs, *Children of the Corn: Field of Screams,* Dimension, 1998.

Also appeared in *Justice Done.*

Film Work:

Producer (with Jack Arnold), *Boss Nigger* (also known as *Boss, The Black Bounty Hunter,* and *The Black Bounty Killer*), Dimension, 1974.

Producer and director, *Adios Amigo,* Atlas, 1975.

Producer and director, *Mean Johnny Barrows,* Atlas, 1976.

Producer and director, *No Way Back,* Atlas, 1976.

Producer and director, *Death Journey,* Unicorn Video, 1976.

Producer and director, *Mr. Mean,* 1977.

Producer and director, *One Down, Two to Go,* Almi, 1982.

Director, *The Big Score,* Almi, 1983.

Director, *The Last Fight,* Best Film and Video, 1983.

Producer and director, *Foxtrap,* Snizzlefritz, 1986.

Producer (with Pier Luigi Ciriaci) and director, *The Messenger,* Snizzlefritz, 1987.

Producer and director, *The Kill Reflex,* Columbia TriStar Home Video, 1990.

Producer and director, *Steele's Law,* Academy, 1991.

Producer and director, *Three Days to a Kill,* HBO Home Video, 1992.

Producer (with Krishma Shah) and director, *South Beach,* Prism Entertainment, 1993.

Director, *Silent Hunter,* New Line Home Video, 1995.

Producer, *Original Gangstas* (also known as *Hot City*), Orion, 1996.

Also directed the film *Justice Done.*

Television Appearances; Series:

Steve Bruce, *Julia,* NBC, 1970-71.

Commentator, *Monday Night Football,* ABC, 1974.

Chester Long, *Half Nelson,* NBC, 1985.

Lowell Carter, *Fast Track,* Showtime, 1997.

Tim Hastings, *BLACK JACK from John Woo,* USA Network, 1998—.

Television Appearances; Episodic:

Anka, "The Cloudminders," *Star Trek,* NBC, 1969.

Julia, NBC, 1969.

"Dangerous Games," *Police Story,* NBC, 1973.

"Johnny Lost His Gun," *The Rookies,* ABC, 1974.

"Thanksgiving," *Police Story,* NBC, 1976.

Lieutenant Mason Warren, "Reign of Terror," *The Equalizer*, 1985.

Also appeared in an episode of *Lou Grant*.

Television Appearances; Movies:
Williams, *Deadlock*, NBC, 1969.

Television Appearances; Miniseries:
Leonard Wingate, *Wheels* (also known as *Arthur Hailey's Wheels*), NBC, 1979.

Television Appearances; Pilots:
Chester Long, *Half Nelson*, NBC, 1985.

WRITINGS

Screenplays:
Boss Nigger (also known as *Boss, The Black Bounty Hunter,* and *The Black Bounty Killer*), Dimension, 1974.
Adios Amigo, Atlas, 1975.
No Way Back, Atlas, 1976.
Joshua, Lone Star, 1976.
The Last Fight, Best Film and Video, 1983.

OTHER SOURCES

Periodicals:
Premiere, April, 1996, p. 43.

WILSON, Colleen Camp
    See CAMP, Colleen

WINNINGHAM, Mare   1959-

PERSONAL

Born Mary Winningham, May 16, 1959, in Phoenix, AZ; raised in California; daughter of two educators; married Bill Maple (a television technical advisor); five children, including: Riley, Paddy, Jack, Calla Louise. *Education:* Attended California State University, Northridge.

Addresses: *Agent*—William Morris Agency, 151 El Camino Drive, Beverly Hills, CA 90212.

Career: Actress. Also singer and songwriter of contemporary folk music.

Awards, Honors: Emmy Award, 1980, for *Amber Waves;* Emmy Award nomination, 1986, for *Love Is Never Silent;* Academy Award nomination, best supporting actress, Independent Spirit Award, best supporting actress, Screen Actors Guild Award nominee, outstanding performance by an actress in a supporting role, all 1996, for *Georgia;* Emmy Award nomination, outstanding supporting actress in a miniseries or special, 1996, for "The Boys Next Door," *Hallmark Hall of Fame;* Golden Globe nominee, best performance by an actress in a supporting role in a series, miniseries, or motion picture, 1997, for *George Wallace.*

CREDITS

Film Appearances:
Modena Dandridge, *One Trick Pony*, Warner Bros., 1980.
Carol Severance, *Threshold*, Twentieth Century-Fox, 1981.
Wendy, *St. Elmo's Fire*, Columbia, 1985.
Pat, *Nobody's Fool*, Island, 1986.
Candy, *Shy People*, Cannon, 1987.
Brenda Carlucci, *Made in Heaven*, Lorimar, 1987.
Julie Peters, *Miracle Mile*, Hemdale, 1989.
Emily Carson, *Turner and Hooch*, Buena Vista, 1989.
Dawn, *Hard Promises*, Columbia, 1991.
Mattie Earp, *Wyatt Earp*, Warner Bros., 1994.
Lois, *The War*, Universal, 1994.
Singer, *Teresa's Tattoo* (also known as *Natural Selection*), Vidmark Entertainment, 1994.
Title role (also song performer of "Hard Times," "If I Wanted," and "Mercy"), *Georgia*, Miramax, 1995.
Bad Day on the Block (also known as *Under Pressure*), Largo Entertainment, 1997.

Television Appearances; Movies:
Janice Gallitzin, *Special Olympics* (also known as *A Special Kind of Love*), CBS, 1978.
Jenny Flowers, *The Death of Ocean View Park*, ABC, 1979.
Marlene Burkhardt, *Amber Waves*, ABC, 1980.
Chris, *The Women's Room*, ABC, 1980.
Michele Johansen, *Off the Minnesota Strip*, ABC, 1980.
Locksley Claitor, *A Few Days in Weasel Creek*, CBS, 1981.
Libby Bellow (song performer of title song), *Freedom*, ABC, 1981.
Kate Bradshaw, *Missing Children: A Mother's Story*, CBS, 1982.
Title role, *Helen Keller: The Miracle Continues*, syndicated, 1984.

Bootsie, *Single Bars, Single Women,* ABC, 1984.

Margaret Ryder, *Love Is Never Silent,* NBC, 1985.

Mary Frances Beaudine/Julia, *Who Is Julia?,* CBS, 1986.

Annie, *A Winner Never Quits,* ABC, 1986.

Ethel Hollars Lee, *Eye on the Sparrow,* NBC, 1987.

Theresa Johnson, *God Bless the Child,* ABC, 1988.

Nicole Rougeron, *Crossing to Freedom* (also known as *Pied Piper*), CBS, 1990.

Kim Paris, *True Betrayal* (also known as *Love and Lies* and *The Kim Paris Story*), ABC, 1990.

Prudence Crandall, *She Stood Alone* (also known as *A Mighty Fortress*), NBC, 1991.

Jamie Hurd, *Fatal Exposure,* USA Network, 1991.

Faye, *Those Secrets,* ABC, 1992.

Kit Kellner, *Better Off Dead,* Lifetime, 1993.

Dana, *Betrayed By Love* (also known as *The Susan Daniels Smith Murder*), ABC, 1994.

Judy Parma, *Letter to My Killer,* USA Network, 1995.

Sheila, "The Boys Next Door," *Hallmark Hall of Fame,* CBS, 1996.

Elaine Hodges, *The Deliverance of Elaine* (also known as *Pen Pals*), CBS, 1996.

Lurleen Wallace, *George Wallace,* TNT, 1997.

Television Appearances; Miniseries:

Studs Lonigan, NBC, 1979.

Justine O'Neill, *The Thorn Birds,* NBC, 1979, ABC, 1983.

Mary Wilkes, *Intruders* (also known as *They Are Among Us*), CBS, 1992.

Television Appearances; Specials:

Nettie Peters, *A Young Pioneer's Christmas,* ABC, 1976.

Aggie Modgelewsky, *Steeltown,* 1979.

Beth, *One Too Many,* CBS, 1985.

Marla (song performer of "Well It's Gone"), *Sexual Healing,* Showtime, 1993.

Television Appearances; Series:

(Television debut, as singer/performer) *The Gong Show,* syndicated, 1975.

Nettie Peters, *The Young Pioneers,* ABC, 1977-78.

Television Appearances; Episodic:

"Button, Button," *The Twilight Zone,* CBS, 1986.

Sarah, the single mom, *Mad About You,* NBC, 1990.

Stage Appearances:

Gilly Brown, *The Genius,* Center Theatre Group, Mark Taper Forum, Los Angeles, CA, 1984.

RECORDINGS

Albums:

(Debut solo album) *What Might Be,* Bay Cities Records, 1992.

Georgia (movie soundtrack), Discovery Records, 1996.*

ZABKA, Billy
   See ZABKA, William

ZABKA, William   1965-
   (Billy Zabka)

PERSONAL

Born October 20, 1965, in New York, NY; son of Stan Zabka (an assistant director); mother, a production assistant. *Education:* Studied advanced guitar and music theory at California State University, Northridge. *Avocational interests:* Surfing, backpacking, rafting, horseback riding, skiing, karate, soccer, swimming, deep-sea diving.

Career: Actor. Appeared in more than twenty television commercials from the age of twelve. Green-belt in karate.

CREDITS

Film Appearances:

Stand-in, *The Island,* Universal, 1980.

(Film debut) Johnny, *The Karate Kid,* Columbia, 1984.

Greg, *Just One of the Guys,* Columbia, 1985.

Jack, *National Lampoon's European Vacation,* Warner Bros., 1985.

Chas, *Back to School,* Orion, 1986.

Johnny, *The Karate Kid, Part II,* Columbia, 1986.

Randy, *A Tiger's Tale,* Atlantic, 1987.

Ruben, *Shootfighter: Fight to the Death,* Columbia TriStar Home Video, 1993.

Howie, *Unlawful Passage,* York Home Video, 1994.

Raymond Vonn, *The Power Within,* PM Entertainment Group, 1995.

Ruben, *Shootfighter 2: Kill or Be Killed,* Columbia TriStar Home Video, 1996.

Alexander, *To the Ends of Time,* Imperial Entertainment, 1996.

Bulldog, *High Voltage,* 1997.

Peyote Brothers, forthcoming.

Film Work; Director:
B-Movie, 1997.
Peyote Brothers, forthcoming.

Television Appearances; Series:
Scott McCall, *The Equalizer,* CBS, 1986-89.

Television Appearances; Movies:
Emergency Room, syndicated, 1983.
Kim Fisher, *Dreams of Gold: The Mel Fisher Story,*
    CBS, 1986.

Television Appearances; Episodic:
(As Billy Zabka) Clarence Mortner Jr., "Space Ranger,"
    The Greatest American Hero, ABC, 1983.
Druggie kid, *E/R,* CBS, 1984.

Appeared on episodes of *Gimme a Break,* NBC, and
The Love Boat, ABC.

Television Appearances; Specials:
Rick Peterson, "Contract for Life: The S.A.D.D. Story,"
    CBS Schoolbreak Specials, CBS, 1984.

Television Appearances; Pilots:
Russell Cooper, *Protect and Surf* (also known as
    Monster Manor), ABC, 1989.

WRITINGS

Screenplays:
Peyote Brothers, forthcoming.*

Cumulative Index

To provide continuity with *Who's Who in the Theatre*, this index interfiles references to *Who's Who in the Theatre*, 1st-17th Editions, and *Who Was Who in the Theatre* (Gale, 1978) with references to *Contemporary Theatre, Film and Television*, Volumes 1-18.

References in the index are identified as follows:

CTFT and volume number—*Contemporary Theatre, Film and Television*, Volumes 1-18
WWT and edition number—*Who's Who in the Theatre*, 1st-17th Editions
WWasWT—*Who Was Who in the Theatre*

Cumulative Index

Craig, Edward Gordon
1872-1966 .... WWasWT
Craig, Helen 1912-1986 .... WWT-17
Craig, Michael 1928- WWT-17
Craig, Stuart 1942- CTFT-12
Craig, Wendy 1934- WWT-17
Crane, Richard 1944- CTFT-6
    Earlier sketch in WWT-17
Crane, W. H. 1845-1928 .... WWasWT
Cranham, Kenneth 1944- CTFT-11
    Earlier sketch in WWT-17
Crauford, J. R. 1847-1930 .... WWasWT
Craven, Arthur Scott 1875-1971 ... WWasWT
Craven, Elise 1898- .... WWasWT
Craven, Frank 1880-1945 .... WWasWT
Craven, Gemma 1950- CTFT-2
    Earlier sketch in WWT-17
Craven, Tom 1868-1919 .... WWasWT
Craven, Wes 1939- CTFT-15
    Earlier sketch in CTFT-6
Crawford, Alice 1882- .... WWasWT
Crawford, Anne 1920-1956 .... WWasWT
Crawford, Cheryl 1902-1986 .... CTFT-4
    Earlier sketch in WWT-17
Crawford, Cindy 1966- CTFT-15
Crawford, Joanna 1942- CTFT-4
Crawford, Michael 1942- CTFT-11
    Earlier sketches in CTFT 3; WWT-17
Crawford, Mimi ?-1966 .... WWasWT
Crawley, Tom 1940- CTFT-2
Creedon, Dennis 1880-? .... WWasWT
Cregan, David 1931- CTFT-6
    Earlier sketch in WWT-17
Crenna, Richard 1927- CTFT-16
    Earlier sketch in CTFT-3
Cressall, Maud 1886-1962 .... WWasWT
Cresswell, Helen 1934- CTFT-15
Crews, Laura Hope 1880-1942 ..... WWasWT
Cribbins, Bernard 1928- CTFT-6
    Earlier sketch in WWT-17
Crichton, Charles 1910- CTFT-8
Crichton, Madge 1881-? .... WWasWT
Crichton, Michael 1942- CTFT-13
    Earlier sketch in CTFT-5
Crinkley, Richmond 1940-1989 .... CTFT-8
    Earlier sketch in WWT-17
Crisham, Walter .... WWasWT
Crisp, Quentin 1908- CTFT-6
Crispi, Ida .... WWasWT
Crist, Judith 1922- CTFT-1
Cristina, Ines 1875-? .... WWasWT
Cristofer, Michael 1945- CTFT-3
    Earlier sketch in WWT-17
Critchlow, Roark CTFT-17
Critt, C. J. 1954- CTFT-1
Croce, Arlene 1934- CTFT-15
Crofoot, Leonard J. CTFT-1
Croft, Anne 1896-1959 .... WWasWT
Croft, Michael 1922-1986 .... WWT-17
Croft, Nita 1902- .... WWasWT
Croft, Paddy CTFT-10
    Earlier sketch in WWT-17
Croisset, Francis de 1877-1937 ..... WWasWT
Croke, Wentworth 1871-1930 .... WWasWT
Croker, T. F. Dillon 1831-1912 .... WWasWT

Croker-King, C. H. 1873-1951 ...... WWasWT
Crommelynck, Fernand
1885-1970 .... WWasWT
Cromwell, James 1940- CTFT-17
Cromwell, John 1887-1979 .... WWT-17
Cronenberg, David 1943- CTFT-14
    Earlier sketch in CTFT-6
Cronin, Jane 1936- CTFT-3
Cronkite, Walter 1916- CTFT-6
Cronyn, Hume 1911- CTFT-17
    Earlier sketches in CTFT-1, 7; WWT-17
Cronyn, Tandy 1945- CTFT-9
    Earlier sketch in CTFT-1
Crook, John ?-1922 .... WWasWT
Cropper, Anna 1938- WWT-17
Cropper, Roy 1898-1954 .... WWasWT
Crosby, Cathy Lee 1948- CTFT-15
Crosby, Denise CTFT-8
Crosby, Gary 1933-1995 .... CTFT-7
    Obituary in CTFT-15
Crosby, Joan 1934- CTFT-12
Crosby, Mary 1959- CTFT-18
    Earlier sketch in CTFT-5
    Brief Entry in CTFT-2
Crosman, Henrietta 1865-1944 ..... WWasWT
Cross, Ben 1947- CTFT-6
Cross, Beverley 1931- CTFT-6
    Earlier sketch in WWT-17
Cross, Julian 1851-1925 .... WWasWT
Croswell, Anne CTFT-1
Crothers, Rachel 1878-1958 .... WWasWT
Crothers, Scatman 1910-1986 .... CTFT-3
Crouch, J. H. 1918- CTFT-1
Crouse, Lindsay 1948- CTFT-4
Crouse, Russel 1893-1966 .... WWasWT
Crow, Laura 1945- CTFT-5
Crowden, Graham 1922- CTFT-9
    Earlier sketch in WWT-17
Crowder, Jack
    See Rasulala, Thalmus CTFT-10
Crowe, Cameron 1957- CTFT-13
Crowe, Christopher 1948- CTFT-14
    Earlier sketch in CTFT-4
Crowe, Russell 1964(?)- CTFT-16
Crowley, Mart 1935- WWT-17
Crowley, Pat CTFT-8
Crowley, Patricia
    See Crowley, Pat CTFT-8
Crowther, Leslie 1933- WWT-17
Croxton, Arthur 1868-? .... WWasWT
Crudup, Billy 1968(?)- CTFT-17
Cruickshank, Andrew 1907-1988 ...... CTFT-7
    Earlier sketch in WWT-17
Cruickshank, Gladys 1902- .... WWasWT
Cruikshank, A. Stewart 1877-1949 .. WWasWT
Cruikshank, Stewart 1908-1966 .... WWasWT
Cruikshanks, Charles 1844-1928 ... WWasWT
Cruise, Tom 1962- CTFT-16
    Earlier sketches in CTFT-3, 9
    Brief Entry in CTFT-2
Crust, Arnold
    See Winner, Michael CTFT-11
Crutchley, Rosalie 1921-1997 .... CTFT-8
    Obituary in CTFT-18
    Earlier sketch in WWasWT

Cruttwell, Hugh 1918- WWT-17
Cryer, David 1936- WWT-17
Cryer, Gretchen 1935- CTFT-4
    Earlier sketch in WWT-17
Cryer, Jon 1965- CTFT-16
    Earlier sketch in CTFT-4
Crystal, Billy 1947- CTFT-18
    Earlier sketches in CTFT-3, 10
Cuka, Frances 1936- CTFT-6
    Earlier sketch in WWT-17
Cukor, George 1899-1983 .... CTFT-1
Culhane, Shamus 1908- CTFT-10
Culkin, Macaulay 1980(?)- CTFT-10
Cullen, David 1942- CTFT-14
    Earlier sketch in CTFT-6
Culley, Frederick 1879-1942 .... WWasWT
Culliton, Joseph 1948- CTFT-2
Culliver, Karen 1959- CTFT-18
    Earlier sketch in CTFT-2
Cullum, John 1930- CTFT-13
    Earlier sketches in CTFT-4; WWT-17
Culp, Robert 1930- CTFT-14
    Earlier sketch in CTFT-3
Culver, Roland 1900-1984 .... WWT-17
Cumberland, Gerald 1879-1926 ...WWasWT
Cumberland, John 1880-? .... WWasWT
Cummings, Bob 1910(?)-1990 .... CTFT-17
    Earlier sketch in CTFT-1
Cummings, Constance 1910- CTFT-4
    Earlier sketch in WWT-17
Cummings, Robert
    See Cummings, Bob CTFT-17
Cummings, Vicki 1913-1969 .... WWasWT
Cummins, Peggy 1925- .... WWasWT
Cundey, Dean CTFT-11
Cuningham, Philip 1865-? .... WWasWT
Cunliffe, Whit .... WWasWT
Cunningham, John 1932- CTFT-10
Cunningham, Robert 1866-? ....WWasWT
Cunningham, Sarah 1919-1986 .... CTFT-3
Cupito, Suzanne
    See Brittany, Morgan CTFT-7
Curel, Viscomte Francois de
1854-1928 .... WWasWT
Currah, Brian Mason 1929- WWT-17
Curran, Leigh 1943- CTFT-5
Currie, Clive 1877-1935 .... WWasWT
Currie, Finlay 1878-1968 .... WWasWT
Currie, Glenne 1926- CTFT-1
Curry, Julian 1937- CTFT-11
    Earlier sketch in WWT-17
Curry, Tim 1946- CTFT-17
    Earlier sketch in CTFT-7
Curteis, Ian 1935- CTFT-10
Curtin, Jane 1947- CTFT-16
    Earlier sketch in CTFT-3
Curtin, Valerie 1945(?)- CTFT-18
    Earlier sketch in CTFT-7
Curtis, Dan 1928- CTFT-10
Curtis, Jamie Lee 1958- CTFT-13
    Earlier sketch in CTFT-6
Curtis, Keene 1923- CTFT-2
    Earlier sketch in WWT-17
Curtis, Ken 1916-1991 .... CTFT-10
Curtis, Richard 1956- CTFT-15

E

F

Gargan, William (Dennis)
　1905-1979 .... WWasWT
Garland, Beverly CTFT-1
Garland, Geoff 1926- CTFT-1
Garland, Patrick 1935- CTFT-13
　Earlier sketch in WWT-17
Garland, Robert 1895-1955 .... WWasWT
Garner, James 1928- CTFT-9
　Earlier sketch in CTFT-3
Garnett, Edward 1868-1937 .... WWasWT
Garnett, Gale CTFT-1
Garofalo, Janeane 1965(?)- CTFT-15
Garr, Teri 1949(?)- CTFT-18
　Earlier sketches in CTFT-3, 10
Garr, Terry
　See Garr, Teri CTFT-18
Garrett, Arthur 1869-1941 .... WWasWT
Garrett, Betty 1919- CTFT-4
　Earlier sketch in WWT-17
Garrett, Joy CTFT-1
Garrick, Gus .... WWasWT
Garrick, John 1902- .... WWasWT
Garrison, David 1952- CTFT-4
Garside, John 1887-1958 .... WWasWT
Garson, Barbara 1941- CTFT-1
Garson, Greer 1903-1996 .... CTFT-8
　Obituary in CTFT-16
　Earlier sketch in WWasWT
Gary, Lorraine CTFT-7
Gascoigne, Bamber 1935- WWT-17
Gascon, Jean 1921-1988 .... WWT-17
Gaskill, William 1930- CTFT-3
　Earlier sketch in WWT-17
Gaspard, Ray
　See Gaspard, Raymond L. CTFT-9
Gaspard, Raymond L. 1949- CTFT-9
　Earlier sketch in CTFT-1
Gassman, Vittorio 1922- CTFT-8
Gassner, Dennis CTFT-11
Gassner, John 1903-1967 .... WWasWT
Gates, Eleanor 1875-1951 .... WWasWT
Gates, Jesse Stuart
　See McFadden, Gates CTFT-16
Gates, Larry 1915- WWT-17
Gateson, Marjorie
　1897-1977 .... WWasWT
Gatti, John M. 1872-1929 .... WWasWT
Gaudet, Christie 1957- CTFT-4
Gaul, George 1885-1939 .... WWasWT
Gaunt, William 1937- WWT-17
Gavault, Paul 1867-? .... WWasWT
Gavin, John 1932- CTFT-2
Gawthorne, Peter A.
　1884-1962 .... WWasWT
Gaxton, William 1893-1963 .... WWasWT
Gay, John 1924- CTFT-9
Gay, Maisie 1883-1945 .... WWasWT
Gay, Noel 1898-1954 .... WWasWT
Gaye, Freda 1907-1986 .... CTFT-4
　Earlier sketch in WWasWT
Gaynes, George 1917- CTFT-8
　Earlier sketch in WWT-17
Gaythorne, Pamela 1882-? .... WWasWT
Gazzara, Ben 1930- CTFT-3
　Earlier sketch in WWT-17

Gazzo, Michael V. 1923-1995 .... CTFT-8
　Obituary in CTFT-14
　Earlier sketch in CTFT-1
Gear, Luella 1899- .... WWasWT
Geary, Anthony 1947- CTFT-18
　Earlier sketch in CTFT-6
　Brief Entry in CTFT-2
Gedrick, Jason 1965- CTFT-14
　Earlier sketch in CTFT-7
Gee, George 1895-1959 .... WWasWT
Gee, Shirley 1932- CTFT-12
Geer, Ellen 1941- CTFT-1
Geer, Will 1902-1978 .... WWT-16
Geeson, Judy 1948- CTFT-8
Geffen, David 1943- CTFT-5
Gelb, Arthur 1924- CTFT-1
Gelb, Barbara CTFT-1
Gelbart, Larry 1928- CTFT-10
　Earlier sketches in CTFT-1, 3; WWT-17
Gelber, Jack 1932- CTFT-5
　Earlier sketch in WWT-17
Geller, Marc 1959- CTFT-1
Gellner, Julius 1899- WWT-17
Gelman-Waxer, Libby
　See Rudnick, Paul CTFT-15
Gemier, Firmin 1865-1933 .... WWasWT
Gemmell, Don 1903- WWT-17
Gems, Pam 1925- CTFT-6
　Earlier sketch in WWT-17
Genee, Dame Adeline
　1878-1970 .... WWasWT
Genet, Jean 1910-1986 .... CTFT-3
　Earlier sketch in WWT-17
Geniat, Marchell ?-1959 .... WWasWT
Genn, Leo 1905-1978 .... WWT-16
Gennaro, Peter 1919- CTFT-4
George, A. E. 1869-1920 .... WWasWT
George, Chief Dan 1899-1981 .... CTFT-17
George, Colin 1929- CTFT-18
　Earlier sketches in CTFT-2; WWT-17
George, Dan
　See George, Chief Dan CTFT-17
George, Gladys 1904-1954 .... WWasWT
George, Grace 1879-1961 .... WWasWT
George, Lynda Day 1946- CTFT-8
George, Marie 1879-1955 .... WWasWT
George, Muriel 1883-1965 .... WWasWT
Gerald, Ara 1900-1957 .... WWasWT
Geraldy, Paul 1885-? .... WWasWT
Gerard, Gil 1943- CTFT-6
Gerard, Teddie 1892-1942 .... WWasWT
Geray, Steve 1904-1973 .... WWasWT
Gerber, Ella 1916- CTFT-1
Gerdes, George 1948- CTFT-4
Gere, Richard 1949- CTFT-13
　Earlier sketches in CTFT-2, 6
German, Edward 1862-1936 .... WWasWT
Germann, Greg CTFT-17
Gerrard Gene 1892-1971 .... WWasWT
Gerringer, Robert 1926-1989 .... CTFT-2
Gerrity, Dan 1958- CTFT-7
Gerroll, Daniel 1951- CTFT-5
　Earlier sketch in CTFT-1
Gershon, Gina CTFT-15
Gershwin, George 1898-1937 .... WWasWT

Gershwin, Ira 1896-1983 .... WWasWT
Gerson, Carlotta
　See Mazursky, Paul CTFT-14
Gerstad, John 1924- WWT-17
Gersten, Bernard 1923- CTFT-5
　Earlier sketch in WWT-17
Gertz, Jami 1965- CTFT-14
　Earlier sketch in CTFT-7
Gerussi, Bruno .... WWasWT
Gest, Morris 1881-1942 .... WWasWT
Gets, Malcolm CTFT-17
Getty, Estelle 1923- CTFT-14
　Earlier sketch in CTFT-6
Geva, Tamara 1907- .... WWasWT
Gheusi, Pierre B. 1867-? .... WWasWT
Ghostley, Alice 1926- CTFT-2
　Earlier sketch in WWT-17
Giagni, D. J. 1950- CTFT-4
Giannini, Giancarlo 1942- CTFT-7
Giannini, Olga .... WWasWT
Gibb, Lee
　See Waterhouse, Keith Spencer .. CTFT-5
Gibbons, Arthur 1871-1935 .... WWasWT
Gibbons, Leeza 1957- CTFT-17
Gibbs, Marla 1931(?)- CTFT-15
　Earlier sketch in CTFT-3
Gibbs, Nancy ?-1956 .... WWasWT
Gibbs, Timothy 1967- CTFT-5
Gibson, Brenda 1870-? .... WWasWT
Gibson, Chloe 1899- .... WWasWT
Gibson, Henry 1935- CTFT-3
Gibson, Mel 1956- CTFT-13
　Earlier sketch in CTFT-6
Gibson, Michael 1944- CTFT-5
Gibson, Thomas 1963(?)- CTFT-17
Gibson, William 1914- CTFT-2
　Earlier sketch in WWT-17
Gibson, William 1948- CTFT-15
Gibson, Wynne 1905-1987 .... WWasWT
Giddens, George 1845-1920 .... WWasWT
Gideon, Melville J. 1884-1933 ..... WWasWT
Gielgud, John 1904- CTFT-14
　Earlier sketches in CTFT-1, 7; WWT-17
Gielgud, Val 1900-1981 .... WWasWT
Gierasch, Stefan 1926- CTFT-10
Gignoux, Regis 1878-? .... WWasWT
Gilbert, Bruce 1947- CTFT-9
　Earlier sketch in CTFT-1
Gilbert, Jean 1879-1943 .... WWasWT
Gilbert, Lewis 1920- CTFT-9
Gilbert, Lou 1909-1978 .... WWT-17
Gilbert, Melissa 1964- CTFT-14
　Earlier sketch in CTFT-5
　Brief Entry in CTFT-2
Gilbert, Olive WWT-17
Gilbert, Ronnie 1926- CTFT-18
　Earlier sketch in CTFT-2
Gilbert, Sara 1975(?)- CTFT-13
Gilbert-Brinkman, Melissa
　See Gilbert, Melissa CTFT-14
Gilder, Rosamond de Kay
　1891-1986 .... CTFT-4
　Earlier sketch in WWT-17
Gilford, Jack 1907(?)-1990 .... CTFT-11
　Earlier sketches in CTFT-2; WWT-17

Cumulative Index

H

I

K

L

M

Menken, Alan 1949- CTFT-11
Menken, Helen 1901-1966 .... WWasWT
Menzel, Jiri 1938- CTFT-12
Menzies, Archie 1904- .... WWasWT
Meppen, Adrian Joseph 1940- CTFT-3
Merande, Doro 1935- .... WWasWT
Mercer, Beryl 1882-1939 .... WWasWT
Mercer, David 1928-1980 .... WWT-17
Mercer, Johnny 1909-1976 .... WWT-16
Mercer, Marian 1935- CTFT-7
    Earlier sketch in WWT-17
Merchant, Ismail 1936- CTFT-13
    Earlier sketches in CTFT-1, 6
Merchant, Vivien 1929-1982 .... WWT-17
Mercouri, Melina 1925-1994 .... CTFT-5
    Obituary in CTFT-13
Mercure, Monique 1930 .... CTFT-11
Mere, Charles 1883-? .... WWasWT
Meredith, Burgess 1909(?)-1997 .... CTFT-4
    Obituary in CTFT-17
    Earlier sketch in WWT-17
Meredith, Don 1938- CTFT-1
Merivale 1882-1939 .... WWasWT
Merivale, Philip 1886-1946 .... WWasWT
Meriwether, Lee 1935- CTFT-2
Merkel, Una 1903-1986 .... WWasWT
Merkerson, S. Epatha 1952- CTFT-16
Merlin, Joanna 1931- CTFT-10
Merman, Ethel 1909-1984 .... CTFT-1
    Earlier sketch in WWT-17
Merrall, Mary 1890-1973 .... WWasWT
Merriam, Eve 1916- CTFT-1
Merrick, David 1912- CTFT-6
    Earlier sketch in WWT-17
Merrick, Leonard 1864-1939 .... WWasWT
Merrill, Beth .... WWasWT
Merrill, Bob 1920- WWT-17
Merrill, Dina 1925- CTFT-15
    Earlier sketches in CTFT-1, 8
Merrill, Gary 1915-1990 .... CTFT-1
Merritt, Grace 1881-? .... WWasWT
Merritt, Theresa 1922- CTFT-8
Merson, Billy 1881-1947 .... WWasWT
Mery, Andree .... WWasWT
Messager, Andre 1853-1929 .... WWasWT
Messick, Don 1926- CTFT-9
    Earlier sketch in CTFT-3
Meszaros, Marta 1931- CTFT-12
Metaxa, Georges 1899-1950 .... WWasWT
Metcalf, Laurie 1955- CTFT-15
    Earlier sketch in CTFT-7
Metcalf, Mark CTFT-8
Metcalfe, James Stetson
    1858-1927 .... WWasWT
Metcalfe, Stephen 1953- CTFT-17
    Earlier sketch in CTFT-7
Metenier, Oscar 1859-1913 .... WWasWT
Metheny, Pat 1954- CTFT-12
Metrano, Art 1937- CTFT-5
Meyer, Bertie Alexander
    1877-1967 .... WWasWT
Meyer, Louis 1871-1915 .... WWasWT
Meyer, Nicholas 1945- CTFT-14
    Earlier sketch in CTFT-1
Meyers, Ari 1969- CTFT-4

Meyers, Timothy 1945-1989 .... CTFT-1
Meynell, Clyde 1867-1934 .... WWasWT
Michael, Gertrude 1910-1965 .... WWasWT
Michael, Kathleen 1917- WWT-17
Michael, Ralph 1907- WWT-17
Michaelis, Robert 1884-1965 .... WWasWT
Michaels, Lorne 1944- CTFT-9
    Earlier sketch in CTFT-2
Michaels, Marilyn 1943- CTFT-8
Michaels, Richard 1936- CTFT-10
    Earlier sketch in CTFT-1
Michaelson, Knut 1846- .... WWasWT
Michell, Keith 1928- CTFT-8
    Earlier sketches in CTFT-2; WWT-17
Middlemass, Frank 1919- CTFT-8
Middleton, Edgar 1894-1939 .... WWasWT
Middleton, George 1880-1967 .... WWasWT
Middleton, Guy 1907-1973 .... WWasWT
Middleton, Josephine 1883-1971 .. WWasWT
Middleton, Ray 1907-1984 .... WWT-17
Midgley, Robin 1934- WWT-17
Midler, Bette 1945- CTFT-11
    Earlier sketches in CTFT-4; WWT-17
Mifune, Toshiro 1920- CTFT-5
Migden, Chester L. 1921- CTFT-11
Mignot, Flore .... WWasWT
Milano, Alyssa 1972- CTFT-14
    Earlier sketch in CTFT-4
Milchan, Arnon 1944- CTFT-12
Miles, Bernard 1907- WWT-17
Miles, Joanna 1940- CTFT-1
Miles, Julia CTFT-12
    Earlier sketch in CTFT-1
Miles, Sarah 1941- CTFT-3
    Earlier sketch in WWT-17
Miles, Sylvia 1932- CTFT-7
    Earlier sketch in CTFT-1
Miles, Vera 1930- CTFT-5
Milford, Gene 1903-1992 .... CTFT-11
Milgrim, Lynn 1940- CTFT-1
Militello, Anne E. 1957- CTFT-3
Milius, John 1944(?)- CTFT-16
    Earlier sketch in CTFT-8
Milkis, Edward Kenneth 1931-1996 .. CTFT-3
    Obituary in CTFT-16
Milland, Ray 1905-1986 .... CTFT-3
Millar, Douglas 1875-1943 .... WWasWT
Millar, Gertie 1879-1952 .... WWasWT
Millar, Mary WWT-17
Millar, Robins 1889-1968 .... WWasWT
Millar, Ronald 1919- WWT-17
Millard, Evelyn 1869-1941 .... WWasWT
Millard, Ursula 1901- .... WWasWT
Miller, Agnes .... WWasWT
Miller, Ann 1919- CTFT-4
    Earlier sketch in WWT-17
Miller, Arthur 1915- CTFT-11
    Earlier sketches in CTFT-1; WWT-17
Miller, Barry 1958- CTFT-17
    Earlier sketches in CTFT-2, 10
Miller, Buzz 1923- CTFT-1
Miller, David 1871-1933 .... WWasWT
Miller, David 1909- CTFT-2
Miller, Dennis 1953- CTFT-17
    Earlier sketch in CTFT-10

Miller, Dick 1928- CTFT-16
    Earlier sketch in CTFT-8
Miller, George 1945- CTFT-15
    Earlier sketch in CTFT-7
Miller, Gilbert Heron 1884-1969 .... WWasWT
Miller, Harry M. 1934- WWT-17
Miller, Henry 1860-1926 .... WWasWT
Miller, Hugh (Lorimer) 1889-? ...... WWasWT
Miller, J.P. 1919- CTFT-7
Miller, Jason 1939- CTFT-4
    Earlier sketch in WWT-17
Miller, Joan 1910-1988 .... CTFT-7
    Earlier sketch in WWT-17
Miller, Jonathan 1934- CTFT-12
    Earlier sketches in CTFT-5; WWT-17
Miller, June 1934- CTFT-4
Miller, Marilynn 1898-1936 .... WWasWT
Miller, Martin (Rudolf) 1899-1969 .. WWasWT
Miller, Nolan 1935- CTFT-8
Miller, Penelope
    See Miller, Penelope Ann CTFT-17
Miller, Penelope Ann 1964- CTFT-17
    Earlier sketches in CTFT-2, 10
Miller, Richard 1930- CTFT-3
Miller, Robert Ellis 1932- CTFT-12
Miller, Ruby 1889-1976 .... WWasWT
Miller, Susan 1944- CTFT-1
Miller, Thomas L. 1940- CTFT-3
Millett, Maude 1867-1920 .... WWasWT
Millett, Tim 1954- CTFT-2
Millian, Andra CTFT-5
Millican, Jane 1902- .... WWasWT
Milliet, Paul 1858-? .... WWasWT
Milligan, Spike 1918- CTFT-6
    Earlier sketch in WWT-17
Milligan, Tuck CTFT-1
Millington, Rodney 1905-1990 ...... WWT-17
Millo, Aprile 1958- CTFT-13
Mills, A. J. 1872-? .... WWasWT
Mills, Alley 1951- CTFT-17
    Earlier sketch in CTFT-10
Mills, Mrs. Clifford ?-1933 .... WWasWT
Mills, Donna CTFT-3
Mills, Florence 1901- .... WWasWT
Mills, Frank 1870-1921 .... WWasWT
Mills, Hayley 1946- CTFT-3
    Earlier sketch in WWT-17
Mills, Horace 1864-1941 .... WWasWT
Mills, John 1908- CTFT-11
    Earlier sketch in WWT-17
Mills, Juliet 1941- CTFT-3
    Earlier sketch in WWT-17
Millward 1861-1932 .... WWasWT
Milne, Alan Alexander
    1882-1956 .... WWasWT
Milner, Martin 1931- CTFT-7
Milner, Ron 1938- CTFT-10
Milstead, Harris Glenn
    See Divine CTFT-7
Miltern, John E. 1870-1937 .... WWasWT
Milton, Billy 1905-1989 .... WWasWT
Milton, David Scott 1934- CTFT-1
Milton, Ernest 1890-1974 .... WWasWT
Milton, Harry 1900-1965 .... WWasWT
Milton, Maud 1859-1945 .... WWasWT

N

O

P

Proett, Daniel (M.) 1953- CTFT-18
   Earlier sketch in CTFT-2
Proft, Pat 1947- CTFT-11
Prosky, Robert 1930- CTFT-3
Provenza, Paul 1957- CTFT-15
Provost, Jeanne .... WWasWT
Prowse, Juliet 1936-1996 .... CTFT-9
   Obituary in CTFT-16
Prussing, Louise 1897- .... WWasWT
Pryce, Jonathan 1947- CTFT-15
   Earlier sketch in CTFT-7
Pryce, Richard 1864-1942 .... WWasWT
Pryde, Peggy 1869-? .... WWasWT
Pryor, Nicholas 1935- CTFT-5
Pryor, Richard 1940- CTFT-3
Pryor, Roger 1901-1974 .... WWasWT
Pryse, Hugh 1910-1955 .... WWasWT
Psacharopoulos, Nikos 1928-1989 .... CTFT-8
   Earlier sketch in WWT-17
Pudenz, Steve 1947- CTFT-2
Pullman, Bill 1954- CTFT-14
   Earlier sketch in CTFT-7
Pullman, William
   See Pullman, Bill CTFT-14
Purcell, Charles 1883-1962 .... WWasWT
Purcell, Harold 1907- .... WWasWT
Purcell, Irene 1903-1972 .... WWasWT
Purcell, Lee 1953- CTFT-4
Purdell, Reginald 1896-1953 .... WWasWT
Purdham, David 1951- CTFT-1
Purdom, C.B. 1883-1965 .... WWasWT
Purl, Linda CTFT-5
Purnell, Louise 1942- CTFT-5
   Earlier sketch in WWT-17
Pusey, Arthur .... WWasWT
Puttnam, David 1941- CTFT-10
Puzo, Mario 1920- CTFT-10
Pyant, Paul 1953- CTFT-16
   Earlier sketch in CTFT-8
Pyle, Denver 1920- CTFT-9
Pyne, Daniel 1955- CTFT-10

Q

Quaid, Dennis 1954- CTFT-13
   Earlier sketch in CTFT-6
   Brief Entry in CTFT-2
Quaid, Randy 1950- CTFT-13
   Earlier sketch in CTFT-6
   Brief Entry in CTFT-2
Quarry, Robert 1924- CTFT-7
Quartermaine, Charles 1877-1958 .. WWasWT
Quartermaine, Leon 1876-1967 .... WWasWT
Quartermass, Martin
   See Carpenter, John CTFT-15
Quayle, Anna 1937- CTFT-4
   Earlier sketch in WWT-17
Quayle, Anthony 1913-1989 .... CTFT-5
   Earlier sketch in WWT-17
Queen Latifah 1970(?)- CTFT-14

Quentin, Patrick
   See Wheeler, Hugh CTFT-5
Quesenbery, Whitney 1954- CTFT-3
Questel, Mae 1908- CTFT-1
Quick, Diana 1946- CTFT-8
Quigley, Linnea CTFT-16
   Earlier sketch in CTFT-8
Quigley, William J. 1951- CTFT-9
Quillan, Eddie 1907-1990 .... CTFT-9
Quilley, Denis 1927- CTFT-14
   Earlier sketches in CTFT-5; WWT-17
Quine, Richard 1920-1989 .... CTFT-8
Quinlan, Gertrude 1875-1963 .... WWasWT
Quinlan, Kathleen 1954- CTFT-5
Quinn, Aidan 1959- CTFT-13
   Earlier sketch in CTFT-6
   Brief Entry in CTFT-2
Quinn, Anthony 1915- CTFT-15
   Earlier sketches in CTFT-1, 7; WWT-17
Quinn, Henry J. 1928- CTFT-2
Quinn, J.C. CTFT-8
Quinn, Martha 1959- CTFT-14
Quinn, Patrick 1950- CTFT-14
   Earlier sketches in CTFT-1, 6
Quinn, Tony 1899-1967 .... WWasWT
Quintero, Jose 1924- CTFT-8
   Earlier sketches in CTFT-2; WWT-17
Quinteros, Joaquin 1873-1944 ..... WWasWT
Quinteros, Serafin 1871-1938 .... WWasWT

R

Rabb, Ellis 1930- CTFT-4
   Earlier sketch in WWT-17
Rabe, David 1940- CTFT-14
   Earlier sketches in CTFT-1, 3; WWT-17
Rachins, Alan 1947- CTFT-18
   Earlier sketch in CTFT-7
Rademakers, Fons 1920- CTFT-8
Radford, Basil 1897-1952 .... WWasWT
Radford, Michael 1950- CTFT-14
Radner, Gilda 1946-1989 .... CTFT-8
   Earlier sketch in CTFT-3
Radnitz, Robert B. CTFT-1
Radosh, Stephen 1951- CTFT-2
Rae, Charlotte 1926- CTFT-2
   Earlier sketch in WWT-17
Rae, Edna
   See Burstyn, Ellen CTFT-13
Rae, Eric 1899- .... WWasWT
Rae, Kenneth 1901- .... WWasWT
Raeburn, Henzie 1900-1973 .... WWasWT
Raedler, Dorothy 1917- WWT-17
Raevsky, Iosif Moiseevich 1900- ... WWasWT
Rafelson, Bob 1933- CTFT-14
   Earlier sketch in CTFT-6
Rafferty, Pat 1861-1952 .... WWasWT
Raffin, Deborah 1953- CTFT-12
   Earlier sketch in CTFT-5
Rafkin, Alan 1928- CTFT-3

Raglan, James 1901-1961 .... WWasWT
Ragland, Robert O. 1931- CTFT-12
Ragni, Gerome 1942-1991 .... CTFT-10
Ragno, Joseph CTFT-2
Railsback, Steve CTFT-6
Raimi, Sam 1959- CTFT-17
   Earlier sketch in CTFT-10
Raimi, Sam M.
   See Raimi, Sam CTFT-17
Raimu, M. 1883-1946 .... WWasWT
Rain, Douglas CTFT-5
   Earlier sketch in WWT-17
Rainbow, Frank 1913- WWT-17
Raine, Jack 1897- .... WWasWT
Rainer, Luise 1912- .... WWasWT
Rainey, Ford 1908- CTFT-18
   Earlier sketch in CTFT-2
Rains, Claude 1889-1967 .... WWasWT
Raitt, John 1917- CTFT-5
   Earlier sketch in WWT-17
Rakoff, Alvin 1927- CTFT-8
Raksin, David 1912- CTFT-12
Raleigh, Cecil 1856-1914 .... WWasWT
Raleigh, Mrs. Saba ?-1923 .... WWasWT
Ralph, Sheryl Lee 1956- CTFT-13
   Earlier sketch in CTFT-6
Ralston, Ken CTFT-14
Ramage, Cecil B. 1895- .... WWasWT
Rambeau, Marjorie 1889-1970 ...... WWasWT
Rambert, Marie .... WWasWT
Rambo, Dack 1941-1994 .... CTFT-5
   Obituary in CTFT-13
Ramey, Samuel 1942- CTFT-13
Ramin, Sid 1924- CTFT-8
Ramis, Harold 1944- CTFT-17
   Earlier sketches in CTFT-2, 10
Ramont, Mark S. 1956- CTFT-15
   Earlier sketch in CTFT-8
Rampling, Charlotte 1946- CTFT-6
   Earlier sketch in CTFT-1
Ramsay, Remak 1937- CTFT-7
   Earlier sketch in WWT-17
Ramsden, Dennis 1918- WWT-17
Ramsey, Alicia ?-1933 .... WWasWT
Ramsey, Logan 1921- CTFT-10
Ranalow, Frederick Baring
   1873-1953 .... WWasWT
Randall, Carl ?-1965 .... WWasWT
Randall, Harry 1860-1932 .... WWasWT
Randall, Leslie 1924- WWT-17
   Earlier sketch in WWasWT
Randall, Tony 1920- CTFT-15
   Earlier sketches in CTFT-1, 7; WWT-17
Randel, Melissa CTFT-2
Randell, Ron 1923- WWT-17
Randle, Betsy CTFT-17
Randolph, Elsie 1904- WWT-17
Randolph, John 1915- CTFT-16
   Earlier sketches in CTFT-2, 8
Randolph, Robert 1926- CTFT-2
   Earlier sketch in WWT-17
Ranevsky, Boris 1891- .... WWasWT
Ranft, Albert Adam 1858-? .... WWasWT
Rankin, Arthur McKee 1841-1914 .. WWasWT
Rankin, Molly .... WWasWT

T

Wordsworth, William Derrick
 1912-1988 .... WWasWT
Workman, C. Herbert
 1873-1923 .... WWasWT
Worley, Jo Anne 1939- CTFT-2
Worlock, Frederic G. 1886-1973 .... WWasWT
Worms, Jean 1884-? .... WWasWT
Woronov, Mary 1946- CTFT-8
Worrall, Lechmere 1875-? .... WWasWT
Worsley, Bruce 1899- .... WWasWT
Worster, Howett 1882-? .... WWasWT
Worth, Irene 1916- CTFT-17
 Earlier sketches in CTFT-3, 10; WWT-17
Worth, Marvin CTFT-12
Wouk, Herman 1915- CTFT-1
Wray, Fay 1907- CTFT-8
Wray, John 1888-1940 .... WWasWT
Wray, Maxwell 1898- .... WWasWT
Wright, Amy 1950- CTFT-9
Wright, Cowley 1889-1923 .... WWasWT
Wright, David 1941- WWT-17
Wright, Fred 1871-1928 .... WWasWT
Wright, Garland CTFT-7
Wright, Haidee 1868-1943 .... WWasWT
Wright, Hugh E. 1879-1940 .... WWasWT
Wright, Huntley 1869-1943 .... WWasWT
Wright, Max 1943- CTFT-8
Wright, Nicholas 1940- WWT-17
Wright, Robert 1914- CTFT-12
Wright, Robin 1966(?)- CTFT-12
Wright, Steven 1955- CTFT-9
Wright, Teresa 1918- CTFT-17
 Earlier sketches in CTFT-3, 10; WWT-
 17
Wright, Mrs. Theodore ?-1922 ...... WWasWT
Wrye, Donald CTFT-12
Wuhl, Robert 1951- CTFT-17
 Earlier sketch in CTFT-9
Wurtzel, Stuart 1940- CTFT-5
Wyatt, Frank Gunning
 1851-1926 .... WWasWT
Wyatt, Jane 1912- CTFT-3
 Earlier sketch in WWasWT
Wycherly, Margaret 1884-1956 .... WWasWT
Wyckham, John 1926- CTFT-6
 Earlier sketch in WWT-17
Wyckoff, Evelyn 1917- .... WWasWT
Wyle, Noah 1971- CTFT-16
Wyler, Gretchen 1932- CTFT-6
 Earlier sketch in CTFT-1
Wylie, John 1925- CTFT-7
Wylie, Julian 1878-1934 .... WWasWT
Wylie, Lauri 1880-? .... WWasWT
Wyman, Jane 1914- CTFT-3
Wymark, Patrick 1926-1970 .... WWasWT
Wyn, Marjery 1909- .... WWasWT
Wyndham, Charles 1837-1919 ...... WWasWT
Wyndham, Dennis 1887-? .... WWasWT
Wyndham, Gwen .... WWasWT
Wyndham, Howard 1865-1947 ..... WWasWT
Wyndham, Olive 1886-? .... WWasWT
Wyner, George CTFT-7
Wyngarde, Peter WWT-17
Wynn, Ed 1886-1966 .... WWasWT
Wynn, Keenan 1916-1986 .... CTFT-4

Wynn, Tracy Keenan 1945- CTFT-8
 Earlier sketch in CTFT-1
Wynne, Wish 1882-1931 .... WWasWT
Wynter, Dana 1930- CTFT-7
Wynyard, Diana 1906-1964 .... WWasWT
Wynyard, John 1915- WWT-16
Wyse, John 1904- WWT-16

X

Xanrof, Leon 1867-1953 .... WWasWT

Y

Yablans, Frank 1935- CTFT-8
 Earlier sketch in CTFT-1
Yablans, Irwin 1934- CTFT-8
 Earlier sketch in CTFT-1
Yaffe, Alan
 See Yorinks, Arthur CTFT-13
Yakko, Sada ?-1946 .... WWasWT
Yale, Kathleen Betsko 1939- CTFT-2
Yalman, Tunc 1925- CTFT-2
Yanez, Michael CTFT-3
Yang, Ginny CTFT-4
Yankowitz, Susan 1941- CTFT-1
Yannis, Michael 1922- .... WWasWT
Yapp, Cecil CTFT-8
Yarde, Margaret 1878-1944 .... WWasWT
Yarrow, Duncan 1884-? .... WWasWT
Yasbeck, Amy 1962- CTFT-17
Yates, Peter 1929- CTFT-6
 Earlier sketch in CTFT-1
Yavorska, Lydia 1874-1921 .... WWasWT
Yeamans, Annie 1835-1912 .... WWasWT
Yearsley, Claude Blakesley
 1885-1961 .... WWasWT
Yeats, William Butler 1865-1939 .... WWasWT
Yellen, Linda 1949- CTFT-3
Yeston, Maury 1945- CTFT-10
 Earlier sketch in CTFT-1
Yniguez, Richard CTFT-6
Yoakam, Dwight 1956- CTFT-17
Yoba, Malik 1967(?)- CTFT-17
Yohe, May 1869-1938 .... WWasWT
Yokel, Alexander 1887-1947 .... WWasWT
Yordan, Philip 1914- CTFT-12
Yorinks, Arthur 1953- CTFT-13
York, Michael 1942- CTFT-13
 Earlier sketches in CTFT-1, 6
York, Susannah 1941- CTFT-5
Yorke, Augustus ?-1939 .... WWasWT
Yorke, Oswald ?-1943 .... WWasWT
Yorkin, Bud 1926- CTFT-1
Youmans, James CTFT-14

Youmans, Vincent 1898-1946........WWasWT
Young, Arthur 1898-1959..............WWasWT
Young, Bertram Alfred 1912-...........WWT-17
Young, Burt 1940-...........................CTFT-5
Young, Chris 1971-...........................CTFT-8
Young. Collier
 See Bloch, Robert....................CTFT-2
Young, David 1928-..........................CTFT-4
Young, Dawn....................................CTFT-4
Young, Freddie 1902-.....................CTFT-13
Young, Freddie A.
 See Young, Freddie.................CTFT-13
Young, Frederick
 See Young, Freddie.................CTFT-13
Young, Frederick A.
 See Young, Freddie.................CTFT-13
Young, Gig 1917-1978....................WWT-16
Young, Howard Irving 1893-..........WWasWT
Young, Howard L. 1911-...............WWasWT
Young, Joan 1903-1984..................WWT-17
Young, Karen.................................CTFT-8
Young, Loretta 1913-......................CTFT-8
Young, Rida Johnson 1875-1926....WWasWT
Young, Robert 1907-.......................CTFT-7
Young, Robert M. 1924-..................CTFT-9
Young, Robert Malcolm
 See Young, Robert M................CTFT-9
Young, Roger 1942-.........................CTFT-3
Young, Roland 1887-1953..............WWasWT
Young, Sean 1959-...........................CTFT-14
 Earlier sketch in CTFT-7
Young, Stark 1881-1963................WWasWT
Young, Terence 1915-1994............CTFT-7
 Obituary in CTFT-13
Youngs, Jim...................................CTFT-7
Yulin, Harris 1937-.........................CTFT-7
Yurka, Blanche 1887-1974.............WWasWT

Z

Zabelle, Flora 1880-1968...............WWasWT
Zabka, Billy
 See Zabka, William...................CTFT-18
Zabka, William 1965-.....................CTFT-18
 Earlier sketch in CTFT-7
Zabriskie, Grace.............................CTFT-16
 Earlier sketch in CTFT-8
Zacconi, Ermete 1857-1948...........WWasWT
Zadan, Craig...................................CTFT-1
Zadora, Pia 1956-...........................CTFT-9
Zaentz, Saul...................................CTFT-9
Zaks, Jerry 1946-...........................CTFT-6
 Earlier sketch in CTFT-1
Zal, Roxana 1969-..........................CTFT-4
Zaloom, Paul 1951-........................CTFT-1
Zamacois, Miguel 1866-1939.........WWasWT
Zampieri, Vittorio 1862-?..............WWasWT
Zangwill, Israel 1864-1926...........WWasWT
Zanuck, Richard D. 1934-...............CTFT-14
 Earlier sketch in CTFT-7

Cumulative Index